FOR REFERENCE

Do Not Take From This Room

Contemporary
Literary Criticism

Guide to Gale Literary Criticism Series

For criticism on	Consult these Gale series
Authors now living or who died after December 31, 1959	*CONTEMPORARY LITERARY CRITICISM (CLC)*
Authors who died between 1900 and 1959	*TWENTIETH-CENTURY LITERARY CRITICISM (TCLC)*
Authors who died between 1800 and 1899	*NINETEENTH-CENTURY LITERATURE CRITICISM (NCLC)*
Authors who died between 1400 and 1799	*LITERATURE CRITICISM FROM 1400 TO 1800 (LC)* *SHAKESPEAREAN CRITICISM (SC)*
Authors who died before 1400	*CLASSICAL AND MEDIEVAL LITERATURE CRITICISM (CMLC)*
Black writers of the past two hundred years	*BLACK LITERATURE CRITICISM (BLC) AND BLACK LITERATURE CRITICISM SUPPLEMENT (BLCS)*
Authors of books for children and young adults	*CHILDREN'S LITERATURE REVIEW (CLR)*
Dramatists	*DRAMA CRITICISM (DC)*
Hispanic writers of the late nineteenth and twentieth centuries	*HISPANIC LITERATURE CRITICISM (HLC)*
Native North American writers and orators of the eighteenth, nineteenth, and twentieth centuries	*NATIVE NORTH AMERICAN LITERATURE (NNAL)*
Poets	*POETRY CRITICISM (PC)*
Short story writers	*SHORT STORY CRITICISM (SSC)*
Major authors from the Renaissance to the present	*WORLD LITERATURE CRITICISM, 1500 TO THE PRESENT (WLC)*
Major authors and works from the Bible to the present	*WORLD LITERATURE CRITICISM SUPPLEMENT (WLCS)*

ISSN 0091-3421

Volume 121

Contemporary Literary Criticism

Criticism of the Works
of Today's Novelists, Poets, Playwrights,
Short Story Writers, Scriptwriters, and
Other Creative Writers

Jeffrey W. Hunter
Polly Vedder
EDITORS

Angela Y. Jones
Justin Karr
Deborah A. Schmitt
Timothy J. White
Kathleen Wilson
ASSOCIATE EDITORS

GALE GROUP

Detroit
San Francisco
London
Boston
Woodbridge, CT

STAFF

Library of Congress Catalog Card Number 76-46132
ISBN 0-7876-3196-5
ISSN 0091-3421

Printed in the United States of America
10 9 8 7 6 5 4 3 2 1

Contents

Preface vii

Acknowledgments xi

Preface

A Comprehensive Information Source
on Contemporary Literature

Named "one of the twenty-five most distinguished reference titles published during the past twenty-five years" by *Reference Quarterly*, the *Contemporary Literary Criticism (CLC)* series provides readers with critical commentary and general information on more than 2,000 authors now living or who died after December 31, 1959. Previous to the publication of the first volume of *CLC* in 1973, there was no ongoing digest monitoring scholarly and popular sources of critical opinion and explication of modern literature. *CLC*, therefore, has fulfilled an essential need, particularly since the complexity and variety of contemporary literature makes the function of criticism especially important to today's reader.

Scope of the Series

CLC presents significant passages from published criticism of works by creative writers. Since many of the authors covered by *CLC* inspire continual critical commentary, writers are often represented in more than one volume. There is, of course, no duplication of reprinted criticism.

Authors are selected for inclusion for a variety of reasons, among them the publication or dramatic production of a critically acclaimed new work, the reception of a major literary award, revival of interest in past writings, or the adaptation of a literary work to film or television.

Attention is also given to several other groups of writers—authors of considerable public interest—about whose work criticism is often difficult to locate. These include mystery and science fiction writers, literary and social critics, foreign writers, and authors who represent particular ethnic groups.

Format of the Book

Each *CLC* volume contains individual essays and reviews taken from hundreds of book review periodicals, general magazines, scholarly journals, monographs, and books. Entries include critical evaluations spanning from the beginning of an author's career to the most current commentary. Interviews, feature articles, and other published writings that offer insight into the author's works are also presented. Students, teachers, librarians, and researchers will find that the generous critical and biographical material in *CLC* provides them with vital information required to write a term paper, analyze a poem, or lead a book discussion group. In addition, complete bibliographical citations note the original source and all of the information necessary for a term paper footnote or bibliography.

Features

A *CLC* author entry consists of the following elements:

■ The **Author Heading** cites the author's name in the form under which the author has most commonly published, followed by birth date, and death date when applicable. Uncertainty as to a birth or death date is indicated by a question mark.

- A **Portrait** of the author is included when available.

- A brief **Biographical and Critical Introduction** to the author and his or her work precedes the criticism. The first line of the introduction provides the author's full name, pseudonyms (if applicable), nationality, and a listing of genres in which the author has written. To provide users with easier access to information, the biographical and critical essay included in each author entry is divided into four categories: "Introduction," "Biographical Information," "Major Works," and "Critical Reception." The introductions to single-work entries—entries that focus on well known and frequently studied books, short stories, and poems—are similarly organized to quickly provide readers with information on the plot and major characters of the work being discussed, its major themes, and its critical reception. Previous volumes of *CLC* in which the author has been featured are also listed in the introduction.

- A list of **Principal Works** notes the most important writings by the author. When foreign-language works have been translated into English, the English-language version of the title follows in brackets.

- The **Criticism** represents various kinds of critical writing, ranging in form from the brief review to the scholarly exegesis. Essays are selected by the editors to reflect the spectrum of opinion about a specific work or about an author's literary career in general. The critical and biographical materials are presented chronologically, adding a useful perspective to the entry. All titles by the author featured in the entry are printed in boldface type, which enables the reader to easily identify the works being discussed. Publication information (such as publisher names and book prices) and parenthetical numerical references (such as footnotes or page and line references to specific editions of a work) have been deleted at the editor's discretion to provide smoother reading of the text.

- Critical essays are prefaced by **Explanatory Notes** as an additional aid to readers. These notes may provide several types of valuable information, including: the reputation of the critic, the importance of the work of criticism, the commentator's approach to the author's work, the purpose of the criticism, and changes in critical trends regarding the author.

- A complete **Bibliographical Citation** designed to help the user find the original essay or book precedes each critical piece.

- Whenever possible, a recent **Author Interview** accompanies each entry.

- A concise **Further Reading** section appears at the end of entries on authors for whom a significant amount of criticism exists in addition to the pieces reprinted in *CLC*. Each citation in this section is accompanied by a descriptive annotation describing the content of that article. Materials included in this section are grouped under various headings (e.g., Biography, Bibliography, Criticism, and Interviews) to aid users in their search for additional information. Cross-references to other useful sources published by The Gale Group in which the author has appeared are also included: *Authors in the News, Black Writers, Children's Literature Review, Contemporary Authors, Dictionary of Literary Biography, DlSCovering Authors, Drama Criticism, Hispanic Literature Criticism, Hispanic Writers, Native North American Literature, Poetry Criticism, Something about the Author, Short Story Criticism, Contemporary Authors Autobiography Series,* and *Something about the Author Autobiography Series.*

Other Features

CLC also includes the following features:

- An **Acknowledgments** section lists the copyright holders who have granted permission to reprint material in this volume of *CLC.* It does not, however, list every book or periodical reprinted or consulted during the preparation of the volume.

- Each new volume of *CLC* includes a **Cumulative Topic Index,** which lists all literary topics treated in *CLC, NCLC, TCLC,* and *LC 1400-1800.*

- A **Cumulative Author Index** lists all the authors who have appeared in the various literary criticism series published by The Gale Group, with cross-references to Gale's biographical and autobiographical series. A full listing of the series referenced there appears on the first page of the indexes of this volume. Readers will welcome this cumulated author index as a useful tool for locating an author within the various series. The index, which lists birth and death dates when available, will be particularly valuable for those authors who are identified with a certain period but whose death dates cause them to be placed in another, or for those authors whose careers span two periods. For example, Ernest Hemingway is found in *CLC,* yet F. Scott Fitzgerald, a writer often associated with him, is found in *Twentieth-Century Literary Criticism.*

- A **Cumulative Nationality Index** alphabetically lists all authors featured in *CLC* by nationality, followed by numbers corresponding to the volumes in which the authors appear.

- An alphabetical **Title Index** accompanies each volume of *CLC.* Listings are followed by the author's name and the corresponding page numbers where the titles are discussed. English translations of foreign titles and variations of titles are cross-referenced to the title under which a work was originally published. Titles of novels, novellas, dramas, films, record albums, and poetry, short story, and essay collections are printed in italics, while all individual poems, short stories, essays, and songs are printed in roman type within quotation marks; when published separately (e.g., T. S. Eliot's poem *The Waste Land),* the titles of long poems are printed in italics.

- In response to numerous suggestions from librarians, Gale has also produced a **Special Paperbound Edition** of the *CLC* title index. This annual cumulation, which alphabetically lists all titles reviewed in the series, is available to all customers. Additional copies of the index are available upon request. Librarians and patrons will welcome this separate index: it saves shelf space, is easy to use, and is recyclable upon receipt of the next edition.

Citing *Contemporary Literary Criticism*

When writing papers, students who quote directly from any volume in the Literary Criticism Series may use the following general forms to footnote reprinted criticism. The first example pertains to material drawn from periodicals, the second to material reprinted in books:

[1]Alfred Cismaru, "Making the Best of It," *The New Republic,* 207, No. 24, (December 7, 1992), 30, 32; excerpted and reprinted in *Contemporary Literary Criticism,* Vol. 85, ed. Christopher Giroux (Detroit: Gale, 1995), pp. 73-4.

[2]Yvor Winters, *The Post-Symbolist Methods* (Allen Swallow, 1967); excerpted and reprinted in *Contemporary Literary Criticism,* Vol. 85, ed. Christopher Giroux (Detroit: Gale, 1995), pp. 223-26.

Suggestions Are Welcome

The editors hope that readers will find *CLC* a useful reference tool and welcome comments about the work. Send comments and suggestions to: Editors, *Contemporary Literary Criticism,* The Gale Group, 27500 Drake Rd., Farmington Hills, MI 48333-3535.

Acknowledgments

The editors wish to thank the copyright holders of the excerpted criticism included in this volume and the permissions managers of many book and magazine publishing companies for assisting us in securing reproduction rights. We are also grateful to the staffs of the Detroit Public Library, the Library of Congress, the University of Detroit Mercy Library, Wayne State University Purdy/Kresge Library Complex, and the University of Michigan Libraries for making their resources available to us. Following is a list of the copyright holders who have granted us permission to reproduce material in this volume of CLC. Every effort has been made to trace copyright, but if omissions have been made, please let us know.

COPYRIGHTED MATERIALS IN CLC VOLUME 121, WERE REPRODUCED FROM THE FOLLOWING PERIODICALS:

Amerasia Journal, v. 19, 1993; v. 22, 1996. Copyright © 1993, 1996 by The Regents of the University of California. All rights reserved. Both reproduced by permission.—**American Book Review,** September, 1995; v. 17, February-March, 1996. © 1995, 1996 by **The American Book Review**. Both reproduced by permission.—**The American Poetry Review,** v. 25, March-April, 1996 for "American Poetry in American Life" by Robert Pinsky; June-August, 1997 for "Story Tellers" by Louise Glück. Copyright © 1996, 1997 by World Poetry, Inc. Both reproduced by permission of the authors.—**Ariel: A Review of International English Literature**, v. 15, January, 1984 for "Narayan's Sense of Audience" by Harsharan S. Ahuwalia. Copyright © 1984 The Board of Governors, The University of Calgary. Reproduced by permission of the publisher and the author.—**The Bulletin of the Center for Children's Books,** v. 47, September, 1993; v. 48, March, 1995. Copyright © 1993, 1995 by The Board of Trustees of the University of Illinois. Both reproduced by permission.—**Belles Lettres: A Review of Books by Women**, Fall, 1991; v. 8 Summer, 1991,1993. Both reproduced by permission.—**Best Sellers,** v. 27, April 1, 1967; v. 32, October 1, 1972. Copyright 1967,1972 by the University of Scranton. Both reproduced by permission.—**Biography,** v. 16, Spring, 1993; v. 17, Summer, 1994. Copyright © 1993, 1994 by the Biographical Research Center. All right reserved. Both reproduced by permission.—**Black American Literature Forum,** v. 18, Summer, 1984 for "Octavia Butler and the Black Science-Fiction Heroine," by Ruth Salvaggio; v. 23, Summer, 1989 for a review of **Dawn** by Adele S. Newson.. Copyright © 1984, 1989 by the author. Both reproduced by permission of the publisher and the author.—**Book World-The Washington Post,** October 8, 1967 for a review of "How Many Miles to Babylon?" by Polly Goodwin; v. XXV. August 6, 1995 for "Mistress of Terror and Torture," by Bettina Drew. © 1967, 1995 Washington Post Book World Service/Washington Post Writers Group. Both reproduced by permission of the authors.—**Callaloo**, v. 14, Spring, 1991. Copyright © 1991 by Charles H. Rowell. Reproduced by permission of The Johns Hopkins University Press.—**Chicago Tribune,** March, 1996. © copyrighted 1996 Chicago Tribune Company. All rights reserved. Used with permission—Chicago Tribune Books, May 25, 1997. Reproduced by permission of the Chicago Tribune.—**Chicago Tribune Books,** May 25, 1997. Reproduced by permission of the Chicago Tribune.—**Children's Literature Association Quarterly**, v. 8, Winter, 1983. © 1983 Children's Literature Association. Reproduced by permission.—**Children's Literature,** v. 11, 1983. Reproduced by permission.—**Commonweal,** v. LIX, October 23, 1953; v. CXII, January 11, 1985. Copyright © 1953,1985 Commonweal Publishing Co., Inc. Both reproduced by permission of Commonweal Foundation.—**The Christian Science Monitor,** June 19, 1985. © 1985 by the Christian Science Publishing Society. All rights reserved. Reproduced by permission from **The Christian Science Monitor.**/ October 2, 1987 for a review of "A Piquant Infusion of India" by Neil Millar; October 2, 1987 for a review of "Lily and the Lost Boy" by Diane. © 1970, 1987 by the authors. Both reproduced by permission of the respective authors.—**Criticism,** v. XXX, Fall, 1988. Copyright, 1988, Wayne State University Press. Reproduced by permission of the publisher.—**Critique: Studies in Modern Fiction,** v. XX, 1978. Copyright © 1978 Helen Dwight Reid Educational Foundation. Reproduced with permission of the Helen Dwight Reid Educational Foundation, published by Heldref Publications, 119 18th Street, N. W., Washington, DC 20036-1802.—**Daedalus: Journal of the American Academy of Arts and Sciences,** v. 118, Fall, 1989. Copyright © 1989 by the American Academy of Arts and Sciences. Reprinted by permission of **Daedalus: Journal of the American Academy of Arts and Sciences.**—**Encounter,** v. LXIV, March, 1985 for "Quiet Quiet India" by Richard Cronin. © 1985 by the author. Reproduced by permission of

COPYRIGHTED MATERIALS IN *CLC* VOLUME 121, WERE REPRODUCED FROM THE FOLLOWING BOOKS:

author.—Wong, Sau-Ling Cynthia. From "Autobiography as Guided Chinatown Tour?: Maxine Hong Kingston's **The Woman Warrior** and the Chinese -American Autobiographical Controversy" in **Multicultural Autobiography: American Lives, by Sau-Ling Cynthia Wong. Edited by James Robert Payne.** Copyright © 1992 by the University of Tennessee Press/Knoxville.

PHOTOGRAPHS AND ILLUSTRATIONS APPEARING IN *CLC* VOLUME 121, WERE RECEIVED FROM THE FOLLOWING SOURCES:

Meena Alexander

1951-

Indian poet, novelist, critic, and autobiographer.

The following entry presents criticism of Alexander's career through 1998.

INTRODUCTION

Alexander is an Indian writer whose poetry and fiction reflect her mulicultural life experiences among diverse ethnic and religious communities on four continents. Generally concerned with the roles of place, memory, and language in identity formation, Alexander's works examine the disparate elements of her heritage and her cultural displacement, concentrating particularly on her status as an educated woman of the South Asian diaspora living and writing in the West. Alexander's search for psychic wholeness through language—a prevalent theme of her poetry—also articulates the concerns facing many postcolonial writers silenced by the dominant literary traditions of the imperial past. Critical discussion of her writings often centers on her contributions to Anglophone postcolonial literature, but scholars also have responded to her feminist perspective on literary and cultural issues. Alexander has remarked: "While I do not think I consciously write as a woman, I have little doubt that some of my deepest emotions and insights spring from having been born into a female body, learning to grow up as a woman in both a traditional Indian culture—South Indian, Syrian Christian, Malayalam speaking—and as part of the complex, shifting South Asian diaspora."

Biographical Information

The daughter of a diplomat, Alexander was born into a socially prominent, Syrian Christian family in Allahabad, India, but was raised in the Sudan, where she attended high school and graduated from the University of Khartoum with a bachelor of arts degree in 1969. She pursued graduate studies at the University of Nottingham in England, writing her dissertation on Romantic English literature which later evolved into *The Poetic Self* (1979). After earning a doctorate degree in 1973, Alexander returned to India and taught at several universities until 1979, when she accepted a visiting fellowship at the Sorbonne in Paris. During her return to India, she also published her first collections of poetry: *The Bird's Bright Ring* (1976), *I Root My Name* (1977), and *Without Place* (1978). Late in 1979 Alexander emigrated to the United States and settled in the New York City area, assuming an associate professorship at Fordham

University. While acclimating to American life, Alexander immersed herself in writing. By the late 1980s she not only had contributed numerous scholarly articles to literary journals and feminist anthologies, but she also published the poetry collections *House of a Thousand Doors* (1988), *The Storm* (1989), and *Night-Scene, the Garden* (1989) as well as the critical study *Women in Romanticism* (1989). A lecturer in the writing program at Columbia University since 1990 and a professor of women's studies at City University of New York since 1992, Alexander produced more prose than poetry during the 1990s, writing two novels, *Nampally Road* (1991) and *Manhattan Music* (1997); an autobiography, *Fault Lines* (1993); another volume of criticism, *The Shock of Arrival* (1996); and a single poetry book, *River and Bridge* (1995).

Major Works

Marked by processes of mediation between and meditation on different literary and cultural traditions, Alexander's imagistic and somewhat romantic poetry attempts to create a sense of identity for the poet and represents a type of psychoanalysis through which different aspects of her personality approach some sort of order. Alexander's early poetry depends on, as often as it reveals, the interstices of memory, history, and ontology; for example, *The Bird's Bright Ring* juxtaposes images of blood, salt, and native flora and fauna with fragmented commentary on the sociopolitical effects of British rule in India. Although Alexander's verse generally favors Indian themes and imagery, feminist issues comprise the majority of her work, including her scholarly studies, and female narrators and characters dominate both her poetry and fiction. *I Root My Name,* for instance, intimates the painful experiences of women, while "A Mirror's Grace," a poem appearing in *Without Place,* recounts Cleopatra's struggle to resist slipping into the margins of patriarchal linguistics. *House of a Thousand Doors* centers on memories and dreams of Alexander's grandmother, whom the poet has described as "a power permitting me to speak in an alien landscape." *The Storm* contemplates the feminist ideal of recreating and rewriting a "pure" female self-identity from fragmentary matrilineal memories. In *Night-Scene, the Garden,* mothers, grandmothers, aunts, and sisters figure prominently in the narrator's memory, which symbolizes a kind of "mother tongue" that encourages the poet to create a "new" self. The poetry of *River and Bridge* explores similar personal and feminist themes, focusing primarily on coping with cultural displacement, but other poems address myriad forms of violence and protest bondage of all sorts, ranging from racial and sexual to economic and religious. Like her poetry, Alexander's fiction carries autobiographical overtones. Centered on literature's relation to life and women's role as healer of communal ills, *Nampally Road* relates the story of a woman writer who returns to her native India following her college education abroad. She plans to create literary order out of India's tumultuous past by writing a book about it, but instead she becomes involved in the resurgent political violence that surrounds her and reluctantly learns that she can do little to stop the suffering. Set in contemporary New York, *Manhattan Music* traces a female immigrant's gradual recovery of her self-identity through a series of interracial, multicultural relationships and intellectual associations.

Critical Reception

Critics often have recognized Alexander's poetry for articulating some of the linguistic dilemmas confronting native writers of formerly British-administered colonies, noting that her imagery and formal structures, though reminiscent of European Romanticism and Modernism, are inflected by complex Indian rhythms, dense syntax, and South-Asian mythology. Consequently, Alexander has engaged the attention of postcolonial literary scholars. Ben Downing has characterized her poetic work thus: "Attracted to both the 'hierarchical unity' of Indian tradition and a modern, Western poetics of rupture, Alexander is faced with the difficult necessity of mediating between them." Alexander's fiction also has received a similar critical response, evinced by John Oliver Perry, who has called *Nampally Road* a "major contribution to South Asian-American literature far exceeding, say, Bharati Mukherjee's novels in cultural richness, psychological complexity, and sociopolitical—not to mention feminist—sophistication." Shilpa Davé, likewise comparing the significance of Alexander's fiction to that of Mukherjee's, concluded that *Nampally Road* represents more than "a narrative of minority victimage, and instead offers a reasonable strategy to incorporate the identity with the past by questioning the relationship between history and our cultural inheritance." Critics also have read Alexander's impulse to question her identity for signs of emergent feminism, responding particularly to her experiences as a woman in both an occidental and oriental context. "Alexander treats her writing as a search for a homeland, which is less physical than psychological, in particular her poetry, as a means of making sense of her multiple cultural, geographical and psychological positionalities," according to Helen Grice, adding that "it is [Alexander's] very ethnicity, gender, and exilic status that make her the person she is, and that it is partly the fault lines that exist between these identities that define her."

PRINCIPAL WORKS

The Bird's Bright Ring (poetry) 1976
I Root My Name (poetry) 1977
Without Place (poetry) 1978
The Poetic Self: Towards a Phenomenology of Romanticism (criticism) 1979
Stone Roots (poetry) 1980
House of a Thousand Doors (poetry) 1988
Night-Scene, the Garden (poetry) 1989
The Storm: A Poem in Five Parts (poetry) 1989
Women in Romanticism: Mary Wollstonecraft, Dorothy Wordsworth and Mary Shelley (criticism) 1989
Nampally Road (novel) 1991
Fault Lines (autobiography) 1993
River and Bridge (poetry) 1995
The Shock of Arrival: Reflections on Postcolonial Experience (criticism) 1996
Manhattan Music (novel) 1997

CRITICISM

John Oliver Perry (essay date Winter-Spring 1986)

SOURCE: "Exiled by a Woman's Body: Substantial Phenomena in Meena Alexander's Poetry," in *Journal of South Asian Literature,* Vol. 21, No. 1, Winter-Spring, 1986, pp. 125-32.

[*In the following essay, Perry examines various manifestations of "exile" in Alexander's poetry, especially in relation to gender, language, and politics.*]

> [If the exile's] body cannot appropriate its given landscape, . . . the substantial body dwindles into phantasm. . . . Language . . . degenerates into a dead script when the bodily power of a people no longer instills it with particularity, no longer appropriates it in the expression of a emergent selfhood. . . . In the battle between the body and the spirit the outworn script of English as we find it here must be made to open its maw and swallow, swallow huge chaosses, the chaosses of uninterpreted actuality.
> —Meena Alexander, **"Exiled by a Dead Script!"** (1977)

Within the developing group of South Asian women struggling with the paradoxes of writing poetry in English, Meena Alexander rises as a solid phenomenon, neither fleeting shade nor faint aroma, but pungent, sure, fully extended in time and space and motion. At age thirty-five, in the middle of the journey of her life, she has, unlike most other poets in India, already produced a substantial amount of poetry: five books in nine years, the last by far the largest and best. Her poems, often reaching beyond a page of narrow lines, have weight and extension individually and accumulate their feelings and significances collectively to build a full body of consciousness. If her just-issued book, **House of a Thousand Doors** (1986), is brought into the wider ken of other women—and one would hope, poets of every sort—also struggling to find their audience and language and subject in India, they will discover a thoroughly defined and exemplary artistry, undeniably contemporary in its increasingly simplified rhetoric and complex developing poetic. Meena Alexander could then very well become an emblem in whose sign others may inscribe their living wholes of experience, no matter how much their cultural condition threatens to make them aliens in their own land, in their own body, in the language thcy are appropriating.

This most recent work is much more convincing in every way than the flailing exploratory wordsmithing of her first two thin Writer's Workshop books, **Bird's Bright Ring** (1976) and **Without Place** (1977), or the eighteen still craftily obscure poems of flame and pain, blood, and vein, **I Root My Name** (1977). As if to prove the continuity of her work, she reprints five of those poems in this last hefty, partly prose volume with forty other poems, all but a dozen previously published in a wide range of journals in India and abroad. From the more mature **Stone Roots** (1980) she reprints only two small poems and a ten stanza dialogue, still somewhat contorted in syntax and symbolism and somehow related to a previously published play about a woman facing a wall, **In the Middle Earth** (1977). In fact, the 1980 book, from a highly regarded commercial press, already engages the forces and values, both social and esthetic, that make Alexander's whole body of work probably the most promising, and, except for Kamala Das', the most fully achieved by any contemporary South Asian woman poet.

Though literally, if not legally, an immigrant now in New York, the "roots" of which she writes are inescapably Keralan, Malayalam, Syrian Christian—not vaguely "pan-Indian"—that common fate of those exiled by the dead script of English and by spending most of their formative years in the shifting life of an Indian administrative family at home and abroad. Without disingenuously complaining of historically enforced social and personal and esthetic alienations, she probes the actualities of her given and constantly changing situations and their relationships to other equally shifting conditions of living, past and present. Her complex personal being feels convincingly exiled not only geographically, linguistically, and phenomenologically, but by the politics of her sexuality with its marginalized gender identity, by her generational modernity with its morally ambiguous liberal-liberated outlook, and by her inescapable

neo-colonial elitism with its guilty and hungry relationship to the so-called impoverished, underdeveloped Third World. All of these potentially abstract, inert conditions she compels into poetry. Not limiting her sphere of importance to feminist poetry, one can say that, except for two or three male poets, Meena Alexander has produced the most substantial poetry yet to appear in the genre of Indo-English poetry—*if* that is a proper term here.

Before this achievement can be placed, however, it is crucial to establish its material origins and its conditions of composition, which are not immediately those of India. Despite overtly declaring in both interviews and several specific poems her allegiance to Jayanta Mahapatra as poetic guru, and despite, indeed, a few painfilled gestures from that fine poet's darkly inward-curling, Orissan movements, Meena Alexander says she began writing poetry with Arabic speakers in Khartoum, where her father, a meteorologist, was stationed. She reports that her first efforts were in French, translated into Arabic for her circle of university friends there. Born in Allahabad, she had done some early schooling in St. Mary's, Poona. Then, continuing to spend part of each year with her maternal grandfather and paternal grandparents in Central Travancore, Kerala, she moved through two English-medium schools to the university in Khartoum; she then completed her formal education with a Ph.D. in English at Nottingham (the scene, with allusions to D. H. Lawrence, of some not inconsequential poems in **Stone Roots**). She also credits Brian Cox, editor of *Critical Quarterly,* with encouraging her poetic efforts in struggling Delhi-Hyderabad years of 1974 to 1979 or so, when as an appreciative "outsider," he told 'her of Jayanta Mahapatra's very relevantly indigenous and by then quite sophisticated achievements in Indo-English poetry that had also appeared in *CQ.*

That her Ph.D. dissertation developed into **The Poetic Self: Toward a Phenomenology of Romanticism** (1979) gives an indication of philosophical strengths that shape both her experiential material and her approach to it, as to poetry itself. For her artistic development reflects her highly intellectualized awareness of historical and literary continuities from Romanticism to post-symbolist esthetics, including, of course, the verbal strugglings and sensory-esthetic derangements of Mallarmé and extending to Marx and Heidegger similar tributes of interpretive incorporation.

So, unlike her ostensible guru, an Orissan college physics teacher who, until recently, has almost continuously lived in his native town, she has been thoroughly trained abroad for international (i.e., Eurocentric) post-modern writing, and, indeed, like several Indian poets in English, she makes teaching English Literature a scholarly, self-defining, relatively liberating profession. After lecturing posts in Delhi and Hyderabad from 1974 to 1979, she came with her American husband, the historian David Lelyveld, to New York City and teaches particularly Romantic poetry at Fordham University there. Thus she has available most of the professional and social and linguistic supports that American poets enjoy for developing their talents. To that extent, then, she cannot be grouped with poets in India who must write in relative isolation not only from this highly productive cultural garden (or is it an artificial green-house?) but also from a dominant English-using circumambience, an audience committed and, on the whole, limited to English and, except for translations, committed to the Amero-English culture which that language, even in its Indo-English variants, inherently embodies. Though obviously living abroad (i.e., self-exiled from India) she and her family of origin and her present family use English predominantly (if sometimes in mixed ways) inside as well as outside the home. Meena Alexander can speak—besides Hindi, French, and Arabic—her mother tongue, Malayalam, but she has not learned that alphabet, and so preserves it in her experience as an oral, never a written or readable, form and medium. That conscious Romantic preservation of innocent childhood vision along with the cultivation of English for capturing a particular Indian family's heritage (as so well exemplified by A. K. Ramanujan) could well extort a cost in nostalgic sentiment, the contradictions of disjunctive cultural revivalism (shown by R. Parthasarathy), and the strains and confusions of alienation from any coherent culture, of which Shiv K. Kumar (her sometime fairly irrelevant poetry friend in Hyderabad) often complains.

Most readers of Indo-English poetry will be alert to those hazards of modern esthetic alienation and the inherent ideology of English, and admittedly such lowered expectations can be met in Alexander, especially in her earlier books, which tend toward mannered modernist-symbolist rhetoric built on highly repetitive patterning of words and sounds with highly ambiguous syntax. While complaining obscurely of being **"Without Place"** they seem without compelling style or independent thought and feeling. Developing toward a simpler, more direct syntax, symbolism and rhetoric, the early "horrible involved poem," she has explained, was " . . . my maiden attempt to pose the problem. It is an attempt to overcome the rhetoric of false problems which are posed. . . . How can you write authentic poetry in India with English?"

In short, in Delhi and Hyderabad she muddled initially with the conventional questions of modern-modish Indo-English criticism until she found her own body of material.

> Poetry is place.
> Reach out and touch your fingernails,
>   your skin
> weep, weep at sightless wings

> that dare
> your quivering body through vacuities
> it cannot image
> cannot name

> to a century
> in her ivory season—
> frail mastodon
> with cracking tusks

> out of whose sinking hooves
> spring
> long-toothed lilies
> flaring mud.

—Part 2, section II, **"She Sings to Herself,"** from "Songs Without Place" in *Without Place* (1977).

Indeed, she is capable of this bald rhetoric even in a passage from a fine recent poem like **"My Grandmother's Mirror":**

> Shall I rinse you
> to an image the moon

> can covet?
> You wince in my eyes.

> Come to me sister:

> my figures cut in a rocking glass
> pitch, then double themselves,
> tragic concupiscence
> that heals nothing.

But, on the whole, the later poetic performance manages to be convincing that its exile status comes from more substantial and particular problems than the inevitable modern one of trying to create a personal identity in poetry. She experiences exile as challenging not simply because of her family and educational and linguistic history, but also because of her elite class and female status. For the latter two conditions of her social being, even more than the former alien emigrant history, deprive her of direct access to the dominant experience of her patriarchal motherland. Yet she does not meekly accept writing from the margins of power, but makes them the frontiers of a feminist and holistic struggle for integration.

The first section of poems in her solidly constructed, but many-faceted *House of a Thousand Doors* is mostly about her beloved, housebound patrilineal grandmother, who spent important contemplative time by the wellside in the lower garden. These are followed by partly imaginary letters of the Gandhian political activist maternal grandmother, whom she never knew and whose good friend was another female national activist, Balamaniamma (mother of Kamala Das)—"numb in the fiftieth year of her life, with the loneliness that can come from living in a woman's body, 'It is a house, a poverty, my flesh is a history,' she murmurs." (It is this woman who is the putative writer of five short prose "Tales of the Emperor" that concluded this volume.) Later poems in the book deal with her relatively innocent, even naive mother's death—**"Narcissus Never Knew Her"**—with her own travails as mother, wife and woman in New York City, and with her attempts to return to, to appropriate a shape for her present identity, her family past on both male and female sides, and their Keralan place, as in **"Poem by the Wellside"**:

> Body, you're a stranger here
> I dare not touch the scars
> of stippled flesh
> milk left when it fled,
> a dry worn belly,
> palms filled with dark water.

(Palms, by the way, are a curiously persistent image from the very first books; perhaps not irrelevantly both the royal palm tree and the hand-palm are political polling signs for the Congress Party.)

To appreciate fully the non-strident, accepting quality of Alexander's feminist focus, it is important to know that Kerala uniquely maintains an archaic form of matrilineal family trees, giving extraordinary status to the female line. That she comes from Syrian Christian stock as well, a fact which accounts for her Anglicized patronymic, compounds her felt separation from her impoverished sisters, also culturally deprived by their extreme economic and sexual marginality which exposes them to terrible abuses:

> Her life and mine are twinned
> blades on a butcher knife
> raised at dream point.
> **("She and I")**

Despite appropriate expressions of outrage and despair at lower caste and outcaste female deprivation—including a powerful prose account of an out-of-state woman raped at a Hyderabad police station—she more often subtly interweaves into more immediate personal memories the feminist position she is centrally developing, of being metaphorically exiled from significant life by her female body, as in this passage of praise and horror about her grandfather as a magnificent, typically oppressive landlord.

> I saw his stiff gold turban
> ivory cane, fit to crack a bullock's back,
> his cushioned chair

> with three foot arms
> drawn to the verandah's edge.
> Three deep in the sand they squatted there
> restless women, stiff with dirt.
> He screwed a silver eyeglass tight
> set tobacco to his lips
> then turned and spat
> past the overseer's shirt
> a woman's left knee scarred with dirt.

This is from a pared-down version of a powerful five-page poem, **"Homeward, to Jayanta and Runu Mahapatra,"** that first appeared in the Summer 1983 *Toronto South Asian Review*. It is a complex evocation of inherited class guilt and deep personal trauma at the death of her grandfather, who, after all, was crucial in encouraging her intellectual development. The predominant emotion actually is not Judaeo-Christian guilt so much as tribal, family, or caste shame alongside awe at the grandfather, all framed by gratitude for the support in making this confession given by her listeners, the dedicatees, in their cosy home in Tinkonia Bagicha, Cuttack. As, in effect, foster father and mother, the Mahapatras help her to "close the wound" of exile years in America and, more important, to own up to the horrible guilty separation she once unquestioningly enjoyed from her even more oppressed sisters. During her birthing pains in New York these women come in dream to deliver her. Cut from the book version, the poem's final threat of violent retribution, though in the key of protest rather than appropriation, deserves reprinting:

> You come armed with ten thousand sickles,
> crossed knives,
> you come under the shelter of flags coloured with
> blood.
> Joined with you
> We uncoil from flesh, station and name.
> Like fern leaves etched on a garden slope
> we rise from the mercy of dark water.

The allusive, densely metaphorical, almost vegetative manner of the final two lines more closely exemplifies Alexander's usual style than the previous pretesting—or the more traditional image that now is left to conclude this major poem:

> I hear the rumour of armies.
> The armies of the night are gathering.

In general Meena Alexander's poems do not suffer from either lack of conciseness or over-directness verging on cliché. In fact, the casual reader may be troubled by the contrary difficulties, of densely compacted allusion and images together with hyper-sophisticated phenomenological observations:

when heat warps the pupil
twisting the eye's dark

trick of overture
so fine, vision is undeceived.
(**"Narcissus Never Knew Her"**)

Such intensely private complexes of sensations and ideas may at first seem dubiously authentic. Implied analogies proliferate readily between various "exiles," especially those from using, perforce, the English language and from living an intelligent, independent existence within a woman's body far from the territory and protection of her family's "house." After we get the whole idea we may wonder whether it is largely a theoretical or poetic ploy; that is, is it mere rhetoric or philosophizing or personal excuse-making without a social and historical and experiential basis that works itself out honestly in the poems as written. She might, I think improperly, be accused of not just being overly ambitious in ideas, but of being intellectually defensive about precisely those forces of alienation because of gender, caste and class, colonialism, English higher education, liberal modernity abandoning oppressive tradition and the like, that she apparently is deploring.

. . . to read her as sending messages, propagandizing for feminism, anticolonialism, or even some merely philosophical stance is to ignore the precise effects which she achieves, not unlike those of John Ashbery.
—*John Oliver Perry*

But to read her as sending messages, propagandizing for feminism, anticolonialism, or even some merely philosophical stance is to ignore the precise effects which she achieves, not unlike those of John Ashbery. Seeking to appropriate poetically the particularity of her consciousness in all its phenomenal being, she abjures finding or creating any general truths in poems or, indeed, in living; and not in poems because not in life (as opposed to the Wallace Stevens estheticist strategy and without quite taking up the William Carlos Williams imagist gambit of "no ideas but in things."). Recognizing the challenges of writing postmodern poetry in English and of dealing in that mode with recent experience in India (though the *House of a Thousand Doors* also opens up her New York City alienations), Meena Alexander has had to give up the role that most Third World writers recognize: very simply, to teach, to bring appropriate ideas, questions, challenges, and supportive attitudes to the still largely traditional and pre-literate masses of people, and moreover, to do so in the languages and forms they understand. In desperation about their cultural

isolation many poets have retreated to estheticism or attempted to interpret "India," that figment of post-colonial imagination, to an international audience. Though living abroad, Meena Alexander has not entirely abandoned a revolutionary stance—or is it only rebellious?—that she early undertook under Frantz Fanon's banner: "a man who could never forget the often retching [i.e., vomitously wrenching?] instability of an art which truly emerges from and through oppression" (**"Exiled by a Dead Script!"** in C. Kulshestra, ed., *Contemporary Indian English Verse, An Evaluation,* 1980). What makes Meena Alexander's poetry authentically of our time and global in significance is her achieving a thoroughgoing sense of oppression *throughout* contemporary existence, whether in exile in America or in the so-called Third World, whether in a male or female body, a marginalized perspective which she knows must be broken until each of us is in her or his own first world. Since that ideal state, that ending is not available to concrete thought, cannot now even be substantially imagined, instead, we can meet in her poetry, given sufficient effort on our part, a substantial history of our contemporary living as:

"A Time of Difficulty"

Why is my mind so nearly blown away,
the far quarter
its rooftops distinct, square-jawed,
alike though in the half mist that covers
our city, doorways
leading to broken stairwells,
the prostitute's cry.
The grandmother kneels in darkness
the cracks in her kitchen wall
sucking in chaos
almost neatly

Are those children then
thumbing marbles, the glass smooth as flesh?
Our minaret is bent,
blue once, lacquered over in glory
the subtle tiles riveting the sky,
the sun unleashed to us.
The mist is a lack
there are soldiers in the mist
one hobbles a little holding his foot,
he sways against the stones
The uniforms are drab
with sweat, with dust
from the uncovered graves
we have cast outside our walls
dug with our own hands
to keep the blackness apart
from day
from light in which the children play

their marbles shining as stars
in a sky milky with cloud.
Slight holes pock the ground
a marble flips, then vanishes;
one cries out, a male child
his voice astounding the soldiers.

Violence is ill use of
small orders; a voice shot free
of the clatter of guns must hurt.
Our precise settlements are blown
as chaff from rice ·
as dross from cotton
the mattress mender heaps
onto my doorsteps, an ancient man
bent almost double, eyes gleaming with
a cataract growth:
his metal hooks glints, untangling,
refurbishing our bedding.

It was harvested not far from here
a freckled stuff that in this winter light
simmers and seethes
spreading its unbreathable aura
till all I see from my narrow chink
is swept into it, mist sky and stone
an excess I cannot word,
a livelihood in a time of difficulty.

Are the soldiers still tramping through?
I cannot see.
Are the graves drinking us?
The walls still hold, I think
a stocky tale bereft,
the crannies widening.
The children must have raced to another alley
to unseen doorways, polished thresholds,
hands with damp rags still labouring.
Will the scorpions hold their sting?

Let me conclude by resuming how this fine poem embodies in a clearly flowing meditation so many feminist issues—the Blakean prostitute's cry among broken stairwells, the grandmother dealing almost neatly with impending chaos, the children's game played without the security of religion, among darkly threatening forces and open wounds only barely held out, the male child's potential for violence "astounding the soldiers"; then a rare generalization:

Violence is ill use of
small orders; a voice shot free
of the clatter of guns must hurt.
Our precise settlements are blown
as chaff from rice
as dross from cotton

Yet rather than a female sifting rice, an ancient male figure "refurbishing our bedding" is expanded into the large concluding symbol of wholeness in living; it is his inclusive activity with cotton that protects as much as can be against the tramping soldiers, the open graves, the widening cracks, the children playing among laboring women, the potential for catastrophe.

Does the poem end with an allusion to Nissim Ezekiel's poetically famous mother, surviving a scorpion's sting to comment: "Thank God the scorpion picked on me / and spared my children"? That would suggest another stage of appropriation still to be achieved for Indian poets in English, that of constituting their own tradition of a truly Indian Poetry, one that will have to be regionally and perhaps religiously, at least attitudinally pluralistic and open. Though she is an immigrant making only sporadic physical returns to India, Meena Alexander has built her "stone roots" and contributed a solid body of work for that long-desired, ever-developing contemporary indigenous tradition. Within her latest poems she has embodied the full particularity of her many senses of exile into a substantial vision of struggling beyond suffering or mere survival toward a dynamic of integration; it is a process inevitably dangerous and destructive in its dialectical play, but solidly phenomenal, respectfully aware of male orbits and profoundly female, thoroughly achieving as poetic work that others, we can hope, will surely learn from.

John Oliver Perry (review date Winter 1989)

SOURCE: A review of *House of a Thousand Doors,* in *World Literature Today,* Vol. 63, No. 1, Winter, 1989, p. 163.

[*In the following review, Perry sketches the thematic concerns and associated characters of* House of a Thousand Doors.]

In a 1986 essay on Meena Alexander for the *Journal of South Asian Literature,* "Exiled by a Woman's Body," I praised the then-forthcoming volume *House of a Thousand Doors* and characterized the author as a substantially developed South Asian immigrant writer. Unhappily in the interim, despite publication of many of the collection's poems and brief poetic prose pieces in over a dozen different, often internationally known journals, the volume has not been widely available to inspire—as could be expected—other Indian women writers. They will find here a richly imaged, sensuously imagined voice that extends the range of Indian English poetry far beyond the ironic parameters of the Bombay poets headed by Nissim Ezekiel. Only Kamala Das, a 1986 Sahitya Akademi Award winner, offers another, rather older, more rebellious, somewhat confessional, but paradoxically restrained feminist model, one that the younger Alexander has recently come to admire. For one thing, they share the matrilineal heritage of Travancore in Kerala, and Das's mother, the Malayalam poet Balamani-amma, was a close friend of Alexander's Syrian Christian grandmother, a repeated inspirational resource throughout *House of a Thousand Doors.*

Alexander frequently visits her family in Kerala, in poetry as in life, but the poetic visitations are commonly at a distance, often as if from New York, her present residence. In the last, long, exceptionally fine poem **"Homeward,"** "I take my turn, closing the wound of America" in the company of her main poetic mentor, Jayanta Mahapatra and wife Runu in their Cuttack (Orissa) home. The main figure here is an oppressive grandfather, a powerful Travancore landlord, dying in fear and excrement yet earning pity and the hope of grace so that in the end his complex guilts and inevitable punishment too are shared. Elsewhere and widely: anxious wariness, perhaps about childhood confusions, unknown resentments, angers, emotional surprises unharbored reluctantly but repeatedly by other family members—sensitive grandmothers, aunts, and mother as well as her American lover-husband and multicultural male child Adam Kiruvella Lelyveld. Thick complexes of feelings are engendered through dramatic imaginative encounters with other local Kerala figures: poor dark women praying, stooping plantation workers, a mattress mender, beggars, a stranger in Hyderabad raped by police, children playing marbles, fleeting goddesses, a girlhood playmate. Naturally, in a more Mahapatran way, the poetry is generated also in and by local Kerala scenes: garden wells, stony landscapes, thorny and fruited trees, silted marshes and paddy fields, boiling brilliant rivers.

Occasionally New York City streets and snows and buildings interact with ghostly Indian awarenesses—or indeed Alexandrian, for Egypt too was an early home for the Alexander family. Ever entwined with these phenomena, mediating their broken shapes, is the haplessly feeling consciousness of a fearing body, the impotent source of unwilled sensations, disturbed and empty desires, cautious affirmations. The poems are substantial, phenomenal, thus eminently feminist and deeply humane, resistant as they should be to other language—or to brief sampling. Nevertheless, here is the next-to-last section from **"Grandmother's Mirror":**

> Wind skims the river
> moonlight mottles the guava bark
> tonight, for the first time
> I feel our childhoods
> would not amount to much
> in any one else's almanac.

> Ash pits where hen feathers quiver
> Bibles filled with darkness
> our dates inscribed inside
> like welts on grandmother's palm
> where boiling oil dropped.
> Odds and ends: worry beads
> smooth as olives
> a starched scarf printed
> with sun and stars,
> an *ayah* who polished chairs,
> bedstead, spitting bowls
> with her flesh
> then strolled backwards
> still waving, into water.
> Three days they searched
> in the black stuff the Pamba river
> throws up and didn't find her.

Ben Downing (review date April 1990)

SOURCE: A review of *The Storm,* in *Village Voice Literary Supplement,* No. 84, April, 1990, p. 9.

[*In the following review, Downing outlines the structure of* The Storm, *centering on the thematic significance of ritual.*]

In her introduction, Meena Alexander compares **The Storm** to "the stiff palmyra fans grandmother had hung to the wall" during Alexander's early childhood in Kerala, South India. The autobiographical poem, by invoking "the poise of a ritualised order," serves as an artifact that rescues the ancestral memory of its creator from oblivion. Elaborating the analogy, Alexander cautions that such recoveries can only be momentary, incomplete: "The severe formal folds in the fan meant that at any one point you only saw several bits of the surface, and those too, only for an instant as any one part fell into its fragmentary concatenation." Alexander's skepticism is not unwarranted given the uprootedness of her youth, with its numerous exiles in the West. Attracted to both the "hierarchical unity" of Indian tradition and a modern, Western poetics of rupture, Alexander is faced with the difficult necessity of mediating between them. It seems, therefore, almost inevitable that she would consider a stroboscopic "bits-and-pieces narrative" to be "the only sort my life can fall into."

Happily, Alexander's life slips into some pretty attractive narrative containers. This is especially true of the first section, entitled **"After the First House,"** which looks through a child's eyes at the systematic dismantling of her grandfather's home, "as if it were a burial." (At this point a certain resemblance to another poem about the shoring of fragments against one's ruin—which also bears a vaguely apocalyptic title, broken into five parts and beginning with a figurative burial—comes to mind. Hmmm.) "[S]ensing her flesh as sheer fall," the girl channels her confusion into a premature awareness of fecundity—"I saw wild ants / mating in heaps"—and of generation—"the centuries swarm through me." Later, she dreams of the house as a desacralized temple, and here Alexander's careful listing of "precious sediments" achieves a splendid, incantatory power:

> rosewood slit and furrowed
> turning in soil,
> teak, struck from the alcoves
> where the icons hung
> bent into waves

Despite Alexander's request to "[l]et me sing my song / even the crude parts of it," the second part—called **"The Travellers"**—is far less effective, relying as it does upon the didactic repetition of terms like "blood," "torment," and "tears" for emotional impact. To Alexander, the miseries of a family living in and out of airports, and those of the war-torn country it left behind, are apparently of a roughly equal magnitude; she speaks of her family's displacement as if it were a diaspora of epic proportions. Our sympathy is not only appealed to—it is demanded. But immigration also brings moments of bittersweet humor:

> Who can spell out
> the supreme ceremony
> of tea tins
> wedged
> under the frozen food counter?

Ritual redeems—this, at bottom, is what *The Storm* has to say. First, however, Alexander must weather a disturbance that—not surprisingly—turns out to be personal rather than meteorological in nature. After a half-successful attempt to align her own life with the *Ramayana* in **"Sita's Story,"** she comes face-to-face with the "bleak / vertiginous source" of her craft. The poem folds back upon itself, retrograde, questioning its own authority. How will she uphold the legends from which her land arises? (In a fascinating endnote, Alexander explains that Kerala is said to emerge from the spot in the ocean where the matricidal Parasurama flung away his bloodied ax.) Finally, she arrives at the climactic realization in **"The Storm"** that "these ceremonial motions / of the damned / healed us of ourselves / all exile ended."

Having tethered *The Storm* to the fixity of ritualization, Alexander finds in **"Aftermath"** all her elements "clarifying as line after line / unpacks into sight." In the crucible

of art, the self that reflects, agonizes, assembles, comes to terms with the earlier self that merely experienced. Suddenly fragments are less sharp at the edges, narrative no longer desultory. The poem that is resolved in itself rings with a specific grace:

> With the bleached mesh of root
> exposed after rainfall
> my bitten self cast back
> into its intimate wreckage
> each jot poised, apart, particular
> lovely and rare.
> The end of life delved back
> into the heart of it all.

John Oliver Perry (review date Spring 1991)

SOURCE: A review of *Nampally Road,* in *World Literature Today,* Vol. 65, No. 2, Spring, 1991, pp. 364-65.

[*In the following review, Perry considers the narrative implications of the feminist sociopolitical perspective of* Nampally Road.]

Based, naturally, on her own experience, ***Nampally Road,*** the first novel by Meena Alexander, India's foremost woman poet in English, for the past decade living in America, was begun in 1979, while she still lived and taught in Hyderabad. Her heroine Mira, who, like Meena, had just spent four years earning a Ph.D. dealing with Wordsworth at Nottingham University, now finds herself trying to understand her relationship as a foreign-returned academic to the ongoing social struggles in India. The classes and college where she teaches—in Sarojini Naidu's old "Golden Threshhold" home—get only one full-fledged scene of their own, but there are abundant descriptions of the nearby streets, monuments (especially the physically isolated and totally ignored Gandhi statue), and public buildings: cafés; "hotel" rooming houses; a sad Divine Life/Hare Krishna temple largely for foreign devotees; a one-room clinic, where Mira's protector-landlady-doctor, called "Little Mother," ministers to India's many miserable, wounded, and ill destitutes. Most of the novel is set in Little Mother's house with its courtyard, roof terrace, overarching pipal tree, and blaring Sagar Cinema hall next door, much frequented by their maidservant and her crass friend from across the way, Laura Ribaldo, who ultimately leaves Hyderabad for the supposedly rich consumer life of Calgary.

The issues raised by the action are complex and multiple, interweaving feminist with other political and social concerns. Mira, said to be resisting an arranged marriage by her mother in Kerala, freely, almost insignificantly, "takes off her sari for" Ramu, her intellectual companion and political conscience. The latter is deeply involved in Leftist-oriented struggles against a tyrannical chief minister of the state modeling his rule on that of the "iron-fisted lady," Indira Gandhi, during the 1975-77 Emergency. Margaret Thatcher also comes in for a brief bashing; so putting women in high political position does not seem a viable alternative to vicious male violence. What occurs as presumably "revolutionary" violence is, first, the burning down of a police station, a spontaneous response by a mob in revenge for police-army attacks on peaceful labor-union demonstrations and most immediately for the beating and gang rape by police of a "detainee," Rameeza Be, and the murder of her husband. Those like Ramu attempting to organize the downtrodden plan the next response carefully and direct the violence against the image of the corrupt leader himself, Limca Gowda, by burning down during his birthday celebration his elaborately erected cardboard city and VIP pavilion. Mira, having twice been brought by Ramu from Little Mother's house to see the scarcely surviving rape victim, first in the burning police station, then in a "safe house," remains largely an aghast, confused, and grief-stricken spectator. In the conclusion she leaves the carnage of the Chief Minister's celebration to find that Rameeza Be is at Little Mother's and is now ready to be nursed back to human life and touching.

Whether, as Ramu once suggests, Mira, as a writer testifying to oppression, exempts herself from participating in revolutionary planning and action, or whether this exemption stems from her bourgeois antipathy toward violence or from her unresolved socially defined gender roles (as another "Little Mother," as an esthete-academic steeped in Wordsworthian irrelevancies, as her lover's mistress), is not determined. She sees her self as divided, escaping commitment by leaping "from one woman's body to another." The action closes before these issues are fully faced by Mira or the author, who, as her poetry reveals, still in 1988, when she finished the novel, married to an American academic, mother of two children, on the verge of tenure and prestigious positions at two universities, was all the more uncertain of her own social obligations to the oppressed—in India, in the Third World, in New York City.

Police gang-rape scandals are an apparently permanent feature of contemporary Indian political and social life, as are the oppressive personality cults and tyrannical behavior of local and national politicians with their elite guards, but neither India nor the Third World has any monopoly on such atrocities. So in all three cultural venues both bourgeois and revolutionary socialist feminists will find Meena Alexander's subtle, deeply evocative, often poetic novel touching their own wounds from generally less violent but

surely politically analogous ravages of body and spirit. A major contribution to South Asian-American fiction far exceeding, say, Bharati Mukherjee's novels in cultural richness, psychological complexity, and sociopolitical—not to mention feminist—sophistication, Alexander's first novel one can suppose represents her renewed initiative toward more socially focused writing about contemporary life, in America as well as India, from a self-exiled multicultural Indian woman's perspective.

Nina Mehta (review date Fall 1991)

SOURCE: "Teaching the Sylvan Swami," in *Belles Lettres*, Vol. 7, No. 1, Fall, 1991, p. 46.

[*In the following review, Mehta praises the ironic tone and confident narration of* Nampally Road.]

When the priest, the butcher, the psychiatrist, and the candlestick maker can't explain and organize the world teeming around us, there's always the poet. Or so Mira Kannadical thinks. After four years of graduate school in England, Mira has found her guru: Wordsworth. She'll return to India, teach a course on her sylvan swami at a local college in Hyderabad and write poetry that will "stitch it all together: my birth in India a few years after national independence, my colonial education, my rebellion against the arranged marriage my mother had in mind for me, my years of research in England."

Nampally Road is Meena Alexander's first novel. It is an absorbing, lyrical story about a twenty-five-year-old who tentatively realizes that her poetic vision cannot accommodate the grim reality and chaos of daily life in Hyderabad. Like Mira, Alexander was born in India in 1951. Like her protagonist, she examines literature's ability to reveal and heal the dislocations that fracture life in a postcolonial, riot-riven land. Like Mira, Alexander is a poet, although unlike Mira she has three elegant collections of verse to her credit.

In 1976, when Mira arrives in Hyderabad, Indira Gandhi's national state of emergency is in full force: Civil liberties have been suspended, and lives are frustrated by new rules and dogmas. Taxes and tempers are on the rise. Mira and Ramu, a fellow instructor at Sona Nivas College, see a peaceful demonstration by a group of orange sellers violently suppressed by the local militia. A woman is gang raped, beaten, and imprisoned by a pack of policemen. Riots erupt and, just as quickly, subside. Against this tumultuous background, officials busy themselves readying Hyderabad for the gala birthday celebrations of Limca Gowda, the city's imperious Chief Minister.

Mira continues her lectures on Wordsworth, but begins to see herself as "a trickster at a fair who swallows pins and plates and apple and struggles to make them all rise up, whole and clean from her guts." A student challenges her by suggesting that Limca Gowda's public relations films are not such a far cry from the sententious poems of the Wye Valley poet.

Mira tries to write poetry, but can't: "The lines sucked in chunks of the world, but then collapsed in on themselves." Wordsworth, she remembers, "hated crowds." He wrote in a state of grace: tranquil solitude. He was able to separate his "inner" and "outer" world. Unable to distance herself from her surroundings, afraid that her poetic impulse is self-indulgent, Mira casts about for a new pundit. Should she follow the example of Ramu, her social activist lover? Durgabai, the selfless doctor with whom she stays? Swami Chari, who promises that nothing exists except Brahmin? In the end, Mira forges her own makeshift world view—one that's still a bit sentimental, but that at least sees individuals where once were "witnesses."

The dialogue in **Nampally Road** sometimes veers toward the bombastic. "The best I can do," Mira explains to Ramu when he tells her she's too quixotic, "is leapfrog over the cracks in the earth, over the black fissures. From one woman's body into another. From this Mira that you know into Little Mother, into Rameeza, into Rosamma, into that woman in the truck on the way to the Public Gardens. A severed head, a heart, a nostril with a breathing hole, a breast, a bloodied womb. What are we?" Ramu may think Mira is histrionic, but he resorts to lofty pronouncements just as frequently: "We shall live in the streets, my love. Like beggars, like birds!"

Alexander is at her most sophisticated when her tone is ironic—when she describes the political machinations of Limca Gowda, the pending birthday festivities, the history of Hyderabad, or Indira Gandhi, "our khaki-clad, iron-fisted Prime Minister . . . of the immaculate lineage and Swiss schooling, who on her New York trips made small type in the *Times* by buying her mascara from Bergdorf's."

Mira maneuvers through a welter of demonstrations, riots, and relationships in **Nampally Road.** And while she struggles to find a voice that can encompass the disorienting events in her life, at least we can rest assured that Meena Alexander has found hers.

Nicola Trott (review date November 1992)

SOURCE: A review of *Women in Romanticism,* in *Review of English Studies,* Vol. 43, No. 172, November, 1992, pp. 569-71.

[*In the following excerpt, Trott examines the methodology and themes of* Women in Romanticism, *noting the defects and strengths of Alexander's views.*]

Meena Alexander takes Wollstonecraft to be a woman *in* Romanticism, rather than a precursor. Her book [**Women in Romanticism**] is most keenly aware, though, of the ways in which the term needs to be redefined if women writers are to have a place of their own within the Romantic estate. The three women in question—Wollstonecraft, Wordsworth, and Shelley, two tragically blood-related, one the sibling of the chief Romantic poet—work surprisingly well together. Alexander exploits their sharp dissimilarities, and sees them partly in terms of historical change, but there are unusual links made, too, as for example between Dorothy Wordsworth, Mary Shelley, and the Lucy poems.

Although she erects a conceptual framework around the ideas of self and subjectivity, the body and maternity, knowledge and power, Alexander's method is essentially biographical. The undogmatic stance is most effective where Dorothy is concerned, and the book might readily have been a monograph. Theoretical feminists will no doubt find the approach tame, even timid; of Dorothy's position in *Tintern Abbey,* for instance, Alexander writes:

> While it is difficult to doubt the acute, pained love the poet bears for his sister, it is equally difficult from a feminist perspective not to acknowledge the sister's symbolic presence as subservient to both genius and desire, gaining power precisely insofar as she is gathered into his vision.

In general, the tone of the book is uneven; this measured justness elsewhere lapses into the gauche, and the introductory quality of the 'Women Writers' imprint militates against Alexander's thematic sophistication. Her theme is the problematic relation of women writers to the central and centralizing assumptions of Romanticism, as it is masculinely defined. Women are seen as tangential to and displaced by the male formulations of the period, including the myths of their own nature, and indeed of Nature *per se.* At the same time, Alexander's project is to relocate these myths in such way that it becomes possible to think in specific terms of a 'Romantic Feminine'. The placing of women in Romanticism also generates a series of qualifying insights into its male practitioners:

> It seems to me that it can only render our reading of Wordsworth more complex, more true, to point out that the centrality of the ego he forged through his astonishing rituals of perception was perfectly in tune with the societal permissions granted the male.

There does remain the distinct problem, never really taken

up by Alexander, of identifying essentialist 'male' and 'female' Romanticisms. On a practical level, however, the book rarely deals in crass oppositions. Alexander displays an awareness of difference among the male Romantics, as well as a desire to see the female in terms of their masculine others and brothers, as the case may be. A wide range of works are examined within a slim volume and with varying success, but the effect is not usually superficial. It is of Dorothy that Alexander has most scholarly expertise, and disappointing, therefore, that the texts themselves, even where relatively unknown or available only in manuscript, are under-quoted. But though at times I found myself impatient with the 'bite-size' sections, with the lack of quotation and alarming distaste for commas, the book offers an enlarged and enhanced view of Romanticism with many suggestions to pursue.

Bruce King (review date Spring 1993)

SOURCE: A review of *Night-Scene, the Garden*, in *World Literature Today*, Vol. 67, No. 2, Spring, 1993, p. 444.

[*In the following review, King situates the themes, structure, and voice of* Night-Scene, the Garden *in the context of Alexander's other poetry collections.*]

A Syrian Christian Indian, Meena Alexander attended university in the Sudan, wrote her first poetry in French, wrote a British doctoral dissertation on German phenomenology, then returned to India, where she published three books of poetry before marrying an American. She now teaches English literature in New York. Someone for whom poetry is more a process—usually consisting of intensely personal, somewhat obscure lyric sequences—than a set of polished artifacts, she early took up a body of basic symbols which recur throughout her verse, symbols which act as images for parts of the self and its desires as well as for the external world. A continual exile moving between countries and cultures, a student of philosophy, she is concerned with the construction of the self and its relationship to memory, history, actuality, and notions of identity, all the while aware that the discovery of the self through the act of writing is equally imaginative and based as much on wishes, false memory, and fantasy as on fact. If some passages of her poems appear facile in sentiment and underworked, others are intense and complex.

The ten-part *Night-Scene, the Garden* is a poetic sequence in several voices and has been performed on-stage. It is less obscure than Alexander's early poetry, and some of its apparently unpoetic lines are strong in speech rhythms. Its focus is mostly on family and local events associated with Alexander's maternal home in Kerala, southern India, and

with her relationship to the past and to her mother. Attention is also given to the father, a grandmother, the fate of several women, the illegal possession of the house by others, its repossession, and its subsequent history as the land is divided among the family. Among the many themes, however, the most significant is a childhood experience in a garden, when Alexander felt she could only possess the world through being a poet—which looks forward to her creation of herself through writing, a process realized by *Night-Scene.* If Alexander is in the tradition of southern Indian poets who often reveal a nostalgia for close family ties and in the tradition of Kerala women poets who in writing of the houses of their mothers and grandmothers affirm the matrilineal rights distinctive of that society, she is also very much a product of a Western literary education. T. S. Eliot's *Four Quartets* is present in some phrasing, rhyming, and construction, but more influentially in the general model of the significance of the garden scene, the various voices and characters, the use of the past, the meditational mode (if more intense and dramatic here), and the way places become a starting point for various experiences that the poem shapes into a comprehensive vision.

Maria Couto (review date 7 April 1993)

SOURCE: "Voices of Empire," in *Times Literary Supplement,* No. 4697, April 7, 1993, p. 22.

[*In the following review, Couto traces the influence and thematic significance of colonialism in* Fault Lines.]

Both these books—one a memoir [*Fault Lines* by Meena Alexander], the other a vivid and enthralling playback of voices [*Unbecoming Daughters of the Empire* by Shirley Chew and Anna Rutherford, eds.]—unfold private lives stamped by Empire and shaped by emerging forces of independence and nationalism. Meena Alexander, an Indian poet, novelist and academic now based in New York, makes clear that the geographical and cultural disruptions in her life compel her to write. She is inspired by a childhood and adolescence full of the contradictions of a feudal Syrian Christian ethos: her grandfather was a theologian and nationalist, her father, a civil servant who had been educated at Imperial College, London, a royalist at heart yet devoted to the secular ideals proclaimed by an independent India. This was a family which valued the social gospel of uplift for the poor but did not question its own privilege, or the system of values familiar to the educated elite in the subcontinent.

From this seedbed, Alexander's poetic narrative develops through her awareness of the growth of the Communist Party in India which successfully ran her home state of Kerala for many years. Despite the upheavals inflicted on the family by the claims of her father's professional life, annual homecomings which sometimes stretched to six months—from Khartoum to the village in Kerala, from English and Arabic to Malayalam, her mother tongue, from desert spaces in the Sudan to the shades of the vast ancestral house and the five-acre garden—drew the child Meena into a sensuous world where her grandfather led her "from sound to sound, from sight to sight, a consonance of sense, a shimmering thing that wrapped us both".

Alexander's deep bond with her maternal grandfather, and her honest appraisal of the histories of the women in her family, underline the intensity of her reflections
—Nicola Trott

Alexander's deep bond with her maternal grandfather, and her honest appraisal of the histories of the women in her family, underline the intensity of her reflections, as they do another brilliant evocation, Sara Suleri's *Meatless Days,* which re-creates her family and society in Pakistan. Both writers are torn by the conflicting demands of the life of the mind and the traditional requirements of femininity. Informing it all is an ancient matrilineal tradition, a fairly widespread grasp of the English language alongside a rich literary heritage in the mother tongue, and a history of Christianity in India which did not come with the Empire but is as old as Thomas the Apostle. Exploring all these factors might have made for a clearer picture of Alexander's complex background. In the event, the episodic form of **Fault Lines** is reminiscent of Michael Ondaatje's *Running in the Family,* his poetic account of growing up in Sri Lanka. Ondaatje joyfully celebrates what Edward Said calls "the reality of hybridity", while Meena Alexander, with the old nostalgias, the talk of wholeness and innocence gone, seeks space for ethnicity to struggle towards social justice and human dignity.

The English language and colonial history link the contributors to Shirley Chew and Anna Rutherford's *Unbecoming Daughters of the Empire,* an account of growing up in the colonies and in Britain which reveals how colonial power in India and Africa meant loss of the mother tongue, loss of self-esteem, struggle and violence. In Australia, the inequality was largely that between Protestant and Catholic. There is hardly a glimpse of the fatal shore. Some writers, Margaret Atwood among them, contribute excerpts from fiction.

The focus on school life, interesting and moving as it is, prevents the essayists from confronting the cultural complexities produced by colonial education, a phenomenon aptly likened to schizophrenia by the Indian novelist Nayantara Sahgal, who does grapple with the issues. The

niece of Jawaharlal Nehru, Sahgal grew up thinking that going to gaol was a career. The Ghanaian novelist Ama Ata Aidoo writes of her grandfather who was tortured to death. The counter-testimony is provided by Marina Warner, who confronts with sensitivity her planter ancestors' complicity in the enterprise of empire. Her exploration goes far deeper than partying on Victoria Day.

Lauren Glen Dunlap (review date Summer 1993)

SOURCE: A review of *Fault Lines,* in *Belles Lettres,* Vol. 8, No. 4, Summer, 1993, p. 43.

[*In the following review, Dunlap notes the stylistic features of* Fault Lines.]

Like Daly and Behar, poet Meena Alexander employs images of weaving and crossing borders in **Fault Lines.** A dizzying multiplicity of threads and borders distinguishes this memoir by an Indian woman who has lived many places and speaks many languages. There is a litany of cities within India: Khartoum, where she entered university at age 13; Nottingham, where she began her doctorate at 18; and that city where she currently lives, "where the whole world swarms," New York. And the languages: Malayalam, Hindi, Arabic, English, French. Of many worlds and of no world, her life in pieces, Alexander confronts radical dislocation and female invisibility. She recounts her struggles to find her voice, artistically and sometimes literally, as she moves in a world where wisdom holds that "The first thing a girl should learn is when to keep her silence," where only boys are taught "to read maps, figure out the crossroads of the world." Alexander's voice is a treasure. Having introduced how the memoir was solicited as part of The Feminist Press's Cross-Cultural Memoir Series, she begins:

> Multiple birth dates ripple, sing inside me, as if a long stretch of silk were passing through my fingers. I think of the lives I have known for forty years, the lives unknown, the shining geographies that feed into the substance of any possible story I might have. As I make up a *katha,* a story of my life, the lives before me, around me, weave into a net without which I would drop ceaselessly. They keep me within range of difficult truths, the exhilarating dangers of memory.

The memoir's consideration of poetic voice, and how it touches on ethnicity and on social injustice, ends with a garden that is a palimpsest. Back with her family for what may be the last time before her father's death, Alexander steals out to the old incense tree in her mother's garden, kneeling to touch her cheek to its roots, taste the raw earth. And beneath the scene in Tiruvella is that still more ancient garden where there is peace erased—but still barely visible, if only for a few moments, in a moonlit garden, back home . . . far from home.

Shilpa Davé (essay date 1993)

SOURCE: "The Doors to Home and History: Post-Colonial Identities in Meena Alexander and Bharati Mukherjee," in *Amerasia Journal,* Vol. 19, No. 3, 1993, pp. 103-13.

[*In the following essay, Davé compares the narrative strategies of Bharati Mukherjee's* Middleman and Other Stories *and Alexander's* Nampally Road, *concentrating on their different approaches to and uses of Western stereotyped definitions of cultural identity.*]

> The very practice of remembering and rewriting leads to the formation of politicized consciousness and self-identity. Writing often becomes the context through which new political identities are forged. It becomes a space for struggle and contestation about reality itself.
> Chandra T. Mohanty, *Cartographies of Silence: Third World Women and the Politics of Feminism*

"How does history make us?" is a question posed in Meena Alexander's novel *Nampally Road.* This question is the basis for my examination of post-colonial inquiry and studies of identity in Asians of Indian descent. The past influences the present and thus Indian cultural heritage is inherently tied to British imperialism. While most people would not deny this relationship, post-Independence Indian writers are still often trapped in the position of a Western colonial subject. Be it Western education, American lifestyle, or the pursuit of the American dream, Indian history is usually marked by what the British did for India and how Western technology and education brought India into the twentieth century. In "Three Women's Texts and a Critique of Imperialism," Gayatri Spivak notes that modern-day writers fall prey to the ever present shadow of imperialism as "attempts to construct the 'Third World Woman' [or person] as a signifier remind us that the hegemonic definition is itself caught up within the history of imperialism." She argues that the imperial narrative overdetermines the re-written post-colonial text in which the "new" narrative is always read in the context of the "primary" text. Thus the written works of immigrant Indian authors or Indian Americans have deep roots in imperialism. The commentary being made on India or immigrant cultures by authors such as Bharati Mukherjee and Meena Alexander is consistently influenced by a history dependent upon Western tradition; in particular, a Western culture that is idealized and where success is measured by assimilation of Western ideals and strategies.

However, Audre Lorde warns that "the master's tools will never dismantle the master's house. They may allow us to temporarily beat him at his own game, but they will never be able to bring about genuine change." And it is Lorde's words that differentiate Mukherjee's and Alexander's approaches towards post-colonial Asian American literature.

I would like to argue that both Bharati Mukherjee and Meena Alexander in their respective works, *Middleman and Other Stories,* and *Nampally Road,* inherit and utilize the traditions of Western education and writing in an attempt to resist imposed stereotypical definitions of different cultures by the West. However, the methods they employ differ. Bharati Mukherjee uses the master's tools of Western narratives to critique immigrant life in the United States, but she does not propose any active processes of change. Instead she becomes a passive recorder of these events and eventually her characters are co-opted by the American dream. Alexander, on the other hand, questions her identity in relation to the past by addressing both her relationship and her main character's to cultural history and to writing itself.

Mukherjee's *The Middleman and Other Stories,* is a panorama of characters who adopt, if not always by conscious choice, Western ideals over the tenets of their own cultural heritage. Two stories that take these post-colonial positions are "Buried Lives" and "Orbiting." "Buried Lives" focuses on the travails of a Sri Lankan school teacher who attempts to illegally immigrate to Canada via Germany. The protagonist, Mr. Venkatesan, is a forty-nine-year old Catholic boys' school teacher who decides to leave Sri Lanka and find refuge in the Western frontier. His identity becomes an invention of his Western teachings, and when he no longer has his school teacher's English lesson plans to guide him, he takes his cues from English novels and Canadian tourist brochures and seeks his fortune in the West. The story "Orbiting," on the other hand, occurs in America and focuses on an Italian American woman surrounded by cultural diversity. The title indicates the position of the narrator as well as the people around her who move "in orbit" around the dominant society. All aspects of foreign culture are judged against the backdrop of white American society. Mukherjee shows that the influence of dominant culture upon identity is not limited only to immigrants but to different pockets of American culture such as the Amish. American culture, like British imperialism, interprets and develops a portrait of the "Other" that manufactures cultural identities as static roles.

Mr. Venkatesan's identity is one of the buried lives referred to in the title, "Buried Lives," and also refers to Matthew Arnold's poem, "The Buried Life," which discusses the wish to act upon pent-up desires. Mr. Venkatesan is buried under colonial influences and the mentality of the British Raj forty years after the independence of Sri Lanka. He measures his own life with the West as the standard of comparison. He desires to study in Oxford where "[h]e'd have studied Law. Maybe he'd have married an English girl and loitered abroad." Marriage to the English would give him access to the power of the British. By possessing a white wife, he would become British. And so, even though Mr. Venkatesan disapproves of activists with "family responsibilities sticking their heads between billy clubs as though they were still fighting the British," he is still obsessed with the British. But instead of fighting them, he seeks to emulate his masters. He participates in the British imperial project to create the domesticated native; a subject who forgoes his/her culture in favor of a superior culture.

He attempts to lay claim to British culture by applying to graduate schools in the West. He pleads in his statement of purpose to be allowed to become one of the English:

> I live my life through their imagined lives. And Hath not a Tamil eyes, heart, ears, nose, throat, to adapt the words of the greatest Briton. Yes, I am a Tamil. If you prick me, do I not bleed? If you tickle me, do I not laugh? Then, if I dream, will you not give me a chance, respected Sir, as only you can?

Venkatesan is a passive figure that cannot act but instead desires to be acted on. He longs for the adventure and the knowledge as only the West can provide. Mukherjee is obviously exaggerating this characteristic by including the letter. Yet what is she endorsing in her writing? Her characters give up their homeland like Venkatesan to pursue adventure and the promises of the West. By doing so, they sacrifice their own identity in favor of the manufactured idealism found in books and travel brochures.

Venkatesan does not end up in America or Britain, instead he remains in Hamburg. The presence of the Germans is particularly interesting because the country is like a middle ground for Asians of Indian descent. At the end of the story, Venkatesan can become a German citizen and thus transform himself into a member of the European community, but the antagonism displayed by the blond German foreshadows his unwelcome reception. The details associated with Venkatesan's colonial subject position draw attention to Mukherjee's sensitivity to identities that are manipulated by Western culture. Yet she does not explore the loss and sacrifice involved in the choices of her characters. Is this ending really a happy one? A shotgun marriage to a naturalized German madam does not seem very promising.

Venkatesan's future stems from a past dominated by the notion that "West is best" and he seems ready to act in any way that will ensure him a place in the West. If Mukherjee is commenting on how Indians and Sri Lankans are influ-

enced by the colonial past, she does not offer any resolutions or any attempt to change the status quo. Instead she highlights the problems, and as a result she falls into the post-colonial trap. In an interview, Mukherjee says, "For me, America is an idea, an abstract entity. America is a frontier that needs constant pushing." In her fiction, the gritty realities are just as important as the dreams of her characters, but in her interviews, the realities take backstage to the "frontier of opportunities" provided by America. Why not offer up a strategy to push post-colonial identities beyond the shadow of imperialism and orientalism?

Like Venkatesan, the characters in "Orbiting" attempt to establish roots and lay claim to American culture. As a second generation Italian American who works within the traditions of the dominant culture, Renata adopts Thanksgiving as a ritual holiday for her family. The cultural icons of the holiday are fleshed out during the story. The gathering of the family is part of tradition as well as the incorporation of new ideas from both Ro and Renata. The turkey in the Frigidaire, carved by an Afghan dagger, accompanied by traditional Italian crostolis marks an infusion of multiculturalism into the celebration of an American holiday as each character seeks to set him/herself as a part of American culture. For example, Renata's father prides himself that he was a fetus in his mother's womb when his parents came to America. Although he claims he feels grounded in the United States, he continually tries to justify his roots by watching sports and drinking liquor, imitating the stereotypical American male he sees on television. Renata's mother, on the other hand, attempts to "find herself" by taking college classes to develop outside of her lower class immigrant identity. Western education is her ticket to acceptance in America.

This dissatisfaction with identity extends to their daughters who change their names. Renata becomes Rindy and Carla becomes Cindi. American culture shapes their identities but in this case, they also choose to make these changes. These fictionalized names becomes a construct for an acceptable ethnicity. The family has an uncomfortable sense of ambiguity about where they fit into society. The adoption of a traditional Thanksgiving dinner becomes an attempt to define themselves as a unified entity in terms of the dominant culture.

The three outsiders who are invited to share in the family ritual comment on American culture by their position as "other." Brent is Cindi's husband, and, as the son of the member of an Amish community, struggles to break out of the stereotype associated with the Amish. He changes his name from Schwartzendruber to Schwartz. Brent is similar to and a more extreme version of Venkatesan, in his desire to be American. Moreover, Brent constructs himself to fit into "normal" definitions of the American male. Yet

Cindi comments, "Poor Brent. He feels so divided. He shouldn't have to take sides." Brent adopts the persona of a successful businessman who drinks hard, follows sports, and dresses well. But according to Renata, Brent seems falsely constructed compared to the distinct difference of Roashan. In Ro, Renata wants to fuse his comforting foreignness and the encompassing dominant society into one:

> I shall teach him how to walk like an American, how to dress like Brent but better, how to fill up a room as Dad does instead of melting and blending but sticking out in the Afghan way. In spite of the funny way he holds himself and the funny way he moves his head from side to side . . . Ro is Clint Eastwood, scarred hero and survivor.

She drapes him in the dominant culture blanket even though she herself is not a fully assimilated American. In order for Renata to fully relate to Ro, she must create a fictional identity for him. However, in this light, an invented identity does not necessarily function in a negative sense. Instead, she attempts to change the boundaries of his relation to the dominant culture. The only problem stems from the fact that she should be concentrating on her marginalized identity. By projecting onto Ro, she is as guilty as the pervading culture, of shaping him into an idealized version of the immigrant. Ro thus becomes subject to Renata's appropriation of his Third World identity.

Mukherjee's stories center around the pervasiveness of the dominant culture in immigrant society. She concludes that the influence of Western society cannot be mitigated, and some sort of assimilation must occur. Her solutions take drastic turns, many times requiring a permanent sacrifice upon the part of her characters. On the other hand, the America portrayed makes room for different cultures, ideals, and individuals within the system which expands the horizons of American culture. The disturbing aspect in Mukherjee's stories is that in order to be culturally accepted in the United States, the "old" culture must be left behind. Mukherjee depicts a world of opportunity but also one that demands a price—in a compromise of identity.

Mukherjee's viewpoint may not always appease critics such as myself, but her words are a launching pad from which cultural definitions may be questioned and modified to offer some practical strategies for transforming identity.

The protagonist of Meena Alexander's *Nampally Road*, Mira Kannadical, struggles to relate her Western education to the political unrest taking place around her in Hyderabad. The narrator and her friends recognize the artificial constructs of the nation and the government and reconstruct their surroundings through their collective vision. The story concentrates on the development of cultural identity as a stabilizing force. The narrator is a writer and teacher who attempts to negotiate her Indian identity with her Western education upon her return to a politically unstable India. During her first weeks back, Mira is caught up in the violence around her: the protest of the gang rape of a young woman, Rameeza, and the murder of Rameeza's husband by the chief minister's corrupt policemen. Mira is unsure where she and her ideas fit in a community that demonstrates and riots against the local government. The circumstances of this novel are similar to Mukherjee's story "Buried Lives," however, instead of fleeing India, Mira strives to express a fluid view of culture through her attempts to write and teach in India amidst the constant political protests. The incisive presence of Mira permeates the novel, piecing together the images and people around her.

Identity is measured through language in this novel. As the novel occurs in India, Mira becomes a member of the dominant society. And yet Indian culture has been modified by Western culture: the government communicates in English, Western schools are considered the best educational opportunities, and America is the land where success is possible. Instead of abandoning her cultural heritage and burying herself in her Western education, Mira seeks to relate her knowledge of Romanticism to the politically explosive situation in Hyderabad. Thus, the ideas she teaches and writes are affected by both Indian and English cultures and influence her expression.

From the onset, Mira's identity is etched in difference:

> Though I tried I really could not write my story. I could not figure out a line or a theme for myself. The life that made sense was all around me in Little Mother and Ramu and the young students, the orange sellers and the violent and wretched, ourselves included. No one needed my writing. It could make no difference . . . I had no clear picture of what unified it all, what our history might mean. We were in it, all together, that's all I knew.

Her inability to write reflects her difficulty in reconciling the historical past and the present in a language of her own making. Trinh T. Minh-Ha, in *Woman, Native, Other*, states: "The structure is therefore not something given, entirely external to the person who structures, but a projection of that person's way of handling realities, her narratives." When Mira questions her use of form and vision she pushes at the boundaries of the traditional narratives available to her. The old narrative structures do not suit her so she tries to find her own answers by relating her class curriculum to a political rally.

Mira seeks connection through her knowledge of language. In the chapter entitled "Wordsworth in Hyderabad," she searches for a new vision with which to interpret her world. She focuses on the optical center with "lenses [that] are all kinds of color, pink, purple, blue, green, gray. See how we can transform the world?" Unlike Venkatesan in "Buried Lives," Mira is not satisfied with her British education. She desires a vision that can bring India and Romanticism together. Her vision is not singular but full of multiple images. Mira slowly recognizes the layered aspects of her identity. The gaze, be it of the reader or the writer, frames a response to the world as an object. This idea fits in with Mira's definition of Romanticism as "the belief in self, the sense that the object has value insofar as it is lit by the gaze." Her attempt to unify the optical center, Wordsworth, the orange sellers, the rape of the imprisoned woman, and the board meeting, is interrupted by her political activist boyfriend, Ramu. The politics of the situation defy any type of coherence of the situation on her part. This lack of unity, however, does not leave the narrator hollow. Instead, an almost positive affirmation of these events unfold in her mind that returns to the "infinite[ly] layer[ed]" identity. Mira is attempting to see several visions through several pairs of eyes. Her gaze is influenced by her different identities as a woman, an Indian, a Western educated teacher, and a writer.

Mira begins to see a form outside of the colonial narrative and essentially *out* of the written word. Instead, dream speech and dream sharing becomes a way to communicate outside the colonized word. By examining the process of narrative, Mira begins to understand the influence of the West upon her innermost identity, her position as a writer. She realizes the way she writes becomes the mold she is constructed in, and that narrative, form, and identity are inter-related, not separate entities. Trinh T. Minh-Ha's suggestion: "It is . . . as if form and content stand apart; as if the structure can remain fixed, immutable, independent of and unaffected by the changes the narratives undergo; as if structure can only function as a standard mold with the old determinist schema of cause and product." Alexander challenges the polar definitions of form and content and attempts to unite them. By the end of the novel, Mira finds expression through a community of women; a dream language that is unique to Rameeza, Durgabai, and Mira. Alexander's solution is to discard the English written word, developed by the West and by men. Instead she embraces a communal dream language that allows the women to express themselves, and escape from the boundaries of Western definitions.

The failure of normal lines of communication is also seen in Rameeza, the woman who was raped by guards in the jail. Verbal language cannot express her pain and anguish and so she resorts to a simple drawing of multiple triangles to express herself. The process, however, is not so simple and serves as a physical metaphor for Mira's inability to write:

> She [Rameeza] picked up the pencil in her fist, a woman unused to writing. But it wasn't just that. The skin had come off on the insides of her fingers, and a fist was better.

Just as Rameeza improvises in her situation, Mira must also change some of her tools to effectively communicate her thoughts. Ramu tries to impose his own meaning upon the drawing as a model of the jailhouse in order to serve his own political agenda; but only Mira is able to interpret the lack of language as intense pain. The translation of Rameeza's pain is Mira's first success in articulating her own identity. By communicating the language of others, Mira begins to understand her own relationship to language. At the end of the novel, Rameeza's mouth is only partially healed, but her healing promises a new accessible language to the women in Mira's life: Durgabai and Rameeza.

The language that links them is dream imagery. Dreaming represents another plane of communication and identity. Mira recognizes this fact when she explains her position to her boyfriend Ramu:

> Look, given the world as it is, there's nowhere people like us can be whole. The best I can do is leapfrog over the cracks in the earth, over the black fissures. From one woman's body into another. From this Mira that you know into Little Mother, into Rameeza, into Rosamma.

In the end, a community of women linked together by shared multiple visions serve as a metaphor for the layered identity. Mira becomes a fluid identity of three different women with three voices. They (the three women in the house and the multiple identities in Mira) reside together, expressing themselves as the situation dictates. This collective identity becomes the catalyst of Mira's writing in the future. Mira sees herself mirrored in the figure of Rameeza at the end of the novel: "As I moved forward the figure advanced. A woman. I knew her from my real life and from my dreams." This connection between worlds begins to break through Mira's writer's block. "She [Rameeza] edged closer to me. Her mouth was healing slowly." The image promises the restoration of language in time. Mira's identity can be drawn out of the collective woman that inspire her, and the language they return to her.

Mira's search for a universal language translates into a vision with multiple possibilities and opens up identity and culture to various influences, not just a monolithic Western culture. Meena Alexander depicts concepts of difference in her novel and supports pluralism as a means of reconciling an individual to a community. Although some may argue that dream imagery is not a realistic form of communication, I argue that dreams offer a hope of a change, a change to see a vision other than what is present. In a paper entitled **"Real Places on How Sense Fragments—Thoughts on Ethnicity and the Making of Poetry,"** Alexander says "My job is to evoke it [her ideas], all of it, altogether. For that is what my ethnicity requires, that is what America with its hotshot present tense compels me to." Writing becomes a way of weaving her past and present into a presentable form that enacts her identity. Meena Alexander's questioning of her past and her writing opens up the definitions of imperialism, post-colonialism, and culture. The influence of environment or culture is integrated into the vision of individual with the intent, and in this novel, success, of modifying a world view. In essence, identity becomes multicultural instead of unicultural.

The major difference between Mukherjee and Alexander involves their individual approaches toward resolution of identity conflicts. Mukherjee's characters constantly chafe on the bit of the dominant society and thereby strain against the stereotyped definitions of identity. Their solution, however, often seems drastic; "murder" of or total disassociation from an individual's past life is necessary in order to be accepted by the dominant society. I believe that Meena Alexander's attitude is more achievable and healthier for "other" cultures. Instead of severing parts of their identities, Alexander's characters add to their identity with visions of Little Mother and Rameeza. Alexander portrays a collective identity to face the turmoil in the environment around her.

The lines of approach toward cultural identity, however, are not clear. There are moments in Alexander's and Mukherjee's fiction where each reverses positions and complicates any concrete establishment of identity. Alexander's collage of cultural icons and use of Gandhian myth is very similar to Mukherjee's tour of New York City in "A Wife's Tale." Alexander's descriptions sometimes function as passive commentary in a guided tour of Hyderabad. And Mukherjee's fiction remains powerful because of its lack of critical judgement upon the characters and situations in her stories. Mukherjee and Alexander do not necessarily present any answers but they do offer important alternative approaches in their fiction. I think, however, it is important to note Spivak's words in "Poststructuralism, Marginality, Post-coloniality, and Value":

> In the field of ethno-cultural politics, the post-colonial teacher can help to develop this vigilance [awareness of societal appropriations of cultural identities] rather than to continue pathetically to dramatize victimage or assert a spurious identity. She says 'no' to the 'moral luck' of the culture of imperialism while recognizing that she must inhabit it, indeed invest it, to criticize it.

Though not discussing Alexander and Mukherjee directly, I believe Spivak identifies the difference between the two authors with pinpoint clarity. Mukherjee remains in the well cut groove of writing about identity conflicts and the exploitation of immigrant cultures, whereas Alexander recognizes her position within the culture and attempts to question herself. Meena Alexander works out a relationship between her writing and her identity that is influenced by the past but not overcome by it. The ability to recognize the powerful impact of the past upon her is one of the strengths of Meena Alexander's protagonist, Mira, in *Nampally Road.* Alexander deftly moves out of painting a narrative of minority victimage, and instead offers a reasonable strategy to incorporate the identity with the past by questioning the relationship between history and our cultural inheritance.

The ongoing processes that emerge from Alexander's and Mukherjee's fiction are just as important as the presence of their fiction. Their struggle to reconcile their Western education with their ethnicity is indeed a leap from the standard Western narratives. Out of their cultural inheritance, each author, in her separate way, contests the role of the Western colonized subject.

Susheela N. Rao (review date Autumn 1994)

SOURCE: A review of *Fault Lines,* in *World Literature Today,* Vol. 68, No. 4, Autumn, 1994, p. 883.

[*In the following review, Rao emphasizes the variety of cultural experiences related in* Fault Lines.]

Traditionally, Indian writers have fought shy of talking about themselves, and of the great classical writers of India like Kalidasa we know very little. Under the increasing impact of the West, however, more and more Indian writers, mostly Indo-Anglian writers, have been recording their life histories. Autobiographies and memoirs of Indian writers who write in English have now become a familiar and accepted fact of twentieth-century India, and the age at which they write their memoirs is decreasing, raising a question about the value of a work which does not record the fullness of one's life's achievements. The author of the present memoir wrote hers when she was about forty-two years old.

Meena Alexander is primarily a poet, though she has written a novel and some essays and is currently a professor of English at Hunter College in New York City. The title *Fault Lines* suggests the impact of her exposure to a number of languages and cultures beginning with her early childhood; it is also a key to her "desperate awareness of [her] femaleness, a sense of shame." She is, in her own words, "a woman cracked by multiple migrations."

Alexander records her experiences as a child in Kerala (in the far southern part of India), in northern India, and later in Khartoum, Sudan, in Africa. Then her life in England is described, and that is followed by a description of her encounter with life in America. Naturally, she was exposed to all the different cultures and languages of these places. Some of the chapters in the book had been read earlier as papers before various groups.

Alexander claims that she began to write poetry even as a child (reminding us of Alexander Pope, who said he lisped in numbers, for the numbers came to him). In these papers there are reflections, reminiscences, self-inquiry, search for identity, and the author's struggle to find a proper expression for a soul trapped in a woman's body. The telling, though simple, is not a straight chronological one but is now and again interspersed with reminiscences of incidents stretching across time and territories, making the whole reading interesting. At times, however, one raises one's eyebrows, as when the author recounts the details of her first journey, made when she was only four months old. Generally speaking, though, **Fault Lines** is an excellent record of a sensitive young Indian woman writer whose poetic expression is the consummate product of colorful experiences with many cultures and countries.

Helena Grice (review date 1996)

SOURCE: A review of *Fault Lines*, in *Amerasia Journal,* Vol. 22, No. 2, 1996, pp. 164-66.

[*In the following review, Grice offers a thematic and stylistic overview of* Fault Lines *in terms of an evolving, multi-ethnic, autobiographical tradition among women of the diaspora.*]

Meena Alexander's **Fault Lines** locates itself in that in-between generic territory already occupied by another Asian American woman, Maxine Hong Kingston. Both subtitled "memoirs," *The Woman Warrior* and **Fault Lines,** are situated in the literal no-man's land of women's autobiographical writings of the diaspora experience. The similarities extend beyond the subtitle. Like Kingston, too, Alexander traverses generic boundaries, incorporating poems, reminiscences and mini-treatises, so that the very texture of the text is fragmented, and these fragments cannot be pieced together perfectly. In her opening chapter, Alexander asks how she can spell out the fragments of such a broken geography as hers, how to represent the fault lines that exist between her disparate existence. Her solution is to write

in fragments, resulting in a fractured narrative that mirrors Alexander's own life. Worlds and words alike are askew. She traces her history across multiple geographical locations (Sudan, England, New York), as well as differing cultural environments, moving from an India in postcolonial turmoil and rupture to the "elite" world of Western academia, where she encounters institutional racism for the first time.

Alexander treats her writing as a search for a homeland, which is less physical than psychological, in particular her poetry, as a means of making sense of her multiple cultural, geographical, and psychological positionalities. In his book, *Design and Truth in Autobiography,* Roy Pascal argues that autobiographical truth arises from the author's attempt to understand the self more completely and to discover the sources of meaning in one's life through the act of writing one's story. Alexander is engaged in a quest for her own autobiographical truth, from diverse sources of meaning. At the start of her narrative, Alexander notes how many different stories she might tell, and how her story is closely entwined with those of others in her life. It is this filial interconnectedness, as that in Kingston's 1976 work, that renders Alexander's memoir epistemologically interesting. For example, Alexander's emphasis on matrilineal connection can be seen in direct contrast to the individualist, self-aggrandizing tendency of more traditional autobiographical works.

> **In *Fault Lines,* there are frequent reminders of the subjective and selective nature of memory recall, and Alexander repeatedly highlights the limitations of memory and the ramifications of this for her narrative.**
> **—*Helena Grice***

In **Fault Lines,** there are frequent reminders of the subjective and selective nature of memory recall, and Alexander repeatedly highlights the limitations of memory and the ramifications of this for her narrative. Of her Grandmother Kunju we are told that Meena never knew her herself, but she reconstructs her through information she has gleaned from her relatives. Again, the similarity to *The Woman Warrior* is evident: like Kingston and her "no-name aunt," Alexander goes on a textual search for an elusive female relative. Grandmother Kunju's biography offers Meena an empowering version of female selfhood to live up to as an educated and well-traveled woman and activist in early twentieth-century India. In common with Kingston's imaginative reconstruction of her deceased aunt's story, what Meena does not know, she imagines, literally spinning a yarn of her grandmother's life for her reader. She writes: "I was filled with longing for an ancestral figure who would allow my mouth to open, permit me a voice. . . . I . . . made up a grandmother figure, part ghost, part flesh." Again, this theme of the female forebear's haunting the text can also be found in such other Asian American autobiographical fictions as Joy Kogawa's *Obasan* and Maxine Hong Kingston's *The Woman Warrior.* Other female relatives who appear to have formative influence on Meena include her mother, Amma, and her maternal grandmother, Mariamma. Meena's mother, in particular, is accredited as a primary referent: "ever since I can remember, amma and I have been raveled together in net after net of time . . . without her, I would not be. . . ." Thus, *Fault Lines* can be seen as part of an emergent autobiographical tradition, exploring not only life at the interstices of racial and gender liminality, but also acknowledging a substantial debt to the power, strength and influence of the various maternal presences in the daughter's life.

In addition to questioning her status as "Indian, Other," Alexander charts her experiences as a woman in both an occidental and oriental context. She interrogates issues and practices such as clitoridectomy, arranged marriage and education for women, through an exploration of her own emerging feminism. From her Khartoum journal entries: "If you want me to live as a woman, why educate me?" to her later recounting of more public oppression: "The trouble was what I was, quite literally: female, Indian," Alexander traces her path towards "a new baptism" of feminist consciousness. Alexander's final recognition is that it is her very ethnicity, gender and exilic status that make her the person she is, and that it is partly the fault lines that exist between these identities that define her. As "a woman cracked by multiple migrations," Alexander's voice joins a growing choir of multiethnic female voices singing the diaspora story. Alexander's text is not as accomplished as *The Woman Warrior*; yet it is nevertheless an important contribution to the evolving new genre of women's autobiographical writing of the diaspora.

Tammie Bob (review date 25 May 1997)

SOURCE: "Three Indian American Writers Examine Cultural Conflict and Identity," in *Chicago Tribune Books,* May 25, 1997, pp. 1, 9.

[*In the following excerpt, Bob highlights postcolonial identity issues explored in* Manhattan Music.]

The issues of identity and cultural displacement are the core of Meena Alexander's novel *Manhattan Music.* She has assembled a large, urbane and angst-ridden international cast of artists, poets, business figures and academics, all partly shaped by terror and violence. The central figure, Sandhya Rosenblum, has come to America as the wife of a

Jewish man and lost herself in the process. She drifts into an affair with an Egyptian post-doctoral scholar who is too numbed by the chaotic state of the world to provide her with real support. He explains this to her by drawing a comparison to Frankenstein's monster.

> [I]mmigrants are like that. Our spiritual flesh scooped up from here and there. All our memories sizzling. But we need another. Another for the electricity. So we can live.

In contrast to Sandhya's helpless depression, her friend Draupati, an American-born performance artist (descent: mostly Indian, part African, Japanese, Chinese, Filipino and a smattering of "low European"), is able to create meaning through her art, in which she represents and attempts to define the "Race-Ethnicity-Gender-CrossTalk thing."

That's what the book attempts to define, too, sometimes a little awkwardly. World events form a constant backdrop without affecting characters or plot. The Persian Gulf war begins, Rajiv Gandhi is assassinated, a bomb explodes in the World Trade Center, the Branch Davidians are incinerated. The characters respond with shock, or bemusement, or philosophical comments, as people do, but these events sometimes distract from the narrative, presented by various characters in fascinating mixes of present, past and dreamed experiences. When Sandhya's cousin, Jay, a globetrotting photographer, briefly encounters a deranged, bigoted Vietnam veteran, the madman's few lines of ravings make a more-pointed and poignant statement about the horrors of war and racism than handwringing recitals of atrocities and speculations about what the world is coming to.

The book suggests hope, through improved communication and technology, a global exchange of art, business, information and experience. Manhattan, the setting for most of the book, is used as a possible model for a polyglot, multicolored, CNN-informed society. "And mightn't one argue," someone says at a cocktail party, "that varied languages altered the structure of consciousness, made one better equipped for life in a world of multiple anchorages such as New York presented?" Sandhya's husband, a typically monolingual American, suggests it might be possible to live a worthwhile life with just one language. "Quite so," the speaker says, "but what of the . . . immigrant in Europe, in America? Who will learn their languages?" The speaker is writing a book on "post-colonial identity. New York City, of course, was the perfect place to put such a book together."

With *Manhattan Music,* Meena Alexander has written such a book.

John Oliver Perry (review date Autumn 1997)

SOURCE: A review of *River and Bridge*, in *World Literature Today*, Vol. 71, No. 4, Autumn, 1997, pp. 867-8.

[*In the following review, Perry considers the principal themes, motifs, and style of* River and Bridge.]

To indicate how difficult book publication is even for important Indian English poets, it may be noted that ***River and Bridge*** was substantially ready in 1988 or at least 1990, the manuscript then opening with an India-referring title poem used later for the fine closing note: **"Deer Park at Sarnath,"** which thoughtfully, not at all sadly, ends, "There is no grief like this, / the origin of landscape is memory." Then in 1995 Rupa in New Delhi published a hardcover edition of ***River and Bridge*** without eleven of the forty-nine poems included in the 1996 TSAR edition. Both the Rupa and TSAR editions begin with **"Relocation"**—"Scraping it all back: // A species of composition / routine as crossing streets / or taking out the garbage / nothing to blow the mind"—clearly a poem for a hip American audience, and they both end with the same poem in the section, "San Andreas Fault," indicating again an American setting for this much-traveled, supposedly "unhoused" or diaspora poet. **"Relocation"** also alludes to the preeminently American W. C. Williams—"The road to the hospital / is contagious already," and "as Broadway thickens with bicycles" presents "the imagination ordering itself." So the initial note of migrancy is struck hard, as again in the very next, newly added poem, **"Softly My Soul,"** with its allusions to "Liberty's torch" and George Washington laughing at "the gazelles on Fifth Avenue / tiny miniskirts hoisted to their thighs." But the improved TSAR version puts first what was Rupa's third section, "Blood Line," including the titular **"River and Bridge."**

The latter poem emphasizes once more the collection's key note: the separated shores of a dividing, life-giving natural flow of liquid energy are crossed by a single, thus comparatively feeble, human creative effort, a birth or rebirth, "a bridge that seizes crossing": "But Homer knew it and Vyasa too, black river / and bridge summon those whose stinging eyes / criss-cross red lights, metal implements, / battlefields: birth is always bloody."

Although it is often clearly feminine/female and occasionally hits a distinctly postcolonial/racial note, Meena Alexander's poetry as well as her prose predicates a distinctly nondualistic sense of herself as sheer energy—and, by extension, others of her sex and indeed the entire human species may be similarly understood. Many almost overt clues bring out of seclusion the still shy sexuality that she recognizes as empowering her creativity. Without denying the importance of her Syrian Christian heritage, she rejects Christian and Cartesian dualisms of mind and body in adopting an intensely personal and expressive English Romantic tradition, with a phenomenological assist from Heidegger. And yet there is something basic here from the Hindu culture as well that pervaded even her diaspora Indian background: a lurking image of the divine androgynous Siva as Destroyer and Preserver (as in Shelley's orientalized West Wind). The ur-goddess Shakti and/or Durga-Kali, imaging the frighteningly powerful female forces driving within all things, is traditionally also evident in Siva—or whatever the god whose name, shape, identity can be invoked for this world that is and is not, that we are of and not.

Again and again the force driving Alexander's poetry and the intense life she imagines arise in the blood of sexuality and passion, as in **"Elephants in Heat."** The rage encompasses beyond mere gender issues a multiplicity of protests against slavery of all sorts—sexual, racial, class- and caste-based, religious, or merely cultural—and against human viciousness, war, political murders, child and woman beatings, natural disasters, suicides, and other deaths by drowning. This last continuing and highly personal fear arises from the poet's childhood experiences with suicides of at least two of the family's servant girls, related or alluded to in several key poems here and earlier. Though a number of these poems are occasioned by external events in Iraq, South Africa, and India as well as Manhattan (the second section is "News of the World"), nevertheless the births of her children, interactions with her beloved (usually identifiable as her husband, quite poignantly in **"The Unexceptional Drift of Things"** and the new **"Generation"**), and especially memories of childhood terrors, deaths, and triumphs, provide primary motifs and materials.

Sometimes both the situation and the significance being wrung from it are rendered in oblique syntax and surrealistic or dream imagery; generally the poems remain at least elusive, unparaphrasable, yet a few social protests are relatively direct. The seven sections (seven pages) of the longest poem here (**"Ashtamudi Lake,"** from part 3, "Mandala") center on a 1986 railroad-bridge disaster in her "home" state of Kerala; over one hundred persons were drowned. These drownings are taken personally, of course, by the poet-speaker retracing that journey, passing by the wrecked rusting train. Then an aborted sexual encounter of twelve years before is recalled, followed by three series of scenes drawn from the train's route or recalled from the past, both personal and historical (Vasco da Gama, Columbus). Although, ironically, it was burning rather than drowning that safety posters warned the train passengers against—using the Hindi word *A-ag*, Agni being the ancient Aryan, now Brahminical sacred flame—the poem's concluding section intensifies the poetic heat into fires of truth, of memories, of the family home being approached, of death seen as "a conquest."

> Rubbing raw the nervous interstices of sense
> Desire's nuptial's lit in us no elsewhere here
> Only a house held by its own weight in the mind's space
> Its elegant portico of polished teak tilting in heat
> As we seize a door with an ivory knob and come upon flames.

Recalling her previous collection, **House of a Thousand Doors** (1988), **"Landscape with Door,"** one of several highly evocative, evasive, private poems—"The iron rose / turns feverish as you stand / beside these trees that have no provenance"—ends with the river of heat localized: "Whole stanzas turn / bewildered, matches held / over torrents of fire. // Your hands / that touched me twice / unpack a square of paper // A child's drawing of a door, / a makeshift house / lacquered in flame." As throughout her writing, the high emotional energy in Meena Alexander's work draws on a kind of conflicted sexuality that has frightened and inspired her to sacramentalize her passions into poetry that will endure migrancy, mixed messages, the world's mire, memory's mendacity.

Susheela N. Rao (review date Spring 1998)

SOURCE: A review of *Manhattan Music*, in *World Literature Today*, Vol. 72, No. 2, Spring, 1998, pp. 456-7.

[*In the following review, Rao admires the narrative technique of* Manhattan Music.]

What purports to be the lives and living thoughts and feelings, and problems and promises of a more recent immigrant group—namely, Indians from India living in the New York/New Jersey area—is orchestrated in the novel **Manhattan Music** by a successful Indian immigrant, who, herself having been exposed to a number of places and countries outside her own home in Kerala in the southern part of India, shows a sensitive awareness of the state of the immigrants. In this story we meet Christians and Jews, Muslims and Hindus, Indians from East India and the West Indies and from Egypt. There is ample sexual stuff (including extramarital affairs) and racial tension. Sandhya, a Syrian Christian (Catholics in Kerala call themselves Syrian Christians and regard themselves as above all other Christians and do not marry outside their group), marries an American Jewish gentlemen and is not exactly happy with

her married life, harried not by any domestic problem but by her own voluptuous fancies (something unthinkable in traditional India). Draupadi, an Indian immigrant from the West Indies, is the other important character who exercises some influence on Sandhya, while the male characters are of secondary importance. The coda, consisting of four poems by Arjun Sankaramangalam, tries to bring the orchestrated music of **Manhattan** to a conclusion through sheer, unbridled fancy in its attempt to coalesce widely scattered events and things, even as the story does, and challenges critics to find in these pages reasoned imagination and imaginative reasoning.

One striking feature of the novel is its narrative technique. While an omniscient narrator reports all of Sandhya's thoughts and doings, assisted by the protagonist's flashbacks and remembrances of things past in India, Draupadi is given the prerogative of speaking for herself. For the epigraphs to the chapters the author uses quotations from a surprisingly wide variety of writers belonging to widely differing time periods, including Shakespeare, Kalidasa, Kafka, and Akka Mahadevi (a twelfth-century Kannada writer). She also shows a knowledge of Indian epic stories, held sacred by the Hindus and sedulously avoided by the more conservative Christians because of the taboo placed on exposure to other religions. There are occasional errors, such as the name "Sandhya" being construed to mean "those threshold hours before the sun rose or set, fragile zones of change before the clashing absolutes of light and dark took hold." In reality, this Sanskrit word means "the conjunction or meeting point of two time periods: night and morning, morning and afternoon, and afternoon and night." Before concluding, we should perhaps ask two questions. With all its Indic terms, baffling to non-Indians, to whom is the novel addressed? Second, granted that the sphere of writing is circumscribed by one's own experience, when do Indian immigrant writers begin to write of a wider experience and make an attempt to merge into the mainstream of American literature?

FURTHER READING

Criticism

Clausen, Christopher. "Romanticism Left and Right." *Sewanee Review* 91, No. 4 (October 1983): 672-80.
    Critiques Alexander's use of "subjectivity" theories in *The Poetic Self*, situating her book in a review of contemporaneous studies of Romanticism.

> **Additional coverage of Alexander's life and career is contained in the following sources published by Gale:** *Contemporary Authors,* **Vol. 115; and** *Contemporary Authors New Revision Series,* **Vols. 38, and 70.**

Kay Boyle
1902-1992

American novelist, short story writer, poet, and essayist.

The following entry presents an overview of Boyle's career through 1998. For further information on her life and works, see *CLC*, Volumes 1, 5, 19, and 58.

INTRODUCTION

Boyle is a renowned American short story writer and novelist. A participant in the expatriate movement of the 1920s, she is acclaimed for her flawless sense of style. Critics cite Boyle's body of work, much of which is semi-autobiographical, as one of the most significant chronicles of the twentieth century. In addition, Boyle is known for her essays, many of which deal with the social obligations of writers, and her poetry.

Biographical Information

Boyle was born on February 19, 1902 in St. Paul, Minnesota to affluent parents. Her mother tutored her at home, and throughout Boyle's youth she traveled extensively in the United States and Europe. Boyle began writing as a teenager under the encouragement and guidance of her mother, and by 1922, she had secured a position at the magazine *Broom*. In 1922 Boyle married Robert Brault, a French engineer, and moved to France. She would remain in Europe until World War II necessitated her return to the United States in 1941. Through the 1920s and 1930s, Boyle lived and worked within the expatriate community in Europe, assisting Ernest Welsh with *This Quarter,* his avant-garde journal which featured the writings of such revisionists as James Joyce, Gertrude Stein, and Ernest Hemingway. By the 1930s, Boyle's fiction was becoming increasingly well known and respected. She won her first O. Henry Award for "The White Horses of Vienna" in 1934 and her second in 1941 for "Defeat." In 1943, Boyle married her third husband, Joseph Franckenstein, an anti-Nazi Austrian baron whom Boyle helped in his escape from Europe. Boyle returned to occupied Germany in the late 1940s as a foreign correspondent for the *New Yorker,* remaining there until the anti-communist hearings of Senator Joseph McCarthy precipitated her final return to the United States. Throughout the postwar period, Boyle continued to write about her experiences and to protest social injustices such as McCarthyism, minority rights, and the American involvement in the Vietnam War. She served a short prison sentence for her involvement in anti-war demonstrations. From 1963 until 1980, Boyle taught creative

writing at San Francisco State University. She died in Mill Valley, California in 1992.

Major Works

Boyle published extensively throughout her career, completing more than forty novels, volumes of short stories, essays, poetry, and childrens books. Through her writings, Boyle advocates an awareness and involvement in social and political issues such as Fascism in Europe, McCarthyism in the United States, and American involvement in the Vietnam War—events which Boyle encountered firsthand. Throughout her career she returned to common themes: the importance of individual accountability and salvation from human destruction in love and fidelity. Her first works, such as "Wedding Day" (1930), *Plagued by the Nightingale* (1931), *Year Before Last* (1932), *Gentleman, I Address You Privately* (1934), *My Next Bride* (1934), and "The White Horse of Vienna" (1936), are set in the turmoil of prewar Europe and center upon independent women who, through their search for their own identity and voice, come into conflict with men and society. Her use of metaphors, experimentations with consciousness and point of view, and powerful descriptions are consistently apparent in these works. Through the late 1930s and 1940s she wrote several novels and short stories about World War II. These include *Death of a Man* (1936), which was misinterpreted as advocating fascism; *Primer for Combat* (1942); *Avalanche* (1944), her only bestseller; and *His Human Majesty* (1949). In the postwar period, Boyle continued to write about social responsibility; among her best known works is an account of a jailed antiwar protester, *The Underground Woman* (1975.)

Critical Reception

The principle question which drives scholarly debate over Boyle's work is why she is not as well known nor as highly valued as peers such as James Joyce, Samuel Beckett, or Virginia Woolf. Early critics such as author Katherine Anne Porter praised her writing style, noting the ways in which Boyle was moving literature away from the traditional novels of the past and towards a period of transition. Consistently throughout the prewar period, critics such as Robert Cantwell, William Carlos Williams, and Struthers Burt praised Boyle's sense of style, skillful use of metaphors, ability to sustain tension, ambitious themes and subjects, and unusual characters. However, many critics noted that despite her skill, many of her stories were inadequately developed, not compelling, and confusing. Louis Kronenberger suggested that Boyle's failure stemmed from attempting too difficult a goal. World War II marked a transition in Boyle's work which irked many critics. Edmund Wilson called her bestseller *Avalanche* (1944) "a piece of pure rubbish" and Betty Hoyenga protested the overpowering role of propaganda in Boyle's work. However, many critics label Boyle a first rate writer, praising her skill at transforming the major events of the twentieth century into powerful, appealing, and personal accounts. As Philip Corwin writes, "At times she succeeds and at times she does not. But whatever the final result her effort is a worthy one, and one thoroughly consistent with those of a writer whose energies have always been expended imaginatively and unselfishly in a constant attempt to enlighten her fellow citizens."

PRINCIPAL WORKS

Wedding Day and Other Stories (short stories) 1930
Plagued by the Nightingale (novel) 1931
Year Before Last (novel) 1932
The First Lover and Other Stories (short stories) 1933
Gentlemen, I Address You Privately (novel) 1933
My Next Bride (novel) 1934
The White Horses of Vienna and Other Stories (short stories) 1936

Death of a Man (novel) 1936
Monday Night (novel) 1938
Primer For Combat (novel) 1943
Avalanche (novel) 1944
A Frenchman Must Die (novel) 1946
1939 (novel) 1948
His Human Majesty (novel) 1949
The Seagull on the Step (novel) 1955
Generation Without Farewell (novel) 1960
Testament For My Students and Other Poems (poetry) 1970
The Long Walk at San Francisco State and Other Essays (essays) 1970
The Underground Woman (novel) 1975
Fifty Stories (short stories) 1980
Words That Must Somehow Be Said (essays) 1985
This is Not a Letter and Other Poems (poetry) 1985

CRITICISM

New York Times Book Review (review date 16 November 1930)

SOURCE: "Kay Boyle's Experiments," in *New York Times Book Review,* November 16, 1930, p. 8.

[*In the following review of* Wedding Day and Other Stories, *the critic argues that Boyle is at her best when she combines experimentation with structure.*]

These short stories and five-finger exercises by Kay Boyle represent both the good and the ephemeral that have come out of the experimental epoch that is now closing. And, because the best of Kay Boyle is quite good (as in **"Episode in the Life of an Ancestor"**), it is easy to forgive the inclusion of the worst of the five-finger exercises (let us choose **"Spring Morning"** as the scapegoat) in this slim volume. An example or so of the ephemeral, indeed, helps to show us how Miss Boyle gets her happiest effects—effects that derive from a wide-open sensibility that enables her to fasten upon amazingly apt images. The merit of the transition experimenters was that their work let the subconscious out, and this subconscious often sees things in sharper, more vivid terms than the conscious mind which is silted over by ordinary ways of seeing, learned by rote. When the garnering of the subconscious is thrown helter-skelter upon the paper (as in **"Spring Morning"**) we get little benefit from it. There is no order, progression, resolution. But, when this garnering is used to enrich a story that has order, progression, resolution (as in **"Episode in the Life of an Ancestor"** or in **"Polar Bears and Others"**), then we do get a great deal of pleasure from the result. Bits like **"Spring Morning"** may be queer jumbles, calling for an alertness at untangling them that is not quite worth the effort, but Miss Boyle's effort in such jumbles to catch all the fleeting impressions of a moment of living have resulted in solid good. By her experimenting she has shed old skins; and the new coat underneath is striped with bright colors, with beautiful designs, with rhythmic curves. For example, in **"Episode in the Life of an Ancestor"** she can talk of the Kansas prairie in terms that set it before you with sensuous brilliance—"all along the edge of it were the Indian fires burning hard and bright as peonies." Would a conventional writer have thought of using peonies, even if in his mind's eye he was dimly aware of such a simile?

Miss Boyle seems to be at home with animals. For example, in **"Polar Bears and Others"** she commences her story by invoking an image of the polar bears cooped up in a warm climate, helpless to change their ways and doomed if man fails to transplant their environment with them in the shape of a few chunks of ice. Then, after a false intrusion on the part of the author (her rapt parenthesis on the subject of romance is out of key), she passes on to an episode which involves two people, man and woman. The thought of the polar bears, open to extreme hurt when they are confronted by a sudden shift in the conventions of their lives, lights up the episode—an episode which is not wholly amenable to statement in a paragraph, but which, nevertheless, is more poignant than many a more obvious triangle situation. (Incidentally, the figure of the polar bear may symbolize the unacclimated reader of Kay Boyle's book.)

Whenever there are animals in Miss Boyle's stories they transmit their grace to the humans who come in contact with them. The grandmother in **"Episode in the Life of an Ancestor"** (she was young at the time of the story) takes on the hardness, the impatience of restraint, the love of swift running in the prairie wind, that characterize the horses which she loves. But Miss Boyle is not dependent on the obvious analogy. Other stories, such as **"Wedding Day"** and **"Summer,"** while they are less substantial than **"Episode in the Life of an Ancestor,"** are successful in their own right; they need no symbolism. However, it is doubtful whether they will remain in the mind as long as **"Episode in the Life of an Ancestor"** or **"Polar Bears and Others."**

Louis Kronenberger (review date 12 November 1933)

SOURCE: "Kaye Boyle's Story of a Moral Crisis," in *New York Times Book Review,* November 12, 1933, p. 9.

[*In the following review of* Gentlemen, I Address You Privately, *Kronenberger states that although Boyle enjoys*

moments of genius in this novel, she fails to sustain the quality.]

It is only recently that we have had much fiction in English whose predominating note is that of sensibility. Our older novelists flirted with the same note; but Meredith, Jane Austen, Henry James impress us, in the long run, as really psychologists or novelists of manners. It is among certain recent women writers—Katherine Mansfield, Elizabeth Bowen, Virginia Woolf and latterly Kay Boyle—that sensibility seems to dwarf all other characteristics. The world they present to us has been refined and smoothed down; it is a world under glass, so to speak. They convey to us a special and overexquisite feeling for life; and it is not life itself we are most keenly aware of in their work, but this special and delicate approach to it. Perhaps even "approach" is an inaccurate description; there is often a kind of withdrawal in their attitude.

> **Whenever there are animals in Miss Boyle's stories they transmit their grace to the humans who come in contact with them.**
> **—*New York Times Book Review***

Among these writers it is Kay Boyle who cultivates the purest order of sensibility. Unlike Bowen and Woolf, she is not, for example, a wit. She throws her whole weight in one direction: toward turning up, with infinite precision, the delicate roots of temperament and interaction. She is a kind of surgeon, though her surgery is always performed with one tool: a scalpel. Her work accordingly has a great deal of inadequacy.

In a book like the present one the finesse displayed only brings out the inadequacy the more sharply. For Miss Boyle has invaded the harsh, dark, tangled precincts of the moral world where whole and merciless vision is demanded, where the attributes of culture can only play a minor part. She has seized one man at a crisis in his development and, pinning him fast, hurled another man into contact with him. Munday, bred in the ascetic ways of the church, has broken with the church when the story opens, and turned to his music for compensation. At that moment (with undue theatrically) the sly, magnetic, effeminate Ayton bursts into Munday's life and insists upon joining it to his own. Munday, his starved body answering before his mind is able, consents; and at once he is drawn into a homosexual relationship with Ayton. Soon he finds himself much more deeply drawn than he could possibly have foreseen: for Ayton has deserted his ship and committed thefts, and Munday is forced into hiding with him. Up to this point, in spite of being overlaid with verbal décor, Miss Boyle's pattern is almost mathematically clear; beyond this point the tracings

grow more and more blurred. A number of other characters move into the narrative, and it loses sight of its major
objective. For Leonie's love for Ayton, her getting with
child by him, Ayton's final diving back into the dark waters
of adventure from which he at first emerged, all seem
strung out as linked-up incidents; they do not give the book
any real plot, any real centre; and they do not constitute a
working out of its theme.

For Ayton is the spectacular figure of this novel, certainly
Munday is the important one. Ayton's character, subtle and
complicated as it is in the nervous sense, is nevertheless a
fairly clear and simple one: he is an inveterate experimenter
with life, a man who lives dangerously, wanting all sensations and all experiences. In naïve hands he would doubtless symbolize some spirit of evil, but realistically (and
Miss Boyle is a realist in her intentions if not always in
practice) he is simply unmoral, unprincipled and mischievous. He is merely the reef against which Munday founders;
the moral issues of the book are centred in Munday. But
once posed, they are never solved. For one thing, Miss
Boyle never carries the book toward its indicated destina-
tion. For another, Munday is hopelessly unreal. He is a collection of fragments that are never integrated. The real
people in the book are two secondary characters: Quespelle
and Leonie.

Because its theme never flowers, because its hero never
breathes, this book for all its minor excellences fails to be
important. And the fault lies, not in a lack of talent, but in
a lack of coordination. Ornament is substituted for architecture. Miss Boyle's writing lives for the moment; each
separate burrowing is more an end in itself than part of
something larger and continuous. The result is a lack of fi-
ber, of weight, which in a book like this one is fatal. Life
cannot be properly revealed through sniffing and snipping;
one must drink and smell.

Yet it would be wholly unjust not to commend Miss Boyle
for what she does give to us. It amounts, at moments, to
revelation; her subtleties of insight are such as no other
writer of our time, in English at least, can match. Her style,
when she has it in control, is enchantingly fluid and lovely;
in some of these pages Brittany comes alive as in a sensitive poem. But the mature novelist gives us something beyond subtleties, beyond style; he makes us see life through
the magnifying lens of the glass, not—as Miss Boyle has
done—through the lens that contracts.

Robert Cantwell (review date 13 December 1933)

SOURCE: "Exiles," in *The New Republic,* Vol. LXXVII,
No. 993, December 13, 1933, pp. 136-37.

[*In the following review which compares* Gentlemen, I
Address You Privately *with Jack Conroy's* The Disinherited, *Cantwell concludes that Boyle's writing suffers from
isolation and unrealistic characters.*]

Kay Boyle has now published three novels and two volumes
of short stories and, with this much evidence on hand, the
character and development of her work is becoming clear.
She is one of the most eloquent and one of the most prolific writers among the expatriates; her work is always finished in the sense that her phrases are nicely cadenced and
her imagery often striking and apt; her characters are almost always highly sensitized individuals who are marooned
or in flight in some foreign country, banding together in
small groups in which the antagonisms often seem intense
beyond their recognizable causes. These small groups of
exiles from their closed circles, the members of which exist on the verge of tears or nervous breakdown, and are often physically ill as well. The drama comes out of their
meetings—it is noteworthy how much Kay Boyle gets out
of the casual coming together of her people, what untold
dangers and mysterious excitement she finds in their first
impressions of each other—out of the tormented relationships and the eventual flight.

Gentlemen, I Address You Privately fits into this pattern.
Here, too, the characters are on the run, not indeed from a
recognizable compulsion, but as though a headlong flight
were the natural course of life and any pause a mere interruption. The hero, Munday, is an American, a former priest,
living in exile in Brittany after having abruptly severed his
connection with the Church. It is characteristic of the writing of the exiles, from Henry James on, that they only begin their stories when the major decisions and the major
conflicts are behind their characters, and devote themselves
exclusively to detailing the experiences which follow. Obviously a career so sensational as Munday's would have led
to its crises and exhaustions, would leave its scars, but as
the story opens Munday is merely contemplating the pleasures that lie in wait for him, and, if he is tormented by his
memories, if his torments in turn infect his new relationships, Kay Boyle does not show him in those moments. A
sailor named Ayton, whose past is also mysterious and
jumpy and who seems equally unscarred by his experiences,
suddenly appears and moves in with Munday. After an elementary resistance on Munday's part, Ayton seduces him,
and the remainder of the book deals with the gradual revelation to Munday of the depths of malice and irresponsi-
bility in his lover. In the end Ayton simply disappears, along
with three Lesbians whose intrigues and disorders typify
the emotional confusion into which Munday's new relationship has led him; they disappear as if by magic and Munday
is left with fresh evidence—which he receives good-
naturedly—of his betrayal.

It is not enough to point out some of the superficial improbabilities in this story, such as the easy changes of sex which the characters make without suffering any drastic psychological punishment. These violations of actuality would be unimportant if they served to heighten some more basic conflict, as comparable inventions are used in Melville and Dostoevsky and Gide. The important point is that, in the world Kay Boyle describes, human beings possess no consistency and no body; they are capable of doing anything, of reversing themselves and shattering the impressions of their own personalities that have been built up out of the complex of their actions and responses; they give expression to extreme moods of affection or despair or distrust, unchecked by apprehension as to the effect of these expressions, never learning the limits within which the others move, never gauging the boundaries of their friends' imaginations or sensing the possibilities that lie before them. Their closest companions grow increasingly mysterious as they absorb more and more information about them; they look upon one another as they might upon some strange wild birds that may be temporarily harbored but can never be understood and are certain in the end to take flight.

This is not a feature peculiar to the works of Kay Boyle; it is a distinctive characteristic of the writings of the American expatriates, from James on to Ernest Hemingway. Those characters in James who makes such baffled attempts to figure out what is going on in the minds of the people about them, and who in the end are only more mystified than when they began, are similar in this respect to the characters in Hemingway who fly to the extremes of antagonism and affection in a moment, confide in strangers and misrepresent their motives and desires to their friends— they are alike in the sense that they are presented as if their actions were unchecked by any barriers save those set up by their fluctuating moods, or as if their actions were somehow inconsequential, incapable of influencing the actions of others. All of these writers—and Kay Boyle more than the rest—present a world made up of insulated groups having only the thinnest contacts with the social life of their environment, being forced to depend on fragmentary acquaintance with servants and bullfighters and hotelkeeper for any knowledge of the life beyond their circle.

Jack Conroy's *The Disinherited* is illuminating by contrast: it is a study of the society from which the exiles have fled, a picture of the life from which they are insulated. Yet Conroy's book is also, in a sense, the story of men in exile. It is the chronicle of a young worker's search for a livelihood, a part of that continual movement Tolstoy described as the wanderings of the workingman over the face of the earth, with its only development the hero's gradual enlightenment as to the character of the society through which he has been moving. As the son a miner,

Larry Donovan has known the meaning of strikes from his boyhood, and after his father is killed in the mine and he has gone to work himself, he learns more of them in terms of his own experience. Half-conscious of his social role, dissatisfied, always reminded of the hardships which his mother and all his people endure, vaguely interested in poetry, he moves from one job to another, from railroad yards to a steel mill, from a rubber-heel plant to an automobile factory, in contact with an ever-widening circle of workers, continually driven by his dissatisfaction to learn from the people around him. He drifts to Detroit, pulled by the magnetic attraction of good jobs, and learns what the speeding-up of labor means; when the depression begins he and the members of his class have known it as a reality before its first consequences have been marked on the stock exchange or in the speeches of government officials. Then he and a friend begin a long trip back home in a wheezy automobile, a trip which seems almost as difficult as the migrations of the pioneers across the plains; the car continually breaks down; they are forced to hunt for work to get enough gas to move a few miles, and to live in a Hooverville while they gather together resources for moving on. There are no swift and mysterious flights in a world so concrete, there is no place for violent fluctuations of mood or long sustained distrust of man for man.

Both of these books are interesting, and both, in their different ways, are well written. The parts of *The Disinherited* which deal with the Monkey Nest Mine, with the death of Larry's father and with the boy's emotion as he watches his mother at work, belong with the best of this literature of first-hand observation. In general Conroy's talent resembles Dreiser's; he reveals a similar unwillingness to doll up an event or an emotion in prose. *The Disinherited* is a first novel, one obviously written over a long period of time, so that the parts often fit together awkwardly; the conclusion, dealing with the stopping of a foreclosure by a group of farmers, when the poor are at last stirred to positive action, seems far less convincing than the earlier parts of the story. And the hero's relations with women belong in another book, in an immature volume in the *Moon-Calf* tradition. Yet it is impossible not to contrast the movement and variety of Conroy's story, the drive and indignation behind it, with the finished care, the sense of fatigue and of labored and artificial eloquence, of Kay Boyle's writing. Unexpectedly, *The Disinherited* suggests one reason for the importance the writing of the exiles has had for us: it suggests that the position of the intellectual in contemporary American society, at least in relation to the kind of life Conroy pictures, is not unlike that of a foreigner in a community he does not understand and with which he has only a fragmentary contact. If Kay Boyle and the other exiles have told us the meaning of isolation, Jack Conroy and a few similar talents are giving us a sense of the richness and strength from which we are isolated.

Edith H. Walton (review date 11 November 1934)

SOURCE: "Miss Boyle's Irony," in *New York Times Book Review,* November 11, 1934, p. 6.

[*In the following review of* My Next Bride, *Walton accuses Boyle of focusing on trivial matters and failing to meet her potential.*]

Several years' ago Kay Boyle published a short story, **"Art Colony,"** which contained the kernel of this ruefully ironic novel. Outlines which she sketched briefly then have been filled in, and Sorrel, the leader of the colony, has moved from the shadowy wings to the centre of the stage. Miss Boyle, incidentally, makes the conventional statement that all her characters are imaginary, but Sorrel, with his tunics and sandals, his craftwork, his dead wife—in the short story she was his sister—who wanted to teach the whole world to dance, so inevitably suggested Raymond Duncan that one may be pardoned a polite skepticism.

The seamier side of idealism receives scant shrift from Miss Boyle, though her wickedest digs are tempered by a lurking sympathy.
—*Edith H. Walton*

The seamier side of idealism receives scant shrift from Miss Boyle, though her wickedest digs are tempered by a lurking sympathy. Sorrel's colony in Paris, sheltered in a dingy and slackly kept house, has disintegrated sadly since the days of his wife, the dancer. The remaining members are a wrangling, ill-fed, second-rate lot; fewer disciples visit him on Sundays to prance rhythmically in Grecian tunics; the sale of hand-made scarfs and vestments and rugs has fallen off in his shop. Sorrel himself, his shining, filleted hair snow-white, is an aging and a rather weary man.

The scheme of Miss Boyle's novel demands that this pseudo-Utopia be viewed freshly from the outside, and the spectator she has chosen is a young American girl who drifts accidentally into Sorrel's orbit. Victoria arrives penniless in Paris and is unable to find a job. She is rescued by two Russian ladies, half-starved, half-crazy remnants of the old aristocracy, who board in the same gloomy house as herself and who know that Sorrel will offer shelter to strays. They introduce Victoria to him, and she is attracted at once by his lean, benignant Middle-Western face. It is agreed that she shall work for a tiny salary in the shop and share the sternly vegetarian meals of the colony.

Victoria is something of an idealist herself and at first she is mesmerized by Sorrel's gentleness and dignity, his air of sweet saintliness. She refuses indignantly to believe that he has been, and still is, a lustful man, and she consoles herself for the disorder of the colony by blaming—quite justly—his unworthy followers. She defends Sorrel, protects him, steals off with him in quest of the ice-cream sodas which he so childishly and pathetically covets. She shuts her eyes to the charge that he has a snobbish, mercenary streak, and only admits it when, instead of relieving the poverty of his colony, he lavishes a sudden windfall of money on a fine new automobile. Even then she but half condemns him. For all his flaws, he has a quality of nobility which cannot quite be denied.

It is a grave defect of **My Next Bride** that Victoria is allowed to steal a story which does not rightfully belong to her. Parallel with her adventures in the colony runs the tale of her love affairs—and it is not a very significant or credible tale. She falls in with a wealthy young man, Anthony, who is really desperately in love with his glamourous wife, Fontana, but who permits himself platonic nocturnal excursions with Victoria and talks a lot of involved poppycock. Knowing he is not for her, Victoria turns in desperation to promiscuity, becomes pregnant, and is rescued, in Anthony's absence, by the understanding, all-wise Fontana. There is something suspiciously Michael Arlen about this pair, and all the episodes in which they are involved are so hollow, false and tinselly that one blushes for Miss Boyle.

IFortunately, what one will remember in the book is the picture of the colony—Sorrel the contradictory; the ribald music hall dancers who live in the same house but who are not among the members, the grave, thin children who bear the astonishing names of Hippolytus, Prosperine, Athenia and Bishinka, the silly American women who flutter round the shop. One will remember also the two starving Russian ladies, with their prim black muffs and fur-pieces, their piteous greediness for food, their fierce pride. Muted humor, tinged with pathos, is the keynote of Miss Boyle's book, and she has contributed some, matchless sketches of fantastic waifs and strays.

IEven when one grants her all this, however, **My Next Bride** raises some sober questions as to the future of Kay Boyle. Her last novel, **Gentlemen, I Address You Privately,** was distinctly a disappointment to most of her admirers. So, presumably, will this one be. That Miss Boyle is an exquisite craftsman few are blind enough to doubt, but one begins to wonder what use she is going to make of her craft. If she continues to spend herself on trivial material, to foster her tendency toward precociousness, to move further and further away from ordinary life, it will be a sad blow to those who have been quick to recognize her as one of the most gifted and interesting of the younger writers.

Alfred Kazin (review date 11 October 1936)

SOURCE: "Kay Boyle's New Novel," in *New York Times Book Review,* October 11, 1936, pp. 6-7.

[*In the following review of* Death of a Man, *Kazin suggests that while Boyle's sense of style is successful, she fails in her narrative.*]

It is some time now since a reviewer was moved to write, concerning a reference to the late Mr. Dillinger in one of Miss Boyle's earlier works, that a reference to Senator Borah in the New Testament could not be more astonishing. Miss Boyle is still far removed from her own, her native land, but she has come to reveal a growing preoccupation with the little tragedies attending the present era of European politics, and no one, I am sure, could ask for a clearer view of the impulses that have driven so many plain folk to Hitlerism than Miss Boyle has conveyed through one of the characters in this novel. The violence is still shadowy, the gust of wind is still but a whiff of smoke, and Miss Boyle is as devoted to the exquisite phrase as ever, but *Death of a Man* has something to say that may be considered above and beyond the precious and the pale.

Miss Boyle's story revolves around the critical events in Austria two years ago that culminated in the assassination of Dollfuss, but it is principally concerned with the tortuous affair between an American girl and a Nazi doctor. It is in the delineation of their respective values, if not in the actual conflict between them, that Miss Boyle is at her best; subtly descriptive, the former offers a literal contrast between the rooted and the uprooted, and composes the memorable portion of the novel. Prochaska himself is a bundle of attitudes, monotonous and warped, but he indicates a philosophy, and it is the philosophy of the many who were led from a revolt against the peace-treaty, the bitter poverty and the humiliation imposed on Austria to faith in a sullen house-painter.

The girl is a spiritual descendant of those unhappy Americans who swarm through the novels of Henry James; in our day a younger sister to the lost generation. Provided with post-war phrases cannot escape, she participates in her lover's activities, but without his passion, and untroubled by his needs. Their affair does not last very long, for she is too conscious of the basic antagonism between them. In her pre-climax soliloquy she repeats the traditional gesture of renunciation, the decade-long complaint of the Brett Ashleys on their European lovers, be they bull-fighters or revolutionaries:

"What he's never said to me is he believes in something; fighting like a fool for something, and I haven't even got that to make me look like a good imitation

of somebody going somewhere and caring where they're going."

The difference between the lovers, however, is not a dramatic difference, for the conflict between them is only stated, prepared for us; it is rarely illuminated by the events in the narrative, and then but fitfully. Prochaska is not a vivid character, but he is sufficiently characterized to make us sense the burden that drives him forward, that allows him to be casual about bombings and cynical about assassination. The girl is even less of a creation, being unintegrated, but we come to understand her predicament. When they draw together, nevertheless, when Miss Boyle attempts to set the basic line of her narrative, the book flounders.

That is largely due, it seems to me, to the fact that the story is built on sand; for all the width and realism of their background, Miss Boyle's characters carry on a private life of their own, full of sudden torments and whispered desires, and her main interest, it is plain, is in the influence of politics on the soul or the temperament, not in its effect on the outward life of men or the pattern of their society. The corners of existence, the mysterious impulse, the silent, tragic act; sex as the joker in the pack—Miss Boyle has used them for her themes over and over again, and it makes little difference here that, considered as a part against the whole, they form little more than a rustle in the drapery.

What it comes to in the end is that we are much too conscious of Miss Boyle's art and not enough of its use toward a significant end; her subtlety is what we remember, not the material through which it is transmitted; and it is a subtlety, in effect, that is reduced to swinging in a void. *Death of a Man* is not simply a book that fails; with all its good points, it decomposes into trivial effects and still-life pictures. Miss Boyle writes a better prose than most of us find nowadays, but it does not conceal the gaping holes in her narrative; it is a prose that comes to be read for its own sake, and we derive our pleasure from its superb diction, its precision and its beat, not from what it arranges in the narrative, or what it reflects of the turns in human character and conduct.

Times Literary Supplement (review date 16 March 1940)

SOURCE: "Springs of Tragedy," in *Times Literary Supplement,* Vol. 39, No. 1989, March 16, 1940, p. 133.

[*In the following review of* The Crazy Hunter, *the critic claims Boyle has found her best literary form in the novelette.*]

Are there varieties of literary talent for which there is no recognized form of aesthetic expression? Young people who "write" or who "want to write" are inclined to think there are. Yet talent is surely specific, a gift for this or that specific form of literature, and what the young people in question may have in mind is only that there are numerous types of literary facility or accomplishment which are not easily adapted to any of the two or three popular forms of literature at the present time. First and foremost, of course, is the novel, and the not very surprising thing is that to an increasing extent abilities of one sort or another that are quite distinct from the novelist's abilities are exercised in novel-writing nowadays. The pressure, both psychological and commercial, of popular taste is here decisive, since so many innocent library fiends will take up a novel who would not cast a look at poetic drama or a travel diary or spend so much as a thought on a treatise on crime or money or psycho-analysis. Under this pressure, as is all too obvious, the dividing line between fiction and biography, for instance, has all but vanished. Even the mathematical physicist, it seems, may now be tempted to cast what he has to say into semi-fictional form. As for the novel itself, clearly it has grown so accommodating in substance and shape as to be aesthetically almost formless.

In the result all sorts of more or less unconventional but not very satisfying novels are turned out which suggest that their authors would show to much better advantage in sonneteering, say, or sermonizing, or pamphleteering—almost anywhere, in fact, except in the literary medium favoured. Perhaps this applies, above all, to the so-called *littérateur*—poet, critic or essayist—as novelist. But it also applies to quite a number of writers of fiction who have excelled in the short story. Miss Kay Boyle, who has one or two volumes of arresting and individual short stories to her credit, is a case in point. As a novelist she lacks variety and, still more, something of robustness, while even some of the best of her short stories seem to set too cramping a limit to her obviously unusual powers. However, in this new volume of hers, which consists of three longish short stories or "novelettes," she seems to have effected a compromise in aesthetic form that comes very near complete success and that matches very happily her gifts of delicately introspective sensibility.

The first of the stories is about a blind hunter and a young girl's dawning perception of tragedy, the second is a curiously Lawrentian tale of a swannery and the parallel strife of passion of human beings and birds, the third is a somewhat more artificial story of an adolescent neurosis and a murder hunt. In each of the three stories Miss Boyle's narrative method is mainly that of the stream of consciousness, in which thought and action, perception and sensation, are simultaneously caught in an instant of experience. It is not at this time a new method, nor has it ever been a spe-

cially resourceful one, but in Miss Boyle's hands in lands itself to a fine-spun but oddly taut awareness, an extraordinary sharpness of imaginative vision that is powerfully communicated to the reader. It is as though her sudden searchings of sense continually stop short at the edge of mystery. This is nowhere more marked than in the passion, almost pagan in intensity, of her feeling for and understanding of animals. In the title-story, much the best of the three, the horse which is condemned to be destroyed is a vividly suggested character, a tensely physical presence, and at the same time a disturbing symbol of the frustrations of the divided household, every member of which is differently concerned in its fate.

The Bridegroom's Body carries a similar suggestion of the springs of tragedy implicit in thwarted passion. This time the symbolism takes shape in the hatred of the old male swan at nesting-time for the young cob, his rival and possible supplanter on the lake. Here also the human characters seem to enact, in a subtler and more obscure fashion, the drama of the swannery. Lord Glourie, for instance, is still the dominant and unsated male. Lady Glourie's serenity of spirit goes with deep earthy passions, the little Irish nurse is shaken and terrified by dimly apprehended desires. Poetical though the conception is, however, the total effect, in this as in the previous story, is clouded almost to the point of incoherence. Miss Boyle has many of the rarer qualities of the good story-teller, but her besetting danger is to try to convey more esoteric intimations than her words or perhaps any words will carry.

Marianne Hauser (review date 8 November 1942)

SOURCE: "Kay Boyle's Primer for Combat," in *New York Times Book Review,* November 8, 1942, p. 6.

[*In the following review, Hauser praises* Primer for Combat *as a powerful portrayal of France in 1940 under Nazi rule.*]

Last year, after nearly two decades in Europe, Kay Boyle returned to America. *Primer for Combat,* her first book since her return, has its setting in France in 1940 during the months that followed Compiègne. It is a novel which in the form of a diary presents an incisive portrait of France after her defeat.

Miss Boyle is no journalist. She does not content herself with a mere enumeration of facts but searches for the human purport behind them, exploring a people's psychological reactions under the immense pressure of a political *force majeure.*

The form of the book is well chosen. No doubt Miss Boyle must have felt that the Battle of France is too recent an event, too much just one chapter of our current struggle, to be made the theme of a broad objective novel. By letting Phyl, American wife of a historian and mother of three children, write down a day-to-day account of what she observes around her in the small Alpine village of the *Haute-Savoie*, Miss Boyle gives her story the fragmentary touch which helps avoid that false ring of melodramatic prophecy so frequent in contemporary war novels.

Phyl relates the conversations she has had with French soldiers, *bistro*-keepers, merchants and aristocrats as well as refugees from Austria, Holland and Czechoslovakia. Small incidents, side glances and casual remarks reflect the common soldier's sarcastic bitterness over his leaders' inadequacies. There is the story about the *poilus* cheering as they were promised shot for their guns. Cautioned that they may not even get near enough to a German, they started laughing. "The Germans?' they said, 'who's talking about the Germans? It's the captain and the lieutenant we want to put away.'" There is the burning fury of the little people as they recognize that France fought nazism with fascism, the coal merchant Lafond's fearless rebellion against the poison of defeatism, and St. Cyr's dandylike submission to the new order as he voices hazy ideas about France's national resurrection, smart in the "uniform of appeasement," the khaki shorts and shirt of the *Compagnons de France*.

Along with true reports about bombings, fleeing refugees and Nazi bestiality, the village is flooded with rumors about German politeness; legends, originating from Goebbels's propaganda mills, about the courtesy and tact of German officers who, "invariably tall, broad-shouldered, clean-limbed and remarkably blond," offer their seats in streetcars and restaurants to French women while "the hollow-chested, seated Frenchmen" do not make a move. One of the reasons, according to Nazi agents, why France lost the war.

Besides specific political observations, Phyl's diary gives a faithful account of the practical difficulties that confront the French daily under the regime of their "liberators." Dunking a dry zwieback into the tasteless liquid of a *café national*, one hardly thinks "about the inconceivable tragedy of France's defeat," but "merely of the speechless misery of these café breakfasts, of the acceptance that was given the dry rusks and the sugarless drinks on the blank marble tables." **Primer for Combat** illuminates the France of 1940 from a hundred different angles. And against the background of snowcapped mountains, the cool, majestic beauty of the *Haute-Savoie*, which Miss Boyle describes superbly, the people's shamefaced depression over their country's fall lays bare the very core of France's misery.

Throughout the broader pattern of the tale runs the intimate story of Phyl's love for Wolfgang. Wolfgang, strikingly handsome Austrian and the husband of Corinne, Pétain's god-daughter, is with the Foreign Legion in Africa. He is no political refugee. He has come to the village as a ski-instructor, and when war broke out was, as an Austrian subject, given the choice of either going to a concentration camp for the duration or signing up as a Legionnaire.

At first, he implores Phyl in his letters to help him escape to Portugal, lest he should be returned to Austria by German authorities. Phyl takes his anti-fascist feelings for granted, as much for an established fact as her unreasoning passion for him. Later, however, the tone of his letters changes. He is still eager to get out of Africa, but does not care to escape nazism. He now turns to his French wife for help, knowing that Corinne, who understands the Nazis as "a new race of man," will, through her close family connections with Vichy, make it possible for him to live on in France.

For the first time Phyl recognizes Wolfgang's true face. Not the face of a villain, but that of the opportunist who lines up with the side which will most likely succeed: the "perfect athlete who understands one thing only; the exact moment to spring from the board." And through this sudden perception, the source of her love reveals itself to her. Her love, she now knows, did not belong to the Wolfgang who exists, but to the one she created. For Wolfgang "is one thing in one woman's language, and another thing in another woman's language, and perhaps he is nothing in anybody's language * * * not even a star, not even a refulgence, but merely nothing."

Phyl's love, incidental and yet conclusive within the tale of a nation's tragedy, is developed with Proustian discernment. Phyl's dream, a woman's dream, brought to an end through the power of her own ethical choice, gives this book its profound human value.

Edith R. Mirrielees (review date 1 December 1946)

SOURCE: "Stories to Remember," in *New York Times Book Review*, December 1, 1946, pp. 9, 72.

[*In the following review of* Thirty Stories, *Mirrielees praises the collection, citing the French section as the best.*]

This most recent of Kay Boyle's short-story collections offers only fact in its title. In the book will be found thirty stories; it is left to the reader to supply any more colorful designation. And Kay Boyle is a writer who can afford to leave it to the reader. Whatever judgment may be passed on her novels, each of her short-story collections thus far has enlarged her following. The present one can hardly fail to do the same.

The present volume is a garnering from "far over a hundred stories, published and unpublished," of the last twenty years. Familiar titles, therefore, are scattered freely along the title page. **"The White Horses of Vienna," "Rest Cure," "Defeat," "Winter Night"**—readers who remember these will not complain at meeting them again. They may complain that some others, equally memorable, are missing. Why one story is taken and another left is a matter of legitimate curiosity. *Thirty Stories* satisfies this curiosity and on the author's own authority:

> On rereading, they held my interest—and I believe this to be one of the primary obligations of the short story. * * * Equally important * * * is that it attempts to speak with honesty of the conditions and conflicts of its own time.

Nobody will disagree with either of these pronouncements nor will many question that both the obligations named are amply fulfilled. The stories, nearly all of them, do hold attention. The volume, in its entirety, speaks for the troublous years of its writing with an unmistakable honesty. What it says comes with special authority by reason of the author's background. If Miss Boyle had stayed in St. Paul, where she was born, instead of becoming halfway native to half of western Europe, she would probably still have written, and written well, but she would have had neither the power nor the privilege of offering the poignant comment on an overturned world that she is now able to offer.

The book is divided into five sections. The first is titled merely "Early Stories: 1927-1934." The others are placed according to national setting as well as time—"Austrian Group: 1933-1938"; "English Group: 1935-1936"; "French Group: 1939-1942"; "American Group: 1942-1946." The French section is by far the longest of the four; the American, the shortest—three stories only and none of these pronouncedly national. Both American and English sections, indeed, lack the rich savor of a special region which is everywhere present in the stories dealing with France and Austria. These latter, it is easy to see, are the countries of the writer's heart.

Most of the stories are war-touched, of course. Given the years they cover, they could not be otherwise. They are not, however, war stories. Bombs and wounds and death in battle, and even hunger, appear, when they appear at all, in retrospect oftener than in immediate happening. What does appear are the histories of noncombatants, those who suffered war without fighting it. And again and again these histories have the ring of something taken straight from observation.

Especially this is true in the French section, which is not only the longest but also the most consistently impressive. Here a France is built up which, whether a true France or not, has the feel of being true. The French countryside, the humble people in it, are lovingly shown. The several aristocrats presented are convincingly French, convincingly aristocratic—also, they are poltroons. Even as poltroons, however, they retain the veneer of a long-established culture, are never quite contemptible. To have succeeded in balancing them so is a not inconsiderable literary feat.

But the most striking roles in nearly all the stories are those played not by natives at all but by foreigners. France, as has been said, is clearly the country of the writer's heart; her head, it seems, does not agree. It is an Englishman who stays by his bombed French village—"there was a name for the people who left France now." It is the same Englishman who constrains an unwilling French mayor to allocate supplies to the children of those who were French by adoption as well as to the pure French. It is a Mexican who gambles away his own safety in behalf of wounded French soldiers. Americans take the honors in **"Hilaire and the Maréchal Petard"**; in **"Let There Be Honor,"** an Englishwoman. There are others—Austrians, a Spaniard—too many to be overlooked, far too many for their placing to have been accidental, though it may well have been unconscious.

This repeated bestowal of the magnificent actions on outsiders might seem to derogate the French, and in a measure it does; the important French, mayors or counts, play groveling parts. But the final emphasis in the collection is not one that has to do with men's failings. What the stories push home is the high-heartedness and faith and daring, the relationship, thicker than blood, of those of all countries whose ideals are more precious to them than their safety. It is itself a high-hearted book.

Virgilia Peterson (review date 17 November 1960)

SOURCE: "There Is No Armistice," in *New York Times Book Review,* November 17, 1960, pp. 4, 26.

[*In the following review of* Generation Without Farewell, *Peterson, a radio commentator and critic, credits Boyle with creating a profound account of postwar Germany which reflects the conditions from multi-perspectives.*]

Always a lyrical troubling writer, Kay Boyle has never written more poignantly, never come closer to absolute pitch than in this new novel, *Generation Without Farewell,* set in Germany during the American military occupation. Miss Boyle has drawn before, for a number of stories, upon her experience as foreign correspondent for *The New Yorker* in post-war Germany. In this latest book she has gone beyond the obvious ironies implicit in the attempt of the victor to establish a *modus vivendi* with the vanquished, beyond the frontiers of nationality, to probe the vulnerability of the modern soul. She does not soften or cheapen her tone by so much as a breath of sentimentality: her bitterness and her anger are as pure as her compassion. She weeps for man without condoning what he does, and in so doing, she has surpassed herself.

For some, however, *Generation Without Farewell* may not be acceptable. The villain of the tale—if Miss Boyle could create so simple a human artifact as a villain—is not a German but an arrogant American colonel. Those of us who look upon Americans as universally harmless are bound to resent and disbelieve him. With his huge shoulders, ruddy dewlaps, unquenchable thirst and instinctive menace to everything that is tentative and tender, Colonel Roberts, commander of all he surveys, is more of an enemy than any German in the book.

Miss Boyle is too truly an artist to force us to meet Colonel Roberts—or, for that matter, anyone on his staff or in his family—head on. We come to know them only through the young German newspaper reporter, called Jaeger, who is at once the narrator of the story and a participant in it, a self-constituted but all too fragile bridge between the occupied and the occupiers, between the Germans and the Americans, to neither of whom he feels he quite belongs. Two years in Colorado as prisoner of war had been enough for Jaeger to learn the American lingo, loosen the knots that regimentation and brutality had so tightly tied. Those two years had allowed buds of hope to swell for the first time; they had been enough to make him a stranger in his own land when he returned to it; but they had not been enough to make him an American.

So it is subjectively, through Jaeger's double vision, that we see the intolerably high-handed American colonel. Through him, we meet the colonel's breath-taking wife Catherine who enters Jaeger's heart like a spear; the colonel's inscrutable and impassioned 18-year-old daughter, Milly; the sycophantic lieutenant on whom the colonel has his eye as son-in-law. Through Jaeger, we evaluate a civilian man-of-good-will, Seth Honerkamp—who is the director of the local America House, dedicated to re-creating a German image for the Germans which not only they themselves but the whole world can respect. (Inevitably, he is doomed to fall victim to a sharp-toothed intelligence officer with whose plans he interferes.)

Others in the book are the stable boy, Christoph Horn, who

has learned from the aristocratic refugee horses—the Lipizzaners—the manners and sensibilities of a prince; the black-marketeer from Brooklyn; the German forester through whom he deals; and the forester's son, Walter, who believes that the forests are bewitched and who cannot forget the little Jewish girl he found trudging the icy road on rag-bound, frozen feet. We also meet the Graf and his Graefin—whose contempt for Hitler is only exceeded by their contempt for Americans; and all the other Germans, the servile and the crafty, the legless and the blind, the ghosts of the dead, and the living in search of dignity and home.

With Jaeger, we attend the colonel's party at which Germans and Americans are supposed to mix. With Jaeger, and the Catherine of his never-to-be-fulfilled dream, we watch the ill-starred child lovers, Christoph and Milly, riding two dancing Lipizzaners, for the last time astride their hopes. With Jaeger, we go deep into the German forest to hunt not only fox and buck and boar but the mythical enemy that the colonel, no less than the German people, needs to envision in order to have something to destroy.

Because of the darkness of the colonel's motives and those of his lieutenant and his intelligence officer, we are sometimes confused as to who shot at whom and how murderous their respective intents actually were. But we are never for a moment confused by the *leitmotif* itself, the age-old battle between principle and blood. To write about Americans and Germans in post-war Germany is still a perilous adventure—and Miss Boyle risks it unafraid. From this nettle, danger, she has plucked the flower of her truth.

Patricia Holt (essay date 17 October 1980)

SOURCE: "*PW* Interviews: Kay Boyle," in *Publishers Weekly*, Vol. 218, No. 16, October 17, 1980, pp. 8-9.

In the following essay based on an interview with Boyle, Holt provides an overview of Boyle's life, concentrating on the author's political activism.]

Climbing the steps of Kay Boyle's four story Victorian home in San Francisco *PW* is greeted by an enormous poster for Amnesty International that has obviously been hanging on the front door for years. It seems a fitting symbol of the long and productive career of this civil rights activist whose personal stand against fascism, McCarthyism and Vietnam exacted a high price: a ruined marriage in the '40s, a blacklisted career in the '50s, a jail term for sit-ins in the '60s, near loss of a job during the San Francisco State College riots and, most recently (and voluntarily), cancellation of her next publishing contract, due to Doubleday's action against Gwen Davis.

It is Boyle's much-acclaimed literary career that prompts our visit, and once inside, we ask to see some of the books she had written since her first collection of short stories was published more than three decades ago. One by one, out they come—novels, short stories, poems, essays, children's titles—no fewer than 32 books by this indomitable figure of American letters, who for many years had been a regular and much-admired contributor to *The New Yorker, Saturday Evening Post, Harper's* and *The Nation.*

At 78 Kay Boyle is still an imposing presence: tall, thin, straight-backed and austere. She is magnificent and angular, her sharp features accentuated by a nose broken in a childhood accident that makes her face appear hatchetlike, aristocratic, imperious. Yet her voice is soft and full of vitality, and her smile disarming. When we place her most recent book, **Fifty Stories,** which Doubleday has just published, on top of the pile, the smile again creases her hawkish visage, reminding us of *PW*'s Forecast observation that in her writing as well as in life, "Kay Boyle wears well."

he daughter of a wealthy Irishman who bungled his inheritance, Boyle remembers that she started out "almost retarded in reading and writing at first" and that if it hadn't been for a grandmother who gave her a book called *Reading Without Tears* she might never have started reading. She was, she says, "raised by strong women." When she was 14 and the editor of *Poetry* magazine wanted her to change a poem slightly, "My mother told me to change it if I wanted to do so, but not to compromise if I didn't want to change it. I didn't and the poem appeared anyway."

Thus began Kay Boyle's image as an uncompromising woman of principle who, though not as inflexible as some critics have suggested, would remain faithful to certain "indestructible values." One of these, ironically, is a belief that "education is a very destructive thing for creative people." Having taught creative writing at San Francisco State College (now California State University at San Francisco) for nearly 20 years, Boyle says, "The academic structure just squeezes it all out of you because that approach is to rely not on your emotions but your *brain,* and that can destroy a creative person. I used to tell my students at State, 'Don't take any more of these creative writing classes. Make this one the last!'"

Boyle's own formal education was haphazard at best. A student of architecture at Ohio Mechanics Institute, she was one of three females in a college of 1000 males and remembers spending much of her two years there "crawling under the pipes in the basement to the adjacent building,

which happened to be the symphony hall, and hiding there listening to rehearsals."

She did not graduate, having fallen in love with a French exchange student. In the early 1920s, she married him, and they moved to Paris. There Boyle began writing immediately (her first short story appeared in *transition*), and she was befriended by American expatriates and international writers—among them, James Joyce, Gertrude Stein, Samuel Beckett, Harry and Caresse Crosby, Sylvia Beach, Janet Flanner, Scott and Zelda Fitzgerald. She also knew Robert McAlmon, whose later autobiography, **Being Geniuses Together,** she was to resurrect in 1968 and reedit with her own memoirs.

What did it feel like to live in a period of such immense literary significance? "Listen," Boyle says flatly, "much of what you read about the expatriates of the '20s and '30s is pure bunk. They didn't sit around in cafés. They were off writing somewhere to make a living. Students have asked me to describe the poetry readings of the time. My god! Nobody dared mention a work in progress, let alone read it aloud."

By this time, however, other writers had discovered Kay Boyle. Writing in The *New Republic* in 1931, Katherine Anne Porter said that Boyle was one of the "strongest new talents" and praised her for "a fighting spirit, freshness of feeling . . . [and] a violently dedicated search for the meanings and methods of art."

But it was her "fighting spirit" that got Boyle in and out of trouble. After divorcing her husband, she drifted into a bizarre commune run by Raymond Duncan (Isadora's brother) and a year later had to kidnap her own child from the commune in order to be free of the place.

Later, in the '30s and into the '40s, living in the Alps with her second husband, Cambridge scholar Laurence Vail, and their children, Boyle began helping Jews acquire U.S. visas—much to Vail's disapproval. "Marriage experts say it's the small things," sighs Boyle, recalling the breakup of her 12-year second marriage. "Someone leaves the cap off the toothpaste, that sort of thing. But with Laurence it was really a monumental political split. He told me that since I had never had a real education I could not understand that history moves in cycles and that the time had come for fascism to sweep across the world. There was nothing you could do about it but accept it, he told me. I have never accepted that premise. Never."

One of those she helped in obtaining a visa was Joseph von Franckenstein—not a Jew but a Roman Catholic, and an Austrian baron at that—whom she was later to marry. Returning to New York Boyle was "completely taken aback" at American anti-French sentiment. She immediately wrote *Avalanche,* a novel she believed was the first ever published to describe the French resistance to the Occupation. Meanwhile, von Franckenstein performed brilliantly as an American OSS agent and was appointed to the diplomatic corps in Germany after the war. It was there that the first rumors of his "Communist leanings" began.

"It was ridiculous, of course," Boyle recalls. "We were *supposed* to mix with people of all political parties, including the Communists." Investigations and hearings were to continue for years, and Boyle herself became the target of similar accusations; every magazine she had ever worked for came to her defense except *The New Yorker,* which, she said, fired her after she had served as a correspondent on retainer for seven years.

Having returned to the U.S. "in disgrace," the couple taught quietly at private schools and worked to clear themselves—which they did after nine years. By that time their life together was essentially over.

Von Franckenstein was reinstated in the diplomatic corps, only to learn he was dying of lung cancer. He had a series of operations, Boyle recalls, and "the doctors told me I had better get a job. San Francisco State had offered me the best position, so I flew there with Joseph in 1963; he died a few months later."

It was with his insurance money that Boyle purchased the Victorian house in which she was to live for the next 17 years. Retired now, she has finally decided to sell the house and move to Ireland, where she will research her next book, *The Irish Women,* which would have been published by Doubleday had Boyle not returned her advance and canceled her contract. This was not an agonizing decision: "I felt that after [Doubleday] turned against Gwen Davis I simply had no choice," she says in her uncompromising way. Then, obviously thinking of her McCarthy experience, she observes quietly, "You never know when it could strike again."

Tom D'Evelyn (review date 19 June 1985)

SOURCE: "Boyle's Moral Essays Chart the Century's Contours," in *Christian Science Monitor,* June 19, 1985, p. 21.

[*In the following review of* Words that Must Somehow be Said, *D'Evelyn claims the book is a valuable record of the twentieth century as Boyle recounts her life experiences artfully and with skill.*]

Kay Boyle is best known for her short stories. *Words that Must Somehow be Said,* which collects her occasional

nonfiction prose of more than five decades, combines the discipline of the short story and the passion of the writer's involvement in the political and social crises of her own time.

The pieces range from book reviews to long, meditative essays of great artistic interest. The earliest piece is a book review of William Carlos Williams's *In the American Grain,* and Boyle recognized it for what it has since proved to be, a classic work of nonfiction prose.

To discover the contours of the American grain, Williams worked with letters, journals, and other accounts of early visitors to America and native Americans—Thomas Morton of Merrymount, George Washington, Red Eric, Hernando De Soto, Sir Walter Raleigh, and others. One of his most impressive pieces, "The Destruction of Tenochtitlan," opens ominously: "Upon the orchidean beauty of the new world the old rushed inevitably to revenge itself after [Columbus's] return." Williams's capacity for fact only strengthens the moral purposefulness of his work.

The same can be said for Kay Boyle. In his prefatory note to *In the American Grain,* Williams claims to have "recognized new contours suggested by old words so that new names were constituted." The stiffness, the oracular obscurity of that announcement, recalls the manifestoes of his and Boyle's compatriots in Paris during the '20s: the old, conventional language was to give way to "new names."

As we know from her contributions to the memoir *Being Geniuses Together 1920-1930,* Kay Boyle felt very much at one with the modern movement in Paris: She, too, conspired in "the revolution of the word." The pieces collected here reveal a maturing and broadening of that spirit.

After a long spell in Europe, Boyle returned to the United States, where she took up the causes that together constitute a crisis in American consciousness: the grass-roots opposition to the Vietnam war, the enormously emotional sense of solidarity of white liberals with black and native Americans, and the ongoing opposition to the scenarios of mutual destruction and hopeless civil defense in the face of the atomic bomb. She published in *The Nation, The New Republic, The Progressive.*

Only rarely does her voice become shrill, the spirit hard. Kay Boyle is first and last an artist. She is capable of passionate tenderness, as in her descriptions of the women she shared prison cells with when she was jailed for joining a demonstration on the steps of the Oakland Induction Center during the Vietnam war. Here as elsewhere she transformed the minutiae of her experience—which, in this case, had a dangerous potential for sentimental or ideological posturing—into the universals of art.

Because she has lived fully in her own time, Kay Boyle's nonfiction prose constitutes a valuable reserve of modern memory. And as an American testimony, *Words that Must Somehow be Said* has benefitted from the authority of her having lived abroad for so long. She knows Vichy France and postwar Germany: The evidence is all here.

Because she has lived fully in her own time, Kay Boyle's nonfiction prose constitutes a valuable reserve of modern memory.
                                        —Tom D'Evelyn

In her essay on the trial of SS Oberscharfuhrer Henrich Baab, Boyle patiently, skillfully, and without mercy exposes the numbing deviousness of evil and its effects on otherwise unremarkable people. And she notes how "the outrageous bombast of official German communications" can be used to "circumvent action, invalidate knowledge, and trouble the essence of truth."

For her part, Kay Boyle has borne eloquent testimony to the unity of action, knowledge, and truth. For integrity, artistic and moral, *Words that Must Somehow Be Said* compares well with *In the American Grain*. They belong together on the short shelf of great American prose works. They are equally, and perhaps uniquely, possessed of "the balm of command."

Susan Slocum Hinerfeld   (review date 29 September 1985)

SOURCE: A review of *Words That Must Somehow Be Said*, in *Los Angeles Times Book Review*, September 29, 1985, p. 10.

[*In the following review of* Words That Somehow Must Be Said, *Hinerfeld, a critic and writer, praises Boyle's writing, but cites the story "Farewell to New York" as a piece in which she falls short.*]

It is not possible to write a line without telling, something of oneself, and in the essay from the very choice of subject speaks.

The person revealed by these essays is clear-thinking direct, sometimes tart, concerned both with fine distinctions and larger meanings. The point of view is principled, liberal, vigorous: Wrongs can be righted through action let us take action now.

A corollary/example: Kay Boyle has no patience with Eliza-

beth Bowen, 'sensitive and distinguished' nor with the central, recurring type of Bowen's fictions, a "pallid and introverted figure. . . ." The tragedy of such a writer in her eyes (in Bowen's case it is reckoned a "minor tragedy") is the failure to locate "a functioning world." The triumph of Boyle as a writer and citizen is that she was born to, belongs to, "a functioning world" intact and nourishing.

We learn in the essay **"The Family"** that Grandfather Boyle, "Puss," founder of The West Publishing Co., was a tyrant and charmer. Perhaps self-confidence came from him.

But it was the matrilineal Evans heritage that mattered, Work, art and ideas could be the center of life. Among the women of that remarkable family there was already a long tradition of civic zeal and high-minded, forthright activism.

Boyle has no time for pale introversion. She was someone who (to borrow from Nadine Gordimer) "always knew what to do and did it." Enabled, she acted when issues seemed to her to call for action. The French would say that she was comfortable in her skin.

The 25 essays here—on literature, politics and human predicaments—span six decades. (It is startling to read a review suggesting the path where Faulkner's future lies!)

Boyle has written novels, short stories, poetry, reportage, criticism and memoirs (notably the major revision of her friend Robert McAlmon's book on Paris in the '20s, *Being Geniuses Together*)—and of course, essays. But that variety was not enough, so she turned to a mutant form.

Perhaps fact and fiction, like oil and water, simply do not mix. A good example is **"Farewell to New York,"** 1947. It is a ghost story, really, its nub that the dead are with us, their voices our conscience.

At 6 on a winter's evening, at a Longchamps restaurant in New York, a Spanish exile remembers a cold night in Paris, 1945. There, in a street called the rue du Palais, was a shop with curtained booths for the taking of identity pictures. "(A)n endless stream of outcasts" passed through its turnstile at 30 francs a throw.

A "strange thing happened . . . suddenly a strip of photographs came out which belonged to no one in the place . . ." The shop girl was annoyed. Then someone said,"I knew him. We came from the same town, we went to school together. He was killed in Durango in 1936." Out come the photographs of dead men, strip by strip, "in spite of death. . . ."

It is a gorgeous fiction, until it ends with quotations from

Pound, Waugh and Eliot, on why they did not fight in the Spanish Civil War. "Spain is an emotional luxury," Pound said in 1937. To repeat his words in 1947 was a luxury of polemics—one the frail story could not afford.

The book closes with the majestic preface from **"The Smoking Mountain,"** which appeared in *The New Yorker* in 1950, reporting the trial of a Gestapo official in a denazification court in Frankfurt. It also reports the moral climate of a courtroom, a city and a country. It is a work of intelligence and subtlety, a preface that is a suitable finale.

Studs Terkel with Kelly Baker (interview date 26 April 1986)

SOURCE: "Studs Terkel: An Interview," in *Twentieth-Century Literature*, Vol. 34, No. 3, Fall, 1988, pp. 304-9.

[*In the following interview, filmmaker Kelley Baker talks to famous social historian and radio personality Studs Terkel about his personal recollections of Boyle.*]

Edited in consultation with Studs Terkel from an April 26, 1986, interview in Chicago with filmmaker Kelley Baker. (From "No Past Tense Permitted," a documentary in progress, courtesy of Kelley Baker, Portland, Oregon.)

[*Baker*]: *What do you remember about the first time you met Kay Boyle? What stands out in your mind?*

[Terkel]: I remember an elegant looking person, at the time Nelson Algren, I believe, introduced me to Kay Boyle some years ago. I remember also having admired her before I'd met her. I remembered some of the short stories she wrote, a good number of them. When I think of Kay Boyle, I think of someone who has borne witness to the most traumatic and shattering events of our century: not simply this particular era, but of the whole 20th century. Starting early. Both as a creative artist as well as being there. We think of Kay Boyle, immediately, as the golden girl of the Twenties in Paris, and the artists who were there. She knew Joyce, you name them, Duchamp, Beckett, she was there, this girl out of Cincinnati and she was writing. You think of Kay Boyle in Europe, pre-Hitler Europe, just as Fascism was about to take over. You think of Kay Boyle being there during the Spanish Civil War that some say was the overture to World War II. She was there, in a sense, trying to celebrate the Republicans who fought Franco as well as Hitler and Mussolini while the rest of the world stood by. She, among others, a few artists, was there. You think of Kay Boyle, you think of Fascism in Central Europe; again, she was there. And always in her stories or whatever reportage she did, she was there bearing witness. When you think of Kay Boyle continuing, post-war, the Cold War, the McCarthy days, she again challenged and defied witch hunters. You think of Kay Boyle in the Sixties teaching at San Francisco State, defying another hunter, Hayakawa, who was the head of San Francisco State. Being on the side of whom? In every event, on the side of the young. And here, just recently, marching in Ohio, a peace march in the mid-Eighties. So we're talking about 60-65 years. All those events that one way or another, for better or for worse have altered all our lives. Kay Boyle, writer, participant, was there.

You know the old black spiritual, "Were You There, When They Crucified My Lord?" Well, she was there for a number of crucifixions, including that of one of her husbands, who was tortured by the Nazis and held his own. She has always been there. And so I think of her, I think of a survivor as well, but not *just* a survivor. We've heard the phrase, "grace under pressure"—the Hemingway. Hers has been grace under incredible pressure; more, I would say elegance under pressure. Kay Boyle is somebody, of whom, if I could use one word, I'd say, elegant.

We talked about politics earlier today, and Kay has been active in politics. You mentioned that a lot of people get disillusioned with politics, especially politics on the left. Do you know why Kay has stayed true to this?

She's the best one to answer that. Think about it now. When times go bad as they are bad now, it is very easy for someone who is older, who has gone through a great deal, to look upon the earth and say, "Oh God, hopeless." Not with her. She maintains a certain kind of, I wouldn't say optimism in a Pollyanna sense, but a certain kind of vision that she hasn't lost. And so she's with the young, forever. She is forever young. I don't mean that in any goofy commercial sort of way. It is something Jane Addams once called the spirit of youth. It's a spirit of being contemporary. She is forever contemporary. She was so in the Twenties, she was in the Thirties, she was in the witch-hunting Fifties, she was in the protesting Sixties, and she is in what you might call the parlous Eighties. She does not have the disillusioned air that some of her few surviving contemporaries might have.

Do you think there's a reason why she has never gotten the respect as a writer that a lot of people think she deserves?

I think there's a reason for that, sure. Since the word elegance was used about Kay Boyle, and there's an elegance to her story telling as well. We live in coarse times. The fact that Reagan is President and popular tells me how coarsened we've become. Not simply in thought, but in language as well. "Make my day." "Mad Dog." "Rambo." You think of Ronald Reagan. You think of a coarsened aspect to our lives that we've accepted as our life. Kay Boyle is precisely the opposite of that. When I spoke of elegance, I meant that. Of a certain gracefulness, in her language as well as her being, as well as I might add, her politics. That's what we're talking about. There's a vision there of something Dorothy Day, the Catholic worker of years ago, said when they once asked her, "Why are you doing what you're doing?" She was arrested and she was active in protesting war and injustice wherever she found it. Dorothy Day replied, "I'm doing it to help in some way make a world in which it would be easier for people to behave *decently.*" In a sense that's the credo of Kay Boyle. We live in a time right now in which *in*decency appears to be the credo of the day. Kay is the outsider in that respect. Because her vision has never been lost. She is perpetually contemporary, and young.

Do you have a favorite story by Kay?"

I have no favorite stories, just seeing her is always a delight. Of course she is ever greenly beautiful. She always seems shocked by coarse behavior. But at the same time recognizing it as being there. I find that kind of funny, I get a bang out of her. And of course as you know Kay is a— how can you describe her?—she's a very attractive woman. I mean she must have been sensational when she was twenty. I mean she's more so now.

Can you talk a little bit more about her looks, her surprise?

There's always an air of surprise about her. Remember her looks now, she has that Grecian profile. John Barrymore had that, as a male. Barrymore and Kay. Looking at her as a young beauty in those photographs, Man Ray, wow! She knew everybody, whether it's in her correspondence with Samuel Beckett, or with Nelson Algren here in Chicago, the air of being astonished. It occurred to me as we're talking, Kay Boyle at a certain age today has never lost that air of wonder. I think the word is wonder. I think a true artist always has this. Something that Charlie Chaplin had. Sometimes you're surprised at her surprise. Why is she surprised at some lousy behavior by someone? Or something that is unexpectedly decent, or nice? I suppose you'd say it's a young girl's air of surprise. I wouldn't say innocence and yet there's an air of innocence too. Because of that vision she has. Not of what is, but of what can be. I think she's afraid, I would suspect she's afraid of nothing. I don't mean there's a sense of bravado going, I don't think she's afraid of the outsider, of that different person. Though she herself lives in this white-dominated society and WASP-dominated society, of which she is part ethnically, you see, she's an outsider: in that she questions, something's gotta be better. Always she spoke for those up against it.

I wouldn't want to cross her. As S. I. Hayakawa found out, when he was head of San Francisco State. When he first met her, he just bowed. I'd known him in Chicago as a semanticist and a jazz fan. He and I both emceed Mahalia Jackson concerts. I didn't know him as he later became what he became. Whether it was a U.S. senator who slept most of the time. When he opened his mouth, you hoped he'd keep on sleeping. But, here came the little tyrant, the little martinet. Kay Boyle was on that campus, and so she spoke out always. The idea of her marching, you know, just a couple of days before this conversation we're having, marching in Ohio, in Bowling Green, or nearby, on behalf of peace, with kids sixty years younger than she is. And she is one of the youngest there marching. As she did in the Sixties, as she spoke out in the Thirties. So it's Boyle forever.

What was it about the short story in New York, "The Ballet In Central Park" that you . . .

One of her lesser known. We always think of Kay Boyle's celebrated stories but there's one, that I read on the air, one the radio show . . . One of her lesser known stories, **"Ballet in Central Park,"** deals with childhood, and a certain loss of innocence. It's this little WASP girl and these Hispanic kids from a different community. They're getting together in this park with other kids. He's pretending he's a matador, and the tragic result. What is here is a tenderness and a gentleness that surely captured childhood. Not just childhood, but the child's visions of two different classes, see, and both merging. A very moving tale. It was a natural for me to put some music to it, a little Flamenco, touching on this kid putting on the act. That story as much as the celebrated **"White Horses of Vienna"** hit me, you see. Before I'd read any of her stories, I saw a piece in the *Nation,* I believe, oh God, centuries ago. It was Kay Boyle's remembering a young drunken poet entertaining at a bar somewhere in London, and it was Dylan Thomas. She was describing this young poet who was drunk and making a fool of himself, yet she, and I believe her husband with her, recognized this, this genius who was being a clown. That was a terribly moving piece. So always there's this common denominator, I think, of her understanding that person outside.

And she didn't have to do the things she did, you see, because I think she could've written her own ticket, she could've been the Belle of Cincinnati. If anybody wants to be the Belle of Cincinnati. I think that's the last thing that Kay Boyle would want. But I think she could have been anything. Or the Belle of Paris for that matter. But naw, there was always that outsider, that outsider she was looking at too.

How do you feel she deals with young writers?

There's nobody better than Kay in dealing with young writers, or young would-be writers. For one thing you can tell from her correspondence with yourself, with me, with scores of others to whom she writes. Longhand of course. You know that hand immediately, when you pick up that envelope and you see that handwriting you know it's Kay Boyle. With Oakland, San Francisco, or Cottage Grove, Oregon, or Bowling Green, Ohio, you know it's Kay Boyle. Or it could be Paris, and you open the letter and there's that handwriting, and there's the detail and that curiosity. I remember the first time I ever heard her talk, it was about young writers. It wasn't about herself, you see. She could've easily talked about the Twenties, the golden girl, Kay Boyle in Paris with the now institutionalized figures. She could've easily talked about being in Central Europe as Hitler was taking over, and as he took over. Or about Spain. No, she was talking about young writers. Some of whom she recognized as possibly serious. And that was always there, and I guess that she's a magnificent teacher because of the interest she takes. And somehow, there's commitment, that's the other aspect of Kay. She's certainly not an art-for-art's-sake writer. Though her work is serious artistically as critics through the years can attest. What's more important, readers who have been influenced by her, whose lives have been touched by her, know it, too. At the same time she is this committed person. She doesn't separate the two. Never a tract, not a political tract, it's a work of art that she offers. At the same time there's the sense of being a part of a time. And participating in that time. Having a point of view. She's not someone who is objectively portraying a scene. I believe she doesn't believe there's such a thing as objectivity.

Kay Boyle also wanted remembrance of some of her contemporaries, some who were younger, who had died. And so she started the Nelson Algren Fellowship because of her admiration for Algren, whom you called the Bard of Chicago, and he was. So she kept going, she wrote to writers and others for contributions for the Algren fellowship. She was the first judge of the Nelson Algren short story contest sponsored by a magazine here in Chicago. Just as she is encouraging young writers, she works hard to keep green the memories of some of her contemporaries, the younger ones who have died. Just as she's part of history herself, as witness and writer, so she wants to maintain it in a literary sense for the other writers she's admired. Who are no longer around.

Why do you think she champions some of the down and out writers, some of the neglected writers?

Why does she? . . . Well, again this is part of the thing that we're talking about. Why wouldn't she, being Kay Boyle? She'd champion the writers being neglected, put down. There has to be talent, I mean the giftedness has to be there.

Why is Kay Boyle not better known? That's another story. Again we come to what we talked about earlier, things are out of joint when someone like Kay Boyle is not as celebrated as she should be.

Suzanne Clark (essay date Fall 1988)

SOURCE: "Revolution, the Woman, and the Word: Kay Boyle," in *Twentieth-Century Literature,* Vol. 34, No. 3, Fall, 1988, pp. 322-33.

[In the following essay, Clark explores the balance between literary and feminist ideology in Boyle's writing.]

Modernist experiments with language have an especially problematic relationship to women's writing which is experimental. Kay Boyle's early work puts the old categories into motion and marks out a new literary space of intense descriptive prose. Yet her impact on literary history has not seemed so powerful as her writing would warrant. In 1929, Kay Boyle signed a manifesto for *transition* calling for "The Revolution of the Word." Other signers included Hart Crane, Harry and Caresse Crosby, and Eugene Jolas. The "Proclamation" asserted, among other things, that "The literary creator has the right to disintegrate the primal matter of words" and that "We are not concerned with the propagation of sociological ideas except to emancipate the creative elements from the present ideology."

Boyle's rewriting of the new word was a different matter from the poetics of someone like Hart Crane, a difference she in fact had signaled herself in a critique of his obsession with the primacy of words, in "Mr. Crane and His Grandmother." Nevertheless, though she prefers the American renewals of Williams and Moore, Boyle shows herself to be in the tradition of Baudelaire and Rimbaud as well. Her innovations in prose style qualify Kay Boyle as a revolutionary of lyric language. In her early works, such as **"Episode in the Life of an Ancestor," "Wedding Day,"** or **"On the Run,"** she swerves her narratives into a language of illumination and intensity that disorders story sequence and the familiar forms of remembering. She experiments in a way that recalls the hallucinatory surrealism of Rimbaud's prose and fulfills the aspiration of the poetic revolution for what the *transition* manifesto calls "the projection of a metamorphosis of reality."

But what does this powerful disintegration of conventional writing have to do with writing as a woman? The strong old forms of the sentimental novel were part of what modernist poetics rejected. And yet, for the modernists, the cultural image of women and writing was deeply involved with that past. A shattering of language seemed to be at odds with writing like a woman. Women writers, too, felt they had to separate themselves from that conventional past. Boyle herself has taken pains to disassociate her work from the older tradition of women's writing as well as from the politics of feminism. Nevertheless, Kay Boyle's reworking of the relationship between time and place, narration and description, may also make the connection between the time of poetic revolution and the place of the woman.

Julia Kristeva, another woman who has complicated relationships with revolution and women's writing, may help us to see the problem. In her essay, "Women's Time," Kristeva redefined Nietzsche's idea of monumental or mythic time, a kind of temporality that is left out of rational discursive history. Kristeva defines "women's time" as "repetition" and "eternity," in contrast with the linear movements of history. Women's time is characterized by

> the eternal recurrence of a biological rhythm which conforms to that of nature and imposes a temporality whose stereotyping may shock, but whose regularity and unison with what is experienced as extrasubjective time, cosmic time, occasion vertiginous visions and unnameable *jouissance*

If the order of production defines the time of history, it is the order of reproduction which seems to define this other kind of time, time which is so bound to the monumental, and the regional, that it is almost a kind of space. The cyclic and monumental forms of time associated with female subjectivity are far from the linear times of progress and project. But we must proceed very carefully, with Kristeva as with Kay Boyle, for it would be very wrong to suggest that either of them advocated a splitting away of a woman's order from human history.

Boyle's early work practices a resistance to extremism in the midst of a modernist extremism about gender. Modernism as it appeared in the 1920s featured an ideological either/or which would either deny the existence of gender difference in the name of equality or, in a move which Catharine Stimpson calls the "modern counterreformation in support of patriarchal law," claim gender difference, as D. H. Lawrence does, for example, to be the final truth.

If Boyle refuses to write polemically, in behalf of an alternative women's reality, she also refuses to omit gendered, female elements from her writing. Working within a culture of gendered extremism, she softly moves to put the contradictions into motion. The word "soft" has a certain significance; in an age which favored the tough over the tender, Boyle uses it so frequently it is almost a stylistic marker. A certain radical fluidity characterizes the forward movement of her narration. She makes visible the movement of what is left unspoken by the controlling enig-

mas of realism. So the luminous otherness of her work might well pass unremarked, since it is "soft," since it is neither an embrace nor a refusal of modernism's radical gendered Other. Boyle's work resists certain categories, traps of ideology, and this includes the categorical oppositions of male and female.

Boyle's work resists certain categories, traps of ideology, and this includes the categorical oppositions of male and female.
—*Suzanne Clark*

Kay Boyle's work might be thought of as revolutionary, then, not only because of the shattering of syntax which connects her experimental writing to the *avant-garde*. She makes the metaphorical connection between individuals, across difference. Her writing subverts the male plot, linear time, by a recursive, anaphoric temporality. And perceptions flow with the voice of the speaker across the boundaries of subject-object, rewriting the Romantic identifications with exterior images which Ruskin criticized as the "pathetic fallacy." Kay Boyle uses the fluidity of poetic forms to wash out the one-track temporality of male discourse and to undermine the singularity of gender ideology by a multiple sympathy. She unsettles the stabilities of identity. Time enters the problematic of space. Women's time enters into history, making it less singular, undoing its regularities.

Three of her early stories will serve as examples of how Kay Boyle's writing might participate in such a project. What kind of narrative time is operating, for example, in the story called **"Episode in the Life of an Ancestor"**? What kind of story is an "episode"? Is it singular or plural? A kind of turning point, or a repeated event?

In the story, a young woman defies her father's conventional desires for her to act like a submissive woman. The masterful way she treats their horses is like the mastery she exercises over her father and would-be suitor, the schoolmaster. But the conflict between the father and daughter is framed by the long view of history. This is the story of an ancestor, of a grandmother as a young woman. The whole shimmers ambiguously between the backward long vision of memory and the immediacy of a present moment: "But at a time when the Indian fires made a wall that blossomed and withered at night on three sides of the sky, this grandmother was known as one of the best horsewomen in Kansas."

The point of view also shifts to produce discontinuities in the linear structure of the plot. It is her father's egoistic will to dominate which provides the conflict in the story:

"Her father was proud of the feminine ways there were in her . . . It was no pride to him to hear [her voice] turned hard and thin in her mouth to quiet a horse's ears when some fright had set them to fluttering on the beak of its head." The daughter/grandmother, however, is not drawn into the conflict. Her perceptions involve the repeated, habitual, physical world and her mode is exclamatory, even joyful: "What a feast of splatters when she would come out from a long time in the kitchen and walk in upon the beasts who were stamping and sick with impatience for her in the barn." From the daughter's point of view, sympathy is a strong recognition of difference, and her "way with horses" is mastery without egotism. Her point of view flows into the animal sensations of the horse:

> This was tame idle sport, suited to ladies, this romping in the milkweed cotton across the miles of pie-crust. Suddenly he felt this anger in the grandmother's knees that caught and swung him about in the wind. Without any regard for him at all, so that he was in a quiver of admiration and love for her, she jerked him up and back, rearing his wild head high, his front hoofs left clawing at the space that yapped under them.

The wildness of the horse seems to represent some kind of primeval vigor and sexuality that might remind us of D. H. Lawrence. It is, however, an energy both shared and directed by the woman. Against this energy, the father's will appears as unreal imaginings: he longs for "the streams of gentleness and love that cooled the blood of true women." He doesn't know what is going on inside her or outside her. As he sees it, she goes off into the unknown for her ride into a night "black as a pocket." The ironic folds in the fabric of their relationship turn about the schoolmaster, a "quiet enough thought" by comparison to the woman and the horses until the father imagines him in the sexualized landscape of her midnight ride. Then his rage produces a paranoid close-up of the schoolmaster's face in his mind's eye—the detail of hairs and pores—in a failure of sympathy which wildly reverses itself again at the end with his unspoken cry: "What have you done with the schoolmaster?" The father's fantasies are chairbound and disconnected from life. In the end, he cannot even put them into words.

The grandmother has hot blood, a heat that spreads and permeates the vocabulary of the story in a membranous action. The women is woven into the fabric of the moment as she is into the words of the text, part of the whole cloth of experience. This displacement of human energy into the surrounding objects of perception makes the descriptions seem luminous, surreal—not imaginary, but strongly imagined. The grandmother's intensity spreads into the landscape with its contrasts of soft and hard, white and red, domestic flax and wild fire: "soft white flowering goldenrod," "Indian fires burning hard and bright as peonies." The deep valleys and gulfs and the blossoming prairies form a topology of pocketing and hollows. The father registers how the daughter is a very figure of thereness: "When she came into the room she was there in front of him in the same way that the roses on the floor were woven straight across the rug." He, on the other hand, is the very figure of absence, speechless, longing nostalgically for some one "of his own time to talk to." On the recommendation, apparently, of the schoolmaster, the woman has been reading the creation of Eve passage from *Paradise Lost*. Milton's lines expose Boyle's poetic figure, the mutuality of flesh and landscape and the spousal emotion. But this revelation of poetic influence offends the father, perhaps as much as the sexuality implied in the passage.

Like Milton, her father takes an accusatory stance toward the woman's sexuality. However, the daughter's refusal to be feminine his way, "the cooking and the sewing ways that would be a comfort to him," undoes his ego-centered plot, an undoing which opens possibilities for the woman to be heroic in more multiple ways. Instead of a single hero dominating a single plot in time, Boyle produces the double figure of the daughter/grandmother and a narrative which circles through episode to a life time. Instead of a hero who would make the woman over in his own image, she produces a heroine who moves through mastery—of the horses, the schoolmaster, even her father—to a sympathy which is not identification with a male voice. The story is contained by long-distance temporality, as if written on a tapestry, a legendary mode which mimics the male heroic modes only to name them "episode." Female desire reshapes the forms of narrative as well as the forms of description: the woman is a hero who changes the forms of the heroic.

But in **"Wedding Day,"** Kay Boyle does not shrink from showing us female power of a less attractive kind, allied with the bourgeois projects of family and possessions, and the literary mode of "realistic" representation. In this story, it is the mother who works to dominate, through organizing the details of the wedding day which will initiate her all too energetic children, the too loving brother and sister, into the empty exchanges of proper social relations. The wedding will initiate them into culture—and separate them. It is the mother who makes the violent cut that institutes order—as if she were founding the very system of culture by preventing the incest of brother and sister—but the gesture is also absurd and grotesque. So it finds its image in the "roast of beef" that "made them kin again" as "she sliced the thin scarlet ribbons of it onto the platter." Not that the mother has, exactly, forced this marriage—she says it was not her idea, and her son defends his sister's choice—whose choice it was is confused. The issue is more primitive; the mother's negativity is on the side of the cut, the ceremonial structure, against any outbursts of trouble or love. She opposes her son with a prayer for "dignity," but, returning from a last excursion together, they find her on her knees tying "white satin bows under the chins of the potted plants."

She must maintain the objects of family life as intact mirrors—so it is that she counts the wedding "a real success, . . . *a real* success" when "no glass had yet been broken." Of course, it is the bride at the wedding who is "broken," but that happens beyond the precincts of the "real" which the mother so carefully maintains. Thus, from the point of view of the mother, the story has a happy ending; if she were the author of it, the incestuous energy of the brother and sister's love would be repressed.

Just as the brother and sister threaten the social order and its objects with their desire, the descriptive intensity of Boyle's style violates the decorum of the ceremony with a contradiction and violence that threatens to flood out the containing devices of concrete objects. What are these images doing at a wedding? The red carpet was to "spurt like a hemorrhage." "No one paid any attention" to the wedding cake, "with its beard lying white as hoar frost on its bosom." What is this negativity? There is the "thunderous NO" of the mother, who refuses to give the copper pans to her daughter as the spirit of a family inheritance might suggest. The mother must keep the pans orderly and unused, the "pride of the kitchen," "six bulls-eyes reflecting her thin face." She wishes, indeed, for the orderly household objects to serve as mirrors for the son and daughter as well, representations of the selves she would have them take on.

The young people challenge the civilizing project. These two are Nietzschean creatures, with "yellow manes," "shaggy as lions," "like another race." Like a refrain, the brother keeps repeating, "It isn't too late." But what else might they do except enter into the schemes laid out for them? Something, this story suggests, as it exceeds and overwhelms the bourgeois "real" of the mother: "in their young days they should have been saddled and strapped with necessity so that they could not have escaped. . . . With their yellow heads back they were stamping a new trail, but in such ignorance, for they had no idea of it."

The necessity of youth, of freedom, of a new race encounters the violence of April, like Eliot's April the "cruelest month," bringing the death, here, of childhood. "Here then was April holding them up, stabbing their hearts with hawthorne, scalping them with a flexible blade of wind." "Over them was the sky set like a tomb, the strange unearthly sky that might at any moment crack into spring." The brother and sister take a ride in a boat together. If the boat ride were solitary, it would be an easy allegory; the wedding would represent the shackling of the poetic spirit. However, they are two; what is between them we are less

likely to see as a visitation of the romantic Imagination than as incestuous desire. Neither they nor we know if they should act on what they feel. "And who was there to tell them, for the trees they had come to in the woods gave them no sign."

The signs of the story produce not a judgment about how the plot should have gone, but a negativity that opens up the forms of the wedding and the story to something else, something which like the sister and brother does not wholly fit in the bourgeois "real," something full of energy, destructive and exuberant. At the end the daughter's "feet were fleeing in a hundred ways throughout the rooms, . . . like white butterflies escaping by a miracle the destructive feet of whatever partner held her in his arms." The wedding, far from locking her exclusively to one person, has propelled her into an anonymity of social exchange. The brother's antagonism scatters the calling cards around the rooms. An exotic, almost romantic energy inhabits the mother's performance as she dances, undermining her decorum, and destroying the very syntax of the sentence: "Over the Oriental prayer rugs, through the Persian forests of hemp, away and away."

In **"Wedding Day,"** Boyle reveals the hidden violence of the social contract and releases the energy of exposure to work on the forms of language itself. At the same time, she does not wholly cast the mother as executioner, the daughter as victim. Rather, she exposes the sacrificial violence of the wedding itself, and the relentless secularity of its bourgeois forms. Boyle resists a "women's writing" which would trap her in an oppositional category identified with the bourgeoisie; she neither endorses nor combats but rather eludes capture in the mother's forms.

Boyle's elusiveness produces an unsettling. She is always in favor of something which illuminates the landscape with significance—call it love—something which bends the narrative plot away from its resolutions, which turns the eye inescapably to the detail, apparently decorative, but now repeating anaphorically the interestedness of the subject who writes. These are not stories about isolated selves, but about the mutual imbrications of relationships among people, and so they do not disguise the complexity of perspectives which our feelings for each other are likely to generate.

Even a story as purely focused as **"On the Run"** shows the contrary motions of resolution coming up against one another and that language of significance breaking closures, keeping the time itself open. The situation is close to biography: two lovers, like Kay Boyle herself with Ernest Walsh, are wandering across the south of Europe, unable to find a place for the sick man to rest—thrown out of hotels because he is dying. In **"On the Run,"** memory is left permeable—fragile, undecided, unpunctuated, determined only by the universal timelessness of death that thus seems everywhere. David Daiches says that Boyle's stories are like parables, with "a special kind of permanence" about them. In our culture, this sense of permanence may be identified with women's time, appearing as a contrary narrative that works across the linear, historical plot. This is especially visible in **"On the Run,"** where the history is known, and the story exists nevertheless not in a past, but in a recurring present, like a parable.

The young couple must deal with a woman who orders them to leave rather than helping them. It is not just a person, but social convention itself which opposes them. The proprietress of the hotel is, in fact, in mourning. She seems to know all about the conventions of death:

> Bereaved in the full sallow of her cheeks bereaved and the tombstones rising politely polished with discreet sorrow bereaved and remembered with bubbles of jet frosted on her bosoms and mourned under waves of hemmed watered crepe. I have mourned people for years and years this is the way it is done.

She seems also to possess a kind of knowledge about religious conventions of sacrifice: there was her "rosary hanging like false teeth," and "the Christ bled with artistry" on her crucifix. But her knowledge has all been projected onto the objects, reduced and transformed to fetishes. So what she says is: "Your husband cannot die here, . . . we are not prepared for death." Here is the terrible irony, that the sick man must keep on going. Like the mother in **"Wedding Day,"** the proprietress does not seem to know what women are supposed to hold in custody: the value of relationship, the cycles of time, of the generations, of biological time. And like the mother, she has translated all of it into the social symbolic.

Thus women's time must return through the narrative of the story. Boyle's writing stops the forward pressing of historical time, like the train stopped at "Saint-André-les-Alpes," and sidetracks it into sensuous, loaded detail:

> As the train stopped a soft pink tide of pigs rose out of the station-yard and ran in under the wheels of the wagon. The crest of little alps was burning across the roofs of the town, with the dry crumbling finger of the church lifted and the sky gaping white and hot upon decay.

She strips the sick man's words of their history to let them fly out as if prophetic, repeated, stripping them even of punctuation:

> Get her out of here he said I am going to cough Christ is this where the death will get me take the cigaret and when I cough walk around the room and sing or something so they won't hear me

There is no period after his words.

The conflict with the proprietress does not appear as a single plot with a conclusion, but as the anaphoric structure of enduring betrayal. The message of betrayal is repeated three times, each introduced by the phrase "The bonne came back to say." It is a sacramental structure. At the end, too, the man's words are stripped of punctuation so that they seem to escape from the symbolic conventions of the story and sound in the mind like stream-of-consciousness, recurring. This is *anamnesis,* a resurrection of the past and not just memory: "Keep on keep on keep on he said maybe I'm going to bleed." Such a resurrection takes place in the process of a narrative dialectic between the linear time of history that is past and the personal time of remembrance, anamnesis. Anamnesis is the form of recollection which Plato associated with eros—and with access to eternal truth. It is the word for the "remembrance" of Christian communion. And it is the unforgetting of the past which Freud advocated, the healing reliving of pain which psychoanalysis could effect. This time which Boyle produces is associated, as well, with what Julia Kristeva calls "women's time."

This resurrection—and not just recollection—of a moment of pain and love inserts difference into the history. The position of difference which we may associate with women's time here is different from the polarized opposition which some of Boyle's characters, like the mother and the proprietress, seem to inhabit. This alternate version of narrative, with its descriptive intensity overwhelming the forward movement of plot, opens language up to the surreal, the hallucinatory. Narrative time gives way to descriptive space.

The energy is not in the story, or the forward movement of plot, but rather in the metaphorical connections among people and place—in relationship. Even though these connections shift and develop through time, so that it looks as though there is an elaboration of plot, the motive force of story is not erotic in the masculine mode. That is, the displacement of desire does not take the form of an adventure. The energy here is moral, even if the situations are unconventional.

And this is true not only for Boyle's early experimental stories, where condensation and stream of consciousness make the form private, intense, and lyrical. As the descriptive and metaphorical qualities of discourse appear in more and more public formulations, from the autobiographical novel, **Year Before Last,** to a best-seller like **Avalanche,** they support more complex and yet more familiar forms of relationship.

Let us look a little closer at this descriptive language which so many of Kay Boyle's readers have noted—which Margaret Atwood cites as one of her most striking attributes. Sandra Whipple Spanier associates it on the one hand with a Joycean project and on the other with the romantic perspective in Boyle: she "depicts the external world as a reflection or projection of the perceiver's consciousness." Like Joyce, Boyle writes a "lyric" novel, which decenters the lyric subjectivity, the image of an ego. Boyle opens language to the pressure of the unspeakable; her words are saturated with the residues of what cannot be said, but can be mutually felt. In doing this, she changes the way we might think about the so-called "pathetic fallacy."

Boyle rewrites the romantic reflexivity, shattering the mirror relationship of self and nature under the pressure of a point of view that flows everywhere and comes from no single or stationary ego, or subjectivity. In this, she eludes the very categories of romantic, unified selfhood, of the "true and false appearances" with which Ruskin had thought through his influential critique of the "pathetic fallacy." Ruskin, let us recall, had argued that it is "only the second order of poets" who delight in the kind of description produced by violent feeling, a "falseness in all our impressions of external things" which "fancies a life" in foam or leaf instead of maintaining distinctions. Ruskin's "great poet" masters feeling:

> But it is still a grander condition when the intellect also rises, till it is strong enough to assert its rule against, or together with, the utmost efforts of the passions; and the whole man stands in an iron glow, white hot, perhaps, but still strong, and in no wise evaporating; even if he melts, losing none of his weight.

This nineteenth-century vision of the strong ego, the whole man, the rational individual has retained its heavy influence in twentieth-century criticism, visible in the work of critics like John Crowe Ransom and Yvor Winters, and visible in the great fear of the "sentimental" which permeates criticism.

Kay Boyle's practice, like Joyce's, breaks open this paranoid logic of the subject. In the place of individual heroic figures, she has the multiple connections of relationships; against the center of a linear plot she brings a counter narrative to bear. Words do not simply mirror subjects; the luminosity of her language tracks the energy of a freed desire to make connections. Hers is the logic of a poetic revolution which makes room for the women, as for others. In this it is not simply experimental, and indeed, the chief characteristics I have observed here are to be found, in slightly different forms, in her later, apparently more conventional work.

Kay Boyle works to rewrite the extreme logic which erases woman from the place of the subject or installs her as the singular Other of male discourse. Hers is instead a lyric refiguring of the story which produces more multiple possibilities. It might simply be called the logic of sympathy.

Whether or not a writing which practices this kind of revolution may be powerful enough to work larger changes in literary culture remains, however, an open question. This is a writer who offers us the possibility of an artistic practice which exceeds the limits of gendered identity, which can say things that could not be said otherwise. As her readers, it is up to us now to find ways to speak about Kay Boyle's words and the revolution of the woman.

Burton Hatlen (essay date Fall 1988)

SOURCE: "Sexual Politics in Kay Boyle's *Death of a Man*," in *Twentieth-Century Literature*, Vol. 34, No. 3, Fall, 1988, pp. 347-62.

[*In the following essay, Hatlen reconsiders* Death of a Man *from a feminist perspective in an attempt to explain why the novel has been misinterpreted as Pro-Nazi.*]

When Kay Boyle's ***Death of a Man*** was first published in 1936, many reviewers, and even one member of Boyle's own family, read the novel as expressing pro-Nazi sympathies. Mark Van Doren, writing in the *Nation,* said that the book tries to "hypnotize the reader into a state of what may be called mystical fascism." In the *New Republic,* Otis Ferguson characterized "Miss Boyle's case for the Nazi spirit" as an instance of "special pleading." As Ferguson read the novel, "Those who plot in the wine cellars and keep the swastikas burning on the mountains at night are the outstanding characters; the author's sympathy and understanding are theirs." The anonymous reviewer in the *Times Literary Supplement* spoke of "the glamour which Miss Boyle casts over the National Socialist movement," and the anonymous reviewer in *Time* described the novel as a "Nazi idyll." In the *Forum,* Mary Colum, prefacing her discussion of ***Death of a Man*** with the statement that "between the tyranny that is fascism and the tyranny that is Communism, there is something more suited to western people in fascism," described Boyle's novel as "a revelation of an almost mystical Nazism that is as startling to us as it was to the American heroine." And Colum quoted with approval, implying that the words represented Boyle's own judgment, a passage in which a Nazi youth describes a speech by Hitler as "like great music, like a poem being sung!"

Finally, Sandra Whipple Spanier reports that even Boyle's own sister apparently read both *Death of a Man* and **"The White Horses of Vienna,"** a widely reprinted short story of the same period, as pro-Nazi, and refused to speak to their mother for a full year "because Mrs. Boyle defended Kay's purpose" in writing these works.

The possibility that Kay Boyle wrote a pro-Nazi novel in the mid-1930s must startle anyone who knows anything about her life. For Boyle has been, as the subtitle of Spanier's critical biography states, an "activist" as well as an "artist" throughout her life, and her politics have been consistently Left. In one of her inter-chapters in *Being Geniuses Together,* Boyle reports that the Sacco-Vanzetti case—one of the great Left-wing causes of the period between the wars—awoke her to political consciousness. During World War II, Boyle wrote two *Saturday Evening Post* serials and many other works designed to bolster American morale in the struggle against Nazism, and after the war she published two novels designed to warn against the danger of a lingering fascism in Europe (*The Seagull on the Steps*) and in American culture itself (*Generation Without Farewell*). In the 1950s Boyle was blacklisted for her presumed "Communist" sympathies. And in the 1960s she became an important figure in the civil rights and anti-war protest movements: her most recent novel, *The Underground Woman,* was born out of this experience. Given the pattern of political commitments suggested by Boyle's life story, it is hard to imagine that she could have become, even briefly, an apologist for Nazism. But if *Death of a Man* is not such an apology, then how do we account for the reaction of the book's reviewers, as summarized above?

I believe that the reviewers of *Death of a Man* generally misread the novel because they saw Boyle's judgment of Nazism as the central issue, whereas in fact the focus of the novel is not the pros or cons of this political movement per se. Alfred Kazin, himself a writer of the Left, seems in retrospect the most perceptive reviewer of *Death of a Man.* Kazin suggested that Boyle's "main interest . . . is in the influence of politics on the soul or the temperament, not in its effect on the outward life of men or the pattern of their society." In the end, I shall here argue, *Death of a Man* does offer a judgment of Nazism. However, in the novel the virtues and vices of Nazism are, I believe, secondary to a larger concern with the effects of the will to power on the lives of human beings, and especially on the relations between men and women. In this respect, *Death of a Man* represents a natural extension of the themes of Boyle's previous novels, all of which were born out of a recognition that power and sexuality are inextricably intertwined. *Plagued by the Nightingale* explores the

tyrannies of nation, culture, and family, which distort and finally destroy the love between a French man and an American woman. The portrait of Eve Raeburn, the Ethel Moorhead character in *Year Before Last,* is a memorable study of maternal-erotic possessiveness; and the portrait of Sorrel, the Raymond Duncan character in *My Next Bride,* provides an equally subtle analysis of the male will to control. Two of the early novels, *My Next Bride* once again and *Gentlemen, I Address You Privately,* offer courageous explorations of the power dynamics of same-gender erotic relationships. Writing to Sandra Spanier in 1984, Boyle insisted that her early novels are pervaded by issues of class and power, and I would fully agree. I would also argue that the strength of these novels lies in Boyle's sensitivity to the way power operates in personal relations, including sexual relations, and her extraordinary ability to bring into focus the point at which the personal and the political meet. So too, I propose, *Death of a Man* explores the ways in which the personal becomes political and the political becomes personal, as Boyle elucidates what might be called the sexual politics of Nazism. In the novel, Boyle explores the ways in which the exigencies of power distort and finally destroy the possibility of love, in a socio-political situation dominated by the Nazi movement. Further, I believe that Boyle here sees Nazism as merely an extreme manifestation of those general patterns in Western culture which current feminist theory calls "patriarchy." In this respect *Death of a Man* seems to me an important text in the emergence of a feminist consciousness, and it is an explicitly feminist reading of the novel that I shall offer here.

> *. . . Death of a Man* **explphs the ways in which the personal becomes political and the political becomes personal, as Boyle elucidates what might be called the sexual politics of Nazism.**
>
> **—Burton Hatlen**

If many early readers saw *Death of a Man* as a pro-Nazi novel, one primary reason is that the central male character, Dr. Prochaska, is an undeniably sympathetic character, and his commitment to the Nazi movement inclines us to see that movement in a positive light. In the opening chapters, Boyle develops a contrast between the vigorous, athletic Prochaska, who climbs about the Austrian Alps with absolute confidence, and the limp, cynical, effete Englishman whom Pendennis, the female protagonist, has recently married. But Prochaska is characterized not only by animal magnetism but by artistic sensitivity; for example, he speaks of Mozart with warm admiration. We also learn that Prochaska's exuberant charm has won him the devotion of the nuns with whom he works, and the children in

Prochaska's hospital also adore him. A lean, strong Nazi, even a Nazi who loves Mozart—this we might have expected. But a Nazi who can charm a lay sister and who romps with a three year old diphtheria victim through a hospital ward—this comes as a surprise. Boyle refuses to let us hate this man. And if we cannot hate Prochaska, how can we hate the movement to which he has dedicated his life?

Prochaska is one of two principal point-of-view characters in **Death of a Man.** As a consequence, we accept, at least provisionally, his view of the world, including his conviction that Nazism is the only alternative to despair. As Prochaska tells Pendennis, the American heroine, "Instead of youth we have been offered despair, but the joke of it is we can't accept it, we really can't. You see we have absolutely no capacity for despair." In some measure, the hope which Nazism offers is material and economic, and at times Prochaska's comments may remind us of the old claim that Hitler "put Germany back to work." But material goals cannot alone account for the fervor of the Nazis, which verges on the religious. Prochaska tells Pendennis that for the Austrians Hitler is a "Saviour" who promises "that it is no longer necessary to despair." And not only to Prochaska but, it would appear, to Boyle herself (for it is the authorial voice that we hear in the following passage), Nazism seems to offer, for Austrians at least, the *only* alternative to despair:

> either a man was blind, his courage and heart had been stifled in him by a defeat too general for individual recognition or else he bore that strong forbidden name for power as . . . Dr. Prochaska and more than half the people of the country secretly and proudly bore it.

The strong forbidden name here is, of course, "Hitler." In the Austria of this novel, there are only two alternatives: Hitler or Dollfuss, who led the clerical-fascist, pro-Mussolini regime which ruled Austria in the early 1930s. That is, we see in the novel no Left-wing alternative to Fascism; and indeed there was no such alternative in the Austria of the mid-1930s, for in 1934 the Dollfuss government effectively destroyed the Left opposition in a military assault on the working class district in Vienna. Given the choice between Hitler and Dollfuss, we can understand Prochaska's preference for Hitler, in those pre-Holocaust days. And we should remember that early Nazism claimed to be a "revolutionary" movement, dedicated to bread and justice. Did Boyle, in the mid-1930s, see Nazism as a progressive political movement? The novel appears to hold open this possibility.

However, Prochaska is not the only Nazi that we meet in **Death of a Man.** In particular, we see a good bit of Praxlmann, proprietor of a *gasthaus* in Feldbruck and the local party boss. Praxlmann is at times a ludicrous figure, as when he laments the destruction of his *biergarten* by a bomb tossed into the yard of a neighboring, anti-Nazi newspaper, and then tossed over the wall into the *biergarten* by an alert night-watchman. But more often Praxlmann is a frightening presence. Boyle describes his "eye" as "shrewd and vicious," and his general demeanor as "violent and strong." Praxlmann's brutality is particularly apparent in his treatment of the women in his life: his wife, his daughter Cilli, and his wife's niece Hella. Hella in particular is the object of Praxlmann's tyrannical will to control:

> "For the love of God!" roared Fati Praxlmann's voice when he saw her talking too long with the men. "Bring me some beer, one of you girls!" he shouted down the room, and he did not speak her name but his heavily-lidded eye was turned on Hella like the eye of a sultan on one of his harem wives.

Praxlmann demands absolute obedience not only from family but also from the party faithful, including Prochaska. A will to power, then, and especially a will to power over women—these are, Boyle's portrait of Praxlmann suggests, another characteristic of the Nazi movement. And ultimately this will to power incarnates itself in the figure of the patriarch, who treats both real daughters and spiritual sons like Prochaska as so many possessions.

Praxlmann's women do not rebel openly against his authority, but they do find ways of asserting their female identities, and in doing so they suggest the limits of patriarchy. Of the three, Hella is most completely victimized by the situation: she comes from the still-peasant branch of Muti Praxlmann's family, and she is beginning to develop a goiter which, she fears, will lose her both her job and any chance of marriage. As a consequence, she cowers, afraid to challenge Praxlmann's authority. Muti Praxlmann, on the other hand, offers a classic example of accommodation. She is indifferent if not hostile to her husband's politics; she even mentions with disapproval an incident in which a Jew is excluded form a ski-jump competition. But Muti is no liberal—rather she is interested only in money, status, and clothes. This indifference, however, gives her a small area of freedom from her husband's will to power. Teen-age Cilli, finally, also begins, if only in a fumbling, instinctive way, to seek out an area of autonomy for herself. She rebels directly against the authority not of her father but of her mother, by refusing to consider marriage to the callow Toni, whom her mother has selected, declaring that instead she wants to "marry a doctor"—thinking, of course, of Prochaska, whom Cilli too loves. In her groping way, Cilli also recoils from the violence which she feels growing in the country: "There is this thing outside and I do not know if it is right or wrong, but it is a thing like war, like death, and I cannot bear it." Cilli's anguish at what is happening leads her to a series of actions which at least indirectly help the Nazi cause, but her motives are always personal rather than political: she loves certain people and wants to help and protect them.

To the oppressively masculine world of the Praxlmann *biergarten*, Boyle also proposes the beautifully sketched world of the *infektionhaus*, the hospital for contagious diseases where Prochaska works. The *infektionhaus* is a world of women and children, for Prochaska himself is apparently the only adult male who enters this region. Boyle begins her description of the *infektionhaus* with a resonant image of birds flying in through the open window and through the children's ward. Three boys in the hospital have been feeding the birds and have "adopted" various species: "the game was to have one's own birds come in the greatest numbers or come first to the sills." The birds are described as fierce creatures: "these birds are savages," says Prochaska later. "They'd take the flesh from your palms if you let them have it." But the birds also evoke a wild, untrammeled life which moves through the prison-like hospital but is never captured by the institutional structure. And indeed, the whole hospital seems to pulse with a wild, free laughter: waiting for the birds, the three boys sit "squeezing the laughter hard and silent in their shivering throats and listening, listening." This world of freedom and spontaneity is available at a terrible price: only the diseased are allowed to enter. But, with a twist that may owe something to Mann's *The Magic Mountain*, Boyle suggests that perhaps only women and children, and only the sick among them at that, are able to break out of the shackles of social convention enough to experience, even momentarily, the wild, free life within them.

Over this kingdom of the wild and the sick, two aging lay sisters, Marianna and Resi, preside. Cut off from a vital relation to the male world, Resi in particular is a twisted human being. Resi is literally "twisted," for she is a hunchback; and her behavior suggests a will-to-power through sacrifice and devotion which is the female counterpart of the male will-to-power that we see working in Praxlmann. In an extended inner monologue, we learn of a series of moments when Resi was momentarily transfigured by a sense of being needed: first by her mother; then, early in her years as a nurse, by a dying man who held her hand and told her, "You are little, Sister Resi. I've always been afraid of women, but you're so little I wouldn't have been afraid;" and then by Prochaska, who told her, "I couldn't get on without you, Sister Resi." The need to be needed, the need to serve: Resi is trapped in this need. And like many women so trapped, Resi is deeply convinced that her devotion has "earned" her the love of others—specifically, the love of Prochaska. Inevitably this love takes a negative twist: when Resi discovers that Pendennis has been staying the night in Prochaska's room, she is left torn and bitter, whispering "Not me, not me." And in revenge she seeks to drive Prochaska from the

hospital, only to find herself driven out instead. The fate of Resi suggests that while the *infektionhaus* may offer a refuge of sorts from the oppressively patriarchal world of the *biergarten*, this world of women and children is itself sick and twisted. But the dialectical relationship between *biergarten* and *infektionhaus*, each breeding the other, also enacts for us the inherent logic of patriarchy, in which the male will-to-power generates, as its inevitable counterpart, the desperate struggle of women to preserve for themselves an area of autonomous selfhood.

When we look at Prochaska through the lens of the woman-centered world of the hospital, he becomes a more ambiguous figure than he may first seem. He moves through the hospital as an alien presence, with "a look of hot-eyed resolution, singularly incongruous in this apparently aimless and languorously drifting tide of pain." "All his life," we learn, Prochaska "had been fearful of becoming as soft as other people were." In the hospital, he can daily demonstrate that he is not "soft": "the children lifted their heads and opened their mouths wide as he bade them and the glittering eye of his instrument pierced the mystery of their throats with a perfect conquering ray." The language here suggests another, darker side to our Nazi hero. And indeed, a careful reading of the novel reveals that from the beginning Boyle portrays Prochaska as a man who, despite his vigor and charm, is so blinded by his male ego and his political obsession that his human responses are paralyzed. Boyle's opening sentence describes Prochaska as a "dark and hot-eyed young man moving quickly and singly . . . alone among the coupled others." He moves, we learn, "as if there were no end to the power he had;" but the erotic energy in him is directed, not toward women, but toward the earth ("these mountains . . . all his life had wooed him . . . as the thought of women wooed him") and toward the Reich, which he sees as a woman. The sense of power and grace which Prochaska gives off is attractive, both to the female characters in the novel and to us as we read, but there is also something ominous about the man. And if we are tempted initially to see Prochaska as a stereotyped romantic lead, we come to see him very differently as the novel proceeds: as a man who has been shaped by the influence of a particular society and a particular social moment, both of which have nurtured in him a kind of "manly" self-confidence which is simultaneously energizing and crippling, since it finally prevents him from the self-surrender that love demands.

Against the figure of Prochaska, Boyle plays off her female protagonist, Pendennis, who is also both liberated and crippled by the culture which has shaped her. Pendennis is a late variation on the James/Fitzgerald theme of "the American girl abroad." Like earlier versions of the American girl, Pendennis is a fiercely independent person. Tearing up a letter from her father, she says, "that's what I do with orders! Every one I've ever had in my life, that's what's happened to it and he ought to know it by this time." And she insists on her own American-ness:

> "I'm Miss America, and I've done everything there is to do in America. . . . I've gone over Niagara Falls in a barrel, and I've got the record for staying the longest time in the air without changing cosmetics. I've been divorced twelve times and I've come to Europe to find a title."

The edge of sarcasm here signals that Pendennis, unlike earlier versions of the American girl, is no innocent: we are a long way from Daisy Miller, or even from some of Boyle's own earlier versions of the American girl abroad. Instead, Pendennis is flamboyantly erotic—and flamboyantly neurotic. She begins to exchange erotic signals with Prochaska as soon as they meet, and before they part "his eyes met hers again and his breath came suddenly short as if she had laid her hand for silence and in caution on his mouth." But at the same time, even during this first meeting, Prochaska (and perhaps Boyle herself, for the voice here is indeterminate) sees Pendennis, for a brief, hallucinatory moment, as "a hard, bitter, cold-eyed old woman, a tight fisted witch, unasking and ungiving." And indeed, Pendennis does sometimes seem a witch, given to decisions which are at best abrupt, selfish, and cruel.

The reasons for Pendennis's neurotic behavior are also clear in the novel: she, too, even more dramatically than Prochaska, is a victim of patriarchy. Pendennis's life has been haunted by her father, who never appears in the novel, but who sends her periodic letters that drive her into wild rages or panicked flights. Like Prochaska's spiritual father, Praxlmann, Pendennis's father embodies "violence and strength," a will to master: "He used to make me do everything I didn't want to do. That's why he stays put together when everyone else falls in pieces." Pendennis has deeply identified with her father. "When I'm fifty," she tells Prochaska, "I'll look like him . . . the sides of my face very full and hard and mottled with drink, except I'll have my pieces of iron hair drawn back like a Lesbian's by that time and a cigar. . . . My father made a man of me. A highball before dinner every night and your friends are my friends. I'd have died with my boots on rather than have an inch of lace on me until a year ago." Pendennis's attempt to "become a man" suggests that she has grown up with no usable models of womanhood. Indeed, Pendennis equates womanhood with nothingness, and much of her behavior is motivated by a flight from the "nothing" that she feels herself to be.

In the course of the novel, it becomes clear that it is Pendennis's American upbringing which has taught her to see herself as "nothing." The status of women in American society is established most forcefully in an extended flashback which is perhaps the most powerful single passage in the novel. Here, Pendennis tells Prochaska about her twin brother Gerald, who early established his masculine power by taming a horse with a reputation for being skittish. This achievement bonds father and son around patriarchal values of strength and power. Pendennis goes on to tell how one day, when the children were eight, they went out riding with their mother, Gerald on "father's big strong horse," and their mother on Gerald's small, skittish horse. Pendennis remembers her mother as looking "severe in her hard hat but at the same time helpless and aging, but not really aging either but as if she'd had enough of it all and she didn't care what happened next, and at the same time a little bit afraid of what was going to happen." The small horse was, says Pendennis, restless, and her mother repeatedly asked Gerald to trade horses with her, but he refused. Her pleas became more and more distraught: alternately, she threatened to tell Gerald's father about his behavior and offered him money, but Gerald persistently tried to bargain her up, demanding seventeen dollars to trade horses. Finally, the small horse reared up and

> shook her down backwards into the stream. The water wasn't deep and mother lay there on her back with her hat still on and the little horse walked quietly after us, shaking his head. I turned around and got to her first and she looked up at me, still looking very severe and she said, "You tell Gerald that if he'll stop and let me down now I'll give him the seventeen dollars," and that was the last thing she said. Gerald rode back into the water but he didn't get off his horse and he said, "All right, you get up then and give me the seventeen dollars," and then in a minute we knew she was dead.

The brutal story of the death of Pendennis's mother tells us all we need to know about the fate of woman within the American version of patriarchy. Pendennis, because of her upbringing, is caught between a model of the female as hapless victim and a model of the male as manipulator and oppressor. Her culture has given her no usable models of how to live as a woman. In the absence of usable models, Pendennis lives by pure whim:

> "And why am I doing it? Something like Marlene Dietrich kicking off her high heels and following Whathaveyou over the desert maybe? Don't you believe it. I'm doing it because I'm sick of the sight of my own face in the mirror and I haven't a book to read and there isn't a show worth seeing."

But these random impulses can only briefly conceal the vacuum where her self should be. After she leaves Prochaska, Pendennis finds herself in a gay cabaret in Vienna, telling the transvestite Jeritza, "I'm nobody, nothing, only the difference is now I know it and it's not going to get me again . . . only if I wasn't ready for it it's because nobody ever told me I'd be nothing but a couple of good dresses and a hat on top." In retrospect, it becomes clear both to us and to Pendennis herself that her abrupt decision to initiate a love relationship with Prochaska represents a flight from her own "nothingness." Yet it is also important to recognize that in this relationship she does become "something," by refusing the passive victimization represented for her by her mother. It also seems clear that Boyle's heart is with Pendennis in this choice; for as Spanier points out, when Pendennis chooses love over social propriety, she joins a line of previous Boyle protagonists, including Munday in *Gentlemen, I Address You Privately,* Hannah in *Year Before Last,* and Victoria in *My Next Bride.*

In the encounter of Prochaska and Pendennis we are witnessing, Boyle suggests, a meeting between Old World and New, Europe and America. Prochaska has been born in a place where every object tells him he is "something really of value, of quality, either to his family or to history or to himself." In contrast, nothing tells Pendennis who she is; or everything around her tells her she is nothing. But despite the difference between the sense of order and tradition which controls Prochaska's behavior and the wild struggle of wills which characterizes Pendennis's America, both cultures represent very different but equally tyrannical forms of patriarchy. Violent, strong fathers attempt to rule the destinies of both these young people. In falling in love, both are rebelling against their fathers. Boyle makes clear how fiercely Praxlmann opposes Prochaska's romance with the American girl. With his "dark seemingly swollen eyes flashing anger and hate as well at her," Praxlmann tells Pendennis that she must "leave this man to what belongs to him, to the thing he has now before him to accomplish and to the wife that will one day come to him." And Pendennis's father comes to Europe to "rescue" her. The disapproval of the fathers suggests that sexual love represents a defiance of patriarchy and of all forms of oppression that issue indirectly out of patriarchy. Sandra Spanier finds throughout Boyle's work "an almost religious belief in love as humanity's only salvation," and this theme is certainly at work in *Death of a Man.* And since the fathers here stand as the enemies of love, then it seems clear that patriarchy, whether it manifests itself in a Nazi or true-born American form, is the enemy.

Pendennis, it seems, fully recognizes the implications of her love for Prochaska. She has no hesitation about repudiating her family and all it represents, in an attempt to create a new world of love. But Prochaska, unfortunately, cannot bring himself to reject so quickly his "father" Praxlmann, or his abstract love of "Austria." Because his feelings for Pendennis run counter to his political commit-

ments, Prochaska experiences his love for her as an implacable destiny. When Pendennis offers herself to him, Prochaska feels, in language that echoes the idiom of D. H. Lawrence, a "keen and powerful tide of blissful torment [sweep] through his blood." The language here suggests a loss of volition and self-awareness, as does another Lawrentian phrase later: "Dr. Prochaska felt the blood swooning in him." A loss of will, an ecstatic melting-away of the self: such is the form which love takes, at least for a willful, masterful person like Prochaska. And as Praxlmann fully realizes, feelings of this sort have no place within a political movement and a social structure dedicated to mastery and control.

However, the opposition between political commitment and love is not absolute. For both can cause a sense of ecstasy, and Prochaska, who loves the Reich as he loves a woman, sometimes has difficulty telling the difference between the two. Climbing into the mountains with Pendennis to light the swastika bonfires, Prochaska feels "a marvelous sense of living, of being alive and of giving life, as if his flesh and the fire in it were rich enough to embrace the world as great music or as the words of a great faith were gigantic enough to give the world a wild and terrible embrace." What unleashes this ecstasy in Prochaska? The mission on which he is engaged? The woman beside him? Both of them? Neither he nor we are sure. And a little later, as they watch the burning swastikas, not only Prochaska but Pendennis too is caught up in this erotic-political ecstasy:

> They stood like children staring, their eyes fixed raptly on it, their lips parted, watching the separate living worms of flame moving tenderly, vulnerably in the balloons that cupped and magnified their light. The girl did not say to him, bewildered, Why are we doing this? Why have we climbed up here? What are we doing this for? Why? And he did not answer, Believe me it is not necessary to think, only to follow and to believe. It is not necessary to reason, only to feel the blood moving and to know. But for a moment their two hearts spoke the same inexplicably youthful and inexplicably terrible words, saying, Nothing having brought us here or together except the flesh of our bodies, the intoxication of movement, the mystery of the darkness together, nothing having any significance except those things we have not done before, our own knowledge of those things to be seized with the hands, the eyes, the lips, the limbs even while the mind is shed as cowardice is shed, disdained like caution, the mind cast off and even the reason for it cast aside and the direction of the body not lost but weaving magically, like a trumpet call unwinding through the flesh, the destination not even questioned, residing as it does in every instance, every breath that's taken, NOW.

In this passage, singled out by several reviewers, the emotions evoked by devotion to blood, race, and land are so compelling that for a moment even Pendennis, the self-centered American, is caught up in them. This passage reminds us that the iconography of Nazism affirmed not only strength but also youth, joy, and action, and that Nazism rejected the intellect as debilitating, "Jewish." But how can we tell the difference between an erotic and a political "swooning" into the bloodstream?

In any case, Pendennis surrenders to the emotional appeal of Nazism only for a moment. Even before she and Prochaska descend from the mountain, Pendennis begins to recognize that this moment of ecstasy has been purchased at the price of her selfhood. The lovers, in flight from the Austrian police, take refuge in a mountain cabin. There Pendennis looks at herself in a mirror and thinks to herself, "I'm nothing, nobody. . . . I am whichever way he's going. I'm not even me." In this passage, Pendennis articulates for the first time that sense of herself as "nothing" which becomes a running motif in the novel. And as soon as the lovers descend the mountain, Pendennis begins to defend herself against this threatened annihilation, by attacking that sense of surrender which she had experienced on the mountain:

> "climbing the mountain they tell you to, believing what they tell you just as it's told to you, and how can you go on swallowing it and swallowing it, why doesn't something start choking you in the middle of every speech they're roaring at you, each one a little bit louder than the other so you won't have the peace and quiet to put two and two together? How can you get it down and keep it down—"

Here it is clear that Pendennis has come to see herself and the party as rivals for Prochaska's loyalty. Both erotic and political ecstasy may entail a loss of rational control, but Pendennis knows the difference between the two; and she knows that one nourishes the self while the other destroys it.

As Pendennis comes to recognize the fundamentally patriarchal and thus anti-erotic character of Nazism, she decides that Prochaska must choose between his love of her and his devotion to the movement. In their final quarrel, Pendennis explicitly links together the authoritarian, militaristic, and anti-Semitic strains in Nazism:

> "One day a man can't jump off a wooden platform and break his neck because he's a Jew and the next day a girl can't go for a walk on Sunday with you and you take your orders, you swallow it all down along with your pride and your sense or what have you! One day they're going to put a pretty little uniform on you with

hearts for sweetness on the elbows and say, 'Now you run along to war, dear,' and won't that be a lot of fun?"

Prochaska replies, "You don't know anything about it! . . . You don't understand for a moment what we're doing—you can't see it—." And at this moment, as Prochaska refuses the choice which Pendennis demands of him, we know that the love affair between the two is over.

Even though Prochaska refuses to give up the Nazi movement for love, he himself later has a moment of recognition. The occasion is a trip into the mountains to meet a courier from Germany, who is carrying money and messages for the Austrian Nazis. The courier, in a passage cited in Mary Colum's review, launches into an ecstatic description of Hitler's speech on the 1934 purge of the Brownshirt faction in the German Nazi party:

> "My God, it was like great music, like a great poem being sung!" said the boy's voice quickly out of the dark. "If you could have heard it down to those last words," and he began saying them aloud in young dramatic exultation, repeating them as if they were sweet to the senses like the taste of wine. . . .

Suddenly, Prochaska finds himself repelled by all this frenzy, which seems to be, as he looks about at the inhuman serenity of his beloved mountains, merely silly. He says to the courier,

> "So what do you think will happen in the end? A lot of uproar and shouting and bloodshed and marching in the streets and then what will we come back to but this quiet, this absolute stillness of the mountains in the end? Where in the world do you think we're going. . . . "

The young courier is, Prochaska realizes, "drunk, stupefied on the thought of death and the rapture of his own fearlessness to meet it;" and with this recognition Prochaska at last becomes able to choose life—and to choose Pendennis.

But Prochaska's recognition of the death-wish in Nazism comes too late to allow him to break the chains of history. For some months, Prochaska mopes in Feldbruck, longing for Pendennis, unable to believe in the movement as he had once believed, but seeing no alternative. Meanwhile, Pendennis mopes in decadent Vienna, hiding from her father, talking obsessively about her "nothingness." Prochaska and Pendennis are released from this paralysis by a sequence of accidents. Cilli tells Prochaska that the Austrian police are on his trail, and shortly thereafter he learns by chance Pendennis's address in Vienna. He goes in search of her, only to learn that Pendennis has already moved on to Salzburg. While she is staying there, she hears the news that Dollfuss has been assassinated by Austrian Nazis in the course of an unsuccessful coup. The assassination leads to a national round-up of known Nazis, and Pendennis decides that now Prochaska will need her. So she boards a train to Feldbrück, in an attempt to find him. And the lovers might indeed have found one another, Boyle suggests, except that Prochaska once again lacks a sufficient faith in love. When he cannot find Pendennis in Vienna, he decides that she is, after all, merely a selfish, faithless human being: "as if," he thinks, "I ever had a girl or as if she was ever anybody's girl or anything better than a taste left in the mouth and in somebody else's mouth the next place she goes and in how many mouths in other places." So Prochaska gives up the search, and as a consequence the trains carrying the two ex-lovers pass (literally) in the night.

Death of a Man seems to me a remarkably prescient and courageous novel. The courage here lies in Boyle's willingness to go beyond stereotypes of gender, nationality, and politics, in creating a male character who is both erotically attractive *and* deeply political, and who is erotically attractive for the very qualities—physical vigor, passionate devotion to a cause, a capacity for ecstatic self-surrender—which have led him to commit himself to the Nazi movement. In Pendennis, Boyle has created a female character who is, in her alienation from her own culture and her uncertainty as to her identity, deeply neurotic, but whose very neuroses dramatize for us the destructive consequences of specifically American forms of patriarchy. (After World War II, Boyle would explore this theme at much greater length in *Generation Without Farewell*.) In flight from the sense of herself as "nothing," Pendennis seizes upon the Nazi doctor, who at least "believes in something." Her love is thus itself twisted, neurotic. Conversely, Prochaska is the product of a culture which equates eros with weakness, and so in the end he is unable to make the final commitment to Pendennis that might have allowed this love to survive. Nevertheless, the love between them allows Pendennis to glimpse an alternative to "nothing," while this love also liberates Prochaska to recognize the death-frenzy within Nazism. As this dialectic works itself out, we come to an understanding of the destructive effects of patriarchy upon both these young people. Their struggle to escape the patriarchal control exercised over them by the Fathers (Praxlmann, Pendennis's father) and by the patriarchal values within their own minds ends, finally, in ironic confusion. Yet we feel good-will for both of them, and in this sense the novel achieves a tragic resonance. Both Prochaska and Pendennis are finally lost creatures, but their struggle nevertheless affirms a sense of purpose in human existence. As read from the feminist perspective which I have here proposed, *Death of a Man* also seems—despite the complaints of early reviewers, who often saw the book as a collection of lyric fragments—an integrated work of art, in which every detail works toward a subtle, complex effect. Fifty years after its initial publication, *Death of a Man* should be read for the delicacy of its art and the power of its insights. It also deserves to be recognized as one of the small classics of twentieth-century American writing, and as an important moment in the emergence of a feminist consciousness.

Ian S. MacNiven (essay date Fall 1988)

SOURCE: "Kay Boyle's High Country: *His Human Majesty*," in *Twentieth-Century Literature*, Vol. 34, No. 3, Fall, 1988, pp. 363-74.

[*In the following essay MacNiven praises* His Human Majesty *as a near perfect novel that is well balanced, with a great tone.*]

When Hugh Ford quoted Glenway Wescott's comment on Kay Boyle, "She was more completely abroad than the rest of us," he wanted to emphasize the extent of her commitment to Europe, the fact that she had gone quickly beyond the role of expatriate to become wife and adopted daughter of France, Austria, Germany. Adopt Europe she did, despite the fact that she took with her for her art the vision of the innocent American woman, female counterpart of Henry James's Christopher Newman, a vision that has never left her. From each of her three husbands Boyle received a portion of Europe. She went to live in France in May 1923 as the wife of Richard Brault, a French aviator turned businessman. The story is told in *Plagued by the Nightingale* (1931): Brault gave her provincial France—protective of its own, tight, bitter, hard, straight-jacketed in the "tailleur gris" her in-laws tried to force upon her. Her French-born American artist and writer second husband, Laurence Vail, gave her the freedom of the great capital, Paris, and subsequently of the Mediterranean (at Villefranche) and of the Alps. Her last husband, Joseph Franckenstein, an Austrian baron before he renounced his title, gave her a vision of Europe in conflict and, paradoxically, gave her back America. It was during World War II and with him that she re-entered the mainstream of American life, and it was due to the attacks she and Franckenstein sustained during the McCarthy era that she came most openly into conflict with U.S. policies and prejudices.

Before their legal troubles began, Franckenstein had provided Boyle the model for the protagonist of the book in which she returned to the United States, the book that may well be her most successful novel, *His Human Majesty* (1949), her powerful evocation of some of the pervasive themes of modernism: exile, expatriation (this time in America), disillusionment, redemption. The book was very important for Boyle: begun in 1943 when she was struggling unwillingly with an "elegant pot-boiler," *Avalanche, Majesty* is a problem novel with a resolution that engaged Boyle's passionate concern: the defeat of xenophobia and the affirmation of love and fidelity. The novel is an exploration of recurring themes important to her fiction. Sandra Spanier lists *Majesty* among those of her novels that contain "several major threads that run through the body of Kay Boyle's fiction: a concern for the gaps in understanding that separate human beings, an almost religious belief in love as humanity's only salvation, and an interest in universalizing particular experience through allegory and myth." Finally, *Majesty* embodies techniques and concepts that reaffirm Boyle's link with such prominent modernists as Joyce, Conrad, and Lawrence. The novel is important both for Boyle's development as an artist and as an achieved work of art.

His Human Majesty, set in army training camps in the Colorado mountains and in Leadville (called Quarry in the novel), is based on Franckenstein's experiences with the U.S. Army mountain infantry in the Rockies and in the Aleutian Islands. It is the fifth of Boyle's war novels, following *Primer for Combat* (1942), *Avalanche* (1944), *A Frenchman Must Die* (1946), and *1939* (1948). Realistically enough, the cast of characters in *Majesty* includes many American citizens plus an assortment of war refugees from almost every European nation where men ski. The volume is divided into what are almost two distinct novellas, **"Enemy Detail"** and **"The Main Drag."** In the first section the hero, Fennington, incurs the guilt of betrayal by making love to Connie Avignon, actress wife of his comrade-in-arms and chess opponent Pater. Fennington is also unsuccessful in his attempt to rescue Connie from exposure after an accident in the mountains. In **"The Main Drag"** the suspicion if not the fact of betrayal is expanded to include all the foreign-born and even the American Indian Sweetwater, when it is bruited about that these men, who might not be "loyal," will be cut from the ranks, with "Only the hundred per centers going overseas." Fennington is redeemed through several generous acts and especially through the love of Augusta, a young barmaid and the namesake of a heroic pioneer, Augusta Tabor, whose diaries Fennington has read. When the unit entrains for the East Coast and Europe it is Cooper from California, the most prejudiced of the critics of the foreign-born, who remains behind, while the refugees have become accepted by the American-born soldiers. This bare outline is fleshed out with a major fire, two accidental deaths, an attempted rape, an attempted murder, blizzard during which seven cars plunge into a canyon, and many reported catastrophes.

Like Franckenstein, Fennington in *Majesty* is a classical scholar and an athlete, and their names have the same number of syllables and the same rhythm. But the similarities

extend far beyond education and skiing ability: Joseph Franckenstein was most evidently a man uncommonly driven by moral imperatives. An aristocrat with well-established connections (his father was a Hapsburg, his mother an Esterhazy), he chose exile from Austria over association with the Nazis. Arrested by the French as an enemy alien, he chose internment over the Foreign Legion, which he scorned as a refuge of felons and other desperate men. Offered a pass to England in 1941 through the agency of his cousin Sir George Franckenstein; then Austrian Ambassador in England, Franckenstein chose to travel by refugee ship to the U.S., perhaps mainly because Kay Boyle was going there. Franckenstein was the model for a male type that enters Boyle's fiction with Sepp von Horneck in *Primer for Combat.* The name is significant: "Joseph Horneck" was an alias later used by Franckenstein for his 1945 OSS mission in Nazi-held Austria. The description of Sepp von Horneck in *Primer* matches Franckenstein perfectly: "Sepp is a big-boned, narrow-faced man with a good profile and darkish, reflective eyes; thirty-five or so, rugged, awkward in movement, but delicate and sensitive in thought and speech." Franckenstein is also the prototype for Ferdl Eder in *1939,* and his moral presence is felt in the daring, fighting French and American protagonists of *Avalanche* and *A Frenchman Must Die.*

Among Boyle's war novels it is in *A Frenchman Must Die* and *His Human Majesty* that the point of view shifts most convincingly from woman to man. The example of Joseph Franckenstein may have helped Boyle break away from the figure of the young American woman so frequently dominant in her earlier novels, with the notable exception of *Monday Night.* Some of the reasons behind the creation of these dominant heroines were certainly biographical. The family members Boyle most admired during her youth were her mother, Katherine Evans, her grandmother, Eva S. Evans (who in 1874 had been one of the first women to receive an appointment in the Land Grant Office in Washington), and her Suffragette aunt, the political cartoonist Nina Allender. The men in Boyle's immediate family, her father, Howard, and her grandfather, Jesse Peyton Boyle, called "Puss," had been the ones she and her sister had rebelled against in their youth. Her father was weak, while Puss, household tyrant though he may have been, was a fussy little man and, worst of all, was racially prejudiced and a fanatical conservative who walked out of the house when Kay Boyle's mother entertained guests whose social or political views he detested. Among Boyle's friends in France were many extraordinary men—Robert McAlmon, Harold Stearns, Harry Crosby, Eugene Jolas, Raymond Duncan, and Samuel Beckett immediately come to mind—but in her first two husbands, at any rate, she does not seem to have found strength of character to match her own. Richard Brault was a generous-minded man, tolerant even of his wife's desertion of him for the poet Ernest Walsh, but he was unable to keep up with her artistic vocation. Laurence Vail, a talented writer and painter, lived with a self-indulgent abandon that precluded the fulfillment of his own promise and interfered with Boyle's work. After years of seeing herself as the stable center of concerted action and of moral judgment in her various relationships—and of transferring that obligation to her women protagonists—Boyle found in Franckenstein a male exemplar of solid political and social virtues. Fennington in *Majesty* is her most convincing portrayal of a virtuous man.

An element that sets *Majesty* apart from most of Boyle's earlier fiction is her exploitation of the humorous possibilities of the macabre.
—Ian S. MacNiven

A comparison of Fenton Ravel, a paragon and the woman protagonist of *Avalanche* (Boyle's one best-seller), with Fennington will show how similar was Boyle's conception of their natures. Fennington is quite consciously, I believe, intended as a complement to Fenton in *Avalanche:* only a middle syllable need be added to her name to arrive at his, and he possesses her virtues of loyalty and innocence to a considerable degree. Fenton's love for Bastineau, the French partisan she travels into the mountains to search for, is apparently grounded on a single circumstance and declaration described by Bastineau: "You were fifteen that spring. . . . That night of the thaw, when the white horse threw you, and I picked you up and carried you home. . . . You said, 'Bastineau, I love you.'" Although Fennington is many years older than Fenton, he too is inexperienced in love: his one romantic attachment before the time-present of *Majesty,* to an English girl he had met after returning her lost dog, is represented only by a photograph of the Irish setter, and when he falls in love it is with the suddenness of Romeo: first with Connie Avignon and then, after her death, with Augusta, the "bar girl," modern embodiment of the frontier heroine Augusta Tabor. Fenton, admirable though she may be, remains two-dimensional, the courageous unblemished Juliet of a mountain romance, a Juliet out of Gottfried Keller rather than Shakespeare. Fennington, however, is rendered credibly three-dimensional by his fall from grace, his individualizing Oxford diction, and his well-developed friendships with Pater and Carmichael, the loquacious son of a mortician from Buffalo. Similar comparisons disadvantageous to *Avalanche* could be made of most of the characters in the two novels.

A comparison of the plots of *Avalanche* and *Majesty* shows how much more subtly *Majesty* has been developed. In *Avalanche* de Vaudois, a secret agent of the Gestapo, is thwarted by the young lovers. Period. While there is plenty of suspense, there are few if any surprises in the actions of the characters, few varying shades of moral judgment. In her novels dealing with war, Boyle is best around the edges of the conflict: her most secure field is the emotions, the psychology, of men and women, not their most violent actions. The violence is arbitrary, melodramatic. De Vaudois stumbles into a steel animal trap; Bastineau leaps down the chimney like Saint Nicholas to rescue Fenton. *Majesty,* although filled with dramatic action as the outline already given suggests, is mainly about interior, private issues (guilt, redemption, love), and these are developed in conversations and interior monologues that are more important than the actions themselves.

An element that sets *Majesty* apart from most of Boyle's earlier fiction is her exploitation of the humorous possibilities of the macabre. The *presentation* of the macabre was not new for Boyle. In *Monday Night* Wiltshire Tobin, patterned after Boyle's friend and Paris familiar Harold Stearns, investigates Monsieur Sylvestre, a famous toxicologist whose testimony, it turns out, has sent innocent men to execution from no other motive on his part than vanity. Boyle does not in *Monday Night* exploit the grim humor potential, for instance, of a murder committed using the poison on flypaper, whereas in *Majesty* Carmichael can hardly speak about corpses without seeing the humor of bodies embalmed and beautified for eternity. *Monday Night* is a good story about an engaging ne'er-do-well and his failure to receive the credit for a brilliant piece of sleuthing, but it is not ennobled by the major themes of *Majesty*. On the contrary, the unwashed and rumpled figure of Wilt Tobin, with a red line across his sweaty forehead where his hat liner cuts in, probably excites more pity and distaste for his condition than admiration for his qualities of mind.

The macabre stories of Carmichael save *Majesty* from the unrelieved earnestness, almost the sentimentality of *Avalanche. A Frenchman Must Die,* and *1939.* His sardonic, balancing look at life from the embalmer's table provides the obverse to the romantic view needed to balance the idealism. Men and women are, after all, at once creatures of nobility and idealism, crass sensuality and baseness—and they become, ultimately, cold meat to be buried with barbaric rituals, their sins forgiven:

> "I gave them the works," Carmichael said. "Erased the lines of greed and lust from their faces and wreathed their lips with heavenly smiles. I closed their eyelids for them forever, filled the empty pouches of dissipation with undertaker's wax, restored youth and innocence. . . ."

The army tries to make men, even the physically inept journalist Pater, into efficient soldiers; the men try to remake one another; and the women try to reform the men. Carmichael mocks all this earnest reforming with the tale of his proud performance as a Pygmalion on one of his first great efforts, the embalming of a girl accident victim, nameless, flattened by traffic: "The state gave her to us, picked her up on the highway one summer dawn after an all-night traffic had passed over her and ironed her out. . . . They brought her in a briefcase, folded over like a paper doll." The story is told during a fire which has resulted in the death of a man, and the juxtaposition is significant: Carmichael uses laughter to fight off the fear of death.

Carmichael's is the voice of a sort of Theater of the Absurd optimism:

> "Now take this war, which I venture to say you could have for the asking," he said, "it offers you two possibilities, the first of which cannot but persuade you of the evanescent quality of hope and all endeavor. There's the possibility that you will die, and the possibility that you won't die . . . and if you die, it's O.K., and if you don't die it's O.K. too, because that still leaves you two possibilities. There's the possibility that you'll be buried in a single grave, and the possibility that you'll be buried in a mass grave, and . . . . "

Carmichael, Irish-American, is kin to Finnegan, and his wake-stories are, like those about Joyce's legendary hero, life-celebrating. Death provides the key polarity of the book: it becomes a subject for laughter in a novel describing the preparation of men and women for war and death—and along the way they make peace with one another and celebrate life. Carmichael closes the book with his last word on promotion, the military, the war: pointing toward a flag-draped coffin, he says, "Speaking of stripes, there's a guy over there that's got thirteen of them." Faced with a world that has much in common with the runaway train Carmichael describes near the end of *Majesty,* the tough-minded assert life with laughter. Carmichael teaches Fennington to reject the talking out of sentiment: when Fennington tries to steer him into a discussion about what his wife means to him, Carmichael parries: "Not here! Not now!" The real lovers choose silence, the lust-driven boast. Cooper carries on about his "air-line hostess" and his "hat-check girl"—and then he is not on the train when the ski troops leave for combat.

Part of the strength of *Majesty* comes from the marvelous set-pieces: in **"Enemy Detail"** the rescue of the German P.O.W. from the ravine by Fennington and the French Desiré Jones, with the temperature at eighteen below zero, which is balanced near the end of **"The Main Drag"** by the comic rescue carried out by the same two men of the drunken soldier, "Felled in the battle of Delirium Tremens . . . overcome by the concerted action of the hot and cold

water faucets," from a bathroom at the North Star Hotel. Boyle's use of counterpoint—stories told concurrently with actions to which they are not directly related—transcends mere entertainment. The rescue of the soldier unable to find his way out of the bathroom and under the delusion that he is in combat is neatly balanced by Carmichael's tale about a man who wrote his way out of the army, after covering "the length of eight tables" with "approximately one hundred and sixty thousand words" and who finished his writing career in the asylum with a "major opus," "Four hundred and twenty thousand words pricked by the point of a pin onto twelve and a half rolls of toilet paper." Some of the important episodes exploit suspense along several lines. In the climax of the book, Don Juan Cooper attempts to rape Augusta in the back seat of a car skidding in a blizzard toward Denver. Henson, a young soldier intent on going A.W.O.L., warns the driver just in time to prevent his driving over the edge of the canyon, and in coming to Augusta's rescue restores his own sense of duty.

The pioneer Augusta Tabor and her modern namesake bring out the virtue already existing in good men, saving them from despair and degradation. The idea of women as the natural protectors of men appears early in Boyle's work. In **"Three Little Men,"** first published in *Criterion* in 1932, the narrator describes her father as a timid man with wrists that were "beautiful, tight and small," a man who "would always tell me that his head pained him, and he would turn it away from use so that we never saw into his eyes." The narrator recalls thinking as a child "that I would place him on my strong wrist, like a falcon, and hood his small bowed head with my fingers so that he need not see the world." In the early work the men tend to be either weak like the father described here, or benevolent tyrants against whom the women scheme and struggle, like Oncle Robert in *Plagued by the Nightingale.* One man who is neither a tyrant nor weak, Martin Sheehan, the Ernest Walsh figure in *Year Before Last,* is rendered dependent on his women by tuberculosis.

In *Majesty* the dependency/support roles alternate: Augusta, "one woman who believes in one man," gives the "child" soldier, Henson, the courage not to desert; Henson, "fighting as Fennington's and Raleigh's deputy," comes to Augusta's rescue during the attempted rape by Cooper; Augusta inspires Fennington to reopen communications with Pater and thus begin his, Fennington's, absolution; Fennington consoles Augusta in her despair on the receipt of the news of her husband, Curly's, death. (Note that Boyle is again playing the echo game with names: Connie's death frees Fennington to love Augusta, Curly's frees Augusta. The good dead give way to the good living. As the irreverent Carmichael says: "They heard we wanted the joint, and they moved out for us. The dead are those who give us elbow room.") Above the buried dead are the mountains that represent peace and purity. Fennington on a lonely ski run near the end of **"The Main Drag"** meets a young bear just awakened from hibernation, and he skis down into Quarry and buys a postcard from Augusta (and realizes his awakening feeling for her), the postcard he sends to Pater that begins Fennington's absolution for the sin of betraying Pater with his wife. The town may be smudged and dirty—the smoke rising, the mud dirtying Fennington's skis—but within that outpost of civilization some men and some women safeguard the virtues of the race, its "Human Majesty."

The conflict between the corruption of the town and the aspirations of some of its inhabitants is reminiscent of D. H. Lawrence, and in other ways as well *Majesty* fits very recognizably into the tradition of the great modernists: of Joyce in the variety of narrative technique, of Conrad in the disclosure of the darkness as well as the better qualities of the human heart, of Lawrence in the emphasis on the power of love. These are subjects for a full discussion elsewhere, but to be brief, there is clearly a Joycean complexity in levels of narration. Often the present narrative time, memory, and an interior voice (given here as often elsewhere in Boyle's work in italics) all operate in the same episode. In the car journey toward Denver in the blizzard, a fourth narrative thread is added, the consciousness of the "Latvians," the generic name given by the native-born to all "foreigners." Although not physically present in the car, "the Latvians had come to take their punishment, dressed up in khaki as if they were Americans, but speaking the language as no native spoke it, and bearing their national griefs and their national betrayals in the government-issue rucksacks on their backs." External scene and interior monologue run concurrently throughout the novel.

While the theme of the darkness within man—his thinly concealed propensity for betrayal, rape, and murder—is common to many modern authors, what seems especially Conradian in *Majesty* is the way in which Fennington's betrayal is concealed from Pater: Fennington, desiring to confess to Pater, lets the truth of his betrayal and of Pater's wife's infidelity stay hidden. It would be "too dark altogether"—Conrad's words—to have told him. Boyle is very conscious of the paradox that a person lives or is faithful until the *news* of his or her death or infidelity is known: Augusta dreads telling her husband's parents of his death, since, as she and Fennington know, her words "would sentence her own husband to die."

Boyle stands much closer as an artist to Lawrence than to either Joyce or Conrad, however. She was much interested in Lawrence, and in 1931 wrote a short story, **"Rest Cure,"** based on his final illness. Spanier has noted Boyle's "romantic preference for intuition" and her association of evil with "the absence or failure of human bonds," and her emphasis in *Majesty* upon the "brotherhood of men," all

very Lawrencian concepts. But Boyle's idealized and understated portrayals of people in love show her to be closer to the standard conception of romanticism than Lawrence is, with his physical descriptions of the sex act, and his insistence on the essential and elemental power of the *body* as an equal partner with the *mind*. Also, while to Boyle war itself is the supreme failing of man as a political creature, *Majesty* holds out hope that on individual terms men and women can triumph; so too Lawrence: man-in-the-aggregate fails in his political novels, in *Kangaroo* and in *The Plumed Serpent*. Boyle's rejection of war is intuitive, impulsive; Connie cries out of Fennington, "Why in the name of God are you fighting a war? What have you, or any other living young men, to do with death?" Lawrence rejects not only war, but the entire exercise of military discipline, as in "The Thorn in the Flesh," in which a young soldier suffering from acrophobia deserts, and in "The Prussian Officer," a story of the sadism underlying physical punishment. On the scale of iconoclasm, Boyle's rejection does not seem to go as deeply as Lawrence's: she finds something worthwhile, even noble, in the exertion of training and in the male camaraderie that grows from it.

It is in her emphasis on tenderness in human relations that Boyle comes especially close to Lawrence, and the relations do not have to be those between men and women: the German-hating Desiré Jones treats the injured German P.O.W. "with impersonal male compassion." Lawrence recognized that tenderness formed a more lasting and ultimately more powerful bond in human relations than raw passion, and indeed Lawrence's title for the first draft of *Lady Chatterley's Lover* was *Tenderness*. Lawrence's statement of the paramount importance of tenderness could apply equally well to *Majesty:* Mellors comes to realize that "It's a question of awareness . . . and that natural physical tenderness which is best, even between men," but only *after* Constance Chatterley has explained his own nature to him: "Shall I tell you what you have that other men don't have, and that will make the future? . . . It's the courage of your own tenderness." One recalls that Constance Chatterley—familiarly called Connie—first loves Oliver Mellors when she observes his tender handling of the pheasant chicks. In *Majesty* another Connie turns to Fennington whose gentleness contrasts with the leering interest of most of his comrades. Finally, his gentle and protective attentions to Augusta when she receives the telegram announcing her husband's death win Fennington her love. The soldiers themselves fear tenderness will unman them: fatigued to the point of collapse by maneuvers, "those who were children among them so close to tears that had the words of tenderness been spoken then, they would have . . . weakly cried." A past war forms the backdrop for *Chatterley,* a novel about men and women crippled physically and/or emotionally by the Great War. In *Majesty* there is no place for physical cripples in the elite ski troops, but the emotional scars are there. All the Europeans carry specters: Hungarian Sergeant Jeno his dead wife, drowned in the Loire while fleeing the Nazis; French Desiré Jones his mother, perhaps dead in Grenoble; Berlin Jew Rudi Mendl his guilt for escaping the slaughter of his people; and so on. The Americans also carry scars, including emotional cicatrices from the invasion of the Aleutian Islands, an attack in which some casualties were caused by friendly fire.

In Boyle's story a human agency, often disguised as accident or luck or fate, often steps in to avert evil: Henson, intending to go A.W.O.L., prevents the rape of Augusta by Cooper; Fennington by appearing in time to cut Mendl down prevents his hanging-murder by Tennyhook. However, there seems to be no sure retribution: Cooper is transferred to a safe ground job in the Army air force—where he will be able to continue his womanizing—and Tennyhook's attempt at murder is never disclosed. Connie Avignon dies trying to help the Afrika Korps prisoner escape because for her a personal loyalty—she had known and loved him at Kreuzeck before the war—transcends public loyalty. Similarly Fennington, after exhorting Henson *not* to go A.W.O.L., does so himself to help Augusta over her grief. However, there seems to be no intervening force for Boyle when human efforts fail or are not made: Sergeant Jeno's wife dies swimming the Loire, seven cars go into the canyon before Henson stops the chain of disaster, Rudi Mendl's family is wiped out. Fragile though mankind's hold may be on life, life itself comes through as far more important than crime or punishment or even justice: hours after the news of Curly's death has been wired to her, Augusta and Fennington embrace, "and the forsaken dead lay quiet as they kissed each other's mouths." "Life!" proclaims Carmichael through all his macabre mortician's tales. "Life and love!" respond Augusta and Fennington. If these are archetypal figures acting out old truths, these truths are nonetheless given memorable expression.

I have tried to show that both Kay Boyle and her art have owed a great deal to Joseph Franckenstein, that her husband eased her return to America. He not only preserved for her the European courtesies and cosmopolitan outlook to which she had become accustomed, but he also let her see the U.S. through the eyes of a foreigner, a refugee, an immigrant. *His Human Majesty* is highly successful in craftsmanship and theme. In it Boyle has demonstrated a near-perfect integration of theme and structure, the counterpoint between action and both spoken and internal dialogue, and in her use of humor she robs death and war of their terror. without reducing them to sentimentality and triviality. *Majesty* contains perhaps Boyle's most balanced statement about guilt and redemption, about the relationship between men and women, a shared trust in which neither party dominates.

Elizabeth S. Bell (essay date Fall 1988)

SOURCE: "Call Forth a Good Day: The Nonfiction of Kay Boyle," in *Twentieth-Century Literature,* Vol. 34, No. 3, Fall, 1988, pp. 384-91.

[*In the following essay, Bell argues that Boyle's essays are proof of Boyle's conviction that writers must be a voice of consciousness and accountability.*]

Noted as a stylist and awarded distinguished recognition for her short fiction, Kay Boyle, in her prodigious writing during the 1930s, earned for her fiction and poetry an enthusiastic and discriminating following. Her later reputation, born perhaps from her reporting of post-World War II Europe and nurtured in the caldron of McCarthy's 1950s, encompasses another element of Boyle's concept of what a writer should be, for Kay Boyle is now additionally recognized as an articulate spokesperson for a variety of political and social issues, a voice of society's conscience, and—not coincidentally—a crafter of the essay as well. Rather than being a separate manifestation of Boyle's writing, the political activism of her recent career is a direct development of the concerns she expressed in her earlier poetry and fiction. Her essays, spanning almost sixty years of this century, reveal the connections that unite her work and chronicle the growth of her artistic vision.

Boyle's essays about literature or writing or writers themselves, those written in Europe before World War II as well as those written after her return to the United States in the 1940s, demonstrate convincingly the growth of Boyle's commitment to and development of the full scope of literature as a profound form of communication between writer and audience and culture. She began with the aesthetic conviction that the writer must draw from deep engagement with his or her themes, but as she saw and experienced the turmoil of the Spanish Civil War, World War II, and the metaphorical McCarthy-era war, she became convinced that writers must become committed crusaders, speaking for those who have no voice and addressing the injustices of contemporary life. While she earlier called for writers to be deeply concerned, she now wants both deep concern and the courage to articulate for a less sensitive world the truth that must be said.

During the late 1920s as neophyte writer in the ferment of Europe's artistic community, Boyle wrote two significant reviews for *transition,* one discussing favorably William Carlos Williams' *In the American Grain* (1925) and the other dealing negatively with Hart Crane's early poetry. The underlying concern she expressed in these essays revolves around the writer's responsibility for accuracy, both that of image or archetype—as she articulated in both essays—and that of language—as she argued more specifically in the Crane essay.

The earlier essay, **"In the American Grain"** (1927), focuses on Williams' attempt in his book of the same name to redefine the American literary heritage. He returned, Boyle tells us, to the documents, court letters, diaries of the past to recapture an unbiased version of life as it was, without the overlay of "borrowed interpretations" based on a perhaps more attractive false image too often attached to any systematic account of the past available in our century. In the process, Williams discovered an authenticity— "sound and color and smell"—that Boyle finds invigorating. Just as Boyle, Eugene Jolas, and their contemporaries in Paris were decrying the limp and inarticulate poetic diction of the late Victorian and Edwardian ages and calling for a Revolution of the Word to inject vitality and meaning into twentieth-century literary language, so Boyle here rejects with Williams the pallid and lifeless portrayal of the American heritage that was contained within "the national American mind."

Her 1928 review, **"Mr. Crane and His Grandmother,"** provides a conjunction of the issues concerning image and language, for Boyle faults Crane on both counts in his poetry. In an extension of her theme from the Williams essay, Boyle's most telling difficulty with Crane comes from the cavalier portrait he painted of his grandmother in "My Grandmother's Love Letters" (*White Buildings,* 1926). She resents the "gently pitying laughter" he granted to his grandmother as he led her through "much of what she would not understand," for Boyle finds the woman "a better bet than he." Boyle abhors Crane's patronizingly chauvinistic portrayal, for it denies real acquaintance with the woman herself and illustrates a profound lack of understanding on Crane's part of the reality of her life—by extension that of all women within the American experience. For Boyle, whose own fiction demonstrates a strong autobiographical thread and an unswerving drive toward recreating in fictional context the real and true, Crane's lack of insight indicates a serious flaw in his poetic vision. In contrast, Boyle's earlier review of William Carlos Williams' *In the American Grain* commends his nod of recognition to the "Pocahuntus tradition" which speaks authentically of the female American experience as the alternate tradition to the "Pilgrim or the Indian polished to bronze."

Yet for Boyle, Crane's writing is ultimately unsuccessful because it lacks vitality and humor; in fact she finds that he uses words to observe truth, finding them useful in "hiding a human fear." She contrasts his poetry with a graphic and visually explicit passage about wild boar hunting from Robert McAlmon and, instead of McAlmon's crisp and clear language, shows Crane's poem to be clouded in essentially incomprehensible images. His meaning is not communicated to his audience because it is not unwrapped in the vital, vigorous language the twentieth century demands.

In attacking Crane's use of highly abstract images, Boyle by definition clarifies her own stance in the matter. In many ways her attack on his imprecise poetic imagery extends the concern she expresses in her review of Williams' work. She craves accuracy of language in much the same sense and with very much the same fervor with which she rejoices in Williams' call for precision in historical image; for her the two demands are, in fact, tightly interwoven. In a later decade, the 1960s, Boyle refers to herself and her earlier compatriots in Europe as resistance fighters in a particular context: "The resistance was against the established English language, and the fight was for the recognition of a New American tongue." In the 1928 Crane essay, she was actively engaged in the validation of this new tongue, particularly in poetic language, and she found Hart Crane's latest book of poetry to be a throwback to a tradition better left behind.

In book reviews produced during the 1930s and very early 1940s, Boyle returns to these two themes, faulting for example Katherine Mansfield for belonging to an older world and Elizabeth Bowen for lacking connection to the real world. Yet she blends her concerns for the writer's precision with a growing demand for passionate commitment to one's themes in the literature one produces. In Mansfield's case, Boyle finds a "lovely, proud, appealing woman" whose best stories and tragic life had kept her immune from a true evaluation of her work. Many of the stories she produced, with only a handful of sparkling exceptions, are shallow and lifeless, "not enough, for what the intent must have been, not love and comprehension for the persecuted young or old, or satire bitter enough for those she would condemn." The passion is lacking, and more sadly, Boyle believed Mansfield knew it. Instead of the issues of life and death, she is confined, according to Boyle, to a world of "irritable and irritating themes." Bowen, too, suffers from a lack of deep commitment, creating a "singularly immature and ungrateful theme." In her earlier books, Bowen's collective protagonist—regardless of name or occupation—seems to Boyle to be too much a victim, too little aware or assertive to engage in meaningful action, too pallid to contain significant insight. Boyle's review contains hope for Bowen's latest effort, *Bowen's Court,* for in her opinion it represents "a truly heroic effort to connect with reality at last," perhaps indicating the birth of a deeper commitment or perception on Bowen's part.

One writer of this period, the years immediately before World War II, whom Boyle finds to be noteworthy is William Faulkner. Her 1938 review of *The Unvanquished,*

"Tattered Banners," praises his "hot devotion to man's courage" and his passion and "fury to reproduce exactly not the recognizable picture but the unmistakable experience." She finds Faulkner's commitment to his themes to be not just the province of *The Unvanquished* or any given of his novels, but of his work in its entirety. He is a risk-taker who explores his themes with insight and conviction, making him "the most absorbing writer of our time." In fact, Faulkner matches Boyle's description of the ideal writer, for he combines precision of image and language with that deep commitment to his themes she believes to be so necessary.

These early essays follow standard formats, concentrating on an individual writer and perhaps specific works of that writer. The prose is clear, the point of view definite, and the persona reasoned. As models of their kind, stylistically and philosophically well-honed, these early essays allow Boyle to deal with writers within the context of their own canons. She looks for internal significance and themes, demanding of the writers a dedication to their individual visions and themes. The revolution she supports during this time is an aesthetic and conceptual one: re-visioning language, reconceptualizing reality, making poetry and literature vital in this twentieth-century world. While her own fiction of this period deals with more political subjects, she does not demand that kind of commitment to social change of her contemporaries.

By the mid-1940s, however, Boyle's world had dramatically changed. From her special vantage point as a newly returned exile of sorts, she observed statewide reactions to the cataclysm in Europe. Her 1944 essay, **"The Battle of the Sequins,"** conveys with almost Swiftian satire the outrage she felt at the societal nonchalance she saw: In the midst of a world gone mad in war, with death and dying everywhere one looked, the scuffle of well-dressed customers for a department store's sale-priced pieces of spangle takes on for some more meaning than the real life-and-death battle going on throughout Europe. The essay's persona magnifies the irony involved by reporting in matter-of-fact tones the grabbing and shoving of the women at the sales counter, while recognizing that moving among them are the ghostly faces of dying soldiers and victims of the war, complete with battlefield and jungle landscapes. The women in the store are cautioned not to look too closely— a needless warning—for "you will see something you do not wish to see." The unexpected juxtaposition of such a trivial setting as a department store with the profoundly moving issues in this essay heightens its ironic effect and demonstrates a new willingness of Boyle's part to experiment with essay form for the sake of communicating a vivid message. Furthermore, although the essay does not deal directly with either literature or writers, it signals a new element in Boyle's philosophy that she would soon attach to her literary essays. After all, Boyle and her generation had witnessed a world-wide loss of innocence: in the post-Holocaust age Boyle knows that no one, especially not the writers, can afford to be as complacent as they had been in the age that existed before.

Boyle's subsequent essay, **"Farewell to New York"** (1947), marks a turning point in her literary commentary. Although the focus of this essay—spoken in the voice of "the Spaniard"—is predominantly socio/political, Boyle uses it to introduce the writer's role in world events. The Spaniard tells her that when a political man is exiled from his country, "he is maimed and mute," but a writer in exile can retreat into "a spiritual terrain of silence which is native to him, and which he can turn to in any country where he is." Because the writer can create this native soil, the writer by nature is not compelled to be silent. Boyle closes the essay by addressing her friend personally, from the perspective of a later, wiser time, to tell him that she feels guilt because so many who had been given the opportunity to speak out "a long time ago" had remained silent or noncommittal or deliberately isolationist. She calls these writers by name—Pound (in 1937 before his involvement in World War II Italy), Waugh, Eliot—and allows their own comments to speak volumes for them.

In technique this essay experiments with time, point of view, persona. Unlike Boyle's earlier literary commentary, it ignores aesthetic concerns directed toward a particular writer's work; unlike later essays it accuses without providing a model of appropriate behavior. Yet the essay establishes Boyle's guiding principle: it no longer will suffice for her to write—even as passionately as she has always done—of deep commitment and precision of language, the aesthetic concerns of a less traumatized world, without adding to those issues a call for involvement on the part of those—the writers—who have access to the pages of world thought. Boyle's philosophy does not so much change its course as that it adds societal cogency and purpose to the elements of commitment, passion, and precision that she has always valued.

In **"Farewell to Europe"** (1953) Boyle explains the personal necessity she felt of returning to America to speak out against McCarthyism. One of her earliest concerns, as explored rather impersonally in her 1927 essay about Williams, is the nature of one's American identity. In 1953, she felt this concern to be even more immediate and its impact far more personal. Her own background, as she tells us, contains many strong voices raised in defense of individual freedom and its corollary, individual responsibility. Yet in the essay she must also chronicle a growing disbelief in American democracy on the part of many Europeans of her acquaintance, for they had heard too loudly and too long the strident voice of "McCartair," the McCarthy who would change the lives and fortunes of many Americans before his day in the sun ended. Boyle tells of her friends who advise her to stay in Europe where she will be freer to speak out than in the suddenly repressed and oppressive America. It is Boyle's recognition of the irony of this situation and her commitment to the values of the democratic country of her heritage that compel her to return to America, against the wishes and better judgment of her friends, to "speak out with those of the other America clearly and loudly enough so that even Europe will hear." Her emphatic defense of American individual freedom coupled with her realization that such defense was not immediately forthcoming leads her to establish a central metaphor that recurs in her essays for the next several decades: the writer's "voice" and the related need for "speaking out."

In **"A Declaration for 1955"** (1955), she turns her passion for commitment into a clarion call for all writers in America, for democracy demands "that one take part in it." Wiser and more determined in 1955 than she had been earlier, Boyle recognizes the enormity of McCarthyism's threat, whether in the voice of McCarthy himself or in the apathy of those afraid to speak, and she calls for the Artist to live up to his or her moral responsibility for changing the world. Recalling that Thomas Mann—who would appear in several of her post-World War II essays—placed the moral and ethical responsibility for any given age on its writers, she urges the Artist to become crusader: "The transforming of the contemporary scene is what I now ask of all American writers."

By 1964, McCarthy had long been discredited, but the silence he engendered was still deafening. For Boyle it was no longer sufficient for just the Artist to speak out, but the young must be given the courage and the insight to do so as well. Boyle writes to teachers of writing in the *NEA Journal* (1964) that learning "how to release reluctant students to speech" must be a major consideration for them. In a later essay, **"The Long Walk at San Francisco State"** (1970), Boyle identifies a writer/teacher/Artist who has done just that—Sonia Sanchez, who urged the students in her creative writing class to use their own language to describe their own worlds, to write "poetry that would have meaning to others in their community, and that is probably one of the things that good writing does." Inherent in the essays of this period is a growing awareness on Boyle's part that those who have traditionally remained silent or been rendered voiceless must be empowered to speak for themselves and for their counterparts. The writers of this period whom she praises are those who have with courage and clarity addressed the issues of contemporary life: James Baldwin, Edward Dahlberg, Dylan Thomas, Emanuel Carnevali, and others.

In many ways these essays, particularly the later ones with

their heavy emphasis on socio/political action and concern for justice, complete a circle, uniting the Boyle of the activist late twentieth century with the young Boyle of the 1920s. She herself makes this connection in **"The Triumph of Principles"** (1972) in which she reminds us, "I remember the days in Paris when we who were writers or painters or composers wrote pamphlets and distributed them in the streets and cafés. I remember when we signed manifestos and read them aloud on street corners, following without any humility whatsoever in the traditions of Pascal, Voltaire, Chateaubriand, Victor Hugo, Zola, so that the world would know exactly where we stood, for we considered ourselves a portion of the contemporary conscience, and we had no pity on the compromiser or the poor in spirit of our time."

The young Boyle wanted writers to express with accuracy and passion the truth that is around them. The mature Boyle can no longer satisfy herself with accurate portrayals of the past or with language to capture the present. She wants nothing less than to spark the voices that will shape the future, and those with the courage to do so must write, must produce a language and a forum for those who find themselves without political power or presence. For herself and with great faith in the integrity of the Artist, Boyle can say with conviction, "It is a good day when the writers speak out loudly and clearly."

Robyn M. Gronning (essay date Spring 1988)

SOURCE: "Boyle's 'Astronomer's Wife'," in *The Explicator,* Vol. 46, No. 3, Spring, 1988, pp. 51-3.

[*In the following essay, Gronning explores the issue of androgyny in Boyle's short story "Astronomer's Wife."*]

Since Kay Boyle's mother, aunt, and grandmother all fought for women's rights, it is not surprising that **"Astronomer's Wife"** is a feminist story. What is surprising, though, is that Boyle, in 1936, not only depicted in one of her characters—the astronomer—the old conception of androgyny as sexless, but also anticipated in the characters of the plumber and Katherine the modern definition of androgyny as sex equality: namely, a condition "in which both sexes share in the positive traits that are now sorted out by gender."

While the old definition of androgyny is a biological one meaning a plant with both stamens and pistils, or in reference to humans, an hermaphrodite, a person who as Mary Anne Warren describes, "has primary and secondary sexual characteristics of both the masculine or feminine sort (or lacks them to an equal extent)," the new definition is a psychological one. Now androgyny means a person who, according to Warren, "possesses both traditionally masculine and traditionally feminine virtues." We see then that androgyny has undergone a change. Although it is not clear exactly when this change occurred, it is clear that androgyny as a psychological condition became fashionable and controversial in the 1970s when some feminists used the term to define a state of sexual equality. It is of note, therefore, that in 1936 Kay Boyle not only explored both the old and the new definitions of androgyny, but that she captured in **"Astronomer's Wife"** the essence of the modern androgynous as the condition in which virtues can be shared by both male and female.

The astronomer is described by his wife as the "mind," whereas the plumber is the "meat, of all mankind." This realization about her husband, which Katherine reaches toward the end of the story, is no surprise to us because we have already recognized the astronomer as being meatless and cerebral. We are aware early in the story that this dreamer, this "man of other things," has no interest in the physical world. He is not aware of the world of women, of spots on vests, of the making of mayonnaise, of the fixing of broken toilets. Rather, he is so involved in the celestial that he transcends these everyday realities and in the process loses contact with himself as a man: he becomes sexless. Eunuch-like, he is, in the old sense of the word, androgynous. He is what is described as "man minus man," the antithesis of the plumber who is the androgynous "man plus woman."

That the plumber is the combination of man and woman—androgynous in the new sense of the word—is clearly stated in the story. He is characterized as "grave and stately" in dealing with matters "as does a woman"; he is admired by Katherine for being a "man who spoke of action and object as simply as women did"; and he performs tasks that the astronomer believes to be worthy only of a woman's "mettle." A man "who likes to know what's what," the plumber possesses the best traits of both sexes. His appearance is masculine; he is tanned and rugged. Yet the plumber's demeanor is feminine; he is "comprehensible" to Katherine.

Katherine can understand the plumber because he is down to earth. A man without his head in the clouds, the plumber shares Katherine's practical, everyday world. He is not like the astronomer whose mind "made steep and sprightly flights, pursued illusion, took foothold in the nameless things that cannot pass between the thumb and finger," but rather he is a man who works with his hands and "likes to know what's what." The plumber is interested in things that Katherine thinks are practical, such as the repair of the underground drain pipe, because he is, like women, interested

in the concrete elements of life: those things which women cling to like "floating debris on the tide." Unlike the astronomer, the plumber is a man who can speak to Katherine about stopped elbows or "madness in a daily shape." She comprehends him because he is a man who shares in her feminine world.

Conversely, Katherine shares in the masculine world of the plumber; thus, she too is androgynous. We understand through her relationship to the plumber that she possesses masculine qualities to the same degree that the plumber possesses feminine qualities. It is not only because the plumber is woman-like that Katherine comprehends him, but it is also because Katherine is man-like that she understands the problems of plumbing. She can handle problems the way the plumber expects her husband to do. She can turn off the water from the meter at night, even in her nightgown. She can go into the drains ("big enough for a man") in order to understand this "study for a man." When she tells the servant that the "trouble is very serious, very serious," Katherine demonstrates that she is comprehensible to the plumber. She expects "true" answers from her queries to the plumber because she shares his world. Separately, Katherine and the plumber are androgynous because they share in the positive virtues of each gender. Together, as a couple, they are also androgynous because, as we see in the closing scene of the story, they complement each other and make a complete union.

The astronomer would never go arm-in-arm into the earth with his wife anymore than he would bother to make a cow a cud out of "flowers and things and what-not" because in his celestial, sexless world he is interested neither in the things of the earth nor in unity. The plumber and Katherine, however, are interested in these "things." The image, at the end of the story, of the plumber and Katherine descending into the underworld, arms linked, knowing that what was said was "true," and leaving the astronomer in his bed to dream his dreams, underscores the androgynous nature of the story. The astronomer is left behind because he is the old androgyny—the sexless, the unfruitful. On the other hand, the plumber and Katherine, both androgynous in the feminist sense of sharing in the positive traits of both sexes, journey to the underground because their life is enriched, made full, by their androgynous natures.

Donna Hollenberg (essay date Winter 1994)

SOURCE: "Abortion, Identity Formation, and the Expatriate Woman Writer: H. D. and Kay Boyle in the Twenties," in *Twentieth-Century Literature*, Vol. 40, No. 4, Winter, 1994, pp. 499-517.

[In the following essay Hollenberg compares the conflicted views on maternity of American writers H. D. and Boyle.]

In memoirs written later in life, when they were self-assured, H. D. and Kay Boyle speak of their respective decisions to leave America for the "freedom" of England and France as if their youthful expatriation were simply liberation from outmoded literary conventions and inhibiting roles as women. H. D. wrote, referring to the anomaly of being a woman writer in the male literary world of America in 1911, "We had no signposts, at that time." In fact, in both cases their anxiety over the conflict between conventional femininity and literary ambition increased soon after arrival abroad. For although expatriation was ultimately crucial to each woman's artistic development, Europe during World War I and its aftermath also proved a place of personal suffering.

Both women were seriously ill and emotionally troubled in connection with pregnancies during the early part of their sojourns abroad: H. D. lost her first child, stillborn in 1915, and almost died of pneumonia in England during her second, illegitimate pregnancy in 1918-1919 (during which her brother and father died). Although she and her daughter survived, a continuing conflict about creativity and procreativity may have contributed to a third pregnancy and her decision to have an abortion in 1928, a year after her mother's death, a choice that exacerbated her psychological pain. Kay Boyle, in addition to bearing a daughter out of wedlock in France in 1927, after the death of her lover before their child was born, underwent two abortions in the twenties. The first, in 1921, at the beginning of her first marriage, before she went abroad with her husband, seems to have been relatively benign. The second, during a period of collapse in 1928-1929, when she was separated from her daughter, coincided with the contraction of spinal meningitis.

Expatriated, bereaved, and separated from their families, both women regressed emotionally during these crises. They reverted to an earlier mode of psychological functioning, a state of mind that H. D. later called the "'jelly-fish' experience of double ego," referring to an unnerving heightening of perception after her daughter's birth, and that Kay Boyle described as a "total disintegration of whatever I was or was not," referring to the period of depression and promiscuity before her second abortion. However, perhaps because their emotional adaptation had falsified them in the first place, this regression led to a penetrating exploration, in their early fiction, of psychological and social patterns that contributed to the repetition of the very gender roles they chafed against.

Both writers record their painfully acquired maternal sub-

jectivity in psychologically specific ways, and they learn to read their personal circumstances as part of larger cultural power structures. In particular, such *bildungsromans* as H. D.'s *Asphodel, Paint It Today,* and *Palimpsest* and Kay Boyle's **Plagued By the Nightingale, Year Before Last,** and **My Next Bride** embody a psychological drama of underlying, problem-ridden mother-daughter attachment that combines with a social drama of exile, with conflicting longings for freedom, and with yearnings for a maternal home. In addition, H. D. in her short story "Two Americans," written shortly after her abortion, uses geographical and racial metaphors to recast her anxiety about motherhood and authorship in cultural terms. Because of their protagonists' position between cultures, the meanings of "home" and "abroad" become over determined and ambiguous in these texts. Each is alternatively oppressive and desirable, so that they cancel each other out as areas outside the self, revealing, instead, an inner region that has been repressed.

Such feminist theorists as Jessica Benjamin, Nancy Chodorow, and Luce Irigaray have analyzed the effects of gender polarity on the formation of identity. For these theorists the view of female development prevalent in general psychoanalytic discourse, in which differentiation from an objectified mother is necessary for successful initiation into heterosexual adulthood, does not adequately analyze the effect of maternal subjectivity, or its lack, on the developing child. Benjamin's investigation of the interplay between love and power considers domination and submission to be the result of a breakdown in equal and mutual human relationships rather than of inevitable aggressive instincts in human nature. Benjamin blames this unbalance on the division of labor, which empowers the male as a subjective agent and sees the female as immanent and unchangeable. She calls attention to the child's need to articulate the mother's independent existence as a factor in the formation of her/his identity, which, she argues, results optimally from mutual recognition, from both attunement and separateness, rather than simply from separation. Chodorow, too, stresses the importance of analyzing maternal subjectivity. In her discussion of the reproduction of mothering, she stresses the differing consequences of women's mothering for girls and for boys. Because girls are the same gender as the mother, she argues, they tend not to develop firm ego boundaries, never separate completely from the mother, and hence are less cut off from pre-oedipal modes of experience. Irigaray claims that because the pre-oedipal relation between mother and daughter is less repressed, women's selves remain more fluid, interrelational, and less split off from bodily experience than men's, a situation that is not yet fully represented in existing (phallocentric) discourse.

These early works of H. D. and Kay Boyle, written in the

context of extreme, even transgressive, maternity, move toward filling in this gap in representation. Here Shari Benstock's point concerning numerous white American women writers is relevant: that because such women were already "ex*patriated in patria*," living abroad enabled them to externalize in their writing the internalized exile they felt at home. Instead of providing an escape from gender roles, expatriation resulted in clarification, so that they could "write out" their sense of exclusion from internalized patriarchal law and self-definition. I would add that, because they were unable to reconcile their artistic ambitions with the conventions of motherhood they had internalized, H. D. and Boyle delineated a threshold of conflicted female affiliation that was crucial in the development of their mature vision.

Like many other women writers, in their early fiction H. D. and Kay Boyle write about fears of self-loss through immersion in the roles of marriage and motherhood. Such fears drive H. D.'s fictionalized autobiographies *Asphodel* and *Paint It Today,* written in the early 1920s, both of which return obsessively to the period 1911-1920, years marked not only by her expatriation but by the attenuation of her friendship with Frances Gregg, the failure of her engagement to Ezra Pound, the failure to her marriage to Richard Aldington after the stillbirth of their first child, her near death during the second, successful pregnancy, and finally, her rescue by Bryher (Winifred Ellerman), the younger woman writer who would become a lifelong friend. As in H. D.'s life, in both novels the heroines' fear of the incompatibility between their literary ambition and the social institutions of marriage and motherhood threatens their integrity. In both, trauma connected with pregnancy causes them to regress.

Since a woman reexperiences her self as a cared-for child when she becomes a mother, her identification with her own mother often revives issues from her childhood that have remained unresolved (Nadelson). As I have written elsewhere, trauma in pregnancy bound up this identification in H. D.'s case, increasing her need to reconcile motherly virtue with intellectual achievement. In these early novels she invented competing imaginative strategies to accomplish this reconciliation, both of which revealed instead the social and emotional constraints that inhibited it. In *Asphodel,* H. D.'s heroine, Hermione, associates writing with virgin birth, thus tacitly acknowledging the power and safety of the patriarchy by excluding men who would make her feel vulnerable. Her affair with Cyril Vane, who takes her to his country home in Cornwall to rest and write poetry after the stillbirth of her first child and the failure of her marriage, is depicted as an idealized compensation for her extreme emotional distress. Her second conception in this magical setting, amid the remains of Druid goddess worship, has a marked parthenogenetic quality: she thinks about

her compelling wish to develop her own genius and welcomes a swallow flying outside her open window as an omen of God's will. A symbol of artistic annunciation, this swallow is associated less with biological conception than with her need to incorporate an omnipotent idealization of herself.

In *Paint It Today* H. D. divorces mothering from heterosexual subordination, replacing it with a lesbian love that enhances the heroine's sense of integrity by enabling her to mother herself. After Midget's friendship with Josepha has been marred by the latter's marriage and motherhood, to which Midget responds with intense anxiety, her rededication to writing takes the form of a more satisfying lesbian relationship with an alter-ego, Althea. This relationship culminates in a veiled allusion to the welcoming of a child, described as an embryonic being, part self, part other, that suggests a desire for personal integration and ownership of her (pro)creativity.

In both novels the voyage away from proper turn-of-the-century Philadelphia to cultural centers in Europe exacerbates the heroines' conflicts. The distance from home enables them to recognize evidences of sexism that riddle the splendor of the historic shrines they visit, but instead of whetting their ambition and anger this new insight provokes more fear and guilt. For example, in *Asphodel,* when Hermione visits the birthplace of Joan of Arc, she considers the risks that her own unconventional ambitions could incur. Like herself, Joan of Arc had "visions"; for this she was burned at the stake as a witch and a heretic, a punishment that Hermione describes in terms of gender roles: "They had trapped her, a girl who was a boy and they would always do that. . . . This was the warning." And her initial rebellion against the institution of motherhood, evident in an irreverent meditation on the story of the Madonna and Child, becomes fraught with guilt as she remembers her own mother, whose conventional life makes her feel ashamed by comparison: "Such a good little Eugenia with a bustle and her hair caught with a diamond arrow. . . . I'm not good."

Similarly, in *Paint It Today* the tension between home and abroad, neither of which satisfies, echoes and intensifies the heroine's sense of self-division. Midget's attempt to escape the stifling effect of rigidly defined sex roles by remaining in Europe with her friend Josepha is thwarted by the latter's mother, who insists that her daughter return to America, a step that leads to Josepha's marriage and motherhood. Midget's own mother's approval of this plan provokes a matricidal fantasy that only increases her guilt, as self-expression becomes associated with devastating hurt and reprisal. Moreover, although Midget does stay abroad, war erupts soon after her own marriage, and she feels estranged from her soldier-husband, who returns from France "with the smell of gas in his breath . . . the stench of death in his clothes." Marital unhappiness, anxiety at the news of her friend's pregnancy, and disillusionment with a culture that could produce world war, cause Midget to develop a new trick of seeing, a mode of perception that transforms the horror of her world to "snow and ash" at great personal cost. This ability to distance herself, reminiscent of the strategy of repression H. D. employed in her Imagist poetry, provides Midget with a means of artistic survival that soon proves unsatisfying.

H. D. gives this conflict over creativity and procreativity resonance in *Palimpsest,* where she takes an archaeological concept as the principle of coherence for three related stories which, taken together, represent a critique of female identity formation in a patriarchy. (A palimpsest is a "parchment from which one writing has been [imperfectly] erased to make room for another" [title page]). Under this rubric H. D. connects "Hipparchia," a story set in "War Rome" (the ancient city she associated with London), seventy-five years before Christ's birth; "Murex," set in "War and Postwar London," the place and period of her pregnancies; and "Secret Name," set in the timeless modernist locale of "Excavator's Egypt." Thus, as Susan Friedman has pointed out, the historical, the personal, and the mythical intersect, and travel through space and time becomes a central metaphor for a woman artist's coming to understand herself ("Exile").

The concept of a palimpsest also allows H. D. to layer the psychological issues that concern her. By presenting the three stories as related "scrapings," she combines the heterosexual romance plot with an underlying story of problematic mother-daughter attachment. "Hipparchia," the story of a woman whose attempts to separate from her mother complicate her relationships with men and with her work, shows the uneasy conjoinment of the two plots; in "Murex," where a woman's poetry encodes maternal loss, the intersecting plots produce artistic inhibition; and "Secret Name," where the heroine is awakened to a buried source of creative power within herself during a visit to the tomb of a dead Egyptian king, implies that integration and artistic independence are contingent upon modifying the androcentric romantic myths that influence women's sense of possibility. In all three, the need to ground creativity in a revised story of female development, and an awareness of the connection between the personal and the political, are central to a cohesive sense of self.

The connection between maternal subjectivity, expatriation, and broader cultural hierarchies of power is most poignantly depicted, however, in a short story that H. D. wrote after her abortion in the late twenties, in which issues of gender, nationality, and race intersect. Not surprisingly, H. D.'s abortion intensified the conflict between

motherhood and authorship, described above, making her struggle for psychological integration and artistic expression increasingly desperate. As she indicates in her short poem "Gift," her "ardent / yet chill and formal" poetics was becoming increasingly untenable. Yet she lacked the positive inner imagery necessary to effect an imaginative breakthrough. In "Two Americans" she resorts to racial stereotypes, in which blacks become the repository of libidinal longings, to clarify her conception of herself as a woman artist in ways which also express her sense of having transgressed gender roles.

It is important to say, here, that H. D.'s use of racial stereotypes to serve her own needs was unconscious and even contradicted her intention. I agree with Susan Friedman that the gender issues H. D. struggled with led her to critique other aspects of the social structure that were inhumane and oppressive. She did indeed identify with all marginal people—Jews, blacks, Indians, homosexuals—who were similarly falsified by racial or sexual stereotypes ("Modernism"). However, I would add that the nature of that identification, at this particularly low point in her life, also led her to participate in a version of "romantic racism" that was prevalent in white Modernist writing. As Aldon Nielsen describes it, this discourse, often admiring in tone, proposes the nonwhite "as an unconstrained libido acting out the sexual and social fantasies of the white subconscious."

More specifically, race became a significant marker of H. D.'s conflict when H. D. met Paul Robeson, whose artistic success in London in the late twenties had made him an international celebrity. She admired Robeson's attempts to portray the dignity and humanity of his race in recitals of Negro spirituals and his ambition to act in films that would controvert the racial stereotypes that were perpetuated by both the American and British film industries (Schlosser). She and her companions, Kenneth Macpherson and Bryher, invited Robeson and his wife Essie to their home in Switzerland to make the experimental film *Borderline* in 1930, in which they wanted to show the connection between white racism, a psychological phenomenon growing out of the deplorable history of race relations, and other noxious psychic states. In particular, they connected white racism with unhealthy repression of the sexual instincts, with "neurotic-erotic suppression" (H. D. "Borderline"). In the film Robeson plays the role of Pete, a black man living peacefully in a mid-European "borderline town" until the arrival of his mulatto sweetheart, Adah (played by Essie), ignites an interracial tangle with a degenerate white couple, Astrid and Thorne (played by H. D. and Gavin Arthur). The "dipsomaniac" Thorne deserts Astrid to have an affair with Adah, which drives Astrid into a jealous rage. The town is disrupted, and Pete and his sweetheart leave unhappily.

In an essay accompanying the film, H. D. draws on racial

stereotypes to denounce both racism and sexism, stereotypes that reappear in "Two Americans." Pete is described as an exemplary creature of the natural environment in stark contrast to the enervated white man, and it is Adah's suspicious sexuality that drives the plot. Thorne acts out his (sexual) "cravings" with Adah, a woman on the "other" side of the social/racial border, who complies. His deserted wife Astrid, "the white-cerebral," finds recourse in an "intemperate fury" that whips her into a state of "dementia" in which she very nearly stabs herself and her husband with a dagger. Astrid's words, "It has all happened because these people are *black*," reveal how much rage between the sexes is concealed behind the ideal of the pure, "cerebral" white woman, who feels robbed by her husband's attraction to the body of another woman for sexual satisfaction, an avenue not openly available to her (H. D. "Borderline").

That H. D. took the role of this self-destructive woman, whose racism also serves an inimical cultural ideal of womanhood, is particularly poignant given her own sense of loss after the abortion. As if in grim self-parody, she is listed in the cast as "Helga Doorn," a pseudonym she chose because of its affinities with Ibsen's melodramatic women (she mentions Hedda Gabler in her essay), whose desperation and debasement similarly reflected widespread discontent. Thus racial fantasies become a vehicle for critiquing the sexual double standard.

Issues of nationality, race, and gender appear to intersect more benignly in "Two Americans," a story based on an informal gathering that may have taken place during the Robesons' visit with H. D. and her friends. A close reading, however, reveals a level of unintegrated anxiety beneath its surface detachment that appears related to H. D.'s abortion. Here H. D. explores the psychological ground between two expatriates—a white American woman poet Raymonde Ransome (based on herself) and a celebrated black American male singer, Saul Howard (Paul Robeson)—who are brought together by Daniel Kinoull (Kenneth Macpherson), the British director in whose film they are working. The story's impetus is Raymonde's troubled response to Saul's easy friendship with Daniel as a fellow artist, despite his racial difference, a camaraderie she cannot share. Though, like Saul, Raymonde admires Daniel's work, her earlier sexual intimacy with the film director has given her feelings of personal defeat that she cannot account for satisfactorily. Her relationship with Daniel has become a burden: he is like a "steel pin," or a "silver thorn" in her side, which she must rid herself of in order to write more freely ("Two"). Saul appears to have successfully used his role as artist to overcome the psychological setbacks of being a black American, so she uses his example to bring the dimensions of her own difference "home" to her.

Henry Louis Gates's point that race is the "ultimate trope of difference," because it is so arbitrarily applied in a racist, sexist society clarifies the meaning of this identification. Because the polarity between black and white persists in culture independent of any significant biological reality (unlike that between masculinity and femininity), the use of racial metaphors in this text allows H. D. to perceive truths about gender that ultimately explode the parallel with race. Again she describes Paul Robeson's presence in mythic terms which float upon the same pool of racial fantasies that are evident in *Borderline*. Again, these fantasies place her protagonist in a double bind. For though her artist-heroine's identification with the celebrated African-American singer is partially self-affirming, in that it confirms her own artistry, her womanhood is still subject to an inimical cultural ideal.

For despite the fact that they are both marginal Americans, Raymonde sees Saul's self-acceptance in terms which ally him with a pagan tradition more conducive to free artistic expression and sexuality than her own Puritan one. He is a dark fertility god, able to inspire the whole company with his talent: "He was no black Christ. He was an earlier, less complicated symbol. He was Dionysus as Nietzsche so valiantly struggled to define him." Unlike her own "crippled song-wing," which was too "shrill," his song "flowed toward all the world, effortless, full of benign power, without intellectual gap or cross-purpose of hyper-critical consciousness to blight it." She would like to be the Apollonian counterpart to his Dionysus, but despite her efforts she can't make this self-representation stick because of guilt connected with her being a woman.

H. D.'s concealment of the causes of Raymonde's "cross-purpose of hyper-critical consciousness" provides clues to her own psychological concerns even as it undermines the story's coherence. Raymonde attributes her "crippled" emotional condition both to an obligation to protect Daniel, who after the war "brought back [her] faith" (we're not told in what), and to war memories that continue to haunt her. Though H. D. does not make the factual content of these memories explicit, she depicts the lingering emotional affect, the monstrous guilt and pain that are the cause of Raymonde's anxiety. Like H. D., Raymonde is suffering from "a certain sort of monster," a deeply punitive sense of self:

> 'Thou shalt kill' reversed commandments for her. She had taken that ever-so-great War too seriously. She had recalled 'thou shalt kill' far, far too personally; it had become for her an actual blood-Minotaur or a sort of blood lust incarnate.

Though these veiled references to killing make the narrative obscure, knowledge of H. D.'s life and earlier, autobiographical fiction accords them psychological credibility and importance. For although in this story she does not fully express her feelings about the transgressive decision to abort, she does inscribe her guilt in the form of her heroine's clouded memory of an earlier wartime death. The narrator's observation that Raymonde had taken "'thou shalt kill' . . . far too personally" conflates H. D.'s abortion with her earlier stillbirth during the war in a way which forgives her agency in the later decision. This conflation makes further emotional sense when we recall that H. D.'s anguish after that stillbirth was increased because she had been ambivalent about the pregnancy. In *Asphodel* she fictionalized her negative feelings explicitly, depicting her heroine's pregnancy as a "deadly crucifixion" and comparing her ordeal in labor with that of a soldier in battle. Thus, though it is not explicitly acknowledged in the text, Raymonde's comparison of herself with an "other" (black male) American artist is implicitly in the service of defending an impugned womanhood.

H. D.'s deep-seated anxiety about her womanhood is operative at a second point in the story when problems of gender role again supersede racial difference or national affinity. For Raymonde identifies with Saul Howard against his light-skinned wife, Paula, whose criticism of her husband, Raymonde suspects, results from feeling overshadowed by his fame, though it takes the form of an apparent racial slur. (Paula accuses her husband of being "lazy.") Dismounting her own suspicion that may be Saul is lazy, Raymonde infers that Paula's criticism of him is related to her attempts to be "Paris and chic," but different "from that tribe who had given jazz to Europe." Though Paula's behavior threatens her racial integrity, it insures her the sexual attention usually accorded a beautiful (white) woman, attention she needs to shore up her self-image as the mere wife of a famous artist. Paula's willingness to sacrifice racial integrity for social gain is an exchange that Raymonde considers anathema.

Finally, Raymonde's inability to identify with *either* Saul or Paula eradicates the parallel between gender and race that has occluded the deeper sources of Raymonde's anxiety, and she is driven into psychological retreat. Though she feels a rivalry with Paula for both Saul and Daniel, Raymonde prefers to detach herself from sexual competition. Instead she allies herself with Gareth (Bryher), whose asexual, "schoolgirlish" interest in Saul is less threatening to Raymonde's fragile artist-identity. Unlike the black singer, whose sexuality coincides with his artistic goals, or his light-skinned wife, who trades on hers, she adopts the asexual mask of "scribe and priestess" to avoid guilt or compromise.

In the mid-thirties, analysis with Freud was a key factor in enabling H. D. to move from this self-protecting emotional stance to a more positive utilization of her maternal sub-

jectivity in her art, a process that has been described more fully elsewhere. Although beyond the scope of this paper, it is noteworthy that H. D. glanced back at the period around her abortion and her friendship with the Robesons in the first section of her last long poem, *Hermetic Definition.* Here the speaker's ability to mediate between opposites in the universe (her connection with Hermes) is dramatized by employing the trimesters of pregnancy as a central trope. Again, infatuation with a young black man is instrumental.

Problematic maternity as a catalyst in the development of authentic, cohesive selfhood, viewed from an expatriated perspective, is also evident in three of Kay Boyle's first four novels, *Plagued By the Nightingale* (1931), *Year Before Last* (1932), and *My Next Bride* (1934). Based on traumatic events in Boyle's life, these novels cover the period between 1923, when she and her French husband, Richard Brault, arrived in France, and 1929, when she began a new life with her second husband, Laurence Vail. In this interval she separated from Brault during a serious illness, conducted a doomed love affair with the dying poet Ernest Walsh, gave birth, out of wedlock, to her daughter Sharon, and joined Raymond Duncan's "artists' colony," where, according to her account in *Being Geniuses Together,* she became increasingly depressed and self-destructive. As in H. D.'s novels, fears of self-loss through traditional female roles determine the atmosphere of these three works, although the heroines of most of Boyle's novels are not fledgling artists but simply bohemian young women in search of definition. Again, troubled motherhood and abortion combine with expatriation to cause self-division and regression. In Boyle this combination leads not only to insight into the way female self-denial is socially constructed, as it does in H. D., but to a more outer-directed thematic focus on her later work, and to political activism upon her return to America.

In Boyle's novels the initial equating of America with convention and entrapment and Europe with freedom and independence is reversed, illuminating both as geographical metaphors for inner struggle. Her heroines come from American families who have instilled a spirit of adventure and individuality that they are inexplicably unable to realize. They experience painful interpersonal relationships in terms of European cultural decadence and class warfare, thus externalizing an inner conflict that has oppressed them. In *Plagued By the Nightingale,* although her own American family has inculcated individualism, Bridget finds the security offered by the inbred, tightly knit family of her French husband, Nicolas, reassuring despite its price. She welcomes the prescribed world of his Papa, Maman, and sisters, although she recognizes the literally paralyzing control they have over her young husband, who is heir to the family bone disease as well as its fortune. Desiring freedom and independence on one hand, she is afraid of being alone on the other. In the end she succumbs to the family's pressure to become pregnant despite her husband's unwillingness to inflict his disease on future generations and his resentment at having to produce an heir in order to receive money from his father. Willing to accept his family's proviso because she can think of no other way to "make a fortune" and get away, she denies her own tears at the unacknowledged exploitation of her body.

Extreme self-abnegation as a condition of motherhood becomes more explicit in the fate of Bridget's favorite sister-in-law, Charlotte, the epitome of womanly graciousness and warmth. Pregnant with her sixth child at the age of thirty-two, Charlotte is unable to imagine any other existence: "One more won't matter," she replies to her brother's worried remonstrance. "It's my life, isn't it?" When she falls ill with a disease resulting from her incestuous union with her husband, a first cousin, and the family tries to deny the seriousness of her illness, she expresses her growing distress as a longing for the nightingale that has disappeared from the ancient acacia tree outside her window. A powerful symbol of violation and enforced silence through its association with the myth of Philomel, and, ultimately, of the transformative power of sisterhood and song, the nightingale here becomes associated with Charlotte's death.

The bird also becomes associated with Bridget's failure to help Charlotte or to learn from her experience. To cheer her up, Bridget buys Charlotte a nightingale in a wooden cage, but it will not sing. When she discusses this problem with Luc, the young doctor who the family has assumed will marry one of Nicolas's sisters, Bridget suggests letting the bird go as a solution. Luc's reply mirrors Bridget's existential dilemma: "You can't just *give* freedom. It's a much more complicated thing than taking it away." Indeed, Bridget's own desire for freedom is played out through her relationship with Luc, whom she manages to free from the grim prospect of marrying into the family. Eliciting his offer of love and then rejecting it, she gives him more freedom from the social script than either she or the nightingale has. Despite her insight, she is unable to extend this freedom to herself.

The emotionally flat ending of the novel becomes explicable when we consider that although Boyle began the novel during her marriage to Richard Brault, father of the first child she aborted, she did not complete it until after the birth of her daughter Sharon, who was conceived out of wedlock during a love affair with Ernest Walsh after she had separated from Brault. In a recent interview, in which she defends these early choices, Boyle poignantly remembers "the passing of the little thing," although she disavows guilt over the abortion, and she is adamant about having wanted Walsh's child, despite its illegitimacy. Perhaps the

"very deep feeling" she recalls, which she associates with the birth of her daughter, was charged with the memory of her earlier loss, and these mixed feelings were displaced onto her first novel, resulting in the novel's ambiguity.

Her next novel, *Year Before Last,* chronicles her love affair with Walsh, omitting any reference to the pregnancy. On the surface a paean to free love and the pure life of the spirit, to bohemianism versus bourgeois philistinism, this novel contains a subtext of moral masochism that may also be a function of the author's internal conflict. Boyle's heroine, Hannah, whose palindromic name underscores her lack of self-definition, is an American woman in an unhappy marriage to a conventional Frenchman, who falls madly in love with a tubercular young Irish poet and editor, Martin, as if commitment to his spiritual force will give her the courage she needs to live her own life. As the novel opens, they are living in a deserted French château with barely enough to eat, having abandoned their respective domestic obligations: she, her husband, Dilly, who has sent her to southern France to recuperate from a lung ailment, and he, his aunt Eve, a glamorous suffragette who bankrolls his literary magazine. The novel follows their life together during the year before Martin's death, as they move from village to village, looking for an inn that will permit them to stay, so that he can recover and put out his magazine. The intensity and instability of their lives, and their sense of homelessness in the face of those who fear contamination, could be read as a metaphor for the plight of pure art and love in an inhospitable world.

Indeed, Sandra Spanier has interpreted the novel as an assertion of the unassailable, transcendent power of love. While I agree that this is its dominant thematic line, I would add that Boyle's idealism is undercut by her depiction of the lovers' ambivalent relationship with Eve, Martin's Scottish aunt, who functions as a mother-figure to both of them. In the psychological dynamics of this ménage-à-trois, Boyle shows the masochism underlying Hannah's social alienation, the sense of fragmentation marked by gender polarity and a diffuse sense of guilt. Eve—the character is based on Walsh's older friend Ethel Moorhead, who was a feminist activist and an artist in her own right—could have been depicted as a strong role model for Hannah. In *Being Geniuses Together* Boyle describes her attraction to Moorhead's independence and commitment to poetry as well as the older woman's jealousy of her affair with Walsh. However, in the novel the narrator stresses the two women's competition for Martin's love, which makes such an alliance impossible. Compared with Eve, who "knew her way and had it," Hannah is a self-effacing presence, "a hesitant wife as frail as a thread . . . who was lingering now, on the outskirts, cringing, and waiting to be bid to go or come."

In fact, the parts played by Hannah and Eve resemble the

splitting of the erotic and the material in conventional representations of femininity, to which Boyle may have resorted imaginatively because of psychological stress. As Suzanne Clark has suggested, Boyle seems to be questioning "whether the erotic young love of Hannah and Martin has any moral force" compared with the stronger older woman's chaste dedication to their common artistic project. Boyle, however, accords Hannah's love for Martin the superior power. At the end of the novel, having fought with Eve about ownership of the magazine, Martin cries out for Hannah's presence. Further, Eve overcomes her animosity toward the younger woman when, desperate for Hannah to save the dying man, she suggests that the three of them start over.

A comparison of Eve's role in the novel with that of Ethel Moorhead in the lives of Boyle and Ernest Walsh confirms the sense that Boyle's punitive characterization of Hannah as weaker than Eve is related to internal conflict over her abortion and illegitimate pregnancy. In *Being Geniuses Together,* where Boyle includes her pregnancy, she not only describes Moorhead's deathbed quarrel with Walsh over the magazine, she also delineates her reconciliation with Moorhead, which occurred under quite different circumstances—after Walsh's death, when she offered to support Boyle and the baby. Boyle's description of her response to Moorhead's offer suggests a role reversal that is a product of intense relief at the older woman's acceptance:

> When I put my arms around her, all strength seemed to leave her, to drain from some fatal wound that could never be staunched and that she wanted no hand to touch, no eye to see. She slipped to her knees, and I knelt with her, holding her in my arms still, rocking and cradling her now as if she were my little child.

Boyle's depiction of the women's affiliation and equivalency here suggests that her omission of the pregnancy from the earlier plot served a struggle with issues of desire and power that devolved from her history of transgressive maternity.

If moral masochism as a result of psychic fragmentation is the subtext of *Year Before Last,* it is the starting point of Boyle's last novel based on her life in the twenties. A much more disillusioned book. *My Next Bride* overtly connects the heroine's painfully acquired maternal subjectivity with her ultimate recognition that expatriation does not provide escape from the inequity of gender roles. The young artist Victoria, whose name reflects her American-Puritan background, comes to Paris with a naive hope of finding love and self-definition abroad: "She was fresh from somewhere else and she did not know yet how it could be. . . . [Hers] was a voice speaking out of a bodily, a national ease that had never been betrayed."

In the novel's first two sections, which chronicle this betrayal, Victoria allies herself unsuccessfully with two fellow male expatriates. Out of a combination of idealism and poverty, she joins an artists' commune run by Sorrel (based on Raymond Duncan), who seems to share her longing for the simple America of the pioneers who lived a life attuned to nature. When she is not working in the colony's store selling scarves and tunics, she paints pictures of the lives of saints, of "angry, good, old men," who she hopes will give her own face definition and strength. But her belief in Sorrel's mission becomes eroded as she sees the inequities and abuse within the group, particularly the way the children are treated, and it is exploded when Sorrel buys an expensive American car for himself with group money from the sale of goods in the shop, instead of the printing press he has always said they needed.

Victoria meets a more subtly corrosive influence than Sorrel, however, when Antony Lister (based on Harry Crosby) appears in the shop. A bohemian American artist like herself, he seems to be a person with a solid identity, who is very much in love with his wealthy artist-wife, Fontana (based on Caresse Crosby, to whom the book is dedicated). But as Victoria comes to know him better, and they fall in love themselves, his own spiritual crisis becomes apparent. The black sheep of a materialistic Boston family, who do not understand his artistic aspirations, Antony is torn between his allegiance to them and his longing for the redemptive beauty of art. He tries to drown his confusion in drink and sex, and ultimately returns to America, where he commits suicide, an act that yields the novel's epigraph, "Knife will be my next bride." One night in a bar, Antony expresses his personal crisis in terms of yearning for a lost, radical Puritan America, in which social and spiritual values took precedence over material concerns:

> Every day I'm in Europe . . . I can see the map of America in my head and the mountain-ranges. I think of State lines and I hear the people talking as well as I hear you and me. Nobody over there sees it or hears it the way I do. . . . They can't hear what is going on the way you and I hear it sitting here in a bar kissing the rock of Plymouth, the stone breasts, the iron mouth of Plymouth, because I'm for Plymouth, I'm for the Puritan women and for the ancestors who were not afraid of beginning there.

This puritanism, part of what Victoria also defines as essential to her self-concept as an American, leads them both to disaster. For by denying Victoria natural access to her sexuality, it sets her up for self-destructive rebellion: she becomes involved in a mindless course of drunken partying that leaves her feeling dirty and dazed. Waking up one day to find herself pregnant, she goes to the vaudeville dancer at the colony to give her pills to "bring it off," and is nearly destroyed physically as well as psychologically. When she collapses in the Metro, her revival is described in terms of national apostasy. As she stands in the street watching the waiters prepare for the Americans who would soon gather for breakfast on the terrace of a nearby café, Victoria realizes that she has nothing left to say to America: "she said America's that way, over there, and her teeth were knocking together. Listen, America, she said, and her nose was running. America, listen, listen, she said, but there was nothing more to say."

Her revival is also depicted in terms of rescue by another woman, Anthony's glamorous wife Fontana, who helps Victoria to get the abortion she seeks. Victoria's relationship with Fontana, to whom she confesses the shame and pain of her inadvertent pregnancy, is crucial to Victoria's survival and to the beginning of self-acceptance at a more fundamental level. For it is in Fontana's company, in the presence of a treacherous *sage-femme*, that Victoria sees the specter of death faced by all the poor women who undergo illegal abortion:

> and all the others, the nameless ones *sans domicile fixe* and *sans profession,* with their heels walked sideways, like Victoria's, and their faces walked long and bony like horses' faces, all of them came forbidden and unbidden out of the darkness of the corners and gathered there around them. . . . There must be something better somewhere else, the thing that was brimming in her eyes was saying. They were out the door, they were on the landing, and behind them in the silence of the *sage-femme's* room they could hear the dripping, the endless dripping of the life-blood as it left the bodies of those others; the unceasing drip of the stream as it left the wide, bare table and fell, drop by drop, to the planks beneath it, dripping and dropping on for ever like a finger tapping quickly on the floor.

Unlike Antony, she comes to realize that neither repatriation nor expatriation will solve her need to be whole because she has been alienated from her own body.

In fact, Victoria's alliance with Fontana, around the pain and agony of the abortion, represents a kind of intrapsychic "rematriation" on the part of Kay Boyle, the beginning of a clearer sense of female kinship that is a turning point in her career. For this alliance develops a motif that has been implicit earlier: the commonality of the heroine's plight with that of other women and her desire for connection (Morse). To sustain her journey abroad, Victoria has carried with her pictures from home of three women who have served as flawed sources of inspiration: her cold, unyielding art teacher, "who had never given a word of herself away," her loving mother, who lacked the courage to finish

what she started, and her vulnerable friend Lacey, a singer who committed suicide rather than return to an abusive husband, whose cynicism prevented her from recognizing Victoria's offer of love. One of the last scenes, in which Victoria and Fontana fall asleep in each other's arms, mirrors an earlier memory of Lacey, but this time Victoria is the needy one. She survives her identity crisis and impulse to self-destruction by taking the comfort that the older woman offers. As Deborah Morse has pointed out, the cultural lesson that Victoria learns leads Boyle to prophesy "a new role *within* society for the artist." In the thirties she became more concerned with communication than with self-expression, more directed toward the social world.

H. D. also ultimately integrated her experiences in childbirth with her poetic practice in ways commensurate with the problems and promise of her early prose, although, unlike Boyle, she never articulated the experience of abortion in either fiction or poetry. This lack of overt representation may reflect an ambivalence that contributed to the lasting power that the trope of childbirth had for her. For both writers, expatriation provided the psychic space in which to explore the impingement of gender roles upon their lives and aspirations. In these early works, they portrayed the effect of inadequate maternal role models upon their developing identity as artists, articulating a tension between motherhood and authorship that they could no longer repress. Driven inward by painful experiences in childbirth in the twenties, H. D. and Kay Boyle delineated elements of maternal subjectivity that became the underpinning of their mature vision.

FURTHER READING

Criticism

Bendall, Molly. A Review of *Collected Poems,* by Kay Boyle. *The Antioch Review* 50, No. 4 (Fall 1992): 780.
    Argues that the poetry in *Collected Poems* are important documents of Boyle's life and the twentieth century.

Cohn, Ruby. "Being Ingenious: A Montage for Kay." *Twentieth Century Literature* 34, No. 3 (Fall 1988): 264-71.
    Chronicles Cohn's experiences as a friend and colleague of Boyle.

Gelder, Robert van. "An Interview with Kay Boyle, Expatriate." *Writers and Writing,* pp. 193-6. New York: Charles Scribner's Sons, 1946.
    An interview with Boyle on her return from Europe during World War II.

Harris, Gale. A Review of *The Crazy Hunter,* by Kay Boyle. *Belles Lettres* 9, No. 3 (1994): 65.

Favorable review of *The Crazy Hunter.*

"The Spirit at Bay." *New York Times Book Review* (26 June 1932): 7.

Reviews *Year Before Last* and argues that while Boyle has written a good novel, she needs to further develop her craft.

Peterson, Virgilia. "Kay Boyle's Craft and Magic in a Moving Novel of Post-War France." *New York Herald Tribune Book Review* 31, No. 39 (8 May 1955): 1.

Favorably reviews *The Seagull on the Step* and summarizes its plot.

Renek, Morris. "Kay Boyle's Victory Over the Frozen Sea." *Twentieth Century Literature* 34, No. 3 (Fall 1988): 294-8.

Praises Boyle's ability to capture the spirit of important twentieth-century events.

Spanier, Sandra Whipple. "Kay Boyle: In a Woman's Voice." *Faith of a (Woman) Writer,* edited by Alice Kessler-Harris and William McBrien, pp. 59-70. New York: Greenwood Press, 1988.

Explores feminist themes in Boyle's work.

Additional coverage of Boyle's life and career is contained in the following sources published by Gale: *Contemporary Authors,* Vols. 13-16R, and 140; *Contemporary Authors Autobiography Series,* Vol. 1; *Contemporary Authors New Revision Series,* Vol. 29; *Dictionary of Literary Biography,* Vols. 4, 9, 48, and 86; *Dictionary of Literary Biography Yearbook,* 1993; *Major Twentieth-Century Writers;* and *Short Story Criticism,* Vol. 5.

Octavia Butler

1947-

(Full name Octavia Estelle Butler) American novelist, short story writer, and essayist.

The following entry presents an overview of Butler's career. For further information on her life and works, see *CLC,* Volume 38.

INTRODUCTION

Best known as the author of the Patternist series of science-fiction novels, which involves a society whose inhabitants have developed telepathic powers over several centuries, Butler explores themes that have been given only cursory treatment in the genre, including sexual identity and racial conflict. Butler's heroines are black women who are powerful both mentally and physically. While they exemplify the traditional gender roles of nurturer, healer, and conciliator, these women are also courageous, independent, and ambitious. They enhance their influence through alliances with or opposition to powerful males. Butler has earned many accolades, including a Hugo Award, a Nebula Award, and a *Locus* Award, all for her 1985 novella, "Bloodchild," which was later published in the collection *Bloodchild and Other Stories* (1995).

Biographical Information

Butler spent her youth in a racially mixed neighborhood in Pasadena, California. Her father died when she was very young, and her mother worked as a maid to support the two of them. Butler has written memoirs of her mother's sacrifices, which included buying Butler a typewriter of her own when she was ten years old, and paying a large fee to an unscrupulous agent so Butler's stories could be read. Butler entered student-writing contests as a teenager and, after attending such workshops as the Writers Guild of America Clarion Science Fiction Writer's Workshop in 1970, she sold her first science-fiction stories. This early training brought her into contact with a range of well-known science-fiction writers, including Joanna Russ and Harlan Ellison, who became Butler's mentor.

Major Works

Four of Butler's novels—*Patternmaster* (1976), *Mind of My Mind* (1977), *Survivor* (1978), and *Wild Seed* (1980)—revolve around the Patternists, a group of mentally superior beings who are telepathically connected to one another. These beings are the descendants of Doro, a

four thousand-year-old Nubian male who has selectively bred with humans throughout time with the intention of establishing a race of superhumans. He prolongs his life by killing others, including his family members, and inhabiting their bodies. The origin of the Patternists is outlined in *Wild Seed,* which begins in seventeenth-century Africa and spans more than two centuries. The novel recounts Doro's uneasy alliance with Anyanwu, an earth mother figure whose extraordinary powers he covets. Their relationship progresses from power struggles and tests of will to mutual need and dependency. Doro's tyranny ends when one of his children, the heroine of *Mind of My Mind,* destroys him and unites the Patternists with care and compassion. *Patternmaster* and *Survivor* are also a part of the Patternist series. The first book is set in the future and concerns two brothers vying for their dying father's legacy. The pivotal character in the novel, however, is Amber, one of Butler's most heroic women, whose unconventional relationship with her brother is often analyzed within feminist contexts. In *Survivor,* set on an alien planet, Butler examines human attitudes toward racial and ethnic differences and their effects on two alien creatures. Alanna, the human protagonist, triumphs over racial prejudice and enslavement by teaching her alien captors tolerance and respect for individuality. *Kindred* (1979) departs from the Patternist series yet shares its focus on male/female relationships and racial matters. The protagonist, Dana, is a contemporary writer who is telepathically transported to a pre-Civil War plantation. She is victim both of the slave-owning ancestor who summons her when he is in danger and of the slave-holding age in which she is trapped for increasingly lengthy periods. *Clay's Ark* (1984) reflects Butler's interest in the psychological traits of men and women in a story of a space virus that threatens the earth's population with disease and genetic mutation. In an interview, Butler commented on how Ronald Reagan's vision of a winnable nuclear war encouraged her to write more dystopic material. This shift in focus is most evident in *Parable of the Sower* (1993), a novel which depicts a religious sea-change, set against the backdrop of a strife-ridden inner city in 2025. Butler has also authored three novels—*Dawn* (1987), *Adulthood Rites* (1988), and *Imago* (1989)—known collectively as the Xenogenesis trilogy; the trilogy has been interpreted as a positive analysis of an evolutionary society in which things are in a constant state of change. Butler's acclaimed novella, "Bloodchild," examines the topic of patriarchal society, and is set in a world inhabited by human-like beings called Terrans who live on "Preserves" which are provided for them by a government run by a monstrous race of creatures known as Tlics. The Terran families are valued by the Tlics because each of them is forced to sacrifice at least one of its sons to the Tlics to function as a "host" for Tlic eggs; the process produces highly desirable offspring but sometimes results in the death of the host. The central relationship in the novella is that between T'Gatoi, a government official who manages the Preserves, and Gan, the Terran boy who serves as the host for her eggs.

Critical Reception

Critics applaud Butler's lack of sentimentality, and respond favorably to her direct treatment of subjects not previously addressed in science fiction, such as sexuality, male/female relationships, racial inequity, and contemporary politics. Hoda Zaki writes: "A constant thread throughout Butler's work is her celebration of racial difference and the coming together of diverse individuals to work, live and build a community. . . ." Several reviewers assert that there is an underlying theme in Butler's narratives dealing with an exploration of slavery, but Butler herself disputes this. In an interview with Stephen W. Potts, she states, "The only places I am writing about slavery is where I actually say so." Critics note Butler's ambiguous endings that leave open the question of the possibilities and limitations of mankind. Jim Miller states, "Whether she is dealing with the role of medical science, biological determinism, the politics of disease, or the complex interrelations of race, class, and

gender, Butler's dystopian imagination challenges us to think the worst in complex ways while simultaneously planting utopian seeds of hope."

PRINCIPAL WORKS

Patternmaster (novel) 1976
Mind of My Mind (novel) 1977
Survivor (novel) 1978
Kindred (novel) 1979
Wild Seed (novel) 1980
Clay's Ark (novel) 1984
*Dawn** (novel) 1987
*Adulthood Rites** (novel) 1988
*Imago** (novel) 1989
Parable of the Sower (novel) 1993
Bloodchild and Other Stories (novella, short stories, and essays) 1995

*Known collectively as the *Xenogenesis* Trilogy.

CRITICISM

Ruth Salvaggio (essay date Summer 1984)

SOURCE: "Octavia Butler and the Black Science-Fiction Heroine," in *Black American Literature*, Vol. 18, No. 2, Summer, 1984, pp. 78-81.

[*Salvaggio is Assistant Professor of English at Virginia Polytechnic Institute and University. In the following essay, she discusses Butler's black, female protagonists in the Patternist novels.*]

A traditional complaint about science fiction is that it is a male genre, dominated by male authors who create male heroes who control distinctly masculine worlds. In the last decade, however, a number of women writers have been changing that typical scenario. Their feminine and feminist perspectives give us a different kind of science fiction, perhaps best described by Pamela Sargent's term "Women of Wonder." In a sense, Octavia Butler's science fiction is a part of that new scenario, featuring strong female protagonists who shape the course of social events. Yet in another sense, what Butler has to offer is something very different. Her heroines are black women who inhabit racially mixed societies. Inevitably, the situations these women confront involve the dynamic interplay of race and sex in futuristic worlds. How a feminist science-fiction character responds to a male-dominated world is one thing; how Butler's black heroines respond to racist and sexist worlds is quite another.

Butler's concern with racism and sexism is a conscious part of her vision. As she herself explains, a particularly "insidious problem" with science fiction is that it "has always been nearly all white, just as until recently, it's been nearly all male." Confronting this "problem" head-on, Butler places her heroines in worlds filled with racial and sexual obstacles, forcing her characters to survive and eventually overcome these societal barriers to their independence. Sometimes her black heroines are paired with white men who challenge their abilities; sometimes they are paired with powerful black men who threaten their very autonomy and existence. And, always, the society in which they live constantly reminds them of barriers to their independence. Tracing the plight of each heroine is like following different variations on a single theme, the yearning for independence and autonomy. That Butler's women, despite all odds, achieve that autonomy makes her science fiction a fresh and different contribution to the genre and makes Butler herself an exciting new voice in the traditional domains of science fiction, feminism, and black literature.

This article is intended to introduce Octavia Butler through her science-fiction heroines—beginning with the defiant Amber in *Patternmaster* (1976), then moving to the confused but powerful Mary in *Mind of My Mind* (1977) and the compromising Alanna in *Survivor* (1978). The heroine I leave until last is one we encounter as the old woman Emma, hovering in the background of *Mind of My Mind.* She later appears as Anyanwu in Butler's most recent science-fiction novel, *Wild Seed* (1980). In Anyanwu we discover the inspiring force of all of Butler's heroines. And in *Wild Seed* we discover dimensions of Butler's fictive world—not the typical feminist utopia, but a flawed world in which racially and sexually oppressed individuals negotiate their way through a variety of personal and societal barriers.

Germain Greer's term "obstacle race" seems particularly appropriate when discussing Butler and her fiction, largely because the women discussed in both situations confront peculiarly social obstacles. Just as women artists, according to Greer, should be seen "as members of a group having much in common, tormented by the same conflicts of motivation and the same practical difficulties, the obstacles both external and surmountable, internal and insurmountable of the race for achievement," so Butler's heroines share in this social and personal struggle for assertion and understanding.

Their particular struggle, however, is accentuated by the extraordinary mental facilities they possess: Each of Butler's four science-fiction novels is built around a society of telepaths linked to each other through a mental "pattern." Thus when Anyanwu, the African woman in *Wild Seed,* is transported on a slave ship to colonial America, she senses the horror of slavery well before she actually witnesses its real-life horrors. Or when Mary, in *Mind of My Mind,* ultimately confronts her oppressive father, she kills him through the machinations of a gruesome mental war game. The violence that accompanies such racial and sexual conflict rarely centers on women in the way that it does in Butler's novels. Here we have females who must take the kind of action normally reserved for white, male protagonists. White males, curiously, play an important role in Butler's fiction—sometimes as enemies, sometimes as foils to the women. We might begin with a discussion of them in Butler's first novel, *Patternmaster.* There they dominate the plot until, as one female science-fiction writer describes in a different context, "a woman appeared." Let us begin, then, with the traditional science-fiction plot, and the sudden intrusion of a woman.

It should not be surprising that *Patternmaster,* Butler's first novel, revolves around that typical science-fiction plot: It employs two of the most traditional mythic structures— the inheritance of sons and the journey motif. Rayal, the Patternmaster, is dying; his two sons, Coransee and Teray, vie for control of the Pattern. This rivalry of sons for possession of the father's empire follows the outlines of an archetypal literary construct: Coransee, the stronger and more obvious heir, is defeated by the young and inconspicuous Teray, who ultimately proves himself—despite all outward appearances—to be the righteous heir. Ostensibly, then, *Patternmaster* is a novel which presents us with a "good-son" hero. We are glad when the honest Teray defeats his sinister sibling; we are glad that this decent young man has overcome the corruption and power lust of the older brother.

But all this is not really what *Patternmaster* is about. Before the adventures of our hero begin to unfold, our heroine appears—Amber. The circumstances of her appearance are just as curious as she is. Teray, captive in his brother's household, calls for a "healer" to treat a woman who has been beaten by a man. Enter Amber—a Patternist with extraordinary mental abilities to mend the human body. Immediately, her strong-minded, judgmental character emerges, and before long she and Teray, both captives in Coransee's household, plot to escape.

The story of their escape, their quest for freedom, now begins to change the typical "quest" motif that defines so much science fiction. For one thing, Teray soon realizes that he cannot physically survive their journey without Amber's healing powers—she may, in fact, be more physically powerful than Teray himself. For another, the fascinating relationship between hero and heroine overthrows all of our expectations about conventional romantic and/ or sexual love. Because Teray is white and Amber black, their relationship continually reminds us of racial distinctions. And because Amber is a woman who refuses to act out traditional female roles (she will not be any man's wife, she is sexually androgynous, she is stronger and more independent than most men), their relationship continually highlights sexual and feminist issues.

Racism and sexism, then, are matters fundamental to an understanding of both plot and character. Coransee's household, for instance, is hierarchically structured so that those who possess power necessarily abuse those who are powerless: "Housemasters" control "Outsiders" who control "Mutes." In this futuristic mental society in which people have the ability to comprehend each other's thoughts, mental understanding gives way to mind control and ultimately mental oppression. The great "Pattern" itself—holding forth the promise of a mentally-unified culture which might use its combined intellectual powers for human advancement—instead has become the prize for Machiavellian power seekers. No wonder Butler continually uses the term "slavery" to describe the "mental leashes" which keep this society in its state of oppression.

Though Teray, the good son destined to inherit the Pattern, is the figure in whom we must place our trust and hope, it is Amber who most dramatically personifies independence, autonomy, and liberation. Forced, as a captive in Coransee's household, to be one of his "women," she nonetheless boasts, "'But I'm not one of his wives. . . . I'm an independent.'" Asked by Teray, whom she truly does come to love, to be his wife, she refuses, "'Because I want the same thing you want. My House. Mine.'" Discussing with Teray her former sexual relationship with another woman, she explains, "'When I meet a woman who attracts me, I prefer women. . . . And when I meet a man who attracts me, I prefer men.'" This is clearly not your typical romance heroine. This is certainly not your typical science-fiction heroine. Ironically, *Patternmaster* makes Amber out to be the perfect prize for two rival brothers. Instead, this "golden brown woman with hair that was a cap of small, tight black curls" turns out to be a model of independence and autonomy.

All ends well in *Patternmaster.* Teray and Amber, with their combined powers, defeat Coransee. And Teray, as the good son, will inherit the Pattern. But it is Amber who somehow stands out as having transcended this political war of wits. In a final exchange between Amber and Teray, she reminds him of how easily she can tip the scales of power. Teray's response is filled with respect, but tinged with fear: "Not for the first time, he realized what a really dangerous woman she could be. If he could not make her his wife, he would be wise to make her at least an ally."

All of Butler's heroines are dangerous women. Perhaps the most conspicuously dangerous is Mary who, in *Mind of My Mind,* has a tremendous potential for destruction. Perhaps the least conspicuously dangerous is Alanna who, in *Survivor,* exerts a subtle but radical influence on a foreign society which she and her parents have colonized. Mary and Alanna, both young black women, sport two very different types of feminism: Mary, a confused and disoriented child raised in the slums of twentieth-century Los Angeles, eventually becomes the leader of a mental empire; Alanna, an orphan in a futuristic Earth society, becomes a unifying force on a foreign planet inhabited by warring tribes. Mary must fight with and ultimately kill her father to achieve "freedom"; Alanna must reject the Christian beliefs of her parents to bring peace and respectability to her new culture. Mary is forced to marry a white man in order to establish and control her mental empire; Alanna chooses to marry the leader of a non-human tribe in order to survive and establish a home on a new planet. Whereas Mary learns to control and dominate, Alanna learns to compromise and survive. In these two women, we discover that the source of female strength can foster very different kinds of feminist power—and very different kinds of human response.

Mary's appeal derives from her brute force. Even as a child, she becomes conditioned to life in a sexist and violent world. The novel opens with threats of male aggression:

> I was in my bedroom reading a novel when somebody came banging on the door really loud, like the police. I thought it was the police until I got up, looking out the window, and saw one of Rina's johns standing there. I wouldn't have bothered to answer, but the fool was kicking at the door like he wanted to break it in. I went to the kitchen and got one of our small cast-iron skillets—the size just big enough to hold two eggs. Then I went to the door. The stupid bastard was drunk.

This same young girl who almost kills one of her mother's "johns" will end up killing her father, a man who forced her to have sex with him and who tries to control her mental powers. Not surprisingly, Mary's opinion of men is filled with bitterness. When her father forces her to marry Karl Larkin, a white man, she can only smirk and reflect how much "Karl looked like one of the bright, ambitious, bookish white guys from high school." When she later questions Karl about their racial difference, her suspicions about his character prove correct: "'How do you feel about black people?'" she asks him, only to hear him reply, "'You've seen my cook.'"

Such racial differences call attention to other forms of enslavement in *Mind of My Mind.* When Doro, Mary's father, tries to explain the nature of "Mutes" to the old woman Emma, she snaps back: "'I know what you mean, Doro. I knew the first time I heard Mary use it. It means nigger!'" Unlike her father, however, Mary comes to sympathize with the people under her mental control. When she kills Doro, patriarchal domination becomes maternal caring. Having the potential for destructive power thrust upon her, Mary learns to control that power, to use it wisely and cautiously. She is Butler's study in brute feminist force.

Alanna's appeal derives from her steadfast character, from intense psychological control and determination. Unlike Mary, Alanna possesses no extraordinary mental abilities. She is Butler's study in the power of human endurance. Instead of combating violence with violence, Alanna accepts the social obstacles which a foreign society imposes on her. Her object is to learn to survive among these obstacles, to accommodate to a culture that is far from perfect.

The most potent of these obstacles is the addictive drug meklah, a drug so powerful that withdrawal from it almost always proves fatal. Forced into addiction, Alanna not only survives withdrawal but also survives as a prisoner taken by one of the warring tribes. Living among this "Tehkohn" group, she confronts and learns to deal with even more obstacles: She proves herself to be a strong huntress (a mark of distinction in Tehkohn culture) and a loyal follower of Tehkohn customs. Ultimately, she marries the leader of the tribe and has their child.

Marriage is often a feminist issue in Butler's novels. Amber in *Patternmaster* refuses marriage; Mary in *Mind of My Mind* is forced to marry. Alanna's marriage to a non-human creature ironically turns out to be the most successful and respectable of all these marriage situations. Her joining with the Tehkohn leader at once liberates her from the enslaving Christianity of her missionary parents and the enslavement of the meklah drug. Moreover, it offers her the promise of establishing a home with people she has come to respect and love. Perhaps the most bitter irony of the novel is that the Christian earthlings, who call their new home "Canaan," cannot accept the marriage of their daughter into a tribe that will offer them their only hope of peaceful existence.

The Christian religion is depicted as notably racist in *Survivor.* As a young, wild black girl, Alanna is adopted by white parents and grows up in a world in which her color is always suspect. On one occasion, a Missionary suggests that Alanna would surely "'be happier with her own kind'" since, after all, "'the girl isn't white.'" When Alanna later asks her mother about this incident, she learns "for the first time how important some Missionaries believed their own coloring to be." Color, in fact, turns out to be one of the major motifs in the novel. The Kohn creatures display a variety of colors as their moods and emotions change: They are gray in sobriety, white in amusement, bright yellow in anger. Their color also indicates hierarchical structure. Only a few of them, for instance, possess the blue, a sign

of honor and power. Yet these colorful, non-human creatures show none of the racial bigotry associated with the Christian Missionaries. Ironically, Alanna's parents can laughingly dismiss the fear that their "black" daughter might mix with "whites," but are repulsed when that same daughter marries the honorable "blue" Tehkohn leader.

As a strong-minded black woman, Alanna submits to a surprising number of social restraints: first to the Christian Missionary code, then to the meklah drug, and finally to imprisonment by the Tehkohn tribe. But in her submission she discovers a source of strength. She learns, as Mary had learned, about herself—and about the different roles she has had to play in order to survive. We see in her an amazing capacity to compromise. Alanna's flexibility allows her to meander around some obstacles, and make other apparent obstacles into real avenues of liberation.

This ability to compromise and survive is what characterizes Butler's most fully-developed and intriguing heroine— Anyanwu in *Wild Seed.* Though all of Butler's protagonists are black, only Anyanwu is born in Africa. Both her African origin and her feminist determination give us every reason to think of her as the ancestress of Amber, Mary, Alanna, and the host of other prominent black women in Butler's fiction. Just as *Wild Seed,* by tracing the origins of Patternist society back to seventeenth-century Africa, provides a foundation for all four of the Patternist science-fiction novels, so does Anyanwu help to explain the yearning for independence and autonomy sought by Amber, Mary, and Alanna.

Before discussing Anyanwu as the character central to Butler's fiction, let me outline briefly the structure and plot of *Wild Seed* to show just how encompassing the novel is— in terms of both the time and space its characters inhabit.

The story spans two continents and nearly two centuries. Meeting in Africa in 1690, Anyanwu and Doro—female and male who have the potential to live forever—travel via slave ship to colonial New England. There Doro, a patriarchal dictator who aspires to breed a race of superhumans such as himself, exploits Anyanwu's abilities as a healer to propagate and maintain his small but growing empire. At first taken in by Doro's mystique, Anyanwu soon comes to realize that she is principally to serve as his breeder and slave. Forced to marry one of Doro's sons, she not only must partake in his animalistic breeding experiments, but must painfully endure their often tragic consequences. After her husband's death, she escapes from the New England colony. In 1840, Doro finds her on a plantation in Louisiana. There, in very real slave territory, Anyanwu has established her own free household only to have it invaded and controlled by Doro. After several of Anyanwu's children meet their deaths because of Doro's intrusion, Anyanwu decides that her only possible escape from his oppression is her own death. When she vows to commit suicide, however, Doro realizes how much the loss of Anyanwu would mean to him. Deprived of his only immortal compatriot, he would be doomed to face eternity alone. But more than that, he would lose the only effective humanizing force in his life. Their reconciliation at the end of the novel brings to a tenuous resolution over a hundred years of intense personal conflict. The ending of this novel, however, is actually the beginning of Butler's three previous novels, since in it we discover the origins of Patternist society.

We might best understand Anyanwu by appreciating the fundamental opposition between her and Doro. Both characters, for instance, are potentially immortal, but their means for achieving this immortality are strikingly different. Doro is a vampire-like figure who must continually kill people and assume their bodies in order to live. Anyanwu is a healer; instead of killing others, she rejuvenates herself. In this sense, she is the direct prototype of Amber in *Patternmaster.* Just as Teray, in that futuristic novel, could not possibly survive without Amber's healing abilities, so the superhuman Doro immediately recognizes in Anyanwu's talents a means to secure his superrace. For all Doro's control over his life and the lives of others, he is necessarily restricted in the physical forms he can assume. True, he may invade other bodies, but the constraints of those bodies are a given. Anyanwu's powers allow far more flexibility and agility: In changing the physical construct of her own body, she can transform herself into various kinds of creatures—both human and non-human. On the slave ship, for instance, when one of Doro's sons tries to rape her, Anyanwu fantastically transforms herself into a leopard and mauls her assailant to his violent death. She also possesses the ability to change from youth to old age back to youth. She may even change her sex, and on one particular occasion when she does so, Anyanwu once again becomes a prototype of Amber—this time by virtue of her androgyny.

The very physical characteristics of Anyanwu, then, highlight her distinguishing qualities. She is flexible and dexterous, compared to Doro's stiffness and dominance. She uses prowess rather than direct, confrontational power. She heals rather than kills, and kills only by assuming a different form and only when she or her children are assaulted. In Anyanwu, we find a woman who—despite her imprisonment by a patriarchal tyrant—learns to use her abilities to survive. In this sense, she is most obviously the prototype of another of Butler's heroines—Alanna in *Survivor.*

The marriage motif in Butler's novels, which I have commented on earlier, is also crystallized in Anyanwu—not only through her willingness to accept husbands forced upon her by Doro, but ultimately through her final reconciliation with Doro himself. Like both Amber and Mary,

Anyanwu has a defiant attitude about marriage, and particularly like Mary in *Mind of My Mind,* she initially refuses to marry a white man whom Doro has chosen for her. Defiance, however, soon gives way to acceptance—and it is here, once again, that Anyanwu closely resembles Alanna, accepting the constraints of her world and trying to make something decent and productive out of the indecent situation in which she finds herself. Left on her own, without Doro's scheming intrusions, Anyanwu is able to produce and raise children possessed of both superior powers and tremendous human warmth. Her aim is to have children who may live with her, not die after a normal life span and leave her to her loneliness. Doro's paternal concerns revolve around his mechanical breeding experiments: He does not create children, but Frankenstein monsters. Anyanwu's maternity, however, is the main source of her being, the principal reason for her existence. As she explains, "'I could have husbands and wives and lovers into the next century and never have a child. Why should I have so many except that I want them and love them?'"

It is this kind of maternal generosity that will finally save Doro. Anyanwu, repulsed by Doro's inhumanity and his enslavement of the very superrace he has fathered, can all too easily kill herself. She can at least escape oppression through death. When Doro asks her why she has decided to die, Anyanwu explains her dilemma: "'It's the only way I can leave you. . . . Everything is temporary but you and me. You are all I have, perhaps all I would ever have.' She shook her head slowly. 'And you are an obscenity.'"

It is tempting to think that Doro pleads for Anyanwu to live not out of selfishness but out of love. We want to believe that, confronted with the possibility of her death, he comes to understand the most important aspect of life—human companionship. Perhaps this is so. Perhaps, however, Anyanwu decides to live not because she is suddenly convinced of Doro's humanity but because she at least sees some hope for a more humane future with him. If Anyanwu lives, she at least has the chance to save their children from Doro's oppression and save the two of them from eternal loneliness. It is the promise of human companionship that finally touches her. When Anyanwu chooses life, in spite of all the horrors which her relationship with Doro has produced and may still continue to produce, she is acting out of generosity both for their children and for him. Her decision reflects the courage and generosity that is in all of Butler's heroines.

Anyanwu is the great African ancestress. She encompasses and epitomizes defiance, acceptance, compromise, determination, and courage. Her personal goal is freedom, but given the obstacles that constantly prevent her from achieving that goal, she learns to make advancements through concessions. By finding her way through that great obstacle course, she is able to bring her best qualities—healing and loving—to a world that would otherwise be intolerable.

Butler's heroines, as I have been trying to show, can tell us much about her science fiction precisely because they are the very core of that fiction. These novels are about survival and power, about black women who must face tremendous societal constraints. We might very well expect them to be rebellious. We might expect them to reverse the typical male science-fiction stereotype and replace male tyranny with female tyranny. This does not happen. Though Butler's heroines are dangerous and powerful women, their goal is not power. They are heroines not because they conquer the world, but because they conquer the very notion of tyranny.

They are, as well, portraits of a different kind of feminism. Amber has the chance to marry the great Patternmaster; instead, she prefers her independence. Mary can easily become an awesome tyrant; instead, she matures into a caring mother. And Alanna, who possesses no extraordinary Patternist powers, learns to survive through accommodation rather than conflict. That very willingness to accommodate and compromise is what allows Anyanwu to endure over a century of oppressive patriarchy. At the end of each novel, we somehow get the impression that the victory of these women, though far from attained, is somehow pending. White men control the war, while black women fight a very different battle.

Octavia Butler with Frances M. Beal (interview date March/April 1986)

SOURCE: "Black Women and the Science Fiction Genre," in *Black Scholar*, Vol. 17, No. 2, March/April, 1986, pp. 14-8.

[*In the following interview, Butler discusses the science fiction genre, her career, and themes in her work.*]

Octavia Butler is a Hugo and Nebula award-winning science fiction writer. One of very few black writers who have selected this genre as their focus, she is a Clarion Science Fiction Writers' Workshop graduate. Her books include, Clays Ark, Kindred, Mind of My Mind, Patternmaster, Wild Seed *and* Survivor. *This interview was conducted by* Black Scholar *Associate Editor Frances M. Beal on October 29, 1985, in East Lansing, Michigan.*

[*Beal:*] *Why did you decide to turn your writing skills to the science fiction genre?*

[Butler:] I didn't decide to become a science fiction writer.

It just happened. I was writing when I was 10 years old. I was writing my own little stories and when I was 12 I was watching a bad science fiction movie and decided that I could write a better story than that. And I turned off the TV and proceeded to try and I've been writing science fiction ever since.

What interested you about science fiction?

The freedom of it; it's potentially the freest genre in existence. It tends to be limited by what people think should be done with it and by what editors think should be done with it, although less now than in the past. In the past, there were editors who didn't really think that sex or women should be mentioned or at least not used other than as rewards for the hero or terrible villainesses.

Blacks were not mentioned without there being any particular reason. Sex was kept out because science fiction began in this country as a genre for young boys. They were either at their girl-hating stage or they had broken out in pimples and had wonderful brains and terrible bodies so they were not wildly beset by the opposite sex.

Some science fiction writers focus on futuristic technological advances and interplanetary plots. Your works, however, often appear to look at the problems of the current society by projecting an alternative ideal society.

I've actually never projected an ideal society. I don't write utopian science fiction because I don't believe that imperfect humans can form a perfect society. I don't really worry about sub-genres or genre really. I write what I have to write and when I finish, I send it off to my publisher and they worry about what genre it falls into.

Now with *Kindred* that was quite a problem. I sent it off to a number of different publishers because it obviously was not science fiction. There's absolutely no science in it. It was the kind of fantasy that nobody had really thought of as fantasy because after all, it doesn't fall into the sword and sorcery or pseudo-medieval and fantasy that everyone expects with a lot of magic being practiced.

One editor thought that it might possibly be converted into a historical romance type of novel. I got all sorts of reaction to it such as, "Well this is awfully good but we don't know what to do with it." So I wound up going back to Doubleday but not to their science fiction section. I wound up going to their general fiction, their mainstream fiction department and being published by them that way. Unfortunately not with as much publicity as I had expected, but at least I was published by them.

Could you briefly explain the plot and conception of your best seller book, [**Kindred**]*?*

[*Kindred*] is the story of a black woman who is pulled back in time to the antebellum South. She is a woman from the present era who is pulled back and enslaved. She has a long association with a pair of her ancestors—one black and one white.

I wrote this book because I grew up during the sixties— that was the period of my adolescence—and I was involved with the black consciousness raising that was taking place at the time. And I was involved with some people who had gone off the deep end with the generation gap. They would say things like, "I would like to get rid of that older generation that betrayed us. I'm not going to do anything because to start, I would have to kill my parents."

EXCESSES OF THE 1960s

My attitude was what the older generations, not just my mother who had gone through enough for heaven's sake, but my grandmother on back had suffered a lot from oppression. They endured experiences that would kill me and would probably kill that guy. He didn't know what he was talking about and there were a great many people who sounded the way he did.

I wanted to deal with my own feelings. My mother was a maid and sometimes she took me to work with her when I was very small and she had no one to stay with me. I used to see her going in back doors, being talked about while she was standing right there and basically being treated like a non-person; something beneath notice, and what was worse, I saw all this.

My mother had almost no education. She was taken out of school at age ten and put to work. Not only that, she had only been in school for a year or two. She was born on a sugar plantation in Louisiana and her mother had no school to send her to. Her mother taught her to read and write, not as well as the school would have but she did the best she could.

So my mother had very little to fall back on. And I could see her later as I grew up. I could see her absorbing more of what she was hearing from the whites than I think even she would have wanted to absorb. I can see from watching her why, for instance, that guy might have thought, "Oh they betrayed us." Without knowing what they had gone through and what it had cost them, some people were making rash judgments.

What are some of the philosophical points that **Kindred** *ends up making?*

Oh I think you would have to read it for yourself. I remember going to a conference in San Diego and having someone read a paper about my work and misinterpreting it badly. I got up and said so. I have the feeling now though that what people get out of my work is worth something even if it wasn't what I intended.

Maybe I should rephrase the question. What were you trying to express?

Various kinds of courage. For instance, there is a woman in the novel who was never called mammy but perhaps she could have been. At a certain point, my character becomes angry at her because she is pushing the other slaves to work. My character says, "Well, they're not getting paid; they are going to get knocked around; why should they work hard?" And the woman says, "Well, do you want to do it? Someone will be made to do it. Do you want to do it? It should be shared if we have to do it."

She has absorbed a lot of the garbage but she is still her own person and she's still doing what she can. She has her own forms of resistance but my character really doesn't see this at first and gradually does come to see this. There's a point in the book when she goes back and forth between the two time periods involuntarily.

Whenever her white ancestor is endangered—and he is a very self-destructive person—she pulls back physically and especially when he's a child, she willingly saves him. Because after all, a child drowning or about to burn to death, you would naturally save the child no matter what color it was.

And later when he's a man and a much less savory person, she saves him because her ancestor has not been born yet. She's not quite sure how these things work, but she is a little afraid. She understands that there is a paradox here. How could everything depend on her. But anyway, she goes on saving him. I've had people come up and ask me why doesn't she just kill him as soon as the ancestor is born.

My attitude when I wrote the book was that TV and movies advertise killing as a very easy thing—how simple to blow somebody away. If it is that easy it shouldn't be, and I didn't want my character to be someone who felt the need to murder somebody. Most of us will never be confronted with that need and the few of us who will be, will generally be confronted by something that demands an immediate decision. He's going to kill you or you are going to kill him. You won't have time to think about it which can be a terrible thing under any circumstances.

Why is science fiction a literary form that black and female writers have not sufficiently explored?

I think part of the reason, as I mentioned earlier, is that science fiction began as a boy's genre. So it was white, it was adolescent and it involved a particular kind of adolescent best described as a need. So this did not make it popular with blacks or adults or women for quite a long time.

Later, I think the movies helped advertise it to the kids and helped turn the adults off. For instance, you go to the movies and there are monsters running around. This is science fiction, suitable for someone that is twelve, not to be taken seriously as a literary form.

But slowly people are being drawn in. Some of the bestsellers, I think, have helped to draw people in who otherwise would never touch science fiction. A lot of the science fiction writers have gotten older, a little bit better accepted and some of them still write very well, and their books bring people in. Science fiction writers come from science fiction readers. I think that as more and more blacks begin to read science fiction, then more blacks will take up writing science fiction, and this is already happening to a certain degree.

Why has there been such an expansion of women writers of science fiction in recent years?

I think that was part of the women's movement. Women were finally asserting their right to write it and define themselves. I think they were sick to death of princesses and witches, which is the kind of role women played in the science fiction I remember when I began.

I came into science fiction when things were opening up for women, when it was okay to notice the fact that the universe wasn't just white or male. So I could write about black women, black heroines and not get anybody upset. I got readers who wrote me letters wondering why there always seemed to be a black person in my work, but most people seemed to either accept it or shut up about it.

Do you think that women find that female writers have brought a different type of perspective to the genre?

I think that they have done a lot for characterization in science fiction. But you can't really talk about "women's science fiction" because there are women writing all kinds of science fiction, from the sword and sorcery to the medieval to hard science fiction to soft science fiction. There is no women's genre in science fiction.

A science fiction writer has the freedom to do absolutely anything. The limits are the imagination of the writer. There are always blacks in the novels I write and whites. In **Quasar** there is a Japanese man and a Mexican woman. In the one I'm working on now there is a Chinese man and a lot of different people are lumped together.

Could you talk a little bit about the work you have in progress now?

I'm working on a trilogy at the present time and the novel that I'm finishing is called *The Training Boar.* It is a story, post Holocaust, of human beings being changed from one generation to another—not entirely human any longer—but human beings who have survived the Holocaust.

They are captured by aliens and this is why they lasted so long as a species. They don't become overspecialized by some conditions. In a way maybe a form of specialization is killing us off now and we don't generally think of it that way. But size may have been a problem with the dinosaurs and we may be about to be killed off by our greatest advantage. My characters are told that human beings have two characteristics that are fine and conducive to the species survival individually, but are a lethal combination.

The first of those characteristics is intelligence and the other is something that can be projected through history—something that keeps showing up in us that has been doing a great deal of harm: It's hierarchical structure/behavior. The combination, because intelligence tends to serve the hierarchical behavior, is what may eventually wipe us out.

Do you think that hierarchical behavior is inborn?

Absolutely. It's not a matter of thinking about it really. I mean look at our closest animal relatives. Look at everything on earth right down to the algae. Two clones of algae are slowly covering Iraq. Eventually only one clone of algae will survive. I mean it's part of life on this planet. So hierarchical behavior is definitely inborn and intelligence is something new that we've come up with and like I said, I happen to think that the combination is lethal.

I think that it doesn't have to be lethal if we deal with it. But unfortunately, the ways in which we tried to deal with it in the past have not really acknowledged the problem. Too often when people start talking about inborn characteristics, they start talking about who shall we eliminate, who has the negative characteristics. And we get to decide what's negative and we get into the eugenics and the real nasty stuff where people use something that could be and is in fact part of behavior science as a reason to put somebody else down to get rid of your enemies, using science for hierarchical purposes.

Do you believe that black writers and their works will become popular to the point where they will be read by everyone and not primarily by blacks?

I'm not read primarily by blacks now strangely enough. Most of my readers are science fiction readers. I don't know. It depends. In this country being black tends to bring out a lot of negative emotions that don't necessarily have anything to do with us.

It's sort of like being Jewish in Nazi Germany. I don't really know if that is the case. It sounds as though it might be. People who are willing to look at all sorts of materials regarding the holocaust get very upset when they hear anything about what's happened here either during slavery or much more recently during the civil rights movement.

For instance, I think most people don't know or don't realize that at least 10 million blacks were killed just on the way to this country, just during the middle passage. People have a hard enough time believing that. They don't really want to hear it partly because it makes whites feel guilty.

RACIAL AMNESIA

Something that I would like to relate illustrates this. Just an anecdote. Another writer during the first *Star Wars* movie had done a review of the movie, a three-page review of it. He praised it very highly and said very nice things about it. Near the last paragraph, he said that one thing about this movie was that it shows every kind of alien, but there is only one kind of human—white ones; no black people were shown. There are no non-whites at all and where are they. He says that he got three pounds of hate mail.

A lot of the mail said that blacks make us feel uncomfortable. We want to see movies with no blacks in them. And this goes back to something that I heard at a science fiction convention. I was sitting next to the editor of a magazine that no longer exists and he was also doing some science fiction writing. He said that he didn't think that blacks should be included in science fiction stories because they changed the character of the stories; that if you put in a black, all of a sudden the focus is on this person. He stated that if you were going to write about some sort of racial problem, that would be absolutely the only reason he could see for including a black.

He went on to say that well, perhaps you could use an alien instead and get rid of all this messiness and all those people that we don't want to deal with. It reflected his view of black people as being other. There's another anecdote that points up this problem. Several years ago I was trying to put together an anthology of science fiction by and about black people. In the first place nobody would buy it. Most of the stories that we got (I was working with another man) were about racism, as though that was the sum total of our lives. Especially, and I hate to say it, all the stories we got from

white people were about racism because that was all they apparently thought that we dealt with.

How did you finally succeed in actually becoming a professional writer?

I had my first short stories published in 1970 when I was 23. I sold my first novel in 1975 but it wasn't published until 1976. That was *Patternmaster.* While *Patternmaster* was out with the publisher, I wrote *Mind of My Mind* and sent it out to another publisher. And while those two novels were both out, I began revising an old novel that I had begun writing while in my teens called *Survivor.*

And while I was working on *Survivor,* I got a rejection from the publisher that I had sent *Mind of My Mind* to and an acceptance from the publisher that I had sent *Patternmaster* to.

I was able to find the time for that kind of output during that time because I had been laid off my job and I had unemployment compensation and I was desperate. I was 27 and I felt that nothing was happening in regards to my writing. I was afraid that maybe nothing was going to happen and that perhaps my relatives were right and that I should go and get a civil service job.

I was really grabbing at straws. I don't think that I could have quit writing, but it would have been very bad for me if I had gone on and written those three novels and had no success. It would have been deadly.

Sandra Y. Govan (essay date Spring-Summer 1986)

SOURCE: "Homage to Tradition: Octavia Butler Renovates the Historical Novel," in *MELUS*, Vol. 13, Nos. 1 and 2, Spring-Summer, 1986, pp. 79-96.

[*In the following essay, Govan delineates the similarities between Butler's* Wild Seed *and* Kindred, *including strong, black, female protagonists, and the use of history and black tradition.*]

Despite the fact that her novels are sometimes difficult to find, Octavia Butler has nonetheless firmly established herself as a major new voice in science fiction. The five published novels of her Patternist saga, depicting over a vast time span both the genesis and evolution of Homo Superior (psionically enhanced human beings) and his mutated bestial counterpart; the one novel, *Kindred,* outside the serial story; and the short stories, all speak exceptionally well for Butler's artistry and growth.

Through the interviews she has given, the articles she's written, the pieces published about her, and of course, her novels, Octavia Butler emerges as a forthright and honest author. She is a writer very conscious of the power of art to affect social perceptions and behavior and a writer unafraid to admit that, when appropriate, she borrows from tradition, that she takes and reshapes African and Afro-American cultural values, that she has heuristic and didactic impulses which she transforms into art. With *Wild Seed* and *Kindred,* for instance, Butler seizes the possibilities inherent in the historical novel and the Black tradition in autobiography. She adapts these forms to produce extrapolative fiction which, for its impetus, looks to an historically grounded African-American past rather than to a completely speculative future. On the surface, this seems indeed a curious connection, this linkage of future fiction to the past. Regardless of the surface appearance, the format itself, extrapolating or projecting from social structures of the past to those possible in the future, is not new (Isaac Asimov's *Foundation* series is a model precursor). What *is* new and distinctive is Butler's handling of the format or frame, her particular choice of past cultures to extrapolate from. She has chosen to link science fiction not only to anthropology and history, via the historical novel, but directly to the Black American slavery experiences via the slave narrative. This is a fundamental departure for science fiction as genre. *Wild Seed* and *Kindred* demonstrate this new configuration aptly. However, before engaging in an immediate discussion of these two novels, it seems appropriate to delay the discussion momentarily in order to better frame it with some critical definitions.

Most of us probably have seen the historical novel as a continuation of the realistic social novel; we associate it with Sir Walter Scott or Charles Dickens, or perhaps with Margaret Mitchell or Margaret Walker. We know that its setting and characters are established in a particular historic context—the age of chivalry or the French Revolution or the antebellum American South. Casual readers of the European or Western historical novel are usually content to forgo the kind of rigorous economic, philosophic, political analysis that Georg Lukács, in *The Historical Novel,* brings to his discussion of the form's origins. Lukács argues, for instance, that of prime importance to the historical novel's development "is the increasing historical awareness of the decisive role played in human progress by the struggle of classes in history." In his analysis, knowledge of "the rise of modern bourgeois society" from "the class struggles between nobility and bourgeoisie, . . . class struggles which raged throughout the entire 'idyllic Middle Ages' and whose last decisive stage was the great French Revolution," is crucial to the historical novel.

Using Sir Walter Scott as his archetypal model, Lukács outlines Scott's principal contributions to the form: "the broad delineation of manners and circumstances attendant upon events, the dramatic character of action and, in close connection with this, the new and important role of dialog in the novel." For my immediate purposes however, Lukács' remarks are most germane when he says the authentic historical novel is "specifically historical," that its history is not "mere costumery," and that it presents an "artistically faithful image of a concrete historical epoch."

Slave narratives, the first Black autobiographies, have a great deal in common with our understanding of the attributes of the historical novel. Each narrative is "specifically historical" (Marion Starling has traced narratives as far back as 1703 and followed them forward to 1944; their peak period was 1836-1860). The historical circumstances of each text are so far removed from "mere costumery" that extensive, often intrusive, documentation of the ex-slave's veracity is quite frequently an established feature of the text, part of what Robert Stepto refers to as the "authenticating" strategy of the narrative voice. And without question, slave narrators strove to produce a powerful yet "faithful image of a concrete historical epoch." Perhaps only a handful of the six thousand extant narratives became artistic successes, works with the strength and quality of Frederick Douglass' *The Narrative of the Life of Frederick Douglass* or Harriet Jacobs' *Incidents in the Life of a Slave Girl* or the dramatic tale of William and Ellen Craft's *Running a Thousand Miles for Freedom.* But successful literary works or not, most slave narratives depicted faithfully and graphically the brutal reality of slave life and each showed the direct impact of slavery, that peculiar institution, not only on the narrator's own life and that of his/her family but also the debilitating and corrupting effects of such an institution on those who held power within it, slaveholders.

Because the slave narrative and the historical novel, especially the historical novel which concerns itself with life in the antebellum South, share some common characteristics, a clear relationship between them may be easily established. For instance, Harriet Beecher Stowe's *Uncle Tom's Cabin* is unquestionably indebted to the life story of Josiah Henson, fugitive slave. But, of more importance than demonstrating a relationship between the historical novel and the slave narrative is our understanding of the specific function slave narratives served. Unlike the novel, whose primary purpose was entertainment, the primary function of the slave narrative was to educate and politicize in no uncertain terms. At the height of their popularity, slave narratives, called "those literary nigritudes—little tadpoles of the press which run to editions of hundreds of thousands," were highly influential tools used by abolitionist societies here and abroad to mold public opinion, to bend the public mind toward the task of eliminating slavery. As a group, slave narratives exhibited these characteristic traits: they focused on the special experience of racial oppression; they were intended to be records of resistance; they employed a variety of literary/rhetorical devices including concrete imagery and diction, understatement, polemical voice, and satire to describe vividly the actual conditions of slavery; they looked at the self outside the typical western perspective of the individual and chose instead to recognize or represent the self in relationship to the oppressed group with ties and responsibilities to group members. Slave narrators were conscious of their own cultural schizophrenia, their burden of blackness in white America, or, as W. E. B. DuBois said in his seminal *The Souls of Black Folk,* their "double consciousness," their two "warring selves in one dark skin."

Slave narrators were conscious, too, that they were presenting objective fact through the filter of their own subjective experience. Taken collectively, their narratives frequently show recurrent patterns. There is a loss of innocence wherein the slave, usually as a child, recollects his or her first awareness of the personal impact of slavery. There are detailed descriptions of various phases of bondage as the slave witnesses them and then experiences them. There is the punishment factor, the resistance motif, the glimpse of life-in-the-quarters. There is also the slave's quest for education, the slave's encounter with abusive sexual misconduct and immoral behavior, the slave's recognition of religious hypocrisy and the adulterated Christianity practiced by "Christian" slave holders, the slave's escape attempts, and, finally, the slave's successful escape. Of course, this pattern varied from narrative to narrative and oftentimes, what was stressed depended upon the discretion and sensibilities of the narrator or, sometimes, on the concerns or dictates of an editor or an amanuensis.

Butler's *Wild Seed* and *Kindred* are rich texts which neatly define the junction where the historical novel, the slave narrative, and science fiction meet. The two novels build upon tenets clearly identified with the expected conventions or norms of the genres she employs. Then, because Butler's forte is extrapolative fiction, we can easily see the melding as each novel moves us through the recreated, historically plausible, viable, yet totally speculative alternative reality which is the realm of science fiction—as distinct from the codified expectations we have of fiction which operates from the realistic or naturalistic realm. To phrase it succinctly, Octavia Butler's work stands on the foundation of traditional form and proceeds to renovate that form.

Wild Seed is not about Arthurian England or the French Revolution. Instead, it is about alienation and loneliness; about needs, dreams, ambitions, and power. It is also about love. Africa provides the cultural backdrop for the initial interaction between plot and character. Although the opening setting of *Wild Seed* is 17th-century west Africa, spe-

cifically the Niger river region of eastern Nigeria, the setting shifts through the course of the novel and we follow the lives of Butler's two immortal central characters, Doro, a four thousand year old Nubian, and Anyanwu, a three hundred year old Onitsha priestess, through the Middle Passage voyage to life in a colonial New England village, to life on an antebellum Louisiana plantation, to California just after the Civil War. In the course of two hundred years of movement we are privy to a broad and vivid historical canvas. Again, however, Butler's use of history and cultural anthropology do more than simply illuminate the text or serve as mere coloration. Both disciplines are intrinsic to our understanding of character, theme, and action. Their use also permits Butler to employ a more original approach to the old theme of the trials of immortality, the theme of the spiritual disintegration of the man who cannot die.

The specifically African segment of *Wild Seed* only occupies four chapters of the text but an African ethos dominates the whole book. The novel opens in 1690. Doro has returned to Africa to look for one of his "seed villages," one of several communities he has carefully nurtured, composed of people with nascent or lateral mutant abilities. They know things or hear things or see things others cannot and so in their home communities, they are misfits or outcasts or "witches" because of their abilities. In his autonomous villages wherein he collects and breeds these people, Doro is their protector; his motives, however, are far from altruistic for he needs his people in a very real way. He "enjoys their company and sadly, they provide his most satisfying kills." Doro's mutant power is the ability to transfer his psychic essence to any human host; thus, he kills to live. And, as he kills, he literally "feeds" off the spirit of the host body. But whenever Doro kills or "takes" his own kind, he gains more sustenance from their heightened psychic energy than he derives from the "taking" of ordinary non-mutant human beings.

The village Doro returns to has been destroyed by slave hunters and as he contemplates the carnage and thinks about tracking and regrouping the captured survivors, his gift of attraction to other mutants, an innate tracking sense or "telescent" subtly makes him conscious of the distant Anyanwu. He finds himself pulled toward her. Butler's narration here adeptly conveys both character and place.

> He wandered southwest toward the forest, leaving as he had arrived—alone, unarmed, without supplies, accepting the savanna and later the forest as easily as he accepted any terrain. He was killed several times—by disease, by animals, by hostile people. This was a harsh land. Yet he continued to move southwest, unthinkingly veering away from the section of the coast where his ship awaited him. After a while, he realized it was no longer his anger at the loss of his seed village that drove

him. It was something new—an impulse, a feeling, a kind of mental undertow pulling at him.

It is a subtle awareness of Anyanwu which attracts Doro and pulls him to a country he has not visited in three hundred years. When he finally meets and talks with her, Doro suspects immediately that they are distant kin, that she is "wild seed," the fruit of [his] peoples' passing by [hers] during one of Africa's many periods of flux. Ironically, Anyanwu herself supports this idea when she recalls a half remembered and whispered rumor that she was not father's child but had been begotten by a passing stranger. Originally, Doro's people were the Kush, an ancient people part of the vast Ethiopian Empire. Anyanwu's people are the Igbo or Onitsha Ibo people of eastern Nigeria. Traditional Onitsha society, explains ethnologist Richard Henderson, was a "community strongly concerned with maintaining oral accounts of the past." Henderson tells us that "Onitsha lacked an elaborate mythology as its cultural charter, and instead emphasized a quasi-historical 'ideology' based on stories tracing the founding of its villages to pre-historic migrations and political fusions." We see an example of this quasi-history when Doro questions Anyanwu, trying to place her in his long personal history. "'Your people have crossed the Niger'—he hesitated, frowning, then gave the river its proper name—'the Orumili. When I saw them last, they lived on the other side in Benin.'" At this point Butler deliberately employs the omniscient narrative voice in conjunction with Doro's to signal the embedded signs of heritage and culture she wants her audience to note. Anyanwu's near poetic reply compresses years of African history, years of tribal warfare and tribal development, years of gradual adaptation to change. "We crossed long ago. . . . Children born in that time have grown old and died. We were Ado and Idu, subject to Benin before the crossing. Then we fought Benin and crossed the river to Onitsha to become free people, our own masters."

Butler's Anyanwu is partly based on a legendary Ibo heroine, Atagbusi, a village protector and a magical "shape shifter." Henderson, whom Butler acknowledges as a source, says that Atagbusi "is said to have been a daughter of the tiny clan called Okposi-eke, a descent group renowned for its native doctors and responsible for magical protection of the northwestern bush outskirts of the town. She was believed capable, as are other persons of Okposi-eke, of transforming herself into various large and dangerous animals, and it is believed that she concocted the medicine that protects the community on its western front."

Like the legendary Atagbusi, Butler's Anyanwu is also a shape-shifter, a woman capable of physical metamorphosis. She can become a leopard, a python, an eagle, a dolphin, a dog, or a man. For self-protection, most of

Anyanwu's powers are hidden from the villagers. And to reduce fear of the inexplicable, Anyanwu alters her body gradually so that she seemingly ages at the same rate as the various husbands she has married over the years, the same rate as the people around her. But whenever she chooses Anyanwu can regain her natural body, that of a sturdy, beautiful, twenty-year-old woman. Anyanwu is the village healer, a doctor for her people. She grows traditional herbs to make the customary medicines even though her power to heal does not always require the use of herbs. A respected and powerful person in the village hierarchy, Anyanwu's place is well defined.

> She served her people by giving them relief from pain and sickness. Also, she enriched them by allowing them to spread word of her abilities to neighboring people. She was an oracle. A woman through whom a god spoke. Strangers paid heavily for her services. They paid her people, then they paid her. That was as it should have been. Her people could see that they benefited from her presence, and that they had reason to fear her abilities. Thus she was protected from them— and they from her—most of the time.

Anyanwu's sense of protection, her maternal instinct of care and concern for her people, is part of the African ethos which pervades the text. Of paramount importance to Anyanwu is the well being and safety of her kin—her children and her grandchildren. This is entirely in keeping with African tradition which holds "children are worth." Henderson affirms this with the observation that the Onitsha are "rooted firmly in notions of filiation and descent. When Onitsha people assess the career of a person, their primary criterion is the number of children he has raised to support and survive him. Children are extolled in proverbs above any other good, even above the accumulation of wealth; 'children first, wealth follows' is a proverb affirming the route to success."

After three hundred years, ten husbands and forty-seven children, Anyanwu's descendants people the land. Their security is the lever Doro uses to pry Anyanwu away from her homeland. He appeals first to her innate sense of isolation and loneliness, proclaiming her place is among her own kind, then he appeals to her maternal spirit, promising children with genetic traits like their mother. "A mother," he tells her, "should not have to watch her children grow old and die. If you live, they should live. It is the fault of their fathers that they die. Let me give you children who will live!" Reluctantly and somewhat apprehensively, Anyanwu agrees to leave the village with Doro. But, when Doro speculates that her children, although they manifest no sign of her mutant ability, are also his peoples' children and that perhaps they should accompany them to the new world, Anyanwu becomes adamant—"you will not touch my children"—and remains so until Doro pledges he will not harm her children.

Unwittingly, Anyanwu's resolute stand in protection of her children gives Doro yet another lever to use against her. Totally devoid of scruples, and possessing a keen insight into her psychological makeup, quite early in their journey to the coast Doro plots the strategy he will use to bind Anyanwu to him. It is a time-encrusted masculine ploy. He will get her pregnant; then, with a new child,

> her independence would vanish without a struggle. She would do whatever he asked then to keep the child safe. She was too valuable to kill, and if he abducted any of her descendants, she would no doubt goad him into killing her. But once she was isolated in America with an infant to care for, she would learn submissiveness.

Doro's power play, his perception of the most immediate method he can use to control Anyanwu reflects his understanding of cultural ties, of the "appropriate manners and customs" which are part of Anyanwu's historical legacy. Though a powerful woman on her own turf, essentially Anyanwu leaves her tribal homeland to protect her kin.

Of course, Anyanwu never does learn submissiveness. Although she and Doro share a link forged in a bygone age, his name means "the east—the direction from which the sun comes" and hers means "the sun," they are not alike. Anyanwu is distinct from any woman Doro has encountered in thirty-seven hundred years. She is his female counterpart with one important distinction—she is not a predator. Her powers have long made her independent not withstanding her emergence from a culture where wives are considered the property of husbands. In one sense, however, Doro assesses Anyanwu correctly; she remains in his compound for years, she even marries as he directs (primarily out of fear and a strong survival instinct); but, she remains, too, for the sake of the children she bears and out of her concern for the strange, sometimes pitiable, sometimes warped or dangerous children who are the products of Doro's mutant communities. Much of **Wild Seed's** tension is controlled by Doro's efforts to break Anyanwu, to use and then destroy her. She resists and fights back with the resources she has—her own strength of will. Again. however, the struggle is not solely for her sake but also for the safety of the children, the kin she forever shields.

African kinship networks seem to be the major structural device Butler uses to build dramatic complexity in this novel. When the principal characters first meet, the question of identity is crucial. Following the customary "who are you?" comes the equally important "who are your people?" The latter question springs from the African sense of connectedness to a specific place, a specific people, or a specific heritage. As indicated above, Doro traces his origins to the ancient Kush, one of the three great sub-Saharan societies. Anyanwu ties the history of her people, through wars and unification, to the powerful kingdom of Benin.

The importance of kinship is demonstrated repeatedly. When Anyanwu embarks on an attenuated version of the slave trade's Middle Passage, she happens upon two captured slaves she can actually help. Fortunately, they have been sold to Doro. It is their good fortune in this sense: Okoye is the son of Anyanwu's youngest daughter. Udenkwo, a young mother stolen from her village and separated from her five-year-old son, is a more distant relative. Anyanwu tells Udenkwo to trace her lineage through her clan and her male ancestry, a process which suggests subtly the value Africans attached to collective identity, familial bonding, and communal history. It happens that one of Udenkwo's ancestors was Anyanwu's eighth son, another, Anyanwu's third husband. (Here Butler slips in a quick feminist thrust: although Udenkwo traces her patrilineage, it is her matrilineal descent, her connection to Anyanwu, literally an earth mother, which saves her.) Because both Okoye and Udenkwo are Anyanwu's descendants, they will be spared the more brutal aspects of slavery. They will not be separated or sold again to some terrifying white plantation master. They will not be assaulted or beaten by Doro or his people. And although they are kinsmen, they will be permitted to marry despite the idea of "abomination" such an act connotes for Anyanwu. The marriage will permit them to offer each other comfort in their new and strange surroundings for as Doro says of his seed people, "our kind have a special need to be either with our kinsmen or others who are like us."

The initial contact with the new world is not quite as traumatic for Anyanwu as it was for true slaves but still, she must cope with complete change. She must reckon with strange and restrictive western clothing, with a new diet (animal milk—another "abomination"), with learning a new language and new customs among a new and foreign people. And she must make all these adjustments in a land where color automatically determines status. The New England village Doro brings Anyanwu to is Wheatley, ostensibly named for an English family Doro supports and a principal cash crop. Butler slips in another quick thrust here for "Wheatley" is an allusion to young Phillis Wheatley, the child stolen from Africa who became known as the "Sable Muse" and was recognized as a significant contributor to 18th-century American poetry. Wheatley, however, is significant for another reason: life in the village cushions the impact of Anyanwu's contact with America's hardening race and color caste system. Doro's villagers are a racial amalgam—Blacks, Indians, mixed bloods, and whites, a mixture not uncommon in the northeastern states before the increase in the slave trade. Anyanwu finds most of the villagers are friendly and also that village society is tight-knit, functioning roughly in a manner that approximates the familiar rhythms of clan life she had known. Relatives within the compound live with or near other relatives. People who share a common language are allowed to group together. Where no blood or tribal ties previously exist, newly formed families function as extended family and the weak, insecure, or unstable are placed with those who will care for them. The villagers see Doro as a guardian spirit who protects them from Indian raids and like disasters even as he controls their lives. They even make blood sacrifices to him for he takes from among them when he needs a new body. Yet despite the death he inevitably brings, whenever Doro is present in his compound he receives all the homage due a titled tribal elder with many children. And in fact, he has several children within the village.

The most serious clash of wills between Doro and Anyanwu is about the value assigned kinship. Doro's genetics program respects no tradition or socially sanctioned belief. He breeds people, related or not, to improve the pedigree of his stock. When in Wheatley he commands Anyanwu to marry and bear children by his son, and suggests that later she will also bear *his* children, Anyanwu withdraws in total revulsion—a greater abomination she cannot imagine. A century will pass, Anyanwu will have escaped Doro and formed her own special protected community (composed of mutants linked by blood and heightened psychic sensitivity) on a Louisiana plantation where she is the master, before she and Doro can come to civil terms again. They forge a new alliance based on respect and compromise. She recognizes he must kill to live but he learns genuine respect for her feelings and abilities and he also realizes that he must cease killing those of his own who serve him best or any of her close relatives. For Doro to regain Anyanwu's companionship, he must salvage what humanity remains to him.

If kinship is an underlying motif contributing to the dramatic tension in **Wild Seed,** it is clearly the focal point of **Kindred,** the motif underscoring the theme. **Kindred** is outside the Patternist saga, yet it shares with **Wild Seed** three common denominators: Black and white characters who move through an historically viable setting, one which explores the tangled complexities of interracial mixing during slavery and beyond; linkage through phenomenal psychic energy; an emphasis on blood ties and the responsibilities that result. The bonds of blood in **Kindred** however are not created by exotic mutation nor genetic engineering. They are the result of plain undisguised lust and the raw exertion of power.

Kindred is a neatly packaged historical novel which uses scenes of plantation life and the techniques of the slave nar-

rative to frame the plot. Dana Franklin, the heroine, is a Black woman, a writer who lives in Los Angeles, California, a woman very much of the present. Her family's roots are in Maryland; a fact made all the more pertinent when Dana finds herself traversing time and geography to move between twentieth-century California and nineteenth-century Maryland. The reason she moves is simple—Rufus Weylin "calls" her to him whenever he gets into trouble he cannot resolve alone, be it drowning, or arson, a bad fall, or a beating. Rufus is a child when he and Dana first meet. He is also white and destined to become her great grandfather, several times removed. The agency which moves Dana is never clear. She never understands *how* it happens. The "why" is easier. Whenever Rufus fears for his life, his subconscious mind somehow reaches out to Dana and transfers her to his setting and his time to meet his need. The only way she can return to her era is if she believes a corresponding threat to her own life exists. Time is totally disjointed for Dana during these transferences. There is no correlation between the time she spends in the past, her own history, and the time which passes while she is absent from her present. Dana's only clue to the mystery surrounding these transfers is the blood tie linking her to Rufus; but even the blood relationship is not, for her, a satisfactory explanation for an inexplicable process.

Once Dana knows Rufus' identity and comprehends what his relationship to her will become, she understands her role more precisely. She is to assure the child's survival until he can father the first branch of her family tree. She must serve as his mentor and be his teacher. The task of trying to mold a humane slave holder, in an era where all the accepted social norms mitigate against the possibility, falls to her. And an awesome responsibility it is considering her circumstances: a modern Black woman periodically surfaces in antebellum Maryland over approximately a twenty-year span, with no free papers, no owner to vouch for her, no way to explain her dress, her speech, or her behavior. Her role is to protect a boy/man who is alternately and erratically "generous and vicious." Immediately, Dana recognizes that she is "the worst possible guardian" for Rufus —"a black woman to watch over him in a society that considered Blacks sub-human, and a woman to watch over him in a society that considered women perennial children." In that age and in that place, Dana is simply a "strange nigger," a fact the child Rufus promptly explains. But because she saves his life and because he realizes they are linked, even though he does not know the extent of their relationship, Rufus, the child, is Dana's unexpected, if unstable, ally.

Quite apart from her role as mentor to Rufus stands Dana's other function. **Kindred,** far more than **Wild Seed,** is an overtly didactic novel, although its artistry is such that one does not realize how much antebellum history gets absorbed. Dana is Butler's tool for sketching a far less romanticized portrait of plantation life from 1815 through the 1830s. She is both a reporter and a respondent for she witnesses and participates in the slave experience. In fact, *Kindred,* is so closely related to the experience disclosed in slave narratives that its plot structure follows the classic patterns with only the requisite changes to flesh out character, story, and action.

Dana's loss of innocence, her discovery that she has slave status is as abrupt and brutal as the same discoveries recorded by Frederick Douglass or Harriet Jacobs in their respective narratives. Tom Weylin is a harsh disciplinarian; he beats his slaves, his horses, and his son with the same whip. On her first visit, he almost shoots the "strange nigger" caught with his son and wife. On her second visit, having seen Rufus' scars, Dana acquires some of her own. Seeking safety away from the big house, she leaves the Weylins to seek help from the black family destined to become her forbears. Patrollers (and Butler carefully identifies them as young whites charged with policing or "maintaining order" among the slave population) arrive at the cabin first. Ostensibly, they have come to see whether a slave husband is meeting illegally with his free wife. The man is. He has no pass permitting his absence from his owner's plantation. For the crime of visiting his family the slave is beaten, then tied to a tree and whipped savagely while his wife and child watch helplessly. Dana is our hidden mute witness. Yet in order to bring her readers closer to the immediacy of the horror we have just seen, Butler moves Dana rapidly from witnessing slavery to experiencing it, from watching, to feeling, to testifying what life was like for a Black woman, even if she were nominally free. After the slave is dragged away, Dana goes to the assistance of his wife. They talk guardedly for Dana cannot explain who she is or where she comes from; nevertheless, the woman grants her permission to stay. Shortly thereafter, Dana steps outside of the cabin and is captured and attacked by one of the patrollers who had returned alone to rape the slave's wife. He realizes instantly that he has not captured the wife but determines almost as quickly that Dana will satisfy his lust. Degradation, brutality, powerlessness, the commonplace violence directed against Black men and women could be no more sharply delineated. Dana's violent struggle to escape the atroller returns her to her own time.

The third time Dana is called into her own history we are privy to a much broader look at life on the plantation from the master's big house to the slave's quarters. She learns that even "favored" house slaves are given a meager diet of table scraps and corn meal mush, occasionally supplemented by what can be stolen from the plantation's larders. Field hands are supposed to work even harder yet are expected to subsist off even less. Just as almost every slave narrative dramatizes the theme of family separation, Butler also brings this theme to life. Dana is sent to the kitchen to learn from Sarah, the plantation's cook. She learns quickly that Sarah has had three children sold away from her; a fourth she was allowed to keep because the child was born mute, therefore "defective," therefore "not worth much" on the slave market. Both in and out of the kitchen Dana discovers what the typical slave's work day is like, first in the big house and later in the fields. She also discovers how slavery can effect a plantation mistress if the woman has no viable authority. Margaret Weylin is described as temperamental, flighty, beautiful, bored, useless. Her husband controls all of the plantation's business affairs and Margaret is left with nothing to do but lavish unreturned affection on her son because "slaves kept her house clean, did much of her sewing, all of her cooking and washing." Margaret cannot even dress or undress without a slave attendant. During her extended third journey into the past, Dana is called to witness another brutal whipping, this time administered for the offense of "answering back." Shortly thereafter, she is the recipient of the same treatment but her offense is far more serious. She has been caught reading to a slave and almost caught teaching slaves thirsty for knowledge how to read and write. An education was, of course, legally denied slaves. Dana's infraction of this rule was both a courageous and dangerous act. The same hostility which fell on Frederick Douglass' attempts to teach his fellowslaves fell on Dana; Tom Weylin seizes her and whips her viciously. He fears a slave who can read and write will escape by forging a pass; for their part, slaves knew being armed with knowledge was freedom and many took great risks in order to learn.

The large, panoramic slice-of-plantation-life we see in this segment of the novel is deftly handled "faction," that blend of authentic verifiable historical fact and well-rendered fiction. Butler treats the recurring themes of casual brutality, forcible separation of families, the quest for knowledge, the desire to escape, the tremendous work loads expected of slaves as effectively as any of the narratives or documentary histories discussing the slavery experience. Her use of these details is more than mere costumery, it is part of the "broad delineation of manners and circumstances" inherent in the historical record and essential for developing plot and character.

Kindred incorporates other devices and themes associated with the slave narrative. These narratives repeatedly demonstrate that slavery as a system displayed little regard for marital status among slaves and no respect for the sanctity of the family unit unless a master chose to recognize a family bond. *Kindred* illustrates this. The narratives record ad infinitum the harsh punishment meted out to any slave who dared evince a sense of self-respect, pride, manhood; but if a slave's spirit would not be broken, it could be sorely tried and his body could be broken. *Kindred* illustrates this extreme as well. Although Butler does not belabor the Christian hypocrisy theme, a popular and effective tactic used in many narrative accounts to arouse moral indignation, she does make the novel's climatic denouement turn on the other principal axis of the formulaic narrative, careful attention to socially sanctioned yet unacknowledged miscegenation, illicit sex and lust behind the facade of law and respectability.

Tom Weylin has sired at least three children by slave mothers who are still on his plantation. On Dana's second trip to the past the patroller who attacks her was actually returning to the cabin to molest a free Black woman; when he found himself with Dana instead, the difference between the two Black women never disturbed him. On her third journey back, Dana's husband Kevin is transported with her. Because Kevin is white, he affords her some measure of protection by posing as her master. Ironically, in 1976, while their marriage must withstand some subtle societal disapproval, it is at least legally recognized. In 1819 Maryland, Dana and Kevin dare not admit their marital bond because such a relationship is illegal, unimaginable, and dangerous. Casual sexual liaisons between white men and Black women were permissible but intermarriage was not. White men were expected to be rakes, or at least their licentiousness was tacitly condoned; white women were expected to be chaste (certainly they dare not openly consort with Black men the way their husbands, fathers, sons took liberties with Black women); and Black women, of course, were often treated as mere sexual vessels. A brief glance at an actual narrative describing the entanglements produced by an absence of moral integrity is pertinent and may make Butler's account of events at the Weylin plantation even more credible. *Incidents in the Life of a Slave Girl* bluntly discusses the moral "corruption produced by slavery." Jacobs records how "the slave girl is reared in an atmosphere of licentiousness and fear." She is "bribed" . . . or "whipped or starved into submission" to the will of her master and/or his sons. "The slaveholder's sons, are, of course, vitiated, even while boys, by the unclean influences everywhere around them. Nor do the master's daughters always escape." At this point the Jacobs narrative discloses the forbidden activities of some white women in response to the moral degeneracy surrounding them. Jacobs' testimony is explicit:

> They know that the women slaves are subject to their father's authority in all things; and in some cases they exercise the same authority over the men slaves. I have myself seen the master of such a household. . . . It was known in the neighborhood that his daughter had selected one of the meanest slaves on his plantation to be the father of his first grandchild. She did not make her advances to her equals, nor even to her father's

more intelligent servants. In such cases the infant is smothered, or sent where it is never seen by any who knows its history. But if the white parent is the father, instead of the mother, the offspring are unblushingly reared for market.

The sexual tension existing at the Weylin home poses both the customary morality/hypocrisy questions and also allows Butler the opportunity to explore another dimension of this tension, sexuality-and-the-white-woman with a little gallows humor. Margaret Weylin discovers that Dana has been sleeping in Kevin's room on a pallet rather than in the attic where other house slaves are expected to sleep. She turns livid with rage. As the Jacobs narrative shows, white men may not be denied their concubines yet they certainly are not supposed to conduct their liaisons in the big house; just down in the slave quarters, out of sight. Margaret slaps Dana, screams at her that she is "a filthy black whore!" and protests loudly that hers is a "Christian house." Of course, Dana cannot retaliate but she does think, rather charitably, that for all her flaws, Margaret Weylin must be a moral woman. However, Dana is soon made privy to an irony she had not anticipated. Margaret, although long married, is smitten by a strong attraction to Kevin; she chases him with a barely concealed ardor and is, therefore, extremely jealous of the near connubial relationship Kevin and Dana attempt to maintain. Jealousy based on the unacknowledged sexual tension between white mistresses and Black slave women linked to white men surfaces frequently in slavery annals.

The most critical sexual relationship in the text however remains the relationship an adult Rufus Weylin forces on Alice Greenwood, a free Black woman on the Weylin plantation. Rufus' feelings for Alice are a mixture of love and lust. He loves her, and he wants her to love him, but he also feels he has a "right" to her and that he is entitled to win her or take her any way he can. Unfortunately, Alice loves a Black man, a slave. Since neither man can openly compete for Alice's affections, this triangle degenerates into an extraordinarily painful relationship, one compounded by rivalry, passion, guilt, love, lust, punishment, pride, power, and implacable hatred. But there are two Black women in young Rufus' life and this adds another level to the sexual tension. Dana and Alice are virtual doubles of each other. Physically, they look alike; intellectually and emotionally, they function as two halves of the same woman, flawed duplicates separated by the dictates of their respective historical time and the resultant sexual-political consciousness each maintains by virtue of their particular social circumstances. In other words, although she is unaccountably displaced in time, Dana retains the attributes of a late twentieth-century woman—knowledgeable, assertive, independent. In contrast, Alice is a nineteenth-century Black woman forced into chattel slavery—by definition her assumed posture is that of ignorance, passiveness, dependence on the will or whim of her owner. Yet even as Butler draws these distinctions they become superficial and the space between Dana and Alice shrinks. For Dana, looking at Alice is like looking at herself, to use Alice Walker's term, "suspended" by historical circumstance. It is as if the folk wisdom of "there but for the grace of God go I" had suddenly been made manifest.

From Dana, Rufus draws a controlled, limited, camaraderie and intellectual stimulation. From Alice he demands sexual attention and actually expects emotional attachment. Although he cannot make her love him, Rufus can and does force Alice to share his bed. And despite the obvious pain that being a witness to (almost a participant in) this crude liaison causes her, Dana abets it until Alice gives birth to Hagar, the woman who is the founder of her family tree. (Distasteful as the situation is, Dana must assist Rufus in his conquest of Alice or her personal history, her present, will be irrevocably altered. This is a variant of science fiction's time travel paradox, the problem of the time-space continuum theme.) Eventually, unable to endure the vicious games of Rufus (he pretends to sell her children), her powerlessness, or her concubinage any longer, Alice commits suicide. Almost immediately, a chastened and tortured Rufus then transfers his entire emotional attention to Dana, seeing her as a replicate of Alice, virtually the same woman, this time whole and complete. Because the insidious institution of slavery has given him virtual carte blanche power over Black lives, Rufus has no misgivings, feels no remorse about attempting to seduce or possess Dana in the same manner he won Alice—that is, by cajolery if possible, force or violence if necessary. It does not matter that Dana has saved his life repeatedly, that she has been, in common parlance, a "good" slave for Rufus. Nor does it matter that the "love" he bears for her borders on incestuousness; after all, Dana has been his protector, his confidant, his mentor, and in some respects his mother and his sister. Since selfish, childish and unstable Rufus can think only of his own immediate needs and wants, and since the system gives him the power to take what he wants—he decides that Dana shall replace Alice and he will not hear her refusal.

Without turning to an actual slave narrative, there probably is no more vivid depiction of life on an Eastern Shore plantation than that found in **Kindred**. The composite rendering is as exact as detailed research could make it. Butler admits to having tempered some of the harshness of the real experience because the slave narratives proved such "grim reading" that she realized she would have to present a "cleaned-up, somewhat gentler version of slavery for there was no entertainment in the real thing." **Kindred,** however, is entertaining and compelling; yet for all the history it enlivens, the average reader absorbs the information without any awareness of an inherently didactic purpose framing an exciting, action filled story. Far from impeding the story line, the didacticism informs it.

Kindred and **Wild Seed** break new ground in science fiction. They are both novels which feature Black characters in major significant roles; they both feature Black women as heroic characters, protagonists who either share power with men or who maintain their right to wield power on an equal basis. Neither of the two women principals yields her basic integrity or submits to male dominance. In each novel we look at a speculative past firmly grounded in an African and African-American social and cultural history. Both **Wild Seed** and **Kindred** mirror Lukács' "broad delineation of manners and circumstances attendant upon events," his insistence upon "dramatic character of action," and his large role voice and dialog within the narrative. Each text is "specifically historical," indeed history is integral to plot, and each effectively welds function to form giving us precise yet "artistically faithful" images of "concrete historical epochs," whole chapters of African-American history, keeping us spellbound all the while.

Butler's works do something else not generally asked of good historical fiction. They reach an entirely different audience, an established science fiction readership which, taken as a whole, is more accustomed to future histories and alien spaces than it is to authentic African and African-American landscapes. That is, I suppose, one of the benefits of renovation: more people are attracted to the old, the historically significant, recreated and redressed in a new light.

Adele S. Newson (review date Summer 1989)

SOURCE: A review of *Dawn* and *Adulthood Rites,* in *Black American Literature Forum,* Vol. 23, No. 2, Summer, 1989, pp. 389-96.

[*In the following review, Newson discusses the subjects of Butler's Xenogenesis series, including prejudice and genetic arrangement.*]

It is a widespread myth that Blacks don't write or read science fiction. The myth is fed by the notion that they cannot afford to indulge in fantasy. Octavia Butler's latest works, **Dawn** and **Adulthood Rites,** prove that Blacks can ill afford to remain ignorant of the genre.

Dawn, Octavia Butler's seventh novel and the first in the Xenogenesis series, introduces new possibilities in the scientific realm of genetic arrangement coupled with observations about the conflicts between the sexes and racial groups. Her canon includes the novels **Patternmaster**

(1975), *Mind of My Mind* (1977), *Survivor* (1978), *Kindred* (1979), *Wild Seed* (1980), and *Clay's Ark* (1984), which treat timescape, mutants, mental telepathy, and genetic rearranging through disease. Thematically they concern themselves with the inevitability of prejudice in human society, with its subsequent oligarchy, the powerlessness of women, and the meaning of humanity.

The narrative of *Dawn* is engaging; the prose flows with a single-minded intensity. Divided into four sections— "Womb," "Family," "Nursery," and "The Training Floor"—, it chronicles the nontraditional science-fiction heroine's (a black woman's) rebirth, development, and adjustment to a foreign environment. The reader roots for Lilith Iyapo's development from the dawn of her new existence as a more complete, compassionate human being and struggles with her as she attempts to champion the causes for all humans who survive a devastating war on Earth.

In *Dawn,* Butler seems intent upon propounding a single didactic message: Until a solution is found (it is not a problem that is likely to be resolved unaided), future societies will be plagued with the same sexual and racial prejudices faced in the present. This suggests that the battle of the sexes and the battle for dominion over racial groups are not battles at all, but rather full-scale wars. Butler's characteristic ambivalence toward her message is also present in this novel. At once the novel gropes for solutions to the problems, while suggesting that wherever there are humans, this discord will be present. The black heroine (Lilith Iyapo) in *Dawn* must choose allegiances between bigoted humans or seemingly bigotless aliens. Through this conflict, many of the heroine's own prejudices (presumably those of the author's as well) are revealed.

The novel is set aboard an alien spaceship, some 250 years after a war on Earth. Lilith Iyapo has survived the war and has been held on board the spaceship. The spaceship is home to the Oankali, a race of gene-swapping extraterrestrials. The Oankali maintain a symbiotic relationship with the "ship"—they serve the ship's needs (it is alive), and it serves theirs (without it the Oankali would be planet-bound and eventually die).

The Oankali rescue Lilith, one of a few to survive the war on Earth created by a handful of people who attempted to commit humancide. The first of the surviving humans to be awakened from the 250-year dreamless and isolated sleep induced by her captors, Lilith confronts very real questions about what it means to be human and the nature of human prejudices. To be human is to thrive in the company of humankind. Lilith explains to the alien Jdahya, "'You shouldn't have isolated any one of us unless your purpose was to drive us insane. You almost succeeded with me more than once. Humans need one another.'" While it may be true that

humans need each other, Butler also demonstrates that, when, a group of humans gather, regardless of the circumstances, prejudice will rear its ugly head. Lilith's own struggles with human prejudices are demonstrated early in the novel through her response to Jdahya, the extraterrestrial assigned the task of acclimating her to the appearance of her hosts:

> She did not want to be any closer to him. She had not known what held her back before. Now she was certain it was his alienness, his difference, his literal unearthliness. She found herself still unable to take even one more step toward him. . . .

> She frowned, strained to see, to understand. Then, abruptly, she did understand. She backed away, scrambled around the bed and to the far wall. When she could go no farther, she stood against the wall, staring at him.

> Medusa.

> Some of the "hair" writhed independently, a nest of snakes startled, driven in all directions.

> Revolted, she turned her face to the wall.

Lilith associates evil, as does the reader, with the Medusa-like aliens, thereby creating a challenge for her to prove herself the worthy/heroic character into which she develops. Ultimately, Butler makes Lilith a champion among weak characters; later she overcomes her repulsion to her hosts, while other characters are unable to. Additionally, this episode serves to illustrate the frailness of the human psyche—the idea that all humans have prejudices taught through one institution or another.

After successfully acclimating Lilith, the Oankali decide it is time to begin to awaken other people to prepare them for the return to Earth—an Earth whose elements are now stable enough to accommodate them. During the process, Lilith becomes the object of the awakening humans' mistrust. They are suspicious of her powers (the Oankali have endowed her with a limited number of powers to ensure her survival). The humans believe her to be alien, because of the dubious liaison she has formed with the grotesque extraterrestrials. After all, she was the first to be awakened and acclimated. Also, the fact that their leader/teacher is a black woman does not help her cause any.

Lilith's task becomes one of convincing the humans that their captors are indeed superior—capable of altering, combining the human gene pool with their own—and that they reside on what roughly translates as a ship. She struggles to maintain her humanness and cordiality towards her hosts, while trying desperately to lead her people and devise a plan of escape.

Here, the plot roughly parallels the historical, albeit self-imposed, function of the Afro-American woman. Substitute blacks for fellow humans and whites for captors, and the parallel becomes clear. Entrapped in a society with different values (the least of which does not embrace her blackness), with the understanding that, no matter how she might want to assimilate, she won't be able to because of her color, she tries to accommodate both her people and her captors. The double jeopardy is familiar, I'm sure, to all black women.

Eventually, more and more humans are awakened—white Americans, black Americans, Oriental, ordinary, and eccentric. In short, Butler provides a microcosm of humankind, equipped with age-old bigotries and prejudices. In this alien world, they ultimately fare no better than they do on Earth. Jdahya, the alien, identifies the problem that caused the destruction of human society on Earth—something that the reader understands will again transpire on a newly replenished Earth, if their genes are not intermixed with those of the aliens. He tells Lilith that humans are endowed with "two incompatible characteristics":

> "You are intelligent. . . . That's the newer of the two characteristics [in the evolution of the human gene pool], and the one you might have to put to work to save yourselves. You are potentially one of the most intelligent species we've found, though your focus is different from ours. . . . You are hierarchial. That's the older and more entrenched characteristic. . . . And a complex combination of genes that work together to make you intelligent as well as hierarchial will still handicap you whether you acknowledge it or not."

There is nothing new in any of the novel's major themes. Indeed, in Butler's 1978 novel *Survivor,* the heroine, Alanna Verrick, is thrust into a similar situation, both in circumstance—"leaving earth settling in a new world of aliens"—and in effect—"I became something else entirely," someone human but above the pettiness characteristic of human prejudices. In the novel *Dawn,* however, Butler seems to want to suggest that gene swapping is the answer to the problems of a hierarchial species—the characteristic from which sexual and racial prejudices grow with their accompanying oligarchy. Her ambivalence is evident in that the most promising of her characters would never sacrifice an ounce of his humanness to improve his lot (i.e., he would never succumb to gene swapping).

What is and remains a hallmark of her work is her deftness at creating the sensual, vis-à-vis unlikely, male/female alliances. In the informal dawning of human society on the space ship, the awakening humans choose mates. Lilith chooses Joseph (an Oriental, shorter in stature than she) as mate. They, in turn, form a physical alliance with Nikanj (an ooli both male and female of the Oankali species):

> Nikanj freed one sensory arm from Joseph's waist and extended it toward her.
>
> She stayed where she was for a moment longer, proving to herself that she was still in control of her behavior. Then she tore off her jacket and seized the ugly, ugly elephant's trunk of an organ, letting it coil around her as she climbed onto the bed. She sandwiched Nikanj's body between her own and Joseph's. . . . She could lift a free hand across Nikanj to take Joseph's cool, seemingly lifeless hand.
>
> "No," Nikanj said softly into her ear—or perhaps it stimulated the auditory nerve directly. It could do that—stimulate her sense individually or in any combination to make perfect hallucinations. "Only through me," its voice insisted.

Joseph and Lilith are not traditional science-fiction heroes. Neither would they be regarded as people likely to form an alliance. This refreshing approach to human relationships makes a good bit of Butler's literature sensuous.

The driving force of the narrative rests with the concept of genetic swapping—trading essence or genetic material. The Oankali trade genes for surviving "as an evolving species instead of specializing into extinction or stagnation." Butler offers the Oankali as the model for fruitful existence. Theirs is a symbiotic relationship with all living organisms. Yet the reader experiences discomfort over the idea that the Oankali are not the species that they originally were. They constantly become something of the organisms with which they trade. Feeling sentimental over this idea, Lilith notes to Jdahya that Jdahya's descendants "probably won't even know one another. They'll remember this division as mythology if they remember it at all." This notion echoes the history or nonhistory of the African in America, who was forced to mix genes and robbed of a history. Yet, the appealing feature of the Oankali heritage is that they are able to pass on memory of a division biologically.

Moreover, Butler is adept at challenging the reader to evaluate his own moral codes. *Dawn* is philosophical in that it asks the reader, by virtue of circumstances surrounding the human characters, to pose the basic question, What does it mean to be human?

The heroine is independent, intelligent, capable, and, in most instances, disliked by her peers—the epitome of heroic womanism. It is easy for the reader to sympathize with her quest for autonomy in the environment of aliens. Again we see Butler's signature—a black heroine thrust into unusual circumstances and compelled to survive. Lilith's life, like that of the black woman's, is a metaphor for the quest which would resolve the problem of her being both revered and despised by those with whom she inhabits society.

Adulthood Rites, the second novel in the Xenogenesis trilogy, chronicles Akin Iyapo's development into adulthood. Akin, the son of Lilith Iyapo, is the first male child born of a human woman on Earth since the war that destroyed Earth some three hundred years before. The Oankali have restored Earth (with the aid of genetic engineering) and returned the survivors of the holocaust to Earth to go about the business of gene swapping to form a hybrid of the Oankali and human species. Akin, part human and part Oankali, is bred to become the champion of the resisters (the humans who would remain childless rather than mate with an alien). He declares his life's work to be the restoration and propagation of a wholly human society.

Dawn ends with the question, Will Lilith Iyapo trade with the Oankali and bear children? Some thirty years and three children later, *Adulthood Rites* begins. Divided into four parts—"Lo," "Phoenix," "Chkahichdahk," and "Home"—, the rubrics designate locations where environment significantly contributes to Akin's development.

The story begins in Lo, a trading village, where Akin is born. There he is nurtured by female and male, human and Oankali entities. As a child, his features are cosmetically altered to give him the appearance of being human. When he is seven months old, he is kidnapped by raiders who hope to sell him to a rich resister village (where there are no children) for goods and a woman. In the hands of his captors, he encounters brutality and violence. By the time he is eight months old, he is sold to a resister couple (Gabriel Rinaldi and Tate—two of the first humans awakened by Lilith in *Dawn*) in the resister village of Phoenix. He spends over a year in the Phoenix village, in which he learns more about the so-called human contradiction that destroyed Earth—"intelligence put at the service of ancient hierarchial tendencies"—and decides that one day he will be the voice of the human resisters.

In part 3, "Chkahichdahk," Akin is twenty years old and anticipating metamorphosis (transformation into adulthood). As a result of his propensity to wander, especially among the resister villages, he is taken with the Oankali nature. His intellect and skills expand, yet he finds the environment of the Oankali sterile and unnatural. He even exhibits signs of repulsion to the Oankali ooli's appearance. By part 4, he has returned home (to Earth) more determined than ever to help the resisters. The people (Oankali adults) agree to permit him to take willing resister humans to Mars to try

again to propagate humanity—"The salvaged Earth would finally die"; left would be little more than a small corpse of a world. Fearing his metamorphosis would repulse the humans, he hurriedly returns to the village of Phoenix to inform the resisters there of his mission. While there, he is prematurely thrown into metamorphosis after which time he resembles a child Oankali, although he is indeed fully grown. A small band of humans joins him, and the novel ends with the larger question—Will human society survive on Mars?—in anticipation of the third and final novel in the Xenogenesis series.

Adulthood Rites is the middle point in the Xenogenesis trilogy. Because of this, it serves an important function as a bridge in the development of both character and story. Yet *Adulthood Rites* is also disappointing. It makes promises that it does not fulfill. It is indecisive in its characterization. It flirts with developing a relationship between Lilith and Augustino Leal (Tino), which is never realized. Other Butler novels feature (mentally and physically) powerful black female heroines. Lilith fits this pattern—she is described as being somewhere between human and construct in ability— but for all her ability, she is mute. Having "deserted" the cause of the resisters to have children, she does little more than sulk silently away, sometimes for days at a time, to appease her aching conscience. Yet she always returns to her children. This is the extent of her wandering (that nontraditional questing of female characters). Tino, the man with whom she might have formed an engaging alliance (as is Butler's trademark/signature), is just as ineffective as she. Were it not for his ooli, he might long ago have committed suicide.

Additionally, the story relies too heavily on dialogue, making it more or less a treatise on the contradictory and often violent nature of humankind. While in Phoenix, Akin encounters two constructs who were also captured by raiders and sold to the resisters. In the following passage they consider the human condition:

> "We are them! And we are the Oankali. You know. If they could perceive, they would know!"

> "If they could perceive, they would be us. They can't and they aren't. We're the best of what they are and the best of what the Oankali are. But because of us, they won't exist any more."

> "Oankali Dinso and Toaht [genetic divisions of Oankali] won't exist anymore."

> "No. But Akjai will go away unchanged. If the Human-Oankali construct doesn't work here or the Toaht, Akjai [full-Oankali] will continue."

"Only if they find some other people to blend with."
This came directly from Amma.

"Humans had come to their own end," Shkaht said.
"They were flawed and overspecialized. If they hadn't
had their war, they would have found another way to
kill themselves."

"Perhaps," Akin admitted. "I was taught that, too. And
I can see the conflict in their genes—the new intelligence put at the service of ancient hierarchial tendencies. But . . . they didn't have to destroy themselves.
They certainly don't have to do it again."

While the dialogue is both engaging and revealing, it appears a bit too laborious. Still, Butler would have the reader
note an independent thinker in the infant Akin, even at this
time. While few constructs would question the omniscient
authority of the Oankali people, Akin questions whether it
is true that humans, if given the chance, would indeed again
try to commit humancide, and he further supports their right
to an Akjai (a species whose genes are not mixed).

And because he is a first, the first male construct to be born
to a human mother, his then will be a marginal existence.
And in this feature of the novel, characterization, Butler's
signature is more than a little evident. She openly acknowledges her task as being that of expanding the range of racial and sexual experiences provided in science fiction. The
Oankali, humans, and constructs (the product of human and
Oankali mating), who inhabit Akin's home, attempt to provide him with the nurturing necessary to ensure his survival.
Early in the novel, Lilith proclaims to Tino, who has come
to investigate the activity in the trading village of Lo, "I
don't want to know what you call us. But spend some time
with us. Maybe you'll accept our definition of ourselves."
This passage is the key to Butler's intention in the novel.
She invites the reader to examine the lives that human nature and fate have dictated for the survivors of the war on
Earth. The reader watches as a myriad of activity whizzes
past. The action of the story begins with the abduction of
Akin and ends with an adult Akin, watching from Gabe's
shoulder as the city of Phoenix (symbol of hope) burns.
The hope for the future of human civilization rests with a
black man, who also happens to be alien.

Frances Bonner (essay date Spring 1990)

SOURCE: "Difference and Desire, Slavery and Seduction:
Octavia Butler's Xenogenesis," in *Foundation,* No. 48,
Spring, 1990, pp. 50-62.

[*In the following essay, Bonner discusses how Butler portrays desire and rape in her Xenogenesis trilogy, and
how the trilogy is still successful despite its lack of hope.*]

Octavia E. Butler's recently completed Xenogenesis trilogy (*Dawn, Adulthood Rites* and *Imago*) is a striking addition not just to her already fascinating body of work, but
also to the field of s[cience] f[iction] trilogies generally.
Too often it seems, especially when the first volume is published as "Book 1 of the whatever trilogy," the reader is prepared for the second-rate and the too heavy-handedly
formulaic. The s[cience] f[iction] reader is often told that
trilogies (and even longer sequences) are preferred by publishers because they enhance the predictability of sales,
rather than being the result of authors desiring a particular
format to enhance the exploration of specific themes or
situations. Fortunately, with Xenogenesis, the lowering
feeling is unnecessary, and indeed, given her predilection
for connected novels evidenced in the Patternist books,
perhaps should not have been felt at all. Yet reception of
the second volume was characteristic of responses to the
second in the less rewarding trilogies—disappointment and
let-down, as if the pleasures of the first could not be sustained. My own first reading of *Adulthood Rites* was no
exception, and it is part of my intention in this essay to explore why this may have been so (re-reading dispelled it)
and where the pleasure in so downbeat a sequence lies,
within a more general exploration of Butler's concerns.

Xenogenesis tells of the activities of an alien race of gene-
traders, the Oankali, and the remnants of humanity they salvage after a global nuclear war for use in their incessant
quest for incorporable genetic diversity. The first volume,
Dawn, is from the point-of-view of Lilith, an Afro-American survivor of the war, who is chosen to train the first
group of humans to be returned, with their Oankali mates,
to the restored but mutated Earth. *Adulthood Rites,* the second, recounts the early life of Lilith's first son, the human-
Oankali construct Akin, as he comes to realize, and then
to convince others of, the need for the humans who resisted
breeding with the Oankali to be given a chance to continue
the (unhybridized) human race, despite the Oankali certainty
that humanity is doomed. The last, *Imago,* is the story of
another of Lilith's children, Jodahs, the first construct
ooloi—the third Oankali sex, whose members are the actual gene manipulators. His acceptance by the polity signals the absorption of humanity into the Oankali (there is
no question of equal partnership) and the eventual complete
destruction of the Earth. The Oankali rescue neither humanity nor their/our planet, they merely delay our demise.

One of the more unusual aspects of the trilogy is that it
has no triumphal conclusion. Humanity has lost before the
story begins, has still lost and is disappearing as it ends,
and their/our short (and we are assured, temporary) victory
occurs, as it were offstage, between *Adulthood Rites* and

Imago. Even more disturbing from a feminist writer is, as Rachel Pollack's review of *Dawn* points out, the centrality and apparent acceptance of rape. This is no easy read; or to put it more precisely, it is quite an easy read, since stylistically it is even less challenging than the Patternist books (the point-of-view only changes between volumes), but it is no easy ingestion. The pleasures are not just fugitive, they are thorny as well, but, to continue the metaphor, once they have hooked in, you cannot readily stop worrying away at them.

Despite a quite ludicrous review in *Publishers' Weekly* which claimed that in *Adulthood Rites* "the author gives us a brief ecstatic experience of this utopian alternative to human society", there is nothing utopian about the societies in Xenogenesis, even for the alien Oankali driven by their need to "trade" for genetic diversity. Butler has herself quite explicitly denied utopian intentions. In an interview given at the time she was finishing writing *Dawn,* she claimed "I don't write utopian science fiction because I don't believe that imperfect humans can form a perfect society." And it is the imperfections that interest, even obsess, her. A recurrent concern, especially of the Patternist books, is with child abuse and child murder (generally explained there as resulting from the pressures of uncontrolled telepathy) and in the interview just quoted she says that the Oankali's diagnosis of what is wrong with humanity is hers too—intelligence and hierarchical behaviour (which latter she believes inborn) is a potentially lethal combination. Not only would it be impossible reasonably to consider Butler's work without reference to her race, it would be improper to do so given her foregrounding of it. The specificity of the Afro-American experience is basic to the Patternist books and the one-off *Kindred,* and central to Xenogenesis. The general absence of black s[cience] f[iction] writers (and readers) has not infrequently been a matter for comment. Kathleen L. Spencer's aside in her review of a combined Starmont guide to the work of Butler, Suzy McKee Charnas and Joan D. Vinge, that Butler was "one of only three Black s[cience] f[iction] writers to date and the only Black woman" led both to protesting letters about the possible existence of "unknown" black s[cience] f[iction] writers and readers and Spencer's admission that she should have written "three recognized Black S[cience] F[iction] writers", but to no new names (the other two given were Samuel R. Delany and Steven Barnes) and not even a comment on Butler's being the only black woman.

Butler has explained the absence of black s[cience] f[iction] writers as derived from the way the lack of black characters in the literature limits its appeal to black readers (and writers of s[cience] f[iction], arguably even more than other genres, come from devoted s[cience] f[iction] readers). Compounding this has been the tendency of editors and publishers to regard the inclusion of black characters as a dis-

traction, acceptable only if the focus of the story is on racism. Even so, there has been the belief that aliens can substitute as all-purpose Others. One big blue extra-terrestrial whose humanity is revealed and accepted can be metaphorically substituted for an examination of any number of actual social divisions, as witness many past discussions on the absence of women/non-Caucasians/homosexuals/disabled people from s[cience] f[iction]. This very point was at the centre of Butler's response in 1980 to a question addressed by *Future Life* to a number of writers: "What role can and should science fiction writers play in working with America's major corporations in planning for the future of society?"

Adele S. Newson has said that the myth that blacks are uninvolved in s[cience] f[iction] is "fed by the notion that they cannot afford to indulge in fantasy" which may help explain why it is that Delany has to keep defending himself against charges by whites that he is not "black enough". It is not, however, a suggestion he advances in his exposition which, no doubt not fortuitously, chimes very well with Butler's exasperation with expectations that the traces of blackness in black writing will be stereotypical and deal unrelievedly with racism.

Concerned as she is with the specificity of the Afro-American experience, it is unsurprising that Butler again and again explores the phenomenon of slavery, in particular the initial stage in which the self—body, soul and subjectivity— is stolen and declared an item of exchange. While most obvious in *Wild Seed* and *Kindred,* people are appropriated by others in virtually all her writings. Furthermore after the appropriation there are usually the issues both of forced reproduction and of love for the captor—the former of these at least, characteristic of the Afro-American slave experience.

It is worth recalling that part of the point of Delany's famous discovery late in his reading of Heinlein's *Starship Troopers* that one of the characters was Filipino was that it had been possible even for a black reader to assume that the character was white. It is unlikely that any reader could get far into Butler's novels in ignorance of the race or ethnicity of any but the most incidental character. To some extent this is a function of the times and the abjuring of the integrationist model. If only in her assertion of the importance and value of difference, Butler is as post-modern as s[cience] f[iction] writers come. In stylistic concerns it is another matter altogether. She is a traditionalist. She is the absent case in Maria Minchin Brewer's suggestion that male writers of what she terms "surviving fictions" are post-modern only in their experimental style, but not in their attitudes and concerns. (Brewer, who I suspect has not read Geoff Ryman, to name just one male writer who should escape her accusation, cites various canonical feminist s[cience] f[iction] works as escaping into thorough-going post-modernity. I am not entirely convinced here either, except, of course, for Joanna Russ.) As well as her insistence on difference, her concern with survival in a (post-)nuclear world and, as I intend to demonstrate later, her attitude to the Oedipal conflict, are characteristically (female) post-modern.

A comparison of Butler's and Delany's treatments of slavery is instructive, for both of them explore the intermingling of slavery and desire in the sexual relationships between slave and owner. The complex meditations on pleasure in perversity, the sado-masochistic game-playing and role reversals of the Nevèrÿona series is not for Butler—he is neither that kind of adult writer, nor that kind of post-modern. She is also constrained by different literary allegiances, especially ones which hold her in some ways closer to the mundane world. Not only does she locate her settings geographically closer to home (and usually on Earth), but temporally they are closer too. The far future is not her domain. Nor does she perceive what she writes as fantasy. Indeed the only one of her books she refers to as fantasy is *Kindred*—the one marketed as mainstream, the one most readily perceived as subject to requirements of historical accuracy.

It may be that it is her gender which is of greater importance to the question of desire, if it is this that results in the various investigations of forced reproduction. In both *Wild Seed* and *Mind of My Mind,* Doro breeds "his" people, without regard for their own wishes; in *Kindred,* the time-travelling twentieth-century heroine, Dana, fears her existence depends on her keeping the nineteenth-century white slave owner Rufus alive to father her grandmother on the black servant/slave Alice; in *Survivor* the alien Garkohn steal humans to breed hybrids; and in Xenogenesis the sole purpose of the Oankali's salvaging of humanity is for breeding, to incorporate some of their genes into the next manifestation of the Oankali. But these are not stories of undiluted outrage. As pleasure and fetishism mut(at)e the power relations in Delany's novels, so love enters Butler's. But love rarely effects her power relations. The moral difficulties such unequal love creates are solved to some extent in Xenogenesis by the announcement that love is chemical. The element of choice has disappeared. Where the slave or captive may have had no choice about bearing the captor's child (or little, if male, in impregnating the designated woman), loving him had been another matter. The Oankali ooloi however create a chemical bond between human and alien. There is still a degree of equivocation however, for while breeders may blame the bond, not all humans succumb. The resisters reject chemical entrapment, even at the cost of infertility and avoidable ill-health.

It is probably fatuous to ask whether gender is less impor-

tant than race in Butler's work. Possibly it is, and given the comparative scarcities of black and female s[cience] f[iction] writers, who would want to suggest it should be otherwise? The conjunction however is what matters; gender articulates race in a most illuminating way. The point is perhaps best made by Adele S. Newson who says that in Lilith's struggle to remain on terms with the Oankali and her fellow humans, the plot of *Dawn* parallels "the historical, albeit self-imposed, function of the Afro-American woman". As mediator, Lilith must bear the odium of her fellows as well as her own guilt over the collaboration, tempered only by her belief that without her, things would be worse. That this too is nothing new for a Butler heroine is revealed by Ruth Salvaggio's comment about the heroines of *Wild Seed* and *Survivor:* "Anyanwu closely resembles Alanna, accepting the constraints of her world and trying to make something decent and productive out of the indecent situation in which she finds herself." The particular articulation can also be seen in the importance of food and the domestic—not just a sign of the female, but, with for example the emphasis on yams, cassava and African agricultural practices, a sign of the black female of African origin.

That we should privilege the viewpoints of the subjugated, and specifically those of women of colour, has long been the argument of the primatologist and historian of science, Donna Haraway. This is not because they are immune from criticism, but because they are more likely to be aware of the various tricks of the dominant in asserting the adequacy, indeed sufficiency, of its knowledge. Haraway argues most persuasively for situated knowledge, for the acknowledged partial perspective rather than for implicit assertions of universalism. In the specificity of the acknowledged position from which Butler writes, she provides just such an example, and Haraway implicitly accepts this in her most recent work which includes an analysis of *Dawn.*

I have already indicated that Butler's works repeatedly assert the value of difference. Haraway too sees this as one of Butler's main themes, saying that *Dawn,* like many of Butler's other fictions "is about resistance to the imperative to recreate the sacred image of the same", and adding that "from the perspective of an ontology based on mutation, metamorphosis and diaspora, restoring the sacred image can be a bad joke". The explicit raison d'être of the Missionaries of *Survivor* is to maintain the sacred (human) image of the Creator. Likewise, Lilith's name, that of Eve's uppity predecessor, while linking her to the Oankali whose tentacles are often referred to as snakes, emphasises her repudiation of the (human) Creator. The transitions of the mutant Doro's people and their descendants, the Patternists, during which they reveal their psychic powers, foreshadow the metamorphoses of the Oankali and their genetic constructs during which their gender is revealed. Both groups are diasporic. Difference is not just a given that is accepted, it is something which is intensified, enhanced and valued, even if not unequivocally—it is, after all, most desired by Doro and the Oankali whose viewpoints the narratives, but not necessarily the narrative intentions, endorse. The shifting points-of-view themselves also present difference.

Haraway notes one point on which difference is not explored, saying that heterosexuality is not questioned.

> The different social subjects, the different genders that could emerge from another embodiment of resistance to compulsory heterosexuality and reproductive politics do not inhabit this *Dawn.*

Yet perhaps she is being too harsh. A concentration on forced reproduction leaves limited space for the non-heterosexual, but the unease of Tino, the human male with his male Oankali mate (the mixed families of Xenogenesis have five members: one male and one female human and a male, female and ooloi Oankali) raises, even if it does not explore, the issue. It may also be that readers find it explored in the relationship between the part-human ooloi, Jodahs, and his male human mate, Tomas. Although the pronoun "it" is used throughout to refer to an ooloi, and this linguistic choice foregrounded by reference to the impossibility of doing so in languages lacking neuter pronouns, the tendency to read as male a character unmarked by specific gender may result in a perception of Jodahs as a male and hence of Tomas's eagerness for sex with it, as homosexual. Certainly with this mating the question of rape does not occur.

Butler's dealing with homosexuality is characteristically oblique. In *Wild Seed,* the shape-shifting Anyanwu spends many years married to a white woman, who is however aware that her husband is really a black woman. Although Denice, the wife, appears only as a photograph, Anyanwu explains to Doro that they married not only to save Denice (who saw ghosts) from an asylum, but also "because after a while, we started to want each other". Earlier, however, Amber in *Patternmaster* quite cheerfully announces her bisexuality. Haraway's comment about *Dawn* does however retain its force for women, not just in that book but in the trilogy as a whole. Women are not there allowed to opt out of heterosexuality and they escape forced reproduction only by accepting no reproduction at all.

Difference is not however Butler's dominant theme. That is power. Slavery is after all the most dramatic manifestation of unequal power. Butler has commented on the effect of her fascination with power. "I began writing about power because I had so little." Writing before the publication of *Clay's Ark* or Xenogenesis, Sandra Y. Govan remarked how in each of the novels to that point "the implicit

struggle for power revolves around explicit conflicts of will and the contests of survival a heroine endures." Certainly this is Lilith's story too and, and if it is modulated a little when the heroine is replaced by her male and ooloi children, then that serves to emphasise how central the gender articulation is.

I referred above to Butler's endorsement of her Oankali creations' perception of hierarchical behaviour as at the root of humanity's problems. Yet, just because the Oankali claim to have avoided hierarchies, it does not mean they have eschewed power. As Haraway says "hierarchy is not power's only shape." They deny humans choice as a matter of course. The exceptions are moments to remark, or are freighted with such negative consequences that they verge on the suicidal. The Oankali know best. As Rachel Pollack notes "this recalls that favorite White American fantasy, the benefits of slavery for the happy Blacks." Yet as Pollack also emphasises, Butler is not pointing an easy ethical lesson, she is examining a "terrible conundrum": at times the Oankali seem right, for the humans have destroyed their planet by their foolishness. The core of the conundrum, and one suspects the crunch for Pollack, is the question of rape.

Other writers on Butler do not foreground the issue; indeed until Xenogenesis (with the notable exception of *Kindred*) neither did Butler—it is subsumed under forced reproduction. In *Dawn,* however, the practice is named, but in circumstances that echo oddly. Lilith, using her Oankali-improved strength, saves one of the women she is preparing to return to Earth from rape by a newly awoken man. The woman questions whether the enhanced Lilith is really human after all. Lilith dismisses the question "If I weren't human, why the hell would I care whether you got raped?" Yet one of the things for which she is preparing her charges is enforced mating with the Oankali. Pollack's paralleling of the ooloi Nikanj's knowing that Lilith's lover Joseph "really" wants to have sex with it, despite his inability to say "yes", with the typical male defense to rape charges, is telling. The unimportance of human verbal consent to Oankali behaviour (and their privileging of what they read the body desiring) recurs when Nikanj makes Lilith pregnant. In a central moment, when asked if she had really wanted a child, Lilith replies "Oh, yes. But if I had the strength not to ask, it should have had the strength to let me alone." The Oankali may have power over the choices of the humans, but over their own mating urge, they are powerless (or choose to declare themselves so). Butler has them revealed as driven by their need to "trade" for genetic diversity as humans are by their hierarchical behaviour.

Yet it remains unclear whether Butler is engaging in her characteristic equivocating, or does not herself regard Oankali sexual behaviour as rape. She certainly calls it by other names. "Rape" is used only of humans—not just on the occasion just quoted, but also intermittently in *Imago* where it serves as part of the revelation of the degeneration of humanity in the absence of Oankali. As far as the aliens are concerned, it seems to me quite reasonable to apply it to the early instances of inter-species sexual activity, when they drug the humans into insensitivity, even insensibility, and submission (the very figures of "white" slavery). Yet the language used would not be all that inappropriate at a getting-to-know-you party. A quite disquieting moment occurs in *Dawn* just after that to which Pollack refers. Nikanj has once again drugged Joseph because it "knows" he really wants to repeat the experience (on the first occasion he did not even get the opportunity to refuse, being anaesthetized at the moment consent could have been asked) and Lilith, instead of joining in the experience which is supposedly better with three, sits back and watches. "She was patient and interested. This might be her only chance ever to watch up close as an ooloi seduced someone." Throughout the trilogy much is made of Nikanj's powers of seduction (in *Adulthood Rites* a human male even makes a friendly joke about it), but this is also our first opportunity to observe an ooloi "seduction" and I for one certainly find the scene, in which a drugged man is subjected not just to casuistry but to a "poor little me" turn from a misunderstood alien, a little hard to take. I wish in some ways that I could say I found it utterly repellent; it would be so much easier. There are points of identification with Nikanj available; the idea that any human would be preferable to the loveable sensitive alien is touching. If only there were not the drugged removal of volition!

It is I think particularly notable that Butler presents this scene with the male rather than the female human and indeed does not show us the scene in which Nikanj first rapes/ seduces Lilith at all. It occurs between the first and second sections of *Dawn* and is not even recalled in memory. It is however a most telling absence. With Lilith there to assure the reader that the sexual experience is pleasurable and something she is all too willing to engage in herself, rape more easily masquerades as seduction. Her own first encounter, devoid of any such commentary, would be difficult to present convincingly as a desirable experience.

The problem of Oankali rape/seduction echoes that in the Patternist books of the sexual activity of Doro and his daughters. The incest is muted not only by Doro's endorsement of it as part of his breeding plans, but by his "wearing" different bodies—the body which sleeps with the daughter is not the one which engendered her. The paedophilic aspect is blurred by the imprecision about the age at which it occurs. The only one of which we are certain is late teenage, but there is a suggestion that this may have been unusual restraint on Doro's part. That the children are not averse, having been brought up to expect it and

having a semi-mystical regard for their father, removes accusations of rape. Certainly Butler presents Doro as a monster and yet there are oddities about the general presentation of sexual relationships between beings of unequal power bubbling away beneath the surface of Butler's fictions. One of the problems I have is in determining the extent to which they are in the books' unconscious or hers.

One obvious seat of power is the family, yet, in common with other feminist writers, Butler is concerned with examining alternatives to the nuclear family, at least in part to relocate power. In the Patternist books, children are often adopted to remove them from actual or potential child abuse, and domestic groupings tend to be larger than currently regarded as normal. In Xenogenesis, Butler goes into considerable detail about the human-Oankali families and their operation. Because the Oankali extend life-spans, particularly the reproductive portion of them, the number of children is great, especially as there are two females both giving birth. (In *Imago,* late in Lilith's life, an aside informs us that in view of her and her mates' age, they are now having "only" a pair of children a decade. Since she is at least 100 and quite possibly 200 or so at this time, the size of her family can only be conjectured.) In any case, Butler avoids Oedipal constructions, with their power determinations, by all the means at her disposal. The incest taboo is rejected both by Doro and by the Oankali, who customarily mate brother and sister through unrelated ooloi. The acceptance of the wandering male, refusing monogamy and family involvement, in both Patternist books and Xenogenesis, not only makes Oedipal passages problematic, but reflects the characteristic asserted to be typical of Afro-American males and in fact increasingly common of males in Anglo-Celtic dominant cultures generally. As a third blow to Freudian normality, in Xenogenesis gender is physically determined by affinity with the same-sex parent, not psychically through rivalry and thwarted desire, or the establishing of Otherness. Although Butler is not one of the female writers of "surviving fictions" that Maria Minich Brewer considers, her comment that they

> link the nuclear narrative to a politics of gender that
> thoroughly displaces the Oedipal narrative-of-conflict
> with the system by inventing new forms of non-hierar-
> chical mediation and community.

certainly applies. (The term "nuclear narrative" here should not be read in a limiting way; Butler's post-nuclear stories are indisputably such narratives.)

My comments so far have been concerned to demonstrate Butler's common concerns in the Patternist and Xenogenesis books. Yet there are discontinuities too. The webs of connectedness that Govan identified as central to the Patternist books, and evident in *Kindred* too, are not so important. Controlled creation has overtaken the mix of attempted control and the operation of chance; mutation in Xenogenesis ceases to be accidental. Because, as Haraway points out, the Oankali differ from humans by engaging in self-formation not through non-living technologies, but on life itself, there is an absence of Oankali art. This is not characteristic of Butler—Anyanwu's Igbo pots and Jan's learning blocks and paintings (in *Mind of My Mind*) testify to this—but it is not an accidental omission. A sustained passage in *Adulthood Rites* details Akin's Oankali-derived distaste for myths and any stories not based on fact; we are repeatedly told how bare the Oankali living spaces are and how only the humans (indeed only women, though this may not be a meaningful exclusion) paint and draw; for quite some time the Oankali deny Lilith even writing materials. In case readers could get to the end of the trilogy still deluded that Butler was depicting an utopia, they should be warned that the society depicted would have no use for the depiction; s[cience] f[iction] along with all the other "lies" (Akin's term for fiction) would disappear.

I said at the beginning that I would attempt to explore my initial disappointment with *Adulthood Rites* and where the pleasure in so downbeat a trilogy lies. I trust I have done the second already; the pleasures in teasing out the patterns and preoccupations of Butler's work are considerable, as is the hard work of reconciliation. I suspect that one of the reasons for my initial personal disappointment with *Adulthood Rites* was something which is not uncommon in Butler's novels, which I think of as the disappearing heroine. Readers of the Gollancz paperback edition graced with John Varley's comment that *Dawn* "Gives us the best heroine I've met in a long time", are likely to be particularly disappointed, for *Adulthood Rites* gives us little of her. I agree with Varley; Lilith is a wonderful heroine—strong, competent, flawed, moody, fighting to make the best of a situation over which she has virtually no control. Childlike, I wanted to read more about her in the second book and watch her win out, but Butler is not concerned with satisfying childish longings in adults. *Adulthood Rites* is from her son's point-of-view and Lilith becomes a comparatively minor character. With *Imago* the shift in point-of-view to the ooloi, Jodahs, and the continuation of Lilith in a minor role is not unexpected. The change is not as startling however as that from *Wild Seed* to *Mind of My Mind* where Anyanwu/Emma not merely becomes a minor character, but also alters in moral evaluation (from heroine-saviour to minor nuisance). Relevant here however are the disjunctions in chronologies—of narration, writing and publication—that do not apply to *Xenogenesis*. In narrative chronology *Wild Seed* precedes *Mind of My Mind* and is followed by *Clay's Ark, Patternmaster* and *Survivor,* yet the publication order is *Patternmaster* (1976), *Mind of My Mind* (1977), *Survivor* (1978), *Wild Seed* (1980) and

Clay's Ark (1984), while *Survivor,* although revised extensively in the light of *Patternmaster* and *Mind of My Mind,* was initially written considerably before.

The problems of disjunctive chronologies have been referred to (though not under that name) by Delany in a complaint about publishers' impositions of narrative chronology on collections of works in a series in a way which obscures if not obliterates the writer's self-critical dialogue with her- or himself. This may give an extra clue as to why series, which may lack pre-determined structures, are often more satisfying intellectually than the more predictably-structured trilogies. Nonetheless a comparison of the reappearance of, for example, Lessa in Anne McCaffrey's Pern series with the reappearance of Lilith in the two later Xenogenesis volumes is an indication that trilogies are not always less surprising. (It is, incidentally, hard to imagine anything more heretical than an authorial re-evaluation of Lessa, who even when not the main focus of a novel can never be other than the dominant character in any scene in which she appears.)

I cannot resist concluding with another quotation from Donna Haraway. No reader, one trusts, could leave Octavia E. Butler's work believing she valued the fixity of the Natural. Whether by mutation, transmutation or direct manipulation, in her fictions nature changes. The most negatively valued groups of humans are those who, like the Missionaries in *Survivor,* attempt to stop variation. Even *Xenogenesis's* resister humans are only allowed to start breeding again on a transformed Mars. As in so many other instances, I concur with Haraway when she says "I am not interested in policing the boundaries between nature and culture—quite the opposite. I am edified by the traffic." Reading Butler is part of such an edification.

Hoda M. Zaki (essay date July 1990)

SOURCE: "Utopia, Dystopia, and Ideology in the Science Fiction of Octavia Butler," in *Science-Fiction Studies,* Vol. 17, No. 2, July, 1990, pp. 239-51.

[*In the following essay, Zaki discusses Butler's work as it relates to the genre of utopian and dystopian science fiction.*]

In an interview published in 1986, Octavia E. Butler stated that there was no "women's genre in science fiction." Women authors, she continued, wrote too many varieties of S[cience] F[iction] for their work to be labeled as one subgenre. Nor did Butler see herself writing utopian S[cience] F[iction]: "I've actually never projected an ideal society. I don't believe that imperfect humans can form a perfect society." I take issue with both of Butler's statements about her own writing. Like other critics of her work, I maintain that Butler is part of the post-1970 feminist and utopian S[cience] F[iction] trend which emerged when writers who were deeply influenced by the second (1960s') wave of the women's movement began to use S[cience] F[iction] to explore issues from a feminist perspective. Collectively, these writers have published over a dozen feminist utopias and have attracted a great deal of critical attention.

The present essay has two objectives. The first is to reveal the dynamic interplay of utopian, dystopian, and ideological elements in Butler's works in the effort to show how one example of popular culture, containing as it does many authentic utopian elements, also includes the less hopeful forces of anti-utopianism and ideology. My second aim is to examine Butler's position within this group of utopia-generating writers by comparing some of her assumptions to those found in the larger body of feminist S[cience] F[iction] utopias. The place that she occupies within this group is unique, for she alone brings to her fiction the experiences of being a black woman. Furthermore, her works chiefly differ from those of her Anglo sisters in that they embody an indirect critique of the liberal feminist imagination and politics expressed in contemporary feminist S[cience] F[iction]—a difference which, insofar as it is attributable to racial considerations, points to certain tensions existing between Afro-American women and the feminist movement.

1. Utopia. For centuries, political philosophers have debated the issue of what constitutes human nature. Often, the heuristic device of a "state of nature"—a pre-social and sometimes pre-political condition—was used to "prove" how certain qualities in humans were either the result of social conditioning or intrinsic to "human nature." Such expositions of the nature of "man" were intricately linked to some vision of political order; they served to rationalize a particular set of social and political institutions. Hobbes, Locke, and Rousseau, for example, each defended a core of human qualities to justify very different notions of the state and the public sphere.

Feminist philosophers have taken up this argument, specifically focusing upon the impact of gender on human thinking. They debate the question by investigating the extent to which gender is a social construction. As in the past, this discussion of "human nature" has a significant link to a vision of politics, and thus has far-reaching implications for feminist strategy and struggle. Differing views of the subject translate into differing critiques of the contemporary social order and differing images of utopia.

Two interpretations have emerged from the feminist debate

on human nature: the essentialist and the materialist. The former argues for the primacy of female anatomy as the central and determining factor in shaping the female unconscious and conscious mind. The female body, in other words, is the locus of difference as well as the basis for unity and social change. The materialist interpretation, to the contrary, prefers to explain the oppression of women by focusing on the social and historical construction of gender and self.

Butler joins the current debate by advancing her particular version of human nature and her particular vision of politics. Her views on both issues are logically consistent, and together serve as a critique of the contemporary social order and as the foundation for her utopian and dystopian vision. I will concentrate primarily on three of her more recent novels, *Clay's Ark (Ark)*, *Dawn,* and *Adulthood Rites (Rites)*.

Ark is the fifth installment of the "Patternist" series, in which Butler traces the evolution of humans into three warring groups. It is her most dystopian work to date. In it she describes the destruction of late-industrial civilization. This destruction, begun by humans, is completed when an extraterrestrial organism is brought to Earth. Humans who survive the alien micro-organism become physically transformed and are no longer Homo sapiens. With *Dawn,* Butler begins her new "Xenogenesis" series by destroying Earth again, as it were, this time by nuclear war. The Oankali, extraterrestrials who happen to be on the scene when this occurs, salvage a few humans and begin the process of rehabilitating Earth. Technologically more advanced than humans, the Oankali's collective vocation involves the trading of genes between sentient species. They are both repelled and fascinated by the human genetic structure. From the perspective of these aliens, humans are fundamentally flawed as they are both intelligent and hierarchical, a lethal combination in the eyes of the Oankali. The Oankali are "driven" by their genetic structure to crossbreed with other life-forms, and they plan to colonize Earth in cooperation with the humans. After studying the individuals they have rescued, they appoint a black woman called Lilith to lead the humans in this collaborative effort. It is Lilith's problem in *Dawn* to convince others of her kind that the unequal relationship between them and the Oankali will work to the humans' advantage. This proves to be an impossible task since the Oankali have transformed humans to the extent that two of the most intimate of acts, sexual intercourse and procreation, cannot be completed without their intervention.

Rites describes the recolonization of an Earth where the unequal relationship between the Oankalis and humans is still a central concern. Some humans, the "resisters," refuse to settle with the Oankali. Unable to procreate, they establish oppositional communities which have no children and therefore no hope. They resort to stealing children from the human-Oankali settlements. Lilith's son, Akin, is one such hostage; he becomes sympathetic to the resisters' plight and champions their rights. Here, as in her other novels, Butler debates the issues of power, unequal relationships between groups, and the constituent elements of human nature.

Butler believes that human nature is fundamentally violent and therefore flawed. The origin of violence, she suggests, lies in the human genetic structure, which is responsible for the contradictory impulses towards intelligence and hierarchy. These two conflicting impulses inevitably propel humans to wage war. In *Rites,* she calls this flaw the "Human Contradiction," or simply, the "Contradiction." Connected to this trait is an inability to tolerate differences, usually physical differences of race and gender. For Butler, there is a pervasive human need to alienate from oneself those who appear to be different—i.e., to create Others. Even when she describes the diminution of racial antagonisms among humans upon encountering a new extraterrestrial Other, she foregrounds how we seize upon biological differences between the two species to reassert, yet again, notions of inferiority and discrimination. For her, the human propensity to create the Other can never be transcended: the end of racial discrimination must coincide with the rise of some kind of similar discrimination based upon biological differences, which accordingly continue to play a role in future social orders.

Butler generally adheres to the notion that men are intrinsically more violent than women. It is true that her women characters occasionally commit violent acts (Anyanwu in *Wild Seed,* for example, often kills), and they sometimes exercise power in an arbitrary and authoritarian way (as Mary does in *Mind of My Mind*). But the violence that her female characters commit is done for survival and defense, either of the self or of the community. Males exercise power for other, less laudable, reasons. In *Rites,* Butler is especially clear about the intensity of the destructive genes peculiar to human-born males. As one Oankali says of males born of human women and Oankali males: "They bear more of the Human Contradiction than any other people." To accept Butler's notion that males are genetically (i.e., inherently) more violent than women is to accept an essentialist view of human nature similar to that of some radical feminists, such as Julia Kristeva and Luce Irigaray. As I will subsequently show, it is also connected to a problematic understanding of the subject which has roots going back to the women's movement of the late 19th and early 20th century.

Another characteristic of human nature as Butler sees it is its static quality, evinced in a human incapacity to change

in response to radically altered conditions. The force by which humans are wedded to their biologically-determined natures and their inability to transcend it she makes clear in her "Xenogenesis" series. Even when extraterrestrials initiate change, humans continue to manifest the same qualities of violence, cruelty, and domination over others. In a crucial debate in *Rites,* Akin argues with his elders about the matter of human independence from the Oankali. He takes a materialist position: if humans were allowed to live in a new and harsh environment, they would be forced to cooperate and transcend "the Contradiction." The Oankali's response is one of informed skepticism: they know the human capacity for self-destruction is unavoidable. Their certainty, Akin realizes, "was an Oankali certainty. A certainty of the flesh. They had read Human genes and reviewed Human behavior. They knew what they knew."

Butler's unmediated connections between biology and behavior have an implicit corollary: that abandoning the human body is a necessary prerequisite for real human alteration. This represents an essentially retrogressive view of politics (i.e., of collective human action), which she never sees as offering the solution to social or political problems. Her conditions for fundamental social change are such as to postpone it indefinitely.

How Butler portrays politics is intimately related to her vision of human nature as a biologically-determined entity. The public arena of politics, where dialogue and dissent occur, is nullified in most of her novels by her construction of permanent states of emergency, which pre-empt any full exploration of the moral and ethical dimensions of political decisions; there can be no room for real debate when the very survival of the individual or group is at stake. Furthermore, the relationship between ruler and ruled is never egalitarian for Butler, but is always a matter of dominance and submission consistent with her essentialist view of human nature. In *Dawn,* for example, the aliens unilaterally appoint Lilith to a leadership position. Since human nature is for Butler a known, finite, and unchanging entity, she cannot view human politics other than deterministically: not as an open-ended series of unfolding events latent with Possibility, but as a process whose result is foregone and predictable. For her, human politics is not an arena for the exercise of choice of freedom, and it offers no opportunities for the improvement of the human condition.

What she denies to humans she invests in her description of alien societies: her aspirations for a more humane community, where consensus is reached through communication and dissent. Alien politics she portrays as being different from and superior to human political activity; indeed, Oankali decision-making (in *Dawn* and *Rites*) figures as utopian. Among the Oankali, true consensus, non-hierarchical communitarianism, and truthful communication can be found. Adults communicate non-verbally by way of their tentacles, a mode of communication which does not allow for deceit or ambiguity; and they achieve consensus by totally coalescing with one another, after which they resume their separate individualities.

Although political theorists from Locke on have expressed reservations about it, the communitarian impulse borne of the merging of individuals with the group often figures as a desideratum in feminist utopian S[cience] F[iction]. Yet that impulse, as it exhibits itself in Butler's "Patternist" and "Xenogenesis" series, is problematic on at least two counts. One of these has to do with the non-verbal communication which serves as the means for resolving differences in points of view and thereby achieving unity. This, after all, is a human impossibility, given the nature of our language and how we use it. The other difficulty pertains to fusion via the creation of a group mind, as Butler depicts it in the Oankali—or as advocated, for that matter, by other feminist S[cience] F[iction] writers. It represents a notion of community which we would do well to approach with caution, as it resonates all too closely with certain ideologies inimical to individual freedom—e.g., fascism.

Is it possible, then, to describe Butler as utopian at all? Though the answer is not clear-cut, the question admits of an affirmative response for two reasons. First, she allows (unique) individuals occasionally to escape the grip of instinct and genetic structure on human behavior. Alanna in *Survivor,* for example, reaches out to other species and decides to make her life with the Terkohn tribe. Other characters, such as the infected crew of Clay's Ark, commit suicide rather than return to Earth and infect their fellow humans with the extraterrestrial organism killing them—an act of considerable self-control. Such examples, indicating that Butler has not completely written off the human ability to change for the better, thus leave open the possibility for utopia.

Second, the various alien societies that she constructs with such imagination and detail not only stand in the sort of political comparison to existing human social arrangements which is typical of utopias, but are also ideal in themselves. Such is the case with the Oankali social order described in *Dawn,* for instance. The Oankali live harmoniously in extended families; and they have developed a post-industrial technology—dependent upon genetic engineering—which makes work pleasurable for them. That technology, moreover, obviates class strife—in which regard, it is significant that Butler decides to link the Oankali organically to tools that are also sentient beings. Appropriating Ernst Bloch's methodology of seeing and decoding the latent utopian alternatives concealed in all cultural objects, no matter how regressive, and using his concept of cultural surplus, we can read Butler's works as expressing hope for unam-

biguous and truthful communication, for long life free of all diseases, for the elimination of racism and the tolerance of differences among people, for pleasurable work, peace and dignity, and for total social communion—all of them authentic and time-honored utopian wishes.

The presence of such yearnings, however, is very much compromised by the fact that their vehicle of agency is other than human. In certain respects, too, any utopian transformation that Butler envisions is far from being radical. Her conservatism surfaces in her description of sexual alternatives made possible by the Oankali: sexual pleasure involves eschewing all contact with human genitalia, and includes monogamy for the aliens. So, too, her utopianism is rendered passive (and even regressive) when she depicts the causes of human strife, leading to nuclear holocaust, as being beyond human control and political intervention. Furthermore, a concurrent dystopian tendency has become evident in her works, most clearly witnessed in *Ark.*

2. Dystopia. Rather than approaching the notions of utopia and dystopia as incompatible opposites, I would suggest that a more valid analysis can be found in a relatively recent article by Soren Baggesen. He introduces the provocative distinction between two kinds of pessimism: utopian and dystopian. Utopian pessimism occurs when dystopian elements in a text are depicted as occurring in, and caused by, specific historical forces. This type of dystopianism is open-ended in its materialism. Dystopian pessimism, on the other hand, assumes that dystopia is inevitable because its origins are ontological or otherwise metaphysical. In this view, the reasons proposed for social degeneration cannot be successfully countered because they are transcultural and transhistorical; pessimistic dystopias are thus close-ended and idealistic. Baggesen's analysis presents a new way of looking at the overlapping boundaries between utopian and dystopian thinking, and suggests that while dystopian pessimism remains anti-utopian and conservative, open-ended dystopias are essentially progressive.

Many dystopian texts serve to warn readers about impending catastrophes; they are involved in what Sheldon Wolin, in a discussion of one function of political theory, calls "posting warnings." These texts in effect warn that if certain social trends go unchecked, the future will exhibit certain specific undesirable qualities. As Wolin writes: "a warning is usually made by a person who feels some involvement with the party or persons being warned; a warning, in short, tokens a commitment that is lacking in [scientifically neutral] predictions." Thus, the overt pessimism of a specific dystopia is often belied by the covert utopian hope that readers will change the trajectory of their society. Such dystopias, then, are intimately connected to utopias in offering oblique hope to the reader.

It seems evident, in the context of Baggesen's and Wolin's arguments, that Butler's dystopianism is pessimistic not because Earth and its civilizations are almost lost, but because the causes of catastrophe are depicted deterministically as unavoidable. For this reason, her critiques of human violence and prejudice are not traced back to their particular social or political foundations. Her dystopianism is therefore anti-utopian in the deterministic definition of human nature. It may be that Butler's sensitivity to the increasing conservatism of the contemporary social and political order, which has made substantial inroads upon Afro-American communities sooner and more systematically than others, has led her to adopt a position of pessimistic, or anti-utopian, dystopianism.

3. Ideology, Feminine Utopias, and Racial Estrangement. To understand the ideological contents of Butler's novels, it is useful to place them within, and compare them to, the post-1970 subgenre of feminist S[cience] F[iction] which was informed by the second wave of the women's movement. Chronologically, Butler belongs to this generation of writers; and inasmuch as her works have many similarities to, as well as some differences from, that tradition, their ideological content can best be understood in its context.

The women's movement of the 1960s, '70s, and '80s influenced a number of women writers to explore Movement ideas and theories in their S[cience] F[iction]. The long and sustained connections between women S[cience] F[iction] writers and their utopian output on the one hand, and the Movement's political theories and practices on the other, has been well documented by Sarah Lefanu. Women writers framed their critiques, demands, solutions, and strategies in light of the Movement's political struggles. One of the key debates in the women's movement and in women-authored S[cience] F[iction] involved efforts to define human nature. Other issues included concerns about the impact of technology on the environment, about child-rearing, about relationships between the sexes, about power, especially in connection with language, and about various notions of family and community.

Taken as a group, feminist utopias appear to share a number of significant political characteristics. One of the most obvious is their elaboration of a basic model of community: a cooperative society which emphasizes the organic nature of its ties and the overriding importance of the common good, enjoys a high degree of unity and cohesion, and is liable to no serious tension between the individual and the larger community. Often these societies represent a conflation of the public and private spheres: personal relationships are foregrounded and less attention is given to descriptions of reorganized economic and political institutions. Many utopias which nostalgically depict agrarian societies show a late-capitalist concern for the ecology. Given the common origin of these texts, it is not surprising that they exhibit similarities in their visions of utopia, their criticisms of existing society, and their suggestions for alternative social and political institutions. Many of the ideals expressed in these works fall fully within the utopian tradition.

It is possible to discern, inhering within the feminist agenda described in these utopias, a number of notions which may once have had revolutionary potential, but which have been coopted by a flexible and tenacious ruling class to negate the opportunities for genuine, radical, social change and to legitimate its position of power. Although there is more than one ideologically-suspect concept in many feminist S[cience] F[iction] utopias—for instance, a concept of leadership which is often ascriptive and non-democratic—I shall focus here on comparing the views of human nature proposed in many of these feminist utopias with that depicted in Butler's works.

Butler's support for the notion of disparate human natures resulting from biological differences is an ideological element which her works share with many Anglo-American feminist utopias. This belief assumes that women have natures dissimilar from men's; and it is expressed in any feminist utopia which depicts women as ontologically nurturing and pacifist and their thinking as nonlinear and circular. It is important to note that this characterization of women's nature is not new, and was probably never a radical concept. As Jean Elshtain points out, the leadership of the first women's movement (at the turn of the century) adopted, for tactical purposes, the idea that women had different, and morally superior, natures. Historically, this notion was formulated and utilized by men to exclude women from the public arena, and it thus developed into an ideology of difference. As it was integrated into the first wave of the women's movement, this ideology permitted that movement's leadership to claim suffrage rights in order that women might "cleanse" and "purify" the arena of politics; but ironically, what the suffragists accepted and perpetuated was male hegemony.

Works such as Charlotte Perkins Gilman's *Herland* (1915), although separated from contemporary feminist utopias by more than 50 years and by a vastly different political landscape, share with post-1970 texts many of the same assumptions about gender differences. It is ironic that the ideology of gender difference, which owes its construction to forces inimical to women's equality, has once again been incorporated into the feminist movement. By espousing the view that women are "naturally" nurturing, strong, and pacifist, these utopias perpetuate an idealist and regressive view of human nature and politics. Butler, in describing her heroines as nurturing, freedom-loving women who employ violence only for the sake of survival, shares with other feminist S[cience] F[iction] writers the same truncated assumptions about women's and men's natures even though she does not place gender concerns conspicuously at the center of her novels.

There is one important difference between Butler's works and those of her Anglo sisters, however, which points to what can only be described as a failure of the liberal imagination of feminist S[cience] F[iction], and by implication, of the second women's movement. Butler's novels contain an implicit and internal critique of and rebuke to one aspect of liberal feminist ideology: its claim to speak for all women, regardless of class or color—a claim founded upon the assumption of a transhistorical and transcultural, engendered unity of all women. Apart from Butler, Dorothy Bryant's *The Kin of Ata Are Waiting for You* (1976), Sally Gearhart's *The Wanderground* (1979), and Marge Piercy's *Woman on the Edge of Time* (1976) pretty well exhaust the examples of S[cience] F[iction] by American women writers who depict futures where populations are not entirely white or where characters of color are portrayed in weakened circumstances; and as Robert Crossley points out, this has been true of the entire genre since the 1940s. All Butler's novels, on the other hand, contain people of diverse races as well as cultures—Africans, Afro-Americans, Anglo-Saxons, and Asians, for example—who function as major characters and whose racial diversity Butler celebrates.

The failure of the feminist imagination that Butler in effect reveals, while it is probably unintentional, is instructive in that it points out the essentially liberal, or non-radical, critique many feminist writers offer of the inequitable, racially discriminatory order of contemporary post-industrial capitalism. In their depiction of all-Anglo utopias, feminist S[cience] F[iction] writers neither criticize racial discrimination nor anticipate a future which would correct the wrongs of a fundamental social, political, and economic injustice. It might be added that the omission is all the more unaccountable in view of the fact that many of the white women involved in the US Civil Rights Movement of the 1950s and '60s subsequently used their experiences and its philosophical framework as the basis for promoting women's rights.

Butler's works thus constitute an implied critique of much feminist S[cience] F[iction] utopian writing, and at the same time represent a more democratic and egalitarian movement in this body of fiction. Her works serve to racially estrange her readers from their environs, and they thereby strengthen and enrich the feminist utopian tradition in S[cience] F[iction]. The inclusion of characters of color, however, does not in itself signify a radical overhauling of

this form of writing, as my discussion of Butler's pessimism has I hope made clear.

In the final political analysis, Butler's vision of the future is a peculiar mix of utopianism, anti-utopianism, and ideology. Expressing as they do many utopian hopes and desires, her works contain a muted critique of the current political order. Yet in denying the possibility of change through political and collective human action, she softens her critique and situates her utopia beyond human reach. This is not to say that the utopian, anti-utopian, and ideological dialectics found in Butler are peculiar to her novels alone. Recent articles by H.-J. Schulz and Carl Freedman, for instance, perhaps indicate a shift towards a more critical evaluation of S[cience] F[iction], whose utopian dynamic theoretical discourse has by and large up to now portrayed as being predominant. As more research on the dynamics of ideology and utopia in S[cience] F[iction] is carried out, the general act specific to S[cience] F[iction]—whether the genre be defined as presenting social alternatives or as incorporating Utopia by virtue of its explicit anticipation of the future's ontological pull—can be interrogated with greater specificity. The existence of anti-utopian forces both in the social order and in texts like Butler's leaves the outcome of that reappraisal in doubt.

Octavia Butler with Randall Kenan (interview date Spring 1991)

SOURCE: "An Interview with Octavia Butler," in *Callaloo*, Vol. 14, No. 2, Spring, 1991, pp. 495-504.

[*In the following interview, Butler discusses her career, her writing style, and her inspiration.*]

Octavia E. Butler is something of a phenomenon. Since 1976 she has published nine novels, more than any other black woman in North America, and even more amazing: She writes science fiction. Having won all the major S[cience] F[iction] awards, (a Nebula and two Hugos), she has gained a substantial cult following, as well as critical acclaim, particularly for her 1979 novel, **Kindred,** *reissued in 1988 in the prestigious Beacon Black Women Writers Series.* **Kindred** *is the tale of Dana Franklin, a black woman from an interracial marriage in L.A. in 1976, who is mysteriously plucked back in time on a number of occasions to 1824 Maryland and to a moral dilemma involving her white ancestor. A book often compared to* Metamorphosis *for its uncannily successful blend of fact and fantasy, it is considered by many to be a modern classic. Butler manages to use the conventions of science fiction to subvert many long held assumptions about race, gender and power; in her hands* *these devices become adept metaphors for reinterpreting and reconsidering our world. Strong women, multiracial societies and aliens who challenge humanity's penchant for destruction inform her work and lift it beyond genre.*

Her works include: **Patternmaster** (1976); **Mind of My Mind** (1977); **Survivor** (1978); **Wild Seed** (1980); **Clay's Ark** (1984); *and the* Xenogenesis *trilogy:* **Dawn** (1987); **Adulthood Rites** (1988); *and* **Imago** (1989). *Butler has also published a number of short stories and novellas, including the award-winning,* **"Bloodchild"** *in 1984. She is working on the first book in a new series.*

Octavia Butler lives in Los Angeles. This phone interview took place on November 3, 1990.

[Kenan:] Do you prefer to call your work speculative fiction, as opposed to science fiction or fantasy?

[Butler:] No, actually I don't. Most of what I do is science fiction. Some of the things I do are fantasy. I don't like the labels, they're marketing tools, and I certainly don't worry about them when I'm writing. They are also inhibiting factors; you wind up not getting read by certain people, or not getting sold to certain people because they think they know what you write. You say science fiction and everybody thinks *Star Wars* or *Star Trek.*

But the kind of constructs you use, like time travel for example in **Kindred,** *or . . .*

Kindred is fantasy. I mean literally, it is fantasy. There's no science in **Kindred.** I mean, if I was told that something was science fiction I would expect to find something dealing with science in it. For instance, **Wild Seed** is more science fiction than most people realize. The main character is dealing with medical science, but she just doesn't know how to talk about it. With **Kindred** there's absolutely no science involved. Not even the time travel. I don't use a time machine or anything like that. Time travel is just a device for getting the character back to confront where she came from.

In earlier interviews you mentioned that there's an interesting parallel between your perception of your mother's life and some of the themes you explore in your work. You spoke of how in your growing-up you saw her in an invisible role in her relationship with the larger society. How have certain ideas about your mother's life consciously or unconsciously affected your work?

My mother did domestic work and I was around sometimes when people talked about her as if she were not there, and I got to watch her going in back doors and generally being treated in a way that made me . . . I spent a lot of my childhood being ashamed of what she did, and I think one of the reasons I wrote **Kindred** was to resolve my feelings, because after all, I ate because of what she did . . . **Kindred** was a kind of reaction to some of the things going on during the sixties when people were feeling ashamed of, or more strongly, angry with their parents for not having improved things faster, and I wanted to take a person from today and send that person back to slavery. My mother was born in 1914 and spent her early childhood on a sugar plantation in Louisiana. From what she's told me of it, it wasn't that far removed from slavery, the only difference was they could leave, which eventually they did.

I was also curious about the amount of research that you do when you're working on a book.

It varies greatly. With **Kindred,** I did go to Maryland and spend some time. Well, I mostly spent my time at the Enoch Pratt Free Library in Baltimore and at the Maryland Historical Society. I also went to the Eastern Shore to Talbot County, to Easton actually, and just walked around, wandered the streets and probably looked fairly disreputable. I didn't have any money at the time, so I did all my traveling by Greyhound and Trailways and I stayed at a horrible dirty little hotel . . . it was kind of frightening really . . . I didn't know what I was doing . . . I had missed the tours of the old houses for that year, I didn't realize that they were not ongoing but seasonal. Anyway, I went down to Washington, D.C. and took a Grayline bus tour of Mount Vernon and that was as close as I could get to a plantation. Back then they had not rebuilt the slave cabins and the tour guide did not refer to slaves but to "servants" and there was all this very carefully orchestrated dancing around the fact that it had been a slave plantation. But still I could get the layout, I could actually see things, you know, the tools used, the cabins that had been used for working. That, I guess, was the extent of my away from home research on **Kindred.** I did a lot more at the libraries.

I'm assuming that entailed slave narratives and . . .

Yes, yes. Very much so. It was not fun . . . It's not pleasure reading. As a matter of fact, one of the things I realized when I was reading the slave narrative—I think I had gotten to one by a man who was explaining how he had been sold to a doctor who used him for medical experiments—was that I was not going to be able to come anywhere near presenting slavery as it was. I was going to have to do a somewhat cleaned-up version of slavery, or no one would be willing to read it. I think that's what most fiction writers do. They almost have to.

But at the same time, I think you address the problem of accuracy and distance with amazing intelligence and depth. In place of visceral immediacy you give us a new *understanding of how far removed we are from manumission. For example, the scene where Dana in **Kindred** witnesses the patrollers catching the runaway, you address this issue straight on; how she was unprepared to bear witness to such horror. So at the same time, you are making the reader aware of how brutal it all is, was, and doubly, how much we're separated from that past reality and how television and movies have prejudiced us or in some cases blinded us to that fact.*

The strange thing is with television and movies, I mean, they've made violence so cartoonishly acceptable . . . I was talking to a friend of mine the other day about the fact that some kids around the L.A. area, on Halloween, kids around fourteen and fifteen, found a younger child with Halloween candy and they shot him and took it away from him . . . Now when I was a kid, I knew bullies who beat up little kids and took away their candy, but it would not have occurred to them to go out with a knife or gun to do that, you know. This is a totally different subject, but it's one that interests me right now. Just what in the world is to be done, to bring back a sense of proportion of respect for life?

*But another thing that makes **Kindred** so painful and artful is the way that you translate the moral complexity and the choices that have to be made between Dana and her white husband and not only in the past but in the present.*

I gave her that husband to complicate her life.

And even though the roles in many ways are more affixed by society in the past, she has to make similar choices in the present; so it's almost as though time were an illusion.

Well, as I said, I was really dealing with some 1960s feelings when I wrote this book. So I'm not surprised that it strikes you that way, as a matter of fact I'm glad. I meant it to be complicated.

Violence also seems to be a part of the fabric of your oeuvre, *in a sense. The fact that Dana loses her arm, in* **Kindred,** *which is inexplicable on one level . . .*

I couldn't really let her come all the way back. I couldn't let her return to what she was, I couldn't let her come back whole and that, I think, really symbolizes her not coming back whole. Antebellum slavery didn't leave people quite whole.

But also, for instance, in "Bloodchild." [Note: *In this story human beings on another planet have entered in a pact with an indigenous species who implant eggs in the humans for incubation. When the eggs hatch, the hu-*

mans are cut open. Not everyone survives.] *I mean, the idea that sacrifice has to be . . .*

Not sacrifice. No, no . . .

You wouldn't call it sacrifice? Cutting people open?

No, no . . . **"Bloodchild"** is very interesting in that men tend to see a horrible case of slavery, and women tend to see that, oh well, they had caesareans, big deal. [*Laughter*].

So really, you wouldn't characterize that as being violent?

Not anymore than . . . well, remember during the Middle Ages in Europe, I don't know what it was like in Africa, if a woman died giving birth, they would try to save the baby.

Over the woman?

In this case, they were trying to save both of them and, I mean, it's not some horrible thing that I made up in that sense. In earlier science fiction there tended to be a lot of conquest: you land on another planet and you set up a colony and the natives have their quarters some place and they come in and work for you. There was a lot of that, and it was, you know, let's do Europe and Africa and South America all over again. And I thought no, no, if we do get to another world inhabited by intelligent beings, in the first place we're going to be at the end of a very, very, very, long transport line. It isn't likely that people are going to be coming and going, you know, not even the way they did between England and this country, for instance. It would be a matter of a lifetime or more, the coming and going. So you couldn't depend on help from home. Even if you had help coming, it wouldn't help you. It might help your kids, if you survived to have any, but on the other hand it might not. So you are going to have to make some kind of deal with the locals: in effect, you're going to have to pay the rent. And that's pretty much what those people have done in **"Bloodchild."** They have made a deal. Yes, they can stay there but they are going to have to pay for it. And I don't see the slavery, and I don't see this as particularly barbaric. I mean if human beings were able to make that good a deal with another species, I think it would be miraculous. [*Laughs*] Actually. I think it would be immensely more difficult than that.

*Fascinating and faultlessly logical. But at the same time—again with the idea of violence—the relationship between Doro and Anyanwu in **Wild Seed**.* [Note: *Set in seventeenth-century Africa, eighteenth-century New York, and nineteenth-century Louisiana, this book is the struggle between Doro, a mindforce, and Anyanwu, a shape shifter, in their attempts, each, to create a new race. A novel of fantasy and science.*] *That takes on a dif-*

ferent paradigm. They are extremely violent to one another.

That's just men and women!

[Laughs] But particularly in their various metamorphoses, when she becomes a leopard, or the sheer number of people Doro kills. It's a sort of natural violence. Or a violence of survival, I should say . . .

It's not something I put there to titillate people, if that's what you mean. [Laughs] I don't do that. As a matter of fact, I guess the worse violence is not between the two of them, but it's around them, it's what's happening to the people around them who are not nearly so powerful.

In your work it does seem to be a given that this is a violent universe and you don't romanticize it in any respect.

I hope not, I haven't tried to. I think probably the most violent of my books were the early ones. A friend brought this to my attention the other day because she was just reading some of my stuff. She said that she was surprised at the amount of violence in **Patternmaster** and casual violence at that. [Note: *The first in her "Patternist" novels, this book initiates the battle between the Patternists (humans with psionic powers) and the Clayarks (disease-mutated human quadrupeds).*] I said it probably comes from how young I was when I wrote it. I think that it is a lot easier to not necessarily romanticize it, but to accept it without comment when you're younger. I think that men and women are more likely to be violent when they are younger.

You have mentioned the African myths and lore that you used in **Wild Seed.** *Can you talk more about that? I didn't realize that you had gone to such pains.*

I used in particular, the myth of Atagbusi, who was an Onitsha Ibo woman. She was a shape-shifter who benefited her people while she was alive and when she died a market-gate was named after her, a gate at the Onitsha market. It was believed that whoever used this market-gate was under her protection . . .

Doro comes from an adolescent fantasy of mine to live forever and breed people. And when I began to get a little more sense, I guess you could say, and started to work with Doro, I decided that he was going to be a Nubian, because I wanted him to be somehow associated with ancient Egypt. And by then his name was already Doro, and it would have been very difficult to change it. So I went to the library and got this poor, dog-eared, ragged Nubian-English dictionary. I looked up the word Doro, and the word existed and it meant: *the direction from which the sun comes; the east.*

That was perfect, especially since I had pretty much got-

ten Emma Daniels, who came before the name Anyanwu, but I had been looking through names for her, Igbo names, and I found a myth having to do with the sun and the moon. Anyway the problem with that is: I lost it. I didn't write it down and I never found it again and all I had was one of the names: Anyanwu, meaning the sun. That worked out perfectly with Doro, the East. So I wound up putting them together.

Such rich etymological and cultural resonance. It's almost as if the African lore itself is using you as a medium.

Which leads me to a slightly different, but related topic. You seem to be exploring the idea of miscegenation on many different levels throughout your work. In Xenogenesis *it seems to reach a new peak. [Note: In the trilogy the alien Oankali join with human nuclear war survivors to create through genetic engineering a new species, better able to survive than both its progenitors.] Over the years you've been dealing with sex, race, gender; but here you're able to raise it yet another complicated step.*

[Laughter]

Seriously. In **Kindred** *miscegenation is quite literal. But in* **Dawn, Adulthood Rites,** *and* **Imago,** *genetics put an odd twist on an old idea.*

One of the things that I was most embarrassed about in my novel **Survivor** is my human characters going off to another plant and finding other people they could immediately start having children with. Later I thought, oh well, you can't really erase embarrassing early work, but you don't have to repeat it. So I thought if I were going to bring people together from other worlds again, I was at least going to give them trouble. So I made sure they didn't have compatible sex organs, not to mention their other serious differences. And of course there are still a lot of biological problems that I ignore.

How many other black science fiction writers do you know personally?

I know two others personally. [Steve Barnes and Samuel R. Delaney]

Any other black women?

I don't know any black women who write science fiction. Lots of white women, but I don't know any black women—which is not to say there aren't any. But I don't know any.

I couldn't compare you to other winners of the Nebula and the Hugo Awards. [Note: The Nebula Award is given by science fiction writers and the Hugo Award by the fans.] When you interact with your fans, how do they react to your being black and a woman? Is there a great deal of interest in the novelty of your being practically the only black women sci-fi writer?

No. If they're curious about that, they tend not to tell me and I'm just as happy to have it that way. No, I've been in S[cience] F[iction] for a long time and I know people. I go to S[cience] F[iction] conventions and no matter where I go in the country, I generally see someone I know. S[cience] F[iction] is kind of a small town and there is no problem with enjoying yourself. Obviously in some places you will meet with some nastiness, but it isn't general. The only place I was ever called "nigger," had someone scream nigger at me in public, was in *Boston,* for goodness sakes. It wasn't a person going to a conference, it was just a stranger who happened to see me standing, waiting for a traffic light with other S[cience] F[iction] people who were headed toward the convention.

In light of that question, how do your readers react to the fact that most of your main protagonists are women and more often black? Does that ever come up?

Yes, as a matter of fact it came up more before I was visible. I wrote three books before anybody knew who I was, aside from a few people here in L.A. And I got a few letters asking why? The kind of letters that hedge around wondering why I write about black people; but there were few such letters. People who are bigots probably don't want to talk to me. I hear signs of bigotry every now and then when someone slips up, someone's manners fail, or something slips out. But there isn't a lot of that kind of thing.

Speaking of women in science fiction, a lot of black women writers whom I've been in contact with lately speak of the ongoing debate between black women and feminism. I'm sure the feminist debate is ongoing within science fiction. Do you find yourself at all caught up within that debate?

Actually it isn't very much. That flared up big during the seventies and now it's a foregone conclusion. Not that somebody is particularly a feminist, but if somebody is it's their business . . . I was on a little early Sunday morning TV show a while back, and the hostess was a black woman and there were two other black women writers, a poet and a playwright and me. And the hostess asked as a near final question how we felt about feminism and the other two women said they didn't think much of it, they assumed it was for white people. I said that I thought it was just as important to have equal rights for women as it was to have equal rights for black people and so I felt myself to be very much a feminist.

And you feel your works then actively reflect feminist ideals?

Well, they do in a sense that women do pretty much what they want to do. One of the things that I wanted to deal with in the Xenogenesis books, especially the first one, was some of the old S[cience] F[iction] myths that kind of winked out during the seventies but were really prevalent before the seventies. Myths where, for instance, people crash land on some other planet and all of a sudden they go back to "Me Tarzan, you Jane," and the women seem to accept this perfectly as all right, you know. We get given away like chattel and we get treated like . . . well, you get the picture. I thought I'd do something different.

There seems to be a movement in your work from a view of continuance to a view of apocalypse. For instance in **Clay's Ark** *the civilization has been attacked by a microorganism. But in* Xenogenesis *there is a postapocalyptic scenario. Has your thinking about that changed? I understand there is a huge debate in science fiction now about writers who tend to wipe the population clean and start over again, as opposed to writers like William Gibson and the other cyberpunk writers, who take as a given that we are going to survive somehow, some way and then extrapolate from that assumption.*

I don't think we are more likely to survive than any other species especially considering that we have overspecialized ourselves into an interesting corner. But on the other hand, my new book isn't a postapocalyptic type of book. I'm not really talking about an earth that has been wiped clean of most people. As a matter of fact earth is as populated as ever and in fact more so because it takes place in the future. The greenhouse effect has intensified and there has been a certain amount of starvation and agricultural displacement. There are real problems. Some of our prime agricultural land won't be able to produce the crops that it's been producing and Canada will have the climate, but on the other hand Canada caught the brunt of the last few ice ages and has lost a lot of top soil, which wound up down here. These are big problems and they are not sexy as problems so they are not the prime problems in the series that I am working on, but they're in the background. It's not a postapocalyptic book, it's a book in which society has undergone severe changes, but continues.

I am really impressed by the way your characters often speak, almost epigrammatically, not to say that it is stiff dialogue, but you achieve a sort of majesty, particularly when you're talking about the human species; how we interact with one another. There is a lot of wisdom in what you have your characters say, without sounding didactic. What are your literary influences to that effect, both science fiction and non-science fiction, what writers?

All sorts of things influence me. I let things influence me. If they catch my interests I let them take hold. When I was growing up I read mostly science fiction. I remember getting into Harlan Ellison's class and at one point having him say, science fiction fans read too much science fiction; and he was no doubt right, but as an adolescent that was all I read except for school work. I guess the people that I learned the most from were not necessarily the best writers (although Theodore Sturgeon was one of them and I think he was definitely one of the best writers). They were people who impressed me with their ideas. I didn't know what good writing was frankly, and I didn't have any particular talent for writing so I copied a lot of the old pulp writers in the way I told a story. Gradually I learned that that wasn't the way I wanted to write.

But as for what influences me now, well, for instance I was reading a book about Antarctica . . . It was a kind of a difficult book to read because it involved so much suffering. Antarctica is probably as close to another planet as we've got on this earth . . . I thought what if I had a bunch of outcasts who had to go live in a very uncertain area and I made it a parched, devastated part of future southern California because there are areas here where the hills fall into the canyons and cliffs crumble off into the sea even without earthquakes to help them along. My characters go to this ruined place as though it were another world and the people they meet there are adapted to their new environment. They won't be savages crawling through the hills. I wanted them to have found some other way to cope because obviously some people would have to. Not everybody would go ape or become members of gangs and go around killing people. There would be some people who would try to put together a decent life, whatever their problems were . . .

Really, I think that's what I mean about something influencing me. The book I read didn't influence me to write about Antarctica but it influenced me to take a piece of the earth as we know it and see what it could become without playing a lot of special effects games.

Are there other literary or nonliterary sources that you see consciously on unconsciously affected your work?

Every place I've lived is a nonliterary influence, every place and every person who has impressed me enough to keep my attention for a while. If something attracts my attention I am perfectly willing to follow that interest. I can remember when I was writing **Clay's Ark,** I would be listening to the news and I would hear something and it would be im-

mediately woven into the novel. As a matter of fact some of the things that I found out after I finished **Clay's Ark** were even more interesting. Down in El Salvador I guess about a year after I finished **Clay's Ark** I read that it was the habit of many of the rich people to armor-plate Jeep Wagoneers and use them as family cars and that's exactly the vehicle that my character was using and I was glad I had chosen well.

Science fiction writers—with a few notable exceptions like Samuel Delaney—are often slapped about the wrists because people feel that their writing styles are wooden and are merely there to get the plot across. Your writing has almost biblical overtones at times. Have you consciously striven for such a style?

I've developed my love for words late in life really. I guess it was when realized that I was writing pulp early on. I realized I didn't want to. I read some of my own writing, which is a very painful thing to do and I could see what was the matter with it, having gotten some distance in time from it. And I realized that there were things that I would have to learn even before that. Back during the 1960 election and the Kennedy Administration, that was when I began to develop into a news junkie. I was very interested in Kennedy and I would listen to his speeches and I guess I was about thirteen when he was elected, and I realized that half the time I couldn't figure out what he was saying and I felt really, really bad about that. I felt stupid. Although I didn't know it at the time, I'm a bit dyslexic. I realized that there was so much more to learn. You're always realizing there is so much out there that you don't know. That's when I began to teach myself as opposed to just showing up at school. I think that there comes a time when you just have to do that, when things have to start to come together for you or you don't really become an educated person. I suspect that has been the case for a lot of people, they just never start to put it all together.

Obviously, you write beautifully. So is it all organic in the sense that all these disparate ideas and themes fit together, that your interests coincided?

No, it's work. [*Laughs*] But you mean style. Yes, and it's something I can't talk about. It's very, very intimate. I make signs. The wall next to my desk is covered in signs and maps. The signs are to remind myself sometimes of things. For instance, a sign from a book called *The Art of Dramatic Writing* by Lagos Egri, it's a kind of a paraphrasing really; tension and conflict can be achieved through uncompromising characters in a death struggle. And just having signs on my wall to remind me of certain things that I need to remember to do in the writing; signs in black indelible ink. That sort of thing, it's kind of juvenile but it really helps me. But there are some things about the writing that are just so personal that you can't even talk about them.

I should ask in closing: Do you have any advice for young writers?

I have advice in just a few words. The first, of course, is to read. It's surprising how many people think they want to be writers but they don't really like to read books.

AMEN!!!!

And the second is to write, every day, whether you like it or not. Screw inspiration. The third is to forget about talent, whether or not you have any. Because it doesn't really matter. I mean, I have a relative who is extremely gifted musically, but chooses not to play music for a living. It is her pleasure, but it is not her living. And it could have been. She's gifted; she's been doing it ever since she was a small child and everyone has always been impressed with her. On the other hand, I don't feel that I have any particular literary talent at all. It was what I wanted to do, and I followed what I wanted to do, as opposed to getting a job doing something that would make more money, but it would make me miserable. This is the advice that I generally give to people who are thinking about becoming writers.

[Laughing] I don't know if I would agree that you have no literary talent. But that's your personal feeling.

It's certainly not a matter of sitting there and having things fall from the sky.

Orson Scott Card (review date January 1992)

SOURCE: A review of *Mind of My Mind, Patternmaster,* and *Survivor,* in *Fantasy & Science Fiction,* January, 1992, pp. 52-4.

[*In the following review, Card praises Butler for her development of the "psi" theme in her Patternist novels.*]

It's odd, I know, to review novels that are out of print or available only in British editions. But Octavia Butler is far too important a novelist—and these books are far too powerful—to be languishing out of print in the United States.

While it's true that her Xenogenesis books (**Dawn, Adulthood Rites, Imago**) are more satisfying as hard science fiction, and show how much power her storytelling has gained in the years of her career, the fact remains that these are wonderful, inventive novels that deserve to be read. They are even worth hunting down from mail-order and specialty stores until such time as a U.S. publisher gets on the stick and reissues them.

Those of you who have read **Wild Seed,** Butler's brilliant novel about Doro, the immortal who lives through the centuries by leaping from body to body as each one dies, and Emma, the shape-changing woman who learns to accommodate him and still find a measure of freedom and respect under his rule, know exactly what Butler is able to do with the "psi" theme that is so easily overdone. Indeed, from the copyright dates on the other novels in this series, one can suppose that she developed this future history during the late sixties or early seventies, when Zenna Henderson and other writers had brought psi stories to a position of temporary dominance in the field, rather the way that cyberpunk brought us a temporary oversupply of stories about computer-brain interfaces and criminal jet-sets.

But because she is Octavia Butler, her psi stories—even the earliest of them—have something special. In many ways, **Patternmaster,** which is the earliest of the Wild Seed books in copyright and the latest in storyline, is more magic romance than hard science fiction, as she follows the younger son of the Patternmaster on his quest to win free of his vicious older brother as he positions himself to succeed their father in control of the network of psionically gifted masters of the civilized world. Yet even in this early novel we can see Butler's keen sense of truth at work, making characters more real than they ever needed to be for this sort of tale. More important, we already can see her touching on the issues of freedom and slavery, power and responsibility that have made all her writings such vibrant studies of the ethics of power and submission. Butler understands as so few other writers do (least of all the libertarians) that some freedom must always be surrendered in order to retain any power to act at all. Her characters are faced with devastatingly difficult choices, and often take the less honorable but more practical choice of surviving in a world where they cannot act on their real preferences.

Survivor is another early work, in some ways only peripherally connected to **Patternmaster** and **Wild Seed,** but again dealing with a character who has to surrender some of her personal choices in order to stay alive long enough to have hope of a final victory. An outcast, she is taken in by missionaries who are leaving an Earth ravaged by war between psis and "clayarks." On another planet they are determined to maintain the purity of the human species, but instead find themselves being used as tools in a struggle between two rival bands of aliens. Only Alanna realizes that they have chosen the wrong side in this struggle, and will surely be destroyed.

Mind of My Mind is the immediate sequel to **Wild Seed,** and for those of us who loved that story (I even used it as my example of how science fiction exposition is handled in my book on writing s[cience] f[iction] and fantasy), it is a *very* satisfying continuation, though I was devastated at the rather callous way she concluded the final struggle between Doro and Mary, the first Patternmaster, and was also disappointed at how little use Butler made of Emma, whom I truly came to love in *Wild Seed.* But those are standard sequel-quibbles—that the author was too heartless with characters who loomed so large in earlier books! The new characters in *Mind of My Mind* are just as alive as any in *Wild Seed,* and Butler's exploration of people who are used to power and suddenly find themselves under someone else's control is clear-headed and brutally unsentimental. As always in Butler's best work, we're never quite sure whom to root for, for when it comes to power, no one who has it is pure, and yet it is easy to lose sympathy or interest in those who *lack* it. You are never quite sure where Butler herself stands on any of these moral issues, as she keeps subverting every moral position you suspect she has taken, until you finally realize that she has no "position" at all, except to observe: This is how power works, and how decent people *try* to control it, and how inevitably they fall short of their aspirations.

I look forward to hearing of all these books being back in print. If you haven't read Butler, you don't yet understand how rich the possibilities of science fiction can be. And the more you read her work, the better you understand how science fiction is the genre of literature *best* suited to teach us about the real world.

Michelle Erica Green (essay date 1994)

SOURCE: "'There Goes the Neighborhood': Octavia Butler's Demand for Diversity in Utopias," in *Utopian and Science Fiction by Women: Worlds of Difference,* edited by Jane L. Donawerth and Carol A. Kolmerten, Syracuse University Press, 1994, pp. 166-89.

[*In the following essay, Green discusses Butler's fiction in terms of its criticism of popular science fiction utopias and its social critique on such topics as racism and sexism.*]

Octavia E. Butler's *Dawn,* the first novel in the trilogy Xenogenesis, is an angry utopian novel, a scathing condemnation of the tendency of human beings to hate, repress, and attack differences they do not understand. It pleads for an end to fear and prejudice, insisting that aggressive social intervention must counteract the ancient hierarchical structures of thought that humans share with their closest animal relatives. The illustration on the jacket sleeve of *Dawn* ironically emphasizes Butler's cause for anger. Though the novel clearly identifies its heroine, Lilith Iyapo,

as a muscular black woman in her late twenties, the cover depicts a slender white girl apprehensively unwrapping what looks like a blanket from the body of a naked white woman. The girl is Lilith, here young, fair-skinned and delicate, peering shyly at the first potential friend she has had in years because she cannot look with eagerness at naked woman. Following Audre Lorde's description of the role of difference within a capitalist economy, the mass-market paperback industry thus puts its desire to reap profits from off-the-shelf sales of *Dawn* over the demands of the novel itself. In redrawing Lilith as a modest white girl rather than the powerful black heroine her creator described, the publishing industry allows forms of sexism, racism, ageism, and homophobia to be perpetuated on the cover of a novel that demands an end to prejudices and acceptance of differences.

I want to look closely at Butler's fiction and the criticism it directs at popular discourse, particularly at science fiction utopias created by recent feminist writers. I also want to consider the transformation of the utopian form when a writer such as Butler, who challenges various forms of cultural hegemony, adapts it for the purposes of social critique. Several of Butler's critics label her work "essentialist"—a term often used pejoratively by poststructuralist feminists to attack biologically based models of human behavior—because of her insistence that humans will behave inhumanely without a series of checks upon them. But Butler's "essentialism" is tricky; her novels focus on the exceptions to the rules she posits as human norms rather than on those who exemplify them.

Many recent women's utopias deal with contemporary problems by defusing the differences that cause conflicts to develop among people. Joanna Russ and Ursula Le Guin experiment with biological androgyny as a means for ending the battle of the sexes. Marge Piercy and Melissa Scott explore futures in which skin color and racial identity are unrelated. Sheri Tepper unites all people under one religion, while Suzy McKee Charnas erases political struggles under a classless anarchy. Feminist utopias of the past twenty years have launched a powerful attack on the ideologies, practices, and textual strategies of the patriarchy, which their authors posit as the principal source of the rejection of differences. Some texts, like Le Guin's *Left Hand of Darkness* and Scott's *Kindly Ones,* have done so by rejecting the binary construction of sexuality, insisting that the gender-defining characteristics of males and females are socially rather than biologically based. Others, like Cynthia Felice's *Double Nocturne* and Pamela Sargent's *Shore of Women,* have rescripted gender relations with the assumption that, even if men and women are fundamentally different, those differences need not lead to the oppression of women under patriarchy. By refusing to allow women to be posited as Other in a binary social and conceptual system, these and many additional novels defamiliarize patriarchy, calling for a world in which men and women can benefit rather than suffer from one another's differences.

Yet many of the texts that challenge that gender status quo ignore, erase, and repress other differences among people. Though Mattapoisett—the utopia in Piercy's *Woman on the Edge of Time*—nurtures people of many different ages, races, ethnic groups, sexual orientations, and interests, the differences among them seem only skin-deep. Some people have Southeast Asian features without any sense of Southeast Asian heritage, while others participate in Jewish religious services without any connection to the thousands of years of Jewish culture that preceded the founding of Mattapoisett. Again, in Charnas's *Motherlines,* because of the emphasis on the vast gulf between the genders, little attention is paid to the material differences between the women protagonists, who at times seem interchangeable. In *The Left Hand of Darkness,* neither race nor sexual preference operate as conceptual categories; if they exist at all, they pass unnoticed. Thus, despite their insistence that patriarchy can be overcome, relatively few utopian feminists seem able or willing to tackle even their own tendency to ignore, erase, and oppress human difference.

This tendency is the focus of Butler's critique of both human society and recent utopian fiction. Difference, disagreement, and diversity provide the life force of her utopias. Though the need to rethink women's roles in human society is a central concern, it is by no means the only problem attacked by Butler. Racism, class oppression, nationalism, religious intolerance, homophobia, and mistreatment of animals and handicapped people are all touched upon in Butler's critique of humanism—itself a form of prejudice here, for "humanism" accepts that human beings should be at the center of their own universes. Butler refuses to categorize people through biology, behavior or even species, demanding new solutions cultivated through a community based on differences. And just as Butler insists upon differences among people, she insists upon differences among utopias. Her work implicitly criticizes utopias by women that avoid conflicts stemming from difference and reject challenges and change from within. Her social critique resembles that of another feminist African-American, Audre Lorde, who writes,

> In a society where good is defined in terms of profit rather than in terms of human need, there must always be some group of people who, through systematized oppression, can be made to feel surplus, to occupy the place of the dehumanized inferior. . . . Institutionalized rejection of difference is an absolute necessity in a profit economy which needs outsiders as surplus people. As members of such an economy, we have *all* been pro-

grammed to respond to the human differences between us with fear and loathing. The future of our earth may depend upon the ability . . . to identify and develop new definitions of power and new patterns of relating across difference. The old definitions have not served us, nor the earth that supports us. The old patterns, no matter how cleverly rearranged to imitate progress, still condemn us to cosmetically altered repetitions of the same old exchanges, the same old guilt, hatred, recrimination, lamentation, and suspicion.

Expanding on Lorde's critique of capitalist society, Butler blames not only human greed for the creation of prejudice, but also the deep-rooted human compulsion to structure societies and thoughts hierarchically. Butler's fictions contain an oft-repeating warning that the human race has long been in the process of destroying itself—a warning that leads several critics to label her work dystopian rather than utopian. Butler's characters often do seem to be living in a nightmare rather than an ideal society; they find themselves trapped among aliens, powerless, angry, and frightened. All of them face the same dilemma: they must force themselves to evolve, accepting differences and rejecting a world view that centers upon their lives and values, or become extinct. In the Patternist books, the Xenogenesis trilogy, and **"Bloodchild,"** such evolution requires pan-human acceptance of alien ideas and values, leading to a merger with the aliens to create a new form of life. In **Kindred, "Speech Sounds"** and **"The Evening and the Morning and the Night,"** evolution involves one group of humans accepting "alien" ideas and values from another group of humans, taking personal responsibility for transforming themselves and the species.

Miscegenation: Bloodchild and Patternist Series

Octavia Butler once told an interviewer that she did not write utopian fiction: "I don't believe that imperfect humans can form a perfect society." But, as any number of texts from Thomas More's prototype onward have indicated, a utopia does not have to be a "perfect" society. "Utopia" is a Greek pun that can be read as "nowhere" (*utopia*) or "good place" (*eutopia*); literary utopias engage the paradox between these two meanings, straddling issues of locality, textuality, and ideology in an attempt to bridge the gap between fictional discourse and everyday life. Thus the utopian form is already a miscegenation of sorts, a blending of pragmatic local concerns with transcendent idealism. For women, utopian fiction permits reimaginings of worlds without patriarchy, without biology-based notions of gender, even without men—all within the context of a critique of contemporary politics. As critic Jean Pfaelzer notes, the question "What if the world were perfect?" is not the same as "What if the world were feminist?"

The latter question seems to interest Butler more than the former, for her utopias are certainly far from perfect. **"The Evening and the Morning and the Night"** relates the events that follow a "cure" for cancer that turns lethal; *Clay's Ark,* the last of the Patternist books, tells of the catastrophic spread of an extraterrestrial virus that transforms human genetics; *Dawn,* the first book of Xenogenesis, begins shortly after the earth has been rendered unhabitable by a nuclear war. Butler's worlds often seem far from feminist as well: few possess egalitarian social structures or communities of women; none has eradicated rape, incest, or compulsory heterosexuality; and the females who inhabit those worlds often rely on threats, coercion, and violence to achieve their own ends. As Dorothy Allison observes, Butler's female characters must "heroically adjust to family life and through example, largeness of spirit, and resistance to domination make the lives of their children better—even though this means sacrificing personal freedom."

Both the utopianism and the feminism of Butler's work are slippery because neither emerges in isolation from a variety of other interests. Butler is not interested in creating a utopia of human beings who seem too gentle to be believed, like those who inhabit Piercy's Mattapoisett and never get into fistfights; nor is she interested in glorifying either women or some abstract notion of the feminine. In fact, despite her insistence that human beings can transform themselves and their world, Butler often seems not to like people—men *or* women—at all. Her works border on the dystopian because she insists on confronting problems that have occurred so often in human communities that they seem almost an unavoidable part of human nature, such as greed, prejudices based on appearances, oppression of women, and might-makes-right ideologies. Rather than create utopias in which these problems have simply ceased to exist, Butler demonstrates time and again in her fiction that they must be worked through—even if that process involves the use of dangerous human tendencies like aggression and coercion to counter similar dangerous human tendencies like violence.

Both **"Bloodchild"** and the Xenogenesis books have one explicitly feminist project: to make male characters experience sex and reproduction from the position of females in male-dominated culture. **"Bloodchild,"** which offers a very short glimpse at a fascinating world, reflects on the extent to which patriarchal cultures find it necessary to use ideology, violence, and oppression to force women to participate in "natural" reproduction. In **"Bloodchild,"** men get pregnant, an ironic twist on a slogan made popular by supporters of abortion rights: "If men could get pregnant, abortion would be a sacrament." In **"Bloodchild,"** an alien race called Tlic require the bodies of healthy young men in which to incubate their eggs. When the eggs hatch inside the men's bodies, the aliens cut the men open to remove the alien grubs.

Although the Tlic attempt to make the process bearable for the men by incorporating them into nuclear families and creating an ideology of spousal love to persuade the men that their participation is voluntary and beneficial, the human male narrator stresses that the men—or, as in his own case, boys—may be "raped," impregnated against their wills, and forced to carry to term fetuses that have never been a part of themselves if they do not submit.

Tlic society is hierarchical, with fertile females possessing the most power—which they use to compete, sometimes violently, for human males. The Tlic who will mate with the narrator is particularly important; she is in change of the Preserve, the human dwelling on the Tlic planet (an animal farm, ghetto, Native American resettlement, and Nazi concentration camp all at once). As such, she is both protector and pimp. "Only she and her political faction stood between us and the horded who did not understand why there was a Preserve—why any Terran could not be courted, paid, drafted, in some way made available to them. She parceled us out to the desperate and sold us to the rich and powerful for their political support." Despite the fact that they are all female, the adult Tlic employ many of the ideologies and practices of patriarchalism: compulsory heterosexuality, reproductive colonization, marital rape, and oppression of the childbearing sex, to name the most deadly. For, like childbirth, Tlic deliveries can be lethal to humans; if the grubs are not removed at the right moment, by the right Tlic, the infants devour their hosts from the inside out.

Though the interference of the aliens has brought about an end to the struggle between the sexes, human women are as subject to Tlic oppression as men; they are not used as Tlic breeders only because bearing Tlic young leaves them too weak to bear the next generation of humans to carry a subsequent generation of Tlic. Familial relationships are quasi-incestuous. The narrator, Gan, and the Tlic whose children he will carry, T'Gatoi, are both children of the same father, whose sperm produced Gan and whose belly carried T'Gatoi. Gan's mother, who is many years younger than his father, grew up with T'Gatoi as a sort of sister; T'Gatoi has thus served as sister and aunt to her future spouse, and has been a second mother to him as well. Gan's relationship to her is laden with Oedipal conflict—he is grateful that he can stroke her as he cannot caress his mother, but feels revulsion and horror at the thought of their eventual mating—and T'Gatoi's desire for him, expressed alternately through parental and romantic clichés, smacks of pederasty. Under Tlic ideology, biology is destiny; none of the beings involved in a human-Tlic mating perceives an alternative.

"Bloodchild" hardly seems a feminist fantasy. It is impossible to perceive the planet of the Tlic as a radical utopia that empowers women, like Joanna Russ's Whileaway in *The Female Man;* Butler's human women are as oppressed as her men, and her female Tlic begin to act like human male oppressors. But **"Bloodchild"** is neither dystopian nor essentialistic. The circumstances that oppress the narrator do not stem from any metaphysical imperative; they are not historically inevitable, and therefore can be altered. The "biology" that complicates human-Tlic relationships is neither transparent nor predictable. The traits of human and Tlic nature that have placed Gan and T'Gatoi in the perverse relationship they negotiate are not "essential"; they are constructed out of social and material conditions that result in the appalling, crisis at the start of the story—the Tlic have changed themselves and the humans before, and can do so again.

More important, Gan's human agency begins a process of reform that may lead to Tlic recognition of the subjectivity of all humans. Gan does not believe or expect that an ideal space of perfect equality can be created, given the material difficulties of life on the Tlic world for humans and Tlic; he does, however, insist on new social structures with the potential for ongoing evolution. Butler's insistence on maintaining a closed family structure, which Haraway and Zaki criticize as a sign of her "conservatism" in sexual matters, serves as her means of emphasizing the vital need for collaboration underlying both the Tlic-human and the male-female relationships of the story; the future of both depends on a joint solution, with mutual extinction the only alternative.

Butler might have chosen to transform reader expectations about "normal" gender behavior by demonstrating how natural giving birth seems to human men, rather than how unnatural. Yet if Butler truly believed that human biology makes rape, compulsory heterosexuality, and enforced childbirth inevitable, she would have no motivation for writing **"Bloodchild"** in the first place. Like the circumstances of Gan's oppression, the production of the story must be situated within a historical framework. Butler published **"Bloodchild"** during a year when controversies over abortion, in-vitro fertilization, and the prevalence of unnecessary caesarean sections—topics cloaked in the metaphors of the story—reached a peak. 1984 also witnessed a political campaign characterized by the polarization of complex constitutional issues into monolithic positions: school prayer versus religious freedom, welfare abuse versus urban poverty, "pro-life" versus "pro-choice," apartheid versus sanctions. Rather than accepting such binaries, which lead neither to productive debate nor to a synthesized answer, Butler insists that individuals consider what is left out of such formulations. The social problems of

"Bloodchild" cannot be broken down into anything so simple as "Tlic versus humans" or "female versus male." The fundamental problem stems from the need for cooperation rather than binarism—and accompanying hierarchialism—to structure an imperfect but just society.

This problem creates the crux of the Patternmaster novels as well. The last book of the series, *Clay's Ark,* constitutes the beginning of a history played out in the earlier volumes. A man returns to earth from a distant galaxy, inadvertently carrying a disease organism that begins the transformation of the human race. "The organisms were not intelligent. They could not tell him how to keep himself alive, free, and able to find new hosts. But they became intensely uncomfortable if he did not, and their discomfort was his discomfort." The organisms invade and recode human DNA, threatening the lives of their hosts if they are not transmitted to other humans. Because transmission requires the breaking of the skin of the uninfected person, the organisms trigger violent behavior and overwhelming lust. The children of the inevitable sexual couplings between infected individuals are not human; they look like catlike, graceful "animals" and mature rapidly into highly intelligent quadrupeds with superhuman senses of smell and hearing. Resistance to the organism's need to spread, which is impossible except in the case of isolated individuals, ensures physical and mental anguish culminating in death.

Clay's Ark—the least utopian of the Patternist books—presents three recently infected individuals attempting to maintain their "humanity," which in this context signifies their control over biological drives. Blake Maslin, a doctor, believes physical strength and medical technology can prevent the disease's spread; his beautiful and brilliant daughter Rane relies instead on mental willpower and morality. Both try to escape the consequences of the disease, refusing to adapt to the physical and psychological changes it demands, and both ultimately lose their lives in the struggle. Only the younger daughter, Keira, who was wasting away with leukemia before surrendering to the new disease, survives. In progressing toward death, she has already begun to transform into something "ethereal not quite of this world," with a vastly different physiology and psychology from her father and sister. Keira survives because she takes the step neither her father nor sister is willing to take: she bonds with the disease and its carriers, willingly accepting the inevitability of the changes necessitated by the organism. Such evolution represents the only possibility for saving Keira's life, for the recently invented epigenetic therapy, a process that has all but eradicated leukemia by reprogramming faulty genes, has failed to correct her cells. Keira may have less of a stake in "protecting" human biology because her own biology has never been normatively human; she has less of a stake in protecting human morality because, unlike her sister Rane, she understands it as a utilitarian construct that can be discarded when its social value ceases to function.

The humans "lose" to the organism and to another group of humans carrying a different mutation. The species divides into three competing groups. The self-destructive, telepathic "Patternists," bred by the ancient patriarch Doro for their psychic skills, develop from victims to oppressors in their struggle against nontelepathic humans and "Clayarks" (the descendants of the characters in ***Clay's Ark***). Telepaths treat the nonpsychic humans as an inferior race, referring to them by the denigrating label "mute." The nomadic Clayarks, considered non-human by the others, are despised and shunned as carriers of the terrifying disease. The Patternist novels share the interest in **"Bloodchild"** in the prevalence of patriarchy, tyranny, and slavery across many different human cultures. None offers a universal utopia, though several characters create utopian spaces within a primarily hostile world. In ***Survivor,*** Alanna resists deep prejudices to join an alien tribe; in ***Mind of My Mind,*** Mary becomes a tyrant with the hopes of single-handedly achieving the peace and group survival her father Doro made impossible. In these books human nature again proves more flexible than some of the characters would like to admit. They cannot preserve an "essential humanity" in the face of mutation and disease; instead, they learn to recognize the extent to which human morality and even human biology are constructed through careful breeding and teaching, and can be changed a good deal.

Ex-communication: "Speech Sounds" and "The Evening and the Morning and the Night"

Donna Haraway writes: "[Competing stories of human evolution] have been bound together in a contentious discourse on technology, often staged in the high-technology media that embody the dream of communication promised by international science and global organization." Having argued against claims for Butler's essentialism, I would like to turn to her two most "essentialistic" worlds, found in the acclaimed short stories **"Speech Sounds"** and **"The Evening and the Morning and the Night."** Both involve the destruction of "the dream of perfect communication promised by international science," to quote Haraway. Each of these fictions is set on earth and begins with a devastating disease that challenges human myths of control over their physical selves and destroys the capacity for traditional verbal expression among victims. Though the diseases are very different—the illness in **"Speech Sounds"** affects all people, while that in **"The Evening and the Morning and the Night"** afflicts only children of drug-damaged parents—both trigger acts of violence capable of destroying entire societies. Butler never explains whether the violence stems from the diseases themselves, or from the rage and

terror felt by the diseased individuals whose bodies no longer respond to their commands, although the latter seems more likely. The stories thus concern methods for interpersonal contact when verbal communication fails, and when the possibility of life-threatening violence is just under the surface of all relationships. Although grounded in the biology of individual bodies, the problems that arise are primarily social in nature.

"Speech Sounds," set in California, follows a devastating worldwide epidemic that, though initially blamed on the Soviets, has no traceable cause or cure. The illness is "highly specific . . . language was always lost or severely impaired. . . . Often there was also paralysis, intellectual impairment, death." Some victims abruptly lose the capacity to read and write; others can still read, but no longer speak; some can do neither, while others can do both but cannot remember what words mean. Of course, one immediate result is the breakdown of late capitalist civilization. The mass communications gone, the vast social apparatus rendered useless, people become like children cut off from parental discipline and love. They are forced instead to struggle for survival against armed criminals, suicidal thoughts, and jealous individuals who will kill for spite those who can speak, read, or write. The protagonist, Valerie Rye, has lost her husband and children to the disease; she can no longer read, write, or remember many things, and her ability to speak can put her life in danger if she demonstrates it in public. Maddened with illness, loneliness, and envy, she is overwhelmed at times with the desire to murder those who can still read; at other times she is overcome by the need for any nonviolent contact with any human being, willing to make love with a man she can never converse with.

Set in Los Angeles—a city where in the 1990s rival gangs fight territorial battles over who has the right to speak which language in which section—**"Speech Sounds"** reflects and explores the relationship between modes of communication and social structures. Like the biblical story of the Tower of Babel, Butler indicates that, deprived of the ability to share a primary language, individuals will leave off building their cities and wander into isolation. Certainly everyone in the story leaves off constructing skyscrapers and focuses on basic survival issues: scavenging for and growing food, finding shelter, establishing defenses against the robbers and rapists who patrol the streets. Although a large series of gestures to represent curses have sprung up, no real sign system has been developed. Violence is a universal language: people take what they can, keep what they defend, and destroy what they resent, without the need for debate or defensiveness.

The loss of speech is less the cause of social breakdown than the loss of literacy. The necessities for remaining alive have continued—food and fuels still circulate, transportation still runs between cities, and apparently firearms are still manufactured—but without the electronic media, capitalist society cannot function. It is in the process of reverting to feudalism when the story begins. **"Speech Sounds"** thus tells the tale of an extremely public society forced to "go private" without any warning. Without the printing press and descendant machines, the public sphere falls part. Everything from government and law enforcement to scientific research and social aid ceases to function, leaving people to an anarchistic state where, although some of the machinery still functions, the superstructure that controls it does not. Society is at best vestigial. Soon the gas will run out, the cars will break down, groups sharing food and protection will begin to disintegrate, men will forget that rape was ever a crime.

Rye, the protagonist, thinks she is lonely because she is not a "private" person; she tells herself she needs people out of a biological need for communication, nurturing, and sex. But she is not a "private" person in a far more important sense: she depends upon a public sphere to satisfy her as a consumer. Not coincidentally, the man she links up with still wears the uniform of the Los Angeles Police Department. Rye finds this anachronism amusing because it reminds her of a little boy playing cop. But it also reminds her of the public life she had before the disease, and she longs for her lover—whom she calls Obsidian, having no way to ask his real name—to protect her, to take her places, to help her get to Pasadena where she may have relatives.

But Rye and Obsidian cannot go back; the world of instantaneous communication, across a room or across the globe, has been destroyed. Obsidian is shot for attempting to interfere in what would once have been called a "domestic disturbance." The police have minimal power because "domestic violence" is still considered a private matter in some areas, but Obsidian is still trapped in a code of ethics from the world before. Rye is as well. Despite her longing for her own lost nuclear family, she feels little sense of social obligation to the two children orphaned in the fight that killed Obsidian, as though she expects a social welfare agency to step in. "She did not need a stranger's children who would grow up to be hairless chimps." But finally the desperateness of their situation reaches her; she realizes that if she does not take them with her, they will die, and she wants no more death on her hands. Then comes the greatest shock: the children can speak normally. Whether the disease has run its course or these two have a rare immunity, they can talk to her.

"Speech Sounds" are not the same things as "speech"; they are less determinate. To those accustomed to a delimited sign system, speech sounds are crude and incoherent; in eighteenth- and nineteenth-century books on American slave and subaltern cultures, for example, the dialects spoken by the oppressed were assumed to be "speech sounds," not language. Butler's **"Speech Sounds"** ends with Rye contemplating what it will mean to be a teacher to the children—to educate them in the use of a skill that may no longer be of any use, that others will envy enough to murder them. What will she teach them? The value of the old language, or the need for a new mode of communication? The hierarchical difference between "speech" and "speech sounds," or the need for a common language between the verbal and the mute? The story ends before such questions can be resolved, but it ends on a hopeful note. Rye knows that, speech or no speech, the next generation will never bring back the world as it was. They will have to create instead a new public order, more diffuse in form and more accepting of difference than the old. They will have to be different.

The disease in **"The Evening and the Morning and the Night"** also leaves different children as the hope of the future. A late twentieth-century "wonder drug," which cures cancer and most viral diseases, causes a genetic disorder in all the descendants of every individual who uses it. The disorder, called DGD (Duryea-Gode disease), initially causes an inability to concentrate, then a psychotic retreat into fantasy; finally, it spurs horrific self-destructive and species-destructive behavior. The father of Lynn, the narrator, killed and skinned her mother completely before dying in an attempt to skin himself alive. This rending of the flesh—"digging out"—is common to all end-stage DGD victims; when they reach this point, they are locked away in exploitative DGD wards, usually chained up, but sometimes allowed to kill themselves if they prove too inventive in attacking their jailers. Although maintaining a medically supervised diet can put off the worst symptoms for several years, eventually the "digging" becomes inevitable. The only alternative to a horrible death in a DGD ward is an innovative private hospital called Dilg, which has a long waiting list. Dilg—named for the Dilg family, which made capital profits from the drug that caused DGD, and then funded research to cure it—also funds scholarships for DGD victims. Lynn is the recipient of such a scholarship. When she visits Dilg, she discovers that the reason has more to do with her biology than her scholarly ability: Lynn is the daughter of two parents with DGD, and as such carries pheromones that enable her to control violent DGD victims.

The Dilg retreat is Butler's strangest utopia, though in some ways her most successful. Under the guidance of "double-DGD" females, patients who would otherwise destroy themselves invent life-saving technology, produce brilliant artwork, and lead otherwise productive lives. Although most of the patients work in isolation because the illness makes collaboration impossible—particularly among members of the same sex—the Dilg community provides a space for education, productivity, and care while protecting DGD victims and their families from exploitation at the hands of high-priced private wards or mismanaged government institutions. The pheremones are both a blessing and a curse. Two females of double-DGD parentage cannot abide contact with one another; Lynn has to fight overpowering urges to inflict violence on Beatrice, the woman who explains Lynn's rare privilege to her. As Lynn acknowledges, she has little choice but to join Dilg, although the thought of spending the rest of her life "in something that was basically a refined DGD ward" does not appeal to her. She shares her lover's suspicion that Dilg's complete control over its patients could lead to exploitation, even though the supervisors are DGDs, too—people who have not yet developed end-stage symptoms. However, she sees little alternative for herself or for the violent victims men like her lover will inevitably become. "If the pheremones were something only men had, you would do it," she tells him.

Like the patients aboard *Clay's Ark,* the DGD sufferers subtly resemble AIDS victims. Butler portrays them as heroic, attempting to commit suicide or quarantine themselves to avoid injuring the healthy. As in the case of AIDS, some people angrily blame irresponsible sexuality for the spread of DGD: "The damned disease could be wiped out in one generation, but people are still animals when it comes to breeding. Still following mindless urges, like dogs and cats." Although this sounds like essentialist rhetoric— "People are at the mercy of their biological urges"—it is important to note that the speaker has undergone voluntary sterilization, proving that biology does not have to be destiny. Lynn's response to his urging that she do the same is to insist on maintaining control of the one part of her biology functioning normally. "I don't want kids, but I don't want someone else telling me I can't have any. . . . [Would] you want someone else telling you what to do with your body?" she asks. The DGD victims also share some parallels with babies born addicted to crack. They suffer from specific motor and speech dysfunctions; some have never met their fathers for their own safety, while others have met only the brain-damaged ruin of their mothers; the "crimes" that cause prejudice against them are not their own.

Butler's appeal for victims' rights, however, shifts dramatically in light of her insistence that the disease may actually benefit society in the long run. Just as AIDS research has led to new discoveries about the immune system and provided valuable information in treating cancer, leukemia, and chronic viral infections, DGD produces highly intelligent individuals who devote their lives to improving life for others; the special value of double-DGD females was discovered by DGD victims, and their own laboratories represent the best hope for a cure. **"The Evening and the Morning and the Night"** would thus seem to offer the most essentialistic position yet in a Butler story, dividing humanity into the haves and the have-nots. But even here Butler demands diversity. The first half of the story focuses on the prejudice still-healthy DGD carriers suffer; although many of them have spectacular careers as scientists (ironically, DGD victims cure many forms of cancer), they are ignored or abused by uninformed and frightened associates. Lynn rooms at college with a DGD victim who becomes a special education major, hoping "the handicapped would accept her more readily than the able-bodied." They share a house with other DGD victims because they have "all had enough of being lepers twenty-four hours a day."

As always, Butler subtly points out the multiethnicism of her character—Lynn is the child of two American fundamentalist Christians, while her lover Alan is half-American Catholic, half-Nigerian polytheistic. Butler also indicates that many of the scientists and doctors are female, black, or another minority. The disease itself trivializes most other forms of prejudice in a transformation similar to that caused by the presence of aliens in the Xenogenesis books.

Dilg is feminist by necessity; females simply handle certain aspects of the disease better than males. But never does Butler consider the possibility of having the females shun male society to protect their assets. In what appears to be a calculated attack on Russ's *The Female Man* and Charnas's *Motherlines,* Butler insists that sexual cooperation is absolutely vital; the segregation of the genders would be deadly for both. Women take on the roles of leader and nurturer not because they are innately more equipped to do so than men, but because the DGD pheremone coincidentally attaches itself to double-DGD females; as Lynn says, if men had the pheremone, they would take on the guidance positions. Women are certainly no less prone to violence than men. Next to Lynn's father, Alan's mother is the most violent character in **"The Evening and the Morning and the Night."**

Similar ideas about gender permeate **"Speech Sounds,"** though the roles are reversed. Left-handed men suffer less brain damage than any other group. Rye kills people more easily than Obsidian. Biology thus is never destiny, even when it seems to be so. Even without the ability to read, Rye has a choice: she can work with people, attempting to create a new society, or become destructive like some of the people she witnesses. And Lynn has a similar choice: she can commit suicide, or live for the moment until the illness takes her, or she can work with Dilg to develop a haven and a cure. The characters in these two stories share some basic similarities, but their best chances for survival come from putting their differences to work.

Re-creation: Kindred

In an essay on fiction set in the antebellum South, Deborah E. McDowell writes: "Contemporary novels of slavery [witness] slavery after freedom in order to engrave that past on the memory of the present but, more importantly, on future generations that might otherwise succumb to the cultural amnesia that has begun to re-enslave us all in social and literary texts that impoverish our imaginations."

Kindred, Butler's fantasy of time-travel into the past of her race and gender, engraves that past into the flesh of her heroine as well as her memory. *Kindred* is Butler's most troubling novel—yet also, in many ways, her most optimistic. The mechanism for the temporal shifts is never explained; this novel is not interested in alien sciences, and can scarcely be described as "science fiction." Rather, the "aliens" in *Kindred* are all too human. They are white Americans from the antebellum South, and they are more frightening than the Tlic. Dana, the black contemporary protagonist, unexpectedly finds herself transported to Maryland before the Civil War. Her great-great-grandfather Rufus calls her there to save his life, which she does several times. Rufus, much to Dana's shock, is not black; her grandmother never told her that not all of her ancestors were slaves.

Dana finds herself faced with a dilemma similar to those of Butler's other heroines: she must decide whether to collaborate with an oppressive agent that threatens her identity as a human being, or whether to cause her own extinction. *Kindred's* particular situation requires that Dana cooperate with her white ancestors as they beat, rape, and murder her black ancestors; if she does not, her great-grandmother may never be born, and she may cease to exist. Rufus, who fathered this great-grandmother, closely resembles Dana's white husband. As he grows from a confused child to a murderous patriarch, Dana finds herself forced to suppress every moral, value, and desire she has ever held dear.

Dorothy Allison's criticism of Butler stems from what Allison perceives as Butler's assumption that children and family always come first. Though Butler's black female characters are aggressive, independent, and in control, they often sacrifice personal freedom and autonomy in order to make the lives of their children better—a tendency that makes Allison "want to scream with frustration." Since utopian thought is optimistic, holding out hope for a better future, Butler does insist time and again on the need for people—especially for women—to make sacrifices for their children. But she indicates that such a demand compromises the present, forcing characters to submit to situations they find unbearable. Women make such sacrifices more often than men not because they are genetically more prone to do so, but because they have been socially driven

to do so. They refuse the consequences of *not* being the ones to take action: the deaths of their children and their future.

If **"Speech Sounds"** and **"The Evening and the Morning and the Night"** may be interpreted as theorizing a biological view of human nature to a greater degree than Butler's other texts, then *Kindred* is their opposite; it insists absolutely that personality and behavior are constructed within a social frame. Rufus beats, rapes, and kills not because white men are inherently more prone to do so than black men or white women, but because white men happen to hold the power in his society and he has been taught from a young age that he *can* beat, rape, and kill. Even Dana insists that the differences between herself and Rufus stem from culture rather than birth.

> Could I make him see why I thought his blackmail was worse than my own? It was. He threatened to keep me from my husband if I did not submit to his whim. . . . I acted out of desperation. He acted out of whimsy or anger. Or so it seemed. "Rufe, there are things we just can't bargain on. This is one of them."
>
> "You're going to tell me what we can't bargain on?" He sounded more surprised than indignant.
>
> "You're damn right I am. . . . I won't bargain away my husband or my freedom!"
>
> "You don't have either to bargain."
>
> "Neither do you."

Rufus is both more reasonable and more impossible than Dana expects: more reasonable because he will listen to her debate, more impossible because he refuses to change even when he understands her. But Rufus shares this flaw with the other men in the novel—including the sympathetic men. On one of her journeys back through time, Dana's husband accompanies her, and she is horrified to discover the extent to which Kevin acts like a patriarchal white man when people treat him as one. In his own time, he is another person. Kevin becomes horrified as well, although he strongly resists acknowledging that the new conditions have altered his behavior; he wants to believe that his personality cannot be changed by circumstance.

Dana is even more horrified to learn that, treated as an enslaved black woman, she will act like one. Her personality, which she always thought of as her fundamental self, modifies in response to Rufus's and Kevin's betrayals until she is no longer sure who she is in her own time or in the past. Dana helps Rufus against her every instinct, not because her nurturing instincts prove stronger than her need for autonomy, freedom, and self-pride, but because she recognizes the strategic importance of doing so. When she does not assist Rufus, she risks not merely her biological ancestry, but the lives of other slaves. Only when he threatens her autonomy by trying to seduce her—only when she realizes "how easy it would be for me to continue to be still and forgive him even this"—does she strike at him: "I could accept him as my ancestor, my younger brother, my friend, but not as my master."

People in *Kindred* do not change because of humanist impulses or moral imperatives. They respond to the agency of others, either immediately or over time. Readers are meant to feel real horror at Dana's periods of complacency as a slave; like her, we respond with a kind of gratitude to the worst excesses of Rufus's behavior because they remind us of the need for action and challenge, no matter how painful. *Kindred* offers a challenge to utopian fictions that value ideals over survival—like *Women on the Edge of Time,* in which the protagonist sacrifices herself (and kills several other people) in order to defend her values, or like the cultures described in *Dawn,* which decide en masse to commit suicide once it becomes clear they will never achieve perfect stasis. Butler instead acknowledges all that has been and remains unbearable in human society, but insists that human agency can change even the most dystopian world over time. It demands patience; Dana must be willing to work, but she must also be willing to wait for substantial change, not to force it in the past at the expense of the future. The work and the waiting pays off. Although Dana is dispossessed of her era, her nation, her family, her belongings, her values, and her beliefs, she gains the understanding that she can make a difference in history. The novel is unfailingly optimistic in this regard. At the conclusion, Dana and her husband return to Maryland in 1976, to mourn those who suffered and to reassure themselves that they have escaped. Utopia in *Kindred* is thus in Dana's own era, when diversity is celebrated in marriage rather than conquered through rape and domination. Not that the scars go away: Dana loses an arm to Rufus's grip, and her knees and skin are marked by the tortures of slavery—just as all descendants of slaves are scarred from America's racist past. But she is still alive and capable of further change. Butler literally engraves the past onto the present by engraving Dana's body as a readable text. As Deborah McDowell predicts, she also engraves the past onto the memory of the future through the act of writing. The text warns people like Dana and like us of the dangers of complacency; it demands utopian thinking.

Contradiction: *Xenogenesis*

Donna Haraway tells us: "Conventions within the narrative field of S[cience] F[iction] seem to require readers radically to rewrite stories in the act of reading them. . . . I want the readers to find an 'elsewhere' from which to envision a different and less hostile order or relationships among people, animals, technologies, and land." This statement could easily describe the project of **Xenogenesis.** Xenogenesis mobilizes human adaptability to reform a species that arrives on earth to reform humanity. The Oankali, whose name means "gene traders," arrive in the Terran system at the end of a nuclear holocaust that has decimated the planet. They bring the remaining humans onto their world-ship with a plan to return them to earth equipped to survive there; the "equipment" will consist of Oankali genes, provided by forcing humans to mate with Oankali partners and evolve into a new species. This crossbreeding is necessary for two reasons. The main one, according to the Oankali, stems from a flaw in human biology: ancient hierarchical tendencies drive humans to violence and self-destruction, and human intelligence only exacerbates the dangers.

But the Oankali have another purpose. They desperately desire to mate with the humans not only to trade genes, but because they find humans extremely attractive. Like the humans with the disease of *Clay's Ark,* the Oankali are driven to spread their organelles or become extinct. Humans particularly attract them because they are susceptible to cancers. If they can understand the cancers and adapt the renegade cells to their purposes, the Oankali feel certain they can make themselves attractive as mates to many new species.

Genetic exchanges occur with the help of ooloi, an Oankali third sex who "mix" the DNA of parents to form genetically desirable children. The ooloi also give enormous sexual pleasure to human and Oankali partners—so much pleasure, in fact, that humans shun all physical contact with humans of the opposite sex without ooloi intervention once they have participated in mating with an ooloi. The ooloi discover what they label the "Human Contradiction":

> You are hierarchical. That's the older and more entrenched characteristic. We saw it in your closest animal relatives and in your most distant ones. It's a terrestrial characteristic. When human intelligence served it instead of guiding it, when human intelligence did not even acknowledge it as a problem, but took pride in it or did not notice it at all . . . that was like ignoring cancer. I think your people did not realize what a dangerous thing they were doing. . . . Your denial doesn't matter. A cancer growing in someone's body will go on growing despite denial. And a complex combination of genes that work together to make you intelligent as well as hierarchical will still handicap you whether you acknowledge it or not.

This incompatible "conflict in their genes—the new intelligence put at the service of ancient hierarchical tendencies," according to many of the Oankali, doom the human race to eventual destruction. Because of the Contradiction, the Oankali never feel remorse about their complete colonization of an independent species; it is for the salvation of the human race as well as for their own purposes that they interfere. The Oankali, who can communicate empathically and work communally, are certain of their superiority. It is never clear that they want anything from the humans other than their cancers and their cooperation, for there is little the Oankali seem to value in human beings except the potential for making them adaptable.

But even the Oankali cannot predict everything. Their "test" group of humans, experimented on while the majority of survivors remain in suspended animation, reveal several surprises: for example, that humans can perform a variety of different identities, that they become uncooperative when information is withheld, that making one human more powerful than others may lead to that person's persecution rather than domination. They also discover that the Contradiction is not equally strong in all people; women, for example, seem to display less of it than men, a fact that the Oankali attribute to male biology, but that the women attribute to conditioning that trains women to demonstrate their skills through nurture rather than force. Most of the Oankali expect Lilith, the strong black heroine of **Dawn,** to choose for a human mate "one of the big dark ones because they're like you"; only her best Oankali friend, Nikanj, is not surprised when she chooses instead a short, soft-spoken Chinese-Canadian man. But the humans shock the Oankali most with the force of their drive to survive. When the humans learn of the plan to breed them, they kill the ooloi who have become their mentors and sexual partners to escape.

For relatively few humans, anti-Oankali feelings arise from racial or sexual prejudices—the Oankali have "ugly" tentacles, and "take men as though they were women"—but for the majority, the desire to survive as a species is the tantamount issue in the conflict with the Oankali takeover of earth. After bonding chemically with humans—only to have the humans flee—several ooloi are forced to admit that their understanding of genetics cannot prevent them from making errors. Many Oankali agree that intelligence might eventually allow humans to conquer their hierarchical tendencies, particularly if they have a new world to conquer, a distraction that would require co-operation and ingenuity. Eventually, after "resister" humans attempt to kidnap and alter "construct" children (half-human, half-ooloi) in order to maintain their species identity, the Oankali are convinced by a construct child that not all humans should be forced to mate with the Oankali. Those who choose not to can be sent to Mars, made habitable by Oankali technology, to continue as an independent race. Of course the Oankali—and some humans—hope that most of the humans

stay. But the Oankali, who have always planned to retain a group of "pure" Oankali in case the Human Contradiction destroys them as well, finally recognize the need for "Humans who don't change or die—Humans to go on if the . . . unions fail."

It is a mistake to interpret Xenogenesis as a serious discussion of essential flaws in human genetics. The novels scarcely seem interested in proving whether or not humans actually suffer from the Contradiction; rather, they illustrate how human agency can triumph over prejudice, violence, and essentialism. The humans in Xenogenesis express absolutely no racial prejudice; the only subset of individuals other than the Oankali who receive any real group hostility are "faggots," for in the postwar world compulsory heterosexuality becomes an important component of the dream of reproducing the species. In **Dawn,** the group of humans who have been dominant—white Christian men—act exactly as the Oankali expect all humans to behave; having lost the most power and prestige, they fight the most strongly against the dominant alien presence. There is also a large, highly xenophobic German resister village. Among the "non-Aryan" groups of humans, there is less violence; Hispanic and Chinese people may choose to go to Mars, but rarely become gun-toting resisters. It is not surprising that a black woman first joins an Oankali family; after years of oppression by other humans, Lilith has less prejudice toward the aliens and a stronger appreciation of the need for change. While she resents the unequal power relationships between Oankali and humans, she resents as well the unequal relationships among the humans she supervises.

Lilith is willing to work with the Oankali to create change. Her son Akin, the hero of **Adulthood Rites** and the first male human-Oankali construct child, is expected by his elders to be nomadic and prone to violence; instead, he bonds strongly with two separate communities and devotes his life to finding a workable solution to the increasing human-Oankali conflict. Jodahs, the human-Oankali construct ooloi protagonist of **Imago,** proves to the Oankali that the aspects of humanity they most fear can be used fruitfully for the benefit of both humans and Oankali. There may be a biological flaw—or there may not—but Butler implies time and again that culture has the power either to reassert the old hierarchies or to triumph over them.

Hoda Zaki has argued that in the Xenogenesis books Butler demonstrates "a pervasive human need to alienate from oneself those who appear to be different—i.e., to create Others." Zaki cites the way humans of different races band together only to oppress the Oankali in the series as proof of this assertion. In fact, I would like to argue that Butler indicates exactly the opposite. The *humans* have been constituted as the colonized Other *by* the Oankali; as Donna

Haraway points out, their reeducation on the Oankali ship resembles the Middle Passage of slaves on their way to America. At this point, the humans are like animals to the Oankali, more interesting for their cancers than their thoughts; their identities have been stripped away, and they are "reduced to flesh"—texts to be inscribed by their oppressors, who identify them as nothing but a package of genes. The human resistance to the Oankali parallels the resistance of a slave to rape by a master who will later claim her child as his property. The agency required to transform this situation into a relationship of equality and trust is staggering, but the transformation occurs. By the end of *Imago,* a group of fertile humans enter an Oankali community of their own free will, after a consensus formed through argument and communication. They can do so because, for the first time, they are not an oppressed minority victimized by the Oankali.

It is interesting that Butler's sympathy for the oppressor leads so many readers to interpret Xenogenesis as a condemnation of humanity. Although she points out that in many ways the Oankali are superior to human beings, Butler insists—through the mouths of many different characters, human and Oankali—that the enforced crossbreeding of an unwilling species is a terrible crime. The Oankali (like the Tlic) commit miscegenation not in their attempt to create a new species, but in an attempt to dominate the old— the humans, who have value in and of themselves. Xenogenesis represents a breakthrough in Butler's fiction in that, for the first time, the protagonists do not have to work alone to achieve their ends. Although Lilith initially resembles Dana, Mary, and other Butler female heroes who take on entire worlds isolated from community support or input, she becomes a member of a large "family" that includes not only humans and Oankali, but animals, plants, and sentient spaceships as well. The world at the end of *Imago* is truly utopian, a society in which all have an equal chance to work together on the construction of a new world. It fulfills Donna Haraway's dream of "an 'elsewhere' from which to envision a different and less hostile order of relationships among people, animals, technologies, and land," and Butler's dream of a world in which differences can be recognized without prejudice and celebrated. "'Human beings fear difference,' Lilith had told him once. 'Oankali crave difference. Humans persecute their different ones, yet they need them to give themselves definition and status. Oankali seek difference and collect it. They need it to keep themselves from stagnation and overspecialization. . . . When you feel a conflict, try to go the Oankali way. Embrace difference.'"

Rebecca O. Johnson (review date February 1994)

SOURCE: "African-American, Feminist Science Fiction," in *Sojourner: The Women's Forum,* Vol. 19, No. 6, February, 1994, pp. 12-4.

[*Johnson is a writer and activist. In the following review, she traces Butler's portrayal of humanity in her Patternist novels and the* Xenogenesis *trilogy, and discusses with the author her* Parable of the Sower.]

I read to escape. Oh, not as often as when I was twelve years old, but my favorite coping mechanism is reading. Mind candy usually. You know the stuff: mysteries, lesbian fantasy, and occasionally science fiction. But when life gets confusing or I am particularly in need of a vacation or a time of reflection, I turn to books that are more than fluff. Books written by authors whose insights stimulate and challenge me. Octavia Butler's books occupy a secure niche in this last and, perhaps, most important category of comfort reading.

Octavia Butler writes science fiction. She is the first African-American woman to write science fiction under her own name. She has written ten books and won many of science fiction's highest awards. Octavia Butler's people (human and alien) shift shapes, imagine they feel other people's pain, actually feel the death throes of people twenty years dead, travel through time and back into slavery, heal themselves and others in amazing ways, and possess a true third gender. They struggle with their own biology and the power it gives them. They struggle with the effect of their genetic tendencies on the world.

The majority of Butler's novels can be grouped into two thematic series. The first series is the Patternist novels. These include *Patternmaster* and *Mind of My Mind* (published in 1976 and '77 respectively and to be reissued this spring), *Wild Seed* (1980), and *Clay's Ark* (1984). These novels are set in Africa and the United States and follow the development of the Pattern, beginning with its long-lived parents, Doro and Anyanwu, to its full manifestation sometime in an unspecified and dangerous future. *Patternmaster* is Butler's first published novel. It chronicles our world in a future overrun by formerly human mutants known as Clayarks. The remnant of the human race is protected by the Pattern, a complex telepathic link that allows the Patternmaster to defend Patternist settlements from Clayark attacks. Nontelepathic humans are called mutes.

The Pattern started centuries earlier with Doro and Anyanwu. Doro takes and uses other people's bodies. In *Wild Seed* he has lived over 3500 years. His work is to build a community of telepathically strong people: to build a family for himself and a race. Anyanwu is younger, about 300 years old. They meet in Africa as Doro is gathering his people, the people he has bred, to take them to North

America and away from the ravages of the slave trade. When we meet them again in **Mind of My Mind,** it is the late twentieth century and Doro is about to succeed in ways that he never imagined. Mary (Doro's daughter), making her transition from latent to active telepath, throws a psychic noose around the necks of five of Doro's most powerful people. The Pattern manifests itself for the first time:

> Others, yes. Five of them. They seemed to be far away from me, perhaps scattered around the country. Actives like Karl, like me. People I had noticed during the last minutes of my transition. People who had noticed me at the same time. Their thoughts told me what they were, but I became aware of them—"saw" them—as bright points of light, like stars. They formed a shifting pattern of light and color. I had brought them together somehow. Now I was holding them together—and they didn't want to be held.

Butler's main characters are always Black women. They struggle with domination, and they struggle to understand their unique powers. Slavery is a recurring and related theme: the actual reality of slavery in the United States as imagined in **Kindred,** a novel in which the protagonist is psychically drawn from the twentieth century back into slavery, as well as the bondage people impose on each other through differential power relationships.

> "White women must be protected," Doro said, "whether they want to be or not."

> "As property is protected." Anyanwu shook her head. "Preserved for use of owner alone. Denice [Anyanwu's white wife who was afraid of having black children by Anyanwu] said she felt like property—like a slave plotting escape. I told her I could give her children who were not related to me at all if she wished. Her fear made me angry even though I knew the situation was not her fault. I told her my Warrick shape was not a copy of anyone . . . I could take the exact shape of one of the white men I had treated in Wheatley."

The exercise of power can save or destroy. Understanding and using The Pattern means agreeing to a kind of domination, initially by one young woman over more powerful others. Existing in that domination gives a disjointed and suffering people a community and ultimately the ability to preserve a portion of humanity.

In the Xenogenesis trilogy, Butler adds even more complexity to these themes. What if humans finally destroy themselves, or attempt to, by launching that final nuclear war? And what if humanity's only salvation is a totally alien species, one that sees themselves as genetic traders and humans as endlessly seductive potential slave partners? In

Dawn (1987), Lilith awakens from a bewildering sleep to meet her "saviors," an alien race called the Oankali. Their bodies are covered with long, writhing, sensory tentacles, and they have three genders. Lilith has been chosen to awaken other humans rescued by the Oankali in the aftermath of nuclear destruction. She is to train them, build a group, and prepare them to meet the Oankali. Each heterosexual human pair is to meet their Oankali mates—male, female and ooloi—and return to earth. The Oankali know some humans will embrace the trade and others will resist, run away, as soon as they return to earth. The trade is not really a free choice. Resisters can leave, but their fertility has been taken away. The Oankali must breed with their new trade partners. They know humans would refuse this if left to their essential contradiction, intelligence at the service of hierarchy. They will not let human resisters reproduce and destroy themselves and the planet again. Humans who submit discover that great physical and sexual pleasure comes with partnership with the Oankali, as well as long life and freedom from pain.

> Yes, Lilith was not free. Sudden freedom would have terrified her, although sometimes she seemed to want it. Sometimes she stretched the bonds between herself and the family. But she always came home. Tino would probably kill himself if he were freed. But what about the resisters? They did terrible things to each other because they could not have children. But before the war—during the war—they had done terrible things to each other even though they could have children. The Human Contradiction held them. Intelligence at the service of hierarchical behavior. They were not free. All he could do for them, if he could do anything, was to let them be bound in their own way. Perhaps next time their intelligence would be in balance with their hierarchical behavior, and they would not destroy themselves.

Lilith is seen as a collaborator by the people she awakens. At times she hates herself because she has been seduced by her ooloi, Nikanj, and the pleasure it gives.

Throughout the rest of the trilogy, **Adulthood Rites** (1988) and **Imago** (1989), Butler imagines life on a seemingly primitive earth. Resisters are as long-lived as trade humans. They steal human-looking offspring of Oankali/Human matings. These children, called constructs, are the receptacle for all that is good and bad in both species. They are also the ultimate salvation for resisters and traders alike.

Science fiction has tended to represent people of color badly. The characters don't feel real or, more frequently, no people of color appear in the story. Butler's characters are African-American, mixed race, Asian, Native American, Latino; she chooses themes that allow her to struggle with the life realities of poor and oppressed people. When I read her books I discover new ways to think about psychic phenomena, violence and self-defense, the growing siege mentality of contemporary society, and the pervasiveness of slavery.

I avoided reading *Kindred* (1979) for years. In this novel, Dana and Kevin have just moved into their first house together when strange things begin to happen. Dana disappears from their living room for a few minutes and reappears soaking wet. She has just saved a boy named Rufus from drowning, a boy who turns out to be her kin and the slaveowner of her ancestors. In discussing this article with a friend, I realized the idea of a kind of psychic slavery was terrifying. Many of us have had relationships that seem to speak to us over time and space. What would happen if a relative, an ancestor, could not only make his or her presence psychically known but also draw us to them, whether we wanted to go or not? And what if that ancestor is a white man in the antebellum South? Of course this isn't possible, but it provides a vivid metaphor for evaluating internalized racism and domination in relationships.

I find *The Parable of the Sower* (1993), Butler's latest offering, more comfortable, in the way a nightmare is familiar. Set in 2025, it follows the coming of age of Lauren Olamina, a young woman living in a walled community in southern California. Walled communities are a fixture of Butler's literary architecture. Humans throw up barricades against assault, to keep out witch hunters, Clayarks, Oankali, and in *Parable,* hordes of desperately poor or drug-crazed people. The walls don't hold, could not hold for families like the Olaminas. They don't have the resources of the rich to buy truly deadly security. They don't seem to have the heart for inflicting that kind of harm. Lauren is on her own, on the road away from the enclosure for the first time in her young life.

Parable imagines the United States after poverty and despair create a truly physical class divide—the poor, naked and on the street; the striving working class struggling to protect the little they have behind inadequate walls; and the rich, with the sea at their back, shielded by armed guards all along the periphery of their lives. To what ends will we go to defend ourselves from each other? At what point does political activism and organizing fail, defeated by conditions we try not to imagine, even though we live with the seeds of that chaos today? Is anything new possible?

Octavia Butler describes herself as prone to pessimism. Her unflagging feminism, however, helps her to create an unflinching view of the best of ourselves and the worst. She shows us choices we might make in a totally alien environment of an Oankali space ship or the more familiar world of the walled cities of Southern California. In the end, her

work allows a great escape from our own daily complexities and a fresh view of our lives when that escape comes to an end.

The following is an except from a wide-ranging interview with Octavia Butler. We talked about all her books. I want to share with you her responses about **Parable of the Sower** *and its relationship to her other novels.*

[*Johnson:*] *Overall, your books tend to focus more on biology and psychic power than on technologies. Why is that?*

[Butler:] Well, biology is just a personal favorite. I tend to prefer it because that's where my interests go. I follow my interests instead of imposing something on myself. What I'm doing in *Parable of the Sower* has less to do with biology and more to do with current events and a kind of extension of current events. I do use some of my love of biology in there [by inventing] some of the drugs that create some of the problems.

What struck me about **Parable** *in terms of current events is the choices one makes around violence. What's self-preservation and what's the cost of survival? That seemed to me to be a theme throughout your books.*

No, it's more like the need to adapt to your circumstances; I mean, I'm pretty explicit about it in *Parable,* but in all of my books there is some need for not only the character but generally the group that she lives with to make some changes. People don't tend to like to do that. As somebody once said, people want things to stay the same, but they want them to change for the better. They would love to get an increase in pay.

They don't like deteriorating conditions?

They don't like changes. Even important ones. For instance, they just tend to want things to stay the same. They're perfectly willing to get more out of it as far as money is concerned as long as nothing else changes.

In Xenogenesis *did the Oankali further exacerbate the worst of human genetics—our tendency toward hierarchy—by taking away people's fertility and taking away people's choice?*

Stress will do that regardless. You can see that happening right now. When people start to see hard times, they immediately look around for someone to blame, and some of them look around for something nasty to do about the problem. Here in California, we've got politicians advocating all sorts of things against foreigners: don't let them use the schools, don't let them use the hospitals, don't let their kids become citizens. All sorts of really dumb things, because they are bound to make for a permanent underclass of un-educated, not very healthy people who are certainly going to share their diseases with the rest of us. And who are going to be very resentful, as they should be, at the way they are being treated.

Parable *takes that to its—*

The governor can get a big rise in his popularity numbers by advocating denying citizenship to the children of immigrants. It wouldn't be that way, I suspect, or there wouldn't be as many people who thought that it was a good [thing]—and certainly no governor would advocate it—if times were better. But we are having a nastier time with the recession here in California than a lot of the country. People are eager to look around for a villain and then to punish that villain. And in the case of the humans and the Oankali, the humans were under terrible stress. They've got a very handy villain who is at least to some degree guilty. I mean the Oankali didn't plot the war that wiped out most of them, but the Oankali are certainly standing in their way for a long time.

Is **Parable of the Sower** *the beginning of another series?*

Yes and no. It is in the sense that I want to take the religion on to the destiny that the character is talking about, and I want to see the ways in which it changes and the ways in which the people change and the interaction. Also I want to play around with the society that grows out of this. So, it is the beginning of a new series in the sense that I want to go on with the ideas, but there are going to be big time gaps, so there are going to be new people.

The part of **Parable** *that I found myself most preoccupied with in relationship to my everyday life was the idea of walled cities or walled neighborhoods, because it feels like that's beginning.*

Oh it's more than beginning; here in the L.A. area, it's very common.

The mindset that allows it to happen—first you fence in your yard—then your neighborhood watch is almost inevitable—

It's not only inevitable, it's down right necessary. I used to be in a neighborhood where there was a neighborhood watch; it didn't become established until about half of us were burglarized. So people wind up acting in self-defense. Really what they wind up doing is about all they can do as individuals who are not wealthy or anything but live in a community where there are natural definitions in the community. There's not that much you can do. So you come together in a neighborhood-watch situation in the hope of at least helping each other.

It seemed in **Parable** *that folks outside the walls never became totally alien to people inside the walls.*

The people who are outside the walls may once have been inside walls that did not survive.

I have a friend who contends that **Clay's Ark** *was written as a commentary on AIDS.*

Oddly enough it wasn't. I didn't know about AIDS at that time. AIDS was around; I just didn't know about it. It was more me playing with biology again. The disease that I used to create the disease of *Clay's Ark* was rabies.

Rabies was the only disease that had a reputation for doing odd things—like the virus could hang around on things for long periods of time and then still infect someone with no warm human body or other body to keep it viable. And it was a disease that had that long incubation period, and also it tended to be an upper before it was a downer—it tended to make you more hyper, more excitable, more attentive before it made you crazy and dead. Not crazy exactly. There are descriptions of people dying of rabies that don't jibe with the idea of ravenous monsters out to bite everybody.

When you wrote **Parable** *did you have to study up on the guns and things you write about?*

Yes, I knew almost nothing. I had to clean out the library. More than that I think, I had to look at comparative religions. What I wanted to do was not to copy any existing religion or philosophy, but on the other hand, not to avoid a thing that I felt was true because it existed in some other religion or philosophy.

I had a lot of trouble writing this because I knew I would have to write about a character who was power-seeking. I didn't realize how much I had absorbed the notion that power-seekers were evil. I find it very difficult to write about a main character with whom I have no sympathy, so I had to find a way of getting around that. I had to come to the realization that like religion, power can be a tool. I mean, power, money, knowledge, religion, whatever is common among human beings, can be beneficial or harmful to the individual and is judged by how it is being used. And also, of course, by the entrenched interests doing the judging.

In **Mind of My Mind** *you are dealing with a character who is eventually power-seeking.*

No, she's not power-seeking in quite the same way. She has been bred to do what she is doing. She doesn't really have a choice, and when Doro tells her to stop doing that she just about dies. So I've done that many times—I put a character in a position where she must seek power or she must handle power whether she sought it or not. This is the first time I've written about a character who was actively power-seeking and didn't have to be. Whose life might even be better if she were not.

Elyce Rae Helford (essay date Summer 1994)

SOURCE: "'Would You Really Rather Die Than Bear My Young?': The Construction of Gender, Race, and Species in Octavia E. Butler's 'Bloodchild,'" in *African American Review*, Vol. 28, No. 2, Summer, 1994, pp. 259-71.

[*In the following essay, Helford analyzes Butler's "Bloodchild" and its implications on our conception of gender, race, and species.*]

"Did you use the rifle to shoot the achti?"

"Yes."

"And do you mean to use it to shoot me?"

I stared at her, outlined in the moonlight—coiled graceful body. "What does Terran blood taste like to you?"

She said nothing.

"What are you?" I whispered. "What are we to you?"

She lay still, rested her head on her topmost coil. "You know me as no other does," she said softly. "You must decide."

Although the invitation is to the character Gan, the questioning human voice in this conversation between human and alien from Octavia E. Butler's 1984 Hugo and Nebula Award-winning story **"Bloodchild,"** I am thoroughly invested in getting to decide who and what the aliens are—aliens so dangerous to humans that T'Gatoi, the gracefully coiled blood-sucker, fears she will be shot. From my perspective as a (human) reader, I work to discover the powerful metaphors which control my understanding of who and what the aliens can be: Their serpent-like quality evokes fears of the dangerous animal realm; the mention of the moon and blood in reference to this female character may allude to a mythic "feminine" power; the debate over the nature of a relationship which includes dependence, exploitation, and threats of violence conjures up a metaphoric representation of the relationship between master and slave. How I decide to read these figures is determined by my own subject positions—primarily that I am a child of popular culture and a white feminist scholar invested in issues of

race and species. However, the conclusions I draw are ultimately less important than is my investigation, inspired by Butler's ability to grab my attention and fire my imagination through fiction written in subtle, provocative language and populated by complex, suggestive characters. The combination of emotional power and conceptual complexity central to **"Bloodchild"** makes this, like all of Butler's fiction, an excellent example of literature which bridges the gap between "high" and popular culture in a manner as complex and unique as her position as science fiction's most prolific—if not only—African American feminist writer.

"Bloodchild" tells of a group of humans who escape antagonism on Earth to arrive on a planet where, generations later, their progeny become the valued property of a powerful alien species called the Tlic. Living on a protected Preserve, human families may be formed and children raised, but each family must offer at least one son to the Tlic. The young boy will serve as a host body for alien eggs which will grow to a potentially lethal larval stage within him before being removed by a female Tlic in a "blood ritual," a process in which the human is sliced open and the grubs are removed by probing Tlic limbs and mouth. The humans will never be free, but the current arrangements are better than those for the first generations, when the Tlic drugged humans and forced them to live in pens as no more than breeding stock.

The story centers on the complex relationship between T'Gatoi, the Tlic government official in charge of the Preserve, who struggles with her need to propagate and the simultaneous friendship with and enslavement of humans which such propagation necessitates; and Gan, the human boy raised from birth to carry T'Gatoi's eggs, who must face both his love for this maternal figure and his growing repulsion from her as a controlling alien being. Through these and other characters, and the setting in which Butler places them, we experience a text which simultaneously explores outer space—in its focus on extraterrestrials and human adventures beyond planet Earth—and inner space, through metaphoric figures which illustrate and invite comment upon the construction of identity. The inner space of **"Bloodchild,"** like that in all of Butler's fiction, is filled with characters who highlight metaphoric considerations of gender, race, and species.

If Barbara Christian is right when she asserts that contemporary African American women write within a long tradition of struggles to represent the self in reaction to external conceptualizations, and Samuel Delany is right to consider science fiction an ideal genre through which to challenge traditional representations of subjectivity, then Butler is the writer to illustrate the best of both worlds. Because her black feminism appears solely in the highly metaphoric genre of science fiction, it is particularly through metaphors that her texts exemplify a meeting point between "high" and popular culture. And the metaphorization of identity, according to critical theorists such as Alice Jardine, Henry Louis Gates, Jr., and Mary Midgley, is central to the postmodern condition, in its emphasis on addressing the tropes and gaps in traditional philosophy and the culture invoked through such discourse. By examining the ways in which Butler's metaphors construct gender, race, and species identity in **"Bloodchild,"** I intend to illustrate some of the problems and promises of the dissolving boundaries between contemporary "high" and popular culture, and between theoretical and literary discourse. But in order to reach the point at which Butler meets "high" culture, we must make a brief journey through the space of critical theory.

Because her black feminism appears solely in the highly metaphoric genre of science fiction, it is particularly through metaphors that her texts exemplify a meeting point between "high" and popular culture.
—Elyce Rae Helford

From the Medusa-like appearance of the alien Oankali in her *Xenogenesis Trilogy* and the archetypal power of the matriarchal shapeshifter Anyanwu in her 1980 novel **Wild Seed** to Gan's "female" reproductive function for the Tlic in **"Bloodchild,"** Butler is deeply invested in science-fictional metaphors for the "feminine" which challenge traditional representations. In this focus, her fiction is closely related to postmodern feminist theory, which is equally invested in examining such metaphors. In *Gynesis: Configurations of Woman and Modernity,* for example, Alice Jardine examines the post-modern preoccupation with rejecting and rethinking Western "master narratives"—humanistic philosophies which propose and rely upon philosophical absolutes such as "Man," "History," and "Truth"—and finds that philosophers who attempt to understand and explain existence and experience through these narratives largely fail to acknowledge their authorial subject positions (most importantly, the fact that they are generally white Western men of a privileged class). Thus, reconceptualizing such narratives necessarily involves a reexamination of the patriarchal politics of Western philosophical thought.

Theoretical approaches, such as feminism, which reexamine master narratives reveal many of the unstated assumptions of humanistic philosophies. However, these approaches often fail as challenges to tradition because they replicate certain universalizing and essentializing tendencies of the philosophical approaches and constructs they reconsider. For Jardine, the most significant problem is the tendency of such theory to replace *denial* of the issue of gender with an *encoding* of what is labeled "feminine," a process she refers to as *gynesis.* "Woman," she writes, "is and always has been, of course, the original problematic object"; and, therefore, "in the search for new kinds of legitimation, in the absence of Truth, in anxiety over the decline of paternal authority, and in the midst of spiraling diagnoses of Paranoia, the End of Man and History, 'woman' has been set in motion both rhetorically and ideologically."

This thesis is central to highlighting the potential limits of contemporary theory, especially for feminists who use the work of master narrative re(en)visionists without acknowledging the *gynesis* in these texts. Yet it is not clear that any linguistic usage of *woman* can be unproblematic. Jardine reasons that

> to refuse "woman" or the "feminine" as cultural and libidinal construction (as in "men's femininity") is, ironically, to return to metaphysical—anatomical—definitions of sexual identity. To accept a metaphorization, a symbiosis of woman, on the other hand, means risking once again the absence of women as subjects in the struggles of modernity.

For this reason, while examinations of cultural constructions of "woman" and "femininity" are proving extremely useful for feminist theorists and activists, and while it may not be possible to transcend the gender implications of language, the limitations inherent in reliance on a "metaphorization of woman" must be acknowledged. Perhaps the most promising rhetorical response involves overt acknowledgment—in the form of critical theory such as Jardine's, and fiction such as Butler's, which foregrounds and problematizes this process. When "woman" emerges through the metaphor of an impregnated young boy, as it does in **"Bloodchild,"** we are invited to examine and challenge our understanding of the construction of gender.

The effects of the process of *gynesis* reach a much wider audience than Jardine considers in her compelling and suggestive study. While she primarily addresses feminists and other academic critics through her readings of French theorists, the prevalence of *gynesis* clearly reaches beyond theory and academia to popular literature and culture. Moreover, the process is suggestive for studying textual representations of groups other than women. Jardine's concise and specific terminology helps me to extend examination of gender and the process of *gynesis* to my concerns with race and species construction through processes I term *ethnesis* and *zoomorphesis.*

Not only women but also members of "minority" races, as

well as non-human animal species, are all labeled and addressed as gaps or spaces in Western patriarchal culture, and slippage between the "real" and the metaphoric often occurs conceptually and textually. Henry Louis Gates, Jr., suggests that "we carelessly use language in such a way as to *will* [a] sense of *natural* difference into our formulations." For him, the term *race* "pretends to be an objective term of classification, when it is a dangerous trope." According to such assertions, textual representations of race are always engaged in a process of metaphorization I call *ethnesis.* The term may be new, but the process is already conceptually familiar to deconstructive race theorists, critics, and race-sensitive creative writers. For example, Butler, in her 1979 novel **Kindred,** examines the construction of race through the story of a black woman who is whisked back and forth through time from the present to the antebellum South. While in the past, she must save the life of a white boy, who is also her ancestor, in order to start her family tree. Through her experiences, we see the complex web of race relations during this period in U.S. history, which included the rape of enslaved women by whites and the arbitrary but intentional labeling of the resulting biracial children as "black"—and therefore "slaves"—by whites. Butler's focus on the historical construction of race encourages our awareness that "blackness" is no more than a construction upheld to continue racist oppression.

Like the study of gender and race, reconceptualization of species can effectively deconstruct the humanist biases of traditional philosophical absolutes; textual representations of this reconceptualization result in the process I label *zoomorphesis.* Denial of the importance of human(e) treatment of animals—and even the fact that humans *are* animals—in many ways echoes the objectification and minoritization faced by women and people of color. Therefore, it is not surprising that animals, too, surface in both contemporary critical theory and popular fiction as lack, absence, and space. Just as women become "woman" through language, so living animals become symbols of "animalness" or that which we label *inhuman.*

Metatheorist Mary Midgley denaturalizes species in ways similar to Jardine's study of gender and Gates's examination of race. Her critical study of the representation of animals in modern Western philosophy, *Animals and Why They Matter,* illustrates that gender, race, and species are inseparable determinants in the construction of identity. In the chapter "Women, Animals and Other Awkward Cases," Midgley draws direct connections between the oppression of animals and women in terms of representation and metaphor:

> The fear of women is a fear of the impulses they arouse and the forces they stand for. They are not seen as actual, limited beings in the world with their own wishes

and problems, but as fantasy figures, angels or witches, elementals with the spiritual powers of whatever emotions they represent.

Both animals and women are most important in terms of their symbolic value. And the most problematic aspect of this symbolism is the reduction to metaphor of animals as well as humans:

> As in the case of women, ambivalence produces a kind of mental squint, splitting the idea of the alien group into compensating half-images, between which the imagination oscillates in an uncontrolled way. The same thing happens about animals.

This oscillation of the imagination well describes the problematic effect of the process of *zoomorphesis* and its similarity to *gynesis.*

Race is also important for Midgley in drawing conclusions about animals. She notes psychoanalyst Carl Jung's tendency to use both animals and race symbolically in his studies of dreams. The presence of "wild" animals in dreams indicates repressed passions, as do images of people of color. Midgley quotes Jung's claim that "certain repressed complexes—i.e., repressed sexuality—are represented by the symbol of a Negro or an Indian; for example, where a European tells in his dream 'Then came a ragged, dirty individual,' for Americans and for those who live in the tropics, it is a Negro." Thus people of color become, like women and animals, significant to philosophical inquiry primarily for their symbolic and metaphoric value to the white, male human subject. From such observations, Midgley concludes:

> It is therefore always dangerous to be an entity which carries one of these loads of significance. Many human beings and also many animals quite harmless to man and even useful, such as toads, spiders and grasssnakes, have suffered a great deal from being draped with unsuitable symbolic values. Carnivores like wolves and lions have been viewed quite unrealistically as deliberate criminals, murdering wildly for the fun of it. The devil himself is seen as half-animal. Even creatures which, to the conscious mind, have no special distinctive symbolism, still always have the general one that they represent a vast non-human realm, in many ways alien to us and beyond our understanding. To many of us much of the time this thought is delightful, but it can also be seen as a threat.

The snake-like alien T'Gatoi, as described in the quotation with which I open this study, is an excellent metaphoric example of the threatening nature of representations of the "vast non-human realm."

The key, according to Midgley, is to attempt to divest animals of the symbolism we place on them and, realizing our inability to "understand" them, to act with the care and respect we show (or *should* show) other humans whom we can comprehend little, if at all, better. This suggestion provides a helpful superficial behavioral response; however, Midgley does not address the political implications of textual representation. All representations metaphorize, and this is as true for animals as it is for women and people of color. The next step is to learn how to understand and use such representations. And this is where **"Bloodchild"** comes in. Reading the characters T'Gatoi and Gan as metaphoric representations of man and woman, master and slave, and animal and human highlights the processes of *gynesis, ethnesis,* and *zoomorphesis.*

Emphasis on the metaphoric impregnation of human males in **"Bloodchild"** makes the process of *gynesis* central to the story. In a 1986 article on Butler in *Ms.* magazine, Sherley Anne Williams reports that Butler "gleefully" describes **"Bloodchild"** as her "pregnant man story." Williams interprets the story as an exploration of "the paradoxes of power and inequality," as Butler portrays "the experience of a class who, like women throughout most of history, are valued chiefly for their reproductive capacities." I'd add that this "class" must be examined through issues of race and species as well as gender; however, Williams describes well the imaginative feminist space which makes the story so compelling a site for the study of *gynesis* in popular culture. Although human women tend to have more body fat—thus reducing their risk of damage or death at the bloodsucking mouths of the Tlic larvae—we learn that only men are "implanted." Human women are left to bear human children, especially sons for future Tlic usage and, at least superficially, human family bonding and happiness. Without such bonding, both species fear humans would become little more than pets or breeding stock.

One of the primary ways in which **"Bloodchild"** encourages a view of the Tlic power structure as a metaphor for human gender relations under patriarchy is through its depiction of men suffering the pains of childbearing (and when "birth" means removing grubs from around your internal organs, the pain can be intense). Even more powerful, however, is the suggestive complication of traditional gender roles during intercourse. Consider a description near the end of the story, as the young human male Gan recounts being drugged and "implanted" with T'Gatoi's eggs:

> . . . I undressed and lay down beside her. I knew what to do, what to expect. I had been told all my life. I felt the familiar sting, narcotic, mildly pleasant. Then the blind probing of the ovipositor. The puncture was painless, easy. So easy going in. She undulated slowly against me, her muscles forcing the egg from her body into mine.

The image of the female penetrating the male and impregnating him clearly complicates the traditional gendering of sexual imagery. The undulating body of T'Gatoi, forcing the egg into Gan's body, recalls human intercourse from both female and male positions: T'Gatoi's action embodies both possession of the female egg and male penetration and ejaculation. To this is added a representation of acquaintance rape in Gan's passivity, despite his agreement to be implanted. This example of popular cultural *gynesis* invites consideration of the gender complexity of the "pregnant man" and the "impregnating woman."

My argument that representation can destabilize the reencoding process, thereby providing readers with images (if not language) to reject limiting and misleading categories of identification, necessitates more intensive examination of these figures. For the metaphoric sex scene in **"Bloodchild,"** the question of destabilization vs. replication becomes whether the "pregnant man" and "impregnating woman" enable readers to reach beyond shock value to consider the scene a complication rather than a simple reversal of traditional gender types.

The image can be read as destabilizing primarily because neither character is clearly identifiable in terms of gender. When we look closely at the figure of the alien T'Gatoi, we see more than a reversal of gender roles. The Tlic's insect-like reproductive cycle (which I will also discuss in terms of species) complicates the gender absolutes of human culture. Tlic eggs are fertilized by the short-lived male of the species, then implanted by the female in a host body, in the kind of reversed sexual act described above. The female raises the infants when they are old enough to exist outside the host. Thus, T'Gatoi can be seen metaphorically to fill all biological and social parenting roles—leaving the Tlic male a less clearly identifiable role—or to problematize the ease with which we ascribe gender roles in terms of parenting at all.

This destabilization of *gynesis* is limited, however, by an emphasis typical in Butler's fiction: Biological roles necessarily lead to the construction of social roles. T'Gatoi is both the government official in charge of the Preserve (filling a dominant and more traditionally "masculine" role, in terms of metaphoric reference to human culture) and caretaker of the humans against other Tlic who wish to return humans to the status of domesticated animals (the role of caretaker illustrating a more traditionally "feminine" role). It may seem merely logical to assign T'Gatoi both "masculine" and "feminine" social roles and personality traits to echo the gender implications of her reproductive functions. However, the emphasis on this parallel within the story evokes a problematic biological essentialism, for the problematization of gender roles seen in the complexity of the reproductive cycle becomes reduced to a simpler and more limiting role reversal when paired with biological determinism. That is, the depiction of reproduction we see in the scene between T'Gatoi and Gan cannot help us to destabilize the construction of gender if social roles reinforce a view of (biological) sex as determinant of subjectivity. Female Tlic dominate in this alien culture; males fill a passive, primarily reproductive function. Through this reversal of traditional human gender roles under Western patriarchy, we see a biologically determined matriarchy whose hierarchical nature limits its effectiveness as a creative textual response to patriarchy. Ultimately, destabilizing social roles would be more effective if biology were not destiny in Tlic culture, regardless of whether it resulted in a patriarchy or a matriarchy.

The issues of power and control which determine human-alien gender relations in **"Bloodchild"** are also suggestive of racial and species metaphors. Throughout the events of the story, Gan becomes increasingly aware of the way humans are controlled and used by the Tlic, enabling a reading of the text through metaphors of enslavement on both racial and species levels. To recontextualize Gan's growing cynicism, T'Gatoi recasts the situation from her perspective:

> "The animals we once used began killing most of our eggs after implantation long before your ancestors arrived," she said softly. "You know these things, Gan. Because your people arrived, we are relearning what it means to be a healthy, thriving people. And your ancestors, fleeing from their homeworld, from their own kind who would have killed or enslaved them—they survived because of us. We saw them as people and gave them the Preserve when they still tried to kill us as worms."

T'Gatoi clarifies that the Tlic must be seen as protectors, to be contrasted, not compared, to the potential murderers or slavemasters the group of humans faced on Earth. The Tlic are fair beings who endured human violence to share in a mutually beneficial relationship. However, when we consider the situation as readers who can see the perspectives of Gan and T'Gatoi from increased critical distance, we also see an outsider faction of humans trading one form of oppression for another. Through Butler's representation of Gan, the product of this exchange of oppressions, we have the opportunity to examine the process of *ethnesis* in a metaphoric figure of the encultured "slave."

My reading of **"Bloodchild"** through metaphors of slavery would not necessarily sit well with Butler. In a 1990 interview, she made clear her concern with claims, such as interviewer Larry McCaffery's, that, "in one way or another, all [her] books seem to explore different forms of slavery or domination":

> I know some people think that, but I don't agree, although this may depend on what we mean by "slavery." In the story **"Bloodchild,"** for example, some people assume I'm talking about slavery when what I'm really talking about is *symbiosis*. . . . Let me tell you an anecdote about slavery. When I was about thirteen I found out on a visceral level what slavery was; before that I hadn't understood why the slaves had not simply run away, because that's what I assumed I would have done. But when I was around thirteen we moved into a house with another house in the back, and in that other house lived people who beat their children. Not only could you hear the kids screaming, you could actually hear the blows landing. This was naturally terrifying to me, and I used to ask my mother if there wasn't something she could do or somebody we could call, like the police. My mother's attitude was that those children belonged to their parents and that they had the right to do what they wanted with their own children. I realized that those kids really had nowhere to go—they were about my age and younger, and if they had tried to run away they would have been sent right back to their parents, who would probably treat them a lot worse for having tried to run away. *That,* I realized, was slavery—humans being treated as if they were possessions.

Butler's response reveals the usefulness of the term *slavery* both as historical experience and as a metaphor for other oppressions, while she apparently struggles with the uses critics make of her fiction as it addresses this issue. While I can sympathize with a resistance to having all of one's novels and short stories reduced to explorations of enslavement, I believe McCaffery is right to point to this powerful theme in Butler's fiction. When aliens control your destiny as fully as the Tlic control the humans, I call it enslavement. Nevertheless, while Butler refuses to label **"Bloodchild"** a story about "humans being treated as if they were possessions," she does offer a definition of slavery that encourages metaphoric readings (abused children as slaves).

As I argue above, a reencoding of race, whether as part of a metaphor for enslavement or "symbiosis," replaces a former philosophical and cultural tradition of denial of race issues. However, if, as Jardine asserts in reference to gender, this tendency is unavoidable in a system in which the alternative to metaphorization is a return to anatomical definitions, the promise of postmodern literary enactments of the process of *ethnesis* will be in their resistance to simple categorization and identification. In the context of

"Bloodchild," the metaphoric representation of slavery between Tlic and humans offers such promise.

Butler's tendency to fall back on biological determinants at times in her representation of gender does not carry over to her depiction of race within **"Bloodchild."** Her approach to literary representations of race is generally similar to that of contemporary race theorists such as Gates, who sees this category as always already metaphorical. In addition, we are exposed to no literal human race relations in the story. T'Gatoi refers to an apparent oppression of humans in generations past which was so intense that it impelled Gan's ancestors to leave Earth, but we do not hear of conflict among humans at any level beyond the familial at the time of the story. Tlic understanding of humanness apparently neither permits nor recognizes racial difference among humans. Race relations become central to the story only in the metaphoric representation of alien-human conflict and the master-slave quality of the relationship between T'Gatoi and Gan.

One way to examine this site of *ethnesis* is to return to the previously discussed implantation scene. As a portrayal of a sexual relationship between dominant Tlic and disempowered human, the scene encourages a reading through the metaphor of white male slavemaster and enslaved female. T'Gatoi makes it clear to Gan that he must submit to her reproductive demands or she will take his sister, Xuan Hoa. She promises to care for Gan and to ensure that the "birth" of her children will not kill or cause him overmuch pain; however, the threat of the rape of his sister is behind this promise. The text seems to play on historical images of slavemasters who achieved sexual cooperation through threats and coercion consisting of simultaneous promises (for example, to free a slave or not to sell her children) and repeated threats (of beatings, death, or the breaking of former promises). Such methods demonstrate in graphic form the slavemaster's control over female slaves' bodies and the slave community.

In **"Bloodchild,"** T'Gatoi literally owns Gan; his mother promised him to their Tlic protector at an early age. Gan's mother considered T'Gatoi a friend when she was young, before she fully understood the nature of their relationship. By the time of the story, however, she realizes that the only way she will escape Tlic domination is through death. She rejects T'Gatoi's attention and the sterile Tlic eggs which are given to humans to drink for their intoxicating and rejuvenating properties.

Gan is saddened by his mother's depression and the distance from her children which this grim emotional state encourages. He knows her attitude is related to T'Gatoi's power in his household, but he is helpless to change the situation. When T'Gatoi wants attention, she gets it. If she doesn't like a family member's behavior, she alters it. Gan's awareness of the power imbalance in human-Tlic relations is made particularly evident when he observes T'Gatoi's manipulation of his mother early in the story. He must watch as she is unwillingly reduced from a defiant state of tension and rigidity to one of drugged tranquillity as T'Gatoi strokes her shoulders, "toys" with her hair, convinces her to ingest the liquid from a sterile egg, and finally stings her to sleep with a scorpion-like tail. Observing this process, Gan thinks:

> I would like to have touched my mother, shared that moment with her. She would take my hand if I touched her now. Freed by the egg and the sting, she would smile and perhaps say things long held in. But tomorrow she would remember all this as a humiliation. I did not want to be part of a remembered humiliation. Best just to be still and know she loved me under all the duty and pride and pain.

Gan seems remarkably aware of the nature of his mother's pain, and respectful of her desire to retain her dignity. After all, it is from his mother that he learned the importance of showing respect. He remembers her words: "It was an honor, my mother said, that such a person [as T'Gatoi] had been chosen to come into the family." But he also recalls that his mother "was at her most formal and severe when she was lying." She has passed on a respectful attitude that will keep her son alive, but cannot hide her true contempt for the oppressive system under which she must live.

T'Gatoi, like slavemasters of the antebellum South, attempts to win cooperation through coercion and contentment through narcotics. Gan's mother knows that humans have no control over their lives, yet she still resists in whatever form possible (without risking further her children's lives). Although Gan longs for the motherly affection that only submission to T'Gatoi will enable, he at least intellectually comprehends his mother's resistance and is, perhaps, inspired by it later in the story.

Gan's intellectual understanding becomes internalized after he witnesses the "blood ritual," which literally refers to the blood T'Gatoi devours as she removes living grubs from the body of an advanced implanted human whose own Tlic female was unavailable. Witnessing this scene, Gan loses his ability to live within the fantasy that humans are truly loved and protected by the Tlic. He had been watching his (human) mother growing daily more angry and resistant to T'Gatoi as the time for Gan's implantation nears. However, only after Gan has seen what this alleged affection can mean in terms of human life does he attempt to face the true nature of human-Tlic relations.

The conversation between Gan and T'Gatoi prior to implantation shows us Gan's growing awareness of his oppression. And through this emotionally charged discussion the ease with which we place these characters in a master-slave opposition begins to destabilize, because here we see T'Gatoi's vulnerability and Gan's strength, challenging the process of *ethnesis* as well as *gynesis*. Gan looks deep into T'Gatoi's yellow eyes and reflects, "'No one ever asks us. . . . you never asked me.'" When T'Gatoi refuses to respond to Gan's statement, he poses the provocative question "'What does Terran blood taste like to you?'" and demands, "'What are you? . . . What are we to you?'" Finally, T'Gatoi answers, "'You know me as no other does. . . . You must decide.'" This enigmatic reply demands that Gan accept responsibility for constructing the terms of a relationship over which he has no control—and he refuses.

Gan cannot escape his destiny as the bearer of T'Gatoi's alien offspring, except at the cost of risking his sister's life; however, he is not content to construct his own image of their bond. He hopes to make T'Gatoi at least acknowledge the coercive nature of the relationship. When she refuses this responsibility by telling him to answer his own questions, he more forcefully demands that T'Gatoi at least *ask* him to carry her children, rather than demanding obedience. T'Gatoi, ever the skillful manipulator, reminds Gan that he is asking her to beg for the lives of her children; however, his demand also reminds her that the Tlic are dependent on humans for their survival. Cooperation is the only way to ensure that humans do not become like the unthinking native animals which destroyed the eggs to protect their lives. Only sentient and rational beings can trust that the grubs will be removed before killing their host. Awareness of this dependence does not prevent the Tlic from using many forms of manipulation to achieve cooperation, yet such awareness challenges a reading of slavery in terms of strong vs. weak or intelligent vs. ignorant. Both Gan and T'Gatoi have conflicted feelings about their relationship. The lives of both peoples are symbolically at stake unless they can come to some sort of agreement.

Humans will always be in a disempowered position in relation to the Tlic. Yet Gan can intervene, finding the gaps in T'Gatoi's apparently dominant position, forcing her to admit the contradictions in Tlic manipulation of humans, reenvisioning himself as more than purely victim. The best T'Gatoi can do when faced with the shock and indignity of having to beg for her children's lives is to ask, "'Would you really rather die than bear my young, Gan?'" Observing Gan's anguish at this manipulative remark, T'Gatoi rises to go to Xuan Hoa, but Gan knows this is the best he will get verbally. He knows he has caused T'Gatoi to feel some of the pain he must live with as a human under Tlic control. Before he agrees to the implantation, however, Gan demands one thing more: that T'Gatoi treat him with the respect he deserves by allowing his family to keep the

(forbidden) rifle which T'Gatoi knows he has. "'If we're not your animals,'" he reasons, "'if these are adult things, accept the risk. There is risk, Gatoi, in dealing with a partner.'" This is the compromise Gan achieves before submitting to implantation. He will have some measure of power to defend himself. *Ethnesis* here addresses and challenges the misleading nature of categories such as "slave" and "master," thereby also complicating race relations and historical understanding in the world outside of the text.

These terms are also challenged at the level of species. When I first read **"Bloodchild,"** I interpreted the story through human/non-human animal relations, as metaphoric commentary on wildlife preserves or zoos. To the extent that enslavement can be argued to reduce the status of human beings to that of animals or "brutes" (to borrow a word from Frederick Douglass and others), much of the complex system of oppression in **"Bloodchild,"** if read through the processes of *ethnesis* and *zoomorphesis,* can help readers to reconsider traditional categories of race and human-animal relations. Tlic reliance on humans for breeding, paternalistic control and manipulation of human destiny, lack of freedom of movement for humans outside of the Preserve—all of these determinants of life for human and Tlic can be read as reencodings of elements of both master-slave and human-animal relations.

There are, of course, significant differences in behavior patterns and rationalizations in the enslavement of humans and that of animals. For example, in **"Bloodchild,"** reference to the protected zone in which humans live as the "Preserve" calls to mind metaphors of human enslavement and colonization (as Southern whites rationalized as appropriate their brutal domination of the lives of enslaved Africans or as the white U.S. government forced Native Americans onto Reservations). But the term evokes animal enslavement even more so (it is closer to "domestication" in this context, despite the more obvious allusion to wildlife preserves), as the term can be interpreted on literal as well as metaphoric levels. However, when the Preserve is also referred to as a "cage," a clear movement into the terminology of species is evident.

One angle from which to clarify more fully the distinctions between race and species, and thus the processes of *ethnesis* and *zoomorphesis* in **"Bloodchild,"** is through further examination of human-Tlic sexual relations. When examined together, two central images in the story complicate traditional categorizations of race and species: the depiction of early Tlic usage of humans for reproduction; and the Tlic's appearance and reproductive cycle. Life on the Preserve did not always allow family living, parent-child relations, or the relative freedom of selecting a human mate. Gan recalls:

Back when the Tlic saw us as not much more than convenient big warm-blooded animals, they would pen several of us together, male and female, and feed us only eggs. That way they could be sure of getting another generation of us no matter how we tried to hold out. We were lucky that didn't go on long. A few generations of it and we would have *been* little more than convenient big animals.

At first, the Tlic treated humans as though they were exchangeable for native animals such as the domesticated *achti*, furry though vicious creatures bred for implantation purposes (which, during the time the story takes place, are used dead as food into which hungry Tlic grubs are thrown after being removed from human bodies). Though the treatment is not incomparable to that of human enslavement, the reference to a "pen" which holds the humans indicates a metaphorization of domesticated animals such as cows and horses, which are often bred in a similar manner (though the taming effect of the eggs is in reality usually the physical binding of the female for the entrance of a male who has suffered prolonged forced abstinence).

Perhaps most intriguing in Gan's statement is his apparently unwitting acknowledgment of the species connectedness of humans and animals. If treated as animals (which we must read here as non-sentient or "unintelligent" beings), humans would in a few generations lose what they consider their unique gift (or legacy) from among the creatures of Earth. When confronted with the Tlic, who are unmistakably animal-like, humans realize the degree to which intelligence (and the value of that intelligence) is determined by those in power.

Gan is apparently unaware of the species implications of his fear that humanity might become "little more than convenient big animals," because knowledge of this earlier predicament does not stop his family from eating the meat of the Terran animals his mother raises (presumably the descendants of animals brought aboard the original spaceship with the escaping humans) or from slaughtering for their fur "several thousand local ones." Awareness of their people's status as (metaphoric) animals causes no change in Gan's and the other humans' problematic treatment of the animals under their control. Yet the tension in this textual reencoding of species enables the reader to problematize the process of *zoomorphesis*, to learn from the humans' unintentional hypocrisy and speciesism.

The "animalness" of the Tlic can clearly be seen in their appearance and reproductive cycle. As the story opens, we get a glimpse of T'Gatoi's species alienness through the sterile eggs her sisters have presented to Gan's family, her "long, velvet underside," reference to her numerous legs, and her coldness, combined with an intelligence that allows her to communicate with humans verbally. Images of amphibians, reptiles, mammals, and insects vie for accurate metaphoric labeling. Elements of all these, but most especially the insect realm, continue as we see T'Gatoi "cage" Gan's mother within her many limbs and sting her to sleep with her tail. Yet we learn even more when Gan describes her in vigorous action:

> T'Gatoi whipped her three meters of body off her couch, toward the door, and out at full speed. She had bones—ribs, a long spine, a skull, four sets of limbbones per segment. But when she moved that way, twisting, hurling herself into controlled falls, landing, running, she seemed not only boneless, but aquatic— something swimming through the air as though it were water.

A fish- or sea mammal-like quality is added to the previous images here, as T'Gatoi flows, despite her boniness, through Gan's living room and out the door.

To this portrait is added an equally inhuman, insect-like reproductive cycle, including eggs which are fertilized by the male of the species, implanted by the female in a host body, and retrieved in order to save the life of the host. Ultimately, it is unimportant which specific (Terran) animals Butler has incorporated to challenge categories of species. The creature's primary significance is its ability to encourage in readers a discomfort in the labeling of any one group or another "animal." Through this destabilizing metaphorization, the complexity of human-alien relations allows us to see the degree to which species, like gender and race, is primarily a matter of who has the power to construct and label whom.

The emotional power of **"Bloodchild"** is barely suggested by such critical analysis. What we may learn from the story—that power relations ultimately determine the construction of identity, that how we see the world depends on how we are allowed or encouraged to see it—is related to but different from what we may feel. Butler manipulates her readers, emotionally even more than intellectually. As the story opens and we begin to read of sterile eggs and the velvet of alien skin, we are likely to be curious, though simultaneously disturbed by the alien's insistent attitude and watchful eye. We may experience further discomfort as we read of the alien female "caging" humans within her limbs to warm her body, and frustration as we watch a woman manipulated by an alien's power. Such reactions, which grow, as the story progresses, to invite feelings of fear, sorrow, and anger, encourage critical interpretation and explanation as we try to understand how and why we are pushed and pulled by Butler's subtle and evocative language.

Even as we reach the conclusion, after Gan has fought with

T'Gatoi to reach what he considers a tolerable compromise, we may still feel ill at ease. T'Gatoi's final words, "'I'll take care of you,'" are an attempt to comfort Gan, yet they only inspire further anxiety and distrust. And this is where Butler leaves her reader—in **"Bloodchild"** as in all of her fiction—in an uncomfortable, compromised space which offers only a superficial and unsatisfying closure. However, this is where she must leave us if our emotions are to support critical interpretation. If we are to leave the story with the disturbing awareness that our understanding of what we label gender, race, and species is entirely relative to the position from which we are permitted to understand these categories, we must feel as well as know it intellectually.

Hoda Zaki (review date July 1994)

SOURCE: "Future Tense," in *Women's Review of Books*, Vol. XI, Nos. 10 and 11, July, 1994, pp. 37-8.

[*In the following review, Zaki asserts the utopian potential of the dystopian society Butler sets forth in* Parable of the Sower, *and ponders the possibility of a sequel to the novel.*]

Octavia E. Butler has not lost her capacity to imagine horrifying societies set in the near future. Her *Clay's Ark* (1984), a work of science fiction set in California, describes the spread of an extraterrestrial organism that changes its human carriers to something other than human. In *Parable of the Sower,* her tenth novel, Butler returns to some of the ideas she explored in *Clay's Ark.* Here, in a novel written in the form of a journal and not billed as science fiction, Butler describes California in the years 2024 and 2025 through the eyes of a young black woman, Lauren Olamina.

It is not a pretty sight; witnessing the decay of California and the rest of the United States is at times a gut-wrenching experience. What makes the book a particularly difficult read is realizing that, in many ways, our own society is not far removed from the one Butler imagines. Her prophetic, dystopian voice carries an urgent message mixed with hopeful signs that make the idea of a future for the human race a tentative possibility.

In 2024 the United States has become increasingly fragmented. Its economy is dominated by transnational corporations owned by Japan, Germany and Canada. Wage-paying employment has become scarce, and many factories use laborers like slaves. Factory jobs are dangerous, wages are low and workers are considered disposable. Overseers, or managers, are not challenged, and companies establish towns that perpetuate the "debt slavery" of the workers, whose children inherit their parents' burden. Workers' children are often sold into slavery. Politicians support large conglomerates, hoping for the creation of new jobs. They practice a politics of nostalgia: they promise to bring back the good old days (the 1980s and 1990s) but cannot, because society is gradually dying. Citizens have lost faith in politicians, the political process and their own ability to change the system.

Lauren Olamina lives with her family in a small interracial community outside Los Angeles called Robledo, where the first half of the book takes place. Like other middle-class communities, Robledo defends itself by holding the world at bay. Much of the day is spent raising food, sewing clothing, educating the young and in self-defense. The inhabitants have devised various measures to defend themselves against the homeless, the poor, gangs of marauders and drug addicts. The community is surrounded by a bulletproof wall topped with wire and bits of broken glass, and all its members over the age of fifteen are taught to use firearms. Nobody ventures outside the compound alone and people do only the essential shopping, although Robledo makes every effort to be as self-sufficient as possible.

Public services have become increasingly ineffective: the police and fire departments are expensive and inefficient; public schools don't seem to exist. The climate exacerbates social problems: it has not rained in years and the resulting shortage of water has made it expensive. Butler is creative in imagining some of the consequences of the water shortage: water peddlers abound; water can be bought in stations like gasoline; clean children are mugged, since cleanliness is a sign of affluence.

Lauren's father is Robledo's leader. He does his best to hold his community and family together, but like the larger society, both are visibly disintegrating. Lauren is one of the few who realize the community is dying and begins to prepare for life on the outside. A remarkable young woman, her close relationship with her father allows her to understand and acquire leadership qualities. Lauren is a "sharer"—she has the ability to share the pain and pleasure of others, a result of her mother's abuse of drugs when she was pregnant with her.

Robledo is destroyed one night in a raid, which Lauren describes vividly:

> Everything was chaos. People running, screaming, shooting. The gate had been destroyed. Our attackers had driven an ancient truck through it. They must have stolen a truck just to crash it through our gate.... They shot us and shot us and shot us. I saw [someone], running, screaming, then pitching backward, her

face half gone, her body still impelled forward. She fell flat on her back, and did not move again.

> I fell with her, caught up in her death. I lay there, dazed, struggling to move, to get up. . . . Someone screamed near me, then tackled me, pulled me down. I fired the gun in reflexive terror, and took the terrible impact in my own stomach. A green face hung above mine, mouth open, eyes wide, not yet feeling all his pain. I shot him again, terrified that his pain would immobilize me when he did feel it. It seemed like he took a long time to die.

The second half of the novel details Lauren's long march northward in search of a haven. She and a couple of Robledo's survivors join the vast stream of humanity walking the highways of California toward Canada. Her leadership in her group is undisputed and is crucial to its survival; it gradually increases as she helps those she knows are the most vulnerable—women with children, former slaves, interracial couples. The newcomers represent various forms of twenty-first-century exploitation: a Black-Hispanic couple with a child, fleeing indentured servitude; two white women forced into prostitution by their father; industrial slaves running away from cruel overseers.

Butler is at her best when she describes the rigors Lauren's group confronts on the trek up Highway 101. They witness countless horrors: decapitated bodies, the rape of women and children, riots, arson, the vandalism of homes, murder, diseases, cannibalism, robbery, feral dogs, half-eaten corpses, drug addicts. Butler is unrelenting in her description:

> The picture of them is still clear in my mind. Kids the age of my brothers—twelve, thirteen, maybe fourteen years old, three boys and a girl. The girl was pregnant, and so huge it was obvious she would be giving birth any day. We rounded a bend in a dry stream bed, and there these kids were, roasting a severed human leg, maneuvering it where it lay in the middle of their fire atop the burning wood by twisting its foot. As we watched, the girl pulled a sliver of charred flesh from the thigh and stuffed it into her mouth.

Butler seems to suggest that the survival of the human race depends on our ability to construct a different society, and to that end she explores three different communities: Robledo, Olivar and Earthseed. Robledo represents a gallant attempt to maintain a sense of decency and community in the face of enormous odds. It is rooted in the past, however, and is dependent on traditional means of bringing people together, such as the teachings of Christianity. It is clear that Butler considers this type of community undesirable: child abuse, incest, racism and suicide happen in Robledo, along with covert slavery practiced under the cover of polygamy.

Olivar is a small coastal town that has allowed a multinational company to move in and run the whole community in exchange for jobs and safety. Lauren's family hears about Olivar on the radio; her parents debate whether to settle there and ultimately decide not to. We are led to imagine communities like Olivar will perpetuate an industrial slavery reminiscent of company towns established in the nineteenth and twentieth centuries.

The third community Butler proposes is based on the principles of Earthseed, Lauren's new religion. It has yet to be established, but we can begin to discern its contours by looking at the group Lauren puts together as she walks California's highways. Earthseed the religion is simple and transformative. It proclaims that God is change, that change is ubiquitous and that individuals can mold God by their actions. Lauren tells somebody she is trying to convert:

> [T]here's hope in understanding the nature of God— not punishing or jealous, but infinitely malleable. There's comfort in realizing that everyone and everything yields to God. There's power in knowing that God can be focused, diverted, shaped by anyone at all. But there's no power in having strength and brains, and yet waiting for God to fix things for you or take revenge for you.

Earthseed allows Lauren to jettison anachronistic values and to formulate new ones that will enable survival of the group and the protection of the young. It permits certain actions previously castigated (such as killing other humans) if they promote group survival. It is not clear whether Earthseed will permit homosexuality; only heterosexual couples are shown falling in love. Lauren herself becomes involved with one of the men in her group. The origins of Earthseed are supposedly eclectic and include the major religious traditions, but it seems most strongly influenced by Christianity and the principles of survivalism. Butler's turn to religion in *Parable* as an important ingredient in human salvation represents a new element in her work.

> **A constant thread throughout Butler's work is her celebration of racial difference and the coming together of diverse individuals to work, live and build community, and *Parable* is no exception.**
> **—*Hoda Zaki***

Butler's future draws heavily and deliberately on African

American history. Throughout *Parable* images of slavery remind us of the U.S. past: slaves hiding their attempts at self-education and literacy, and fleeing cruel overseers; Lauren's band of survivors, which recalls the Underground Railroad; the pervasive feeling that freedom, work and security lie to the north.

A constant thread throughout Butler's work is her celebration of racial difference and the coming together of diverse individuals to work, live and build community, and *Parable* is no exception. In *Survivor* (1978) and the Xenogenesis trilogy (1987, 1988, 1989), for example, she addressed the need for overcoming prejudice by having different sentient species live together in a symbiotic relationship. In *Parable,* as elsewhere, Butler portrays men and women of different racial backgrounds in roles not usually found in fiction about the future. In a world increasingly polarized ethnically and racially, her work contributes a needed critical element to the genre of science fiction.

Fiction about imminent apocalypses cannot be dismissed as mere dystopian fantasy. The slowly disintegrating society of *Parable* is an exaggerated reflection of what is occurring today. Newscasts of California's National Guard quelling the Cinco de Mayo disturbances, television advertisements for new car and home security mechanisms, and newspaper articles on the present boom in companies offering armed security to wealthy communities all acquire a special resonance after one reads Butler's book.

Dystopias commonly imply solutions, and it is highly possible that Butler will flesh out hers in a sequel to *Parable.* Butler took the image of the sower from the Christian Gospel, where it is said that among many scattered seeds, a few will be fruitful. It is clear that Earthseed is one of these, its utopian promise as yet unfulfilled.

Cathy Peppers (essay date March 1995)

SOURCE: "Dialogic Origins and Alien Identities in Butler's Xenogenesis," in *Science-Fiction Studies*, Vol. 22, Part 1, March, 1995, pp. 47-62.

[*In the following essay, Peppers studies how Butler's* Xenogenesis *trilogy uses our three common stories of origin—Biblical, sociobiological, and paleoanthropological—to make us look at human identity in new ways.*]

Octavia E. Butler's post-apocalyptic trilogy Xenogenesis is about a new beginning for the remnants of humanity, those few humans who are still alive after a nuclear apoca-lypse to be "rescued" by the alien Oankali. In order to continue to survive, the humans are offered the "choice" of reproduction only if they engage in a species-order version of miscegenation with the Oankali. As the title of the trilogy suggests, Xenogenesis is an origin story, a story about the origins of human identity, but it is a story with a difference. Xenogenesis means "the production of offspring different from either of its parents"; this is reproduction with a difference, the (re)production of difference. And the "xeno" of this genesis comes from the Greek *xenos,* which in its original bivalence meant both guest/friend and alien/stranger. As an origin story, this trilogy tells about the genesis of an alien humanity, of a humanity which will survive not, as Donna Haraway puts it, by "recreat[ing] the sacred image of the same," but because Lilith, the African-American heroine of the first novel, will become the progenitrix of the new race of "constructs" (children born of Oankali and human parents). She will give birth to herself as other. As she asks the Oankali, "What will our children be?" Their answer: "Different. . . . Not quite like you. A little like us."

The focus of my reading is to see how Butler's trilogy enacts what Donna Haraway calls a "cyborg" origin story. While Haraway claims in "A Cyborg Manifesto" that "the cyborg has no origin story in the Western sense," it is important to note that she does not say that cyborgs have no origin stories. She makes a distinction between traditional Western origin stories, which are based on "salvation history," and are "about the Fall, the imagination of a once-upon-a-time wholeness before language, before writing," and cyborg origin stories, which "subvert the central myths of origin of Western culture" by focusing on "the power to survive, not on the basis of original innocence, but on the basis of seizing the tools to mark the world that has marked them as other." This distinction is important because it offers a way out of the double-bind "feminism" often finds itself in when it encounters the "postmodern."

In general, postmodern critics/theorists exhibit an allergy to origin stories, seeing them, as Lyotard sees "master narratives" in general, as outmoded reifications of humanist, essentialist notions of identity. The various versions of the postmodern "anti-aesthetic, anti-essentialism" offered by such critics as Brian McHale and Larry McCaffery tend to construct an image of postmodern fiction as dismantling master narratives wherever it finds them, eschewing the "individual" as a sentimental attachment, and replacing the nostalgic search for origins with a sometimes grim, sometimes gleeful insistence on Baudrillard's simulacrum (which tells us that we live in a world of copies with no originals). In the postmodern/s[cience] f[iction] critical tradition (which has its own origin stories), this has led to a privileging of cyberpunk as "apotheosis of the postmodern." It has also led to claiming a "post-gender," origin-less cyborg as the new ideal for our posthumanist bodies and identities. In the process, as postmodern s[cience] f[iction]'s other, feminist s[cience] f[iction] is characterized as being mired in essentialist humanism, nostalgically longing for maternal origins.

For a feminist, for this feminist, the anti-essentialist, anti-origins attitude taken up by mainstream postmodernism needs to be challenged, in order to recognize that those whose stories have been written out of the dominant accounts have different stakes in the desire to rewrite origin stories. As a way out of the dichotomy set up between the postmodern allergy to origins and the (supposed) feminist recuperation of essentialist origins, one might merely out-Foucault Foucault. It is, after all, to Michel Foucault's 1971 article, "Nietzsche, Genealogy, and History," that we might look to establish the "origin" of contemporary postmodern attitudes about origin stories.

In that article, Foucault claims that we should "challenge the pursuit of the origin" because "it is an attempt to capture the exact essence of things, their purest possibilities, and their carefully protected identities; because this search assumes the existence of immobile forms that precede the external world of accident and succession." To challenge this discourse about origins, and the lack of value in origin stories it implies, one need only turn to Foucault's *History of Sexuality,* in which he notes that "discourse can be both an instrument . . . of power, but also a hindrance, a stumbling block, a point of resistance and a starting point for an opposing strategy."

There's an ambivalence in Foucault here, one I'd like to exploit in order to open up the discourse on origin stories to questions of gender and race. As a feminist, I can recognize the problems in how traditional origin stories are used to reproduce the logics of domination by positing "natural, original" gender and race differences. At the same time, it's important to read how alternative/rewritten feminist origin stories destabilize, contradict, and contest the traditional discourses of origin on their own turf. These origin stories are powerful precisely because they not only denaturalize the dominant accounts, but also because they partake of the enabling power that marks all discourse about origins.

Xenogenesis, as a "cyborg" origin story, partakes of these qualities. It "seizes as tools" our culture's most powerful origin stories, those stories which are at the origin of what it means to be human in the Western order: the Biblical story of our genesis as "Male and Female, created He them"; the sociobiological story, which situates our identities in our genes; and the paleoanthropological story of our evolution from our Stone Age ancestors. To these dominant discourses, the trilogy adds what Foucault might call a "subjugated knowledge," a genealogy often written out of the dominant accounts, and therefore a powerful tool for

resistance: the narrative of the African diaspora and slavery (a/the origin story of African-American identity). Xenogenesis, as an origin story and as s[cience] f[iction], is not about denying the discourses of science (biology, anthropology), nor the discourse of Biblical genesis; rather, it's about changing them from within, using the very power of these discourses to help us imagine the origins of human identity in other ways.

Xenogenesis resists "recreating the sacred image of the same," not by merely retelling one origin story with a difference, but by putting the four originary discourses I mentioned above into a dialogic relation with each other. As Mikhail Bakhtin sees it, while monologic discourse, or a traditional Western origin story, might pretend to the illusion that there is one Truth to tell, "any living discourse" cannot escape its existence in a "dialogically agitated environment . . . entangled with alien" contexts. Just as the surviving humans in Xenogenesis cannot escape being entangled with the alien Oankali, the origin stories retold in the text exist only in dialogic relation to each other, and it is in this excess of genealogies that oppressive ideologies are exposed and resisted, and simple essential identities are contested.

So here I want to map the four originary discourses/origin stories which Butler makes use of in *Xenogenesis:* the Biblical, the sociobiological, the paleoanthropological, and the slave narrative. My point will be not simply to see how each traditional narrative is changed, but also to consider the changed meanings made from their dialogic interaction with each other. As I hope to show, the kinds of identities we can imagine are dependent on the kinds of origin stories we can tell. Ultimately, Butler's trilogy exposes the relationships between gender/race and genealogy, showing us how to acknowledge difference without necessarily resorting to "essentialist," traditional humanist, bounded-self identities.

1. Adam's Others: Biblical Genesis and Slavery. A quotation from Bakhtin on the (almost) inevitably dialogic nature of any living discourse:

> Every discourse . . . cannot fail to be oriented toward the "already uttered," the "already known". . . . Only the mythic Adam, who approached a virginal and as yet verbally unqualified world with the first word, could really have escaped . . . this dialogic inter-orientation with the alien [word, self, language].

In place of this "mythic Adam," Xenogenesis begins with one of Adam's others, Lilith, which reminds us that even "our originary ancestor" in Biblical discourse did not stand alone at the start of the human story.

Adam himself is "created" in two slightly different versions of Genesis: in 1:27, "God created man in his own image; male and female created He them"; in 2:7-25, God creates Adam from dust, Adam gives names to the animals, and then Woman (Eve) is created from Adam's rib. Lilith's genesis story, however, happens off-stage between these two chapters. Originally a Sumero-Babylonian goddess, she was assimilated into the Biblical genesis by Hebraic tradition as Adam's first wife; however, because she refused to submit to his rule (in particular, would not lie beneath him in sex), she was repudiated and cast out of Eden. Her "fate" was to couple with "demons" and give birth to a monstrous brood of children. Clearly, in a genesis story that begins with Lilith as first ancestor, we have a text which does not pretend to have the privilege of escaping a dialogic relation with the "alien" or with the "already known" stories of the origins of gender and race.

But this re-telling of genesis from Lilith's point of view is not a simple utopian revaluing of maternal origins. This "reconstruction" of Lilith is not innocent of the power dynamics of the history of race and gender. While some feminist revisions of Lilith's story insist on her heroic agency, Butler's African-American Lilith is forced to live the "choice" enforced during slavery. Lilith is "awakened" by the Oankali in order to "parent" the first group of humans who will be returned to the reconstructed post-apocalyptic Earth. Once there, they will only be allowed to reproduce and survive if they engage in "miscegenation" with the "demons"/the Oankali. Lilith sees her role as being a "Judas goat" leading humanity to an undesired mutation, and her hope throughout the first novel is to prepare the humans for escape once they reach Earth. In short, she is anything but eager to embrace the power of being the progenitrix of the new human race. In a conversation with the first Oankali who tells her what will be, she says, "It is crossbreeding, whatever you call it. . . . Then she thought of grotesque, Medusa children. . . . Snakes for hair. Nests of nightcrawlers for eyes and ears." Lilith's use of Medusa imagery here is not only a reference to what the Oankali look like—their sensory organs are tentacles—but also an echo of the serpent-like demon children of the Biblical Lilith.

This re-creation of the black woman's "choice" under slavery—that is, the non-choice of being permanently "available" to the sexual desires of the slave owners—reminds us not only that any historically accurate genealogy of African-Americans must acknowledge the spectre of coerced miscegenation at its origins. It also reminds us to take racial history into account in any recreation of Lilith. As Sondra O'Neale notes, while earlier religious iconography included "the black woman . . . as a glorious archetype . . . these images of black women as equally acceptable cultural standards of beauty" began to change, until, by the 16th century, "art created to accommodate the emerging slave trade" presented black women "as icons of evil rather than . . . divine beauty." For example, "the black woman was introduced as Lilith . . . made responsible for [Adam's] sin." Here, because the text puts the origin story of African diaspora and slavery into dialogue with Biblical discourse, we are led to see how a recovery of black women's identity must also take into account the fact that a potentially empowering goddess like Lilith was "racialized," "became black" as part of aesthetic representation in the service of slavery. Thus, while Lilith in Xenogenesis does eventually "concede" to mating with the Oankali, and while she does gain power from this "choice" (physically—the Oankali enhance her strength and memory; and narratively—she becomes the "mother" of the new race of "construct" children whose lives are chronicled in the second and third novels), Lilith is still a "slave" to the negative connotations of her name. Throughout the rest of the trilogy, she continues small resistances to her life with the Oankali: her construct children note that she clings to writing things down, even though she's been given an eidetic memory; she continues to touch her human husband's hair, even though mating with the Oankali leaves the other partners unable to stand physical contact without mediation by the ooloi (the third sex of the Oankali). And she repeatedly "escapes" temporarily to be alone as much as she can, even though mating with the Oankali makes one physically dependent on being near the ooloi.

Further, in **Adulthood Rites,** she tacitly approves of the desire of the Resisters—those humans who, on Earth, have escaped mating with the Oankali even though it means their continued sterility and eventual extinction—to be allowed to settle a human-only colony on Mars. This, despite the fact that the Resisters have, in their legends, recreated Lilith as the traditional Biblical icon of the evil mother. As one of the Resisters tells her:

> You should change [your name]. It isn't very popular.
>
> I know . . . I'm the one who made it unpopular. . . . I awakened the first three groups of Humans to be sent back to Earth. I told them what their situation was, what their options were, and they decided I was responsible for it all. . . . Some of the younger ones have been taught to blame me for everything—as though I were a second Satan or Satan's wife.

They further accuse her of having "sold out" humanity like Judas, and even speculate that she did so because she's lesbian.

The second novel's narrative shows how, in the struggle to remain "pure, essential humans," the Resisters retell the traditional Biblical story to narrate their new "origins." The third novel, *Imago,* includes a group of Peruvians who escaped being found by the Oankali, and they also use the Biblical story of Mary to narrate their origins and to remain "pure." In both cases, putting the origin story of African-American diaspora and slavery into dialogue with traditional Biblical accounts does not deny the enabling power of the genesis origin story, but rather asks "enabling for whom?" by resisting it on its own turf, opening it up to accounts of the origin of gender and race.

2. (Eu)Gen(et)ic Engineering: Sociobiology and Slavery. From the beginning of *Dawn,* Lilith's perception of her situation echoes the discourses of both the slave narrative and sociobiology. Her "awakening" to discover that she has been taken from Earth to be kept captive on an alien ship orbiting beyond the moon reconstructs the African slave's Middle Passage. Like the African slaves in America, she is (at first) denied access to reading or writing materials, those things "humans need . . . to help us remember." Hence, while the Oankali can tell Lilith the "stories of the long, multispecies Oankali history," the most Lilith can do is scratch Nikanj's name in the dirt with her finger. And, like Harriet Jacobs describing the moral contradictions fundamental to life under slavery—"There may be sophistry in all this; but the condition of a slave confuses all principles of morality, and, in fact, renders the practice of them impossible"—Lilith, too, realizes that "She was a captive. What courtesy did a captive owe beyond what was necessary for self-preservation?" She perceives the morality of "her job . . . to prepare [the other humans] to be the Oankali's new [reproductive] trading partners" as "impossible."

At the same time, the slave master Oankali are also figured as the ultimate sociobiologists. One of the meanings of "Oankali" is "gene traders," or, as one Oankali puts it, "We do what you would call genetic engineering . . . naturally." Because the very essence of the Oankali compels them to "acquire new life," to mate with and thereby use and manipulate other species' genes, Lilith perceives herself as a "genetic experiment." While the "genetic engineers" insist that their gene trading is not about "slavery," the narrative of Xenogenesis relentlessly keeps the discourses of slavery and sociobiology in continuous dialogue.

But this dialogue is not about using the story of slavery to flatly deny the explanatory power of biology to construct our human identity; it is about changing the sociobiological story from within, using its very real explanatory power to help us imagine the origins of humanity in alien ways, ways more open to including our "imperfections," our differences within. In this way, Xenogenesis is a "cyborg" origin story in two senses: discursively, it's not a monologic "salvation history," but a dialogic hybrid, creating another human identity by "seizing the tools to mark the world that

has marked" everyone except white men "as other"; and it's also a story of our origins as cyborgs. As Donna Haraway claims, "we are cyborgs. The cyborg is our ontology." Though the cyborg generally indicates a hybrid of machine and (usually human) organism (e.g., Robocop or Terminator), Haraway expands it to encompass a broader notion of boundary-crossing identity, an ontology within which, in general, the boundaries which have separated "organic/natural" from "technological" have grown porous. In this sense, we are reminded that what we know of the "natural body" is the product of the culturally powerful discourse of biology. And biology is a "logos," a discursive technology, and such "technologies [are] instruments for enforcing meanings" about the individual.

Where the African-American narrative of slavery finds its origin in miscegenation, rather than in the "purity" of the races, the cyborg narrative of human identity might find its origin in a sociobiological determinism. But rather than reinforcing the story of the "pure, bounded individual" who "evolves" through a competitive "survival of the fittest," it finds our origins in genetic "miscegenations"—mutations, symbiosis. Perhaps we are "biologically determined" ("our fate is in our genes"), but not in the ways we usually think.

Butler's use of sociobiological explanations for human identity in her s[cience] f[iction] tends to focus on "imperfections," and she continues this focus with a vengeance in *Xenogenesis.* For example, the Oankali are particularly attracted to Lilith's "talent" for cancer, which they are able to genetically engineer to enable the regrowth of lost limbs, and eventually to create construct children who are shapeshifters. Seeing cancer in this way not only puts a positive spin on something we normally find hideous (and fatal), it also disrupts the usual sociobiological story of human evolution, which assumes that every biological characteristic has a clear purpose either favoring or disfavouring survival. And, as I've had reason to come to understand, cancer is a particularly frightening disease because it doesn't allow for the usual medicalized use of military language to describe it. We cannot "battle" cancer as a "foreign enemy" which has "invaded" us and must be "expelled"; cancer cells are not wholly other, but exist precisely on the border of me/not me. In revaluing cancer, the text is also therefore valuing "mutation" and "boundary-crossing" identity.

Beyond the use of cancer, the Oankali themselves are represented as completely symbiotic beings: originating from a single-celled organelle ancestor which proved itself capable of mutating enough to mate with virtually any other organism (even ones which "were unable to perceive one another as alive,") the Oankali have gone on to grow and change in interbreeding with species across the galaxy. Some of the new "species" of Oankali which have resulted are embodiments of Oankali technologies (e.g., their ships and transport vehicles)—they do not make non-living technologies—and all the Oankali, including these, are able to link up in a sort of embodied version of the internet and communicate together in "the closest thing to telepathy" Lilith has ever seen. But it's not just the Oankali who are symbionts; enforced contact with them makes humans see how we, too, are already symbiotic beings. As Nikanj (an ooloi) explains:

> Examine [a human]. Inside him, so many different things are working together to keep him alive. Inside his cells, mitochondria, a previously independent form of life, have found a haven and trade their ability to synthesize proteins and metabolize fats for room to live and reproduce. We're in his cells too now, and the cells have accepted us. . . . Even before we arrived, they had bacteria living in their intestines and protecting them from other bacteria that would hurt or kill them. They could not exist without symbiotic relationships with other creatures. Yet such relationships frighten them. . . . I think we're as much symbionts as their mitochondria were originally. They could not have evolved into what they are without mitochondria.

Here we see Butler making use of sociobiology to tell a story not only of Oankali origins, but of ours, as well. And yet, it is not quite the usual sociobiological story, nor is there a simple, unquestioned acceptance of this idea of symbiotic identity. Despite the fact that the humans' relations with the Oankali are marked by a powerful erotic desire, "such relationships [still] frighten them," and with good historical reason.

As an African-American writer of s[cience] f[iction], Butler's use of the discourse of sociobiology is similar to that of the minority writers examined by Nancy Stepan and Sander Gilman in "Appropriating the Idioms of Science." As the discourse of science in the late 19th century rose to become "an especially weighty discourse of identity," and in particular, as science was (and still is) marked by the ideology of racism as a reinforcement of slavery, many minority writers, who were constructed as raced objects of study by this very science, "reacted by actively seeking . . . to seize and control . . . the idioms" of science, "to use its tools and techniques to define and defend themselves."

Butler's appropriation and redeployment of the idioms of sociobiology involves recasting the usual origin story of the evolutionary rise to dominance of the heroic individual (that first organelle floating in the primeval soup) through ruthless competition and survival of the fittest, by privileging instead the "marginally acceptable" story of Lynn Margulis, the microbiologist who collaborated with James Lovelock on the Gaia hypothesis. Her "symbiotic theory

of the origin" of the species remains "controversial." Margulis' theory that many of the microbiotic components of our cells, like the mitochondria, evolved from free-living species which later entered into symbiotic relationships, posits a human identity which suggests that "All of us are walking communities." As Jeanne McDermott describes the implication of this alternative origin story: "Margulis challenges the . . . myth of the rugged individual—alone, self-contained, and able to survive." If, as Margulis suggests, "our concept of the individual is totally warped," and "we . . . are [really] composites," or symbionts, "living together in intimate association of different kinds of organisms," then our usual notions of "individuality" and "independence" are really "illusions." In addition, "the traditional view of a cutthroat Darwinian world," in which the mechanics of evolution justified "exploitation, since it was natural, [as therefore] morally acceptable," is also an illusion. It becomes "a fallacy" to think that "evolution works at all times for the 'good of the individual'"; instead, there is a "thin line between evolutionary competition and cooperation . . . guests and prisoners can be the same thing, and the deadliest enemies can be indispensable to survival."

It's hard to think of a better representation of the relationship between the Oankali and the humans in *Xenogenesis.* As Lilith and the other humans are forced into an intimate alliance with the Oankali, these "deadliest enemies" become "indispensable to human survival." In choosing to privilege Margulis' symbiotic story of origins over the traditional Darwinian one, Butler is able to expose and contest the eugenic aspirations driving the latter. The eugenics movement, born at the turn of the century, xenophobically reacting to immigration and nostalgically carrying forward the logic of slavery, dreams of a recreation of the (imagined) racially "pure" origin of the species. Eugenic dreams were both supported by the Darwinian logic that "exploitation" of "inferior races" by "superior" ones is "natural" and therefore "morally acceptable," and in turn supported the scientific use of biological discourse to construct "race." And they still function in this way. Currently, eugenic dreams of creating a "pure and perfect humanity" continue to supply the logic for our contemporary uses of the prime technology of sociobiology, genetic engineering.

Butler's representation of genetic engineering in Xenogenesis is complex because she insists on restoring the originary history of this science to its contemporary manifestations. Thus, the Oankali genetic engineers are neither simply "indispensable" aids to human evolution nor "deadliest enemies"; the dialogue between these two versions is never neatly resolved. Early in *Dawn,* here is Lilith's reaction to the Oankali plan:

> In a very real sense, she was an experimental animal

Experimental animal, parent to domestic animals? Or
. . . nearly extinct animal, part of a captive breeding
program? Human biologists had done that before . . .
used a few captive members of an endangered animal
species to breed more for the wild population. Was
that what she was headed for? Forced artificial insemi-
nation. Surrogate motherhood? Fertility drugs and
forced "donations" of eggs? Implantation of unrelated
fertilized eggs. Removal of children from mothers at
birth. . . . Humans had done these things to captive
breeders—all for a higher good, of course.

Notice how this paragraph traces a genealogy of genetic
engineering back to its origins in slavery. From the apparently laudable goal of saving species from extinction, to
the contested use of reproductive technologies on women,
to the use of slave women as captive breeders is indeed a
slippery slope.

And yet, we are reminded, the Oankali genetic engineers
don't trade on the basis of slavery. What humans have done
historically in the interest of eugenic control (mired in
what the Oankali call our "Human Contradiction," which
puts intelligence at the service of hierarchical behavior),
the Oankali do "naturally." And in contrast to Lilith's negative description above, when we later see examples of
Oankali use of genetic engineering, we clearly see the intense, usually erotic, pleasure involved in their manipulations, and, on the whole, the Oankali seem to be engaged
in biophilic, not eugenic, uses of technology.

The unresolved dialogic relation between the discourses of
slavery and sociobiology in Xenogenesis exposes the racist and sexist genealogy of the traditional biological origin story, but, by including Lynn Margulis' alternative story
of our symbiotic microbiological origins, Butler's text also
shows us the possibility of imagining less reductive notions of individual identity. In this, Butler's narrative functions like the other narratives of women scientists
described by Haraway: "In dispersing single meanings and
subverting stable narratives of sex [and race], they . . . open
degrees of freedom in their culture's constructions" of
identities. But this dispersion of meanings of "the biological individual" does not lead to what Susan Bordo calls
deconstructionist postmodernism's "imagination of
disembodiment: a dream of being everywhere." Butler's
s[cience] f[iction] contestation of sociobiology's story of
the individual does not argue that biology is irrelevant and
human identity only the reflection of a disembodied culture. What is being argued instead is that our choice of biological stories makes a difference; as "cyborgs" whose
"organic" identities are produced in part through an "interface" with the "technology" of meaning which is biology,
we (or some of us) might have good reason to choose the
alternative story offered by the Oankali.

However, as for other feminists trying to imagine the nature of identity in the face of a relentless ideology of
"anatomy is destiny," for Butler, too, the problem of "essence" will not simply go away with the advent of an alternative story for microbiological anatomy. If the essence of
human nature resides only in our genes, then the Oankali
have already taken this essence before the trilogy begins;
they have already read and copied all the genetic codes of
the humans before awakening them to set up human-
Oankali settlements. Taking E. O. Wilson's (frightening)
promise that sociobiology can "monitor the genetic basis
of social behavior" as a caution, the text also raises the
question of how far our biological nature determines our
cultural structures and human behaviors. As even the Oankali
genetic engineers know, there's more to human evolution
than genes; as they say, "we need cultural as well as genetic
diversity for a good trade."

**3. Resisting a Paleoanthropological Recreation of the
Same.** As a postapocalyptic story, Xenogenesis has wiped
the cultural slate clean in order to retell the story of human evolution. This enables Butler to question just how
biologically determined the most "interesting" aspects of
"human nature" are. As Stephen Gould notes, debates about
biological determinism engender no controversy when it
comes to such biological constraints as our inability to pho-
tosynthesize, but the social and political stakes involved in
the paleoanthropological story are exposed when we come
to the "interesting" "specific behaviors that distress us and
that we struggle to change (or enjoy and fear to abandon):
aggression, xenophobia, and male dominance, for example."
The traditional story of human evolution from the trees to
the development of technology and civilization has tended,
as Misia Landau notes, to tell the same story over and over
again: these "interesting" cultural structures and human
behaviors find their origins in the logic of a Darwinian
teleology, where natural selection determines them as
most fit for survival. Thus we are told, especially by the
likes of Desmond Morris and Robert Ardrey, that "ter-
ritoriality" (read: aggression, violence), "xenophobia"
(read: racism), and "gross sexual dimorphism" (read:
sexism) are "innate" features of human nature, and therefore biologically inevitable, both in the past and into the
future.

> That Butler chose to title the ultimate
> volume of her trilogy *Imago*—which means
> the "perfect stage" of an animal at the end
> of its evolution—suggests that she is indeed
> telling a story of evolution in which the
> "most fit" will survive.
> —*Cathy Peppers*

That Butler chose to title the ultimate volume of her trilogy *Imago*—which means the "perfect stage" of an animal at the end of its evolution—suggests that she is indeed telling a story of evolution in which the "most fit" will survive. But there is an irony to this title, and to its teleological implications as well. This evolutionary use of the term "imago" was coined in Linnaeus' taxonomy for insects to name the final and perfect form after metamorphosis. In terms of the trilogy as a whole, what metamorphosis will humanity, and the paleoanthropological origin story, undergo before reaching "perfection"? And what will happen to those "innate" and "interesting" qualities of human nature, aggression, xenophobia, male dominance?

Hoda Zaki reads Xenogenesis as reflecting Butler's belief that "human nature is a biologically-determined entity"; the trilogy's representation of "unmediated connections between biology and behavior" mean "Butler believes that human nature is fundamentally violent," that xenophobia is "innate," and that "men are intrinsically more violent than women." For Zaki, the trilogy posits "a human incapacity to change in response to radically altered conditions." To be sure, we do see characters recapitulate those behaviors which traditional paleoanthropology tells us are the naturally-selected-for products of our evolution. The first human male Lilith meets after being awakened tries to rape her; in the Resister colonies it is not long before some humans create weapons and begin raiding and killing each other; and some of the Resister colonies divide themselves by race and react xenophobically to others.

But I don't think the text rests this easily with the traditional story. As with the other origin stories it retells, Xenogenesis puts this "already known" story into dialogue with an "alien" story of another evolution, redeploying the idioms of paleoanthropology in order to contest the "innateness" of a human nature based on violence, xenophobia and male dominance.

This dialogue begins in *Dawn,* staged as a "debate" between first Lilith and Paul Titus (the first awakened human she's allowed to meet), and then between Lilith and Tate Marah (the first human Lilith awakens to prepare for resettlement with the Oankali). In the largest sense, it's a debate about whether or not humans can rewrite the "Stone Age" origin story/script. Lilith, by virtue of her personal history as an African-American woman who has studied anthropology as a means of knowing cultural difference, and as one who has already lived with the Oankali, represents a version of the paleoanthropological story Haraway calls "Woman the Gatherer," as opposed to characters like Paul Titus and some Resisters who recapitulate the "Man the Hunter" story.

In the Man-the-Hunter story, human culture is built on innate aggression, dominance structures, and xenophobia, reflected in hunting, weapon-making, and traffic in women. As Haraway notes, in this story, "the crucial evolutionary adaptations making possible a human way of life" were those associated with "male ways of life as the motors of the human past and future. . . . Hunting was a male innovation . . . the principle of change." In contrast, Woman the Gatherer (a contestatory story told by such scientists as Adrienne Zihlman, Sarah Hardy, and others) is about "female mobility [as gatherers and] the transformative power of . . . mother-young relationships"; in this version, instead of meat-eating produced by hunting, the crucial evolutionary change was about becoming better gatherers—"the shift was not from plants to meat, but from fruits to tubers"—where "a sharp sexual division of labor was not" crucial. Altogether, the Woman-the-Gatherer story is about "the deconstruction of staples in the narrative of . . . technological determinism, masculinism, and war: e.g., male-female sexual bonding, male-male agonism, home bases as hearths for nuclear families, and the trope of the tool-weapon."

We see several of these competing story elements being debated in the scene between Lilith and Paul Titus. Paul Titus, embodying the Man-the-Hunter story, dreams of hamburgers, and assumes that human life back on Earth will be like the (Desmond Morris version of the) "Stone Age," where giving birth in the jungle will be brutish and likely lead to death (and keep women in their place), and Lilith will end up living "like a cavewoman"; men will "drag [her] around, put [her] in a harem, beat the shit out of [her]." In contrast, Lilith claims, "we don't have to go back to the Stone Age," or at least not that version. Lilith does not miss eating meat (the Oankali don't eat it, nor do they encourage hunting) and sees the value of subsisting primarily on cassava and other roots/vegetables. And for her, "natural childbirth" (which she has already undergone in her pre-apocalypse life) may not be "fun," but it is preferable to pregnant women "being treated as though they were sick."

Lilith sees the possibility of living an alternative story of human evolution with the Oankali, and, when we see her and others living this story in *Adulthood Rites,* it is indeed a life which "deconstructs the staples in the narrative" of Man the Hunter. Hunting has been replaced by agriculture and gathering, which in turn obviates the sexual division of labor, weapons production, aggression and hierarchy, and leads to the displacement of the nuclear family. In short, the behaviors and social structures which traditional paleoanthropology tells us are innate and therefore ineluctable can be changed, not only by changing the story of our biological identity, but also by the processes of cultural evolution.

Still, as Lilith knows, there will always be those who choose to relive the same old story. There is Paul Titus, whose "caveman" logic leads him to attempt to rape Lilith. There are the men Lilith awakens who attempt to reinstate male violence, dominance, and harem building. And there is Tate Marah, a white woman, who at first believes that "human beings are more alike than different" and are therefore doomed to keep repeating the mistakes of the past. In *Adulthood Rites,* this is essentially what the Resisters do. In their desire to remain "pure, essential humans," they recreate the traditional story of Man the Hunter, with various villages divided along racial lines, the (re)manufacture of guns and Bibles, raiding between villages, and social structures built around nuclear (albeit sterile) families and the traffic in women. As one Resister puts it: "That's the way human beings are now [again]. Shoot the men. Steal the women." But the narrative makes clear that humans are not biologically determined to restore the sacred image of the same.

While a xenophobic reaction to the alien Oankali is figured in the text as a biological revulsion, so is attraction to them, and Lilith and others learn to overcome their revulsion. While human males, in particular, seem most invested in maintaining a Man the Hunter way of life (and, indeed, according to the Oankali, "human males bear more of the [tendency to hierarchical behavior] than any other people," we see various male characters resist this presumably biological imperative. And Tate, who becomes a leader of the Resisters, is finally shown to be both adaptable and dedicated to changing the "Stone Age" script of violence and male dominance. Thus the narrative implies that it is not necessarily biology that determines these behaviors and cultural structures, but social and political vested interests. Perhaps this is why it is characters in the middle of the sexual/racial (and species?) hierarchy of privilege—Tate, a woman but white; and Akin, Lilith's construct son, who is male but bears the mark of race and species otherness—who convince the Oankali that the Resister humans should be given a chance to begin their evolution again on Mars. Perhaps because these characters gain some privilege from their places in the traditional evolutionary story, they are also in a position to question it most effectively. In any case, the Oankali do relent, although the "fitness" of this colony to survive on Mars is left ambiguous. Akin cannot decide whether the Oankali represent a necessary symbiosis ensuring human survival or predatory enemies blocking human evolution, and while he is convinced, as are the Oankali, that human evolution is biologically determined, at the same time, "chance exists. Mutation. Unexpected effects of the new environment," so that perhaps the new genesis of humanity on Mars may not replicate the same old nuclear apocalyptic future.

While Butler questions the biological innateness of the Man-the-Hunter paleoanthropological story, she also turns the trope of evolutionary inevitability against itself by showing how the cultural structures and human behaviors produced by this story may themselves be evolutionary "dead ends," making humans unfit for survival. By the end of *Adulthood Rites,* several of the Resister villages have committed mass suicide, and the escalating weapons production and raiding have killed many more. In a particularly ironic and funny scene, the Resisters' archeological salvage operation of a Catholic church turns up a plastic icon of Christ which Akin determines to be poisonous and nonbiodegradeable. While Tate suggests that humans need these icons as reflections of their identity, it is also clear that as long as humans cling to this recreation of the same, this is how "people poison each other. . . . In a way, that's how the war started." And, while the Oankali do relent and allow the Resisters to begin again on Mars, this part of the story happens off-stage, between *Adulthood Rites* and *Imago,* and is therefore a "dead end" in the trilogy's narrative of evolution. Apparently, Xenogenesis is not very interested in yet another story of origins which will probably only replicate a logic of purity and produce human identities which are (willfully?) "innocent" of the possibilities inherent in the "pollution" of symbiotic, cyborg identities.

Overall, as a story of origins, Xenogenesis contests our culture's most powerful originary discourses (Biblical, biological, anthropological), which are also therefore our most weighty discourses of identity, by insistently keeping each one in dialogue with the others, and with the African-American origin story of slavery as well. In this way, the text offers a reading lesson for keeping feminism in dialogue with postmodernism in the context of origin stories. If the Oankali are figures for postmodern anti-origins ("going back . . . is the one direction that's closed to us," and the Resisters are figures for an insistence on an essential notion of identity, neither comes away unchanged from the encounter. The text offers a third choice between: 1) a postmodern call to "forsake the pursuit of the origin" (as Foucault recommends) or to reveal science as yet one more meaningless master narrative (in the Lyotardian sense), and 2) an essentialist desire to claim some gender/race identity based in a "biology" outside history or cultural construction (as feminists are accused of doing). We can, as cyborgs, choose among alternative stories of our biological inheritance (themselves technologies of meanings) with which to interface.

The trilogy itself privileges this third choice, represented by Lilith's origin of a new "race" of "constructs": her children with the Oankali are the hero(ine)s of the second and third novels, and these constructs, being constructed out of the complex discursive dialogue I've described above, carry with them both the desire to reclaim potentially powerful origin stories which marks "feminism," and the recognition, which marks "postmodernism," that traditional origin stories have historically been oppressively reductive in their creation of identity. By the time we get to the third novel, the text fully embodies in its construct ooloi hero(ine) Jodahs a cyborg identity which breaks down the boundaries between human/nonhuman, male/female, and natural/technological. This "genetic engineer" is both the scientist and the laboratory (it is the ooloi who manipulate the genetic exchanges of reproduction within their own bodies); both (and neither) male and female (Jodahs is a shapeshifter, and we see it become both genders in different scenes). While Lilith's presence doesn't allow us to forget the erotic violence of forced reproduction at the hands (tentacles?) of the Oankali, the text still seduces us into a reading dialogue with the alien, partly by "romancing" Jodahs (note the use of romance discourse in a scene where it seduces a human mate, but more importantly by showing how, with the creation of Jodahs, the trilogy has come to the "perfection" of a new species which, while it may not be entirely "safe," seems preferable to the notions of identity we hold now).

It is this desire for the alien, the other, for difference within ourselves which, more powerfully than forsaking origin stories altogether, can allow us to recognize the value of origin stories while resisting and changing them from within. As Lilith says, "Human beings fear difference. . . . Oankali crave difference"; by putting readers in intimate association with the Oankali, Xenogenesis generates xenophilia in place of xenophobia.

Jim Miller (review date February/March 1996)

SOURCE: "The Technology Fix," in *American Book Review*, Vol. 17, No. 3, February/March, 1996, p. 28.

[*Miller is the author of the short story collection,* Las Vegas Everywhere. *In the following review, he asserts that Butler is "not just a good science-fiction writer, but also one of the most interesting and innovative political writers around today."*]

At a recent speaking engagement in Ann Arbor, Michigan, Octavia Butler told the story of how she was hassled by the police in L.A. for trying to pay for her groceries with a hundred dollar bill her mother had given her for Christmas. The money was hers, but she was black with no I.D. and that was all that was needed to make the store manager and the police suspicious enough to confiscate the money. She followed the cops to the station and waited to get the hundred dollars back, but paid a price in pain and humiliation. This was a story about power and perseverance as are most of the fictions in ***Bloodchild and Other Stories,*** Butler's most recent collection of award-winning tales. Whether she is dealing with the role of medical science, biological deter-

minism, the politics of disease, or the complex interrelations of race, class, and gender, Butler's dystopian imagination challenges us to think the worst in complex ways while simultaneously planting utopian seeds of hope.

> **Whether she is dealing with the role of medical science, biological determinism, the politics of disease, or the complex interrelations of race, class, and gender, Butler's dystopian imagination challenges us to think the worst in complex ways while simultaneously planting utopian seeds of hope.**
>
> —*Jim Miller*

The title story, **"Bloodchild,"** interrogates the paradoxes of patriarchy by thrusting us into a world where "Terrans" live on "preserves" provided for them by the "Tlic government." The Terrans are human-like creatures who must serve as "hosts" for the "eggs" of the disturbingly inhuman Tlic creatures. When the male Terran narrator must serve as a host, we are treated to a defamiliarizing view of "sexual" relations that raises interesting questions about how natural or inevitable our present, "human" gender relations are. The presentation of the "preserves" in the story also begs the question of whether or not even the most benign-seeming protectionist social policies are ever completely innocent. Running underneath these themes is a horror of the blood and guts reality of human existence.

"The Evening and the Morning and the Night" investigates the role genetics plays in making us who we are. It posits unsettling questions about biological determinism, Social Darwinism, and the status of medical science in an inescapably political world. The horrible "Duryea-Gode disease" is the side-effect of a wonder drug that cures cancer, and a figure for the double-edged sword of the technology fix. Those who suffer from it are held in "concentration-camp rest homes and hospital wards," kept open by "greed and indifference." The cure is foreseeable, but progress is slow. One cannot help but think of our current problems with AIDS while reading this complex and disturbing story.

In **"Near of Kin,"** Butler's only non-science fiction story, she gives us a sympathetic portrayal of incest. The story deals with family tensions and issues of love, power, and responsibility, but, despite the startling theme, it lacks the imagination and vitality of the other pieces in the volume. In principle, the idea is interesting, but the tale is told with a flatness that fails to deliver any impact. The cunning, defamiliarizing strategies of the other stories work far more effectively.

"Speech Sounds" is the finest story in the volume. Like Butler's brilliant novel, *Parable of the Sower,* this fiction thrusts us into a post-apocalyptic L.A. where "There was no more LAPD, no more any large organization, governmental or private. There were neighborhood patrols and armed individuals. That was all." Most of the people in this world have fallen victim to "an illness" which may be the result of global conflict, "a new virus, a new pollutant, radiation, divine retribution" or something else. The "illness" takes away speech or reading skills, making for profound difficulties in communication that result in frequent conflicts and acts of random violence. Unlike most of the worlds brought to us by cyberpunk, this world is unplugged. The technology fix has failed and people are left to learn new, more human ways of surviving. The narrator, an ex-university professor who has lost the ability to read, negotiates the mean, Social Darwinist streets, finds and loses a lover, and ends up adopting two small children against her own best interests, because the children need a "teacher and protector." This is what makes Butler's work stand out. She does not, as many others do, play with the idea of cool new technologically sophisticated toys or revel in the dystopian world she creates. There is a utopian seed of hope in her often dark vision, a lesson on compassion and the value of regarding the other as part of one's greater self.

The final story in the volume, **"Crossover,"** is a good explication of the psychological costs of shitwork, an investigation of what causes people to lose it. In this case, the female narrator has to deal with the stress and drudgery of work as well as the scars of an abusive relationship and the hard life of the street. All of this pushes her too far and she crosses over into the bizarre, dark corners of her imagination. Butler's portrayal is sympathetic without being sentimental; it is both emotionally compelling and intelligent.

Two essays, **"Furor Scribendi"** and **"Positive Obsession,"** comprise the rest of *Bloodchild and Other Stories.* Of these two, only one, **"Positive Obsession,"** should have been included. **"Furor Scribendi"** is a list of suggestions for beginning writers which might be interesting to some, but doesn't go much past a Creative Writing 101 lecture. This essay and the afterwords which follow each story struck me as filler, and the small commentaries might bother readers who prefer not to be given a packaged meaning after each story. On the other hand, those interested in Butler's work do get some interesting tidbits of information about the inspiration for each story. **"Positive Obsession"** is a far stronger essay that conveys how Butler's background and past experiences speak to her writing. Here she discusses personal fears, work issues, and race among other things. Perhaps the most interesting part of the essay is her response to the question of what good is science fiction to black people:

What good is science fiction's thinking about the present, the future, and the past? What good is its tendency to warn or to consider alternative ways of thinking and doing? What good is its examination of the possible effects of science and technology, or social organization and political direction? At its best, science fiction stimulates imagination and creativity. It gets readers off the beaten track, off the narrow footpath of what "everyone" is saying, doing, thinking—whoever "everyone" happens to be this year.

Octavia Butler's work is science fiction at its best. The fictions in *Bloodchild and Other Stories* get us off the beaten track and encourage us to think differently about the way we live, the way we treat ourselves and each other. This makes Octavia Butler not just a good science-fiction writer, but also one of the most interesting and innovative political writers around today.

Danille Taylor-Guthrie (review date 31 March 1996)

SOURCE: "Writing Because She Must: Octavia Butler's Stories, Essays," in *Chicago Tribune Books,* March 31, 1996, p. 5.

[*Taylor-Guthrie is assistant professor of Afro-American Studies at Indiana University Northwest. In the following review, she praises the stories in Butler's* Bloodchild and Other Stories *as "vintage Butler."*]

Octavia Butler is the only woman among the four most prominent African-American science-fiction writers, a group that includes Samuel R. Delany Jr., Steven Barnes and Charles R. Saunders. Her grounding in African-American culture, concern for feminist issues and ability to imagine the future make her work unique, and were presumably factors that brought her a well-deserved MacArthur Fellowship in 1995.

Bloodchild and Other Stories should delight Butler devotees and attract new readers. The volume contains five previously published stories, each with its own afterword, and two essays, one autobiographical and the other on writing. The author's commentaries on her works are as pleasurable to read as the fiction itself.

Butler is a writer by vocation not merely profession: She writes because she must. In her nine novels Butler explores questions and issues that have spurred her intellectual curiosity, whether of a scientific, sociological or psychological nature. Her cultural orientation manifests itself not in anything that might be identified as racially specific but rather in deeper questions: What is the essence of human nature? Are there fundamental and absolute roles for the sexes? What type of communities and families are possible, and how compatible would humans and another species of life be?

She has culled the essential issues of an African-American experience and projected them into other worlds.

"Bloodchild" and **"Near Kin"** are two of the most provocative stories in this collection. The first describes how Terrans (Earthlings) have fled to another planet where they have been welcomed by the Tlic, a sickly and dying species. Not only have the Terrans found a new home but the Tlic have found a new host to procreate within. Butler, in her afterword, says that interpretations of this as a story about slavery are wrong; it is a love story, speculating on the compatibility and possibility of strong emotional ties between humans and another species of life.

The "alienness" of the Tlic physical form, as well as the role human males play in "carrying" the Tlic children, is a wonderful leap of imagination on the part of Butler. Why shouldn't a male be able to nurture and incubate the young if the physical requirements of gestation do not call for a womb? And why couldn't love exist between species?

"Near Kin" is not a science-fiction story. Readers will discover that Butler places a story in whatever world an issue is best probed. This story of a young woman's alienation from her mother is inspired by the Bible. "The stories got me: stories of conflict, betrayal, torture, murder, exile, and incest," Butler writes. "I read them avidly . . . and when I began writing, I explored these themes in my own stories."

How does one recognize the self versus inherited behavior patterns? **"Near Kin"** has a surprising twist within a tight narrative that propels the reader. Butler creates characters that readers care about, and she is especially adept at throwing in the unexpected.

Bloodchild and Other Stories is not only vintage Butler, it permits the reader to look behind the pen. In her autobiographical essay, **"Private Obsession,"** for example, Butler says she had no models for her work and received little encouragement, but she persisted because she could visualize her goal. ***Bloodchild*** whets our appetites for Butler's sequel to her award-winning novel, ***Parable of the Sower.***

Octavia Butler with Stephen W. Potts (interview date November 1996)

SOURCE: "'We Keep Playing the Same Record': A Con-

versation with Octavia E. Butler," in *Science-Fiction Studies,* Vol. 23, Part 3, No. 70, November, 1996, pp. 331-38.

[In the following interview, Butler discusses the science-fiction genre, responses to her work, and themes her work addresses.]

For readers of this journal, Octavia E. Butler literally needs no introduction. Her exquisite, insightful works—especially the three Xenogenesis novels, (***Dawn, Adulthood Rites, Imago***) and her award-winning story **"Bloodchild"**—have been discussed and analyzed more than once in these pages.

One usually has to get up early in the morning to reach Ms. Butler. A private person, she prefers writing in the predawn hours and by eight AM is frequently out of the house on the day's business. She has other claims to uniqueness: she is a native of Los Angeles who does not drive; she is a woman of color working in a genre that has almost none, and she is a science-fiction author who has received a prestigious literary award, to wit, a 1995 grant from the MacArthur Foundation.

The following conversation took place by telephone early one morning in February 1996. It has been edited only to eliminate digressions, redundancies, and irrelevancies and to bridge some technical difficulties; Ms. Butler was given the opportunity to review and amend the finished version.

[Potts:] Your name has been turning up with increasing frequency in journals . . . devoted to the serious study of science fiction. Do you read reviews or literary criticism of your work?

[Butler:] I do, but I tend to get angry. Not when I disagree with someone's interpretation, but when people clearly have not read the whole book. I'm not too upset when they are factually wrong about some incident, which can happen to anybody, but I am when they are inaccurate about something sweeping. For example, somebody writing a review of ***Parable of the Sower*** said, "Oh, the Earthseed religion is just warmed over Christianity," and I thought this person could not have been troubled to read the Earthseed verses and just drew that conclusion from the title.

I ask because a substantial part of modern literary theory dwells on relationships of power and on the human body as a site of conflict: between men and women, among classes and races, between imperial and colonial peoples. These issues intersect nicely with the subject matter of your fiction. I was wondering if you were at all familiar with cultural theory.

Ah. No, I avoid all critical theory because I worry about it feeding into my work. I mean, I don't worry about nonfiction in general feeding in—in fact, I hope it will—but I worry about criticism influencing me because it can create a vicious circle or something worse. It's just an impression of mine, but in some cases critics and authors seem to be massaging each other. It's not very good for storytelling.

The first work of yours I read was the story "Bloodchild" in its original printing in Asimov's. I remember being particularly impressed that you had taken the invading bug-eyed monster of classic science fiction and turned it into a seductively nurturing, maternal figure.

It is basically a love story. There are many different kinds of love in it: family love, physical love . . . The alien needs the boy for procreation, and she makes it easier on him by showing him affection and earning his in return. After all, she is going to have her children with him.

In fact, she will impregnate him.

Right. But so many critics have read this as a story about slavery, probably just because I am black.

I was going to ask you later about the extent to which your work addresses slavery.

The only places I am writing about slavery is where I actually say so.

As in **Kindred.**

And in **Mind of My Mind** and **Wild Seed.** What I was trying to do in "Bloodchild" was something different with the invasion story. So often you read novels about humans colonizing other planets and you see the story taking one of two courses. Either the aliens resist and we have to conquer them violently, or they submit and become good servants. In the latter case, I am thinking of a specific novel, but I don't want to mention it by name. I don't like either of those alternatives, and I wanted to create a new one. I mean, science fiction is supposed to be about exploring new ideas and possibilities. In the case of "Bloodchild," I was creating an alien that was different from us, though still recognizable—a centipede-like creature. But you're not supposed to regard it as evil.

Something similar is going on in the Xenogenesis trilogy, isn't it? While teaching the books in my university classes, I have encountered disagreement over which species comes off worse, the humans or the Oankali. Humanity has this hierarchical flaw, particularly in the male, but the Oankali are the ultimate users, adapting not only the entire human genome for its own purposes but ultimately destroying the planet for all other life as well. Are we supposed to see a balance of vices here?

Both species have their strengths and weaknesses. You have small groups of violent humans, but we don't see all humans rampaging as a result of their Contradiction. For the most part, the Oankali do not force or rush humans into mating but try to bring them in gradually. In fact, in **Adulthood Rites,** the construct Akin convinces the Oankali that they cannot destroy the human beings who refuse to participate. The Oankali decide that humans do deserve an untouched world of their own, even if it's Mars.

In the case of both humans and Oankali, you offer sociobiological arguments for behavior: humans are bent toward destroying themselves and others; the Oankali are biologically driven to co-opt the genome of other species and to literally rip off their biospheres. Do you largely accept sociobiological principles?

Some readers see me as totally sociobiological, but that is not true. I do think we need to accept that our behavior *is* controlled to some extent by biological forces. Sometimes a small change in the brain, for instance—just a few cells—can completely alter the way a person or animal behaves.

Are you thinking of Oliver Sacks's books, such as The Man Who Mistook His Wife For a Hat?

Exactly. Or the fungus that causes tropical ants to climb trees to spread its spores, or the disease that makes a wildebeest spend its last days spinning in circles. But I don't accept what I would call classical sociobiology. Sometimes we can work around our programming if we understand it.

The exploitation of reproduction and, by extension, of family arises in a number of your works. Doro in the Patternist novels is breeding a master race and uses family ties with heroines like Anyanwu in **Wild Seed** *and Mary in* **Mind of My Mind** *to help keep them under control. Family ties control the problematic bond between Dana and Rufus in* **Kindred.** *Reproduction and family lie at the crux of the relationship in "Bloodchild" and between the humans and Oankali in* **Xenogenesis.** *Do you intentionally focus on reproductive and family issues as a central theme, or did this just happen?*

Perhaps as a woman, I can't help dwelling on the importance of family and reproduction. I don't know how men feel about it. Even though I don't have a husband and children, I have other family, and it seems to me our most important set of relationships. It is so much of what we are. Family does not have to mean purely biological relationships either. I know families that have adopted outside individuals; I don't mean legally adopted children but other adults, friends, people who simply came into the household and stayed. Family bonds can even survive really terrible abuse.

Of course, you show the power of such bonds operating in either direction; for instance, Anyanwu in **Wild Seed** *and Dana in* **Kindred** *both ultimately take advantage of the fact that their respective "masters" need them.*

They don't recognize these men as their masters.

I was putting the word in quotation marks. Are you suggesting that people in subordinate positions should recognize and exploit what power they do have?

You do what you have to do. You make the best use of whatever power you have.

We even see that humans have more power than they realize over the Oankali. Especially with the construct ooloi in **Imago:** *they have no identity without human mates. Aaor devolves into a slug.*

The constructs are an experiment. They do not know what they are going to be, or when it is going to happen. And they do not need humans specifically, even though they prefer them; they can bond with anything. But they have to bond.

I would like to go back a bit in your literary history. Who were your authorial influences as an apprentice writer?

I read a lot of science fiction with absolutely no discrimination when I was growing up—I mean, good, bad, or awful [laughs]. It didn't matter. I remember latching onto people and reading everything I could find by them, people like John Brunner, who wrote a lot. I could pick up Ace Doubles at the used book store for a nickel or a dime, so I was always reading John Brunner. And Theodore Sturgeon—by the time I was reading adult science fiction, he had a considerable body of work. Of course, Robert A. Heinlein. I can remember my very first adult science fiction, a story called "Lorelei of the Red Mist." If I am not mistaken, it was Ray Bradbury's first published story. Leigh Bracket began it and he finished it.

Can you think of anybody outside of science fiction?

I tended to read whatever was in the house, which meant that I read a lot of odd stuff. Who was that guy that used to write about men's clubs all the time? John O'Hara. It was Mars for me. I like British between-the-wars mysteries for the same reason. They take place on Mars; they're different worlds.

Might we suggest that since John O'Hara writes about upper-class white culture, his world would be almost as alien to you as the worlds of science fiction?

Absolutely. There was a book of his stories in the house, as well as books by James Thurber and James Baldwin. I did not read any Langston Hughes until I was an adult, but I remember being carried away by him and Gwendolyn Brooks. When I was growing up, the only blacks you came across in school were slaves—who were always well treated—and later, when we got to individuals, Booker T. Washington and George Washington Carver. Booker T. Washington started a college, and Carver did something with peanuts; we never knew what. We did not read anything by a black writer except [James Weldon] Johnson's *The Creation,* and that was in high school. We managed to get through adolescence without being introduced to any black culture.

I was in that same generation, and I remember that it wasn't really until the seventies that we started opening up the canon. Actually, the issue is still controversial, judging from the so-called "culture war" over how inclusive the canon should be or whether we should even have one.

Yes, it's too bad when . . . well, there was one person I had a lot of respect for, but he could not find a single black person to put into the canon, so I lost my respect for him rather badly.

On its surface, **Parable of the Sower** *looks like a change in direction from your earlier work.*

Not really. It is still fundamentally about social power.

But it is much more a close extrapolation from current trends: the increasing class gap, the fear of crime, the chaos of the cities spreading to the suburbs, the centrifugal forces tearing our society apart.

Yes. It really distresses me that we see these things happening now in American society when they don't have to. Some people insist that all civilizations have to rise and fall—like the British before us—but we have brought this on ourselves. What you see today has happened before: a few powerful people take over with the approval of a class below them who has nothing to gain and even much to lose as a result. It's like the Civil War: most of the men who fought to preserve slavery were actually being hurt by it. As farmers they could not compete with the plantations, and they could not even hire themselves out as labor in competition with the slaves who could be hired out more cheaply by their owners. But they supported the slave system anyway.

They probably opposed affirmative action.

[laughs] Right. I guess many people just need someone to feel superior to make themselves feel better. You see Americans doing it now, unfortunately, while voting against their own interests. It is that kind of shortsighted behavior that is destroying us.

Are these problems somehow unique to American society?

Oh no, of course not.

I was sure you'd say that.

We are seeing a particular American form here, but look at the Soviet Union. When capitalism took over, it is amazing how quickly they developed a crime problem. Unfortunately, the most successful capitalists over there now seem to be the criminals.

Which is ironic because in classic Soviet Marxist theory the capitalist class was associated with the criminal class.

That may be the problem. We are getting into murky territory here: I heard about an old man in Russia who tried to turn his farm into a successful private enterprise, but his neighbors came over and destroyed his efforts. He was not a criminal, but to them that kind of individualistic profit-making was criminal behavior. I guess to succeed in Russia you have to be someone who (a) doesn't care what the neighbors think and (b) has a bodyguard. And if you're in that position, you probably are a criminal.

To get back to **Parable of the Sower,** *Lauren Olamina is empathic—*

She is not empathic. She feels herself to be. Usually in science fiction "empathic" means that you really are suffering, that you are actively interacting telepathically with another person, and she is not. She has this delusion that she cannot shake. It's kind of biologically programmed into her.

Interesting. So what is happening, say, when she feels the pain of the wounded dog she ends up killing?

Oh, even if it is not there, she feels it. In the first chapter of the book, she talks about her brother playing tricks on her—pretending to be hurt, pretending to bleed, and causing her to suffer. I have been really annoyed with people who claim Lauren is a telepath, who insist that she has this power. What she has is a rather crippling delusion.

So we should maintain some ironic distance from her?

No.

We should still identify with her.

I hope readers will identify with all my characters, at least while they're reading.

Through Earthseed, Lauren hopes to bring back a sense of communal purpose and meaning by turning people's eyes back to the stars. It made me think: the space program of the sixties really was part of the general hopefulness of the decade, part of our sense that anything was possible if we strove together as a people.

And that was the decade of my adolescence. We keep playing the same record. Earlier I was talking about it: we begin something and then we grow it to a certain point and then it destroys itself or else it is destroyed from the outside—whether it is Egypt or Rome or Greece, this country or Great Britain, you name it. I do feel that we are either going to continue to play the same record until it shatters—and I said it in the book, though not in those words—or we are going to do something else. And I think the best way to do something else is to go someplace else where the demands on us will be different. Not because we are going to go someplace else and change ourselves, but because we will go someplace else and be forced to change.

Do you think we will be better for that change?

It's possible. We could be better; we could be worse. There's no insurance policy.

I gather that we can expect another book to pick up where **Parable of the Sower** *left off.*

Parable of the Talents is the book I am working on now.

It will be interesting to see where you go with the story.

Well, in **Parable of the Sower** I focused on the problems—the things we have done wrong, that we appear to be doing wrong, and where those things can lead us. I made a real effort to talk about what could actually happen or is in the process of happening: the walled communities and the illiteracy and the global warming and lots of other things. In *Parable of the Talents* I want to give my characters the chance to work on the solutions, to say, "Here is the solution!"

Parable of the Sower *was published by a small press (Four Walls Eight Windows), as was your collection* **Bloodchild and Other Stories. Kindred** *was republished* *by a small press (Beacon). As a successful science-fiction author, what made you turn to less commercial publishers?*

I had probably reached some kind of plateau in science fiction, and I couldn't seem to get off it. I knew I had three audiences at least, but I couldn't get my science-fiction publisher to pay any attention. I could tell them all day and all night, but they would answer, "Yes, that's right," and then go off and do something else. You know, the best way to defeat an argument is to agree with it and then forget about it. I had wanted to try one of the big publishers not normally associated with science fiction, and then my agent came up with this small publisher. I thought I would take the chance.

Would you like to break down some of the walls between generic marketing categories?

Oh, that's not possible. You know how we are; if we kill off some, we will invent others.

*I ask in part because I noticed that Beacon Press published **Kindred** as a book in its "Black Women Writers" series.*

Yes, I mentioned having three audiences: the science-fiction audience, the black audience, and the feminist audience.

And being marketed through such categories doesn't trouble you.

Well, they're there, as I was just saying, and there's nothing you can do about it.

I remember that during the New Wave of the Sixties—

Oh, where is it now?

—I was among those who believed that science fiction was moving to the forefront of literature.

Well, parts of it did move into the mainstream. In other cases, people simply did not call what they were doing "science fiction." I mean, Robin Cook did not announce that he was doing medical science fiction, and Dean Koontz does not publish his work as science fiction. And there are a lot of people who write science fiction although the word does not appear anywhere on the cover or inside. It doesn't mean they don't like science fiction; it means they want to make a good living.

As I pointed out initially, your treatments of power, gender, and race coincide with many of the interests of cur-

rent literary theory, and your own race and gender inevitably come into literary critiques of your work. Has being an African-American woman influenced your choice of theme and approach?

I don't think it could do otherwise. All writers are influenced by who they are. If you are white, you could write about being Chinese, but you would bring in a lot of what you are as well.

I cannot help noting—as you yourself observe in your essay—"Positive Obsession"—that you are unique in the science-fiction community. While there are more women working in the field than there were thirty years ago, there are few African-Americans, and I still cannot think of another African-American woman.

I have heard of some who have published stories. The ones who are actually writing books are not calling themselves science-fiction authors, which is right because they are actually writing horror or fantasy. For instance, the woman who wrote the lesbian vampire stories, the Gilda stories, Jewelle Gomez—she's not science fiction but she is fantasy, and that's in the family. But I don't think she even presented her work as that.

Do you think many people are still under the impression that science fiction is primarily a white male genre?

Yes. In fact, sometimes when I speak to general audiences they are surprised there are a lot of women in science fiction. Because people do have a rather fixed notion of what science fiction is; it either comes from television or they pick it up somehow from the air, the ambience.

Any last words to the science-fiction critical community about how to approach your work?

Oh, good heavens, no!

[laughs]

As far as criticism goes, what a reader brings to the work is as important as what I put into it, so I don't get upset when I am misinterpreted. Except when I say what I really meant was so-and-so, and I am told, "Oh, but subconsciously you must have meant this." I mean—leave me alone! [laughs] I don't mind attempts to interpret my fiction, but I am not willing to have critics interpret my subconscious. I doubt they are qualified.

Madelyn Jablon (essay date 1997)

SOURCE: "Metafiction as Genre," in her *Black Metafiction: Self-Consciousness in African American Literature,* University of Iowa Press, 1997, pp. 139-65.

[*In the following excerpt, Jablon analyzes how Butler has transformed the science-fiction genre by subverting its standard formula with* Parable of the Sower.]

Linda Hutcheon identifies detective fiction, fantasy, and erotic fiction as genres of metafiction. Although she omits science fiction from her list, it is included here, for it best exemplifies the self-reflexiveness resulting from the invention of an alternate reality. Furthermore, much of what Hutcheon says about fantasy literature is applicable to science fiction, a classification that is often considered a subgenre of fantasy. In these genres of covert diegetic self-reflexiveness, the "act of reading becomes one of actualizing textual structures." Because the reader is familiar with the "story-making rules" of these genres, his or her understanding of a work results from appreciation of it within the context of its class from its concurrence with and deviance from standard formulas best evident in the genres of popular romance and pulp fiction.

From her analysis of fiction by Jorge Luis Borges, Vladimir Nabokov, Alain Robbe-Grillet, and Dorothy Sayers, Hutcheon identifies three techniques characteristic of the genres of metafiction. The first is the presence of the detective or sleuth, who acts as a reader or interpreter of events. This character's role duplicates the reader's efforts to make sense of both fiction and "reality." The detective story thematizes the "hermeneutical paradigm" and serves as an "allegory of reading." A second strategy is the presence of a detective (or other character) who is also a writer and/or the presence or absence of manuscripts or other important written documents, as in Edgar Allan Poe's "Purloined Letter." Third is the belief—expressed by the detective or another character—that certain occurrences are part of real life, while others are present only in fiction. I expand this category to include all references to the imaginary and the real. Lauren, the protagonist of Octavia E. Butler's *Parable of the Sower,* explains this category when she says: "I've never felt I was making any of this up. . . . I've never felt it was anything other than real: discovery rather than invention: exploration rather than creation." . . .

Octavia E. Butler's *Parable of the Sower* also relies on social and political ideas to extend the boundaries of fantasy. In *Fantasy and Mimesis,* Kathryn Hume outlines four types of fantasy: escapism, expressive literature, didactic literature, and perspectivist literature. Butler's novel fits Hume's classification of didactic literature or "the literature of revision." This classification of fantasy literature "calls attention to a new interpretation of reality" as it "tries to force the readers to accept the proffered interpretation

of reality and to revise their worlds to fit this interpretation." The authors of didactic fantasy literature offer "at least a token program of reform," which may be religious or moral, as in Bunyan's *Pilgrim's Progress,* or social and political, as in John Steinbeck's *The Grapes of Wrath.* Butler addresses moral, religious, social, and political themes. One lesson she teaches is that there is a continuum from personal to political, from religious to social and communal. As Mosley revises categories of the personal and collective, so does Butler. The second revision of genre is evident in Butler's use of positive and negative examples for instruction. She presents both utopia and dystopia, encouraging readers to imitate the actions of some and refrain from imitating the actions of others. Butler's heroine, Lauren, also defies classification. Hume distinguishes between "stories which center on a hero" and "stories which use a superhuman saint or messiah." Lauren combines characteristics of both. Like the folk hero, she has imperfections and personal idiosyncrasies that make her human. Like the messiah, she espouses "new interpretations of the cosmos" and "assigns new meanings to life." Through the introduction of a new religion, Lauren fits Northrop Frye's definition of a hero in the "high mimetic mode" (she is superior to other people but not to her environment), but the plot in which she appears is that of a romance. It commences with her living with her family as a member of a walled community. The dissolution of that society at the hands of villains who live outside the walls begins her journey and entry into a non-rational world governed by violence. She undergoes tests and trials, survives, and emerges a triumphant new leader. The story also fits the pattern of a tale of initiation. The novel traces Lauren's development from a fifteen-year-old girl living under the watchful eye of an overprotective father to an independent eighteen-year-old woman who is beginning her life's work and a mature relationship. The novel employs a variety of archetypes for the purpose of demonstrating that romances tell the story of the ego gaining control over the id. In Butler's novel, the unconsciousness is the world beyond the wall, outside the community, and the people residing on either side of the road that Lauren travels. The Satan worshipers in Butler's tale are cannibals, scavengers, thieves, and drug users whose survival depends on the destruction of others. Arrival at Bankole's farm represents a return to order, a celebration of community values and hope for future generations, and, of course, a subsuming of the id to the control of ego and superego.

Freedom is the subject of this, Butler's tenth science-fiction novel. Like her earlier novels, it integrates historic elements to introduce this subject. There are references to slavery and to the African Diaspora. The novel can be read as an allegory of the slave narrative. In this apocalyptic tale, Lauren Oya Olamina, the daughter of a Baptist minister, leads a diverse group north to establish Earthseed. The story Lauren records in her diary begins in 2024 and describes the destruction of the walled community in Robledo, California. It describes the three-year journey north on Route 101 toward the freedom represented by the land owned by Taylor Franklin Bankole on the coastal hills of Humbolt County. Lauren describes her group as the "crew of the modern underground railroad." She figures as a Sojourner Truth leading the way north, persevering because of her own stubborn refusal to live "as some kind of twenty-first century slave."

Bankole's observation that the "country has slipped back 200 years" is validated by the histories of those who join the group. Emery's sons have been taken from her and sold for payment of debts owed to the company store. Allison and Jillian Gilchrist run away from a father who is trying to sell his daughters. Grayson Mora and Doe Mora are runaway slaves, as are Travis, Gloria, and Dominic Douglas, whose flight to Canada is assisted by the wife of the slavemaster who knows of her husband's desire for Gloria.

In her discussion of **Wild Seed** and **Kindred,** Butler's previous novels, Sandra Y. Govan observes that the writer "links science fiction to the Black American slavery experiences via the slave narrative." In an interview, Butler explains how history affects her writing. She begins by recalling a visit to Mount Vernon, where she listened to the presentations of tour guides whose memorized speeches obscured the historical truth by referring to "slaves" as "servants." As preparation for writing science fiction, Butler read slave narratives but realized that she "was not going to come anywhere near presenting slavery as it was. [She] was going to have to do a somewhat cleaned-up version of slavery, or no one would be willing to read on." Although she may refrain from portraying the African-American experience of slavery as history, her cleaned-up science fiction version provides a frightening degree of verisimilitude. Govan describes Butler's references as follows: "Butler treats the reoccurring themes of casual brutality, forcible separation of families, the quest for knowledge, the desire to escape, the tremendous work loads expected of slaves as effectively as any of the narratives or documentary histories discussing the slavery experience." Butler rescues the past from the obscurity that results from identifying "slaves" as "servants."

When Christopher Charles Morpeth Donner assumes the office of president in 2024, he dismantles the space program, suspends "overly restrictive worker protection laws," and encourages foreign investments in company towns such as Olivar. This former middle-class suburb of Los Angeles has been purchased by Kagimoto, Stamm, Frampton, and Company, a Japanese-German-Canadian enterprise, which has taken control of municipal utilities such as the desalination plant that provides the town's water and corporate-owned power and agriculture industries. Because most people are unemployed, the company is able to staff its operations with highly qualified workers who soon become in debt to the company. This is what happens to the Solis family. Emery's husband, Jorge Francisco Solis, becomes ill with appendicitis and dies as a result of inadequate medical care. Emery must work to pay off the debt that her husband, a company-town employee, has incurred. Because she is unable to do so, her two sons are taken from her and sold into slavery. Afraid that her daughter will also be taken, she flees.

When Cory, Lauren's stepmother, urges her father to consider applying to Olivar, her father echoes the words of the Bible and the ex-coloured man who said he had sold his birthright for a mess of pottage when he crossed the color line: "This business sounds half antebellum and half science fiction. I don't trust it. Freedom is dangerous, Cory, but it's precious, too. You can't just throw it away or let it slip away. You can't sell it for bread and pottage."

Unlike the ex-coloured man, Lauren's father, a dean, professor, and Baptist minister, knows the cost of freedom and is unwilling to relinquish it for the safety and security that company towns represent. This is Butler's special blend of fact and fiction, the historical past and the imagined future. Addressing this issue of fact and fiction in the creation of Olivar, Lauren says:

> Maybe Olivar is the future—one face of it. Cities controlled by big companies are old hat in science fiction. My grandmother left a whole bookcase of old science fiction novels. The company-city subgenre always seemed to star a hero who outsmarted, overthrew, or escaped "the company." I've never seen one where the hero fought like hell to get taken in and underpaid by the company. In real life, that's the way it will be. That's the way it is.

Lauren distinguishes between science fiction and reality. Reference to the "company-city subgenre" sets the fictional world apart from the real world. Her plot summary develops a set of oppositions between "real" and "fictive" worlds. Fiction features a hero who outsmarts or escapes the company town. "Real" heroes succeed in gaining admittance to these towns. Cory, Lauren's stepmother, debuts for this role of hero when she urges her husband to apply to Olivar. Her daughter, Lauren, will fulfill the destiny of the fictional hero. **Parable of the Sower** sets up this dichotomy between real and fictive worlds, leading the reader to expect that once the definitions of "real" and "fiction" have been established, the novel will attempt to traverse the boundaries. Contrary to these expectations, the novel follows the plot outline of the subgenre. Lauren, the hero, establishes the first Earthseed community. This community, aptly named Acorn, is a cooperative rather than a corporate venture. The novel announces its "fictionality" and meets all the necessary criteria of the subgenre.

These definitions of fiction and reality are complicated by Lauren's own discussions of them. This hero-character, a writer and reader, defends the belief that imaginary and real worlds intersect. As an initial effort to convert others to Earthseed, Lauren asks her followers to read and think about how what they read can assist them in improving their lives. Lauren agrees that the good old days that their parents discuss will never return, but she feels that the future is not devoid of hopeful possibilities. The past cannot occur again, but the future can be good. Joanne asks what can be done to prepare for the future. As if eagerly awaiting an opportunity to address this question, Lauren answers by instructing her to read all the books she can. Joanne scoffs, "Books aren't going to save us," and Lauren responds:

> "Nothing is going to save us. If we don't save ourselves, we're dead. Now use your imagination. Is there anything on your family bookshelves that might help you if you were stuck outside?"
>
> "No."
>
> "You answer too fast. Go home and look again. And like I said, use your imagination. Any kind of survival information from encyclopedias, biographies, anything that helps you learn to live off the land and defend ourselves. Even some fiction might be useful."

Lauren reconciles fictive and real worlds by stressing the importance of imagination to survival: "Use your imagination," she tells Joanne. "*Even* some fiction might be useful" (italics for emphasis). Of course, fiction, as the previous passage suggests, is exactly what Lauren is engaged in, and it has already assisted her by providing her with important information about the character she is playing. Lauren defends her author and the genre of science fiction against the argument that it has no bearing on "reality." Even though we may know the story before we finish or even begin the book, because fiction engages our imaginations, it is useful to our individual and collective survival. Keith, Lauren's stepbrother, leaves the walled community to enter the real world outside. Before he is killed, he returns home several times with such valuable commodities as chocolate candy bars and currency. When Lauren inquires into his procuring of these items, he confides that he lives in an old, deserted building with thieves, prostitutes, and drug addicts and that he is valued by this group because he can read and write: "They stole all this great stuff and they couldn't even use it. Before I got there they even broke some of it because they couldn't read the instructions." So, as Lauren correctly surmises, Keith reads for a living, help-

ing his friends learn to use their stolen equipment. This would seem to suggest that reading—in and of itself—will not help us to survive. To be an effective tool in our salvation, reading must be accompanied by imaginative thought. The evidence that suggests this is Keith's brutal murder. Lauren teaches her traveling companions to read by way of the exercise book she created to explain Earthseed. This book—which we shall look at shortly—requires imagination to assist with survival.

After disclosing the meaning of Earthseed, Lauren says, "I've never felt I was making any of this up. . . . I've never felt that it was anything other than real: discovery rather than invention, exploration rather than creation. All I do is observe and take notes, trying to put things down in ways that are as powerful, as simple, and as direct as I feel them." By referring to her discovery of something that already exists, Lauren advances the platonic descriptions of artistic invention. Earthseed is a component of Lauren's religion, and the title of a book she is writing on the subject. In this passage, she embellishes her ideas concerning the interplay of real and imaginary worlds:

> "You believe in all this Earthseed stuff, don't you?"
>
> "Every word," I answered.
>
> "But . . . you made it up."
>
> I reached down, picked up a small stone, and put it on the table between us. "If I could analyze this and tell you all that it was made of, would that mean I'd made up its contents?"

Elsewhere she explains that she is discovering or imagining something that already exists. She says: "I never felt that I was making any of this up—not the name, Earthseed, not any of it. I mean I've never felt it was anything other than real: discovery rather than invention, exploration rather than creation."

Imagination is a gateway to truth. And Lauren's book, *Earthseed: The Book of the Living*, exemplifies this idea. She contrasts it with the Tibetan and Egyptian Books of the Dead by saying that there may already be a book of the living, but she doesn't care. As a collection of verse, it explores the nature of God and the role of humankind. It is her own book of Psalms. Thirty-one excerpts are interspersed in the diary that serves as the frame.

According to Hume, literature is the product of two impulses: fantasy and mimesis. Although the mimetic has been celebrated and studied, while fantasy has been regarded with suspicion or trivialized (she reminds us that Plato banned it from the Republic)—Hume believes it is an equal component in the creation of literature and "an impulse native to literature and manifest in innumerable variations from monster to metaphor." Butler's novel investigates these ideas about literature by transforming them into fiction. Lauren never told her father that she was not a Baptist. He was a minister, and she didn't want to hurt his feelings, especially since the family jeopardized their lives by practicing their religion. When the novel opens, a group is traveling to a church outside the city wall in order to be baptized in a church rather than at home with bathwater. Although Lauren finds comfort and consolation in her religion, especially the community it fosters, she also takes issue with its portraiture of God. Rather than believe in "a big-daddy-God or a big-cop-God or a big-king-God, . . . a kind of superperson," she sees God as change. "From the second law of thermodynamics to Darwin evolution, from Buddhism's insistence that nothing is permanent and all of Ecclesiastes, change is a part of life." Lauren believes that "God *is* change" and that humans can affect the changes that occur. She compares her beliefs to those of Benjamin Franklin, Thomas Jefferson, and the Deists. She says they believed God was something "that made us then left us on our own." Lauren disagrees with this image of God as "a big kid, playing with toys." Instead, she believes that people have control over their lives and that "God exists to be shaped." She calls this "godshaping," and when things don't go well she admonishes herself, "Poor Godshaping. Lack of Forethought." Lauren's religion celebrates the role of the individual in shaping his or her destiny. In this context, prayer becomes a way of imagining things into occurrence:

> God can't be resisted or stopped, but can be shaped and focused. This means God is not to be prayed to. Prayers only help the person doing the praying, and then, only if they strengthen and focus that person's resolve. If they're used that way, they can help us in our only real relationship with God. They help us to shape God and to accept and work with the shapes that God imposes on us. God is power, and in the end, God prevails.

> But we can rig the game in our own favor if we understand that God exists to be shaped, and will be shaped, with or without forethought, with or without our intent.

The supreme will of the individual is set against a backdrop of Agamemnon. As the reader travels with Lauren along Route 101, he or she sees the destruction of civilization: scavengers profit from the demise of others, children and women are victims of the lawless activities of men, three-year-olds and seventy-three-year-olds are raped to death by outlaws. The biggest threat are the paints, men and women who shave their heads and paint their faces blue, green, or yellow. Paints take a drug—pyro (also known as blaze, *fuego,* flash, and sunfire), which affects their neurochemistry and makes watching the "leaping changing patterns of fire a better, more intense longer-lasting high than sex." Lauren says, "It's like they [the paints] were fucking the fire, and like it was the best fuck they ever had." At the close of the novel, Lauren's tribe of converts cover their bodies with wet rags to protect themselves from the "orgy of burning" that is consuming "dry-as-straw Southern California."

Cory compares the discord to Babylon, while Joanne compares the devastation to Jericho, but Lauren consoles herself with the parable of the widow and the story of Noah, focusing on the "two-part nature of this situation": "God decides to destroy everything except Noah, his family, and some animals. *But* if Noah is going to be saved, he has plenty of hard work to do." This fictional world ends as the Bible predicts, and the salvation of humankind takes place with the birth of the Earthseed community and the resurrection of Bankole's farm.

Unlike the old world, where race was a barrier and interracial relationships were condemned, the world that Lauren creates welcomes people of all races and ethnicities. The children of Earthseed are part white, Mexican, Japanese, Black, and Black Latino. When Lauren looks at them she sees the future of humankind. Thelma Shinn discusses the role of race in Butler's utopian future. She says, "By combining Afro-American, female, and science fiction patterns, she can reveal the past, the present, and a probable future in which differences can be seen as challenging and enriching rather than threatening and denigrating and in which power can be seen as an interdependence between leader and those accepting that leadership, each accepting those limits on freedom that still allow for survival of the self."

The title of the novel announces its fictionality: it is a parable, a story with a religious or moral slant, but unlike the original biblical tale, it suggests hope for the future. The sower's seed doesn't bear harvest, but Lauren's Earthseed "falls on good ground," bearing "fruit a hundredfold."

. . . ***Parable of the Sower*** . . . introduce[s] history into genres that are often thought to be ahistorical . . . [and] introduce[s] black history, as "unrecorded history" or the history inspired by visits to Mount Vernon and reading slave narratives. By introducing the issue of race, . . . Butler transform[s] genres traditionally viewed as entertainment for a general audience. Tani and Hume suggest that this audience can be educated while it is being entertained. . . . Butler take[s] advantage of this opportunity, and the result is the modification of . . . the science-fiction genre. . . . [C]haracterizations of science fiction and fantasy are unable to account for Butler's work. African-American writers transform these genres by introducing inquiry and commentary about standard practices, formulas, and norms into the works themselves.

FURTHER READING

Criticism

Armitt, Lucie. "Space, Time and Female Genealogies: A Kristevan Reading of Feminist Science Fiction." *Image and Power: Women in Fiction in the Twentieth Century,* edited by Sarah Sceats and Gail Cunningham, pp. 51-61. London: Longman, 1996.

    Applies a psychoanalytic analysis based on the work of Julia Kristeva to Octavia Butler's writing and other feminist science fiction.

Campbell, Loretta H. "Planting a Seed." *Belles Lettres* 10, No. 1 (Fall 1994): 86.

    Praises Butler's "dazzling apocalyptic visions" and "straightforward prose" in her *Parable of a Sower.*

Card, Orson Scott. Review of *Wild Seed, Dawn, Adulthood Rites,* and *Imago,* by Octavia Butler. *Fantasy & Science Fiction* 78, No. 2 (February 1990): 40-3.

    Praises Butler's writing, but asserts the need for another novel to continue the story told in the latter three books.

Lee, Judith. "'We Are All Kin': Relatedness, Mortality, and the Paradox of Human Immortality." *Immortal Engines: Life Extension and Immortality in Science Fiction and Fantasy,* edited by George Slusser, Gary Westfahl, and Eric S. Rabkin, pp. 170-82. Athens, GA: The University of Georgia Press, 1996.

    Explores the relationship between biological and spiritual immortality in Butler's *Xenogenesis* trilogy and Dorothy Bryant's *The Kin of Ata Are Waiting for You,* and the commonality between theology and science fiction.

White, Eric. "The Erotics of Becoming: *Xenogenesis* and *The Thing.*" *Science-Fiction Studies* 20, Part 3 (November 1993): 394-408.

    Discusses the evolutionary theory posited by Butler's *Xenogenesis* trilogy of novels and John Carpenter's film version of *The Thing,* which treat humanity as a stage of evolution as opposed to its conclusion.

Additional coverage of Butler's life and career is contained in the following sources published by Gale: *Authors and Artists for Young Adults,* **Vol. 18;** *Black Writers,* **Vol. 2;** *Contemporary Authors,* **Vols. 73-76;** *Contemporary Authors New Revision Series,* **Vols. 12, 24, and 38;** *Dictionary of Literary Biography,* **Vol. 33;** *DISCovering Authors Modules: Multicultural Authors* **and** *Popular Fiction and Genre Authors; Major Twentieth-Century Writers;* **and** *Something About the Author Autobiography Series,* **Vol. 84.**

Andrei Codrescu

1946-

(Has also written under pseudonyms Betty Laredo, Tristan Tzara, and Urmuz) American poet, short story writer, memoirist, essayist, journalist, novelist, and travel writer.

The following entry presents an overview of Codrescu's career through 1995. For further information on his life and works, see *CLC,* Vol. 46.

INTRODUCTION

Romanian-born poet Andrei Codrescu is celebrated for his spare, proto-surrealistic verse, his keen observation of contemporary culture, his affection for his adopted homeland, and his mastery of American idiom. Although best-known as guest commentator for the program "All Things Considered" on National Public Radio, he has published more than 20 volumes of poetry, fiction, essays, and autobiographical works. His themes deal largely with life in communist Romania and his experiences as an expatriate living in Rome, Paris, and the United States. His writing ranges from introspective verse on urban themes as in *The History of the Growth of Heaven* (1971) to a collection of short stories, *Monsieur Teste in America* (1987), in which English becomes a "toy box" of colloquialisms, to his Gothic thriller, *The Blood Countess* (1995), based on the life of a Dracula-like figure from history. Although Codrescu's poetry has been influenced by Romanian avantgardists such as poet and essayist Tristan Tzara (whose name Codrescu has used as a pseudonym) and dramatist Eugene Ionesco, it has also been compared to the works of American poets Walt Whitman and William Carlos Williams. His prose fiction has been compared to the works of Zoe Oldenbourg, Anne Rice, and Franz Kafka.

Biographical Information

Born in Romania shortly before the communists came to power, Andrei Ivanovitch Goldmutter, (he changed his name to Codrescu while attending university) spent his first four years living amiably in his grandmother's castle in the hills of Transylvania. A precocious child, he was unpopular with other children. At age 16, he began to write poetry and became involved with his country's literary intelligentsia. Unfortunately, his poems, critical of the communist Ceausescu regime, caused his expulsion from the University of Bucharest. After receiving his master's degree from the University of Rome, he and his mother emigrated to the United States in 1966. He arrived in New York with no knowledge of English, but learned to speak the language on

the street from hippies, poets, rock music, and other sources. He moved to Detroit, joined John Sinclair's Artist Workshop, and eventually went to California. With the publication of his first collection of poetry, *License to Carry a Gun* (1970), he was hailed as a promising young talent. This success was followed by his second collection of poetry, *The History of the Growth of Heaven,* and two autobiographical volumes of prose, *The Life and Times of an Involuntary Genius* (1975) and *In America's Shoes* (1983). In 1982, he founded a new journal, the *Exquisite Corpse,* a monthly magazine of "books and ideas" which combines opinion, satire, and commentary on current events. A year later, he began broadcasting weekly commentary on the American scene and world events for National Public Radio's "All Things Considered". *A Craving for Swan* (1986), a collection of two years of his broadcast essays, resulted. In the same year, he also published *Comrade Past & Mister Present,* a blend of prose, poetry, and journal entries, considered one of his finest works. In 1990, he was invited to drive cross-country and record his experiences. A compilation of these adventures, *Road Scholar,* came out in 1993 as both book and film. Codrescu is a professor at Louisiana State University and lives with his wife Alice and two children.

Major Works

Codrescu's first published volume, *License to Carry a Gun,* won him the Big Table award and established him as a promising young poet. In it are three personae who represent the confrontational philosophy of his early poetry: a jailed Puerto Rican poet, an ex-beatnik turned "mystical Fascist" in Vietnam, and a woman who wants to "touch something sensational / like the mind of a shark." His second collection of poetry, *The History of the Growth of Heaven,* is a mix of surrealism and introspection about contemporary events and personal experience. Most significant is the re-creation of his childhood in Sibiu, Romania, and Ceausescu's feared Securitate, which was housed there. Two autobiographical volumes of prose followed, *The Life and Times of an Involuntary Genius* and *In America's Shoes* (1983). *The Life and Times* deals with his longing for self-expression in his homeland behind the Iron Curtain and the culture shock he suffered when he arrived in the United States. *Shoes,* written in a warm, humorous tone, details his emergence into the American way of life. His *Selected Poems, 1970-1980,* was also published in 1983. In 1982, Codrescu became editor of a new journal, the *Exquisite Corpse,* a monthly magazine which combines opinion, satire, and polemics on contemporary culture. A year later, he began broadcasting weekly commentary on the American scene and world events for National Public Radio's "All Things Considered." This resulted in the publication *A Craving for Swan* a collection of 150 of his broadcast essays. In the same year he published *Comrade Past & Mister Present,* which includes several long poems as well as prose and journal entries. The volume, considered one of his finest works, is a collection of memoirs and opinion on moral, sexual, and political issues. In 1987 he published two books, a collection of essays entitled *The Disappearance of the Outside,* and a collection of short stories entitled *Monsieur Teste in America,* a *tour de force* on the American vernacular. His *The Hole in the Flag* (1991) documents with awe and revulsion the Romanian revolt of 1989. Lighter themes are encompassed in *Road Scholar* (1993), a compilation of Codrescu's adventures while driving cross-country in a 1968 Cadillac. The book was also made into a film. *The Blood Countess* is Codrescu's first novel. The book is a Gothic thriller based on Codrescu's real-life Hungarian ancestor, Elizabeth Bathory, who is depicted as a sadistic, Dracula-like tyrant of the 16th century.

Critical Reception

Although Codrescu's earliest poems caused his expulsion from the University of Bucharest, critical reception in the West has been generally favorable. From the publication of his first collection of poetry, *License to Carry a Gun,* for which he received the Big Table award, reviewers have considered him a rising talent. His self-denigrating sense of humor, his keen insight on contemporary culture, and his mastery of American idiom in his essays and memoirs such as *A Craving for Swan* and *The Hole in the Flag* have also won him accolades. Reviewing *A Craving for Swan,* Charles Bishop calls Codrescu a "witty and insightful commentator whose unique background, gift for language, and radical common sense make this a recommended book." Alex Kozinski says in the *New York Times Book Review* that *The Hole in the Flag* is "a work of great complexity and subtlety . . . a gripping political detective story." While Codrescu's first novel *The Blood Countess* has received mixed reviews, *Kirkus Reviews* calls it an "expertly crafted first novel . . . that merits comparison with the fiction of Zoe Oldenbourg and Marguerite Yourcenar."

PRINCIPAL WORKS

License to Carry a Gun (poetry) 1970

The History of the Growth of Heaven (poetry) 1971

The Life and Times of an Involuntary Genius (memoirs) 1975

In America's Shoes (memoirs) 1983

Selected Poems, 1970-1980 (poetry) 1983

A Craving for Swan (essays) 1986

Comrade Past & Mister Present (poetry and prose) 1986

The Disappearance of the Outside (essays) 1987

Monsieur Teste in America (short stories) 1987

American Poetry since 1970: Up Late [editor] (poetry) 1988

The Hole in the Flag (memoirs) 1991

Road Scholar (travel essays) 1993

The Blood Countess (novel) 1995

The Muse is Always Half-Dressed in New Orleans (essays) 1995

Alien Candor: Selected Poems 1970-1995 (poetry) 1996

The Dog with the Chip in His Neck (essays) 1996

Blood Countess (novel) 1998

Hail Babylon!: In Search of the American City at the End of the Millennium (essays) 1998

A Bar in Brooklyn: Novellas and Stories 1970-1978 (short stories) 1999

Ay Cuba!: A Socio-Erotic Journey (travel essays) 1999

Messiah (novel) 1999

CRITICISM

Marcel Cornis-Pop (review date Spring 1987)

SOURCE: "Escape into New Languages: The Avant-Gardist Ideals and Constraints of Andrei Codrescu's Poetry," in *Sagetrieb*, Vol. 6, No. 1, Spring, 1987, pp. 21-39.

[*In the following review, Cornis-Pop discusses the experimental, proto-surrealistic style of Codrescu's poetry.*]

> Having avantbiographed the world
> To make another come right out of it
> I have certain scribbler's rights
> On the next one—endlessly impregnate
> The self about to be designed.
>
> I praise the lava holes
>
> whence issued my first passport.
>
> (*Comrade Past & Mister Present* 34)

A RISKY, EXPERIMENTAL STYLE?

Andrei Codrescu, "the Involuntary Genius of American surrealism," defies easy description. In his case the very label of "surrealism" seems partly inappropriate and confining. As his newest book, *The Disappearance of the Outside* makes clear, Codrescu has little patience for the watered down, domestic variant of surrealism "adrift/today/ in the Mall"; and even less for the international "poetic sludge used by translators and mandarin poets to sculpt the sad shape of the present." His real interest goes with the proto-surrealistic spirit that, before the days of universal collage and "ecriture automatique," imbued everything (including its own procedures) in the acids of deconstructive wit.

Codrescu's aggressive, "schizoactivist" style has grown subtler, its ideological and poetic intents more articulate . . .
—Marcel Cornis-Pop

Critics, especially upon the publication of *Selected Poems 1970-1980,* regarded Codrescu's avant-gardist beginnings with a certain melancholic relief: " . . . It is interesting to see that, yes, Codrescu did have a poetic youth and a risky, experimental style which fits his times. What is more interesting is how he developed certain aspects over the years." There is, undoubtedly, significant poetic development from *License to Carry a Gun* (1970) to *Comrade Past & Mister Present* (1986): but not necessarily away from experimentation towards some "consolidation of gains" and closure. Codrescu's aggressive, "schizoactivist" style has grown subtler, its ideological and poetic intents more articulate (consider the **"The Juniata Diary"**). Codrescu's recent poems still make a somewhat discordant

and eccentric figure in contemporary poetry. At a time when American poetry seems content to follow a cautious notion of "risk" (as poetry editor for the *Paris Review,* Michael Benedikt welcomed "poems that are coherently risky, that take risks that succeed"), Codrescu has consistently walked a jagged edge of risk, pushing the imaginary borderline between poetic freedoms and constraints further out. A most difficult task, to be sure, given the increasing pressures that work on poetry at present: " . . . In 1967, I was experimenting with all sorts of looseness, riffing, rhythm. (I had a different accent everyday). Then I tightened up a bit for my masters, the publishers. First, Paul Carroll raised my capitals & raped my text with punctuation. Then Mike Braziller with his insistence on the elegiac. Then my surrealist fans with their insistence on recognition (i.e. orthodoxy). All of these insistences, even when strenuously or successfully resisted, left some of their fingerprints, if not the shape of their pressure, on my work. Of course, one evolves that way too, nobody's a frozen CB" (*Comrade Past & Mister Present* 92).

Codrescu's biography as a poetic "mutant" is in many ways representative: the story of a Central European expatriate in pursuit of his mythic America, that slowly receding boundary of the imaginative *outside.* "He arrived in New York (Stephens recounts) not knowing a word of English, and once told me how the taxi driver who drove him from the airport into Manhattan charged him $17 for the trip, leaving him $3, a bundle of Romanian poems, and a good knowledge of Italian his first time in the Village." His next trip was to Ginsberg's apartment in the Lower East Side, to join the great American scene of experiment about which he had read in books; but to his amazement, he found that scene on the wane. In only a few more years poetry entered the "Age of Confusion" at the hands of a "generation of neo-academics who turned out a quasi-surrealistic product culled from the numerous bad translations that mushroomed under the urinary inflationism of Robert Bly." Codrescu still spent a euphoric intermezzo in the wide-open culture of the San Francisco Area before his dream of a free and borderless Idea-State subsided: "Suddenly, all around me, the people fell silent. They put their shoes back on. The chill of mortality was in the air. . . . "

Codrescu also brought with him the secret aspirations and nostalgias of another interrupted avant-garde, the Romanian: "I had natural Surrealistic sympathies and was determined not to let the Balkans down: after all we had originated Dada and gave voice to the absurd. Proto-Surrealisms of various kinds floated about us since the Symbolists. I was temperamentally and genetically suited for New York in the 1960s." The Romanian avant-garde fits better than any other modernistic trend the description of *Avantgardismus Interruptus.* Emerging on the European scene at a time when Western culture allowed itself to be off-centered and deconstructed with greater ease, the first wave of Romanian avant-gardists (Brancusi, Tristan Tzara, Marcel Iancu, Victor Brauner) contributed their share to the modernist revolution. But this phase ended soon with the transplantation of Tzara, Brauner and Fondane mainly to France; also with the symbolic suicide of Urmuz (in 1923). After 1924, with the absent Urmuz acting as a genuine "semaphore" for literary experimentation, a new wave of Romanian avant-gardists tried to pick up the scattered pieces and participate in a reconstruction of modern art in a post-Dada age. Finally, soon after the war, a third generation of Romanian avant-gardists made one last attempt at revitalizing the experimental scene. In their "Message Addressed to the International Surrealistic Movement" (1945), Gherasim Luca and Trost called for a new "revolution of the spirit" to replace the mere "verbal revolution" of their predecessors. A sense of urgency and bleak foreboding filled their message: only a year later, under the pressures of Stalinization, the Romanian historical avant-garde was forcefully dismantled. It barely had time to relocate some of its representatives (Eugen Ionesco, E. M. Cioran, Gherasim Luca, Isidore Isou, Paul Paun) in the center of the European (post)modernism.

Under "normal" circumstances the avant-garde periodically exhausts itself, or is detoured and absorbed by mainstream culture. If we add to this the fact that the avant-garde's capacity for "cyclic" recovery has been seriously impaired in the last twenty to thirty years, we have an explanation of—in Lyotard's words—the current "period of/artistic/ slackening. . . . From every direction we are being urged to put an end to experimentation, in the arts and elsewhere." Where the "power assumes the name of a party, realism and its neoclassical complement triumph over the experimental avant-garde by slandering and banning it"; where "power is that of capital," "postmodern" eclecticism (a kind of "degree zero of contemporary general culture . . . ") is substituted for the old avant-gardist radicalism.

But the case of the Romanian avant-garde can be called anything but "normal." To this day, the "historical" avant-garde has not been fully assimilated and *canonized* by Romanian critics. Its violent interruption in the fifties, before it could run a complete course, predictably enhanced its appeal in contemporary literature. Several generations of postwar Romanian writers have used the half-mythical pursuits of the earlier avant-gardists as "a necessary filter" in their own literary exploration. It is not, therefore, surprising to find Codrescu's American poetry connected to this fourth (utopian) cycle of the Romanian avant-garde. The title of his first book (reminiscent of Geo Dumitrescu's 1945 *License to Fire Rifles*), confessed to a symbolic continuity of intentions: after Tzara and Fondane, Ionesco and Gherasim Luca, here was another expatriate member of an "insomniac generation" (the first born in postwar Romania) trying to carry on that experimental legacy and stir the dormant waters of international postmodernism.

If genealogically Codrescu belongs to Romanian (European) avant-gardism, in language, thematics and overall preoccupations he is indisputably an American poet. As a perceptive reviewer wrote, "Codrescu's influences range from European poets (Tzara, Ponge, Eminescu, Lautreamont, Rimbaud, Villon, Cavafy) to American poets (Ashbery, Berrigan, Creeley, Spicer, etc.). His poetry has an international base, but the uniqueness of his voice is in his uses of the American idiom. . . . " Codrescu's main effort has been to relocate American surrealism at the intersection of two experimental traditions (European protosurrealism, and the Williams-New York School line of poetry); he has significantly expanded and enriched that intertextual space in American poetry which makes such a poetic dialogue possible.

"I COUNTED SO MANY LANGUAGES IN THE DARK"

As an aspiring Romanian poet in the sixties, Codrescu's secret dreams (shared with other members of his generation) were those of Poetic Subversion and Exile. These two ideas loomed large as myths: "In school we had whispered the names of our great exiles. They had replaced the smaller national heroes. The names of Tristan Tzara, Eugen Ionesco, Mircea Eliade, Emil Cioran—sent shivers up our spines. For me, the meaning of their exile overshadowed by far the meaning of their creations. . . . Exile was the unifying idea and, in my mind, it assumed the proportions of *a place*." But what he was to find soon after his expatriation is that Exile is not a "vast/outer/territory" with "distinct boundaries," but a shifty, elusive country of the mind.

His predecessor in the mythical limbo "between statelessness and naturalization," Mircea Eliade, defined the exilic province as a decentered, dynamic world with the nostalgia of a center. But he also endowed it with a redeeming feature: "Wherever one is, there is a *center of the world*. As long as you are in that center, you are at home, you are truly in the real *self* and at the center of the cosmos. Exile helps you to understand that the world is never foreign to you once you have a central stance in it." What Eliade does not make clear enough is how one accedes to that central stance. Exilic experience endows one with an "extra cognizant," "extra territorial" perspective, but also leaves him in an unsettled tension. By definition the exile is a *homo duplex*, inhabiting one place and remembering or projecting another. Through the exilic "jump" (*ex-salire*), the artist comes to know otherness and strangeness, but his arduous task remains that of transforming a figure of rupture into one of connection. According to Eliade he can do this through *myth* and a unifying *language:* "In exile the road home lies through language, through dreams. . . . "

But what language? An Ur-language of universally applicable symbols? The mother-tongue in which "one still dreams"? Or the adoptive idiom? These are questions that subtend much of Codrescu's poetry. Language-intercrossing and poetic myth are his keys to the "outland" of imagination. But they also serve to fill the void of his real exilic limbo. Unlike the orthodox avant-gardists, Codrescu has never tried to develop a language beyond languages, a kind of poetic esperanto like Khlebnikov's Zaoum idiom, Marinetti's "degree 4," Virgil Teodorescu's "leopard" language, or Isidor Isou's "lettrisme." Codrescu has sought *home* in a real poetic language, though one uncertainly balanced between native and foreign, rational and irrational, learned and unlearned. Ronald Sukenick has praised Codrescu's language achievement in the following terms: **The History of the Growth of Heaven** is another leap from the sinking ship of Newspeak into the life boat of the living word. What's interesting about this book is that it reads as if Codrescu is really beginning to write in a new language as though someone in the middle of a conversation started speaking in multi-colored bubbles instead of words." There remains, however, a tension between the new and old languages, or between the "diurnal" and "nocturnal" aspects of the poet's idiom: "The acquired language is permanently under the watch of my native tongue, like a prisoner in a cage. Lately, this new language has planned an escape to which I fully subscribe. It plans to get away in the middle of the night with most of my mind and never return. This piece of writing in the acquired language is part of the plan: while the native tongue is (right now!) beginning to translate it. . . ." (**"Bi-Lingual"**).

Codrescu's literature explores other language tensions as well. One is the incongruity between an imaginative poetic idiom and the debased "T.V. vernacular" of present-day culture (a theme provocatively addressed in his N. P. R. commentaries—recently collected in **A Craving for Swan**). Another is the tension inherent in all languages between signifiers and signifieds, those "breches" and "decalages du sens" that interested also the early surrealists. Without overstating the poet's capacity to bridge all these gaps, Codrescu still imagines (*pace* Derrida) a way back to the redeeming roots of language. Consider this splendid passage from his recent **"Dear Masoch"** (**Comrade Past & Mister Present** 7):

> . . . No chilly languages, no translations
> from chilly texts. No translators catching colds
> from opening windows between languages, no
> crossroads,
> only real stammerings, true hollows where the tongues
> stand in their cases heavy with the awkward honey
> of the first spoken, the as-yet-unsaid. . . .

The most perplexing gap, however, remains that between language and self, mask and identity, voice and silence. In **Craving for Swan** (39), Codrescu ironizes the exorcism of silence that goes on in this country: people drowning their anxieties in the drone of TVs or the noise of their own "voices that have taken on the eeriness of speaking machines." Yet he is equally suspicious of the postmodern celebration of silence, absence and self-cancellation. Today,

> in psychoanalysis and other therapies, people pay for
> what
> they are missing, but not in order to recover it, only to
> be
> confirmed in their lack, to be reassured of the
> normality of
> absence, of the utter popularity of the abyss, the
> sanctioned
> nothingness, the triviality of death. . . .
> Well, I prefer the mask to the well-thought
> nothingness . . . (**Comrade Past & Mister Present**
> 52)

The multiplication of masks and assumed identities becomes Codrescu's way of coping with Silence and Exile. He combats the perceptual poverty of contemporary culture with his own (surrealistic) version of *imitatio dei:* "unleash fantasy machine, populate being with images, populate earth with schizobeings" (**Comrade Past & Mister Present** 76). His strategy resembles in certain ways Nabokov's: "Whereas so many other language exiles clung desperately to the artifice of their native tongue or fell silent, Nabokov moved into successive languages like a traveling potentate. Banished from Fialta, he has built for himself a house of words. To be specific: the multi-lingual, cross linguistic situation is both the matter and the form of Nabokov's work." Codrescu's poetry seeks a similar cross-linguistic, cross-cultural space, a kind of Derridian *in-between*; its intercrossing of voices and languages has both aesthetic and ideological implications. As one speaker in **Comrade Past & Mister Present** (49) announces, his great discovery after thirty is *plurality:*

> . . . In other
> words, all other words, not just the tolerance
> of difference, but the joyful welcoming of differences
> into one's heart spread out like the pages
> of a newspaper. . . .

"WRITE DOWN MY LIFE/THAT COULD BE MY LIFE IF/ I INSISTED"

The "pursuit of a/plural/dialectic" is central to most of Codrescu's poems (also to his essays, despite their personal, strongly opinionated nature). Codrescu "has more respect for the voices inside him (as his many assumed characters attest) than any other poet I can think of. . . . "

Most of his collections published so far are organized in thematic cycles, each experimenting with a voice, an identity, a state of mind. Codrescu is, in the space of a single book (his first), a jailed Puerto Rican poet, "scout into a political future of prison reality, a sacrificial lamb"; an ex-Beatnik ex-Vietnam mystic writing about America from Istanbul; or his wife Alice Henderson Codrescu and the archetypal "woman in man." Or he can become, with equal ease, a monk in his barren cell, an opium eater, Masoch, Tristan Tzara, a political refugee, etc. Through these invented personas, Codrescu maps a wide range of experiences and cultural milieus (especially of the sixties and seventies), redefining recent history in dialogical terms as a confrontation between Eastern and Western models. Like much exilic literature that begins with an imaginative "leap" in space, with a "what if," his poetry has a projective, hypothetical dimension: it probes the very domain of the *possible* through these added identities. In many of his poems, the dramatic persona functions as an imaginative "grid," providing Codrescu with a consistent view from "inside the cheese holes" of reality, with a paradoxical self-definition:

> "*tout ce qui existe est situe*" said max jacob and
> one
> day my situation was such that only a detached,
> religious
> and ecstatic perspective could bring home all that i
> was.
> since i was nothing in particular at the time i became a
> monk because it seemed to me that monks had no
> ego, only
> visions and a sense of humor. i am still a monk to the
> extent that this is true. my professional services when
> i am in robes consist of techniques for sabotaging
> history with the aid of god. so to speak. (*The
> History of the Growth of Heaven*)

In other poems the technique of the persona is used ironically, with the speaker behind the mask trying to adjust himself to his new role or exit it when it becomes too constricting. The quixotic attempts made by the jailed Puerto Rican in *License to Carry a Gun* to escape prison parallel Codrescu's own efforts to disencumber himself from his poetic mask:

> rain cuts an exit in the wall
> for him who is of rain a square hole
> westward. through which the men of rain
> will fly.
> they prayed to water for a long time,
> they sold what they could.
> . . . . .
> rain cuts an exit   wet like cunt
> in lonely nights from very left
> (*Selected Poems* 7)

Codrescu's more recent poems make this effort very problematic. The poetic persona gets entangled in an insidious network of roles, in a web of language; the "man of face" (Codrescu's self-definition) is caught in his own game with face realities and masks.

"I SELL MYTHS NOT POEMS"

As Codrescu explains in **"De Rerum Natura"** (*Selected Poems* 71): "With each poem goes a little myth. . . . These myths appear at the end of the magazine under the heading ABOUT CONTRIBUTORS or above my poems in italics. Very soon there are as many myths as there are poems and ultimately this is good because each poem does, this way, bring another poet into the world. With this secret method of defying birth controls I populate the world with poets."

There has always been an almost imperceptible borderline between fiction and reality, myth and its parody in Codrescu's poetry. The compilers of "Books in Print," taking Codrescu's authorial set-up *ad literam,* listed his name not as author, but as editor of *License to Carry a Gun.* One of the many personal myths that Codrescu's life and poetry illustrate is that of "clandestinity": the young man who stole across the Romanian-Hungarian border in the spare-tire compartment of a car, seemed predestined for a career as an avant-gardist poet. It might be argued that not all young Romanians who sneak across the borders stowed away in ingenious *caches* (car trunks, empty bass viol cases, refrigerator trucks) have in effect become experimental poets. But in Codrescu's case, there is a deep metaphoric continuity between his life and poetry. With poetry itself reduced nowadays to quasi-"clandestinity," what we need most is a versatile originator, "a rogue and a magician, a hustler and a monk; in short, a protean creator continually creating himself." Codrescu seems in many ways ideally qualified for that role. In Morton Marcus' words, "Andrei is the first truly existential personality . . . in literature," an incarnation of Camus' absurd man "who dreams himself into an unending series of identities in order to live as fully and meaningfully as he can in a meaningless universe and who thereby continually attempts to humanize an unhuman world."

**In *Comrade Past & Mister Present* [the] interplay of fiction and reality, textuality and life becomes the predominant theme. Codrescu stages ample dialogues in which real and fictitious literary figures mingle.
—*Marcel Cornis-Pop***

Codrescu's use of masks and personas seems akin to the surrealistic principle of *metamorphosis* and game with "one in the other." But Codrescu ascribes to this kind of metamorphosis a more complex function: at once disruptive, "unlacing" the rigid structure of language and reality; and constructive, filling the fissures created in the conventional order of things with a paradoxical, multidimensional life (see *Comrade Past & Mister Present* 52). Where Breton would have looked further for a "fil conducteur" to rearrange the pieces of the puzzle into a coherent "*champ magnetique*," Codrescu is content to keep his poetic field in a state of active, provisional equilibrium. His "sermonettes for all the interlocking/tremors in the land" cannot promise more than an illusion of presence, a mental bridge:

> My next book will have a poem for each
> Saint dropped by the Church,
> 33 poems in all . . .
> I will put a little cross by each poem
> meaning 'here lies,'
> a very deceptive move since no one
> will lie in there,
> no one, not even the Monk
> who will be out thinking of girls
> what are poems? (*Selected Poems* 23)

In *Comrade Past & Mister Present* this interplay of fiction and reality, textuality and life becomes the predominant theme. Codrescu stages ample dialogues in which real and fictitious literary figures mingle. In **"The Fourth of July,"** for example, he debates the question of poetry with a Romanian exile in Germany and an American poet with a degree in versification. This piece ends significantly with a confusion of roles and styles, and a surrealistic-grotesque vision in which the poet's head and the breast "of reality" seek reciprocal adjustment:

> . . . But then a miracle happened.
> The head began to shrink. No, the other breast began
> to grow.
>
> No, the head began to shrink. No. And so on. I
> could care less. (16)

This is, I trust, Codrescu's version of the permanent (poetic) revolution. We sit back and wait amusedly to see which of his two spheres will explode first.

"SOMETIMES A WORD BLOWS UP LIKE A BOMB"

Semantic explosion, verbal fissures, existential division are characteristic motifs in "postsurrealistic" European poetry. Codrescu accompanies the deconstructive poetics of his French colleagues (Ponge, Deguy, Garelli) with an explosive, aggressive attitude, more akin to the early dadaists. Julio, the jailed Puerto Rican poet, is visited by an updated version of Don Quixote, expert in existential guerrilla tactics:

> they will forever refuse you the license to carry a gun
> but i am a gun . . .
> . . . . .
> the license to carry a gun is a license to be.
> patricius, brutus, don quixote come naked
> to my mind vs. target! (**"the license to carry a
> gun,"** *Selected Poems* 6)

Passages like this abound in Codrescu's early poems, contaminating even his erotics: the poet's heart is "a bomb with a fine trigger," his mind is restructured to look like a gun, his "woman shoots / him with her fresh body / of winter." Even "the Virgin holds a gun / not the baby" in a "Flemish-style, late 17th century" icon. Codrescu's bellicose vocabulary and unexpected associations (or rather, dissociations) of images have made some of his critics uneasy, taking their attention away from other aspects of his poetry. For Abbott "there was too much shotgun and not enough target" in Codrescu's early poems. Other reviewers seem to better understand the essentially antithetic (oxymoronic) nature of Codrescu's poetry, "yoking together" the mundane with the imaginative, the concrete with the abstract, the profane with the elevated. Morton Marcus, for example, believes he can hear echoes from the surrealistic proverbs of Eluard in the terse, aphoristic contradictions of Codrescu's poetry.

But Codrescu's verbal and metaphoric audacity has a deeper purpose than that of "startl / ing / the reader into thought or out of it." In his more recent poetry he clearly moves beyond surrealistic contradiction, exchanging a type of "oneirocritique" (Apollinaire) for a broader cultural critique. In a poetic culture like the American, emphasizing the iconic, imagistic aspect of language, Codrescu's "eccentric image vocabulary" is bound to become noticeable. By smuggling "exotic," European layers of vocabulary into his American poetry, he disrupts the continuity of both imagistic traditions. As his most recent essay on *The Disappearance of the Outside* proves, Codrescu is engaged in a Baudrillardian critique of today's inflationary image culture. In his effort to subvert the "T.V. newspeak" or the self-reproductive iconography of pop culture, he often invokes the example of other champions against visual simulacra: Breton, Dali, Ted Berrigan, or the Romanian fairy tale.

There is, behind the superficial clash of images, a genuine dialectic of conflict, a confrontational philosophy. In a poem from the Peter Boone section of *License to Carry a Gun,* the persona rejoices at the universality of conflict:

> what happened to me.
> it isn't only this war in Vietnam.

it's the war of my blood,
the small wars in immaculate labs,
the war of children in the flesh of assaba,
the wars in cosmos over the heads of philosophers.
(***Selected Poems*** 10)

Codrescu himself echoes this notion of conflict in ***In America's Shoes*** (80) when he announces: "What America needs right now is a good war . . . I mean a poetic war." His half-serious proclamation recalls the traditional battlecry of avant-gardists against philistine culture; or the similar injunctions of the recent theorists of the post-avant-garde: "Let us wage a war on totality; let us be witnesses to the unpresentable; let us activate the differences and save the honor of the name." Given Codrescu's Romanian background, it is not surprising to find him engaged in a battle against totalistic forms of thought. As he reflects in ***The Disappearance of the Outside*** (166): "all people under the gun invent ways of escaping history through language," through a recasting of poetic tropes and existential concepts.

The prime conflict in Codrescu's poetry is that between a free-wheeling, wide-ranging imagination and the superficia of everyday reality. Abbott recognizes in Codrescu's poetry "a sense of deep, unfolding thought, but crosscut with a precise sense of falsity, a relentless mind that will not allow a pose to pass unexamined." The two faculties, that I would call *analytical* and *deconstructive,* collaborate to make his poems true "voyages of discovery (unlike most poems by Eshleman and Bly, the two who claim to do this, but who never surprised me with anything but the breadth of their pre-tested thought)." At times, when the analytical (reflexive) faculty proves stronger, Codrescu's poetry moves toward existential and metaphysical self-definition. At other times, when the playful, deconstructive type of thought prevails, his poetry becomes a comedy of contradictions, or a "schizoactivist" definition of our postmodern condition:

Poetry-on-condoms parachuted on cities, . . .
increase in man-machine, woman-machine relations,
food & air agents causing
sterility, the inability to love—all these added to
psychocryogenics are propelling 85 percent of my
generation to
IBM (Imminent Mental Breakdown). IBM =
Imminence of
Bored Matter. Flight of Styrofoam cups around a
malfunctioning humming Xerox. Nostalgia. Nostalgia
& the
Machine.
(***Comrade Past & Mister Present*** 72)

On the whole, Codrescu's poetry communicates an almost

Blakean sense of the insurmountable obstacles a poetic mind encounters in today's world:

The many windows framed in yellow light
are pulled together making
mind structures, more mind chains
around the masses falling through the season.
(**"Drowning Another
Peasant Inquisition,"** *Selected Poems* 116)

"A GRAMMAR" OF DIFFERENCES

Contradiction and antithesis move also the syntactic level of Codrescu's poetry. His texts have given at times the impression of disconnectedness, especially to critics more accustomed to follow a poem with a tight, argumentative structure. "In the early poems," Abbott complains, "the image/thoughts tended to peter out in 'of-of' phrases and not fold into each other. . . . " It might be argued that in many of Codrescu's poems this syntactic discontinuity and jagged phrasing has an aesthetic function. Codrescu's unexpected syntactic and ideatic shifts in the middle of a line have dadaist and surrealist antecedents. Within the Romanian tradition of the avant-garde, one could mention not only Urmuz' or Tzara's early use of *noncontiguity* and semantic "suspense," but also the more subtle "grammar of poetry" theorized in the twenties by Ilarie Voronca (Codrescu also has a collection of poems entitled ***Grammar and Money,*** 1973). For Voronca, "The poem is not only made of words, but also of blanks, of gaps over which the step hangs suspended, slips and follows the infinite embrace." As this passage and others suggest, Voronca advocated not only a radically new syntax, but also a new poetic epistemology. Likewise in Codrescu, the syntactic discontinuity is related to his philosophy of (anti-) interpretation. As he confesses in one of his later metapoetic pieces (**"Against Meaning,"** *Selected Poems* 126):

Everything I do is against meaning.
This is partly deliberate, mostly spontaneous.
Wherever I am, I think I'm somewhere else.
This is partly to confuse the police, mostly to
avoid myself especially
when I have to confirm
the obvious which always
sits on a little table and draws a lot
of attention to itself.
So much so that no one sees the chairs
and the girl sitting on one of them.
With the obvious one is always at the movies
The other obvious which the loud obvious
conceals
is not obvious enough to merit a
surrender of the will.
But through a little hole in the boring report

God watches us faking it.

Codrescu's polemics with the category of the immediately *obvious* (an aesthetic category created by our postmodern age), is accompanied by a subtle textual and syntactic movement that disrupts the "given" and opens unexpected windows in it for the not-so-obvious or supra-sensible. Two very different concepts of "grammar" clash here: one is the "official grammar" ironized in **"Cohere Britannia"** (*Comrade Past & Mister Present* 29):

> coherence in its own bag is being home
> coherence in a double bag at the supermarket is being
> in prison
> you boys better cohere here by the window
> a coherent view of the yard leads to a better and
> more coherent
> vision of things to come in a fine coherent world
> cells cohere
> coheres *ceolli mundum*
>
> lemme give you the coherent version of our position
> several
> years ago me and a country i've never been in
> meshed whereby
> I cohered into a society of former strangers and was
> reduced
> to coherence not to speak tears having to constantly
> enforce my
> and their coherency with cliches I got so much shit
> together to
> uncohere my anus to reflect the universe was one all
> this time

Against this iron-clad coherence, Codrescu mobilizes a personal "grammar" of discontinuity, contradiction and identity shift:

> I was dead and I wanted peace
> then I was peaceful and not quite dead yet
> then I was in my clothes
> and I took them off and then
> there was too much light
> and night fell
> then I wanted to talk to somebody
> and I spoke ecstatically
> and I was answered on time in every language
> in a beautiful way
> but I felt unloved and everyone
> Came to love me
> (*The History of the Growth of Heaven* 7)

OF POETIC IMAGINATION AND "TRANSCENDENTAL IRONY"

Codrescu's technique of "deep-frying/the/visual material,"

adding, subtracting, overlapping the details until an entirely new "reality" emerges, has baffled those critics more accustomed to find "something objective, and plenty to see" in a poem. In place of the mundane shorthand that often passes for poetry today, Codrescu promises something short of an *epiphany:*

> With the collapse of the vocal cords and through
> the graces of laryngitis, a new perception of reality
> knocked me off my divan and twisting my arms,
> delivered me dripping at the gates of heaven.
> (**"Ode to Laryngitis,"** *Selected Poems* 118)

The trivial or innocuous everyday is thus transformed into "an occult new beauty" through a technique that reaches perfection in *For the Love of a Cat* (Four Zoas Press, 1978). But even earlier, in *The History of the Growth of Heaven* (1973), Codrescu created similar epiphanic moments in which the ice-box of domestic reality lit up with an eerie, transcendental light:

> Dear God, Cauliflower & Broccoli are so Beautiful
> Together!
> And the frozen ducks in the cracked cellophane
> pushing
> a slice of pizza into the side of a clam can!
> And the cheese singing!
> Oh I believe that all of us
> are ready! (**"Us,"** *Selected Poems* 49)

From this point of view, Codrescu (who does not hesitate to quote Blaga with his theory of poetic "mystery": "Our job is not to uncover it, but to increase its mysteriousness") seems closer to the expressionist poetry of Lucian Blaga or to the Beats whose "sandwiches of reality" still allowed a peep "at the back of the real," than to the present-day textualists who celebrate universal opaqueness and lack of transcendence:

> Truly, there is no perfect opaqueness in nature.
> Someone is looking through me at you just as
> through you
> someone is staring at me.
> Ah, to be a beautiful narcissist wrapped
> like Christmas paper around
> a gentle voyeur!
> This is what I want, Seigneur!
> And then to glide out of focus (**"Ode to Curiosity,"**
> *Selected Poems* 115)

But Codrescu is not a naive utopianist, to be sure. His tentative forays into an *outside* or *beyond* are often suspended halfway, blocked by the carapace of immediate realities:

> late night, san francisco

so few things to write about
when there is a sky full of the electric lights
        of san francisco

stilling the lights in your head from the left
and the sea some two feet away filling the other ear
with the sounds of all things you ever wanted to say

. . .

there is nothing here now.
the whining after the unplugging of the world.
(*The History of the Growth of Heaven* 71)

He knows that the category of the *outside* (understood, in almost romantic terms, as the domain of the spontaneous, imaginative, organic) is gradually vanishing. "Great areas of language are being colonized today by technocrats, propagandists, double-speak politicians. When the words re-emerge from such use, they have been devastated, vampirized and drugged" (*In America's Shoes* 186). Under these circumstances, imagination itself can no longer afford to remain idealistic; it must become anti-utopian, anti-imagistic, ironic. Many of Codrescu's "revelations" are tentative, spoken through a problematic persona, like the monk fallen from grace in *History of the Growth of Heaven.* More often than not humor and a kind of "transcendental irony" fill his poems "like creme/de menthe" ("**Irony as Nursery,**" *Selected Poems* 134): Codrescu seems to half-heartedly imply the existence of a higher pattern (a deeper scenario) behind things. But his "religion" works both ways, transfiguring the mundane everyday, and debunking the sacred beyond. It is not always clear whether what we read is an epiphany or a parody of a desecrated myth. Consider this passage on today's commerce with symbols:

did you ever have a grey knot topped symbolically
with lightning
bolts and mounted in the middle of yourself like a
pagoda? of course
not. but I have. I have the only one in the world or
rather I had
because i've traded it for a scarf. this scarf is from
god. you can see
smears of cheese on it . . . yes, god's feet are made
of cheese.
whenever he walks he leaves smears, that's how he
walked upon the
waters. . . . the water went into the holes in the
cheese and the whole
thing swole up . . . like floaters . . . rubber balloons
. . . well, anyway,
that's how I got the scarf, but I will trade it to you for
a paddle board. do
you need a paddle board? no, but I know someone
who does . . . he'll

trade his gum wrappers for the paddle board. do you
need gum
wrappers? no, I will give the gum wrappers to a tall
man . . . he knows
me . . . /etc./
(**"Port of Call,"** *Selected Poems* 76)

A similar "swapping," reshuffling of planes takes place in Codrescu's poetry to the bewilderment of the reader who finds a piece of heaven in the refrigerator, a "barren cell" in the monastery, and snatches of divinity "breezing through the assholes of angels." Still, Codrescu's antithetical irony never ends with a wholesale cancellation of meaning, in a total blank. There is, as Marcus observes, "violence, anger, sex/in this poetry/,but no death. Codrescu's whole poetic seems built as a construct to transport seeds. He is concerned in his poems with living. . . . " This statement needs qualification. If it is true that a volume like *Necrocorrida* (1980) directly exorcises the death impulse in Codrescu's imaginative biography, survival through writing is never unproblematic. Consider this splendid ironic elegy on life, death and books:

books

death covers me with fine dust.
I love used fat books. they are
like used fat bodies coming out of sleep
covered with fingerprints and shiny
snail trails.
I wish to read the way I love:
jumping from mirror to mirror like a drop of oil
farther and farther from my death.
but god gives us fat books and fat bodies
to use for different reasons
and less a metaphor I cannot say
what is that haunts me
(*Selected Poems* 40)

This poem outlines an entire poetic ontology, *in nuce:* moving between promise and incertitude, fragility of life and weight of textuality, it encircles reality with a metaphor. In itself that metaphor may not be much; then, again, it might turn out to be the very image Codrescu has been looking for, the "great healing metaphor"

. . . invented by my first exiled self in Nueva York
in the great year 1966 when the whole world was a
disease
only the brilliant metaphor of my young body could heal
as it hurtled through Nirvana Village and Central Park
open
like a gold sieve to the wonder of possibility!
(*Comrade Past & Mister Present* 88)

John Krich (review date 10 January 1988)

SOURCE: "Premises as Pretense," in *The New York Times Book Review*, January 10, 1988, p. 17.

[*In the following review, Krich gives mixed reviews of* Monsieur Teste in America and Other Instances of Realism. *He lauds Codrescu's mastery of American idiom, but faults his overuse of simile.*]

"America can be taken for granted," counsels Andrei Codrescu near the outset of his latest prose flight. "The obvious is very serious about itself here." The point can hardly be argued in a country where morning papers carry headlines like "Study Reveals Unreality May Be Good for You." It is with healthy doses of such medicine that the Romanian-born poet seeks to treat his adopted homeland. If these stories are termed "instances of realism" that's only because this eternal emigre views American reality as the outdated passport each new arrival carries in his vest pocket. As in his weekly musings for National Public Radio's "All Things Considered," Mr. Codrescu succeeds in carving out his place as an American voice by failing to heed his own advice. In his work, not a single advertising jingle is taken for granted, the obvious is subverted through carefully aimed barrages of obscurity and no punditry is ever handled more seriously than a trip to the 7-Eleven.

Still, this volume will baffle a listening audience who have come to expect a cross between Andy Rooney and Andre Gide. Out of artistic integrity or self-indulgence, Mr. Codrescu chooses here to abandon mass taste, along with linear thought and most literary conventions. "He was irony, she was subjective mysticism" is about as much character development as we get. While *Monsieur Teste in America* offers copious servings of poetic observation, it skimps on the everyday detail that makes Mr. Codrescu's radio musings so affecting.

The title novella in this collection of short fiction offers an intriguing premise. On his 29th birthday, Mr. Codrescu summons Monsieur Teste, the Paul Valery creation who represents his intellectual conscience, to help him make sense—or better yet, nonsense—of American symbology. But premises are mere pretense, as is writing about how all writing is pretense, and Mr. Codrescu's dialogue soon makes the two alter egos sound like dueling Zen roshis: "'The point is that you can't trust the world with your understanding of it.' 'But how then . . . can you entrust the world to your understanding?'" The story meanders off into the birth of a hermaphroditic love-child named Maximum, a discourse on "crypto-morons" and the cataloguing of American schools of poetry in the form of a luncheon menu. ("Aktup, Metabolism, the Bowel Movement and Syl-

logism. All have me as one of the founders.") It comes as no shock when the piece concludes about Mr. Codrescu's European shadow, "I had learned nothing from him and he who knew everything had taught nothing."

In **"Samba de los Agentes,"** the ramblings and cadence of a Colombian immigrant named Jose sound suspiciously Slavic. Everyone in Mr. Codrescu's universe, including this ex-cop protagonist, is a poet and knows it. And all gain acceptance in America by sending some packaged piece of their souls to market. "I have an agent, therefore I am," seems to be one of many subtexts in this odd regurgitation of the crime story genre. The six shorter pieces in the collection are scattershot affairs united solely through the use of female narrators who are hip, sassy and, once again, familiarly literary in their obsessions. The only voice individuated from the author's is faint indeed, emanating from the disembodied spirit of a spacey grad student channeled through a Brooklynese medium named Madame Rosa.

> **Like Nabokov's, Mr. Codrescu's greatest strength lies in his outsider's appreciation for the succulence of American idioms.**
> **—John Krich**

Like Nabokov's, Mr. Codrescu's greatest strength lies in his outsider's appreciation for the succulence of American idioms. Where language is reinvented daily on billboards, it offers liberation from the chains of connotation. "Contagious words imbued with mass-market meanings like a sponge full of ink crowded my mind to dictate their grammar to me!" the narrator confesses. "The words of America's language brought me an incalculable dowry."

Unlike that strain of American writing that seeks authenticity through spareness, Mr. Codrescu proves he's comfortable with the American idiom by taking colloquialisms out for every possible spin. For him, English is not a tool chest but a toy box—and there is playing in every page here. By now, Mr. Codrescu has become a master at mixing ontological speculation with such random bits of Americana as "flying K-Mart lawn chairs." But the author remains too enamored of purple prose for purpleness's sake. "My dreams are dotted with the dance of psychopatia sexualis in the graveyard of the planet," is one of many sentences that read like bad sendups of beatnik prosody. And Mr. Codrescu would do well to sign up for the 12-step recovery program at Simile Addicts Anonymous. A sampling: New York is said to lie "under the general strike like an actress under a Foreign Legionnaire"; "Vague regrets coursed through him like phosphorus through protozoa"; "'I'm stuffed up with thoughts like a swan with pomegranates'"; "Truth sits in an autobiography like a bird dog in an underground hospital."

At this rate, America will need Andrei Codrescu the way a cement mixer needs a parakeet. *Monsieur Teste in America* opens with the author's admission that he's "bored in heaven"—and what follows is both a celebration and a frantic evasion of that delicious fate that unites the assimilated and the lunatic. Perhaps Mr. Codrescu can't admit aloud that there's as little to becoming an American as he feared—or that, for all his wealth of associations, America may yet prove too small a subject.

Stuart Klawans (review date 28 May 1988)

SOURCE: "Embarrassed Palefaces," in *The Nation*, Vol. 246, No. 21, May 28, 1988, pp.756-60, 62.

[*In the following review, Klawans criticizes the works featured in* American Poetry Since 1970: Up Late *for their unworldliness and absence of emotion, although he notes their wit and clever observation.*]

Randall Jarrell once remarked that the poet in our time is like a maker of stone hand axes. That was forty years ago. From the vantage point of the 1980s, most poets would agree that Jarrell didn't know how good he had it. Contemporary poetry, according to the conventional wisdom, is that which goes unread. It is, however, argued over, and with a vehemence that sometimes seems livelier than the poems themselves. Consider this sampler of recent invective.

Mary Kinzie: "Ashbery is the passive bard of a period in which the insipid has turned into the heavily toxic."

Louis Simpson: "Most American poets lack a theme. . . . After a while they are reduced to making casual remarks about matters of no importance."

Robert Dana: "'Tired' is the word for most contemporary poetry. 'Competence' *ad nauseam.* Minor brilliances. . . . [Much] of our present poetry seems the product of a single, generalized voice and mind. Poet copying poet."

And here, in a now-legendary example, Diane Wakoski attacks John Hollander for his apostasy against free verse. Through his sin, Hollander became a figure like Milton's Satan, "full of spite from lack of recognition and thinly disguised anger, one who was frustrated and petty from that frustration."

One begins to envision poetry, like the contested estate in *Bleak House,* as having long since disappeared, while the arguments over it continue to rage. Thus, it is with a sense of relief that I recommend Andrei Codrescu's plump new anthology, *American Poetry Since 1970: Up Late.* Here are real, live poets, 104 of them.

And here, too, is an argument. Introducing his book, Codrescu gets into the spirit not by praising the poets but by attacking David Perkins, the Harvard professor who recently brought out *A History of Modern Poetry: Modernism and After.* Perkins, says Codrescu, is one of those professor-poets guilty of maintaining "the proposition that poetry, like all things, has been getting worse since the days of the gods, in this case Ezra Pound and T. S. Eliot but mostly Eliot."

Against this version of American poetry—whether it really is Perkins's version remains to be seen—Codrescu puts forth an anthology of outsiders. It is a forthrightly exclusive selection, which does not try to summarize all the poetries of the past two decades but rather takes a stand for some of them. Thus, there are no rhyme-and-meter mongers here. Although the so-called New Formalists have been at the center of recent debates, you would not know from Codrescu that they even exist. Nor does Codrescu include the Creative Writing poets—the ones with the carefully controlled voices, reciting carefully graded lists of images that drop away to a carefully pained *aperçu.* Neo-Surrealists *are* included, but not the ones who practice an artful, Ashbery-style verse. Codrescu's Surrealists are closer to the original models, who disdained art itself. "The majority" of the poets, Codrescu writes, "are anti-literary, as avantgardists have always been. This is, however, an avantgarde without a single program, in a country where the term 'avantgarde' never even took root, having been supplanted by the more academic and ambiguous 'modernism.'"

In other words, these are the poets who say no—no to professionalism, no to inclusion in a canon, no to quibbles about form, no to literature itself. If they feel allegiance to any tradition, it seems to be one not of writing but of generalized opposition: "New American Poetry, since Whitman, has been at odds with official culture over the facts of America," Codrescu writes; and that's as much of an appeal as he gives to any figure earlier than Frank O'Hara. These up-late poets do not intend to have their measurements taken and compared with those of other known specimens, because they suspect they're being fitted not for their laureates' robes but for a casket. Whatever their various purposes, they do not write to be judged by David Perkins. I suspect they shouldn't be subjected even to the indignity of this review.

Nevertheless: Having noted the principal negative virtues

of these poets, let me mention the positive as well. The first is rapidity. You don't have to wait for anything to happen in these poems. Sometimes it's the writer's feelings that come at you in a rush, as in Maureen Owen's "African Sunday":

> Fuck I want to be bound by
>   devotion!   Tortured
> by passion!
>   just like the ad says
>   for d h Lawrence's
> Sons and Lovers   in today's
>   Sunday Times   instead I'm
> here with you . . .

Sometimes the rushing you hear is language itself blowing by. Here is the start of "Redo" by Lyn Hejinian:

> Agreement swerves
> a sonnet to the consonants.
> Sparrows. As a wind
> blows over the twigs of a rough nest
> entered by a bird that impales
>
> a vowel on its beak . . .

One way or the other, these poets seem determined to step on the gas and go.

Despite this insistence on contemporaneity, this passion for writing in the moment, a few of the up-late poets retain their sense of history, literary or otherwise. Ed Sanders is represented here with his long and lovely "Yiddish Speaking Socialists of The Lower East Side":

> Oh they failed
> but I can hear their ghosts
> walk down the cobbles
> outside the St. Mark's church

Sam Abrams contributes "The World Is With Me Just Enough," a tribute to being tickled by a 7-year-old, which contains his declaration, "i'd rather be a pagan/tickled in a creed outworn."

Another virtue appears: lightness of tone. The poets here who prefer personal statement avoid the deep, hollow tones of sincerity; the collagists, the Surrealists, and the more impersonal writers manage to avoid the drone, the boom, the bardic wheeze. Even the explicitly political poems—Michael Brownstein's "Declaration of Independence," Bernadette Mayer's "The Tragic Condition of the Statue of Liberty," Codrescu's own **"A Petite Histoire of Red Fas-**

cism"—tend toward the quick, the satirical, even the burlesque.

On first glance, then, the Codrescu-Perkins split is the latest skirmish in that old war of redskins against palefaces. Given that it is now fifty years since Philip Rahv identified the combatants, back when Jarrell was a mere youth, one might mutter, *"plus ça change"* and go home. If you *do* intend to leave now, I hope you will do so with a copy of ***Up Late*** under your arm. But if you suspect, as I do, that something else is going on, turn with me now to *A History of Modern Poetry.*

Granted, this book comes with the full backing of Harvard University, which in this case means it costs $25 in hardcover and has a typo on every page. Perkins, for what it's worth, goes by the title of John P. Marquand Professor of English and American Literature. If you don't hold that against him, you will quickly discover that he's far from the single-minded bore Codrescu portrays. In fact, he is generous, sympathetic, sensitive, inquisitive and has a goodly streak of common sense.

These are the virtues one hopes for in a literary historian; and that may be one reason Codrescu treats Perkins so harshly. Literary history itself has become something of a lost art in recent years. People who have studied literature—and I would bet that includes every one of the up-late poets—used to be drilled in the explication of texts. That went on from the 1950s through the early 1970s; since then, literary theory has taken over. (All right, this is a caricature and doesn't even mention feminist and Third World criticism—but as a picture of official literary studies, it's close enough.) Thus, for two or three generations, students have been told only in passing that literature might be an object for history. Witness Terry Eagleton's little book on literary theory, which has become a one-volume *Cliff's Notes* for the deep-thinking set. The names Auerbach and Curtius appear only once in it, and then as symbols of a quaint, half-forgotten past.

Perkins, evidently, has not forgotten. He approaches his subject with an initial impartiality, knowing that his own judgments cannot alter the facts: These were the poets who wrote during these years. Though Codrescu would have you believe that Perkins's interests are narrow, his focus in fact is as wide as he can make it, and his first effort is always to understand. Here is Perkins quite far afield from T.S. Eliot, explaining the open form of Charles Olson and Robert Duncan:

> At least in theory, writing a poem was for these poets
> not different from any spontaneous act of living. Like
> most modern artists, moreover, they were impressed
> by the formal differences between life and the tradi-

tional work of art. The work was organized for an aesthetic purpose, selective in its use of experience, delimited and meaningful. Life, on the other hand, is unselective, for it presents anything and everything. It flows on and on, and nothing within it is isolated, nothing exists as a completed entity.

In this sense, Perkins writes, open form was not an aesthetic strategy but rather "a matter of faith." This is as clear and meaningful an explanation as I've found. It is so good, in fact, that it elucidates much of the poetry in *Up Late.*

One can find passage after passage like this in Perkins. On the poets of the counterculture: "When a poet's transvaluations dramatically challenged the accepted norms of society, and his way of life proved his sincerity by what it sacrificed, immense moral power accrued. Allen Ginsberg and Gary Snyder sometimes write very well, but their great influence has derived from the image we have of their lives in conjunction with their poems." And here is Perkins explaining how Pound and Williams became the great influences on American poetry after World War II: "Pound and Williams were of the high Modernist generation. They carried the prestige of the 1920s and could hand it on, as the ancient fathers of Israel passed the tribal blessing to their sons. They were in the United States. You could visit them. They were interested in your work. You could write them, enclosing poems, and Williams, at least, sent enthusiastic replies."

Clearly, Perkins has a talent for getting under the skins of different styles and into the heads of people who lived in the recent past. It is also clear that his history is not a traditionalist's polemic. His discussion, through the 1960s, is wide-ranging. Only when he gets to the 1970s does he narrow the field; and then he does so to give in-depth analyses of two poets, John Ashbery and James Merrill, who have firmly established their reputations.

This is where Codrescu begins to quarrel with him in earnest. One can say in Perkins's defense that it may be too soon for a historian to deal with poets of the 1970s and 1980s. One might add that Perkins praises Ashbery and Merrill highly, but not past reason. But this, I suspect, is just what bothers Codrescu. It is Perkins's moderation, his broad sympathies, that set off the argument against him. Why?

The answer may be that Perkins is capable of absorbing even the up-late poets into the body of literature. His fault lies not in having ignored them now but in showing a willingness to understand, sort and label them twenty years from now. This is precisely what these poets fear. The real question, then, is why they should be afraid—why bother to write poetry if you don't want to be part of literature?

Till now, I've taken the up-late poets at face value, as hotheads in full revolt. Now it's time to question them more closely.

"The making of community against anti-social technology is the chief object of the poetry gathered here," Codrescu writes. But what sort of community is being made? Think for a moment of the places where people come together. They form communities where they work; but there is not a single poem in *Up Late* about labor. Nobody sells insurance; nobody doctors in New Jersey. Bernadette Mayer writes about not living on a farm, and that's it for the world of work. People also get together through sports. Sometimes, in fact, I think sports is the only unifying element in American society. There is only one poem that involves sports (a very good one, by Elinor Nauen). People get together through voluntary associations: They attend church, form political groups, play in garage bands. But they don't do any of those things in *Up Late.* Then there is the street where one lives, the neighborhood, the town. Nobody writes about those places, either, although Jim Gustafson has poems on the *idea* of San Francisco and Detroit. Ethnic groups are communities, but the poets in *Up Late* who bother to think about that form of society are, not surprisingly, Lorenzo Thomas, Alberto Rios and Victor Hernandez Cruz. Finally, there is the most obvious form of community, the family. In 568 pages of text, I found only three poems that had anything to do with families.

To complete my survey, I then checked how many of the poets in *Up Late* write about being poets. The answer is roughly a third.

It becomes obvious, then, that Codrescu is talking about making a community of poets. That, I believe, is the guilty secret of *Up Late.* In the old battle, the writers of sensibility and tradition were the palefaces; the writers of raw experience were the redskins. But here the rebellious, risk-taking poets are forming, of all things, a republic of letters. In 1988! No wonder they become uneasy when David Perkins walks into the room—they've already done half his work for him. These are not redskins—they are embarrassed palefaces.

I have characterized the poetry here as rapid and light in tone, even when its subjects might invite a weightier treatment. Those are indeed virtues, in the better poems. In the worse, one begins to get a sense of skimming along. It is then that one feels how little the poetry is engaged with the world at large, and how much it cares about the world of poetry. Here, for example, is a poem by Bill Berkson, "Star Motel," in its entirety:

> Inside I could hear
> a party of people

the aimless cars
and in the middle distance
inexorable murmurs
of the ice machines.

Well, it's a poem. It's not bad. But think of it this way: If you were to come on with this intensity on a date, you would be home, alone, by about 10:30.

People who are interested in literary history may discern the genealogy of poems such as this, with their pretense of worldliness masking a priestly disengagement. They are the offspring of Frank O'Hara, in particular the poems he referred to as "I do this I do that." Now, I do not mean to disparage O'Hara, an admirable poet, but merely to point out a fact of literary inheritance: It is often the weakest part of a writer's work that becomes the most influential. That's because the weakest part is the most easily imitated; and in O'Hara's "I do this I do that" poems one may find the beginnings of the living-in-the-moment in much of *Up Late,* and of its accompanying fault—an absence of deep emotion.

Of all his "I do this I do that" poems, probably none pulls off the trick so well as "The Day Lady Died." The bulk of it runs on from mundane detail to detail:

and for Mike I just stroll into the
  PARK LANE
Liquor Store and ask for a bottle of
  Strega and
then I go back where I came from to
  6th Avenue
and the tobacconist in the
  Ziegfeld Theatre and
casually ask for a carton of
  Gauloises . . .

And so forth. The poem departs from thisness-and-thatness only in its last lines, when O'Hara, having picked up a copy of the *New York Post,* sees that Billie Holiday has died. Then, all at once, he feels himself back at the Five Spot,

while she whispered a song along
  the keyboard
to Mal Waldron and everyone and I
  stopped breathing

So the accumulation of ordinary detail gives way at last to the memory of a moment of transcendence, a sudden loss of breath. The poem works. But for all O'Hara's unpretentious, plain speech, I feel there's something dishonest going on here. The moment of transcendence wasn't his creation; it was the work of Billie Holiday. O'Hara points

to her and says, "See, *she* was great," and then takes credit for her art.

Why shouldn't poets give their readers what Billie Holiday gave her audience every night? They used to. Indeed, even today, there are poets who can deliver something very like her electric charge. As evidence, here in its entirety is an early poem by Rita Dove (who is not included in *Up Late*). It is called "Nigger Song: An Odyssey," and it doesn't just point to Billie Holiday, it *embodies* her.

We six pile in, the engine
  churning ink:
We ride into the night.
Past factories, past graveyards
And the broken eyes of windows,
  we ride
Into the gray-green nigger night.

We sweep past excavation sites;
  the pits
Of gravel gleam like mounds of ice.
Weeds clutch at the wheels;
We laugh and swerve away, veering
Into the black entrails of the earth,
The green smoke sizzling
  on our tongues.

In the nigger night, thick
  with the smell of cabbages,
Nothing can catch us.
Laughter spills like gin from glasses,
And "yeah" we whisper, "yeah"
We croon, "yeah."

You remember this, don't you? It's poetry, the real stuff. Some of the poets in *Up Late* remember it, too. A lot of them don't. Instead of poetry, they provide good company, wit, clever observation, the occasional puzzle to solve. That's a lot, certainly enough to make the book worth your while. But the best thing I can say about *Up Late* is also the worst: It's the fastest read of any poetry anthology I've seen.

I expect that someday, David Perkins will indeed write a history that includes many of the poets in *Up Late.* He will bring out all their best qualities and probably deal more gently than I have with their shortcomings. He also will thank Andrei Codrescu, as he should, for assembling them and for having the courage and intelligence to be their advocate. By that point, of course, Codrescu and his fellow poets will have flown off into some new and still-unnameable realm, from which they will view Perkins's efforts with derision. And that, too, is as it should be. I only hope that by then, this useless railing against literature will have ceased. There is nothing cowardly about wanting to write literature—Rita Dove and thousands of others have proved that. Problems arise only when people are too sure of what they mean by literature. In that sense, as an anthologist of the contemporary, Codrescu is every bit as timid as he accuses Perkins of being. Where are the song lyrics? Where is August Darnell of Kid Creole and the Coconuts—a true Surrealist if ever there was one—or that plain-spoken populist Springsteen or all those adversarial rappers? Where is American folk poetry, such as "Here I sit, all brokenhearted"? And has no one noticed that David Mamet, singlehandedly, has brought back verse drama? Contemporary poetry, in some of its guises, is indeed marginal to American life; but in other guises, it has come very close to the heart. *Up Late* and *A History of Modern Poetry* might both have benefited from including the truly popular forms of poetry. With their somewhat incompatible virtues, though, they deal very well with what they attempt to cover. My advice is to read them both, then set out into the wider world, with Providence, Rita Dove and Kid Creole as your guides.

Albert Mobilio (review date 9 August 1988)

SOURCE: "Pick a Peck of Poets," in *Village Voice*, Vol. XXXIII, No. 32, August 9, 1988, pp. 49, 53.

[*In the following review, Mobilio faults* American Poetry Since 1970: Up Late *primarily for packing too many poets into too few pages, resulting in a poor presentation of the poets' individual voices.*]

These are strange days for American verse. The community of poets has never been bigger or more professionally published, yet poetry has never been more neglected by serious readers. Consider the sheer volume of verse seeing print each year. There are tens of thousands of published poets in the U.S., and they vie for space in hundreds of university- and state-funded journals. A few dozen small presses kick in with shelves of chapbooks, collecteds, and selecteds. If even poets can't keep track of all this, no wonder lay readers can hardly get their bearings.

But who really reads? A guess might include newly minted MFAs checking out the competition, poetry editors, poetry program directors, perhaps poets—in short, the middle management and workers in the cottage industry poetry has become. If you visit the Gotham Book Mart—the mecca for poetry magazines (few other book stores will carry them)—you'll find thousands of issues stacked in ragged rows in the back, lushly produced or xeroxed, old and unread. On occasion a poet disturbs the crowded shelves, not to buy, but to crib submission addresses. Marxists would call this a crisis of overproduction.

Out of the multitude, there are perhaps a thousand professional poets—published books, government grants, tenure, a modest reputation. And that intimate bunch is splintered into a Beirut of factions and counterfactions. If an audience is to be drawn from outside the initiates, somehow this welter of voices must be made to cohere, or at least seem to do so. The best means to this end has traditionally been the anthology. Verse has always reached its largest audience in collections that end up in public libraries and, most important, school curricula. No other genre is served so well in anthology. From the increasingly isolated precinct of contemporary poetry, the anthology ventures out, a missionary among the masses.

The impact can be considerable. Donald Allen's *New American Poetry* (1960) became a fixture on classroom booklists and introduced a generation reared on Frost and Eliot to an alternative tradition in the making. The effects still resonate. In providing the first widespread exposure to Beat, Black Mountain, and New York School verse, *New American Poetry* sired the next new wave of poets and critics as it redrew the boundaries of the American tradition. No volume by an individual poet, Ginsberg's *Howl* included, matched the depth and range of its influence. Allen's selections—Olson, Creeley, Duncan, O'Hara—infiltrated the canon in the Trojan horse of a compact, smartly built anthology.

In the polemical introduction to *Up Late,* Andrei Codrescu wastes no time proclaiming its descent from *New American Poetry.* The first sentence pays homage to "one of the most influential books in the history of American poetry." Codrescu, however, views the affinity in terms of a shared oppositional stance toward what he calls the "poet-professor." The derision distorts Allen's pronouncement that his collection coalesced around "a total rejection of all those qualities typical of academic verse." Allen wrote this fully aware that many of his poets held academic jobs; in fact, Olson had been president of Black Mountain College. While Allen objected to the aesthetic implications of poetry written for or within the academy, Codrescu's pique finds its source in the sociological aspects of the poet-professor's life. Poets have undergone "mandarinization" at the hands of the colleges that co-opt them with jobs. Their radicalism has been muted by the National Endowment for the Arts—"Avowedly apolitical, the NEA is anything but." Codrescu keeps one eye on the *Morrow Anthology of Younger American Poets*—his chief competitor in laying claim to the under-40 generation. He parodies *Morrow's* characterization of its own typical poet: "married, has two children, has received a National Endowment for the Arts or a Guggenheim grant, and teaches in a college where he edits a small magazine." In rejecting the mandarins, Codrescu challenges not a kind of poetry, but a kind of poet.

Reflecting no identifiable poetics, cultural movement, or desire to include once-excluded voices, Codrescu's selections appear to be chiefly determined by biography, a grab-bag assortment of folks connected to alternative or avant poetries over the past 20 years. At nearly 600 pages, featuring over 100 poets, *Up Late* qualifies as an official tome. The bulking up most likely responds to *Morrow's* 784 mainstream pages. If so, Codrescu has massed a Persian army to dismantle a straw man, his "poet-professor." *Morrow's* editorial guideline was both arbitrary and meaningless—poets under 40. Why not poets under 46, or poets beneath contempt? By virtue of his grounding in a strong, authentic, alternative tradition, Codrescu didn't need the horde. The legacy of O'Hara, Duncan, and Zukofsky is sufficient. Nonetheless, even this assembled multitude will elicit complaints—oversight, cliquishness, and axe-grinding—from the ranks of the uncollected; that's a given. What distinguishes *Up Late* is that many of those ingathered have good reason to gripe.

> **Reflecting no identifiable poetics, cultural movement, or desire to include once-excluded voices, Codrescu's selections appear to be chiefly determined by biography, a grab-bag assortment of folks connected to alternative or avant poetries over the past 20 years.**
> **—*Albert Mobilio***

The anthology does provide an earnestly comprehensive vita for the alternative poetry scene since 1970. Every tribe and its mutations are charted. Codrescu gleefully runs down the list:—"second and third generation New York School Poets . . . California Zen Surrealists, performance and 'new wave' poets, erotic lyricists and 'language' poets, in short, all that is new now." The cadence of a sales pitch is appropriate. So numerous a cast gives the reader the sense of a crowded K-Mart where you must do your shopping quickly or risk being overrun; 100-plus means a slim, hurried sample and then on to the next. No anthology can present a poet's collected works, but it should offer a sample that is both representative and engaging. When the most generous spread, 13 pages, hardly hints at Ted Berrigan's energy and scope, how can lesser-known but intriguing poets like Marjorie Welish or Robert Grenier make substantive impressions in five pages? Even Berrigan's allotment of 11 poems (some merely a few lines long) hardly does justice to his central role in whatever poetics *Up Late* may be trying to document—a fair number of the chosen are friends and students of Berrigan's, their work clearly, sometimes excessively, influenced by his flair for converting the everyday into the epic.

The cramping together of much-published careers—Ron Padgett in five pages, Anselm Hollo in nine, John Godfrey in just two—doesn't allow individual voices to register. What you get is a snippet of Padgett's playfulness ("I have always laughed / when someone spoke of a young writer / 'finding' his voice.' I took it / literally: had he lost his voice?") or Hollo's blunt lyric ("I bring you / this head, / full of breath- / takingly beautiful / images of yourself / & put it in / your lap"). A polyphonic blur starts humming in the head about midway.

The traffic jam is especially unaccommodating to poetic styles closely identified with St. Marks and the New York School (a sizable chunk of the book). Maureen Owen, Michael Brownstein, Bernadette Mayer, Jim Brodey, and Alice Notley work in a tradition and method pioneered by Frank O'Hara and Paul Blackburn in the early '60s. They approach their own personalities as objets trouvés and conduct a self-reflexive investigation in a tone of calculated, often beguiling offhandedness. A certain brinksmanship is a prerequisite, imparting, for example, an emotional charge to the repeated "I" in the closing lines of Alice Notley's "In Ancient December"

> Can you worship loss? I can't
>   remember it, I forgot to
> sing it off from happening I had to
>   arrange the flowers,
> thousands everywhere, & thinly & it
>   being purple I forgot
> to see it ten thousand times . . .

Deceptively cool and discursive, the surface invites and then betrays a rapid reading. The second take reveals a vivid tableau evoked in stuttered sadness. The repetition of the first-person pronoun—an often imitated New York School trademark—affirms the privacy of poetic grammar and gesture while undermining that closure through overuse. It is poetry of tension played against grace, poetry of personality rather than ideation, and it is served best in extended selections—you must get to know the poet. *Up Late,* however, provides too little breathing room and the result is a collision of half-realized sensibilities.

The only significant poetry movement to take shape since 1970—language poetry—is well represented by Clark Coolidge, Susan Howe, Michael Palmer, Lyn Hejinian, Leslie Scalapino, and others. Drawing on ideas that informed the writing of Stein, Zukofsky, and the French Surrealists, language poets insist we look hard at what poems are actually made from—not images, plot, voice, or character, but language itself. Their texts are designed to be nonreferential, to display their own vocabulary and mechanics rather than wintry days, lawn chairs, and the smell of steak in passageways. A fragment from Michael Palmer's

"Baudelaire Series" gives some notion of the aesthetic's debt to both Stein and the French:

> She says, You are the negative—
> Behind you an horizon in red
> and the horizon a question
> a mark in final red
> your eyes are sealed against
>
> She says, You do not know when
>
> She says, You are counter
> You are degrees only
> and now in summer a mouthful of
>   blood
> and sutured nylon thread

Juxtapositions of language poets' disengaged, sometimes austere meditations with poems relying on persons and emotional appeal produce some instructive flashes. Following Anne Waldman's casual chant, Leslie Scalapino's textbook rhythms feel less like a means to a clarified end than a parody of the rationality that explanatory prose must manipulate. Codrescu wisely chose not to schematize authors by categories, allowing whatever laughs or lessons there are to emerge unexpectedly.

The surrealist bent in his own poetry explains Codrescu's fondness for new surrealists like John Yau, Jack Skelley, Elaine Equi, and Harrison Fisher. Turning a French predilection for distance and dislocation on classic American tropes, they thread familiar material through deranged synapses. Jack Skelley's mock lover's ode "To Marie Osmond" is lacquered in media buzz ("your crystal-perfect face / on the cover of the *Enquirer*") and refried Western myth ("movie star men stand upright among beasts, / holding tokens of serpents, sunglasses, electric guitars"). John Yau's methodical dream measured prose poem, "The Kiss," offers a mirror-warped detective tale that might have been dictated from the car radio in Cocteau's *Orpheus*. Laced throughout the anthology is a good start on an anthology tracing the Surrealist influence on American verse.

Complaints about overabundance aside, poets warranting inclusion—Gustaf Sobin, Nathaniel Mackey, August Kleinzahler, Hugh Seidman, Charles Simic, and Charles Wright—come to mind. Unfortunately, Simic and Wright cut figures perilously close to the poet-professor's profile. Still, a good number of Codrescu's selections are inarguably apt. He mixes established names—Ed Sanders, Tom Clark, Eileen Myles, Lewis Warsh—with younger, less familiar poets: Amy Gerstler, Chuck Wachtel, Jeff Wright. There are also several lost gems from the early '70s, like Brownstein's prose poem "Floating."

The frequent glimmerings, however, cannot redeem the dross. By jam-packing this anthology, Codrescu not only dilutes its impact as an aesthetic summary of the second wave in alternative poetry, but renders it nearly useless as an educational text. Part of *New American Poetry*'s appeal in this setting was its concision—a mere 45 poets. Exclusion and hierarchy lie at the heart of the anthologist's task. Ideally, it's not an opportunity to make new friends or reward old ones.

Poetry anthologies roll off the press shrink-wrapped in controversy and disappointment. Failure is presupposed, the format's obbligato, largely because no one knows precisely what would constitute success. Like physicists pursuing the unified field theory, poets long for an ultimate synthesis, an anthology so complete, so definitive that it stands above any faction or carper's reproach. Short of that, we settle; this collection is a good band on a distant station that just doesn't come in clear. Perhaps in retrospect, **Up Late** will represent these decades in verse well enough—there was too much poetry given too little time.

Alex Kozinski (review date 30 June 1991)

SOURCE: "Romania's Big Bamboozle," in *The New York Times Book Review,* June 30, 1991.

[*In the following review, Kozinski commends Codrescu's* The Hole in the Flag: A Romanian Exile's Story of Return and Revolution *for its accurate description of Romania and its people during the 1989 revolt.*]

Like the panorama of life in post-revolutionary Romania, which the poet and essayist Andrei Codrescu describes with both awe and revulsion, **The Hole in the Flag** is a work of great complexity and subtlety. For everyone who watched as the Romanian revolution unfolded, Mr. Codrescu provides a gripping political detective story.

Mr. Codrescu, a regular commentator for National Public Radio who had been fiercely critical of the Ceausescu regime, arrived in Bucharest with a radio crew in the days of the December 1989 revolt. On one level, his book is a travelogue. In crisp, often humorous detail, he describes his experiences and reactions on returning to a land he had left as a teen-ager.

We learn a great deal about the harsh conditions in Romania that induced Mr. Codrescu and his mother to leave their homeland, and about the subtle and not-so-subtle changes brought about by 25 years of Ceausescu rule and a few days of revolution. These observations provide the background against which the other, more unsettling, themes of the book are woven. Foremost among these is the dark and still-unsolved mystery of what exactly *did* happen during those eight fateful days when Nicolae Ceausescu was toppled and a new Government took control.

Like most everyone else, Mr. Codrescu starts out convinced that the Romanian revolution was the result of a spontaneous popular uprising by an oppressed people against a tyrannical, narcissistic dictator. Early chapters describe the images of the revolution as portrayed in the media: a peaceful protest in Timisoara; machine guns firing into a crowd of unarmed civilians; the flight, capture and execution of the Ceausescus; a protracted battle between the Army and the shadowy forces of the Securitate; the deaths of tens of thousands and destruction reminiscent of World War II; the defeat of battalions of fanatical Ceausescu loyalists; and the final victory of the people under the benign leadership of a spontaneously created caretaker Government. A euphoric and ingenuous Mr. Codrescu—like much of the rest of the world—accepted this melodrama as the revealed truth.

Having skillfully carried us with him, he starts planting seeds of doubt by pointing out inconsistencies and improbabilities in the official account of the revolution. He winds up dissecting it event by event, image by image, assumption by assumption. The glorious, pure, idealistic vision of the Romanian revolution gives way to an ugly and misshapen thing, the product of a grotesque masterpiece of deception, "a process of mass hypnosis."

> **Everyone, of course, recognizes tyranny in a monster like NicolaeCeausescu. But Mr. Codrescu explores the ways in which government can accomplish its tyrannical ends by misdirection, without need of force.**
> —*Alex Kozinski*

Everyone, of course, recognizes tyranny in a monster like Ceausescu. But Mr. Codrescu explores the ways in which government can accomplish its tyrannical ends by misdirection, without need of force. He argues that the revolutionary Government bamboozled the Romanian people through its control over the country's only television station. By manipulating televised images, Mr. Codrescu believes, members of the new Government managed to etch themselves into the minds of the Romanian people so deeply that no other party stood a chance of dislodging them. Much of the evidence the author marshals to support his thesis consists of deduction and speculation; it will be up to the reader to decide which vision of the Romanian revolution to believe.

What seems unassailable, however, is Mr. Codrescu's touching, painstakingly accurate description of Romania and its people, the good and the bad, the pristine and the hideous. Romania is one of the most beautiful places on earth. With a loving eye, Mr. Codrescu fills his book with the rich texture of Romanian culture, from the noble, turn-of-the-century buildings of Bucharest to the peasant shrines of his Transylvanian birthplace. He contrasts these with the unsightly rows of boxcar apartments built by Ceausescu and the ghastly pollution generated by mindless industrialization.

The Romanian people, too, present a series of disquieting contrasts. They are portrayed as generous, friendly, cosmopolitan and politically savvy, and as mean-spirited, grim, ethnocentric and politically naive. Drawing from the country's violent and often tragic history, Mr. Codrescu explains how the contradictory images are both accurate. Indeed, one cannot understand Romanian society, or grasp the magnitude of the problems it faces on its way to a Western-style democracy, without understanding paradoxes such as these in a country that has guarded the gateway to Europe for two millennia.

The most significant lesson of the Romanian experience may be that he who controls the media controls the course of events. This underscores the conviction that the ultimate guarantee of our own freedom lies not in our system of checks and balances, nor in our constitutional protections against unreasonable searches and seizures, nor in many of the other protections afforded by the Constitution—important though they all be—but in the First Amendment, which puts private individuals, not the Government, firmly in control of our political and social discourse. It is a lesson well worth keeping in mind.

Alfred Stepan (review date 9 October 1992)

SOURCE: "In a Sultanistic State," in the *Times Literary Supplement*, No. 4671, October 9, 1992, p. 26.

[*In the following review, Stepan states that the chief merit of Codrescu's* The Hole in the Flag: A Romanian Exile's Story of Return and Revolution *is its documentation of how myths are replaced by counter-myths.*]

What do the current presidential and parliamentary elections in Romania tell us about the nature of its "transition" from communism, or, indeed, about the "revolution" of 1989?

To get a feeling of the elation, fear, confusion, uncertainty and disillusionment that surrounded the fall of Ceausescu in the winter of 1989, one couldn't do better than read the account by the poet Andrei Codrescu of his return to Romania at the time, after a twenty-five year exile in the United States. One of his best chapters, entitled **"Seize the Means of Projection"**, describes the young activists, peasants and former officials in front of the television cameras, urgently presenting their views of what was happening to an electrified country and to the world. Securitate terrorists were still believed to be a counter-revolutionary threat. Rumours of deliberately poisoned water supplies, of 10,000, 60,000, even 100,000 dead, filled the news channels and the streets. Codrescu even then had his doubts about the sincerity of many of the new converts to revolution from the old regime, but he, like everyone else, was swept up in the events.

Six months later, on a return visit, Codrescu's euphoria turned to despair. The old communists, now the neo-communists organized in a National Salvation Front, had "captured the revolution"—the government itself, led by Iliescu and his former communist allies, but also the words and the meanings of the revolution. President Iliescu had called out vigilante miners to smash the students (who represented to Codrescu the most authentic part of the revolution in Bucharest). Codrescu was distressed to find that many of his friends hailed Iliescu for thanking the miners publicly for their patriotic and disciplined rampage. Then, too, the body count at Timisoara had apparently been inflated by digging up bodies from nearby paupers' graves. Codrescu was thoroughly disillusioned and disorientated. It seemed to him the whole revolution had been a fake, a film scripted by the Romanian communists, with a "beautifully orchestrated piece of Kremlin music conducted by Maestro Gorbachev".

Codrescu's difficulty in knowing what happened is ours too. We do know that the number of people killed in the collapse of Ceausescu's regime was probably closer to 2,000 than 60,000. We also know that Codrescu is probably right in thinking there was an element of a staged counter-revolution, even to the extent of simulated gunfire, and that disinformation played an important role in the events. To this day, rumours are encountered more in Bucharest than in any other Eastern European capital. On recent trips, I find myself using "archaeological" sources for information on the recent past. If, during the uprising, Iliescu's supporters in the Central Committee Building in Bucharest's main square were under siege by Securitate loyalists, why are the surrounding buildings destroyed, and the Central Committee Building virtually unscarred by bullets?

The Rise and Fall of Nicolae and Elena Ceausescu by Mark Almond and *Romania in Turmoil* by Martyn Rady lack the immediacy of Codrescu's account, but their broader historical scope provides better balance. Almond's biography is the best we now have. It is particularly astute about the physical (and ideological) architecture of the fi-

nal years of Ceausescu's regime, such as the schematization plan to eliminate rural-urban distinctions by the forced relocation of peasants into multi-storey buildings, and the razing of many of Bucharest's historic churches in the Old Town, to make way for the approaches to the most brutal building project in Eastern Europe, the House of the Republic. Finally, Almond deals well with the international dimensions of Ceausescu's fall, especially the impact of the collapse of hardline communists in other parts of Eastern Europe in making Ceausescu seem more isolated and vulnerable. Rady has three chapters on the pre-Ceausescu period, followed by five on post-Ceausescu developments, and for most readers his book is perhaps the single most useful introduction available to present-day Romania.

Codrescu's idea of a "scripted" revolution, implying a sinister plot written in advance, whose enactment allowed its authors to "capture" the revolution, is still probably the most widely accepted framework for analysing the events in the country. But of all the transitions from communism that occurred in Eastern Europe, Romania's is the one where we are least able to know "what really happened"; and of all the narratives, that of a scripted revolution allows for the fewest ambiguities and contradictions. The value of *The Hole in the Flag,* then, lies not in its account of connected events as they occurred, but as a document of how myths are replaced by counter-myths. For Romania, more than for any other transition in Eastern Europe, any primarily narrative approach is inherently unsatisfying; what we need, rather, are studies of the dynamics of myth-creation and the functions of disinformation—a deconstruction of revolution itself. The best effort along these lines is the piece by Katherine Verdery and Gail Kligman, in *Eastern Europe in Revolution,* edited by Ivo Banac. They too, have sifted through the supposed facts and evidence, they know all the literature, but their concern is with the very terms by which the events in Romania were experienced, described and understood: "the miners", "the demonstrators", "the front", "the revolution", "neo-communism". This makes for a lot of quotation marks, but is illuminating.

Another way to approach the Romanian transition is to think more deeply about the nature of the Ceausescu regime and to place Romanian politics in comparative perspective. Of the Warsaw Pact countries in Eastern Europe, Romania had the weakest organized opposition and the bloodiest transition. It is the only one where nothing remotely close to a round table took place and the only one where high Communist Party officials from the previous regime currently run the country. Civil society is so weak that many members of the two most innovative centre-left organizations, the Civic Alliance and the Group for Social Dialogue, want the monarchy back, in order, they say, to give civil society a chance to develop. Middle Eastern associations of the term are unfortunate, because regimes as geographically diverse as Kim Il Sung's in North Korea, Bokassa's in the Central African Empire, and Somoza's in Nicaragua all approximate Weber's sultanistic ideal type. Understanding the combination of sultanistic and totalitarian tendencies in Ceausescu's Romania clarifies much that is distinctive in Romania's past, present and foreseeable future. It was precisely the sultanistic quality of Ceausescu's regime that enabled Iliescu to present Ceausescu as the embodiment of the system, and to imply that he, Iliescu, had changed the political and economic system completely by "decapitating the hydra-headed monster". In no other Warsaw-pact country would this rhetorical trick have had such weight.

Where do we stand now in our understanding of present-day Romania? To answer this question we have to go beyond the conceptual framework provided by the "script", "revolution", the "captured revolution" or "neo-communism". To speak of scripted uprisings in Timisoara and Bucharest is to underestimate the critical importance of the "movements of rage" (to use Ken Jowitt's memorable phrase) in undermining Ceausescu's coercive power. "Revolution" over-estimates the degree to which these movements of rage represented organized opposition groups with their own leaders and programmes. "Captured revolution" misses the extemporaneous opportunism and weaknesses of Iliescu. "Neo-communism" overstates the principled cohesion of the government that followed Ceausescu's downfall, and in particular does not take into account the profound divisions within the National Salvation Front that emerged in 1991. In fact, in the last twelve months the anti-Iliescu wing of the NSF, faced with a crisis of governance in September 1991, formed a coalition government that included some of the traditional liberals, supported Prime Minister Stolojan's courtship of the IMF and, in late March 1992, won control of the party label.

But as the current elections show, sultanistic rule has still left behind a flattened political and social landscape. Civil society remains incipient, the rule of law fragile, political coalitions turbulent, most political tendencies compromised. In this context, the Romanian opposition was not able to mount a Chilean-style, principled and united democratic campaign, led by a prominent political figure, and carry its message into every corner of the country. The weakness of the opposition, as much as the strength of Iliescu, explains why Iliescu will no doubt win the presidential run-off on October 11. But since no clear pro-Iliescu or anti-Iliescu group of parties has emerged with a majority in parliament, the outcome could well be a series of unstable coalitions, whose explanation will take us even further beyond the framework of "captured revolution" or "neo-communism", but not, unfortunately, beyond the framework of sultanistic legacies.

Francis X. Clines (review date 9 May 1993)

SOURCE: "They See America Rolling," in *The New York Times Book Review*, May 9, 1993, pp. 1, 22.

[*In the following review, Clines praises* Road Scholar: Coast to Coast Late in the Century *as full of "wit, discovery, and self-deprecation."*]

In their separate careerings in time among American epiphanies, Walt Whitman and Jack Kerouac went beyond self-concoction to achieve an originality that made it all look easy: hit the road, get to the core, bang us in the heart with words that access the routine beauty and pain of daily life. Their work remains so readable and so indelibly American that it's no wonder that fresh attempts at wandering the nation and mapping its presumptive soul go forward with the inevitability of book advances.

Lately, a formula seems to be overtaking much of the wandering. It often features a narrator using the internal combustion engine as Muse, with highway subbing for plot line, and dialogue bites from grizzled, terse denizens as American chorus. The exercise seems preoccupied with climacteric more than climax. For it often involves a restless, mid-something male deciding he must go off alone in America driving his favorite stripped-down or optioned-up vehicle—generically, a 19-ought-something four-cylinder Testosterone will do, with a pint of Anomic stashed in the glove compartment—and searching for at least that minimum of surprise and originality to fulfill a book contract, with maybe a fender-dent of transcendence thrown into the bargain.

The genre is no replacement for the lost American novel, at least not yet. But a reader does begin itching for a clearer line between uncanny reportage and not-so-creative fiction, considering how some of the latest examples pack in long coils of conversation in folksy contracted dialects that would seem too complex to be totally retrieved from the memory of a truly guileless wanderer. Contrarily, some of the better writing includes perfectly realized fragments of lives so burnished and broken that Flannery O'Connor's peacocks might be set to preening with envy.

Then again, there is Andrel Codrescu, a naturalized American and the most American writer of all in the current offerings of motorized searchers. Mr. Codrescu, a poet who is best known as an essayist on National Public Radio, takes this drive-time script and turns it inside out into a fine trick bag of wit, discovery and self-deprecation in a book badly titled **Road Scholar: Coast to Coast Late in the Century.**

From the outset, he is smart enough to anticipate the main pothole in driving a 1968 red Cadillac and retracing his own racy immigrant roots (he was born in Romania and came to the United States in the 1960's) through the locales of Hippiedom "I expected to find nothing in those places," he concedes, "partly because there would be little time to discover anything genuine, and partly because I never found anything of interest deliberately; the best discoveries of my life have been by accident." Fortunately, he changed his mind upon being advanced "a ridiculously small amount of money that was, however, more than my poetry had earned me in a lifetime of practicing its dangerous pinturns."

Mr. Codrescu takes off with a television documentary crew and a photographer, David Graham, who complements the author well in glimpsing the random nonsense and unreliable reality of things in general. It is a measure of Mr. Codrescu's talent that such an orchestrated mission manages to produce an unpretentious, wry journey in the art of essay writing, from light to sparsely serious. Once at the wheel of America's "banal instrument of carnage," the writer buys fuzzy dice and a drink holder and begins driving from his New Orleans home to the Lower East Side digs of Allen Ginsberg. There they lightly agree to plot for the reburial of the poet Ted Berrigan's remains in the St. Mark's Church grave of Peter Stuyvesant, documented in passing from Mr. Codrescu's interesting store of American antihistory as a founding anti-Semite.

Thus does he putter in a kind of countertravelogue about the land, all the way to San Francisco, via the "Kingdom of It," Las Vegas, with rarely a dull page in this simple book. It is mainly about the fun of writing and reading and meandering, rather than self-conscious synthesizing. Better for the reader to have Mr. Codrescu philosophically accepting a fax about the next city's lodgings from a cemetery attendant in Camden, N.J., who intrudes as the writer tries to have a special thought at the grave of Whitman, "sexually manifold and optimistic, the spokesman of liberty in all its guises."

Non sequitur, no harm. We're soon visiting the Burned-Over Patch region of surviving zealotries in a narrow swath of rural western New York. First, the Hutterians, the Christian communist and pacifist refugees who fled Hitler to live in Amish like aloofness in a Bruderhof, or "place of brotherhood." Then the descendants of the Oneida Perfectionists, who lived in a community conceived in free love, where the poet pines for the lost spirit of "continual flirtation as in a medieval court of love." Mr. Codrescu is the sort of writer who feels obliged to satirize and interplay with reality and not just catalogue impressions. He can redeem flagging curiosity in a single sentence, as when, returning to Detroit haunts he loved as a student, he finds he must wax more Mad Maxish than Whitmanesque; "I see that when a city becomes extinct, its last inhabitants go crazy."

> **Mr. Codrescu is a reminder that locomotion is not the heart of the matter; a decent imagination is. Opinionated travelogue inventories of Americana won't do.**
> —*Francis X. Clines*

Mr. Codrescu is a reminder that locomotion is not the heart of the matter; a decent imagination is. Opinionated travelogue inventories of Americana won't do. Nor will serial compilations of unforgettable characters suffice, as Pete Davies proves in "Storm Country: A Journey Through the Heart of America." Mr. Davies, a British novelist, is tireless as a lepidopterist in netting what feels like each and every flitting Midwesterner he spies in his travels (13 states, 1981 Ford pickup) in the heartland "with its savage weather and its sentimental music." He packs his pages with characters, and the friends and relatives of these characters, each of them with a story to tell and each story pretty much told in his book to the point of Chaucerian overdrive. "It's the nearest thing I know to going to the moon—*and I love it!*" he exults as he wheels about, trying to document the withering of "the whole mythic notion of what America is" and capturing individual lives "fresh out of a country song." It is the latter quality that intoxicates the book all too well. He concludes his 7,449 miles by comparing America to "that girl you had that thing with when you were 20," an experience "bigger than good or bad, bolder than right or wrong." Well, I guess. . . .

Karen Stabiner (review date 9 May 1993)

SOURCE: Review of *Road Scholar: Coast to Coast Late in the Century,* in the *Los Angeles Times Book Review,* May 9, 1993, p. 6.

[*In the following review, Stabiner favorably reviews Codrescu's* Road Scholar: Coast to Coast Late in the Century.]

National Public Radio commentator and poet Codrescu came to the United States from Romania when he was 19, in 1966, believing, among other things, that dogs in America carry pretzels on their tails (that, from his grandmother). He was quickly disabused of most of his preconceived ideas, but was not fully Americanized until 1990, when television producer Roger Weisberg asked him the question that would change his life: Would you like to drive? More to the point, would Codrescu like to learn and then drive across the country, recording his observations on film and, as it turns out, in print. The author was quite

comfortable in his role as eternal passenger, but the proposal was irresistible. He enrolled at the Safe Driving
School in New Orleans, bought himself a 1968 Cadillac and
set off on his adventure. Codrescu is the print equivalent
of character actors who like to chew up the scenery just a
bit, to get themselves noticed, but he has found some tasty
morsels: everything from fellow poets to his gun instructor in Las Vegas.

Ileana Alexandra Orlich (review date Fall 1993)

SOURCE: "Song of My Emerging Self: The Poetry of
Andrei Codrescu," in *MELUS,* Vol. 18, No. 3, Fall, 1993,
pp. 33-40.

[*In the following review, Orlich describes Codrescu's*
Comrade Past & Mister Present, *the story of his self-in-
tegration into his adopted culture, as intensely personal
and powerful.*]

For almost thirty years, since 1966, Andrei Codrescu has
lived in the United States, absorbed a new culture, published
more than twenty books, taught American university students, and broadcast weekly essays on National Public
Radio's "All Things Considered" on the American scene or
world events from a peculiar perspective and in accented
English. Now that knowledge of what has been happening
in Eastern Europe is suddenly available, we might attend
more carefully to the words of one who returned from
those depths and is in a position to tell how the accumulation of the thousand miniature pictures of the two worlds
can impress the memory and shape of the poetic self.

Codrescu's poetic universe is a compound of the Romanian
experience since World War II, of the cold war climate as
felt in an East European country, of his own status within a
distinguishable minority, and of his own unique psychological development within this context and the new world experience that followed it. His childhood spent in Romania,
in the Transylvanian town of Sibiu, is epitomized in a poem
like "history" in *The History of the Growth of Heaven,*
which typically blends contemporary events and personal
experience:

> in 1946 there was my mother inside who
> i was still hiding.
> in 1953 i was small enough to curl behind a tire
> while the man with the knife passed.
> in 1953 also i felt comfortable under the table
> while everyone cried because Stalin was dead.
> in 1965 i hid inside my head
> and the colors were formidable
> and just now at the end of 1971

> i could have hidden inside a comfy hollow in the
> phone
> but i couldn't find the entrance. (54)

Citizens of Sibiu, however, in one of those unforeseen historical ironies, had nowhere to hide because the town
housed a concentration of the greatly feared Securitate,
which, in the last throes of recent upheaval, turned its devastating artillery on the town's people.

But the compound of his Romanian past and American
present is best illustrated in the volume **Comrade Past and
Mister Present** published in 1986. It chronicles Codrescu's
development through the forty years of the poet's life, divided equally between Romania and the United States, often focusing on the poet's emerging self, which becomes
both the subject and the implement of artistic expression:

> History: in 1967, I was experimenting with all sorts of
> looseness, riffing rhythm. (I had a different accent ev-
> ery day.) Then I tightened up for my masters, the pub-
> lishers. First Paul Carroll raised my capitals and raped
> my text with punctuation. Then Mike Braziller with his
> insistence on the elegiac. Then my surrealist fans with
> their insistence on recognition (i.e. orthodoxy). All of
> these insistences, even when strenuously or success-
> fully resisted, left some of their fingerprints, if not the
> shape of their pressure, on my work. Of course, one
> evolves that way too, nobody's a frozen CB. (***Com-
> rade*** 92)

This *juif érrant* who left postwar Eastern Europe in 1966
feels that "being an outsider is not a misfortune, it is a
blessing and, what's more, a script for freedom. It's not the
suffering that's good for you, but the *thinking*. Thinking is
impossible inside, where everything serious has already
been thought for you by others" (**Comrade** 86). He aims
at integration and self-acknowledgment in an adopted culture:

> I think, I made myself a peculiar niche in American lit.
> Perlmutter used to be my name, fallen angel my
> vocation.
> Permutit, pearl mother, wanderer, pearl nipple, Jew
> tit.
> Roving tit, migrant mother, vagabond breast, nipple
> bum.
> (***Comrade*** 96)

As a former "Romanian who translated himself into an
American" (***Raised by Puppets***), the poet strides through
the streets of New York on a Monday morning when "parts
of the Sunday newspaper still covered the city" and invokes
his consciousness through his senses: "The smell of pastry
and coffee was being attacked by ginger / & Mongolian pep-

per / from inside red restaurants" (**Comrade** 9). While eating pirogis in a Ukrainian restaurant he learns of John Lennon's death and reminisces in Proustian fashion:

> I remembered that it was here
> in the Kiev
> ten years ago
> that I'd heard of Bobby Kennedy's death
> which at the time struck me like the free winds of doom
> with apocalyptic illuminations
> of anarchist Jew
> I owe to myself. (**Comrade** 21)

The personal sublimation of history and his role as dissenting outsider entitle him to constant renewal of self, for poetic identity is always Other:

> Having avantbiographed the world
> To make another come right out of it
> I have certain scribbler's rights
> On the next one—endlessly impregnate
> The self about to be designed. (**Comrade** 34)

To understand the present and one's self is to live in history, and Codrescu feels free to reminisce. The memories are often presented in compact organic capsules that explode into surrealistic prisms:

> a city that isn't sexy is like ropes lying there
>   in the old Black Sea port
> after all the longshoremen died of clap
> & the dusty statue of Ovid applauds all by itself,
> some Roman joke floating in from the Turkish coast.
> (**Comrade** 39)

By summoning his personal and private past the poet defines and explores an emerging sense of self, separated from the rest by the uniqueness of the remembrance. Passionate, involving relationships between Codrescu as a viewer and the natural scene, often filled with sexual innuendos, serve as further attempts to reveal the poetic self:

> I did enjoy the pale winter sun.
> I made the most of the spring breeze that lifted minis.
> I let my tongue wag into the summer heat and collected
> a whole urn full of lovely sweat
> In the fall I fell with the leaves and felt *désuet*.
> (**Comrade** 50)

Codrescu learns from his readings of *I migliori fabbri*, Baudelaire, Apollinaire, Lorca, Nerval and from the paintings of Goya and Dali. From "brother" Blaga, a twentieth-century Romanian poet whose work Codrescu has recently translated into English, he understands that attachment to the immediate senses is only the first step before the mystery begins to burn "giving off only enough light for the enormous job of making oneself." The job, however, becomes complete only when the poet is able to "stumble . . . out of the box of self," past the self-created monads ("the perfectly selfish little globes of soap") brought about by egocentric preoccupations ("I have thought, along with babies, bishops, Copernicus, and Sartre, / that one's job in letters and in life / was to express a self attached to a head / which can then be detached, cut off, *tu sais*") into "Point Plurality . . . a landmark that's been here all along, on which / Mr. Jefferson grounded us" (**Comrade** 49). Redefined to conform with contemporary norms, Codrescu's Point Plurality is

> not just the tolerance
> of difference, but the joyful welcoming of differences
> into one's heart spread out like the pages
> of a newspaper. (**Comrade** 49)

From the standpoint of a fervent advocate for pluralism— "the great discovery of my thirties is plurality" (**Comrade** 48)—Codrescu is fascinated by the manifold, individually distinguishable leaves of grass of America rather than the indistinguishable proletarian masses, often hungry, often cold, he once knew in Communist Romania. He unhesitantly introduces himself as "the sole mumbling interpreter of / an older art lost to the anxiety of the milieu, / a man from history in a position to know and to tell" (**Comrade** 42). What he tells, with the full awareness that "the infinite and the political do not exclude each other" (**Comrade** 52), is a conscious utterance directed to the twentieth-century readers of two worlds—the East and the West—which swarms to the poet's mind, inundates his senses without hierarchy of admission and disregards geographical separation for, in Codrescu's poems, the East and the West intermingle and are absorbed as one entity.

From his personal past, this cultural émigré recalls "a country without directories." Communism, or "Red Fascism," has annihilated the individual who is now turned into a "Nobody and Not Self," also known as "inert proletarian matter," whose sole claim to fame lies in the production *en masse* of brass Bolshevik statues. The ruling classes employ themselves "to know the statues" (i.e. study Marxist-Leninist dialectic) and impart such knowledge into the "inert masses" (i.e. the proletariat). An articulate prophet, Codrescu watches the masses gathered on February 11, 1984 in Red Square to look at the corpse of "Andropov of Russia," but also

> to tug at their zippers,
> to tug at the big zipper of history unzipping
> the Nylon Curtain and the Leather Wall. Sheer nylon
> stockings

atop a leather jacket. (*Comrade* 59)

In the same journal entry, and clearly benefiting from the favoring circumstances of his new status as a citizen of a democratic and open society, the poet's voice speaks with further, almost uncanny foresight:

> Ah,
> the prophetic powers once so miraculous seem only
>   tawdry now
> when the only things to prophesy are miserable things,
>   in and of themselves a great bitter value.
> Only a fool would now be proud of being a seer.
> (*Comrade* 59)

As the former Eastern European identity of a "comrade past" is left behind, Codrescu redefines himself as a "mister present," a man of the West. The experience is regenerative even if the West sometimes seems to cooperate with forces that promote alienation (the IBM machines, for instance, Imminence of Bored Matter, threaten their users with "imminent mental breakdown" and place them under a "heat of persecution"—a condition which succinctly but accurately defines the collective status of Americans mastered by technology). The modern American, Codrescu feels, suffers from a lack of imagination, is a prisoner behind "a Berlin Wall of television, fridges, and stereos / blaring out tears, pent-up signs, wordless senti-mentality" (*Comrade* 43). Cracks in this wall portend economic dysfunction. Falling demand must be restored by a doctrine of required excess and trashy material over-sufficiency. Remnants of the Eastern wall find buyers in the West, while remnants of the Western wall clog available landfills.

Like Pound's age demanding "chiefly a mould in plaster," the America Codrescu sees is a place where "the new things are mostly like the new writers, things molded to conform" (*Comrade* 109). And the rules for conformity are dictated by an assortment of systems, philosophical, cultural and political, brought about by "art museums, literature of mobile homes, trailer parks, squatter burbs, suburbs" (97) meant to annihilate the self.

The evils of the two worlds, ascetic communism and a capitalism of conspicuous consumption, fold the poet in, suffocate him, while "sprouting all round him." Presiding over this latter-day Waste Land is "the cardboard body of a huge Stalin growing out of all proportion" (*Comrade* 43), pointing to its one-dimensional character, suggesting its heroes, "hate-filled stars," and touching off the flying "doves with bullets in their heads." Reminiscent of the personae in *The Waste Land,* a few characters populate the desolate landscape. Notable among them is Masoch, a Molloch of the '70s, "doodling with contracts" (*Comrade* 1), which are

dehumanizing closed systems, and reminding us that everything in our world is spelled out in material form and available for a price. (Codrescu's criticism of Masoch and his world of "standard contracts" repeats what Pound said as early as 1913 in *Patria Mia* when he accused Americans of being obsessed by money and material acquisitions.) There is also a deaf woman, a Madame Sosostris of the 70's whose clairvoyance is rather cryptically revealed in her sign language cards. To complete this gallery, a former Bulgarian ambassador, who was a Communist member of the police before his defection, acts as a maitre d' and cook and is, secretly, a poet engaged in a fruitless "pursuit of the dialectic" (*Comrade* 42).

Questions about what the poet is doing in this hellish environment provide Codrescu with an identity. Subscribing to the idea that a genuine poet should stimulate the quality of life, Codrescu becomes blatantly outspoken. Echoing the Emersonian call in "The Poet" to which Whitman so avidly responded, he lashes out against his contemporaries who seem timid talents rather than "children of music" or "liberating gods": "The New American writer is a timid soul, a solicitous academic or a terrified lackey" (*Comrade* 109). It is as if the poet's emerging self has come full-circle to accept its challenge of putting "a whole new set of fantasies in the myth basket of the race" and identify itself with its ambassadorial role. The nightmarish modern world "with monstrous fleur-du-mal painted with human blood and brains on the ceiling of cheap hotels" (*Comrade* 3) becomes suddenly escapable as the poet is trumpeting his message:

> The job always, the only job
> is to be an ontological reminder, a real pain in the
> ass, reminding every one why we took up the pen
> in the first place, to scratch ourselves on the wall
> or under the aching arm, to kick open the lid, to set
> the water free, the hair loose, the spirit flowing.
> Make you hear again that metarooster crowing!
> (*Comrade* 52-53)

Codrescu presents the anatomy of hell and chaos only because these speak of the necessity for a change and of the need for the poet's "ability to make all hear again." This ability is Codrescu's "figure in the carpet": it reveals that "the content that fills the flowing shapes / of my heart's pure yearning is communal like the city" (*Comrade* 52). His is a distinctly East European voice that nevertheless contains a fleeting vision of Whitman's vistas, the passion of Pound railing about the crassness of his contemporary culture, and a less patrician echo of Eliot's condemnation of the moral violence and exhaustion of modern man. It is also the voice of a forward thrusting individual, of a poet who—for all uncompromising criticism—is a "caresser" of American life which he celebrates and sings:

O great healing metaphor invented by my first exiled
        self in Nueva York
in the great year 1966 when the whole world was a
        disease
only the brilliant metaphor of my young body could
        heal
as it hurtled through Nirvana Village and Central Park
        open
like a gold sieve to the wonder of possibility!
(**Comrade** 88)

With a keen sense of humor, Codrescu speaks of an
America miraculously located "at the psychointersections
of cities" where

> At the U. of the Future, Professor Mayakovski
> is discussing with Professor O'Hara
> the pleasure of belonging somewhere. (**Comrade** 59)

This poet's "Love Song" is sincere and does reverberate
amid the bounty of the West:

> So using the conveyance
> of the "I" to get us through the streets I came
> to the exact meeting place of a thousand "I"s
> clamoring for attention with an uninterrupted
> belief in culture and the Pie. (**Comrade** 50)

In the process, the poet also defines and explores his
emerging self:

> I rolled through my new country healing first my ills with
> poetry, then others', until at least a shaman, I stood
> looking at the two oceans simultaneously and knew
> beyond the shadow of a doubt that I invented it all,
> just as I made myself. (**Comrade** 89)

Through all the intervening layers of **Comrade Past and
Mister Present** the poet's self leaves husks of past identity as he encounters the multiform experiences of life. In
a process of social and psychological ecdysis, he is propelled by his uninhibited imagination, his personal experiences, and his vivid recollections. Basic to his progress is
the testimony of his own senses, without which he could
not transform such intensely personal material into a powerful and nearly universal message. In a way that he could
not have foreseen, Codrescu has anticipated the struggle of
his native country to emerge from its nearentombment, has
warned his American contemporaries of the dangers inherent in the obsession with the mechanical and the material
while exalting the Nirvanic quality of America, and has
worked inward to his consciousness through his senses and
his insights and outward to his American audience to create his new poetic self, conscious that "each time, every
night, all experience must be renewed" (**Comrade** 51).

Kirkus Reviews (review date 15 April 1995)

SOURCE: A review of *The Blood Countess*, in *Kirkus Reviews*, April 15, 1995, pp. 487-88.

[*The following review commends Codrescu's historical
novel* The Blood Countess, *comparing it to the works of
Anne Rice, Zoe Oldenbourg, and Marguerite Yourcenar.*]

An expertly crafted first novel uncovers the roots of contemporary Eastern European carnage in the lurid story of
a notorious 16th-century murderess.

Romanian-born poet, essayist, and NPR commentator
Codrescu (**Road Scholar,** 1993, etc.) abandoned plans for
a factual book about Elizabeth Bathory, his real-life ancestor, a beautiful Hungarian countess convicted and imprisoned for torturing and murdering more than 600 young
girls—and has instead produced a compulsively readable
fiction in which the story of Elizabeth's life and crimes is
juxtaposed with a parallel narrative describing the agonies
of conscience suffered by her 20th-century descendant: an
Americanized journalist whose reluctant return to his
homeland exposes him to Elizabeth's aura and influence—
with catastrophic results. Drake Bathory-Kereshtur, testifying before a judge from whom he begs punishment,
recounts his enlistment by a patriotic group bent on restoring Hungary's aristocracy and monarchy to their former
grandeur, and repeats the tormenting question ("In what way
were the people of Elizabeth Bathory's time like us?") raised
by this paralyzing plunge into his, and his country's, past.
Its counterpart story traces the welter of violent influences
that shape the young countess's steely character and documents her phlegmatic savagery with a perversely amusing
articulation of droll understatement and feverish Grand
Guignol excess. Though Anne Rice might indeed be warned
to look to her laurels, this exciting book offers rather more
than a racy few hours' reading pleasure. Codrescu has expertly blended convincing period detail and colorfully grotesque folk materials with a riveting characterization of a
woman who was doubtless never understood even by those
who loved and feared her most. Furthermore, he persuasively links such familiar horrors as "ethnic cleansing"
with his modern protagonist's vision of "Older things that
now stirred from their slumber, blind creatures that lived
in the deep mud of ancestral memory, things with horns
and tails."

A wonderful historical novel that merits comparison with
the fiction of Zoe Oldenbourg and Marguerite Yourcenar.

Nina Auerbach (review date 30 July 1995)

SOURCE: "Haunted in Hungary," in *The New York Times Book Review,* Vol. CXLIV, July 30, 1995, p. 9.

[*In the following review, Auerbach faults Codrescu for his depiction of Elizabeth Bathory and other female characters as either virgins or vamps in* The Blood Countess.]

In his buoyant 1993 film, **Road Scholar,** the Romanian expatriate Andrei Codrescu emulated the American odysseys of Walt Whitman and Jack Kerouac. Stopping along the way west to scrutinize quaint national divinities, from hamburgers to crystals, Mr Codrescu, grinning in his red Cadillac, fulfilled his immigrant's pledge "We were done with the Old World, liberty was ours."

In his new novel, **The Blood Countess,** a Hungarian emigrant goes back to his bloody Old World, with no red Cadillac in which to escape crazy faiths. Drake Bathory-Kereshtur, a journalist in America, returns to an "anxious and unsettled" Budapest swarming with skinhead fascism, anti-Semitism and medieval magic from the fairy tales—or horror stories—that Communist indoctrination had suppressed. He sees that "the lightly settled soil of democracy and atheism was rapidly turning over, releasing dormant agents."

Awakening after a burial that seems long only to mortals, these ancient agents of savagery overwhelm modernity and its representative, the bemused Drake. The most tenacious monster is a woman: the 16th century Countess Elizabeth Bathory. Drake's ancestor and the personification of his national past, who is said to have preserved her youth by bathing in virgins' blood, Elizabeth erupts into the present when a monarchist coterie declares Drake King of Hungary.

At the climax of the novel, Drake travels with these motley believers to ancient Bathory castles. In this nightmare journey, characters and country revert to their haunted past. Elizabeth returns as various strange apparitions, instigating a murder, which Drake accuses himself of before a high-minded American judge.

This parable of atavism and possession is chilling, but unfortunately, it is not the only story; interwoven with Drake's journey is a historical novel about Countess Bathory herself. Though she does not bathe in maidens' blood, she showers in it with the help of an ingenious cage. Menstruating, marrying, studying herself in mirrors, biting little pieces out of her maids, experimenting with baroque sexual refreshments, Elizabeth Bathory supposedly embodies the demonic past.

Alas, she is too silly for that. On her wedding night she arouses herself with dreams of spurtings and spoutings and whippings fit to prmt only on the walls of a boys' locker room. As an incarnation of history, Elizabeth is closer to pornographic Victorian biters like Swinburne's pagan goddesses than she is to the cold hate at the heart of Mr. Codrescu's historical horror. Her supposed perversions distract from and diminish the authentic abominations of our own chilling times.

***The Blood Countess* is an ornate novel, thick with dense symbolism and decorative violence. It reveals a more ambitiously literary Andrei Codrescu than the popular commentator on National Public Radio, who is a wry and realistic political observer flaunting his dissociation from all countries, relishing quirks and denouncing all specimens of stupidity and tyranny.**
—Nina Auerbach

The Blood Countess is an ornate novel, thick with dense symbolism and decorative violence. It reveals a more ambitiously literary Andrei Codrescu than the popular commentator on National Public Radio, who is a wry and realistic political observer flaunting his dissociation from all countries, relishing quirks and denouncing all specimens of stupidity and tyranny. As a novelist, Mr. Codrescu borrows Kafka's enigmatic dream mode. He no longer aims to observe nations, but to create fantastic national allegories. His novel is so drenched in elaborate (if studiously metaphorical) sadism, in obscure fairy idles and legends, that I longed for his incisive radio voice to tell me what was going on.

The problem in this novel, as in its version of history, is women. They are virgins or vamps, victims or furies, who mess up an effective thriller. In the course of *The Blood Countess* the spirit of Elizabeth possesses all the modern characters, including a glamorous female professor who studies the Bathory archives, beats her adoring students and finally turns into a ridiculously overdrawn emanation of the Countess. Elizabeth also inhabits a comatose woman, allegorically named Eva, who prowls ominously around Hungary at the end, getting younger and younger. The arousal of women, this ending suggests, is the death of civilization.

I don't believe that, and I don't think Mr. Codrescu does either. *The Blood Countess* gets lost in lurid symbolism and bizarre sexual embellishments. Its operatic women become scapegoats for all social viciousness, but in the best parts of the book hatred is a pervasive, even casual motivation to everyone. I wish Mr. Codrescu had written a sparer, tighter novel about his bedeviled King of Hungary without trying to resurrect Elizabeth. As a specter, she is wonderful; as a character, she is ludicrous. Mr. Codrescu writes splendidly about women as remote agents of fear, but when he tries to depict them, campy posturing undermines political dread.

Bettina Drew (review date 6 August 1995)

SOURCE: "Mistress of Terror and Torture," in the *Washington Post Book Review*, Vol. XXV, No. 32, August 6, 1995, pp. 3, 10.

[*In the following review, Drew lauds Codrescu's* The Blood Countess *for making comprehensible to the West the hatred and violence of modern Eastern Europe by exposing its bloody past.*]

What makes Andrei Codrescu's voice on National Public Radio so distinctive is the way it mixes American vernacular with a Transylvanian accent so rich it conjures up sophisticated counts about to do evil in gloomy hilltop castles. Happily, his new novel skillfully exploits this cultural bilingualism. In it, Codrescu weaves the story of an infamous 16th-century Hungarian countess who murdered, and bathed in the blood of, some 650 young girls with the trials of her modern-day American-immigrant descendant, who has recently returned to post-Communist Hungary. Based on extensive research in old Hungarian archives and on Codrescu's keen impressions of contemporary Eastern Europe, the novel links feudal Europe's mania for torture with the hatred, chaos and savage butchery that has followed the collapse of communism in the region.

Countess Elizabeth Bathory (1560-1613) was born into a world of torture racks and disemboweling pokers, a world where miscreants were hung from hooks or had their breasts cut off, where the services of German torture-machine maker Philip Imser were heavily in demand. "Her corner of Europe was soaked in the blood of countless commoners who had not done the bidding of their nobles," Codrescu writes. "Death was the common punishment for almost any infraction, even petty theft. Peasant rebellions were suppressed so severely that they passed into folktales because straightforward accounts were too gruesome to tell."

Though beautiful, educated and exceedingly wealthy, the countess had plenty of early experience with horror. As a young girl she witnessed the rape and hanging of her two sisters in a peasant uprising, then saw their captured murderer placed upon a hot iron throne and melted to death. Ignored by her mother, abandoned by a husband who submerged his life in the daily barbarism of far-off wars against the Turks, the intelligent and curious Elizabeth took comfort in the nobility's life-and-death power over the peasant and became addicted to violence. At first her craving for the pain of others was linked to sexual pleasure, but in the end blood was all. She especially enjoyed a cylindrical cage with sharp iron spikes inside, which, when suspended from the ceiling, rotated and contracted, driving the stakes into the flesh of the victim within. Finally, as the numbers of young women disappearing from the villages kept mounting, Elizabeth's infamous reputation forced her supporters to imprison her.

Her descendant Count Bathory-Kereshtur provides a welcome counterpoint to this bloody tale. A divorced New Yorker sent to cover Budapest by his newspaper, Kereshtur, shocked by the city's skinheads and political instability, is sought out by monarchist elements eager to have him resume his noble role. At a hilarious cocktail party of long-irrelevant Hungarian noblemen, genealogical calculations, performed by sticking hors d'oeuvre toothpick flags of Hungary into an improvised chart, reveal that he is the next in line for the throne.

The absurdity of the situation is in no way lost on the count. "The whole solemn business of staring at a bunch of dirty toothpicks with grains of rice and meat juice sticking to them in order to ascertain my rights to the kingdom was more than I could bear," he avers before going home to drink himself to sleep with a bottle of Jack Daniels. His more pressing problems involve guilt over a sexual aggression he feels was probably rape, his infatuation with the twenty-something daughter of his former lover Eva, and the way all the people he meets keep turning into modern-day counterparts of Elizabeth Bathory's twisted inner circle.

If this plot sounds a bit farfetched, it is, but somehow it doesn't seem to matter all that much. In this blend of historical fiction, confessional and fairy tale, Codrescu has done more than tap into a Western fascination, whipped up by Hollywood Draculas and vampires, with the bloody past excesses of Central Europe. He has written a vivid narrative of the 16th century that even accuses Martin Luther of sexism and invites Kepler to the castle for dinner; he has made the history of Hungary and its shifting contemporary situation entertaining and compelling. In digging down to the "older things now stirred from their slumber, blind creatures that lived in the deep mud of ancestral memory, things with horns and tails," Codrescu has found a forceful way of making the mayhem and hatred now reigning in so much of Eastern Europe more historically and emotionally comprehensible to American readers.

Robert L. McLaughlin (review date September 1995)

SOURCE: "Blood & Guts in Budapest," in *American Book Review,* Vol. 17, September, 1995, pp. 16, 23.

[In the following review, McLaughlin commends The Blood Countess *for its historical foundation and commentary on current world events, but pans it for its repetition of themes, poor narrative technique, and sloppy treatment of details.]*

Not far into **The Blood Countess,** Andrei Codrescu's new novel, it occurred to me that this book wants to be *The Name of the Rose.* Prominent intellectual combines history and mystery, past and present, to popularize complex ideas in the form of a can't-put-it-down page-turner. Indeed, there is much about the ideas in **The Blood Countess** that is compelling and its narrative is intriguing, but in the end the novel is not as successful intellectually or narratively as one would wish it to be.

The novel, in alternating chapters, tells stories of late-sixteenth-century and contemporary Hungary. The former is the story of Elizabeth Bathory, an actual historic figure, whose reputation as a near monster who bathed in the blood of virgins has survived to the present day. According to the novel, this reputation is both exaggerated (as one character says, "One may drink blood, in the belief that it's an elixir, or suck it, in an excess of passion, but bathe in it? The sticky mess. The quick coagulation.") and an understatement.

Elizabeth is an extraordinary child born into a violent world. Still a baby, she exhibits the abilities to remember and repeat everything she hears and even to mimic the speakers' voices, thus unnerving her maids but attracting her wet nurse, Darvulia, a practicing witch who sees much potential in Elizabeth for subverting the man-made world. Her earliest shaping experience is a peasant revolt at her family's Ecsed Castle, during which she sees her two sisters raped and murdered and after which she sees the rebels forced to eat the roasted flesh of their leader before they are killed. The novel then follows Elizabeth closely from the ages of nine to fifteen as she observes and then participates in a world of contradictions. She is educated by a Catholic monk and Lutheran pastors. She attends the coronation of her cousin, prince of Transylvania, and visits a Pest slum. She is married to Franz Nadazdy but lives alone as he fights perpetual wars. From the world around her, she comes to four conclusions: that because of her position, people will do pretty much anything she wants; that abstractions are worthless and that to understand something, one must observe it; that the human soul is visible only when pain brings it to the surface; and that time, subtly but constantly attacking her body, is her enemy.

These conclusions result in Elizabeth's creating a dark underside to the palace life her position forces her to lead. While during the day she functions as administrator for her and her husband's estates, diplomat with Hungary's conflicted royal families, and pupil to her religious instructors, at night, in her private quarters, she rages at, tortures, and frequently kills the endless supply of peasant maidens Darvulia recruits to her service. Convinced that the maidens' blood restores the youth of her skin, she installs a cage over her bath, in which young girls are pierced to death while their blood showers on the Countess.

Elizabeth finally goes too far. On the last day of the sixteenth century, resigned to her lost youth, she orders all the mirrors in her house broken and thrown out, stands a young church singer in their debris, and has water poured over her, freezing her into a statue representing the effect of time on beauty. The public, religious, and royal outcries are so great that Elizabeth's cousin, the palatine Thurzo, dispenser of justice, is forced to take action. He confines Elizabeth to one of her castles, holds hearings in which the witnesses tell of Elizabeth's deeds and are subsequently put to death, and, while never officially charging Elizabeth with any crime, has her walled into her suite of rooms, leaving only an opening to pass in food.

The contemporary story takes the form of a confession to murder by Elizabeth Bathory's direct descendent, Drake Bathory-Kereshtur. Standing in a New York City courtroom, Drake narrates to the judge (surely the most indulgent judge in history; she makes Lance Ito seem like Roy Bean) stories of his childhood in Soviet bloc Hungary, his emigration to the United States after the failed 1956 revolution, and his return to post-Warsaw Pact Hungary. Sent by the newspaper he works for to report on the capitalist transformation of his homeland, Drake is soon manipulated by forces only some of which he comes to understand. Klaus Megyery, a childhood friend and former secret policeman, summons him, a member of a royal family, to become a representative of a new monarchist party in the politically volatile country. At a gathering of royal descendants, it is decided that Drake has the best claim to be the new king of Hungary. Drake is suspicious that the party is supported mainly by skinhead storm troopers and eventually learns that the party is actually the brainstorm of Klaus's former employers as a means of establishing a fascist government.

Nevertheless, Drake becomes fascinated by the thought of himself as royalty and by the connection between himself and the historically remote yet strangely present Elizabeth Bathory. He develops a companionship with a former lover's daughter, Teresa, who is a historian specializing in the Early Modern period. Through her, he meets Lilly Hangress, biographer of Elizabeth Bathory. Ditching Klaus and his skinheads, Drake and Teresa rent a car and search for his family's estates. But this escape becomes another trap as they are mysteriously guided from estate to estate, to a meeting with a 400-year-old alchemist seeking the secret of perpetual youth, and eventually to a snowbound evening in Elizabeth's chambers in Lockenhaus Castle, where Drake helplessly enacts a ritual sacrifice that apparently returns Elizabeth Bathory to the world just in time for the millennium.

These parallel plots support several interesting and pessimistic theses about the development and state of Western society generally and Eastern European society in particular. Both Elizabeth's and Drake's Hungarys are emerging from long periods of totalitarian culture, the totalized systems of social, political, and intellectual life of, first, Roman Catholicism and, later, Soviet communism. These monolithic systems, by tolerating no heresy, were able to establish virtually unquestioned order and stability for a period of time. But when these periods end, the societies are thrown into chaos. Various monolithic systems war to establish totalizing control; the Roman Catholic Church vs. the Lutheran Church; Christian Europe vs. the Islamic Turks; religious faith vs. science; Western capitalism vs. socialism; fascism vs. democracy. Each of these systems will go to any lengths, including horrific episodes of violence, in order to suppress instability, lack of order, and any relativity that might challenge its exclusive claim to absolute truth.

What Elizabeth learns from the conflicts of her society and what she comes to represent to Drake's society is violence as *raison d'être*. That is, for Elizabeth, violence becomes an outward thrust into a chaotic reality, an attempt to objectify and stabilize that reality so that the individual can define herself in relation to it. This novel's unhappy conclusion seems to be that in Elizabeth's world and in ours violence is the necessary response to an otherwise indeterminate reality. Even the systems we might look toward to subvert the evolution of violence in the service of control are implicated in that same evolution. When they get the opportunity (a revolt, a plague, or the breakup of parliament), the exploited lower classes—the peasants and the skinheads—are capable of the same defining violence as the upper classes. And Darvulia and her witches (now they would be ecofeminists), though dedicated to promoting women's arts and powers and to subverting male systems, are active participants in Elizabeth's violence against other women. Elizabeth's return to the world and Drake's seduction into murder seem to offer little hope for release from a pattern of violence against people, animals, and the world. All that has changed from Elizabeth's time to ours is the technology of killing.

What's unsatisfying about all this is the novel's presentation of its ideas. The novel is thematically episodic. That

is, an idea is introduced, then set aside as other ideas are introduced. Eventually, we'll come back to the first idea again, but then it's a restatement, not a development of the idea. One gets little sense of the novel's themes modifying or growing as the plots go on and as the ideas come in contact with each other. As an intellectual juggler, the novel can't keep all its balls in the air at the same time.

There are similar problems with the novel's narrative technique. The subject matter ends up not being as absorbing as it ought to be, primarily because of its presentation. The setup of plot points is clunky and, eventually, predictable. At one point we are told that one of Elizabeth's Lutheran tutors has a pet monkey. Many pages later, the monkey is reintroduced, and we are told, "Pastor Ponikenuz felt for his monkey the absolute maximum of affection he allowed himself toward any living creature." The reader reacts, "Oh yeah, he *did* have a monkey," and, simultaneously, "Whoa! Something's going to *happen* to that monkey." Indeed, on the next page Elizabeth's pet jaguar (don't ask) bites off its head. And so it goes. Does a young alchemist prepare a beaker of acid? Whoops! There it goes into somebody's face! A novice maid scratches Elizabeth in her bath? Where's that cage? While we are given many incidents, neither Elizabeth's nor Drake's worlds ever become completely present to us.

Connected to this, the novel seems to have a lot of trouble with dialogue. Much of Elizabeth's story is told in indirect discourse, even when it seems that direct discourse would be more appropriate and effective. Drake's first-person narration works the same way. As a result, at any given point, what happened, what was said, and what the characters thought are presented as three different items; they are rarely integrated in a way that connects the reader emotionally to the moment.

There is also some annoying sloppiness in the novel's treatment of details. Fires blaze, then blow out, then blaze again in a matter of paragraphs. Elizabeth is walled into her rooms in 1611 and dies, we are told, five years later—in 1613.

The result of all this is that we never share the other characters' fascination with Elizabeth. We are emotionally distanced from her and increasingly unaffected by her punching and scratching and murdering. I suspect that we are supposed to be simultaneously attracted to and repulsed by Elizabeth, as Drake is, but the novel doesn't pull it off. In fact, Drake, due, no doubt, to his first-person narration, becomes much more real for us and interesting to us than Elizabeth.

The Blood Countess, then, has much to recommend it as a late-summer beach book: its historical foundation is interesting; the incidents of its parallel plots keep one turning the pages; it has much to say about our world. But I can't help wishing that it were better than it is, that its narratives were better accomplished and that its ideas dived deeper.

Kirkus Reviews (review date 1 June 1996)

SOURCE: A review of *The Dog with the Chip in His Neck: Essays from NPR and Elsewhere,* in *Kirkus Reviews,* Vol. 64, June 1, 1996, pp. 797-98.

[*The following review identifies Codrescu's best essays in this collection as those which deal with the most personal subjects.*]

Prolific belletrist, novelist, and NPR commentator Codrescu offers his trademark benign-oddball perspective on a broad array of cultural topics in another scattershot collection.

Codrescu grew up in Communist Romania and came to America in 1966, and most of the essays here are either explicitly or implicitly about the experience of exile, whether linguistic, political, or geographical. The subject of computers and the Internet prompts several Luddite out-bursts about the failure of communication; the titular pet's surgically implanted ID tag inspires a brief technophobic fantasy poised between humor and genuine uneasiness. Codrescu cocks an eye at young lesbians in San Francisco, a Japanese game show, Brancusi's life and sculpture, airline travel, and the faithful in Jerusalem. But he's at his best when his subjects are most personal. He anchors a diffuse piece about the complications and rewards of communicating across language barriers with a single perfect anecdote about arriving in Detroit without speaking any English and being befriended in a ghetto coffee shop. A pilgrimage to Mexico with his Castaneda-obsessed 14-year-old son sparks a splendid piece that poetically conflates his son's adolescent volatility and Mexico's tempestuous history. And his takes on life in Eastern Europe after the fall of Communism are acid reminders that the adoption of "freedom" and "democracy" has by no means solved most problems there. But when Codrescu riffs on abstractions, he tends to strain his whimsy to the point of opacity. From a piece on walls as metaphors: "The only creature worthy of respect is the wallflower. A creature is a wall. Respect is space. Therefore, worth is the space one accords a wall." Whatever.

Newcomers to Codrescu may be put off by some of his slapdash indulgences here, but his many fans will welcome the opportunity to roam around again in his quirky mind.

Additional coverage of Codrescu's life and career is contained in the following sources published by Gale: *Contemporary Authors,* Vols. 33-36R; *Contemporary Authors Autobiography Series,* Vol. 19; *Contemporary Authors New Revision Series,* Vols. 13, 34, and 53; and *DISCovering Authors Modules: Poets.*

Paula Fox

1923-

American novelist, essayist, and author of children's books.

The following entry presents an overview of Fox's career through 1996. For further information on her life and works, see *CLC*, Volumes 2 and 8.

INTRODUCTION

Fox is one of the most highly acclaimed contemporary American writers of children's and young adult fiction. Her writing for children has earned her numerous industry awards, including the Newbery Medal and the Hans Christian Andersen Medal. Additionally, Fox has been praised for her novels for adults, many of which explore the small, private moments of despair and alienation in everyday life.

Biographical Information

Fox was born in New York City to Paul Harvey and Elsie de Sola Fox in 1923. Her parents rarely lived in one place for very long, and as a young child Fox was sent to live in New York's Hudson Valley with a minister and his invalid mother. There she developed a love for stories that later influenced her decision to become a professional writer. In 1931 Fox went to live with her maternal grandmother on a sugar plantation in Cuba, where she attended a one-room school and became fluent in Cuban Spanish. She returned to New York City three years later, when the revolution led by Batista y Zaldivar made Cuba socially and politically unstable. After high school Fox held many jobs, working as a machinist at one point and moving on to low-level positions at publishing companies and newspapers. After World War II she took a job with a leftist British news service, which sent her to cover post-war Poland. When she returned to the United States, she married and had children, but the marriage ended in divorce. Fox then attended Columbia University but never received her degree because of financial difficulties. Nonetheless, she worked as an English teacher for Spanish-speaking children. In 1962 Fox remarried and spent six months living in Greece while her husband, an English professor, held a Guggenheim fellowship. It was then that she decided to make writing a full-time career. Fox resides in Brooklyn, New York.

Major Works

Fox's writing for children and young adults is highly regarded because of the way Fox deals with difficult, often

tragic, situations with neither sentimentality nor condescension toward her readers. Her second major work, *How Many Miles to Babylon?* (1967), is considered a classic in the young adult fiction genre. Ten-year-old James Douglas, an African-American child living in the inner-city, is left with three great-aunts after his mother enters a mental institution. In order to cope, James creates a fantasy life in which his mother is really a queen returned to Africa. He is drawn into a group of young thugs with a dog-napping scheme, taken to a Coney Island funhouse where the dogs are hidden, and, using his ingenuity and intelligence, escapes and rescues the dogs. When he returns home, he finds his mother there waiting for him. *The Slave Dancer* (1973), Fox's most acclaimed and most controversial book for young adults, tells the story of a kidnapped white child trapped on a slave ship. Thirteen-year-old Jessie is taken from his home onto a ship bringing slaves to the United States and forced to play his fife while the slaves are forced to dance to amuse their captors. Thrown into these nightmarish circumstances, Jessie attempts to retain his sense of morality and humanity. Fox's novel is a meticulously researched tale of innocence forced to face violent experience. *One-Eyed Cat* (1984) depicts the guilt a boy feels after shooting a cat in the eye. The complicated story that develops deals with family secrets and ultimate attempts at reconciliation. In *Monkey Island* (1991) a formerly middle-class boy finds himself abandoned and homeless in the city. In *The Eagle Kite* (1995) a teenager must come to terms with his parents' separation because of his father's homosexuality and later death from AIDS. Similarly, in Fox's fiction for adults, complex situations lead to alienation and often despair as characters attempt to find meaning and focus in their lives. In *Desperate Characters* (1970) a middle-class couple in New York are complacent about the distance between them, but the story gradually reveals deeper and more violent feelings destroying their relationship. Annie, the protagonist of *The Western Coast* (1972) drifts among people she cares little about, all of whom leave a bigger impression on her than she leaves on anyone. Finally, her search for meaning leads her to an unknown future in Europe. *A Servant's Tale* (1976) features a similar protagonist whose actions are often inscrutable. The illegitimate child of a servant and the son of a wealthy plantation owner in the Caribbean, Luisa spends her entire adult life quietly insisting on working as a servant, although her decision is misunderstood by everyone around her.

Critical Reception

While Fox is generally considered one of the most important authors of fiction for children and young adults, her work is not without detractors. *The Slave Dancer*, in particular, has received negative commentary from some critics who claim that Fox portrayed the captured Africans as weak and dispirited and the captors as victims of circumstance themselves. Nonetheless, the book won the prestigious Newbery Medal and is widely hailed as classic of children's literature. Fox's other works for young people, especially *How Many Miles to Babylon?*, are also praised for their integrity and honest presentation to children of complex social and personal issues. Fox's novels for adults have not been as well received, although many critics admit that the works are brilliant, if not likeable. Both *The Western Coast* and *A Servant's Tale* have been harshly reviewed because of the ambiguous, obscure natures of their protagonists; but other critics have found the novels appropriately weighty for their subject matter. *Desperate Characters* is Fox's most successful novel for adults. Pearl K. Bell observed that the book is "a small masterpiece, a revelation of contemporary New York middle-class life." Of the judgment that her works are "depressing," Fox has stated: "'Depressing,' when applied to a literary work, is so narrow, so confining, so impoverished and impoverishing. This yearning for the proverbial 'happy ending' is little more than a desire for oblivion."

PRINCIPAL WORKS

Maurice's Room (juvenilia) 1966
How Many Miles to Babylon? (young adult novel) 1967
A Likely Place (juvenilia) 1967
Poor George (novel) 1967
Dear Prosper (juvenilia) 1968
Hungry Fred (juvenilia) 1969
The King's Falcon (young adult novel) 1969
Portrait of Ivan (young adult novel) 1969
Blowfish Live in the Sea (young adult novel) 1970
Desperate Characters (novel) 1970
The Western Coast (novel) 1972
The Slave Dancer (young adult novel) 1973
The Widow's Children (novel) 1976
A Servant's Tale (novel) 1976
The Little Swineherd and Other Tales (juvenilia) 1978
A Place Apart (young adult novel) 1980
One-Eyed Cat (young adult novel) 1984
Lily and the Lost Boy (young adult novel) 1986
The Moonlight Man (young adult novel) 1986
The Village by the Sea (young adult novel) 1988
In a Place of Danger (young adult novel) 1989
Monkey Island (young adult novel) 1991
The Slave Dancer (novel) 1991
Western Wind (young adult novel) 1993
The Eagle Kite (young adult novel) 1995
Desperate Characters (novel) 1999
Widow's Children: A Novel (novel) 1999

CRITICISM

Nicholas J. Loprete, Jr. (review date 1 April 1967)

SOURCE: A review of *Poor George*, in *Bestsellers*, Vol. 27, No. 1, April 1, 1967, p. 5.

[*In the following review, Loprete offers a negative assessment of* Poor George.]

George Mecklin, the hero (or anti-hero, if you prefer) of this slim and over-priced first novel [***Poor George***], is a teacher in a private school in Manhattan to which he commutes by train from his rented Westchester cottage. George is married to Emma, a part-time librarian at Columbia. Immediately the reader suspects that here is another academic novel dealing with the inner workings of the teacher's world. But the reader is wrong. George Mecklin the man engages Miss Fox's attention, not George Mecklin the teacher. When George discovers a teenage delinquent-in-the-making hiding in his home, he offers to tutor him.

Ernest the adolescent is the catalyst of this book. By the time you have finished reading, you have met the hypocritical Devlins; a narcissistic actor and his alcoholic wife; George's sister Lila and her son, Claude; and an assortment of type-teachers. Nor is this all. Emma, who has resented George's interest in Ernest, deliberately allows Ernest to seduce her. At the conclusion, the Mecklins have separated; George is recovering from a bullet wound inflicted because of an incredible adventure as a Peeping-Tom; Ernest is dead—the victim of a beating by a young hoodlum.

Poor George is a pretentious book filled with self-analysis and self-pity. In an outrageous example of dust-jacket hyperbole, we are told that the novel "carries to a new depth a permanent theme in American literature—the theme of innocence." I disagree. It is boredom that is carried to a new depth. There is no communication among the flat people in this novel. They address words to each other, but no one seems to listen. They are on different wave-lengths; they speak in tongues to disguise true feelings. They do not respect each other as human beings because they are nothing more than cardboard characters cut from the same pattern. My sympathies to the "poor reader" if he chooses **Poor George.**

Polly Goodwin (review date 8 October 1967)

SOURCE: A review of *How Many Miles to Babylon?,* in *Washington Post Book World,* October 8, 1967, p. 24.

[*In the following review, Goodwin praises the uncanny realism in* How Many Miles to Babylon? *but expresses reservations about the book's appropriateness for young readers.*]

Paula Fox has demonstrated an almost uncanny insight into young boys in two earlier stories, **Maurice's Room** and **A Likely Place.** Now, with equal skill [in **How Many Miles to Babylon?**], she takes a highly imaginative, lonely Negro boy of "barely 10" through a nightmarish day. James knows what is real—that his father is gone and he is living in a small, shabby room in Brooklyn with three old aunts who are caring for him while his mother is in the hospital. But what James feels is very different—that his mother has gone to Africa to tell people he is a prince and to "fix everything."

One day James walks out of school and goes to the empty house where he acts out his fantasy. He paints his face, dons a feathered headband and a piece of red curtain, lays at his feet the ring he thinks is a sign from his mother, and dances by candlelight in the cold, dark basement. Suddenly three jeering boys appear. Tall, thin Stick, short, plump Blue and

small, mean-looking Gino seize the terrified boy and force him to help them in their dog-stealing racket. James tries to run away but fails. He rides for miles on the back of Gino's bike to Coney Island, where he sees the ocean for the first time and is confined with three small dogs in the Fun House. That night the boys return to the empty house and he escapes at last. When he returns home and finds his mother waiting for him, James' fear and his world of pretense are ended.

It is a disturbingly realistic tale, but I wonder if this is indeed a book for children. Perhaps it is for perceptive adults instead, who will appreciate it as a superb study of a child under emotional stress, a story through which runs a strong thread of sadness.

Times Literary Supplement (review date 16 October 1969)

SOURCE: "Doing Their Own Thing," in *Times Literary Supplement,* October 16, 1969, p. 1198.

[*In the following review, the anonymous critic praises* The Stone-Faced Boy *but recommends it for mature readers.*]

. . . Gus, the hero of **The Stone-Faced Boy,** is something of a lone wolf, although he is the middle child of a family of five. As a protection against the teasing of other children, he has learnt never to show his emotions. Now he finds he is unable to do so, even when he wants to, and this worries him. He develops a habit of feeling his face to see if he is smiling. "Pretty soon he would have to start carrying around signs—signs that read: *laughter; scowling; puzzlement; curiosity; anger*—which he would have to hold up over his head." If, however, the reader thinks this book is going to be the story of how he solves this problem, he is mistaken, for Gus remains stone-faced to the end.

Instead, by relating the incidents of one night as they appear to Gus, a keen insight is given into his real feelings. Those incidents are curious enough. First the children find a strange dog in the snow, and then arrive home to find an equally strange woman in the kitchen. She turns out to be their eccentric great aunt from Italy. Obliquely she seems to understand Gus's predicament and, perhaps symbolically, she gives him a geode, a stone seemingly as featureless as his own face, through a crack of which he can see sparkling crystals inside. Through her, indirectly, he learns how to master his young brother, the biggest thorn in his flesh, and he overcomes his irrational fear of the well.

This is a strange book that can be read at several levels. Superficially it is an entertaining and at times chuckle-making story, but the depths will probably be seen and appreciated only by the maturer, discerning few. Donald Mackay's almost dreamlike illustrations very satisfactorily complement the story. . . .

Peter S. Prescott (review date 25 September 1972)

SOURCE: "Taken in Hand," in *Newsweek,* Vol. LXXX, No. 13, September 25, 1972, pp. 25-26.

[*In the following review, Prescott finds* The Western Coast *stylistically interesting but its plot and purpose unclear.*]

Other fiction writers will appreciate the formidable technical hurdles that Paula Fox set for herself in this, her third and most ambitious novel [*The Western Coast*]. There is almost no plot, for one thing, no story line strong enough to sustain suspense or even to indicate an inexorable direction; the novel instead consists of a series of events, some quite dramatic, which involve a large but continually changing group of characters. For another, the story so scrupulously re-creates a particular place in a particular time, and kinds of people who have often been written about badly before, that the novel serves as a kind of social history, convincing us that this is the way it must have been. Most difficult of all: the heroine is an entirely neutral person, a blank upon which others leave their prints, and in this way we come to know them, but not her. This is a useful device, but I am not sure there is any way it can be brought off entirely successfully.

"Don't you know anything?" people ask Annie Gianfala. "I need to be taken in hand," Annie admits. The time, as the book starts, is 1939 and Annie is "not quite 18," living on her own because her father has taken a woman to New Mexico. Annie attracts drunks, homosexuals, misfits, drifters, crazy people; the affinity between the maimed and the innocent is now firmly entrenched in American letters, and Annie, who is quite bright, is aware that she encourages in others expectations that she cannot fulfill. Annie fends the others off until Walter Vogel, a Communist, unemployed actor and sometime sailor, tells Annie he doesn't like virgins. Annie thinks Walter holds the world's secrets, he can take her in hand, and so, with another boy, she makes the necessary adjustment.

Alone, hungry, purposeless, Annie settles into a dreary room and a drearier job somewhere between Hollywood and Los Angeles. She falls in with jobless film writers, apologists for Stalinism, a kindly homosexual. "Like beads from a broken string," she thinks, "rolling senselessly all over Southern California." She becomes married, abused, promiscuous, divorced, deathly ill, bored by the Communist

claptrap people tell her to read. In time, she will simply throw it over, grow up a little as she cares for a dying relative, and then set out for Europe, realizing "how often she'd known people she really hadn't liked, had spent hours and days and months with them."

> **Miss Fox is an excellent satirist and a superb observer who can, in a paragraph or a page, bring a character or an incident vividly alive.**
> —*Peter S. Prescott*

Most of them, indeed, are not likable—particularly the Communists. Paula Fox is very good at showing their insufferable rigidity, their boring diatribes, their internecine nit-picking, even the way they look: "In his gray little face the tiny jawbone flexed with purpose and self-love, the delicate nose pointed at heaven." Miss Fox is an excellent satirist and a superb observer who can, in a paragraph or a page, bring a character or an incident vividly alive. Here, however, because she is determined to get so much into her book, there is a side effect: after their brief parts are played, the characters are thrust aside so that others may take their place. Even toward the end of her book, with Annie for no clear reason about to go to Europe, Miss Fox brings on new people, which leads me to think there may be more novels about Annie (who is just her author's age) to come.

If so, perhaps Annie will become less of a catalyst for others and more clearly herself, whatever that self will be. One of the characters here, thinking about Annie, felt that "she was, in an essential way, without self" and he was "faintly repelled" by her. So are we.

Carolyn Riley (review date 1 October 1972)

SOURCE: Review of *The Western Coast,* in *Best Sellers,* Vol. 32, No. 13, October 1, 1972, pp. 296-97.

[*In the following review, Riley compares Fox to contemporary writers such as Joan Didion and Grace Paley but asserts that Fox is ultimately worthy of praise for her own literary achievements, notably because of her work in novels like* The Western Coast.]

Reading *The Western Coast,* one is reminded of the sociopsychological sensibility of Joan Didion or Grace Paley and one sees in the prose the fine sure hand of Doris Lessing. But Paula Fox has that pure talent for fiction which, though it suggests other excellent writers at every turning, emerges complete in itself, endowing her fiction with its own discrete energy.

The Western Coast is a bildungsroman of the best sort. The novel is a chronicle of Annie Gianfala's effort (sometimes passive, sometimes wrenchingly conscious) to grow—not up, but down, "to the small patch of earth [she'd] marked out as [her] own." It is the "marking out" that is the story here, the effort to define one's place of being and the resources behind one's responses to a frightening and complex environment. In the beginning, Annie sees herself "among people who saw the world she hastened through so nervously, so uncomprehendingly, having meanings, categories, explanations that made it possible for them to know where their next thought was coming from," while "in her closet of terrors, Annie picked up words in the dark, hoping they would not turn out to be serpents." As Annie's friend shrewdly warned: "What one is afraid of becomes one's only real life."

Annie still thought that "there's a world of grown-ups somewhere—a place, a way of being, a message, that will reveal the nature of things." And "somewhere in the back of her mind hung pale abstractions, motionless as painted clouds, God, orderliness of meals, gravity of mien, classroom papers, one's name neatly written on the upper-right-hand corner, families grouped around the dining table, the elders teaching the young, undying love, music of the spirit, not of the kisses and deaths of movies stars." Hence it is Annie's job, just as it is everyone's, to reconcile the abstractions and real world, the grown-ups and herself, her idea of marriage and her own peculiar relationship with her husband, the notion of orderly meals and the hunger pains in her gut, and on and on. Annie's struggle is, of course, everyone's struggle—that of finding a personal equilibrium in a world of disparity between real and ideal. Paula Fox's genius, then, is her ability to present for our recognition a quality of life which hovers, unarticulated, on the edges of our minds.

Annie herself, however, has perhaps more to be afraid of than most—sickness, suicide, homelessness, poverty, Communism, war. And it is the very plethora of fearsome surroundings that demonstrates Miss Fox's only weakness as a novelist. Anxious to provide Annie with sufficient numbers of mirrors and indices with which to identify and measure her own emergent sensibility, she has over-appointed Annie's living room and thereby burdened her novelistic method with overtransparency.

But in the end, Miss Fox has achieved for Annie a perfect sense of conclusion, real in that no "answers" have been found, no "ending" defined. Annie has moved into a kind of maturity in which she looks clear-eyed at "ordinary life" with "its ordinary powerful truths," not with any particular

"knowledge," but rather with a "way of knowing," a stance, a resolution—in sum, an identity. Paula Fox (unbeknownst to the author of the dreary and untantalizing jacket copy) is a wonderfully able novelist—certainly one to watch for future work but, more important, a writer who has already made a significant contribution to contemporary fiction.

Peter S. Prescott (review date 27 September 1976)

SOURCE: "Distress Signals," in *Newsweek*, Vol. LXXXVIII, No. 13, September 27, 1976, pp. 100, 102.

[*In the following review, Prescott praises the artistry of Fox's novels but finds them too deliberately difficult to be enjoyed by readers.*]

Paula Fox is so good a novelist that one wants to go out in the street to hustle up big audience for her.

> "Here. Read this novel. Please."

> "Is it any good?"

> "First rate."

> "Will I like it?"

> "Not a chance. It's for admiring, not liking."

> "Oh. Well, I like to like a book."

There's the problem. Most readers of novels want to be entertained, not subjected to art. For them, art without entertainment is difficult. They know very well that novelists long ago agreed that families are hell and marriages something worse, that characters in novels come in varying degrees of pathos and despicability. All this they will accept if the novel is *likable*. Paula Fox, whose novel *Desperate Characters* was made into a movie, does not indulge such weakness. She makes difficulties for herself in writing fiction, approaches a novel like a spelunker; hunching slowly over real rocks, the searchlight on her forehead describing delicate arcs in the darkness; her beam makes pleasing patterns, but there's not much room for an audience. Story being of little use to her, she focuses on a situation that darkens and intensifies. Her characters play against each other, but none is a whole person; each reveals only that edge of his personality which can be wedged tight into the scene that occupies his author at the moment.

[In *The Widow's Children*] Desmond and Laura Clapper, about to embark on a boat to Africa, throw a tiny party the night before the sailing. Laura knows, but tells no one, that her aged mother died that afternoon in a nursing home. It is this concealed event that charges the evening with electricity. Desmond, who through Laura's intervention has inherited a business that he does not understand, drinks himself in a truculent stupor. Laura's daughter Clara, who describes herself as a boarder in the house of Atreus, succumbs to a chronic ache of self-disgust. Also present are Laura's brother Carlos, a homosexual, and Laura's friend Peter, an editor who no longer likes to read, for whom "the sight of a printed page filled him with a faint but persistent nausea."

Drinks flow, cigarettes burn. Laura, feared by everyone, forgives everyone his fear. The guests speak but no one listens; each falls into his private reveries. Such a freeze-frame approach to narrative is detrimental to an orderly story, yet Fox's purpose is not to move from here to somewhere else, but to turn each scene into a compression chamber: "Clara had trouble breathing—the air was leaking out of the room, draining color from everyone's flesh, faces, and hands and the room furnishings had gone the same ashen color, nothing left to live on but a sweated smoky heat. They were all dying to the vigorous sound of the rain outside." .

Mortification, humiliation, unattended gasps for recognition—Fox spares her characters no distress. Peter, who recognizes that the terrible grip of the family must be broken, protests only in "prig's squeaks." A mother's smile at her daughter is translated into the language of pathology: "Clara could see the three plump cushions of her lips, the large somewhat dingy teeth, and behind them the quivering mucosity of her tongue." Just so, no doubt, but how is a reader to rise to this story? Fox's brilliance has a masochistic aspect: I will do this so well, she seems to say, that you will hardly be able to read it. And so she does, and so do I, who admire her work, find myself muttering in the street—"admirable, not likable."

Edith Milton (review date 15 January 1977)

SOURCE: "Books Considered," in *New Republic*, Vol. 176, No. 3, January 15, 1977, pp. 27-28.

[*In the following review, Milton finds* The Widow's Children *to be a brilliant and accurate portrayal of the suffocating nature of contemporary life.*]

Years ago, I heard Elizabeth Bowen give a lecture on the difficulties of writing a novel. Describing the Retreat from Moscow, she inferred, was nothing compared to getting people to move from one room to another: why were they moving? how much should one go into why and how? I seem to recall her saying that Virginia Woolf, having once spent

three months separating her characters from their *boeuf en daube,* was stuck with them for another six, hanging about in the passage.

Elizabeth Bowen implied that this problem of short-distance transit was an artistic nuisance; but I think she meant one to accept it also as a cultural fact which the artistic difficulty merely reflected; as a cogent paradox for our times, when moving from country to country and from world to world has become easy, but getting to the airport is still the worst part of the trip. Being stuck seems to be as much one of our myths as being lost was for the Ancient Greeks: Ulysses' wandering translates for us into a day of circling Dublin, and hell is the locked room of Sartre's *No Exit* or the mindless after-dinner paralysis of Buñuel's *Exterminating Angel.*

Paula Fox's most recent novel, **The Widow's Children,** is about being stuck. It is spare and understated, and so intensely cool that it becomes sometimes unpleasant to read. Its first 150 pages are an experience of pure claustrophobia. But it is also the most elegant exploration I have read of the chaos of modern life, and of the inertia and deprivations on which that chaos rests.

The plot is almost non-existent: two of the characters are about to leave for a trip to Africa, and three others have come to have a farewell supper with them. There are three Maldonadas (a name which my atrocious Spanish tempts me to read as "recipient of evil"). Laura, who is extravagant and ruthless, her rejected and timid daughter, Clara, and her brother Carlos, a gentle, feline failure, full of affection and social warmth. There is also Desmond Clapper, Laura's second husband, who, like her first, lives mainly to get drunk, and Peter Rice, an old friend, who works in a publishing house.

They talk about Moroccan dancing girls and Ecuadorian profiles; Laura, who is described as *"una viajera,"* has traveled over several continents, but insists there are only six of them. In image and in memory, the characters comprehend the world. But in fact they are in a hotel room and doomed to get little further. Far from reaching Africa, they will be lucky if they can struggle out of the room, through the passage, and to the restaurant where they expect to eat. The restaurant is called *Le Canard Privé,* which translates equally well into *The Caged Duck* or *The Private Illusion.*

That pun informs the novel. Illusion and the state of being caged are synonymous, so closely interwoven that it is impossible to say where cause becomes effect. What Paula Fox describes is the human animal removed from its natural habitat and placed in the artifice of contemporary life. The atmosphere of this environment leaves the hotel room without air, and causes the potted ferns in the lobby to be plastic; when she says she is dizzy from lack of oxygen, Clara is dissuaded from going outside, and told instead to imagine a pond in spring. Nature has been subverted into the fake equivalents of a zoo landscape, and the zoo animals prowl about deprived, perverted and confused by this alien, captive existence. But still, their animal nature clings to them like nostalgia; all the Maldonadas are fond of apes and monkeys, Carlos walks like a cat, Peter makes noises like a seagull, Clara pretends she is a brood of baby possums nestling in a spoon, and recalls how her father, dead drunk, barked like a dog. It is her mother, Laura, however, whose jungle needs remain paramount and obvious, despite their perversion from natural grandeur into a sort of mean anarchy. She derogates human dignity: "'Tell me about the dignity of leopards! Of cockroaches! But don't tell me about the dignity of man!'" She is a bigot. She throws tantrums and glasses. She is not entirely human: "She felt that . . . she was cut off forever from speech, that if she spoke, there would be no words, only a barbaric gibbering. . . ." But even she has been trained into a gross version of civilization, and in the sequence where we see her most intimately, wild with grief, soaked with rain, she is also desperate to urinate, her jungle wildness pathetically at odds with her inability to satisfy this simple impulse.

As with other animals shut up in zoos, the outstanding danger of captivity is infertility, disruption of mating and breeding habits. The race is dying out. Carlos is homosexual; Laura, who has had four abortions, seems eager to devour the one child she allowed by accident to be born; the daughter herself is involved in a presumably unreproductive exercise in adultery, while the editor, Peter, is turning from fleshly appetites to the mineral endurance his name suggests.

The result of their captivity, then, is simple: there are unlikely to be survivors. But the causes of their bondage are manifold and reach from their own numbed wills to the crime-besieged city where they are having the farewell dinner. The five *bon voyage* celebrants are occluded from celebration by almost everything: by poverty-marred childhoods, and histories touched with political violence and displacement, by a death in the family, by slow elevators, by buses which may be late, and food which is not what they wanted. As they make their uncertain way from the hotel room down to the street, they are stopped in the corridor by a publisher's party for Randy Cunny, the pornoqueen. Their passage past, strewn with false recognitions and specious invitations, is as fraught with dangers as Christian's road through the Slough of Despond. But Paula Fox is infinitely subtle in her definitions; it takes a moment to realize one has met with allegory.

And the book as a whole has an edge of allegory. Like all of us, the characters are most closely confined in their in-

escapable bondage to each other: "Families hold each other in an iron grip of definition," says Peter to Clara. And of the grandmother who brought her up, Clara says "She was like a locked room I had escaped from." But Clara has not escaped. The single real event in the novel's progress, the grandmother's death, happens before the narrative begins, and only Laura knows about it. Children and grandchildren describe the old woman in their memory of her as a joyful and beautiful innocence, decaying into tired, poor, and painful old age, and meeting the solitary death of Everyman. She is called Alma (the human soul, perhaps, or am I being too simple minded?) and the book's climax is really about nothing more than a decision whether Clara should go to her funeral, and about nothing less than modern man's chance of cutting his losses, turning away from history, the strength of his delusions, and the mad downhill race toward chaos, to remain recognizably human.

By the end of the book one understands that Paula Fox has been writing gently and uninsistently about the rule of chaos and its hold on her characters and our imagination. Peter recalls Laura recurrently as he first saw her on a spring morning, a vision of freedom and possibility, the joys of disorganization. He becomes, in the course of the novel, its protagonist, and he reaches the recognition that his spring epiphany was a sweet delusion. Her friends and relations refer often to Laura's lawlessness, and she becomes the emblem, the raw material of the city's chaos and the anarchy of modern life. She is fond of the word "nothing." "'What you've done is nothing . . . nothing!'" are her last words to Peter. They comprehend all there is.

But she may be right. Without the illusion of freedom inherent in lawlessness, not much seems to be left. Only a sort of modest obedience to human decency and ritual order, exemplified in the funeral itself and in an image of Hassidim on the way there. The book ends with another memory, fragile, fading, Victorian, replacing Peter's golden vision of Laura: " . . . another spring morning . . . when he'd . . . heard, below in the kitchen, the voices of his mother and his sisters, as they went about making breakfast, known the cat and dog had been let out . . . and felt that day, he only wanted to be good." It would be hard to say if that vision is closer to the truth than the other, or further away.

Fox leaves us with an ambiguous solution. She restricts herself in writing to rigors which equal those to which she restricts her characters. When we meet a squeezed lemon on page 12, we know we will encounter it again because otherwise it would not be there. She extends the limitations she describes in her fiction to include the fact of her writing it. There is something marvelously honorable in her work. Meticulous in observing the unities, she moves through a corner of New York as if she were moving through Thebes. With great economy, she extends five characters to six, then seven, and brings in an occasional messenger, voices of the city, waiters, taxi drivers; the chorus, in short. And in the last chapter, as we cross the bridge to Queens and it is tomorrow, the release from those tight and airless regions in which she has held us is so enormous it feels almost like a promise of redemption.

Bruce Bassoff (essay date 1978)

SOURCE: "Royalty in a Rainy Country: Two Novels of Paula Fox," in *Critique,* Vol. XX, No. 2, 1978, pp. 33-48.

[*In the following essay, Bassoff discusses issues of deformation and paralysis in* Desperate Characters *and* The Widow's Children.]

At the end of Plato's *Phaedrus,* the urban man, Socrates, delivers a beautiful pastoral prayer that includes the request: "May the outward and inward man be as one." Having shown that both erotics and rhetoric are arts of acting on somebody when you have full knowledge and the other does not, Socrates asserts a new kind of erotics—of the living word of face to face dialogue—and prays for that word's adherence to what is present and what is personal. In Paula Fox's *Desperate Characters* (1970), Sophie Bentwood, whose last name suggests the crookedness against which Socrates is arguing, makes a statement that seems almost parodic of Socrates' prayer: "God, if I am rabid, I am equal to what is outside." Besides sickness, "rabid" also suggests the dissociated quality of raving. In the same novel the animadversions against contemporary civilization uttered by one of the characters, a college professor and an erstwhile socialist, are described as "an old habit of words." In *The Widow's Children* (1976), Peter, an editor for a publishing company, takes exception to Laura's use of the word "nigger," to which she responds, "All right, my dear Peter. I know your sensibilities. They're all about *language,* aren't they?" If at one point in that novel Fox seems to parody the ambition to have words adhere to what they designate— a group of women have badges "inscribed" with their names pinned to their gowns—in *Desperate Characters* Otto (Sophie's husband) tells of a man who takes apart and reassembles used typewriters so that the keyboards spell out "mystic nonsense words." The idea is an enormous commercial success, which the man justifies by saying that "the destruction of a typewriter and its reconstitution, its humanization, as a kind of oracle, was a direct blow at American Philistinism." He begins to buy things, but, in order not to be corrupted by his success, he deforms these luxurious objects enough to ruin their function. This "revolutionary" aesthetic is, interestingly enough, accompanied by a brutal authoritarianism toward his wife, whose least creative gesture he suppresses.

Such deformation is a theme of both *Desperate Characters* and *The Widow's Children.* In the former novel Sophie buys a radio for her lover, Francis Early, who then seems to replace it with a better, more powerful radio, about which he says: "I can get the world," which allows him to crowd out Sophie. Instead of smashing the new radio, which is what Sophie wants to do, she smiles: "She didn't know how to violate that mutual smile of theirs. It was miasmic. It stayed on her face while she undressed. It would not go away, and she bore it home with her, a disfiguring rictus." Smiles are always disfiguring in Fox's novels because they are masks used to disguise intent, to ward off aggression, or to play at one's own feelings: "At the thought, she felt her mouth contort into what she could only imagine as a hideous smile of malice." Sophie also notes of her relation with Francis that it has shoved her violently into herself, a turnabout that relates to both novels' theme of crookedness. In *Desperate Characters,* for example, Charlie Russel talks with Sophie about the breakup of his partnership with Otto. Suddenly he mutters, "Why do I feel like a crook?" One character says of Charlie that he is "a bleeding heart, dying to be loved. He has the face of a handsome baby, doesn't he?" What another character calls Charlie's "impeccable attitudes" stem from his desire, above all, for innocence, a desire that falsifies his "virtuous opinions." Charlie, however, points to the same kind of crookedness in the culture at large. Everything, he says, is a business: "the having children business, the radical business, the culture business, the collapse of old values business, the militant business . . . every aberration becomes a style, a business. There's even a failure business." Francis Early's personality is interesting in this respect: "He couldn't seem to help himself—even his bitterness was somehow turned to personal profit. It added to his mystery, it gave his smile an elusive sadness, and it was an element in that quality he had of always recognizing the *real* meaning that lay behind people's words, as though his soul attended in the wings of a theater, ready to fly out and embrace them in universal awareness." Despite her own awareness, however, Sophie is taken in by Francis, whom she sees in the same way as Charlie sees himself. In this society irony becomes a kind of cancer that makes it almost impossible to distinguish between reflecting and reacting against cultural phenomena: "Whether she was celebrating their new affluence, or making an ironic comment, I don't know." When Leon, erstwhile socialist, says to his former wife, Claire, "I'd take my shopping sack all over the city before I'd settle for sour grapes," he reveals in Aesopian fashion the anxiety with which the middle class tries to certify its experience as genuine. Charlie, talking indignantly about the problems of the poor, says, "You just wait"—as if he identifies with them and against his own class. Immediately, however, he excludes Sophie also from that warning: "I didn't mean you, Sophie. I don't know what I mean." Because he feels "murdered" by Otto's refusal to recognize his virtue, he becomes murderous by class proxy. Similarly, Charlie's letting go of Sophie's arm as she stumbles—"as though by stumbling she'd forfeited her right to his support"—shows how understanding can be a means of evasion—as if virtuous opinions exempted one *a priori* from the judgments they implied.

Following an exchange in which Francis Early notes that his wife is indifferent to things but wants to know the name of everything and Sophie claims, disingenuously, not to know the names of anything—as if a shell game were being played with reality, Sophie points out that she and Francis have "both been crooked." One can appreciate why problems of order (like the theme of entropy in Thomas Pynchon's works) are so crucial in contemporary fiction. Since outer, perceivable order tends to manifest an underlying order, whether physical, social, or cognitive, one must evaluate orderly form in terms of the organization it signifies: "The form may be quite orderly and yet misleading, because its structure does not correspond to the order it stands for." The statement reminds one of the opacity of rhetoric decried by Socrates in the *Phaedrus*. At one point in **Desperate Characters**, Sophie observes Otto as he sleeps: "Even in sleep he looked reasonable, although the immoderately twisted bedclothes suggested that reason—in sleep—had been attained at a cost." Late in the novel Sophie discovers a passage underlined twice by Otto: "To vindicate the law." Having learned that young boys have been hanged for the vindication, Sophie thinks: "How had Otto felt, reading those lines sometime during the night? Had the hanging of young boys appalled him? But why had he underlined the words? Did he mean that the horror of law is that it must be vindicated? Or had he thought of himself, of his own longing for order? Or was the double line an expression of irony? Or did he think law was only another *form* of that same brute impulse which it was directed toward restraining?" Such lucidity concerning the law is fatal in primitive societies which depend on a scapegoat mechanism to relieve them of their immanent violence. A profound deception allows them to expel their own violence and then to confound it with other natural forces. A judiciary system, on the other hand, limits violence by rationalizing it—by investing it in a judiciary authority. Sophie's concern with the legitimacy of the law is part of the concern Fox's characters express with the validity of values in general. Otto, for example, unlike Charlie, wants to be "left out" because he does not want to be "taken in." As Sophie says to him, "You're so full of cunning, catching everyone out ... the American form of wisdom!" When he looks back at his brownstone house, he wants "to catch the house empty," as if to indicate that he is not duped even by his own sense of security. Otto formulates a reciprocal paradox to the one concerning the law when he says of the young, "They are dying from what they are trying to cure themselves with." Otto, however, wants the security toward

which he seems ironical, which is why he expresses such respect for the legal process that Charlie sees as "an ironic joke." Accused of being a "square" and thought of as being "reductive," Otto tells Sophie that she does not "draw enough lines." His desire for rational limits is seen in the following description: "Telephone cables, electric wires, and clothes lines crossed and recrossed, giving the houses, light poles, and leafless trees the quality of a contour drawing, one continuous line." Sophie, who has lost all real interest in work and bemoans her own inertia, seeks an illusory redemption in her relationship with Francis. If Otto tries "to catch the house empty," she tries to force from her consciousness the realization that the room in which she lies with Francis is "except for her own presence ... empty." When she assures herself, however, that she is "going to get away with everything" (her affair with Francis and her being bitten by a cat), she begins to cry and finds the following sentence in a book: "Illnesses do their work secretly, their ravages are often hidden." During her affair, that she is getting away with it is "harrowing" to her, that such a "violation" of her habitual intimacy with Otto should leave so little evidence. When she looks at Otto, who is unaware of her "violation," his forehead is "furrowed" as he eats some applesauce. Such imagery occurs also in **The Widow's Children**, where Peter has "a worrying sense that a day had passed without leaving a mark," and where problems of intimacy tend to be "harrowing." In *The Crying of Lot 49*, Pynchon uses images like these in a context that recalls lines from *Oedipus the King* "How, how could the father's furrows, alas, bear to keep silence for so long?" In an "infected city" Oedipa Maas (whose last name means "loophole" in Dutch) imagines an "unfurrowing of the mind's plowshare" as a "special relevance to the word" that will liberate man from relations of sterile rivalry. Fox's characters suffer from the same sense that real existence is somehow elsewhere and that their acts have no real consequences.

Otto's drawing of lines—which sometimes result in excluding Sophie also: "He had closed her *out* into the house"—is not in itself sufficient: "I wish someone would tell me how I can live," he says. But Charlie's sentimentality is no solution, as one parodic figure in the novel indicates: "She was staring down at a copy of *Life* magazine, her mouth open." In a subtle way Fox associates Charlie with the dissolution that contrasts with Otto's fastidiousness. The trigger for the novel's plot is a cat's biting Sophie as she tries to show it affection. The words "edge" and "ledge," repeated frequently throughout the book, help to convey the sense of violation committed by the cat. At first the creature is described rubbing its half-starved body with "soft insistence" against the door of a house that seems "powerfully solid" to Otto, but when it turns against Sophie's insistently friendly hand, it is a "circle of barbed wire." The cat's head, moreover, is described as "massive, a pumpkin, jowled and unprincipled and grotesque." When Charlie knocks on the door early in the morning, Sophie holds her bitten hand "stiffly against the soft folds of her nightgown," and before she recognizes Charlie, she sees a large body swaying on the other side of the door and a "large head" veering toward it. In addition, Charlie turns on Sophie later and says, "You don't know what's going on. . . . You are out of the world, tangled in personal life." The cat's attack brings home the same point to her. "Life had been soft for so long a time, edgeless and spongy." The association of Charlie and the cat is compounded by another "beast" in the book. Sophie's friend Claire tells her about Leon's new wife, a "dull girl who's convinced herself she's a creature of unbridled lust." Having deceived Leon with a thesis on Henry James, she now waits for him "behind the door, stark naked, liberated from intellectual concerns, his beast, she calls herself." The mention of James and "beast" suggests "The Beast in the Jungle"—his story about a man who spends his whole life waiting for something extraordinary to happen and then discovers that the extraordinary thing is that *nothing* has happened. When Sophie is bitten by the cat, she feels shame—as though she has been caught "in some despicable act"; she feels "vitally wounded" though she tries to tell herself that it is only her hand; and when she tells someone that she has been bitten before, she stammers slightly as if she has "tripped over her lie." Her statement, "I'd been feeding the damned beast and it turned on me," sounds like a line from *The Libation Bearers,* but here the "beast" is her own inertia and sloth—the good sentiments that substitute for the half-starved reality of the cat—and the bite is a "small puncture" in her "fatuity."

The problem of personal sovereignty is accompanied in Fox's novels by various kinds of lighting and indications of weather.
—*Bruce Bassoff*

The beast in the jungle is a deception—like *Le Canard Prive* ("the decoy") visited by the restaurant goers in *The Widow's Children.* That novel also contains a significant lie. When Laura asks her daughter, Clara, whether her dress is French, Clara replies, "No . . . I got it on sale." Fearing Laura's judgment of her extravagance—and of the self-assertion that it represents—Clara passes her original off as a copy. The problem of personal sovereignty is accompanied in Fox's novels by various kinds of lighting and indications of weather. In *Desperate Characters* "brilliant wall lights" give the appearance of a sale in progress although no "copy of anything on the premises" can be found. In keeping with the theatrical imagery of both novels, the host of that house (a psychiatrist) looks like "a man preceded into a room by acrobats," and Sophie holds up a mirror to his face after reciting these line of Baudelaire: "Je suis

comme le roi d'un pays pluvieux, / Riche, mais impuissant, jeune et pourtant tres vieux." In this "rainy country" light has some peculiar qualities. Although Sophie, for example, criticizes Otto for examining everything "in the light of what Charlie would have to say," she admits to having seen her lover, Francis, in the same way Charlie sees himself. In her recollection of being with Francis, "Light seemed everywhere at once" although the room seems empty of his presence. Light and seeing are deceptive: At first Sophie finds Francis "touching," but he cannot really touch anyone—Otto, with unintentional ambiguity, says that Francis does not take him in. Francis' apparent responsiveness to people is the "only provision" he carries. Similarly, when Mr. Haynes says of his family, "We're here for all the world to see," he is repudiating the city folks with an exaggerated image of "country folks" who "do love their kitchens." During the episode in the country, Haynes's truculence is described as "gleaming through his smile like a stone under water." A stone, we recall, has been thrown through the window of a house belonging to friends of the Bentwoods, and Sophie experiences her momentary but powerful detestation of Otto as she assumes a "Medusa's face," which, of course, turns people to stone. In *The Widow's Children,* Peter thinks of "something hopeless . . . embedded like a stone at the heart" of his failed marriage and shortly afterwards enters a bookstore in which a mirror is being installed to prevent thefts. The proprietor complains, "Who's supposed to watch that mirror all the time?" These images have occurred in another important scene: when Clara is taken to one of the Hansens' "borrowed apartments" to see her father and mother, she looks up to see "Laura standing in a doorway, holding a glass in which ice cubes floated, looking at her. It was as though a stone had looked at her. Suddenly Laura had hurled the glass into the room." The "glass" is also a mirror that Laura is trying to smash as she sees her reflection in Clara—excluded by Laura as Laura has been excluded by Alma, her own mother. As far as theft is concerned, Laura accuses Clara of stealing her voice (the aural counterpart to her image). Such imitation is pandemic in the novel—like the shadows of Plato's cave. At one point a "sober ventriloquist" seems to have taken charge of Desmond's voice. Laura does crude imitations of the Jewishness she repudiates in her own past, and her first husband, Ed Hansen (whose "charm," like Charlie's in *Desperate Characters,* is a kind of mask), is said to have imitated Laura's mother wonderfully. Alma, in turn, was also a good mimic, especially good at imitating one of her sons, Eugenio, who says of his whole family what Plato says of opinion: "We have all learned by imitation. . . . In my family we could never do anything but imitate. We never *knew.*"

Desperate Characters begins with an image reminiscent of Shelley's neo-Platonic "Life, like a dome of many-coloured glass, / Stains the white radiance of Eternity, / Until Death tramples it to fragments." If light seems "everywhere at once" with Francis, and if a painter friend can describe his life with "the calm zealotry of one who has received truths from the sun," the Bentwoods' experience of life is somewhat different. The "strong light" at the beginning is "softened by the stained glass of a Tiffany shade." In their "living" room, moreover, is a standing lamp, "always lit," with a "shade like half a white sphere." These elements of transcendent unity and immanent dispersion occur throughout the book. Over the windows of the "houses on the slum street" are rags or sheets of "transparent plastic." Later on, cream from a "plastic container" spills all over Otto, who wants to be "left out," and Sophie nurses her memories of Francis "like an old crone with a bit of rag for a baby." Francis tells Sophie how a "glass worm" can be sectioned, and the sections will survive. When someone shatters the window of the house that seems so perfect with all its original things that a sale seems in progress, Sophie and her psychiatrist friend find "a few shards of broke glass." Charlie, who wants to identify with the poor and be part of the solution, says, "Do you know that when people change slowly and irrevocably and everything goes dead, the only way to cure them is a bomb through the window. I can't live that way, as though things were just the same." When Sophie visits her friend Claire, she notes that the whole surface of the building is covered with "dollops of some substance" that looks like "solidified guano," and only a trickle of light seeps through "filthy stained-glass windows." In Claire's apartment, where the light coming through the window is so murky it seems "to have texture," Leon complains that his privacy has been violated in the "age of baby shit." The novel is so full of garbage and dreck that Fox's characters often feel as if they are drowning in a tide of refuse, which also includes debased language. Donald Barthelme has been said to construct "a single plane of truth, of relevance, of style, of value—a flatland junkyard—since anything dropped in the dreck *is* dreck, at once, as an uneaten porkchop mislaid in the garbage." He "has the art to make a treasure out of trash, to see *out* from inside it, the world as it's faceted by colored jewelglass." No one in Fox's novels is making treasures out of dreck. The closest we come to such transformation is cooking. Leon, having looked back nostalgically on the days when he and Claire had nothing but when, handing out leaflets on Sixth Avenue, he felt that he knew the answers to everything, now shares an interest with Claire in cooking: "It's all that's left. . . . It's what is left of civilization. You take raw material and you transform it. That is civilization." In *The Widow's Children,* Peter recalls his first cooking lesson, which his uncle gave him on the day of his mother's death. Their pie, we learn, "tipped over . . . and then simply exploded." Their sense of futility reminds us that the artist alone concocts foods "so purely spiritual and momentary they leave scarcely any stools," creates works that "insist more than most on their own reality." As Peter shambles "toward disintegration" in an el-

emental state of fear, he sees a model ship, a "work of skill and patience, an imitation of reality that was itself a realization." A more ironical moment of transcendence occurs in *Desperate Characters* when Sophie finds Otto standing at the window—the curtains of which are "gritty" in the "monochromatic dullness" of the morning—and staring at a Negro who, as he reels silently along the sidewalk, holds a "green plastic airplane" and collapses "in violent genuflection."

In *The Widow's Children* the "foreignness" of the Maldonadas provides an unfamiliar view of the familiar. Carlos and Laura use "comic strip words," and when Eugenio says that his family could never do anything but imitate, he could be talking of the culture at large where imitation and rivalry are what we mean by individuality. Also revealing is the contrast between Laura's "thrilling displays of temperament" and Madame de Bargeton's "ambition and poignant ineptitudes" in the novel by Balzac that Sophie is reading. Whatever the ineptitudes, the ambition of Balzac's characters implies the "conversation, work, solutions" that Sophie finds in the hospital—where an old woman, soaking her hand as Sophie has soaked hers, parodies her sense of futility and puns ironically on "solution." Laura, on the other hand, whose eyes are described as "drowned," relates stories with "a strange shallowness" which implies the irresistible fascination of certain appearances. The parasitism which this fascination engenders is suggested by the story Francis tells of a larva that insinuates itself into the brain of a songbird in order to complete its metamorphosis In *The Widow's Children* we learn that Peter's friendships with both Laura and Violet have really been a "mindless feeding on someone else's personality." Violet herself is "nebulous" and "indescribable" to herself, and the "increasing materiality" of her life makes her feel more and more abstract. Sophie, who is described as "abstracted" at one point, thinks of her preoccupations as "nebulous" and experiences the materiality of her life as the "shadowy, totemic menace" of the things around her. Despite the "profound spiritual indolence of the Maldonadas," which includes Laura's own "inertia," the self-doubts of Clara and Peter mean that the former believes "no one but Laura" and the latter betrays other people as "his gift to her." The vicarious nature of Peter's and Clara's experiences is conveyed when Peter marries in that he feels that he is "marrying the Hansens, too"; his wife is important only in so far as she allows him to imitate these models. As for Clara, when Peter asks her what she gets out of an affair she is having, she replies, "I feel his pleasure." Peter recalls his father, a man "unadorned by temperament," as a "shelter," a "silent place," but he and Clara cannot "see things in a plain way." Peter knows that Laura arouses men "to empty purpose," and Clara knows that the "self-betraying part of her nature" awakens "in her mother's presence, compelling her to submit to a profound intent in Laura to destroy certainty," but the only "shelter" they find at the end (as they try to break Laura's spell) is in a "family sepulcher." Laura is not "a point in a continuing line of human descent but the apex of a triangle," and an "iron triangle" is the shape of Clara's fate. The irony, however, is that Laura's difference from everyone derives from the same sense of exclusion from which the others suffer. Laura treats Clara as she feels she has been treated by Alma, her mother, and she uses her mother's death to exclude Clara further. If Alma becomes "the old child of her own daughter," Laura views *her* daughter as a rivalrous sibling: "But she didn't leave Clara. . . . She never left Clara." When Peter and Clara drive to the funeral, hoping to break the grip of the past, they see a group of Hasidim whom they take to be an omen. Earlier, Eugenio, who has been described like Atropos as he draws thread through a fabric and then bites it off, says, "When one forgets the past, there is nothing, is there?" Like Charlie in *Desperate Characters,* however, Eugenio can only parody true ideas since the past for him (as for Clara) is only something he continually trips over. Clara thinks to herself, "Perhaps something had really happened, at last," while Sophie thinks, as she contemplates Otto's insistence on vindicating the law, "There was no end to it." Musing over Baudelaire's notion of "spleen," Walter Benjamin says that "the man who loses his capacity for experiencing feels as though he is dropped from the calendar." If Baudelaire "holds in his hands the scattered fragments of genuine historical experience," our modern sense of *duree* "has the miserable endlessness of a scroll. Tradition is excluded from it." Where "degree is shaked" and "truth" is denuded of the consistency of tradition, illusions of authority flourish. For example, people fear Laura because of her basic deficiency: "She's dead cold inside, half born. She doesn't really know that anyone else is alive. The world—it's only an expanded bubble of herself—what she hates is part of herself. . . . She never gets *outside* anything." Although such imperialism is only a variation of their own sense of exclusion—of living hypothetically—it is the source of her authority over people like Peter and Clara. One recalls the loathing that Otto in *Desperate Characters* feels for Tanya, a woman who, with her long succession of love affairs, remains "grossly virginal." These inconsequential affairs caricature Sophie's own affair with Francis: "She had chosen him at a late moment in her life when choices were almost always hypothetical. It was a choice out of time." Tanya, when staying once with Otto and Sophie, used "every drawer in an immense bureau for the few articles she'd brought with her that weekend," as if personal resources were in an inverse relation to abstract possibilities. Tanya is also related to Sophie's mother, who used to wake Sophie each morning with "derisive applause": "Early risers are the winners." Sophie has never discovered "the prize her mother's words had once led her to believe existed." During the Depression her mother drove with her through the streets where "poor people"

lived in order to vindicate their middle-class existence. When Sophie repudiates Tanya over the phone, she says, "You think because somebody's husband sticks it in you, that you've *won.* You poor dumb old collapsed bag! *Who are you kidding!*" As opposed to the "prize" the man across the way exposes to Sophie, and which eventually includes his baby, winning in these instances seems an abstract assertion of superiority. In one of many uses of cold in her novels, Fox has Tanya "recovering from a cold" when she calls Sophie, and when Desmond asserts his superiority in a restaurant, "His tone was cold with the tyranny people display in an environment shaped by their ability to pay." The irony is, however, that the environment reflects their own anonymity.

Both *Desperate Characters* and *The Widow's Children* are also replete with animal images. Laura, who has kept the news of her mother's death from everyone as her own possession and who has left the restaurant in a rage at Clara's "theft" of her voice, bemoans "the old beasts of her life"— her mysterious impulses. Longing for the "utter quietness of animal being," she remembers how she once undid a knotted string in front of a lion, whose rapt attention she maintained. If we recall that Laura has stolen Clara's inheritance when she has been deprived of her own, we can see that the knotted string resembles the more Gordian knots of R. D. Laing. And when we recall Laing's animadversions against a society that destroys experiences inconsistent with its cliches, we can see that a sense of dispossession is also a more general problem of culture:

> So long as a culture maintains its vitality, whatever must be renounced disappears and is given back bettered; Freud called this process sublimation. But, as that sage among psychiatrists Harry Stack Sultan once said, "if you tell people how they can sublimate, they can't sublimate." The dynamics of culture are in "the unwitting part of it." Now our renunciations have failed us; less and less is given back bettered. For this reason, chiefly, I think, this culture, which once imagined itself inside a church, feels trapped in something like a zoo of separate cages.

And characters in Fox's novels are described as "performing bear[s]" or "sluggish beasts." To complicate matters, the bars are constantly moving so that one can never be sure whether he is inside or outside, observer or observed. The failure of Western culture is expressed in various ways in *The Widow's Children.* If our systems of symbols organize both moral demands and the expressive release from such demands, the two functions have fallen apart in a more remissive culture. At one point Peter and Laura "understood each other; she was ruled by impulse, he, by constraint. And each pitied the other for their subjugation to opposing tyrannies." The erotic, which, as Plato reveals in the *Sympo-*

sium, is supposed to reconcile love of oneself (or of one's own) with love of the other, is parodied here by the pornographic. Clara uses obscene jokes to awaken a response in her relatives, even if it is the aggressive response of laughter. She thinks, "Yet what jokes took the place of, with their abject mangling of the ways of carnal life, their special language more stumps than words, she could not fathom." These "stumps" occur earlier in Laura's description of beggars in Madrid, who shake their stumps at her and laugh. Peter, in turn, describes the characters in the book as "beggars, pinching each other." Hours are "mutilated, debauched"; all things are "pinched, poor, broken, worn ragged"; and Peter's possessions are "shadowed clumps." The obscene joke Clara tries to recall has to do with a woman and a doorknob, and later Desmond, who is "always suspecting crooks"—and whose own narrowness he experiences as a lie, checks the doorknob of the room several times. Like the porn queen, Randy Cunny, who appears in one sequence, Laura also arouses men "to empty purpose" and conveys a false promise of intimacy. If Laura, however, cannot get outside herself, Clara's problem is that she cannot get *inside* herself to experience her own pleasure. We are told, moreover, that Clara's "not wanting" is an "effort to fend off a huge collapse" against Laura's indifference— as if she is playing possum in order to avoid death. Later, she imitates Laura by imitating a possum, as if partial identification with her avoids a more complete one.

While in ***Desperate Characters*** the problem of exchange between inner and outer is conveyed by the theme of excretion, in ***The Widow's Children*** it is conveyed by the theme of incorporation. As Freud teaches us, the aim of incorporation is derived from the biological aim of feeding and can occur in other systems besides the digestive one. The eyes, for example, can be involved in such a derived aim. Clara has "the startling impression" that her mother's eye sockets are empty—"like mouths, opening to scream." The sexual relations in the novel reveal relations of autonomy and heteronomy. Laura, for example, swings away from intimate contact with Clara "like an accomplished old adulterer." Carlos, Laura tells us, becomes a homosexual "to avoid supporting a woman." Clara, who has hoped futilely for "rescue" by Carlos, thinks about her visits to him and her father: "They had barely acknowledged her presence, as though she'd been one of Carlos' young men whom she sometimes found there with them." As Peter and Laura talk about Peter's sisters, who excluded him as a child, Laura refers to them as "sister dykes"; and Peter, whose existence has become more and more exiguous, is described as "an old nanny." When Clara cannot find a cartoon that Alma, who uses them to communicate with all the family, has sent to Laura, she thinks: "Had Laura chewed it up and swallowed it?" Among other images suggesting cannibalism, Carlos alludes to the sow that eats its farrow, "I'm becoming an old sow." The "widow" whose children these

are has been taught to betray her own experience and to exclude her own children, whom she later comes to dominate "through the tyranny of her pathos." The epigraph of the novel is from Rilke's "Widow": "Deprived of their first leaves her barren children stand, and seem, for all the world, to have been born because she pleased some terror." Alma has "pleased" the "terror" of convention that has become divorced from reality—"La Senora had warned her that she must not notice such things." Eugenio, the child who has suffered most from his family's "fall" from privilege, has a poster on his wall of a castle in Spain: "It was a twelfth-century fortress; the mist enveloping it did not conceal its brutality." The interface between the self and the world recurs throughout the book. With drunken sentimentality, a "kind of mist" settling over his mind, Desmond thinks of the "style" that separates Laura from the middle class. Clara talks of Alma as a fog that surrounds her. Laura and Desmond, like the fortress, are both referred to as "brutes," and Laura's face, when she expresses loathing for the "self-regarding sentimentality" of the Jews, looks "brutish and empty." Laura is like the person in ***Desperate Characters*** who says, "I started out with you and ended up with myself," since the "Jew" against whom she fulminates is herself. When Violet (the other woman on whom Peter depends for her temperament) tries to reassure Peter about what she assumes to be his homosexuality, her "conventional language" is "inane, brutal and mawkish."

At the end of the novel, Laura denies the effectiveness of what Peter and Clara have done to liberate themselves from her. In response to Clara's "questioning glance," Peter wants to cry out, "Wait! It's not nothing. . . . I've almost got hold of it!" The name "Maldonadas," however, which suggests a kind of nihilistic disease, implies that Peter has got hold of nothing. In ***Desperate Characters*** the hippie son of the Bentwoods' friends wears an army fatigue jacket "on which were pinned buttons shaped and painted like eyeballs, staring from nothing, at nothing," and in ***The Widow's Children*** Carlos, whose inertia is extreme, wears someone else's spectacles. Laura is thought to be able to "see through people," as if a diagnosis were possible among these optical distortions, but all Laura can see through are the "manners" she induces people to assume. What Laura is really good at, as she says herself, is "makeup." We learn at the very end that Peter's revelation is only a reversal of the case: his mother's manipulation of appearances into "some tangled thing" and Laura's own knotted strings hold *him.* One recalls the girl in ***Desperate Characters*** who says of the anklet she wears: "It hurts me to wear it. . . . Every time I move, it hurts." When Peter says of his mother, "No intelligence at work, and no feeling except vindictiveness toward me because I was *hers,*" he could almost be describing Laura as well. Denied by both of them at the end, Peter is bound as victim to a kind of psychological vendetta. He recalls a morning in childhood when, hearing his mother and sisters in the kitchen and seeing the paw marks of animals "braiding the snow"—an image associated with the "thick plaited design in gilt" (or "guilt") that frames a mirror in Laura's hotel, all Peter wants is "to be good." If, as Peter notes, "Families hold each other in an iron grip of definition," that happens because families can no longer reinforce the purposes of a traditional community or resist the manipulations of its contemporary counterpart.

Fox's characters seem to suffer from a Midas touch. Violet feels "nebulous, indescribable," and the "increasing materiality" of her life seems to deprive her of any real security. Eugenio says of himself, "Beggars can't be choosers" and laughs a "grinding, metallic chuckle." Having lost his patrimony as a child and having actually been "thrown out of people's homes," Eugenio "still waits to be thrown out" as if that alone validated the worth of what is inside. What Eugenio seeks is the "blissful oblivion of wealth," which corresponds to the mindless imitation he sees as characteristic of his family. Laura's voice, similarly, is "metallic, serrated" as she contemplates the "futility" of her mother's absurd wisdom. Her own presence, however, her "elaborate killer's manners," causes only betrayal in others. Her compliment to Clara, for example, is unjust because wounding. That this Midas touch has a cultural dimension is revealed in Peter's remark: "Culture makes one bitter." When Alma comes from Spain to Cuba in order to marry an older man whom she has never met, she experiences a "strange, bitter, piercing smell everywhere— it seemed green to her, like the new bitter green leaves of spring." The bitterness suggests the betrayal implicit in the promise. La Senora has warned Alma that she must not notice certain things, and this gesture of suppression is repeated twice: when Clara visits Laura in one of the "Hansens' borrowed apartments," her father puts his fingers to his lips, "warning her to be silent as though someone were sleeping"; and in the restaurant Laura makes a similar gesture when Clara claims that she is "really full." One of the rules by which we often abide is the denial that we live by rules. Laura, for example, is thought to be lawless, but the principal rule suggested by these gestures is: "Thou shalt not implicate thy mother in matters of fullness or emptiness." The same sense of promise is conveyed in Peter's first meeting with Laura and Ed Hansen: "It had been a spring day, the room smelled of the unthawed earth and the first fresh greenness outside . . . the light had been so sweet, so clear!" "Sweetness" is associated with hope and rescue. Carlos, who is "sweet" but ineffectual, cannot "do much for anyone" although Clara has looked to him for rescue. The old man who bakes a cake with Peter after the death of Peter's mother is also described as "sweet." The pie Peter makes with his uncle tips over and then explodes—like the empty form of self-realization associated with Laura. In the restaurant Clara has "a bittersweet recall of the outside natural world, the coarse shifting earth upon

which squatted these hotel and restaurant strongholds, so close, muffled, airless." For these city people, whose longing resembles that of Socrates' pastoral prayer, the "natural world" is the name given to their disappointment with "culture." The word "coarse" is crucial in both novels because it refers to the material dimensions of culture. In a culture which trivializes ideals by the sheer weight of its material means and which also turns ideals into fads by means of its tolerance, one can either take "visible pleasure" in one's coarseness or make capital out of one's disappointments. Although Francis "coarsens" a bit in **Desperate Characters,** his "limpidity of expression" derives from his ability to turn everything, even bitterness, to personal profit. In **The Widow's Children** Clara experiences a sense of "bitter triumph" at being deprived of her inheritance, and "being broke" conveys an "inherent promise" of "sudden dramatic reversal" although it never comes. The disappointment of success, however, is irreversible. In the "rainy days" of March, Desmond recalls, he had dreams in college which he cannot now recall. In their rainy country Paula Fox's characters feel deprived of their sovereignty—the inevitable result, perhaps, of each man having become his own king.

John Rowe Townsend (essay date 1979)

SOURCE: "Paula Fox," in *A Sounding of Storytellers: New and Revised Essays on Contemporary Writers for Children,* J. B. Lippincott, 1979, pp. 55-65.

[*In the following essay, Townsend provides an overview of Fox's works for children.*]

Of the new writers for children who emerged in the United States in the later 1960s, Paula Fox was quickly seen to be one of the most able. Her books were unusually varied; each had a distinct individual character, but at the same time each was stamped with her own imprint. And they had an air of newness: not merely the literal contemporaneity which almost anyone can achieve but the newness that comes from looking at things with new eyes, feeling them in a new way.

In the 1950s and early 1960s, a traditional and generally reassuring view of children and their role had run through the work of the leading and well-established children's writers. Childhood was part of a continuing pattern—the orderly succession of the generations—and children were growing up to take their place in a known and understood world. As the 1960s went on, it was perceived increasingly that this pattern did not reflect reality. Families and societies were not stable; the older generation was not regarded, and did not even regard itself, as the repository of all wisdom, and it could not be assumed that young people were anxious to grow up and join it. The generation gap had opened up, and before long writers for young people were trooping into it, often in a worried, heavy-footed and anxious-to-be-with-it way.

Paula Fox was one of the small number of writers who brought quick sharp perceptions to the new and in many ways uneasy scene, and also an instinctive sympathy for the young who (just as much as their parents) had to deal with it.
—*John Rowe Townsend*

Paula Fox was one of the small number of writers who brought quick sharp perceptions to the new and in many ways uneasy scene, and also an instinctive sympathy for the young who (just as much as their parents) had to deal with it. A recurrent theme in her work of the late 1960s, and again in *Blowfish Live in the Sea* (1970), is that of non-communication and lack of understanding between young and old. But she is not a writer who could be content to mine a single narrow seam. She has written both adult and young people's novels; she has produced picture books and younger children's stories; and her most substantial work on the children's lists up to the time of writing, the award-winning *The Slave Dancer* (1973), is a historical novel of weight and intensity which stands on its own, at a distance from her other books.

Her early books for children have central characters aged from about eight to ten, but one would hesitate to say that they are 'for' readers of such an age. The audience and the author's position in relation to it seem curiously fluid. One has no sense that the writer, as an adult, is *here,* in charge, handing it out, while the audience of children is *there,* duly taking it. If there is a message in the air, it is probably for someone quite different. The first two, *Maurice's Room* (1966) and *A Likely Place* (1967), are not telling children anything except a story, but seem rather obviously to be saying something to parents: don't fuss the child, let him grow in his own way. The two books are humorous, even witty, but in a way that one would expect to appeal to readers rather older than their heroes. And the third and best of the early books, *How Many Miles to Babylon?* (1967), whose hero is barely ten, was one of only two books specifically recommended for teenagers by Nat Hentoff in the *Atlantic* for December 1967. The conventional wisdom is that children and teenagers don't want to read about children younger than themselves, and this generally appears to be true. But it could be that discussion of the question betrays a more fixed attitude than Paula Fox would adopt. Who says who is to read what? Like many other writers, she raises the question 'For whom?', and as with many other writers I can find no answer except 'For whom it may concern.'

Maurice's Room is in fact a blessedly funny book; and as for readership, one can only try it on and see if the glove fits. Maurice at eight is dedicated to his collection of junk, which spills over everything. His parents feel he needs more constructive interests, and often discuss him with their friends.

> Some visitors said that collections like Maurice's showed that a child would become a great scientist. Many great scientists had collected junk when they were eight years old. Other visitors said Maurice would outgrow his collection and become interested in other things, such as money or armies. Some suggested to the Henrys that they ought to buy Maurice a dog, or send him to music school so that his time might be spent more usefully.

And his parents, with the best intentions, get everything wrong. The dog they borrow to be a companion to Maurice is in fact a dreadful nuisance to him, yet Mother is soon convinced that 'Maurice and Patsy are inseparable.' An attempt to get Maurice to learn an instrument is disastrous. The beautiful sailboat that Mr Henry buys Maurice for his birthday is forgotten while Maurice and friend grope for some old bedsprings lying on the bottom of the pond. 'If I had known you wanted bedsprings instead of a beautiful three-foot sailing ketch, I would have gotten you bedsprings,' says poor Mr Henry in despair. Finally, Maurice's parents decide to move to the country, where they hope that everything will be different. And this time at least all is well, for although Maurice isn't terribly interested in the country as such, there is an old barn that already holds the nucleus of a promising new junk collection. It's a hilarious, subversive book, full of casual joys. One can see that Maurice will survive the well-meant but uncomprehending intrusions of adults, just as will Lewis in *A Likely Place.* Lewis, too, is fussed by the grown-ups, but is fortunately left by his parents in the charge of eccentric Miss Fitchlow, who goes in for yogurt and yoga, calls Lewis 'pal', and lets him off the lead. Which is just what he needed. It is a short, dry, subtle book; and if there is a lesson in it, then I suspect that, as in *Maurice's Room,* it is really a lesson for parents.

Paula Fox's third book, *How Many Miles to Babylon?,* is a longer novel of much greater depth and complexity. Its hero, James, is a small black boy living in Brooklyn, whose father has disappeared and whose mother has gone into hospital, leaving him in the care of three elderly aunts. One day he walks out of school and goes to play by himself in an empty house. In his mind is a story that his mother has really gone to her own country across the seas and that he is secretly a prince. Three small boys, not much older than James but tougher, capture him and make him help them work their dog-stealing racket. James travels frightening miles with them on the back of a bicycle, goes to a deserted funhouse on Coney Island, sees the Atlantic. At night he frees the stolen dogs, runs away, gets home to the old aunts, and finds his mother there. She is back from hospital; she is no princess and he no prince. 'Hello, Jimmy,' she says.

On the surface it is a straightforward story, with its strong plot about the fearful boy and the tough gang and the dogs and the juvenile racketeering. But there are strange undertones: the symbolic voyage, the 'other' story of James which is only hinted at. The action, although shadows are cast before and behind it in time, takes place within a day and a night. 'Can I get there by candlelight? Yes, and back again.' Both action and setting are almost dreamlike; the landscape an intimately-known landscape yet glimpsed as if in shifting mists. Everything is experienced through James; and James himself is wandering in a mist of illusion, though eventually compelled by what happens to grasp at rough reality. It is felt in every page, but never said in crude terms, that James is a member of a submerged race and class, and isolated even within that. He is not a sharply-drawn character, nor meant to be, for the reader will suffer with him rather than observe him from the outside; but the minor characters—the three old aunts, the three young racketeers—are clear in outline, defined by the words they speak.

In one sense the outcome of *How Many Miles to Babylon?* is plain. James has proved himself, has faced the actual world, found and accepted his actual mother. He has come through. But to say that is not enough. Illusion and reality, the symbolic and the actual, are not to be so neatly separated. There is much in the book that the mind cannot simply deal with and eject. The inner mystery is something to be carried about and wondered at from time to time rather than be resolved.

The same might be said of *The Stone-Faced Boy* (1968), whose hero Gus—the middle child of five, about ten years old, timid, vulnerable, shut-off—goes out into the snow at night to free a stray dog from a trap. Gus, too, proves himself; finds the key that will help him to overcome his problems. But again this is not quite all. *The Stone-Faced Boy* is a winter's tale, with the quiet, real-yet-unreal feeling of a white landscape. There is a shiver in it, too: a ghostliness. The trap in which the dog is caught belongs to an old man, who takes Gus home to his cottage, full of the debris of the past, for a cup of tea with his equally old wife. And at one point the old man tells the old lady to show Gus how spry she is.

> She made a strange little jump and then, holding her

skirt out with her two hands, she did a little dance in front of the stove, smiling, wobbling slightly, kicking one foot out, then the other. Then she fell back softly into the rocker, like a feather coming to rest.

On the previous page we have heard that the old lady 'had a light, free laugh, and to Gus's surprise the sound reminded him of Serena'. Serena is his younger sister, aged about eight: nice, dreamy, imaginative. Gus feels it is impossible for Serena to get so old. But of course she will; this delicate tying together of the two ends of life makes one of the book's many quiet yet admirable achievements.

Portrait of Ivan (1969) does not have the mysterious depths of *How Many Miles to Babylon?* or *The Stone-Faced Boy,* but has subtleties and satisfactions of its own. It is a brief novel about a boy of eleven who leads a dull, lonely life, walled in by well-to-do, conventional, adult-dominated surroundings. The walls about him begin to crack when he meets the painter Matt and the elderly reader-aloud Miss Manderby, and start collapsing rapidly as he potters about in a boat with a barefoot girl called Geneva. There is a key sentence to the understanding of one aspect of Paula Fox when Ivan realizes that in his life in the city

> he was nearly always being taken to or from some place by an adult, in nearly every moment of his day he was holding on to a rope held at the other end by a grown-up person—a teacher or a bus driver, a housekeeper or a relative. But since he had met Matt, space had been growing all around him. It was frightening to let go of that rope, but it made him feel light and quick instead of heavy and slow.

Ivan has needed space in which to open out, yet by a near-paradox, in order to open out he needs a framework, a context for his own life, a sense of who and what he is and how he got here. He has been living in what might be called a cramped void. It is something important when his friend draws for him the imagined sledge on which his mother, whom he never knew, left Russia as a child, a little girl who 'did not know she had begun a journey that led right to this room where her son now lay, half asleep'. That is a link that Ivan needed.

Ben, in *Blowfish Live in the Sea,* is eighteen and although the book is largely about him, the viewpoint is that of his half-sister Carrie, aged twelve. Though Ben is older than Ivan, his emotional position is somewhat similar, in that, just as Ivan needed the link with his mother in order to orientate himself, Ben needs to find his father. But Ben's father is not dead; he is a drifter, a pathetic, unsatisfactory person. Ben's mother has divorced and remarried, and Ben has a stable, prosperous home, but he is totally alienated.

He has dropped out of school, got rid of all his possessions, and Carrie sees him as

> a tall thin person in a droopy coat with the collar up. The person's hands are shoved into the coat pockets; the threads that stick out from the places where buttons used to be are a different color from the cloth of the coat. When he walks, the person looks down at his feet as they move forward in cracked muddy boots.

'Blowfish live in the sea' is the message that Ben writes on brown paper bags, on unopened letters, in dust on window-panes; and the explanation is that his father once sent him a blowfish—round as a soccer ball, stiff with varnish, orange and yellow and shiny—with a letter describing it as a souvenir from the upper reaches of the Amazon. Ben's graffito is a comment on this shabby deception. But when his father turns up, a perennial failure with nothing to his name but a seedy rundown motel, Ben decides to join him: 'He needs some help to get it into shape. He doesn't have hardly any money. . . . The place is a wreck.' We leave Ben starting on the carpentry, keeping his father off the drink; we don't know how long it will last, but we know it is something positive for Ben at last and will be the making of him.

This is the principal strand of the book, but there are others. Running through it all is Carrie's affection for Ben. As she looks at him, dusty and sad, with the rawhide thong round the hair that he won't get cut, Carrie remarks, 'Sometimes I thought I loved him better than anyone.' And in his desultory way Ben returns the affection; in fact there are traces everywhere of a loving, more open Ben. Although Ben belongs strictly to his time, and although people of his age already look different and behave differently, he is not in the least invalidated as a character by subsequent change. The underlying human nature can be seen quite clearly within the pattern formed by its interaction with outward circumstances.

Paula Fox is obviously much concerned with relationships between children and adults. She is conscious that in a complicated and rapidly changing society it is hard for the generations to live together satisfactorily.
—*John Rowe Townsend*

Paula Fox is obviously much concerned with relationships between children and adults. She is conscious that in a complicated and rapidly changing society it is hard for the generations to live together satisfactorily. It will not do for grown-ups to think in terms of feeding a child into the production line and in due course drawing off an adult from the other end; but neither can young people really write off the older generation, ignoring it as irrelevant or hating it as the enemy.

Her books for younger children are a mixed collection, and in my view have not always been successful. They include a curious, way-out picture book *Hungry Fred* (1969), about a boy who eats his way through the contents of a house, the house itself and the backyard, and is still hungry. Then he makes friends with a wild rabbit as big as himself. 'The rabbit leaned against Fred. Fred smiled. He felt full.' It is difficult to see what young children will make of this. And although one accepts that a picture book, like a poem or story, does not have to be understood in literal terms in order to make its impact, there needs to be an imaginative power and unity which I do not find in *Hungry Fred,* and which the artist, understandably, could not supply. *Good Ethan* (1973), about a small boy who ingeniously solves the problem of retrieving his new ball from the wrong side of a street he has been told not to cross, is a simpler and more satisfactory conception, and benefits from pictures by Arnold Lobel which are exactly in key with it. Paula Fox is also the author of *The Little Swineherd and Other Tales* (1978); a group of short, folk-type stories set in the odd framework of an attempt by a duck—yes, a duck—to succeed in show business. The duck is promoting the actual storyteller—a goose who simply likes to tell stories—and there is dry satiric humour in the account of the duck's attempts at exploitation and his uncomprehending interventions in the creative process. But the book as a whole does not quite work. Russell Hoban would have done this kind of thing better. The title story, however, about the half-starved and neglected boy who takes over a small holding when its owners disappear and has vastly improved it by the time they come back to reclaim their property, is a touching and memorable one; it would have been preferable, I believe, to present it on its own.

I have left until last the book which, so far, is Paula Fox's finest achievement. I do not think it could have been predicted from her earlier work that she would write such a book as *The Slave Dancer.* It is the story of Jessie Bollier, a boy who is pressed into the crew of the slave ship *Moonlight* in 1840 for a voyage to Africa, picking up a cargo of blacks to be sold in Cuba. This is a case where the discipline of writing for the children's list has been wholly to the benefit of the book as a work of art. The 'young eye at the centre' is no mere convention of the adventure story for children; it is the one perspective from which the witnessing of dreadful events can be fully and freshly experienced, and at the same time the moral burden be made clear. Jessie is horrified by the treatment of the slaves, but he is powerless to prevent it; moreover he is young, white, and one of the crew, and the oppressors are his fellow-countrymen.

Jessie plays the fife, and his job is to make music to which, for brief periods daily, the slaves can exercise. This is called dancing the slaves. The aim is to keep them (relatively) healthy and therefore marketable, in spite of the crowded and filthy conditions in which they live. A slave has no human value but has a financial one: a dead slave is a lost profit. As the voyage goes on, the slaves, crammed together in the reeking hold, become sick, half-starved and hopeless, most of them suffering from 'the bloody flux', an affliction that makes the latrine buckets inadequate. And Jesse finds that 'a dreadful thing' is happening in his mind:

> I hated the slaves! I hated their shuffling, their howling, their very suffering! I hated the way they spat out their food upon the deck, the overflowing buckets, the emptying of which tried all my strength. I hated the foul stench that came from the holds no matter which way the wind blew, as though the ship itself were soaked with human excrement. I would have snatched the rope from Spark's [the mate's] hand and beaten them myself! Oh, God! I wished them all dead! Not to hear them! Not to smell them! Not to know of their existence!

The Slave Dancer is not a story solely of horror. It is also a novel of action, violence and suspense, culminating in shipwreck (which was indeed the fate of a slaver called *Moonlight* in the Gulf of Mexico in 1840; the actual names of her crew are used). Jessie and a black boy named Ras with whom he has made a precarious friendship are the only survivors; they reach land and there is a limited happy ending. Ras is set on the road to freedom; Jessie gets home to his mother and sister, is apprenticed, lives an ordinary, modestly-successful life, and fights in the Civil War on the Union side.

> After the war my life went on much like my neighbors' lives. I no longer spoke of my journey on a slave ship back in 1840. I did not often think of it myself. Time softened my memory as though it was kneading wax. But there was one thing that did not yield to time.
>
> I was unable to listen to music. I could not bear to hear a woman sing, and at the sound of any instrument, a fiddle, a flute, a drum, a comb with paper wrapped around it played by my own child, I would leave instantly and shut myself away. For at the first note of a tune or of a song, I would see once again, as though they'd never ceased their dancing in my mind, black men and women and children lifting their tormented limbs in time to a reedy martial air, the dust rising from their joyless thumping, the sound of the fife finally drowned beneath the clanging of their chains.

Those are the closing sentences of *The Slave Dancer.* Ul-timately the book is not depressing; the human spirit is not defeated. But it is permeated through and through by the horror it describes. The casual brutality of the ordinary seamen towards the slaves is as fearful in its way as the more positive and corrupt cruelty of the captain and mate and the revolting, hypocritical crew member Ben Stout. For the seamen are 'not especially cruel save in their shared and unshakable conviction that the least of them was better than any black alive'. They are merely ignorant. Villainy is exceptional by definition, but dreadful things done by decent men, to people whom they manage to look on as not really human, are a reminder of our own self-deceit and lack of imagination, of the capacity we all have for evil. There, but for the grace of God, go all of us.

Is such knowledge fit for children? Yes, it is; they ought not to grow up without it. This book looks at a terrifying side of human nature, and one which—in the specific manifestation of the slave trade—has left deeply-planted obstacles in the way of human brotherhood. The implication was made plain by Paula Fox in her Newbery acceptance speech in 1974. We must face this history of evil, and our capacity for evil, if the barriers are ever to come down.

Anne Tyler (review date 9 November 1980)

SOURCE: "Staking Out Her Territory," in *New York Times Book Review,* November 9, 1980, p. 55.

[In the following review, Tyler praises Fox's realistic handling of teenage problems in A Place Apart.*]*

I know a teen-age girl who seems to spend most of her library time opening books, reading their end flaps and slamming them shut. "Fourteen-year-old Mary and her alcoholic mother...." Slam. "When fifteen-year-old Laura learns she's pregnant...." Slam. What she wants, she says, is a book about somebody ordinary. It could be somebody with a problem, if necessary, but does the problem have to be the most important part of the book?

The 13-year-old narrator of *A Place Apart* has several problems. Her father has died, she and her mother have moved to an unfamiliar town, and the boy who befriends her often confuses and troubles her. But the center of the novel is Victoria herself, not her problems; and Victoria makes a truly wonderful heroine—"ordinary" enough to win over any young reader, but also reflective, observant and articulate.

"I had a dream last night," she tells her uncle. "I dreamed I was a queen, and my crown was a circlet of those little brown pears you can buy in the market in the fall. And I was floating over land that was covered in mist."

"Your dream means that what you must do is find your own country," her uncle tells her.

In a sense, that's Victoria's biggest problem, and one that most adolescents will understand—locating her territory, naming it, making sense of what's happening around her. She used to believe, she tells us, that "If I could describe one entire day of my life to someone, that person would be able to tell me what on earth life was all about." But that was before her father died, and the year that's covered by *A Place Apart* is the period of time it takes her to regain, however shakily, some sense of order and security.

The issue of her confusing friend—a boy who enjoys manipulating people—is a major part of the plot, but it doesn't seem essential. Far more important is Victoria's grief for her father, which is palpable—fading, reviving unexpectedly and fading again. There's a moment, very shortly after his death, when Victoria's mother wakes her in the middle of the night and the two of them sit staring at each other. There's another, just before a vacation trip, when Victoria is stricken by the sight of two suitcases where once there were three.

Victoria's mother is beautifully drawn—a woman floundering but doing her best. When she thinks of remarrying, later in the story, Victoria doesn't approve; but the man is sympathetic and he tries hard, and Victoria realizes that. It's a relief—no black-and-white characters here, but the stuff of real life.

Her readers are complimented, you might say. Paula Fox trusts them to appreciate a story—without gimmicks or exaggerations. She writes a honed prose, avoiding all traces of a gee-whillikers tone, and her language is simple and direct. *A Place Apart* is a book apart—quiet-voiced, believable and often very moving.

Paula Fox (essay date 1981)

SOURCE: "Some Thoughts on Imagination in Children's Literature," in *Celebrating Children's Books: Essay on Children's Literature in Honor of Zena Sutherland*, edited by Betsy Hearne and Marilyn Kaye, Lothrop, Lee and Shepard Books, 1981, pp. 24-34.

[*In the following essay, Fox reflects on the ability of books to fuel the imagination, especially of children.*]

Literature is the province of imagination, and stories, in whatever guise, are meditations on life.

Goethe wrote that supreme imagining is the effort to grasp truth through imagination. It does not consist in making things different but in trying to discover them as they are.

Imagination is random and elusive. We deduce its presence by its effects, just as we deduce that a breeze has sprung up, a breeze we can't see, because we hear and see the rustling of leaves in a tree. It is the guardian spirit that we sense in great stories; we feel its rustling.

Imagination can be stillborn; it can be stifled. But it can be awakened. When you read to a child, when you put a book in a child's hands, you are bringing that child news of the infinitely varied nature of life. You are an awakener.

Few have attested so passionately to the power of books as the Russian writer Maxim Gorki. As a child, he lived in a remote nineteenth-century village, Nizhni. When he was ten, he was farmed out as a servant to a provincial family. Here is how he describes it in *Childhood*, the first volume of his autobiographical trilogy:

> Those winter evenings in that little cramped room with my master and mistress were quite unbearable. Outside there was nothing but deathly night. Sometimes I could hear the frost crackling. People sat at the table, as silent as frozen fish. Sometimes a blizzard would buffet the window and the walls, roar down the chimneys and make a banging noise in the dampers. The babies would start crying in the nursery and one felt like sitting down in some dark corner, hunching oneself up and howling like a wolf.

But Gorki didn't howl like a wolf. Instead, he learned to read. And although there were very few books in that woebegone village, he managed to get hold of most of them. But he was punished for reading, and so he read secretly at night. The books, he writes,

> . . . made the world a larger place, beautifying it with fabulous towns, showing the high mountains and wonderful seashores. Life blossomed miraculously, the earth became more attractive, richer in people and towns and many different things. And now as I looked at those distant fields beyond the Volga, I knew very well they were not just a desert. . . . The earth had seemed empty and lonely. And as a result my heart became empty . . . . All desire would disappear and there would be simply nothing to think about. . . . As I read, I began to feel healthier and stronger, and I worked rapidly and skilfully, as I now had a purpose, the sooner I finished my chores, the more time would

be left over for reading. When they took books away from me, I became listless and lazy, and a morbid forgetfulness which I had not known before would take hold of me.

Gorki soon tired of stories in which there was a simple-minded, shadowless confrontation between pure good and pure evil, with evil inevitably routed and good inevitably triumphant. At ten, he knew better. He knew that good and evil were often inextricably tangled in the same person, the same event. But what had originally excited his imagination in those early fables he read was a sense of a world utterly unlike Nizhni.

Although those fantasies had begun by leading him away, out of his own life, they also had the extraordinary effect of helping him to discover his own life, as though up until then it, too, had been an unknown country beyond the Volga.

Books awakened Gorki's imagination, not only about different people and places, but about himself. And instead of "morbid forgetfulness," instead of brutish resignation, Gorki began to perceive with imaginative vision that there was more to his grandfather than his cruelty, more to his grandmother than her lunacy, and that the people of his village were not merely fools, or dangerous beasts, or drunken sots, but were, as he was, baffled and fearful and struggling to endure.

Gorki discovered another marvel about stories—their power to bring comfort to people, to divert them and make them merry, to enchant them. He found that he, himself, could invent such stories, and he told them even to those people who had jeered at him for reading. He saw that he could make them laugh, make them forget, for a little while, the meagerness of their daily lives and bring them into the realm that William Wordsworth described as: "That twilight when we first begin to see this dawning earth . . . "

The first intimations of "this dawning earth"! I do not have to make an effort to recollect how the beginning of certain books affected me when I first read them, because they still do. Such beginnings as: "Call me Ishmael." Or, "An angry man—there is my story: the bitter rancour of Achilles, Prince of the House of Peleus, which brought a thousand troubles upon the Achaian host." Or, "Alice was beginning to get very tired of sitting by her sister on the bank, and of having nothing to do. . . ." Or, "Emma Woodhouse, handsome, clever, and rich, with a comfortable home and happy disposition, seemed to unite some of the best blessings of existence; and had lived nearly twenty-one years with very little to distress or vex her." Or, "Happy families are alike but an unhappy family is unhappy after its own fashion." Or, "Midway in our life's journey, I went

astray from the straight road and woke to find myself alone in a dark wood."

But along with the literature of imagination, there has always been tract literature. Stories that once strained to instruct young readers in how to attain virtue and the happiness of virtue have been replaced now by stories that strain to teach children how to manage life by merely naming such "problems" as disease, physical anomalies, and even death, and assuring them there is nothing to be afraid of, nothing to suffer about, nothing complex.

Samuel Taylor Coleridge attacked the old didactic literature for its debasement of human pity and passion 190 years ago when he heard from a friend a description of a children's book typical of that period. He writes: "A child is to come home and tell its mother, 'The sixpence you gave me I gave to a beggar. Did I do right, Mamma?'—'O! yes my dear,' cries the mother, kissing him, 'you did,'—thus blending one of the first virtues, charity, with one of the basest passions of the human heart, the love of hearing oneself praised."

And Coleridge goes on to say, "[I] sought no praise for giving to beggars, and I trust that my heart is not the worse, or the less inclined to feel sympathy for all men, because I first learnt the powers of my nature, and to reverence that nature—for who can feel and reverence the nature of man and not feel deeply for the afflictions of others possessing like powers and like nature?"

Recently, I saw a letter an acquaintance received from a television producer of programs for children that suggests the fashion of the new didacticism. In turning down my acquaintance's book for television adaptation, the producer wrote that it was a "superior" work, but that it did not "fall into the rigid guidelines set forth by our network personnel," who, said the producer, are now "tending toward crisis stories . . . concerning diabetics, suicides, teenage pregnancies, etc."

The "etc." speaks powerfully of the way in which the most profound and painful difficulties of living have become trivialized.

A choice of subject matter has never made writing. And it has not been the function of literature to show people of any age how to deal with problems or how to solve social and sexual dilemmas. The implicit instructions of contemporary "realistic" books may vary from those of 1810, but they have the same sequel: they smother speculation, they stifle uncertainty, they strangle imagination.

It is difficult to believe the authors of such books, of any era, believe that children possess "like powers and like nature," to be reverenced, to be respected. They are rather like W. H. Auden's social worker: "Writers can be guilty of every kind of human conceit but one, the conceit of the social worker," he writes, then goes on to characterize his social worker's view of life: "We are all here on earth to help others: what on earth the others are here for, I don't know."

I suggest that if, in literature, we are given nothing to think about, to imagine, outside the external trappings of our own lives, we are likely to remain motionless and ignorant. And the earth will, indeed, seem empty and lonely as it was to Gorki when he was deprived of books.

We are all born provincials, but there is in us that push against the constraint of circumstances, of the given, that we show in our first efforts to stand up on legs that are not quite ready to support us, in that struggle toward a larger life we make in our first attempts at human speech.

If we make the effort, the imaginative effort, we can sometimes see the inherent imaginative energy in a child's astonishment at fire, at thunder, at birds and cats and wheels, at colors and shapes and the texture and taste of things— at all, in fact, which is always in peril of becoming commonplace to us because we are "grown-ups" and because we have ceased to venerate life, and have "solved" its puzzles.

Any passing observations of infancy and growth can tell us about the discomfort and joy of being alive, sorrow and joy, bound together from the beginning.

But often we want to forget, to swathe our seminal awareness in comfort. And we present children with cozy books about divorce and desertion and death and sex, promising them that, in the end, everything can be made all right. Thus we drown eternal human questions with contemporary bromides, all mechanics and sanctimony, filled with a ruinous complacency.

Just as junk food can dull pangs of hunger, so can junk books dull the hunger of a child's mind, stuff it with unearned certainties, those straws, Henry James wrote, that "we chew to cheat our appetites."

A characteristic of such literature is that it tends to promote and vindicate adult predispositions toward children and childhood. Another is that these books deliver us from the responsibility, the effort of self-knowledge without which we cannot really think about and understand children, who are not a race apart but ourselves when new.

But the truths we sense in great imaginative literature send us back to the earliest, most essential memories of our own lives, and, at the same time, direct our vision outward toward other lives, toward life itself.

I was taught to read when I was five. The old house where I lived in those days was filled with books and not much else. The roof leaked, the well was always going dry, the wallpaper peeled, the furniture was patched and mended, the driveway up the long hill to the house was impassable in heavy rain or snow, and there was never enough money for repairs.

But the books! They lined the walls of the rooms; they stood in columns on the floor; they were piled up in the attic on top of a river of *National Geographics* that cascaded down the crowded attic stairs.

In bad weather, when I couldn't go outside, I used to sit on those stairs and extract a *Geographic* as carefully as if I were playing pick-up-sticks, so I wouldn't bring the whole attic down on myself. Among the glossy pages of the magazines, I met up with pygmies and Balinese dancers, cities built on water, mountain peaks yet unscaled, desert people and people who lived amid eternal snow, dragonflies and anacondas. On those attic stairs in an old house that seemed always on the verge of collapse, I began to sense huge possibilities.

Some years later, I went to live on a sugar plantation in the middle of Cuba—a far distance from an old Victorian wreck on the Hudson River! I had no books there except for one or two ragged textbooks passed among the students, of which I was one, whose school was one room attached to the rear of a small church. Still, there was a man who came to our village once a month from the city of Cienfuegos. He came on one of the dusty roads that led to the plantation, pushing a handcart in front of him. In it were piles of two-sheet "books" that reproduced songs that were current and popular in Havana. The paper, I recall, was a harsh and acid pink. The sheets were so poorly printed that sometimes whole lines were blotted out. A child would buy a few pages for a *centavo* or two and I, along with the other children of the plantation, would memorize all the words and sing them to each other. Some of the songs told real stories with beginnings and middles and ends, stories that were often sad, but comic now and then, too. One, I remember, was about a garbage man whose sweetheart deserted him, and he grew so melancholy, he lost all interest in his work! That particular song had the lyrical title *El Cantino Arabal*. Such was our longing for stories that we made up still others of our own, inventing for ourselves a kind of mythology of which those coarse pink sheets of paper were the text.

When I returned to the United States, I went to live in a small community on Long Island. A few other little girls and I found an abandoned shed in the neighborhood and decided to start our own library. We pooled our books, and somewhere we dug up a few sticks of furniture. Until the cold drove us out, along with the awful depredations of a neighborhood gang of small boys who regarded us as enemies, we spent many charmed hours after school in our library. By the time we had to abandon it, I had a real library card.

When I was in the seventh grade, we had to memorize a good deal of poetry, especially William Wordsworth's poetry. No one I knew then, except a born actor or two, really liked to memorize poems. It was hard work. But we did it. And the poems stayed in my mind, within reach for many years. As I got older, I began to read poetry for my own pleasure, and among the poets who seemed to me to be magician-saints, Wordsworth towered, difficult, dense, as remote and unimaginable a human being as Pericles.

A few years ago, I spent some weeks in the Lake Country in England. I went to visit Dove Cottage where Wordsworth and his family lived from 1800 to 1808. It was a clenched little house full of dark passages and tiny rooms. In the kitchen, there was a black, rusted coffee grinder the Wordsworths had used. I could hardly tear my glance from it. It had never occurred to me that Wordsworth had been real!

Later, I went on to Rydal Hall, a few miles away from Grasmere. It was a lovely Georgian house Wordsworth had rented when he became a little prosperous. It stood on a hill, and all around it were his gardens, just as he had planted them. The house had only recently returned to the Wordsworth descendants. Two elderly women from Grasmere kept guard over it and took the few pence it cost to explore it.

As I passed by one of them, she whispered something to me. I leaned forward. More loudly, she said, "Miss Wordsworth! She's in there!" And she pointed to a narrow door next to her chair.

I thought she was speaking of a ghost. I nodded. She smiled. "His great-great-granddaughter," she explained.

At that moment, the narrow door crashed open into the little hall where I stood, and out came a large, handsome middle-aged woman in a fierce tweed suit. A cigarette drooped from her lips, and she was smiling with immense good humor. I was introduced. She shook my hand vigorously and asked, "Are you enjoying the house?"

I don't remember what I replied. I do remember that I remained rooted to the spot as she swept out the front door, hurled herself into a dilapidated station wagon, reversed violently, knocked into a fence, laughed, waved to me out the car window, cigarette ashes flying, and disappeared down the driveway.

It is not memory alone, but imagination that brings back to me the palpable presence of that car-banging, tweedy woman, her amiable face afloat in the smoke of her cigarette, and hovering behind her, spectrally, the lineaments of her ancestor.

William Wordsworth wrote in Book XIII of *The Prelude* (which he titled *Imagination*): ". . . each man's mind is to herself witness and judge; and I remember well that in life's every-day appearances I seemed about this time to gain clear sight of a new world."

Imagination is the great witness. Without it, there is no past, only, as Gorki wrote, morbid forgetfulness.

Hamida Bosmajian (essay date Winter 1983)

SOURCE: "Nightmares of History–The Outer Limits of Children's Literature," in *Children's Literature Association Quarterly*, Vol. 8, No. 4, Winter 1983, pp. 20-22.

[*In the following essay, Bosmajian discusses the "historical nightmares" of slavery, the Holocaust, and the atomic bombing of Hiroshima as depicted in children's books, including Fox's* The Slave Dancer.]

In the last two decades the ironic mode—the depiction of the human condition as limited by realistic historical time and space—has made definite encroachments on children's literature, particularly in stories about familial or social trauma. Though reviewers often question if works about child abuse, family disintegration, sex, violence, drug addiction, and prejudice can still be called children's fiction, perceptive adults would agree that such works can both have therapeutic value for young victims and raise the consciousness of youngsters whose environment is stable. There is, however, another category of the ironic mode in young people's literature: literature about historical trauma.

The nightmare of history is de-creation by adults, a nightmare that always includes children, be they enslaved Africans, Nazi holocaust victims, or survivors of Hiroshima. Historical trauma is a collective inundation of a culture; it affects the life, not just of the individual or the small group, but of the entire social order, its past, present, and future. The reader of literature about such traumas can no longer comfortably apply us/them dichotomies, for this literature universalizes moral problems, choices, and consequences. The image of the child in such literature, as recalled by a survivor-witness, is often a devastating ethical challenge, for children have often been singled out to suffer special brutalities.

We are loathe to shape our collective sin and guilt through the genre of children's literature. Perhaps we fear that to depict the children within the nightmare of history will both taint our own image of innocence and deny young readers trust in the future we shape; for is not children's literature a seduction of children into our symbolic structures and values? Yet children have lived and do live in historical time and voice their concerns today about the next possible nightmare—global nuclear war.

Three works that confront the themes and horizons of historical trauma in children's literature are Paula Fox's *The Slave Dancer,* Hans Peter Richter's *Friedrich,* and Toshi Maruki's *Hiroshima No Pika.* In my discussion I will point out how the three cardinal sins of Western civilization—the enslavement of Africans, anti-Semitism and the holocaust, and the atom bomb as apocalypse—affect the child characters in these stories, and how they might influence the young reader's reaction to our civilization's discontents, crimes, and guilts. I contend that if such literary works are shared within a context where youngsters can voice their concerns and where adults are ready to engage in dialogue rather than diatribe, rationalization, and assuagement, they cannot but be therapeutic. They define and thereby set limits to the anxieties of young readers.

In each narrative the main character is a victim-survivor. In *The Slave Dancer* and *Friedrich* the narrator writes a confession because he witnessed and participated in historical crimes. Seven-year-old Mii in *Hiroshima No Pika* is a portrait ostensibly intended for the pre-analytical reader. The impact of her story, told in the third person, comes through the great simplicity of the text and its powerful illustrations.

The Slave Dancer seems removed in time for some young readers, who have read it as an adventure story comparable to *Treasure Island,* but others are moved by the suffering depicted and find in this fiction an historical understanding of the oppression of black people. They can identify with the ethical problems of thirteen-year-old Jessie Bollier, who is kidnapped in New Orleans in 1840 and commanded to play his fife for the dancing of the slaves on board *The Moonlight.* Even though this book won the Newbery Award, Fox received negative criticisms, especially for her portrayal of blacks and Jessie's reactions to them. Yet when we compare *The Slave Dancer* with autobiographical accounts of concentration camp survivors, we find that Fox is accurate in depicting the psychology of human beings in extreme situations. Her fictional autobiography springs from Jessie's need to confess, for he finds

no relief when he confesses to a runaway slave, and when Jessie tries to share his feelings with his mother, she cries, "I can't hear it! I can't bear it!" Jessie then decides that he will "do nothing that was connected ever so faintly with the importing and sale and use of slaves." He soon discovers, however, that everything he "considered bore, somewhere along the way, the imprint of black hands." Even after writing his confession, he finds no relief from his memory of the nightmare of history.

> ... when we compare *The Slave Dancer* with autobiographical accounts of concentration camp survivors, we find that Fox is accurate in depicting the psychology of human beings in extreme situations.
> —*Hamida Bosmajian*

Jessie's trauma is especially focused in the central chapter "Nicholas Spark Walks on Water." Here we see the chaos and rigidity of the life of victims and victimizers in the concentrated space of *The Moonlight.* The crew is unable to tolerate any human impulse toward the captive blacks. In Jessie's memory the captives are, with one exception, an undifferentiated mass, and the crew members are fixed into specific stereotypes. Mass and stereotype prevent Jessie from identifying himself with either. When the slaves are pulled from the hold after a few days at sea, their trauma has deprived them of will: "The adults ate mournfully, the food dribbling from their lips as though their spirits were too low to keep their jaws firm." Nevertheless, their very helplessness is a threat to Jessie, who reacts with self-defensive aggression: "I hated the slaves! I hated their shuffling, their howling, their very suffering...! I hated the foul stench that came from the holds..., as though the ship were soaked with human excrement. I would have snatched the rope from Spark's hand and beaten them myself! Oh, God! I wished them all dead!"

Jessie's feelings are very much comparable to those of Tadeusz Borowski in *This Way for the Gas, Ladies and Gentlemen.* He, too, is outraged at the victims: "I am simply furious with these people—furious because I must be there because of them. I feel no pity. I am not sorry that they are going to the gas chamber. Damn them all ... I could throw myself at them and beat them with my fists." *The Moonlight* and the camp are images of the *anus mundi,* a world of sin and waste whose stench will stay with Jessie or Tadeusz for the rest of their lives. Jessie is so frightened by his hate for the blacks that he refuses to play his fife. A severe beating is to be his punishment, and as he steps to the railing to receive his blows, he notes, "The sea was blue today." Borowski observes: "The sky grows translucent and opens high above our heads." From slave ship and camp human cries rise high into the indifferent universe.

Jessie tries "to get used to it" and develops the inmate's characteristic split consciousness. He co-operates, sees, pretends not to see, and develops a contrasting vision: "I found a kind of freedom in my mind. I found how to be in another place." Reality, however, bears down on him when a black, whom Spark gratuitously tortured, attacks the sailor and is flogged to unconsciousness. Jessie escapes into the kitchen only to find the cook picking "worms out of a piece of crusted beef," a microcosm of ship and crew. The enraged Spark shoots the black and is himself bound and thrown overboard for having deprived the captain of profit. Before he drowns, he seems to take three steps on water, a grotesque parody of Christ. In keeping with the ironic mode, Fox often inverts the religious value of images. Jessie's name reminds us of the child as savior, now lost in a totally fallen world. The shape of the slave ship is like that of a cathedral nave (*navis*) and the harmony of the cosmic spheres becomes in Jessie's memory and last words "a joyless thumping, the sound of the fife finally drowned beneath the clanging of their chains."

Both the point of view of the novel and the circumstances of history make it impossible to name the slaves. Only after the shipwreck can Jessie exchange names with Ras, the sole black survivor. In Hans Peter Richter's *Friedrich*, however, it is the narrator and his family who remain nameless, for this narrator cannot even experience the memory of guilt—he has implicated himself too much. There is safety in remaining nameless, and the anonymity adds a universality of guilt to the story, which could be the story of many a German family. The victims here are named, as if to rescue them from the vast anonymity of the millions who were murdered.

Friedrich is the story of the friendship between two boys during the time of the Third Reich, but Richter does not show a child being led to the gas chamber. There has been no depiction of the final solution in a book written for children, though there are many accounts, poems, and drawings by children who were in the camps. As of now the ultimate extremity is censored by adult writers as too horrible to depict. Because writing is as therapeutic for the writer as reading can be for the reader, the writer, especially of children's literature, may even be afraid of subliminally expressing aggression against children.

Friedrich Schneider and his parents, who live in isolation in their urban apartment, believe that they are accepted as Germans, and are thus caught in the "illusion of reprieve." When the narrator's father, a Nazi for expediency's sake, advises Herr Schneider to flee Germany, Schneider cannot imagine slavery and injustice, much less pitiless murder in

twentieth century Germany: "Perhaps we will put an end to our wandering by not seeking flight any more, by learning to suffer, by staying where we are." Bettelheim's criticism in *Surviving* of Anne Frank's family for wanting to maintain the *status quo* is corroborated in Richter's book. The author's emphasis is always on individual human suffering resulting from human choices. He reveals graphically the ransacking of the Schneiders' apartment, the death of Frau Schneider, and the arrest of Herr Schneider by the Gestapo.

Present or not, the Schneiders will always be the focus in the narrator's world, even as his consciousness splits, objectifies conflicting worlds, and finally allows itself no reflection. Caught in the historical moment he becomes a member of the *Jungvolk*, yet still maintains his friendship with Friedrich. Awareness of otherness begins harmlessly enough when the narrator's mother notes while bathing both boys: "Well, Fritzchen! You look like a little Jew." The word *Jew* will be repeated with increasing vehemence on placards, on park benches, and in speeches and songs of the Nazis. Still, the narrator tries to get an eager Friedrich into a *Jungvolk* meeting, where Friedrich is made to say, "The Jews are our Affliction." Occasionally there is a humane teacher or righteous judge, but anti-Semitic myths turn more and more into gruesome reality. During the famous night of broken glass, the narrator finds it "strangely exhilarating" to be drawn into the crowd. Almost accidentally he picks up a hammer, almost casually he breaks a glass pane; then he immerses himself in an orgy of vandalism, until spent, tired, and disgusted, he walks home to find that the Schneiders' apartment, too, has been demolished. His tears come too late.

While Friedrich grows in moral courage and self-awareness, the narrator is infantilized by the totalitarian system, in which ego and superego identify with the state. At the end he can no longer express his feelings for Friedrich. After Friedrich is refused entry into the shelter and dies during the air raid, the narrator can only clutch "the thorny rosebush" in front of the apartment house to let physical pain somehow replace the anguish he dare not express. The Nazi landlord notes, "His luck that he died *this* way," implying the other end that would have been likely for Friedrich. The book ends with this "lucky" death and only Richter's chronology at the end shows that the Third Reich collapsed on May 8, 1945. Richter wants to show the young reader that we do make choices and even have the choice to give up our freedom to choose until there is no choice left.

While choice is severely curtailed in *Hiroshima No Pika*, the book's last sentence, spoken by Mii's mother, presents the ultimate choice: "It can't happen again . . . if no one drops the bomb." Maruki decided to create the picture book after she listened to the spontaneous testimony about

Hiroshima by a woman who came to see her picture exhibition about the atomic bomb. Her story is about a mother and daughter whose emotions and reflections are indirectly expressed through textual and pictorial images that are appropriate for a pre-school book. Japanese readers are likely to respond quite differently from American readers, the latter's heritage being that of perpetrator of this historical nightmare. Furthermore, the last sentence is more likely to be interpreted positively by Japanese, who view human beings as basically good whereas our tradition defines us as fallen and out of tune with nature and, therefore, more likely to drop the bomb.

Maruki's evocation of the sudden intrusion of "Little Boy," on August 6, 1945, into the life of ordinary people creates neither the apocalyptic myths nor the survival fantasies Ira Cherms discusses in "Mythologies of Nuclear War." The bomb drops while the family breakfasts. Mii's mother resolutely leaps into the flames to rescue her husband, bandages him with her obi, and carries him on her back out of the house and toward the river. At the same time she is always concerned about Mii, as fire and water constantly threaten to engulf the family. Mii sees heaps of dead and wounded, but the image that remains most in her consciousness is that of "a swallow. Its wings were burned, and it couldn't fly. Hop . . . hop. . . ." The harbinger of spring has been denied and will forever become part of Mii's sorrow.

After reaching the relative safety of an island, Mii and her parents fall asleep for four days. When mother and daughter return to Hiroshima, they find "A burnt out wasteland stretched before them as far as the eye could see." In contrast to the firestorm, distinct pieces of rubble fill the field of vision where mother and daughter stand in an aura of relatedness. But the book does not end with a consolation: Mii's father dies of radiation sickness, and radiation keeps Mii from further growth, a fierce parody of the small child's secret wish. Mii will always be her mother's little girl since that fateful August day. "Sometimes Mii complains that her head itches, and her mother parts her hair, sees something shiny, and pulls it out of her scalp with a pair of tweezers. It's a sliver of glass, imbedded when the bomb went off years ago, that has worked its way to the surface." Mother and daughter do not dwell on their trauma, but those splinters are a shockingly novel image of memories that cannot be repressed.

Annually, mother and daughter express their emotions and memories through a communal ritual as Mii, along with others, mourns the dead by setting lanterns adrift in the seven rivers of Hiroshima to float to the sea. She marks one lantern "father" and the other "swallow" as her mother watches sadly. Maruki's final picture expresses serenity as brightly clad mourners set afloat warm-colored lanterns with their flames contained, spiritual symbols without the threat of

conflagration. This picture also complements the last sentence, in that fire must be contained, and that can only happen if no one drops the bomb.

These three books do not project survival fantasies onto the nightmare of history, for each survivor-victim receives lasting physical, moral, or psychological damage. Each of the three child characters is denied wholeness through the process of individuation. We, who live in the fearful symmetry of the world of experience, would like our children to sing songs of innocence, but it is difficult to delude children who have intimations of nuclear war. By breaking with the convictions of children's literature, these stories open spaces or blanks for the young readers' thoughts. Young readers will fill the blanks and appropriate the text in ways not necessarily acceptable to adults. Yet, the damage will not come from books, for these books impress order on historical chaos. Stories that we hear or read are stories that can be told. While on the outer limits of children's literature, these books, too, share the subversiveness of children's literature written by adults. Through them we communicate to the child our suffering, sins, and guilts. A child character is central in each, and bears much of the burden, as a young scapegoat whose consciousness and conscience is to awaken to what our civilization lacked. Do we still expect children to redeem us even after we dropped "Little Boy" on Hiroshima?

Lois R. Kuznets (essay date 1983)

SOURCE: "The Fresh-Air Kids, or Some Contemporary Versions of Pastoral," in *Children's Literature*, Vol. 11, Yale University Press, 1983, pp. 156-68.

[*In the following essay, Kuznets examines the use of the pastoral fantasy in children's literature—particularly Fox's* How Many Miles to Babylon?—*as a rite of passage for young protagonists.*]

Pastoral literature traditionally demonstrates the human need for the healing powers of the simple, rural, or rustic life, by contrasting that life with the complex, urban, or urbane one. Such traditional pastoral needs and contrasts can be seen not only in adult literature but also in children's literature, including contemporary books such as Jean George's *Julie of the Wolves* and Betsy Byars's *The Midnight Fox* and classics such as *At the Back of the North Wind, The Adventures of Tom Sawyer, The Wind in the Willows, The Secret Garden, Heidi,* and of course *Alice's Adventures in Wonderland,* seen by Empson as prototypically pastoral, with Alice as "swain."

Even the contemporary children's books that I examine

here—Felice Holman's *Slake's Limbo* set in modern Manhattan and Paula Fox's **How Many Miles to Babylon?** set in modern Brooklyn—evoke pastoral contrasts within urban settings. The two books manage to arouse and satisfy our need for pastoral reconciliations in different ways: the first through a story of primitive survival that reaches back to seasonal myths promising pastoral rebirth, and the second through a story of a dangerous journey that echoes pastoral romance. Both books treat Manhattan and Brooklyn realistically yet avoid the bitter irony that usually pervades adult books in which protagonists seek pastoral healing in an urbanized world.

These urban novels—whose protagonists perhaps will never have the opportunity to visit the country except as fresh-air kids, temporarily breathing, as Holman says of her hero, "someone else's fresh air"—initially seem to vary in important ways from those children's books that are set primarily in wilderness or country. The two books considered here have buried the pastoral imagery deep within the psyches of the protagonists and similarly buried the pastoral plot of retreat and renewal deep within the structures of the novels themselves. When the pastoral imagery emerges from the individual psyche in dream and fantasy, it often does so in exaggerated and distorted forms. And it is the problem of the novel as a whole to bare the *essential* aspects of the pastoral plot itself, giving the protagonist an opportunity to turn pastoral dreams into an urban reality devoid of ironic overtones.

This process is clearest in *Slake's Limbo,* the strange and wonderful story of thirteen-year-old Aremis Slake, virtual orphan, who made his home for one hundred and twenty days of winter in a cave off the subway tracks under the Commodore Hotel, and who was there transformed from a "worthless lump" into a "vendor of papers, a custodian of a small thriving coffee shop and a discriminating scavenger. And he was also a hobbyist."

Slake's potentiality for transformation is first expressed in his propensity to dream, usually of "somewhere else. Anywhere else." But these dreams seem impotent and essentially debilitating in the context of tenement, street, and school: "Dreaming thus led him into lampposts, up to the ankles in puddles, up to the elbows in spilled things, sprawling down stairways while teachers scolded and classmates scoffed, pushing him down again as soon as he gained his feet." His fantasies are also distortions of pastoral images, turning natural, cyclical gardens into desperate illusions of eternal Gardens of Eden. So, though we may applaud, we also grimace at Slake's attempt to climb a tree in Central Park, to tie back on to it the last of the autumn leaves in order to fulfill "an old fantasy that this year the leaves would stay on the trees."

The ways in which well-meaning people have hoped to give

him a brief taste of pastoral life are satirized in Slake's nightmare during his first night in his subway cave. He dreams that he is back as a terrified fresh-air child being chased by his "family's" pet pig. Later, noticing a man helplessly caught in a subway rush, he is reminded of a trip to the beach, during which he first got sick in the bus and then was knocked over and nearly drowned by the surf. A day at the shore, a fortnight in the country—neither was a healing experience.

Paralleling Slake's distorted pastoral fantasies and indicating their pervasive nature among urban dwellers are the distorted pastoral dreams of a subway driver, Willis Joe Whinny, who once saw a movie about Australian sheepherders and longed to become one, until he traded in his dream for the promise of a motorman's pension—in spite of the fact that Willis, unlike Slake, had country connections, a grandmother whom he used to visit in Iowa. She actually once had known a Montana sheepherder. By the time we met Willis, his dream has resumed but has been distorted into an image of his subway passengers as soulless sheep whom he herds from station to station.

Throughout the book, the middle-aged Willis and the young Slake are moving toward each other as inevitably as Bloom and Stephen Dedalus in Dublin, but we are most immediately aware of the contrast between the two. The first becomes more and more alienated from humanity in the distortion of his pastoral dream, becoming, as Holman says, not really the herder but simply the "lead sheep"; the second becomes more human, more connected, more far-sighted in establishing his underground home, changing from an "outlander in the city of his birth (and in the world)" to one who is "oddly in touch with the flow of the world."

The motif of renewal pervades the novel, but it is so realistically implemented, and renewal is so rarely elsewhere exclusively associated with the underground, that we may not initially recognize this motif as outlining a pastoral story of retreat and regrowth. It is not usual for us to accept a freshly cleaned public bathroom as an omen of a new life, nor are we accustomed to thinking of the recycling of urban waste as a basically pastoral image. Yet Slake's first business is the reselling of secondhand newspapers, and his first meal is the restaurant leftovers of a hurried businessman. By the time a cleaning woman to whom he talks daily gives him her son's old jacket, mended, and he makes for himself a pair of adequate glasses from among the many dropped lenses he has scavenged, we know that recycling applies to wasted human possibilities as well as to trash and garbage: we are witnessing an example of true urban renewal.

Holman continually pushes in the direction of the pastoral discovery and settlement theme by her similes: "He began to know the signs of the subway as a woodsman knows the wilderness," and "surely as any explorer who had first set foot anywhere—the Arctic, the Moon—Slake was certainly at least one of the few and only settlers in this piece of dark continent." Slake thus takes his pastoral place among frontiersmen.

Holman also pushes underground imagery back to its origins in nature myths. We have tended recently to associate the underground with death, hell, or insanity from which modern heroes are rarely able to emerge. Holman disassociates the underground from its hellish finality and reassociates it with the cyclical wintering place of Persephone from which she is annually reborn, albeit with struggle, into the arms of her earth mother. In these terms, the one hundred and twenty days that Slake spends underground clearly constitute a period of germination. He experiences anxiety that makes him actually sick when he discovers that his cave will probably be covered over in much-needed subway repairs, but his being pushed out of his underground home in the spring is as cyclically inevitable as his going down into it in the fall. When Slake lies ill upon the tracks, holding a sign that says "Stop," it is also inevitable that Willis will be driving the train that screeches to a halt a few feet from the fallen Slake. Willis himself reconnects with humanity, holding Slake "as he once held his new son and daughter." Mothered by the cleaning woman, Slake, the orphan, is in his rebirth fathered by the motorman.

If we now think of *Slake's Limbo* in terms of its relationship to children's literature in general, we see that, although the urban reality depicted in the book in some ways serves to mask the pastoral allusions, the very detailed and circumstantial nature of that reality also links it with certain emphases characteristic of children's novels, particularly those with rural settings.

The emphasis on practical means of survival in a new environment is particularly evident in this context. We are fascinated by Slake's stratagems for survival, his transformation from ineffectual dreamer to effective actor. The practical survivalist aspect of *Robinson Crusoe* and *Swiss Family Robinson,* strong elements in their fascination for young and old alike, generally have been carried over into books more specifically directed toward the child reader. There seems to be an understanding on the part of writers and publishers of children's books, both classic and modern, that the more urban becomes the experience of the child-reader, the more fascinating become the details of feeding, clothing, and sheltering oneself. The relative simplicity, directness, and recent novelty of doing these things in a rural environment account for some part of the enormous popularity of Wilder's *Little House in the Big Woods,* with its detailed description of processes of meeting ba-

sic needs, processes in which even the very young can participate in some capacity.

For older children, the idea of being able to survive alone becomes more attractive and tenable, although frighteningly formidable in modern times. Erik Erikson describes the seven-to-twelve-year stage of development as a period in which "industry" attempts to overcome "inferiority" and "the child becomes ready to handle the utensils, tools, and weapons used by the big people." How attractively reassuring it is to read about Karana in *The Island of the Blue Dolphins* and Julie-Miyax in *Julie of the Wolves* who, forced to put into practice the ancient lore and skill of their peoples, are able to survive through the use of relatively simple tools (in contrast to the complex machinery of modern industrial society). Slake makes it look relatively simple, too—recycling the waste of this society in a way not unlike Mary Norton's Borrowers!

Over and over in children's books, we find practical details of living in a simpler society emphasized and fulsomely described, whether this society exists in rural fields, desert islands, or big woods. Sometimes in this existence, direct experience and experimentation are specifically contrasted to booklearning. This is certainly true in Slake's case since the newly alert Slake is, of course, playing hooky from school, in which he had wandered in a daze: he is Wordsworth's "growing boy" on whom "Shades of the prison house begin to close." Such a contrast also is surely part of the pastoral element in *Alice's Adventures in Wonderland.* Alice, one recalls, tries frantically to bring to mind some imperfectly mastered booklearning that would serve her underground, but only reasoning from experience and experimentation will get her into the garden she first glimpses. In *A Wild Thing,* a modern young-adult book that resembles *Slake's Limbo* in many interesting ways, Morag, a runaway who has been deemed retarded by the school system, is capable of learning to survive, at least temporarily, alone in the Highlands.

The simple order that Slake imposes on his daily life signifies an understanding and control of diurnal rhythm that is also characteristically emphasized in other children's books that partake of the pastoral. Eating, sleeping, and working begin to become meaningful activities—no longer imposed from above—once Mary Lennox gets into the secret garden. Morag, too, in *A Wild Thing,* experiences the need for meaningful orderly activity in her life, even if it is no longer dominated by the clock (or perhaps because it is not).

Moreover, we are not at all surprised in *Slake's Limbo* to discover, in keeping with a pastoral convention well honored in children's books, that Slake's growth underground includes the nurturing of an animal (that the creature should be a rat seems both inevitable and weirdly pastoral in the identification of child keepers with their animal charges). In adult traditional pastoral, of course, shepherds and shepherdesses do not engage in much practical care of sheep. Shepherding simply seems to provide a leisure for the composition of poetry. But animals and birds do have symbolic functions there, especially in pastoral romance, where they serve as guides into the gardens and forest groves where the hero will experience whatever epiphanies he is meant to experience. The robin for whom Mary Lennox feels the first glimmerings of positive emotion functions not only initially to stimulate her nurturing instincts, but also as the traditional pastoral guide into the garden. In children's pastoral, animals require nurturing and provide companionship, serving in both roles as guides into the essential pastoral experience. The use of animals is even more true of **How Many Miles to Babylon?,** which will be discussed below, than of *Slake's Limbo.* It is certainly true of Tom's midnight fox in Byars's novel, the wolves and bird in *Julie of the Wolves,* the wild dogs, birds, and others of *The Island of the Blue Dolphins,* and the nanny goat and kid of *A Wild Thing.*

Linked still further with developmental ideas of children's literature is the *rite of passage* suggestion in Slake's age, thirteen. Slake can be seen as having won his entrance into adulthood by the trial of his underground independence. The pastoral experience in children's books can often be seen as such a testing-ground for life in the wider world, presaging a reentry into society and into a larger maturity. As in Tom's return to the city after his experience with the midnight fox in the country, the protagonist often emerges not only wiser but often sadder. Some of this sadness clearly is related to a loss of innocence that marks the return from a pastoral world.

Be that as it may, Slake (who is not necessarily sadder, but certainly wiser) has won his independence as well as his right to society through his experience underground. After being briefly cosseted in the hospital and having his existence in the minds of others confirmed by the receipt of a card from Willis, Slake slips away at the suggestion that the "juvenile authorities" will step in to help him. We are once again reminded that, in literature if not in life, when orphans finally find their parents they usually no longer need them as *parents,* having found an identity that first incorporates and then transcends them. Indeed, the parents themselves are often in need of the help of their children: Slake rescues Willis as surely as Willis rescues Slake; James of **How Many Miles to Babylon?** calls his mother back to real life from a mental institution—facts that certainly contribute to the theme of pastoral healing in these two books.

The experience of James, the ten-year-old black protago-

nist in **How Many Miles to Babylon?,** shares these urban pastoral characteristics in a less pervasive and concentrated way, but the pattern of distortion and transformation of the pastoral through urban experience is similar. Although the three aunts who take care of virtually orphaned James are clearly more attentive and concerned than Slake's vaguely present aunt, James's life prior to the main experience of the book is just as fragmented, dream-dominated, and haunted by failure.

He has Willis's nostalgia for a pastoral life known by his ancestors and solicits stories from his aunt of country days gone by:

> But James wanted to hear all about that—about the country store where you could buy everything from a pork chop to a hoe, about the long dirt roads where the soft dust slipped around your bare toes, about the black stove in the kitchen where pine wood burned all winter long.

His longing takes the form here of creation of imaginary "felicitous space," such as Slake finally creates for himself in the subway cave. The pastoral fantasy that he conjures up to make his tenement, street, and school existence tolerable is one in which we find fragments of traditional pastoral romances of the sort that Shakespeare used in *The Winter's Tale:* royal babies left to be brought up by rustics, their identity to be revealed only in the crisis of adolescence:

> He was being guarded by those three old women so that no harm would come to him. His mother had gone across the ocean to their real country, and until she came back, no one was supposed to know who he really was. She had to fix everything. . . . He knew he was not the only prince. He knew there were others. When everything was all right, all the princes would come together in a great clearing, dressed in their long bright robes and their feathers, and after that everything would be different.

James's version of the pastoral romance is obviously derived from stories of African ancestry that James's mother had told him before his father left them and before she herself disappeared one night into a mental hospital. It is not much different from Geeder's fantasy about Zeely in Virginia Hamilton's *Zeely.* But James has started to act out his fantasies—when he finds a dime-store ring in the dirt, he is sure it is a sign from his mother that she will send for him soon. By the time we meet James, we can see that the fantasy has taken over even those parts of his life that are not particularly unpleasant. His teacher, though pastorally named Miss Meadowsweet and demonstrably concerned about him, is unable to reach him through his fog of daydreaming. He, like Slake, plays hooky, slipping away from the school to the basement of an old condemned brownstone, where he has worked out an elaborate ritual designed to bring home again his queenly mother. Urban reality breaks into his dance in front of a cardboard figure of Santa Claus left behind in the household debris; three young dognappers find him, make fun of his ring and ritual, and put his innocence to work for them in conning the dogowners.

James's experience is much more like the pastoral journey-return plot than is Slake's four-month sojourn in the underground. (Comparing their titles—*Slake's Limbo* and **How Many Miles to Babylon?**—confirms their respectively different emphases on stasis and movement.) After acquiring Gladys, a small white poodle with a red bow, Stick, Gino, and Blue force James to accompany them on their bicycles out to Coney Island, where they are already hiding another expensive dog in the funhouse. James's growing feeling of responsibility for Gladys, although he has hitherto been afraid of dogs (just as Slake had hitherto been afraid of rats) is a central part of his maturing experience, and, of course, a pastoral convention of animal companionship. When they first pick her up, he is annoyed by this responsibility—"With what he had on his mind why should he fuss about a dog?"—but by the time they arrive at Coney Island his concern about her overshadows his own anxiety:

> James felt terrible about Gladys at the moment. She must be frightened and homesick. He felt he cared more about Gladys than anything in the world except his mother. The thought of his mother surprised him. He hadn't had a picture of her in his mind for awhile. Well, she couldn't help him now. He was completely alone.

The projection of his own fear onto Gladys, his immediate association of Gladys with his own mother, his ensuing feeling of responsibility for his own fate are all neatly tied together in this paragraph. Reality is overtaking fantasy.

Still another true pastoral image acts as a corrective to the old one. Arriving at Coney Island in the evening, James experiences the ocean for the first time; it is appropriately invigorating: "James felt almost hopeful, smelling the water, listening to the sound of the waves breaking." But he also learns something about the distorted nature of his fantasy: "No matter what he pretended, he knew she couldn't have gotten across the Atlantic Ocean."

Like Slake, James moves from dreaming incompetence to alert competence, and does it in a similarly incongruous place, not a subway cave but the Coney Island funhouse.

Once upon a time, back in the classroom, James had been admonished by Miss Meadowsweet, who claimed that he was such a dreamer that he couldn't "find his way out of a paperbag." Yet, after they are locked in the funhouse by a passing security guard, it is James who, as a result of a previously aborted escape attempt, knows a possible way out behind the merry-go-round. When they crawl among the painted horses, Blue shouts, "Get those horses in the corral," reminding us of still another type of pastoral fantasy.

James's ultimate escape, after spending part of a tense night in the brownstone (during which we acquire some sympathy for his young exploiters as well) seems sure. We also expect him to fulfill his responsibility to Gladys by taking her home first—which he does at the expense of a long and frightening walk. James has earned the name "Prince," which the boys have begun to call him, in earnest before the long journey is over.

His return to his own tenement is also celebrated by his aunts and neighbors in the traditional heroic way: "We thought you was dead." "He's back. Look! He came back." And, of course, his mother is there waiting for him, brought back from *her* "funhouse" by his ordeal. Again, the Persephone myth of the return from a trip to hell and back into the arms of a parent is invoked, at a number of different levels. And again, by the time he finds his parent, he is as ready to help his parent as his parent is to help him. James enters the room and walks toward his bed:

> A small woman was sitting on it. . . . She was hardly bigger than Gino.
>
> James stood still. But where were her long white robes? Her
>
> long black hair? Where were her servants, her crown? . . .
>
> Why, she was hardly any bigger than he was! . . .
>
> How *could* she be his mother?

The process of role reversal can begin even at the age of ten, but his mother still has the power and responsibility, in this case, of granting him the birthright of his own identity:

> He thought, who am I? I'm not a prince. How can I be a prince? Who am I?
>
> As though she had read his mind and heard his question, his mother held out her hand.

"Hello, Jimmy," she said.

Slake and James are both heroes, not anti-heroes. The city is not the end of them. Take away their fresh air, lock them in the funhouse, and yet they have the internal strength to make it anyway. If there is an irony in these endings, it is not a bitter one but a gentle irony—and the joke is on the cosmos, not the protagonists.

And what is this strength inside? It's the same strength of which pastoral dreams are made, albeit at first distorted. It is no mere chance that our heroes are at first incompetent, bumbling dreamers. James has a moment early in his captivity by the boys when he realizes the power of his own mind:

> They hadn't known what he had been laughing about, James realized. They couldn't tell what he was really thinking. They could make him go where they wanted and they could search him. But they couldn't get inside his head where his thoughts were. Maybe he'd have a great thought that would show him how he could get home.

James gets home. Again, *Slake's Limbo* carries out this theme in a more encompassing way. Holman shows us that she is concerned with the concept of the human soul when Willis's country grandmother tells him an anecdote about the Montana sheepherder who, when she complained that he smelled like his sheep, replied: "'The only difference between me and a sheep, ma'am, is that I've got a soul.'" Willis is about to lose his soul in distorted fantasies. Slake has a soul that is developing, it appears, as it does in much traditional literature, in the metaphor of a bird. The bird first gnaws our hero from within and then, being freed, becomes a talisman and a leader. From the beginning of the story, and even after his rebirth, Slake felt hunger combined with anxiety, and then anxiety alone, as if a bird had settled in his gut and was pecking him from within. In the hospital, he feels a release from this bird, as if he has finally coughed it up. And then, when he leaves the hospital, he envisions it soaring above him toward the rooftops and wants to follow where it leads him. The last words of the novel, as upbeat as James's mother's greeting, are, "Slake did not know exactly where he was going, but the general direction was up."

I should reemphasize that the concern here with baring both the pastoral skeleton and the soul has largely ignored the very interesting urban flesh with which both are clothed. This depiction of the city is not only interesting but extremely realistic. These are urban novels written by urban writers who know New York, in all its terror, its shabbiness, and its wit, very well indeed. They are also writers who clearly, consciously play with specific types of settings—the underground subway, the Coney Island funhouse—that, in adult literature, have served as metaphors for the disturbed minds of anti-heroes, beginning with Dostoevski's narrator in *Notes from Underground.* Such settings are, in adult literature, permeated with bitter irony.

This bitter irony, which neither Holman nor Fox evokes, is not particularly suitable for a child audience, but it has certainly not been avoided entirely in pastoral books for children or young adults such as *Julie of the Wolves* and *A Wild Thing,* where the female protagonists learn pastoral skills to no seeming, lasting avail in the modern world. Holman and Fox, however, seem determined to confirm the value of the pastoral dream in an urban reality and to assert the possibility of realizing it, even when growing up poor and/or black in a polluted city that has already obviously defeated many adults. It is a message that is conveyed not just by the relative triumph of the protagonists, but by the assertion that the young protagonist can redeem some of these defeated (or corrupted) adults, as Slake, in some way, saves Willis, and James, in some way, saves his mother. In classic children's pastoral, as in pastoral romance, the old can be redeemed by the young, as is Colin's father by Colin and Mary, and Heidi's grandfather by Heidi. Part of the irony of *Julie of the Wolves* and *A Wild Thing* comes from the fact that neither Julie nor Morag can influence the old, who may, or do, respectively destroy them.

Both Slake and James move from distortions of their pastoral needs into living out, within an urban context, true pastoral adventures of primitive survival or dangerous journeys—seemingly to redeem some adults along with themselves. Holman and Fox know that both children and adults are haunted by such frightening questions as "Where has all the fresh air gone?" Yet these authors also seem to say that we still must breathe and can even be *in*spired.

Blair T. Birmelin (review date 3 November 1984)

SOURCE: "Novel Conditions," in *The Nation,* Vol. 239, No. 14, November 3, 1984, pp. 459-60.

[In the following review, Birmelin praises Fox's ability in A Servant's Tale *to render the perspective of social powerlessness but finds her choice of narrative style too opaque.]*

Nadine Gordimer has described black South African playwrights as being concerned not with the development of actions but with the representation of conditions. In her latest novel, *A Servant's Tale,* Paula Fox, who is one of our most intelligent (and least appreciated) contemporary novelists, clearly has represented conditions. Fox's earlier novel *The Widow's Children,* about several generations of Cuban-born Spaniards in America, reverberates with much more than family history, though it is also marvelously specific as to time, place and character. In *A Servant's Tale,* the conditions represented are those in the life of a Hispanic woman named Luisa. Born and raised on a small island in the Caribbean, she emigrates with her parents to New York City in 1936 and grows up to spend the rest of her life cleaning other people's rooms.

Luisa tells her own story, which begins with her increasing awareness of the scandal of her illegitimate birth in Malagita, a tiny village employed down to the last soul on the coffee plantation of the de la Cueva family. Her mother, a kitchen maid in the de la Cuevas' *vivienda,* is in time-honored fashion seduced by the son of the house, Orlando. Oddly, their liaison lasts: Orlando refuses to marry the heiress of a neighboring plantation, and his mother cuts him out of the family fortune. Eventually Luisa's parents marry, but their union is a bitter one. He is violently contemptuous of his wife, who humbly continues to work at the big house in order to support him and their child.

Despite this domestic hell, Luisa's memories are precious to her. Small and poor and decaying, Malagita yet contains all the aspirations as well as the fears of its inhabitants. Their imaginations do not stray. It is Luisa's father who threatens this world, not because he is brutal and a wastrel but because he is educated and knows something of a world beyond. When revolution is imminent, Luisa and her family emigrate, exchanging their cabin for a damp basement in the barrio of upper Broadway. And so Luisa comes of age in isolation, her community shrunk to her poor parents and a series of even poorer boarders, all seeking refuge from hard times and the confusion of the city.

From this point on, Luisa's tale is a lament:

> My work, done and every day undone—was the dull, mechanical movement of a treadle. I dreamed of another life. I wondered if I had become the ghost of the plantation, if the people of the village, walking along the dirt roads at twilight, gazing up at the slowly darkening sky, would, sensing my presence, shiver and retreat indoors. Yet it was the very monotony of my servant's life that freed me to return in my thoughts to Malagita.

After a brief marriage and divorce, she goes back to work in order to support herself and her son. Though she gains the good will of her employers, she has only one real friend, a black girl who becomes a lawyer and later goes south to work in the civil rights movement. But Luisa is not touched by her friend's ambition or her idealism, and a servant she remains. Fox refuses to allow her heroine a resolution to this struggle; nor does she permit the reader the luxury of empathy and catharsis. Luisa's voice, objective as it seems, also makes her opaque. Regarding her relationship with her first employer, Luisa writes (and in tone and judgment, the title notwithstanding, this book is *written,* not spoken), "I sensed I must relinquish nothing of my secret life." Fox, having established this need for her character, respects it. We know Luisa only indirectly—her oval face through someone's compliment, her stubbornness and Cinderella-like decency through her role as maid and mother. And if Fox is careful to diagram the historical conditions of her protagonist's world, she is also careful to communicate the peculiar quality of Luisa's social and political unawareness—less simple ignorance than a refusal to understand the complexities of an alien society.

With this novel as with an earlier one, *The Western Coast,* Fox demonstrates an interesting attitude toward what fiction can and cannot impart about a particular life and its relation to history. Admittedly we can never know the full extent to which a person affects or is affected by public events. But the author implies that our perception of a given period can be altered by the respectful study of an individual. It is in this way that her work is didactic. One is reminded of Flaubert's use of history in *L'Education Sentimentale* as something to be reseen, rewoven through individual perspectives, and of such American writers as Theodore Dreiser, Frank Norris and William Carlos Williams, who struggled to reinterpret the orthodoxies of American history through their tales of individual people.

In *The Western Coast,* Fox represents the Depression years through the eyes of the ignorant young loner, Annie Gianfala, who moves through the end of the 1930s and the war years like a female Virgil winding through the circles of hell. Annie and Luisa perform something of the same function, which is to create a historical context that allows the reader to see events from below, as it were—with an objectivity that derives from powerlessness. And yet the earlier character, Annie, is finally the more effective catalyst, perhaps because Fox tells her story in the third person rather than the first. Luisa's perceptions can render psychologically detailed portraits of her parents and her employers—charming, lying Mrs. Burgess, or the Millers, whose two demanding children "had their secret lives [too], refuges from the weight of that love that seemed to measure and record every breath they drew." But what we get to know of Luisa herself is more conventionalized and finally less interesting. "I sensed . . . a shapeless lump of obduracy in myself," she writes. "But I could not lift it up into light." That diffident monotone, which Fox has purposefully chosen, insures that her servant will remain in shadow.

Anne Tyler (review date 11 November 1984)

SOURCE: "Trying to Be Perfect," in *New York Times Book Review,* November 11, 1984, p. 48.

[*In the following review, Tyler calls* One-Eyed Cat *a "book of real value" because of its honest portrayal of the parent-child dynamic.*]

In Paula Fox's 20-odd years of writing for children, she has distinguished herself as a teller of mingled tales. Let other authors underestimate their young readers' intelligence however they will, creating entirely villainous villains and entirely heroic heroes—but Miss Fox trusts that even children know life is a complex, inconclusive, intriguingly gray-toned affair.

One-Eyed Cat is a story about an introspective 11-year-old boy, the only child of a minister and his wife, who is immobilized by arthritis. The year is 1935, the place is a small town in New York State, and Ned Wallis is the boy attempting to be the perfect person his parents believe him to be. Or perhaps we should say the person he *imagines* they believe him to be, for his mother confesses straight out that she's not your standard saintly invalid, and his father is a fine enough minister to be unsurprised by ordinary human error.

In Ned's case, the error is thoughtless cruelty. It so happens that a maternal uncle has brought him a loaded Daisy air rifle for his birthday. His father confiscates it, explaining that while the uncle's earlier presents—archeological treasures of various sorts—provided material for the imagination, all that one can imagine with a rifle is "something dead." The rifle goes to the attic. But in the dark of night, Ned sneaks it outdoors for just one shot, and that's what sets the plot in motion. He shoots at a sort of shadow, although semiconsciously he knows it may be more than a shadow. His target is a cat, which loses an eye to Ned's bullet.

For Ned, the knowledge of his guilt marks the beginning of a new distance from his parents. "It was with the gun that his trouble had started. Yet the gun hardly seemed to matter now. It was as if he'd moved away, not to the parsonage next to the church, or to Waterville, but a thousand miles away from home. What did matter was that he had a strange new life his parents knew nothing about and one that he must continue to keep hidden from them. Each lie he told them made the secret bigger, and that meant even more lies. He didn't know how to stop."

Luckily, he has a chance to redeem himself. While he's helping an elderly neighbor with his chores, he sees the cat again and takes steps to feed and shelter it, all the while

continuing to keep his guilt a secret. How he finally confesses—and to whom—makes for a genuinely affecting scene.

The story moves slowly at times, perhaps too slowly for younger readers, and it suffers on occasion from a sense of indirection. The uncle who brought the rifle, for instance, invites Ned to take a trip with him. With some reluctance, Ned accepts the invitation, but eventually he changes his mind and stays home. One feels that the author herself may have changed her mind; what was introduced as an important element of the plot peters out without having served much purpose.

Generally, though, *One-Eyed Cat* succeeds. It's full of well-drawn, complicated characters—Mrs. Scallop, the insensitive housekeeper who means well nonetheless; the lonely old man who waits for his grown daughter's postcards, even though she just sends him the same one over and over; and two very appealing parents. There's integrity in the plot, as you'll realize when the housekeeper tells Ned that his mother's disease was caused by Ned's birth. In a slicker story, Ned would have brooded over her words throughout the rest of the book and never let his mother know why. In *One-Eyed Cat,* he tells his mother at once, and she dismisses the notion conclusively—and anyhow, he never really believed it from the start.

Most important, though, is what the story can teach young readers about grown-ups' expectations of them. If I had a child right now in his middle years—old enough to land himself in some sort of mess, young enough not to know yet that his parents themselves are imperfect—I would offer him this book. It says clearly, but never too baldly, that parents are not so easily scandalized as all that, that what disturbs them more than their children's mistakes is the sense that their children are concealing serious worries: This is what makes *One-Eyed Cat* a book of real value.

Paula Giddings (review date 18 November 1984)

SOURCE: A review of *A Servant's Tale,* in *New York Times Book Review,* November 18, 1984, p. 9.

[*In the following review, Giddings asserts that while* A Servant's Tale *begins with a well-developed sense of purpose and character, the novel loses focus when Fox moves her characters to an urban setting.*]

Luisa, the heroine in Paula Fox's fifth novel, *A Servant's Tale,* is born, out of wedlock, to a father who comes from a wealthy, plantation-owning family, the de la Cuevas. Her mother, whose family was reduced to peonage by the de la

Cuevas, works as a kitchen servant in their *vivienda*, or "big house." Luisa, however, escapes the fate common to children of such unions when her father spurns a bride-to-be of his own station to marry Luisa's mother. For his impetuousness, he is disinherited. For her untimely birth and working-class bloodline, Luisa will never be more than "a bedbug" in the eyes of La Senora, her paternal grandmother.

Malagita, the island town where the de la Cueva sugar plantation lies, is a worthy setting for such passions. Even its flora—gleaming palm fronds, "blossoms of climbing vines and tangled creepers twined around the branches of mango trees"—becomes a metaphor for the ironies and betrayals of its history. Through Miss Fox's skillful evocation of the island's lore and superstitions, Malagita emerges as a place vibrant with restless spirits—murderous bones and flesh turning back to earth. Against this backdrop, using the impressionistic perception of the young Luisa, Miss Fox creates a host of vivid characters. We meet the sycophantic town priest, who has a cloven foot "like a goat's hoof," and a woman, thought to be a witch, whose face is "splotched with raw pink patches as though parts of it had been peeled like a fruit." These and others make the array of players Miss Fox introduces reminiscent of the archetypal characters found in the works of many contemporary Latin American writers.

One of Miss Fox's narrative strengths is the ability to deftly portray her main characters through a single action or incident. We gain much insight into Luisa's mother, for example, when she smuggles home some flan from the kitchen of the de la Cuevas, for whom she works. Stumbling back to her cabin, she is close to apoplexy for fear of dropping the expensive platter that holds the dessert. Why didn't she just remove the flan and place it on one of her own dishes? Because of the beauty of the dessert's original form. "I couldn't bear to empty it into the bowl," she says. For her, bringing home the flan was an act of unaccustomed daring, its terror made worthwhile by her effort to preserve the integrity of the only art form she knew.

Early in the novel, however, it is Luisa's maternal grandmother, Nana, who dominates the story. She is the child's nurturer, a delightfully wise old woman who has managed to extract wisdom from the tragedies of peasant life. She passes the emotional remnants of her past to Luisa—the abandonment and suicide of a husband who could not bear being a sharecropper on land once his; her bowing to others' wishes and allowing her own daughter to work in the de la Cueva kitchens. But what makes Nana's recounting more than the bitter complaints of a old woman is her consummate skill as a storyteller, her words given weight by the pathos of her own experience. When Luisa's mother cautions that stories and lies are the same thing, Nana tells

Luisa that there is indeed a difference. "A lie hides the truth," Nana tells Luisa, "a story tries to find it."

An impending revolution abruptly changes the path of Luisa's life. Her father must take the family away from the island, but first there are poignant exchanges with Luisa's two grandmothers: Nana tries, unsuccessfully, to "kidnap" Luisa so that she won't lose her. La Senora, on her deathbed, will hardly acknowledge Luisa's existence. Then, suddenly, Luisa finds herself on the hardened streets of New York's Spanish Harlem.

There are no storytellers or devil's disciples in the city. The pavements hold no traces of the old traditions, and Miss Fox does not exploit the barrio's inherent drama. Consequently, the characters must stand on their own. While the prose style does not falter, the novel is less successful in this urban setting.

As in the earlier sections of the novel, there are vivid minor characters, such as the menagerie of boarders that Luisa's family takes on as they move from tenement to tenement and the varied employers Luisa works for. Luisa's development, however, seems to stop at this point in the tale. Even though she marries, bears a son and is divorced, there is no evidence of her growth or change. The absence of knowledge about the inner drives of the adult Luisa becomes evident when she makes the decision for which the novel is titled. She quits school and resigns to become a servant—"a maid," she announces with "sour triumph."

Luisa's decision defies the entreaties of her parents and her closest friends—a black, racially conscious brother and sister who are determined to rise above the station of their own mother, who was a maid. And the reader, of course, wonders why Luisa has chosen to become a servant on the eve of World War II, a time when better jobs are opening up for women. She speaks of wanting to leave the barrio, of a kind of freedom in maid's work, and talks about the inevitability of her station. But there is no adequate explanation of her motives, of why she feels that being a maid is the only path to her goals. Is it something in her blood?

Later, Luisa finds that servitude does not provide freedom from betrayal. She discovers that her teen-age son has been seduced by an otherwise endearing middle-aged divorcée for whom she works. This revelation prompts her to return to Malagita. The return to the island seems to promise that Luisa is searching for answers to her own life by coming to terms with her past, and the reader hopes that this voyage may clarify Luisa's motives for insisting on becoming a servant.

When Luisa arrives on the island, she encounters an old friend of her deceased Nana. Their uneasy meeting leads to a bitter exchange, and Luisa is told that Malagita was never hers, and "now it is ours." It is then that Luisa finally reveals a smoldering, subliminal thought. Ever since that day she last saw La Senora, her dying paternal grandmother, she had been "awaiting an inheritance . . . promised only in dreams." Is this then the deeper motive or the hidden psychological impulse that sustained her even as she dedicated herself to the role of servant? But again there is no indication that this "dream" has been a conscious or unconscious influence in her life.

A Servant's Tale, which begins with provocative characters and sharp narrative perceptions seen through the keen eye of the young Luisa, becomes listless under the weight of a protagonist who, as an adult, is less interesting and less clear than many of the novel's other characters. Despite Paula Fox's excellent prose, which is sustained throughout the book, the character Luisa does not evolve. She fails to transcend the stereotype of a woman—and one of color at that—who submits to a station in life preordained by others.

Linda Simon (review date 11 January 1985)

SOURCE: "Valet Girl," in *Commonweal,* Vol. XCII, No. 1, January 11, 1985, pp. 22, 24.

[*In the following review, Simon finds in* A Servant's Tale *a deftly handled examination of the individual power and purpose of the marginalized under-classes.*]

Servants know their masters' secrets. From their posts upstairs, downstairs, backstairs, they have a privileged view of the privileged classes. Anonymous, invisible, flies on the wall and the pitcher's ears, they are able to observe a reality closed to the rest of us: private vanities and foibles, hidden trials and unspoken troubles. As a literary device, the perceptive servant is a useful character in the hands of a skilled novelist. In Paula Fox's hands [in *A Servant's Tale*], the Hispanic maid Luisa de la Cueva emerges as one of the most memorable characters in contemporary fiction; her tale is a delicately wrought study of the sources of oppression and liberation in our own time.

Luisa de la Cueva, illegitimate daughter of the kitchen maid Fefita Sanchez and Orlando de la Cueva, her employer's son and heir, grows up on the tiny Caribbean island of San Pedro, in a village dominated physically by the de la Cuevas' sugar mill, and psychologically by poverty, ignorance, and superstition. Malagita seems frozen in time, with traditions held not so much to affirm a sense of community, as out of fear of change. It seems a place forgotten by the outside world—until there begin rumors of political unrest,

of an uprising. "A revolution was a pitiful thing," Luisa reflects. "It made people think something different was going to happen."

When the revolution threatens to depose the de la Cuevas from their lofty state, Luisa's father (who in a moment of passion married his plump, passive Fefita) decides that the three must emigrate to the United States. Fefita is horrified. She cannot conceive of existing anywhere but in tiny Malagita; she cannot conceive of any existence for herself except that of servant.

It is 1936. In New York, the family moves from tenement to tenement, taking in boarders so that they can manage to pay their rent. Fefita can hardly venture out without her daughter. She cannot learn English. She cannot assert herself into a world she sees as threatening and alien. Orlando cannot find a job, then finally—shamefully for him—becomes a street-sweeper. Luisa goes to school.

She is forced to memorize Wordsworth and Emily Dickinson, while she longs for Malagita, the simpler life, her beloved grandmother. Her friend Ellen Dove, a black girl with enormous drive and high aspirations, tries to instill in Luisa a sense of possibility. She must stay in school, she tells her; she must go to college, must free herself from the world of her parents. But Luisa wants to work, to save her money, and to go home.

> . . . Fox is concerned with the cataclysmic moments of private lives, and the quiet desperation of ordinary people.
> —*Linda Simon*

Her barrio, she decides, is just another village, only dirtier and noisier than Malagita. She is no less isolated from the outside world, no more effective. When America enters the Second World War, Luisa sees soldiers and admits, "I couldn't imagine where they were going, what might happen to them." She reads Hollywood gossip, stops reading war news. She quits school and becomes a live-in maid.

To Orlando it appears that Luisa is following in her mother's timid, ineffectual footsteps. "I had no reason to hope for more," he tells Luisa. "But I did hope." Even her first employers, the ideologically liberal Millers, think Luisa should do something "better": "You could go to night school, you know," Mr. Miller offers. She could make something of herself. But Luisa replies coolly, "I'm glad to be working for you." At last she feels she has control over her life. Her choice is a deliberate act.

For Luisa, work—and she sees a life as a servant as decent,

honest work—is liberating. She is treated with respect and maintains her dignity and independence. After her marriage ends (her husband, a magazine editor, tries to make her over according to his own expectations), she patches together several jobs and manages to support herself and her son, Charlie.

And being a servant has another attraction for Luisa: she believes it may enable her to penetrate the mystery of a society that seems unfathomable, a society populated by men and women oppressed by forces within themselves and without, suffering, complicating their lives, and rarely connecting on anything but a superficial level.

Fox portrays Luisa's many employers as sympathetically as she does Luisa herself. The flighty, hard-drinking Phoebe Burgess and her cranky son Brian; the eccentric Mrs. Justen, tireless rescuer of stray animals ("As long as people are cruel to animals, they'll be cruel to each other," she righteously tells Luisa), whose capacity for love excludes her own mother; Gerda Mortimer, an aging hippie, and her seductive husband; a homosexual antique dealer, whose gentleness wins Luisa's affection—all are deftly etched, palpable characters with desires, dreams, agonies, and fears. Yet their essential mystery baffles Luisa and convinces her that she is an outsider. She tries to understand, reading "signs" in unmade beds and messy bureau drawers. But the world remains elusive.

When Mrs. Burgess seduces Charlie, Luisa is shattered and uncomprehending. "What are you doing with my son," she implores Mrs. Burgess. Phoebe Burgess's simple "I don't know," and Mrs. Justen's "She can't help herself," don't satisfy Luisa. She decides she must leave New York, and returns to San Pedro with the "intention that everything in my life would become clear when I set foot in Malagita." But Malagita has changed, with a huge plastics factory replacing the sugar mill, and a community that shuts her out. The child whose intrepid wanderings earned her the nickname "Luisa, *la viajera loca*"—the mad traveler—has become a woman without a home, a woman forever on the outside looking in.

Luisa's history coincides with large changes in the modern world—one great war and several smaller ones, the depression of the thirties, the civil rights movement, the disaffected sixties—but these are peripheral to Fox's interest: the eternal, pervasive needs of human existence. As in her previous novels, **The Western Coast, Desperate Characters, A Widow' Children,** Fox is concerned with the cataclysmic moments of private lives, and the quiet desperation of ordinary people.

Darryl Pinckney (review date 27 June 1985)

SOURCE: "A Not-So-Simple Heart," in *New York Review of Books*, Vol. XXXII, No. 11, June 27, 1985, pp. 27-29.

[*In the following review, Pinckney finds* A Servant's Tale *to be an examination of the subversion of expected values and actions by an outsider to the dominant culture.*]

The freakishness of innocence gives the pessimism of Paula Fox's domestic plots an unexpected ambiguity. ***Poor George*** (1967) is the story of a schoolteacher who brings about the collapse of his marriage by taking a sullen youth under his wing. ***Desperate Characters*** (1970) depicts a childless, middle-aged couple fending off the destabilization strategies of friends and strangers. ***The Western Coast*** (1972) chronicles an unprotected girl's forced march toward experience during World War II. ***The Widow's Children*** (1976) relates the efforts of a spinsterish daughter to shake loose from her oppressive family. Fox's main characters are odd-balls, restless without being rebellious, and appear somewhat culpable in their unhappy discoveries of what makes others tick. They miss crucial pieces of the puzzle and yet are not altogether blameless for the shabby luck that awaits them behind every wrong door.

Though **Desperate Characters** was something of a success, the others seem to have fallen like the philosophical tree with no human ear around in the forest. These novels are very accomplished, tightly constructed, sometimes hard to the point of cold. One feels they come from a precise intention that prevents any relaxation in the prose. Setting and character are firmly in place but their clean surfaces are deceptive, and put one in mind of children who have, under their fine Easter clothes, clenched fists. The sense of the suppressed gives a biting quality to Fox's dialogue, and what may begin as an examination of familiar American themes ends as something a little different because her characters have been merely *passing* for normal.

Fox's work is in many ways a portrait of New York, where she was born in 1923 of half-Cuban parentage. Her novels have the native's savvy for which detail to choose from the metropolis of potential data overload. Even *The Western Coast,* with its Party members and writers exiled from the East, is Manhattan not Hollywood in tone. Hers is the New York of neither the highest nor the lowest. Husbands and single women report to work and get by in the spirit of treading water. Divorcées look upon alimony checks as booby-trapped tokens of remembrance. Family trees are likely to hold tales of alcoholism, of capital unwisely spent, of inheritances that do not help matters much. No one has roots in the immediate society or is much at home in the present, and yet there is little nostalgia typical of those who have come down in the world.

Fox's city dwellers worry about money not in the newfangled sense of it as a means of expression or liberation, but in the old-fashioned way, as a measure of security, as so many sandbags against the unknown. Middle-aged couples wake up to find that the neighborhood has gone downhill, that the summer house has been burgled, and that the loud-mouthed hippies, the blacks with blaring radios on the corner, are up to no good. Disaster comes from outside the home, out of the urban night, out of another class, and is presented as a temptation to test their received assumptions of ordinary life. Perhaps this wariness of the accidents lurking in a more open society is what denies Fox's novels a contemporary atmosphere. Her work belongs to a tradition in which realism is a more than inadvertent method of social inquiry.

A Servant's Tale seems at first a shift from Fox's previous novels. If the characters in her other books come to suspect that their promises to themselves or their contracts with others have something of the swindle about them, then Luisa Sanchez, a cleaning woman, has taken on in her life heavy obligations which she struggles to keep, but she is cheated anyway. The third-person speculative interior of the earlier novels, complete with instructions to the jury, has here been replaced by a controlled, first-person laying out of evidence. Unlike the New York of Fox's earlier work, the city in *A Servant's Tale* is seen from the underside, while the displaced, troubled characters to whom Fox is drawn are looked at from a distance, from Luisa's point of view. Although Fox's dual background has always been present—all her characters are foreign in some way, fear isolation, take little about America for granted—this novel makes direct use of it.

Luisa is a daughter of the plantation economy, articulate about the migration from her island, San Pedro, to the railroad flats of the big city where she will work for years as a maid. But her story is different from other books about immigrant life, of fighting to make it, or of becoming American. Luisa's is a history of refusal and this premise serves as a device to set up a tale about a wholly unprotected soul. Fox's portrait of San Pedro, Luisa's lost idyll, is schematic, dour, laid on rather thick, piece by lacquered piece. Luisa's childhood there is remembered through the sifting intelligence of the stoical adult. It is an imagined place, presented as a real country, but it emerges as a fantasy, a picturesque invention. San Pedro is where Luisa is from, and coming from someplace else is the condition that defines her working life. That Luisa has such unexplained romantic longings for a gloomy paradise adds to the sense one has of her as a deeply peculiar creation. Nothing she does conforms to our expectations.

Life on the plantation, Malagita, where Luisa was born in 1926, is filled with lore, not incident. Everything has already happened in this depressed, insular place—the con-

quest of the Indians, the importation of slaves, the Spanish-American War, the rise of the sugar latifundio. The last act was the ruin of the small farmers, and at a young age Luisa knows, like catechism, the story of how her maternal grandfather left a note, abandoned his family, and while searching for new land, died in a swamp.

Luisa's status as a bastard is also fixed, though her father, Orlando, younger son of the plantation owner, jilted his official financée to live with Fefita Sanchez when Luisa was four months old. Luisa's maternal grandmother, Nana, does not speak to Fefita because Fefita "gave them the only thing she had a right to withhold." Luisa finds Nana's cabin on her own, and hears the gossip, the oral history of the village. Nana is her only companion. Luisa's paternal grandmother, the widowed "La Señora," has no more connection with her grandchild than "a hen with the egg it drops in the straw." Luisa gazes with hate on her privileged cousins. "'What's mine?' I asked. 'Nothing!' cried Nana fiercely."

The men drink, fight, play pelota or the lottery when the fields and cane mill are "dead." "There were many old men in our village who had little to do except find people to listen to them. But the women, even the oldest ones, tended the chickens and pigs and goats and their gardens." Often the men are seen as idlers, almost irrelevant. Luisa's father may be a de la Cueva but he is, like a woman, fallen, disinherited, marked by the misalliance. He cannot lift his woman and child out of their *bohío*. Fefita continues to work in the kitchen of La Señora's *vivienda*, as if no union with a son of the house had taken place.

> "Who should I love better? God or you?" I once asked Papá.
>
> "I am the one who feeds you," he had answered. "I am the one who is here."
>
> It was a lie. My mother fed me. I knew that from the beginning. But his lie pleased me, and I often repeated it to myself as though it had been a kindness, a kind touch on my hair.

On Luisa's birthdays her mother recalls her labor, during which she thought the screams of a pig as its throat was cut were her own. Malagita has a graveyard full of babies; Luisa finds a worm in the belly of a rag doll.

Though La Señora owns the land, Malagita is not a matriarchy. Machismo asserts itself through the violence of powerlessness. Fefita sits on a stool near the cabin door in order to get out quickly when her husband goes into one of his "white-faced rages." Prayer, witchcraft, and fetishistic post cards of the Sacred Heart are for women. Political matters belong to men, and take the form of following rumors from the capital. The revolution that forces Orlando to move his family north is, for Luisa, bewildering, like a Victrola or a moving picture, something brought in from the outside. "The United States was a great hole to the north which would swallow me."

The New York barrio is also depressed, insular, but the vividness of Fox's rendering of its claustrophobia and anxiety contrasts with her painstaking, worked-up portrait of San Pedro. When Luisa and her parents arrive in 1936 they have two boxes and at the time of their last move as a family in 1943 they have fourteen. This slow accumulation of sad belongings, "each a relic of struggle," is as close as they will get to the American dream. They have, through Orlando's father, citizenship, but it makes no difference. This, like Orlando's refusal to desert Fefita, is another quirky adjustment Fox makes in a familiar outline.

Fefita is unable to learn English; they are treated with contempt by relatives who have scraped toward a measure of material comfort and cultural assimilation. Even the food from the bodega, the smell of which was once consoling, is reduced to what the Irish children call "spic grub." Luisa remembers meals when there was scarcely enough.

> The flat was a place I never wanted to be. Walking home from school, always hungry, always angry because I was hungry, I imagined the dark hallway, the blue painted walls, the swollen lumps of plaster, the narrow, stale, silent rooms.

The correlation between menial work and survival is not lost on Luisa when her father, after years of not working, finds a job as a street cleaner and they begin to eat meat. The division of labor within the family is unchanged until then: Fefita works for a time in a perfume factory, but Orlando, still the landowner's son, takes in boarders whose defeat and terror are like an incurable viral strain. Luisa resents her father's weaknesses and feels "an irritable pity" for her mother, who eventually wastes away from cancer.

> When I watched Mamá ironing a shirt of Papá's as she bent over the sheet-covered plank balance on two straight-backed chairs that she used for an ironing board, her own dress unpressed, her lips moving as she talked to herself, I wanted to kick away the plank, its clumsiness and inadequacy proof that I would never be able to enter the world which I had begun to suspect lay beyond our barrio.

The news of La Señora's death and that Orlando has inherited nothing is a turning point in Luisa's inner life. "The death of a hope I'd not known I'd had, so nebulous, I couldn't put a word to it, but knew it had been hope by the desolation which followed its loss, made me feel faint and ill."

Luisa takes an afternoon job at a variety store. "A tide was carrying me away from the life my parents had made. . . . I felt a joy that was nearly vengeful." It is not a surge toward improvement, but an escape, a refusal to participate. This refusal takes the form of a life of drudgery.

Fox would have us believe that Luisa has made the choice to become a servant only out of temperament or as an act of mourning or revenge for the loss of Malagita, an abstraction, an idea, that one feels Fox has imposed on the observed life of work. She does not adequately convince us of Luisa's chaste but perverse decision to be a maid, though it is central to the moral problem Fox seems to be working out in the novel. Though Luisa is articulate with herself, she is, like the serving girl Felicité in Flaubert's *A Simple Heart,* mute with the world. To make Luisa speak without violating the recessiveness necessary to her character is Fox's challenge and the boldness of her creation. It may be also why the book seems at the same time so deliberately withholding, and so literary. Luisa's choice is asserted, and part of the strategy of the book is to set her up for this choice.

Fox is careful to show that Luisa is aware of the other means by which people get out of poverty. Ellen Dove, an ambitious black girl, is a shrewd insertion as Luisa's life-long friend because it takes into account the lives of women busting suds and sweating in the big house to give their children a better future. Ellen's mother also works as a maid, and she is the only one who never asks why Luisa wants to be a servant. The Dove children have the determination to seize the opportunities available during World War II. Ellen applies herself at school because she does not want to be "some woman's *girl.*" Ellen's brother, who is later killed in the war, tries unsuccessfully to infect Luisa with the romance of possibility.

> "I'm going to be a servant. I'm not good in school the way Ellen is. I'm going to have to get real work soon. . . . And—oh, I have to get away!"
>
> . . . What I had said so loudly, so boldly, had taken me by surprise. . . . But something had come together in my mind the minute I'd spoken, fragments of a picture of myself in a black uniform with a white apron. I felt a sour triumph.

Luisa is unmoved by arguments that the uniform is demeaning, is forbearing when Ellen treats her jobs as if they were "a sickness about which it would be indelicate to speak." Independence, a quick way out of the barrio—beyond these partial explanations Luisa's choice has the force of renunciation. "They wanted to drag me across the line into a life that required an effort I was unable, or unwilling to make."

Luisa moves neither upward nor downward. She is immobile. The oddity of Luisa's contract with the world accounts for the hold she has as a character on the imagination. *A Servant's Tale* may be about immigration, marriages between unequals, or class relations, but it is most effective as a meditation on the pride in humility, and on the astonishing will of the masochist.

Perhaps Luisa's escape is from herself. Newsreels of bombings make Luisa long for a situation in which she is "released from doubt, set only on survival." It is as if she suffers the kind of breakdown that expresses itself as an unwillingness to contend, as a paralyzing blend of being superior while also being fearful. Perhaps it is also an unconscious attempt to take up her mother's burden. Fefita warns Luisa to watch out for the sons. Luisa points out that her employers' son is eight years old. "Watch out for the father, then," Fefita replies. If Luisa is spitefully embracing the state she was born to or conforming to the image America has of her, then her first employers urge her to go to night school and, being Jewish, are sympathetic to her as a "foreigner." But Luisa cannot respond. She is on hold, ruled by a fixed idea. "The very monotony of my servant's life . . . freed me to return in my thoughts to Malagita."

Where Luisa's employers are open, lacking in caution, she is secretive, closed. "I was a pair of hands, a household nurse." From austere furnished rooms Luisa travels to her growing list of clients—a businesswoman, a middle-aged couple, an anarchic proofreader, an actress who wants Luisa to call her by her first name: "I called her Miss Grant." Or: "I didn't care what they called me." Luisa's aloofness appears, at times, aristocratic, and she takes pride in the discarded clothes, in the serenity of anonymity.

> I shopped for my employers, occasionally served meals, changed their linen, got to know dry cleaners . . . took telephone messages, played their radios, poured Lysol into their toilet bowls, and from their soiled sheets and plates, their wastebaskets and garbage cans, found traces of their human passage through the nights and days from which I was able to deduce their habits, their pleasures and aversions, even their pretensions. Rising to their apartments in the service elevators to which I was ordered by doormen, I felt the kind of repose that comes, I imagined, during the recovery from a long illness.

Exotic to some, a comfort to others, Luisa learns bitter lessons about being a servant. The power she finds in efficiency, in being depended on, in knowing more about them than they do about her has its price.

> A servant can disrupt the order of her employer's life

only in dire emergencies, but it is her connivance in bringing them about that is the accusation made against her. A servant's face must be blank. I shouldn't have shouted at her and let her hear my private voice.

Luisa has no delusions about equality and accepts the unfairness of life.

> Jaded, clammy with fatigue, I washed the slats of Miss Mathes' venetian blinds. The grime I rinsed from them settled beneath my fingernails. It didn't matter. It was a token of my intention.

Behind it all is the longing to return to San Pedro, but when Luisa realizes how long it will take to save the fare she experiences a "commotion" of spirit that coincides with a glimpse of another way of life.

Ellen introduces her to City College students whose "anger could speak." Luisa meets Tom Greer, a tall, blond radical in tweed who is writing a book about cocoa plantations. Here Fox has recourse to the Jane Austen Maneuver: across a crowded room a dashing, eligible man sets aside more suitable matches to fall for the beleaguered but somehow superior girl whose moral sense and perfect manners inspire him to declare himself in a courtship no longer than a stroll around the garden. Yet Fox's description of this marriage is memorable, since it comes from something truly observed in life—the husband ashamed of his wife. "Who wants to be a domestic if they can be something else?" Luisa leaves the room when company is present because she had been taught that men "were supposed to be left alone together."

> "Stop cleaning up," he demanded. He took a glass from my hand. "You're not the maid," he said patiently.

When they divorce, Tom marries a colleague of his own class. But Luisa is left with a child, an object of sacrifice outside of herself. Luisa's marriage illustrates the depths of her inability to express herself and her refusal to become an American. Tom's reluctance to support the child restores her to the labors that distract from or conceal her vulnerability. "I knew what I knew. Work was a hook I had to swallow to be saved." Luisa goes back to work in the way a streetwalker does what has to be done. She lavishes attention on her son Charlie that is almost erotic in its intensity. Luisa's life now has two components: her work and her son. The boy is as reserved and elusive as his mother and through the years they come to seem like siblings.

Though much time passes in the book, Luisa's single-mindedness makes her seem ageless. She has an affair with one of her employers, but it is mostly a painful example of the mortifications, the degradation inherent in being a servant. Luisa has no friends among her own class, doesn't even seem to know any of the other maids in the buildings where she spends her days. It is impossible to imagine her going to bingo games or devoting her free time to a church choir. Other than Charlie, the only person she seems to trust is an antique dealer for whom she works, a homosexual who understands the damage and dispossession of the alienated. Much of the book involves "the small comedies of behavior" of Luisa's employers, but it is not merely an outsider's picture of middle-class life because the drift of Luisa's concerns is in the foreground. "I realized that I hadn't believed in the possibility of justice, only in fits of mercy."

The climax of the book comes as a crack in Luisa's rigidly held routine. Luisa has been caught up in the tangled life of Mrs. Burgess. Divorced, with a spoiled, dishonest son, Mrs. Burgess is capricious, destructive, selfish, but the messiness of her life tempts Luisa to let down her guard. Mrs. Burgess, however, oversteps the formality of the employer-servant relationship: she has an affair with Charlie.

> What I remembered were the faces of Señora de la Cueva's servants. They had belonged to her, too, and to her son. They flocked to my mind, my mother's face among them, and they seemed to look at me with contempt. . . . They had known better than to trust La Señora, to imagine the bond between them was more than that of mistress and servant.

The betrayal of Luisa's intimacy brings her working life to an abrupt end, as if a contract had been canceled. The period of torpor and disorder that follows is meant as a kind of collapse, although in fact the years of silence and discipline may seem in many respects more like a breakdown. The realization that Charlie is not entirely hers causes Luisa to return to Malagita, the memory of which has sustained her like a painkiller.

Malagita has changed, but it is the desolation of revolutionary change. The *vivienda* has become a state-owned hotel and a maid there angrily tells Luisa that Malagita belongs not to her but to the people. "'I never thought that,' I whispered, even as I knew I had thought only that all through the years of my servitude. I had been waiting." She is spoken to as a de la Cueva, not a Sanchez. Perhaps Fox intends Luisa's solitary, childlike dream of Malagita to explain her lack of desire for anything in America. Her somewhat mysterious servitude now seems to have been a kind of exile and penance, and an act of revenge, which she can endure because her sense of being superior has kept her from being devalued by others in the way, in a Victorian novel, the bastard in the stable lives out a humble position in the hope of one day assuming his proper place.

The scenes of Luisa's life as a servant are intense, thor-

oughly convincing, but the motives for her choice remain abstract and they somewhat overwhelm the book. One wonders why Fox did not make Luisa a servant from necessity, but the nagging presence of the question may be part of Fox's point. There is a deep eccentricity in trying to imagine what it must be like to be someone like Luisa, and in this sense *A Servant's Tale* is an extension of Fox's examination of peripheral lives, of those who have few resources and little right of appeal. The conception is original, daring, and unnerving.

Anita Moss (essay date Fall 1985)

SOURCE: "Varieties of Children's Metafiction," in *Studies in the Literary Imagination,* Vol. XVIII, No. 2, Fall 1985, pp. 79-92.

[*In the following essay, Moss includes* How Many Miles to Babylon? *in a discussion of the effectiveness of self-referential qualities in children's fiction.*]

> "It's because she wants it told," he thought, "so that people whom she will never see and whose names she will never hear and who have never heard her name nor seen her face will read it and know at last why God let us lose the War: that only through the blood of our men and the tears of our women could He stay this demon and efface his name and lineage from the earth."

So ruminates Faulkner's brooding Quentin Compson as he listens to the aged and tiny Miss Rosa Coldfield tell him of the demonic Thomas Sutpen's violent struggles to establish a dynasty and to beget an heir no matter how. Quentin does not quite have it right. The point for Miss Rosa, as it is later for Quentin and Shreve as they piece together the fragments of Sutpen's saga, is not just to "get it told" but in the telling itself. Quentin and Miss Rosa struggle to tell their stories in an effort to make sense of their lives and the histories of their families. Quentin serves as both teller and intense listener in Faulkner's powerful novel which is more about the process of making story than it is about Sutpen's tragedy, more about the telling and the listening and finally getting it told. As critic Barbara Hardy writes in *Tellers and Listeners:* "Humankind cannot bear very much abstraction or discursive reasoning. The stories of our days and the stories in our days are joined in that autobiography we are all engaged in making and remaking, as long as we live, which we never complete, though we all know how it is going to end." Miss Rosa knows the end all too well; that's one compelling reason why she has to tell it to a sensitive listener.

Many novelists have been acutely concerned with the process of creating narrative and with the narrative forms of ordinary life which are embedded throughout fiction. The nature of narrative itself often becomes the real concern in novels and stories. So too, many children's writers have created stories about the making of stories. Why characters tell stories and how they tell them, as well as to whom, become major themes in Paula Fox's *How Many Miles to Babylon?* (1967), Natalie Babbitt's *Knee-Knock Rise* (1971), Charles Dickens' *A Holiday Romance* (1868), and E. Nesbit's *The Story of the Treasure Seekers* (1899). To a greater or lesser extent all of these books may be considered as "metafictions," works in which the imagined process by which the story is created becomes a central focus of the book. This metafictional quality is implicit in the first two works and explicit in the last two, as both *A Holiday Romance* and *The Story of the Treasure Seekers* actually feature fictional child authors as narrators.

How stories within stories interlace to form an overarching structure; how characters function as both tellers and listeners; how children's writers choose to end their stories; and how they conceive of the process of storytelling itself through their fictional child authors are literary issues which recent narrative theory has addressed in significant ways. Paula Fox is deeply interested in how her protagonist, James, uses story to endure emotional trauma, learns to tell stories to an audience other than himself, and thus somehow comes to terms with the unremittingly grim realities of his life. Natalie Babbitt reveals her fascination with the abuses of narrative and with the nature of endings in *Knee-Knock Rise*. Finally Charles Dickens and E. Nesbit have created rare examples of children's metafiction, in which fictional child authors must struggle with difficult narrative and rhetorical choices as they create their stories. In the case of both the Dickens and Nesbit books, the investigation into the nature of narrative raises important questions about the specific nature of children's writers—adults who must somehow address child readers. Both Dickens and Nesbit are concerned with creating a new kind of children's story, different in mode and manner from pious Victorian children's literature.

Fox calls attention to the nature of narrative and examines its effect upon ten-year-old James, the hero of *How Many Miles to Babylon?* A ten-year-old black child who lives in one room with three aged aunts in a tough New York ghetto, James is happiest when either telling a story or listening to one. His engagement with story in fact becomes the only way that he can endure the rather harshly realistic story of poverty, abandonment, and kidnapping which his author creates for him. The stories within stories in the novel become a significant way whereby Fox shapes her fiction and achieves a satisfying sense of closure at the end. When James returns from his ordeal with the dog-napping street kids, Stick, Blue, and Gino, he is able at last to connect in-

ner and outer story when he tells his neighbors his adventure.

In James' neighborhood most of the stories are sad; even the beginnings are sad, probably the reason why these stories are seldom finished. As Mr. Hedge remarks to James, "I've gotta story that'd wring your heart. . . . They broke my wheel. The man backed up his big ugly car right into my wheel. Smashed it. . . ." James does not hear the end of Mr. Hedge's story, nor does he expect to: "Stories were always beginning in his building, loud stories that filled up the halls with shouting and then fizzled out like damp firecrackers."

In the shabby and cramped room, rendered ghostly and strange by the flickering television set, James lives with three great aunts. Aunt Grace tells him "awful warning" stories about the dire actions of truant officers if he does not go to school. But James likes Aunt Paul's tales about the three aunts' childhood in the rural South—long ago, faraway stories about the regular and dependable rhythms of farm life that connect James to his family's past and to nature as well. He can repeat the story himself like a comforting litany: "On Mondays we washed . . . On Tuesday we ironed. On Wednesdays we scrubbed the floor with potash. . . ." Aunt Althea, however, discourages stories about the past. She is far more interested in the story of James's future. From the surging details of ghetto life and the serene scenes from his family's past, James gathers narrative materials. Going downstairs, he hears fragments of conversation "like pieces of string he could tie together."

James's ability to piece together stories helps him to endure both emotional pain and boredom: "He was a good walker. He had discovered that if he told himself stories, he could cover a lot of ground without noticing how much time it took." Listening to his inner stories also intensifies and clarifies James's experience. Each time he tells himself a story, he can "remember more clearly what things had felt like and tasted like, how they had looked . . . whether they had really happened or not."

Standing squarely in the midst of unrelenting gray pavement and surrounded by images of waste—the skeleton of a car, heaps of junk, and wasted people, James knows the sad story of his father's abandonment. Haunted by the vision of his mother standing by the window and sadly whispering, "Gone, gone, gone . . . ," James realizes that his mother had to go into the hospital. But this is one sad story which James cannot bear. Because his author has created a story too harsh for him to endure, he counters it with an inner story of wish-fulfillment. Like Scheherazade, James's very survival depends upon the story he can tell, one which he can also listen to, one that he desperately needs to believe: "James had discovered another story hidden just beneath it.

It was different from the first, but if he felt it, wasn't it true?"

James imagines that he is a prince in disguise, left by his regal mother with three old aunts. His mother had gone to Africa to prepare a place for him, "to fix everything," And she would return and take him there, dressed in feathers and robes.

Situated in an unendurable present, James must imagine stories from the past and from the future. Although the story he imagines is not literally true, it is nevertheless a fantasy which ultimately contributes to his identity and security. When the right time comes, James will be able to let go of the fantasy and to tell another that integrates the actual conditions of his life with his wishes and dreams. This dreamlike fantasy, inspired by a magical ruby ring and enacted in the basement of an abandoned building, allows James to come to terms with the history of his race and to right the wrongs of the people who "had been made to march for days and weeks through the wild forests, with their hands chained and their necks in ropes, until they came to a river where they were put in boats that carried them across the water."

The sad story of the captured Africans is significantly the only story his mother had ever told James. Aunt Paul's story, then, connects him with the past of his family, while his mother's story puts him in touch with the social history of his race. Both of these tales exert a moral, social, and psychological force upon James and help him to shape an identity for himself, a life story he can bear to tell himself and to tell others. His central problem is to connect his fantasy identity which restores him both to his true mother and to his true homeland with the setting and situation of his actual existence. The narrative materials he needs to revise his story come to him when his ritual in the deserted house is interrupted by Stick, Blue, and Gino.

Stick and Blue inject their own vivid elements into James's story. They call him a "dwarf" and refer to the mysterious figure on the wall as a "cardboard Sandy Claus." Inventive abusers of narrative, Stick and Blue tell imaginative lies in the interest of perpetuating their dog-napping scam. To protect his inner story from these tough boys, James experiments with new forms of narrative: he must make secret plans; he must learn to lie inventively; and he learns to select details for withholding from his listener. James also learns that he cannot escape from all problems by telling himself stories: "He wished he could make a story out of what was happening to him right now—pretend he was just walking home to his Aunts, to his bed in the corner. . . ." James's fake ruby ring becomes an evocative emblem of James's failed attempts at narrative: "The ring! In his pocket, it was magic, but lying in the dusty corner, it was

just what Stick had called it, a candy-box ring, good for nothing." Likewise James's fantasy about his mother's preparing an African kingdom for her son James, the Prince, loses its rich and resonant luster outside the dark shelter of the damp basement. James's terrifying adventure with Stick, Blue, and Gino forces James to revise his visionary "song of himself." At the same time, the dangerous encounter provides him with enlarged narrative possibilities. First these new characters inspire him to perceive reality through arresting figurative language: "Gino's eyes looked like holes burnt in oilcloth." And "Everytime Gino spoke it was as if a door with a rusty hinge was swinging in the wind."

More significantly, James encounters a new and exciting setting. On his adventure to Coney Island, he sees the Atlantic Ocean for the first time. The ocean's vastness overwhelms him and causes James to question his cherished story: "How could she have taken enough food to last her? As for her getting her own boat, no little rowboat could get all the way to the other beach on the other side." As a storyteller, James must thus come to grips with the necessity for narrative plausibility.

As James revises the story of his mother's African journey, he apprehends a truer sense of her emotional situation. She is not a regal African queen preparing a home for her son. Her actual story is closer to her own tale about the captured Africans. Weighed down by poverty and responsibilities she cannot handle and abandoned by her husband, James's mother had collapsed in a corner, succumbed to a nervous breakdown, and entered a hospital. When James looks out over the Atlantic Ocean, he thinks "of it rolling all the way to Africa and breaking into waves on another beach." As he contemplates her journey, he thinks, "It was terrible to think of his mother out there in the black night bobbing around on top of that water, by herself." The revised story which James imagines provides him with a vivid symbol of his mother's lost emotional state; she is indeed temporarily at sea in the black abyss of a nervous collapse.

Exploring these new possibilities for story enlarges James's sympathies not only for his lost mother but also for the kidnapped dogs. Lost in the darkness of a "crazy funhouse in the middle of the night, he felt he cared more about Gladys than anything in the world—except his mother."

When James rescues the dogs and runs away from Stick, Blue, and Gino, he heads home, trying to invent a story convincing enough to tell his aunts, recognizing at last, "No story was good enough. He would have to tell them what had really happened." When he arrives at home amid the joyous reception of the entire tenement, James narrates the story of his adventure:

"They wouldn't let me go," said James as loud as he

could. He looked up the stairwell where all the people were, dressed in their nightclothes, leaning over the railing, looking down, "They made me ride for miles. I went to Coney. I saw the Atlantic Ocean. They stole dogs. Listen, all of you. They kept watch on me. But I got away even though there were three of them."

In the new story of his life, James does not function as both teller and listener. James, the teller, addresses an audience deeply interested in his story. Moreover, he does not function as a passive character waiting for his mother to solve the problems. He has used his powers of invention to solve his own problems. In his new story he conceives of himself as the resourceful and successful hero of a dangerous adventure, one who saves both himself and the helpless homesick dogs.

In the final scene of the novel James must revise his story still further. He had pictured his mother as a tall and regal queen with long black hair in white robes. In reality she is a tiny woman with short hair in a dark dress. Looking at her, he thinks, "Why she was hardly any bigger than he was! How *could* she be his mother?" He also thinks, "Who am I? I'm not a prince. How can I be a prince? Who am I?" As if she had heard his thoughts, his mother speaks to him, "'Hello, Jimmy,' she said."

In pronouncing James's true name, his mother helps him to find the best of all possible endings for a children's story—reunion with one's mother, a safe return home, and a sure sense of identity. James's story, however, does not merely end. The novel achieves what narrative theorists refer to as "closure"; as one critic expresses the notion, "the sense that nothing necessary has been omitted from a work." In *How Many Miles to Babylon?* this sense of closure is achieved through a process described by Marianna Torgovnick as "circularity." That is, the ending of the novel clearly resembles the beginning: James is at home with Aunt Grace, Aunt Paul, and Aunt Althea. Once again the family gathers around a boy who tells a story. In the beginning, however, one significant character was missing. The mother's presence at the end achieves the effect of circularity, but it also suggests an "open" ending. The reader has a sense that James has acquired the skill to revise his story in the future.

Perhaps an even more pronounced version of a children's metafiction is Natalie Babbitt's *Knee-Knock Rise*, which announces its concern with the nature of narrative in its prologue:

Facts are the barren branches on which we hang the dear, obscuring foliage of our dreams.

In a "countryside that neither rolled nor dipped but lay as flat as if it had been knocked unconscious," the people of the village of Instep have invented a monster, a Megrimum, around which they can create deliciously terrifying stories. Narrative in many varieties appears in Babbitt's spare little fable: gossip, superstition, fantasy, dream, narrative poems. The book also examines the intricate collaboration between tellers and listeners necessary for stories.

When the central character, Egan, arrives in Knee-Knock Rise to attend the autumn fair, he meets his haughty cousin, Ada, who delights in befuddling him with terrifying tales: "'Uncle Ott ran off up there and the Megrimum ate him!' She smiled rapturously and pointed again."

For the first half of the narrative, then, Egan functions as attentive listener. He hears Ada's inventive tales about the Megrimum. When Ada's father, Uncle Anson the clockmaker, brings home a cunningly-made clock with feathered knee-knock birds on it, Sweetheart the cat pounces on it and destroys it. The incident is puzzling. What has it to do with Egan's quest for the Megrimum or Ada's scary tales? Apparently Babbitt wants her readers to see that Uncle Anson is an excellent clockmaker, but he is no storyteller. His wife and daughter do not give him the chance. The fact that he cannot tell stories accounts for his inability to predict outcome. As Ada importantly explains, "I guess he forgot about Sweetheart.'" When Aunt Gertrude asks Anson to "tell" Egan why the incident had happened, the poor clockmaker can only utter a "strangled noise." While her father struggles with his inarticulateness, Ada quickly fills the silence with her tale about knee-knock birds, cats, and, as always, the Megrimum.

Babbitt suggests that Ada misuses her narrative powers: she establishes her superiority over others and imposes her will through her stories. She warns Egan, for example, "'The Megrimum likes cats. . . . And if people are mean to a cat, the Megrimum comes down and eats them up.'" In the end Ada uses her inventive powers to deceive herself and others and to undermine the only story Egan tells. Like Uncle Anson, Egan is rendered silent. His attempts to attain heroic identity through story fail. Even his account of climbing the Rise and finding no Megrimum fades in the radiance of Ada's colorful imagined explanation.

Like her young daughter, Aunt Gertrude possesses powerful storytelling abilities. While Ada concentrates her narrative energies on the Megrimum, Aunt Gertrude's specialities are gossip and superstition. When Aunt Gertrude sees the Megrimum at the window, she cannot wait to hold "court to a stream of eager visitors." Like Ada, Aunt Gertrude also knows how to capture her audience by including terrifying details. Listeners, Babbitt implies, delight in mysteries and terrors.

Before his climactic (or rather anticlimactic) journey up the Rise in search of the Megrimum, Egan encounters two other important sources of story: he reads Uncle Ott's verses, and he experiences a prophetic dream. Uncle Ott's verses mostly recount stories of disillusionment. In one poem the speaker climbs a hill to find the secret at the top only to discover "Another hill."

Egan's dream represents a microcosm of the entire story. In most literary works, Barbara Hardy observes, "Dreams . . . are images which express the waking lives of the dreamers more lucidly and rationally than the real dreams of our sleeping lives outside fiction." In Egan's case the dream foreshadows the story he eventually enacts.

Egan's next experience with story appears in the form of an inner fantasy. Egan imagines himself at the center of a traditional hero tale: "'What would it be like,' he wondered, 'if he himself were to climb to the top and slay the thing that dreamed there?' He would come down again with its head on a stick and they would be so proud of him. He would be famous."

However, when Egan reaches the top of the Rise, he finds no Megrimum—only Uncle Ott, who explains that the moaning is nothing more than a hot spring whistling through the narrow hole in a cave. Egan does not immediately realize the significance of his discovery. If there is no Megrimum, the tiny town of Instep has no story, no identity, no way to relieve the tedium of its existence. Egan still cherishes the fantasy that he is a hero. As he makes his way back down the Rise, he whispers, "'I'll be famous.'"

Egan's inner story, however, never coalesces with reality. One of his difficulties is that he fails to engage his audience. When Ada, Aunt Gertrude, and Uncle Anson finally hear him out, Ada counters at once with a far livelier tale: "'He didn't want you to see him. . . . He hid in the cave in the mist!'" Egan, like Uncle Anson, lapses into bewildered silence, his attempts at narrating having failed. Babbitt thus underscores the necessary collaboration between tellers and listeners. Listeners like secrets more than revelations and embrace tantalizing questions more than flat bland answers.

As Egan's attempts to kill the Megrimum end in disillusionment, so too do his efforts at storytelling. At the end of the book the reader finds Egan once more in the cart with the chandler. Although the situation contains elements of a circular ending, the pattern is incomplete. In the beginning Egan had hoped to climb the Rise and to make discoveries. At the end, however, he knows no more than he had at the beginning. The force of Ada's telling has not only silenced him; he also doubts his own experience. Poet Robert Frost admonishes us to "Provide, provide . . . " or

someone else will do it for us. So it is with stories; Egan lacks the power to tell his own story and must accept Ada's instead. He is dissatisfied because the adventure has not ended as he had hoped and expected. Closure appears to be incomplete. Indeed this sense of incompleteness invites readers to question their own assumptions about narratives and their endings. Babbitt has aroused her readers' expectations only to deflate them. In so doing she appears to assert her independent powers as a storyteller, her rebellion against the constraints of convention.

If Babbitt fails to deliver the promised story, however, she has provided clues which point to the novel's ending; that is, she presents narratives within the narrative whose endings are structurally parallel. An alert reader, Babbitt thus implies, would have predicted the outcome correctly. Finally, Babbitt suggests, the most powerful story will prevail even if it isn't true. Though Ada and Gertrude abuse their narrative skills, they do tell more interesting stories than Egan.

Babbitt also seems to call into question the usual assumption that children's stories exhibit happy endings. She has herself argued that "the happy ending" is perhaps the most universal identifying characteristic of a children's story. In distinguishing a story for children from stories written for adults, she explains:

> And yet it seems to me that there is a tangible difference when you apply one rather simple sieve to the mass. It does not work for every children's story, but perhaps it does apply to all that we remember longest and love best and will keep reading aloud to our children and to our children's children as a last remaining kind of oral history, a history of the essence of our own childhood. I am referring, of course, to The Happy Ending.

It would almost seem that Babbitt's ending contradicts her opinions on the importance of a happy ending in a children's story. At the same time, perhaps she implies that the saddest stories are those in which a dream dies. Egan after all almost has his belief in the dream restored. Babbitt implies, then, that we need the inventive liars like Ada to keep the dream alive and to titillate us with tantalizing terrors.

Perhaps the most extreme examples of narratives concerned with the nature of story are those works in which the process of creating the story becomes a central theme. *How Many Miles to Babylon?* and *Knee-Knock Rise* deal with the making of story, with the relationships between tellers and listeners, and with the uses and abuses of narrative. In the following examples of metafiction, however, the "primary concern is to express the novelist's vision of experience by exploring the process of its own making."

Metafiction appeared early in the history of the novel. One finds evidence of it in Cervantes' *Don Quixote* and in Laurence Sterne's *Tristram Shandy*. In Sterne's novel, the fictional author struggles, sometimes comically, with essential narrative problems: the narrator's role and function in relation to the story and the reader, matters of literary conventions, and rhetorical choices. In works of metafiction the function of what critics have called "implied authors," narrators, narrative, and "implied readers" are self-consciously explored. According to Christensen, this concern in metafiction assumes a larger significance: in the author's investigation of the essential narrative situation—the complex and intricate collaboration of narrator, story, and reader (or listener), the work of metafiction explores the nature of human communication in general.

Although many children's books have explored the development of a child author—Alcott's *Little Women,* Mollie Hunter's *The Sound of Chariots,* Eleanor Cameron's *Julia* books, among many others, relatively few can actually be said to concentrate upon the process of their own making. In the two examples discussed here, both Dickens and Nesbit seem anxious to explore the nature and function of children's literature generally as they reveal their child authors in the process of creating children's stories.

A nineteenth-century example of children's metafiction is Charles Dickens' *A Holiday Romance* (1868). In this work Dickens portrays the conversations of four young children—Alice Rainbird, William Tinkling, Robin Redforth, and Nettie Ashford. Alice Rainbird, the most sensible, intelligent, and inventive of the group, suggests that each child tell a story to educate adults who write stories making children ridiculous. According to Alice, educating the grownups will be presented under a "mask of romance," while "pretending in a new manner" means that children will no longer pretend to be grownups:

> "We will pretend," said Alice, "that we are children. . . .
> We will wait ever constant and true till the times have
> got so changed as that everything helps us out, and
> nothing makes us ridiculous, and the fairies have come
> back."

Dickens reveals the children in the process of creating stories not for their own amusement but for didactic purposes; he thus slyly reverses the more usual procedure of adults writing for the moral education of children. At the same time, Dickens fails to convey a genuine and spontaneous sense of the child's voice. Ironically, he succeeds in making his child characters ridiculous (except for Alice Rainbird). William Tinkling, Robin Redforth, and Nettie Ashford

tell silly and uninteresting stories. Tinkling coyly recounts the details of his marriage to Alice, vainly insisting that his story is the best and the most important. Redforth narrates the adventures of Captain Boldheart, dwelling on the pleasures of pursuing and punishing the Latin Grammar Master. Nettie Ashford describes a country where the children are in control. The children spend their time eating sweets and punishing their foolish "children," adults who make silly speeches in parliament and who refuse to smile as they dance. Tinkling, Robin, and Nettie, Dickens suggests, abuse storytelling just as much as adult writers for children. Once they possess the power to create their own stories, they make them just as silly and contrived as the stories they wish to reprehend and to correct. Only Alice Rainbird succeeds in creating a coherent and interesting story. In this way Alice, the fictional child author, resembles in some respects the historical author, Dickens. Just as Dickens had advocated the fairy tale as the best kind of children's story and had written essays in *Household Words* defending the value of the form, so Alice chooses the fairy tale for her tale, "The Magic Fishbone." At the same time, Alice treats some fairy tale conventions with humorous irony. Both Dickens and his child narrator are aware that the usual "fairy business" may sometimes be silly: the magical talisman in Alice's story is not a golden apple, a cap of darkness, a ruby ring, or an enchanted purse, but a lowly fish bone. Prince Certainpersonio is not a dashing handsome hero, but a shy, passive young man who sits by himself, "eating barley sugar, and waiting to be ninety." Dickens and his child author modify romance with a little realism. Alice, a sensible narrator, understands her conventions and manipulates them for the desired effect upon her audience. Dickens, then, reveals both Alice and her story as superior to the other children in *A Holiday Romance* and the tales they tell.

By underscoring the processes by which stories are created and by emphasizing the character of the teller, Dickens invites his reader to examine the nature of children's stories in order to conclude with him and his child author that fairy tales are the best of all possible stories for children. When Alice promises to "pretend in a new way" and "to bring back the fairies," she echoes her historical author's words written fifteen years earlier:

> We may assume that we are not singular in entertain-
> ing a very great tenderness for the fairy literature of our
> childhood. What enchanted us then, and is captivating
> a million young fancies now, has, at the same blessed
> time of life, enchanted vast hosts of men and women
> who have done their long day's work, and laid their
> grey heads down to rest. It would be hard to estimate
> the amount of gentleness and mercy that has made its
> way among us through these slight channels.

The best and most famous instance of children's

metafiction is E. Nesbit's *Bastable* series, including *The Story of the Treasure Seekers* (1899), *The Wouldbegoods* (1901), and *The New Treasure Seekers* (1904). Nesbit had undoubtedly read Dickens's *A Holiday Romance,* and she adopts his rhetorical device of a child narrator who is also the child author. Her narrator also pretends to conceal his identity and then proceeds to give it away almost at once.

Nesbit's child author-narrator addresses his reader directly and explains his narrative choices. Throughout the three books Nesbit reveals her child author in the process of discovering his technique as a writer. Oswald Bastable, who learns much of his craft from a mentor, Albert's Uncle, affirms the principle of careful selection of incident, noting that he will omit dreary prefaces and description. He experiments with tone and diction, at times deliberately imitating "goody books" often given as school prizes, only to give up such elevated language for his own casual colloquial idiom, which includes such expressions as "It was Al . . . " or "It was no-go."

In revealing Oswald's struggles to become an author, Nesbit perhaps shows herself in the process of finding her own role as children's writer and in developing an appropriate tone and voice to address her child reader. Oswald's narrative choices may also reflect Nesbit's attempt (a successful one) to create a new and modern kind of children's story.

One of the choices Oswald defends is his method of ending *The Story of the Treasure Seekers.* After the Bastable children have explored several unsuccessful ways to restore their fallen fortunes, they find that the financial problems of their family are finally solved by a wealthy maternal uncle. The novel ends with a bounteous and cheerful Christmas scene at the uncle's comfortable mansion. Oswald admits that his ending resembles that of a fairy tale or a Dickens novel but argues that it is nevertheless what happened, noting that life is after all sometimes "rather like books."

Oswald's assertion that life is "rather like books" suggests some important characteristics shared by these four examples of children's metafiction. By its nature metafiction underscores the distance between actuality and fiction, between nature and art. To one degree or another each of these works explores perennial critical issues of narrative theory. Is literature an imitation of nature? Is the literary imagination a mirror or a lamp?

Indirectly Paula Fox comments upon this controversy in *How Many Miles to Babylon?* The story James narrates at the end undoubtedly reflects the actual conditions of his life more accurately than his imaginative romance about ruby rings and African Queens. The new story, however, somehow lacks the imaginative energy of James's earlier

story. Fox thus adroitly dramatizes the tensions between psychologically realistic fiction and romance. She manages to show, however, that as both kinds of story enable James to resolve his emotional conflicts, so human beings need both the mirror and the lamp. Babbit, on the other hand, apparently rejects the mimetic function of narrative. Ada's imagined version of reality becomes more "real" than Egan's actual experience. In the end even Egan starts to believe her vivid and dramatic story rather than his disillusioning experience.

While Fox and Babbitt embed their critical concerns about the nature of narrative in the dramatic and emotional conflicts of their characters, Dickens and Nesbit self-consciously explore these matters through their fictional authors. Dickens' child narrators do not imitate nature; they imitate other stories. Only Alice Rainbird, however, is wise enough to choose the right literary model. In imitating silly stories, Robin Redforth, William Tinkling, and Nettie Ashford fail to reach their child audience.

Nesbit's child narrator and fictional author relies upon many literary models as he makes narrative decisions. Oswald's example of blending the structure of the fairy tale with the texture of realistic children's stories was to become one of Nesbit's major contributions to the history of children's fiction. Nesbit's metafiction reveals both herself and her child author in the process of discovering their identities as children's writers and of discovering conventions and techniques which would influence many children's writers in the twentieth century. Oswald's exploration of literary convention, his awareness of his relationship to the implied reader, his use of diction, tone, and his process of selection and arrangement become ways by which Nesbit herself explores the nature of children's stories. Nesbit's self-conscious use of metafiction, however, produced a classic of children's literature, a work which was to usher in modern children's literature. Most critics of Dickens' fiction, however, emphasize how slight *A Holiday Romance* is in comparison with his great novels. Most readers detect a condescending tone in Dickens' treatment of the childish cuteness of his narrators; his attempts to render the child's voice strike many readers as affected and strained. Critics praise Nesbit's authentic presentation of the child's voice through Oswald as narrator.

Both Dickens and Nesbit clearly use these children's metafictions to explore the nature of children's fiction. Writing much earlier in the nineteenth century than Nesbit, Dickens composed *A Holiday Romance* at a time when the moral tale still dominated British children's literature. Also by this period British novelists were creating few metafictions. Part of Laurence Sterne's task in creating *Tristram Shandy* was to convince the reading public of the novel's validity as a literary form. Similarly Dickens clearly felt that he must justify the kind of children's story he was writing. Apparently *A Holiday Romance* fails as literature because of Dickens' confused sense of audience. The book clearly does not address the child reader; rather Dickens admonishes the adult critic of children's literature to embrace fairy tale, romance, and the imagination and to avoid moral and matter-of-fact tales. Perhaps his needs as a critic divide and thwart his creative purposes.

Nesbit was writing at the very end of the century when the influence of pious Victorian literature had already diminished considerably. While she wished to explore the nature of children's fiction through her child author, she did not need to make her case so vehemently as Dickens since the battle for imagination and the fairy tale had been won. Oswald explains that he is simply trying to write the kind of story he would like to read. He knows his literary models thoroughly. He understands the tensions between romance and realistic fiction. Chaotically comic realistic episodes which imitate "life" and which strive for mimesis, do not easily come to an end. Human beings must blunder through such episodes until nature provides its own efficient and definitive ending. But literature, specifically the fairy tale, provides Oswald with a way to end the Bastables' ineffectual attempts to restore their fallen fortunes. Oswald explains his reason for choosing a fairy tale ending: "'. . . I think it was much jollier to happen like a book, and it shows what a nice man the Uncle is, the way he did it all.'"

Judith Sheriff (review date August-October 1986)

SOURCE: A review of *The Moonlight Man*, in *VOYA*, August-October 1986, p. 142.

[*In the following review, Sheriff praises Fox's handling of her characters' ambiguous feelings for each other in* The Moonlight Man.]

[In ***The Moonlight Man***], twelve years after her parents' divorce, 15-year-old Catherine Ames has the opportunity for a seven-week visit with her father, with whom she has had only brief visits since the divorce. Her 50-year-old father, however, is three weeks late picking her up at her Montreal boarding school. Finally, just as both Catherine and the headmistress agree that Catherine's mother must be contacted, her father calls, full of apologies, and arranges for Catherine to meet him in Nova Scotia. Catherine, so very eager to be close to her father, immediately forgives and travels to join him. Within two days Mr. Ames and friends are drunk and Catherine takes care of them. Soon she discovers that the vacation was instigated by her stepmother: "She said—if you never got a close look at me,

you'd be wondering about me all your life." And Catherine does wonder. Why does her father, a writer with two novels to his credit, earn his living by writing travel guides? Why does he live so much in a literary and alcoholic fog rather than in touch with the real world and his own daughter? Why his abrupt mood changes, his chauvinism, his lies and broken promises? But despite all the questions, the answers to which she only partly understands, it is a good visit in that Catherine really does come to know this stranger. Two days before their vacation is over, Mr. Ames again gets very drunk, precipitating a very honest and very painful quarrel.

As in Fox's Newbery Honor book, ***One-Eyed Cat,*** the story is not so much about *what* happens as it is about what the characters perceive about the events and their own actions. Fox's characters have great depth, and Catherine especially is notable for her realistic, yet ambiguous, feelings for her father. Her father's alcoholism is not treated in clinical detail but with great emotional sensitivity. When Catherine returns to her mother's home in New York, she realizes how glad she is to be there—and how glad she will also be to return to school: they all, indeed, do have lives elsewhere. In short, this is another artistic beauty, and surely another award winner from the talented Ms. Fox.

Sarah Hayes (review date 28 November 1986)

SOURCE: "Breaking the Rules," in *Times Literary Supplement*, November 28, 1986, p. 1344.

[*In the following review, Hayes applauds Fox's break with conventional teen-novel themes in* The Moonlight Man, *noting the complexity of emotion and mild didacticism of the novel.*]

Catherine's father is late picking her up from boarding school—three weeks late. And instead of spending the summer in Rockport, as she had expected, he takes her to an odd little house in Nova Scotia at the back end of nowhere. Catherine knew her father would turn up eventually. She knew he would charm and entertain her in unexpected ways. She knew she would be disarmed. She did not know that her father was an alcoholic.

The word alcoholic is never used. Mr Ames is a drunk, a lush, a moonshine man; not a "problem". This is not a novel about learning to live with alcoholism, but a portrait of a wonderful, charming, doomed man who happens to drink. He drinks in a wild, blind, obsessional way. Catherine is only fifteen, but she is forced to turn out in the middle of the night and drive her father and his drinking cronies home. On one occasion, after a tour (for research purposes) round various local illicit stills, Catherine thinks he is dying. In his sober periods he goes on fawning and grovelling and charming and "drowning his daughter with language".

By the end of the summer Catherine can take no more. She is glad to return to her ordinary, tidy mother and her careful, caring stepfather. But she has changed. She sees the world differently: not as a place in which people are hopelessly flawed, and not even as a place in which weakness requires understanding and forgiveness. Paula Fox is not concerned with homilies. By the end of the summer Catherine has seen through her father's sickness to the person underneath, and he has opened her eyes and ears. Mr Ames bombards his daughter with books and words and ideas. He bullies her: "Don't be victim. It rots the brain." "Find a better word." "Be dignified." "Don't be a prig." "Don't condescend." Gradually Catherine learns to be true to herself, to trust her reactions and throw off the shackles of convention and fashion. She even learns to respect the humble sandwich.

The novel is painful; there is the suffering and self-hatred of the drunk, and the pain of living with him—with the broken promises, the lying and the charades of renunciation. But it is not an unhappy or depressing novel. Good times as well as bad lodge in Catherine's memory. Mr Ames is an exciting man to do very ordinary things with. And the landscape of Nova Scotia steals up imperceptibly to anaesthetise the hurt.

The Moonlight Man breaks all the rules for teenage novels. It has a cast of two, both of whom are bookish; there is no romance, no sex, no action: and the author dares to preach (though her sermon has a strange theme). Paula Fox challenges the reader to take another look at her or his assumptions, using the tragedy of the adult to break through the complacency of youth. Despite its sombre story and serious intent, her book remains quirky, humorous, intimate and readable—a triumph against the odds.

New York Times Book Review (review date 10 December 1986)

SOURCE: A review of *The Little Swineherd and Other Tales,* in *New York Times Book Review,* December 10, 1986, p. 86.

[*In the following review, the anonymous critic finds* The Little Swineherd and Other Tales *"luminous" and comic but also appropriately sober.*]

To open a children's book by Paula Fox is to be in the hands of a master storyteller. Rarely do writers bring such lumi-

nous prose to the old-fashioned "tale," and Miss Fox's characters, whether they be animal or human, are affecting. Best of all, she has the kind of humor that plays over words as sunlight plays on water. She is funny, witty and urbane, and a joy to read.

The teller of these particular tales [*The Little Swineherd and Other Tales*] is a Canadian goose, and the listeners are a duck and a random number of frogs. The duck, who is a failed theatrical manager, has been looking for a new client since his last one (a cat) disgraced him by devouring an audience of mice. The duck hopes to hire the goose and revive his career. The goose is only interested in weaving stories.

As her stories unfold we meet a small, ill-treated swineherd who grows into a compassionate youth; a rooster who falls madly in love with his own image; a raccoon who finds happiness in life by learning to play the flute; and many more. Interspersed with the tales is a running dialogue between the duck, who would like to doctor the goose's act and get it on the road, and the goose, whose, ambitions are nonexistent. Anyone who has ever been involved in theater will find these discussions hilarious, but in the midst of the comedy sadness stands like a somber guest at a party. As with all good fables, the human condition becomes more poignant when we can see it in a different form.

Leonard Lubin's black-and-white illustrations for *The Little Swineherd* are graphic, elegant and show a deep understanding of the stories.

Diane Manuel (review date 2 October 1987)

SOURCE: "Adventures to Remember," in *Christian Science Monitor,* October 2, 1987, p. B4.

[*In the following review, Manuel writes that* Lily and the Lost Boy *is "a coming-of-age story that will be remembered both for its emotional impact and for the sensory impressions that linger long after the last page is turned."*]

Quick now—what was your favorite book as a child, and why? Did you love *Winnie the Pooh* for the sharing it taught—or because you never tired of visualizing Pooh Bear pretending to be a small black rain cloud, with all those bothersome bees buzzing about?

Did you read *The Five Little Peppers and How They Grew* under the covers at night because it was about family togetherness—or because you wanted to savor the smells and sounds of an old-fashioned Christmas?

Very often it's the details we remember best—the vivid evocations of time and place and character—that made our favorite books so real and believable, that gave them staying power.

A preview of this fall's new titles for children indicates there will be writing rich in detail. They come from both well-known and first-time authors, representing a number of popular genres: high fantasy and science fiction, historical fiction and humor, mystery and survival tales, as well as picture books.

One bold newcomer to children's publishing features a list that's strong on all counts. In its remarkable debut, Orchard Books, a division of Franklin Watts, Inc., of New York, is a microcosm of the best that's to come this season. Three intriguing titles prove the point.

Newbery Medalist Paula Fox, author of **The Slave Dancer, Blowfish Live in the Sea,** and **The Stone-Faced Boy,** is known for her sensitive portrayals of youngsters' often conflicting emotions.

In her first book for Orchard, **Lily and the Lost Boy,** Fox explores the jealousies that can crop up between an older brother and adoring younger sister, and also the idealistic tenderness that can rise above sibling rivalries. In the process she comes up with a strong story of tested friendship and compassion.

The setting is the Greek island of Thasos, where wild thyme blooms in the hills and fresh-caught octopus is hung to dry on clotheslines. Eleven-year-old Lily Corey and her 13-year-old brother, Paul, become fellow explorers for three months one spring while their professor father is on sabbatical. They dig for shards and coins at the local acropolis, and Paul even allows Lily to read aloud to him from her book of Greek myths.

Enter Jack Hemmings, a troubled American teen-ager who reminds Lily of "an engine racing, with no place to go." As Paul gradually turns his back on his family to spend more time with Jack, the tension builds. It culminates in a tragic evening that ends with the accidental death of a young Greek child.

It's grim ground in many ways, but author Fox balances the anxious moments with overflowing images of place and time—of weathered fishermen in sturdy caiques, of mandolin-like bouzouki music floating up from the village wharf, of ancient amphitheaters filled with today's applause.

Like another recent teen novel set in Greece, *The Morning of the Gods,* by Edward Fenton, **Lily and the Lost Boy** is a coming-of-age story that will be remembered both for its emotional impact and for the sensory impressions that linger long after the last page is turned.

Penny Blubaugh (review date February 1988)

SOURCE: A review of *Lily and the Lost Boy,* in *VOYA,* Vol. 10, No. 6, February 1988, pp. 279-80.

[*In the following review, Blubaugh admires Fox's portrayal of village life and of complicated emotional themes in* Lily and the Lost Boy.]

[In **Lily and the Lost Boy**], Lily, 12, and her 14 year old brother Paul are living on the small Greek island of Thasos where their father has taken the family with him while he's on sabbatical from his teaching job in Massachusetts. He's picked Thasos as a temporary home because not many English-speaking tourists visit and he's determined to learn as much about Greece and the Greeks as he can first hand.

Both children seem to love the island, are progressing well in Greek and are happy with each other's company for the first time in several years. As the day to day frustrations begin to die down and the Coreys become more attuned to the pace of the island, it begins to be almost a paradise except, as Lily says, for the vipers.

Then one morning as the children are visiting the Acropolis, they see a strange boy about Paul's age. Excited and curious Paul goes over to meet him, but Lily feels herself drawing away. Once met, Jack Hemmings, an American living with his father further up the island, begins to draw Paul in and Lily watches their new-found closeness drift away. At first she's angry with Jack, but as she watches and listens, as she sees Paul closing his family out and turning to Jack, she begins to wonder. Why is Jack never with his father? Why does his mother pay money to keep him away? Why do the islanders dislike Mr. Hemmings in spite of their admiration for his dancing?

Jack begins to spend more and more time with the Coreys and in spite of his ideas, things that drag Paul into delinquent situations, Lily starts to feel how much pain Jack carries. Finally Jack's recklessness takes the life of another child and after he runs away Lily feels that she must be the one to find him. Their return to Thasos makes her even more aware of his loneliness, but there's little she can do to help him. And finally, as the Coreys leave the island, Jack and Mr. Hemmings stand at the quay and watch, more separated together than they ever were apart.

This is a warm, poignant story that shows life in both its simplicity and its complexity. It paints a beautiful picture of village life in Greece, shows the goodness of life itself, but offers no easy solutions to the difficulties of living.

Ellen Fader (review date September-October 1991)

SOURCE: A review of *Monkey Island*, in *Horn Book Magazine*, Vol. LXVII, No. 5, September-October 1991, pp. 596-97.

[*In the following review, Fader praises Fox's deft handling of serious social issues in* Monkey Island.]

[In *Monkey Island*], eleven-year-old Clay Garrity awakens in the welfare hotel where he and his pregnant mother have lived for the last month to find his mother gone. His search for her leads him to a nearby park, where he becomes part of an encampment of homeless people, but a bout with pneumonia brings Clay's situation to the attention of the social service agencies, which place him with a foster family while they continue the quest for his absent mother. Although he is well cared for in the foster home, Clay especially misses the two homeless men who had become his surrogate family and who had helped him survive. He repeatedly visits the park until he meets up with one of the men, who has taken significant steps to better his life. In a poignant and promising ending, Clay, his new baby sister, and his mother, who now has a job, move into their own apartment. They have hope that Clay's father, who had deserted them after becoming depressed and defeated about his inability to find a job, will eventually reappear. Fox's story is neither an indictment of society nor a vehicle to proffer solutions for a growing national problem. It is instead an emotionally powerful story of one family's travail, one child's anxiety and fear, and the people who help that child until he and his mother are reunited. These are characters readers will understand and care about; Clay's universal struggle with the issue of what constitutes a home, his bewilderment over his abandonment by both his parents, and his ambivalence at his reunion with his mother are expertly and honestly played out. The novel individualizes the problems of homeless people and puts faces on those whom society has made faceless; readers' perceptions will be changed after reading the masterfully crafted *Monkey Island.*

Dinitia Smith (review date 10 November 1991)

SOURCE: "No Place to Call Home," in *New York Times Book Review*, November 10, 1991, p. 52.

[*In the following review, Smith assesses* Monkey Island *as*
an honest portrayal of homelessness, particularly the rarely dealt with issue of homelessness as it affects members of the middle class.]

One autumn morning 13-year-old Clay Garrity wakes up in a welfare hotel in Manhattan and discovers that his mother has left him. Clay's father, who has also disappeared, is an unemployed magazine art director. His mother, until recently, had a job working with computers. Clay is white, he has been to good schools (he can read *Robinson Crusoe*)—an atypical homeless child. He is the hero of *Monkey Island,* Paula Fox's delicate and moving novel, one of the first describing middle-class homelessness for young readers.

The sight of homeless people pushing shopping carts down the street or sleeping on benches in local parks has become a fact of life, and for children they are the ultimate representation of a terrifying fantasy—of parents leaving, of loss and displacement. How does a writer make the unbearable bearable without violating the basic truth of the situation?

Ms Fox, who has won an American Book Award for children's fiction for her novel *A Place Apart,* the Hans Christian Anderson Medal for her collected children's work and a Newbery Medal for the young adult novel *The Slave Dancer,* has written a relentless story that succeeds in conveying the bitter facts.

She depicts life in a welfare hotel precisely the way Clay's pregnant mother needs the sound of a portable radio all the time to drawn out her increasing despair, the way the woman next door cares—alone and lovingly—for her retarded son who sits all day watching television, "his feet turned out like a duck's feet." The elevator is a "a poison box," the halls are littered with trails of coffee grounds from leaking garbage bags. A trip to the bathroom can be a dangerous journey.

Eventually, Clay makes his way to a city park—called *Monkey Island* by thugs who prey on homeless people there. Like most of the newly homeless, Clay has trouble sleeping. The recent arrivals "were in a panic for days," one character observes. "They were also the angriest if someone or something woke them up in the middle of the night." Life is a constant, primal search. A portable toilet at a construction site is a gift, a broken water fountain means no way to wash that day. For an old woman, counting her few possessions over and over again is "a kind of housekeeping."

Although the focus of Ms. Fox's story is a middle-class family, she never lets us forget the way race and class affect destiny. When Clay catches pneumonia, his black friend, Buddy, wants to take him to a hospital but knows a taxi probably will not stop for him "*Nigger* is the longest word I know," says Buddy.

Eventually, Clay is placed in a foster home where people are kind. But, one wonders, how will Ms. Fox ever resolve Clay's abandonment? Will she stage a scene of false forgiveness? When Clay and his mother are finally reunited, his mother doesn't ask Clay to forgive her. "Sorry can't erase all that," his mother says. She can only hope that one day she and Clay will find a way "to go on caring for each other that's . . . beyond *sorry*."

Connie C. Rockman (review date July 1993)

SOURCE: A review of *Amzat and His Brothers: Three Italian Tales Remembered by Floriano Vecchi* by Paula Fox, in *School Library Journal,* Vol. 39, No. 7, July 1993, pp. 90-91.

[*In the following review, Rockman finds* Amzat and His Brothers: Three Italian Tales Remembered by Floriano Vecchi *too realistic and disturbing for children.*]

Fox retells three Italian folk-tales that were told to her by a friend who heard them from his grandfather when he was a child growing up in a pre-World War II Italian village. The tales are variations of familiar stories: "Mezgalten," for example, contains elements of "The Brementown Musicians" and "The Wolf and the Kids." Acts of violence may disturb some adults, as in the title story when Amzat and his wife trick his brothers into murdering their wives and then cause the drowning of the brothers. The third story shows the prejudice of villagers toward a woman and her son because of their habit of never bathing and the dull wits of the son. While the woman and son end their days living in a palace (and eventually learning the art of bathing), and the worst of their tormentors end up poorly, the depiction of the heckling is harsh. The people in these stories seem to be more rooted in real life than the usual archetypal folktale characters. A good welcome, but this isn't the one. McCully's pen-and-ink sketches add little.

Horn Book Magazine (review date July-August 1993)

SOURCE: A review of *Amzat and His Brothers: Three Italian Tales Remembered by Floriano Vecchi* by Paula Fox, in *Horn Book Magazine,* Vol. LXIX, No. 4, July-August 1993, pp. 468-69.

[*In the following review, the anonymous critic admires the traditional fairy tale tone and themes of* Amzat and His Brothers: Three Italian Tales Remembered by Floriano Vecchi.]

Explaining in her preface how these stories have come down to her "as a kind of unwritten library that is passed from generation to generation," Paula Fox has added her own distinctive voice before sending them on their evolutionary way. In the first tale, clever Amzat and his wife foil his greedy brothers' schemes to cheat him out of his property. The second story is a variation of "The Bremen Town Musicians," in which a rooster, ewe, donkey, cat, and dog band together to kill a wolf who has tormented them. And in the final story, this one in the noodlehead tradition, the author introduces Olimpia and her simpleton son Cucol, for whom a thought was a "beautiful cloud of meaning that he liked to study for a long time." Hounded out of their home by their neighbors, they go off into the woods, where through a series of slapstick misadventures they end up with an enormous bag of gold. Mother and son live out the rest of their days in wealth and luxury, while those villagers who had been the cause of their exile are reduced to living in the hovel that the two had abandoned. Paula Fox has retained the darker elements that are as much a part of folktales in their original forms as the humor. Justice is imposed with harsh and obliterating finality. Amzat's revenge on his brothers results not only in their deaths but in the death of an innocent shepherd as well. Emily McCully's drawings, with their heavy deep brown lines and animated characters, pick up both aspects of these intriguing tales.

Betsy Hearne (review date September 1993)

SOURCE: A review of *Western Wind*, in *The Bulletin of the Center for Children's Books,* September, 1993, Vol. 47, No. 1, pp. 9-10.

[*In the following review, the critic admires Fox's spare but evocative prose in* Western Wind.]

[In *Western Wind*], eleven-year-old Elizabeth Benedict believes the reason she's being sent to spend August with her grandmother in a primitive Maine island cottage is the newly born brother on whom her parents lavish attention. Paula Fox uses an isolated situation, as she has done before, to delve into a child's deepening awareness—here, of her grandmother's value as a person, a painter, and an elder facing death with dignity. Through interactions stripped bare by a simplified life devoid of electronic distractions or electric conveniences, the two characters replace their formal connection with an affectionate respect that contrasts ironically with the one other family on the island, who comprise an odd mix of overprotection and underestimation of each other. Elizabeth, her grandmother, and the vulnerable young island boy whom Elizabeth rescues in more ways than one, are fine portrayals of individualistic independence at different stages of a life spectrum. Always spare, Fox's style especially suits this taut narrative, into which she slips similes that are frequent but consciously plain to suit the setting: a bay is "like a tray holding bits of land on its metal-blue surface"; "the family is really like a small country"; "birds swooped and rose like torn strips of paper"; Elizabeth sees "a yellow bar of sunshine like the light at the bottom of a closed door" or stifles "a laugh that was rising in her throat like a bubble in a bottle" or watches interest fading from someone's face "like light dimming in a room." These are primarily visual images—almost cubist like some of Gran's paintings—but they become less decorative than inherent to plot and pace, as when Elizabeth realizes that the cottage room seems "beautiful, almost like a person she had begun to love" or when the supporting posts in the same room, which "had suggested trees or columns to Elizabeth, now looked like the stout wooden bars of a cage" around the island family fearful of having lost their little boy. It's seductive to start quoting a good writer, but perhaps Fox summarizes her own book best: "Make it up," orders the boy in soliciting Elizabeth to play his imaginative game. "You just need a little bit of a thing to start a story. Pretty soon, there's everything!"

Cyrisse Jaffee (review date 10 April 1994)

SOURCE: A review of *Western Wind*, in *New York Times Book Review*, April 10, 1994, p. 35.

[*In the following review, Jaffee finds* Western Wind *slightly melodramatic but admires the book's probing of human relationships without offering simplistic solutions.*]

[In *Western Wind*], to her dismay, 11-year-old Elizabeth Benedict has been sent to stay with Gran for a month by her parents, who have just brought home a new baby. Not surprisingly, Elizabeth is resentful and sullen, and the prospect of spending August with her "unpredictable and ungrandmotherly" Gran only adds to her unhappiness.

Gran—Cora Ruth Benedict—a painter whose attitudes and words are often as sharp and pointed as the rocky landscape she loves, has left the picturesque but tourist-ridden charm of Camden, Maine, to settle off the coast on rustic Pring Island. Unsentimental, proud and opinionated, Gran is a stickler for proper English usage, honesty and clean living.

So Elizabeth must grapple not only with the lack of electricity and indoor plumbing and with Gran's silences, but also with loneliness and boredom, fueled by the anger she feels about being abandoned by her parents. Meeting the only other family on the Island—John and Helen Herkimer

and their children, Deirdre and Aaron—doesn't seem to offer any solace, either.

Deirdre is sarcastic and unfriendly, and Aaron is a precocious, hyperactive child whose antics earn him a lot of attention. (It's no coincidence that the dynamics of the Herkimer family echo those of Elizabeth's.)

It is Aaron who animates the story. Like Elizabeth, he knows that his behavior alienates other people. "Sometimes when someone hugs me," he tells her, "I feel like an eagle has got me in its claws" It is the boy's disappearance one foggy night that reveals and tests the intricate ties—and love—that have bound these people together.

Despite the weakness of its minor characters and its somewhat melodramatic plot, *Western Wind,* in the tradition of the best young-adult fiction, manages to capture the essence of Elizabeth's transformation from a self-absorbed adolescent to a more tolerant, loving person. The lessons she learns are about making connections, which, as the skillful Paula Fox eloquently demonstrates, is what life, and art too, are all about. "We cannot forswear our integral connections with other people," Ms. Fox said in 1974 when she accepted the Newbery Medal for her novel *The Slave Dancer.* "I write to discover, over and over again, my connections with myself, with others. Each book deepens the question. It does not answer it." Within its familiar framework, *Western Wind* will gently lead the reader along the unsteady path toward discovery.

Paula Fox (essay date 1994)

SOURCE: "About Language," in *Ohio Review,* 1994, pp. 7-19.

[*In the following essay, Fox explores the ability of language and stories, at their best, to concretize the ephemeral and ambiguous nature of universal experience and what Fox considers the unfortunate bastardizing of language in contemporary parlance.*]

Great stories give us metaphors that flash upon the mind the way lightning flashes upon the earth, illuminating for a instant an entire landscape that had been hidden in the dark.

In some sense all stories are metaphors. There is mystery in the way they make recognizable what we think we have not experienced. Four hundred years ago, Edmund Spenser, the English poet, wrote: "The story of any man's real experience finds its startling parallel in that of everyone of us." It is as though at the core of humanness, at least in young humans, there is a readiness for news not only from the world apprehended by the senses but from those other worlds reached through imagination.

In an essay on story, a contemporary writer, Carol Bly, has written: "The human mind recognizes a feeling only when it has words for it—which means someone else has conversed in it. When Conrad Aiken in his story *Silent Snow, Secret Snow* tells the reader how much the boy loves his beautiful imagined inner life—the snow—we recognize the same love in our own inner life. If we hadn't had his story, and others like it, we might never recognize how dear we hold our private perception of the universe."

A writer gathers up all the seemingly random elements of life, stares into the roiling mass of feeling and thought that is at once the affliction and peculiar blessing of being human, and finds a design—that is, a story.
            —*Paula Fox*

A writer gathers up all the seemingly random elements of life, stares into the roiling mass of feeling and thought that is at once the affliction and peculiar blessing of being human, and finds a design—that is, a story. If it is a good story, if it is after truth, it intimates what is beyond words. If it is a poor story, no matter how skilled its use of language, it is *only* words, and a reader senses in it an intrusive self-congratulation like that suggested by a Buddhist homily that tells of a man who pointed at the moon but wanted the onlooker to notice only his pointing finger.

Everyone's story matters. Each story is, one might say, a word in a larger story, the intimations of which can reach us in myriad ways, through religion and philosophy, or in a sudden tremor of sensibility that, for an instant, can penetrate the fog of our ignorance not only of why we are here, but where *here* is.

"Maybe we're here," wrote the poet Rainer Maria Rilke, "only to say: house, / bridge, well, gate, jug, olive-tree, window— / at most, pillar, tower—but to say them, remember, / oh! to say them in a way that the things themselves / never dreamed of existing so intensely." Rilke's words make me think of the immense silence into which we hold up our small bundle of words. It is like the blue light of our small planet glimmering in the darkness all around.

The language of great poets and writers alludes to what we cannot speak. It enables us to question the surface of life. Robert Louis Stevenson said there aren't enough words in Shakespeare to express the merest fraction of human experience in one hour. But, he wrote, "a particular thing once said in words is so definite and memorable that it makes us forget the absence of many which remain unexpressed, like a bright window in a distant view."

The urgency with which we describe our passages through life appears involuntary, as though the impulse to record the journey is as powerful as the impulse to speak—a thing embedded in the genetic make-up of our species. "To begin my life with the beginning of my life, I record that I was born (as I have been informed and believe) on a Friday at 12 o'clock at night. It was remarked that the clock began to strike and I began to cry simultaneously," so David Copperfield announces his birth. When I first read that opening passage—after all, the simple statement of arrival anyone who has lived and anyone alive at this moment could make—I was 10, and I was electrified. I've since then read it to students, some very young, some old, and I've seen on most of their faces that startled attention that gripped me when I was a child. It is downright and plain, but the stroke of art in it, I think, lies in the word *believe*. It is exactly the light word to convey David Copperfield's nature, and to suggest his destiny, which is to unfold in the hundreds of pages that follow. It is a humorous word in its context, faintly, in fact, *disbelieving*.

Record-keeping began millennia before Charles Dickens was born, in cave paintings, in the lists on shards of the pottery of vanished civilizations, in the accounts, journals, logs, and diaries discovered in those first written languages of which we have any knowledge. There is the unwritten library too, what used to be called the oral tradition, tales passed from generation to generation; generations that lived before the blind poet we call Homer told of wily Odysseus, of Hector, the great warrior, of the mischief of Paris and Helen's beauty—a library that we must hope will endure long after our own time, long after the life and death of another blind poet, Jorge Luis Borges, who died in 1986, 2700 years after Homer spoke his poem.

Poetry and imaginative literature are record-keeping of all that animates what we name, variously, the soul, the psyche, spirit, mind, and heart. But words are not the things they name. They are things themselves, potent and galvanizing, that can arouse and disturb, provoke laughter or murder, and even instruct us as to their limitations when, after we think we have explained everything, we are confronted by existence itself.

Language can only point at reality, like a mute gesturing frantically at the unnameable. Still, we are driven to speak, to try to understand, to try to penetrate mysteries, to interpret the not altogether reliable news we receive from our senses, to "get it." And in some fashion, if insufficiently, we *can* get it, such is the power of language.

But it is fragile, too, and always at risk. It is so much easier to resort to the day's catch-words, its jargon, when one is in the grip of fear and confusion, startled by the intimation of the chaos that can turn life upside down on any sunny morning.

There is a great affair now in this country about dialects, about their right to claim equal standing with the English that has dominated written and spoken discourse for centuries. Yet English itself is a dialect. It belongs to a Germanic sub-family of Indo-European, whose vast range includes such disparate sub-families as Arcadian Greek, Old Norse, Celtic, and, far far back, hieroglyphic Hittite. All languages are dialects, constantly in flux, shrinking or swelling, subject to the migrations and settlements and conflicts of human history.

Years ago, among the many jobs I had in my youth was one that involved reading South American and Mexican novels for a movie studio. I was paid $6 to $9 for each book, depending on its length, and I was obliged to summarize plots to present to producers who would judge whether or not they were movie material. I was hired because I could speak Spanish. Or so I thought. What I discovered, after my first attempts at reading these works, was that what I spoke was Cuban, itself composed of dialects, with words absorbed from Africa and China, from native Carib, as well as the varied Latin-rooted Spanish, colored by idioms from all the provinces of Spain from which colonizers came to Cuba. For the novels of Chile and Bolivia, Argentina, Ecuador, and Peru, I needed Quechua, or at least some familiarity with a few of its 28 sub-groups. The job didn't last long, and I was careful after it to qualify what I meant when I said I could speak and read Spanish.

What interests me as a working writer are the ways in which we use language to elucidate reality or to falsify it in whatever dialect we claim as ours, and another way in which we don't use it for anything except as vocal padding around nothing at all, as in a brief exchange I overheard as I walked on the street behind two men.

"It's going to rain. You know what I'm saying?" asked one.

"I hear you," replied the other.

Then there are those dry-as-dust phrases that seduce speaker and listeners into thinking something important is actually being said, as in an interview of a sociologist on a radio program I listened to. The sociologist became so unhinged by his use of the phrase "in terms of" that it seemed to take on physical properties, like a maze, from which he was unable to escape. At last he actually said, "in terms of . . . in terms of. . . ." There was a broken giggle, silence, then a burst of vapid music during which, I imagined, the sociologist was led away to rest for a while.

It is not hard to find words that have been so mauled that their original meanings have leaked out of them like air from punctured balloons, words, for example, like *creative* and *concept,* that are applied recklessly to all manner of human endeavor, and are used to characterize not only the effort involved in the deployment of armed rockets in space, but also the latest design in running shoes for the middle-aged jogger.

The French poet Paul Verlaine said one hundred years ago, "When you hear the word *concept,* get up at once and leave the room."

It is the lingo of psychology and sociology, initially devoted to the exploration and explication of human community and behavior, that has made singular contributions to the disintegration of meaning in language. I think of a middle-aged woman I knew, who, when she learned her father was close to death, said at once that death could be a "very enriching experience." Before her emotions could be engaged by this momentous event in her life, she had sped away from it, staking out a claim for the enrichment of her own soul before the anguish of a death could get the drop on her.

Even in minor matters we are too impatient to permit ourselves to be as puzzled as, in truth, we are. We rush to define events before we begin to sense what we feel about them. We are astonished, then chagrined and frightened at the fluid, shifting nature of our own feelings. We refuse to put up with uncertainty. So we write off continents of human mysteries with feeble clichés; we reduce the living person standing right in front of us to a heap of sociological or psychological platitudes.

Of course we put names to things to help ourselves begin to understand them, and, in the social sciences, to establish reference points from which to construct theories about human behavior. But there is a counter-tendency. We also name them so as to dismiss them and rid ourselves of the hard work of reflection. It appears to be the tendency of these disciplines to grow rigid in time if an opposing impulse does not come into play to break up the frozen mass of certainties.

The most cursory glance at changes in thinking about psychology over the last 50 years suggests we can only hypothesize about the nature of human personality. New information is always arriving. It may be partly that because we do not have the steadying forms of older cultures to fall back upon, we are, as a nation, more open to the new. And it is a great thing not to be sealed into the tombs of the past, a great thing to resist the impulse to ransom openness in order to preserve dead tradition. But the danger is to hail what is new as absolute truth—until the next *new* comes along to displace it.

Nietzsche observed that everything absolute leads to pathology. A contemporary physicist, Dr. David Bohm, writes that "most categories are so familiar to us that they are used almost unconsciously . . . it is possible for categories to become so fixed a part of the intellect that the mind finally becomes engaged in playing false to support them."

What I am thinking about is the deadening of language, an extreme alienation from living experience which manifests itself in words that have no resonance, a language of labels that numbs our power to feel, our sensibilities, and stifles our innate capacity to question, to turn things over in our minds and reflect upon them. During the Vietnam war, the phrase *body count* entered the American vocabulary. It is an ambiguous phrase, inorganic, even faintly sporting. It distances us from the terrible reality of the dead and mutilated.

The language of labels is like money issued with nothing of intrinsic value behind it. And it is dangerous. George Orwell wrote that if thought corrupts language, language can also corrupt thought. A while ago I saw an appalling instance of language gone berserk in the words of a woman interviewed in the parking lot of a small office building in which a man had just shot 7 people to death. Yes, she had seen it all, she told the television reporter, just as she was about to get into her car. For a moment she ducked out of camera range, then reappeared clasping in her arms her son, a boy of 5 or 6. "He saw it all, too, and it was a real learning experience," she said.

Last fall, as schools were opening, a series of interviews brought another child and his mother before the camera. The mother smiled dotingly and ruefully as she confessed she had paid nearly $100 for the running shoes her 8-year old was wearing to his first day in school. No, she replied to the reporter's question, she really couldn't afford them but felt she had to buy them. Whereupon the 8-year-old piped up, "You have to do what your peer group does," a non-thought he may have picked up from television, that great forum of shiftlessness and banality.

Why has the word *indicate* taken the place of *said,* as in "The journalist indicated the building had been bombed"? What is the gain? And consider "like," which has broken loose from hip talk, once its main province, and taken root in the daily language of observation and emotion, so involuntary as to seem a neurological tic. "I feel like sad," said a youth after the shooting murder of a classmate in a gun- and gang-beleaguered Brooklyn high school.

There is to me a significant shade of difference between *sad* and *like sad.* Perhaps "like," meaningless and automatic, served to postpone, if only for a split-second, the realization of a real death. To say *I feel sad* is concrete. But as Orwell observed in 1949, the whole tendency of modern prose is away from concreteness. I think of *loving, caring, sharing, healing,* the four new horsemen—or horsepeople—of a limp apocalypse. I think of the vast range of human emotion and need which is to be packaged by them, its paradoxes and contrarieties smoothed flat. I think of the way their deep meaning has been made meager by mindless use. They have become formulas. In a publisher's ad I saw in the *New York Times,* a plug for a murder mystery began, "lovingly written. . . ."

Picture, if you will, Macbeth and Othello, the Karamazov brothers, David Copperfield, Anna Karenina, Tess of the D'Urbervilles, Lady Chatterley, and even Scarlett O'Hara, in the waiting room of a contemporary therapist, desperate to discuss their problems of low self-esteem. "Self-esteem," its presence or absence, is to guarantee success or abysmal failure, as it seeks to explicate all human behavior, as though human beings have not waked in the mornings to do the daily drudgery of the world, made art and science, built up civilizations, and given charity and hope and love to each other in famine and war and pestilence, when they were half-mad with suffering and bewilderment.

Should we not honor and esteem the life in the self as well as the self in life?

In a book whose title I have forgotten, I recall reading that American English as it is routinely spoken—and apart from the often impenetrable jargon of specialists—consists of about 142 words, and that this number is shrinking rapidly. The world may end as T. S. Eliot intimated, not with a bang but with a whimper, at least the world of mind.

The rock-bottom significance of language, its organic nature, can be exemplified in the difference between the German of Goethe and Heine, and the German spoken in the concentration camps of World War II. The latter speech was totally barbarized to fit the circumstance. While he was a prisoner in Auschwitz, the Italian-Jewish writer, Primo Levi, noted that the German infinitive, to eat, when applied to the feeding of prisoners, was rendered as *fressen,* which in good German is applied only to the feeding of animals. When violence is done to people, it is preceded by violence done to and in language.

A few months ago, a representative of Louis Farrakhan's Nation of Islam asserted during a speech he made at Kean College in New Jersey, that Jews have stolen rubies, pearls, and diamonds from every country in the world, which, he said, explained the word, *jewelry.* He used his own gross ignorance to invent an etymology that incites to murder.

As we grow up, we learn to make distinctions between what we call real and what we call *imagined,* almost always at the expense of the latter. Yet it is imagination that brings us intimations of the elusive truth of being, and of what Carl Jung called "the terrible ambiguity of the moment." Imagination is as stifled by obscure and ornate language as it is by psychological and sociological cant. And there are too many experts in those fields who believe there are answers to anything, and anything is defined by them as that for which they have answers.

I read the following statement in a newspaper column: "The youngest sibling in a family unit, encouraged by her role models, has begun to communicate interpersonally." Is this illuminating about the onset of speech? Is there a way to communicate other than interpersonally? What is a role model? A person? A call to Central Casting? Is life a performance? Recently I reread E. M. Forster's novel *A Room with a View,* and this passage struck me: "She gave up trying to understand herself and joined the vast armies of the benighted, who follow neither the heart nor the brain, and march to their destiny by catchwords. The armies are full of pleasant and pious folk. But they have yielded to the only enemy that matters—the enemy within. They have sinned against passion and truth, and vain will be their striving after virtue."

Now we have arrived in a time where the summoning of imagination to put the self in another's place, that most fundamental function of writing, perhaps of human community itself, is under siege.

—*Paula Fox*

A sculptor acquaintance, who teaches art at the Pratt Institute, told me about a student in her class who announced, "I can't relate to him," when the sculptor began the semester with a lecture on Leonardo da Vinci. The student, adept at ideological bullying, went on to say, "Da Vinci has no relevance for today's artists." Used in such a manner, relevance can only be capricious, a thing that can change from month to month as fashion does, a powerful constraint on the effort to see beyond the immediate and opportune.

An implication underlying this phrase *relate to* is that what one doesn't recognize as directly pertaining to one's own life is, at best, of no interest and, at worst, menacing. How are people to learn with an attitude that is so inimical to spiritual growth, to the spirit of inquiry that has wrung from our species its best thought and art? "I can't identify . . . I can't relate to. . . ." What is the consequence of these notions, if not their intent, but to consign to oblivion all that is unlike us, all that we are not habituated to?

The literature of imagination cannot survive such strictures as these. It is a paradox that in this most "now" atmosphere, where only the "new" is supposed to engage us, the opposite occurs. Novels must substantiate what we think we already know. How like the affliction borne by contemporary composers: If it isn't Mozart, if I can't whistle it, burn it! The ungenerous, narrow ideas of relevance, of self-identification must be reinvented. They perpetuate the provincialism of self. They banish the interesting from life.

When I was young, I, and the people I knew, read novels for news. *News* is the very meaning of the word *novel.* We read for the transforming experience of losing ourselves in a great story, and when it ended, turning our still dazzled eyes and attention to daily life, of finding our lost selves returned to us, consoled and deepened.

It was the tail-end of the Depression. War was imminent. A person who had been to college was an oddity. We were poor. The circumstances of most of the people I knew were like mine: grim. Yet we read and exchanged books. I still have a worn copy of *Tender is the Night* by F. Scott Fitzgerald that may have been given to me, or else which I pinched. And I remember with what inexpressible delight I found in "Ode to a Nightingale," by Keats, the very words of that title. I read the novel while I looked for miserable jobs and cheap places to live. I read *The Idiot,* too, and *A Passage to India,* and novels by D. H. Lawrence and Faulkner and Hemingway and O'Hara and Tolstoy, and Chekhov's stories. And I and the people I knew, as we scrounged to live, talked and talked about them.

For some of us, it was the way we began to learn about the world. The novel, unlike other art forms, contains things that are, in a sense, alien to it—science and history, religion, music, art, and above all, psychology.

"People in a novel need not be like real ones," Ortega y Gasset wrote. "It is enough they are possible."

What great novelists and poets try to imagine is truth. And truth is like the light that falls, without prejudice or judgment, on the French Riviera of the '20s, 19th-century Russia, a mining town in England, the snows of Kilimanjaro, and the narrow dusty roads of a southern hamlet. The light fell, too, on me, on the people I knew, who were like beads from a broken string, rolling about the country, trying to find places where we could exist. Literature and poetry gathered us up.

Reading was healing. It went with love and caring. Books were shared.

Now we have arrived in a time where the summoning of imagination to put the self in another's place, that most fundamental function of writing, perhaps of human community itself, is under siege. I heard an interview on the National Public Radio in which the interviewer, a woman, asked a male novelist, in a disbelieving voice, "You're writing about a woman? From the inside? How fascinating!"

She may have been simply ignorant of all that literature has aspired to. I suspect not. I suspect her posture was disingenuous, dictated by the new truth squads among us who command writers to write only about their own genders and ethnicities and circumstances. She had lost, or never attained, that ordinary sense, that it requires an imaginative leap over the fence of one's gender to understand the opposite sex, and that that leap is propelled by the same kind of imagination needed to understand anything.

The ideology of these truth squads sanctifies the differences between people, attributes only virtue to one group, only villainy to another. The squads have been always a part of the human community, ordering people about, telling them how to think, and in extreme instances, cutting out their tongues when they were displeased.

That fence I spoke about is turned into a metaphysical wall, impossible to scale. Even to try is an offense, or, as was suggested in the interview, peculiar. People who claim that no one has the authority to write about them except themselves are really asserting that they are unimaginable.

I cannot conceive of a more devastating isolation than that suggested by the idea that I am unimaginable except to someone of the same sex and background, the same age and experience of life. That is—a clone of myself. What unutterable boredom!

There is no such clone. We are as individual as our thumb prints, a perception that ought not be confined to police stations. Writers have always known it. They have been obliged by the nature of their work to break through the arbitrary barriers erected by that tribalism which may be yet another original sin. Or so it would seem from its consequences today and throughout human history. Writers have been obliged to go against the sulk of passing ideologies, to reveal, as great clowns do, the underside of our nervous certainties, our crippling and murderous follies.

Hard and unremitting labor is what writing is. Yet it is in that labor that I feel the weight and force of life. That is its nettlesome reward. It is not usually easy to convince people in writing courses just how much unremitting labor is required of a writer. Gene Tunney, a writer of the '40s, said: "Writing is easy. You just sit there staring at a blank sheet of paper until drops of blood form on your forehead."

Sentimentality, as opposed to sentiment, is another enemy of writing. Sentimentality says: only feelings matter, thought doesn't matter; words don't matter. That's like telling a pianist that it is of small consequence if you play B-flat instead of the C-sharp that is written on the score. It's the feeling that counts. Tell that to a musician. Tell a writer language doesn't matter. Words, like notes, have tempo and color and innate sequence, and they are as elusive as will-o-the-wisps—the right words, that is, the ones we must struggle to find.

None of us, or very few, I think, are partial to slow, ruthless wearying effort. Yet there comes a time when you know that ruthless effort is what you must exert. There is no other way, and along that way you will find such limitations in yourself as to make you gasp with the knowledge of them. Yet, still, you work on. If you have done that for a long time, something will happen to you. You will succeed in becoming dogged. You will have become resolute about one thing—you go to your desk day after day, and you try to work. You give up the hope you can come to a conclusion about yourself as a writer. You give up conclusion.

A critic of the '20s, John Middleton Murry, wrote a definition of the writer's work: "A writer does not really come to conclusions about life, he discovers a quality in it. His emotions, reinforcing one another gradually form in him a habit of emotion; certain kinds of objects and incidents impress him with a peculiar significance. This emotional bias or predilection is what I have ventured to call the writer's mode of experience; it is by virtue of this mysterious accumulation of past emotions that the writer . . . is able to accomplish the miracle of giving to the particular the weight and force of the universal."

My Spanish grandmother told me stories of her life in Spain before and after she was sent at the age of 16 to marry a man she had never seen. Some stories were comical, some were filled with dread. My grandfather, a man from Asturia, owned a plantation far from Havana. His very young bride was plunged into a 19th-century colonial world that is now gone forever. He died just after the Spanish-American War. Her life was changed violently again when she left the plantation, most of which had been burned to the ground during the war, and came to the United States.

What I recall about her stories, told to me in fragments over the years I lived with her in a rather mean little suburb on Long Island, was an underlying elegiac note, a puzzled mourning for the past. Every story, as substantial, as palpable, as the kitchen table where we often sat, or in the tiny living room where sunlight fell upon a worn carpet through the rusted bars of a fire escape, had a subtext, and it was its melancholy note I can still hear.

Concrete stories, transcendental meanings; surface and depth. Writing is a struggle to understand the mystery of human life. Writers—real writers—do not claim the discovery of truth. What they attempt to arrest is that reality we embody so that we can bring it closer to the light of consciousness. Stories re-invent the world so that we can look at it. Stories are those bright windows of Robert Louis Stevenson's, shining in the darkness that ever threatens to shroud them.

"It sometimes seems to me," Franz Kafka begins a letter to his friend, Max Brod, "that the nature of art in general, the existence of art, is explicable solely in terms of making possible the exchange of truthful words from person to person." Such a claim for language, for story, for writing that holds both writer and reader accountable to each other, reminds us that reading is the great answering art to the art of fiction.

The Greek word for reading means: recognition.

Roger Sutton (review date March 1995)

SOURCE: A review of *The Eagle Kite*, in *Bulletin of the Center for Children's Books*, Vol. 48, No. 7, March 1995, pp. 234-35.

[*In the following review, Sutton finds* The Eagle Kite *too ambiguous in its handling of the subject matter.*]

When Liam's mother Katherine tells him that his father Philip contracted AIDS from a blood transfusion, Liam knows she's lying. He knows from his school sex ed classes that such a risk has become near-impossible, but he also suddenly remembers, "clearer every moment like a photograph negative in a developing tank," the time three years ago when he saw his father secretly embrace a young man on the beach near the family's summer cottage. Now Philip has moved back to that cottage, leaving Liam and Katherine in New York with many secrets between them. This is a tough portrait of a family in crisis, each member struggling between love and the betrayals of that love, lying to themselves and each other about what is really going on. But while Fox must be commended for avoiding didacticism or sentimentality, she seems reluctant to tackle either her subject or story head on, substituting metaphor for emotional engagement. Too much is outlined or off-stage, with past events and memories rendered in a pluperfect tense that has a distancing effect ("During the year he'd

been away, Liam had had no desire to see him at all"). The best scenes are those where Liam visits Philip at the cottage and confronts him ("You killed our family") only to be answered in equable manner ("Nobody is killed except me"). Even here, though, the conversations often turn fuzzy and ponderous about time and light-years, and readers are likely to get lost in the ambiguities. When Liam asks, in a conversation that had, we think, been about Philip's now-dead lover Geoff, "Can you say how it was? What it was?," we're not sure what he's asking; when Philip answers, "It breaks over you like a huge wave. You go under. Some people swim out of the wave. I couldn't," we don't know what to think. What is "it"? Love? Betrayal? Homosexuality? The book gets better and clearer in its last third. Philip's death scene is written with compassion and a restraint that never turns into remove; here Fox reveals her gift for showing, in brief and simple language, the ways people discover each other and themselves.

Claudia Morrow (review date April 1995)

SOURCE: A review of *The Eagle Kite*, in *School Library Journal*, Vol. 41, No. 4, April 1995, pp. 150, 153.

[*In the following review, Morrow praises* The Eagle Kite *for its honest portrayal of both deeply personal and socially charged contemporary family issues.*]

[In *The Eagle Kite*], Liam, a high school freshman, learns that his father is dying of AIDS. Suddenly, his comfortable family is in pieces, and his father has gone to live in a seashore cottage two hours from the family's city apartment. Distanced from both parents by secrets each of them seems compelled to keep, Liam remembers having seen his father embrace a young man years before—a friend, his father had said. In the remainder of the book, Liam and his parents wrestle with truths that encompass not just disappointment and betrayal, but intense love. This is far more than a problem novel. AIDS is integral to the plot, the issue is handled well, and the character who has AIDS is portrayed sympathetically, but the book's scope is broader than that. It is a subtly textured exploration of the emotions of grief that will appeal to the same young people drawn to Mollie Hunter's *A Sound of Chariots* (1972) and Cynthia Rylant's *Missing May* (1992). Dramatic tension is palpable, sustained in part by a dazed, timeless quality in Liam's slow reckoning with loss. The characters are neither idealized nor demonized, and Fox's take on Liam as a confused, seethingly angry, tight-lipped, surreptitiously tender teenager has the ring of authenticity. Some in the target audience may find the action too slow or the mood too dark, but those who persevere will be rewarded by the novel's truthfulness.

Nancy Vasilakis (review date September-October 1995)

SOURCE: A review of *The Eagle Kite*, in *Horn Book Magazine*, Vol. LXXI, No. 4, September-October 1995, pp. 608-9.

[*In the following review, Vasilakis asserts that, although the themes in* The Eagle Kite *may be difficult for teenagers to absorb, the book is ultimately worth the effort.*]

Liam Cormac was ten years old when he saw his father on the beach embracing another man. He has never spoken of the incident and has repressed the memory of it—until now, in his first year of high school, when he learns that his father is dying of AIDS. The family, unable to confront the truth of Philip Cormac's homosexuality, enters a period of denial and individual withdrawal. Philip leaves their apartment and moves into a small cabin on the New Jersey shore. Liam and his mother speak little to each other and visit Philip once a month. The time spent with him is awkward, silent, and ultimately unfruitful. Liam makes frequent treks to the public library where he furtively hunts up information about the disease. He suppresses his questions and fears and knowledge from everyone, and his resentment grows until he feels compelled to hurl at his father the full force of his anger. He travels alone to his father's cabin on the day before Thanksgiving, and the two finally begin to talk. To his surprise, Liam learns that his father feels as powerless as he, and that he is in the midst of his own search for understanding. Philip's dying becomes a time of dignity and reaffirmation for all three members of the family. Paula Fox has taken on a difficult subject and suffused it with a beauty of form and style that is distinctively her own. The evolution of Liam's emotions from voiceless anger and an abiding sense of loss to acceptance and love, a journey paralleled by his mother's, is described with painstaking honesty. This will be a hard novel for teens to absorb, but well worth the effort.

English Journal (review date November 1996)

SOURCE: A review of *The Eagle Kite*, in *English Journal*, Vol. 85, No. 7, November 1996, p. 88.

[*In the following review, the anonymous critic finds* The Eagle Kite *a "haunting exploration of guilt."*]

Although **The Eagle Kite** is probably the shortest and easiest of the Honor Books to read, its haunting exploration of guilt may make it one of the most complex. First, is the guilt that thirteen-year-old Liam feels for hating his parents. He hates his mother for lying to him about how his father got AIDS. She said it was from a blood transfusion his father had during an appendicitis operation, but Liam knows from sex education class that blood transfusions have "been safe for years." Liam hates his father for loving a young man named Geoff and getting AIDS from him, and Liam hates himself for joining in the web of lies by pretending that he believes his mother and by telling his friends that his father has cancer.

Liam is shocked to realize that he and his father and mother aren't a family anymore; they are like strangers mouthing words that someone else has written for them. One night after supper when "there had been no conversation at all," Liam's dad announces that he's "going away for a bit. Not far," just to a cottage on a beach that's about two hours away. "It's better for all of us," says Liam's mother, and Liam suddenly realizes "They're enemies."

Liam and his mother pay monthly courtesy visits to his father, but during the second Thanksgiving weekend that the father is at the cottage, Liam decides to go by himself for a visit. His aunt who has come for the holiday is horrified at the idea, but Liam's mother defends his decision, and Liam "was suddenly happy! He'd forgotten what it was like—to be with his mother in this way, united, defended."

The visit itself isn't so happy. Terrible words are exchanged in which he tells his father what he knows, but instead of feeling better, he feels worse and decides that "The best thing was to know nothing. And he'd given up the second best, to know and not tell." This was the darkness before the dawn, and by the end of the story Liam is able to confess to his mother that the reason he never told her that he knew how his father had gotten sick was that "If I had told you, then it would have been really true." However, at this point, it's a truth that Liam can face even if he can't fully understand it.

From a literary standpoint, it is interesting that Fox's title of **The Eagle Kite** is so much like M. E. Kerr's *Night Kites* (1986). In both stories, young boys are given a special kite to fly at the beach, one by a big brother who is gay and one by a father who is gay. The kites come to symbolize the loneliness and the bravery of the individual men as they combat both societal prejudices and the devastating effects of their illness.

Additional coverage of Fox's life and career is contained in the following sources published by Gale: *Authors and Artists for Young Adults*, Vol. 3; *Contemporary Authors*, Vols. 73-76; *Contemporary Authors New Revision Series*, Vols. 20, and 36; *Children's Literature Review*, Vols. 1, and 44; *Dictionary of Literary Biography*, Vol. 52; *Junior DISCovering Authors*; *Major Authors and Illustrators for Children and Young Adults*; *Major Twentieth-Century Writers*; and *Something about the Author*, Vols. 17, and 60.

The Woman Warrior

Maxine Hong Kingston

(Born Maxine Ting Ting Hong) American autobiographer, novelist, journalist, essayist, and short story writer.

The following entry provides analysis and criticism of *The Woman Warrior*. For further information on Kingston's life and career, see *CLC*, Volumes 12, 19, and 58.

INTRODUCTION

A highly acclaimed memoirist, Kingston integrates autobiographical elements with Asian legend and fictionalized history to delineate cultural conflicts confronting Americans of Chinese descent. Frequently studied in a variety of academic disciplines, her works bridge two civilizations in their examination of social and familial bonds from ancient China to contemporary California. As an American-born daughter of stern immigrant parents, Kingston relates the anxiety that often results from clashes between radically different cultural sensibilities. Her exotic, myth-laden narratives are informed by several sources: the ordeals of emigrant forebears who endured brutal exploitation as they labored on American railroads and cane plantations; the "talk-stories," or cautionary tales of ancient heroes and family secrets told by her mother; and her own experiences as a first-generation American with confused cultural allegiances. From these foundations, Kingston forms epic chronicles of the Chinese immigrant experience that are esteemed for their accurate and disturbing illumination of such social patterns as Asian cultural misogyny and American institutional racism. Her 1976 autobiography, *The Woman Warrior: Memoirs of a Girlhood among Ghosts,* which won the general nonfiction award from the National Book Critics Circle, is a chronicle of Kingston's confrontation with her dual heritage.

Plot and Major Characters

The Woman Warrior is a personal, unconventional work that seeks to reconcile Eastern and Western conceptions of female identity. Kingston eschews chronological plot and standard nonfiction techniques in her memoir, synthesizing ancient myth and imaginative biography to present a kaleidoscopic vision of female character. The narrative begins with Kingston's mother's brief caveat concerning No Name Woman, young Maxine's paternal aunt, whose disrepute has rendered her unmentionable. Left in their village by her emigré husband, No Name Woman became pregnant—perhaps by rape—and was forced by the villagers to drown herself and her baby. Affirming traditional attitudes, Maxine's

mother, Brave Orchid, describes such practices as foot-binding and the sale of girls as slaves, and she threatens Maxine with servitude and an arranged marriage to a retarded neighborhood boy. Subsequent chapters, however, provide sharp contrast to these bleak visions, for Brave Orchid also recites the colorful legend of Fa Mu Lan, the woman warrior who wielded a sword to defend her hamlet. Kingston then describes Brave Orchid's own incongruent character; independent enough to become one of rural China's few female doctors, she returned to her customary submissive role upon joining her husband in America. The book is divided into five sections; Kingston's character is central to the second and fifth sections, in each instance identifying herself with Fa Mu Lan.

Major Themes

The Woman Warrior was described by Paul Gray as "drenched in alienation," and is also characterized by ambiguity, because, as Gray pointed out, it "haunts a region somewhere between autobiography and fiction." The memoir concerns both issues of culture and gender, and illustrates the various forces that shaped Kingston's childhood experience. The book's subtitle, *Memoirs of a Girlhood among Ghosts,* alludes to the ghosts that abounded in Kingston's childhood—not only the ghosts of her ancestors that peopled her mother's stories, but the Americans who, because they were "foreigners," were considered "ghosts" by her mother. Jane Kramer commented that young Maxine, "in a country full of ghosts, is already a half-ghost to her mother." Kingston's narrative delineates the conflicting images of womanhood handed down to her by her mother, illustrated by the myths of heroic women that stand in sharp contrast to the long-standing system of female oppression in China. Diane Johnson remarked that "messages which for Western girls have been confusingly obscured by the Victorian pretense of woman worship are in the Chinese tradition elevated to epigram: 'When fishing for treasures in the flood, be careful not to pull in girls.'"

Critical Reception

Critics lauded Kingston's fanciful description and poetic diction, through which she imparts her fear and wonder of Chinese legacies. Her memoir has been praised as a masterfully written, exceptional testament to the rich heritage that is often lost or forgotten by emigrants and their children after they settle in the United States and must adapt to American society. *The Woman Warrior* aroused some controversy among critics who maintained that Kingston was presenting a false impression of Chinese culture and traditions. Critics particularly took issue with Kingston's depiction of Chinese men and society in general as misogynist and what they deemed her loose, inaccurate renderings of Chinese myths, which, they argue, she presents as fact. Critics also faulted Kingston for taking liberties with the traditional genre of autobiography, including fictional elements in her narrative that are offered as fact. Other critics defended Kingston's narrative, and argued that it was not the author who classified her work as nonfiction. William McPherson called *The Woman Warrior* "a strange, sometimes savagely terrifying and, in the literal sense, wonderful story of growing up caught between two highly sophisticated and utterly alien cultures, both vivid, often menacing and equally mysterious." Jane Kramer remarked: "[*The Woman Warrior*] shocks us out of our facile rhetoric, past the clichés of our obtuseness, back to the mystery of a stubbornly, utterly foreign sensibility. . . . Its sources are dream and memory, myth and desire. Its crises are crises of a heart in exile from roots that terrorize and bind it."

PRINCIPAL WORKS

The Woman Warrior: Memoirs of a Girlhood among Ghosts (autobiography) 1976
China Men (autobiography) 1980

Hawaii One Summer (essays) 1987
Through the Black Curtain (essays) 1987
Tripmaster Monkey: His Fake Book (novel) 1989

CRITICISM

Deborah Homsher (review date Autumn 1979)

SOURCE: A review of *The Woman Warrior,* in *Iowa Review,* Vol. 10, No. 4, Autumn, 1979, pp. 93-8.

[*In the following review of* The Woman Warrior, *Homsher lauds the volume and analyzes Kingston's fictionalized approach to autobiography.*]

Reading **The Woman Warrior,** one gets an immediate impression that its writer has worked hard to form the book. Her memories of a Chinese-American girlhood in California are spliced with myths and anecdotes told by her imposing and thoroughly Chinese mother. Chapters are arranged in blocks against opposing chapters, some gaps bridged with cries of self-doubt or victory, while others are left for the reader to interpret. Kingston breaks up time as she breaks up the usual distinctions between fact and fantasy, and in doing so, separates her book from more traditional, chronological autobiographies. Her first chapter relates and then embroiders a story that was told by her mother, Brave Orchid, when Kingston first menstruated. It is a cautionary tale about a real aunt in China who bore an illegitimate child, brought down the village's violence on her house, drowned herself and was then excluded by the retaliatory silence of the family from the comforts that family ghosts expect. Her name was suppressed, all talk of her forbidden. Kingston's second section relates an entirely different tale about Fa Mu Lan, the mythical Warrior Woman. This "talk-story," which was repeatedly chanted by Brave Orchid and her daughter, told of a girl taken to the mountains by a magic bird, who trained herself to become strong in self-discipline and magic and later returned to wreak vengeance on her family's and country's enemies. These introductory myths juxtapose a woman who, as an outlaw, became a victim against a second woman, dutiful and heroic. Kingston jumps from these stories to the central history of her mother in China, then to the tale of another aunt, Moon Orchid, a delicate and giggling old woman who emigrated and ended in madness, broken by the U.S., which Kingston's mother had survived.

Kingston, the narrator, the expected subject of this autobiography, never set foot in China, where her mother was a medical student, nor was she present in Los Angeles, when her fragile aunt received the rebuff that led to her madness. This *distance* of the narrator, this self-effacing quality, contrasts with the intimacy one can sense in reading the book. Kingston links inherited stories with explications and memories of her own. She also works to see these people clearly, trying to construct a picture of her relatives from fragments and to enter their world in much the same way that a sympathetic reader would. She is as involved in this process of learning as we are. Her labor becomes most apparent when we compare the writer's detailed, scenic conjectures about the crises that overwhelmed her aunts in China and Los Angeles with the bare tales which were actually given to her. Her outlawed aunt was raped . . . or no, she was in love, a flirt, who combed her hair into wisps and burned out a freckle; none of these details can be found in the scare story told by Brave Orchid. Kingston's expansion of that story comes very close to the work of fiction, but it is always done as part of the effort to make her own past and her kinfolk real.

The act of speech is real. It sometimes burned the throat of Maxine, the shy Chinese-American, to speak aloud. The Chinese are taught to keep misfit emotions silent, but words suppressed gain heat; the release of "unspeakables" becomes an act of aggression against the community. Kingston's first action in *The Woman Warrior* is a defiant telling. Her mother said, "You must never tell anyone," yet here the author records the secret story of her No Name aunt, thus breaking the silence which was a deliberate act of punishment against an offender with whom the narrator feels a frightening kinship. With her name forbidden to relatives, the aunt might as well never have lived, for words are vehicles of memory, respect and finally creation; in words Kingston has reclaimed her.

Shared words have also comforted the author. A chant of one's descent line can call the wandering Chinese spirit home. Mother and daughter sang the chant of the Woman Warrior, Fa Mu Lan, as they worked. This was an act of fellowship, and the prose style of the White Tiger chapter beats with confidence. Sentences are comparatively short and frequently begin with the "I" of the strongly active hero, who walks in a supernatural world made familiar by concrete natural objects—water gourds with fibers, rabbits, tree bark, squirrels. The Woman Warrior menstruates, defecates, has a baby and strings up the umbilical cord as a red flag.

Kingston recognizes the power of concrete details embedded in tales of faraway places since her own mother, the shaman, used this technique in order to build China in Stockton, California. To prevent her daughter from becoming a foreign ghost, a non-human thing like the monsters in Stockton who delivered newspapers and picked up garbage, but spoke no recognizable human language, the mother had to raise a China up around her child verbally. This created China had to be enough like the real place so that the child could return smoothly to her homeland. Ev-

ery Chinese child raised in America tends to become part ghost in the eyes of its immigrant parents: part un-Chinese, unfamiliar, untraditional. There is no linguistic distinction made between ghosts who appear as smokey columns and the flesh and blood American "ghosts" who read gas meters and work at the drug store. What then is real, what is just talk? The question troubles Kingston. She recognizes that the violent Chinese villagers who pillaged the home of her pregnant aunt helped one another "maintain the real" by eradicating misfits, and that her mother's myths tested "our strength to establish realities." Reality is constructed by people acting and speaking. "I continue to sort out what's just my childhood, just my imagination, just my family, just the village, just movies, just living."

When a mother tries to construct China in a foreign place, there are bound to be terrifying gaps waiting for the daughter when she begins to explore a larger world. Gaps, distances, the separations that accompany adolescent rebellion, and secrets, which are gaps in speech, all frighten and challenge Kingston. The beginning and ending of the book deal with separations. The violence of the No Name woman story speaks for the difficulty of binding adolescents and shows a disobedient girl cast out. In the final chapter, young Maxine tortures a silent Chinese girl whom she sees as a partial image of herself; she wants to separate from and punish "herself." Then she attempts to bridge a division by telling all her guilty secrets to her mother. A person must talk out loud to join the community, but somehow the thoughts this girl has alienate her nearly as often as they tie her. She hates the shared phrases about girls—"Feeding girls is feeding cowbirds." "Better to raise geese than girls, "—and hates her parents' ink drawings of villagers, after a flood, "snagging their neighbor's floatage with long flood hooks and pushing the girl babies on down the river." She cannot digest the whole of this Chinese system as her mother did: her mother had once bought and owned a girl slave.

It's to be expected that an autobiography of a second-generation American would track down the ramifications of distance, but in *The Woman Warrior,* problems of distance expand beyond topic to influence form. Kingston's use of inherited stories to begin or center most of her chapters creates ambiguity between the close personal and the distant impersonal. Passed through generations, the Fa Mu Lan chant is "impersonal" or "suprapersonal"; it has gained an existence and form of its own, and speaking brings it to life. But what happens when the chant is written down? Kingston, the adult, retrospective writer, is not the confidently chanting child; she sees the child from a distance and remembers her real hope that the magic bird would take her away. It never did. The warrior's story is simultaneously hers and not hers, an influence but also a disappointment. Writing can be a sneaky form of suppressed speech. Kingston writes forbidden secrets, but a reader rarely hears the character of Maxine speaking. As she works with the stories of her relatives, she dramatizes the sense of distance and silence which frequently oppresses her even as an adult. The author has subtitled her book "Memoirs of a Girlhood among Ghosts," rather than "Autobiography of My Girlhood." Memoirs traditionally concentrate on descriptions of meetings with other, famous people. Kingston sometimes regrets, but also employs her role as onlooker, at one point stepping back to look through the eyes of her visiting aunt and examine the messy, ink-stained child, herself. This situation recalls the situation of a fiction writer, who also stands apart from the story by using a narrator to "speak" and judge.

The form of the book is dramatic. Kingston enacts the central problem of her life, that she is not completely Chinese, she is part hovering ghost. Unlike an armchair autobiography told by an older man or woman who has reached a comparatively secure and contemplative stage in life, this is a laboring book which depends on the act of writing, the juxtapositions of words and tales, to crystallize meanings. The writer gathers concrete objects. She also removes herself a little in order to give the stories a kind of objectivity which she knows to be part illusion. Most important, however, is her method for making people real, which she does by juxtaposing contradictory personality traits of the most important and complex person in the book aside from the narrator—her mother. Brave Orchid tells ugly and good stories, draws pictures of rejected baby girls floating downriver, yet also loves her daughter. She once defended a weak madwoman whom the villagers eventually stoned; she also bought a girl slave. The author presents these contrasts as stories which are blocked side to side and often left without reconciling explanations, a structure that mirrors many of Kingston's own childhood experiences with her mother. Brave Orchid is an artist, a creator, an accomplished eater of carp eyes, a woman capable of standing as a substantial individual while at the same time fitting in with a culture that calls girls "maggots." Unable to imitate her perfectly, Kingston nonetheless imitates many of her techniques.

Norman Holland argues that a reader cannot distinguish fiction from autobiography by internal evidence. However, once a person has been told to expect "truth" or "fiction," one's relationship to the text changes, and this change is partly a matter of distance. Readers "reality test" autobiography by comparing it with their own opinions and experiences. Roy Pascal argues similarly that readers make moral judgments of autobiographical narrators. Autobiographies are at their best, Pascal writes, when they show individuals in "successive collisions with circumstance," so that in the process of reading such a book, one can gain practical wisdom in living. Those events outside the range of the author's experience are outside the range of autobiography, and the critic counsels young men to turn instead to the autobio-

graphical novel for investigations of potential situations. Kingston obviously circumvents these fatherly suggestions by exploring the lives of her female relatives, lives that run far beyond her own experience. This freedom to explore fantasy dramatically many would simply call fiction.

According to Pascal and Holland, readers do not tend to unite with autobiographical "heroes" as they do with fictional heroes; an element of judgment intrudes, so that the "dream alliance" between a reader and a character in fiction becomes much more difficult, or impossible, with autobiographies. This situation creates a paradox important for the discussion. A fiction writer's invisibility and distance from the work allows it to stand on its own; at the same time fiction, thus freed from its progenitor, seems much more intimately adaptable to the involvement of readers. The feeling I get from *The Woman Warrior* is that Kingston constructs a partly fictional world in order to be able to re-enter it imaginatively as a reader, someone who is distant enough to see clearly but is also emotionally involved in the story. This move is very similar to the adaptation of focus any adult must make when looking at someone who was once completely "mother," but who is now a "person," with all the hitches and complexities that implies.

A more precise definition of the distinctions between autobiography and fiction, which usually parallels the distinctions between informative as opposed to more artful prose, has been suggested by Kenneth Burke. His analysis of the "psychology of information" as opposed to the "psychology of form" leads him to examine the ways in which art depends on dramatic manipulation of the audience by means of sequential and often juxtaposed forms that are patterned after "psychological universals" like the enjoyment of rest after exertion or the involvement in a mounting crescendo. According to Burke, the more a work depends on psychology of form rather than information, the more it bears repeating; thus music keeps fresh after many repetitions. The point to be made here is not that most autobiographies are artless; certainly what I've tagged as a traditional autobiography uses a satisfying form as it moves from childhood to a more firm and often generous old age. But Kingston is more artist than most, and this is partly because of need.

Kingston's preoccupations with forms and living symbols can be discovered by a simple comparison of chapters. She begins by embroidering the violent story about the nameless aunt who was both outlaw and victim, then follows with the White Tiger myth of Fa Mu Lan, which offers an emotional alternative to the threats and dangers that accompany adolescence. This chant encourages Kingston, for it offers her a new interpretation of her own writing, which does not challenge the laws of the community in this case, but acts with them instead. Like the Woman Warrior, she carries words carved into the skin of her back and will now tell vengeance for her family.

These two different lessons were told by one mother. How does one explain the inconsistencies? Brave Orchid stands in the center of the book and her chapter, the third, ends with a tense and loving dialogue between the nervous daughter and the great, bearish, worried older woman. Kingston has moved regressively from her adolescence, to childhood, to life in China before she was born. Her fourth chapter shifts to a skyscraper in Los Angeles where she has never been. By occasionally taking the viewpoint of her aunt, Moon Orchid, the narrator gains the vision of someone who has stepped fresh off the plane from China; she may now be able to see how her own mother views her. Kingston also manages to compare two immigrants, one a survivor who can heft hundred pound sacks of Texas rice and who works in the dust and steam heat of a laundry, and the other, Moon Orchid, a giggling lady who was crushed by the determined plans of her own strong sister. The author watches the bullying and subsequent tender concern of her mother towards her aunt. She draws conclusions about justifications for force—people must "get tough" to survive here—so she can accept the methods used on her as a child.

The explosion finally comes when Maxine tries to communicate her secrets to her mother, and the simultaneous, babbling screams of the two females recall the dialogue that ended the central section. Her analysis of the difficulties of survival in the U.S. has helped Kingston move towards sympathy; after relating how her mother ordered her to stop "whispering, whispering," she theorizes that this was probably her mother's own quiet time, the one cool space available in the schedule of a hot day. And the book ends with a Chinese singer who, after being captured by barbarians, finally sang love of her lost country. Ts'ai Yen, this singer and poet, part mythic, part historical, offers the narrator an alternative to the Woman Warrior who partly failed her as a child. The poet is also a warrior, so the two mythic forerunners blend.

Kingston constructs her memories into patterns that will educate her to go on. She relies on artfulness and felt comparisons partly because she had been required to build a world from contradictory pieces, but even more, because understanding how the Chinese world fits together means understanding Brave Orchid, the magician who raised the fence around her. People evade explanation, they have many faces and must be examined in layers. A great deal of fiction has been created from the search for "ghosts." Lily Briscoe tries to paint Mrs. Ramsey, who can be found somewhere in the connections between varying personal impressions. Marlow follows the rumors to Kurtz. Nick Carraway hears stories of Gatsby and touches them up to flesh out the man for the sake of his own survival.

It has become commonplace to say that novels do not ask for judgment of characters so much as they try to develop sympathy. Sympathy implies acceptance of complexities, contradictions, social influences. This autobiography embodies the labor of a young woman to develop a large sympathy for her mother, a woman who was able to stride across the ocean when forty years old and then bear six children. Once Kingston can see her mother, she can turn and see herself as an entire and complex adult, rather than as a crazy mosaic of mutually exclusive pieces. Her combinations of fictional and autobiographical techniques make this book quite an experience for the reader, who is invited to participate emotionally in the dramatic scenes and then finds the author sitting alongside, talking and crying. If it is true that we stand back slightly from autobiographies and "reality test" them, it must also be true that the willingness of a person to offer her life to such scrutiny has to be accepted as an act of generosity. Kingston invites singing.

Carol Mitchell (essay date January-June 1981)

SOURCE: "'Talking-Story' in *The Woman Warrior:* An Analysis of the Use of Folklore," in *Kentucky Folklore Record,* Vol. 27, No. 1-2, January-June, 1981, pp. 5-12.

[*In the following essay, Mitchell delineates Kingston's integration of oral storytelling into her written narrative in* The Woman Warrior.]

The Woman Warrior: Memoirs of a Girlhood Among Ghosts, by Maxine Hong Kingston, is one of a number of novels that have explored various aspects of the immigrant experience in the United States. The novel is autobiographical and focuses not on those who themselves immigrated to the U.S. from China, but rather on the first generation born in this country. Through her stories the narrator draws us into her problems of growing up in an immigrant community and her struggle with various aspects of her Chinese heritage: her fear of being sold as a slave if she should return to China, her fear of ghosts, her fear of insanity, and her continual fear of being worthless just because she was born female.

Although the author was brought up in Stockton, California, the narrator never mentions the name of her hometown; it is only clear that the town is in California and probably close to San Francisco. What is important is that the narrator grew up in a Chinese community surrounded by a larger American community. Many, if not most, of the people in the community came from New Society Village in China, a peasant village seemingly rather isolated from the mainstream of Chinese culture and speaking one of the more obscure dialects of the Chinese language. Since the narrator's parents, as well as many of the other immigrants, assume that they will return to China when they have made enough money, the parents and the community are attempting to teach the children the traditional village values. Ties with the village are still continued through the exchanges of letters with relatives, and the children are sent to Chinese school as well as to the American school.

There are, of course, pressures that are antithetical to the continuance of village traditions, for instance, the American schools that the children are required to attend where they must speak English and where they learn to question many of the old beliefs. The secretiveness of the Chinese parents themselves also plays a part in this loss of tradition. Some of the secrecy is because of the immigration authorities and the fear of deportation, but not all of it is for that reason.

> The emigrants confused the gods by diverting their curses, misleading them with crooked streets and false names. They must try to confuse their offspring as well, who, I suppose threaten them in similar ways—always trying to get things straight, always trying to name the unspeakable. The Chinese I know hide their names; sojourners take new names when their lives change and guard their real names with silence.

> How can Chinese keep any traditions at all? They don't even make you pay attention, slipping in a ceremony and clearing the table before the children notice specialness. The adults get mad, evasive, and shut you up if you ask. You get no warning that you shouldn't wear a white ribbon in your hair until they hit you and give you the sideways glare for the rest of the day. They hit you if you wave brooms around or drop chop-sticks or drum them. They hit you if you wash your hair on certain days, or tap somebody with a ruler, or step over a brother whether it's during your menses or not. You figure out what you got hit for and don't do it again if you figured correctly.

With the Chinese peasants as with many other peasant groups there is a reticence about speaking of certain subjects for fear of making the gods jealous or for fear that mentioning a subject may make it happen. And although it is not mentioned in the novel, another probable reason for the parents' reticence in speaking of some traditional customs is the embarrassment the immigrant parents feel if their Americanized children laugh at them for continuing old customs that the children believe to be unimportant and silly in America.

The children too may be uninterested in learning the old ways. As the narrator says: "I think that if you don't figure it out, it's all right. Then you can grow up bothered by neither ghosts nor deities. Gods you avoid won't hurt you. I don't see how they kept up a continuous culture for five thousand years." However, the narrator is not really able to dismiss the old traditions so easily, and the novel itself becomes a way of integrating Chinese and American traditions, attitudes and experiences.

It is on the author's integration of oral story telling into the written story telling of the novel that I will focus, for the author uses the oral stories to structure the novel as well as to show the character of the narrator. During the narrator's childhood her mother "talks-story," telling the children myths, legends, family narratives and other memorate from China. Just as those narratives were used to help structure and explain life experiences, so the novel is talking-story in order to explain the past. The narrator interweaves her mother's traditional legends and family narratives with her own additions and interpretations in an attempt to understand herself, her mother and her other female relatives, and Chinese and Chinese-American women in general.

The novel does not follow the life of the narrator chronologically, but rather our understanding of the narrator gradually becomes clearer as we learn about her reactions to the stories she heard in her youth. Each of the five sections of the novel tells the story of a woman with whom the narrator has identified herself either because she fears becoming like the woman or because the woman gives her hope for her future self. During the course of the novel the narrator moves closer to her material as fewer and fewer fictional distancing techniques are used to interpret her past, and it is only in the last section of the novel that the narrator talks-story about herself.

In the first three sections of the novel the narrator retells oral stories that her mother had told to her during childhood. These oral stories contribute to the fictional distance the author has from her material, but in the last two sections the narrator tells the story primarily from her own experience which means that most of the fictional distance has been removed. Basically the progression from fictional distance to immediacy is as follows:

Section I tells the story of a third person which was told by a second person to the narrator who then tells the story as a narrative in the third person.

Section II also tells the story of a third person which was told by a second person to the narrator, but this time the story is told as a first person narrative.

Section III tells the story of a second person which was told by that person to the narrator who then tells the story in the third person with many first person quotations.

Section IV tells a second person's story as it was seen and participated in by the narrator.

Section V tells the narrator's own story.

The first section, "No Name Woman," tells the story the narrator has heard from her mother, of a young aunt whose husband left China to find work. More than a year after he had left she became pregnant. The villagers raided the house on the night the baby was to be born. After the raid the aunt gave birth to the baby in the pigsty and then drowned herself and the baby in the well, and the family from then on acted as if the woman had never been born.

> Whenever she had to warn us about life, my mother told stories that ran like this one, a story to grow up on . . . Now that you have started to menstruate, what happened to her could happen to you. Don't humiliate us. You wouldn't like to be forgotten as if you had never been born.

The story was briefly told by the mother and focused on the horrors of the raid and the condemnation to oblivion without giving any details about the kind of woman the aunt was or what her motivations might have been. However, the narrator feels haunted by the ghost of this forgotten aunt, and she feels the need to better understand the aunt. Since the aunt has officially been forgotten she cannot ask her parents for more information about her, so she speculates: "Unless I see her life branching into mine, she gives me no ancestral help." The narrator imagines the aunt to be somewhat similar to herself but placed in the misogynic and superstition ridden peasant Chinese village.

The story's impact on the narrator is primarily two-fold. First, her speculations about the aunt's desire to be attractive and its disastrous consequences lead her to fear being attractive to boys, so even though she would like to go on dates she decides that being sisterly makes more sense. Perhaps more important is that she realizes that the real punishment for the aunt was being forgotten, for since she receives no offerings from her living relatives her ghost is condemned to wander hungry and alone forever. The support of the family is necessary not only in life but in death as well.

The aunt's story is a part of the narrator's invisible or ghost world that she must come to terms with during the course of the novel: "Those of us in the first American generations have had to figure out how the invisible world the emigrants built around our childhoods fit in solid America." The narrator must deal with the question of whether such a thing could happen to her or not, even in America. Her aunt's marriage was arranged; will hers be? The villagers raided the aunt's family for the aunt's wrong doing; might the villagers in America do the same kind of thing to her family? If the narrator steps outside the traditional Chinese woman's role and acts like an American woman, will she hex her family here in America? Just which ones of the Chinese customs pertain to American life? It is also in this short section that the narrator first discusses arranged marriages, foot binding and the importance of a woman bearing male children—customs that show the secondary importance of women in Chinese society and that make the narrator fear returning to China.

The title of the novel, *The Woman Warrior*, comes from this legend, for the narrator needs this heroic role model to help her feel a sense of her own worth in a culture that frequently emphasizes the worthlessness of girls.
—Carol Mitchell

The second section of the novel, "White Tigers," tells the legend of a famous woman warrior, Mu Lan: "She (the narrator's mother) said I would grow up a wife and a slave, but she taught me the song of the warrior woman, Fa Mu Lan. I would have to grow up a warrior woman." This legend, along with other legends of Chinese women warriors, showed an exciting and glamorous role for women. Mu Lan became a woman warrior in order to save her elderly father from conscription and in order to right the wrongs that had been done in her village. Because she did her deeds out of filial respect, not just for personal glorification, she is an acceptable role model for a woman. Mu Lan's story is told at greater length than the story of the no name aunt. The narrator, imagining herself as the warrior woman, tells the legend in the first person. The title of the novel, *The Woman Warrior,* comes from this legend, for the narrator needs this heroic role model to help her feel a sense of her own worth in a culture that frequently emphasizes the worthlessness of girls. It is in this section of the novel that the narrator juxtaposes the heroic swordswoman with the folk sayings she continually heard about women.

> 'Girls are maggots in the rice.' 'It is more profitable to raise geese than daughters.'

> 'When fishing for treasures in the flood, be careful not to pull in girls.'

The sayings hurt her feelings and made her angry, but the woman warrior gave her hope that she too could be valuable to the family.

She also felt ambiguous about the woman warrior. How could a little girl be heroic if no magic birds showed her the way to gurus as they had shown Mu Lan the way? So she worked hard at school:

> I got straight A's Mama.
>
> 'Let me tell you a true story about a girl who saved her village.'
>
> I could not figure out what was my village and it was important that I do something big and fine, or else my parents would sell me when we made our way back to China. In China there were solutions for what to do with little girls who ate up food and threw tantrums. You can't eat straight A's.

Success for a girl was not considered as something that brought credit to her own family since in China a girl would marry and go to live with her husband's family; thus, her successes were considered as minor when compared with her brothers' successes which did bring credit to the family since when brothers married they stayed with the family.

The woman warrior who is independent contrasts with the ideal wife who is passive, obedient and dependent, and since the narrator cannot be both, she feels caught in another trap.

> Marriage and child birth strength the swordswoman, who is not a maid like Joan of Arc. No husband of mine will say 'I could have been a drummer but I had to think about the wife and kids. You know how it is.' Nobody supports me at the expense of his own adventure. Then I get bitter: no one supports me; I am not loved enough to be supported. That I am not a burden has to compensate for the sad envy when I look at women loved enough to be supported.

Thus even her attempt to be heroic is not entirely satisfactory. Her American successes are some comfort: "I *am* worthy of eating the food." Also, she can believe that fundamentally her parents love her, but the constant repetition by her parents and other villagers of proverbial sayings which emphasize the worthlessness of girls force her to constantly prove to herself and others that she has some value.

The third section, "Shaman," focuses on Brave Orchid, the narrator's mother, during her years in medical school and during the time she practiced medicine in China before coming to the United States. The narrator learned these stories, along with the stories of the no name aunt and the woman warrior, from her mother's talking-story, and the narrator has mixed feelings concerning the stories about her mother as well as the other stories. On the one hand, her mother has been able to be an active—even heroic, at least in her

ghost fighting—and independent woman; on the other hand, her mother accepted the slavery of girls and bought a slave, and her mother wants to return to China, where the narrator feels she might be sold as a slave. In addition, the narrator needs to understand her mother better than she has in the past, so the talking-story of the novel is an attempt to make her mother's personality and life intelligible.

Probably because Brave Orchid's husband had been gone from China for some years. Brave Orchid was able to go to a two year school of mid-wifery. Thus even prior to her emigration she was actively making her own living rather than helplessly remaining at home being waited on Additionally her mother was a ghost fighter both at the school and in the countryside where she sometimes was waylaid by ghosts as she went to visit patients. Brave Orchid was a very practical woman with much common sense who was able to combine the folk medicine and magic which her patients demanded with the Western medicine she learned at the school. She refused to treat patients she could tell were dying so that she would be untainted by death and her reputation would be that of a doctor whose patients only got well. While she believed to a certain extent in the reality of ghosts, she believed a strong mind could fight against them.

Her mother's ability to fight ghosts and to call people's spirits back when they had been frightened by ghosts is some consolation to her daughter, for America is full of ghosts. There are Garbage Man Ghosts, Police Ghosts, Social Worker Ghosts; in fact, all non-Chinese are ghosts since the Chinese believed that there were no real humans but themselves and maybe the Japanese who were about half human. Fortunately, the American Ghosts are not quite as bad as the ghosts in China, for at least American Ghosts have familiar shapes while ghosts in China come in all sorts of frightening shapes—from hairy blobs that expand and contract to pillars of smoke like whirlwinds. Thus while the subtitle of the novel, *A Girlhood Among Ghosts,* refers to the ghosts of women ancestors and legendary women, it also refers to the American Ghosts among whom she grew up.

But her mother's talents in China are not necessarily talents the daughter wants in a mother in America. Ghost Fighters in China were big eaters and could eat anything, but the daughter finds repulsive some of the items her mother serves to her family. She is horrified by her mother's talking-story about eating monkey brains from a living monkey—supposedly a great delicacy.

The story of her mother's slave girl also bothers her, first, because it is frightening to think that girls were frequently sold as slaves, and, second, because she feels that her mother may have valued her slave more than she does her daughter. The slave knew how to bargain; the daughter not only did not know how to bargain but was also embarrassed when she had to translate her mother's bargaining in American stores. Even though her mother assured her that she paid more to the hospital when her daughter was born than she paid for the slave in China, the daughter suspects that her mother resents it.

The fourth and fifth sections of the novel focus on first hand experiences of the narrator rather than on stories that were told to her, so the following discussion of these two sections is much briefer than the discussion of the other sections since the integration of these two women's stories into the narrator's is more direct.

The fourth section of the novel, "At the Western Palace," tells the story of Brave Orchid's sister Moon Orchid who arrived in the U.S. when she was about 65 years of age and was unable to adjust to this new world and became insane. Again, the focus is on arranged marriages and helpless dependency, for Moon Orchid was married without her consent to a man considerably younger than she. For years she had lived alone in China after he emigrated. He sent her money, and she could afford to be taken care of in the traditional style of the upper class Chinese woman. But this was no preparation for moving to a new country; here she becomes paranoid, believing that Mexican Ghosts are after her, and she is only happy when she is placed in a mental asylum where she feels the other women are like her and where she feels protected.

In Moon Orchid's story the narrator tells of what she has herself seen and participated in unlike the previous women's stories which had been told to her by her mother. However, the author still keeps a considerable fictional distance in the story by using the omniscient author voice because the fictional distance corresponds with the emotional distance that the narrator needs to keep from her aunt. The narrator must come to terms with her aunt's insanity and her own fear of insanity: "I thought every house had to have its crazy woman or crazy girl, every village its idiot. Who would it be at our house? Probably me." There had been the crazy woman in the village in China who was stoned to death that her mother talked story about, and there were several crazy women all in village families who lived close to her. Was this the result of Chinese attitudes toward women, or the result of the pressures caused by the conflict between American and Chinese attitudes toward women, or just the pressures of poverty? The narrator cannot answer the question except by showing all of these pressures as they impinge upon the life of the narrator, and the narrator's way of coming to terms with the pressures is to externalize the pressures by writing about them in the novel.

In the last section of the novel, "A Song for a Barbarian Reed Pipe," the narrator talks-story about her childhood, her

problems of adjusting in the American school, her fears that a marriage is being arranged for her, her guilt over her breaches of only partially understood Chinese customs, her embarrassments over her mother's Chinese behavior in the American community, and her inability to tell the difference between "true stories" and "just stories" when her mother talks-story. It is this last problem that has been explored all through the novel as the narrator remembers all of the stories about various women that her mother told. Finally it makes no difference whether the no name aunt was really her aunt or whether Mu Lan was real, for they had a real impact upon her development as a woman.

The narrator ends with the legend of Ts'ai Yen, a Chinese woman who was abducted by barbarians and lived with them for some years. While she was there she heard the music of their flutes and composed a sad and angry song which she took back to China with her, and the song was handed down among her Han descendants. In many ways the narrator feels like Ts'ai Yen, living among barbarians and composing her sad and angry song, although whether the barbarians are the Americans or the Chinese immigrants is not so clear.

However, the narrator is also Mu Lan, and her novel is the revenge of the Woman Warrior since it is not longer practical to go around beheading people. For Mu Lan too used words which were carved in her back counting the injustices that she was to avenge: "The ideographs for *revenge* are 'report a crime' and 'report to five families.' The reporting is the vengeance." Her revenge is on those who feel women are worthless, those who restrict women and especially on those who teach women to see themselves as helpless and worthless.

Linda Hunt (essay date Fall 1985)

SOURCE: "'I Could Not Figure Out What Was My Village': Gender Vs. Ethnicity in Maxine Hong Kingston's *The Woman Warrior*," in *MELUS,* Vol. 12, No. 3, Fall, 1985, pp. 5-12.

[*In the following essay, Hunt examines Kingston's treatment of the conflict and confusion created by her various roles as a woman and as a member of separate and distinct cultures and classes.*]

Feminist theorists have argued about the extent to which women share a common culture. In *Three Guineas* Virginia Woolf has a character assert, "as a woman I have no country. . . . As a woman my country is the whole world." This has a fine ring to it, but if the sentiment were wholly true we would not find in women's lives so much pain, confusion, and conflict. Temma Kaplan explains the complexity of the subject: "It is impossible to speak of 'women's culture' without understanding its variation by class and ethnic group. Women's culture, like popular or working class culture, must appear in the context of dominant cultures."

The truth of Kaplan's statement is borne out by reading fiction and autobiography written by women from different backgrounds. Such books not only show the great cultural diversity women experience but also evoke the incompatible definitions of femininity and the irreconcilable demands a woman is likely to encounter as she attempts to live in more than one cultural world at the same time.

Women's worlds may vary widely depending on ethnic background and social class, but in the societies from which we have written literature, male dominance is a common denominator. Maxine Hong Kingston's autobiographical *The Woman Warrior* suggests that we need to pay attention to the contradictions male dominance creates for women who are at one and the same time subordinated by a culture, and yet, embroiled in its interstices; such women may be painfully at odds with themselves. A woman like Kingston, who is doubly marginal (i.e. not a member of the dominant race or class) is likely to feel this conflict with particular acuteness because an affiliation with a minority culture tends to be particularly strong.

Maxine Hong Kingston's personal struggle is fought—and resolved at least partially— on the battlefield of language.
—*Linda Hunt*

Explaining to the reader one of the many contradictions which are part of the legacy of her Chinese-American girlhood, Kingston comments bitterly, "Even now China wraps double binds around my feet." The most difficult doublebind has been the need to reconcile her loyalty to her Chinese-American heritage, a background which devalues and even insults women, with her own sense of dignity as a female.

This paper is about Kingston's attempt to resolve the war within herself, a struggle that is exacerbated by the tremendous emphasis Chinese culture puts on social cohesion. She has been raised to experience and require a powerful identification with family and community, and yet, as a woman, she cannot simply accept a place in a culture which calls people of her sex "maggots," "broom and dustpan," "slave."

Maxine Hong Kingston's personal struggle is fought—and resolved at least partially—on the battlefield of language.

The words used against her sting, and, unable to find the right words and the right voice to express her own point of view, and indeed, unsure of that point of view, she is rendered nearly voiceless for much of her youth. She speaks inaudibly or in a quack, and once physically assaults another Chinese girl whose silence reminds her of her own. The core of the problem is that by being simultaneously insider (a person who identifies strongly with her cultural group) and outsider (deviant and rebel against that tradition), she cannot figure out from which perspective to speak. It is only through mastery of literary form and technique—through creating this autobiography out of family stories, Chinese myths, and her own memories—that she is able to articulate her own ambivalence and hereby find an authentic voice.

Kingston begins with an aunt back in China whose name the family tried to forget, telling her story in such a way that she artfully shifts point of view and sympathy in order to convey her divided loyalties. The aunt became an outsider to her village by getting pregnant while her husband was in America. The enraged villagers, terrified by her behavior, drove her to suicide: any lust not socially-sanctioned was seen as disruptive of the social order.

The author identifies with the rebellious aunt, whom she calls "my forerunner," creating from her imagination various detailed scenarios, first of rape and then of romantic attraction, alternative versions of what might have happened, which are narrated in the omniscient third person. Kingston hypothesizes that her female relative might have succumbed to her impulses as relief from the burden of being "expected . . . alone to keep the traditional ways, which her brother now among the barbarians in America could fumble without detection." She expands on her theme, beginning to imagine in sensuous detail the pull that an attractive man might have had on this aunt "caught up in a slow life."

But Kingston's allegiance is abruptly withdrawn. Interrupting her sensuous description of the imagined lover, the narrator exclaims, "She offered *us* up for a charm that vanished with tiredness, a pigtail that didn't toss when the wind died" (emphasis mine). The word "us" is starting because Kingston has abruptly shifted from third person the first person plural and from identification with the aunt, the outsider, to being one of the villagers, an insider.

The aunt's story is resumed in a more objective vein, and we are given an explanation of the motives of the avengers of the social code:

> The frightened villagers, who depend on one another to maintain the real, went for my aunt to show her a personal, physical representation of the break she had made in the "roundness." . . . The villagers

punished her for acting as if she could have a private life secret and apart from them.

While the remainder of the tale emphasizes the events which befell the persecuted woman, her thoughts and feelings, the narrative remain riddled with ambivalence. Kingston's recounting of her aunt's story been a defiant act of recompense towards the forgotten relative, a desire not to participate in her punishment. Yet, one more twist occurs in the last sentence of the chapter:

> My aunt haunts me. . . . I alone devote pages of paper to her. . . . I do not think she always means me well. I am telling on her, and she was a spite suicide, drowning herself in drinking water.

Suddenly the aunt is seen as an enemy, and Kingston's own act writing her story appears in a different light.

Kingston's profound conflict about where her loyalty lies regarding the experience of this aunt she has never met serves to convey her own agonized indecision about what stance to take towards her own Chinese-American upbringing. If she identifies with the community, she must accept and even endorse her own humiliation at their hands; if she allows herself to fully experience the depths of her alienation, she is danger of being cut off from her cultural roots. Thus she juxtaposes an exploration of the legend of Fa Mu Lan, a tale her story-telling mother used to chant, against the story of the outlaw aunt. The purpose is to tell whether her culture's myth about a heroic woman who defends her village will provide a way for Kingston to transcend the degrading female social role, and yet, be loyal to the community.

Kingston retells the story, casting herself as the swordswoman who through magic and self-discipline is trained to bring about social justice while at the same time fulfilling her domestic obligations. Significant a good part of her training involves exercises which teach her how create with her body the ideographs for various words: in Kingston's universe it is through mastery of language that a warrior is created. Language is again important in that before Fa Mu Lan sets out, dressed as a man, to lead her male army against the enemies of her people, the family carves on her back the words which suggest their endless list of grievances.

When the narrator, Kingston's fantasy of herself as Fa Mu Lan, returns home the villagers "make a legend about her perfect filiality." This myth, combining heroism and social duty as it does, is explored to see if winning the approval and admiration of the Chinese or Chinese-American community can provide so much gratification that Kingston will be persuaded to repress her injuries at the hands of the community. However, she subverts her own attempt by embedding within her tales of the female avenger certain elements which bring forth once again the theme of the injustices women suffer as a sex and the issue of female anger.

Hunting down the baron who had drafted her brother, she presents herself as defender of the village as a whole: "I want your life in payment for your crimes against the villagers." But the baron tries to appeal to her "man to man," lightly acknowledging his crimes against women in a misguided attempt at male-bonding:

> Oh, come now. Everyone takes the girls when he can. The families are glad to get rid of them. "Girls are maggots in the rice. It is more profitable to raise geese than daughters." He quoted to me the sayings I hated.

Since this version of the swordswoman's story is Kingston's own creation, she is surely introducing the baron's sexism at this juncture to show the reader that, try as she does, she *cannot* simply overlook the patriarchal biases of Chinese culture. The enemy of her village seeks to create an alliance with the defender of family and community on the common ground of misogyny. No wonder Kingston exclaims just after the swordswoman's tale is finished, "I could not figure out what was my village."

Even more subversively, in the process of spinning out her tale of the dutiful defender of the village, Kingston briefly indulges in a digression about a different kind of warrior woman. She has herself (the swordswoman) released from a locked room in the baron's castle a group of "cowering, whimpering women." These females who make "insect noises" and "blink weakly . . . like pheasants that have been raised in the dark for soft meat" are utterly degraded:

> The servant who walked the ladies had abandoned them, and they could not escape on their little bound feet. Some crawled away from me, using their elbows to pull themselves along. These women would not be good for anything. I called the villagers to come identify any daughters they wanted to take home, but no one claimed any.

As creator, Kingston allows herself to respond with hostility to her own fantasy of the ultimate in female humiliation by turning these pathetic creatures into "witch amazons" who "killed men and boys." Unlike Fa Mu Lan, who is impelled to be a warrior by idealism and disguises herself as a man, these women are mercenaries (i.e. *self* interested), ride dressed as women (i.e. *female* identified), and buy us girl babies from poor families; slave girls and daughters-in-law also run away to them. Kingston reveals her intense discomfort with this anti social story she has used to deconstruct the socially-acceptable swords woman myth by distancing herself from it. She falls into the conditional "it would be said," "people would say," and concludes, "I myself never encountered such women and could not vouch for their reality."

Despite such subterfuges, the reader has not been allowed to forget that any Chinese woman who seeks to identify exclusively with the injustices experienced by the entire "village" at the hands of outsider will be denying the damage she herself and others of her sex have suffered at the hands of outsiders and insiders alike. The term "female avenger" becomes ambiguous: can Kingston be satisfied with being a avenger who is a female or does she need to be the avenger of females.

Not ready to answer this question, Kingston uses the third and fourth chapters of *The Woman Warrior* to probe even further the implications of her culture's sanctioned way for a woman to be strong. Brave Orchid, Kingston's mother, has lived a life that conforms quite closely, within the limits of realistic possibility, to the woman warrior model. Le behind in China when her husband went off to America to improve the family's fortunes, she entered medical school and became a doctor Through rigorous self-discipline she triumphed not only over her studies but over a "sitting ghost" who serves as the symbolic embodiment the fear and loneliness she must have experienced. "You have no power over a strong woman," Brave Orchid asserts to the ghost.

After completing her studies Kingston's mother returned home to serve her people as a practitioner of medicine. For some years she braved the terror of the dark woods as she went from village to village on her rounds as a physician. Like the swordswoman of the legend who returns from public life to do farmwork, housework, and produce sons, Brave Orchid accepted the next, more mundane, phase of her life without complaint; when summoned by her husband to the United States she became his partner in a laundry and had six children (including the author) after the age of forty-five.

Kingston is being as fair as possible. Her mother's story shows that the warrior woman model could work for some women. Proud of her past achievements, Brave Orchid has turned them into materials to draw on when she "talk-stories." Yet Kingston follows the narrative of Brave Orchid with the experience of Moon Orchid, Brave Orchid's sister, whose emigration to the United States leads to her madness and death. This aunt is not a strong person—and it is important that Kingston remind us that not all women have access to the remarkable reserves of strength and inflexible will that have served her mother. Also, Brave Orchid is responsible for her sister's breakdown in that she insists that Moon Orchid aggressively pursue her Americanized and bigamously remarried husband. She assumes her sister's

husband and his second wife will accept their obligation to Moon Orchid since she is "Big Wife" (first wife), and bolsters Moon Orchid's faith by reminding her of family stories from China in which the first wife had no difficulty reclaiming her position in the family after a lapse of time. Brave Orchid's advice is dangerous because she is holding onto a myth of reality structured around laws and traditions that regulated marital interaction in China and offered some protection to women but which is useless in America. Thus Kingston reminds us that new situations require new myths. The warrior woman legend may have been the best Chinese society could offer her mother, but if she herself is to use it, fundamental modification will be necessary.

It is in the final chapter, "A Song For A Barbarian Reed Pipe," that Kingston articulates most explicitly both her fury at her Chinese heritage and the strategies she has found for making peace with that heritage and salvaging from it what she can. She tells of how as a teenager she stored up in her mind a list of over two hundred truths about herself, bad thoughts and deeds to confess to her mother. When she tried to tell one item a day only to find Brave Orchid simply wasn't interested, she "felt something alive tearing at [her] throat."

Finally, one night when the family was having dinner at the laundry, her "throat burst open." Instead of confessing her own disloyalty to family and Chinese tradition, Kingston found herself bitterly cataloguing her own numerous grievances:

> When I said them out loud I saw that some of the items were ten years old already, and I had outgrown them. But they kept pouring out anyway in the voice of Chinese opera. I could hear the drums and the cymbals and the gongs and brass horns.

The transmutation of sins into grievances is significant: the fact that Kingston conceptualized these items first one way and then the other reveals again the ambivalence about whether she is insider or outside which caused her muteness. This outburst is an important breakthrough in that she is impelled to make a choice, and choosing to identify a injured outsider frees her to speak. At this stage what she articulate with that new found voice is the need to get away from the Chinese American community: "I won't let you turn me into a slave or a wife. I'm getting out of here. I can't stand living here anymore."

At the same time, Kingston's list of grievances is certainly an echo of the grievances the legendary swordswoman had had carved on her back, the difference being that Fa Mu Lan's list was not personal. Kingston's autobiography becomes her way of being a woman warrior on her own behalf and perhaps on behalf of other Chinese girls and women. She had found a way to exact revenge against her background (one idiom for revenge being to "report a crime") and yet to honor it. In crying out to the world about her culture's mistreatment of women, she has in a sense taken on the warrior role her culture recommended to those of its women most capable of heroism. In finding a literary form and techniques which allow her to give voice to the conflicts and contradictions which almost silenced her, Maxine Hong Kingston is paying tribute to the importance her family and culture have always placed on the verbal imagination.

Kingston's autobiographical masterpiece, with its theme of diverse cultural realities, reminds us to be careful about embracing a universal notion of what it means to be a woman. At the same time, however, the book raises the possibility that an important link not for all but for many women is the *disjunction* between female identity and the other aspect of cultural heritage. Agonizing contradictions between allegiance to gender and fidelity to some other dimension of one's cultural background—and this might be race or class instead of or as well as ethnicity—may be a commonplace of the female experience. From an artistic point of view the result may be an anxiety of *identity* that is at least as debilitating as the "anxiety of authorship" that Susan Gubar and Sandra Gilbert argue takes away women's sense of legitimacy as writers. Maxine Hong Kingston found a way to break out of the silence created this anxiety, but the alienation which stems from such a rupture at the very center of their beings may be one of the most profound obstacles women face in finding their voices.

David Leiwei Li (essay date Fall 1988)

SOURCE: "The Naming of a Chinese American 'I': Cross-Cultural Sign/ifications in *The Woman Warrior*," in *Criticism,* Vol. XXX, No. 4, Fall, 1988, pp. 497-515.

[*In the following essay, Li surveys how Kingston establishes a uniquely Chinese-American female identity in* The Woman Warrior.]

In a span of twelve years since the publication of her first book, **The Woman Warrior,** Maxine Hong Kingston has established herself in the American literary canon. Initial recognition of her success is evidenced in such prestigious book awards as the National Book Critics Circle Award for **The Woman Warrior** (1976) and American Book Award for **China Men** (1980), fellowships as NEA and Guggenheim, and the appearance of her works in popular college readers as *Crossing Cultures, The Conscious Reader* and *The Bedford Reader.* Through the years, we have been witness-

ing a steady accumulation of critical articles and chapters of scholarly anthologies that express at once a continuous interest in her work and a consensual acknowledgement of her as a major American talent. Recent editions of *The Norton Anthology of Literature by Women* and *The Harpers American Literature* have allotted space to selections from **The Woman Warrior.** Kingston's position in American literature has now been further confirmed by the most current attempt at canonical authorization, the *Columbia Literary History of the United States.*

Kingston's canonization results from the agreement among the emergent forces in literary criticism. As a consequence of feminist and civil rights movements, women and minority writers have been active in exploring their experiences and developing their voices in the literary scene. To theorize such phenomena comes the feminist and new historicist critical cadre that has powerfully influenced the interpretive community, awakening it to the narrowness of the canon of "masterpieces" and calling for recognition of a corpus of female and ethnic authors. **The Woman Warrior** seems a perfect sample of the issues in debate, and the current literary "dissensus," to use Bercovitch's term, has actually framed topics for most critical responses to the book: the female protagonist as victim or victor, versions of the American dream, and autobiographical narrative as a kind of fiction summoning a collage of genres.

Though perceptive in their own rights, these criticisms appear to be insufficient approaches to **The Woman Warrior,** for hardly any of them provides a clear language for Kingston's self inscription. Kingston's is a situation far more complex than James's international theme. If Daisy Miller is caught in an encounter with the unmanageably foreign, a distinctive binary opposition of the innocent American versus the sophisticated European can be drawn. After all, both share a large portion of the Western culture and Daisy's is a sojourner experience. Kingston, however, addresses neither the experience of being Chinese in America nor American in China but rather the experience of being a Chinese-American growing up in the United States. The book demands of the reader, as life demands of its heroine that he/she wade through strands of cultural forces, to understand what is being Chinese, what is being American, and what is being Chinese-American.

Clifford Geertz says [in *The Interpretation of Cultures: Selected Essays,* 1975]:

> Becoming human is becoming individual, and we become individual under the guidance of cultural patterns, historically created systems of meaning in terms of which we give form, order, point, and direction to our lives.

This furnishes us with an encompassing perspective appropriate to our analysis of *The Woman Warrior.* The individuation of the girl Kingston can thus be viewed in light of the choices she made from the cultural repertoires: her public gestures and private dreams conflict and converge to weave a web of social significances that constitute her being. While ethnic origin makes her acculturation problematic, gender becomes a compounded complication for her formation of the self. An examination of *The Woman Warrior* hence invites our attention to the specific issues of race and gender as they are embodied in the broader categories of culture in relation to which the individual defines or dissolves his/ her identity. Kingston's literary representation of this intriguing experiential process is stunning—she renders the most abstract cultural programming in the most material significations of language. Her conscious interplay of the linguistic differentia and modes of fictional characterization among cultures opens a field of ideological contention, and it is to her negotiations with names, pronouns, and narrative/generic conventions in *The Woman Warrior* that we turn.

"talk stories"

"'You must not tell anyone,' my mother said, 'what I am about to tell you,'" begins *The Woman Warrior.* As enigmatic as it is plain, Kingston breaks the covenant of the previous story community only to establish the confidence in the new one. So self-reflexively fore-grounded by the narrator, the method of telling is typically one of Chinese "talk story." It was not uncommon in the pre-television days of China for parents to entertain and educate their children by talking stories to them. This oral tradition served to transmit values and reinforces models of behavior in an unobtrusive yet effective way.

The structure of *The Woman Warrior,* in turn, is a Chinese box of "talk stories," through which Kingston conceives and perceives herself. Determinant in the interrelationships of these stories is then the concern of gender identity both corporate and individual. The "No Name Woman" story of her aunt plunging into the family well with her illegitimate newborn epitomizes the doom of many women in old China; the "White Tiger" chapter with its Fa Mu Lan legend portrays a miraculous woman warrior who is a Chinese predecessor of Joan of Arc; "Shaman" presents a narrative account of her mother, Brave Orchid, whose astounding valor exorcises the sitting ghost and whose professionalism in her medical career offers an alternative of another possibility of female existence; the episode of how Aunt Moon Orchid's submissiveness leads to abandonment and madness unveils "At the Western Palace," contemporary Los Angeles; finally, the comparatively straightforward and relatively full autobiographical exposition of the author's girlhood culminates in the tale of the ancient Chinese woman poet,

Ts'ai Yen, whose "Song for a Barbarian Reed Pipe" has earned her a name in history.

> **The hide-and-seek game of naming Kingston plays with her audience is a deliberate one. The purpose is to show that her "writing has many layers, as human beings have layers."**
> **—David Leiwei Li**

It is not difficult to observe here that the "talk stories" as a whole constitute a unique kind of semiotic system exemplifying different levels of female existence. These levels complement and contrast with one another to form a vigorous dialogic process of moulding femininity. "Here is a story my mother told me," Kingston remarks toward the end of the book, "not when I was young, but recently, when I told her I also talk-story. The beginning is hers, the ending, mine." When the story fan turns into the story talker, Kingston has completed her rites of passage: the girl has become a woman.

naming

If "talk story" is Kingston's measure of reinscription of the female self at a macrocosmic narrative expanse, she enriches her strategy by deploying the semantic entity of naming at a microcosmic plane. In his discussion on personal naming, Geertz maintains the following:

> The everyday world in which the members of any community move, their taken-for-granted field of social action, is populated not by anybodies, faceless men without qualities, but by somebodies, concrete classes of determinate persons positively characterized and appropriately labeled. And the symbol systems which define these classes are not given in the nature of things—they are historically constructed, socially maintained, and individually applied.

The character names in *The Woman Warrior* provide an insight into the construction of gender and person in both Chinese and Anglo-American cultures and the presentation as well as the coinage of these names always bear with them Kingston's hidden ideological agenda.

Of the six main female characters in the book, we observe that two are referred to by their full names, two are addressed by their first names, and another two are not given proper names. Kingston's confessed "twisted design" has gone beyond the mere labyrinth to a conglomeration of meanings: we note that the first set of names are her transcription of phonetic symbols from the Chinese characters whose value stays at the referential but not the semantic level; the second set of names are translations of the Chinese characters which have conveyed meaning but lost the original sound; and the last set of names are no names yet these unnamable beings are powerful presences that permeate the work.

The hide-and-seek game of naming Kingston plays with her audience is a deliberate one. The purpose is to show that her "writing has many layers, as human beings have layers." Further, the manipulation of Chinese and American naming conventions is an effort to bring into consciousness the cultural ignorance that surfaces, in cross-cultural exchange. The basic category of naming is, therefore, a lead, for author and audience alike to discovery and self discovery.

1. *Names transcripted from Chinese characters*

In both Chinese and American cultures, the use of full names connotes social formality, the practice of which is itself a public recognition of one's societal identity. The names of Fa Mu Lan and Ts'ai Yen, with their respective martial and poetic feats, have been engraved in the pages of Chinese history. They thus become the most wishful self-imagining of the nameless persona of the girl Kingston who yearns to grow out of her anonymity to stand side by side with her temporally and spatially remote ancestresses. As she venerates them by presenting their names in full, so she loves them by concealing the stereotypical nuances their given names carry. Unlike the Anglo-Americans who draw heavily upon biblical sources to name their children, the Chinese have the utmost creativity in combining characters to form a first name (customarily, it is either a single-character named called "Dan Ming" or a double-character name, "Shuang Ming"). In addition to the usual function to classify and distinguish, each name has a unique meaning and certain functions. In traditional Chinese society, such naming performs at least three tasks. First, it expresses a wish; for instance, it is not uncommon for a female to have a name meaning "succeeded by brothers" as a favorable token for the son-thirsty parents. Second, a person's fate is believed to be changeable if a certain character is placed in his name. An example of this would be to include "Water" in his name, if his constitution at birth is, according to the folk concept, deficient in the element, so that he may achieve balance in his life. Third, a name signifies the social status of the namer and the gender of the named, for character/word choice tells at once the family's educational level and its attitude toward the infant. As the naming of the male child is often-times elaborate, the case with a female is simple. Consequently, female names are likely to be less expressive and more stereotypic.

Equipped with some basics about naming, we now go back to Fa Mu Lan and Ts'ai Yen. We need to be reminded here that a Chinese has his/her last name first, Fa and Ts'ai are thus last names. That a family name precedes a given name is indicative of the culture's emphasis on the membership of a person in the family lineage as opposed to the valuing of the individual suggested in the name order of the American. Mu Lan can be literally translated as "Sylvan Orchid," and Yen as "Well-wrought Jade." It is no coincidence that a recent anthropological study of Chinese naming in Hong Kong reports that "Splendid Orchid, Morning Flower, Resembling Jade" are among the most frequent types of female names. Flowers and jewelry have become commonplaces attached to the notion of femininity. And it is natural that Kingston would hate to see her heroines put in a vase or stored in a vault. By rendering Fa Mu Lan and Ts'ai Yen in sound symbols and by emptying the semantic content the characters originally have, Kingston has discarded the patriarchal reinforcement of woman as sexual/aesthetic object and material commodity. Kingston's counteraction against the male power of naming both contains and transcends the textual level. In fact, Yen is widely known in China by her other name, Wen Ji, meaning "Civil Beauty" or "Cultured Slave." The deliberate withholding or rather suppressing of this piece of information is at once an attempt at the annihilation of the dominant male chauvinist consciousness and a manifestation of the female power of emancipation via renaming.

2. *Names translated from Chinese characters*

Renaming operates on different planes to correlate a variety of social and historical conditions. If Fa Mu Lan and Ts'ai Yen are names of Chinese antiquity, Brave Orchid and Moon Orchid are names in and for the American reality. The meanings are translated and the family name of the sisters dropped. This negotiation is a step of cultural adjustment not abandonment. Addressing by the first name may be regarded as the characters' desire to mingle with the Toms and Kathys, but it appears more likely to be a remainder of our author's realization of the American social milieu where everybody is supposed to be equal and familiar. But, the word "Orchid" at least denotes the family connection of the mother and the aunt if it does not further indicates the extended family of the orchid with its banal orchidaceousness. Yet, "Brave Orchid" can hardly be a Chinese name given its inherent contradiction in terms. "Bravery" is allegedly a masculine quality, which a Taoist would designate as "Yang" (the sun), and the character that stands for its a frequent emblem on the front of the uniform for dynasties of royal soldiers. "Orchid", with its tender floweriness, however, is a conventional equivalent of femininity, a quality always affiliated with "Yin" (the moon). Such a name combination as "Brave Orchid" is then not to be licensed in real life circumstances because of its deviation from both cultural and linguistic norms. Nevertheless, the name becomes fictionally viable and even convincing because Brave Orchid turns out to be a living exemplifier of the paradoxical appellation. She is at once a female vanguard of the self-reliant rugged individual and a version of traditional motherhood. The name tellingly replicates the person's contradiction of cultural expectations or rather it serves as a transitional token that Kingston means to transcend.

If the violation of the naming system befits Kingston's design of working toward an ideal womanhood, her conformity to it serves to expose the smothering status quo of women that demands change. Moon Orchid, a perfect female name by traditional judgment, foreshadows the sorry destiny of its bearer. The "Moon," the Chinese cosmic correspondence of "Yin" or femaleness, is also the home of the Roman goddess Luna. East and West, Lunacy is coded female. Once a victim of patriarchal order in rural China, Moon Orchid is at a total loss in America, confronting her husband's marriage with another woman without the slightest bravery to claim her man. So, she sings her song with the cuckoo and enters the crammed attic of mad-women, living in a world no better than the well in which her sister-in-law, the no name woman, has found her permanent rest.

3. *No names*

While the namelessness of a person generally implies one's lack of individual identity, it does not, I would argue, always blur one's representative possibilities. The rebelliousness or rather the anti-nomianism of the no name woman aunt is so pointedly invoked that one cannot help recalling Hester Prynne in the woods and Edna Pontellier heading for the open sea. Denying the no name woman aunt of her name is a community measure to safeguard its values and exercise its mechanisms, whereas one consequence of such a denial is to impart a collective identity to the aunt who has now joined the forces of the rejected women and has become a type and a sign. Similar to the father whose name has never been mentioned in the text yet whose authority is extant, the no name woman has exhibited the potential power of her gender.

That the narrator of the book has no name is a different case. One way of reading this fact is to see her as a composite of all the five characters so far analysed: they are her mothers who personify for her the meanings of constructing femininity in various historic times and socio-cultural contexts. Another way of looking at it is to regard the narrative as a traffic of symbols whose flow defies the codification of naming until the very moment when the reader is shocked into awareness of who the woman warrior actually is. Her name is in the making.

personal pronouns

The process of attaining a name commences with enormous bewilderment for the girl of our book. She must first of all come to terms with the symbols that represent her:

> I could not understand "I." The Chinese "I" has seven strokes, intricacies. How could the American "I," assuredly wearing a hat like the Chinese, having only three strokes, the middle so straight? Was it out of politeness that this writer left off strokes the way a Chinese has to write her own name small and crooked? No, it was not politeness; "I" is a capital and "you" is a lower-case. I stared at that middle line and waited so long for its black center to resolve into tight strokes and dots that I forgot to pronounce it. There is a Chinese word for the female *I*—which is "slave." . . .

Here the girl's problem with the English and Chinese pronouns is very striking, for it underscores the conflicting cultural brigades fighting for her allegiance. The antithetical interplay rests first in the generic Chinese "I" and the English "I." Her bafflement at the latter sign results from her immersion in the Chinese culture from which she originates. Note, for example, the Chinese have not only the Confucian stress on the communal worth of the self, but also the Juang Jouian resistance to categorical schemes that results in the downplay of an "i." Contrarily, however, we have in the American cultural heritage the Emersonian divinity in man and the Whitmanian celebration of the absolute individual that eventuate in the "I" being bigger than anything else.

Her second perplexity seems to hinge on another parity, namely, the one between the traditional Chinese female "I" and against the English "I." Even though the English language does not contain a specially designated pronoun for the second sex as the ancient Chinese obviously has, the Anglo-American "I" in the male-centered English language poses similar tribulation for female holders of the same pronoun. Kingston's uneasiness with the English "I," as we may see, is a reiteration of an age-long concern of female writers. Virginia Woolf contemplates after having done an exhaustive comparative reading of male and female authors:

> Indeed, it was delightful to read a man's writing again. It was so direct, so straightforward after the writing of women. It indicated such freedom of mind, such liberty of person, such confidence in himself. . . . But after reading a chapter or two a shadow seemed to lie across the page. It was a straight dark bar shaped something like the letter "I." [*A Room of One's Own*, cited in Patricia Meyer Spacks, *The Female Imagination*, 1976]

The assertive English "I" has an alien effect on the female

bearers of the language, who are barred from such an assured stance that the pronoun suggests. Woolf and Kingston seem to have shared a feminist vision that ironizes the inequalities of gender inherent in the double standard culture. Together, they implicitly challenge the dominantly male "I," so "insanely egotistic," that finding a means of representing themselves is rendered incumbent.

re-visioning myths & cross-dressing genres

The issue of personal pronouns in naming is central to Kingston because these linguistic entities always mirror the condition of people they personate, and this issue is closely connected with the problem of narrative voice. If the "I" in the confessional mode of Western autobiography seems presumptuous by Chinese thinking, the traditional self-effacement of the Chinese has provided almost no model to its Western counterpart. If the "I" in both languages upsets the female well being, the narrator's adoption of the given, be it personal pronouns or narrative strategy, will make inevitable her susceptibility to imprisonment by the established male category. To forge an "I" under the extreme burden of history-culture and gender-genre, Kingston has formulated her own copying device in what Alicia Ostriker terms as "revisionist mythmaking" [in "The Thieves of Language: Women Poets and Revisionist Mythmaking," in *The New Feminist Criticism: Essays on Women, Literature and Theory*, 1985]. The ideas is that an appropriation of a previously acknowledged myth for some altered ends "confers on the writer the sort of authority unavailable to someone who writes 'merely' of the private self" and "ultimately mak[es] cultural change possible."

The woman warrior myth of the "Whiter Tiger" chapter is a case in point. To understand Kingston's re-visioning, we need first of all to contextualize the prototext. Originated in a Chinese folktale, "The Ballad of Mu Lan" had its first written reification as early as the fifth century. The narrative verse relates the story of Mu Lan's substitution for her senile father for conscription, her military triumph, and her eventual return home, shedding her armor only to put on her old dress. The popularity of the poem with both the ruling and the ruled for centuries of feudal history can be explained in terms of the very cultural resources the poem derives from. For the emperor, Mu Lan has performed the duty of a subject and paid tribute to his royalty, while for her father, Mu Lan has fulfilled her obligation of being a daughter and displayed proper filial piety. The wish to perpetuate the social hierarchy as well as male hegemony, as expressed in the Confucian maxim of "emperor as emperor; lord as lord; father as father; and son as son," is embodied in this particular myth so that the cultural capital is reinvested.

Undermining such a valorized myth for Kingston involves

transfiguration and disguise. Like the Mu Lan who puts on male attire to be sanctioned for battle, Kingston codes her material with cherished American values in order to win her readership. Yet, unlike the Mu Lan who does not even have a place in the feudal order but volunteers her service for the king/father, Kingston creates a rebel whose fight for justice is also a process of affirming her identity. Therefore, from the outset, the woman warrior is combating her foes with a double-edged sword.

Kingston rewrites the Mu Lan story with substantial additional material. The sixty-two line, six stanza original myth has a battle scene depicted succinctly in six lines:

> Travelling thousands of miles in wars,
> Time flies among mountains.
> Wintry gust cuts golden arms,
> Cold light shines on iron armors.
> The general engages in hundreds of battles,
> And the hero returns in ten years.

Kingston, in her reconstruction, however, has fleshed out this basic plot with the ritual trials and training, the supernatural aid of the immortals and the nurturing of the natural elements or animals before our heroine embarks on her journey to conquer the ultimate evil. In effect, the audience of the book experiences the text in very much the same way the movie-goers react to a cinematic intercutting. Within the premise of the myth in discussion, we notice yet another level of negotiation. With the addition of material, the myth itself undergoes a structural change: it has been transformed into a version of the Kung Fu movie interspliced with a Western.

The re-visioning of a valorized myth, it seems, involves a process of "cross-dressing as re-dressing" [Susan Gubar, "Blessing in Disguise: Cross-dressing as Redressing for Female Modernists," *Massachusetts Review*, Vol. 22, 1981]. Kingston's artistic match-making of the Kung Fu and the Western in the re-presentation of the Chinese myth is an exploitation of the general audience who will be, one may argue, more responsive to formulaic genres. The American TV series entitled "Kung Fu" has in fact its setting in the American west with Chinese Buddhist and Taoist monks alike giving psychic concentration workouts to their disciples and bestowing upon them miraculous marital arts and moral axioms. More than one hundred years of American fascination with oriental mysticism from the Transcendentalists to the Beats and Hippies has found its most salient expression in mass media. Though Kingston's myth is not located in the fictional west, she certainly capitalizes on the perennial American enchantment for the new, the exotic and the endless horizon. In an effort to draw her power from the mass culture, she is simultaneously celebrating the very ideological matrices underlying the culture, for her story outlines the same Western frontier thesis that promulgates "democratic mobility" and American individualism.

General Mu Lan combating on horseback in the revised myth gives an alternate version of the Western pop hero, the Lone Ranger, if you may. Her disguise enables her to experiment and reverse the traditional role models and establish a new set of relationships based on equality and individual fulfillment. While waging war against the oppressing and exploiting emperor across the country, Mu Lan also finds a husband, begets a son, and creates a mobile home of her own. The empire is overthrown and the emperor beheaded, but full justice will not be done until the final shoot-out. The archenemy is the baron whose favorite saying is: "It is more profitable to raise geese than daughters." Mu Lan "attack[s his] stronghold alone," and finding him there "counting his money," she "rip[s] off [her] shirt" to show her statement of vengeance tattooed on her back: "When I saw his startled eyes at my breasts, I slashed him across the face and on the second stroke cut off his head." This Amazonic flourish consummates her epic journey and signals the victory of good over evil, justice over injustice and feminists over chauvinists.

In "Myth and the Production of History" [in *Ideology and Classic American Literature*, edited by Sacvan Bervotich and Myra Jehlan, 1986], Richard Slotkin points out that "Myth does not argue its ideology, it exemplifies it. It projects models of good or heroic behavior that reinforce the values of ideology, and affirms as good the distribution of authority and power that ideology rationalizes." Kingston's marriage of the Kung Fu and the Western in her myth is no accident: she is enunciating the power and toughness of her gender to partake of any endeavor her male correspondent is capable of.

words, voice & song

The desire expressed in the myth marks the lack of such fulfillment in the reality of the mythmaker. "My American life has been such a disappointment," our narrator admits. Racism, sexism and corporation capitalism continue to shackle her in every conceivable way. From the Mu Lan myth, the narrator confides in us. "I've learned exactly who the enemies are. I easily recognize them—business-suited in their modern American executive guise, each boss two feet taller than I am and impossible to meet eye to eye." The identification of the baron in the tale with the boss in life is a movement from mythic fantasy to harsh reality. For Kingston, such a movement begins and always proceeds with the mastery of words. If naming, pronoun usage, reshaping of myths reflect stages of the self communicating and coping with language, a full articulation will betoken the pinnacle of self

empowerment. "The swordswoman and I are not so dissimilar," the concluding paragraph of the "White Tiger" chapter goes:

> What we have in common are the words at our backs. The idioms for *revenge* are "report a crime" and "report to five families." The reporting is the vengeance—not the beheading, not the cutting, but the words. And I have so many words—"chink" words and "gook" words too—that they do not fit my skin.

The words here are heavily loaded. If the keyword for Kingston's Mu Lan Myth is "revenge," the word not only reminds us of the historic context behind "The Ballad of Mu Lan" but also leads us to another historic/mythic story of General Yue Fei (1103-1141) from which the carving of the back emanates. What is blatant in both Chinese narrative accounts but latent in Kingston's is the distinctive ethnocentrism that propels the historical heroes to defend their country, Zhong Guo (China), literally translated as the "Central Kingdom," from the harassment of the barbarians. Now that the WASPs are buzzing us "chinks," we might as well call them "ghosts": when the drug for Crazy Mary is mistakenly delivered to her house, Brave Orchid fumes, "That ghost! That dead ghost! . . . Revenge. We've got to avenge this wrong on our future, on our health, and on our lives." Simple labels, in their condensed form, represent a complex cluster of values overlapping racial, sexual, social, economic, and political categories and they carry considerable cultural information. The usage of "ghost" for foreigners became a common practice probably in the late nineteenth century when Western imperial powers invaded the Chin Empire of China with guns and opium. For the first time in history the citizens of the "Central Kingdom" were decentered and they strove to retain their centrality by defining their oppressor as the other, the "ghost," the "Kuei" which takes on the meaning of "devil" and "demon." Such negative connotations associated in the English language with Satanic forces are more or less dropped as Kingston opts for the word "ghost" which accentuates the insubstantiality and neutrality of a specter. Notice that the word "ghost" has its highest frequency in Brave Orchid's speech, a first generation immigrant who speaks little English and who probably finds it sufficient to release her frustration by showering "Kuei"s on her foes, therefore achieving some allegorical solution to problems in reality. The easy way out is insufficient for the American-born Kingston who is yet to actualize the phantasmic world by co-option of its symbolic dynamics, the "ghost" words.

There are always double binds on the pronunciation of words for the American-Chinese Kingston. She is first confronted with the pull of two cultures. Corresponding to her previous confusion with the pronoun "I" in both English and

Chinese, Kingston finds that discrimination against female speech in both cultural patterns exacerbating. The Chinese saying, "a ready tongue is an evil," is echoed by the example of talking "American-feminine." This dual social-cultural pressure culminates in the torturing of her six-grade alterego, another wordless Chinese girl. She cannot make her speak either by reasoning or by force. The aftermath of this event is our narrator's eighteen months confinement to bed "with a mysterious illness." A brief citation of her monologue to her unfortunate Doppelgänger will help us come up with a diagnosis of her malady—another double bind that her appropriation of American mainstream culture seems to entail, "Do you want to be like this, dumb . . . your whole life? Don't you ever want to be a cheerleader? Or a pompon girl? . . . You've got to let people know you have a personality and a brain." The model she exhorts and the quality she admires generates a dilemma. The popularity conferred on the cheerleader lies in the secondary position that her role typifies and her "rah-rah" shout is less a product of brain than an acquiescence to male power. Again, the ritualistic demonstration of the footballer and the cheerleader on the playground is arguably a modern instance of the knight and lady in the field of ancient chivalry. The roles assigned to the female seem to have undergone little change despite the passage of time. A cheerleader occupies only the sideshow: she is not even close to Mu Lan who commands an army of male soldiers. The girl Kingston is ironically locked into, as the narrative so delicately captures for its reader, the hegemonic cultural categories that she needs to disentangle herself from.

The female malady gets its partial cure when our heroine has gained literacy in the "ghost" language. The fluency in language is accompanied by a cultural competence the language constitutes. Her zero IQ in kindergarten, owing to her Chinese-speaking parents' innate deprivation in the target culture, has been reversed. She proclaims her success with pride:

> Do you know what the Teacher Ghosts say about me? They tell me I'm smart, and I can win scholarships. I can get into colleges . . . I know how to get A's . . . I can make a living and take care of myself.

The revelation of the above passage seems to go beyond the power of assertion with which the sharing of the verbal system endows her. Her gain in the English language is balanced by the loss of her traditional Chinese values. Indeed, the girl Kingston's proclamation marks her departure from the Confucian paradigm of social relationships that emphasizes the family/interdependence to an American archetype of individuality/independence. The girl Kingston is also aware that the appropriation of the linguistic resources marks nothing more than an initiation into modes of domi-

nation. To better realize the potential of the words, she appears to have an intuitive grasp of the law governing the exchangeability of cultural competence to cultural capital by becoming part of a specific set of objective relationships, i.e. the educational system. Her smartness proven by her previous A's will enable her to have scholarships in college and the A's she makes there will earn her a living. The girl Kingston's declaration of independence is endorsed by the very system at once encouraging the mobility of those individuals who are able to fit in and turning back those who cannot. Her actual attainment of a degree and a certificate is an indication of her success via participation in the system, be it linguistic, educational, economic, or cultural. Once silenced by the invisible and indominatable forces, she now becomes part of the very forces and augments them with her voice, so high, like "an icicle in the desert."

Kingston orchestrates her voicing with another mythic story, the capture of the second-century Chinese woman poet Ts'ai Yen, which intensifies her closing narrative to the highest possible note. Conceivably, the historic and literary documentation is again revisioned by Kingston to effect a settlement—the settlement of the writer/narrator's past with her present, the settlement of her place of belonging and the settlement of her identity. In her autobiographical verse, the ancient poetess Ts'ai Yen expressed ever so poignantly her anger and humiliation at being made slave and wife by the invading nomadic tribe. The note of exasperation and despondency pervades the poetry of Ts'ai Yen who complains of her plight of being a female captive. The tone of fury is notably absent in Kingston's version. Instead, we see Ts'ai Yen riding on the horse of the barbarian chieftain and receiving a gift of a mare when impregnated by him. She fights with him, charging into villages and encampments. She becomes the baffled Ts'ai Yen living among the understanding noble savages. One day, Kingston tells us, she is so struck by the music of barbarian reed pipes filling the desert outside her tent that she starts to sing

> a song so high and clear, it matched the flutes . . .
> Her words seemed to be Chinese, but the barbarians understood their sadness and anger. Sometimes they thought they could catch barbarian phrases about forever wandering . . . she left her tent to sit by the winter campfires, ringed by the barbarians.

The poet in exile is no longer alienated. The ethnicity that once seems a handicap is now her strength. She merges into the "ring" with a revitalizing energy. Her voice in the chorus is not mere integration. It has made a difference, creating an interface of cultures upon which new knowledge generates. The recorded myth of Ts'ai Yen with her minority voice accepted by a majority audience becomes a self-fulfilling prophecy that signifies Kingston's own canonicity. "It translated well," as our narrator asserts in the last sentence of *The Woman Warrior,* and her book is indeed a translation *par excellence.* It translates a cross-cultural experience into words, a hyphenated Chinese-American into a non-hyphenated Chinese American, and a no name woman into the woman warrior, Maxine Hong Kingston.

Joanne S. Frye (essay date 1988)

SOURCE: "The Woman Warrior: Claiming Narrative Power, Recreating Female Selfhood," in *Faith of a (Woman) Writer,* edited by Alice Kessler-Harris and William McBrien, Greenwood Press, 1988, pp. 293-301.

[*Frye is an American educator and the author of* Living Stories, Telling Lives: Women and the Novel in Contemporary Experience. *In the following essay, she argues that in* The Woman Warrior, *Kingston portrays an image of female selfhood that is both imaginative and realistic.*]

One of the compelling insights of feminist literary criticism has been the recognition that the literary traditions we inherit have often denied women the power of naming and the power of narrative: women have inherited a sense of story in which action and affirming self-definition seem precluded not only by social environment but also by expectations of how stories work. Neither the mythic nor the realistic mode, as traditionally used, has seemed capable of adequately portraying the possibilities for a strong female selfhood.

In response to this apparent preclusion, recent women writers have sought to develop alternate narrative modes for the literary interpretation of female experience. And, as Suzanne Juhasz points out in her analysis of form in feminist autobiography [in "Towards a Theory of Form in Feminist Autobiography: Kate Millet's *Flying* and *Sita;* Maxine Hong Kingston's ***The Woman Warrior,***" in *Women's Autobiography: Essays in Criticism,* 1980], some particularly fruitful development of form has been done by women autobiographers. Associating these formal responses with versions of reality that are "characteristically" female, Juhasz identifies two possible patterns of response to female experience: the personal, factual, diary-like form chosen by Kate Millett and the imaginative, fantastic, novelistic form chosen by Maxine Hong Kingston in ***The Woman Warrior.*** Kingston's style, argues Juhasz, develops "from the notion that fantasy, the life of the imagination, creates female identity." The argument is as follows: Millett's choice of the diary-like form is appropriate to women because "women's lives are traditionally private lives"; Kingston's choice of the fantastic is appropriate because "women also live, traditionally, another kind of private life, an inner life of the imagination that has special significance for them due to the outright conflict between societal possibility and imagina-

tive possibility." "Kingston's approach," Juhasz says, "makes creating rather than recording, the significant autobiographical act."

> **In my view, Kingston's reaction to female experience is centered in simultaneously claiming new possibilities and integrating a knowledge of actual lived reality—claiming fantasy not as a separate inner world of the imagination but as a powerful tool for reshaping lived experience beyond the repressions of personal daily life.**
> **—Joanne S. Frye**

Juhasz's assertions and her analysis are perceptive, particularly her assessment of the formal restructuring which women are developing in response to claiming and recreating their own lived experience. But, without disputing the overall argument, I want to point out the dangers implicit in building an analysis on the antithesis between the fantastic and the realistic and to argue that Kingston's achievement lies rather in her use of the narrative process to refuse this antithesis and to develop a female identity within a social context. To claim fantasy as an autobiographical mode—i.e., to withdraw into what Juhasz calls the "inner life of the imagination" as a reaction to an oppressive reality—is to risk leaving the oppressive reality untouched, unaltered, and also to leave one's shaped identity without a basis for action within that reality. Kingston, I think, is *not* withdrawing from reality. Rather, by drawing upon they possibilities of Chinese narrative tradition as well as the English language tradition to which she contributes, she is offering both an imaginative construction of self and also a realistic affirming of self within a societal context.

In my view, Kingston's reaction to female experience is centered in simultaneously claiming new possibilities and integrating a knowledge of actual lived reality—claiming fantasy not as a separate inner world of the imagination but as a powerful tool for reshaping lived experience beyond the repressions of personal daily life. For it seems to me that the power of ***The Woman Warrior*** lies not in the invisible force of fantasy as distinct from reality but in the powerful interaction of fantasy with reality—without refusing to differentiate—in determining new possibilities for female selfhood. Through this interaction, the narrative process, then, enables Kingston to develop a strong female identity, grounded—as is narrative itself—in the capacity to choose and to interpret and in the ability to act in a social context.

The most immediate reality in Kingston's childhood is extremely oppressive: not only the isolation of a bi-cultural context in which she can claim neither Chinese identity nor

American identity but also the immediate misogyny of much of that context. Kingston grows up haunted by a vague fear of being sold into slavery or wifehood and a more immediate awareness that her brothers are more valued than she and her sisters, as is clearly evidence in the rituals and celebrations of their lives. She knows fully the traditions of feet-binding and the capacity of the language to reinforce self-hatred; as she says, "There is a Chinese word for the female I—which is 'slave.' Break the women with their own tongues!" She is surrounded, too, by the villagers' voices sadly noting, "One girl—and another girl," and her great-uncle's voice roaring his refusal: "No girls!" And the misogynist sayings fill the air around her: "Feeding girls is feeding cowbirds"; "There's no profit in raising girls. Better to raise geese than girls"; "when you raise girls, you're raising children for strangers."

Her own femaleness thus becomes itself a negation to be overcome. At times in her childhood. Kingston attempts resistance by trying to deny her femaleness, especially by breaking the established codes for female behavior: achieving academic success, behaving clumsily, breaking dishes, refusing to cook. And her resistance to the norms gives her reason to gloat when accused of being a "bad girl": for, she says, "Isn't a bad girl almost a boy?" But the resistance is difficult, if not impossible, to achieve when immersed in daily reality since she is confronted not only with the repressive norms from her Chinese heritage but also with the conflicting and differently repressive norms of American femininity.

The attempts to reject her own femaleness imply a kind of self-hatred, which is even more evident in a story of factual reality from her childhood, told in the final section of the autobiography. Following the portrayal of her own shrouded childhood silence in American public schools, she tells of her physical and psychological abuse of another Chinese American girl with whom Kingston herself obviously identifies, for the "quite one" shares Kingston's own earlier refusal to speak aloud in public and her inability to participate in American life. But Kingston is also making every effort to differentiate herself from this girl by claiming her own hatred of neatness and pastel colors, her own desire to be tough rather than soft. The actual abuse is clearly an effort to expunge those parts of her Chinese-female identity which she abhors and to mark out her own possibilities for strength in resisting that identity. The experience is followed by a "mysterious illness" and with it an eighteen-month period of social isolation, after which she must relearn "how to talk" and come to recognize that the other girl has different ways of surviving, different protections than are available to Kingston. The painful retelling of the abuse and of her subsequent healing solitude becomes the attempt now to reinterpret her own past, to free herself from both the silence and the aggression, to alleviate the evident guilt she

feels, and to understand the sources of the person she has become, somehow straddling Chinese and American realities and accepting her female identity.

But this effort cannot succeed through simple documentation of either the repressive reality or her attempts to resist it. Rather she must claim her female identity by shaping her narrative interpretation of self through the interpenetration of fantasy with reality. The dominant fantasy in the autobiography is, of course, that of the woman warrior, told in the second section, titled "White Tigers." The tale is a retelling of the story of a legendary Chinese woman, Fa Mu Lan, who replaced her father in battle, fought with courage and strength, and then returned to live peacefully in the village. Kingston uses it as an old legend with roots in reality; but she also uses it as a powerful personal story, transforming the legend of Fa Mu Lan—which, as a child, she had sung over and over with her mother—into a personal myth of being herself chosen to be the salvation of her people. Telling it in the first person indicative, she claims for herself all the mythical powers of Fa Mu Lan. But in the final paragraph, she returns to the subjunctive—no longer "I did," but rather "I would"—and concludes the tale: "From the words on my back, and how they were fulfilled, the villagers would make a legend about my perfect filiality."

The framing of the legend-as-personal myth—introduced and concluded in the subjective mood but told throughout in the indicative—is confusing to some readers: students have asked me, "What really did happen? What does she mean, she carried her baby inside her armor? Did she really meet an old man and woman who taught her magical survival techniques?" The power of the fantastic event told as actual; is hard to resist. But the tale gains its real power through the simultaneous knowledge that it is not actual and that it is grounded in what *is* actual: though the tale itself is framed in the subjunctive mood, its larger frame is the highly conscious narrative of lived experience both preceding and following it. The section begins, for example, with a clear assessment of the uses of fantasy: "When we Chinese girls listened to the adults talk-story, we learned that we failed if we grew up to be but wives or slaves. We could be heroines, swordswomen. . . . Perhaps women were once so dangerous that they had to have their feet bound." And the presentation of the legend is followed abruptly by the statement, "My American life has been such a disappointment" and the reiteration of the misogynist sayings which surrounded her childhood.

The tale becomes her protection against her hostile surroundings, but it is not a fantastic escape from a harsh reality, as might be implied in the contrast between "slaves" and "swordswomen" or in the allusion to women's once dangerous powers. Rather the tale is itself rooted in her harsh daily reality and assumes for itself and for her a reality of its own. Early in the section she recalls the stories of her childhood: "Night after night my mother would talk-story until we fell asleep. I couldn't tell where the stories left off and the dreams began, her voice the voice of the heroines in my sleep." And then, "At last I saw that I too had been in the presence of great power, my other talking-story.... She said I would grow up a wife and a slave, but she taught me the song of the warrior woman, Fa Mu Lan. I would have to grow up a warrior woman." This reality then—the power of her mother as a real woman and as a story-teller—is the source of the knowledge present in the subjunctive become indicative, the impetus for the personal legend, and the basis for creating a powerful selfhood rooted in reality, strengthened through fantasy, and evolved through the narrative process. She understands the limits of the real—"I mustn't feel bad that I haven't done as well as the swordswoman did; after all, no bird called me, no wise old people tutored me. I have no magic beads..."—but she also understands the strength available through both the mythic perception and the lived reality.

The conclusion of the section draws fully on this integration of a painful reality and an infusion of strength. Kingston evokes her present distance from the American-Chinese villagers of her childhood: "When I visit the family now, I wrap my American successes around me like a private shawl; ... I refuse to shy my way anymore through our Chinatown, which tasks me with the old sayings and the stories." But the concluding paragraph reveals precisely how this refusal has become possible—and it is not simply a question of "American successes," but rather of finding a use for the Chinese legend in the context of a successful American reality:

> The swordswoman and I are not so dissimilar. May my people understand the resemblance soon so that I can return to them. What we have in common are the words at our backs. The ideographs for *revenge* are "report a crime" and "report to five families." The reporting is the vengeance—not the beheading, not the gutting, but the words. And I have so many words—"chink" words and "gook" words too—that they do not fit on my skin.

The woman warrior, with the words of vengeance carved into the skin of her back, and the mother's daily talking-story merge for Kingston into a powerful source of female identity—beyond the bound feet and the cries of "maggot" which haunt her childhood on the other side of this reality.

This use of fantasy is not precisely an "inner life" as distinct from "societal possibility." Rather it is a restructuring of societal possibility through the dailiness of stories told and stories remembered. The fantasy, in other words, is not distinct from the reporting of fact—it is itself a kind of re-

porting from the dailiness of both childhood and adulthood: vengeance for the abuse inherent in "chink" words and "gook" words—the claiming of the power of language through a heritage of power in fantasy. In this way, Kingston can merge her "American successes" as a writer with the heritage of the fantastic from her Chinese-American childhood: as a writer she claims the power to avenge the wrongs done to her people and to herself—to be the woman warrior. In claiming, the power of the legend, she has simultaneously claimed her own personal strength and her ability to act in a social context.

The centrality of narrative and the power of imagination are established even before the introduction of the central fantasy of the woman warrior. The book opens in a section titled "No Name Woman" with Kingston's mother telling her a story in confidence, a real life story of an aunt who had been expunged from the family history for her sexual sins, her illegitimate pregnancy. Kingston's mother concludes her narrative with a warning: "Now that you have started to menstruate, what happened to her could happen to you. Don't humiliate us. You wouldn't like to be forgotten as if you had never been born. The villagers are watchful." Kingston calls this narrative "a story to grow up on" by which her mother "tested our strength to establish realities." She goes on, "Those of us in the first American generations have had to figure out how the invisible world the emigrants built around our childhoods fit in solid America." Kingston's own immediate response to the problem is to recreate for herself in vivid detail the story of her aunt, thereby making it her own to experience fully, to live out for her aunt. In the midst of this narrative Kingston, somewhat incongruously, addresses her own specific problems in growing up and trying "to turn myself American-feminine"; but the conclusion brings her back to the imagined subjective experience of the aunt and the painful recognition of outsiderness focussed in her aunt's suicide and the family's denial. The issue of femininity and more, of female sexuality, however, finally does provide a kind of coherence: it is because of her sexuality that Kingston's mother tells her the story, and it is through the knowledge of her own sexuality that Kingston creates the story of her aunt's painful death. The need for a female heritage by which to assess and develop her own female selfhood is the driving force: "Unless I see her life branching into mine, she gives me no ancestral help." Through telling the aunt's story and thus rescuing her from the family silence which had denied her existence, Kingston has created the branches of her own female ancestry.

There are other women, too, both real and fantastic, whose stories shape Kingston's emerging female identity: another aunt, Lovely Orchid, who does not, cannot, endure the culture shock in her arrival in America; the other "crazy women," who in various ways have lost their control over language as a shaping force—"Insane people were the ones who couldn't explain themselves"; her sister, whom she wants to protect from the marriage-making assaults on her selfhood; the other Chinese girls in her school, hated for their shared silence in public; her grandmother who loved the theater and refused to fear the bandits; and finally the legendary poet Ts'ai Yen. Each provides yet another lens on Kingston's own immediate reality: the possibility of seeing it more clearly and claiming it more forcefully. And each participates in establishing an awareness of female vulnerability to cultural expectations and female strength through language and especially through narrative power.

The stories, then, become interpretive strategies for her own lived experience as a female and are never severed from that experience. Each story—legendary fantasy or imaginative construction of another's life—interacts profoundly with the foundation narrative of her own immediate experience: the autobiography of fact, of daily lived reality. As she has told us in the opening section, her mother explicitly gave her stories—both fantastic and actual—in order to heighten her awareness of perceived reality.

The third section thus assumes a pivotal significance as Kingston's sympathetic reconstruction of her mother's own story of her life in China as a woman alone and independent, a woman who establishes her identity through her work as a student and then a doctor but who also engages in fantastic encounters with ghosts and monsters. The experience, as told, is both alien to the teller and personally real and powerful to her. Through telling her mother's story, she understands her own Chinese roots, the reality of a deeply misogynist heritage which nonetheless has fed her mother's strength and autonomy. The conclusion of this section provides us with the most recent event in the autobiography: a conversation between mother and daughter—"when I last visited my parents"—a conversation in which they affirm a shared identity in being both Dragons, born in dragon years, and in being both fully committed to the work they do, however different it is: "She sends me on my way, working always and now old. . . ." As the most direct branching of ancestral lives, Kingston's mother provides the personal integration of fantasy and reality through which Kingston can claim her strength in femaleness.

But before she can claim the strength she shares with her mother, she must find the uses of narrative which will effectively assess her own reality; and these cannot be the same as her mother's easy blend of fantasy and reality. The process by which she works this through for herself is analogous to the writing of the autobiography itself: the taking on for herself the story-telling and the listening functions which she has previously attributed to her mother. In the final section of the book she tells of a childhood confrontation with her mother, based on her own need to gain absolution through confessing to her mother: "I had grown inside me a list of over two hundred things that I had to tell my mother so that she would know the true things about me and to stop the pain in my throat." When she actually undertakes this confession process, she and her mother end up shouting at each other from the confusion of Kingston's need and their difficulties of cross-cultural, cross-generational communication: "And suddenly I got very confused and lonely because I was at that moment telling her my list, and in telling, it grew. No higher listener. No listener but myself." Thus she confronts her own essential aloneness and attempts to overcome it through the imposition of language and explanation, the naming of realities and the imagining of possibilities: making herself the confirming listener and integrating her mother's reality into her own become the basis of her autobiographical process.

While claiming the listening function for herself, she must also claim and redefine the story-telling function. She ends one segment of her childhood confessional outpouring by saying, "And I don't want to listen to any more of your stories; they have no logic. They scramble me up. You lie with stories. . . . I can't tell what's real and what you make up." Her mother's story-telling—which so clearly branches into her own life and her own identity—must be redefined for her own uses, but it cannot be entirely relinquished. Where her mother had felt no need to distinguish between fantasy and reality in her narratives, Kingston feels impelled to begin with reality and to hold onto the distinction and yet to allow them to interpenetrate as a part of the truth-telling process. The necessity of defining her reality and her cultural roots, the need to contain and overcome the negations of her culturally perceived femaleness drives her to write the autobiography—to be teller, as well as listener—and in it to claim the power of narrative explanation: "Be careful what you say. It comes true. It comes true. I had to leave home in order to see the world logically, logic the new way of seeing. I learned to think that mysteries are for explanation." And two pages later: "Perhaps . . . what I once had was not Chinese-sight at all but child-sight that would have disappeared eventually without struggle. The throat pain always returns, though, unless I tell what I really think. . . ." The need to make sense of her life—lived reality and imaginative construction—is what motivates the autobiography and what defines the rich and complex form it takes: "I continue to sort out what's just my childhood, just my imagination, just my family, just the village, just movies, just living." And the sorting out is a new integration of her mother's uses of fantasy with her own lives reality.

The final story, then, is a merging of these needs from an adult perspective, and, significantly, a merging of her mother's story-telling with her own. She introduces it, saying, "Here is a story my mother told me, not when I was young, but recently, when I told her I also talk-story. The beginning is hers, the ending, mine." Like the story of the woman warrior, this story focuses on a woman from Chinese legend: Ts'ai Yen, a poet. But this story is given Kingston's own family history, as related by her mother, and is given its "branches" into Kingston's own life through the implicit meaning of the narrative rather than through the narrative transfiguration of selfhood, as with the woman warrior. Captured by the barbarians, Ts'ai Yen gave music and form to her experiences among them, thus communicating to both the barbarians and her own people, somehow bridging those cultural differences and also transmitting meaning in a different language eighteen centuries later. Kingston ends the story and the autobiography with the meaningful understatement about one of the songs, which survives in modern China and in Kingston's personal history: "It translated well"; like Kingston's own story, the verse has bridged the cultures and infused the experience with meaning for its listeners.

Thus does Kingston claim for herself the power of Ts'ai Yen, the power of language both to shape and to convey reality: the power of narrative to bridge cultural barriers and to reinfuse the female identity with the strength of an affirmed selfhood. In merging the realistic with the fantastic, *The Woman Warrior* demonstrates the centrality of the narrative process to interpreting lives and its special capacity to overcome the isolation of being an outsider—without a cultural identity and refusing identity in femininity as prescribed by either culture. Through the interpenetration of fantasy and reality in a multi-layered narrative, she has moved beyond her misogynistic heritage and overcome what she elsewhere calls her own "woman-hatred." In her autobiography. Maxine Hong Kingston has been able to use the narrative process itself to refuse the cultural negations she describes and to claim her femaleness as a source of strength both rooted in her cultural heritage and affirmed beyond that heritage. In doing so, she enriches her bi-cultural literary heritage and makes it truly her own.

Malini Schueller (essay date Fall 1989)

SOURCE: "Questioning Race and Gender Definitions: Dialogic Subversions in *The Woman Warrior*," in *Criticism*, Vol. XXXI, No. 4, Fall, 1989, pp. 421-37.

[*In the following essay, Schueller provides an analysis of* The Woman Warrior *as a work that offers insight into issues of racial, national, and gender identity.*]

Ever since its publication in 1976, Maxine Hong Kingston's *The Woman Warrior* has been praised as a feminist work. But while critics have written extensively about the articulation of female experience in *The Woman Warrior,* they have been unable to deal simultaneously with the questions of national and racial identity that the book so powerfully raises. However, if we approach women's writing as centrally concerned not strictly with gender but with oppression, we can fruitfully examine the conjuncture and relationship between female and ethnic identity, an important issue not only for this text but for feminist theory as well. I will briefly examine the politicization of female identity offered by some feminist critics and then examine *The Woman Warrior* as a dialogic text, one which subverts singular definitions of racial and ethnic identity and which valorizes intersubjectivity and communication.

In "The Laugh of the Medusa" [in *New French Feminism*, 1981] Helene Cixous proclaimed a manifesto for women's writing: "A feminine text cannot fail to be/more than subversive. It is volcanic;/as it is written it brings about an/upheaval of the old property crust,/carrier of masculine investments." Feminist critics have long recognized that what constitutes female experience is not biological gender or a specific female psyche but the constraints and limitations felt by women as a result of the cultural constitution of gender and the phallocentric organization of society. To write socially and politically as a woman is therefore to question the truth status and ostensible ideological neutrality of cultural norms and institutions. The feminine text, Cixous continues, "shatter[s] the framework of institutions." Kristeva has similarly argued that women's writing should "reject everything finite, definite, structured, loaded with meaning, in the existing state of society." Even though Marxist feminists like Monique Wittig have criticized the apparent lack of recognition by feminists of "women" (as opposed to mythical "woman") as an oppressed social class, it is obvious that Cixous and Kristeva are in fact very aware of this oppression. The subversions of institutions and cultural norms that Cixous and Kristeva call for in women's writing are goals for all marginal and oppressed groups. Marginal groups have little investment in concepts of unity, coherence, and universality because their own political efficacy depends upon forcing a recognition of the value of difference and diversity upon the dominant culture. Third world feminists have in fact challenged the presupposition of feminists who speak in the name of a singular womanhood and whose own analyses are blind to racial difference. The danger of theorizing about marginalized groups—women and racial minorities—is actually that of positing an essential blackness and femininity. What is politically important for women and racial minorities is not to frame correct definitions of female and ethnic identity but to question all such definitions. Above all it means to reject the concept of a stable and autonomous self upon which such definitions depend.

Bakhtin's privileging if the dialogic rests upon a similar awareness of the dangers of unified thinking and the liberative potential of dialogic subversions. Dostoevsky, the exemplar of dialogic thinking, succeeds not by creating a single consciousness at the center of the text but by presenting "a whole formed by the interaction of several consciousnesses, none of which entirely becomes an object for the other" [Mikhail Bakhtin, *Problems of Dostoevsky's Poetics,* 1984]. Dialogic thinking is based on intersubjectivity. It celebrates the Otherness of language, the potential of words to always carry echoes of other words. That is why feminist critics are increasingly beginning to use Bakhtin's theories as sites of women's resistance and women's voicing. Kristeva was the first to see the productive challenge of dialogic thinking. "Bakhtinian dialogism," according to Kristeva, "identifies writing as both subjectivity and communication, or better, as intertextuality" [*The Kristeva Reader,* 1986]. Dialogic forms such as the carnival challenge "God, authority, and social law." Dialogic subversions, as Patricia Yaeger has usefully demonstrated, are emancipatory strategies in women's writing. Few contemporary American writers are as aware of the need to question and subvert accepted cultural definitions as Maxine Hong Kingston. *The Woman Warrior* is a sustained subversion of cultural, racial and gender definitions and an affirmation of a radical intersubjectivity as the basis of articulation.

The Woman Warrior is a collection of "memoirs" of Kingston's experiences of growing up in an immigrant family in Stockton, California. Kingston reveals the squalor and poverty of Chinatowns, the endemic racism, the traumas of acculturation in a hostile environment, and her own attempt to subvert gender hierarchies by imaginative identification with the woman warrior. But although Kingston writes polemically against the subjugation of women and the racial hostility experienced by Chinese Americans, she does not do so from a position of stability or unity. Articulation itself is a complex issue in the text. The very act of speaking involves breaking through the gender and race barriers that suppress voicing from the margins. But the voice Kingston speaks through is not isolated and autonomous. It refracts, echoes, and is creatively conjoined with the numerous voices with which it interacts. This undefined basis of narration dramatizes Kingston's determination not to create singular definitions of ethnic identity in order to combat the impoverishing stereotypes to which Chinese Americans are subject, not to postulate the foundations of a new hierarchy. It is clear at the very outset that the act of articulation itself will be a major concern in the book. Kingston begins her memoirs with a secrecy oath imposed on her by her indomitable mother: "You must not tell anyone," and a moral drawn from the story of the adulterous aunt who has been banished from family memory. "Don't humiliate us. You wouldn't like to be forgotten as if you had never been born." Kingston is aware of the temerity involved in the very act of her writing. To articulate herself she must break through the numerous barriers that condemn her to voicelessness.

The unnamed narrator thus begins her recollections with the act of listening rather than speaking. Sworn to silence, she hears the tale of the unnamed aunt who gives "silent birth" to "save her inseminator's name." This initial story establishes the denial of expression women are condemned to in patriarchy and the cultural stranglehold the narrator must fight in order to express herself. The narrator here is a present day prototype of the "madwomen" of the Nineteenth Century, whispering their secrets from patriarchal attics. "Go away and work," her mother tells her. "Whispering, whispering, making no sense. Madness. I don't feel like hearing your craziness. . . . I shut my mouth, but I felt something alive tearing at my throat." She feels the agony of silence, the "pain in [her] throat" that comes from holding back the two hundred things she has to tell her mother.

But the anxiety of articulation is also peculiarly a racial one. Kingston is sensitive to the brutality and degradation experienced by Chinese immigrants. *China Men* records the heroism of Chinese railroad workers and sugarcane planters who survive hostility and violence. Living in a culture that had for long grouped Orientals with imbeciles and denied Chinese immigrants legal and naturalization rights, the present-day immigrants in *The Woman Warrior* still live in fear. Immigrants thus "guard their real names with silence" and even after years of living in America avoid signing innocuous permission slips for their children at school. The narrator realizes that "silence had to do with being a Chinese girl." In the American school she is overcome by dumbness, her voice reduced to a whisper. In the Chinese school she finds her voice but it is a strained one: "You could hear splinters in my voice, bones rubbing jagged against one another."

These vivid accounts of being tortured by silence are metaphors for the particular limitations the marginal writer must overcome in order to be heard. African-Americans had to demonstrate their very humanity by being able to write when public strictures expressly forbade schooling for them. Ralph Ellison felt compelled to "prove" his artistry by emulating the modernists. His unnamed, invisible narrator of *Invisible Man* could only discover his identity underground, in a Manhattan city sewer. Alice Walker's heroine, Celie, finds herself unable to speak to anyone but an abstract God; Toni Morison's Pecola remains trapped within a racial silence that condemns her to look forever at her image in the mirror. Kingston's voicelessness is a symbolic expression of the culture's refusal to give her voice legitimacy. But the alternative to this disempowerment, Kingston knows, is not to create a "true" Chinese woman's voice or to define a singular Chinese identity to celebrate, but to question the very political structures that make positions of power and powerlessness possible. Kingston deconstructs oppositions between American and Chinese, male and female, and most importantly between Self and Other by articulating herself through a language in which opposed and diverse voices constantly coexist. By doing so, Kingston questions the values of the autonomous self and definitions of racial and sexual identity, and simultaneously presents dialogic intersubjectivity and community as the realm of hope and possibility.

The tale of Fa Mu Lan, the legendary swordswoman who took her father's place in battle, fought gloriously, returned victorious, and lived obediently thereafter with her parents, is a fascinating and complex narrative of multiple voicing and gender reconstruction. Like most of the stories in the book, this one is not an "original." But Kingston reveals in retelling tales, deriving her inspiration from the community of tellers before her rather than from defining her own singular voice. The tales of swordswomen become part of the imagination of children as they listen to the adults "talk-story." Brave Orchid, the narrator's mother, recreates for her, in turn, the most adventuresome of the swordswomen tales. "Night after night my mother would talk-story until we fell asleep. I couldn't tell where the stories left off and the dreams began, her voice, the voice of the heroines in my sleep." The narrator remembers her own participation in the continuation of folklore. ". . . As a child I had followed my mother about the house, the two of us singing about Fa Mu Lan. . . . I had forgotten this chant that was once mine, given me by my mother, who may not have known its power to remind." The origins of the tale are communal and familial and the narrator's continuation of it attests to the relatedness of her voice to other voices. It is obvious that the intents of Brave Orchid's and the narrator's tales vary greatly; but the fascinating aspect of the tale is the narrator's ability to tell her own tale both in opposition to, and in harmony with Brave Orchid's tale.

The folkloric intent of the tale is the strengthening of the institution of the family. Girls are reminded that growing up as wives or slaves is a mark of mediocrity, failure. They have the potential to be "heroines, swordswomen." But the task of the swordswomen is similar to that of a wife: maintaining the family honor. The swordswoman "got even with anybody who hurt her family." Brave Orchid's version emphasizes filiality and obedience to the patriarchal order. Fa Mu Lan is "the girl who took her father's place in battle . . . and returned alive from the war to settle in the village." The narrator will both dialogically challenge certain familial values and retain others. The conflictual role of the narrator within the institution of the family is evident from the beginning. The girl (with whom the narrator identifies) decides to begin her tutelage under the old man and woman of the mountains after hearing their arguments. The old man challenges her: "You can go pull sweet potatoes, or you can stay with us and learn how to fight barbarians and bandits;" The old woman continues: "You can avenge your village. . . . You can be remembered by the Han people for

your dutifulness." A complex structure of oppositions is built up here. The girl leaves her family to seek her future alone but finds solace in a substitute household; the new family invites her to transgress her traditional role as a female and become a fighter, but the purpose of this transgression is to fight barbarians (read: outsiders); and she must always maintain strict filiality.

But soon within the tale, gender oppositions and family structures become less clear. The old man and woman become, for instance, an embodiment of perennial, natural forces, always changing but always in harmony. They are the dancers of the earth everywhere, two angels, perhaps an infinite number of angels. "They were light; they were molten, changing gold—Chinese lion dancers, African lion dancers in midstep. . . . Before my eyes, gold bells shredded into gold tassels that fanned into two royal capes that softened into lions' fur." Kingston here seems to attempt a move beyond gender difference to a higher "unity" beyond gender. But this vision is only an initial move in the attempt to question traditional definitions of gender and deny gender hierarchies. The couple often appear like young lovers. He appears as a "handsome young man" and she as a "beautiful young woman" who in spring "dressed like a bride." But to the girl the manner of the couple suggests that "the old woman was to the old man a sister or friend rather than a wife" because they do not reduplicate patriarchy. Having problematized traditional gender roles, Kingston presents the complex figure of the swordswoman ready for battle. As the swordswoman leaves her village she is at once the knight in shining armor who rides on her talismanic white horse and the departing bride who receives gifts like wedding presents. She wears men's clothes and ties her hair back in manly fashion and is complimented on her beauty. "How beautiful she looks." Her husband appears before her during battle not as a titular head of the family, but as the lost part of the androgyne, "the childhood friend found at last." With her pregnancy, the swordswoman's gendering is finally most complicated. She looks like a powerful man, carries the inscription of her family's revenge on her back and her baby in the front.

Through her retelling of the tale, Kingston, in addition to questioning gender roles, also recreates the role of avenger for her purposes. She needs to be the female avenger *and* the avenger of the family. Thus the woman warrior out in battle avenges not only the wrongs to her village but the hierarchical genderizing she has been subject to. In a scene of ironic misspeak, the swordswoman alights at the house of a rich baron and announces herself as a "female avenger." The baron, misunderstanding the appellation tries to appeal to her "man to man." "Oh come now. Everyone takes the girls when he can. . . . 'Girls are maggots in the rice.' 'It is more profitable to raise geese than daughters.' He quoted to me the sayings I hated." The legend of the swordswoman becomes the personal story of the Chinese-American girl enraged at the misogynist proverbs she constantly hears in the immigrant community. But Kingston does not separate herself from the community. She also wishes to avenge the hardships of her family, their loss of their laundry in the process of urban renewal, and the pervasive racism to which the Chinese are subjected. "The swordswoman and I are not so dissimilar," the narrator realizes. "What we have in common are the words at our backs.... And I have so many words—'chink' words and 'gook' words too."

Kingston deals with the necessity of maintaining and creating multiple ideological positions, of always letting the numerous voices echo in her own articulations. For Kingston this refraction of other voices is an affirmation of community and diversity. Thus it is appropriate that the final story of the book emphasizes differences and communicative interaction. "Here is a story my mother told me . . . recently, when I told her I also talk story. The beginning is hers, the ending, mine." As opposed to the beginning of the book where the mother silences her, here the narrator emphasizes how their voices are inextricably and dialogically linked, even if they are different. This relationship of mutuality becomes even more interesting in view of the fact that what the narrator presents as a single story is, compositionally, two stories. The first, in all probability the mother's story, is about the indomitable grandmother whose word is inevitably proven right, and therefore obeyed by the community. She fearlessly commands the household to accompany her to the theater, and true to her prediction, the bandits attack the theater that night, leaving the house safe. Brave Orchid and the grandmother, we guess, are spiritual as well as physical kin. Kingston's story, based on the songs of Ts'ai Yen, is about the importance of achieving mutually creative understanding of the Other. Ts'ai Yen, the embodiment of marginality, perseveres, even in an alien environment to understand and be understood by her captors. "Her words seemed to be Chinese, but the barbarians understood their sadness and anger." But Ts'ai Yen also seems remarkably similar to the mother that has so vigorously been fleshed out in the book—captive in a strange land, who fights when needed, and whose children do not speak her language. "She spoke it to them when their father was out of the tent, but they imitated her with senseless singsong words and laughed." These strong resemblances suggest that the two stories are integrally related to each other. Brave Orchid is both an indomitable matriarch, protector of the family, and a captive in a strange land, straining to be heard.

The narrating voice as it emerges in *The Woman Warrior* is thus highly provisional, always full of echoes of other voices, and never autonomous. Kingston does not merely wish to appropriate power and write an authoritative "marginal" text. She wishes to celebrate marginality as a position of writing and not to postulate a new source of authority or a new hierarchy. [In *Women's Autobiography: Essays in Criticism,* 1980] Estelle Jelinek has suggested that personal narratives of men and woman are fundamentally different. The emphasis by women is on "the personal, especially on other people, rather than . . . their professional success, of their connectedness to current political or intellectual history." Men, on the other hand, "tend to idealize their lives or to cast them into heroic molds to project their universal import." Reviewing the history of women's autobiography [in "Women's Autobiographical Writings: New Forms," *Modern Selves: Essays in Modern British and American Autobiography,* 1986], Carolyn Heilbrun has noted that till recently in women's narratives, the "public and private life [could] not be linked, as in male narratives." Jelinek and Heilbrun's points are well taken although one could argue that the refusal of women to cast their lives into heroic molds or to universalize their experiences is in fact a radical form of resistance to patriarchal values. Virginia Woolf, certainly the progenitor of modern women's writing consciously tried to avoid the traditional stable and authoritative "I." In *A Room of One's Own* which Kingston echoes, Virginia Woolf said: "'I' is only a convenient term for somebody who has no real being . . . call me Mary Beton, Mary Seton, Mary Carmichael or by any name you please." Denying universality, absolute values, and an autonomous self are crucial to writings of all marginal groups.

Just as it is important for Kingston to treat gender as a site of difference, it is vital for her to treat race too as a play of differences. Indeed to view *The Woman Warrior* as a book about an essential, abstract, female self beyond culture and society is to miss the point entirely. The immigrant experience is an integral part of the book. Kingston is sensitive to the dehumanizing definitions Chinese Americans are subject to and is determined not to perpetuate the same by merely inverting the hierarchies. At the base of such definitions is the destructive binary logic which hierarchically divides male and female, self and other, white and non white. Edward Said has compellingly demonstrated how such hierarchies have operated in depictions of the "Oriental" as the passive and denatured Other. In *The Woman Warrior* Kingston questions and undoes oppositions that make such sterile racial definitions possible.

The narrator of *The Woman Warrior* is uniquely positioned to dialogically question racial oppositions. She is the daughter of Chinese immigrants for whom America is temporary exile, and China home, but who nevertheless will stay in America. Her only reality is America, but it is the America of the margins (Kingston makes no bones about Stockton being a racial and economic ghetto). She goes to Chinese school and to American school. Her own undefinable position is a metaphor for the way in which ethnicity will operate: "I learned to make my mind large, as the universe is large, so that there is room for paradoxes.... The dragon lives in the sky, ocean, marshes, and mountains; and the mountains are also its cranium. . . . It breathes fire and water; and sometimes the dragon is one, sometimes many."

Reed Dasenbrock [in "Intelligibility and Meaningfulness in Multicultural Literature in English," *PMLA*, Vol. 102, 1987] describes **The Woman Warrior** as a "multicultural" text, one that is not only explicitly about a multicultural society, but one which is implicitly multicultural in "inscribing readers from other cultures inside [its] own textual dynamics." Kingston's questioning of racial and cultural oppositions is multicultural in the latter sense—implicitly so, and highly fraught with political significance. On an obvious level Kingston obviously creates clear cultural oppositions, indeed as if she were speaking in the voice of the monocultural reader. American life is logical, concrete, free, and guarantees individual happiness; Chinese life is illogical, superstition-ridden, constricted by social roles, and weighted down by community pressures. The American school teaches that an eclipse is "just a shadow the earth makes when it comes between the moon and the sun"; the Chinese mother prepares the children to "slam pots and lids together to scare the frog from swallowing the moon" during the next eclipse. American culture promises the young girl opportunity for excellence if she gets straight A's. She can go to college. But she also has the freedom to be a lumberjack in Oregon. In China the girl fears she will be sold as a slave; or within the immigrant community she will be married off to a Fresh Off the Boat Chinese. Indeed the structure of hierarchical oppositions is so cleverly set up that the narrator's growth might be equated with being fully "American."

But Kingston sets up these hierarchies only to subvert and make undecidable these singular oppositions. "To make my waking life American-normal, I turn on the lights before anything untoward makes an appearance. I push the deformed into my dreams, which are in Chinese, the language of impossible dreams." But just as the conventional American reader might begin to feel at ease with the comfortable hierarchy (American-normal, Chinese-deformed), Kingston challenges it. "When the thermometer in our laundry reached one hundred and eleven degrees on summer afternoons, either my mother or my father would say that it was time to tell another ghost story so that we could get some good chills up our backs." American-normal reality gets so nightmarish that Chinese ghost stories are needed to chase it away into imaginary chills. Not only is the cultural hierarchy subverted but the traditional associations of logicality and dreams are suspended. Similarly, Kingston questions other oppositions. If revolutionary China is a nightmare of ruthless disciplinary violence, Stockton, California has its own gratuitous slum violence. "The corpses I've seen had been rolled and dumped, sad little dirty bodies covered with a police khaki blanket." The No Name aunt, who is punished for transgressing her social role as wife and daugh-

ter-in-law, has her American counterpart in another aunt. Moon Orchid comes to America at the behest of her sister Brave Orchid to claim the Americanized husband who has abandoned her. Her fate: insanity.

In fact the very subtitle of the book, "Memoirs of a Girlhood Among Ghosts," is designed to question cultural oppositions. Reed Dasenbrock sees the use of the term "ghost" in the book as a "Shlovskian defamiliarization not so much of the word as of our self-concept" because as non-Chinese readers we are forced to question our perceptions of ourselves. Ghosts is perhaps the most dialogically used term in the book because it describes the experience of living within both Chinese and American cultures. Kingston has said that ghosts are "'shadowy figures from the past' or unanswered questions about unexplained actions of Chinese, whites, and Chinese in America." Ghost is an appellation used for any concept that defies clear interpretation. The narrator lives in a double ghost world—that of the China of legends, rumor, history, ancestors she does not know and that of an American world full of its own ritual ghosts. Thus we have Brave Orchid, at once conjurer and Shaman, the exerciser of ghosts; the No Name aunt whose wandering ghost the narrator is drawn to; and the numerous American ghosts—Taxi Ghosts, Bus Ghosts, Police Ghosts, Fire Ghosts, Garbage Ghosts. The continued use of the term across cultures does not deny the idea of difference but that of hierarchical separation and thus definition.

Kingston's questioning of oppositions and her resistance to definition are intensely political strategies. For the marginal writer who is often the subject of singular definition, such a dialogic stance is often a strategy of survival. Kingston thus problematizes and subverts racial definitions in order to reveal the dangers of maintaining them. Ironically, many of the early reviews of the book reflected the very essentialized definitions Kingston was fighting. The appraisals reflected a familiar "Orientalism." A *Publishers Weekly* critic praised the book for its "myths rich and varied as Chinese brocade" and prose that "achiev[ed] the delicacy and precision of porcelain." Another critic claimed to be confused by the depiction of some Chinese women as aggressive and others as docile, suggesting that Chinese women have a singular identity. Suzanne Juhasz, writing for a scholarly journal, saw Kingston's retention of a "traditional literary style" a result of her need, as a daughter of immigrants, to prove her English language skills. As these reviews suggest, Kingston's position in the literary world is more clearly implicated in her marginality, more political than are the positions of many other women writers.

Kingston operates out of this position to insert indeterminacy into cultural definitions. She presents Chinese culture as a conglomeration of diverse, multiple, often contradictory values that she does not attempt to unify into an easy explanation. Such unities, for Kingston, are the hallmarks of tourist propaganda, not lived culture. Kingston does not believe in the possibility of representing Chinese culture because that assumes that there is a simple "Chinese" reality and culture easily available for representation. As Kingston puts it, "There are Chinese American writers who seek to represent the rest of us; they end up with tourist manuals or chamber of commerce public relations white-wash." In *The Woman Warrior* every aspect of Chinese culture and Chinese immigrant life is so diverse that it resists generalization. The striking contrast between the strength of the narrator's mother, Brave Orchid, who becomes a doctor in China and fights for her rights in America and Moon Orchid who accepts the role of abandoned wife, is only one of several. Immigrant Chinese range from the wealthy, Americanized husband of Moon Orchid, to the Stockton Chinese who maintain their native village affiliations, to refugees from the revolution. And the difference between the immigrant Chinese and the Chinese from the narrator's village is so vast that to the untutored eyes of Moon Orchid, the former appear like foreigners. "I'm glad to see the Americans talk like us" says Moon Orchid to her sister. "Brave Orchid was . . . again startled at her sister's denseness. 'These aren't the Americans. These are the overseas Chinese.'"

In addition to presenting a diverse variety of Chinese characters, Kingston uses traditional cultural material to question the concept of a unified culture. Thus she uses well known myths to write a narrative that is deliberately antimythic. Myths, as many of the modernists saw, could play the conservative function of creating and preserving cultural unity. In his essay on Joyce [in *Selected Prose*], T. S. Eliot explained the mythic method as "a way of controlling, of ordering, of giving a shape and significance to the immense panorama of futility and anarchy that is contemporary history. . . . a step toward making the modern world possible for art, toward . . . order and form. . . ." It is possible for the mythic method to create order, shape and form because myths conventionally serve a stabilizing function in society. Kingston, well aware of the traditional function of myths, uses them in order to subvert this function.

Kingston begins with the story of No Name Woman to suggest that all myths and legends are contingent upon some cultural necessity. Brave Orchid relates this family myth as a warning to her daughter, but the narrator realizes its fictitious aspect. There is the logical improbability of her mother having witnessed the attack when she and the aunt were not living in the same household. But this ambiguity does not trouble Kingston. Such an uncertainty allows her the freedom to continue the process of recreating the myth. With this initial move Kingston questions the privileged access to truth that myths claim and sets the stage for further destabilization of the function of myths. The choice of the story is also significant: "She observes the custom of ancestor worship in such a way as to destroy its fundamental principle, that of maintaining patriarchal descent intact." Similarly Kingston narrates the legend of Fa Mu Lan through her own identification with its and makes its patriarchal moral about filial piety incidental. The purpose of the tale in Kingston's text, is to create uncertainly. Fa Mu Lan can represent the female avenger but she can also represent a continuation of patriarchy as Brave Orchid, to an extent, does. Ts'ai Yen's tale about her captivity by barbarians and her return home becomes a tale of intercultural understanding rather than, as is traditionally received, an ethnocentric tale about Chinese cultural superiority.

More importantly, in *The Woman Warrior* myths do not solve moral and cultural conflicts but create them. Chinese myths abound with misogynistic rituals—smearing bad daughters-in-law with honey and tying them on ant nests, keeping ash ready near a birthing bed in order to suffocate a potential female child and so on. Kingston deliberately presents historical facts and exaggerated legends as if both are equally true and thus questions the truth status of both myth and history. Thus she uses the occasion of describing her mother's adventures as a doctor in China to talk about the rope bridges used by Chinese laborers in Malaysia and about the ghosts her mother encounters while walking on similar bridges in China; she writes about Chinese myths about Japan—the Japanese having descended from an ape that raped a Chinese princess or from the first Chinese explorers of Japan—in the midst of describing the Japanese occupation of China and relating the story about the crazy village woman lynched by refugees because she wears a shiny hat, possibly visible to the Japanese pilots. Kingston keeps up the uncertainty by blurring the boundaries between myth and history and never settling on the validity of either. Like the cryptic appellation "Ho Chi Kuei" which means anything from "centipede," "grain sieve" to "good frying," all that the narrator can glean from her mother about the social validity of myths is that Chinese people "like to say the opposite."

The Woman Warrior thus subverts all forms that have the potential of providing cultural stability and unity. Myths here create contradictions and confusions. Kingston writes polemically as a Chinese-American woman confronting and battling with the patriarchal, white American culture but she does so from a position that is radically unstable. She writes as a woman, but destabilizes the concept of gender; she speaks as a Chinese-American, but questions racial definitions. Authorship therefore becomes a complicated question because Kingston refuses to give us a traditional position from which she articulates. This does not mean that the text is apolitical or socially meaningless. Gender and race are important to Kingston, but not as transcendent and true categories. Kingston does not dismiss or destroy these categories, but radically transvalues them by making them dialogically interactive. And because she subverts these categories only in relation to the singular definitions imposed by the dominant culture and does not attempt to lay the foundations of another (more pure or true) set of categories, she resists impoverishing the issues of gender and race.

Wendy Ho (essay date 1991)

SOURCE: "Mother Daughter Writing and the Politics of Race and Sex in Maxine Hong Kingston's 'The Woman Warrior,'" in *Asian Americans: Comparative and Global Perspectives,* edited by Shirley Hune, Hyung-chan Kim, Stephen S. Fugita, and Amy Ling, Washington State University Press, 1991, pp. 225-38.

[*Ho is an American educator. In the following essay, she studies the interplay between mother and daughter in* The Woman Warrior, *and discusses how this interaction illuminates racial and gender-based concerns.*]

In the autobiographical novel *The Woman Warrior,* by Maxine Hong Kingston, a young daughter attempts to bridge the gap among different and often conflicting cultures, generations, languages, and gender roles. She talks with a mother who tells her stories of the past and present; the stories are a complicated mixture of truths and lies by which she attempts to navigate her own life. The important factor is that mother and daughter talk-story, each struggling to reassess, translate, and articulate an authentic self-identity that is rooted in their needs for individuation/disengagement, mutual respect, and attachment to each other and their communities. In talking, they discover commonality and difference, weaknesses and strengths, anger and love.

In the book, the psychic bonding between mother and daughter through gender, socialization as women, and talk-story traditions is used to work through and express the new psychic landscape of the Chinese American daughter-writer in America. As her mother's daughter, she rejects, brutally critiques, and lovingly transforms her mother's life and stories. Through this personal struggle, she learns to speak and write a new language which is deeply rooted in the life and fictions of her mother, the champion talker in a Cantonese oral tradition. Talk-story becomes an important fluid, interactive mode of communication and discovery for the daughter as well as the mother. It becomes a way of ordering and fighting symbolic and real "ghosts," of learning ways to reclaim through language and image the cultural processes of achieving one's identity as a woman, writer, and individual in society. In the novel, the daughter learns to break her own suffocating silence in creative, subversive ways and thereby vindicates the ancestral women in her family/culture, reclaiming their names and their stories for herself and other women in America.

The mother, Brave Orchid, is a preserver of many different and often conflicting messages to her daughter. She speaks in a multiple- or double-voiced discourse often consisting of "dominant" and "muted" registers. The daughter also learns to speak, write, and live in multiple registers as a Chinese American woman writer. Showalter [in "Feminist Criticism in the Wilderness," *Feminist Criticism: Essays on Women, Literature, Theory,* 1985] provides one illustration of the complexity of this model for some minority women: "A black American woman poet, for example, would have her literary identity formed by the dominant (white male) tradition, by a muted women's culture, and by a muted black culture. She would be affected by both sexual and racial politics in a combination unique to her case; at the same time . . . she shares an experience specific to her group." There is a similar entanglement for Asian American women. Both Brave Orchid and her daughter are affected by the similarities and differences in their social and material circumstances, interpretative systems, written and talk-story strategies, which have been influenced by China and America. The ways mother/daughter talk, bond with each other, and reach psychological maturity are based on issues of gender as well as on issues of class and race. It is a negotiation among complex choices of discourses involving a mother who hides and reveals truth; a Chinese mother and father who pass on Chinese culture in the mother's talk-story; and a New World culture. All have positive and negative impact on the life of a Chinese American daughter.

On one level, Brave Orchid as a traditional Chinese woman feels the need to preserve her family and Chinese traditions against the dominant culture of Western "ghosts" in America. She is the keeper of the secrets, stories, male descent lines, culture, rituals, food. Because of the importance of preserving ties with their own history, culture, and family, Brave Orchid attempts to pass to the daughter the puzzling remnants of Chinese culture, which are half-embedded in silence and contradiction, despite the often oppressive, inequitable circumstances for women within traditional Chinese family structure and society. [Evelyn Nakano] Glenn [*Issei, Nisei, War Bride: Three Generations of Japanese American Women in Domestic Service,* 1986] provides a possible understanding of this type of behavior: "When individuals and their families confront economic deprivation, legal discrimination, and other threats to their survival . . . conflict over inequities within the family may be muted by the countervailing pressure on the family to unite against assaults from outside institutions . . . the family [becomes] a 'culture of resistance.' The locus of conflict . . . lies outside the household, as members engage in collective attempts to create and maintain family in opposition to forces that undermine family integrity."

Dual powerlessness as a woman and as a minority—the intersection of sex and race—burdens the relationship between Brave Orchid and her daughter. The personal relationship of mother or daughter and their families is intimately intertwined with the history of an immigrant race in America, a country which has a long, ugly history of discriminatory behavior against the Chinese and other minorities. The internal world of family is oppressive to women, but the external world is often perceived as the greater common enemy to the family collective, inhabited by non-Chinese "ghosts" who present a whole layer of problems/tensions in languages, cultural systems, and survival in America. These "ghosts" seem to threaten the physical, socioeconomic, and psychological well-being of Brave Orchid and her Chinese family. Kingston's memories are filled with her parents' fears of being sent back to China or being jinxed by white "ghosts"; with the silencing of Chinese women, and men, by the white patriarchy; and with the socioeconomic hardships of their shared life. To survive as a distinct ethnic group and family, minority women are often caught in a double bind between their own needs and concerns as women and those of their Chinese American communities in America.

Like her mother, the daughter negotiates the preservation and the subversion of aspects of traditional Chinese culture against the pressures of mainstream Western society. However, she is in a precarious position of her own: she is not Chinese enough for her mother, father, and ethnic community and not American-feminine enough to find a home among the white "ghosts." She therefore lives life on the edges of these communities, juggling complicated sign systems, languages, experiences. Her mother does not entrust the whole story of the family or their names or rituals to her. The intimate communications—the literal silences and talk-story—between mother and daughter are valorized and problematized in this book. She is half Chinese, half ghost-barbarian, taught and raised among the ghosts who might threaten her parents and their traditional way of life.

In her work of preservation, Brave Orchid is implicated in the culture or Law of the Father, the patriarchal ("official") stories and non-stories (silence) about fallen women and useless girl children in traditional Chinese society. The power of patriarchy is strong and demands filiality even from feisty survivalists who can talk-story like Brave Orchid, Fa Mu Lan, and Ts'ai Yen. For example, in the opening chapter the valuable work of preservation of family, culture, and society is linked physically and symbolically with women. The villagers fear that if women stepped out of the boundaries of their assigned roles as daughters, wives, and mothers, it would lead to the disruption or destruction of family, culture, language, and society. Women are valued according to their obedience, passivity, and maintenance of the traditional ways. And the Chinese mother and family attempt to instill in the young daughter (even in America) the virtues and habits that are considered ideally feminine in traditional Chinese culture [Helen Bannan, "Warrior Women: Immigrant Mothers in the Works of Their Daughters," *Women's Studies,* Vol. 6, 1979]. In such a societal framework, one can see how No Name Woman's private life as a woman—her desires, sexuality, dreams, needs— are silenced violently. As Cixous bluntly states. "Either the woman is passive; or she doesn't exist. What is left unthinkable, unthought of" [Elaine Marks and Isabelle de Courtivron, editors, *New French Feminisms: An Anthology,* 1981].

At home, Maxine is confronted by prejudices her parents brought from old China—the image of girls as useless maggots, stink pigs, or cow-birds, fit to be killed or sold. Her own mother's words and actions devalue her worth as a woman, crippling and silencing her. At school and work— the outside world—she is silenced not only by sexist but also racist stereotypes that haunt her childhood and womanhood. Maxine describes the pain of transforming her squeaking, quacking, ugly duckling voice. As a child, she speaks of years of silence and withdrawal, enjoying the silence and the world of her imagination, Chinese operas and crazy women, until she realized she had to talk in school to establish an "I" identity or be a non-person with no language to define herself. She is considered retarded by some of her teachers, handicapped and silenced in her second language English; her voice sounds "brittle." Later, she describes her voice as "a crippled animal running on broken legs," "a small person's voice that makes no impact." She says there were "splinters in [her] voice, bones rubbing jagged against one another." She protests typing invitations for her boss in a "voice unreliable." She accuses her mother of cutting her frenum, destroying her ability to speak, to acquire language. In her crippled voice, she struggles to explain to her mother "true things" about herself and to get rid of her throat pain; her mother, caught up in her own world of private frustrations and patriarchal stereotypes, fails to understand the crazy, lonely babbling of her awkward daughter. The daughter's throat pain is the struggle to articulate how she really thinks, feels, and acts—to make known the invisible and to come against her mother again and again though the power of language.

The daughter is warned by her mother not to tell anyone the secret about her father's sister, No Name Woman. This disobedient woman had "crossed boundaries not delineated in space." For this reason, no words, name, or memory is allotted her. It was as if she had never been born. Thus, the daughter's learning of patriarchal relationships within the family and other cultural institutions coincides with her learning of the names and non-names and rules of naming and non-naming implicit in the system of language. To have no name is the punishment; to be remembered as a patriarchal caveat to other women is the punishment.

Brave Orchid has seen with her own eyes that the consequences of disobedience to this Law of the Father can literally mean isolation, exile, insanity, or death. There is the haunting terror for a communally-oriented individual of being "a bright dot in blackness, without home, without a companion, in eternal cold and silence." The mother tells her daughter that "what happened to her [No Name Woman] could happen to you. Don't humiliate us. You wouldn't like to be forgotten as if you had never been born." It could be a mixed warning that is based on fear, love, acquiescence to tradition, or even survival for herself and daughter.

The lesson is not totally lost on the daughter: "The work of preservation demands that the feelings playing about in one's guts not be turned into action. Just watch their passing like cherry blossoms." The patriarchal tradition often determines that women inhabit silence—non-verbal, non-written—inhabit a confined boundary where internal/external, hardly visible reaction/action is deemed appropriate feminine behavior. She has more than enough models of "slaves" in her memory: No Name Woman, Moon Orchid, silent Chinese schoolgirls, crazy women. Even dragon-mother is reduced in her power in America. The "slave mentality" of women is just below the surface, waiting to make an appearance; even as an adult, the daughter feels that "China wraps double binds around [her] feet." For example, Maxine wants to feel independent and yet she finds herself feeling envious, bitter, and unloved because she is not supported by a man. Despite the example of the fabulous woman warrior Fa Mu Lan, she learns that there is a Chinese word for the female "I" which means slave—*mui*. Women are powerless in this discourse; they are being defined, classified, and forced to articulate themselves in relationship to male perspectives—master/slave. The patriarchal structure of society and language appears to be set up to "break women with their own tongues!"

Kingston is not out to valorize or privilege a seamless form of communication between mother and daughter; instead, I think she shows us the conflicting layers of this communication. Brave Orchid's voice, her talk-story, is not simply an unambiguous mirror for patriarchal Chinese discourse. There is, I think, indication of a muted subtext which seeps through the text, making for intricate knots, wrinkles, circles, and holes in her stories and injunctions. Mother speaks with a forked tongue. Her discourse is implicated in and hidden with other modes of discourse; thereby, her maternal subtext is very difficult to locate, evermore ambiguous, double-edged, and ambivalent, fraught with danger at best. On one hand, it would seem that she reinforces the laws of society by repeating the caveats of patriarchal society in talk-story. Yet despite the fact that Brave Orchid tells her daughter she will end up "a wife and a slave," the daughter distinctly remembers following her mother around the house chanting the song of the warrior woman. She learns

that she fails if she becomes just a wife or a slave. Brave Orchid also tells the secret of No Name Aunt to her daughter, providing her with a small but tantalizing bit of information about her women ancestors. This ambiguous, ambivalent gift of a secret is raw material through which, in her own written, talk-story text, the daughter imaginatively resurrects this rebellious dead aunt after years of silent fear and neglect.

In opening her book with this story, the daughter makes visible the secret that her mother, father, and the Chinese village have kept hidden. She demonstrates and asserts her affinity for this ostracized aunt by exploring possible reconstructed versions of the truth where there had been only silence or one absolute patriarchal version of the story. Kingston restores the aunt through musings on her imagined lives, feelings, and motivations. She provides herself and her readers the dynamic opportunity of choice between the interstices of patriarchal privilege. It is a subversive form of ancestor worship which would not have the approval of the father; and it takes its form not with paper boats, clothes, or money to honor the dead—those decorative and ephemeral things burned—but with the enduring power and memory of the written word (the power of authorship) which had been predominantly the preserve of males in Chinese society. It is a double transgression of patriarchy: No Name Aunt was erased from family memory by the taking away of her name and place in society and by the family's silence about her very existence. In this way, Maxine breaks the complicitous, vicious cycle of silence with her mother and the Chinese community against this outcast woman. But consequences of the neglect and resurrection of her aunt after so many long years, as well as her rebellion against the fathers, haunt Kingston. To resurrect the restless dead—the spite suicide, the wild woman—into living memory as well as to speak so boldly in a patriarchal society is a serious act with many possible consequences for Kingston: "The Chinese are always very frightened of the drowned one, whose weeping ghost, wet hair hanging and skin bloated, waits silently by the water to pull down a substitute."

The other voice is Brave Orchid's private (coded/indirect) language as a woman and the example of her own life as a doctor, which is "secret and apart from them." She lives two years without servitude, acquiring a job, a room of her own, and new women friends. These women called Brave Orchid back from the spirit world by shouting out (non-vertical/hierarchical) directions for her spirit to follow: "They called out their own names, women's pretty names, haphazard names, horizontal names of one generation." It is akin to what Showalter means when she talks about the muted culture of women, "the boundaries of whose culture and reality overlap, but are not wholly contained by, the dominant (male) group." It is Brave Orchid's own marginalized/repressed woman space, seeping indirectly through the cracks and fissures of the malestream as well as mainstream Western and Eastern thought about definitions/roles for women. For it is the same mother who suffers not only sexism in two cultures but also racism in her adopted country. She suffers racism in America where she is reduced to work in a laundry and in tomato fields. The woman warrior, the mythical dragon-mother, who ghostbusted, who made herself strong in China, is reduced to fending off, rather unsuccessfully, the mundane "ghosts" (such as shopkeepers, mail carriers, police, winos) that occupy her ordinary life in America. Mother, as well as daughter, develop multiple voices to encode or signify in language as a way of surviving in a racist, sexist world; similarly, they must develop the capabilities to decipher and pass on this intricate encoded language.

Thus a remaining source of power for this displaced woman warrior is her magical stories about transformation, heroic swordswomen, and female doctors; these signify or suggest a woman's freedom and potential. The mother exercises her daughter's mind beyond daily limits: "I learned to make my mind large, as the universe is large, so that there is room for paradoxes . . . The dragon lives in the sky, ocean, marshes, and mountains; and the mountains are also its cranium . . . it breathes fire and water; and sometimes the dragon is one, sometimes many." It is no surprise that mother and daughter in this magic real world are dragons born fierce and powerful in the Year of the Dragon. It is the mother who sings her "out of nightmares and horror movies" and makes her feel safe and loved. The daughter feels the presence of great power in her mother's talking-story.

Chinese heroic motifs are preserved through oral or talk-story traditions: talk-story, however, is transformed in Kingston's work into a history from a personal and communal standpoint. She participates in and directs the history of her people, a position she inherits from her mother. The daughter attempts to speak with the communal voice of assorted legendary and real-life characters: the voices of ancient heroines, the Fa Mu Lans and Ts'ai Yens; the ceremonial voice of the family scop rehearsing and reclaiming biographies of worthies and genealogies from the collective family memory; the shamanic voice that chants magical incantations and women's names to keep away ghosts, demons, and nightmares; as well as the more impersonal voice of history.

In this book, heroism is constantly being redefined in myths/fantasies and real life experiences. For on one level, the talk-stories of mother/daughter are about inner psychological, imaginative quests or adventures which are often invisible or closed to readers, to outsiders. And yet the borders they challenge—cultural, social, and psychological—and their specific discoveries should be of central importance not only

to the writer herself but also to us. Mother/daughter engage in painful struggles with languages, cultures, inherited oral/literary traditions, and with each other to find more adequate ways of telling about women's experiences, fighting their way out of silence, out of traditionally sanctioned roles and stereotypes, to project more authentic images of how they feel, think, and act.

As a Chinese American woman, the daughter-writer is carving out new territory in alien lands (literally and figuratively) which would marginalize her, her family, and heritage. With time, she realizes her own power as a storyteller; she is not simply a storehouse for her mother's stories, life, and secrets. Neither is she simply an extension or double for her mother. In working out her identity, there is as much active collaboration/bonding as there is brutal resistance/disengagement between mother and daughter.

In terms of mother/daughter collaboration/bonding in process, Kingston says, "Here is a story my mother told me, not when I was young, but recently, when I told her I also talk story. The beginning is hers, the ending, mine." The ego boundaries between mother and daughter are not clearly defined even in adulthood, but there is a sense of separation, of a new voice branching out from mother. For the Chinese American daughter's fictions insistently seem to challenge and/or reject the authority of patriarchy/imperialism as well as mother, paying attention to what has been traditionally seen/unseen as marginal. She questions the stereotyped images and fictions of her mother, their split cultures as well as the language of their value judgments. The daughter, as her mother before, and each in her own challenge and degree, attempts to disrupt and subvert the discourses which confine their potential. Both their stories and voices generate an interactive and multiple sense of their similarities and differences as mothers/daughters, of their possible complicity in traditional/dominant power configurations and strategies of appeasement, and of their subversive signifying strategies for survival. Brave Orchid jam-packs, pries, crams, funnels her daughter with continual harping, advice, and stories. She will marry off or sell this useless, squeaky, duck-voiced, bad girl. In contrast, the young daughter is later associated with Ts'ai Yen's singing voice.

The need and search for self-expression—to break the silence of oppression and victimization in terms of sexism and racism within the dominant Western culture and the sexism in her own Chinese culture—becomes a way to hold on to sanity and to find identity. As the protagonist says in *The Woman Warrior* to another silent Chinese girl, "If you don't talk, you can't have a personality . . . talk, please talk" or "I thought talking and not talking made the difference between sanity and insanity. Insane people were the ones who couldn't explain themselves." Yet, what to say?

In the search for a personal voice and self, the daughter's awkward first steps are mirrored in her voice, the self-conscious, awkward voice of an immigrant daughter attempting to assess—to make sense of no sense—her mother's contradictory statements: her truths and lies. The frustrations between daughter and mother are very evident. There is a point in the story that the daughter wishes to escape the "hating range" of home and her mother's stories which appear to have no "logic." These Chinese stories scramble her up. She tells her mother, "You lie with stories. You won't tell me a story and then say, 'This is a true story,' or, 'This is just a story.' I can't tell the difference. I don't even know what your real names are. I can't tell what's real and what you make up." There is no unified, centered tradition in her communities in America that allows her as a Chinese American woman to speak easily and forthrightly in her own person. The self is often fragmented, split and invisible to the self and is defined indirectly by a conflicting web of interpersonal relations and roles. It is more a constant struggle to break from the community of "we"; whether with mother, family, or society, to reach an understanding of oneself as an individual "I" in community.

Maxine is caught then with her weak voice in this hyphenated position between cultures/languages, parents: Paula Gunn Allen notes that people caught between two cultures are often "inarticulate, almost paralyzed in their inability to direct their energies toward resolving what seems to them insoluble conflicts" [King-Kok Cheung, "'Don't Tell': Imposed Silences in *The Color Purple* and *The Woman Warrior*," *Proceedings of the Modern Language Association*, Vol. 103, 1988]. She has definite handicaps. She is excluded from mainstream culture and from centers of power in her own racial community. She is faced with social prohibitions and language barriers that silence her authentic experiences, and she is confused by her own mother's mixed messages in patriarchy. As a child in school, Maxine paints layers of black paint over pictures of houses and flowers and suns. And when her confused parents take them home, she "spreads them out (so black and full of possibilities) and pretended the curtains were swinging open, flying up, one after another, sunlight underneath, mighty operas." There is indeed a rich life even under what appears to be black/lack—absence.

Writing becomes a heroic form of verbal expression for this silent, but imaginative, young girl: it is a way to defend herself with words—potential is discovered in the process of learning to articulate herself—to write talk-story. It becomes a courageous act that leads to transformation and discovery. Through the book, she is training, disciplining herself to control the voice and pen before she can be a writer. At first, she appropriates patriarchal rhetoric and codes of behavior; she fights as a woman in the guise of a male warrior, with bloodthirsty warring and lopping off of heads. To become a boy is an early rebellion against her mother and her mother's harping on the uselessness of girls. It is a way of denying her connection with what is devalued in her society. Fa Mu Lan wears armor while pregnant, which makes her look like a "powerful, big man." She gives up her child to fight in the wars as a "slim young man." Upon her return home, she impresses her son not so much as a mother but as a war general. In this male disguise, she learns to articulate and redress her rage and grievances; at the same time, she wins the love and respect of her family and community as a warrior. For a time, she leads the life of the privileged male sex—the apple of her mother's, father's, country's eye. And then she returns to filial servitude as a daughter, wife, and mother.

Alas, the nightly legends, movies, and dreams of the fabulous swordswomen do not change Maxine into a precious boy. Even heroines and mothers, it seems, return to lives as filial daughters, wives, and mothers. The daughter discovers that there are no easy ways to resolve contradictions or to be all things to all people and to herself. Life in fantasy movies or myths/legends is hard to translate into real-life experiences. The slave mentality attacks even the brave with the fear of isolation, loneliness, and danger. To take a sword to her lousy boss is a comic, pathetic scenario. There are no supporting casts of eighty pole fighters, self-sacrificing bunnies, or psychic kung-fu training for the kind of social and cultural wilderness a Chinese American woman must negotiate in America. Not even straight A's at Berkeley or working for change in her daily life can make her a loved boy, or American-pretty, or the fabulous swordswoman of old. Mother's stories are not easily translatable in a daughter's life.

In her anger and frustration, Kingston gradually discovers one good similarity: the Chinese idiom for revenge literally means to "report a crime"; to report—witness and record—the injustices suffered by her Chinese women ancestors and to herself as a Chinese American woman. It is the *language* of contradiction and the *language* of sexism and racism—painful, ugly words which maim and kill—that she as a warrior attempts to purge, to decapitate with violent vengeance: "Girls are maggots in the rice" or "It is more profitable to raise geese than daughters!" If there is a group of women she could identify with in this episode, it would be those amazon swordswomen who "did not wear men's clothes," but "rode as women in black and red dresses. They bought up girl babies so that many poor families welcomed their visitations. When slave girls and daughters-in-law ran away, people would say they joined these witch amazons. They killed men and boys."

The image of wilderness, inherited from her own mother's stories and life, is reclaimed and adapted by the daughter with her "witch amazons." She uses it to describe the "wilderness" of her Chinese American experiences as a woman in the territories of patriarchal language, descriptions of the world, and definitions of personal experience. She even tests her growing voice by undermining her mother's voice and stories. It is an adventurous journey of survival, testing, and knowledge as a Chinese woman in America. Maxine's perception of the wilderness begins to shift to the unexplored space beyond the patriarchal prison house—the symbol of the wild territory to be appropriated and transformed into a rich and imaginative female space that displaces male power.

This awareness of such potential female space for the private self problematizes and enriches the daughter's sense of identity: instead of the self ever being fully solid, unified, or defined, it becomes a more shifting, fluid, decentralized notion of selfhood without hard, finite boundaries. Wilderness can provide the perfect image of the wild-zone, the "the mother country of liberated desire and female authenticity," which Showalter calls the repressed area of women's culture that can never be fully known. (It may even bear connections to Kristeva's semiotic space.) There is in this female space the potential for a new feminist mythology centered on matriarchal principles at once biological and ecological in contrast to much of patriarchal history. Such writing may signal the potential of the feminine voice as an alternative source of power and exorcism of the past; the image of wilderness provides textual space for such revisionary play. The young girl is learning to traverse this wilderness territory—at home, in America, in barbarian lands, in writing, in self—as a woman not disguised as a male warrior.

As the novel progresses, Maxine processes different models such as No Name Woman, Moon Orchid, mother Brave Orchid, woman warrior Fa Mu Lan, and finally Ts'ai Yen, the poet. She takes back their stories and experiences with her imaginative power as a Chinese American woman writer. Cheung notes that, "In reshaping her ancestral past to fit her American present, moreover, Kingston is asserting an identity that is neither Chinese nor white American, but distinctively Chinese American. Above all, her departures from the Chinese legends shift the focus from physical prowess to verbal injuries and textual power." In this endeavor, she fights the invisible hurts—the prejudices, the sexism and racism against her and her community. She fights the suffocating aspects not only of mainstream ideals of beauty/behavior (American-feminine) but also of her mother's traditional views of female children: that she is a bad girl because she refuses to cook, cracks dishes. She is rebellious, silent, surly, clumsy, ugly—wanting to be a boy—not to marry. She expands the fight not only as a woman but as a Chinese American woman against racism in America: "The swordswoman and I are not so dissimilar . . . What we have in common are the words at our backs.

The reporting is the vengeance—not the beheading, not the gutting, but the words. And I have so many words—'chink' words and 'gook' words too—that they do not fit on my skin."

From Chinese mothers and female relatives, the daughter brings to her writing coded, talk-story language such as secrets, dreams, myths, folk wisdom, legends, incantations, paradoxes, singing/chanting, gossip, jokes, crazy talk, and parables. The descent lines of this daughter-writer are located in matriarchal bonding, with slave women and with heroic, rebellious, trail-blazing women who step outside the circle of the known and approved status quo of patriarchal society. In terms of form, Kingston's realistic fiction registers the surface details of her daily life; yet, on another level, the conventions of realism are frequently disrupted by shifts into magical, visionary moments, fantasy, and myth, often reappropriated from her mother's talk-story tradition, which may be truer to her new sense of reality and self beyond patriarchal discourse.

In such ways, her writing becomes split-level/multiple discourses where alternative ways of seeing are contained within the same fictional structure. This is reflected not only in her retelling and rewriting of myths, but also in her use of mixed genres, such as autobiography, poetry, legend, ghost story, dream vision, and oral tradition. This style disrupts the story line of rigid, structured classifications or of traditional power. It opens to question and executes disarrangements and defamiliarization, which demand new perspectives and solutions to questions of power, gender, socioeconomic, and cultural order. The emphasis is on process and revision so that absolute truth is only provisional and writing is not transparent but something to be decoded and reconstructed through the reader's or listener's collaborative efforts. In other words, the text is not finalized meaning or a mere recording of actual life or interpretation, but the self-talking story, an enactment of the continual dynamic struggle to construct and deconstruct meanings.

As much as her mother puts her down, Maxine as an adult finally comes to terms with her Chinese heritage and her mother. Stifled and frustrated, she leaves home and mother in order to see the world differently. She needs breathing space outside of her Chinese world. She explores the other parts of America "where the 'I' is a capital and 'you' is lower case." It is no wonder that Maxine is fascinated by the potential in the language of the New World: the American "I" is straight, assertive and capitalized; it is not written in small, crooked strokes as in Chinese. The symbolic language of the barbarians—the "ghost" fathers—suggests a new language in which to talk about self in a new way, other than as a slave. What she learns is that there is also a logical world: "I learned to think that mysteries are for explanation. I enjoy the simplicity. Concrete pours out of my mouth to cover the forests with freeways and sidewalks . . . shine floodlights into dark corners: no ghosts." Hannah Arendt has noted that intellectual freedom or a new sense of reality can exist only in the context of psychic space, while psychic space can be created only between distinct and contrasting points of view. In this space between viewpoints, the daughter continues to "sort out what's just my childhood, just my imagination, just my family, just the village, just movies, just living." She can return to the ambiguous, ambivalent facts and fictions of her life and her mother's for raw material and find creative inspiration without losing her developing sense of a separate self in her split communities in America.

From a qualified distance, she can begin to see her mother as an intelligent, energetic, feisty, and courageous woman who transmits complex messages in difficult social and historical circumstances; not simply as a repressive, egotistical, insensitive tyrant who is quite capable of victimizing and destroying other women (sister Moon Orchid, her daughter Maxine, servant girls) in the name of bully love. Brave Orchid is a very powerful role model and hero to her daughter, who acknowledges her affiliation: "I am practically the first daughter of a first daughter." Brave Orchid, after all, was a ghostbuster in her own time, a doctor, a survivor, and fellow dragon. Kingston had blamed her mother for cutting her frenum to stop her from talking, but the mother says, "I cut it to make you talk more, not less, you dummy. You're still stupid. You can't listen right." Her mother has untied her tongue in order for her to "speak languages that are completely different from one another." She senses the point of the duplicity: "The emigrants confuse the gods by diverting their curses, misleading them with crooked streets and false names. They must try to confuse their offspring as well, who, I suppose, threaten them in similar ways—always trying to get things straight, always trying to name the unspeakable. The Chinese I know hide their names; sojourners take new names when their lives change, and they guard their real names with silence." Duplicity is again evident when the daughter accuses her mother of calling her ugly all the time. Her mother protests that she did not actually call her daughter ugly: "That's what we're supposed to say. That's what Chinese say. We like to say the opposite." Duplicity is a way of life that protects the powerless, that ensures survival when one feels threatened or has something to hide from the powerful—whether we are speaking of jealous ghosts or a racist/sexist community or country.

In this autobiographical novel, Kingston has begun to counter the earlier destructive, limited male warrior guise with the woman warrior. There is discovery and reclamation of psychic territory and of connections for the daughter-writer between the Old and the New World; between the individual and her mixed communities; between mother and daughter. She challenges social and symbolic codes which delineate the position of women in society as an absent presence. Her corrective is a collective female vision of talk-story, of open-ended, multiple loads to truth and meaning, of transforming art. Her challenge is the voice of the Chinese woman singing of her sadness and anger in a barbarian land: hers is a voice that continually orders and reshapes meaning through art. This is one way out of psychic paralysis, silence, separation, or death. The daughter-writer has begun to achieve a confidence and power in her own distinctive Chinese American voice; as she says, Ts'ai Yen's songs from the savage lands translated well in Chinese and in barbarian terms. As she frees her own voice, she also frees the oppressed women who have haunted and still haunt her. She is, after all, the one escaping to tell. Like mother and No Name Aunt, the daughter-writer pieces "together new directions," following them "instead of the old footprints." From the position "not to tell" to "tell," she is a hopeful voice singing in the desert.

Khani Begum (essay date 1992)

SOURCE: "Confirming the Place of 'The Other': Gender and Ethnic Identity in Maxine Hong Kingston's *The Woman Warrior*," in *New Perspectives on Women and Comedy*, edited by Regina Barreca, Gordon and Breach, 1992, pp. 143-56.

[*Begum is an educator who has taught literature and feminist criticism at Bowling Green State University. In the following essay, she surveys the manner in which Kingston establishes her own identity as a woman and as a Chinese American in* The Woman Warrior.]

The personal quest motif appears frequently in the literature of occidental societies, but rarely surfaces in that of oriental cultures, where integration with the community and family takes precedence over individuation of self. Maxine Hong Kingston's ***The Woman Warrior: A Memoir of a Girlhood Among Ghosts,*** analyzed by most critics as a quest for identity, is perceived also as "oriental," exotic, and mysterious because it expresses the Chinese American experience. Even when critics evaluate its literariness within the tradition of American literature, they cannot resist marginalizing it. Kingston's narrative, on the one hand, lends itself to analysis as a quest narrative precisely because it is concerned with questions of self-definition and identity. On the other hand, it resists categorization as individual autobiography because it concurrently interweaves myth, fiction, and reality to create its own unique tapestry of form. It refutes facile distinctions of form that place it as representative of either occidental or oriental literature. While Kingston's memoir is not strictly autobiographical (its subtitle, "Memoirs of a Girlhood Among Ghosts," indicates ambiguity of both form and content), it still deals with a journey or quest. More specifically, it explores the quest of a unique and *particular* self, one that is female and one whose experience of growing up is both Chinese and American. Caught between two cultures and the product of both, Kingston's protagonist Maxine, in order to find her authentic self, must negotiate the contradictions between her two worlds before discovering and valorizing her individual cultural uniqueness and otherness from each.

Kingston's and/or her protagonist Maxine's quest for identity actually occurs on three levels, those of gender, ethnicity, and nationality. It involves confronting her Otherness—first, as a woman in patriarchal society (both Chinese and American societies being patriarchal in structure); secondly, as a member of an ethnic minority in America; and finally, as an English speaking (and writing) American within a "real Chinese" family ("my parents did not understand English"). It is only through painfully confronting, acknowledging, and validating her Otherness at all three levels that she discovers her true individual self and its connections with and place within community and family. It is as a daughter of another disenfranchised Chinese woman in American society, Brave Orchid, that she journeys toward self actualization. Bonding with her mother while at the same time tearing herself apart from her, Maxine re-evaluates her relationships with her mother, Chinese American culture, and America. The mother/daughter relationship with both its bonds and its tensions becomes crucial to her search for ethnic and gender identity.

Kingston's and/or her protagonist Maxine's quest for identity actually occurs on three levels, those of gender, ethnicity, and nationality.
—*Khani Begum*

Employing feminist psychoanalytic approaches drawn from Luce Irigaray concurrently with Gayatri Spivak's notions about the disempowerment of minority cultures, I wish to explore issues of 'Otherness' and notions of Subjectivity from a Marxist/psychoanalytic perspective in *The Woman Warrior*. While Irigaray, claiming that any theory of the Subject has been appropriated by the "masculine" [*The Speculum of the Other Woman,* 1985], defines empowerment for women in terms of an essential feminine or as "the sex which is not one," Spivak opposes the essentialist position by emphasizing Marxist views grounded in Third World experience that concentrate on exploitation [*In Other Worlds: Essays in Cultural Politics,* 1978]. Spivak's argument is deconstructive rather than psychoanalytical. She develops the experience of the female body as the object of male censorship and exploitation. Pointing out that any understanding of the 'subaltern classes' (Third World and/or Asiatic societies) in terms of their adjustment to Euro-

pean models is destructive, she sees the political project as being that of allowing the subaltern to speak. This translates to feminist issues as well, for women too function as a subaltern class that has been defined and silenced by the dominant culture, which in most cases is both male and white.

Paralleling and contrasting the tasks of the historian and the teacher, Spivak says:

> A historian confronts a text of counter insurgency or gendering where the subaltern has been represented. He unravels the text to assign a new subject-position to the subaltern, gendered or otherwise.

> A teacher of literature confronts a sympathetic text where the gendered subaltern has been represented. She unravels the text to make visible the assignment of subject-positions.

In examining texts like Kingston's, texts that reflect a subaltern culture's struggle for recognition and empowerment amidst or adjacent to a dominant culture, the critic is both historian and teacher, for he/she must unravel the text to both assign new subject-positions as well as make visible the assignment of existing ones. Despite the fact that over the last decade or so Maxine Hong Kingston's place appears to have been established within the American literary canon, too many American as well as Chinese American critics, reviewers, and readers continue to perceive Kingston's *The Woman Warrior* in terms of marginal experience because it represents for them an experience that *appears* marginal from *their* own subject-positions. Kingston, maintaining that it is an experience shared by many Chinese Americans and because the Chinese American is a *type of American,* wants it to be considered within mainstream American literature. With the exception of a few progressive curriculums, however, her books more often continue to be taught in multicultural, ethnic literature, or women's studies courses rather than alongside works by mainstream American writers like Thomas Pynchon, Saul Bellow, and such. As long as this is the case, the critic and teacher cannot ignore the subalternity of her texts; instead, they must begin by recognizing these texts as reflecting varieties of subaltern experience and then proceed to illuminate not only their uniqueness and Otherness but also their bonds with and roots within the dominant cultural experience.

The first step toward self-actualization and identity requires a facility with language and the power to speak. All oppressed and disenfranchised societies and groups have achieved their goal of freedom and recognition only after they articulated their situation and defined themselves. Spivak finds that the disempowerment of minority cultures is often achieved by the dominant culture through the denial of language or the power to speak out. By silencing the Subaltern, the dominant group maintains power. Irigaray too writes about the need for woman to speak in her own tongue or tongues and not become, like the Pythia, a vehicle for patriarchal opinion. Two Asian American writers, Frank Chin and Jeffrey Paul Chan, voice their anger over what they consider the castration of Chinese American males through the denial of a "legitimate mother tongue." They perceive the erasure of the Chinese American male's manhood as resulting from the concept of dual personality; being both Chinese and American, the "Chinese-American is never completely accepted by either the Chinese from China or the white Americans. Considered a foreigner and an alien by American society, he is expected to be at home in the Chinese language, while the "real Chinese" refuse him acceptance as Chinese because his birthplace is the U.S.

> The concept of dual personality successfully deprives the Chinese American of all authority over language and thus a means of codifying, communicating, and legitimizing his experience. Because he is a foreigner, English is not his native tongue. Because he was born in the U.S., Chinese is not his native tongue. Chinese from China, "real Chinese," make the Chinese American aware of his lack of authority over Chinese, and the white American doesn't recognize the Chinese American's brand of English as a language, even a minority language, but as faulty English, an "accent." . . . the development of Chinese American English has been prevented, much less recognized. The denial of language is the denial of culture.

> ["Racist Love," in *Seeing through Shuck,* edited by Richard Kostelanetz, Ballantine Books, 1972, pp. 65-79]

Finding deprivation of language to be a contributing factor "to the lack of a recognized style of Asian-American cultural integrity . . . and the lack of a recognized style of Asian American manhood," Chin and Chan claim: "On the simplest level, a man in any culture speaks for himself. Without a language of his own, he is no longer a man."

Chin and Chan, perceiving this denial of language as affecting essentially Chinese males, consider the literary success of Chinese American women authors as yet another form of emasculation of the Chinese American male: "The mere fact that four of the five American-born Chinese-American writers [Jade Snow Wong, Diana Chang, Virginia Lee, Betty Lee Sung, Pardee Lowe] are women reinforces this aspect of the stereotype [stereotype of the Asian male as completely devoid of manhood]." While their point that the deprivation of language contributes to the Chinese American male's crisis of identity is a valid one, their implication that

it devastates only Chinese American males is disturbing. Such gender differentiation over the effects of language deprivation apparently arises out of Chin's and Chan's conviction that literary creativity belongs in the domain of men. This bears out Irigaray's claim that any theory of the Subject has been appropriated by the "masculine." To perceive the Chinese American woman's (only relative) publishing success as emasculating, indicates that the Chinese American male is assuming a gender exclusive claim on creative subjectivity. And, he in turn, by denying the Chinese American female the right to creative subjectivity and identity as co-subaltern, relegates her to a doubly subaltern position. Moreover, in most oriental cultures, women are expected to remain silent and are discouraged from voicing their opinions. In fact, silence in women is considered a virtue reflecting shyness and inner beauty, qualities considered embodiments of femininity.

For Kingston, the importance of speech, of being able to express oneself to others in a common language is crucial in asserting one's subject-position. Its significance becomes almost overwhelming in the scene where Maxine in the sixth grade, both verbally and physically harasses the "quiet" Chinese girl to get her to talk: "If you don't talk, you can't have a personality. . . . You've got to let people know you have a personality and a brain." The violence with which Maxine attacks the girl, pinching her cheeks and screaming at her, is motivated by her own fear of losing identity, and it is directed as much at herself as it is at the quiet Chinese girl, who stands for every Chinese girl in America. Unlike the Japanese kids, who "were noisy and tough," Maxine, like other Chinese girls, finds talking agonizing: "It was when I found out I had to talk that school became a misery, that the silence became a misery. I did not speak and felt bad each time that I did not speak." She soon realizes the connection between silence and being Chinese: "The other Chinese girls did not talk either, so I knew the silence had to do with being a Chinese girl." Recognizing the subalternity of her Chinese American and gender positions, she painfully confronts her Otherness in American society. Even though Maxine herself has "a terrible time talking" and burns with embarrassment when she hears her own voice splinter and sound like "bones rubbing jagged against one another," she valiantly tries to overcome her shyness.

The conflict here is between her Chinese sense of female identity, which requires women to be shy and voiceless, and her American identity which insists that without a voice you have no personality. "Sometimes I hated the ghosts for not letting us talk; sometimes I hated the secrecy of the Chinese." Maxine recalls the first time she became silent and her disgust at the sound of her own voice.

> When I went to kindergarten and had to speak English for the first time, I became silent. A dumb-

ness—a shame—still cracks my voice in two, even when I want to say "hello" casually, or ask an easy question. . . . A telephone call makes my throat bleed and takes up that day's courage. It spoils my day with self-disgust when I hear my broken voice skittering out into the open.

She perseveres in making herself talk because she knows that she must talk to get a job, make a living, and "speak up in front of the boss"—in short to survive in America. She recalls that her silence was thickest during the three school years when she covered her school paintings with black paint and for the first year spoke to no one at school. Evidently the conflicts and contradictions of her two worlds that have been tearing Maxine apart throughout her childhood, finally erupt in her venomous outburst inside the girl's washroom. Her paintings, covered over with black paint, are the external evidence of the young Maxine's schizophrenic condition. Hiding her paintings with black paint points to a desire to conform to the codes of at least one of her worlds and a wish to end the conflict going on within herself. The black paint serves as a shade or curtain pulled over the person she is becoming, and thereby silencing whatever personality her paintings may be trying to express.

Paul John Eakin points out [in *Fictions in Autobiography: Studies in the Art of Self-Invention,* 1985] that the encounter with the quiet Chinese girl represents the making of the self and even though Maxine fails to make the girl speak, she succeeds in voicing herself with awesome power. After this experience, Maxine spends the "next eighteen months sick in bed with a mysterious illness." Her attempt to negotiate between her Chinese Otherness and the need to have a personality takes this physical toll, and when she returns to school she has "to figure out again how to talk." Torn between the need to be a Chinese woman, and hence silent, and an inborn desire for personal autonomy, it is Maxine's *American* self that surfaces in the washroom incident allowing her to acknowledge that speech and language are instruments of power.

Kingston's memoir begins with an example of another silenced woman, namely the story of No Name Woman, the aunt who was shunned by family and community for committing adultery and who eventually drowned herself and her newborn child in the family well. No Name Woman's narrative is meaningful at all three levels of gender, ethnicity, and nationality within the context of Kingston's own experience. As Eakin suggests, the retelling of this tale makes Kingston's narrative a

> . . . symbolic analogue of not only the aunt's initial defiance of tradition in search for a private space in which individuality could dwell "secret and apart," but also of the aunt's subsequent plea for the

observance of tradition in the endless search of her ghost for the place and recognition of a name.

Even though No Name Woman's battle occurred in China, it parallels Maxine's situation symbolically. For Maxine too is seeking a private space where she can dwell as an individual—as a Chinese American woman. Like No Name Woman, who is an alien in her community because of her nonconformity, Maxine, who also is Other and outcast in her family through the fact of having been born in America and for having established bonds with her environment, an otherwise alien culture, must find her own private place and identity. No Name Woman's Otherness and alienation stems from the rape or act of sexual indiscretion (Maxine wonders whether her aunt was victim or rebel), which in either case makes her a *pariah* by virtue of the stain of immorality it implies and because her "aunt crossed boundaries not delineated in space." Since the traditional definition of what it means to be a Chinese woman categorically rejects anyone marked with a 'scarlet letter,' so to speak, Maxine's aunt has no other identity except that of outcast and no recognizable place within the traditional family structure. Unlike Maxine's, her choices are limited. She chooses to die with one last bid for identity by drowning herself in the family well. This becomes an act of protest, of "speaking out" and it forces the oppressor to take notice, even if it is only by way of forbidding further mention of her name and story.

The fact that No Name Woman's suicide is actually an act of vengeance—by drowning herself and her child in the family well she effectively pollutes their water supply—indicates that she re-assigns her own subaltern position from that of female victim, one whose body has been exploited by the patriarchal culture, to that of active Subject. Rather than allow the males to appropriate all subject-positions, woman (No Name Woman through her suicide and Maxine through her reportage of the forbidden tale) re-appropriates for herself the subject-position. Actually No Name Woman is both victim and victor, for she in turn victimizes the entire family—men and women—by temporarily denying them drinking water.

Her own victimization and subsequent act of vengeance continue to haunt the family. The men declare that her story never be told, but it is passed on to the next generation of women by another subaltern, Brave Orchid. Though the tale is told the young Maxine as a warning, it only succeeds in empowering her, for it is not only a cautionary tale about the victimization of those who defy tradition, but also about their strength and the power of protest. By spreading the story to the next generation, Brave Orchid re-assigns subject-positions for both No Name Woman and herself, involuntarily empowering herself and Maxine. She exacts her own vengeance by repeating the forbidden tale and, as the storyteller, assumes subjectivity for herself. Her's too is an act of insurgence against the will of the patriarchy. The tale, instead of warning Maxine into compliance with patriarchal wishes, motivates her to defiance by reiterating what she has begun to realize, namely the subalternity of woman's existence in patriarchal culture. Her resistance, resembling her mother's act of insurgence, takes Brave Orchid's "talk story" a step further. She begins her memoir with No Name Woman's story, and inscribing it as historical record, she re-assigns subject-positions for both No Name Woman and herself. By making it a part of her own memoir, she also succeeds in empowering future generations of women in her family.

Loss of a name implies loss of identity, of familial continuity, and even personality. The story of No Name Woman echoes the struggle of all Chinese Americans in establishing their right to be counted as Americans in the face of Chinese Exclusion Acts, deportations, and laws denying them citizenship. They all have been, in a sense, 'No Name Persons.' Many had to change their names either to avoid deportation or to facilitate the processing of immigration papers. Maxine notices "The Chinese I know hide their names; sojourners take new names when their lives change and guard their real names with silence." Margaret Miller too points out that often in Chinese culture children are not aware of their parents' and grandparents' names, as it is the position occupied by each family member within the family unit that takes precedence over their individuation as personalities ["Threads of Identity in Maxine Hong Kingston's *The Woman Warrior*," in *Biography,* Winter, 1983]. In the case of immigrant families the real names were often not disclosed in order to keep children from inadvertently giving away any secrets about illegal immigrant relatives. Many Chinese Americans often had several different names for different purposes, and identity was often flexible—a Chinese name for use amongst the Chinese community and an American name for immigration purposes.

In *The Woman Warrior,* when the rumor goes around that the U.S. Immigration authorities have set up headquarters in San Francisco, parents warn their children:

> Lie to Americans. Tell them you were born during the San Francisco earthquake. Tell them your birth certificate and your parents were burned up in the fire.

Just as No Name Woman is denied identity within her Chinese community, Kingston is denied identity as an American writer by some critics within the literary community. Speaking of the reviews about her book, Kingston finds the "exotic-inscrutable-mysterious-oriental reviewing" ["**Cultural Mis-readings by American Reviewers**," *Asian and Western Writers in Dialogue: New Cultural Identities,* edited by Guy Amirthanayagam, 1982] offensive. She feels

that to say Chinese Americans are inscrutable, mysterious, and exotic "denies us out common humanness, because it says that we are so different from a regular human being that we are by our nature intrinsically unknowable" and "to call a people exotic freezes us into the position of being always alien." She also objects to the ignorance about her nationality displayed in most of these reviews:

> Another bothersome characteristic of the reviews is the ignorance of the fact that I am an American. I am an American writer, who like other American writers, wants to write the great American novel. *The Woman Warrior* is an American book. Yet many reviewers do not see the American-ness of it, nor the fact of my own American-ness."

They do not see its American-ness or recognize Kingston as an American writer because of the subject-position from which they read the book, and because of the positions they assign it as a representation of a marginal or subaltern experience and Kingston as a Chinese-American writer (Chinese-American with the hyphen). They thus classify both her and the representations in her work as subaltern material. Even as Kingston attempts to establish her identity as a young Chinese woman growing up in America, she is denied her national identity by those reviewers who orientalize her work by praising it for its "strange and brooding atmosphere inscrutably foreign, oriental" [**"Cultural Mis-readings by American Reviewers"**]. Kingston, reacting to such praise with, "How dare they call their ignorance our inscrutability," finds that even those critics who perceive it as mainstream American literature (for example, Michael T. Molloy), criticize her for stepping out of the "exotic" role. Spivak's point, that in approaching works of cultural history one needs to be conscious of the assignment of subject-positions, applies also to the critical apparatus brought into play, which too employs its own set of subject-positions. On the one hand, critics who see Kingston's work as oriental, inscrutable, and foreign, do so because they have already assigned themselves a subject-position and Kingston and her work a subaltern one. On the other hand, Kingston's annoyance with such reviews indicates that, perceiving herself as a type of American, she assigns herself and her work subject-positions. Thus the delineation of what is true and real and what is imagined and illusory changes constantly depending upon what subject-positions are being assigned and adopted by author, reader, and critic.

Within Kingston's narrative too subject-positions are always shifting. The demarcation between the real and the illusory or the mythic is never clear, and the reader is continually forced to examine the assignment and re-assignment of subject-positions within the text. The subtitle, "Memoirs of a Girlhood Among Ghosts," emphasizes the shifting ambiguity of narrative form and content. While the work proposes to be autobiographical, the word "memoir" allows it to take liberties with the objective factuality and chronology of events. The use of the word "ghosts" throws into question the objective reality of the characters, who are being represented intermittently through memory and the imagined recreations of reality and myth by the author.

The other "ghost" features in the narrative belong to Maxine's dreams and also originate from her mother's "talk story." They are the tales of the woman warrior, Fa Mu Lan and the epic poet, T'sai Yen. The stories of these two mythic characters run contrary to the reality of women's lives in Chinese culture, as both Fa Mu Lan and T'sai Yen are heroic figures who not only forge their individual destinies and personalities, but also locate themselves within familial and communal bonds. Maxine finally pulls together her differences from the ethnic community, her family, and American society and draws her connections with these mythic characters by insisting that she too can have a place within the ancestry of her Chinese family and still remain an individual in both her American-ness and her Chinese-ness.

The mother/daughter relationship, crucial for Kingston's final self actualization, directs the movement of the entire narrative. Kingston, having been raised in America, derives her experience and understanding of China and its culture through her parents, with her mother functioning as the primary source of information about her cultural heritage. As females and as members of subaltern classes, women of ethnic minorities find their valuation limited by the dominant culture as well as by the patriarchal structure of their own ethnic society. Maxine's early recognition of these limitations almost devastates and silences her. For example, the onset of the eighteen month mysterious illness results as the consequence of her inner conflict over confronting the quiet Chinese girl—an act of insurgence defying the patriarchy's silencing of woman. Instead of being silenced either by suicide, as in the case of No Name Woman, or by madness, as in the case of Moon Orchid, Maxine recovers from her illness and learns to talk again. Maxine establishes both her connection with and her distance from her mother by itemizing all the things she feels the need to tell Brave Orchid. Listing her grievances in this way allows Maxine to recognize the powerful role language plays in the oppressed individual's quest for identity.

Language finally allows Kingston to establish her identity as neither specifically Chinese nor specifically American, but rather as a Chinese American Woman. She owes her empowerment to her mother, who taught her the art of "talking story" and who also cut her frenum when she was little to allow her to speak in many tongues. As with the other tales in the narrative, where the distinction between reality and fiction is obscured continually, this tale too is fraught with ambiguity. Uncertain whether her mother cut her fre-

num to allow her to speak or to silence her, Maxine examining her frenum in the mirror, wonders if the whole incident isn't yet another "talk story." Nevertheless, in spite or because of the cut frenum, Maxine learns to speak with power and transcribes her mother's stories in a language foreign to their origins. Thus, by recreating these Chinese tales in English and paralleling them with her own story, she makes them her own; she makes them representative of her individual Chinese American identity. By speaking out about the truths forbidden her as a woman of Chinese culture, she empowers herself. Her mother's transgression of patriarchal ways through "talking story" the unspeakable and the forbidden, is taken beyond the oral tradition by Maxine who speaks these forbidden truths and myths out on paper.

Through the act of writing she understands and defines exactly who she is, someone that society, both Chinese and American, has not yet defined accurately—a Chinese American, whose experiences, while sometimes common with those of the Chinese, the Americans, and the men among whom she has grown up, differ greatly from all three groups to make her a unique individual, a Chinese American woman. She belongs to the true subaltern class, one that frequently has been silenced not only by the dominant culture, the dominant sex, and the males of her subaltern class, but also has been made invisible. Spivak's political project, that of allowing the subaltern power to speak, is played out in this narrative of a young woman, who as a member of a subaltern class, inherits both the limitations and the tools for her survival from her mother and learns the lesson of speaking out. To speak out and define herself and her rightful place, she, of necessity, has to distance herself from her mother. Realizing her separateness and Otherness from men, from the Chinese, and from the Americans, she affirms her individual identity only by confirming her Otherness at all these three levels.

Despite her attempt to pull away from her mother, Maxine is more like Brave Orchid than she is willing to admit while growing up. Brave Orchid, despite patriarchal limitations imposed upon her, became an individual who exorcised ghosts, delivered babies, immigrated to America, worked the family laundry, and raised a family in a foreign country. The grown-up Maxine finally recognizes the great debt she owes her mother and her own instinctive connection with her before closing her narrative with the story of T'sai Yen: "Here is a story my mother told me, not when I was young, but recently, when I told her I also talk story. The beginning is hers, the ending mine." It is impossible to distinguish where Brave Orchid's story ends and Maxine's version begins, for Maxine intertwines the stories and thus connects herself back with her beginnings. She, like her mother, also "talks stories"—only hers are written ones. Following in her mother's footsteps, she too is a pioneer who has exorcised her own ghosts and broken bonds of silence. Despite their differences, and possibly because of them, they are both engaged in a similar quest for individuation, for self, and for identity as woman, as Chinese, and as American. The evolution of Maxine's identity holds larger significance for all Asian Americans who, as [Frank Chin and Jeffrey Paul Chan,] the editors of *Aiiieeeee! An Anthology of Asian American Writers*[, 1974] explain, have been separated by geography, culture, and history from their land of origin. As a result, the identities they will carve out for themselves will reflect cultures and sensibilities that are distinctly not Chinese, Japanese, Indian, Korean, or white American, but that are distinctly original and unique.

Sau-ling Cynthia Wong (essay date 1992)

SOURCE: "Autobiography as Guided Chinatown Tour? Maxine Hong Kingston's *The Woman Warrior* and the Chinese-American Autobiographical Controversy," in *Multicultural Autobiography: American Lives,* edited by James Robert Payne, University of Tennessee Press, 1992, pp. 248-79.

[*Born in Hong Kong, Wong has been a professor in the Asian American studies program at the University of California, Berkeley, and is the author of* From Necessity to Extravagance: Contexts and Intertexts in Asian American Literature. *In the following essay, she surveys the controversial critical reaction to* The Woman Warrior.]

Maxine Hong Kingston's autobiography, *The Woman Warrior,* may be the best-known contemporary work of Asian-American literature. Winner of the National Book Critics Circle Award for the best book of nonfiction published in 1976, *The Woman Warrior* remains healthily in print and on the reading lists of numerous college courses; excerpts from it are routinely featured in anthologies with a multicultural slant. It is safe to say that many readers who otherwise do not concern themselves with Asian-American literature have read Kingston's book.

In spite—or maybe, as we shall see, because—of its general popularity, however, *The Woman Warrior* has by no means been received with unqualified enthusiasm by Kingston's fellow Chinese Americans. A number of Chinese-American critics have repeatedly denounced *The Woman Warrior,* questioning its autobiographic status, its authenticity, its representativeness, and thereby Kingston's personal integrity. Though often couched in the emotionally charged, at times openly accusatory, language characteristic of what the Chinese call "pen wars," the critical issues raised in this debate are not merely of passing interest. Rather, they lie at the heart of any theoretical discus-

sion of ethnic American autobiography in particular and ethnic American literature in general. It would therefore be instructive to set out the terms of the controversy and explore their theoretical ramifications, with a view to understanding the nature of Kingston's narrative enterprise in *The Woman Warrior.*

The most fundamental objection to *The Woman Warrior* concerns its generic status: its being billed as autobiography rather than fiction, when so much of the book departs from the popular definition of autobiography as an unadorned factual account of a person's own life. Responding to a favorable review of the book by Diane Johnson in the *New York Review of Books,* Jeffery Chan notes [in "Jeff Chan, Chairman of SF State Asian American Studies, Attacks Review," *San Francisco Journal,* May 4, 1977] how "a white reading public will rave over ethnic biography while ignoring a Chinese American's literary art" and attacks Knopf, "a white publishing house," for "distributing an obvious fiction for fact." The thrust of Chan's message is that the autobiographical label is a marketing ploy in which the author, to her discredit, has acquiesced. Chan's stricture is echoed by Benjamin Tong, who finds *The Woman Warrior* "obviously contrived," a work of "fiction passing for autobiography" ["Critic of Admirer Sees Dumb Racist," *San Francisco Journal,* May 11, 1977]. By way of contrast, while the unusual generic status of *The Woman Warrior* is also widely noted by non-Chinese-American critics, it is seldom cited as either a weakness or a matter of personal, as opposed to artistic, purpose.

How far is Kingston personally responsible for the nonfiction label on the covers of *The Woman Warrior*? According to her, very little:

> The only correspondence I had with the publisher concerning the classification of my books was that he said that Non-fiction would be the most accurate category; Non-fiction is such a catch-all that even "poetry is considered non-fiction."

And poetry is something in whose company she would be "flattered" to see her books. The entire matter might have rested here—but for some theoretical issues raised by the controversy which command an interest beyond the topical.

Although Kingston's detractors do not use the term, at the heart of the controversy is the question of fictionalization: to what extent "fictional" features are admissible in a work that purports to be an autobiography. The Chinese-American critics of *The Woman Warrior* focus their attention on the social effects of admitting fictionalization into an autobiographical work. Their concern, variously worded, is summed up most concisely, if baldly, by Katheryn Fong:

I read your references to mythical and feudal China as fiction. . . . Your fantasy stories are embellished versions of your mother's embellished versions of stories. As fiction, these stories are creatively written with graphic imagery and emotion. The problem is that non-Chinese are reading your fiction as true accounts of Chinese and Chinese American history. ["To Maxine Hong Kingston: A Letter," *Bulletin for Concerned Asian Scholars,* Vol. 9, No. 4, 1977]

Thus stated, the **Woman Warrior** "problem" is seen to rest ultimately on the readers, not the author; the basis for denouncing **The Woman Warrior** is pragmatic, response-contingent, and reader-specific. Why, then, has Kingston been implicated at all in the misreadings of her audience? It is possible to reject the very question as irrelevant, in that authors have little control over how their published works will be read. On the other hand, when critics like Chan, Tong, or Fong hold Kingston responsible for her readers' failings, they do so from a set of assumptions about ethnic literature that are grounded in a keen awareness of the sociopolitical context of minority literary creation. Such an awareness is precisely what is missing in many white reviewers' remarks on **The Woman Warrior**; moreover, the autobiographical genre, with its promise (perceived or real) of "truthfulness," by nature encourages preoccupation with a work's sociopolitical context. Thus the charge of unwarranted fictionalization must be addressed.

The Woman Warrior can be considered fictionalized in a number of ways. On the most obvious formal level, it violates the popular perception of autobiography as an ordered shaping of life events anchored in the so-called external world. It aims at creating what James Olney calls "a realm of order where events bear to one another a relationship of significance rather than of chronology" ["Some Versions of Memory/Some Versions of Bios: The Ontology of Autobiography," *Autobiography: Essays Theoretical and Critical,* 1980]. According to an early student of the genre, autobiographies must contain, "in some measure, the germ of a description of the manners of their times" [Roy Pascal, *Design and Truth in Autobiography,* 1960]. Although recent scholars have found the referential grounding of autobiography much more problematic and its defining essence much more elusive [e.g., Olney, "Autobiography and the Cultural Moment: A Thematic, Historical, and Bibliographical Introduction," *Autobiography*; Elizabeth Bruss, *Autobiographical Acts: The Changing Situation of a Literary Genre,* 1976; John Paul Eakin, *Fictions in Autobiography: Studies in the Art of Self-Invention,* 1985], the term *autobiography* usually does evoke, at least among general readers, a chronologically sequenced account with verifiable references to places, people, and events. As one critic puts it, in more abstruse language: "Texts bound by the real insist upon an epistemological status different from works of the imagination in which the real is more nearly hypothetical" [Arnold Krupat, "The Indian Autobiography: Origins, Type, and Function," *American Literature,* Vol. 53, No. 1, 1981]. But what if the "real" that an autobiography is bound by is the "imagination" of the protagonist? This is the thorny problem of generic differentiation posed by **The Woman Warrior.**

By an outwardly oriented definition of autobiography, **The Woman Warrior** is at best only nominally autobiographical: to borrow a phrase from Pascal, it is a work "so engrossed with the inner life that the outer world becomes blurred," told by a narrator who, as a child, regularly sees "free movies" on "blank walls" and "[t]alks to people that aren't real inside [her] mind." The prose slips from the subjunctive to the declarative with but the slightest warning: the No Name Woman story begins with *perhaps*'s and *could have been*'s but soon dispenses with these reminders of conjecture. Likewise, while the Fa Mu Lan segment in "White Tigers" is initially marked as an enumeration of the possible and desirable—"The call *would* come from a bird. . . . The bird *would* cross the sun. . . . I would be a little girl of seven. . . ." (my italics)—the bulk of the narration is in the simple past tense, as if recounting completed events in the actual world. Two divergent accounts are given of Brave Orchid's encounter with the Sitting Ghost, neither of which could have been definitive since the event (or alleged event) predates the birth of the daughter/narrator. "At the Western Palace," presented as a deceptively conventional, self-contained short story, is revealed in the next chapter to be a third-hand fiction. In short, the referential grounding of **The Woman Warrior** is tenuous and presented in a potentially misleading manner. A few public places and events in the "outer" world are recognizable from what we know about author Kingston's life; all else is recollection, speculation, reflection, meditation, imagination. Verifiability is virtually out of the question in a work so self-reflexive. Presumably, then, readers who do not pay sufficient attention to the narrative intricacies of **The Woman Warrior,** especially white readers with biased expectations, will mistake fiction for fact.

The critics of **The Woman Warrior** also detect fictionalization—in the sense of "making things up"—in the way Kingston has chosen to translate certain Chinese terms. A central example is the word *ghost,* based on Cantonese *kuei* or *gwai,* a key term in the book appearing in the subtitle as well as several important episodes. Kingston renders *kuei* as *ghost.* Chan and Tong ("Critic of Admirer"), while conceding that the character can indeed mean "ghost" (as in "spirit of the dead"), insist that it be translated as *demon* (or *devil* or *asshole*). They object to the connotations of insubstantiality or neutrality in Kingston's translation, finding it unsanctioned by community usage and lacking in the hostility toward whites indispensable to true works of Chinese-American literature.

Tong further elevates the rendition of *kuei* as *ghost* into a "purposeful" act of pandering to white tastes and adds another example of "mistranslation" ("Critic of Admirer"): referring to "frogs" as "heavenly chickens," which should have been "field chickens" in Cantonese. (*Tien,* "sky" or "heaven," and *tien,* "field" or "meadow," differ only in tone, which is phonemic in Chinese dialects.) Tong suggests that Kingston must have knowingly selected the wrong term, the one with the "familiar exotic touristy flavor" relished by "whites checking out Chinese America" ("Critic of Admirer").

A more serious charge of fictionalization concerns the way Kingston handles not just single Chinese terms but Chinese folklore and legends. The story of Fa Mu Lan, the woman warrior invoked as the young protagonist's patron saint, is recognizable only in bare outline to a reader conversant with traditional Chinese culture. The section on the girl's period of training in the mountains draws extensively on popular martial arts "novels" or "romances" (*wuxia xiaoshuo*) as well as from traditional fantasy lore on *shenxian* ("immortals"). As for the way Kingston makes use of the traditional Fa Mu Lan story, at least the version fixed in the popular "Mulan Shi" or "Ballad of Mulan," deviations from it in *The Woman Warrior* are so numerous that only a few major ones can be noted here. The tattooing of the woman warrior is based on the well-known tale of Yue Fei, whose mother carved four characters (not entire passages) onto his back, exhorting him to be loyal to his country. Also, the spirit-marriage to the waiting childhood sweetheart, a wish-fulfilling inversion of the No Name Woman's fate, is utterly unlikely in ancient China, considering the lowly place of women. The traditional Fa Mu Lan is never described as having been pregnant and giving birth to a child while in male disguise. The episode of the wicked baron is fabricated. The Fa Mu Lan of "Mulan Shi" is a defender of the establishment, her spirit patriarchal as well as patriotic, a far cry from a peasant rebel in the vein of the heroes of *Outlaws of the Marsh.*

Because of these and other liberties Kingston has taken with her raw material, *The Woman Warrior* has been criticized by a number of Chinese Americans varying in their knowledge of traditional Chinese culture. Chinese-born scholar Joseph S. M. Lau dismisses the book as a kind of mishmash, a retelling of old tales that would not impress those having access to the originals ["The Fictional World of Chinatown," *Ming Pao Monthly,* Vol. 173, 1980]. Writer Frank Chin, who is fifth-generation, attacks Kingston for her "distortions" of traditional Chinese culture. In a parody of *The Woman Warrior* filled with inversions and travesties, Chin creates a piece entitled "The Unmanly Warrior," about a

little French girl growing up in Canton and drawing inspiration from "her imagined French ancestor Joan of Arc."

> [Her] picture of Joan of Arc . . . was so inaccurate as to demonstrate that the woman has gone mad, the French people of Frenchtown on the edge of the port city said. The French girl is writing not history, but art, the Chinese who loved the book said, and continued: She is writing a work of imagination authenticated by her personal experience. ["The Most Popular Book in China," *Quilt,* Vol. 4, 1984]

Clearly, the personal authority of an autobiographer is not easy to challenge. Perhaps sensing this, some of Kingston's critics concede it but blend the charge of fictionalization with that of atypicality. Again, the projected reactions of the white audience are kept constantly in sight. Speaking of the protagonist's account of not knowing her father's name, Chan calls this experience "unique" and expresses fears that Kingston "may mislead naive white readers" by not giving any background on the system of naming unique to Chinese Americans. Fong complains: "Your story is a *very personal* description of growing up in Chinese America. It is *one* story from one Chinese American woman of one out of seven generations of Chinese Americans" (italics in original). Like Chan, she feels that a narrative as personal as Kingston's must be made safe for white consumption by means of a sobering dose of Chinese-American history; the historical information to be incorporated should emphasize the "causes" behind the "pains, secrets, and bitterness" portrayed in *The Woman Warrior.* Fong lists various excerpts that she finds especially dangerous and glosses each with a summary of experiences considered canonical to an ideologically correct version of Chinese-American history. Without such a corrective, she suggests, Kingston will reinforce the white readers' stereotype of Chinese Americans as eternally unassimilable aliens, "silent, mysterious, and devious." Tong feels that Kingston's upbringing in the one-street Chinatown of Stockton, an agricultural town in California's Central Valley (instead of in a bigger, geographically more distinct and presumably more "typical" Chinatown) disqualifies her from attaining "historical and cultural insight" about Chinese America ["Chinatown Popular Culture: Notes toward a Critical Psychological Anthropology," in *The Chinese American Experience: Papers from the Second National Conference on Chinese American Studies (1980),* edited by Genny Lim, 1980].

According to Kingston's critics, the most pernicious of the stereotypes that might be supported by *The Woman Warrior* is that of Chinese-American men as sexist. Some Chinese-American women readers think highly of *The Woman Warrior* because it confirms their personal experiences with sexism (e.g., Suzi Wong, Nellie Wong). Others find Kingston's account of growing up amidst shouts of "Maggot!" overstated, yet can cite little to support the charge besides *their* own personal authority. Contrasting **The Woman Warrior**'s commercial success with the relatively scant attention received by books like Louis Chu's *Eat a Bowl of Tea* and Laurence Yep's *Dragonwings,* both of which present less negative father images, Fong implies that Kingston's autobiography earns its reputation by "over-exaggerat[ing]" the ills of Chinese-American male chauvinism. She is willing to grant that a more understanding response from white readers might have given Kingston more creative license but finds the existing body of Chinese-American literature small enough to justify a more stringent demand on the Chinese-American writer, especially the woman writer.

If Chinese-American women disagree about the accuracy of Kingston's portrayal of patriarchal culture, it is hardly surprising to find male Chinese-American critics condemning it in harsh terms. Chan attributes the popularity of **The Woman Warrior** to its depiction of "female anger," which bolsters white feminists' "hallucination" of a universal female condition; and Tong calls the book a "fashionably feminist work written with white acceptance in mind" ("Critic of Admirer"). If Chinese-American literature is, according to the editors of [*Aiiieeeee! An Anthology of Asian American Writers* (1974)], distinguished by emasculation [Frank Chin, Jeffrey Paul Chan, Lawson Fusao Inada, and Shawn Wong], then Chinese-American writers cannot afford to wash the culture's dirty linen in public. Frank Chin declares that personal pain—merely a matter of "expression of ego" and "psychological attitudinizing"—must be subordinated to political purpose ["This Is Not an Autobiography," *Genre,* Vol. 18, No. 2, 1985].

For Chin, the very form of autobiography is suspect because of its association with the Christian tradition of confession. Although **The Woman Warrior** does not deal with Christianity, Chin places it in a tradition of Christianized Chinese-American autobiographies from Yung Wing's *My Life in China and America* through Pardee Lowe's *Father and Glorious Descendant* to Jade Snow Wong's *Fifth Chinese Daughter.* His rationale is that all autobiography, like religious confessions and conversion testimonials, demonstrates "admission of guilt, submission of my self for judgment," for "approval by outsiders." "[A] Chinaman can't write an autobiography without selling out." In fact, claims Chin, the autobiography is not even a native Chinese form, and Chinese-American writers have no business adopting it. Unfortunately, however, "[t]he Christian Chinese American autobiography is the only Chinese American literary tradition" ("This Is Not an Autobiography").

Some of the generalizations made by Kingston's critics, such as the exclusively Western and Christian origin of autobiography, may be called into question by existing schol-

arship. According to one student of the genre, a complex autobiographical tradition does exist in Chinese literature, its origins traceable to the first century A.D., in the Han Dynasty [Wendy Ann Larson, "Autobiographies of Chinese Writers in the Early Twentieth Century," 1984]. Moreover, the confessional mode attributed by Chin solely to a guilt-obsessed Christianity can also be found in traditional Chinese writing [Pei-Yi Wu, "Self-Examination and Confession of Sins in Traditional China," *Harvard Journal of Asiatic Studies,* Vol. 39, No. 1, 1979]. This does not invalidate Georges Gusdorf's important insight [in "Conditions and Limits of Autobiography," translated by James Olney, in Olney's *Autobiography,* 1980] on the cultural specificity of the modern Western autobiography: the point is not to claim that the modern Western autobiography as we know it was practiced in ancient China (it was not) but merely to point out the oversimplification in many of the statements that have been made about **The Woman Warrior.** When Chin links the genre with Christian self-accusation, he overlooks the possibility that the late medieval *breakdown* of Christian dogma might have been responsible for the emergence of autobiography as an autonomous literary tradition (Gusdorf). Furthermore, emphasis on the confessional element represents only one school of autobiographical scholarship, the Anglo-American; there are others (Eakin). Even if autobiography were an entirely Western phenomenon, according to Chin's own pronouncements on the unique, nonderivative nature of Asian-American literature (especially on its separateness from Asian literature), Chinese-American writers have a right to appropriate a genre not indigenous to the Chinese in China but indigenous to the Chinese in America. As Chin and his *Aiiieeeee!* co-editors put it in their prefatory manifesto on Chinese and Japanese-American literature, an "American-born Asian, writing from the world as Asian-American," should not be expected to "reverberate to gongs struck hundreds of years ago."

Other more or less self-contained disputes on isolated assertions by Kingston's critics could be explored. On the whole, however, one may say that the entire Chinese-American autobiographical debate touches on articles of ideology so jealously held that the existence of a variety of opinions, scholarly or otherwise, may itself be seen as a problem rather than as a possible source of solutions. Given the peremptory tone in which much of the criticism of **The Woman Warrior** has been conducted, it is important that the tacit assumptions of the critics be articulated.

The theoretical underpinnings of the hostile criticism may be summarized as a series of interlocking propositions, some concerning the nature of autobiography as a genre (regardless of the author's background), others generalizable to autobiography by all American ethnic writers, still others peculiar to Chinese-American autobiography.

First of all, autobiography is seen to be self-evidently distinguishable from fiction. If the two genres blur at all at the edges, the interaction merely takes the form of fiction providing "techniques" to render the mundane material of autobiography more attractive; the epistemologies status of the narrated material is not affected. In the same way that language is considered a sort of sugarcoating on dry nuggets of fact, the autobiographer's subjectivity is seen as having little or no constitutive power; rather, it is a Newtonian body moving about in a world of discrete, verifiable—and hence incontrovertible—facts, its power being limited to the choice between faithfully recording or willfully distorting this external reality. In principle, therefore, autobiography is biography which just happens to be written by one's self. It claims no special privilege, poses no special problems. Finally, the *graphe* part of *autobiography,* the act of writing, the transformation of life into text, is seen by Kingston's critics as a mechanical conveyance of facts from the autobiographer's mind to the reader's via a medium in the physical world, the process pleasant or not depending on the author's literary talents. In the case of the **Woman Warrior** debate, correspondence between word and thing is deemed so perfect that a Chinese term, *kuci,* is supposed to be translatable by only one English equivalent, with all other overtones outlawed. The arbiter here is to be the individual critic backed by the authority of "the Chinese American community" (as if Kingston herself were not a member of this community).

Recognition of a preexisting external reality, however, imposes a special obligation on the ethnic American autobiographer: to provide a positive portrayal of the ethnic community through one's self-portrayal. At the very least, the autobiographer's work should be innocent of material that might be seized upon by unsympathetic outsiders to illustrate prevalent stereotypes of the ethnic group; the author should stress the diversity of experience within the group and the uniqueness and self-definition of the individual. Ideally, an ethnic autobiography should also be a history in microcosm of the community, especially of its suffering, struggles, and triumphs over racism. In other words, an ethnic autobiographer should be an exemplar and spokesperson whose life will inspire the writer's own people as well as enlighten the ignorant about social truths.

The collective history of the ethnic community—one does not speak of *a* history in this theoretical framework—provides the ultimate reference point for the ethnic autobiographer. Here is where the Newtonian analogy begins to break down, for the self proves, after all, to be subjective in the everyday sense of "biased" or "unreliable." Handicapped by its interiority, it cannot be the equal of other "bodies" which can be summed up as a bundle of externally ascertainable properties. The self is epistemologically underprivileged, not privileged, to discover the validity of its

private truths, it must appeal to the arbitration of the community (however defined). The history of the collectivity is ballast for the ethnic autobiographer's subjectivity; it is a yardstick against which the author can measure how representative or how idiosyncratic his or her life is, how worthy of preservation in writing. Should individual experience fail to be homologous to collective history, personal authority must yield to ideological imperatives, and the details of the narrative must be manipulated to present an improved picture. According to this logic, the ethnic woman autobiographer victimized by sexism must be ready to suppress potentially damaging (to the men, that is) material; to do less is to jeopardize the united front and prostitute one's integrity for the sake of white approval. *Bios* is of little worth unless it is "representative"—averaged out to become sociologically informative as well as edifying.

A series of mutually incompatible demands on ethnic autobiography follows from the tenets outlined above. Initially, ethnic autobiography is thought useful because its focus on the uniqueness of the individual establishes a minority's right to self-definition; a sufficient number of autobiographies will disabuse white readers of their oversimplified preconceptions. Autobiography's allegedly pure factuality is also prized for its educational value: unlike fiction, it can be counted on to "tell it like it is" and resist charges of artistic license made by doubting readers. Nonetheless, autobiography cannot, by definition, be more than *one* person's life story; thus it cannot be fully trusted. What if the single individual's life happens to confirm or even endorse white perceptions instead of challenging them? Hence the insistence that ethnic autobiography be "representative." The requirement would have been easily fulfilled if the autobiographer happened—that vexatious word again!—to have already been "representative," in the sense of conforming to a view of the group agreed upon by the members making that determination. Short of that, the "representativeness" will have to be formed out of recalcitrant material, through an editorial process true to the spirit but not necessarily the letter of the "ethnic experience."

The minute this is done, however, the attempt to make absolute the generic distinctions between autobiography and fiction ends up dissolving the boundaries altogether: autobiography loses its putative authority in fact and turns into fiction. Language loses its innocuous transmitting function and assumes the unruly power of transmutation. The individual loses his or her uniqueness and becomes a sociological category. From the effort to counter homogenization by offering depictions of diversity, a new uniformity emerges: one set of stereotypes is replaced by another. In the final analysis, the main reason the critics attack *The Woman Warrior* is not that it is insufficiently factual but that it is insufficiently fictional: that the author did not tamper more freely with her own life story. And ironically—given the critics' claimed championship of self-definition and literary autonomy—the kind of fiction they would like Kingston to have written is closely dictated by the responses of white readers.

Only when safeguards against misreadings are supplied may the autobiographical label once more be affixed with confidence, the benefits of the genre now purged of the inconvenient admixture of potential harm. The ignorance of white readers seems to be taken for granted as immutable by Kingston's critics. The possibility that the less unregenerate readers may learn to read the allusions in *The Woman Warrior,* just as generations of minority readers have learned to read the Eurocentric canon, is never once raised; nor is the possibility that a Chinese-American writer may by right expect, and by duty promote, such learning in his or her audience.

These issues naturally have their counterparts in other ethnic American literatures. The differing versions of Frederick Douglass's early life found in his autobiographies provide a classic example of how a black autobiographer might feel compelled to edit "factual" details in the interest of anticipated social effect [e.g., Henry Louis Gates, Jr., *Figures in Black Words, Signs, and the "Racial" Self,* 1987]. It is worth noting that, while critic Henry Louis Gates, Jr., justifies the "crafting or making [of a 'fictive self'] by design," citing the urgent need to establish the black man's right to speak for himself, he also finds a certain flatness of aesthetic effect when Douglass begins to substitute "one ideal essence for another." "Almost never does Douglass allow us to see him as a human individual in all of his complexity."

Though the dilemma is shared by other ethnic American autobiographies, the conflicting claims of typicality and uniqueness take a particularly acute form in Chinese-American autobiography: at stake is not only the existence of the minority writer's voice but the possible perversion of that voice to satisfy the white reader's appetite for exoticism. Indeed, it is only within the context of the Chinese-American autobiographical tradition that both the vehemence of Kingston's critics and the novelty of the narrative undertaking in *The Woman Warrior* can be understood.

To borrow a phrase applied to early African-American writers, Chinese-American writers "entered into the house of literature through the door of autobiography" (Olney, "Autobiography and the Cultural Moment"). Autobiographies predominate in Chinese-American writing in English. Some autobiographies are by Chinese-born writers who grew up in China (Lee, Yung, Kuo, Su-ling Wong, Wei); others are by writers born and brought up in the United States (Lowe, Jade Snow Wong, Goo, Kingston). An autobiography from the former group typically focuses on the protagonist's early experiences in China, often ending very

abruptly upon his or her arrival in the United States. The author tends to believe the life depicted as representing Chinese life of a certain period or social milieu, and of interest to the Western reader chiefly for this reason rather than for its uniqueness; such a conviction may easily degenerate into the accommodating mentality of a friendly guide to an exotic culture. The autobiographies in the second group, those by American-born writers, are primarily set in the United States. Given the distressing tendency of white readers to confuse Chinese Americans with Chinese in China, and to attribute a kind of ahistorical, almost genetic, Chinese essence to all persons of Chinese ancestry regardless of their upbringing, the pressure on American-born writers to likewise "represent Chinese culture" is strong. Removed from Chinese culture in China by their ancestors' emigration, American-born autobiographers may still capitalize on white curiosity by conducting the literary equivalent of a guided Chinatown tour: by providing explanations on the manners and mores of the Chinese-American community from the vantage point of a "native." This stance has indeed been adopted by some, and, in a sort of involuntary intertextuality, even those works that do not share it will most likely be read as anthropological guidebooks. The curse is potent enough to extend at times to nonautobiographical literature; for a book like *The Woman Warrior,* then, it would be all but impossible to prevent some readers from taking the autobiographical label as a license to overgeneralize.

A few examples will characterize the stance of the cultural guide found among both Chinese-born and American-born autobiographers. In Lee Yan Phou's *When I Was a Boy in China,* personal narrative slows at every turn to make room for background material; seven of the twelve chapter titles—"The House and Household," "Chinese Cookery," "Games and Pastimes," "Schools and School Life," "Religions," "Chinese Holidays," "Stories and Story-Tellers"—could have come out of a general survey of Chinese society. The individual's life serves the function of conveying anthropological information; the freight, in fact, frequently outweighs the vehicle. Lee directly addresses white American readers as "you" throughout the book and consciously assumes the persona of a tour guide: "The servants were . . . sent out to market to buy the materials for breakfast. Let us follow them"; "Now, let me take you into the school where I struggled with the Chinese written language for three years." In Helena Kuo's tellingly titled *I've Come a Long Way,* the tour guide role seems to have become second nature to the author. Like Lee, Kuo addresses her audience as "you" and constantly takes into account their likely reactions. Her descriptions of place are filtered through the eyes of her white readers; the similes she favors are pure *chinoiserie.* In the midst of a narrative about her journalistic career, Kuo solicitously inserts a mini-disquisition on traditional Chinese painting, to ensure that her charges will not be lost in the future when she is no longer around.

It is perhaps no accident that a good number of the autobiographies by Chinese-born writers are rather abruptly cut off soon after the author's arrival in the United States, in apparent contrast to the structure of immigrant autobiography described in William Boelhower's typology [*Immigrant Autobiography in the United States,* 1982]. Unlike the European works cited by Boelhower, these do not chronicle the author's experience of encountering and coming to terms with American culture. While only further study can elucidate this observed difference, one might venture a guess on its cause: the Chinese authors may have sensed how far American interest in their life writings is based on the image of otherness, on exotic scenery and alien cultural practices. As the autobiographers become Americanized, the fascination they hold for the reader would fade; hence the sketchy coverage of their experience in the United States.

Some American-born Chinese autobiographers also seem to have adopted the narrative stance of a cultural guide, though the presence of the audience is more implicit in their works than in Lee's or Kuo's. *Father and Glorious Descendant,* by Pardee Lowe (a contemporary and friend of Kuo's), abounds in descriptions of Chinatown customs and rituals, such as *tong* banquets, Chinese New Year festivities, celebration of the father's "Great Birthday," preparation of unusual (by Western standards) foods, and funeral practices. The name of the Lowes' ancestral village in China, Sahn Kay Gawk, is periodically rendered by the quaint circumlocution "The-Corner-of-the-Mountain-Where-the-Water-Falls," although that etymological information has been given on the first page of the book. Two chapters are devoted to a series of letters between Father and his cousin, written in a comically florid, heavily literal prose purporting to be a translation of classical Chinese. Lowe's handling of the English language betrays a habitual awareness of the white audience's need to be surprised and amused by the mystifying ways of the Chinese. Jade Snow Wong's autobiography, *Fifth Chinese Daughter,* shares with Lowe's an emphasis on Chinatown customs and rituals; with Lee's and Kuo's, a tendency to intersperse the narrative of her life with discursive segments of information on Chinese culture. A description of a dinner party for her American friends includes a step-by-step record of how egg foo young and tomato beef are cooked; an account of a visit to a Chinatown herbalist for her cough is interrupted by a clarification of the Chinese medical theory of humors.

Although there is much else in Lowe's and Wong's books besides these gestures of consideration for the sensibilities of white readers, it is undeniable that both of these authors, like their Chinese-born counterparts, are conscious of their role as cultural interpreters who can obtain a measure of recognition from whites for the insider's insight they can offer. The title of a chapter in Wong's book, "Rediscovering Chinatown," aptly epitomizes one way American-born Chinese may make peace with their cultural background in the face of intense assimilative pressures: to return to one's ethnic heritage with selective enthusiasm, reassessing once-familiar (and once-despised) sights and sounds according to their acceptability to white tastes.

As a form characterized by simultaneous subjectivity and objectivity, simultaneous expression and documentation [e.g., Albert Stone, "Autobiography in American Culture: Looking Back at the Seventies," *American Studies International,* Vol. 19, Nos. 3-4, 1981; Kathleen Mullen Sands, "American Indian Autobiography," in *Studies in American Indian Literature: Essays and Course Designs,* edited by Paula Gunn Allen, 1983], autobiography easily creates in its readers expectations of "privileged access" (Olney, "Autobiography and the Cultural Moment") to the experience and vision of an entire people. From an intraethnic point of view, the writing of autobiography may be valued as a means of preserving memories of a vanishing way of life, and hence of celebrating cultural continuity and identity; in an interethnic perspective, however, the element of *display,* whether intentional or not, is unavoidable. Many "outsiders" will thus approach ethnic autobiographies with the misguided conviction that the authors necessarily speak for "their people." The practice of reading autobiography for "cultural authenticity" may be a particularly serious danger for Chinese-American autobiography, given the group's unique situation in United States society. The ancestral land of Chinese Americans, due to its long history, sophisticated civilization, and complex encounters with American imperialism in recent history, casts an inordinately strong spell on the white imagination. Moreover, Chinese Americans, who have been subjected to genocidal immigration policies, are placed in the situation of permanent guests who must earn their keep by adding the spice of variety to American life—by selectively maintaining aspects of traditional Chinese culture and language fascinating to whites. In the terminology of Werner Sollors, if the essence of the American experience is the formation of a society based on "consent" rather than "descent," Chinese Americans have clearly been (and still are) excluded from participation in "consent" by the dominant group's insistence on the primacy of their "descent." The irony is that many readers from within the ethnic group itself have, like the detractors of *The Woman Warrior,* inadvertently contributed to this simplified and often condescending view by likewise positing a direct pipeline of cultural authenticity between the collectivity and the individual. The idea of overdetermination by "descent" is thus left unchallenged. Demanding "representativeness," the Chinese-American critics of Kingston differ from the white literary tourists only in the version of cultural authenticity subscribed to.

This tension between "consent" and "descent" is reminiscent of W. E. B. Du Bois's well-known concept of "double consciousness." The writers are aware of themselves as "insiders" with unique experiences that cannot be fully captured by ethnic categories alone. On the other hand, they cannot but sense the "outsiders" constant gaze upon their skin color, their physiognomy, their "difference." Their American right of "consent"—here taking the form of the freedom to create literature true to their felt lives—is perpetually called into question or qualified by reader expectations based on "descent." Some Chinese-American autobiographers have, indeed, sought distinction in their exotic "descent," allowing the dominant group's perceptions to define their identity. However, it is important to recognize that Kingston has taken an altogether different path in *The Woman Warrior*. The protagonist has eschewed the facile authority which self-appointment as guide and spokesperson could confer on her. The discursive space occupied by *The Woman Warrior* is between the two poles of the "double consciousness"; the audience the narrator addresses in the second person is composed of fellow Chinese Americans sharing the protagonist's need to establish a new Chinese-American selfhood:

> Chinese-Americans, when you try to understand what things in you are Chinese, how do you separate what is peculiar to childhood, to poverty, insanities, one family, your mother who marked your growing with stories, from what is Chinese? What is Chinese tradition and what is the movies?

Boelhower writes:

> In the mixed genre of autobiography, . . . the question of identity involves matching the narrator's own self-perception with the self that is recognized by others, so as to establish a continuity between the two (self and world), to give a design of self-in-the-world. ["The Brave New World of Immigrant Autobiography," *MELUS,* Vol. 9, No. 2, 1982]

If the "others" are the potential "misreaders" among her white audience, Kingston is in truth far less obsessed than her critics with "the self that is recognized by others." There are, of course, other "others" in the protagonist's lonely struggle: her Chinese family, relatives, fellow "villagers," whose perceptions of her do not match her self-perceptions either. "Descent" notwithstanding, connection to them has to be forged, which can take place only after an initial recognition of difference. Neither American nor Chinese culture, as given, offers a resting place; the protagonist of *The Woman Warrior* has to discover that there is "[n]o higher listener. No higher listener but myself." Her project is to reach "an avowal of values and a recognition of the self by the self—a choice carried out at the level of essential being—not a revelation of a reality given in advance but a cor-

ollary of an active intelligence" (Gusdorf). This project is so bold, so unfamiliar, that even her fellow Chinese Americans sometimes mistake it for the accommodationism of earlier autobiographers. For resemblances can indeed be found between *The Woman Warrior* and its predecessors—like Lee, Kingston retells Chinese tales heard in childhood; like Kuo, she makes general remarks on Chinese culture; like Lowe, she speaks of unusual Chinese foods; like Wong, she recounts experiences of sexist oppression. The crucial question is whether these resemblances are merely superficial or whether they bespeak a basic commonality in autobiographical stance. Only a careless reader, I submit, would be able to conclude that Kingston's stance in *The Woman Warrior* is that of the trustworthy cultural guide.

For the "native" in this case, having been born and raised in "ghost country" without benefit of explicit parental instruction in cultural practices, is barely more enlightened than an "outsider" would be: "From the configuration of food my mother set out, we kids had to infer the holidays." Quite unlike the generalizations about Chinese culture in *I've Come a Long Way* or *Father and Glorious Descendant,* which are meant to be encapsulations of superior knowledge, those in *The Woman Warrior* bespeak a tentative groping toward understanding. From fragmentary and haphazard evidence, the protagonist has to piece together a coherent picture of the culture she is enjoined to preserve against American influence. The effort is so frustrating that she exclaims in exasperation: "I don't see how they kept up a continuous culture for five thousand years. Maybe they didn't; maybe everyone makes it up as they go along." But the point, of course, is that the Chinese who remain in Chinese-dominant communities would have no trouble at all transmitting culture through osmosis. It is the protagonist's American-born generation who must "make it up as they go along." The emigrant parents' expectation of a "continuous culture" is, if entirely human, ahistorical and therefore doomed. (So, one might add, is the critics' similar demand for cultural authenticity. Purity is best preserved by death; history adulterates.)

Given *The Warrior Woman*'s situation in the broader cultural timescape of Chinese America, then, the so-called distortions of traditional Chinese culture found in the text are simply indications of how far removed from it the protagonist has become. As Deborah Woo rightly observes, "where culture is problematic as a source of identity, cultural ignorance itself is part of what is authentic about the experience." Thus the substitution of "heavenly chicken" for "field chicken" is not exoticization but an example of how a young Chinese child in an English-dominant society may misunderstand a tonal language. The protagonist's cosmological speculations on the omnipresent number six, involving a misinterpretation of *dai luk* (which in Cantonese pronunciation can be "the big six," a nonexistent collocation, or "the big continent/the mainland"), betray her "craving for coherence" in the face of a bewildering mass of unexplained cultural data [Vivian Hsu, "Maxine Hong Kingston as Psycho-Autobiographer and Ethnographer," *International Journal of Women's Studies,* Vol. 6, No. 5, 1983]. It is not an actual Chinese fortune-teller who confuses the homophones, which might have justified the charge of willful distortion on Kingston's part; the phrase "the Big Six" is framed by the young girl's meditation on her mother's life, the fortune-teller a fictive one whom she imagines her mother consulting.

It is, in fact, essential to recognize that the entire *Woman Warrior* is a sort of meditation on what it means to be Chinese American. To this end, the protagonist appropriates whatever is at hand, testing one generalization after another until a satisfactory degree of applicability to her own life is found. As she says of the differing versions of the No Name Woman's story: "Unless I see her life branching into mine, she gives me no ancestral help." The aphoristic statements about Chinese ways interspersed in the narrative—"Women in the old China did not choose"; "Chinese communication was loud, public," "Among the very poor and the wealthy, brothers married their adopted sisters, like doves"—are not offered for the benefit of readers hungry for tidbits of anthropological information. Rather, they are threads in a larger tapestry of inferences, some sturdy, some thin, which the protagonist weaves for her own use. Rejecting the theory that the aunt is a "wild woman" or a passive rape victim, the narrator decides on a version relevant to her life in an immigrant family: a story of assertion of "private life" against the harsh demands of group survival.

Even with material that tempts with its air of certainty, the protagonist finds it necessary to tailor-make meanings from altered details. Thus she spurns the simplistic lesson of the traditional Fa Mu Lan tale, creating instead a potentially subversive woman warrior to whom even traditions yield. While the heroine of "Mulan Shi" sees herself merely as a second-best substitute for an aged father (there being no elder son to take his place), the little girl in "White Tigers" is a *chosen* one, destined to be called away by "immortals." Martial artists typically pass on their skills to sons or male disciples; the old couple in the mountains, in contrast, devote years exclusively to her training. For the traditional Mulan, the campaigns are but a detour; at the end of the poem, the erstwhile general puts on makeup, ready to resume her interrupted feminine life. Kingston's Fa Mu Lan chooses wifehood and motherhood in the midst of battle. Her fellow villagers know of her identity before her triumphant return from battle; their relinquishment of their precious sons to her army is thus an affirmation of faith in her female power. Of course, the very necessity of male disguise means that the narrator's fantasized challenge to patriarchy

can never be complete; in the last analysis, she would like to be remembered for "perfect filiality." Yet even Fa Mu Lan's return to her parents' house has an element of active choice. All in all, working within the constraints of internalized values, the protagonist has done her best to make of unpromising material an inspiring, if not entirely radical, tale.

The treatment of the T'sai Yen story follows much the same pattern of sifting out details to arrive at a relevant meaning. Kingston's retelling omits a crucial scene in the original "Eighteen Stanzas for a Barbarian Reed Pipe": T'sai Yen's painful leave-taking from her half-barbarian sons. Though by now attached to her captor and heartsick at the prospect of never seeing her children again, T'sai Yen nevertheless chooses Han lands as her real home, negating the twelve years spent in the steppes as a mere unfortunate interlude. Herself a half-barbarian to her China-obsessed parents ("Whenever my parents said 'home,' they suspended America"), the narrator might have found such a detail too close for comfort, and too contrary in spirit to her own undertaking of forming a Chinese-American self. Thus we find a shift of emphasis: the last pages of *The Woman Warrior* celebrate not return from the remote peripheries to a waiting home but the creation of a new center through art. Singing a song that transcends cultural boundaries, T'sai Yen can now leave "her tent to sit by the winter campfires, ringed by barbarians."

As with the "Eighteen Stanzas," the moral that the protagonist draws from the assorted Chinese ghost stories diverges from the one intended by the source. No automatic authority on Chinese culture simply by virtue of "descent," the protagonist must resort to public, written texts in her quest for meanings not forthcoming in her mother's private oral tradition. (Contrary to one critic's judgment that the Mandarin transliteration of some names in *The Woman Warrior* betrays how Kingston passes library research for her Cantonese mother's bedtime stories, Kingston does not attempt to cover her trails, as any self-respecting cultural guide would. She provides dates with the Mandarin names and identifies the source, "the research against ghost fear published by the Chinese Academy of Science" [Zhongguo Kexueyuan Wenxueyanjiusuo, *Stories of Those Who Are Not Afraid of Ghosts,* 1961]. The lesson she constructs to make sense of her experiences in a frugal immigrant family—"Big eaters win"—bears little relation to the political allegory of the Communist-compiled anthology. But what matters is not the fit (for which Procrustean beds are notorious). The most useful lesson the protagonist can learn from her research is that a passive staking of her life on some preestablished reality, like looking up *Ho Chi Kuei* in a dictionary filled with decontextualized definitions, will always prove fruitless.

The narrator's methodology of self-redemption is thus remarkably consistent. Over and over, we find her forgoing the security of ready-made cultural meanings, opting instead to painstakingly mold a new set suited to her condition as a Chinese-American woman. The many questions about "facts" plaguing the narrator—Were there an Oldest Daughter and Oldest Son who died in China? Did Brave Orchid cut her frenum? Did the hulk exist or was he made up?—function much like a series of Zen *koan,* frustrating because impossible to answer by appeal to an external authority (mother, in this case). In the end, realization of their very impossibility frees her to explore the fecund uncertainties of her Chinese-American existence.

The readers who fault *The Woman Warrior* for not being more responsible toward "facts" would do well to meditate on their own *koan.* To read departures from traditional material found in *The Woman Warrior* as Kingston's cynical manipulations of naïve white readers, as her critics have done, is not only to fly in the face of textual evidence but to belittle the difficulty and urgency of the imaginative enterprise so necessary to the American-born generation: to make sense of Chinese and American culture from its own viewpoint (however hybrid and laughable to "outsiders"), to articulate its own reality, and to strengthen its precarious purchase on the task of self-fashioning. The Fa Mu Lan story itself, which many of Kingston's critics take to be a fixed and sacred given, actually exists in a multitude of Chinese texts differing from each other in purpose as well as detail.

Kingston's critics have been measuring *The Woman Warrior* "against some extra-textual order of fact," not realizing that this order is "based in its turn on other texts (dignified as documents)" (Eakin): an ideologically uplifting version of Chinese-American history revising earlier racist texts, a version of the Fa Mu Lan legend sufficiently hoary to be considered "historical." The critics' concern is understandable in view of widespread ignorance about the sociopolitical context of Chinese-American literary creation, the inherent duality of the autobiographical genre (which encourages reading for "cultural authenticity"), the existence of autobiographies by both Chinese-and American-born writers promising privileged glimpses into the group's secret life and the apparent similarities between them and Kingston's work. These issues are, indeed, vital ones generalizable to other ethnic American autobiographies, even to all ethnic American literatures. Nevertheless, intent on liberating Chinese-American writers from one set of constraints, Kingston's detractors have imposed another, in the meantime failing to take note of the most fundamental freedom of all that *The Woman Warrior* has wrested from a priori generic categories and cultural prescriptions: the freedom to create in literature a sui generis Chinese-American reality.

Sue Anne Johnston (essay date Spring 1993)

SOURCE: "Empowerment through Mythological Imaginings in *Woman Warrior,*" in *Biography,* Vol. 16, No. 2, Spring, 1993, pp. 136-46.

[*In the following essay, Johnston explores Kingston's use of myth in* The Woman Warrior.]

In *The Woman Warrior,* Maxine Hong Kingston explores the relation between a mythic, three-dimensional reality represented by China of the mind, and a flat literal reality equated with America. In its exploration of the shifting line between history and memory, fiction and nonfiction, dream and fact, Kingston challenges western rational ways of seeing, classifying, ordering. Indeed, the very difficulty of categorizing Kingston's work (fictive autobiography?) may cause us to question the very notion of categories, the dichotomous classifications upon which our systems of logic depend. French feminist critics have reminded us of the subversive potential of new ways of saying: "To put discourse into question is to reject the existing order. . . . It means choosing marginality (with an emphasis on the margins) in order to designate one's difference, a difference no longer conceived of as an inverted image or double, but as alterity, multiplicity, hetereogeneity" [Josette Feral, "The Powers of Difference," in *The Future of Difference,* edited by Hester Eisenstein and Alice Jardine, 1980]. By laying claim to her own language, her own voice, Kingston refuses the role of racial or sexual Other and invents herself as speaking subject. While dramatizing the movement from silence to articulation, she may appear to be moving away from her roots in the Chinese and Chinese-American tradition, moving toward an essentially American "logic" that seems a necessary part of her American success. In actuality, however, she synthesizes her own idiolect, an intensely personal language neither Chinese nor American, nor simply Chinese-American, but a way of seeing that draws from, and challenges, all the traditions she has inherited. Chinese myth and tradition, western literary styles and American popular culture—all are the raw material for Kingston's alchemical imagination.

In Kingston's world, east and west, like yin and yang, female and male, define themselves against each other. The American reader of *Woman Warrior* who sees her own culture from the vantage point of a marginal outsider may also look at the Chinese society and see her own culture in a glass darkly. For both Chinese and American cultures have this in common: both seek to contain or nullify the Other, the different, the female. Yet the misogynist Chinese traditional culture is itself objectified as Other by the dominant American culture in which it struggles to define itself. Furthermore, especially seen within the context of American culture, the qualities of Chinese culture which we symbolically associate with femininity are highlighted. If we define the word "feminine" in a broader sense than the biologically restrictive word "female," if we regard it in its connotative sense, as a way of seeing that focuses upon the intuitive, emotional, and symbolic, America's antipathy toward the feminine is seen as more soul-destroying than traditional Chinese misogyny. Kingston's America, in the name of efficiency and individualism, sacrifices the kinds of ambiguity, paradox, metaphor, and *relationship* that is the essence of Kingston's poetic vision. In juxtaposing American and Chinese ways of seeing, Kingston reveals to us the inadequacy of the masculine "Logos" deified in Western culture. "In the beginning was the Word, and the Word was with God, and the Word was God. He was in the beginning with God," begins John's gospel. For the author of **Woman Warrior,** as for other Chinese girls, the beginning is not a masculine Logos, but the mother's talk story. Although she rails against her mother for telling confusing stories with no clear line between truth and falsehood, we cannot help but observe that her memoirs are modeled upon her mother's talk story, in style, structure, and content. At the very moment she seems to be lashing out at her mother, and boasting of her American successes, an irony becomes apparent. Brave Orchid's stories are the richest heritage she has bequeathed her daughter—not for the social prescriptions they embody, but for the habit of poetic seeing they have instilled. As transmitter of Chinese tradition. Brave Orchid gives a double message, saying that she will "grow up a wife and a slave" but teaching "the song of the warrior woman." Just as the China which oppresses women also teaches that women can be "heroines, swordswomen," Kingston's mother too is a "confounding contradiction" [Linda Morante, "From Silence to Song: The Triumph of Maxine Hong Kingston," *Frontiers*, Vol. 9, No. 2, 1987]. Even her unlikely name, Brave Orchid, connotes the paradox of masculine courage in a delicate feminine flower. Her mother attempts to silence her; yet the effort of overcoming silence makes Kingston's story. The fantasy that the frenum of her tongue has been cut by the mother reflects the ambivalence the girl Kingston reveals toward her mother. Perhaps Kingston's mother meant to silence her by cutting her tongue; then again, perhaps she meant to free her, to cut her tongue loose. "'I cut it so that you would not be tongue-tied. Your tongue would be able to move in any language. You'll be able to speak languages that are completely different from one another. You'll be able to pronounce anything. Your frenum locked too tight to do those things, so I cut it.'" It is her mother who, by giving her the talk story, also gives her the mythos of who she is and where she came from.

What the girl Kingston absorbs from the talk stories is not necessarily what Brave Orchid intends on a conscious level. Stories like that of the no-name Aunt, for instance, are clearly admonitory, illustrating what dire consequences await the female who is a sexual maverick. Yet the conspiracy of silence surrounding this woman calls up in the girl Kingston imaginative forays into a Chinese village far away in time and space, into the mind of this unnamed aunt, into a tutelary identification with her. The whispered story of this outcast aunt haunts the author, who writes into it what she wants, needs to believe. "Unless I see her life branching into mine, she gives me no ancestral help." She makes of her an implausible romantic; she makes of her a complying victim to the man. In the end, she images her aunt not as victim, but as one who, like another rape victim—Ts'ai Yen—on one level triumphs over victimization. The no name aunt acts: she shows love for her baby by drowning it. She has the last silent word; by drowning herself in the drinking water she has revenged herself on the community which condemned her; a "spite suicide," a "weeping ghost," she waits later by the well to pull in a substitute. In hearing this talk story, Kingston listened for metamessages of power in the most seemingly hopeless situation. Like Ovid's raped and silenced Philomela, Kingston's no-name aunt finds, as a hungry, haunting ghost, the dark power of revenge in a seemingly hopeless situation.

> **In Kingston's world, east and west, like yin and yang, female and male, define themselves against each other.**
> **—Sue Anne Johnston**

Like her no name aunt, Kingston too breaks rules. Simply by revealing the scandal of the aunt, Kingston is betraying a confidence, breaking the mother's command to silence. "You must not tell anyone . . . what I am about to tell you." This memoir, which is so deeply personal in its content, is political in its import. Just as the speaking out of a caterpillar or a playing card in *Alice in Wonderland* unsettles any a priori expectations we may have about how animals and things behave, the speaking out of a Chinese-American female overturns our assumptions about the quiet, passive nature of Chinese-American females. The autobiographical act is potentially subversive in a communal tradition which commands filial duty, family and clan loyalty, female silence: it is also subversive in the context of a larger America.

Perhaps it is easier, however for us to see, and accept revelations about Chinese-American culture than about our own. The candor with which Kingston disarms us at the outset is deceptive. At the same time she wins our trust by establishing an intimate confidentiality she also fulfills her filial duty by protecting or camouflaging the "truth." By suggesting alternate versions of what the aunt's story might have been, she undercuts the usual autobiographical claim of verisimilitude. It is significant that Kingston here merges the subjunctive and indicative moods, as throughout her memoirs she will continue to flesh out, color and deliberately twist the stories she has heard "into designs." By warming remembered, fragmentary, recounted stories in the caldron of her imagination, Kingston undermines the very notion of nonfiction as documented, eye-witness "truth"—a notion identified with scientific, western, masculine rationalism.

Kingston's memoir questions the line between fiction and non-fiction, examines the relation of poetry to prose. It does this by way of metaphor. It contrasts what Alexis de Tocqueville once referred to as the "anti-poetic" life in the United States with imaginative and mythical habits of thought represented by China. For all its associations with the deformed, with a misogynist tradition, with maddening indirectness, China is the land of rich and fertile myth; in contrast, American rationalism, which explains an eclipse of the sun scientifically rather than as the "frog-swallowing the moon" seems poverty stricken. Learning the American outlook means learning to see surfaces rather than depths, explanations rather than mysteries. "Now colors are gentler and fewer; smells are antiseptic. Now when I peek in the basement window where the villagers say they see a girl dancing like a bottle imp, I can no longer see a spirit in a skirt made of light, but a voiceless girl dancing when she thought no one was looking." The ability to see spirit, light made visible, is something lost not only with growing up, but with moving away from her Chinese world into the American one. The Chinese secrecy which exasperates her at times also lends itself to rich nuance in a way that American directness does not. Chinese is the language of dreams and impossible stories, of metaphor and paradox. In America, "Things follow in lines at school. They take stories and teach us to turn them into essays." American schools, with their neatly formulated essays rather than open-ended stories, are the repository of American values. The American Teacher Ghosts recognize her talent by saying she "could be a scientist or mathematician"—two possibilities for which she seems precisely unsuited. She in turn grabs at other, equally unlikely occupational possibilities: "I want to be a lumberjack and a reporter." With her slight physique and her bookish propensities, Kingston is clearly not telling a literal "truth" in this "truthful" confrontation with her mother, but an imaginative one. What Kingston is really saying is that she will not be hemmed in by convention. The image of the lumberjack, like the image of the woman warrior, is a romantic one, but what is strikingly incongruous about this image is its gender. Ironically, it is tradition-bound China which provides the romantic myth of a female warrior while America offers a practical career alternative for girls. "'Learn to type if you want to be an American girl,'" advises Brave Orchid. We must realize that when Kingston says "Give me plastic, periodical tables, TV dinners with vegetables no more complex than peas mixed with diced carrots" she is really saying the opposite, as the mother has indicated is the Chinese custom. Despite its readily apparent misogyny, Chinese culture is seen to allow for mystery in a way that American reductiveness does not.

In the story "White Tigers," Kingston learns, in the final stages of her training as a woman warrior, how to infer the immense, unknowable dragon from its parts. Like China, like the self whose story she tells, the dragon can never be seen "in its entirety"; understanding the dragon, like understanding a *koan,* requires a Chinese way of knowing—indirection, intuition, paradox. "The dragon lives in the sky, oceans, marshes, and mountains; and the mountains are also its cranium. Its voice thunders and jingles like copper pans. It breathes fire and water; and sometimes the dragon is one, sometimes many."

The paradox which is the dragon is the paradox of Kingston's China of the mind. Oppression as a female within the Chinese culture, and the double oppression of race and gender within America, is only part of the truth. Her ethnicity, her sex, and her special vantage point just outside two cultures, nourish the poetic vision that is her empowerment. Kingston has remarked upon how myth in the women's stories, unlike myth in the men's stories of **China Men,** is integrated into the warp and woof of the women's lives. "In **The Woman Warrior,** when the girls and women draw on mythology for their strengths, the myth becomes part of the women's lives and the structure of their stories" [Paula Rabinowitz, "Eccentric Memories: A Conversation with Maxine Hong Kingston," *Michigan Quarterly Review,* Vol. 36, No. 26, 1987]. On the surface China preaches a shrill misogynist message: "Girls are maggots in the rice!" The covert message, however, is different. Chinese-American girls learn silence as a survival tactic, but "Normal Chinese women's voices are strong and bossy. We American-Chinese girls had to whisper to make ourselves American-feminine." Ironically, it is the apparently more emancipated American culture that teaches Chinese-American females to subdue and modulate their voices.

Her experiences in both Chinese and American societies have fired her with anger—yet the enemies of capitalism, racism, sexism are far less tangible than the Sitting Ghost her mother wrestled with in China. She cannot direct her anger as the swordswoman does, and yet, if reporting is indeed vengeance, there is a sense in which her autobiographical act is too. Just as her mother burns out the Sitting Ghost with alcohol and oil, Kingston exorcises her demons through writing. Kingston uses her anger rather than allowing it to cripple her. In contrast, a witchwoman she remembers from childhood represents impotent female anger. The woman called Pee-A-Nah "was an angry witch, not a happy one. She was fierce; not a fairy, after all, but a demon." Kingston fears that she too may be a crazy outcast; she dreams of a vampire self. "Tears dripped from my eyes, but blood dripped from my fangs, blood of the people I was supposed to love." By writing her story, by breaking the silence enjoined upon her, Kingston may feel she betrays a trust, feeds on the life blood of her family and community. Yet the vampire is also a powerful figure, and Kingston's "report to five families" constitutes a powerful claim for recognition by Chinese and American societies.

Without denying the bitterness of the double oppression Kingston describes, we see that, through myth, she turns her oppression inside out. Like the ancient woman warrior Ts'ai Yen with whose story Kingston ends, cultural marginality has been turned to artistic advantage. Like Ts'ai Yen, Kingston has drawn from the Chinese and "barbarian" cultures she stands beside and between. The mythical Ts'ai Yen set her song of China to a song as high and clear as the barbarian flute music which haunted her in the desert. Kingston too has communicated an essentially Chinese way of seeing in an American idiom, and in the autobiographical process of self-creation, has won the admiration of the barbarians themselves.

Whether she is telling the story of her woman warrior's revenge, her mother's defeat of the sitting ghost, or the story of Ts'ai Yen, whose song reaches both barbarians and Chinese, Kingston shares with the reader the gift of seeing mythically rather than logically, a gift that is implicitly Chinese. The apparent powerlessness of the author's marginal status within American culture is curiously liberating. Confronted with cultural contradictions, Kingston's mind does not shatter like Moon Orchid's or Crazy Mary's; rather it stretches to accommodate the paradox it finds. Anger galvanizes not only the swordswoman, but the poet. As Nina Auerbach remarks within the context of Victorian culture, "Woman's freedom is no longer simple initiation into historical integrity, but the rebirth of mythic potential. The mythologies of the past have become stronger endowments than oppressions." As Kingston has demonstrated in her work, the woman, the minority writer, the artist, may, like the artist, lover, and lunatic, be of an imagination all compact. They may draw on the very myths which have been a historical instrument of oppression, teasing out new meaning through poetic reshaping. Like writers Toni Morrison and Leslie Silko, Kingston draws magic and aliveness from her ethnic rootedness, from her "connection with people who have a community and a tribe" (Rabinowitz).

Bonnie TuSmith (essay date 1993)

SOURCE: "Literary Tricksterism: Maxine Hong Kingston's *The Woman Warrior: Memoir of a Girlhood Among Ghosts*," in *Anxious Power: Reading, Writing, and Ambivalence in Narrative by Women*, edited by Carol J. Singley and Susan Elizabeth Sweeney, State University of New York Press, 1993, pp. 279-94.

[*TuSmith has been an professor of English at Bowling Green State University and is the author of* All My Relatives: Community in Contemporary Ethnic Literatures. *In the following essay, she considers Kingston's narrative strategy in* The Woman Warrior.]

When an ethnic female writer publishes an "autobiography," she is immediately confronted with inappropriate expectations. As readers we must realize, for example, that neither the Ben Franklin paradigm nor the exotic world of Suzie Wong are valid points of reference for interpreting *Woman Warrior.* Ultimately, we must read the work on its own terms. In reading Kingston's "autobiography," we must recognize that the writer is a creative artist who consciously uses a strategy of narrative ambiguity to tell her story.

When Kingston says in an interview that literary forms "reflect patterns of the human heart" [Timothy Pfaff, "Talk with Mrs. Kingston," *New York Times Book Review,* June 18, 1980], she tells us how she views herself as a writer. By connecting form with "heart" rather than "life," she refers to the artist, not the sociologist. For Kingston, artistic form is organic rather than artificial: it is part and parcel of the human spirit. This position directly contrasts with the stated premise of a major study on Asian American literature, which deliberately "emphasize[s] how the literature elucidates the social history of Asians in the United States" [Elaine H. Kim, *Asian American Literature: An Introduction to the Writings and Their Social Context,* 1982]. When applied to an artist who consciously manipulates form in order to be true to "patterns of the human heart," the belief that a literary text can and should be used to document an ethnic culture seems misguided. Because many critics have made the same assumption, they tend either to blame or praise *the author* for her naive narrator's interpretation of Chinese American culture.

In *Woman Warrior,* Kingston uses a narrator who has a child's passion for knowing. What is Chinese and what is American? What is real and what is make-believe? Do the Chinese despise women, or do they see them as potential warriors? Since we have an impressionable protagonist/narrator who feels bombarded by confusing stories in her childhood, this desire for definition is appropriate. However, because the young protagonist singlemindedly pursues either/or options and because her voice dominates the book's first part, the unwary reader is easily lulled by her simplistic pronouncements. Due to her confusion, limited knowledge, desire for absolutes, and total subjectivity regarding people and events, her narration is unreliable.

In an interview, Kingston clearly distinguishes herself from this narrator: "Oh, that narrator girl. It's hard for me to call her me. . . . She is so coherent and intense always, throughout. There's an intensity of emotion that makes the book come together. And I'm not like that" [Phyllis Hoge Thompson, "This Is The Story I Heard: A Conversation with Maxine Hong Kingston and Earll Kingston," *Biography*, Vol. 6, No. 1, 1983]. The distinction between the "I" and "that narrator girl" is revealing. The reader must understand that the writer is, in her daily life, neither coherent nor intense, even though her narrative persona epitomizes these traits.

Had Kingston limited her narrative to the protagonist's naive point of view, she might not have advanced significantly from Jade Snow Wong's *Fifth Chinese Daughter* (1945). In contrasting Wong's and Kingston's literary forms, Patricia Lin Blinde categorizes Wong's autobiography with the Horatio Alger paradigm of American success ["The Icicle in the Desert: Perspective and Form in the Works of Two Chinese-American Women Writers," *MELUS*, Vol. 6, No. 3, 1979]. According to Blinde, Wong simply "'repeat[s]' the white world's articulations and expectations as to what Chineseness is or is not." Consequently, autobiography becomes "a public concession as to her place (and by extension the place of Chinese-Americans) in the world and mind of Americans." On the other hand, Blinde says, Kingston belongs to a generation with fewer illusions. The pre-World War II faith in a coherent world, "a world that still believed in the truths of its own imaginative constructs," is no longer possible. In fact, the coherence of Kingston's "narrator girl" is drastically different from that presented in Wong's work. Kingston creates an ambivalent narrator who compensates for her insecurities by reaching for absolutes, while the literary artist transcends her naive narrator's limitations through technique. Before delving into these artistic strategies, however, we must first understand Kingston's definition of autobiography.

Blinde's perception that literary form separates Kingston from Wong is provocative. What does it mean to say that two autobiographies are worlds apart because of their forms? According to Thomas Doherty, autobiography is a literary form particularly suited to Americans' "individualistic and optimistic" self-image. Therefore, Franklin's self-portrait as "an aggressive actor in a society of possibilities" is considered the prototype for "autobiographies in the American tradition" ["American Autobiography and Ideology," in *The American Autobiography: A Collection of Critical Essays*, edited by Albert E. Stone, 1981]. Given this definition, ethnic women's stories are anything but "American" autobiographies. The self as a confident actor selecting among various possibilities simply does not reflect the experiences of most women in America. In order to write a prototypical American autobiography, then, the ethnic woman must either conform to the Eurocentric male definition of the genre and produce a seemingly self-effacing, assimilationist work like *Fifth Chinese Daughter*, or she must subvert and redefine "autobiography" in some way. Kingston's own

viewpoint on the subject is revealing. In an essay exposing her reviewers' racist assumptions, she explains: "After all, I am not writing history or sociology but a 'memoir' like Proust." She quotes one reviewer who understood this and said that Kingston was "slyly writing a memoir, a form which . . . can neither [be] dismiss[ed] as fiction nor quarrel[ed] with as fact" [**"Cultural Mis-readings by American Reviewers,"** *Asian and Western Writers in Dialogue: New Cultural Identities*, edited by Guy Amirthanayagam, 1982].

This distinction between autobiography and memoir is crucial to the Kingston controversy. By evoking Proust's massive *A la recherche du temps perdu*, which Lillian Hornstein calls "an autobiography of the mind" [*The Readers Companion to World Literature*, 2nd edition, 1973], Kingston challenges the static notion of autobiography in the "American tradition." The Proustian memoir emphasizes fluidity and the presentness of psychological time. Memory is a private code of freely-associated images triggered by seemingly insignificant details in one's environment. As such, the memoir is exploratory. Rather than positing a coherent, already-constituted self which only has to be "revealed" through the autobiographical act, it views identity as fluid and constantly evolving. This alternative understanding of the function of autobiography is particularly suited to women. Unlike their male counterparts' texts, as Leslie Rabine points out, there is no "lost paradise" in **Woman Warrior** and other ethnic women's "semiautobiographical works" ["No Lost Paradise: Social Gender and Symbolic Gender in the Writings of Maxine Hong Kingston," *Signs*, Vol. 12, No. 3, 1987]. In addition, since there is no "it" to return to, the absence of an Edenic past actually structures ethnic women's stories. But how can absence provide structure? In place of a linear, backtracking approach based on community-decline and nostalgia, works like **Woman Warrior** depict continuity through change and creative adaptation.

In identifying her literary form with Proust's, Kingston not only refutes traditional definitions of autobiography and non-fiction but also legitimizes genres such as memoirs, diaries, and journals (all "female" forms, according to some feminist theorists) which have been considered—at least in America—less "literary" than *the* autobiography. Given the value judgments implicit in issues of literary genre, the publication of Kingston's first book as an autobiography, with "memoirs" in its subtitle, suggests conscious manipulation. As we have seen, the two terms are not synonymous. If Kingston believes she has written an exploratory, quasi-fictive memoir, why did she allow her book to be published as autobiography without qualification? If the general public tends to view autobiography as gospel truth, is Kingston somehow responsible for misleading the reader? After all, the absolutist position implicit in "American autobiography" and the text's dominant narrative voice seem a perfect match. When the narrator tells us that her ethnic culture denigrates women—equating females with "slaves" and "maggots" and thus forcing her to "get out of hating range"—should we not take her word for it? And if we do, can we then conclude that Kingston defends the lone female against her oppressive ethnic community?

To address this question, we might consult Ralph Ellison. "America is a land of masking jokers," he informs us. Franklin posed as Rousseau's Natural Man, Hemingway as a nonliterary sportsman, Faulkner as a farmer, and Lincoln as a simple country lawyer—"the 'darky' act makes brothers of us all" [*Shadow and Act,* 1953]. Ellison asserts that the smart-man-playing-dumb role is not the unique province of black culture. Rather, "it is a strategy common to the [American] culture," and "might be more 'Yankee' than anything else." The historian John Ward corroborates this point when he identifies Franklin as a social and literary trickster. In *The Autobiography,* says Ward, when Franklin offers himself as Representative American, he acknowledges his awareness of this self-conscious pose ["Who Was Benjamin Franklin?," *Retracing the Past: Readings in the History of the American People,* Vol. 1, edited by Gary B. Nash, 1986]. This observation suggests that the prototypical American autobiography already has the markings of an "invented self" and does not provide the "straight goods" which the general public expects from the genre.

If we realize that masking is, in Ellison's sense, an *American* cultural phenomenon, and that tricksterism is prevalent in American literature, we can then approach a writer like Kingston without misconceived notions of her "difference." Given that autobiography, like any other genre in literature, is an artistic construct, Kingston's ethnicity should not make her work "social history." If we can accept Franklin's pose in this supposedly non-fictional genre, we should be able to read autobiographies by ethnic women writers with the same understanding. Otherwise, our approach is both racist and sexist. The parallel between scholarship on Frederick Douglass and Kingston illustrates this point.

In an enlightening analysis, Henry Louis Gates demonstrates that virtually all of Douglass' biographers have misconstrued their subject by taking the autobiography literally. The self that the famous abolitionist describes in his three autobiographies is a public image carefully crafted to promote his cause [*Figures in Black: Words, Signs, and the "Racial" Self,* 1987]. As such, it is "fictive" in the sense of "made by design." "Almost never," Gates points out, "does Douglass allow us to see him as a human individual in all of his complexity." In using an intentionally constructed persona as "fact," biographers can only present an external view of their subject, a view which is the conscious manipulation of its trickster creator. In a sense, Douglass and

Franklin are Representative Men today because we still believe their autobiographical constructs. While the misreading of both Kingston's and Douglass' autobiographies stems from the same misunderstanding of the nature of literature, Kingston's situation is complicated by the writer's non-great-man status. If we cannot get quick facts about her ethnic culture from her autobiography, as we can from writers like Wong, then why should we even bother with Kingston?

Yet, from the wide readership that **Woman Warrior** enjoys, it seems that many people find the work of value. This, we contend, has a great deal to do with its artistry. In devising a narrative strategy of ambiguity which captures her multivariate ethnic reality, Kingston is a "literary trickster" in the best American tradition.

Critics accurately identify her various boundary-crossing strategies in **Woman Warrior** as ambiguous or ambivalent. Ambiguity plays a prominent role in the text. They miss the mark, however, when they attribute these strategies to the necessity of "bridging two cultures." If we understood that, as they say, "cultures are made, not born" [Dale Yu Nee, "See, Culture is Made, Not Born. . . ," *Bridge, An Asian-American Perspective,* Vol. 3, No. 6, 1975], we would know that Chinese America as an ethnic culture is not a "bicultural" dualism of either/or possibilities. Rather, it is a *new entity* which is neither Chinese nor European. Because many people have difficulty with this concept (since we are so used to thinking in stereotypes and polarities), they sort between "Chinese" and "American" along with the naive narrator. As mentioned earlier, the narrator's sorting does not reflect Kingston's worldview; it is an artistic device used to create thematic tension between the female individual as protagonist and the ethnic community as antagonist.

A key element of Kingston's strategy of ambiguity is to offer alternative, often contradictory versions of a story without value judgment. The narrator usually tells us when she invents; however, we must sort through her various "truths." Because we are on shifting sand, a convenient anchor is a naive narrator who seeks absolutes with life-and-death urgency. The young protagonist's desire for easy answers when confronting her mother's "talk-stories" about China reflects the reader's need for firm ground. This is a literary "trick," though. Active participation in the text almost requires a level of confusion like the protagonist's. In an essay on fiction and interpretation, Naomi Schor defines the relationship between "interpreter" (interpreting critic or reader) and "interpretant" (interpreting character in the text) as one of "narcissistic identification" ["Fiction as Interpretation/Interpretation as Fiction," in *The Reader in the Text: Essays on Audience and Interpretation,* edited by Susan R. Suleiman and Inge Crosman, 1980]. When a literary work features an interpretant, such identification makes distance difficult to maintain. In reading Kingston, however, distance is crucial.

In *Woman Warrior,* the surface discourse is misleading because the struggle between the protagonist and the immigrant community of Stockton is narrated from the protagonist's point of view. This view, as we have said, is naive due to the narrator's limitations. While anti-female attitudes and unusual practices of "the Chinese" are emphasized, limited space is devoted to the cultural mores of European Americans. In addition, the protagonist's white male oppressors are never identified as such; instead, they are given the generic name "boss" and described as "business-suited in their modern American executive guise." Because the narrator identifies her mother's vivid and grotesque stories as Chinese, the reader might conclude that the Chinese are truly barbaric. This unbalanced presentation of cultures should serve as a warning signal to the discerning reader. Why, one might ask, are white male oppressors "bosses" and ethnic male oppressors "Chinese"? In order to understand such seeming distortions, we must examine the text.

In *Woman Warrior,* verbal articulation is necessary to survival. The protagonist shows how acutely she feels this when she tortures the quiet girl. "If you don't talk," she exclaims, "you can't have a personality." People deprived of speech, as are the various crazy women cited in the text, do not survive. Here is the primary dilemma of the Chinese American experience. It is in *America* that survival is an issue for ethnic Americans, where deprivation of speech (a direct result of racist laws) leads to a lack of personality and even the lack of will to live. Storytelling is thus an essential skill in a hostile environment, a skill which ensures the survival of the tribe as well as its individual members. To arrive at this interpretation, the reader must piece together various elements in the text, or what might be called the "subtext." What makes Kingston's "memoirs" so slippery is the implied author's refusal to spell out connections for the reader. Words such as "talk-story," "personality," and "survival" are linked by juxtaposition rather than cause-and-effect logic. The reader must fill in the gaps.

Forcing active reader participation is, of course, a prevalent modernist technique. Nevertheless, a major problem for ethnic writers is the audience's lack of knowledge regarding ethnic American histories and cultures. In *Woman Warrior,* this is problematic since historical information is scattered throughout the text and often is not attached to specific issues. When the narrator tells us that Chinese people are secretive, for example, we might not understand why until the fear of deportation is mentioned. Thus, the reader is expected to suspend judgment and not jump to conclusions as the narrator does. Kingston's technique of ambiguity, then, requires reconstructive reading skills. While illuminating contexts for the story can be found in the text, only the alert reader can make the necessary connections.

Given the memoir's nonlinear form—that is, its achronological ordering—when Brave Orchid declares, "That's what Chinese say. We like to say the opposite," and the naive narrator inserts "It seemed to hurt her to tell me that," readers need to step back and reconstruct an appropriate context for the exchange. We must realize that we are not witnessing a cultural clash; actually, *both* mother and daughter are Chinese Americans who share a common culture—though of two successive generations—in America. Brave Orchid calls herself Chinese when she wishes to rationalize her behavior. The evasiveness which both the narrator and her mother attribute to the Chinese, as if it were a racial characteristic, is easily explained within the context of Chinese American history. Even the protagonist's grudge against the "emigrant villagers" must be viewed in the appropriate context.

The misogynistic sayings which are repeated throughout the text must be understood in relation to the Chinese bachelor society in America. As a result of the Chinese Exclusion Act of 1882, Chinese women were extremely scarce for several generations in this country. Immigration laws toward the Chinese became somewhat more liberal only with the advent of World War II. This historical fact might have contributed to a brand of male defensiveness (a solidified posture against female encroachment) which is unique to the Chinese American experience. In other words, negative male attitudes toward women—at least as the protagonist experiences them—are partially American-made and, as such, cannot be attributed to the Chinese without locating them in their specific social and historical contexts.

Why is *Woman Warrior* so ambiguous in both its rhetoric and ideology? Some critics attribute the work's ambiguity to Kingston's "bicultural" background. Not all ethnic texts employ ambiguous narrative strategies, however. For Kingston, ambiguity is a conscious choice which has little to do with bridging cultures. In various interviews, she comments on the need to play literary tricks in "nonfictional" works. On a pragmatic level, she wanted to protect her subjects from immigration officers and police; "but what happened," she admits, "was that this need for secrecy affected my form and my style" ["This is the Story I Heard"]. In other words, ambiguity was necessary as a "cover." A second consideration has to do with the attempt to capture oral culture on the printed page.

As an ethnic female writer, Kingston aligns herself with the Chinese oral tradition of storytelling or talk-story. "Oral stories change from telling to telling," she points out. The written word, on the other hand, is static and finite. "That really brothers me, because what would be wonderful would be for the words to change on the page every time, but they can't. The way I tried to solve this problem was to keep ambiguity in the writing all the time" [Arturo Islas, "Maxine Hong Kingston," *Women Writers of the West Coast: Speak-*

ing of Their Lives and Careers, edited by Marilyn Yalom, 1983]. This structural ambiguity allows us to *experience* Brave Orchid's changing the story with each telling.

Walter Ong argues that there is no such thing as "oral literature," because "you can never divest the term 'literature' of its association with writing. This association inevitably deforms the study of oral performance" ["Oral Culture and the Literate Mind," in *Minority Language and Literature: Retrospective and Perspective,* edited by Dexter Fisher, 1977]. Ong warns us against the habit of viewing oral performance as literature *manqué.* Since Kingston is, above all, a writer, can she be placed in Ong's category of offenders? As she views it, the vitality of her ethnic heritage resides in oral storytelling. The ability to talk-story is equated in both **Woman Warrior** and **China Men** with communal survival and affirmation: it gives talkers like Brave Orchid "great power" (**Woman**). For Kingston, to claim her cultural status, the ethnic female writer must make words "change on the page" in the manner of oral performances. Thus **Woman Warrior,** a work which is literary in many respects, thematically privileges orality. Here ambiguity is the creative compromise of a literate mind conveying the improvisational immediacy of oral culture.

By maintaining fluidity throughout the text, Kingston assumes a nonparadigmatic stance and challenges the frequently monolithic Western tradition. In **Woman Warrior,** fluidity between immature and mature perceptions is maintained through two narrative voices: one child, the other adult. "You lie with stories," the child screams at her mother. "I can't tell what's real and what you make up." This accusation suggests that the young protagonist wants certainty in her life. The narrative's conscious, forward thrust seeks clarity—a release from confusing stories and nightmares. This seemingly clear position is undercut, however, by an adult narrator who admits, analyzes, and condones her own fabrications.

After describing in elaborate detail her aunt Moon Orchid's confrontation with her husband, the narrator comments, "What my brother actually said was. . . ." In other words, the story she just told is her own creation. Her next concession—"His version of the story may be better than mine because of its bareness, not twisted into designs"—implies that the reader has the right to choose among versions of the text. The adult narrator's own position, however, is clearly conveyed through a parable:

> Long ago in China, knot-makers tied string into buttons and frogs, and rope into bell pulls. There was one knot so complicated that it blinded the knot-maker. Finally an emperor outlawed this cruel knot, and the nobles could not order it anymore. If I had

lived in China, I would have been an outlaw knot-maker.

Why would she have been an outlaw knot-maker? For the mature narrator, simplicity and clarity no longer seem important. Contrary to the "narrator girl's" anxiety about confusing ethnic stories, her unconscious penchant for telling stories "twisted into designs" like complicated knots is now a virtue. The adult protagonist has attained a tolerance for ambiguity.

While presenting herself as an "outlaw," an exile from the Chinese American community in which she grew up, the adult narrator yet seeks a way to return to the fold *on her own terms.* She had to leave, she claims, because she thought that "the Chinese" despised females. Psychologically and spiritually, however, she has not given up her ethnic community. The cycle of departure and return is, as the narrative shows, a new and welcome possibility for ethnic females. Ultimately, women warriors do not ride off into the sunset.

Structurally, each story of the woman warrior—whether of the legendary Fa Mu Lan, the narrator's mother Brave Orchid, or the narrator herself—tests the potential for reconciliation between the individual and her community. The narrator declares, for example, that both she and the legendary swordswoman have "the words at our backs." That is, if she uses her verbal ability to avenge her oppressed ethnic community, might she not also be loved and admired by her people? The parallel between the two "warriors" seems perfect until we realize that Kingston's Fa Mu Lan story is a Chinese American myth and not Chinese history. In the classics, Fa Mu Lan's parents do not carve words of vengeance on their daughter's back. In Chinese culture, the legend serves as an example of a daughter's filiality toward her parents. Kingston's fantasy tale, on the other hand, emphasizes the hazards of crossing gender boundaries: "Chinese executed women who disguised themselves as soldiers or students." Assertion of womanhood—by secretly having a lover and bearing a child in battle—is made a heroic act. These details do not correspond to legendary Chinese heroines who fulfilled the "neuter" role of warriors without strong sexual identification [Mary Backus Rankin, "The Emergence of Women at the End of the Ch'ing," *Women in Chinese Society,* edited by Margery Wolf and Roxane Witke, 1975]. Hence, the narrator/author's "'chink' and 'gook' words," as well as Fa Mu Lan's tattoos and male/female assertions, are creative constructs made in America.

Once we realize that the sense of Chinese historical "truth" conveyed in the "White Tigers" section is an illusion, we can question the narrator's next formulation in the same chapter. When she declares, "My American life has been such a disappointment," rather than falling into the bicultural trap of counter pointing "Chinese" heroism against an unheroic "American" life, we might ask: what other life does the narrator have? Since she has never had a Chinese life outside her imagination, the word "American" is meaningless and merely designates "reality." By the same token, when the narrator uses the term "Chinese," the reader needs to substitute "illusion." Because the swordswoman myth is mostly a child's wish-fulfillment, it cannot serve as catalyst for change. The "woman warrior" of the book's title is possibly the trickster's first joke.

Kingston herself has stated that Fa Mu Lan is *her* myth: "But I put ['The White Tigers' chapter] at the beginning to show that the childish myth is past, not the climax we reach for. Also, 'The White Tigers' is not a Chinese myth but one transformed by America, a sort of kung fu movie parody" [**"Cultural Mis-readings by American Reviewers"**]. Within the text, the mature narrator exhibits the same awareness when she says: "Perhaps I made him up [the retarded man from her childhood], and what I once had was not Chinese-sight at all but child-sight that would have disappeared eventually without such struggle." In a single stroke, all of the naive narrator's insights are dismissed as "child-sight." The titanic struggle between "Chinese" and "American" is now seen as a made-up story. Given this interpretive reversal, what is left?

Portrayals of women in **Woman Warrior** seem to alternate between positive and negative depending on the narrative point of view. Both Fa Mu Lan and Brave Orchid are heroic when the naive narrator describes them, as evidenced in the "White Tigers" and "Shaman" sections. These positive portraits of privileged, exceptional individuals suggest that the warrior image is indeed promoted in the book. When we move to the omniscient narrative of the fourth chapter, however, we find a different view of strong women. Just as we gradually realize that Fa Mu Lan exists only as a fantasy, here we view the "real life" warrior as less than perfect. While the episode between Brave Orchid and her sister Moon Orchid is humorous, it also exposes the destructive side of the rugged individualist. In this chapter, Brave Orchid drives her sister insane. She is culpable, the implied author seems to say, because she cannot empathize with those weaker than herself. This negative judgment is periodically inserted into the text from the third-person point of view: "But Brave Orchid would not relent; her dainty sister would just have to toughen up." There is also intrusive commentary: "She looked at her younger sister whose very wrinkles were fine. 'Forget about a job,' she said, which was very lenient of her."

Even though the text embeds the negative aspects of heroic women such as Fa Mu Lan and Brave Orchid, it also includes an alternative community of women with whom the narrator is identified. In the Fa Mu Lan story, "cowering,

whimpering women" on "little bound feet" later form a mercenary army of swordswomen called "witch amazons." While these women are described contemptuously from Fa Mu Lan's point of view ("They blinked weakly at me like pheasants that have been raised in the dark for soft meat"), they also present a vivid image of the downtrodden who ultimately prevail. Throughout the text, a string of oppressed, misunderstood women—including the no-name aunt, the witch amazons, Moon Orchid, the quiet girl, various crazy ladies, and the narrator herself with her "bad, small-person's voice that makes no impact"—counterbalances the superwomen. The protagonist waivers between the weak and the strong, as she does between her outlaw status and her ties to the ethnic community. Her fear of insanity causes her publicly to denounce the rejects, the "Crazy Marys" and "retards," of society. On the other hand, she is closely identified with them in the text—she asks her sister, "do you talk to people that aren't real inside your mind?"—and, in contrast to Brave Orchid, exhibits a deep understanding for this segment of society.

Halfway through **Woman Warrior,** the adult narrator returns home for a visit. The familiar tug-of-war between mother and daughter resumes until the daughter confronts her overpowering mother with the confession, "when I'm away from here, I don't get sick" and Brave Orchid responds with "It's better, then, for you to stay away. . . . You can come for visits." Then the mother calls her daughter "Little Dog," a term of endearment. In this crucial scene, not only does a mother learn to let go of her child, but the two women establish grounds for mutual respect. This hint of reconciliation is extended to the books' symbolic ending. The final story is a collaboration between her mother and herself, the adult narrator informs us. Rather than the usual vying over which version of a story is "truer," we now have two storytellers enjoying equal time without, as Sidonie Smith puts it, "the privileging of one before the other" [*A Poetics of Women's Autobiography: Marginality and the Fictions of Self-Representation,* 1987]. This final juxta-position suggests the recognition and acceptance of human diversity, mutual respect, and communal sharing.

As an ethnic woman writer, Kingston employs the narrative strategies of a "trickster" to tell her tale. This approach allows her to explore a naive narrator's ambivalence toward her mother's confusing stories without equating the narrator's viewpoint with her own. If we recognize that **Woman Warrior** is a complex work of art and not a social document, we might begin to appreciate Kingston's attempt to make words "change on the page."

Bonnie Melchior (essay date Summer 1994)

SOURCE: "A Marginal 'I': The Autobiographical Self

Deconstructed in Maxine Hong Kingston's *The Woman Warrior*," in *Biography*, Vol. 17, No. 3, Summer, 1994, pp. 281-95.

[*In the following essay, Melchior explores the issues of identity, the traditional Western concept of self, and the American tradition of autobiography raised by Kingston's rendering of her memoir in* The Woman Warrior.]

Autobiography has been called the "preeminent kind of American expression" [Robert F. Sayre, "Autobiography and the Making of America," in *Autobiography: Essays Theoretical and Critical*, edited by James Olney, 1980], perhaps because its autonomous "I" is strikingly congruent with the "I" of American ideology. Many critics see this genre as arising from the conscious awareness, in Western culture, of the "singularity of each individual life," a singularity that induces a sense of the self as individual rather than communal. The history of autobiography, says Mary Mason, is "largely a history of the Western obsession with self and at the same time the felt desire to somehow escape that obsession" ["The Other Voice: Autobiographies of Women Writers," in *Autobiography*, edited by Olney]. In other cultures, individual existence may be seen as interdependent, its rhythms asserted "everywhere in the community" ["The Conditions and Limits of Autobiography," in *Autobiography*, edited by Olney]. Western culture is preoccupied with the idea of "self-making," and in autobiography, individuality accounts for itself as made and gives the how of the making. A logically coherent, stable self emerges, a self that has been caused by prior events and choices. Such a self is congruent with the American gender biases reflected in our adulation of the self-made man.

Another assumption of autobiography is that information and events in the text are supposed to be more or less consistent with evidence found in other valid documents; the author promises not to lie, consciously at least [Elizabeth Bruss, "Eye for I: Making and Unmaking Autobiography in Film," in *Autobiography*, edited by Olney]. Autobiography, then, supposedly presents a truth not found in fiction, the truth of brute fact. Such a stance often implies a dichotomy between fiction and fact, leading to a conviction that the text means one and only one thing, a kind of "textual fundamentalism" [Robert Scholes, *Protocols of Reading*, 1989].

Maxine Hong Kingston's autobiography *The Woman Warrior: Memoirs of a Girlhood among Ghosts* (1976) challenges the assumptions of the genre and the shared assumptions of American culture. In doing so, it explores the distinctions between oral and written discourse, distinctions mirrored by the oppositions between the Chinese traditions of her immigrant parents and the influences of her American environment. While the oral traditions of Chinese immigrants privilege the communal memory and promote a sense of the self as defined by affiliations with others, traditions which are influenced by the technology of writing privilege, instead, "history" (linear, sequential time) and promote a sense of the self as singular [G. Thomas Couser, *Altered Egos: Authority in American Autobiography*, 1989]. Written texts, unlike oral stories, can have individual authors, and reading them is a private act.

Kingston's challenge to American ideologies does not, however, translate into an easy affirmation of the oral or the "Chinese." For one thing, she is *writing* an autobiography. Also, as a native-born American, she cannot return to being Chinese. Furthermore, both Chinese and American traditions denigrate females in the sense that they deny them the identity and potency enjoyed by males. To be male is to be autonomous and active; to be female is to be passive and dependent. A heroine is not a female hero; she exists, usually, to further or impede the development of the hero. When she is the protagonist of the work, what she seeks differs. These different goals problematize the assumptions of autobiography. For instance, men, according to [Patrocinio P.] Schweikert, "define themselves through individuation and separation from others, while women have more flexible ego boundaries and define themselves by their affiliations with others" ["Reading Ourselves: Toward a Feminist Theory of Reading," in *Gender and Reading: Essays on Readers, Texts, and Contexts*, edited by Elizabeth A. Flynn and Schweikert, 1986]. The male hero sets out on a "night sea journey" to slay the dragon of the not-self (which might lurk perhaps within the self), while the female hero seeks the cave in order to retrieve the lost and give birth [Sandra M. Gilbert, "The Parables of the Cave," *The Critical Tradition: Classic Texts and Contemporary Trends*, edited by David H. Richter, 1989].

Kingston deconstructs autobiography and the male American ideologies associated with it by problematizing its assumptions about the nature of the self and the nature of "fact." Reading her text implies that *I* is not causal; it is a textual construct, open-ended, that exists only paired with *you*. A self is not a product that is made, but a participatory process. Neither is the meaning of a text (or a life) linear. Her text constantly folds back on itself, reflexively contradicting meanings it had seemed to support, as the very title illustrates. This is autobiography that inhabits a postmodern world.

The book has no preface or prologue explaining its plan, but begins with a chapter titled "No-Name Woman," supposedly a cautionary tale the narrator heard from her mother. No-Name Woman, an aunt in China whose illicit pregnancy led to dishonor and suicide, seems to represent the negative pole in this bildungsroman, the opposite of a "woman warrior," since her story and even her name have been "erased." However, the chapter, as it continues, encourages a proliferation of non-coherent interpretations, almost as if we are looking at simultaneous worlds all occupying the same space. The narrator's speculations concerning motive and action are contradictory, yet her verb tenses (alternating between the expected hypothetical and the simple past) convert speculation into actual history. The story does not seem to be functioning as a cautionary tale, and even whether the mother meant it as such becomes problematic. By telling the story to her daughter, she has given the aunt a history that binds one generation to the next and a name that names this chapter. No-Name Woman may be an avatar of the woman warrior instead of her opposite.

In the next chapter, "White Tigers," the narrator says that the same mother who told her the story of No-Name Woman and who said she should grow up to be "a woman and a slave" also taught her "the song of the woman warrior" (Fa Mu Lan) and the empowerment that comes from "talking-story." At the beginning of the chapter she says, "Night after night my mother would talk-story. . . . I couldn't tell where the stories left off and the dreams began." Her text, which slips from one kind of discourse into another, similarly affects the reader. It begins as a mythical tale of "heroines" and "swordswomen," then fuses author and heroine with an *I* that transforms legend into personal history. It ends back in the everyday, where the narrator, no longer a warrior/hero who "has it all," worries that, unless she does "something big and fine and figures out what is her village," her parents might sell her as a slave. Straight A's in school do not seem to transform the female *I* (which means slave in Chinese) into a swordswoman.

Still, this chapter seems to present a model for achieving female identity and self-worth if only the narrator can find a modern equivalent, and that problem might be solved by the equation of action and writing. Kingston has grafted the legend of a male general who had his back tattooed onto the legend of Fa Mu Lan [King-Kok Cheung, "'Don't Tell': Silences in *The Color Purple* and *The Woman Warrior*," *PMLA,* Vol. 103, 1988], so that the woman warrior herself becomes a text: inscribed on her back are all the grievances of the people. The narrator asserts that the *reporting* is the revenge—"not the beheading, not the gutting, but the words." The author, then, can act by writing this autobiography. Nevertheless, the reader is nagged by little doubts. How can this woman warrior represent female identity and self-worth when she can act only by disguising herself as a man? How can we trust the "truth-claim" of an autobiographer who presents legend as personal history?

The third chapter, "Shaman," implies that Brave Orchid, the narrator's mother, is a modern woman warrior. The narrator recounts how, alone in China, her mother became a successful healer and exerciser of ghosts. In the United States,

however, she is a laundress, a drudge. At eighty, she is dyeing her hair so that she will be hired to pick tomatoes. These contrasts (and her many denigrating remarks about females) make Brave Orchid a problematic role model or "shaman." The narrator makes no attempt to reconcile these discrepancies either, ending the chapter, instead, with still another twist: in a scene reminiscent of her battle with a Sitting Ghost in China, the mother who makes her adult daughter feel sick and threatened at home (she has to "lock the doors against the ghost sounds") sits in the dark by her sickbed and heals her by "naming" her with an endearment of childhood and freeing her to go. The mother is at once mentor and alien, sickness and cure. Her story supports and at the same time controverts the American Myth of "pulling yourself up by your own bootstraps."

Ghosts, this chapter implies, have something to do with becoming a successful woman warrior. (Their importance is also emphasized by their mention in the book's subtitle, *Memoirs of a Girlhood Among Ghosts.*) The hairy amorphous thing the mother defeated in China is not the only kind, either. The mother calls all native-born Americans, even her own children, "ghosts." (There are Garbage Ghosts, Urban Renewal Ghosts, Scientist Ghosts, and more.) People from the past are also ghosts. At the end of the chapter on No-Name Woman, the narrator says, "My aunt haunts me, her ghost drawn to me." Her rendering of the Chinese word *kwei* as *ghost* rather than the usual *demon* [David Leiwei Li, "The Naming of a Cross-Cultural American 'I': Cross-Cultural Sign/ifications in *The Woman Warrior*," *Criticism,* Vol. 30, 1988] directs attention toward concerns of reality and selfhood rather than good/evil and suggests a paradoxical truth: the past is present and ghosts *are* real in the sense that they do affect our choices and our lives. Being a person to another person, however, is more than just being "real."

The fourth chapter, "At the Western Palace," is about another aunt, Moon Orchid, who is a double of No-Name Woman. This aunt, who has been comfortably supported in China for years by a brain-surgeon husband living in Beverly Hills, is bullied by Brave Orchid into coming to this country and claiming her rights as "First Wife." When the Americanized husband rejects her, the uprooted wife goes crazy and ends up having to be institutionalized. Not every woman, apparently, is capable of being a "woman warrior." In this chapter, the autobiographical narrator disappears completely, replaced by an omniscient-sounding, unidentified "author." Despite this strange point of view, we assume the "author" had the facts of her story from her brother and mother. However, the next chapter indicates that everything in this chapter is, in a sense, a lie. The narrator admits that all her detailed descriptions were spun from one brief comment by a witness. This admission threatens her autobiographical authority because she is "making up a story" rather than "telling the truth."

Each chapter, so far, has provided an avatar of the woman warrior and moved closer in time and space to the autobiographer's life. The sequence seems governed by analogy and point of view. As the subject has moved closer and the time-span contracted, the *I* has proliferated and then disappeared completely. In the last chapter, "A Song for a Barbarian Reed Pipe," the *I* returns. This chapter deals overly with the narrator's adolescent search for an identity— a search for language. She cannot talk, she says, because her mother cut her tongue when she was a baby. Her mother responds that she cut her tongue so that she *could* talk The climax of her struggle is a scene in a lavatory where she tries to torture a doppelganger into talking (threatening her all the while that she "shouldn't tell") (Cheung). (Elise Miller [in "Kingston's *The Woman Warrior:* The Object of Autobiographical Relations," *Compromise Formations: Current Directions in Psychoanalytic Criticism,* 1989] points out that her actions parallel her mother's efforts to force Moon Orchid into asserting her "self"). Following this incident, she is stricken with a mysterious malaise that keeps her in bed until, after a year, her mother decides it is time for her to get up.

The chapter ends with her finding her voice in a "duet." She tells a story her mother told her when she told her mother that she also "talks-story": "The beginning is hers," she says, "the ending mine." Her "ending" is the story of Ts'ai Yen, a Chinese princess who had to live for years in an alien land among barbarians. She thought they lacked music until one night when she saw hundreds of them sitting on the sand blowing on flutes and heard a yearning high note "like an icicle in the desert." Soon afterwards, a high clear voice that matched the flutes came from her tent. Eventually, her children, who spoke no Chinese, "sang along." How this parable "branches" into the narrator's life and whether the singing princess is mother or daughter is not explained.

By focussing the book on an "autos" that is created by and through stories, Kingston affirms its communal nature, for stories live and are modified in the communal memory. She questions individual autonomy and originality and suggests that meaning demands risk and a commitment to the unknown, a commitment that might be short on congratulations and long on suffering. Birth rather than "making" seems her metaphor. The book teems with stories of dead and deformed babies and female madness. She asks whether the difference between sanity and insanity is talking. Are insane people "the ones who can't explain themselves?" Or is it that sane people "have variety when they 'talk-story?' Mad people have only one story that they talk over and over." Her use of the pronoun *I* dramatizes a self that is not self-contained. It merges with the *I* of the protagonists in "No-Name Woman" and "White Tigers."

This ambiguously individual/communal selfhood is, accord-

ing to linguist Emile Benveniste, structured by language itself. *I* and *you,* he points out, differ significantly from all other pronouns. They do not refer to a concept or an individual; they are embedded in the unique moment of discourse. They dramatize the difference between "language as a system of signs and language assumed into use by the individual," between "langue" and "parole." *I* and *you* are the only "subjects"; third person (*he's* and *she's*) are nonpersons because they are never participants in the discourse. This distinction might indicate how the Chinese Sitting Ghost resembles the American ghosts: without "language," neither can be an "I" in a discourse with the mother. Meaning always depends on who speaks and who listens. Despite the supposition that *I* is a "stable sign, the product of a complete code whose contents are recurrent," the *I* in a speech act is "always new," even if repeated [Roland Barthes, "To Write: An Intransitive Verb?," in *The Structuralists: From Marx to Levi-Strauss,* edited by Richard and Fernande De George, 1972].

By talking-story to us, Kingston draws us into an ongoing discourse of "I's" and "you's." In an interview, Kingston said, "I do not give boring exposition. Readers ought not to expect reading to be as effortless as watching TV" [**"Cultural Mis-Readings by American Reviewers,"** *Asian and American Writers in Dialogue: New Cultural Identities,* edited by Guy Amirthanayagam, 1982]. By forcing the reader to construct an interpretation of who she is, she dramatizes the conception that the self is not a stable entity: it is constructed and reconstructed in a continuing social process. The narrator's list of 200 grievances that grows even as she tells it illuminates the nature of the autobiographical act, an act that ends not with explication but with yet another story.

There is no sense in this text of linear, causal time, a sequence of chronologically ordered events that leads us to understand why the person is what she is. Instead, time loops: the past is not distinct from the present but part of it. We see people weaving themselves into each other's stories. Repeated yet varied patterns replace "cause." Roles are simultaneous, making us aware of the recursiveness of revision in writing and of how this defines the self. From a psychoanalytic perspective, such an organization argues that identity formation is "circular and regressive," that "a quest for women warriors and shamen must also include a recognition of weakness and madness" [Elise Miller].

That there is a fixed objective truth about the self is further challenged by unusual combinations of verb tenses and by varying points of view. They deconstruct fiction/fact and subject/object dichotomies. Robin Lakoff makes the point that verbs do not always indicate objective time: instead, they sometimes indicate the speaker's attitude toward the event. The narrative in a chapter like "Western Palace" seems objective because it is third person, but it does not have the omniscience and authority that this point of view implies. Instead, the narrator has merged her identity with her mother's in order to invent the detail and the emotional reactions that convince us of the story's truth.

The third person, according to Barthes, does not necessarily indicate an impersonal point of view. If *I* can be substituted for the third person (the name Brave Orchid, for instance) and the discourse still "makes sense," it is "personal." Most traditional narrative, he says, rapidly alternates the personal and the impersonal, producing "a proprietary consciousness which retains the mastery of what it states without participating in it." This criterion suggests that this chapter is Brave Orchid's *personal* narrative since the text can be changed to first person without producing any sense of strangeness. Here is Kingston's third-person version:

> Brave Orchid would add her will power to the forces that keep an airplane up. Her head hurt with the concentration. The plane had to be light, so no matter how tired she felt, she dared not rest her spirit on a wing but continuously and gently pushed up on the plane's belly.

Here is the same passage presented in the first person:

> I would add my will power to the forces that keep an airplane up. My head hurt with the concentration. The plane had to be light, so no matter how tired I felt, I dared not rest my spirit on a wing but continuously and gently pushed up on the plane's belly.

The narrator is neither trapped in the illusion of the autobiographical "I," nor is she Barthes' manipulative writer of traditional fiction. Her discourse does not recapitulate either the self-illusions of autobiography or the "bad faith" of other discourse but "unites the writer and the other, so that . . . each moment of discourse is both absolutely new and absolutely understood." The chapter's funny yet painful double sensibility makes it a duet, a sound like an "icicle in the desert."

Belief in an objective "truth" is further challenged by the indeterminacy of the "facts" in this autobiography. What is the mother's age—76 or 80? Was she 36 or 26 in medical school? Is the narrator her eldest child or did two older siblings die in China? *Did* her mother cut her tongue when she was a child? The narrator cries,

> I don't want to listen to any more of your stories; they have no logic, They scramble me up. You lie with stories. You won't tell me a story and then say,

"This is a true story," or, "This is just a story." I can't tell what's real and what you make up.

The mother responds, "That's what Chinese say. We like to say the opposite." Secrecy and silence throughout counterpoint talking-story. Adults are so secretive that the narrator wonders how they kept up a continuous culture for five thousand years: "Maybe they didn't," she says; "maybe everyone makes it up as they go along." Her mother's adjuration that "You must not tell anyone" begins this book of telling. Even as the narrator examines the difficulties she had in interpreting her mother's stories, she is talking-story to us, posing us with the same problems of truth that she had in interpreting her mother's stories.

Comparing Kingston's autobiography with Richard Rodriguez' *Hunger of Memory* (1982) is illuminating because in many ways the two have the same concerns. Both authors were "minority" students who got "straight A's" and struggled with two cultures to finds a coherent identity. Both autobiographies focus on language (Rodriguez explicitly says his does). Both are "ghostridden" and "ghostwritten" in ways related to their authors' ethnicity (Couser). However, Rodriguez' book, subtitled *The Education of Richard Rodriguez,* self-consciously situates itself in the tradition of American autobiographies by men of letters. Like Henry Adams, Rodriguez will write an intellectual autobiography organized as a "series of essays." In response to his New York editor's plea for more "Grandma," he asserts that his "most real life" lies necessarily in public issues: "My writing is political because it concerns my movement away from the company of family and into the city." This statement makes his history representative of the nation's. Earlier, he states, "This is my story. An American story." Such an emphasis on the public and the universal, according to feminist critic Estelle Jelinek, is typical of male autobiography ["Introduction: Women's Autobiography and the Male Tradition," *Women's Autobiography: Essays in Criticism,* 1980]. I do not mean to undermine the complexity and insight of Rodriguez' text. I do mean that Kingston's marginality as a woman poses her with conflicts she can deal with only by subverting the assumptions of a male-dominated genre. To be female and Chinese, after all, is to be "a maggot in the rice." Rodriguez' statements about the nature of literacy and education imply a belief in the author's autonomy, his authoring of the meaning of his life. He defines education as an effort of the will that requires "radical *self*-reformation": "[I was] haunted by the knowledge that one *chooses* to become a student. (Education is not an inevitable or natural step in growing up)." In fourth grade, he developed what he himself called a "grandiose reading program" (it included *The Iliad, Moby Dick,* and the "entire first volume of the *Encyclopedia Britannica*"). A "scholarship boy," he says, *uses* education to "remake himself."

Since knowledge is constructed from reading and reading is a private act, education itself is self-administered and non-communal. This belief in self-making is interestingly contradicted by his definition of education as imitative: "The best synonym for primary 'education' is 'imitation.'" His discussion of "the scholarship boy" vacillates between contempt and applause. On one page he seems to agree with Hoggert's criticism that the boy is a "blinkered pony" who views life as a "permanent examination," while on the next he is presenting the boy as a model for coping with "the general predicament." Students must, he says, "develop the skill of memory long before they become truly critical thinkers." But how does imitation develop a "point of view"? His assertion that assimilation is "necessary" and "valuable" is similarly contradictory:

> There are *two* ways a person is individualized. . . . while one suffers a diminished sense of *private* individuality by becoming assimilated into public society, such assimilation makes possible the achievement of *public* individuality.

Whereas Kingston makes her written autobiography an extension of the interaction of oral story-telling (the *I/you* of discourse), Rodriguez describes the written and oral as incompatible. To have a social identity—an identity in the larger community—he must give up the communion of oral language and be alone with abstractions and dead authors. Reading, described as sitting in a library and turning pages like "stiff layers of dead skin," is an act of social withdrawal: "I *hoarded* [my emphasis] the pleasures of learning. Alone for hours. Enthralled." Enjoyment of the "lonely good company of books" means he no longer can talk to his parents about anything of importance—"only small, obvious things." His description of a family Christmas at the end of the book comes from a yearning ghost who sees through a glass wall, but cannot hear and cannot speak.

Although both Kingston and Rodriguez share a sense that time is not linear, that the past somehow inhabits the present, Rodriguez' organization is analytic rather than analogic. Meaning implicitly stems from a sequence of his individual choices and the consequences of those choices. Chapter I recalls the intimacy of his early family life—an oral life—and the loss of that intimacy when he begins to identify with the English version of his name. The next three chapters deal with his acculturation as an "American," focussing respectively on mental, spiritual, and physical components. Chapters 5 and 6 concern his mature roles as political activist and then as autobiographer/historian. Chapters 2 and 6 from a crucial pair: the first defines the nature of reading and its relation to education, the second the nature of writing. Reading is cause, writing consequence. His doubts about linearity are indicated by his syntactically fragmented style (single-word sentences and frequent interruptions with dashes and quotes) and by his looping between past and present. (He describes his own writing as "six chapters of sad, fuguelike repetition"). Nevertheless, he seems to propose a progress, though one that necessitates a cruel loss: one "matures" from apprentice to public man to introspective historian. When he returns, in the last chapter, to immediate family relationships, he is the public man, the outsider. G. Thomas Couser describes *Hunger of Memory* as a "linear conversion narrative" based on "canonical authors." Crucial to producing a sense of causality and progress is his discussion of the nature of literacy in Chapter 2 (called "The Achievement of Desire"):

> The ability to consider experience so abstractly allowed me to shape into desire what would otherwise have remained indefinite, meaningless longing. . . . If, because of my schooling, I had grown culturally separated from my parents, my education finally had given me ways of speaking and caring about that fact.

Rodriguez' autobiography asserts, unlike Kingston's (which does not assert anything), that there is a fixed, objective truth about the self and that language can tell it, despite the fact that his narrative seems radically deconstructed by its own tropes: "In writing this autobiography," he says,

> I am actually describing the man I have become—the man in the present. . . . I write under the obligation to make myself clear to someone who knows nothing about me.

Assuming the separation of subject and object, he "vacuums" his past life for insights into his present pain as he has vacuumed the books he has read for "anything to fill the hollow within me and make me feel educated." "The existence of a question," he says, "implies the existence of an answer."

Like Kingston, he explores the nature of the self as defined by language. For him, however, learning public language means the loss of music rather than the gain implied by "Song for a Barbarian Reed Pipe." His opening chapter, "Aria," recalls a world as alive with magical sound as the island in *The Tempest*:

> Voices singing and sighting, rising, straining, then surging, teeming with pleasure that burst syllables into fragments of laughter.

Then, however, he learns public language, and his profit on it is silence and isolation, only his own "echoing voice . . . resembling another's." "Aria" ends with a funeral. The public self, "Rich-heard Road-ree-guess," says,

I write today for a reader who exists in my mind only phantasmagorically. Someone with a face erased; someone of no particular race or sex or age or weather. A grey presence . . . (*un gringo*).

He writes for a ghost.

Both Kingston and Rodriguez struggle, as a minorities, to find a public self, a voice. "If my story is true," Rodriguez says, "I trust it will resonate with significance for other lives." For most of us, it is true, though not entirely in the sense he means. In our desire for a public identity, we *have* sacrificed the personal. Robert Sayre asks whether we are "a nation of individualists or a nation of conformists, each scrambling to imitate somebody else." We look oddly homogeneous driving along in our similar cars, living in our similar houses, and eating our fast foods. When strangers call each other by first name, what does "personal" mean? According to John Adams, our conformity stems from "the instinct of emulation": lacking inherited titles and aristocratic rank, everyone competes fiercely for the "'distinction' that can only by received from, other people." Kingston seems to work out a more promising reconciliation, perhaps because her gender prohibits her access to the American Dream.

American myth seems to imply that "reality" and the self are as simple as the bold stroke of the capital *I* with its tiny modifying addenda, but this simplicity, according to Kingston, is an illusion:

> I could not understand "I." The Chinese "I" has seven strokes, intricacies. How could be the American "I," assuredly wearing a hat like the Chinese, have only three strokes, the middles so straight? Was it out of politeness that this writer left off strokes the way a Chinese has to write her own name small and crooked? No, it was not politeness; "I" is a capital and "you" is lower-case.

The graphic ambiguity of the written *I* suggests the ambiguity of individuality and the self-contradiction of autobiography. To write autobiography, the language of self-reference, is to make knots, she says—and knots blind the maker. Is such a blindness the blindness of Tiresias and the "fallen" Oedipus?

Names and what they mean are crucially important in both autobiographies. Both Jacques Lacan and Jacques Derrida make the point that proper names inscribe and individual into an already existing social discourse. Rodriguez, by accepting the public, *gringo* version of his name, silences the part of himself that is private, Mexican. He celebrates that name, although he admits that his individuality is now "tenuous—because is depends on my being one in a crowd." The narrator of **Woman Warrior,** however, never tells us either her first name or her proper name. This marked absence, perhaps, contributes to the desperation with which she exhorts her doppelganger (in the lavatory scene) to

> "Say your name. Go ahead. Say it. Or are you stupid? . . . You're so stupid, you don't know your own name, is that it?"

In the first chapter she had complained that the Chinese "guard their real names with silence" (Chinese children do not know them). She supposes that children "threaten" their parents by "always trying to get things straight, always trying to name the unspeakable." Parents, on the other hand, advise giving a new name every time so "ghosts won't recognize you." A woman's proper name, according to [Sandra M.] Gilbert and [Susan] Gubar, effaces her identity because it is never proper in the French sense of being "her own" either to have or to give [*No Man's Land: The Place of the Woman Writer in the Twentieth Century,* Vol. 1, 1988].

At the end of the book, the reader finds that the narrator's name is as secret as her mother's secret name yet as public and communal as No-Name Woman's, as stable and as unstable as *I*. Like No-Name Woman, she has no name but the one inscribed by the discourse itself, a name, a "self," created by the interaction of writer and reader, storyteller and listener—a duet. Her story is and is not her mother's story.

Laura Riding's ambiguous poem on names seems an appropriate epigraph to Kingston's fictive autobiography:

> I am because I say
> I say myself
> I am my name
> My name is not my name
> It is the name of what I say.
> My name is what is said.
> I alone say.
> I alone am not I.
> I am my name.
> My name is not my name,
> My name is the name.
> [quoted in Jane Marcus, "Laura Riding
> Roughshod," *The Iowa Review*, Vol. 12, 1981]

LeiLani Nishime (essay date Spring 1995)

SOURCE: "Engendering Genre: Gender and Nationalism in 'China Men' and *The Woman Warrior,*'" in *MELUS*, Vol. 20, No. 1, Spring, 1995, pp. 67-83.

[*In the following essay, Nishime traces Kingston's treatment of gender and ethnicity in* The Woman Warrior *and* China Men, *and discusses how genre illuminates the author's concept of identity.*]

China Men, Maxine Hong Kingston's book on the history of Chinese-Americans, followed close on the heels of the publication of her much acclaimed autobiography *The Woman Warrior.* Kingston has said that she first envisioned the two volumes as one book; yet if we view these books as companion works, then it is curious how differently they represent what might be called the Chinese-American experience [Stephen Talbot, "Talking Story: Maxine Hong Kingston Rewrites the American Dream," *San Francisco Examiner,* June 24, 1990]. While the first, most obvious divide may be at the level of gender, as evidenced by the two books' titles, another equally important division takes place at the level of genre. When Kingston allies generic distinctions, i.e., history and autobiography, with particular genders she both explores and exposes that underlying alliance, raising questions about the role genre plays in defining both gender roles and Chinese-American identity. At the same time, she raises questions about the meaning of the public and private in relationship to history and autobiography and how notions of public and private give those genres a gendered status. By locating gender in Kingston's manipulations of genre and mythology and looking at the gendered categorization of generic forms, we can also locate the place of Chinese-American identity in her conception of gender and genre.

Much of the power of these two works lies in Kingston's attempt to intervene in and undermine a "master narrative" of history and identity in America. Although Kingston does skillfully parody and disrupt accepted notions of history and autobiography and destabilize those categories with her introductions of gender and race, her ability to escape the boundaries of genre remains in question.

Perhaps the question that must be asked is: How complete is the connection between genre and the ideology that gave rise to it? Does Kingston's repetition of these genres, albeit in altered forms, merely contribute to reinforcing those forms or, as Judith Butler claims, can there be "repetition with a difference?" In other words, as Gayatri Spivak might ask, "Can the subaltern speak?" Kingston never fully escapes genre because she must write within and against the constraints of generic forms in order to comment upon them and manipulate them. If she abandons the forms completely, the cultural resonances so crucial to her disruption of hegemonic conceptions of Chinese-American identity, gender and history, would be lost, but her adherence to those forms raises questions about her ability to fully subvert or escape the ideologies that inform those genres.

Whether Kingston speaks without being consumed by the "epistemic violence" of her writing tools, namely language and genre, is my central question. My search is not for Kingston's "authentic" voice hidden within these forms, but an examination of how she engages with and uses these forms to her own ends. By examining Kingston's deconstruction of the opposition between fictional and non-fictional forms, such as autobiography and history, her use of mythology to explore issues of national identity, and her manipulations of genre and mythology through the introduction of race and gender, I hope to delineate constraints of genre and the meaning of the subversion of these forms at the intersection of gender and Chinese-American identity.

Looking at the opposition between these two books' genres proves to be no easy matter, as Kingston rarely lets any clear opposition stand. Instead, what was a matter of black and white, autobiography and historiography, slips away into a hazy area where generic boundaries are difficult to define. Although both books blur the boundaries between the two genres, they do not find a common third term, and instead they present examples of two very different approaches to both history and autobiography.

These unstable oppositions are apparent even before one cracks the binding of either book. Although both books now can be found in the fiction or Asian American literature section, the generic distinctions given to them by their publisher betray their earlier distinctions. *The Woman Warrior* falls under the rubric of autobiography while *China Men,* a work of history, is categorized as nonfiction/literature. But the books do not remain within the two distinct genres of autobiography and history, much less maintain their mutual exclusivity. Perhaps some of the loudest uproar over *The Woman Warrior* centered upon Kingston's blurring of the boundary between non-fictional autobiography and a fictional retelling of her life story. She insists on an eccentric voice, telling her memoirs from a highly personal point of view and making no attempt to "objectively" review her subjective, skewed vision of her world. *China Men* also participates in this transgression of generic boundaries, for this history makes room for fables, myths, family lore and personal accounts as well as official laws and documents. In both cases, Kingston questions and undermines the status of "truth" and "facts" by questioning the concepts of universality and objectivity.

The problem of generic distinctions appears endemic to Asian American literature, since "ethnic histories" almost always threaten the boundaries between genres, because the term is traditionally seen as an oxymoron. In some senses, all minority writing is considered to be always/already autobiographical. Trinh T. Minh-ha reminds us that, "the minority's voice is always personal; that of the majority, always impersonal" [*Woman, Native, Other: Writing*

Postcoloniality and Feminism, 1989, original emphasis]. Asian American writing, like much minority writing, is perceived as autobiographical in the sense that writing by Asian Americans is "about" their experience as Asian Americans in a way that Anglo-American writing, with its assumption of universality, is never "about" being white. Thus Michael Fischer, despite his otherwise careful reading of several Asian American novels, claims to research "the range or historical trajectory of autobiographical writing within each ethnicity" while unselfconsciously citing clearly fictional, non-autobiographical works by Frank Chin and Shawn Wong ["Ethnicity and the Post-Modern Arts of Memory," in *Writing Culture: The Poetics and Politics of Ethnography,* edited by James Clifford and George Marcus, 1986]. The history of the dominant, unlike that of the minority, is perceived to be universal or unmarked. An ethnic history, following this logic, is a private, personalized history than cannot transcend to the level of the general and the public.

By blurring the distinction between autobiography and history, Kingston at first appears to be repeating and encouraging a common misreading of writings by Asian Americans as always autobiographical. Donald Goellnicht begins his article on *China Men* saying, "Maxine Hong Kingston's second (auto) biographical fiction, *China Men* . . . ", although this book has few "(auto) biographical" markers, (for instance, Kingston rarely appears as a character in the novel, and the stories she tells more closely resemble short stories or anecdotes than biographies) ["Tang Ao in America: Male Subject Positions in *China Men,*" *Reading the Literatures of Asian America,* edited by Shirley Geok-lin Lim and Amy Ling, 1992]. Still, this categorization of *China Men* as (auto) biographical rather than historical seems, in fact, to be encouraged by the way Kingston crosses genres in this book. Instead of rushing to shore up the distinctions in Asian American writing between autobiography, fiction and history, Kingston chooses a different strategy. In *China Men* rather than attempting to rid Chinese-American history of the "taint" of the personal or autobiographical, Kingston revises notions of what makes an experience historical, by asking by what standards we decide what can enter into history and the public realm.

Kingston contrasts the "private" (read: non-representative and therefore non-historical) stories of the "Grandfathers" to the official public (read: objective and historical) documents of the time. For example, Kingston follows the story of the "Grandfather of the Sierra Nevada Mountains" with a recitation of the restrictive laws against Asian Americans that basically legalized racism. The chapter, which simply recounts the laws, appears midway through the book, yet, as Goellnicht says, "This centric authority of American law is subverted and contested by the 'eccentric' or marginal, but richly imaginative stories of *China Men* that surround it." Her juxtaposition of the two versions of history points out the inaccessibility of that official history in comparison with the "Grandfathers'" story. The narrated, and perhaps fictional, stories of the "Grandfathers" allow a more meaningful view of the history of Chinese-Americans and provide a space in which to write the history that had been left out of the exclusionary laws. This use of official documents also emphasizes the fact that the documents are only available in an already interpreted form, and they do not provide a transparent look into the past. They frame the narrative of the Chinese in America by the stories they leave out, stories such as Kingston's. Although the documents masquerade as objective, they are not necessarily more true or real than the history we receive through the Grandfathers' story.

China Men at first appears to be a private family history populated by the narrator's grandfathers, but soon it becomes clear that she has more grandfathers than is biologically possible. While the "Grandfathers" are individual people with their own personalities and personal histories, they also are a type or a generic forefather whose story is representative of many Chinese-American immigrants. Kingston gestures towards a history of Chinese-Americans in America that is beyond her family history, yet the quirkiness of each individual characterization prevents the creation of a single individual who represents the norm of Chinese-American experience. One cannot gauge the authenticity of one's family by measuring how closely one's history conforms to the stories Kingston tries to create a new definition of history for Chinese-Americans by foregrounding the individuality of the stories, yet the book also documents their role in history as Chinese-Americans.

Homi Bhahba has asked "Whether the emergence of a national perspective-of an elite or subaltern nature—within a culture of social contestation, can ever articulate its 'representative' authority in that fullness of narrative time." This difficulty in both being within a "culture of contestation" and trying to speak with authority is reflected in *China Men* by the placement of the "Grandfathers" as both the object and subject of a national identity ["DissemiNation: Time, Narrative, and the Margins of the Modern Nation," in his *Nation and Narration,* 1990]. While they may be acting as subjects by expanding the definitions of Americaness, they also act as objects of that nationalistic discourse so that they may speak as Americans, thus gaining a "representative authority." Their history cannot be separated from the "public" national history of America. In this way, Kingston simultaneously claims a "representative authority" for her history in the service of creating a space for Chinese-Americans in Anglo-American history while remaining "within a culture of social contestation" by refusing to fall back upon notions of authenticity and origin. The experiences of the book's characters do not stand apart from history, just as what we know as history is caught up in social, cultural, and "private" perceptions. This book asks us to question what facts we deem real and what experiences are "historical" and, in so doing, makes explicit the connection between individual identity and history without reverting to the paradigm of history as a point of origin.

The attack on Kingston over the autobiographical status of her book *The Woman Warrior* is well known. Frank Chin, perhaps Kingston's most well known critic, describes Kingston's transgressions by saying, "[Her] elaboration of this version of history, in both autobiography and autobiographical fiction, is simply a device for destroying history and literature," because Kingston does not "accurately" portray the experience and history of Chinese-Americans ["Come All Ye Asian American Writers of the Real and the Fake," in *The Big Aiiieeeee!: An Anthology of Chinese American and Japanese American Literature,* edited by Jeffrey Paul Chan, et al., 1974]. To her critics, Kingston violates the commitment to "factuality" that the name autobiography implies and, in doing so, confronts two differing traditions of autobiography. She challenges, on the one hand, the non-fiction appellation of autobiography, and, on the other hand, the anthropological information retrieval concept of ethnic autobiography.

The anxiety over Kingston's book centers upon the role of and expectations for ethnic autobiography. Kingston writes against a tradition of Chinese-American autobiography that gave an ethnographic treatment of Chinese-American society. As Sau-ling Wong says, with a great deal of irony, in "Autobiography as Guided Chinatown Tour," "Ideally, an ethnic autobiography should also be a history in microcosm of the community, especially of its suffering, struggles, and triumphs" [*Multicultural Autobiography: American Lives,* edited by James Payne, 1992]. Autobiography has a long history in Chinese-American writing, beginning with early "conversion" narratives prompted by Christian missionaries, and many of the better selling, earlier works do fit into Wong's pattern. In her article about the reception of her book, Kingston notes the tendency of critics to review her book on the basis of how good a "tourguide" she proves to be, judging her by how well she recreates the "mystery" of Chinatown and how "authentically" she displays its exotica. The concern over Kingston's book relies on a notion of ethnic autobiography as a learning tool for the projected white audience. Kingston's book would seem to be a failure if ethnic autobiography is to be read as a type of ethnography, but her success lies in a reworking of this tradition.

This, then, is the tradition within and against which Kingston is writing. Yet instead of a total rejection of the ethnographic impulse in ethnic autobiography, *The Woman Warrior* does, in many ways, uphold the concept of ethnic autobiography as an exploration of what it means to be a Chinese-American. At the same time, Kingston still insists upon the singularity of her view and does not attempt to speak for all Chinese-Americans nor represent them completely. In the book she admits that she cannot speak for Chinese-Americans because she is not even sure what exactly is the Chinese-American experience.

In the book, the narrator's isolation from other members of her community does not allow her to hear the stories of others to provide a scale by which to measure her own experience. The narrator tells us that she could never tell if what she was experiencing was typical of Chinese-Americans or simply a family eccentricity, so that when she leaves her hometown she must read anthropology books about China to look for hints about her life. Her alienation is so complete that she must read books written by outsiders to find out about herself and try to find a self that she can recognize. This ironic situation prevents the protagonist from taking a position of absolute or sole authority on Chinese-Americans or acting as a source of information retrieval, since she learns about Chinatown from books instead of the "ultimate" referent of experience. She cannot act as the symbol or representative of Chinese-Americans for the outsider who wants to learn about the "true" culture of a Chinatown since her experience is so personalized. Kingston must expand the boundaries of ethnic autobiography in order to explore her identity as a Chinese-American and create an alternative authority rather than formulating a complete definition of that identity for the imagined outsider reader.

Kingston also plays with other conventions of autobiography, conventions that are not limited to ethnic autobiography. As I mentioned earlier, autobiography is often assumed to be factual and empirically true. In the book, the clear distinctions between fiction and non-fiction are not made so; what the protagonist recounts as her subjective experience may or may not exist in an "objective" account of her life. Yet the truth of her life is more clearly represented through the fictions she tells since she lives in a world where her own reality is bound up with half truths and fictions. In a telling scene in *China Men,* Kingston and her sister remember the same event completely differently, and they never find out which version was true, yet for each of them her own memory was true. The narrator has had to create her own reality and says, "She [her mother] tested our strength to establish realities." When the protagonist narrates her life, she must include the non-truths that make up her reality; sticking to empirical truth would falsify her experience.

In *The Woman Warrior,* the convention of the singular individual in autobiography is also dismantled, and the author plays with the assumption of the centrality of the individual in autobiography. The typical American autobiography, with *Autobiography of Benjamin Franklin* as its archetypal example, emphasizes the theme of individual struggle and triumph, often in the face of community resistance. *The Woman Warrior* concerns itself less with the individual character of the narrator than with her place within a social structure. In fact, the book's protagonist never actually gets named, questioning the immediate identification of the protagonist with the author and allowing the protagonist to participate in the narrative as a character rather than claiming the ultimate authority of authorship.

The story does not function as a tale of individualism. Rather it details her search for her place within the community and her family and the meaning of her identity as a Chinese-American. The story of the protagonist is intertwined with her relationship with her mother, and *The Woman Warrior* tells the story of the protagonist's mother and is as much a story of her relationship to her mother as it is "about" the protagonist. Kingston, by emphasizing the social aspect of an individual identity, broadens the scope of autobiography to include the constant negotiations with different social structures that make up the shifting ground of ethnicity. As Michael Fischer tells us, "Ethnicity is not something that is simply passed on from generation to generation, taught and learned; it is something dynamic. . . ." Ethnicity, in *The Woman Warrior,* cannot be understood as an individualist experience but has meaning only within a social context. It resides within a social dynamic. The book's protagonist says, "[We] have had to figure out how the invisible world the emigrants built around our childhoods fits into solid America." Ethnicity, and by extension Kingston's identity, is constantly being created through the competing discourses of the emigrant's "invisible world" and "solid America."

A close examination of the function of mythology in *China Men* and *The Woman Warrior* makes clear the breakdown of generic distinctions and the performativity of ethnicity in those books. While Kingston's use of mythology has raised objections from other members of the Asian American community, her manipulations, or distortions, of those myths enable her to question the basic assumptions of the generic forms of history and autobiography. The use of myth helps her to find a way to write Chinese-Americans into American history and to search for her own Chinese-American identity.

As I mentioned earlier, Kingston undermines traditional notions of history by questioning the meaning of objectivity and neutrality in the narrative of history. By inserting Chinese-American mythology and Chinese-American people into Anglo-American history, Kingston does not merely augment the existing history. She also exposes the mythological roots of Anglo-American history, putting its claim to objectivity and truth into jeopardy. Richard Slotkin calls myth "the primary language of historical memory" which

functions to "assign ideological meaning to that history" ["Myth and the Production of History," *Ideology and Classic American Literature,* edited by Sacvan Bercovitch and Myra Jehlen, 1986]. Yet myth, like history, is a symbolic production that acts like a transcendent truth by effacing its ideological use value. In Slotkin's elegant aphorism, "[Myth] transforms history into nature." Myth is the narrative that gives meaning to history, that allows history to function as truth rather than as just another story.

In her story in *China Men* entitled "The Adventures of Lo Bun Sun," an auditory pun on the story of Robinson Crusoe, Kingston exposes the ideological underpinning of the traditional story. Like Robinson, Lo Bun Sun is a shipwrecked pirate, and the story is a familiar one, but the use of a Chinese name is different enough to defamiliarize the story and cast it in a new light. The story depends upon the assumption that the sailor is white, so that it can plug into the myth of the Great White Adventurer civilizing the "native." However, when the two characters are both "natives," the naturalness given to the story by the power of myth is lost, and the story appears both ludicrous and brutal. Kingston's revisioning of the Robinson Crusoe story demonstrates the ability of myth to naturalize and normalize to such an extent that the gaps and fissures in a story that should mark the fault lines of the "master narrative" are glossed over. The gaps that mark where certain histories were left out disappear behind the familiar myths of Anglo-American history.

Kingston reveals and reopens those gaps by reinstating the Chinese-Americans who were erased from Anglo-American history. She does not reject the notion of a Chinese-American history along with all history but emphasizes its constructed nature. In fact, she uses the American mythology of the West to help her write Chinese-Americans into the history of the frontier. Linda Hutcheon characterizes the postmodern relationship to the use value of the past when she says, "It puts into question, at the same time it exploits, the grounding of historical knowledge in the past real" [*A Poetics of Postmodernism: History, Theory, Fiction,* 1989]. After showing how mythology enters into history, Kingston does not abandon the project of history but, instead, attempts to create a new mythology for Chinese-American history. Kingston depicts a certain "heroic dominance" in terms of the land. The first job of the character Ah Goong is to fell a redwood and, in the end, he conquers the mountains through which he has to tunnel. Kingston firmly places the Chinese in the American landscape and enumerates the ways in which he has participated in forming and creating that landscape in order to further her goal of "claiming America" and creating a Chinese-American history and identity. It is crucial to note that their part in the building of America is couched in legendary and epic terms, unlike the "factual" empirical tone of traditional history books. Kingston exploits rather than naturalizes the power of mythology in her histories.

The Woman Warrior describes a very different relationship between the female protagonist and mythology than is found in *China Men.* The former focuses much more narrowly upon Chinese myth rather than exposing the mythology of Anglo-American history. After the short first chapter, Chinese myth forms a frame around the account of a Chinese-American girl's childhood in a small town Chinatown. The mythical figure of Fa Mu Lan, "the girl who took her father's place in battle," haunts the book and her childhood. Like the myths of *China Men,* the story of Fa Mu Lan offers a chance of escape, not the "China men's" escape from historical obscurity but an escape from the anonymity that is her gender's fate. The protagonist remembers her mother's stories and says, "She said I would grow up to be a wife and a slave, but she taught me the song of the warrior woman, Fa Mu Lan. I would have to grow up a warrior woman."

Much of the controversy surrounding *The Woman Warrior* revolves around the issue of Kingston's revision of classical Chinese myth, yet this very revision is the means by which she can write her own history. Through her rewriting of Chinese myth she can include her own voice within a Chinese—and, since she learned these stories from her mother in America, a Chinese-American—tradition. The protagonist of *The Woman Warrior* inserts herself into the stories of Chinese myth and, thereby, participates in the narrative of the community. She rewrites Fa Mu Lan in such a way that Fa Mu Lan speaks with her voice, and she can identify and recognize herself in the stories of Chinese America and claim a Chinese-American identity. Unfortunately, she is left with the problem of getting others in the community to recognize her version of the myth and confirm her voice and place within the community, a difficulty I will discuss later.

Thus, in the words of Homi Bhabha, Kingston "acknowledges the status of national culture—and the people—as a contentious, performative space of the perplexity of living in the midst of the pedagogical representation of the fullness of life." Kingston negotiates between a fixed, complete, "pedagogical" definition of Chinese-American culture and her lived experience of national identity, an identity that is continually being defined, redefined and "performed." The main character now has a history and a legacy that gives her authority to act as more than a "wife and slave," but, by not effacing her participation in the act of creating that history, she avoids the trap of origins and the trap of biological determinism. So while the main character still "could not figure out what my village was," she was able to carve out a space for herself through the act of narrative by mak-

ing her "village" the world of Chinese myth. Unlike the work done with myth in *China Men,* the protagonist's involvement with myths does not rework Anglo-American history, but, instead tries to find her a place within her family and community not only as an individual but also as a Chinese-American.

The Woman Warrior and *China Men* both challenge assumptions about the nature of history and myth in the Anglo-American tradition, yet their similarities cause their differences to stand out in bold relief. *China Men* subverts notions of a seamless, "factual" history, untouched by either mythology or particularity, in an effort to write Chinese-Americans back into the history of America. *The Woman Warrior* examines and undermines similar concepts, yet the protagonist never succeeds in fully reconciling her gender and her identity as a Chinese-American and never enters into "history" like the "Grandfathers" in *China Men.* Thus, her ability to speak as a national remains threatened, since nationalism is not a quantifiable trait but exists in a fluid relationship to society, and her identity as a Chinese-American is tenuous as long as her place within the community does not allow her view to be as "universal" as any other voice. Her struggle has a different location from the struggle in *China Men.* The two books explore different boundaries between myth and history and the public and the private, highlighting the difficulty of finding an identity that encompasses both nation and gender.

In Sau-Ling Wong's discussion of the intersection of nationalism and gender for Chinese-Americans, she coins the term "ethnicizing gender," contrasting it to gendering ethnicity. The assignation of gendered characteristics according to ethnicity is a familiar trope, but Wong proposes a flip side to this analysis. Instead, the enactment of gender leads to an ethnic labeling. In America a strict gender demarcation of Asian ethnicities as feminine, as opposed to the more masculine "Americans," operates to bind notions of gender to ethnicity and nationalism. In Wong's example of Chinese-American immigrant writing she says, "Thus the characters' actions, depicted along a spectrum of gender appropriateness, are assigned varying shades of "Chineseness" or "Americanness" to indicate the extent of their at-homeness in the adopted land" ["Ethnicizing Gender: An Exploration of Sexuality as Sign in Chinese Immigrant Literature," *Reading the Literatures of Asian America,* edited by Shirley Geok-lin Lim and Amy Ling, 1992].

In *China Men* the crossing of the boundaries between the public and private spheres has implications in terms of the gendered connotations of those two terms. The conception of Chinese-American history as essentially private as opposed to the public Anglo-American history also genders that history feminine since the private sphere has long been associated with the female. By bringing the "private" Chinese-American history into the public sphere, Kingston moves its story into the traditionally masculine public sphere of American history. In **China Men,** the claim to a Chinese-American identity and history necessitates this move from the feminine private sphere into the masculine public discourse. Since, in Wong's formulation, American ethnicity, as opposed to Chinese ethnicity, means masculinity, the assertion of the place of the Chinese in America is, by definition, also a move towards confirming Chinese-Americans' masculine "Americanness."

This is not to say that Kingston whole-heartedly embraces a masculine ideal for Chinese-Americans. The ambiguity of her response to this split between a "feminine Chineseness" and a "masculine Americanness" may be best exemplified by **China Men**'s opening chapter, "On Discovery." The short chapter resembles a fairy tale about a man named Tang Ao who sails to the Gold Mountain, which is another name for America, where he is captured and dressed and treated like a woman. At first glance this seems merely to be about the trauma of the feminization of Chinese men who came to America, yet the story also is concerned with the suffering of Chinese females. Tang Ao's ear piercing and painful footbinding were both practices of Chinese women, and the story appears to be as much about the constraints of women's roles as the "emasculinization" of Chinese men in America. Still, despite Kingston's recognition of the pain of fulfilling these gender roles for women, she still celebrates a masculine ideal to counteract the stereotypes of Asian males and to assert their "Americanness." Although Kingston often maintains a playful tone, the irony of aspiring to a masculine ideal that ultimately traps Asian American males cannot seem to overcome the immediate appeal and power of that ideal.

This re-writing of American myth and history to create a masculine, and therefore Chinese American, ideal for Chinese men raises difficult questions about the role of Chinese-American women in this new history. While it is true that due to exclusionary laws women were largely absent from early Chinese-American history, the images and terminology that Kingston uses in relation to the land do not leave a space for women trying to find their voice in this history. While one might argue that it is unfair to hold Kingston responsible for articulating a female voice in a book specifically focusing on Chinese-American males, the question remains as to why Chinese-American males and females must speak their history through different genres and with a different vocabularies. Kingston, through the character Ah Goong, configures the land as something to be conquered and overcome. He has a highly erotic relationship to the whole landscape and, in one unforgettable scene, is so overcome by the beauty of the scenery that he ejaculates out of a hanging basket into a valley yelling, "I'm fucking the world" (**China Men**). This type of language, that sexualizes

and feminizes the land and puts it in terms of possession, is characteristic of a great deal of the writing about Western expansionism and the Frontier. Not only is it troubling in terms of the environment, but it raises concerns about finding a place for women when this male centered language underlies Kingston's version of Chinese-American historical myth.

While Kingston treats these visions of Chinese-American masculinity with irony and humor, she does, nevertheless, celebrate them as symbols of Chinese-Americanness. She juxtaposes Ah Goong's view of Chinese men as "pale, thin Chinese scholars and the rich men fat like Buddhas" and the positive ideal of "these brown muscular railroad men" (**China Men**). Ah Goong tells himself, "He was an American for having built the railroad" (**China Men**). By participating in this visible, public part of American history, by "fucking the world," and by becoming an American masculine ideal, Ah Goong can claim a place as a Chinese-American, but where does that leave Chinese-American women? Perhaps a partial answer can be found in the relationship of a woman to nationalism in **The Woman Warrior.**

In the controversy surrounding **The Woman Warrior,** one of the most often heard accusations charges Kingston with an alliance with white feminism and denying the cause of Chinese-American nationalism. Her detractors read her criticism of Chinese and Chinese-American men as another display of pandering to a white audience and a betrayal of Chinese-Americans, more specifically Chinese-American men. The strong reaction to Kingston's book recalls the injunctions of the ethnicizing of gender described by Wong. Wong analyzes a short story by Yi Li and says, "In Huang's eyes, strength in a Chinese woman is not only unwomanly but tantamount to ethnic betrayal" ("Ethnicizing Gender"). Since Americanness translates into masculinity, Chineseness for Huang suggests femininity, and a Chinese woman's deviance from prescribed gender roles connotes an abandonment of femininity and, by extension, Chineseness. Within this logic of ethnicity and gender, **The Woman Warrior** tells the story of a woman who rejects her feminine roles and thereby rejects her identity as a Chinese-American.

The Woman Warrior can be read as Kingston's attempts to reconcile the opposition between feminism and nationalism through her reworking of the genre of autobiography. Jean Franco argues that the study of gendered subjects who exist in the periphery and "off center" forces us to alter hierarchical thinking and "challenges the often unexamined assumptions that yoke feminism with bourgeois individualism" [*Plotting Women: Gender and Representation in Mexico*, 1988]. Kingston does challenge those assumptions and deviates not only from the convention of ethnic autobiography but also from the "bourgeois individualism" of many feminist autobiographies. Rita Felski in *Beyond Feminist Aesthetics* plots what she sees as the usual trajectory of feminist autobiography and relates it to the masculine tradition of the Bildungsroman. In feminist autobiography of the 1970s and 1980s, according to Felski, women move from the private to the public sphere and break away from their place in patriarchy, emphasizing "internal growth and self-understanding rather than public self-realization." In contrast, the protagonist in *The Woman Warrior* eventually moves away from the Chinese-American community, "out of the hating range," but her purported goal is always directed towards the community. Her search for self-understanding and for her identity is invested in a recognition by the community since her identity cannot be fully realized outside of a social relationship. By insisting on a feminist view while maintaining the centrality of community, Kingston attempts to link feminism with community and nationalism rather than individualism.

By incorporating issues of nationalism and community into the autobiographical form, Kingston further complicates the public/private divide suggested by that form. Autobiography, often seen as a private form of writing about the individual, seeps into the public arena in *The Woman Warrior* as I noted above. Notions of the public and private shift from those in *China Men*. In *China Men* I defined the public as the Anglo-American discourse as opposed to Chinese-American history that was, by that definition, private. But in *The Woman Warrior,* that world of the private sphere shrinks even smaller. While Chinatown may represent a private world to the "public" world of the American metropolis, in this book Chinatown is the public world that shapes the protagonist's "private" or personal identity. The dichotomy of the public and private becomes even more vexed because of the uneasy place that the protagonist in *The Woman Warrior* occupies within the Chinese-American community. Rather than viewing that community as her private sphere, the community also functions as the public sphere to the much tighter circle of her family. Instead of grappling with Bhabha's question about "representative authority" as an oppositional force within dominant culture, the book's protagonist must struggle with her ability to even speak as a Chinese-American in her own community.

Before the protagonist can participate in the public debate over Chinese-American history, she tries to find "public" recognition as a Chinese-American within her community. Once again she attempts to negotiate this public/private divide with a manipulation of genre.

Jean Franco tells us that, "nationalism demands new kinds of subjects invested with authority to define the true and the real." The protagonist of *The Woman Warrior* attempts to obtain this authority through the interruption of the genre of autobiography with mythology. By interspersing the au-

tobiographical sections with mythology, Kingston stresses the importance of myths in creating the narratives of our daily lives and the necessity of new stories to tell ourselves. Only through a fantastic rewriting of the myth of Fa Mu Lan can the protagonist reconcile the opposition between feminism and nationalism. By rewriting the fable, she creates a Chinese myth that allows her to subvert gender roles and still be a national hero. Through Chinese myths she begins to realize a Chinese-American identity and says, "The swordswoman and I are not so dissimilar. May my people understand the resemblance soon so that I can return to them."

That recognition never fully arrives so she cannot be "invested with the authority to define the true and the real," and she cannot redefine nationalism along the lines of her invented heroine. As we are reminded by the mother in the first chapter, one does not exist without recognition from the community. "You wouldn't like to be forgotten as if you had never been born." She remains distanced from Chinatown in a world where, "the colors are gentler and fewer, smells are antiseptic. Now when I peek in the basement window where the villagers say they see a girl dancing like a bottle imp, I can no longer see a spirit. . . ." Still, the last pages perform a fictional resolution, and she tells her mother's story, "The beginning is hers, the ending mine." She shares a story with her mother and, by writing the ending, she makes it her own and writes herself into a communal myth. In the final utopian moment we can imagine that her story, like the songs Ts'ai Yen brought "back from savage lands," can be understood by her childhood community since "It translated well."

In the end, Kingston never gives us the ultimate solution to the conflict between nationalism and gender. Despite her attempts to subvert or write alternatives to the many master narratives of Anglo-American history, Chinese-American nationalism, feminist autobiography, and Chinese-American autobiography, among others, she can never completely escape those narratives. While she decenters these narratives and calls into question the gendered assumptions that enable them to function, she still remains inscribed within their discourse and writes in reaction to those discourses. Nevertheless, Kingston's project cannot be read as either a complete failure nor a complete triumph. Her manipulation of generic forms opens up a space for her to explore Chinese-American identity and to imagine the different shapes it can take.

Marlene Goldman (essay date 1995)

SOURCE: "Naming the Unspeakable: The Mapping of Female Identity in Maxine Hong Kingston's 'The Woman

Warrior,'" in *International Women's Writing: New Landscapes of Identity,* edited by Anne E. Brown and Marjanne E. Goozé, Greenwood Press, 1995, pp. 223-32.

[*Goldman has taught women's studies at the University of Victoria and Canadian literature at the University of Toronto. In the following essay, she assesses* The Woman Warrior *as a postmodern work that offers a distinctive sense of female identity.*]

In *A Room of One's Own,* Virginia Woolf raises questions concerning women's identity and the problem of inscribing this identity in literature. Such questions must be addressed if women writers are to convey a sense of their own experience, rather than simply reiterate a male perspective. In particular, Woolf argues that, due to the differences between men and women's experience, women cannot expect to utilize traditional literary forms: there is "no reason to think that the form of the epic or of the poetic play suit a woman any more than the [traditional, male] sentence suits her." Although Woolf claims that the novel form is still young enough to be "soft" in a woman's hands, contemporary women writers have shown that even this form must be reconceptualized if it is to represent their unique understanding of identity and its relationship to gender, race, and class.

Maxine Hong Kingston's work *The Woman Warrior* provides a powerful example of one author's experimental treatment of the novel form. For reasons that I will outline, *The Woman Warrior* can be classified as a "postmodern" text. Blending "fact" with fiction, autobiography with folktale elements, the work maps out the contradictions that arise from a collision between two distinct cultures. As a Chinese American, Kingston refuses to portray her identity as unified. She refuses to dismiss the complexities generated by the clash between cultures. Instead, she weaves these contradictions into her text to arrive at a more expansive, although precarious, inscription of identity.

In describing the work as "postmodern," I am suggesting that it shares certain features common to postmodern literature. For one, the text demonstrates an awareness of the "constructed" nature of meaning—an awareness that meaning is developed and produced within particular systems of representation. For instance, the narrator's mother tells her children stories to test their "strength to establish realities." Thus, realities do not exist preformed out there in the world. Instead, they must be "established" by each individual. As Patricia Lin Blinde puts it in her essay on Kingston, life as portrayed by the novel is "a complex network of fictions" ["Icicle in the Desert: Form and Perspective in the Works of Two Chinese-American Women Writers," *MELUS*, Vol. 6, No. 3, 1979].

A second feature of a postmodern text concerns its para-doxical relationship to literary convention. These works challenge the conventions even as they exploit them, and they also depend on the reader's familiarity with these conventions [Linda Hutcheon, "The Politics of Representation," *Signature,* Vol. 1, 1989]. Third, as a "memoir," *The Woman Warrior* shares yet another feature common to postmodern texts in that it foregrounds a concern regarding the ability to understand the past or, more specifically, "to know the past in the present" (Hutcheon). In blending "factual" subject matter with folktales, for example, the text presents a radical challenge to traditional assumptions regarding the process of constructing both personal and public history.

Finally, in its exploration of history, the text, like so many postmodern works, does not represent typical historical figures: the warriors and victors. Instead, it gives voice to the "story and the story-telling of the non-combatants or even the losers" (Hutcheon). In fact, all five chapters in Kingston's work portray the experience of women. The first chapter effects a reinscription of a woman so marginalized by her community that she has no name. The fourth chapter treats the fate of a woman who cannot withstand the rifts between subject positions generated in the East and West; unable to map out her identity, she goes insane. Kingston's memoirs are also populated by the mentally deranged, retarded, and grotesque—individuals whose "difference" from the norm usually precludes their appearance in history (Blinde).

Fredric Jameson, a critic who is highly skeptical of postmodern literature, might well dismally categorize *The Woman Warrior* as a typical postmodern text: a "heap of fragments" produced by a fragmented self. In many ways, it could appear as if the self, or narrator, arranging the memoirs has lost its capacity to organize its past and future into "coherent experience" ["Postmodernism, or the Cultural Logic of Late Capitalism," *New Left Review,* Vol. 146, 1984]. But what if this capacity to organize past and future—a capacity inextricably linked to the ability to generate a coherent identity—were not simply "lost" but consciously problematized by the text?

In the conclusion to his attack on postmodernism, Jameson discusses the phenomenon of mapping and links the ability to create spatial maps with the ability to map out identity. He cites Kevin Lynch's description of the alienated city as a space in which "people are unable to map (in their minds) either their own positions or the urban totality in which they find themselves." Disalienation, by contrast, involves the "practical reconquest of a sense of place, and the construction or reconstruction of an articulated ensemble which can be retained in memory and which the individual subject can map and remap along the moments of mobile, alternative trajectories." Operating, as he does, with this binary opposition of alienation and disalienation, Jameson predictably views texts that resist the call to "practical reconquests" (in this case, not of place, but of a coherent self) as poisonous signs of cultural entropy and relativism. In doing so, he fails to recognize that a postmodern text such as *The Woman Warrior* could offer another model for the mapping of "past and future."

Kingston's text can be best understood as an "interrogative text," to use Benveniste's term [Emile Benveniste, *Problems in General Linguistics,* translated by Mary Elizabeth Meek, 1971]. This text enlists the reader in contradiction, lacks a single course that contains and places all others, and refuses to offer a single point of view. Kingston's novel constitutes an alternative system for organizing experience, an activity directly related to the inscription of identity. Further, this alternative model addresses specific, feminist concerns that spring from an awareness of the contradictions inherent in the discourses that structure female identity.

According to Jacques Lacan, upon entry into language (which Lacan refers to as the symbolic order), the child becomes subject to structures of language that are marked with societal imperatives. With respect to women, Catherine Belsey points out that the two fairly standard Western discourses, liberal humanist discourse and feminist discourse, offer contradictory subject positions to women. Thus, even when a person is located within a single culture, the attempt to adopt a noncontradictory position can create "intolerable pressures" [*Critical Practice,* 1980]. Understandably, then, the contradictions and resultant fragmentation of identity are multiplied when an individual must contend with discourses emanating from not one, but two cultures, each governed by a separate language or symbolic system.

This is precisely the position in which Kingston's narrator, Maxine, finds herself. Not only must she struggle to locate herself within the diverse and contradictory discourses of the Western tradition, but she must also wrestle with the positions afforded by her Chinese heritage. If, as Benveniste argues, language provides the possibility of subjectivity by allowing the speaker to say "I," then the inscription of subjectivity is doubly problematized when there are two "I's" to choose from. As a child, the narrator is mesmerized by the English word for "I." She asks, "[H]ow could the American "I," assuredly wearing a hat like the Chinese, have only three strokes, the middle so straight?" She is startled by this articulation of selfhood, which seems so foreign: "I stared so long at that middle line and waited so long for its black center to resolve into tight strokes and dots that I forgot to pronounce it." The American word for "here" presents a similar difficulty. It lacks "a strong consonant to hang onto and so flat, when 'here' [in Chinese] is two mountainous ideographs." With no fixed position in either symbolic system, Kingston's identity remains divided and in flux. Her tongue, having been "cut," symbolizes this division, which

enables her to speak languages that are "completely different from one another." Yet the positive implications of this ability are seemingly counterbalanced by negative outcomes. Her "broken" voice, which "cracks in two," becomes a source of pain and humiliation because it prevents her from achieving a form of coherence recognizable by traditional standards.

Yet, as suggested earlier, Kingston refuses to ignore the multiple contradictions resulting from the demands of two symbolic systems. She does not map out a polarized position either in the form of a solid identity or in the form of a "solid" genre such as autobiography. In many respects, her decision to utilize traditional narrative forms to suit her aims corresponds to the feminist strategy outlined by Teresa de Lauretis. According to de Lauretis, feminists view narrative and narrativity as mechanisms to be employed "strategically and tactically in the effort to construct *other forms of coherence,* to shift the terms of representation, to produce the conditions of representability of another—and gendered—social subject" (emphasis added).

With an awareness of this feminist strategy, Kingston's rejection of traditional forms of coherence does not necessarily imply the valueless incoherence and schizophrenia posited by Jameson. In fact, *The Woman Warrior,* with its transgeneric form and fluid boundaries, where genre spills into genre, constitutes a tenuous new model for the construction of identity. In particular, the final chapter, entitled "Song for a Barbarian Reed Pipe," offers a means of reconciling different discourses based on incorporation rather than denial.

The text specifically addresses the proliferation of contradictory subject positions afforded to women, and it articulates the difficulty women have in mapping out a subject position in the face of these contradictions. In Kingston's case, these contradictions relate specifically to an author whose rural Chinese culture, combined with her American experience, affords particular subject positions for women. In a discussion of Chinese culture, Margery Wolf clarifies the well-established discourse sanctioning control over the female sex. Wolf states that the Three Obediences by which women were to be governed were common knowledge: as an unmarried girl, a woman must obey her father and her brothers; as a married woman, she must obey her husband; and, as a widow, she must obey her adult sons [Margery Wolf, *Revolution Postponed: Women in Contemporary China,* 1985].

In Kingston's book, one of the most obvious challenges to this discourse sanctioning control over women is found in the story of the Woman Warrior. Tension immediately arises as a result of the juxtaposition of the book's title, *The Woman Warrior,* and the figure presented in the first chapter, "No name woman." These two figures, the warrior and the unknown aunt, and their respective stories, generated by a single culture, reflect the antithetical subject positions available to women. On one hand, as suggested by Wolf and illustrated in the story of the no name woman, the community demands that women remain subordinate as "wives and slaves." Adherence to this discourse of submission is imperative. As the narrator explains, the rural Chinese community's notion of the real is threatened when an individual's drives, whether sexual or narrative, challenge this discourse of submission. When the aunt disobeys this discourse, "the frightened villagers, who depended on one another to maintain the real . . . show her a personal, physical representation of the break she had made in the roundness . . . The villagers punished her for acting as if she could have a private life."

To rebel against the discourse of submission constitutes an act of violence against the community: "one human being flaring up into violence could open up a black hole, a maelstrom that pulled in the sky." The mother's first words to Kingston warn her against committing just such an act of violence: "You must not tell anyone . . . what I am about to tell you." After she tells Kingston the story of the aunt, Brave Orchid repeats this warning, "Don't tell anyone you had an aunt. Your father does not want to hear her name." As a result of these admonitions, Kingston decides that "sex was unspeakable and words so strong and fathers so frail that 'aunt' would do my father mysterious harm." But the very fact that the story has been published makes it clear that the mother's injunction to silence has been broken or, more accurately, evaded. Kingston does not tell *anyone* about her aunt; she tells everyone. Aware that, in retelling her aunt's story, she may be as dangerous and controlling as those who sought to punish her ancestor through silence, Kingston subverts her authority by offering several versions of the tale. Sensing the pernicious aspect to the desire to "get things straight," she must resist the urge "to name the unspeakable."

But Kingston must break the silence. She must write in order to locate herself, to determine how the "invisible world the emigrants built around . . . [her] childhood fits in solid America." Her parents, more thoroughly Chinese, are not faced with this problem of psychic orientation. Whenever they said home, "they suspended America." Kingston must rebel if she is to make sense of her cultural heritage, the "invisible world," which informs her identity. In disobeying the community, however, she risks injuring herself because the community that she betrays is already a part of her; she has been constituted according to the community's discourse. Nowhere is this made clearer than in the section entitled "White Tigers." Here a father and mother "carve revenge" on their warrior-daughter's back. They inscribe their oaths and their names in her flesh, so that even if she were killed, the text would still be legible; people could use her dead body as a weapon.

Body, as text, records the iterable marks of a community—marks that can be used by others. In this portrait of body-as-text, Kingston not only self-consciously foregrounds her activity as a storyteller/writer producing a text that has an independent existence from her but also indicates that her own identity and sense of place have been inscribed by her community: "[T]hey had carved their names and address on me, and I would come back." Thus, when she breaks her silence to take revenge by "reporting," she takes vengeance against herself and the people she loves. In her nightmares, she becomes a vampire: "[T]ears dripped from my eyes, but blood dripped from my fangs, blood of the people I was supposed to love." The tensions generated by her self-division—her awareness of the discourse that demands submission combined with her need to retell the stories in order to understand herself—suffuse the stories she narrates. Even the idealistic portrait of the woman warrior, which challenges the traditional role of female subservience, still includes traces of the discourse that designates women as inferior.

The story of the woman warrior, in contrast to the story of the no name aunt, emphasizes that women "failed if they grew up to be but wives or slaves" because they could be "heroines, swordswomen." The folktale celebrates women's power and their ability to perform heroic deeds on behalf of the community. In telling the story, Kingston inscribes herself into Fa Mu Lan's tale, just as she actively entered into the story of her aunt because, as she says, "unless I see her life branching into mine, she gives me no ancestral help." As a warrior, she trains body and mind, finally learning dragon ways—how to infer the whole from the parts, how to make her mind large, "as the universe is large, so that there is room for paradoxes." Her female body, rather than seen as a hindrance, becomes an advantage in battle against larger, clumsier males. Bodily functions, including menstruation, become acceptable. Even the capacity to reproduce is celebrated. Kingston recognizes that, in giving birth, women write history through their bodies. As she says, women who engaged in sex "hazarded birth and hence lifetimes." Therefore, in the depiction of Fa Mu Lan as a mother, the story portrays an integral part of the historical process as experienced by women.

While the discourse that celebrates the female remains dominant, elements of the opposing discourse are evident throughout; the text does not efface contradictions. Admitting that she hid her identity from her army, the narrator explains that the "Chinese executed women who disguised themselves as soldiers or students." The evil Baron voices misogynist sayings: girls are "maggots in the rice. It is more profitable to raise geese than daughters." When she returns home, the warrior woman tells her husband that now that her public duties are finished, she can stay with him doing farmwork and housework and giving him "more sons." Essentially, she conforms to the role of wife and slave. In general, as the story of the warrior nears its conclusion, the intrusions of the opposing discourse become more frequent, until finally, the folktale collapses under its weight.

At this point, the sayings previously cast into the mouth of the evil Baron are recontextualized. The enemy is revealed to be her father and mother and other emigrant villagers. No longer a heroine, the narrator sees herself at the mercy of a symbolic system that renders her subservient: "[T]here is a Chinese word for the female 'I'—which is 'slave.' Break the women with their own tongues!" Despite the power of the discourse advocating subservience, the story of the woman warrior is never completely repressed. In fact, it resurfaces in the second chapter, entitled "Shaman," which describes her mother's training and experience as a doctor.

Like the mythic warrior, Kingston's mother is afforded a respite from slavery. Brave Orchid lives for two years "without servitude." After completing her training, she returns home as triumphant as any female avenger. Like the female warrior, she, too, is familiar with "dragon ways." Brave Orchid is also victorious in battle. While the woman warrior of the folktale struggles against evil Barons, Kingston's mother contends against "ghosts." Ultimately, Kingston reveals that this ability to do battle with ghosts is a skill that is necessary for the development of a sense of identity.

In the novel, ghosts (as well as barbarians) occupy the shifting territory outside the borders of "reality," as designated by the Chinese. Yet the supernatural continually encroaches upon daily existence. For instance, the baby of the no name aunt is called a "little ghost." When Brave Orchid's sister, Moon Orchid, confronts her Americanized husband, they are both unreal and insubstantial to each other: "[H]er husband looked like one of the ghosts passing the car windows, and she must look like a ghost from China." The land of ghosts, America is filled with specters—Taxi Ghosts, Bus Ghosts, Police Ghosts. As Kingston says, "[O]nce upon a time the world was so thick with ghosts, I could hardly breathe, I could hardly walk, limping my way around the White Ghosts and their cars."

Brave Orchid's ability to overcome ghosts resides in her capacity to *incorporate* the supernatural: "[M]y mother could contend against the hairy beasts whether flesh or ghost because she could eat them." This ability to incorporate what lies outside the subject—the not-I—is linked to her strong sense of identity. During an encounter with the Sitting Ghost, Brave Orchid boasts, "I do not give in. . . . You have no power over a strong woman." Unlike her daughter, Brave Orchid is not caught between two symbolic systems; there-

fore, she identifies herself more solidly as Chinese, as one of the Han. Even when she emigrates, she is not divided. She kept her Chinese name, "adding no American nor holding one in reserve for American emergencies."

Although Brave Orchid's identity appears stable, Kingston is at pains to show that identity is never a solid construct. Even Brave Orchid's spirit is divided, sometimes wandering in the past with her dead children in China and her husband in America, sometimes keeping her sister's plane aloft and her son's boat in Vietnam afloat. The fragility of identity is constantly brought to the reader's attention. Moreover, the necessity of mapping out identity is revealed to be a crucial process.

After her encounter with the Sitting Ghost, Brave Orchid's classmates must help her spirit locate the To Keung School as "home" by reciting its geographic location. Here the mapping of identity involves both geographic and ancestral trajectories. Brave Orchid also gives a map of China to her children—she "funneled China into our ears: Kwangtung Province, New Society Village, the river Kwoo . . . 'Go the way we came so that you will be able to find our house.'" The narrator recalls how her mother led her children "out of nightmares and horror movies" by singing her name along with the names of her mother, father, brothers, and sisters. However, as barbarians born in America, the children have difficulty understanding how to use these maps to construct personal identities.

The dangers associated with an inability to orient oneself, to map out one's identity in the presence of the not-I, are dramatically illustrated in the story of Moon Orchid. Brave Orchid paid for her sister's fare, enabling Moon Orchid to leave China and come to America. But Moon Orchid, finding herself forcefully uprooted, can make little sense of the barbarians among whom she finds herself. Her nieces and nephews appear to her as "wild animals," and while she assumes that they must have "many interesting savage things to say, raised as they'd been in the wilderness," she cannot comprehend them. The encounter with her estranged husband reinforces the fact that she does not belong in America. He tells her, "You can't belong. You don't have the hardness for this country." Hardness, or solidity, is associated with America (Kingston refers to "solid America"). Solidity is a trait that Moon Orchid lacks. Shortly after the encounter with her ghost-husband, Moon Orchid gives up trying to understand the American barbarians and retreats into madness.

The story of Moon Orchid's failed attempt to leave China and live in the West illustrates Jameson's point regarding the connection between the ability to make a cognitive map of a city and the ability to map one's identity. Brave Orchid realizes that in "whisking her sister across the ocean by jet" and making her "scurry up and down the Pacific coast," Moon Orchid had misplaced herself. Her "spirit (her 'attention' Brave Orchid called it) scattered all over the world." In trying to help her sister locate herself and regain her identity, Brave Orchid chants her sister's new address to her. She tries, to no avail, to help Moon Orchid create a map that would "anchor [her] . . . to this earth."

In effect, Moon Orchid's madness represents one way of dealing with multiple discourses. Rather than effect a more positive exchange with the not-I, in this case, Western culture, Moon Orchid rejects it altogether. As a result, her discourse ceases to include variety. As Brave Orchid explains, "[M]ad people have only one story that they talk over and over." At the asylum, Moon Orchid is content because difference has been abolished: "no one ever leaves . . . we are all women here." She delights in the narcissistic belief that the world is one and that everyone understands each other: "[W]e speak the same language, the very same. They understand me, and I understand them." Her madness reflects a primary desire for nondifferentiation. This extreme form of narcissism involves the "impossible, imaginary attempt to totally integrate the self" [Dominick LaCapra, *History and Criticism*, 1985]. Within the novel, Moon Orchid's fate functions as a warning, illustrating that attempts at denying the existence of contradictory discourses and self-division are dangerous. As Suzanne Juhasz states, the association of women with madness in Kingston's text is shown as "the alternative to their achievement of self-identity" ["Maxine Hong Kingston's Narrative Technique," *Contemporary American Women Writers: Narrative Strategies,* edited by Catherine Rainwater and William J. Scheick, 1985].

Throughout the text, polarized and reductionist stances of any kind are revealed to be unsatisfactory methods for grappling with the presence of contradictions. The narrator takes up such a position when she tortures her weak, silent schoolmate. Determined to fit into solid America, Kingston rejects her Chinese self and projects it onto the "soft" Chinese girl who refuses to speak. Kingston divides herself, viewing with contempt the bonelessness and liquidity of her victim, who seems to be all tears and snot. But Kingston's binary stance ultimately collapses when she finds herself "crying and sniffling," behaving exactly like the girl she despises. A similar attempt to eradicate difference occurs when Kingston determines to confess her "secret list" to her mother. Her motive stems from a narcissistic desire similar to Moon Orchid's desire for sameness. As Kingston says, "[I]f only I could let my mother know the list, she—and the world—would become more like me, and I would never be alone again." But Kingston can never regress to this state of original oneness.

In the story of the poet Ts'ai Yen, an alternative model is offered for the construction of identity. This model affords

a more positive engagement with what lies beyond the world designated by a particular symbolic system—an engagement that does not eradicate discontinuity and separateness. Kingston first alludes to this model in the preamble to the story of her grandmother who loved opera. In introducing the tale, the narrator recalls that the story was told to her recently by her mother: "[T]he beginning is hers, the ending, mine." This model of assimilation and incorporation has, in fact, been operative throughout the novel. The stories Kingston overheard as a child have all been translated, elaborated on, and finally passed on to the reader.

As indicated before, the most powerful articulation of this model of incorporation is conveyed through the final story of Ts'ai Yen. According to the story, the poet, who lived in the first century, is captured by barbarians. Carried far from home, she lives among the barbarians in the desert for twelve years and bears the chieftain two sons. Her sons do not speak her language, and they mock her. One night, she hears the barbarian's music. Until this time, she had thought that the death whistles that emanated from their arrows were the only music they were capable of producing. While playing their flutes, the barbarians strive to produce a high note beyond the range of possibility—an icicle in the desert. After hearing this music, Ts'ai Yen retires to her tent and begins to sing a song "so high and clear, it matched the flutes." Her words "seemed to be Chinese but the barbarians understood their sadness and anger . . . Her children did not laugh, but eventually sang along." Later, when she is rescued and reunited with her people, Ts'ai Yen brings her songs back from the savage lands: "'Eighteen stanzas for a Barbarian Reed Pipe' . . . It translated well."

The poet's position as exile among barbarians is analogous to Kingston's position as Chinese American. Kingston, like Ts'ai Yen, is dislocated and must struggle to make sense of contradictory discourses if she is to comprehend her identity. Ts'ai Yen's ability to incorporate the music of the barbarians corresponds to Kingston's ability as "outlaw knotmaker." Her power to weave together the contradictory elements of Chinese and American discourses represents a more positive engagement with the not-I—an engagement where the not-I, far from being excluded and repressed, is able to recognize itself. The high note captured in the poet's voice can be likened to the stories Kingston narrates—stories begun by her Chinese mother and concluded by the American daughter. These hybrid narratives enable Kingston to represent her identity. Yet the structure of the narratives implies a more fragile "form of coherence," an unstable form with the tenuous existence of an icicle in the desert.

Ultimately, Kingston's text, with its depiction of the narrator's unstable subject position, offers an alternative model for portraying female identity—one that resists organizing "past, present, and future into coherent experience," to use Jameson's words. As I have illustrated, rather than dismiss the complexities generated by her dual heritage, Kingston foregrounds these difficulties and allows them to inform the design of the work as a whole. She does not take up a polarized position in an attempt to "name the unspeakable." Instead, Kingston reconceptualizes the traditional form of the novel to create a postmodern text—a transformation that lends support to Virginia Woolf's claim that women writers must abandon traditional literary forms if they hope to inscribe their own conceptions of female identity in literature.

Sheryl A. Mylan (essay date 1996)

SOURCE: "The Mother as Other: Orientalism in M. Hong Kingston's *The Woman Warrior*," in *Women of Color: Mother-Daughter Relationships in 20th-Century Literature*, edited by Elizabeth Brown-Guillory, University of Texas Press, 1996, pp. 132-52.

[*In the following essay, Mylan examines what she terms as elements of Orientalism in Kingston's portrayal of her mother in* The Woman Warrior.]

In the time since Edward Said's *Orientalism* was first published in 1978, the investigation of Western society's attempts to contain and represent non-Western cultures has become even more important. Postcolonialist studies have increased attention to the imperialist and ethnocentric spirit which underlies the discourse of so-called advanced societies. Since such discourses mask their ideological intentions to dominate, it is essential that they be interrogated to see the ways in which non-Western societies are cast into the role of Other. Denigrating non-Western belief systems, the West sets up its own values and standards as right and natural, which justifies its will to power. Long before Said, anthropologist Francis Hsu speculated about why Western society was governed by its need to dominate: "Can Americans afford to allow any other people, especially a non-Western people, to better them in any way? My conclusion is that they probably cannot because active superiority over others is essential to a people with the individual-centered way of life" [*Americans and Chinese,* 1970]. The Western sense of individuality is bound up with the need to vanquish. It is odd to think that someone who has suffered the misrepresentations of monoculturalism might regard her own heritage from such an interpretive position. In a sense, however, that is what happens between the Westernized daughter, Maxine, and her Chinese mother in *The Woman Warrior.*

Just as Britain, France, and the United States represented non-Western cultures in ways to assert their cultural hegemony, Maxine portrays her mother in a way to gain strength over her. Although Edward Said's *Orientalism* focuses on the Anglo-Franco experience with Arabs and Islam, it discusses characteristics of Orientalism which work well to describe Maxine's view of her mother, who represents all that is baffling and repugnant about Chinese culture to her daughter. Said states that "Orientalism was the distillation of essential ideas about the Orient—its sensuality, its tendency to despotism, its aberrant mentality, its habits of inaccuracy, its backwardness." He is interested in Orientalism as a school of interpretation in which the culture, its history, and textuality intersect and by which non-Western cultures are studied and judged. As such, these large cultural issues may seem to bear little relation to the personal struggles of a daughter and her mother. However, if the personal and public are inseparable and if all acts are political and public expressions, then Orientalism can be seen in everyday struggles as well as in global contexts. Then it no longer will seem so odd to accuse the heroine, Maxine, of such a Western monocultural perspective. Out of ignorance and misunderstanding of her mother's life in China, Maxine constructs a framework by which to judge her; her standards for judging her mother are, if not manifest Orientalism, at least latent or unconscious demonstrations of Orientalism.

To admit the possibility that Maxine sees her mother and the Chinese culture she represents as the Other helps to explain the negative responses *The Woman Warrior* received from Asian American critics like Katheryn Fong, Benjamin Tong, and Frank Chin. It also reflects the continuing concern in the Asian American community about who has the right to represent their experiences. Complaining about the fakery of the text and its complicity in a racist, imperialist enterprise in "This Is Not an Autobiography," Chin argues for the authentic representation of Chinese culture [*Genre,* Vol. 18, No. 2, 1985]. Tong agrees with Chin that Hong Kingston sold out with her exotic stereotypes, created to please a white audience ["Critic of Admirer Sees Dumb Racist," *San Francisco Journal,* May 11, 1977]. Certainly such critics are right in decrying the misrepresentations and caricatures of the Chinese as a superstitious, enigmatic, and devious people; these stereotypes have a lengthy history in American writing, not only in the popular press, but even among respected writers such as Bret Harte, Jack London, and John Steinbeck [Elaine Kim, *Asian American Literature: An Introduction to the Writings and Their Social Contexts,* 1982]. However, Hong Kingston never intended *The Woman Warrior* to be a documentary portrayal of Chinese culture and insists that it is "an American book"; she also states that her own "American-ness" has often been ignored and misinterpreted [**"Cultural Mis-readings by American Reviewers,"** *Asian and Western Writers in Dialogue: New Cultural Identities,* edited by Guy Amirthanayagam, 1982]. While some Western writers have represented Asian cultures as Other to dominate and appropriate, it is a mistake to view Hong Kingston primarily as a Chinese writer who willfully misrepresents and betrays her cultural legacy.

In part, this problem of the Asian-Americanness of *The Woman Warrior* stems from reading the text as Western autobiography, with its demands for factual accuracy. It is not merely that the West, unlike more communally based cultures, has different concepts of individuation, the self, and the individual's relation to the community, as Margaret Miller has demonstrated in "Threads of Identity in Maxine Hong Kingston's *The Woman Warrior*" [*Biography,* Vol. 6, No. 1, 1983]. Miller's points about autobiography are important, but it is also important not to overlook the fact that Hong Kingston planned to publish the work as a novel—which, in itself, counters classical Chinese literary tradition and its devaluation of fiction. However, she was convinced by her publishers to market the text as an autobiography, which has obviously led some readers to confuse the main character with the writer. The result of this confusion is that instead of seeing that Maxine behaves like a Eurocentric American who exoticizes Asian culture as a means of containing the threat of its power, some critics equate Hong Kingston with Maxine the daughter. Such an equation easily leads to the charges of inauthenticity and cultural betrayal against which Hong Kingston has protested. She is trying to capture the truth of her own psyche, to the extent that this is ever possible, not the documentary truth of Chinese culture. If Hong Kingston is allowed her rights as an author, though, and Maxine is read as a fictional construct, then the monoculturalism she exhibits is less a willful rejection of Chinese heritage than an unconscious way of subduing her mother's power over her.

Besides the charge of cultural distortion, another problem results from equating Maxine's monoculturalism with Hong Kingston's presentation of it. This is the complication of the mother-daughter relationship which arises because Maxine, the fictional character, is the autobiographer in Hong Kingston's "autobiography." Lynn Z. Bloom analyzes the dynamics of such relationships in women's autobiographies, noting that the autobiographer/daughter figuratively becomes her own mother as well as the "recreator of her maternal parent and the controlling adult in their literary relationship. . . . This may be an unfamiliar position for the daughter; it is certainly a reversal of the power and dominance" that has plagued her during the formation of her identity as a young woman. Maxine as autobiographer has a vested interest in presenting her mother in such a way that her power is diminished. No undistorted presentation is ever truly possible, despite the desires for cultural accuracy; writers are always re-presenting. It must be noted that Maxine is a writer, representing her mother and her stories. Orientalizing her mother and Chinese culture is one such way for Maxine to create her own self. Although it is cer-

tainly true that all people struggle to create a separate identity from their parents, as Nancy Chodorow has demonstrated, it is more difficult for girls since they identify with their mothers longer than boys do.

Making the break is even more complicated for young women whose cultural legacies are in sharp conflict. Amy Ling notes that "a minority individual's sense of alienation results not only from rejection by the dominant culture but also rejection of parental strictures" [*Between Worlds: Women Writers of Chinese Ancestry,* 1990]. Because of Maxine's need for personal autonomy, she aligns herself with Western culture, even though the West will always stigmatize her on the basis of race. It certainly seems strange that Maxine, in effect, takes up with the enemy and rebels against her mother, the one who tries to provide examples of strong Chinese women. It would seem more reasonable for Maxine to rebel against the patriarchal, patrilineal, and patrilocal Chinese culture—still alive in her Asian American community—which devalues women. After all, the important kinship relations, *liu ch'in,* all involve men—relationships between fathers and sons, between brothers, and between the brothers' children, their grandchildren, and their great-grandchildren [C. K. Yang, *The Chinese Family in the Community Revolution,* 1958]. She should also take aim at the Confucian doctrines which oppress women, such as the three obediences—a woman's obedience to her father, then to her husband, and finally to her sons when she is widowed—and the four virtues—woman's ethics, teaching a woman her place, woman's speech, telling her to speak little, woman's appearance, telling her to please her husband, and woman's chores, teaching her to do her housework [Henry Staid Shih-Shan, *The Chinese Experience in America,* 1986]. But instead, Maxine makes her mother the target. She sees her as Other to carve out some psychic space for herself, both as a young Chinese American woman and as an artist.

To distance herself from her mother and her Chinese ways, Maxine must come to terms with sexuality, an excess of which, as Said demonstrates, has long been ascribed to non-Western cultures. In the first story, "No Name Woman," Maxine is a young woman on the verge of her own sexual awakening. She may be inexperienced and unknowledgeable about sex, but she is very curious and imaginative. Her mother tries to give her some advice by telling Maxine her aunt's story. Maxine, however, rejects the lesson—or, rather, she recasts it into her own version of Chinese sensuality. It is important to remember that this is an orientalized version of uncontrolled passion since romantic love is a Western concept, which even required the "linguistic creation of the term lien ai" (Hsu).

Brave Orchid's version for Maxine is the simple account of her aunt's adultery and the murder of her newborn baby, whom she held when she leapt into the well to her death. She tells her daughter this story of suicide and murder as a cautionary tale to prevent Maxine from disgracing the family. Although widows' suicide among the gentry brought honor, especially for a childless woman who would no longer be of any value to her husband's family and whose only other option would be a second marriage to a man of lower status, such was not the case here. No-name aunt was from the country, and, as Margery Wolf notes, "among peasant women the act is not exotic" ["Women and Suicide in China," *Women in Chinese Society,* 1975]. It brought only horror, disgrace, and a warning that redounds on her niece fifty years later and in a different culture. The fact that Brave Orchid's warnings are so dire is some indication of the power of sexuality, once unleashed. Brave Orchid, whom Maxine sees as motivated by necessity, rather than as driven by passion, constantly presents a culture in which sexuality is a danger to be guarded against.

Maxine says she has difficulty imagining her aunt being sexually uninhibited, yet she immediately imagines her aunt at her dressing table, trying to arrange her hair in "heart-catching tangles" to attract her lover's gaze. Maxine embellishes her mother's simple tale, perhaps imagining her aunt as more wild and sexually unrestrained than she was. Whether or not the picture is accurate is irrelevant. Accuracy and knowledge of a culture count for nothing in Orientalism, which makes it particularly pernicious. The Other culture is appropriated—restructured and re-presented to fit the so-called advanced culture's need for superiority and domination. So, even though Maxine views her aunt as a kindred spirit—passionate and rebellious—when she recasts her story, sexualizing it more than her mother does, she is commenting pejoratively both on Chinese culture and on her mother.

In "White Tigers," Maxine sexualizes the ancient story of Fa Mu Lan as another effort to distance herself from her mother. The story of Fa Mu Lan or Lady Mulan has constantly been retold in genres as different as the ballad and the opera; it appears during the seventh to ninth centuries of the Tang dynasty with its great flowering of literature and art, during the fourteenth to seventeenth centuries of the last such ruling family, the Ming dynasty, and during the modern period. Various versions exist, with different characters and events. One of the biggest changes in this version—the lengthy apprentice-training in martial arts, deriving from *wuxia xiaoshuo,* the martial arts novel—emphasizes woman's power; the most important change, though, is the new combination of mother and soldier here, because it bespeaks Maxine's fascination with power and motherhood. Attitudes toward menstruation and childbirth, in particular, are a crucial part of the story for Maxine. When Fa Mu Lan begins to menstruate, the advice she receives from her surrogate mother is quite different from the warning Maxine

received from her own mother when she learned the story of her no-name aunt. Instead of using the occasion to tell Fa Mu Lan not to disgrace her family by getting pregnant, her surrogate mother merely asks her to delay having children so that she can fulfill her role as warrior. She tells her not to worry about the blood, but to let it flow.

In many of the traditional versions of the story, Fa Mu Lan reveals to her fellow warriors only in the final moments that she is a woman. In the version Maxine relates, soldiers agree to fight alongside Fa Mu Lan, even after they learn that she is a woman. Though she is dressed as a man and wearing armor, the crowds cheer her on as a beautiful woman. The detail devoted to her pregnancy and the first month of her son's life further sexualizes the story. Note, for instance, how Fa Mu Lan regards her pregnant shape: "Now when I was naked, I was a strange human being indeed—words carved on my back and the baby large in front." When the baby is born, Fa Mu Lan and her husband discuss what they should do with the umbilical cord, deciding to tie it to a flagpole to dry so they can save it in a box, just as their parents had done with their children's.

Fa Mu Lan's story is not only so fantastic that Maxine cannot use it as a model for her own development, but also so eroticized that she can dismiss her mother and her Chinese culture along with the story. She dismisses it so thoroughly, in fact, that it remains forgotten until long into her adulthood, although mother and daughter had chanted it together as they worked around the house. Brave Orchid had told Maxine the story of Fa Mu Lan—a name which is translated Sylvan or Wood Orchid, emphasizing their sisterhood—to help her daughter grow up as a powerful woman, despite her fears that Maxine wouldn't be able to avoid becoming a wife and a slave. Her fears about slavery are realized when Maxine is too weak to resist the racism of her boss, when he tells her to order "nigger yellow" paint and to book a banquet hall being picketed by CORE and the NAACP.

Maxine's inability to combat racism stems, in part, from orientalizing her Chinese culture, which leaves her with no inner resources upon which to draw. It is little wonder then that she whispers her protest to her boss, her "voice unreliable." By regarding her Chinese heritage as Other, she has effectively silenced her own voice. In telling Maxine the story of Fa Mu Lan, Brave Orchid was trying to give her daughter a precious gift to inspire and strengthen her. In trying to find strength apart from her mother, Maxine rejected this story as inapplicable to the racist power struggles of the twentieth century. As a young woman trying to form her own identity, she finds that the story of Fa Mu Lan simply does not translate well, unlike the story of Ts'ai Yen—the second-century poet, scholar, and musician held captive for twelve years—whose songs of both barbarian and Chinese culture "translated well." Before Maxine gets to the point where she can appreciate how two cultures—or two very different people—can meet in a spirit of mutual appreciation, she has to come to terms with her own needs to orientalize her Chinese heritage.

One of the needs Orientalism fulfills is the need for dominance. Power is gained by seeing the non-Western culture as weak and female, for implicit in Orientalism, Said notes, is a male "power-fantasy." Through her interest in a woman warrior such as Fa Mu Lan, Maxine shows her desire for power. But by re-presenting a powerful and more sexualized Fa Mu Lan who, at the end of the story, nevertheless returns to her village, gives her son her helmet and swords, kneels before her in-laws, and assumes her duties as housewife and the bearer of more sons, Maxine thwarts her acquisition of genuine power. Brave Orchid was once a scholar and doctor, but now lines up with transients, alcoholics, and drug addicts for part-time farm work in addition to working long hours in the laundry. Looking at her mother as an example as well as the stories she tells, it is little wonder then that Maxine is conflicted about her real possibilities for power. She wants nothing so much as to get away from the chief reminder of what a Chinese woman is—her mother.

One way that this conflict is manifested is Maxine's desire to be like a boy. Constantly aware of the privileges of manhood, she rebels against traditional female tasks. She won't cook for her family, and she breaks dishes when she is forced to wash them. Her mother's reprimands for this behavior please Maxine; after all, "Isn't a bad girl almost a boy?" She questions why there are elaborate month-long celebrations for the birth of a boy and none for the birth of a girl. When Maxine and her sisters visit their three cousins, the girls' great-grandfather screams at all six of them, calling them maggots and reproaching them for not giving him grandsons, but Maxine, who wants the privileges accorded to men, is nevertheless quick to condemn such patriarchal views. When her cousins explain that their great-grandfather behaves that way at every meal, Maxine and her sisters console them by saying, "Our old man hates us too. What assholes." When she grows up and attends Berkeley, she refuses to be passive and marches for political causes, but still, "I did not turn into a boy." Although as an adult Maxine continues to long for the independence which she associates with being male, her disgust with someone calling girls "maggots" shows her appreciation for female worth. Her readings in anthropology teach her that the Chinese believe that "'girls are necessary too,'" although she says that no Chinese she ever met conceded this point. But still she is willing to allow that "perhaps it was a saying in another village." This growing acceptance of her own femaleness and her admittance of the possibility that not all Chinese disregard women reflect her movement away from

Orientalism, which sees non-Western culture as sensual, feminine, and weak.

It is interesting, though, that Maxine usually associates China with femaleness and dependency since her mother, who represents everything Chinese that she wants to flee, is so strong. In some ways, Maxine views her mother as despotic—another characteristic of Orientalism. Perhaps the incident which best reflects the tyrannical power Maxine invests her with is the cutting of her daughter's frenum. With the understandably characteristic ambivalence of an Asian person who orientalizes her culture, she says, "Sometimes I felt very proud that my mother committed such a powerful act upon me. At other times I was terrified—the first thing my mother did when she saw me was to cut my tongue."

Perhaps this mutilation subconsciously reminds Maxine of the mutilation most associated with the Chinese— footbinding, a practice introduced during the Five Dynasties period of the tenth century among court dancers [Ono Kazuko, *Chinese Women in a Century of Revolution 1850- 1950*, edited by Joshua A. Fogel, 1989]. Men praised the "golden lotus," finding it erotic to see women sway like willows. And so, for a thousand years, breaking the arches and bending the foot so that it would curve into a three-inch bow was a sign of gentility, soon imitated by all but lower-class villagers who had to work. By the late nineteenth century, intellectuals saw it as an "out-moded vestige of the past which crippled half the population and caused loss of 'international face'"; Natural Foot Societies started springing up in the early twentieth century [Elisabeth Croll, *Feminism and Socialism in China*, 1978]. Still, footbinding is an image that resonates in Maxine's mind: "Even now China wraps double binds around my feet." Like footbinding, the mutilation that Brave Orchid inflicts on Maxine suggests that her mother wants to help break her power—to destroy her voice. Just as footbinding suggests contradictory images of women, the cutting of her frenum causes Maxine to feel ambivalent. Kay Ann Johnson notes that in Chinese culture "while women were seen as naturally weak and submissive, they were also often portrayed as dangerously powerful" [*Women, the Family and Peasant Revolution in China*, 1983]. So the image of binding and the actual cutting of her frenum coalesce in Maxine's mind, making her feel that her mother is trying to weaken her, despite her reasonable explanations.

Maxine is unable to accept Brave Orchid's reasons for cutting her frenum. She tells her daughter that she cut it so that she would not be tongue-tied and so that her tongue would be able to move in any language. Despite this explanation, Maxine repeatedly asks her mother to explain her motives and questions why she didn't cut her brothers' and sisters' tongues. Maxine believes her mother is lying to her; in fact, any explanation Brave Orchid gives her daughter is immediately suspect: "If my mother was not lying she should have cut more, scraped away the rest of the frenum skin, because I have a terrible time talking. Or she should not have cut at all, tampering with my speech." Although Maxine often accuses her mother of being irrational and finds her actions incomprehensible, she is the one who is behaving irrationally in rejecting her mother's explanations. Instead of believing that her mother is acting on her behalf, Maxine attributes her difficulty speaking to her mother's mutilation of her tongue, an action which she can only read as willfully cruel.

This cruelty could have only one objective, according to Maxine—to dominate and silence her. As proof, she recalls her early years when she found it almost unbearable to speak. She thinks about how, even as an adult, her voice cracks and she feels dumb when she speaks But her youth was the worst: she was silent at school for a year; for three years both she and her sister were completely silent, Maxine's only expression being her totally black paintings. She associates this domination with Chinese culture, observing that the other Chinese girls were also silent, so she knew the silence had to do with being a Chinese girl. Maxine struggles with English at school, where she speaks it for the first time. When she recites in class, her voice sounds splintered. But it is not merely that English is a new language for her. One of her classmates whispers, "You can't entrust your voice to the Chinese, either; they want to capture your voice for their own use. They want to fix up your tongue to speak for them." Despite her mother's statement that she wants her daughter to communicate freely, Maxine is silenced both in English and in Chinese.

Because Maxine cannot overpower her mother, she dominates one of the girls in school. She torments a girl who cannot even speak up in her Chinese school, perhaps because in the girl's timidity Maxine sees an image of her own powerlessness. By torturing another Chinese American girl, Maxine reveals her own self-contempt. Frank Chin and Jeffrey Chan note that such "self-contempt is nothing more than the subject's acceptance of white standards of objectivity, beauty, behavior, and achievement as being morally absolute, and his acknowledgment of the fact that because he is not white, he can never fully measure up to white standards" ["Racist Love," *Seeing Through Shuck,* edited by Richard Kostelanetz, 1972]. So Maxine—barely able to communicate herself—pinches the girl, squeezes her face, pulls her hair, and demands that she talk. Maxine tells her to say her name, to call for her sister, to ask Maxine to leave her alone, to say anything—even "a" or "the"—and she promises she will relent. But the girl can only sob and make choking noises. Finally, in language that partially echoes her mother's admonition to Maxine when she tells the story of her aunt, she tells the girl that she is doing this for her own

good and that she must never tell anyone she has been bad to her. She badgers the girl to talk. But the girl never really does talk; even as an adult, she remains sequestered in her family's home. The prospect of being silent and closed up—one of the crazy women that Maxine imagines every Chinese house has—increases her desire for independence from the oppressive Chinese culture her mother represents.

Unless she breaks away, Maxine knows she will go crazy. This prospect terrifies her because she has seen craziness up close in her aunt, Moon Orchid, as well as in the mad Chinese women in her neighborhood. Like the moon, her aunt is a reflective surface, but what she reflects are the traditional Chinese beliefs about women and their relations to their families, which Maxine finds so repellent. When Moon Orchid comes to the United States to reclaim her husband, Maxine sees a cultural clash which convinces her more than ever that China is the Other. At her sister Brave Orchid's prodding, Moon Orchid begins her quest. Her husband abandoned her and her daughter thirty years ago. Now, however, Brave Orchid persuades her that she can once again enjoy her status as first wife, although her prosperous physician-husband is married to a Westernized nurse and has a son. The plans, so incomprehensible from a Western point of view, but so reasonable to Brave Orchid, leave Moon Orchid humiliated. She begins her descent into madness. Soon she has paranoid fantasies; she thinks that Mexicans are plotting to kill her, so she stays in the house, with the windows and drapes closed and the lights off. When she refuses to let anyone else leave for fear they will turn into ashes, Moon Orchid is finally institutionalized. The plight of her aunt is not lost on Maxine. To be Chinese is to go mad; it is to be trapped in an alien, irrational world. Not surprisingly, Maxine notes that all of Brave Orchid's children decided to major in science or mathematics.

Maxine values the orderly, rational world represented by science since, through the lens of Orientalism, she sees nothing but irrationality in Chinese culture. A prime example is Brave Orchid as shaman. The song of her experiences at the To Keung School of Midwifery should serve as an example to Maxine of an independent woman with her own career. Certainly she is a model to the group of students who are like daughters to her as well as to her colleagues and friends. Instead, her experiences set her further apart from her daughter. Of all the incidents that surely happened at the medical school, the ones Maxine focuses on are all supernatural, like Brave Orchid's exorcism of a ghost. Dared by the other students, Brave Orchid sleeps in a haunted room where she battles a sitting ghost: "She grabbed clutches of fur and pulled. She pinched the skin the hair grew out of and gouged into it with her fingernails. She forced her hands to hunt out eyes, furtive somewhere in the hair, but could not find any. She lifted her head to bite but fell back exhausted."

Although a knife is just beyond her reach, Brave Orchid defeats the ghost not through physical violence but through words. She speaks to the ghost throughout the night, insisting that it has no power over a strong woman. When the students gather around her the next morning to find out what happened, her story becomes even more strange and wonderful. She tells them that she was gone twelve years in all, during ten of which she was lost. She says that she walked back to the To Keung School from the Gobi Desert and that once she died Had she not willed the monster to shrink, it would have fed on both her and the others. Finally she says that it waits to feed on them unless they attack it first. After they burn it out, one of the students finds a piece of wood covered with blood.

After retelling this story of her mother's medical training, Maxine says, "She had gone away ordinary and come back miraculous, like the ancient magicians who came down from the mountains." Once she becomes Doctor Brave Orchid, her experiences are hardly the sort that would make her a credible scientist in the West. When she goes to work in the villages, she sees ghosts falling out of trees and coming out of cervixes because "medical science does not seal the earth, whose nether creatures seep out, hair by hair, disguised like the smoke that dispels them." One night she encounters an ape-man which has escaped; she is undaunted, though, telling it to go home. Supernatural events like these do not trouble her because she "was midwife to whatever spewed forth . . . sometimes babies, sometimes monsters."

Most irrational of all is the fact that Brave Orchid refuses to treat people who are dying. This, however, only improves her reputation and increases the number of her patients. She will not deal with the dying because she insists on bringing only health from house to house. The last picture of Brave Orchid as doctor is her turning her back on a woman who has been stoned by her villagers. Fearful of strafing by Japanese airplanes in 1939, they are alarmed by the village crazy lady, who has put on a head-dress with small mirrors. As she dances, the light glints off these mirrors, which the villagers fear are signaling the planes. They stone her to death while Brave Orchid turns and walks to the mountains. Neither these experiences nor her medical expertise would be valued, much less comprehensible, in the West.

In fact, in the United States Brave Orchid's medical skills completely fail. It is not merely that her Chinese diploma is not recognized: she cannot even help her family. She tells Maxine that her diet is too yin, which is causing her to catch colds so frequently. In fact, she mistakenly thinks one of Maxine's cold pills is LSD but takes it anyway. Maxine tells her mother it is a simple over-the-counter cold tablet and also reprimands her for taking pills that are lying around. It is curious that a medically trained person would need to be told such things, but she does. Brave Orchid's medical expertise obviously does not translate well into the West-

ern world that Maxine knows and accepts as right and normal So, although Brave Orchid's knowledge and professional accomplishments should connect mother and daughter, they do not. Because the experiences are so alien to Maxine's cultural perspective, they make the chasm between mother and daughter even greater.

Not only are Brave Orchid's experiences in medical school and as a doctor alien, but so is her behavior in ordinary life, which Maxine finds baffling. When a delivery boy from the drug store mistakenly brings some pills to the Hong household, Brave Orchid is enraged and swears vengeance. She forces Maxine to go to the store and demand that they stop the curse. She feels their house has been tainted by the medicine and can only be remedied by free candy. Maxine recognizes that the druggist will no doubt think she is begging. But since her mother will not be dissuaded, she tells the druggist, "'My mother said you have to give us candy. She said that is the way the Chinese do it.'" Interestingly, she does not say, "That is the way we do it." She separates herself from what she sees as her mother's bizarre ideas and behavior. When the druggist presses her further—"'Do what?'" he asks—she responds, "'Do things.' I felt the weight and immensity of things impossible to explain to the druggist." After that discussion, he does give the family candy, but it is leftover candy from holidays just past. Brave Orchid thinks she has triumphed, but Maxine is sure that the druggist is merely taking pity on them. The confrontation that is supposed to show power and victory only reinforces Maxine's belief that the Chinese way is weak, inappropriate, and irrational.

As if these traits were not enough to stigmatize the Chinese culture and its people as Other, its inaccuracy, another characteristic of an orientalized culture, troubles Maxine. The West, with its penchant for dominating the world through definition, precision, and fact, rejects ambiguity, imprecision, and mystery. It is not surprising that Maxine, in her efforts to reject her mother, is so bewildered and frustrated by her mother's inattention to fact. For example, when they are discussing age, Brave Orchid tells her daughter that the last time she saw her she was still young, but now she is old. Maxine tries to point out to her that they visited only a year ago. But her mother won't change her opinion; she simply notes that during that year Maxine became old. Then, talking about death, she mentions that she is eighty. Maxine says that according to her papers she is seventy-six. They argue about the exact age for a while; Brave Orchid says that her papers are wrong and that she's eighty, eight one in Chinese years. She says she may be seventy or eighty and that numbers do not matter. To her, exactness is simply unimportant. There is a truth beyond fact, and a way of knowing beyond reason. Brave Orchid's is a different way of knowing, but Maxine makes no room for alternate visions of reality.

Nor does Maxine recognize that she sometimes mistakes ambiguity for inaccuracy. It is only as she develops, both as a person and as a writer, that she sees that there can be richness and beauty in ambiguity, especially in the Chinese language. As an adult she begins to look up the meanings of "Ho Chi Kuei," which immigrants call her and the others who have lived in the United States for a while. She does not know Chinese, but instead of orientalizing the culture to reject it, she begins exploring the language—the basis of any culture. She learns that "Ho Chi Kuei" translates in various ways, from one of a number of insects to "non-eater," a term which relates to Brave Orchid's notions of heroism. But she does not make this realization, which allows her to move away from her Western monoculturalism, until adulthood.

As a girl, she also fails to recognize that there might be serious, practical reasons for the inaccuracy, outright lies, and "the secrecy of the Chinese"—not *our* secrecy—which she detests. "Don't tell" is her parents' constant refrain, although, as Maxine notes, "we couldn't tell if we wanted to because we didn't know." As an adult, of course, Maxine recognizes that "they would not tell us children because we had been born among ghosts, were taught by ghosts, and were ourselves ghost-like." But when she was growing up and trying desperately to divorce herself from her mother and her Chinese heritage, she did not realize how serious the possibility of deportation was and, therefore, how great the need for secrecy about one's background was. Although the worst of the deportation fear was over by the 1950s when Maxine was a girl, the fearful memories from earlier years surely must have remained strong in the tightly knit Chinese communities. The Immigration Act of 1924, passed to halt further Japanese immigration, also prohibited Chinese wives from coming to the United States to join their husbands. This act effectively stopped the growth of Chinese families, which typically had from six to a dozen children. Women who tried to enter the country were detained at Angel Island Immigration Station in the San Francisco Bay, where they might be held up to two years [Judy Yung, *Chinese Women of America: A Pictorial History,* 1986]. The Chinese had good reason for guarding their identities even from their children, who might blurt out information that could lead to deportation for their families, but all Maxine could see was a legacy of lies, of which she wanted no part.

Maxine sees the Chinese as inaccurate or deceitful not only in matters with potentially serious consequences, but also in ordinary situations. She says that she and the other children in the family never really had a sense of when holidays occurred. There was no anticipation or excitement, only a vague awareness that they had eaten a certain food which deemed it a holiday. If anyone had the temerity to ask for explanations the adults got angry and evasive and

silenced the annoying child. Maxine finds all the secrecy about these events doubly puzzling. She is confused not only about the actual dates of holidays, but also about how Chinese traditions, which her mother seems so insistent about honoring, are ever maintained or how they maintained a continuous culture for five thousand years. Once again, it is interesting to see that she refers to the Chinese as "they"— the Other—to distance herself from a culture that seems irrational from a Western perspective.

Though Maxine is often curious about how a culture that seems so strange to her could have lasted for so long, she also says she has no desire to understand it. In fact, she says that "if you don't figure it out, it's all right. Then you can grow up bothered by 'neither ghosts nor deities.'" But, of course, she is tormented by Chinese ghosts. Although Maxine may have learned from Brave Orchid and other members of the Chinese American community to refer to all non-Chinese people as ghosts—Meter Reader Ghosts, Garbage Ghosts, Urban Renewal Ghosts, Public Health Nurse Ghosts, Burglar Ghosts, and Wino Ghosts—for her, the real ghosts are Chinese, those shadowy, inexplicable presences that haunt her life. And she expends considerable effort to understand why her mother uses language in a way that bewilders rather than clarifies.

One such instance regards the birth of babies, who must be named and described as other than they are in order to protect them from the jealous gods. Despite her avowed desire for accuracy, Maxine is, however, pleased when her mother calls her "Little Dog," even though she, like her mother, is a Dragon. "Little Dog" is "a name to fool the gods." This name signifies a loving connection, rooted in a cultural heritage that Brave Orchid hopes her daughter will eventually accept with pride. This sense of connection, however, will come only in time. When she is younger and prone to orientalize Chinese culture, Maxine is frustrated to the point of rage by what she regards as duplicity.

Maxine's frustration leads to one of the most memorable battles between mother and daughter. Because she believes Brave Orchid does not really know her, Maxine feels compelled to recite a list of "over two hundred things . . . so that she would know the true things about me." She wants the truth to bring them closer, but unlike Brave Orchid, who wants their Chinese heritage to unite them, Maxine wants their union grounded in a Western sense of fact and accuracy. So she says, "If only I could let my mother know the list, she—and the world—would become more like me, and I would never be alone again." One night when mother and daughter are alone in the laundry, Maxine begins to tell her the items on the list—how she killed a spider, how she hinted to a girl that she wanted a doll. When Brave Orchid doesn't respond to these revelations, Maxine thinks she must be more explicit. But to Brave Orchid, such precision and details are not the means to truth. In fact, telling her to go away, she adds, "I don't feel like hearing your craziness." What is taking place in this scene is a clash of cultures arising from two different ways of knowing. Viewing her mother from a Westernized perspective, Maxine misunderstands what her mother values as truth. Consequently, she sees her disregard of the "truth" as a sign of Chinese primitiveness and inferiority, from which she must dissociate herself. Maxine recalls that she had to leave home to view the world logically, as a place filled with simplicity and without ghosts. She equates the West with order, logic, and rationality—a way of knowing superior to the byzantine complexities of a culture that she herself has orientalized. It is a way for her to escape her ghosts, for it is the Chinese culture which seems foreign to her. She also equates China with darkness, the West with a light that can illuminate the error of non-Western societies.

But Chinese society is only "backward" from a Eurocentric point of view in which progress is the domain of the West. The stories about her mother's cooking and eating as a strategy to combat ghosts are one such case in point. Maxine attributes Brave Orchid's ability to win over the sitting ghost to her ability to eat anything; "all heroes," she says, "are bold toward food." Maxine notes that her mother kills and cooks raccoons, snakes, and skunks for her family and gives them five-day-old leftover squid eyes. She doesn't want to know the reasons why her mother cooks the kinds of food that she does; she evidently does not realize the privation which the Chinese suffered for many years and which had driven them to the United States since the 1850s. So thrift and inventiveness in the face of privation, which would ordinarily be praiseworthy qualities, do not make such a cuisine acceptable to her. Her rejection is far more than children's usual dislike of exotic foods, though. It is the exotic culture represented by the foods which Maxine rejects. This is suggested by her linking her mother's cooking with the fantastic stories of warriors who are heroic eaters: Kao Chung, "who in 1683 ate five cooked chickens and drank ten bottles of wine that belonged to the sea monster," Chou Yi-han, who ate a fried ghost, and Wei Pang, who ate a "ball of flesh entirely covered with eyes."

Maxine makes the sorts of equations that set up China as Other, which she can then reject. She thinks that all she is rejecting is weirdness, not heroism. Out of ignorance, she is cutting herself off from a tradition of courage. Sau-ling Wong discusses the semiotics of eating in Asian literature, the importance of the ability to "eat unpromising substances and to extract sustenance, even a sort of willed enjoyment, from them; to put it symbolically, it is the ability to cope with the constraints and perceptions Asian Americans have had to endure as immigrants and racial minorities." But

rather than really face these problems, Maxine would rather ally herself totally with Western culture. In fact, so total is her denial that she refuses to cook for others and apparently cooks very little for herself, since her mother is so concerned that Maxine hasn't fattened up. But Maxine wants nothing to do with the heroics of eating. After recounting the mythic stories about eating, she says she would live on plastic, a perfect metonym for the greed and unnaturalness of Western society.

Eventually, however, Maxine rejects the plastic society of the West, but, more importantly, she rejects her Orientalism. She realizes that she understands little of her Chinese legacy, but now, instead of exoticizing it so much that she can dismiss it out of hand, she longs to discover this part of her culture. She knows now that to fix one particular image of a culture is to falsify it; she is open to fluid interpretations which allow and appreciate cultural difference. Though she once said she never wanted to go to China, she ultimately changes her mind and plans a visit as she continues to sort out what was real and what was imagined.

The Woman Warrior concludes with a collaborative talkstory by mother and daughter. Brave Orchid begins the story, telling about her grandmother and how she foiled thieves that struck the homes of theater patrons who were watching plays. Leaving the doors and windows open, the family went to the play. Because the bandits struck at the theater, the family's home and their possessions were safe. This segues into Maxine's portion of the story. She begins: "I like to think that at some of those performances, they heard the songs of Ts'ai Yen, a poetess born in A.D. 175." For twelve years, Ts'ai Yen was a captive of a barbarian chieftain by whom she had two children. At night the barbarian warriors played music on their flutes—a high, disturbingly beautiful music that contrasted with the deathly music of the arrows which flew during the daytime. Ts'ai Yen begins singing in a voice which matches the flute music, her pain and anger about being separated from her family and China evident in her song. When she is ransomed, she brings her "songs back from the savage lands," one of which is "Eighteen Stanzas for a Barbarian Reed Pipe," a song that the Chinese sing to their own instruments. Maxine notes that the barbarian songs translated well, a comment usually seen as a reconciliation of the conflicts that have divided mother and daughter. But such a reading is in danger of sentimentalizing the reconciliation, of making it seem that the two cultures can meet in a happy fusion or assimilation. Maxine's Chinese heritage is not neatly compatible with her American culture, as suggested by the fact that mother and daughter each tell different stories with only the slightest of connections. The two cultures can only touch; each must stand separate, its difference accepted rather than stigmatized as Other.

More importantly, Maxine is no Ts'ai Yen, a sojourner in barbarian cultures, longing to return to her native land. The United States is her native land, not China. Like Ts'ai Yen, she is, of course, an artist, reinterpreting the stories her mother tells her in the light of her American experiences. As Frank Chin notes, it is important to distinguish between being Chinese and being Chinese American. In a racist society, both are lumped together because of skin color and physical characteristics. But, Chin notes, "We're not interchangeable. Our sensibilities are not the same" [*Bridge* Vol. 2, No. 2, December, 1972]. It is Maxine's mother, Brave Orchid—also a consummate storyteller—who has spent long years away from her homeland in an alien culture. Unlike Ts'ai Yen, though, she is not returning home. And even if she were to try, it would not be the China she knew—but instead a tissue of the fact, fantasy, and endlessly retold myths that would form her own memoir among ghosts. Though mother and daughter's collaborative talk-story does not signal an assimilation of Chinese and American cultures—which would not be desirable, even if it were possible—it does suggest that Maxine has stopped duplicating the hegemonic cultural values and assumptions of the West. She is free to find meaning in a cultural heritage that has a vital presence in her life and, finally, can put to rest the ghosts of her past.

FURTHER READING

Criticism

Bischoff, Joan. "Fellow Rebels: Annie Dillard and Maxine Hong Kingston." *English Journal* 78, No. 8 (December 1989): 62-7.

Examines Dillard's *American Childhood* and Kingston's *The Woman Warrior* as portraits of teenage rebellion appropriate for study by high school students.

Chan, Mimi. "'Listen, Mom, I'm a Banana': Mother and Daughter in Maxine Hong Kingston's *The Woman Warrior* and Amy Tan's *The Joy Luck Club*." In *Asian Voices in English,* edited by Mimi Chan and Roy Harris, pp. 65-78. Hong Kong: Hong Kong University Press, 1991.

Examines *The Woman Warrior* and Tan's *Joy Luck Club* in terms of their representation of Chinese and American culture.

Cheung, King-Kok. "Self-fulfilling Visions in *The Woman Warrior* and *Thousand Pieces of Gold*." *Biography* 13, No. 2 (Spring 1990): 143-53.

Analyzes *The Woman Warrior* and Ruthanne Lum McCunn's *Thousand Pieces of Gold,* illustrating how the authors' imaginative rendering of Asian myth forges their protagonists' identities.

Clemons, Walter. "East Meets West." *Newsweek* LXXXVIII, No. 15 (11 October 1976): 108-09.

Laudatory review of *The Woman Warrior.*

Garner, Shirley Nelson. "Breaking Silence: *The Woman Warrior.*" In *The Intimate Critique: Autobiographical Literary Criticism,* edited by Diane P. Freedman, Olivia Frey, and Frances Murphy Zauhar, pp. 117-25. Durham and London: Duke University Press, 1993.

Assesses Kingston's use of the feminist practice of breaking free of imposed silence in *The Woman Warrior.*

Geok-lin Lim, Shirley. "The Tradition of Chinese American Women's Life Stories: Thematics of Race in Gender in Jade Snow Wong's *Fifth Chinese Daughter* and Maxine Hong Kingston's *The Woman Warrior.*" In *American Women's Autobiography: Fea(s)ts of Memory,* edited by Margo Culley, pp. 252-67. Madison: University of Wisconsin Press, 1992.

Geok-lin Lim "attempts to recover the tradition of 'lifestory' behind Chinese American women's writing, and to read these works in light of ideas raised in feminist critical theory," using *The Woman Warrior* and Jade Snow Wong's *Fifth Chinese Daughter* to illuminate her premise.

Goellnicht, Donald C. "Father Land and/or Mother Tongue: The Divided Female Subject in Kogawa's *Obasan* and Hong Kingston's *The Woman Warrior.*" In *Redefining Autobiography in Twentieth-Century Women's Fiction: An Essay Collection,* edited by Janice Morgan and Colette T. Hall, pp. 119-34. New York and London: Garland Publishing, Inc., 1991.

Compares and contrasts *The Woman Warrior* and Joy Kogawa's *Obasan* to illustrate their treatment of culture, language, gender, and identity.

Quinby, Lee. "The Subject of Memoirs: *The Woman Warrior*'s Technology of Ideographic Selfhood." In *De/Colonizing the Subject: The Politics of Gender in Women's Autobiography,* edited by Sidonie Smith and Julia Watson, pp. 297-320. Minneapolis: University of Minnesota Press, 1992.

Quinby declares: "I examine the ways in which . . . *The Woman Warrior* subject[s] modern power formations to the scrutiny of one who has been subjected by them. . . . [and] constructs a new form of subjectivity, what I call an *ideographic selfhood.*"

Thompson, Phyllis Hoge. "This Is the Story I Heard: A Conversation with Maxine Hong Kingston and Earll Kingston." *Biography* 6, No. 1 (Winter 1983): 1-12.

Interview with Kingston and her husband in which the

author discusses fiction, nonfiction, biography, and viewpoint.

Wang, Veronica. "Reality and Fantasy: The Chinese-American Woman's Quest for Identity." *MELUS* 12, No. 3 (Fall 1985): 23-31.

    Explores Kingston's treatment of Chinese American women's quest for identity in *The Woman Warrior.*

Woo, Deborah. "Maxine Hong Kingston: The Ethnic Writer and the Burden of Dual Authenticity." *Amerasia Journal* 16, No. 1 (1990): 173-200.

    Considers the controversial reaction to *The Woman Warrior,* that Woo asserts points to "a more general dilemma which faces ethnic minority writers" who are viewed as "spokespersons for the 'ethnic' experience."

Additional coverage of Kingston's life and career is contained in the following sources published by Gale: *Authors and Artists for Young Adults,* **Vol. 8;** *Contemporary Authors,* **Vols. 69-72;** *Contemporary Authors New Revision Series,* **Vols. 13, and 38;** *Dictionary of Literary Biography,* **Vol. 173;** *Dictionary of Literary Biography Yearbook,* **1980;** *DISCovering Authors Modules: Multicultural and Novelists; Major Twentieth-Century Writers; Something about the Author,* **Vol. 53; and** *World Literature Criticism Supplement.*

R. K. Narayan

1906-

(Full name Rasipuram Krishnaswami Narayan) Indian novelist, short story writer, essayist, memoirist, travel writer, journalist, critic, and editor.

The following entry presents an overview of Narayan's career. For further information on his life and works, see *CLC*, Volumes 7, 28, and 47.

INTRODUCTION

R. K. Narayan is considered one of the three best Indian authors writing in English; the other two are Rao Raja and Mulk Raj Anand. Narayan's fiction contains a unique blend of Indian mysticism and English form. His fictional world, Malgudi, is one of everyday concerns and common language set in southern India, which he successfully portrays through subtle prose and humor.

Biographical Information

Narayan was born in Mysore, India, in 1906. His father was an administrator and headmaster at several government schools and instilled in Narayan a love of literature. He did not have much academic success, however, having difficulty with his college entrance exam in English. In 1926, he enrolled in the B.A. program in English in Maharaja College, Mysore, after which he embarked on a short-lived teaching career. Finding the academic life was not for him, Narayan turned to writing. After being turned down by several publishers, Narayan gave the manuscript of his first novel, *Swami and Friends* (1935), to a friend and gave him permission to destroy it. The friend showed the novel to Graham Greene, who was impressed and found a publisher for the book. Narayan's writing career was born and the prolific writer went on to publish novels, several volumes of short stories, collections of essays, and his memoirs, entitled *My Days* (1974).

Major Works

Narayan's fiction inhabits the world of everyday events and common people in a fictional place called Malgudi. He incorporates traditional Hindu mythology and legends in stories of modern events. He tells stories of ordinary people who rely on Hindu principles to guide them through the ethical dilemmas and problems of modern life. Narayan's fiction avoids being overtly political or ideological. His early novels focus on the conflict between Indian and Western culture. *Swami and Friends* chronicles an extroverted

schoolboy's rebellion against his missionary upbringing. *The Bachelor of Arts* (1937) depicts an idealistic college student who attacks the bourgeois order but eventually reconciles himself to an obedient, lawful existence. In *The English Teacher* (1945; published in the United States as *Grateful to Life and Death*), an educator who endures the premature death of his wife overcomes his grief through religion and philosophy. After 1945, Narayan's fiction portrays middle-class characters who must reconcile Western ideals of financial and personal success with the everyday reality of Indian life. *Mr. Sampath* (1949; published in the United States as *The Printer of Malgudi*) chronicles a village printer's unsuccessful attempt to become a film producer. Narayan's most obviously political novel, *Waiting for the Mahatma* (1955), recounts the adventures of a man whose love for a young woman leads him to attempt to sabotage Mahatma Gandhi's peace movement. *The Guide* (1958) is Narayan's most popular and accomplished novel. This work is the tale of Raju, a former convict who is mistaken for a holy man upon his arrival in Malgudi. Implored by the villagers to avert a famine, Raju is unable to convince them that he is a fraud. Deciding to embrace the role the townspeople have thrust upon him, Raju dies during a prolonged fast and is revered as a saint. In *The Sweet-Vendor* (1967; published in the United States as *The Vendor of Sweets*), a merchant abandons his profession and his family concerns for a life of tranquillity and meditation. In *A Tiger for Malgudi* (1983), Narayan makes use of Indian legends and folktales to suggest that beasts may be as capable of thought and feeling as human beings. Narrated by a tiger, this novel traces the animal's spiritual development in overcoming its potential for violence. Narayan's collections of stories, such as *Gods, Demons and Others* (1965) and *The Grandmother's Tale* (1992), encompass many of the same themes as his novels in the tighter form of the short story.

Critical Reception

Critics often classify Narayan as arising out of the tradition of oral storytelling. Reviewers note his gift for wry, subtle humor, which he uses to expose the foibles of being human. Shashi Tharoor asserts that "Narayan at his best [is] a consummate teller of timeless tales, a meticulous recorder of the ironies of human life, an acute observer of the possibilities of the ordinary: India's answer to Jane Austen." Narayan's comedy is the focus of many reviews, and it is commonly held that his is a gentle humor. Hilary Mantel says, "At the heart of Narayan's achievement is this: he respects his characters, respects their created natures. This is why he can make jokes about them and stay friends with them." Critics also point out his ability to give individual stories arising out of a unique cultural experience, universal significance. Reviewers assert that the creation of the fictional Malgudi helps Narayan portray the flavor of Indian life without worrying about the specifics of a real city. Critics attribute much of the popularity of Narayan's work to his ability to successfully use the English novel form to portray Indian life and Hindu culture. Chitra Sankaran says, "With Narayan's works . . . the deceptive simplicity of his fiction very often obscures his superb capacity to blend traditional Indian modes with the English novel form."

PRINCIPAL WORKS

Swami and Friends: A Novel of Malgudi (novel) 1935

The Bachelor of Arts (novel) 1937

The Dark Room (novel) 1938

Mysore (travel essay) 1939

Malgudi Days (short stories) 1941

The English Teacher (novel) 1945; published as *Grateful to Life and Death*, 1953

An Astrologer's Day and Other Stories (short stories) 1947

Mr. Sampath (novel) 1949; published as *The Printer of Malgudi*, 1957

The Financial Expert (novel) 1952

Waiting for the Mahatma (novel) 1955

Lawley Road: Thirty-Two Short Stories (short stories) 1956

The Guide (novel) 1958

My Dateless Diary: A Journal of a Trip to the United States in October 1956 (travel journal) 1960

The Man-Eater of Malgudi (novel) 1961

Gods, Demons and Others (short stories) 1965

The Vendor of Sweets (novel) 1967; published in England as *The Sweet-Vendor*, 1967

A Horse and Two Goats and Other Stories (short stories) 1970

The Ramayana: A Shortened Modern Prose Version of the Indian Epic [translator] (novel) 1972

My Days: A Memoir (memoirs) 1974

The Painter of Signs (novel) 1976

The Emerald Route (travel essay) 1977

The Mahabharata: A Shortened Prose Version of the Indian Epic [translator] (novel) 1978

Old and New (short stories) 1981

A Tiger for Malgudi (novel) 1983

Under the Banyan Tree and Other Stories (short stories) 1985

Talkative Man (novel) 1987

A Writer's Nightmare: Selected Essays, 1958-1988 (essays) 1988

A Story-Teller's World: Stories, Essays, Sketches (short stories and essays) 1989

The World of Nagaraj (novel) 1990

The Grandmother's Tale [with sketches by R. K. Laxman] (short stories) 1992; published as *The Grandmother's Tale and Other Stories*, 1994

Salt & Sawdust: Stories and Table Talk (short stories) 1993

CRITICISM

Anne Fremantle (review date 23 October 1953)

SOURCE: "The Nearness of Two Worlds," in *Commonweal*, Vol. LIX, No. 3, October 23, 1953, pp. 70-71.

[*In the following review, Fremantle calls Narayan's* Grateful to Life and Death *"a tour de force, as perfect as it is pure."*]

Mr. Narayan's first novel, **The Financial Expert,** was a delicious comedy, subtle and gay. His second book, [**Grateful to Life and Death,**] about a teacher of English in a college in India, is one of the rare novels dealing with marriage which suggests the truly sacramental nature of the physical relationship. The hero, Krishna, his lovely wife, Susila, and Leela, their little daughter; his parents, her parents, the old family retainers; his colleagues, his friends, the little dusty town where they all live, are delicately chiseled, and the over-all impression is of a filigree carving, in sandalwood or ivory. We see, and smell, the jasmine that Susila always wears, and that is her own identification, the delicious meals she cooks, the horrible stench of the filth that gives her the typhoid from which she dies, and the garlands his friends hang on Krishna when, at the tale's end, he resigns his job, and decides to devote himself to running an eccentric school for small children.

Susila's long illness and death are heartbreakingly described, as are Krishna's stupid, tender clumsiness, and, at the last, his tragic unawareness. Because the fever has fallen he thinks Susila will now recover. So he takes their child for a walk with a small, chattering companion. When they return, the doctor's car is at the door. After telling the distraught husband to "expect a change in about two and a half hours, the doctor turned and walked off. Krishna stood stock still, listening to his shoe creaks going away, the starting of his car; after the car had gone, a stony silence closed in on the house, punctuated by the stentorian breathing, which appeared to [him] the creaking of the hinges of a prison gate, opening at the command of a soul going into freedom."

The dull emptiness, the true hell that is the pain of loss, are movingly recounted. Not since Jules Romains' *Le Dieu des Corps* has any novel attempted to express the intimacy of the souls of those whose bodies are married. And Mr. Narayan conveys this without ever alluding, even indirectly, to physical love: it is a tour de force, as perfect as it is pure.

The second part of the book describes Krishna's gradual return to life. One day he gets a letter from a stranger "for Krishna whose wife Susila has recently passed over." She wishes to communicate with him, and has chosen this way to do it. Later she teaches her husband how she can reach him directly, and, when he has learned by experience how near the two worlds are, and yet how far apart, he realizes that Susila's nearness, their child's happiness, and a life of recollection are all he needs. So, when his grandmother takes the child to rear her, he and his friends decide to live together as *sannyasis,* devoted to teaching small children and the effort to live daily an ever more interior life.

The loss of Susila, found again on another level, is echo of the first Krishna's love for Sita and also of Orpheus and Eurydice in our own tradition. Mr. Narayan has written a story for which we, like his hero, may be "grateful."

Donald Barr (review date 19 May 1957)

SOURCE: "Three Minds in Trouble," in *New York Times Book Review,* May 19, 1957, p. 4.

[*In the following review, Barr lauds Narayan's* The Printer of Malgudi *for its comedy and subtlety.*]

The town of Malgudi, fermenting with dreams, is the setting R. K. Narayan has devised for his novels of life in modern India. They have all been charming novels—modest in dimensions, gentle both in laughter and in pain, alive with an easy eccentricity—and the latest of them, *The Printer of Malgudi,* is something more than charming.

It is the subtle story of three minds and six wild universes. These universes of philosophy, influence, art, love, sudden glory and vainglory have a kind of unearthly abundance. They keep no books. They are made of hopes. Kipling's puritan *God of Things as They Are* does not preside over any of them. The three minds are not geniuses but the brains of little bubbling, faltering fellows with complaining families and the ordinary male's mixture of remorse and absent-mindedness.

Srinivas, over whose shoulder we watch the story, is an editor, or rather a weekly philosopher, who is enabled to write his provincial magazine only by vigorously neglecting his wife and refusing to open any letter that might be a bill. Srinivas' young friend, Ravi, is a love-torn accountant with a brilliant talent for drawing one picture, the image of a girl with a gem in her earlobe and a highlight on her cheek whom he once saw and has never been able to find again. Srinivas' printer, Sampath, is a masterly first-impressionist, in whose spacious gestures and rich evasive words a creaky press and one exhausted boy somehow become a big establishment, and who moves among the imaginations of his friends like some minor deity.

These three are seduced from their own dreams into another, more vivid and less innocent hallucination: they go into producing a film. Each finds here an awful, prosperous travesty of his desires. Passion leaves Ravi mentally deranged; success leaves Sampath morally deranged; only the philosopher Srinivas escapes, and he is not unscathed.

The story is very tidy, but it is not intellectually dapper in the fashion of a French novel. It is worked out in the English style with seemingly unstudied detail that covers the almost allegorical outline. And there is in the writing something that is distinctively Mr. Narayan's, though it may be a trait of his Hindu origins: he moves so naturally and unapologetically into strange incidents and speeches that he seems without our noticing it to enlarge our powers of fancy. His is a delightful and as yet not wholly recognized talent.

It is a comic talent of a special kind. Conventional comedy shows us a world where there is no real and present pain and where every man has his price. In ordinary farce there are thwacks and betrayals and even death, but we are kept at an ironical distance from the characters, so that blood is merely red ink and agony merely a grimace. In ordinary dramatic or sentimental comedy we are close to the characteristics but real pain is not. In Mr. Narayan's world there is farcical violence and dismay, and we are deeply involved in the characters, yet we never go beyond a certain buoyant pathos into tragedy.

Life in ordinary comedies is continually making good men shrug and retract what they thought were their principles; only villains and fanatics and sour fools adhere to their stated purposes. Mr. Narayan's dreamers do preserve their principles, or at least they recover them, but they are not contemptible. He accomplishes in his mild way what Cervantes and Dickens did, a comedy of innocence.

Donald Barr (review date 12 February 1961)

SOURCE: "A Man Called Vasu," in *New York Times Book Review,* February 12, 1961, pp. 5, 16.

[*In the following review, Barr praises the delicacy of Narayan's comedy in* The Man-Eater of Malgudi.]

Each artist—if he is a true artist,' and not just a utensil by means of which people gratify themselves according to the habits they have already—has to educate an audience for himself. This is not so difficult for a writer who is unusual in the usual ways: perversity, obscurity, syntactical tricks. Yet it has taken a quarter of a century for Americans to learn the meaning of R. K. Narayan's bland, sly, important genius. Why? Perhaps if we know why we have been so obtuse about his other books, we may be a little more perceptive about *The Man-Eater of Malgudi.*

Narayan's first novel, *Swami and Friends,* was the beguiling comedy of a Hindu schoolboy. It was oblivious of the class struggle, and it was unsuspicious of love; there was a cricket club in the book, but it was only a cricket club, and there was pain, but it was only a fact; not a word would have had to be different if Karl Marx and Sigmund Freud had never lived. This story was published in England in 1935, a time when young writers were supposed to search, either in the sharpening crisis of the social order or in the unhealthy recesses of the human personality, for the causes

of the monstrous evil that was then spreading across the world.

Graham Greene, for instance, had gone beyond Marx and Freud to an older and more radical apocalypse; he seemed to write with his face stiffened against the smell of all the men who had gone through the world to Hell before him, and no one could possibly have been less like Narayan, in whose work innocence grows like a weed. Yet it was Greene who first saw the significance of the young Indian's work and who encouraged him while, slowly, reviewers and readers became aware of what was going on beneath the gentle simplicities of Narayan's tales.

Not until 1953 did these tales appear in America, and then it was the Michigan State College Press that brought them out. At last, in 1958, Viking took Narayan over. He now has a critical reputation and a following; but even now there are many readers who miss the point. We are used to a certain kind of comedy, in which characters are trapped or tricked into violating their principles—the pure man is seduced; the clever man loses his head; the bachelor gets married. This fits our view of the universe as being slightly malicious toward us personally and our view of human nature as being less virtuous and intelligent than it tries to look. Narayan's is likewise a comedy of inadvertence, but it works the other way round: it is innocence that spoils corruption; a kind of rich, wild sanctity will suddenly break out and wreck someone's grubby enterprise; in the midst of a whole fugue of evasions one thoughtless act of courage will ruin everything. It implies an unusual philosophy.

Not that Narayan thinks the world is an easy place or thinks pain and guilt are unreal. *The Man-Eater of Malgudi* tells of the invasion of a quiet and faintly incompetent civilization by a competent barbarism, and the effect is genuinely terrifying. The civilization in question is a ramshackle print-shop in South India; it is the hangout of powerless politicians and unpublished poets; there is an air of anxious self-deception here, but there are also order and courtesy. One day, Vasu appears, gigantic, angry, uncontrollable, endlessly roaring and jeering. He can smash a door or a man with a blow. He scatters the poor talkers and dreamers in the anteroom, and he takes over the attic of the print-shop rent free. He is a taxidermist, an excellent craftsman.

Soon the neighborhood is filled with the reek of dead animals; the inhabitants, Hindus with a reverence for all life, are appalled but too frightened to act. The back stairs creak with the comings and goings of prostitutes. Vasu's jeep comes and goes with its pathetic cargo. A child's pet dog is slaughtered in the street and added to the pile of raw material. The rumor begins to form—incredible and obviously true—that there is a plot against the temple elephant. There are pompous conferences and foolish plans; there is the cruel intuition of defeat.

Suddenly the feral man is dead. And the suspicion of murder hangs over the house just as the stench of the taxidermist's vats had hung over it before. It is characteristic of Narayan that the truth about Vasu's death turns out to contain the only solution to the problem of evil that pretends to be a final solution; yet the author is much too polite to pretend to anything bigger than a quiet ending to a story.

Vasu and the print-shop might be the West and India, might be science and humanism, might be totalitarianism and liberal civilization. They are all of these things and none of them. For Narayan's comedy is not a mere sprightly allegory any more than it is a mere anthropological anecdote: it is classical art, profound and delicate art, profound in feeling and delicate in control.

Santha Rama Rau (review date 8 November 1964)

SOURCE: "It's All in the Telling," in *New York Times Book Review,* November 8, 1964, pp. 4, 56.

[*Rama Rau is the author of* Remember the House *and other books about her native India. In the following review, she asserts that Narayan is like a revered village storyteller in his presentation of stories from Indian mythology in* Gods, Demons, and Others.]

R. K. Narayan, writing about that cherished and revered figure in Indian life, the village storyteller, displays all the gifts of wit, insight, moral inquiry and teaching possessed by— well, the expert Indian village storyteller. His latest book is quite different in form, though not in attitude, from his much-admired novels of modern Indian life. ***Gods, Demons and Others*** is a carefully grouped collection of ancient tales taken from the vast and complex mythology of India and presented as they might be told in their traditional setting—except that, unmistakably, the author's urbane and affectionate style informs his descriptions of the narrator and the texts of the stories. Mercifully, he spares us the expected didactic interludes which most of his colleagues use to give weight to their efforts.

In Mr. Narayan's skillful hands each story engages and enlightens the reader on at least three levels. The first and most obvious comes from the universal essential of all storytelling combined, in this case, with the special nature of the audience. Illiterate, but not uneducated, the Indian villagers naturally demand narrative excitement—remarkably difficult even though the storyteller has splendid plots

to use for raw material. He belongs to a country that still depends, for the most part, on an oral transmission of learning. His listeners have often heard the legends and the wisdom and philosophy they contain, and are well able to judge his expertise. He must hold their interest with an actor's sense of timing, a poet's ability to evoke a mood, a good teacher's ability to instruct and entertain.

Beyond sustaining the what-happens-next suspense by his own differences in emphasis or elaboration of adventures, the storyteller must, in some way, seriously explore the human predicament. As Mr. Narayan explains it, "Each tale invariably starts off when an inquiring mind asks of an enlightened one a fundamental question." Even more challengingly he must use his rich inheritance of tradition and literature to illuminate the philosophy it expresses.

> **Each tale invariably starts off when an inquiring mind asks of an enlightened one a fundamental question.**
>
> **—*R. K. Narayan***

"No one," declares Mr. Narayan's storyteller, "can understand the significance of any story in our mythology unless he is deeply versed in the Vedas [the Hindu scriptures]." Since stories and scriptures are all interrelated with matters as diverse as ethics and grammar, or equally with semantics, mysticism, astrology, astronomy, philosophy and moral codes, the storyteller's position in village life acquires a daunting and imposing stature. No wonder the villagers assemble at his ancestral home after the day's work, decorate his sacred images with garlands of jasmine, join in his prayers, until the valley is full of their chanting and even the howling jackals cannot be heard. Then they settle back to hear the kind of stories concerning the gods, demons and others that Mr. Narayan has recorded.

He has made his selection from only those stories that center on outstanding personalities, because they alone make sense in any age or idiom. However surprising, they remain somehow familiar, filled with magic, yet recognizable types, fabulous and human, known from the nursery but always open to change, re-evaluation and fresh understanding.

While a story like **"Chudala"** may end imperturbably with the astonishing assurances that the king "ruled happily for 10,000 years" still its hero is a troubled man of action, apparently endowed with every worldly blessing but unhappy and restless because he cannot understand his inner being and struggles with a feeling that "everything seems unreal." He tries listening to philosophers, scholars, priests; he tries elaborate rituals; he tries contemplation. "But when the effect of it all wore off he was back in his solitude, fumbling for security." A not unusual modern condition. Even the attempted alleviations are of a sort that people have sought out all through history for a comparable malaise.

Similarly, one of the timeless questions that plague both the narrators and the listeners in the Ramayana, the great Indian epic, is how far a virtuous man should be ruled by duty and by public demands on him when they are opposed by humane considerations and private loyalties. So central is this problem to India's famous epic, and so various the interpretations and feelings about it, that in some parts of Southeast Asia where the Ramayana was spread, presumably by traveling storytellers and priests, the heroic King Rama is seen as a self-righteous egoist, insensitive to the point of cruelty, so concerned with his public image that he will unhesitatingly sacrifice his devoted wife to its enhancement and given to shameless tantrums if he is thwarted in any way.

Although, as a storyteller, Mr. Narayan could have this latitude of approach, he prefers to follow the orthodox Indian view that Rama was a perfect man—on the surface. With a kind of wry helplessness he comments on Rama's less appealing traits and unobtrusively manages to guide the reader into an indignant sympathy with his wronged heroine.

In one way or another Mr. Narayan gives vitality and an original viewpoint to the most ancient of legends, lacing them with his own blend of satire, pertinent explanation and thoughtful commentary; and meeting the exacting criteria set by centuries of professionals in his field. His brother, R. K. Laxman, complements the texts most admirably with decorative chapter-heads of gods, demons and others, in traditional poses and time-honored scenes painted with a bold modern brush.

S. C. Harrex (essay date June 1969)

SOURCE: "R. K. Narayan's *The Printer of Malgudi*," in *Literature East and West,* Vol. XIII, Nos. 1 and 2, June, 1969, pp. 68-82.

[*In the following essay, Harrex analyzes Narayan's use of comedy in* The Printer of Malgudi.]

The Printer of Malgudi was first published as **Mr. Sampath** in 1949. It is not the most accomplished of R. K. Narayan's novels, and its action, though very funny at times, is a little inadequate as a representation of life which is both amusing and true. However, considered from the point of view of Narayan's development as a comic artist, **The Printer of Malgudi** is an interesting transitional work;

and it complements the enlarged consciousness of life evident in his previous novel, **Grateful to Life and Death,** in which he explored through a newly sharpened tragicomic style the metaphysical implications of an anguishing experience. In devising a parabolical setting for the comedy of **The Printer of Malgudi,** Narayan extended his imaginative horizons. Thus, by the penultimate chapter the author is viewing the story in terms larger than itself—archetypally, in fact.

Up to this point the story has been fairly straightforward. Srinivas, a university graduate who had been undecided about his professional future, became a newspaper proprietor-editor. His printer, Mr. Sampath, came to regard the paper (*The Banner*) as his personal responsibility; and, although Srinivas had to discourage him from dabbling in editorial matters, their relationship was soon amicably involved. When Sampath abandoned his trade to become an entrepreneur-director of Sunrise Pictures, Srinivas reluctantly suspended publication of *The Banner* but before long found himself, at Sampath's instigation, writing the script for the company's first production, *The Burni of Kama.* To the disappointment of Srinivas, a philosophical purist, the film's mythological integrity (it was about the love and marriage of Shiva and Parvathi and his destruction of Kama, the Lord of Love) was sacrificed. Also involved in the production of this extravaganza were: a kind of Cecil B. De Mille Chief Executive, De Mello of Hollywood; Somu, part financier-producer-director and former Malgudi district board president; Shanti, the femme-fatale leading lady; V. L. G. or Shiva, a devotee of the god, who has played the same role in Indian cinema for a quarter of a century; Ravi, a neurotic young artist whom Srinivas had befriended and found a job for in the studios.

The relationships of these people becomes increasingly complicated. Srinivas is disenchanted when his script is mutilated in the interests of romance, music, dance routines, and comic relief. Somu and Sampath resent each other's influence. Sampath falls in love with Shanti; V. L. G. is impatient of Shanti's temperamental turns and the pampering she receives; neurotically fixated about a girl whose portrait he had started to paint but couldn't finish because she left Malgudi, Ravi identifies this dream girl with Shanti and is driven out of his mind by his hopeless passion for her. This "chaos of human relationships and activities," particularly the erotic mix-up, results in catastrophe. During the filming of the last scene, Ravi goes beserk; rushing onto the set, he violently embraces Shanti, carries her off, and is not finally subdued until the studios have been reduced to a shambles. The film is ruined, Shanti hysterically throws over Sampath and her movie career, and Ravi is released from jail an incommunicative nervous wreck.

The plot is a deliberate parody-pastiche of conventional

situations in popular romantic fiction, and *The Burning of Kama* pokes fun at the Hollywood and epic fashions of Indian cinema. ("Golden opportunity to see God himself" is one of the poster advertisements for the film.) On this basis Narayan entertainingly exploits the more external and dramatic qualities of comedy, especially farce, burlesque, satire, and caricature. The description Ravi's fatal disruption of the film, for example, is straight-out humorous romp:

> It was going to be the most expert shot taken. The light-boys looked down from their platforms as if privileged to witness the amours of gods. If the camera ran on for another minute the shot would be over. They wanted to cut this shot first where Shiva's arms went round the diaphanous lady's hips. But it was cut even a few seconds earlier in an unexpected manner. A piercing cry, indistinguishable, unworded, like an animal's, was suddenly heard, and before they could see where it originated, Ravi was seen whizzing past the others like a bullet, knocking down the people in his way. He was next seen on the set, rushing between Shiva's extended arms and Parvathi, and knocking Shiva aside with such violence that he fell amidst his foliage in Kailas in a most ungodly manner. Next minute they saw Parvathi struggling in the arms of Ravi, who was trying to kiss her lips and carry her off. . . .

They soon realized that this scene was not in the script. Cries rang out: "Cut." "Power." "Shut down." "Stop." And several people tried to rush into the scene. Ravi attempted to carry off his prize, though she was scratching his face and biting his hands. In the mess someone tripped upon the cables and all the lights went out. Ravi seemed to be seized with a superhuman power. Nobody could get at him. In the confusion someone cried: "Oh! Camera, take care!" "Lights, lights, fools!" Somebody screamed: 'The cobra is free; the cobra is creeping here, oh!" People ran helter-skelter in the dark. While they were all searching and running into each other they could hear Ravi's voice lustily ringing out in another part of the studio. And all ran in his direction.

Here Narayan uses some of the more popular devices of comic style. Appropriately, the account reads like a film-script conception of the kind of fast-moving abortive situation dearly beloved in the film industry. Although "this scene was not in the script," it would fit nicely into a slapstick comedy. Hence the clichés—"piercing cry . . . like an animal's," "whizzing past like a bullet," "ran helter-skelter"; hence also the stock situations—the disruptive agent (Ravi), sudden incongruity and deflated dignity (Shiva as victim of violence, his ungodly fall), and general confusion (darkness, rampage, a cobra loose). If the comedy of *The*

Printer of Malgudi operated only on this obvious level, however, the novel would be less interesting than it is and not nearly so relevant to an appreciation of Narayan's comic art.

But the comedy does function at a deeper level as well, largely because the two central characters, Srinivas and Sampath, are portrayed as real-life people and because comedy for Narayan is a means of revealing the sorrows and many of the serious moral issues beneath life's surface. During the course of the narrative Srinivas phases out of comic involvement into the detachment of "a mere spectator," and as his consciousness more comprehendingly engages some of the fundamental problems of existence, he increasingly becomes identifiable with the narrative point of view. Sampath also changes. Srinivas observes that the printer's "old personality . . . is fast vanishing"; his former jovial vitality is suffocating beneath the vulgar "prosperity" and "new rotundity" of his tycoon exterior and being consumed in his desire to complement his domestic marriage with a social marriage to Shanti. Thus, while the comic action develops, the characters do not remain static.

Furthermore, here is an implicit universality in this story of men who bring destruction upon themselves by losing their heads over a beautiful woman. Unlike Shiva, they have neither the power nor the will to resist Kama and his piercing arrows. And, by the penultimate chapter, we find that *The Printer of Malgudi* is a fable as well as a farce, that it is conceived, like life, against a legendary background.

In an atmosphere of "hypnosis," "chants," "rhythmic beats," and "pungent incense," Srinivas witnesses a magician's attempts to cure Ravi through exorcism. A "sweep of history passed in front of his eyes":

> Srinivas suddenly said to himself: "I might be in the twentieth century B.C. for all it matters, or 4000 B.C." . . . His scenario-writing habit suddenly asserted itself. His little home, the hall and all the folk there, Anderson Lane and, in fact, Malgudi itself dimmed and dissolved on the screen. . . . Presently appeared . . . Sri Rama, the hero of Ramayana. He was a perfect man, this incarnation of Vishnu. Over his shoulder was slung his famous bow which none could even lift. He was followed by his devoted brother Laxman and Hanuman, the monkey-god. Rama was on his way to Lanka (Ceylon) to battle with evil there, in the shape of Ravana who abducted Sita. . . . He . . . would wipe out wrong and establish on earth truth, beauty and goodness.

Requiring water, Rama made the river Sarayu; subsequently the hamlet of Malgudi sprang up. Thus, modern Malgudi has links with a central Hindu myth, and *The Printer of Malgudi* is a comic distortion of it. Ravi's abduction of

Shanti hilariously parallels Ravana's abduction of Sita, and Srivinas plays a Laxman role in his relationship with Sampath (an ironically identifiable Rama, not a worthy hero) and with Ravi. Whimsically, Srivinas' imagination, which had been dedicated to transliterating the Shiva myth on celluloid, now automatically responds to legend cinematically.

As the camera of time rolls, Malgudi is seen to have microcosmic associations with the major phases of India's past.

> When the Buddha came this way, preaching his gospel of compassion, centuries later, he passed along the main street of a prosperous village. Men, women and children gathered around him. He saw a woman weeping. She had recently lost her child and seemed disconsolate. He told her he would give her consolation if she could bring him handful of mustard from any house where death was unknown. She went from door to door and turned away from every one of them. Amongst all those hundreds of houses she could not find one where death was a stranger. She understood the lesson. . . . A little crumbling masonry and a couple of stone pillars, beyond Lawley Extension, now marked the spot where the Buddha had held his congregation. . . .

> The great Shankara appeared during the next millenium. He saw on the riverbank a cobra spreading its hood and shielding a spawning frog from the rigor of the midday sun. He remarked: "Here the extremes meet. The cobra, which is the natural enemy of the frog, gives it succor. This is where I must build up my temple." He installed the goddess there and preached his gospel of *Vedanta;* the identity and oneness of God and His creatures.

> And then the Cristian missionary with his Bible. In his wake the merchant and the soldier—people who paved the way for Edward Shilling and his Engladia Bank.

The Buddha episode, with its moral of compassion based on the universality of human suffering, reminds the reader of Srivinas' humane and comic endeavours, both as an editor who within "twelve pages of foolscap . . . attempted to set the world right," and as a friend to Ravi whom the "fates seemed to have chosen . . . for their greatest experiment in messing things up." The fable of the extremes meeting in the cobra and the frog provides an analogy, humorously discrepant, of some of the relationships in the novel. Srivinas seeks peace, but the hood of discord spreads over him: "Here I am seeking harmony in life, and yet with such a discord at the start of the day itself." On another occa-

sion he interprets a trivial hurt he gave his wife as "the original violence which has started a cycle . . . the despair of Gandhi," and sees nonviolence "with a new significance, as one of the paths of attaining harmony in life." However, Srinivas's domestic discord seems slight compared with that of the trio—Sampath, Shanti, and Ravi. Significantly, Shanti is very attached to her cobra-head handbag, which, Srinivas remarked to Sampath, "seemed such a symbolic appendage for a beautiful woman."

Especially meaningful from a Hindu standpoint is the involvement versus nonattachment situation in which Srinivas finds himself for most of the novel. Sampath is in octopus of gregarious affection. When having lunch in a restaurant he brightens up everyone who goes near him and keeps "the whole establishment in excellent humor." "When a person becomes my customer he becomes a sort of blood relation of mine," he tells Srinivas. He introduces Shanti as his cousin!

As Srinivas watches Ravi being exorcised he experiences a revelation—the necessity for a person to achieve his "true identity"—and now puts his adventures in Hindu perspective. Reflecting on fate and reincarnation, Srinivas is convinced that to equate the moment with the eternal is absurd; and this realisation frees him from the bonds of involvement:

> Dynasties rose and fell. Palaces and mansions appeared and disappeared. The entire country went down under the fire and sword of the invader, and was washed clean when Sarayu overflowed its bounds. But it always had its rebirth and growth. And throughout the centuries, Srinivas felt, this group was always there: Ravi with his madness, his well-wishers with their panaceas and their apparatus of cure. Half the madness was his own doing, his lack of self-knowledge, his treachery to his own instincts as an artist, which had made him a battle-ground. Sooner or later he shook off his madness and realized his true identity—though not in one birth, at least in a series of them. "What did it amount to?" Srinivas asked himself as the historical picture faded out. "Who am I to bother about Ravi's madness or sanity? What madness to think I am his keeper?" This notion seemed to him so ridiculous that he let out a laugh.

> . . . The recent vision had given him a view in which it seemed to him all the same whether they thwacked Ravi with a cane or whether they left him alone, whether he was mad or sane—all that seemed unimportant and not worth bothering about . . . in the rush of eternity nothing mattered.

At the end of the novel, when Srinivas "was once again in

danger of getting involved" with Sampath, he achieves his freedom without conceding any more than a gesture of "bare humanity." Although Srinivas has had a surfeit of Sampath and is rediscovering the enchantment of working on his newspaper, he had felt earlier much more than bare humanity towards the printer. Narayan obviously shares the fascination felt by the editor for the magnetic personality; and as involvement is the stuff of his novels, as it is the stuff of human life, the author's fascination with life is not likely to stop at the extreme of detached harmony. Such fascination is less consistent with withdrawal than the hope of reconciliation between the cobra and the frog. Sampath's character, however pathetic at the end, was too intriguing to be totally surrendered, and he made good sense when he told Srinivas "man's heart is not a narrow corner."

The Printer of Malgudi then, ends with the two central characters going their divergent ways; Srinivas has survived the encounter and seems to have glimpsed his "true identity." As has been suggested, this denouement has been precipitated by the formal synthesis of story and parabolical or archetypal setting whereby Narayan relates comedy, at its deepest levels, to life. Accordingly, it is hardly surprising that Srinivas retrospectively regards his movie associates as "figures out of a nightmare," that he says "They all belong to a previous life," and that "'Nonsense—an adult occupation' was one of the outstanding editorials he wrote after *The Banner*'s rebirth." Adept at humorously revealing the general in the particular, Narayan achieves his parabolical comedy in characteristically Indian terms. This comic method has a parallel in the intention underlying the "Life's Background" feature in *The Banner*:

> He had tried to summarize, in terms of modern living some of the messages he had imbibed from the Upanishads on the conduct of life, a restatement of subjective value in relation to a social outlook. This statement was very necessary for his questioning mind; for while he thundered against municipal or social shortcomings a voice went on asking: "Life and the world and all this is passing—why bother about anything? The perfect and the imperfect are all the same. Why really bother?" He had to find an answer to the question. And that he did in this series.

Another Narayan quality which complements his comic imagination is the capacity to experience "great wonder at the multitudinousness and vastness of the whole picture of life"; at the same time it is a capacity which he is capable of treating ironically:

> . . . tracing each noise to its source and to its conclusion back and forth, one got a picture, which was too huge even to contemplate. The vastness and infiniteness of it stirred Srinivas deeply. "That's clearly too big,

even for contemplation," he remarked to himself, "because it is in that total picture we perceive God. Nothing else in creation can ever assume such proportions and diversity. This indeed ought to be religion. Alas, how I wish I could convey a particle of this experience to my readers. There are certain thoughts which are strangled by expression. If only people could realize what immense schemes they are components of!" At this moment he heard over everything else a woman's voice saying: "I will kill that dirty dog if he comes near the tap again."

Such is the flexibility of Narayan's comedy that it accommodates Srinivas's "questioning mind" and his own in conjunction with the exposition of serious themes, particularly the identity of the Self, the intricacy of human relationships, the nature and problems of art.

Srinivas' decision to found *The Banner* resulted from philosophical preoccupations about the Self, and his jocular earnestness is nicely in keeping with Narayan's comic tone. When asked by his future landlord "Who are you?" he replies: "It is a profound question. What mortal can answer it?" Srinivas realizes that, to begin with, man has to be more than a mere economic unit if he is to know himself, and he later comes to the conclusion that to understand oneself is to "understand everything." He examines this "big problem" in the light of the following Upanishadic text: "Knowing the self as without body among the embodied, the abiding among the transitory, great and all-pervading—" *The Banner* is to be his means of searching

> . . . for an unknown stablizing factor in life, for an unchanging value, a knowledge of the self, a piece of knowledge which would support as on a rock the faith of Man and his peace; a knowledge of his true identity, which would bring no depression at the coming of age, nor puzzle the mind with conundrums and antitheses.

Srinivas's connection with the "Sunrise Pictures" group makes him acutely conscious of the "very intricate mechanism of human relationships." He marvels at what he imagines to be a cosmic principle of "balance" which obtains in all matters of existence, particularly human relationships. A comprehensive view shows, for example, that there are

> . . . things being neither particularly wrong nor right, but just balancing themselves. Just the required number of wrongdoers as there are people who deserved wrong deeds, just as many policemen to bring them to their senses, if possible, and just as many wrongdoers again to keep the police employed, and so on and on in an infinite concentric circle.

The relationship between Ravi and Srinivas is a "concentric circle" which encloses some pertinent observations about the relationship of life to art. As writers, Srinivas and his author both aspire to an impartial and objective artistic ideal, an externalization of emotion, an objective correlative:

> By externalizing emotion, by superimposing feeling in the shape of images, he hoped to express very clearly the substance of this episode: of love and its purification, of austerity and peace.

Thus, in his conception of *The Burning of Kama,* Srinivas is a poetic artist:

> Srinivas's imagination was stirred as he narrated the story. He saw every part of it clearly: the God of Love with his five arrows (five senses); his bow was made of sugar cane, his bowstring was of murmuring honeybees, and his chariot was the light summer breeze. When he attempted to try his strength on the rigorous Shiva himself, he was condemned to an invisible existence. Srinivas read a symbolic meaning in this representation of the power of love, its equipment, its limitation, and saw in the burning of Kama an act of sublimation.

Appropriately, Narayan's ·comic style has effective "cinematic" qualities. When describing the editor's inspired vision of the film medium, Narayan may well have been giving expression to his own consciousness of the artistic limitations of language as well as of the basically dramatic nature of comedy. "Ideas," Srinivas reflects, "were to march straight on from him in all their pristine strength, without the intervention of language: ideas, walking, talking and passing into people's minds as images."

The Srinivas-Ravi relationship also gives rise to a witty play upon the maimed genius and empathetic patron conventions. Thus melodramatic romanticism is expertly turned to comic account:

> He was no longer a petty, hag-ridden bank clerk, or an unwelcome, thoughtless visitor, but a personality, a creative artist, fit to take rank among the celestials.

> Srinivas knew what silent suffering was going on within that shabby frame. He knew that an inspiration had gone out of his life. He had no doubt a home, mother, and brothers and sisters, but all that signified nothing. . . . Srinivas very well knew that he came there only in the hope of news about his lost love. . . .

Ravi also serves to demonstrate the unreliability of the woman element in artistic creation, particularly the anarchic consequences of passionate intensity.

In fusing action, fable, and theme into a comic whole Narayan uses Srinivas as a unifying agent, a sensitive consciousness at the heart of the novel. Accordingly he employs a limited third-person point of view, one of his favorite narrative devices. The author is not as austere as his main character wants to be; for his comedy is liberally spiced with the entertainment equivalents of dance, music, and light relief to which Srinivas objects in *The Burning of Kama.* On the other hand, the author infuses Srinivas with his own comic spirit as is shown by the characterization in the opening pages. The editor is well aware of the "comicality," "an odd mixture of the sublime and the ridiculous," in his "bombast."

And in the final analysis *The Printer of Malgudi* entertainingly reveals R. K. Narayan as a comedian of the sublime and the ridiculous.

Neil Millar (review date 19 February 1970)

SOURCE: "A Piquant Infusion of India," in *Christian Science Monitor,* Vol. 62, No. 72, February 19, 1970, p. 10.

[*In the following review, Millar discusses the character studies in the stories of Narayan's* A Horse and Two Goats.]

Mother India has many gentle children. This book [*A Horse and Two Goats*] is written with the gentleness of strength.

R. K. Narayan is a novelist of distinction who follows no trend but humanity, no vision but his own—kindly, level, comical, moved.

A Horse and Two Goats is a collection of short stories, all (one suspects) wholly Indian in spirit. Each of them is a character study, a glint of mankind, an infusion of India.

The surface is comedy and tragicomedy. Sometimes grief lies under it, but never despair. And each story deserves to be read at least twice—in an age when much contemporary fiction may not deserve to be read once.

Mr. Narayan's quiet, almost insidious prose makes it clear that his world is not ours, although part of ours may be part of his. But his world is available to us, an achievement made possible by his skill and by the common humanity of both worlds.

Not that the author's people are especially common; his

main actors are all eccentrics in one way or another. (Who isn't?) They teach us lessons for or about ourselves. Perhaps all credible tales of possible people do that.

Some of the lessons are incidental. In the tale which names the book, a destitute goatherd is given 100 rupees—$7.50 in United States currency—a sum which seems to him almost a fortune. (How enormously wealthy are we who can afford to buy a book every week and a full meal every day!) But this story's light is made to glance off many subjects other than destitution and riches—success and failure, for example, India and America, sculpture in public places, courtesy, and the failure to communicate.

Poverty hangs on the bright Indian air, but nobody seems to be polluted by it—at least, not to the point of self-pity or opting out of the world. Most of Mr. Narayan's characters are eager to opt in.

In the longest story, **"Uncle,"** a man looks back on his childhood and the fat, mysterious guardian who cherished him. There have been sinister mutterings about the uncle's past, but the nephew does not investigate them, does not even want to know if they are true. Did the uncle—if he was an uncle—gamble away his protégé's inheritance? Did it matter? One thing was certain in the fog of doubt: the man loved the boy.

To read this story is to walk or dart through infancy again, viewing the strange and sometimes terrifying adult world through childhood's bold or anxious eyes.

The next story is a character study of the gardener Annamalai, grumpy, loyal, pathetic, an elderly strong man sorely tried by a distant brother and a near neighbor, a comic figure, and a mystery in his own right. This tale has a half-hidden villain, and it is the narrator.

"A Breath of Lucifer" concerns a hospital attendant, a male nurse, a man of imagination. Although probably a fraud, he is a competent artisan at his noble craft and an incompetent amateur of the ignoble bottle. We never see him, but we know him.

And lastly Krishna, a young man deeply in love with his wife. She is ill: her cheerfully inept physician is unconcerned. Her husband consults an astrologer, who suggests therapeutic immorality in order to appease the wrath of Mars. In loyalty to his beloved, Krishna should be unfaithful to her.

Hapless Krishna! He does his best to do his worst, to dishonor his marriage in order to save his wife, but miserably fails to find a partner in well-intentioned sin. Mournfully

he returns home. The story ends there. So does this calm, delicate, adult quintette of poignant comedies.

They open windows into one man's half-invented world. They handle their strength gently. If their sorrow comes gift-wrapped in a smile, the smile is genuine and the sorrow unemphasized, almost unacknowledged.

Every one of Mr. Narayan's unconscious comedians is believable and even likable. Their author loves them all.

This illumines them.

Bhagwat S. Goyal (essay date 1977)

SOURCE: "From Picaro to Pilgrim: A Perspective on R. K. Narayan's *The Guide,*" in *Indo-English Literature: A Collection of Critical Essays,* edited by K. K. Sharma, Vimal Prakashan, 1977, pp. 141-56.

[*Goyal was a book reviewer for the* Hindustan Times *and has published several books analyzing literature. In the following essay, he traces the metamorphosis of the main character, Raja, in Narayan's* The Guide.]

He chiefly relies on a resilient and multidimensional irony to expose the human follies and absurdities generated by a blind adherence to obsolete custom, mechanical ritual, and belittlingsuperstition.
—*Bhagwat S. Goyal*

R. K. Narayan's literary imagination has the same dazzling comicality, the same vigorous mask-stripping as the creative genius of his brother, R. K. Laxman, the celebrated cartoonist. Narayan, however, does not resort to exaggeration, distortion, or caricature to achieve his comic effects. He chiefly relies on a resilient and multidimensional irony to expose the human follies and absurdities generated by a blind adherence to obsolete custom, mechanical ritual, and belittling superstition. He is well-acquainted with the powerful hold of traditional values and attitudes on the psyche of middle-class Hindus and skilfully portrays the subtle operation of vague, amorphous and mystifying beliefs in their lives. His major themes and techniques are defined by the exigencies arising out of the conflict between middle-class morality and individual aspiration and between human endeavour and its unexpected consequences, by his human and social concerns, and by his intense preoccupation with man's need and desire to achieve salvation through the realization of a symbiotic relationship between the individual and society.

The Guide occupies a unique position in the Narayan canon. It is the eighth novel written by him and is an obvious manifestation of his thematic brilliance and stylistic sophistication. In this novel, Narayan seems to be particularly fascinated by the ubiquitous presence of swamis and saints, gurus and guides, charlatans and philistines, cobras and concubines in India's colourful society. With the aid of his characteristic, indulgent humour, he is able to capture the captivating spectrum of Indian life, with all its superstitions and hypocrisies, its beliefs and follies, its intricacies and vitalities, its rigidities and flexibilities.

One fruitful way of looking at this fascinating novel is to see it as a vivid and vitally comic variation on the Kafkaesque theme of metamorphosis. Whereas in Kafka's terrifying story, Gregor Samsa finds himself metamorphosed into a gigantic insect, in Narayan's novel a "picaro" finds himself transformed into a "pilgrim", a criminal changed into a saint. The central experience at the heart of both these pieces of fiction is, however, spiritual. In both the cases the protagonists have been parasites, have always let others decide for them, and have always postponed the claims of the human self, till a stage is reached when these can't be put off any further. But while Gregor's "metamorphosis is a judgment on himself by his defeated humanity", Raju's metamorphosis is a judgment on himself by his victorious humanity. What kills Gregor is "spiritual starvation", but what fills Raju with glory is "spiritual fulfilment".

The action of the novel proceeds in two distinct streams, presenting two different aspects of Indian culture. One stream flows in the legendary Malgudi (a miniature India) with its rich tradition of classical dances offered by Rosie-Nalini and the breathtaking cave-paintings that embellish Marco's *The Cultural History of South India.* Another stream flows in the neighbouring town of Mangala, where the spiritual dimension of Indian culture is presented through Raju's growth into a celebrated swami. Raju's presence in both these streams indicates the close affinity between art and spirituality in India. Thus Raju, Rosie and Marco become temporal symbols of India's cultural ethos. While Marco's aspirations seek their fulfilment in unearthing the buried treasures of India's rich cultural past, Rosie's longing seeks satisfaction in the creative channels of classical dancing in the midst of an ever-present, live audience. Raju is all the time dreaming of an elusive future till a time comes when he is irrevocably committed to a definite future by undertaking a fast in the hope of appeasing the rain-god. While Marco is a cultural historian of the past, Rosie is a cultural ambassador of the present, and Raju is a cultural prophet of the future. Before reaching the supreme

excellence in their respective fields, however, they are debased and tainted by the exclusiveness of their passions. Marco's obsessive devotion to the pursuit of India's cultural heritage keeps him tied down to a sterile, dry intellectualism, affecting his human wholeness. Similarly, Rosie's quest for stardom makes her compromise with the purity of her art, resulting in her submission to mixed dance-forms like the cobra dance. Raju is able to achieve a new spiritual status only when the dross of his unholy desires is burnt away in the fire of self-purification achieved through discipline and rigorous self-control.

One of the basic themes of the novel is the acquisition of genuine humanity by a man through the realization of his human and spiritual selfhood. The novel traces the growth of Raju from a spurious, no-good fellow to a genuine human being. Throughout his life he has remained a fake romantic individualist, only to realise in the end that his one chance of redemption lies in becoming a real martyr to the needs of the people. The pattern of Raju's life is determined by his inability to say "I don't know" under any circumstances. From a petty shopkeeper he becomes a tourist guide, popularly known as "Railway Raju". He is fired with ambition and his fame and reputation as a seasoned guide spread far and wide. For him his new vocation becomes both a source of earning and self-education: "I learned while I taught and earned while I learned, and the whole thing was most enjoyable." Perhaps he would have remained a tourist guide, if he had not met a girl who called herself Rosie and who changed the whole course of his life. The moment she sets foot in Malgudi, she asks to be shown a king cobra which can dance to the music of a flute. Her husband, whom Raju chooses to call Marco (because he is dressed like an eternal traveller) is repelled at the idea and it is obvious that the husband and wife have diametrically opposite tastes and interests. Raju is so fascinated by the girl's loveliness and elegance that he grooms himself with extra care in order to be more presentable. He doesn't find her very glamorous, but her sparkling eyes and dusky complexion fire his senses and he finds himself irresistibly drawn to her. When he takes her to see the cobra dance, he immediately realizes that she is a born dancer. Later, when Marco wants to go to see the cave paintings, Raju is surprised to see him alone. Marco asks Raju to try his persuasiveness on Rosie. Raju is happy to get such an assignment. Embellishing his talk with charming flattery and romantic effusiveness, he is able to persuade her to accompany them to the caves. Raju takes them to the Peak House whose natural surroundings and exotic charm fill Rosie with ecstasy. But when Raju goes there next morning he finds that Marco and Rosie have again had a quarrel. He thinks of Marco in relation to Rosie as "a monkey picking up a rose garland." He is unable to understand Marco's obsessive interest in ancient relics, and says, "Dead and decaying things seemed to unloosen his tongue and fire his imagination, rather than things that lived and moved and swung their limbs." He is bored with Marco's "ruin-collecting activities". Rosie, too, doesn't like to see the "cold, old stone walls". Raju learns that Rosie belongs to a family "traditionally dedicated to the temples as dancers", which means she was a *deva daasi* (god's maid). Though her caste was not looked upon with respect, she decided to pursue higher studies and took Master's Degree in Economics. After seeing a matrimonial advertisement announcing "No caste restrictions", she got married to Marco. She found that her wealthy husband was more interested in books, papers, painting and old art than in being a "real, live husband". When Marco decides to stay on to explore the cave paintings fully, Raju takes charge of Rosie and soon becomes her ardent lover.

Marco accepts Raju as a member of his family. Analysing the causes of Marco's failure with Rosie, Raju says: "Marco was just unpractical, an absolutely helpless man. All that he could do was to copy ancient things and write about them . . . Perhaps he married out of a desire to have someone care for his practical life, but unfortunately his choice was wrong—this girl herself was a dreamer if ever there was one. She would have greatly benefited by a husband who could care for her career." Marco, of course, does not have the least suspicion regarding any kind of physical relationship between Rosie and Raju. He seems to have full confidence in his wife's fidelity and trust in Raju's sincerity. He is, perhaps, unable to gauge the extent of his wife's passion for dancing and her sense of emotional suffocation. Rosie can't share her husband's enthusiasm for old cave paintings and other relics. Marco thinks that the very fact of his having provided respectability, security and wealth to Rosie should keep her satisfied. But Rosie dreams of having her own career as a dancer and Raju is able to perceive the intensity of her desire which he fully exploits: "I found out the clue to her affection, and utilized it to the utmost." For Raju, Rosie becomes the only reality in his life and consciousness. He is, however, unable to understand the strange conflict going on in the heart of Rosie. In spite of her submission to Raju, she continues to have regard for her husband. As Raju puts it, "She allowed me to make love to her, of course, but she was also beginning to show excessive consideration for her husband on the hill." Perhaps the strong pull of middle-class morality and the Indian woman's traditional subservience to and worship of her husband as a god makes her feel drawn to Marco. "After all, he is my husband. I have to respect him. I cannot leave him there." Obviously, it is not out of any genuine love or regard for her husband that she wants to pay attention to him; it is just because of the accepted social conventions that she *has* to do it. She possibly wants to have the best of both the worlds: the name, honour and wealth of her husband, and physical love and fulfilment of her ambition to dance from Raju. There doesn't seem to be any sincere or genuine conflict in her heart, even though she tells Raju: "Is this right what I am doing? After all, he has been so good to me, given me comfort and freedom." When Raju asks her why she doesn't stay with him and take interest in his activities like a good wife, she merely sighs.

Aided by Raju, Rosie begins to practise *Bharat Natyam.* She reads *Natya Shastra of Bharat Muni* in order to acquaint herself with the purity of the classical forms of dance. She also begins to teach Raju the elementary things about this dance form. Raju is able to see that Rosie is a very talented dancer, so much so that "when she indicated the lotus with her fingers, you could almost hear the ripple of water around it." He also feels the sublimating power of art: "While I watched her perform, my mind was free, for once, from all carnal thoughts, I viewed her as a pure abstraction."

Things, however, take a sudden, dramatic turn. When Raju interferes too much in the affairs of Marco and Rosie, he is asked to keep away from them. He finds himself in a strange dilemma. Neither has he broken off completely from Rosie, nor does he have any meetings with her. He "never bargained for this kind of inexplicable stalemate." He had got used to "a glamorous, romantic existence" so much that he feels "bored and terrified by the boredom of normal life." He is depressed to think that Rosie will soon go away from his life for ever. But he finds himself in the seventh heaven when Rosie comes back to him. She is highly depressed as her husband has refused to take her with him. Raju soon learns about the cause of her present plight. Rosie had sought Marco's permission to dance because she thought she would be very happy if she could do that. She would like to make experiments in dancing in the same way as Marco had been doing in his field of historical research. This equation between an intellectual discipline and an athletic exercise inflamed him and he said: "This is a branch of learning, not street-acrobatics." Marco told her exactly what Hazlitt says about the nature of mechanical performance in his celebrated essay, *The Indian Juggler:* "An acrobat on a trapeze goes on doing the same thing all his life; well, your dance is like that. What is there intelligent or creative in it? You repeat your tricks all your life. We watch a monkey perform, not because it is artistic, but because it is a monkey that is doing it." Even this did not dishearten her totally. She asked him to see a dance piece and then make up his mind. Marco saw it but told her that there was nothing artistic in it. But she committed a blunder by saying that everyone liked it except him. She referred to Raju and Marco probed her more deeply about what she had been doing all the time. He was soon convinced of her infidelity and decided to leave her behind. He told her plainly: ". . . you are not my wife. You are a woman who will go to bed with anyone that flatters your antics."

Now that Rosie has nowhere to go, she comes to depend on Raju. Raju's mother is suspicious of her from the very beginning. She warns her son: "She is a real snake-woman, I tell you." Raju finds himself deeply sunk in debt. His career as a well-known guide has almost come to an end. He begins to apply his mind to the possible exploration of Rosie's passion for dancing for commercial purposes. With a businessman's shrewd instinct he thinks of her as a gold-mine and tells his friend Gaffur: "You know *Bharat Natyam* is really the greatest art-business today". As Rosie continues her practice sessions, Raju realizes that for her her art is foremost. "She was a devoted artist, her passion for physical love was falling into place, and had ceased to be a primary obsession with her."

Another dramatic turn comes in the novel when Rosie is given a new name, Nalini, and she is introduced as a new dancing sensation. Raju invites the Secretary and the Treasurer of Albert Mission School Students' Union to see the performance of Nalini, so that if they like it they can have her dance recital in their annual function instead of the usual Shakespearean tragedy. The boys are enchanted and say that "watching this lady is an education". And so the meteoric rise of Nalini as a dancer begins. Raju becomes a shrewd impresario, handling all Nalini's assignments. While Nalini acquires fame as a great dancer, Raju accumulates wealth and with that a prominent social status. He is "on back-slapping terms with two judges, four eminent politicians of the district whose ward could bring 10,000 votes at any moment for any cause, and two big textile mill-owners, a banker, a municipal councillor, and the editor of *The Truth*." Through his intimacy with all sorts of people, he knows "what was going on behind the scenes in the Government, at the market, at Delhi, on the racecourse, and who was going to be who in the coming week."

Raju, however, exploits Rosie for his own advantage and narrow, selfish ends. He says, "I had a monopoly of her and nobody had anything to do with her. . . . She was my property." And a little later, ". . . I did not like to see her enjoy other people's company. I liked to keep her in a citadel." This narrow monopolization of her makes her suffer from a "dangerous weariness." Raju had practically forgotten about Marco's existence. One day he receives a parcel containing Marco's book, *The Cultural History of South India*, in which the author has acknowledged Raju's help in locating the caves. Soon after, a letter addressed to Rosie alias Nalini arrives which Raju opens. Learning that Rosie's signatures are required on a document for the release of her jewellery-box, Raju's foolish impulse gets the better of his judgment and he forges Rosie's signatures and waits for the arrival of the box. What he receives instead is a warrant for his arrest. In spite of the best efforts of his adjournment-expert lawyer, Raju is sentenced to two years' imprisonment.

Once inside the jail, Raju turns into a different sort of person. Perhaps what had happened was all to his spiritual good. He is considered "a model prisoner". He becomes a *Vadhyar* or teacher to the other prisoners and tells them "stories and philosophies and what not". He even gets to love his life in the prison. Narayan's irony and sarcasm get into full play when he makes Raju say: "If this was prison life, why didn't more people take to it? They thought of it with a shudder, as if it were a place where a man was branded, chained, and lashed from morning to night! Medieval notions! No place could be more agreeable; if you observed the rules you earned greater appreciation here than beyond the high walls." This last comment goes to the very heart of the paradox of freedom. The life "beyond the high walls" doesn't care for the observation of rules—it only brings chaos and anarchy. But life inside the prison gets full appreciation for the observation of rules. Raju, however, is galled to think of Rosie's rise to new heights of stardom and popularity without him. "Her empire was expanding rather than shrinking. It filled me with gall that she should go on without me." Even though a perceptible change has occurred within him, his basic egotism remains. It's only in the end that he is able to conquer it and achieve salvation.

When Raju is released from the prison he takes shelter in an old ruin of an ancient shrine in Mangala, where the process of his spiritual rebirth begins. In this ruin, Raju sits on a granite slab cross-legged "as if it were a throne". Immediately after his release from the prison, he had gone to a barber's shop where he was made to "look like a *maharaja*". Now both these words "throne" and "maharaja" indicate that this shrine will become his new-found kingdom where he will acquire a new stature, a new authority and a new awareness. Of course, Raju himself is blissfully unaware of any such prospect at the moment. Right now his main worry is not to let his shady past be known to the people. The innocent village-man, Velan, who takes Raju to be a swami, assigns him a role which eminently suits Raju's histrionic genius. When Velan states that he has a problem, Raju asks him to tell him about it, his "old, old habit of affording guidance to others asserting itself". Raju impresses Velan, with his clever talk, but when the grateful man tries to touch Raju's feet, Raju recoils and doesn't permit him to do so. His simple humanistic instinct revolts against this act of debasement. There is a mixture of hard irony and bitter truth when he says: "God alone is entitled to such a prostration. He will destroy us if we attempt to usurp His rights."

When Velan brings his rebellious sister for Raju's guidance, Raju tells him that the time is not yet ripe to think of his problems. With a brilliant broadside on Indian holymen's tricks, Narayan shows how they shift the matters requiring immediate attention to the realms of eternity, as Raju does when he tells Velan: "We cannot force vital solutions. Every question must bide its time." Then exercising a sort of hypnotic spell on Velan's "difficult" sister through a fixed stare, he says: "What must happen must happen; no power on earth or in heaven can change its course just as no one can change the course of that river." This has a desired effect both on Velan and his sister for we learn later that all his worries are over and his sister has agreed to do exactly as she is told to do. Raju's trick is only to utter high-sounding platitudes before these simple, gullible people, whose unshakeable faith in the miraculous powers of the swami makes them take every word spoken by him as a word of God. With a little application of his knowledge of human psychology which he acquired during his work as a tourist guide and later as a leading socialite, he can create an impression of profundity and greatness on his admirers. That he comes to acquire almost a mesmeric hold on the minds of the simple village folk is obvious when Velan's sister tells everyone about him: "He doesn't speak to anyone, but if he looks at you you are changed." The reputation of his miraculous powers begins to spread all around, but Raju himself is disturbed by his unexpected popularity. Feeling ill-at-ease in his present role he thinks of fleeing the place. But when he ponders over the matter more seriously he realizes that he has nowhere to go and possibly he could not find a better place. Moreover, he has not trained himself to make a living out of hard work. His fundamental parasitism makes him realize that he has no alternative, "he must play the role that Velan had given him."

The deserted shrine occupied by Raju soon begins to hum with activity. It becomes the site of a children's school in the evening, which gives Raju "a chance to air his views on life and eternity before the boys". He speaks to them "on godliness, cleanliness, on Ramayana, the characters in the epics; . . . on all kinds of things." The elders also seek to be enlightened by his discourse, but Raju cleverly evades it by saying, "All things have to wait their hour." Does Raju really believe in what he says here? Or, is he merely mouthing the mystic jargon of the swamis? Do the events occur in a pattern predetermined by the mysterious Spirit of Time? The spirit in which the author wishes us to take Raju's homilies becomes clear when he comments: "The essence of sainthood seemed to lie in one's ability to utter mystifying statements." Not only this. Raju should also grow a beard and long hair if he wishes to enhance his spiritual status. The swamihood becomes a matter of glib talk and a particular kind of physical make-up. By the time Raju arrives at the stage of stroking his beard thoughtfully, his prestige has grown beyond his wildest dreams. He finds that he can no more afford a private life. "He seemed to belong to the world now. His influence was unlimited." He soon finds himself becoming a multi-purpose swami as he begins to discharge the functions of a medical man, legal adviser, spiritual healer, chanter of holy verses and discourser on philosophy.

Raju's enforced sainthood leads him to a state when he finds it unnecessary to maintain a calendar. Having lost count of time he passes into the realm of timelessness. It is obvious that playing the role of a swami has affected his inner being as well as refined his human sensibility. "His eyes shone with softness and compassion, the light of wisdom emanated from them." He receives so many gifts from the villagers that he loses interest in accumulation. He even protests to Velan one day. "I'm a poor man and you are poor men; why do you give me all this? You must stop it." But who can stop these credulous illiterates from giving gifts to a swami?

Things would have continued to be rosy for Raju, had not a severe drought created the conditions of scarcity and famine in Mangala. The natural rhythm and flow of time seemed to have been disturbed and Raju quickly perceived it. When Velan described the grim situation to Raju, he consolingly said: "Such things are common; don't worry too much about them. Let us hope for the best." Though the doubts and cares of the people are not stilled by these words, they dare not challenge the sacred authority of the all-knowing swami. The continued absence of rains evokes fantastic speculations from the villagers. One villager wants to know if the "rains fall" because "the movement of aeroplanes disturbs the clouds", while the other seeks to know if "the atom bombs are responsible for the drying up of the clouds". This reveals a peculiar aspect of Indian life: the remarkable co-existence of science and superstition, knowledge and ignorance, mythology and weather-prediction. Raju tries his best to console and amuse the villagers with his purportedly solemn but actually light-hearted explanations, but even comforting words and "discipline of thinking" lose their power in the face of a grim struggle for survival. As the fast depletion of the material resources of sustenance leads to harrowing conditions of existence, "philosophical attitude" loses all meaning. When cattle stop yielding milk and fail to drag the plough through the furrows, when sheep look scurvy and bony and when wells and earth dry up, the harmony of human relationships is acutely disturbed. "They quarrelled over the water-hole for priorities, and there was fear, desperation, and lamentation in their voices."

The villagers begin to lose their heads and enter "a nightmare phase". They ask Raju to accompany them and see for himself the dying cattle. When he does go, however unwillingly, he is repelled by the sickening odour emitted by the dead buffalo. He knows that he cannot mitigate the foul smell by "soothsaying" but when he learns that the buffalo doesn't belong to anyone known, Raju offers consolation by saying that probably it was a wild buffalo and was bitten by a poisonous insect. To the desperate villagers this explanation comes as a great relief. But with famine conditions persisting, the village shopman begins to demand higher prices for grain, which leads to his quarrelling with a person who can't pay the enhanced price and soon it flares up into a full-scale battle between two groups, in which Velan is also badly hurt. When Raju, the arch-escapist, hears the shrieks and cries of the fighting villagers, he begins to think of leaving the place: "At this rate, I think I'll look for a new place." The heart-rending scenes of drought and famine leave him cold and so long as he can be fed free he doesn't mind staying there. He doesn't feel involved at all in the suffering and tragedy of the people. He represents the countless fake swamis in India leading a parasitic life. Raju's crass cynicism and heartlessness become glaringly evident when in his characteristic, but grimly humorous vein, Narayan comments: "Personally, he felt that the best thing for them would be to blow each other's brains out. That'd keep them from bothering too much about the drought."

When Velan's brother comes to Raju to report that Velan is hurt and that the two groups are preparing to fight again, Raju tells him that "It is not right." The stupid brother of Velan begins to argue and Raju gets annoyed. Raju asks him to go and tell Velan to stop the fight. "Tell your brother, immediately, wherever he may be, that unless they are good I'll never eat." Velan's brother is completely mystified and he is unable to see any connection between the fight and Raju's food. He promises, however, to deliver the message, but when he actually does so he gives a garbled version, "He wants no food until it is all right." The villagers think that Raju is undertaking fast to appease the rain-god. One of them says: "He is like Mahatma. When Mahatma Gandhi went without food, how many things happened in India! This is a man like that. If he fasts there will be rain." Thus the victims of the great Gandhian hoax begin to feel elated without realizing that if a man's fast could affect the pitiless elements and could produce rains or stop floods governments would have saved millions of rupees spent over huge irrigation projects!

Enthused by the implication of Raju's fast, the people of Mangala forget about their quarrel and decide to go and pay their respects to "Swami, our Saviour." But the person whom they think as their saviour is really an inhuman monster who even now, in the midst of a black famine, waits "for his usual gifts and food". He cleverly extracts the food of his choice from these simple, superstitious villagers. Narayan's tongue-in-cheek irony explodes in full blast when he tells us Raju managed to relate "some principle of living" with a particular variety of delicious food, and "he mentioned it with an air of seriousness so that his listeners took it as a spiritual need, something of the man's inner discipline to keep his soul in shape and his understanding with the Heavens in order." Even while he

discourses on *Bhagvat-Gita*, the gospel of selfless action and detachment, he thinks of eating *bondas*. He is disappointed when he finds that the people haven't brought any food for him. When they praise him for his fast he tells them that it is good that they have patched up and that he will take his usual food next day. Velan asks him if he expects it to rain and he tells him what his brother has told people in the village. The village community, which has been feeding Raju and worshipping him as a saint, can legitimately expect him to do this saintly service for the people—a little penance and fasting for two weeks to bring down rains. Raju realizes that he has been caught in the trap of his own smartness. He decides to take his own words more seriously and the first thing he does now is to come down from his high pedestal. "He now saw the enormity of his own creation. He had created a giant with his puny self, a throne of authority with that slab of stone." He asks Velan to give him a day to think over the whole matter. His first impulse is to run away from the whole stupid *tamasha*. But then he recollects the crowds of faithful men, women and children touching his feet reverently and putting their great trust in him. He thinks that if he could keep food in reserve and be left alone at night, he could come off the ordeal of the fast successfully. He believes that the rains would descend in their natural course sooner or later, and then everything would be all right.

Raju asks Velan, "What makes you think that I can bring the rain?", and Velan replies that they have full faith in what he had told his brother. Even now Raju avoids stating plain truth. He, however, has decided to tell Velan the whole story of his life. He tells him that he can undertake the fast but it will not have any meaning because he is not a saint. When he concludes his story a new day has dawned. Raju thinks that Velan will react angrily to his being an imposter, but to his utter surprise Velan addresses him as Swami and assures him that he will never utter a word of what he has heard to anyone.

Raju's fast soon begins to assume great public importance. Even the Government is compelled to send a commission to enquire into the drought conditions and to suggest remedies. A press correspondent sends a telegraphic message, "Holy man's penance to end drought", and public interest is at once aroused. Daily dispatches are sent about the Swami's fast with detailed descriptions of his penance. Soon the whole thing assumes the spirit of a carnival. Raju finds himself turned into a big celebrity. At the same time, however, he loses his privacy and he feels sick of the whole thing. He wants to shout at the people to tell them that he cannot save them. No power on earth can save them if they are doomed. But he also realizes that there is no escape for him now. He should therefore face his trial as best as he can. This proves to be the final turning point of his life. He begins to think about his fast more seriously. Realizing that the famine doesn't allow him to get any food, why shouldn't he try to live up gracefully to his role? "Why not give the poor devil a chance, Raju said to himself, instead of hankering after food which one could not get, anyway?" This resolution gives him a peculiar moral strength. He begins to reflect upon the significance of his fast. "If by avoiding food I should help the trees bloom, and the grass grow, why not do it thoroughly?" This does not mean, however, that Raju suddenly becomes a religious convert and that he sincerely believes that his fast would bring rains. He decides to observe fast in a genuine spirit more as a concession to people's belief and as an act of self-discipline rather than in expectation of causing a miracle. His whole life has been a ceaseless record of deception, trickery and sexual licence, and now he wishes to confront his naked, real self. "For the first time in his life he was making an earnest effort, for the first time he was learning the thrill of full application, outside money and love; for the first time he was doing a thing in which he was not personally interested." Rising above a narrow, selfish individualism, Raju seeks to discover his true human identity through the identification of his fate with that of the whole humanity.

The sleepy village of Mangala is thrown into sudden limelight. Crowds of picnickers, journalists, thrill-seekers, devotees and all sorts of people begin to converge at this small village. Almost a new township springs around the place. This peculiar feature of the Indian way of life—how people turn even a grim thing like a famine into an occasion for a festive gathering is dramatically highlighted here. Malone, an American T.V.-man comes with his whole paraphernalia to shoot the event. His interview with Raju is a remarkable piece of Narayan's sustained irony.

"Tell me, how do you like it here?"

"I am only doing what I have to do; that's all. My likes and dislikes do not count."

"Can fasting abolish all wars and bring in world peace?"

"Yes."

"What about the caste system? Is it going?"

"Yes."

"Will you tell us something about your early life?"

"What do you want me to say?"

"Er—for instance, have you always been a Yogi?"

"Yes; more or less."

It is obvious from this interview that while Raju makes an honest statement in answer to the first question, his answers to other questions are meant more as a snub to the foolishly inquisitive American. We know that Raju has always been a *Bhogi* (a hedonist) rather than a Yogi. The whole tripe about the abolition of wars by means of fasting is nothing short of a biting satire on the Gandhian philosophy of fasting and non-violence. Even the Government seems to be more worried about saving the life of the fasting swami than about providing relief to the famine-stricken villagers. The novel ends with Raju's completion of the last day of his fast. Having become extremely weak owing to his fast, he is hallucinated and he mumbles, "Velan, it's raining in the hills. I can feel it coming up under my feet, up my legs," and with that he sags down. It is natural for him to feel the cold water of the river rushing under his feet making his legs numb. The rains, of course, have not come and even Raju's sagging down doesn't indicate that he dies. The fact is that Narayan leaves his ending deliberately open. The coming of the rains would have meant triumph of superstition over reason, while Raju's death would have reduced his entire penance to a glorious absurdity. What is really important at the end is neither the rains nor the question whether Raju lives or dies, but that Raju has achieved salvation and real human status through his integration with the life of the community.

Prajapati P. Sah (essay date 1980)

SOURCE: "R. K. Narayan's 'Gateman's Gift': The Central Theme," in *Literary Criterion,* Vol. XV, No. 1, 1980, pp. 37-46.

[*In the following essay, Sah asserts that the central theme of* Gateman's Gift *is Govind Singh's role as a socio-economic animal.*]

What is the central theme of R. K. Narayan's story **"Gateman's Gift"?**

In asking this question I assume that a good story is written not purely for entertainment, or for the sake of an interesting and amusing description of an event or a character, but for communicating something to the reader over and above the simple facts of description. By this I do not mean that every good story has a 'message' or a 'moral,' but I do mean that every good story has a perception of reality—be it social or individual, and this is the writer's own perception which he wants to communicate to the reader. The reader of course is at liberty to read the story at any level he likes, and in most cases it may not include the level of the writer's perception of reality, but a good story does not become a good story till it includes this level.

R. K. Narayan, for whom the world of social relations is as important as the inner universe of man and who often reaches great heights in depicting the interaction of the two, is a man of comprehensive vision.
—*Prajapati P. Sah*

When asked to describe the central theme (the main idea, the motivating factor, the writer's intended communication, of **"Gateman's Gift,"** students often quote the opening sentence of the story which is a layman's statement of the psychological principle of suggestion:

> 'When a dozen persons question openly or slyly a man's sanity, he begins to entertain serious doubts himself.'

It takes some time to disabuse the students' minds of the idea that a story is not written to illustrate or 'prove' a principle, whether the principle is a psychological one or a sociological, economic, or scientific one. A story is written because a writer comes across some event, character, episode, etc., in his experience which suddenly forces into his attention some half-recognized truth about the reality of the mental, physical, or social world with a fresh and renewal urgency. The truth may concern any of the various areas which impinge on man's existence—his relations with himself or a transcendental power, his relations with fellow human beings, his position in the psychological, sociological or economic universes of which he is a part, or his relation with the physical universe including nature. Each writer differs in his choice of the areas according to temperament or historical circumstances. R. K. Narayan, for whom the world of social relations is as important as the inner universe of man and who often reaches great heights in depicting the interaction of the two, is a man of comprehensive vision. For an incidental reader this comprehensive vision often tends to get lost in the rich details of person, place and circumstance which first entitled Narayan to the high critical attention as a novelist that he attracted. But, for me at least, the loss in missing the wood for the trees in the case of R. K. Narayan is as great in significance as perhaps it was in those cases of loftier concern for which the metaphor was first devised.

In **"Gateman's Gift"** too, it is easy to lose one's way in the detail. Having dismissed the psychological suggestion theory, one still has to tackle proposals like the following: the complex character of Govind Singh, the subtle psychological workings of his mind which lead him finally to give

up making toys—a depiction of this is the author's main concern. And, of course, there is the chiaroscuro of characters—the invisible business-like Bank Manager with a God-like presence hovering on the scene, the affable and genial Accountant, and the whole lot of very visible bank workers that crowd around Govind Singh's every work of art. The answer is not quite satisfactory: psychology is, of course, present, but it is not mere psychology. Narayan is not interested in complex characters for their own sake, for basically he is a writer, not a psychologist. He is too much interested in the society to be completely absorbed into the psyche of the individual—and this of course is no original statement about Narayan. In any case, psychology alone never made a writer a significant one.

Is it then a sociological study? Are we being invited to witness the effects of class-division? Is it a study of the undesirable effects of premature retirement on able-bodied (and may be not so able-bodied) men with too much leisure? The absurdity of these suggestions becomes quite apparent if we ask the simple question 'Do these factors, either alone or jointly, explain the powerful effect the story has on the reader?'

I do not think one needs to labour the obviously negative answer to this question. Whence does, then, arise the power of the story, the absolute authenticity of the totally unexpected conclusion which signals the unfailing touch of a master? In what follows, I shall attempt to provide an answer.

The answer that I provide to the question raised at the beginning of [the essay] is stated briefly as follows:

The central theme of **"Gateman's Gift"** is neither the psychological working of Govind Singh's mind nor the sociological factors which perhaps give rise to them, nor both of these together; and of course, it is not the psychological principle of suggestion. The central theme of **"Gateman's Gift"** is the tragedy and the irony involved in man's perennial (and perennially unsuccessful) efforts to break free of the vice-like grip in which the attitudes, his own and those of others in the society, born of the social and socio-economic institution of man's own creation, hold him permanently.

Having made this ponderous-sounding pronouncement, let me explain why I think there may be a grain of truth hidden under these ponderous coverings which a better stylistician may succeed in expressing more simply and elegantly.

Sociologists tell us that man is a social animal, and they sometimes put it as if there were an element of necessity in man's social character. I need not labour the point, since

I think most people will agree that the social character of man's existence is an offshoot of the purely contingent desire on most people's part for a reasonably peaceful and happy, and reasonably long span of survival. The acceptance of social, or socio-economic, institutions, and the willingness to let one's attitudes and beliefs be maximally shaped and determined by the requirements imposed by such institutions, certainly characterise the behaviour of most people most of the time, but equally certainly they do not characterise the behaviour of all the people all the time. If they did, human existence would be much poorer, and the nobler aspirations of man would find no expression. Literature, art, philosophy, and music would either not exist or would have different meanings. Life would be wholly mechanical and the distinction of mind and matter, with the full range of its consequences, would not have been thought of.

However, the fact remains that man needs socio-economic institutions and they are essential, if not indispensable, for his survival. And since they are so important, they cannot but shape his mental and emotional life too. In fact, it should not surprise us if most people, most of the time, think, feel, and react as if the social compulsions of man were necessary and not contingent. It is enough for the purposes of our argument that some people most of the time and most people some of the time do not think, feel, and react in this way. Among some people who do not, I would include poets, artists, musicians, painters, and some novelists and philosophers. There may be others, even among lay people, who deserve to be included in this list but generally, lay people would fall in the second category (most people— some of the time).

In the context of the present story, I will need to say very little about the first category. I will not take up discussion of the point, which someone may well raise, in what sense can the efforts of the persons falling in the first category be said to be 'perennially unsuccessful', although the pervading disenchantment and sense of loss which characterises the world of art and literature may well be traced to it. More significantly, the queer logic of the human situation by which tragedy, loss, and failure have, over the years, come to be associated with the noblest efforts in art, literature, music, and philosophy indicates a possible explanation along the above lines. It is possible that arguing along these lines we may come to the paradoxical conclusion that all great works in art and literature are failures, and may even say that the greater the failure the greater the work of art. The paradox would be more apparent then real, for there is a level where great works of art are great successes and there is a level where they are great failures. And if the greatness of a failure is to be measured by the greatness of the efforts, it may also be true that the greater the failure the greater the work of art.

But I must return to my immediate concern. The theme of **"Gateman's Gift"** is concerned with the people of the second category, ordinary people who in the very simplicity of their existence are creatures of the socio-economic institutional framework, which once created, exists independently of their will. It is to this level of existence that all the characters in the story belong—Govind Singh himself, the Bank Manager, the Accountant and the whole lot of bank workers that hover in the background. A sociological explanation may try to make much of the distinction of economic class between the gateman and the Bank Manager, but it is important to realize that in the writer's perception they both belong to the same level of existence: both are in the vice-like grip of the socio-economic framework; the reactions of both, and the perceptions which determine these reactions, are determined by their relative positions and orientation in the same framework, and they both behave mechanically according to the standards for their positions prescribed by that overriding framework.

Till, that is, one of them, gateman Govind Singh, breaks through the constricting hold of the framework (with of course only as much willed effort on his part as was involved in his acquiescence in the framework in the first place). Part of the irony also arises from the fact that even the effort to break free is not always so much of an effort, but a compulsion, the real nature of which is not clear even to the agent. In fact, the realization of its real nature may never come to the 'agent' at all. As with Govind Singh, he may simply follow the urge, not realizing that he is set on a collision course with the societal framework and his own 'social' nature; the 'realization' finally comes in the form of the actual collision, when only two possibilities remain open: either, if he is 'lucky', the collision is a 'beneficial' one in the sense that it corrects his deviation from the orbit, and he is again safely back in his original position with little 'harm' done; or, if he is 'unlucky', the collision may destroy him. It is another matter that the greatest successes in art and literature are often the results of such 'malevolent' collisions.

What is the nature of Govind Singh's breakthrough? Having had spent twenty five years of his active life in passive acquiescence in the societal system, Singh his little awareness of the special gift with which he is endowed—that of toy-making. It is no small indictment of the dehumanizing nature of the framework that, fixed in its well-oiled grooves, a man may never discover the creative side of his personality. It is only when retirement from service brings a major one of Govind Singh's lifewheels to a stop, that he has time and opportunity to discover his true talent, the fulfilment of which would have been considered the major objective in a system which gave priority to man's freedom. Such an unconstrained system being somewhat inconceivable, one could even settle for a slightly less fair system which would at least allow people who wish to follow their creative urge, as and when they wish it, to do so without thereby setting them on a collision course with the system. But in the system in which we live, even that is almost inconceivable.

One may well ask what prevented Govind Singh from following his creative urge unimpeded? He was retired and had all the leisure he wanted; his work was admired by the people among whom he had lived and whose opinion he valued, and since he did not very much care for financial rewards, (and was anyway getting a pension), what was it that eventually forced him to the conclusion that 'doll-making was no occupation for a sane man'? In what way, one may particularly ask, can one hold the societal system responsible for the break-up of Singh's mental life? One may discover a lack of understanding on the part of the Bank Manager, who, a perfectly satisfied cog in a machine, reacts in an absolutely predictable style to Singh's offerings, and is in actual fact responsible for the registered letter which was the immediate cause of the breakdown. But even if we grant it that the Bank Manager was either a fool, or a perfect product of the system (inasmuch as he was never 'without' it), to have been unable to appreciate that when you enter the temple of the Muse, you leave your sociological ribbons of 'status' and 'role' outside, even if one grants it, is it sufficient to explain the derangement of Singh's mental faculties?

My answer is 'No.' There is a telling passage in the story which gives us the clue. When the Accountant reads out the contents of the Manager's appreciatory letter, couched though it is in the typically official language which the Bank Manager after years of grinding in the well-oiled grooves of the institutional machine wears as the voice of his soul, Singh is not elated: 'He beat his brow and wailed'. Why? After all, Singh was an illiterate, who 'scrawled' his signature and needed to have the letter read out to him, and the officialese would not matter to him, and at any rate, the letter carried the sanction of a very concrete reward of one hundred rupees which in an ordinary person of Singh's status would have condoned many a greater vice. Why then did Singh not jump for joy and who was he not shaken out of his mad state?

The clue lies in the remaining part of the incomplete quotation: 'He beat his brow and wailed: Tell me, Sir, am I mad or not?' And when the affable Accountant assures him that he does not look at all mad, 'Singh fell at his feet and said with tears choking his voice, 'You are a god, Sir, to say that I am not mad. I am so happy to hear it', and on the next pension day he turns up as spruce as ever at the office counter firmly convinced that doll-making is 'no occupation for a sane man.'

The tragedy and the irony of it! Even the well-meaning Bank Manager must have been baffled by the outcome of his generous gesture and it would perhaps remain as one of the numerous mysteries of life and character which his well-trained mind has learned to shut out in a corner till the flames of the funeral pyre reach them. For if even Singh himself, who had 'reached out to infinity', even if for the briefest while, could fail to take the measure of the divine stirrings in him, what chance did the lowly Bank Manager stand in this game, which is played not by the sociological counters of status and role where he could beat Singh hollow, but where the soul of man in God's image talks to its maker across the heavens in a tone of equality?

But leave the Bank Manager to his fate, and ask of Singh: What was the nature of his 'beneficial' collision with the societal system which sent him spinning back to his 'right' orbit—the orbit no longer that of a gateman, for which one could find a few mitigating things to say, but that of an ex-gateman! Truly enough, Singh lives off the pension he has earned during his active life as a gateman both financially and spiritually! When you have lived most of your life pretending that eternity does not exist, and you have been well-rewarded for doing so, an encounter with eternity must be the most frightening thing that can happen to you. Singh had all his life stuck to the societal role assigned to him; he had done well; his work as a gateman had been appreciated. In this role, he had followed the rules meticulously: he was always smart and alert, but most relevantly, he had maintained his distance from the Bank Manager. The Bank Manager was like a God to him; sitting behind multiple layers of walls and floors in his *sanctum sanctorum*. When he moved out, he took a few quick steps, ringed by his underlings as if the fresh air would foul him, and was promptly enclosed again in the safety of the car, and you could hear him heave a sigh of relief as if the exposure had been an avoidable danger. During all this, Singh's role was only to present a smart salute from a distance which perhaps the Sahib acknowledged with a barely perceptible movement of his hand. During the twenty five years of Singh's service, the Sahib had spoken to him only twice—and, mind it, it was the Sahib who had spoken to him, he had never dared speak to the Sahib! He knew what his role required of him, and he observed the rules. As a result, he led a smooth life, quite undisturbed by any registered letters, those harbingers of disaster which the lawyers specialize in sending. But, come retirement, and his insane dabbling in doll-making, and the corrupting admiration of the bank people, Singh was beset with vanity, *ahamkara*, and he dared do what he had never dared in the twenty five years of life as a gateman: he tried to bridge the gulf their respective social roles as a gateman and Bank Manager imposed between them by sending gifts to the god! How dared he think that the lowly creations of his menial hands could merit the attention of the mighty Bank Manager! He did not even stop at that! The foolish admiration showered on his work by the ignorant office-workers egged him on to ask if the Bank Manager had liked his work! Egged on further by the 'stock reply' of the Accountant, 'He said it was very good.'—one more corrupting influence sending his *ahamkara* soaring—he dared the ultimate profanity, he made a model of the office frontage in which—horror of horrors—he modelled himself alongside the great god! What check! What defiance! Has anyone ever broken so many rules, such profundity of barriers, at one stroke without paying for it? Can the society, at one stroke, go back to its origins and forget the history of so many thousands of years? Can you strip the man naked and say that civilization has given him no coverings of custom and hierarchy? True enough, poets and artists do often try the impossible, but has not tradition neutralized and sequestered them? In the business of living, what role do they play? Great sages, philosophers, and saints wasted years in penance so that men may see each other as human beings, but did not tradition apotheosise them till they became the sanction for the very things they had forbidden? And where so many great men had failed, could an ordinary gateman, and that one too motivated by the lowest of motives, that of *ahamkara,* succeed? The very idea was preposterous.

Retribution comes in the form of the registered letter. It is a visitation from a different world; an emissary from the nether world come to wreak vengeance on Singh for his sins against the social system. He crumbles and cringes before it: 'Please take it back, I don't want it', but the punishment for 'wrongdoing' and for violating the system from which one has drawn nourishment is not so easily evaded. The emissary follows him like a spectre: it will not be exorcised and it will not reveal its secret. One hardly needs to say that the spectre, in Singh's eyes, is actually his own sins come home to roost. He has violated the code of the society; he has tried to reach above his station, he had dared glimpse man in the 'primitive' state of absolute equality. And the price must be paid.

Thus it is that the social-economic institutions of our own creation establish their absolute mastery over us: they rule us through ourselves. We are free, if we so claim, only with their permission. We may enjoy this conditional freedom, but no more. Even to try to get a glimpse of what lies beyond is to invite retribution, and the retribution comes to us not through an agency outside, but from ourselves. We are our worst enemies.

But this is of course to view it from the outsider's viewpoint. For the reformed Singh, as for most people, the brief period of his encounter with infinity, the short exposure to humanity in its essence, is the period of insanity, of excruciating pain and disaster. From such encounters, people rarely return whole to 'sanity', but Singh's encounter had

barely begun, and the presence of the-gateman-for-twenty-five-years was much too overpowering. He managed to return to 'normalcy'—the normalcy not of course of a human being, but of an ex-gateman!

"Gateman's Gift" is a sad story, for it reminds us that it is our destiny to live against our true selves, that man must remain a creature of the socio-economic convention, that we must always play games till the soul becomes estranged with itself and speaks a voice which it itself does not recognise, till, in brief, our whole existence becomes phoney. If, in the midst of all this darkness, there is any reason for living, it is that the defeat does not crush man, and though one Govind Singh may be vanquished and crushed, other Govind Singhs will arise and keep up their defiance of the abominable principle that man is a socio-economic animal and *necessarily* so.

C. N. Srinath (essay date Summer 1981)

SOURCE: "R. K. Narayan's Comic Vision: Possibilities and Limitations," in *World Literature Today,* Vol. 55, No. 3, Summer, 1981, pp. 416-19.

[*In the following essay, Srinath asserts the importance of the fictional Malgudi in Narayan's fiction.*]

R. K. Narayan's Malgudi has not changed much since 1935 when he wrote his first novel. It is the same pace of life, same locale, same topography, which should naturally amount to monotony; but thanks to the novelist's craftsmanship in not resorting to descriptions of the place, Malgudi is alive as a character. In novel after novel we find the familiar landmarks such as Nellappa Grove, the Lawley Extension, Kabir Road, the Albert Mission school, the spreading tamarind tree, the river Sarayu, the Mempi hills—all these are presented realistically, but what makes it a living reality in art is the ability of the author to give a mythical aura to factual details. Any attempt of the novelist to be realistic in the narrow sense in presenting the changing circumstances of the technological world would have meant ruin to Narayan's art, which thrives on familiar characters in limited surroundings, the life of a small town that refuses to grow into anonymity but like his characters strives toward self-identity. Hence the mythical realism becomes essential for Narayan to communicate the spirit of the place.

It is interesting to watch how, while Malgudi remains more or less the same, there is a gradual development in the protagonists of the novels—from Swami of the first novel to the bachelor of arts to the English teacher and the guide to the sweet-vendor "Philosopher" Jagan. It is a world of commoners and ordinary folk, but these people possess extraordinary qualities that lend themselves to the very stuff of Narayan's comic art. Not all the characters are mild and vague about their future. We have Margayya and Raju, who hold dynamic notions of themselves, and in wanting to achieve their private goals, which are opposed to the norms of society, they fail; but their failure is an essential process of self-exploration leading to self-knowledge. Narayan achieves this without any rhetorical consciousness of the deep traditional rhythm that pulsates through the Indian scene. The way Narayan does it, one wonders if his awareness is any deeper than that of one of his own characters. It gives one a feeling of limitation, but for Narayan's art it is immensely supportable, this delicate, implicit sense of tradition in the very common men he creates. What Narayan told Ved Mehta about himself is relevant here: "To be a good writer anywhere you must have roots—both in religion and in family. I have these things." We find both religion and family have had an impact, one subtle, the other direct, on men and women in Malgudi that has found sometimes queer, sometimes meaningful manifestations in novel after novel.

If in Narayan there is no trace of intellectuality, it has never endangered the integrity of his art, for the stuff of his fiction is life as it is lived on the road, in markets and homes. The individual merges into the society without much ado, implying a philosophical acceptance. This amounts to the traditional emphasis on the community, which is the ultimate principle in governing the destiny of individuals. In a country where all the arts, literature and philosophy are geared to a realization of the values of the community, which are placed always above the individual interests, Narayan's work sounds so natural, authentic. But paradoxically, it is the same tradition which has produced extraordinary individuals whose personal aspirations ultimately nourished the community and its well-being. And the frontiers of Narayan's art are visible and concrete, which is the secret of his success and the source of his strength and his limitations as well.

Swami and Friends, Narayan's first novel, is undoubtedly one of his best works, and as a boy's classic it has very few parallels in English fiction either in India or abroad. While we are initiated into the Malgudi world for the first time, we are also introduced to the typical Narayan character, Swami, who is also Chandran of ***The Bachelor of Arts,*** Krishnan of ***The English Teacher,*** Sampath of the same title, Margayya of ***The Financial Expert,*** Raju of ***The Guide.*** It is a buzzing world of schoolboys, their mischiefs, envies, anxieties, fears, wishes and wishful thoughts. In such an atmosphere where cricket and cricket-talk permeate, Swami and his friends form a coterie: Somu, the Monitor of the class; Mani, the mighty good-for-nothing, absolutely nonchalant in the matter of studies and a terror

to his teachers; Shankar, the most brilliant of the boys, who evokes much jealousy in one section of the class, which accuses him of currying the teachers' favor by washing their clothes; and Samuel, called the Pea because of his size. The group is complete when Rajam the aristocrat joins the gang. Narayan evokes male adolescent psychology through an authentic presentation of the attitude toward studies and examinations of both the bright boys and the indifferent, ever-playful lot, who come across perhaps most colorfully and vividly due to the novelist's secret predilection for them. The description of the enormous nonacademic preparation for the examination provides ample opportunity for Narayan's humor and gentle irony. Here is an inventory of the stationery items listed by Swami to be handed over to his father:

Unruled white paper	20 sheets
Ruled white paper	10 sheets
Black ink	1 bottle
Clips	...12
Pins	...12

While Narayan makes fun of the misplaced enthusiasm and easy-to-afford devotion of Swami and his group, he brings out the wisdom of innocence in the boys when, for example, Swaminathan is worried about the ripeness and sweetness of mangoes that figure in an arithmetical problem. It is only an adult mind that indulges in the maze of figures and numbers to arrive at a meaningless solution. What does Swaminathan care if one gets ten mangoes for fifteen annas or ten annas for fifteen mangoes? The crucial thing is whether they are ripe and sweet at all.

The excitement and tension that prevail in a boy's world are authentically portrayed by the novelist when we see Swami's group itching to start a cricket club and wrangling over the choice of a name for it; Friends Eleven, Jumping Stars, Excelsiors, Champion Eleven and finally Malgudi Cricket Club because of its irresistible magical associations with M. C. C. Then these nonentities called "M. C. C. Malgudi" write to the sports dealers in Madras in a language and an easy confidence behind which there is neither cash nor credit prompting the dealers to honor the letter.

Dear Sir,

Please send to our team two Junior Willard bats, six balls, wickets and others quick. It is very urgent. We shall send your money afterwards. Don't fear. Please be urgent.

Yours obediently,

Captain Rajam
(CAPTAIN)

That Narayan, who employs the comic-ironic mode when dealing with the limits of the common man's world, should see ample scope for recognition of the source of all these adult fears and anxieties, aspirations and actions in the world of boyhood here reveals both the pervading human folly and his own comic sense in probing deep into the less explored regions of human consciousness. The way Narayan presents human folly makes one begin to wonder whether by shedding it one is not depriving oneself of the "naïveté of being human," to use Walsh's phrase.

Chandran of *The Bachelor of Arts* combines the adolescent mood and temper of Swami and the maturity of Krishnan in *The English Teacher*. The episodes depicting his college life, his relationship with teachers, his extra-curricular activity, his love life—all these suggest a natural development of the Swami period in man's life. *The English Teacher* is a logical development of *The Bachelor of Arts,* where we find evidence of settled life and the poise of family harmony, which unfortunately is short-lived.

The flow of the quintessential comic sense of Narayan is thwarted by the tragic death of Krishnan's wife, and artistically, in a way, the limits of the comic vision turn out to be subjective in excluding the tragic and letting it stay apart. The comic vision has a sufficiently mature accommodative sweep to include the tragic in it, but for Narayan the artistic distancing or detachment seems to be a luxury at a time of personal loss, the more so as we know the novel to be autobiographical.

Coming to *The Financial Expert,* Narayan's sixth novel, one is struck by the ingenuity of craftsmanship in projecting the rise and fall of the protagonist Margayya in five sections, corresponding to the five acts of an Elizabethan tragedy. Narayan's treatment of Margayya, monetary wizard that he is, is comic but not without a tinge of sadness. The strength of Narayan's comic art is to present even a rogue from human angle and thereby shed light on his likable weakness as well. It is just such a low-key, twinkle-in-the-eye attitude to life's little ironies that can produce both Margayya, with his mystique of wealth amassed at society's expense, and also his son Babu, who can ruin his father's career. Narayan seems to believe in the wheel of life's moving, making many adjustments with the axle, pins and ball bearings; it is this movement that is presented, without any rhetorical embellishment.

The next important novel of our study should be *The Guide,* which is perhaps the most widely discussed of Narayan's

works. The book, which has all the ingredients of a commercial film (indeed it was made into one), both in the maturity of the comic vision and in the novelist's artistic sophistication shown in the treatment of his theme (a sophistication which was lacking in the earlier novels), transcends the limits of a seemingly bizarre story. The authenticity in the treatment of Raju, an ordinary tourist guide with no extraordinary qualities except a certain cunning with which he plays on the gullibility of the village folk and Rosie the dancer, shows Narayan's artistic restraint in projecting Raju as a saint. It is this restraint which makes Raju's character and Narayan's art look credible.

The growth of self-knowledge in Raju, interestingly enough, comes mainly through Rosie, though his time in jail might have contributed its share to the maturing of the erstwhile railway guide into a Swami. Similarly, though on a different plane, Ramaswamy in *The Serpent and the Rope* needs Savithri for his self-knowledge (however corrupt she may be in aping the external features of Western civilization), for she represents essential Indian womanhood. It is true that Raju does not show the same kind of awareness of which Ramaswamy is capable, but the tone that Raju employs while narrating the story of his life to Velan has an undercurrent of maturity and wisdom born of experience.

Raju achieves this maturity only toward the end and by an arduous path, however, and one sees the paradoxical element in his character from the beginning. As a guide, he can speak eloquently about a waterfall or a temple or a hilltop, though he is not really interested in it; he speaks like a connoisseur of dancing, shows a sensitive appreciation of Rosie's art and does everything to promote her, but turns out to be a mercenary manager who craves only fame; he is put in prison on a charge of forgery but leads a profitable life there, winning loyalty from fellow prisoners and respect from the superintendent; he holds forth on the philosophy of the Bhagavad Gita yet craves for a *bonda* right in the middle of the discussion. We realize that Raju does not take himself seriously while the entire village is hanging on his every word. Ironically, it is that faith the villagers have put in him that at first infuriates him but touches him too.

> Lying on his mat he brooded. He felt sick of the whole thing. When the assembly was at its thickest, could he not stand upon a high pedestal and cry, "Get out, all of you and leave me alone. I am not the man to save you. No power on earth can save you, if you are doomed."

But soon a change takes place in him, and he resolves to chase away all thoughts of food. This resolution gives him a peculiar strength, and being encouraged by the very purity of his thought and motivation, he feels like pursuing it; indeed, his character develops on these lines.

> "If by avoiding food, I should help the trees bloom and the grass grow, why not do it thoroughly?" For the first time in his life he was making an earnest effort, for the first time he was learning the thrill of full application outside money and love; for the first time he was doing a thing in which he was not personally interested.

So ultimately it is the community around him that becomes the focal point in the novel, not the tourist guide to Malgudi, Rosie's lover and patron/promoter, not even the night guide to the skies. For he is moved by the recollection of the big crowd of women and children touching his feet. Raju is no longer a private man. He has lost all his privacy and has been feeling miserable about it for many days, but now he draws strength and sustenance from the very people whom he has detested having hang around him. Raju, the imposter, impresario and ex-convict, has in spite of himself become a kind of saint. Indeed, he has transformed "a slab of stone to a throne of authority," and the novelist's feat in bringing out this remarkable change in the character amounts to a growth, a certain maturity of vision in the writer no less than in the character. That Narayan has achieved this in terms of comedy, by working out a smooth transition between the comic and the tragic, is the merit of this novel.

The Sweet-Vendor, while continuing the line of *The Guide* in presenting the ambivalent development of its protagonist, is significant in fusing the comic with the serious, and to achieve this Narayan resorts to such familiar themes of his as the father-son relationship, domestic life, Gandhism, the Indian paradox of attachment to wealth and a desire for total renunciation. Added to these in *The Sweet-Vendor* is a kind of East-West encounter, as Mali brings his girlfriend from America to assist him in his machine-story-writing adventure.

Jagan, the sweet-vendor, is presented comically as an astute businessman and a Gandhist who is simple and frugal in his habits, the author of *Nature Cure and National Diet,* a regular reciter of the Gita. If his "oddities"—such as taking only twenty drops of honey per day instead of sugar, or using margosa twigs for brushing his teeth and having only ten-watt bulbs in the house—provide ample scope for comic portrayal, we are also made to see another, more human, side: namely, his love for Mali, his remembrance of his early married life, his generosity toward Mali's wife. Narayan shows us the potential of his comic art to achieve the profound when in the end we see Jagan, who has hitherto believed in the sweetshop or Mali as his sole salvation, reach a higher level of perception and detachment by recognizing the responsibility of each individual for his own salvation.

Narayan's ever-alert eye for the comic does not spare even the epics—the Ramayana and the Mahabharata. His *Gods, Demons and Others,* an earlier work, is not really noted for any reinterpretation of myth or legend, but neither is it a mere paraphrase of the stories found in the Indian Puranas. There is an unmistakable freshness of approach and insight in the presentation of some characters. It is interesting to note that Narayan, more than any Indian novelist except Raja Rao, has been inspired to a considerable extent by the Puranas, not merely in the ingenious way one of the legends is adapted in *The Man-Eater of Malgudi,* but also in the art of storytelling. His essay **"The World of the Storyteller"** reveals the secrets of his own success as storyteller. The essay has a poetic appeal while it evokes an atmosphere by creating the widening circles around the focal point—namely, the storyteller. The seeming naïveté of such an approach should serve as a corrective to the high-strung intellectual of modern times who is eager to present a theory of fiction.

The choice of material by and large suggests a writer's vision, and that Narayan has chosen such characters as Narada and Ravana in his *Gods, Demons and Others,* who reappear in his *The Mahabharata* and *The Ramayana,* only defines the contours of his comic vision. The characters and situations that lend themselves to comic treatment are the very stuff of Narayan's art. Narayan has strayed outside fiction to everyday life, which is after all full of fictional possibilities. His *Dateless Diary* and *Reluctant Guru,* the latter a collection of fascinating essays on a variety of subjects such as the postman, cows and milk, and on educational policies, and his autobiography *My Days,* which brings out vividly his painful college days and their demand of much effort and preparation for examinations (Narayan was not a serious student known for any academic distinction while in college, and his term as a schoolteacher lasted only one day)—all these are recollected in a tone which is pleasantly reminiscent, and because of the novelist's preoccupations in life and fiction, one does not see anything surprising in the autobiography. A lively interest in the family and domestic life and an aversion to academic and scholarly things which we find in the autobiography are also true of a typical Narayan character in fiction.

If Narayan does not believe in any systematic and critical study of his own work, it is because he as a storyteller is in the tradition of the *bhagavatar,* the traditional Indian storyteller of his own essay **"The World of the Storyteller,"** who expects an instant response from his audience to his stories or descriptions of a puranic character and incident. It is a live art medium which engages the attention of the public constantly; Narayan himself, a lover of Carnatic music, knows that a tradition of instantaneous, simultaneous performance and response (which is true of our music concerts) exists, and he may be happy if his work is responded to in a more or less similar manner. A writer like Narayan does a service to criticism as well in freeing it of its jargon, which is a tribute to the "naïveté" of his art.

When we take stock of Narayan's entire work, we do come across novels and short stories which really are naïve and poor, such as *Waiting for the Mahatma* or *The Painter of Signs,* but that is the price a writer has to pay for being prolific and also for having produced such fine works as *The Guide* and *The Sweet-Vendor,* which have set such a high standard, making consistency a casualty.

Anita Desai (review date 7 March 1982)

SOURCE: "Narayan Country," in *New York Times Book Review,* March 7, 1982, pp. 1, 14-15.

[*Desai is the author of such books as* Clear Light of Day. *In the following review, she presents an overview of the setting and characters found in Narayan's* Malgudi Days.]

When R. K. Narayan was recently made an honorary member of the American Academy of Arts and Letters, he said in his acceptance speech that he had created the town of Malgudi in order to play the despot. Had he chosen to write about Calcutta or Bombay, he would have had to step carefully, confine himself to observation, whereas in the imaginary town of Malgudi he could set up a statue wherever he liked, demolish the town hall if he wished, put up a tea shop without the permission of the municipality, banish old residents and introduce strangers, just as he pleased.

Anyone who reads this new collection of stories[, *Malgudi Days,*] will laugh at the notion of Narayan as a despot, for there could be no one less tyrannical and more amiable. The town he has created on the sandy banks of the Sarayu River, with its Town Hall Park, its Albert Mission School, Lawley Road, the ineffably named Boardless Hotel and the Matchless Stationery Mart, is small, uncrowded and unpretentious; its residents appear to be bound together by ties of long familiarity and neighborly curiosity rather than the spirits of envy, malice and rivalry that rule the residents of larger, more congested cities. Its ruling temper is one of kindliness. Witness the postman Thanappa, who not only contrives to arrange the marriage of a young girl he has known since she was a baby but takes the responsibility of holding back a letter about her father's uncle's illness and then the telegram announcing his death rather than postpone or ruin the girl's wedding. Although the girl's father is shocked to learn of the postman's subterfuge, he readily forgives him, and the postman feels no guilt. The two unforgivable sins are unkindness and immodesty. When a

blind man ill treats the dog that leads him about the town on his begging rounds, the other denizens of the pavements think nothing of cutting the leash that attaches the hapless animal to the tyrant and setting him free. But even a dog in Malgudi cannot bear to be unkind, and he soon returns to his master and his duty.

Another characteristic of Narayan's creations is their innate humility. In "Gateman's Gift" a retired civil servant discovers he has a talent for modeling realistic figures in clay; his success crazes him, and he returns to normalcy only when he renounces his gift and swears he will never indulge in anything so "childish" again. The more immodest and imprudent sculptor in "Such Perfection" nearly wrecks the town by making an idol so perfect that it attracts the vengeance of the gods since "such perfection is not for mortals." The sin of hubris has been committed and must be punished; a great storm descends to play havoc with the town. Yet even the gods above Malgudi are kind-hearted. Since the sculptor cannot bear to mutilate his statue as the frightened villagers beg him to, the storm does it for him and severs the toe of the image, thus pacifying the gods and restoring calm. As for the sculptor, "He lived to be ninety-five, but he never touched his mallet or chisel again."

Narayan appears to feel that he can play the tyrant only so long as he remembers to be just, compassionate and humane. The characters he creates must be unassuming, their lives and endeavors small in scale so as not to invite the sin of vainglory or the retribution that will surely follow. Does this make Malgudi a utopia where the weather is mostly benign, the fields fruitful, the people content? No, Narayan is neither so deluded nor so unobservant as to allow that. Malgudi may be an appealing little town, but it has enough blind beggars, starving dogs, unscrupulous landlords and open gutters to ward off the most malevolent of evil eyes. Nor has Narayan any illusions about its residents. A pickpocket who is caught returning an empty wallet resolves not to abandon pickpocketing but never to return stolen goods, while the astrologer who sits under the boughs of a tamarind tree in the park admits to having attempted murder in his youth.

Apart from the compassionate realism with which Narayan observes life in this teeming microcosm, it is his sense of humor—fresh, sharp and wryly ironic—that prevents *Malgudi Days* from crumbling into the sugary crystals of sentimentality. He is like the father in a story called "Father's Help." Perfectly aware that his son is only making excuses for not going to school by claiming that his teacher Samuel is a sadist who will cane him till he draws blood, the father calls his son's bluff and warns him: "Don't come to me for help even if Samuel throttles you. You deserve your Samuel." Malgudi is peopled with characters whose company is pleasantly undemanding: not for them the hunt, the chase or the prize. A sense of detachment envelopes them comfortingly, and time meanders through their lives as somnolently as the river Sarayu. They know neither the pressure of the present nor the lure of the future, their lives and homes are complete in themselves, suspended in the auric amber of timelessness. Yet Narayan never belittles his subjects; he conveys the full measure of their dignity. In **"God and the Cobbler"** the cobbler who sits under a margosa tree that sends flowers down on his head all day cannot impart his calm fatalism to the fascinated hippie who talks with him while his battered sandals are being mended. "You must be blessed to have a rain of flowers all day," says the hippie. The cobbler retorts, "Can I eat that flower?" But he possesses a quality that the hippie recognizes and covets but cannot capture: a steady awareness of another dimension to his shabby existence. "God punishes us in this life," the cobbler tells the hippie. "In my last birth I must have been a moneylender squeezing the life out of the poor, or a shopkeeper cornering all the rice for profits—till I render all these accounts, God'll keep me here. I have only to be patient."

All Narayan's characters share this awareness: a melody or a stroll on the river bank transport them into the other realm; an idler, leafing through Plato's *Republic* and *The Life of Ramakrishna,* reflects, "Whatever they might have meant, they all seemed to hold forth the glory of the soul, which made me survey myself from top to toe and say 'Sambu, who are you? You are not the creature with a prickly stubble on his chin, scar on the knee-cap, with toenail splitting and turning blue . . . you are actually made of finer stuff.' I imagined myself able to steer my way through the traffic of constellations in the firmament, in the interstellar spaces, and along the milky way."

This is hardly the India that is to be found in the daily newspapers, in television reports, or in news magazines. Nor is it the India of the terrifyingly overloaded cities or even of the drought-stricken and forgotten villages. Where is Malgudi to be found? In the speech he gave at the American Academy of Arts and Letters ceremony, R. K. Narayan said that this was the question put to him most frequently. "It is actually on West 23rd Street in Manhattan, in and around the Chelsea Hotel, where I used to stay at one time and still visit whenever I can," he confessed. "I have been seeing the same tobacconist and barber there for 50 years: it never seems to change." The Americans in his audience were delighted with this information, but of course no one quite believed him. Malgudi is everywhere—in Manhattan, on the banks of Indian rivers, and probably in the plains of Siberia and the swamps of Africa as well, "I find it wherever I go," he said. A happy fate, one feels, for both writer and reader.

Harsharan S. Ahluwalia (essay date January 1984)

SOURCE: "Narayan's Sense of Audience," in *Ariel,* Vol. 15, No. 1, January, 1984, pp. 59-65.

[*In the following essay, Ahluwalia discusses how Narayan's awareness of his audience influences his writing.*]

R. K. Narayan is one of those creative writers who make a living out of their writing. He has struggled very hard to establish himself, i.e., to make himself and his works acceptable to a particular audience in the English-speaking world. Narayan's awareness of his audience is matched by his acute understanding of the commercial aspect of imaginative writing. Describing the book buying situation in his home town (Mysore) in an article published in 1953 he says that among a population of two hundred and seventy-five thousand persons capable of reading and appreciating his books and financially able to buy them, only 200 copies of his novel, **The Bachelor of Arts,** had been sold. In another essay, Narayan says, "The commercial aspect of literary life is alien to our culture; and book-buying and book-keeping [*sic*] are not considered important. Our tradition is more 'Aural,' that means a story-teller is in greater demand than the story-writer. The story-teller who has studied the epics, the Ramayana and the Mahabharata, may take up any of the thousand episodes in them, create a narrative with his individual stamp on it, and hold the attention of an audience, numbering thousands, for hours, while the same man if he sat down to write his stories would hardly make a living out of his work. Being ideal listeners by tradition, our public are not ideal readers." Because of this non-commercial outlook on writing, the writer is considered above wants; he writes to please himself. On the other hand, in the West the commercial outlook on writing has never been looked down upon. Narayan would agree with Dr. Johnson: "No one except an idiot ever wrote but for money." Because of the apathy of Indians to book buying, Narayan published almost all his books first abroad and then in India. After their acceptance in the West, his novels have of late been prescribed in Indian Universities on undergraduate and postgraduate syllabuses. As a result, his sales increased in India in the sixties and the seventies. Even so it cannot be said that Narayan has become popular with Indian readers.

In this connection, certain facts throw interesting light on the relative standing of Narayan in India and the English speaking world. Between 1935 and 1952 his novels appeared first in England. Indian reprints came several years later. From 1953, he caught on in the United States when Michigan State College Press published six of his novels during a period of three years from 1953-1955. After 1955 Narayan's novels have been first published in America, then in Britain and lastly in India. To consider commercial publication of his novels in England and America alone, *The Financial Expert* was published by Noonday (six editions) and Time; *The Guide* by Signet and Penguin; *The Man-eater of Malgudi* by New English Library (Four Square); *The English Teacher* by Pyramid; *Printer of Malgudi* by Arena; *The Vendor of Sweets* by Avon; *Swami and Friends* by Fawcett and Oxford. Paperback editions of all his novels are now being reissued in America by Chicago University Press and in England by Heinemann. Some of his novels have also been translated and published in Russia, Poland, France, Israel, East and West Germany, Sweden, Norway, Finland, Holland, and Yugoslavia.

Narayan shows keen awareness of the demands put on him by the Western readers and publishers. Foreign publishers, he writes, expect an Indian writer "to say something close to the image of India that they have in mind." This problem is not faced by writers writing in Indian languages for Indian readers because both have the same values and they participate in the same range of experience. Foreign readers crave the Indian flavour and for them this flavour is exotic. Most of the articles published about India in American and British newspapers and magazines bear out this view. Narayan himself has succumbed to the temptation of producing pot-boilers such as **"New Role for India's Holy Men,"** **"Ghee is Good,"** and **"Why Go Matha is Loved"** which he wrote with an eye on the audience of *New York Times Magazine.*

Narayan's own limitations reinforced by his desire to write for the reading public in England and America have clearly demarcated the frontiers of his art. When asked in an interview how he "picked up" themes for his novels and stories, he replied "that he waits for 'some propitious moment'—an incident, a report in the papers, an eccentric he stumbles across. Any of these becomes 'a jumping off ground for a chain of ideas.'" Almost all his novels start with a situation or character which seems to come straight from life, after which the novels develop in the writing. Narayan is not the novelist who conceives the whole novel in advance. It is not to be wondered at that most of his novels are not well made.

Narayan has an eye for the absurd in Indian life. With the observation of eccentric characters in absurd situations, he is entertaining. He is a gifted caricaturist. By careful selection and exaggeration of details, the characters are made to look entertainingly grotesque. Let us take up just one character: Jagan, who is a sweet vendor in the novel to which Narayan gives the same title. Jagan is a Gandhian but he does not pay the sales-tax. "If Gandhi had said somewhere, 'Pay your sales tax uncomplainingly,' he would have followed his advice, but Gandhi had made no reference to the sales tax anywhere to Jagan's knowledge." Narayan describes at length his comic fads and theories of living.

Jagan plies charkha which was Gandhi's prescription for the economic ills of the country as well as for any deep agitation of mind. His *jibba* and the *dhoti* are both made of material spun with his own hands. He wears "non-violent footwear" made from the leather obtained from cows that have died naturally. He makes excursions to remote villages where a cow or a calf was reported to be dying. When he secures the hide he soaks it in some solution before giving it to a cobbler for making his sandals. He brushes his teeth with a twig from the margosa tree because the nylon of the brush has an adverse effect on the enamel. He has given up salt, sugar, and rice and cooks for himself according to his theories. He has only a ten-watt bulb in his room because light rays should soothe the optic nerves and not stimulate them. He believes that socks should not be worn because they heat the blood and because you insulate yourself against the magnetic charge of the earth surface. He has written about his life-giving theories in his book on Nature Cure and Natural Diet which is lying with Nataraj waiting to be printed. His wife refuses to associate herself with any of his life-giving activities. Even when she lies dying, he talks about Nature cure.

Some of the delightful comic episodes in Narayan's novels read like short stories, others like cartoons or comic strips. To give just one example: the switching on ceremony of the film "The Burning of Kama" at the Sunrise Theatre in *Mr Sampath.* At the appointed time the Pandits rise, light the camphor, and circle the flame before the gods, sounding a bell. Then they go to the camera and stick a string of jasmine and a dot of sandal paste on it. Then the president gives his speech. There is comedy in the sudden twist in the speech. He begins by criticizing the mythological and ancient subjects for movies; but when he is told that the movie that he is inaugurating also has a mythological subject, he begins to extol the Indian epics as the storehouse of wisdom. Narayan presents various shades of humour from gentle irony to parody. If his comedy has any purpose, it is the purpose of a cartoonist, i.e., not to let life become too solemn. Narayan's comic vision, which is his strength, also makes his art limited.

Documentary details of social and religious customs of India are given in his novels clearly with foreign audiences in mind. Sometimes such a description is too long and is not integrated well into the story. There is a perfect picture of the joint family in *Mr Sampath* where the elder *brother* of Srinivas provides for everyone. On the other hand, the joint family has broken down in *The Financial Expert.* Margayya's relations with his elder brother were quite warm till his marriage after which their wives could not get along. When their father died they got involved in litigation, divided the house and partitioned everything which he had left. Marriage is arranged after comparing horoscopes. In *The Bachelor of Arts* marriage cannot take place because the horoscopes do not match. There is a long flashback in Chapter 12 of *The Vendor of Sweets* when Jagan thinks of his own marriage. Narayan describes in detail the code which is observed when a boy goes to see his would-be wife. Since he is not expected to show too much personal interest in his marriage, he depends on his younger sister who eavesdrops and brings news as the boy pretends to study. The demand for dowry, wedding feasts, and, later, visit to the temple of Santana Krishna to remedy barrenness are described at such length that the whole chapter seems to be intended for the special benefit of the foreign readers. In *Waiting for the Mahatma,* rites connected with death are presented with a touch of comedy. There is a long description of an exorcist as he tries to cure Ravi of his madness in *Mr Sampath* and a short description as he cures Susila of typhoid in *The English Teacher.* Lakshmi Pooja and a pilgrimage to Tirupathi in *The Financial Expert* and religious procession in *The Man-eater of Malgudi* are described at great length. These pictures of traditional India have an exotic appeal for the western readers.

For the same reason, Narayan draws upon Indian myths and legends in his novels. Indeed they have become a part of his style. He makes use of the story of Shiva and Parvathi and the burning of Kama by Shiva's third eye in *Mr Sampath,* the cosmic dance of Shiva in *The Vendor of Sweets* and the stories of Savitri-Satyavan in *The English Teacher,* Santhanu in *The Painter of Signs* and Bhasmasura in *The Man-eater of Malgudi.* The exotic appeal of such stories for the American audience can be seen from the fact that when Harvey Breit and Patricia Rhinehart adopted *The Guide* for Broadway, they incorporated into the play the story of Santhanu and Ganga which is not there in the novel. It is only in *The Man-eater of Malgudi* that Narayan attempted to treat consciously a realistic story in terms of a myth. Vasu, who dominates life around destroys himself in the manner of Bhasamasura. No doubt, Narayan is commenting in this novel on the tyranny of the strong, the corruption of power, helplessness of the good when confronted by evil but the traditional Indian idea of evil destroying itself sounds too simplistic. He does not seem to understand the forces which underlie the making of a modern Rakshasha.

Narayan generally tends to be traditional in his vision of life. His art, therefore, does not show that exploratory quality which gives to a creative work depth and range. In most of his novels, he sticks to the traditional Indian values of endurance, detachment, and withdrawal. *The Dark Room* presents the loveless marriage of Savitri with the tyrannical Ramani. When the husband refuses to give up his mistress, she tries to commit suicide, but is saved. Unable to live without children and without the security and comfort provided by the marriage, she comes back home. One can

speculate how Hardy or Lawrence would have explored the theme of loveless marriage. Again, in *Mr Sampath,* Srinivas has been getting involved in the life of everyone around. Towards the end, however, Srinivas has a vision of history in which he sees the rise and fall of kingdoms and realizes that an individual does not count in the scheme of life. So he can take a detached view when his friend Ravi is beaten by the exorcist to drive out his madness. One gets the impression that the attitude of Srinivas is perhaps endorsed by the novelist. In Narayan's novels the tragic potentialities of a situation or a theme are never grasped. His characters never question the gods. *Punarjiwan* (rebirth) either before death (as in the case of *The Vendor of Sweets*) or after death (as in the case of *The English Teacher*) comes handy as a solution to the muddles of this world, or to death itself.

To conclude, Narayan's peculiar genius as a comic entertainer has helped him win a large audience in the English-speaking world. This reading public, in turn, has not allowed him to venture out into other areas of human experience. He has got along prosperously with one little spot called Malgudi to the almost complete exclusion of any concern with socio-political forces at work in the country. What need has he to look at the vast panorama that India has been and is!

G. S. Amur (essay date 1985)

SOURCE: "The River, the Lotus Pond and the Ruined Temple: An Essay on Symbolism in R. K. Narayan's Novels," in *Indian Readings in Commonwealth Literature,* edited by G. S. Amur, V. R. N. Prasad, B. V. Nemade, and N. K. Nihalani, Sterling Publishers, 1985, pp. 94-105.

[*In the following essay, Amur traces Narayan's use of the symbols of the lotus pond, the garden, and the ruined temple in* The English Teacher, The Financial Expert, *and* The Vendor of Sweets.]

An interesting episode in R. K. Narayan's autobiography, *My Days,* relates to his brief role as editor and publisher of *Indian Thought,* a journal which was started with the grand design 'to phrase our culture properly', to utilise the English language as medium for presenting our cultural heritage'. *Indian Thought* failed, as a similar venture by Shrinivas, the fictional hero of *Mr. Sampath,* was to fail later, because Narayan soon realised that what he needed was a five thousand page encyclopaedia and not a hundred and twenty page journal and he was trying to 'pack an elephant into a demi-octavo carton'. In spite of the characteristic irony Narayan employed in both the contexts however, he has been carrying out his ambitious design not only through works like his English adaptation of Kamban's *Ramayana* or *Gods, Demons and Others* where he retells some of the Hindu myths, but through the novels themselves which, as V. S. Naipaul has recognised, have a distinctly Hindu quality in their content as well as form. Narayan borrows the form of the novel from the West, but in his creative use of it, he subverts it from within by introducing elements from the Indian narrative tradition. This is particularly true of his symbolism.

The most obvious iterative symbol in Narayan's novels is the river Sarayu, an integral part of the Malgudi landscape and a unifying presence in Narayan's fictional world. Narayan derived the name from *Ramayana*. The very first verse of Kamban's *Ramayana,* which Narayan has retold in English, mentions the river 'which flows through the country of Kosala'. Rama, Sita and Lakshamana spend a night on its banks on their way to the forests. In Shrinivas's vision in *Mr. Sampath* too the river is associated with Rama but a new myth is created:

> He rested on a sandy stretch in a grove, and looked about for a little water for making a paste for his forehead marking. There was no water. He pulled an arrow from his quiver and scratched a line on the sand, and water instantly appeared. Thus was born the river.

This account has its parallels in Indian mythology, but here the shape of the myth is determined by the quality of Shrinivas's imagination and Narayan's comic evaluation of his vision. The river in this myth of genesis marks the beginning of time for Malgudi and assures it of continuity ('The river flows on'). In Narayan's novels, as in *Ramayana,* the river Sarayu divides experience into two areas—the active day-to-day world of men and women and a green world beyond. The two are separated but continuous. Sarayu can always be forded at a point near Nallappas Grove which not surprisingly is close to the cremation ground. The world beyond the river always necessitates a kind of rebirth or assumption of a new role for the protagonist.

The sacred rivers of India, like the Ganga, are rivers of prosperity (sukhada) and salvation (mokshada). Thus they are intimately concerned with the well-being of man on earth as well as his liberation from it. They are agents of purification and transmutation. As Zimmer observes:

> Physical contact with the body of the goddess Ganga has the magic effect of transforming . . . the nature of the devotee. As if by an alchemical process of purification and transmutation, the base metal of his earthly nature becomes sublimated, he becomes an embodiment of the divine essence of the highest eternal realm.

The river thus is a communal as well as a personal symbol.

As a communal symbol Sarayu is 'the pride of Malgudi'. Its sands are 'the evening resort of all the people of the town.' The historic events in the life of the town happen on the banks of the river. On 15th August 1930, we learn from *Swami and Friends,* that 'two thousand citizens of Malgudi assembled on the right bank of the Sarayu to protest against the arrest of Gauri Shankar', and it is here that the crowd waits for the Mahatma. But Sarayu is a silent witness to much smaller events like the abortive duel between Mani and Rajaram which ended happily.

Sarayu plays even a more significant role in relation to the inner life of the Malgudi characters, and is associated with some of the most intense moments of their experience like Chandran's meeting with Malathi which results in love at first sight or Savitri's attempt at suicide after she leaves her husband's house. For Krishnan, the frustrated English teacher, the plunge in the river provides 'a new lease of life'. On the fateful day she caught the typhus fever, Susila insists, rather whimsically, on a visit to the river: ('I must wash my feet in the river today') and her desire is fulfilled. This proves to be Susila's last visit to the river and her act of washing herself in the river assumes in retrospect a ritualistic significance. The river also prompts literating confessions. Mr. Sampath, to Shrinivas's utter surprise ('I didn't know you cared for the river'), chooses the banks of the river Sarayu as the scene for his revelations regarding his relationship with Shanti. And it is here again that Daisy tells the secret story of her life to Raman. But perhaps the most intimate relationship that Sarayu has with the life of an individual is in *The Guide.* Raju's career as a holy man begins on the banks of the river and ends on the river bed. Sarayu has had no appeal to Raju in his earlier life in Malgudi. The traditional Hindu symbolism of the river as an agent of purification, as a destroyer of sin, is most relevant to Raju's transformation.

The other side of the Sarayu is a land of new possibilities, usually symbolised by a garden. Krishnan discovers the occult world and establishes transcendental connections with his dead wife in a garden house beyond Sarayu. Margayya's search for the red lotus takes him, much against his will, to a garden also on the other side of the river, and Jagan, the vendor of sweets, chooses the ashrama as shrama-like garden beyond Sarayu to begin a new life. At a much lower level, beyond the river offers images of illusory life like the studio which Somasundaram builds in *Mr. Sampath,* or symbols of a different way of life, as the village where Mari and Ponni live.

A more striking example of Narayan's use of symbols is that of the lotus pond, invariably associated with a garden and a ruined temple. Though not as ubiquitous as the river, it figures in at least three of his novels—*The English Teacher* (1945), *The Financial Expert* (1952) and *The Vendor of Sweets* (1967)—where it occupies a position of great structural significance. In these three novels, the symbol is related to a crisis in the soul of the protagonist, and its occurrence is controlled by this factor. It figures early in *The Financial Expert,* when Margayya's precarious career under the Banyan tree is interrupted by his own impulsive verbal attack on the powerful Secretary of the Cooperative Bank and the loss of the vital accounts books through an equally impulsive act of his spoilt son Balu, who throws them into the gutters. In *The English Teacher* it occupies the middle of the action and follows immediately after the crisis in Krishnan's life precipitated by his wife's sudden death through illness. It connects the two parts of the novel. The symbol makes a late appearance in *The Vendor of Sweets* almost at the end of the novel, where it is related to a deep crisis in Jagan's life following his struggle with his son Mali.

Narayan's observant eyes must have picked up this symbol from the familiar Indian landscape, particularly of the south but it is a symbol which is deeply embedded in Sanskrit literary tradition. In Bana's *Kadambari,* one of the most famous of the early Sanskrit prose narratives for example, the lake Achchoda ('clear water'), at the foot of the Kailasa mountain in the heart of a forest, and the Shiva temple built on its northern bank provide the setting for Mahashveta's encounter with Pundarika and also for Chandrapida's chance discovery of her which leads to his union with Kadambari. Pundarika ('white lotus') was born of Lakshmi, the lotus goddess, and the lotus motif is the dominant element in Bana's elaborate presentation of the lake. As Chandrapida approaches the lake, he is struck by the beauty of the beds of blue lotus. He touches the lotus with his fingers, tastes lotus fibres, places lotus leaves on his bosom, adorns his hand with a lotus, and relaxes on a bed made of lotus leaves. The lake impinges on Chandrapida's consciousness as a symbol of timeless existence:

> . . . What, before this world was created, existed as
> the watery cosmos, in the form of Brahma's egg . . .
> is lying here, under the guise of this lake.

Achchoda lies on the edge of the known world, Bharatavarsha, and it provides Chandrapida with the threshold experience which ultimately leads to transcendence. Mahashveta, whom Chandrapida meets in the temple of Shiva on the northern bank of the lake, initiates him into the superhuman world of the *gandharvas* and brings about his union with Kadambari, *a gandharva kanya*. Chandrapida himself is a human incarnation of the Moon and his initiation into the new world leads him to the discovery of his own divine identity.

In Bana's story, Achchoda is a symbol of transformation as well as initiation. For Mahashveta and Pundarika, it provides the natural background for a momentous transfiguration with the rapturous and overwhelming discovery of the power of love. Pundarika goes through a series of transformations—he is reborn as Vaishampayana, the Brahmin, and later as a parrot—before he is reunited with Mahashveta. The significance of the lotus lake as transforming agent is further brought out by the metamorphoses of Kapinjala, Patralekha and others.

Bana derived his symbolism from Hindu mythology. As Zimmer points out, water in the Hindu myths is an ambivalent symbol of existence as well as non-existence. In the Narada myth of *Matsya Purana,* as Zimmer tells it, water as pond is existence and Narada's plunge into it, which results in his metamorphosis into a woman, is a ritual of initiation. 'In the symbolism of the myth,' Zimmer explains, 'to dive into water means to delve into the mystery of Maya, to quest after the ultimate secret of life.' The lotus, similarly, is a central symbol in the Indian—Hindu, Buddhist and Jaina—philosophical and literary tradition. According to the Atharva Veda, the body itself is 'the lotus shaped mansion'. The 'thousand petaled lotus of pure gold, radiant as the Sun' is the first product of the creative principle and, associated as it is with Parajapati, contains in itself all creation. The lotus symbol is also associated with Shri or Lakshmi, the consort of Vishnu and the goddess of beauty and wealth.

Narayan's use of the lotus pond symbol in his novels acquires special significance when it is viewed against the background of the Hindu mythological and literary tradition. The symbol makes its first appearance in *The English Teacher* where it is directly related to the process of the hero's achievement of transcendence. Krishnan receives a call from a stranger, who as medium has received a message from Krishnan's dead wife, and goes to meet him at his garden house in Tayur. The garden, across the river Sarayu and separated from Malgudi, represents the green world ('green haven') where Krishnan is able to renew his self through an experience of transcendent love which comes to him from the supernatural world and initiates him into the mystery of life and death. *The English Teacher,* as Narayan himself has said, is largely autobiographical and Krishnan's experience corresponds to Narayan's own as he describes it in *My Days.* There is, however, a very significant change. If in Narayan's real life, the communion with the spirit of the dead takes place in a closed chamber (in Rao's house,) here it is located at the lotus pond in the heart of the garden, suggesting a literary source. Like the Achchoda lake in Bana's *Kadambari* hidden in 'a very extensive grove of trees', the lotus pond of *The English Teacher* lies in the midst of a dense cluster of trees, shrubs and orchards and, like the Achchoda again, it is 'lovely with blue lotus', a religious symbol as old as the Rigveda. The resemblance between the two extends to 'the small shrine' on the edge of the pond which corresponds to the Shiva temple on the banks of the Achchoda lake. In Narayan's novels temple is often a ruined or a neglected temple, though they do take note of the fact that new temples continue to be built—the Subramanya temple in *The Dark Room* and the Srinivasa temple in *The English Teacher* for example—and old ones continue to receive support from the community, as in *The Man-eater of Malgudi.* The temple that Krishnan sees is 'a small shrine, its concrete walls green with age, and its little dome showing cracks', suggesting antiquity and contemporary neglect simultaneously. His friend's approach to the temple is more aesthetic than religious. ('The most lovely ruin you ever saw,'), though he is fully aware of the nature of the divinity it represents and knows the legend surrounding it:

> It is said that *Sankara* when he passed this way built it at night, by merely chanting her name over the earth, and it stood up because the villagers thereabouts asked for it. The Goddess is known as *Vakmata* the mother who came out of a syllable.

Krishnan's friend himself does not worship at the temple, but an old priest visits it occasionally, out of piety as the friend puts it, and offers worship to the Goddess. For Krishnan and his friend, however, the temple is only a part of their consciousness. When the friend offers to have the temple opened, Krishnan says: 'No, don't worry 'about it now.' The ruined state of Narayan's temples, as contrasted with the splendour of the temple in Bana's story, is indicative of the erosion of Hindu religious culture which has survived through the ages but has lost much of its glory. Krishnan's initiation into the occult world and his communion with the dead, which in some measure corresponds to Chandrapida's initiation by Mahashveta, is mediated by the friend, who assumes a priest-like role and the 'helpers' from the supernatural sphere, as well as the lotus pond which affects him in an indirect way. Like Chandrapida, Krishnan too has an experience of the timeless reality:

> It gives one the feeling that it is a place which belongs to Eternity, and that it will not be touched by time or disease or decay.

Narayan's treatment of the symbol in *The Financial Expert* is ambivalent and ironic, though in externals it conforms to the archetype. Unlike the introspective and idealistic Krishnan, Margayya, the self-centred and materialistic hero of *The Financial Expert,* lacks a capacity for spiritual experience and his response to the lotus pond, a symbol which figures again in association with a garden and a ruined temple, is divided and sceptical. In obedience to the commands of the priest who gives him a *mantra* and prescribes a ritual for acquiring wealth, Margayya sets out

for the lotus pond in search of a red lotus but he does so not in the spirit of a seeker but with the purposefulness of the practical man who is keen on accomplishing a task. Here too the lotus pond is in 'a large wood, semi-dark with sky-topping trees—mango, margosa and what not'. But for Margayya it is far from being a 'green haven':

> His legs ached with this unaccustomed tramping and his feet smarted with the touch of thorns. He passed through the thicket expecting any minute a cobra to dart across and nip at him.

Unlike Krishnan, Margayya refuses to lend himself to the experience of the lotus pond. Though the blackened stones in the corner of the *Mantap* are a confusing time image ('it might be last year or a century ago'), for Margayya the lotus is a reminder of finite time: 'They know better than we do that it's nearing sun set'. He avoids the plunge in the water, resisting initiation, and employs Dr. Pal, the mysterious stranger, to pluck the red lotus for him. The lotus pond offers no transcendental experience for Margayya. On the contrary, it draws him even closer to the earth by bringing about an encounter with Dr. Pal, the author of *Bed-Life.* It is also significant that unlike Bana's hero who adorns himself with lotus, Margayya reduces the red lotus to ashes to be mixed with ghee. The priest's words about the lotus: 'It is a great flower. The influence it has on human beings is incalculable' do not affect him in any profound sense. Margayya's relationship with the priest, unlike Krishnan's with the 'friend', is one of tension and lacks harmony. Margayya does not share the priest's sorrow over the loss of the lotus in the modern world.

The triple symbol of the garden, lotus pond and temple attains its maximum complexity in *The Vendor of Sweets,* where it is presented from two distinct points of view— the bearded image-maker's and Jagan's—which in the end merge together. Here too the garden is located on the other bank of the Sarayu river and presents a distinctly separate though not discontinuous world from that of Malgudi. Unlike in the other two novels, in *The Vendor of Sweets,* all the three parts of the symbol receive extended attention, and are realised in full particularity. The garden, for example, merely suggested in terms of a cluster of trees in the earlier novels, is here transformed into a symbol of primeval creation:

> Over this little building loomed banyan, peepul and mango trees and beyond them stretched away a grove of casurina, the wind blowing through their leaves creating a continuous murmur as of sea waves. The surroundings were covered with vegetation of every type: brambles, thornbushes, lantana and oleander intertwined and choked each other.

The garden is inhabited by a variety of creatures—lizards, chameleons, birds, frogs and monkeys.

The temple, similarly, is not just a ruined temple of the earlier novel, a static symbol of an eroded religious culture. It has acquired a new dynamism through its association with the master image-maker and his dream of making a new god to replace the stolen image. It is also a symbol of creativity and light. The image which the Master could not complete is that of Gayatri. The bearded man explains to Jagan the significance of the goddess:

> Since she is the light that illumines the sun himself, she combines in her all colours and every kind of radiance, symbolised by five heads of different colours She possesses ten hands, each holding a conch which is the origin of sound, a discus, which gives the universe its motion, a goad to suppress evil forces, a rope that causes bonds, lotus flower for beauty and symmetry, and a *kapalam,* begging bowl, made of a bleached human skull. She combines in Her divinity every thing we perceive and feel from the bare, dry bone to all beauty in creation.

The temple is surrounded by incomplete images—the pedestal of Vishnu, arms of Saraswati, and other places of sculpture—endowing the place with an aura of pervasive divinity, remindful of the beautiful idols of Shiva lying on the banks of Achchoda. The bearded man's continuous narration recreates several legends like that of the dancing figure of Nataraja, yet another of Narayan's favourite symbols, 'which was so perfect that it began a cosmic dance and the town itself shook as if an earthquake had rocked it.

In *The Financial Expert* the initiator, the mysterious priest who guides Margayya in his quest for wealth, remains in the background, but in this novel as in *The English Teacher,* he plays a vital role. The bearded man, the little master image-maker turned hairdyer, is completely at home in the old-new world of the garden. Jagan notes the transformation: 'Ever since they had stepped into this garden, the man had become more authoritarian'. He almost merges into the atmosphere and assumes the appearance of 'a statue of many thousand years' antiquity'. The image-maker and the image are one. The bearded man is essentially a primitive and can slide into the past at will: 'He reached up to a branch of a guava tree, plucked a fruit and bit into it with the glee of a ten-year old-child.'

Jagan's response to the lotus pond experience is more complex and more dynamic than either Krishnan's or Margayya's. Jagan's personality is a curious blend of strong native shrewdness like that of Margayya, and an acquired Gandhian idealism which offers an interesting parallel to Krishnan's cultivated refinement. In the course of his ini-

tiation into the new life, he passes from doubt and uncertainty to certitude and determination. Jagan's entry into the garden results in a dislocation of his sense of reality: 'The edge of reality itself was beginning to blur: this man from the previous millennium seemed to be the only object worth notice'. The bearded man opens out a new world for him and he now realises how narrow his own world had been. 'Am I on the verge of a new *janma?*', Jagan wonders, but his surrender to the new experience is not total at this stage. Obsessed with his own idea on dietics, he does not eat the guava fruit offered to him by the bearded man and allows it to drop to the ground. His initiator invites him to enter the pond but Jagan is held back by doubts and fears: 'perhaps he is going to throw me down into the pond. . . . ' When he actually takes the plunge he is fascinated by the blue lotus and experiences 'a sense of elevation' and fulfilment: 'it would be such a wonderful moment to die, leaving the perennial problems of life to solve themselves', he says to himself, but he is still scared by the persistent invitation of the bearded man to approach him in the water and wonders whether he should 'turn back and rush away'. Jagan's fear causes a ripple of comedy:

> Jagan plunged his arms into the water, and shuddered when something clamped its jaws on his hand. 'Oh,' he screamed. It was only the other's hand grip.

The lifting of the stone from the water presents no problems to the bearded man but it leaves Jagan exhausted. But this however marks the beginning of his involvement. Back in his own house, Jagan is again bothered by doubts and suspicions, 'How could he trust him? On what basis?' But gradually he undergoes a conversion and accepts the bearded man and the new life he offers: 'I don't care what he does. I am going to watch a goddess come out of a stone'.

Thus, Narayan's use of the archetypal symbol of the garden-lotus pond-temple while absorbing its mythic significance, as a symbol of initiation, transformation, transcendence and self-renewal, through the protagonist's participation in a symbolic world by images of beauty, creativity, timelessness, and divinity, reveals his talent for original experimentation. Though the role of the symbol in all three novels examined is similar, its presentation in terms of its components and its relationship with the protagonist vary from novel to novel. The garden, the lotus pond and the temple are drawn only in broad outline in the earlier novels, but in *The Vendor of Sweets* they acquire fullness and solidity. The symbol as it appears in *The English Teacher* is a direct approximation to the mythic archetype in terms of the protagonist's response. Its presentation in *The Financial Expert* is ironic, while in *The Vendor of Sweets* it moves from irony to affirmation. The role of the initiator too varies. In *The English Teacher* he is just a gifted medium. In *The Financial Expert* he emerges from the traditional religious background and retains his sacred mystery. In *The Vendor of Sweets,* he is a magus figure, with several dimensions—secular, religious and artistic.

Richard Cronin (essay date March 1985)

SOURCE: "Quite Quiet India," in *Encounter,* Vol. LXIV, No. 3, March, 1985, pp. 52-9.

[*In the following essay, Cronin looks at V. S. Naipaul's appraisal of the religious and the political in Narayan's work by analysing* Waiting for the Mahatma *and* The Painter of Signs.]

I know of only one substantial attack on R. K. Narayan's achievement. It might be of some interest simply as a novelty, but, coming as it does from a man who has claims to be the best living writer in English, it deserves more serious attention than it has received. V. S. Naipaul admires Narayan, and his admiration survived, he tells us, the rainy season in India during which he slowly re-read *Mr Sampath, the Printer.* It survived, but the account of the novel that follows leaves us in little doubt that it did not survive intact. Before the monsoon Naipaul had admired Narayan as a comic realist: after it he was left with an uneasy appreciation of Narayan's skill in disguising religiose fables to make them look like novels. *A Tiger for Malgudi* would not seem to him a retreat into quasi-philosophical whimsy forgivable in a writer near the end of a distinguished career, but the predictable outcome of tendencies present even in Narayan's strongest work.

Naipaul's problem has to do with the status of Malgudi. He knows that Narayan's fiction depends on the creation of Malgudi: his "comedies were of the sort that requires a restrictive social setting with well defined rules," and he knows too that Malgudi is not Bangalore or any other real South Indian town: it is "a creation of art." But for Naipaul the value of fictional worlds depends on their maintaining a vital connection with the real world that they mirror. When he had read Narayan's novels in Trinidad and in London he had not doubted that connection: when he read *Mr Sampath* in Bombay, in Delhi, in Kutch, his sense of it snapped. He could not connect the India he read about with the India he saw around him. The cool sympathy with which Narayan views his characters and their doings, his "ironic acceptance" of the oddity of men and women and the oddity of their ways, no longer seemed evidence of a Chekhovian sophistication, but an expression of a weary indifference to human pain, not the less offensive because it is presented to the reader as sanctioned by Narayan's religious sense of life, his Hinduism.

Towards the end of *Mr. Sampath,* Srinivas, the central character, experiences a vision in which he sees the history of India pass before him, stretching back into the prehistoric past, forward into the unimaginable future. The vision leaves Srinivas in a state of elevated philosophical calm, a mood in which "madness or sanity, suffering or happiness seemed all the same." He then witnesses a primitive exorcism ritual in which a friend of his, a young artist called Ravi who has been driven mad by unrequited love, is beaten with a cane by an old priest. Srinivas has an impulse to protest against this cruelty, but finds himself "incapable of any effort": "The recent vision had given him a view in which it seemed to him all one whether they thwacked Ravi with a cane or whether they left him alone. . . ." Ravi has, he now sees, all eternity to regain his sanity, "though not in one birth, at least in a series of them." All the same, Srinivas is troubled by the noise of the thwacking: he goes outside.

Mr. Sampath was written in 1949, and, as Naipaul notes, it expresses a sense of India that had been fixed before Independence. Srinivas, dependent on his brother for money, on his wife for domestic comfort, is left free to cultivate his interest in the lofty spiritual doctrines of the *Upanishads.* His spirituality is a flower of idleness. His character is less a product than a symbol of stultifying colonial dependence. When Narayan published *The Vendor of Sweets* India had been independent for twenty years, and the economic achievement of independent India could no longer be ignored. India had laid itself open to Western technology, and had become a major producer of industrial goods. Naipaul reads *The Vendor of Sweets* as Narayan's report on the new India, Jagan, the sweet vendor, is a Gandhian. That is to say, when he was a young man Gandhi gave him, as he gave millions of his countrymen, a vision of citizenship, its dignities and responsibilities. Since then Jagan's vision has narrowed, and bifurcated. He sits in his shop reading the *Gita* and listening to the tinkling of coins on the counter. Gandhi had shown him how he might become a whole man, how his religious and practical sense might each vitalise the other, but he has long since forgotten the lesson. His Gandhianism has become a harmless variety of nostalgia.

When Jagan's son returns from America with a foreign girl-friend and a business project based on a fiction-writing computer, Jagan, the old India, is forced to recognise the new. His response is bafflement, anger, and at last panic. He decides to become *sannyasi,* but his decision is only a mockery of Hindu orthodoxy, and not only because Jagan takes his cheque-book with him into his new life as a mendicant. He gives up the world not because he has completed his worldly duties but because he can no longer deal with them. The Indian ability to absorb and to direct Western technology is coarsely parodied in the representation of Jagan's son and his fiction-writing machine: "You see these four knobs? One is for characters, one for plot situations, one for climaxes." Narayan evidently has no notion how such a machine might work. He ridicules machines from a position of invulnerable technological innocence. He is unable to see in the person of a young Indian educated in the West anything other than decadence—alcohol, girlfriends, unscrupulousness, a trivial aping of Western manners and dress, and a pathetic interest in machines that owe more to Heath Robinson than to the micro-chip. Narayan laughs and Jagan panics, but Narayan is only apparently more sophisticated than his character. At bottom their responses are much the same.

So ends Naipaul's critique, and for all his insistence that he remains an admirer, it is damning. His Narayan shelters from the fact of pain by cultivating a religiose indifference, and responds to change only with uncomprehending mockery. At moments of crisis he retreats, as Srinivas retreats from the noise of Ravi being thwacked, into a visionary India, a pastoral land, eternal, free from pain, an India that can only be seen in a vision, for it is a country that never existed. Such places of imaginative refuge are perhaps necessary for a colonial people, a people deprived of responsibility for their own lives, but in modern India they are a harmful luxury, for they get in the way of the duty to see the real world and to see it clearly, which the citizens of a self-regulating nation must accept if ever they are to make a better life.

India: A Wounded Civilization records two visits made by Naipaul to India, the second, the visit with which the book is mainly concerned, during the Emergency. Naipaul makes no mention of *The Painter of Signs,* and this is odd, because *The Painter of Signs* is an Emergency novel. In it, Narayan responds to the same crisis that Naipaul records. Here, if anywhere, the truth of Naipaul's critique may be tested.

The Painter of Signs is a rewriting of a novel which Narayan had published 22 years earlier—*Waiting for the Mahatma.* The point is too obvious to need detailed justification. Sriram and Bharati in the earlier novel become Raman and Daisy in the later. Sriram and Raman are both of them impelled by love to become campaigners, and both are sign-writers. Sriram roams the countryside daubing on every available wall Gandhi's ringing demand. "QUIT INDIA." Raman is a professional calligrapher, and the message has changed: "We are two; let ours be two; limit your family." The relationship between the two novels signals Narayan's acceptance of an argument that occupies Naipaul throughout his book. With the Emergency, the pattern of India's development as an independent nation decisively changed. Gandhianism had run its course, and the Emergency was the suitably dramatic signal that it had been re-

placed by a new political philosophy, led and articulated, ironically enough, by someone also called Gandhi.

Waiting for the Mahatma is the story of Sriram growing up. At the beginning of the novel he is "comfortably reclining on the cold cement window-sill" of his grandmother's house. It is his favourite posture: "The window became such a habit with him that when he grew up he sought no other diversion except to sit there, sometimes with a book, and watch the street." By the end of the novel he has broken his adolescent habit of disengagement from life, and prepares to set up home with his bride, Bharati, and to shoulder the responsibility of looking after 30 children, orphans of the partition riots. But Sriram's growth into adulthood is entangled with the development of India into nationhood. All through his adolescence Sriram is fascinated by a picture hanging in the sweet-shop opposite his house, a "portrait of a European queen with apple cheeks and wavy coiffure." Before he can become a man he must free himself from this vague Western ideal of womanhood and fall in love with Bharati, whose beauty is Indian, who is what her name means, the daughter of India. Bharati is a disciple of Gandhi, and Gandhi, though only an occasional actor in the story, is the novel's dominant presence. Through Bharati he superintends Sriram's emergence into independent manhood just as he presided over India's progress to independent statehood. The novel ends with the assassination of Gandhi and the marriage of Sriram and Bharati. The coincidence is symbolic. Gandhi is not so much murdered as translated: his work done, the children of the new nation safely given into the hands of young India, Gandhi feels free to shrug off the burden of existence. It is not the death of a man, but of a saint, foreseen by Gandhi and calmly accepted by him. *Waiting for the Mahatma* is a weird hybrid, at once a comic *Bildungsroman* and a religious fable of national origin.

At times, the two work well enough together. A sharply observed detail like the portrait of the apple-cheeked queen is weighted by its significance within the fable. The portrait allows Narayan to treat a potentially ponderous theme, the escape from emotional and imaginative dependence on the colonial power, without disturbing the deft ease of his narrative. The fading of the old imperial roll of honour and its replacement by a new nationalist martyrology is caught in the contrast between Sriram's father, killed in Mesopotamia, whose memorial has shrunk to the meagre proportions of the buff envelope that brings his monthly pension, and Bharati's father, killed in the Congress agitation of 1920, whose death is proudly remembered.

Even the representation of Gandhi is not monotonously fabular. It is enlivened occasionally by the novelist's sharp perceptions. Narayan seems quietly amused by Gandhi's penchant for delphic utterance—"How do you know he means that and not something else?" The spiritual weight of Gandhi's presence, though awesome, can become oppressive: "The Mahatma's silence was heavy and pervasive, and Sriram was afraid even to gulp or cough, although he very much wanted to clear his throat, cough, sneeze, swing his arms about." But more often than not the effect secured by the mingling of fable and novel is evasion. Narayan turns to the novel when he wants to evade the consequences of his fable, and to the fable when the novel starts to drift into dangerous areas. *Waiting for the Mahatma* is an evasive book, and what it is most anxious to evade is politics.

The most striking instance is Narayan's representation of Gandhi. Few would deny that Gandhi's success had to do with his ambiguous status as the leader at once of a religious movement and a political campaign. When he returned to India from South Africa he found a country with deep and continuous religious traditions, but a country that was governed by Britain, and was in consequence, politically underdeveloped. His achievement was to take those religious traditions and to make them serve in place of absent traditions of political association. Narayan's effort is to undo Gandhi's project; to salute Gandhi as a saint while leaving as vague as possible his other role, as a statesman.

Narayan offers a Gandhianism with the politics left out. The *charka*, for instance, functions in Narayan's fable as a religious implement, like a rosary. In the novel it is a wickedly frustrating little machine. Sriram's attempts to master it are rendered with all Narayan's comic flair. What no one would guess is that hand-spinning had a crucial place in Gandhi's economic programme, freeing India from dependence on the Lancashire cotton mills, and indicating that the best means for India's economic development was through village industries. Even giving oneself up to imprisonment scarcely seems a political act. Gandhi instructs Bharati to surrender herself at the nearest police station. He does not tell her why. She accepts his instruction as a religious command, inscrutable, not to be questioned. She obeys, not because she is Gandhi's follower, but because she is his disciple. Obedience in this religious view of things is not a means to the successful outcome of a project, but an end in itself.

Sriram does not go with Bharati to prison. He decides, conveniently, that Gandhi has left his followers free each to continue the struggle as he thinks best. There follows the most enigmatic section of the novel. Sriram falls in with Jagadish, a photographer with ambitions to make movies, always a danger signal in Narayan. Jagadish is a supporter of Chandra Bose and the INA, less a Gandhian than a guerrilla, and, under his direction, Sriram himself becomes a terrorist. [Cronin adds a footnote explaining that the Indian National Army was largely recruited from Indian prisoners of war. Chandra Bose believed the Germans and the Japanese to be India's natural allies in their struggle against the British. He planned to invade India with the cooperation of the Japanese, oust the British, and establish an independent government.] There is a detailed account of his taking some leaflets to distribute at a nearby military barracks, and deciding, after he has scratched his arm on the barbed-wire perimeter, to make a dignified retreat. He tosses the leaflets into the compound: "The boys may pick up and read the messages at their leisure tomorrow morning."

Sriram's subsequent career—he becomes an arsonist, a bomber, he derails trains—is narrated in a single paragraph. The reason is clear. The first episode is available for treatment in the dry, comic manner that Narayan favours, but the later incidents are not, and so they must be glossed over. Sriram is a dreamy young man. Nothing much in the outside world except for Bharati impinges on his dreaminess. Narayan is well practised in the depiction of such characters, and Sriram is utterly convincing. But the chief function of the novelist's skill, here, is to save the fabulist from the need to offer any serious account of the political implications of Sriram's career. Narayan suggests clearly enough that Sriram is wrong to be diverted from Gandhi's kind of nationalism to Chandra Bose's, but since Sriram is scarcely represented as a responsible moral agent, Narayan avoids the obligation either to indicate why Sriram is wrong or to assess the gravity of his error.

At the end of the novel Sriram asks Gandhi's permission to marry Bharati. Gandhi asks Bharati if she finds the proposal agreeable:

> Bharati bowed her head and fidgeted.

> "Ah, that is a sign of the dutiful bride," said the Mahatma.

After her parents' death Bharati was "practically adopted by the local Sevak Sangh." Her life has been devoted to the Independence struggle. She is strong-minded, fearless, and ignores most of the traditional restrictions placed on the behaviour of Indian women. She walks alone through rough countryside to meet Sriram at the ruined temple where he has his hide-out. She handles his inept sexual advances quite unhysterically. She gives herself up to imprisonment without fuss, and she risks death in the partition riots calmly. It is curious to see such a woman at the very end of the novel revert to the stereotype of the coyly blushing Indian bride.

This is just one example of what is surely the oddest fact about *Waiting for the Mahatma.* Narayan contrives to celebrate India's independence, because he can represent it as having changed almost nothing. When Sriram is released from prison, the waiter in a local restaurant and Jagadish both complain of the country's disorganisation and the government's ineptitude:

> "We ought to rejoice that it is our own people that are blundering, isn't that so?" Sriram asked, some of his irresponsible spirit returning.

The tone of this whole passage is odd. There is the novelist's wry amusement at the dashing of millenarian hopes; but there is also, one senses, a queer satisfaction, as though Narayan is reassured that what was a muddle when the British ruled will go on being a muddle now that they have left. Walking down his own street Sriram sees life going on as it always had done. He thinks:

> Why could he not have lived like these folk without worries of any kind or any extra adventures: there seemed to be a quiet charm in a life verging on stagnation, and no change of any kind.

This is a moment of lassitude, and yet one feels that Narayan's strange achievement is to invest what might seem the most dramatic moment in recent Indian history, India's accession to independence, with something of that quiet charm.

The surprising transformation of Bharati into a traditional Indian bride is one aspect of this: it is a somewhat desperate stratagem by which Narayan reassures himself and reassures the reader that the process by which India won its independence has not unloosed any uncharming forces for social change. But crucial to the whole enterprise is the representation of Gandhi. It seems obvious that Gandhi, apparently despite but in fact because of his claim to be an orthodox Hindu, threatened a radical, for Narayan an alarming, reorganisation of Indian society.

Throughout the novel Narayan contrives at once to celebrate Gandhi and to defuse his threat. One example must suffice. When he visits Malgudi, Gandhi politely declines an invitation to stay at the municipal chairman's luxurious house, and chooses instead to stay in the outcaste colony, among the sweepers. It is a symbolic challenge to the caste system and Narayan unambiguously applauds it. But caste is the principle on which traditional Indian society, the society that Narayan sees as possessed of a quiet charm, relies for its stability. Narayan's response is to enclose Gandhi's symbolic challenge within the fabular life of a saint. Incidents in such a life are contemplated with religious awe, but they are invested with an autonomous rather than an exemplary value. Gandhi's action is proper, saintly: it is admired, but with an admiration that does not have uncomfortable social consequences. That is why Gandhi's

response when Sriram confesses his terrorist activities is not at all surprising:

> "We will hear if there has been anything so serious as to warrant my going on a fast again. Do you know how well a fast can purify?"

Narayan's Gandhi shows no concern to establish whether Sriram has killed or maimed, no concern for his victims. His worry is that Sriram may have polluted himself: his concern is to fix on the appropriate purification ritual. It is a response explicable only in terms of the caste feeling that, earlier in the novel, Gandhi has seen it as his business calculatedly to outrage, and it is appropriate to the novel's benign conclusion, in which Narayan salutes the birth of a new nation, the moment when everything has changed, and yet magically, charmingly, everything stays just the same.

In *The Painter of Signs* Bharati becomes Daisy, Sriram becomes his near-namesake Raman, and the place of Gandhi is taken by—no one. Narayan is not a rash man. Like Sriram, Raman is an orphan. He lives not with his grandmother but with an old aunt, and like Sriram's grandmother the aunt leaves Malgudi to live out her last days in Benares. Raman shares Sriram's detachment. In *The Painter of Signs* it is signalled by Narayan's use of a narrative technique in which Raman's actual words are supplemented by unspoken speeches in which Raman expresses those feelings that he is too polite, too timorous, or too canny to voice. Like Sriram, too, he is impelled by love to give up his familiar life for the uncomfortable lot of the political campaigner. He accompanies Daisy as she tours the surrounding villages spreading the message of birth control.

Bharati, whose name proclaims her Indianness, is replaced by Daisy—"What a name for someone who looked so very Indian, traditional and gentle!" She has many of Bharati's best qualities. She is careless of physical comfort, self-assured, independent, and utterly committed to her mission. But Bharati's struggle was to secure India's independence; Daisy's is to control the growth of India's population. Whereas the one project secures Narayan's hearty—if, as I have tried to show, oddly complex—approval, the other seems to him not so much mistaken as sacrilegious. Bharati is a disciple of the Mahatma, Daisy of some unnamed missionary who has appointed her an officer in his campaign to spread propaganda for birth control throughout India. But there is no need for me to imitate Narayan's reticence. Daisy is a Sanjayite. *Waiting for the Mahatma* is transformed into *The Painter of Signs* to mark the difference between the idea of nationhood inspired by Gandhi, and the idea that replaced it, the idea most strikingly embodied not in the person of Indira Gandhi, but in that of her son. Raman carries the tools of his trade in a shoulder bag decorated with a "bust of Gandhi printed in green dye." It is a bag that the reader knows from another of Narayan's novels, *The Guide,* where it is carried by Raju's uncle, but here it bears an added significance. It signals that Gandhi has, as it were, been assimilated into the fabric of Indian life, that Gandhi's achievement was to enrich without damaging the complex web of social relationships in which Narayan finds his Indian identity incorporated. Narayan represents the new Gandhianism as an attempt to rend that fabric, to cut it with a surgeon's knife.

There is much that Narayan admires in Daisy and, by implication, in the social campaign that she represents. He is aware, as Raman's survey of the venalities of Malgudi's public and business life makes clear, of the corruption that it opposes. He can admire, too, Daisy's steely idealism, her energy, her willingness selflessly to give herself up to a cause. She is, after all, a Sanjayite, and Sanjay Gandhi's achievement had this in common with the Mahatma's, that he activated the social consciences of a sizeable proportion of India's best young people. He took an idealism which a few years before might have dissipated itself in the futile and ugly violence of Naxalite revolution, and disciplined it, gave it an outlet in the service of the state rather than in its destruction. In his characterisation of Daisy, Narayan accepts as much. To understand why Daisy, in some ways so admirable, is at last bitterly repudiated, we must understand Narayan's response to sex and to children.

In *Waiting for the Mahatma* nothing about Gandhi is stressed more than his love of children. He distributes the fruit and flowers he is given to the children that he meets. In Malgudi, at the municipal chairman's house, he shares his couch with a little sweeper boy and feeds him the chairman's oranges. The orphan children, victims of the partition riots, are his special care. Almost his last thought before he is killed is to ask after the health of one such child, a girl he has named Anar, pomegranate bud, and to give Bharati apples and oranges to take to the children. His love of children is not so much an aspect of his character as one of the proper badges of his saintliness. He is not like Marx, writing *Das Kapital* with children balanced on his knees. That image works to characterise Marx, to supplement his austere identity as a political philosopher with the human qualities of the family man. Gandhi's love of children is more like Christ's. He savours the frisky energy of young life with a holy relish, as a way of marking as movingly as possible his loving care of all humanity. Daisy is carefully established as his antitype:

> She never patted a child or tried any baby-talk. She looked at them as if to say, You had no business to arrive—you lengthen the queues, that's all.

At Malgudi station the stationmaster assembles his children before Gandhi "as if on a drill parade." "Why don't you let

them run about and play as they like?" asks Gandhi. When Daisy leaves a village the children are assembled to bid her goodbye:

> Daisy looked at them critically. "Don't suck your thumb, take it out, otherwise you will stammer," she said to one. To another one she said, "Stand erect, don't slough." She turned to their mother and added, "Correct posture is important. Children must be taught all this early in life." She was a born mentor, could not leave others alone, children had better not be born, but if born, must take their thumbs out of their mouths, and avoid slouching.

The contrast needs no underlining, nor, perhaps, does what it implies. Daisy's resistance to the growth of India's population is represented as a perverse refusal to accept and to rejoice in the processes of life, an attempt to substitute a stiff, sterile angularity for the prolific, leaping spontaneity that is found at once in the movements of playing children and in the patterns of Indian dance and architecture, and signifies in all three the divinely generous creativity that assures us of the presence of the gods within the world.

Narayan plays fair by Daisy. The spokesman for the religious point of view is a cantankerous, boastful, and thoroughly unattractive old priest, keeper of an image of the Goddess of Plenty: "Be careful, you evil woman, don't tamper with God's designs. He will strike you dead if you attempt that." But Narayan's distance from the priest's style does not mark any serious disagreement with his point of view. Raman's aunt, as Narayan's old women often are, is the mouthpiece of the traditional wisdom: "Isn't it by God's will that children are born?" Raman responds with a joke: "But our government does not agree with God." It is a serious joke.

But what follows? Daisy visits a village where the population has increased by 20% in a year. She responds vigorously:

> "Has your food production increased twenty per cent? Have your accommodations increased twenty per cent? I know they haven't. Your production has increased only three per cent in spite of various improved methods of cultivation. . . ."

Narayan pokes fun at this display of statistical earnestness, but to mock the style of Daisy's speech is not to challenge its substance, and what Daisy spells out in her gauche, bureaucratic manner is the fact of starvation. Narayan has nothing to say to this. He can offer in reply only Raman's bland assurance that though the children may be starving they appear perfectly healthy:

Malgudi swarmed with children of all sizes, from tod-
dlers to four-footers, dust-covered, ragged—a visible
development in five years. At this rate they would overrun the globe—no harm; though they looked famished,
their brown or dark skins shone with health and their
liquid eyes sparkled with life.

One remembers Naipaul's weighty charge that in Narayan
religion is an excuse for indifference to the sufferings of
others, that his Hindu piety breeds, and is a disguise for,
callousness.

To Narayan, sexuality is first of all a threat, a dangerous
impulse that must be struggled against, Sriram and Raman,
pricked by sexual desire, both try to follow Gandhi's remedy for the control of lustful thoughts: "Walk with your
head down looking at the ground during the day, and with
your eyes up looking at the stars at night." But both fail.
Raman tries to rape Daisy, and Sriram is only saved from
raping Bharati by his sexual inexperience. When she visits
him in his temple refuge, he notices "her left breast moving under her white Khaddar sari," and makes a clumsy, frantic, sexual assault on her. After it is over she rebukes him
hesitantly, unhappily: "He had never seen her so girlish and
weak. He felt a momentary satisfaction that he had quashed
her pride and quelled her turbulence." Male sexuality is
darkened, Narayan believes, by other desires—sadism, the
urge to dominate. More than Bharati is threatened, for desire releases even in the mild and diffident Sriram impulses
which, if unrestrained, would make impossible the continuation of any society that Narayan could recognise as
civilised.

But Narayan is no ascetic. Sexuality threatens social stability, but it is also true that a test, possibly the crucial test,
of a society's value is whether in restraining the sexual instinct it allows that instinct to be fulfilled. Lust must first
of all become love. In *The Painter of Signs* the process is
beautifully traced. "Do you ever recollect the face of the
woman whose thighs you so long meditated on at the river-
steps?", Raman asks himself, and then he visits Daisy in her
office:

> A side glance convinced him that the full sunlight on
> her face made no difference to her complexion, only
> he noticed a faint down on her upper lip and the ves-
> tige of a pimple on her right cheek.

When Raman notices that pimple it is the proof that his
generalised capacity for lust has yielded a particular incli-
nation to love. But love, even love genuine enough in its
way, like Raju's for Rosie in *The Guide,* is still a dangerous and a destructive emotion. It is redeemed only within
marriage, when it is constrained within the larger social
organisation.

Bharati agrees to marry Sriram only if Gandhi gives the
couple his permission. Gandhi stands to her in place of father, and so Bharati does no more than show proper filial
duty in requiring his consent. But for Narayan the convention embodies a deep truth: that love can be fulfilled only
through an act of submission in which the lover submits his
love to the higher duty of obedience. It follows that love
is redeemed only within a society that exerts over its members a traditional authority. Daisy becomes Raman's mistress, and promises to be his wife. But the novel ends when
she hears of a dramatic increase in the population of Nagari,
packs her bags, and leaves Malgudi and Raman both. She
could not behave otherwise. She is unable to make that
obeisance to traditional authority without which, Narayan
believes, love can never be other than a capricious and a
destructive emotion, and she cannot do so because she has
committed her life to a cause that requires her to view such
authority as an obstructive and antiquated set of prejudices.

Like *Waiting for the Mahatma, The Painter of Signs* is
both a novel and a fable. It is a novel about a love affair
that goes wrong, and a fable about Sanjayism. At the end
of *Waiting for the Mahatma* Sriram and Bharati prepare
to marry and accept responsibility for the upbringing of 30
orphans. The life that they embark on so happily is Gandhi's
proper memorial, for this achievement was to instil in his
followers a sense of social responsibility, of the duty a man
owes his fellows, that, before Gandhi, had scarcely figured
as a part of the Hindu tradition. But Narayan could celebrate Gandhi's success only because it had been accomplished without disrupting that subtle interweaving of
familial duty, proverbial wisdom, custom and religious law
which constitutes the authority that guarantees the most
precious of human freedoms, the freedom to love. At the
end of *The Painter of Signs* Raman, abandoned by his aunt
and abandoned by Daisy, cycles towards the Boardless Hotel, "that solid, real world of sublime souls who minded
their own business." That is, I think, the only bitter sentence
in the whole of Narayan's *oeuvre.* Daisy is left to devote
her life to the expression of a social concern unschooled
by love, and such a concern breeds inevitably hatred and
violence. Raman is left with the shrunken view that the
sublimest state to which a human being can aspire is that
of minding his own business. It is a personal tragedy for
Raman and Daisy, but it figures a national tragedy for India.

Shiva Naipaul, V. S. Naipaul's brother, ends a vitriolic assessment of Sanjay Gandhi's achievement by quoting these
sad words spoken by a sociologist at Delhi University:

> "Sanjay did express a certain dark side of the Indian
> personality. I recognize that darkness in myself. Some-
> times," he said slowly, deliberately, "when you look
> around you, when you see the decay and the point-

lessness, when you see, year after year, this grotesque beggarly mass ceaselessly reproducing itself like some . . . like some kind of vegetable gone out of control . . . suddenly there comes an overwhelming hatred. Crush the brutes! Stamp them out! It's a racial self-disgust some of us develop towards ourselves . . . that is the darkness I speak about. . . ."

Daisy is a zealot not a Kurtz, but for all that there is much in the anonymous sociologist's words to remind us of *The Painter of Signs.* One thinks, for example, of Daisy's ill-concealed contempt for the villagers whose lives she is trying to improve. That it is a racial contempt is lightly indicated by her name, and by the impudent transformation of her mentor into a Christian missionary. But Narayan is less concerned to apportion blame than he is to lament the outcome of a story in which Daisy and Raman are both of them the losers.

It is odd that V. S. Naipaul, who, in recent years, has travelled the world as a self-appointed missionary intent on the destruction of all human illusions, and has found everywhere material to feed his capacity for bleak and unforgiving disdain, should find in the Emergency glimmers to inspire a wan hope, whereas Narayan, whose temperament seems of all major modern writers the sunniest, should contemplate the same events and arrive at last at a mood very like despair.

The contrasting responses are the product of profound differences between the two men. They are differences of temperament and of religious belief: they are also political differences. "Narayan," William Walsh insists "is not a political novelist," and there is obvious truth in his contention. Raman speaks for Narayan in finding Daisy's lack of humour wearing ("Why shouldn't we also laugh a little while preventing births?") and a lively sense of humour does not fit easily with disciplined political commitment.

Political writing characteristically flattens language in an effort to render it a medium fit to communicate unambiguous meaning. Narayan loves language for its playfulness, its mischievous tendency to subvert the flat, univocal intentions of its user. "QUIT INDIA," writes Sriram on every available wall. What message could be plainer—until a passing Indian asks why he is being asked to leave his own country, and another, troubled by the uproar that Sriram's arrival has caused, suggests that he add an "e" to his message, and appeal instead for a little quiet. Raman is an artist in his way. Calligraphy is a joy to him: he delights in "letters, their shape, and stance, and shade." Narayan shares with his hero the belief that art has an intrinsic value as unrelated to any extrinsic purpose the artist might serve as Raman's pleasure in his craft is to the motives of the businessmen who commission his signs. When Raman abandons

all his other trade and binds himself to the endless reproduction of Daisy's single message, he is, among other things, a type of the artist who puts his talent at the service of a political campaign, and Narayan feels any such decision as constricting. But George Orwell reminds us that for a writer to choose to be nonpolitical is itself a political act; and it seems clear that in Narayan's case the rejection of politics is the expression of a deep-rooted conservatism, a comprehensive hostility to radical change.

Narayan's novels begin when Malgudi is threatened by some newcomer, which may be the Mahatma or the movies, a taxidermist or a dancing girl. Narayan flirts with the danger, but the novel ends only when the threat has been removed, when it has been blunted by the repressive tolerance of traditional India, or when it has been exposed as a *rakshasha,* an evil demon that, because it is evil, necessarily destroys itself. The admiration that Naipaul felt for such a writer was never likely to be other than fragile, puzzled, for Naipaul's achievement is as clearly built upon his sense of himself as deracinated, his painful and proud insistence on living in a free state, as Narayan's is founded on his participation in the values, the prejudices, the culture of the society that he depicts.

The vision of two writers so essentially opposed could never tally. We can ask of each only that he submit his vision honestly to the test of an undoctored reality. In *Waiting for the Mahatma* Narayan studiously, and with considerable flair, avoids so difficult and dangerous a procedure. In *The Painter of Signs* he does not. There is reckless honesty in his refusal to counter Daisy's statistics with anything more substantial than Raman's dogged insistence that starvation is perfectly compatible with glowing good health. And there is honesty, too, in the flimsiness of the consolation he offers—to himself, to his readers, and to those suffering from the ministrations of Daisy and her less scrupulous real-life colleagues. It is written on a ribbon-wide slip of paper, and offered for sale at a price of five *paisa* by a "professor" who sits each day by the fountain outside the Malgudi town hall. It consists of just three words, "This will pass."

Alfred Kazin (review date 21 July 1985)

SOURCE: "A Calm Eye on Daily Disasters," in *New York Times Book Review,* July 21, 1985, p. 19.

[*Kazin teaches English at the City University of New York Graduate Center and the author of* An American Procession. *In the following review, he praises Narayan's use of the short story form in* Under the Banyan Tree.]

Rasipuram Krishnaswami Narayan is on the threshold of 80 still India's most notable novelist and short-story writer in English. Quite apart from the beautiful traditionalism of his middle name, there is good reason to note his full Indian name. Mr. Narayan is an elegant, deceptively simple stylist who cleverly reports—or translates—the speech of his Indian characters into inflated schoolroom English. "How can we blame the rains when people are so evil-minded?" "A good action in a far-off place did not find an echo, but an evil one did possess that power." Yet everything he describes is intensely local, reflecting his long residence in Mysore and the intricacy of continuing and conflicting traditions throughout modern India.

Mr. Narayan's strength is that his material seems inexhaustible. He clearly feels he has only to look out his window, take a walk, hire a servant, to pick up story after story. The American reader may not know exactly where all this is taking place, but the world is so intensely visualized and comprehended—without any particular judgment made on so many daily uproars and disasters—that he finds himself surrounded by brilliant pinpoints of life in the vast, steamy, unknowable land mass that is the foreigner's India.

Storytelling becomes inevitable in such a world, and storytellers themselves become characters. In the most arresting piece of the collection[, *Under the Banyan Tree*], **"Annamalai,"** Mr. Narayan returns to his favorite subject, the uneasiness of educated English-speaking Indians in relating to their "inferiors." Mr. Narayan shows himself overwhelmed by the servant whose character he has been trying to decipher for 15 years. In the title story, the last in the collection of 28, the great spreading banyan tree is the ritual setting for an illiterate but highly professional village storyteller who always takes 10 days to narrate a tale to the villagers. Perhaps reflecting Mr. Narayan's awareness of age, this storyteller suddenly finds himself unable to carry on and makes a public profession of weakness that is of course another story, his last.

> **What usually interests Mr. Narayan is the chance to make a story, not a point, out of anything that comes his way. His is a cult of observation for its own sake. . . .**
> —*Alfred Kazin*

Mr. Narayan is an almost placid, good-natured storyteller whose work derives its charm from the immense calm out of which he writes. It has all happened before, it happens every hour, it will happen again tomorrow. But there are levels of irony, subtle inflections and modulations in his easy, transparent style, meant to show the despair—usually economic panic—driving his characters. In **"A Horse And Two Goats,"** Muni, an old peasant who has lost everything

but his goats, tethers them to the trunk of a "drumstick tree that grew in front of his hut and from which occasionally Muni could shake down drumsticks. This morning he got six. He carried them in with a sense of triumph. Although no one could say precisely who owned the tree, it was his because he lived in its shadow."

Muni and his wife are straight out of the Brothers Grimm—Muni "always calculated his age from the time of the great famine when he stood as high as the parapet around the village well, but who could calculate such things accurately nowadays with so many famines occurring?" In the morning of the day covered in the story, before Muni meets the red-faced American who will apparently change their fortunes, his wife scolds him: "'You are getting no sauce today, nor anything else. I can't find anything to give you to eat. Fast till the evening, it'll do you good. Take the goats and be gone now,' she cried, and added, 'Don't come back before the sun is down.'"

They have no children. "Perhaps a large progeny would have brought him the blessing of the gods." But the American passing through their village mistakes the statue of a horse on the outskirts for Muni's property and buys it for 100 rupees. Muni returns with the money to his incredulous wife, believing he has sold his goats to the foreigner. They turn up bleating at his door, and the old woman to whom he has been married since they were both children some 60 years earlier threatens to go off to her parents.

The story is totally without condescension or sentimentality, does not even linger satirically on the acquisitive American. But the transparency with which it discloses the totally abject condition of Muni and wife is all the more striking because there is no visible moral. What usually interests Mr. Narayan is the chance to make a story, not a point, out of anything that comes his way. His is a cult of observation for its own sake, and his stories are always even-tempered and benign in a way that reflects the author's lack of political edge and his "British" culture. Reading him, I remember Nehru saying "I am the last Englishman to rule India." Mr. Narayan's stance is not what you get from the so much more penetrating and politically sharp mind of V. S. Naipaul. But of course Vidiadhar Surajprasad Naipaul, in spite of the name, is not from India.

"Annamalai," the most troubled and dramatic story in this collection, shows Mr. Narayan transcending himself under the pressure of a character not to be contained by routine observation. Annamalai is presented as the author's gardener, watchman, "and general custodian of me and my property." He is of course illiterate "in any of the fourteen languages listed in the Indian Constitution"; he dictates wild unfathomable letters for the village scribe to write down. He is sensitive to names and wants his master to remove his own name from the gate: "All sorts of people read your name aloud while passing down the road. It is not good. Often urchins and tots just learning to spell shout your name and run off when I try to catch them. The other day some women also read your name and laughed to themselves. Why should they? I do not like it at all."

Annamalai, a demon for work, "came in only when he had a postcard for me to address. While I sat at my desk he would stand behind my chair, suppressing even his normal breath lest it should disturb my work, but he could not help the little rumbles and sighs emanating from his throat whenever he attempted to remain still." Anything Annamalai relates (he often talks for the pleasure of talking aloud, needing no listener) becomes a story in itself. He recounts Japanese brutalities during the war, and tells a long story about a tailor and his sewing machine that I did not understand and that, I suspect, is meant to be understood as a reflection of Annamalai's capacity for storing grievances.

Sometimes, however, one of his tales is sufficient unto itself:

> I was sitting in a train going somewhere to seek a job. I didn't have a ticket. A fellow got in and demanded, "Where is your ticket?" I searched for it here and there and said, "Some son of a bitch has stolen my ticket." But he understood and said, "We will find out who that son of a bitch is. Get off the train first." And they took me out of the train with the bundle of clothes I carried. After the train left we were alone, and he said, "How much have you?" I had nothing, and he asked, "Do you want to earn one rupee and eight annas a day?" I begged him to give me work. . . . The lorry put me down late next day on the mountain. All night I had to keep awake and keep a fire going, otherwise even elephants came up.

After 15 years, the author loses him. "Why do you have to go away like this?" . . . "He merely said, 'I don't want to die in this house and bring it a bad name. Let me go home and die.'" Nowhere else in this fine book does Mr. Narayan so interestingly submit to his material. He claims in his foreword that "the short story is the best medium for utilizing the wealth of subjects available. A novel is a different proposition altogether, centralized as it is on a major theme, leaving out, necessarily, a great deal of the available material on the periphery. Short stories, on the other hand, can cover a wider field by presenting concentrated miniatures of human experience in all its opulence." But the opulence of India includes a lot of misery and confusion. Though a miniature, **"Annamalai"** bursts the bonds of that predictable form, the short story. It brings a human strangeness home to us, as only a novel usually does—and that is the unexpected effect of Mr. Narayan's collection.

Cynthia Vanden Driesen (essay date Autumn 1986)

SOURCE: "R. K. Narayan's Neglected Novel: *Waiting for the Mahatma*," in *World Literature Written in English*, Vol. 26, No. 2, Autumn, 1986, pp. 362-69.

[*In the following essay, Driesen analyzes Narayan's* Waiting for the Mahatma *by tracing the main character's relationship to Gandhi.*]

By the time **Waiting for the Mahatma** was published (in 1957), R. K. Narayan had already established an international reputation as a novelist. It is therefore somewhat surprising that in the steadily accumulating volume of critical commentary on Narayan's work in Western literary journals, no detailed study of this particular novel has yet appeared. Some general discussions of Narayan's work hardly mention the novel, while those that do evince a variety of contradictory impressions. For example, Keith Garebian objects to the portrait of Gandhi in the novel as being "sketchy, and at worst, clichéd," while another critic sees it as one of the novel's strengths, "a sure and delicate description of saintliness whose equal is perhaps only to be found in the great Russian novelists." Again, where this latter critic finds the novel's central irony lies in the Gandhian disciple's inability to abide by the rules of conduct set for him by his guru, Shirley Chew finds that Sriram is "pleasingly bold in following his ideal." As the one novel in which Narayan appears to have drawn very directly on one of the most turbulent phases in India's political and social history, it has a special interest. It certainly merits more discussion and comment than has been accorded it.

As the title itself implies, the focus of the novel is not so much on Gandhi himself as on the Indian reaction to Gandhi. The plot traces the adventures of the youth Sriram, his sudden removal from a quite, apathetic existence to a life as adventurously varied as that of any picaresque hero, events brought about by his involvement in the campaign of Mahatma Gandhi against British rule in India. Garebian comments that "politics is not Narayan's forte," but it is soon apparent that, in fact, politics is not his main interest in the novel. While some incidental political comment could, perhaps, be extracted, on this momentous phase in Indian history, the novel is more remarkable for the typically low-keyed manner in which Narayan shapes a work with much more than a local and limited significance. The novel presents a study of the bewilderments, the uncertainties, the struggles and the human failures of the disciple who only imperfectly understands his master, and whose attempts to follow the latter's teaching involve a battle not only against external circumstances but also against deeply ingrained unsaintly aspects of his own imperfect nature. What the novel dramatizes, then, is Narayan's continuing concern with the idea of spiritual perfection and the difficulty of its attainment by "average" humanity.

As a devout Hindu, Narayan reveals that the philosophical preoccupations are, not surprisingly, closely aligned to Hindu religious belief, although it is Narayan's peculiar achievement to successfully embody those preoccupations in issues that evoke a sense of their broad human relevance. It is interesting to note that the three novels which followed each other in a particular decade, *Mr. Sampath* (1949), *The Financial Expert* (1952) and *Waiting for the Mahatma* (1957), might each be regarded as a parable on one of the three cardinal sins mentioned in the Bhagavad Gita as representing the "triple gates of Hell, the sins of lust, of greed and of anger." *Mr. Sampath* dramatizes the disastrous consequences of indulgence in the sin of lust; *The Financial Expert* the Nemesis which overtakes avarice; while in *Waiting for the Mahatma* the hero's particular failing (among others) is a proneness to the sin of anger.

The novel has five discernible phases, each coinciding with distinct developments in the discipleship of Sriram. The first portrays Sriram's thoroughly self-centred uneventful existence until his encounter with Bharati leads to the contact with Gandhi and the beginning of a new life. From the beginning, Gandhi's exhortations towards non-violence and self-discipline are shown to register but vaguely on Sriram, whose mind is filled mostly with his sensual longings for Bharati. The second section focuses on the personality of the Mahatma himself and his impact on those around him, particularly Sriram, who is now an accepted member of his band. Though his main reason for joining Gandhi has been his attraction to Bharati, Sriram is "desolate" when the time comes for bidding his master goodbye. Part three shows Sriram's dedication being tested in his lonely mountain hideout. As long as he is sustained by Bharati's encouragement and example, he remains faithful, but loneliness, physical hardship, and sheer boredom are steadily eroding his dedication. When, in obedience to Gandhi's injunction, Bharati departs voluntarily to prison, his fall becomes only a matter of time. This comes about in part four, when Bharati's place as guide is filled by the terrorist Jagdish. Sriram is easily dominated by him, the more so because his doctrines are much more in tune with the natural promptings of Sriram's own temperament. Part four also shows Sriram imprisoned for his crimes. While he is himself too obtuse to realize the full extent of his betrayal of the Gandhian ideals, the point is underlined by the remark of one of the other criminals. "You call yourself the Mahatma's disciple, and you have derived no good from it." The fifth and last section of the novel shows Sriram free in an independent India. The final irony is that though the British have now left India, the country has been thrown into chaos with the violent conflict between Hindu and Moslem; the Gandhian ideals appear to have gone down in defeat and Gandhi himself is assassinated. Yet, through the preparations for the marriage of the two young people, Bharati, the perfect disciple, and Sriram, the fallen one, duly blessed by Gandhi, the novel concludes on a note of hope.

Unlike most of Narayan's other works, this novel has a markedly picaresque quality. The central character shows basically little change in himself, but is presented against a constantly changing background, and this succession of different settings cumulatively builds up an impression of an entire society, of Indian under the impact of Gandhi—a time of revolutionary social and political change. Sriram's quiet, even somnolent existence in Kabir Street, at the beginning of the novel, affords the reader a glimpse of this world before the advent of the saintly reformer. Subsequently, through the peregrinations of the hero, the reader is offered an impression of a cross-section of the kinds of responses evoked by Gandhi—sceptical, hypocritical, frankly hostile or simply indifferent.

While Gandhi himself is not the central focus of the novel, he remains a persuasive influence. As though well aware of the innate difficulties of rendering the saint himself interesting as a fictional subject, Narayan concentrates rather on the portrait of the sinner who aspires to follow his teachings. Yet the saint himself needs to be portrayed with sufficient power and conviction if the disciples' attraction to him is to be rendered credible and convincing. Narayan's portraiture preserves a delicate balance between the humanly appealing and the mysteriously awe-inspiring. The externalized presentation is important in preserving a sense of mystery, of spiritual power and grandeur. The reader first observes the Mahatma (the great soul) through the eyes of Sriram, one of a crowd of many thousands gathered to hear him and do him homage. The crowd's respect for him is underlined humourously by their impatient ridicule of their own local dignitaries. Gandhi's own complete assurance, the authoritative ring of his injunctions, his uncanny prescience in singling out and dealing with the disturbing elements in the crowd, convincingly establish him as a figure worthy of respect. His very physical presence appears to be a source of some kind of grace, so that after his arrival in Malgudi, office workers, children, all feel happy when "They saw him pass . . . a white-clad figure, fair-skinned and radiant," and when he takes up residence in the meanest quarter of the town, "the men left off fighting . . . the whole place looked bright . . . with lamps and green mango leaves." When in the presence of the Mahatma, who shows an uncanny ability in reading people's thoughts as it were, Sriram finds himself incapable of lying. Although he first joins Gandhi because he is physically attracted to Bharati, when the time for Gandhi's departure arrives, not even the proximity of Bharati seems to mitigate his (Sriram's) misery.

This is a saint who remains attractively human and approachable. If given sometimes to sober silences, more often he is shown smiling and good-humoured. He smiles as he speaks to the municipal chairman, softening the fact of his refusal of the latter's hospitality and laughs happily at his own quip. While talking with Sriram, "he laughed in a kindly manner" and again while listening to Sriram's perorations against the British "regards him with a smile." Right at the end of the novel, amid all the violence and chaos, again he greets the young people with a smile. There is considerable skill in the manner in which Narayan evokes the impression of a man deeply conscious of great responsibilities, a public personality whose presence "had the effect of knocking down the walls of a house and converting it into a public place," surrounded by sycophants, disciples and hangers-on, yet possessed of a completely unself-conscious humility and a capacity for concern with the most minute problems affecting his numerous protégés. So he keenly follows Sriram's progress in the art of spinning, and his concern for the latter's grandmother provokes Sriram to reflect, "What made the Mahatma attach so much importance to Granny when he had so many things to mind? When he had the all-important task of driving the British out he ought to leave simple matters like Granny to be handled by himself."

Yet the Mahatma is shown, most effectively, to be no soft-headed and unpractical idealist, but a shrewd (if kindly) observer of men and matters. His singling out of the sweeper's boy for special attention and his choice of dwelling in the sweeper's village are calculated gestures designed to have the maximum possible effect in protesting discrimination against this oppressed section of the Indian community. Again, refusing the orange juice pressed on him because of his own austere regimes, he is careful to please his influential host by admiring the fruit, "turning it slowly between his fingers. The Chairman felt as happy as if he himself were being scrutinised and approved." The terms in which he refuses the man's ostentatious hospitality show the same diplomatic grace: "would you rather not spare an old man like me the bother of walking through those vast spaces? I'm a tired old man." The Mahatma's kindness has a strongly practical bent. Although he invites the sweeper's boy to sit with him, he does not permit him to be slovenly. He shows the boy how to peel an orange in a socially acceptable way: "What to do with the pips, how to hide the skin and what to do with all the superfluous bits packed within an orange."

Poised against this portrait of the perfect spiritual leader is that of his highly imperfect disciple. Since Sriram's is the central consciousness through which most of the events in the novel are mediated, his emotions and predicaments, the constant inner struggle incurred as a result of his commitment to ideals which go so directly against the grain of his own nature, are presented with a particular sense of immediacy. Contrasted with the almost supernaturally prescient Gandhi, Sriram appears more than ever a very average and undistinguished young man. Even his grandmother seems to have very little respect for his mental abilities, while Sriram himself reflects, "I am a fool. It is a wonder that a girl like Bharati cares for me at all." Unlike the central figures of other Narayan novels, like Krishnan (*The English Teacher*) or Srinivas (*Mr. Sampath*) he has no penchant for philosophical questioning. When, on a solitary occasion, he is moved to consider the problem of life on earth. "This philosophical trend he immediately checked. . . ."

Narayan's criticism of this inadequate disciple is registered mainly through the play of a gentle comic irony. Typically with Narayan, the harsher note of satire is avoided. At every point, Sriram is a contrast to his mentor. Against Gandhi's consistent kindliness and gentleness, shown in his efforts to spare the feelings of even the most shallow and hypocritical, one measures Sriram's short-tempered violence. His old grandmother is shown little consideration, and he shouts at her "in a great rage" when she ridicules him about his new enthusiasms. He is annoyed by Bharati's teasing and even becomes so impatient at her own attachment to the Gandhian teachings that "he wanted to shout at her . . . he wanted to threaten her." Early in his career as a Gandhian volunteer he becomes disenchanted by the unspectacular nature of non-violent resistance. Only when, under the tutelage of the terrorist Jagdish, he commits arson, derails trains, plants bombs he finds "he was actually beginning to enjoy the excitement . . . It gave him a feeling of romantic importance." On one occasion, suspecting Jagdish might be playing a practical joke on him, he thinks, "I will crush his skull with a big stone, and he revelled in visions of extraordinary violence." So Sriram transgresses constantly against the primary Gandhian rule of non-violence.

Neither does he find it easy to adhere to other Gandhian injunctions. Chastity of thought and action seem impossibilities to a young man hopelessly in love. He is constantly distracted by sensual desire whenever he is close to Bharati. It is her strength of character rather than his own self-discipline that keeps his impulses under control. Gandhian austerity in matters of food and personal comfort impose a great strain. In Gandhi's camp he misses the soft pillows of his bed at home and finds himself frequently yearning for the delicate morsels with which Granny used to indulge him.

As though to underline further his backslidings, Sriram is counterpoised against the figure of Bharati. Narayan's portraiture of the young woman succeeds in establishing the conviction that the rules of existence laid down by the Mahatma can, in fact, be adhered to by the sincerely dedicated. Not only is it possible to follow in the footsteps of the master, one might almost become like him. A close personal relationship exists between the Mahatma and Bharati. Conveying his instructions directly, or confidently interpreting them, she acts as the visible and continued extension of Gandhian influence on the young man's life. Occasionally she seems to be touched by the same quality of grandeur as Gandhi himself. Sriram recognizes this when he feels, "He was frightened of her. She seemed to be too magnificent to be his wife." With her, private and personal claims weigh little against her dedication to the Gandhian ideal. She goes to prison unquestioningly at Gandhi's behest. Like her mentor also, she is compassionate and good humoured, yet possessed of a shrewd knowledge of human foibles and weaknesses. She can speak sharply enough on occasion, moving Sriram to remark, "You have the same style of talk as my grandmother. She is as sharp tongued as you are." Her austere idealism does not preclude a mischievous sense of humour and Sriram finds her teasing sometimes difficult to bear. Hers is one of Narayan's most attractive and authentic portraits of a woman.

These characters are convincingly established as convincing individuals yet they also appear to be invested with a wider representative significance, the cumulative result of subtly evocative detail. Sriram's name, for instance, recalls that of the great hero of the Indian epic the *Ramayana*. While there is some irony here, considering the nature of this particular hero, the detail is significant. The novel could be read as a kind of parable with Sriram as a figure representative of the Indian nation, attracted to the Gandhian teachings but lacking the moral fibre necessary for faithful and continued adherence to them. The novel indeed provides the reader with an understanding of how it was possible for Indians, so shortly after their hard-won freedom from British rule under Gandhi's guidance, to become entrapped in fratricidal strife, with bloodshed and violence on a scale that made it one of the darkest periods of Indian history. This aspect of the novel's significance is registered through other delicately suggestive details. Sometimes it appears as a result of syntactic structure or phraseology. For instance, the description of Sriram's abandonment of his early apathetic existence has a deeper resonance, as of a national awakening. He is only a young man, but he is presented as waking from an "age-long" slumber. Again, the description of his house invokes recollections of India's ancient heritage:

> The walls were two feet thick, the doors were made of century-old teak planks . . . the tiles were of burntwood which had weathered the storms and rains of centuries . . . Here the family lineage began years ago and continued still. . . .

Interestingly, Sriram's immediate family remain shadowy, they are "figures in a legend." Unlike the typical Narayan hero who usually gains in solidity from being depicted against a background of intertwining domestic relationships and routines, Sriram appears curiously homeless. Bharati too, like Sriram, appears in some sense both anonymous and representative. She, indeed, has even less family and domestic background than Sriram. There is a rather magnificent freedom about her as she moves about quite untrammelled by the usual taboos that should surround a young Indian woman of her age. Like Sriram's, her name is significant. She could stand as a figure representative of Mother India. It would be crude of course to attempt to trace these parallels too rigidly, but certain details recur suggestively. For instance, earlier in life, Sriram had paid "homage" to the portrait of a foreign queen, but when he discovers Bharati, "she looked so different . . . he realized how shallow was the other beauty, the English queen. . . ." Yet while carrying this broader representative significance, these characters still preserve their conviction as authentic individual portraitures, contributing indeed thereby to the success of the enclosed parable.

Most of the other characters in the novel are presented in terms of their response to Gandhi. There are the conservative and the sceptics like Sriram's grandmother, to whom Gandhi is only a disturber of the peace, "one who preached dangerously, who tried to bring untouchables into temples." Yet the old woman, as Narayan presents her with his characteristic gentle irony, is an austere, conscientious, unselfish and deeply religious woman. She is actually much closer to the Gandhian ideal than her frivolous nephew, who affects to be Gandhi's disciple. There are other conservatives, like the village schoolmaster, who believe that "what we need is not a Quit India, but a Quiet India," or like the timid villager who asks, "Why should we irritate the Sircar?" At the opposite pole to these are those like Jagdish the terrorist who feel that Gandhi's stance is not revolutionary and militant enough. Then there are the hypocrites like the timber merchant who attends Gandhi's meetings but supplies the timber to the British war effort, or the municipal chairman who wears homespun clothing and flaunts the pictures of national heroes in his home only for the occasion of Gandhi's visit. To complete the picture are those frankly indifferent to Gandhi, carelessly co-operating with the forces he is aligned against, like the villagers of Solur and the vendor of English biscuits. These are those to whom the great issues of the day mean nothing, immersed as they are in the mundane routines of their daily lives like the neighbours Sriram watches, "sitting by the window reading an evening paper, comfortable folk." The comprehensiveness of Narayan's picture of an India under the impact of Gandhi is surprising in a novel apparently so slight in structure.

Partly perhaps because of this aim of the writer's, to use a broader canvas, as it were, there is a less strong sense of place in this work than in the other novels of Malgudi. One wonders whether this could partly account also for the fact that this novel appears also to have had less of an impact, for this sense of place has certainly been a potent factor in the success of others of Narayan's works. Graham Greene, for instance, attempting to elucidate his response to them, speaks of "those loved and shabby streets of Malgudi. . . ." Certainly some of those landmarks reappear, evoking that peculiar sense of recognition familiar to the reader of Narayan's novels: Market Road (where Sriram's old home is situated), the cremation ground across the river from Nallappa's Grove, the River Sarayu, the sweepers' village "outside the town limits . . . where nobody went." Sriram's adventures, however, necessarily involve a disjunction with the routines of Malgudi, and travel away from its environs.

While its plot is connected with well-known events in Indian history, the novel also demonstrates another continuing and characteristic strength of Narayan's work, a sense of broader, deeper and more subtle changes gradually overtaking an entire way of life. *Khadi* (homespun fabric) is now the right patriotic dress to wear and the municipal chairman is careful to remove the portraits of English royalty from his home. Bharati's activities exemplify a revolutionary new ideal for Indian women and an "untouchable" is permitted to sit on a Kashmir counterpane in the house of the municipal chairman. Strong as are the currents of change, the forces of conservatism are not easily routed, and typically Narayan also demonstrates the strength of their appeal. The exchanges between Sriram and his grandmother show one aspect of the conflict between youth and age, change and tradition, which is again a recurring interest in Narayan's work. The reader is often left with the awareness that there is much to be said for the traditional virtues and the integrity of the traditional way of life. Here, as in other ways, one is made aware that finally, at its deepest level, the interest of the work transcends the narrowly parochial.

India's experience under Gandhi is used then to demonstrate a truth of universal application—the perennial difficulty of fundamentally altering human nature and how narrow and difficult the path to spiritual perfection is. Yet in the peculiar note of hope which still remains at the end of the novel (through the proposed union between Sriram, the inadequate reality, and Bharati the possible ideal) the impression is also established that the effort has to be continued, in spite of drawbacks. The example and teaching of the saint, the power of his spiritual example transcends his death and retains its power to shape individual lives. In spite of setbacks, the struggle for the ideal must continue.

David W. Atkinson (essay date Winter 1987)

SOURCE: "Tradition and Transformation in R. K. Narayan's *A Tiger For Malgudi*," in *International Fiction Review,* Vol. 14, No. 1, Winter, 1987, pp. 8-13.

[*In the following essay, Atkinson discusses Narayan's depiction of Hinduism and its relationship to everyday life in* A Tiger for Malgudi.]

R. K. Narayan is often labeled "a small town ironist," who, with gentle humor, lays bare the weaknesses, foibles, and incongruities of ordinary people. As well, Narayan addresses fundamental questions about human existence, creating in Malgudi a fictional microcosm of India that embraces the organic wholeness of the Hindu tradition. Here Narayan is especially sensitive to how humankind falls short in its religious ambitions, as his characters repeatedly settle for less than the ideal and are frustrated by the fundamental limitations of being human. In Narayan's most recent novel, *A Tiger for Malgudi* (1983), these limitations emphasize the unsettling disjunction between the philosophical underpinnings of Hinduism and their relevance to everyday life.

Central to *A Tiger for Malgudi* is how the individual, fettered by his own self-delusion, works within a framework established by the Hindu concepts of *dharma* and *karma*. *Dharma* is a word having many meanings, but in essence it points to how the individual, possessed of particular abilities, functions in society. How these come about results from the law of *karma,* which determines that every action produces an effect manifested in a present lifetime or a future one. Subject to the inevitable working of *dharma* and *karma* is the struggle, through the course of countless lifetimes, to break through ego-derived ignorance to realize the oneness of reality. While it might seem that one is trapped in a predetermined cycle, in which *dharma* and *karma* are linked, the individual always retains freedom of choice, and therefore the ability to break free of *samsara* (i.e. cycle of existence), difficult though this task might be.

In *A Tiger for Malgudi,* then, Narayan aims to explode man's principal delusion that he "is all-important, that all else in creation exists only for his sport, amusement, comfort, or nourishment." To this end, the human characters of *A Tiger for Malgudi* are presented as trying to manipulate the natural world for their own ends and failing miserably in the process. By using a tiger as his central character, and by allowing the reader to see through a tiger's eyes, Narayan portrays man as selfish and insensitive to the world, as well as totally unaware of his role in the great scheme of things. That Raja's thoughts and activities are superior to anything he observes of humankind affirms just how much the individual is immersed in egocentric ignorance.

A Tiger for Malgudi is developed in three parts, each recounting a period of Raja's life, and each expressing some aspect of the *dharma-karma* theme. The first section focuses on Raja's life in the jungle, where as a hunter and predator he feels no remorse for what he does. It is, Raja confesses, "a time of utter wildness, violence, and unthinking cruelty inflicted on weaker creatures." Raja is completely resolved to this role in the divine plan, and accepts that some things are beyond question and cannot be changed; as he says, "I don't know why God has chosen to give us this fierce make-up, the same God who has created the parrot, the peacock, and the deer." Here the nature of *dharma* is presented, not only as determining one's actions, but also as imposing certain expectations realizable only through individual initiative and action. Raja does not therefore automatically become "King of the Forest": the submission of other creatures is worth nothing unless it is earned.

The second part of the novel begins when Raja's mate and cubs are killed by hunters. Raja's response to his loss is predictable and natural. There arose within him "a blind impossible anger" in which he "just wanted to dash up, pounce upon every creature, bite and claw and destroy." But Raja also finds that preying on domestic animals is much easier than pursuing creatures in the wild. Crucial in Raja's make-up is his pride in being a tiger; now, however, he takes pride in carrying off the defenseless villagers' sheep. Much after the fact Raja recognizes his mistake in turning away from what he is by nature. "Looking back," Raja says, "I feel that I should not have chosen the easy path—of raiding villages." It is because Raja forgets who he is that he becomes careless and is transformed into the unnatural creature who performs for circus patrons and film directors.

Revealed, as well, in Raja's circus and film experiences is the important distinction between what one has control over in one's life and what one does not. Raja can, for example, do little to prevent the destruction of his cubs and mate; and, similarly, Raja, once captured, can do little about what Captain inflicts upon him. Nevertheless, one must look inwardly to determine how best to respond to the events of one's life. As well, it does not mean that *dharma* can be changed. Thus Raja, although admitting that he is well kept by Captain, admits, "I was still a prisoner." One can never drive from the tiger his tiger's nature, and, when Captain finally pushes Raja too far, Raja kills him, albeit inadvertently, and his essential nature is reasserted. What occurs here anticipates the Master's observation that the spiritual process leading out of ignorance requires that one discover one's real self. One must get in touch with the *vasana* (i.e. seeds) of one's past lives, which is "never lost, but is buried in one's personality and carried from birth to birth." That Raja returns once more to being a tiger suggests the positive orientation of Hinduism, pointing to the dynamic nature of the human personality, which can be deceived but which eventually overcomes this deception.

The connection between ignorance and egocentricity is further developed in *A Tiger for Malgudi* when Raja addresses why the villagers fear him. "It was due," Raja says, "to their general lack of a sense of security and an irrational dread of losing their assets." Narayan points to how possessions affirm self-importance and how humankind's greatest fear is having that self-importance compromised. There is the implication, too, that the freedom Raja regains is the freedom toward which all creatures, and especially humankind, should aspire. Instead humankind surrounds itself with prisons of its own making. What comprises this prison the Master makes clear when he tells the frightened villagers, "Never use the words *beast* or *brute*. They're ugly words coined by man in his arrogance. The human being thinks all other creatures are 'beasts.' Awful word." It is pride that lies at the root of human delusion and suffering. Also suggestive is when a villager asks the Master. "Is this the occasion to discuss problems of vocabulary?" When the Master answers, "why not," he indicates how language expresses human egocenteredness, for it makes a statement about reality, not in any objective sense, but only in the sense the speaker sees it.

Significant in Narayan's development of the general theme of spiritual transformation is Raja's statement, made while he takes refuge in the local school, "I was enjoying my freedom, and the happy feeling that the whip along with the hand that held it was banished forever. No more of it; it was pleasant to brood over this good fortune." Freedom brings happiness, and freedom for Raja is to be his natural self. But at the same time, Raja's freedom is not absolute, and whatever happiness he enjoys is ephemeral. This "natural freedom" is important because it leads to the further end of absolute freedom from self delusion, to which Raja commits himself in the third and final section of the novel. Having been saved from the angry villagers by the Master, Raja becomes the *sadhu*'s (i.e. wise man's) devoted disciple, learning much about his own nature, his place in the order of things, and his relationship with God. In this regard, the Master, in saying to Raja, "Understand that you are not a tiger, don't hurt yourself. I am your friend," points to the ultimate freedom transcending the apparent freedom from conventional labels.

The last part of *A Tiger for Malgudi* makes explicit what is largely implied in the novel's earlier sections. The Master describes God "as the Creator, the Great Spirit pervading every creature, a source of power and strength." This contrasts with Raja's perception of God as "an enormous tiger, spanning the earth and the sky." The Master's suggestion is that man, and for that matter the tiger as well, makes God in his own image, and that neither perception of the divine corresponds to what the divine is in its fullness. Rather they are objectified conceptions of the divine which is internal to us, and are conditioned by who and what we are. Thus Narayan connects the notion of the divine with that of *dharma.*

Concerning the quest to realize the divine within, the Master makes the further point that the goal is not easily realized. The Master's message is that, consistent with the law of *karma,* one must work to move through various stages of increasing spiritual awareness until one consciously turns away from the world to achieve *samadhi* (i.e., enlightenment). In this struggle, one must stress, not one's failures, but one's successes, small though they might be. Underpinning what one does is that one must aspire in one's actions to live in the world without being consumed by it. The Master describes to Raja how we become too "busy and active and living by the clock," preoccupied with being "respectable" in society. One must realize that one must live in the world without being fettered by it. As the Master says, one must take care not to be "overburdened with knowledge, facts, and information—fetters and shackles for the rising soul," which, "like food, must be taken within limits." One must further understand that to grasp after the world is to affirm one's egocenteredness and to perpetuate a fiction that can only bring suffering. It is with this in mind that the Master says, "No relationship, human or other, or association of any kind could last forever. Separation is the law of life right from the mother's womb. One has to accept it if one has to live in God's plans."

While *A Tiger for Malgudi* dwells on changes in Raja, it also, by stressing the static nature of other characters, suggests how they are victims of their own ignorance and spiritual inertia. Most obvious in this regard is Captain, who sees himself in total control of his own life and all that he touches. It is not that there is anything especially wrong with this attitude, for, after all, Hinduism teaches that one is responsible for the fruits of one's actions. What is wrong is that Captain is consumed by his own self-importance, which is manifested in the power he holds over both the animals and the people with whom he comes into contact. The entire Grand Malgudi circus, which Captain inherits, but then transforms to his own liking, is a central symbol of the fictional reality with which he surrounds himself. The extent of Captain's deception is expressed in several other ways as well. Raja observes how Captain's sole aim for him was to run "round and round in circles in pursuit of nothing." Even tigers have purpose, something Captain fails to realize. Captain also introduces Raja to the circus audience as "not an ordinary, commonplace tiger but an intelligent creature . . . almost human in understanding." Ironically, what Captain says is true, as Raja possesses far more understanding than Captain himself. Finally, Captain is presented as a skilled linguist, capable of speaking to the audience in Hindi, English, and Tamil. The implication is that, while Captain speaks the words, he does not understand what he is saying. He neither appreciates how language is inherently deceiving, nor does he try to use it correctly.

Captain's self-importance is most flagrantly revealed in his relationship with Madan, the film director, who approaches Captain about having Raja perform in his film. Captain has no interest in the film, except that it offers him another way of controlling and manipulating others. Madan is forced by Captain to draft and redraft agreements, can only do with Raja what Captain allows, despite the "artistic" demands of his film, and is driven to desperation in "securing an audience with the great man." Captain is doing little more than playing power games with Madan, which give him a false sense of his own importance and enmesh him even further in the deception coming from such selfishness.

Madan is not, however, without fault, for he is equally insensitive in the way he treats Jaggu, his leading actor. Just as Captain manipulates Madan, so Madan treats Jaggu, first threatening him with punishment and then offering him a bedmate. It hardly needs saying that all Madan's plans break down: the film is never completed and Madan himself is reduced to hysteria. In having no relationship with reality, the film, like the Grand Malgudi Circus, symbolizes the fictional baggage humankind creates for itself.

One other character also serves to highlight the theme of self-deception. Jaggu is an innocent, who had, previous to his movie role, made what little money he could performing feats of strength; certainly he is neither actor nor hero. But Jaggu is also tempted by riches, which, in his own slow-witted way, he sees as a way of affirming his own importance. As well, Jaggu is totally out of touch with reality; nothing could be clearer than when Narayan describes the process of transforming him into a film hero. The makeup men, for example, touch "him up here and there as if he were inanimate." When Jaggu is described as giving "no sign of being alive," it is suggested that he is totally unaware of what is going on around him, and, like both Captain and Madan, unable to break through his own ignorance.

The Master is, of course, intended to serve as the ideal. When initially asked who he is, his answer signifies the basic goal that all the other characters, except Raja, ignore. "You are asking a profound question. I've no idea who I am! All my life I have been trying to find the answer." His instructions to Raja when he leads him to safety are equally suggestive: ". . . the eye is the starting point of all evil and mischief. The eye can travel far and pick out objects indiscriminately, mind follows the eye, and the rest of the body is conditioned by the mind." The Master suggests how one, while attracted to the world, is incapable of distinguishing what has meaning and purpose and what does not. In clattering one's mind with the ephemera of life, one needlessly complicates it and loses sight of the true goal beyond particularity. Finally, the Master embodies the ideal in his action; he sees himself as nothing special, and rejects any attempt to treat him as a "holy" man. He says to those prostrating themselves in front of him, "I am not different from you, we are equals and [you have] no need to pay homage to me. It has no meaning."

There seems, then, a very clear assertion in *A Tiger for Malgudi* of very basic Hindu teachings. Not all, however, is as clear as it appears. It is relevant here that the less admirable characters such as Captain and Madan are much more fully developed than the Master, who is a shadowy and unconvincing figure for a good part of his relationship with Raja, and who, when his wife appears at the novel's end, becomes a very contradictory one. Narayan is far more interested in the characters that fall short of the ideal, and one is therefore left wondering to what degree Narayan is committed to the Hindu world view that *A Tiger for Malgudi* seems so clearly to espouse. While to some the closure of *A Tiger for Malgudi* might seem contrived and weak, it is possible to see Narayan consciously placing the novel against an ironic backdrop which brings into question its religious and philosophic underpinnings.

Crucial to this approach is the sudden introduction into the novel of information concerning the Master's early life. In contrast to his present life as an ascetic in a loincloth, the Master's early life was committed to satisfying his own selfish appetites. The Master's wife describes how "others may take you for a hermit, but I know you intimately": she talks of his "inordinate demands of food," and of how he insisted on her "total surrender night or day" whenever passion "seized" him. Thus the reader is presented with two radically different views of the Master, with the portrait of his earlier life suggesting what must be overcome to attain the stage of *sannyasin* (i.e. ascetic) and ultimately the achievement of *samadhi* (i.e., enlightenment). This juxtaposition of past and present, however, also presents problems, for it begs the question of how and why this radical transformation came about. All the reader is told is that the Master left his wife and family without warning and without ever telling them of his intentions. For the Master to say as he does that his past does not count is not sufficient to satisfy the reader's curiosity.

There are other ambiguities in the Master's character as well. The role of *sannyasin* demands that one fulfill one's responsibilities as a householder before embarking on the single-minded pursuit of enlightenment. In calling the Master's act of "renunciation" one of "desertion," his wife suggests that the Master may not have done as he should, and thus who and what he is comes under suspicion. The

same can be concluded when she says to him, not without a hint of irony, "one has the right to show one's veneration for a sublime soul, a saint perhaps." The "perhaps" adds an unsettling note that cannot be ignored. In attempting to distance himself from his wife, the Master insists that his wife refer to him as "he" rather than "you"; he rebukes her saying, "You are beginning, I now notice, to use the word 'you,' which is not proper; keep to 'he.'" Such unnatural expression conflicts with the Master's overt claims about truth, and suggests that the Master is not as honest as he thinks either with himself or others. The most troublesome feature of the novel is what finally happens to Raja. When the Master goes off to release himself "from all bondage," Raja, rather than returning to his natural state a wiser tiger, is sent to a zoo because, as the Master says, "he is only a tiger in appearance . . . He is a sensitive soul who understands life and its problems exactly as we do." If this is truly the case, then it hardly seems appropriate that he be reduced to a zoo animal taking a "tonic" each day to improve his coat. As in both the circus and the film, Raja is trapped in a totally alien environment. That the Master talks of it as a "new life," in which Raja will make hundreds of people happy, does not change the incongruity of the situation. That the Master is directly responsible for Raja's new life, with all its similarities to those imposed on Raja by Captain and Madan, seems more than a coincidental parallel, and generates yet more questions concerning the Master's so-called wisdom.

It is difficult to accept the unresolved conclusion of *A Tiger for Malgudi.* This lack of resolution need not be seen, however, as an artistic flaw. Rather it enhances what is already evident from the rest of the novel: that man is a complex creature with complex problems for which there are no absolute answers. From Narayan's point of view, traditional religion purports too often to provide absolute answers that are taken far too seriously. The aesthetically unsettling way in which the novel is left hanging is therefore an effective counterpoint to the implied inadequacies of the world view which it espouses.

R. K. Narayan with Stephen R. Graubard (interview date Fall 1989)

SOURCE: "An Interview with R. K. Narayan," in *Daedalus*, Vol. 118, No. 4, Fall, 1989, pp. 232-37.

[*In the following interview, Narayan discusses Indian writers, India, and criticism of his work.*]

[*Graubard:*] *What can one say, in brief compass, about Indian literature? How do you see it?*

[Narayan:] This is a vast field—Indian literature—ancient, modern. There are so many languages in India. To know the literature of each is very difficult, and yet there are few translations from one language into another. It is difficult to judge the literature of so many languages. I can judge only Tamil; I cannot read literature in Kannada but I understand it, and English, of course. About literature in the other languages I would not be able to tell you very much. Yet there is so much literature and literary criticism in each of these languages.

Yes, that is true. What is read by one group may not be read by others. But what about Indian English literature—writers like Anita Desai, . . . Mulk Raj Anand, and Vikram Seth?

Anita Desai and Vikram Seth are good writers. I very much enjoyed reading *The Golden Gate Bridge.* In fact, I reviewed it.

What about poetry in English?

I don't read modern poetry. I confine myself to old English poetry. And to T. S. Eliot.

But looking at Indian writing in English, is it very innovative?

It is difficult to make a judgment. Publishers bring out all kinds of things in English. I get books from publishers, particularly American publishers, asking for my opinion. But most of the stuff is inferior. What do you feel about the situation?

Since there appears to be a market abroad for Indian writing in English, the publishers are stepping in. There is a lot of interest in Indian writing.

I don't know about other forms, but in fiction, I think, there is a lack of judgment. I base this impression entirely on what the publishers send me.

Is the treatment of books meant for the Indian market different from those intended for a foreign market?

I don't know; I don't think about it.

Is it possible to generalize about Indian life or about Indians?

I know only about my part of the country, a little; and, of course, Mysore. I don't know rural Mysore. I don't like villages. I don't even know the whole of Karnataka, though I have visited all parts of the state. I have written about Karnataka, but not as fiction. My fiction is set in my own background, though Malgudi is imaginary. Malgudi is fixed in the 1930s, and that gives me extraordinary freedom. I can even put a lighthouse there if I want to, though there is no coast near Malgudi.

Do you read reviews of your books? To what extent are you affected by criticism?

Earlier, I never read reviews of my books because I did not want to become self-conscious. Now, I may occasionally read them, but they do not bother me. Critics say that I don't talk of the aspirations of the people, of the political agony that we have gone through, and of all those plans for economic growth. I am not interested in that. I am interested in human characters and their background. That is important for me; I want a story to be entertaining, enjoyable, and illuminating in some way.

I visited the towns of Belur and Halebedu yesterday and found them absolutely fascinating.

Yes. You must have noted that much of Indian art is anonymous. Perhaps that is how it should be. I like a work of art that has a life of its own independent of its creator. When I write, I write for myself. While writing, I don't think of readers' reactions. A book, a piece of writing, even a paragraph, has an organic life of its own, and people are free to view it in any manner they like. I would like to be free of responsibility for my fictional characters.

I am interested to know that you rarely read criticism, that you are not much moved, even by harsh criticism.

As I said, I do not read criticism because I do not want to be self-conscious. Perhaps the whole basis of life is to be oneself and not to be self-conscious. When I am writing, I don't read much because I do not wish to be influenced. When I write, I don't know what is coming next. But it grows as I write, and when I read it at night, I am sometimes surprised by what I have written in the afternoon.

You really don't know the details when you sit down to write?

I have a general idea of what I want to write, but the details come only when the writing is in progress. They well up from some depth within me.

Do you also read nonfiction?

Yes. Biography, science subjects, travelogues, and things like that.

I would like to talk about another aspect of contemporary India. Many Indians grow up in one part of the country and then move elsewhere. Indians are peripatetic. Even within the country large numbers are on the move all the time. Is this reflected in your life, your thinking, your writing?

I do not think so, though I do travel a lot. I go to Europe for pleasure, but also to work, to see my publishers. They are only excuses for visiting New York or London.

So you go to Europe or America to work and enjoy yourself. But does the time you spend in New York or elsewhere not become part of your imaginative life? The reason I ask this is that I wonder whether Indians can move to the West and yet retain their Indianness.

They can live anywhere because they create their own surroundings. They do not complain, however difficult it may be. But they create their own environment; they spend most of their time with their relatives or countrymen. On a Saturday or Sunday they may travel fifty miles to meet other Indians and have *Idli* or *Dosai*. They create a little India wherever they go. A small number go outside their own community and get to know others. But, then, in New York you have Americans living on West 23rd Street who do not know what life is like on West 25th Street. I used to go to a store on 23rd Street to buy my provisions; the storekeeper had never gone beyond 23rd Street. Every time he met me he said, "It must be fun going through Times Square at night. Someday I'll do it."

Is the difference between Westernized, modern India and traditional India a real difference for you?

Traditional India is very strong. Modern India is very dynamic; the people are different; they are more Westernized. Again, life in the home may be different from life outside. One can be traditional at home and modern outside.

Do you yourself put a great deal of emphasis on the differences between traditional India and modern India? What do you feel?

Probably you can find it in my stories. Their background does not change. The society in my stories remains static. That makes it more convenient to tackle. When you go to Bombay, you find it is different from Delhi or Calcutta. It is impossible to talk about an urban India, and even more so, a rural India. I cannot stay in a village. I like to watch villages while I am passing by in a car or train, but I would not like to live there. I cannot write about Bombay. It is a different society.

What about Calcutta?

I was in Calcutta for a while some years ago. I liked it. Calcutta is an interesting city. There are some impressive old buildings. Calcutta has a great deal, but of all the cities I like Madras.

Apart from the fact that you like New York, London, and Paris, why do you like Madras?

I like Madras because I was born there and because in Madras the ancient and the modern coexist. Madras is both old and new, and you can find lots of things there—drama, theatres, lectures, religious discourses, musical concerts. Some Madrasis is are very orthodox. There are parts of the city where people with a traditional background in Sanskrit are still living. I like talking about Madras much better than talking about India.

What book are you writing now?

It is a novel, *The World of Nagaraj.* It is being serialized in *Frontline,* published by the Hindu newspaper group. The novel is in progress; some eighteen installments have come out.

What is your day like?

I get up at the stroke of eight. I wake at four or five, but I do not care to get up before eight. I would like to sleep till nine, if possible. I have breakfast at eight-thirty and then some *pooja,* some prayer and meditation for an hour. I write from three-thirty to about five-thirty in the afternoon. At night, before I go to bed, I read what I have written during the day and make corrections, which is a much longer and more tedious process. The days when I could write continuously for long periods are over.

Michel Pousse (essay date 1990)

SOURCE: "R. K. Narayan as a Gandhian Novelist," in *Literary Criterion,* Vol. XXV, No. 4, 1990, pp. 77-90.

[*In the following essay, Pousse delineates how Narayan "separated the obviously ephemeral implications of [Gandhi's] philosophy from what was eternal in it and he gave literary existence to the latter."*]

It has proved difficult to separate Gandhian novelists from the Mahatma himself, the Freedom Fighters, or the first years of India's independence. Gandhi and the school of literature he inspired seemed to be so much at one with each other that many a literary critic assumed that the school which had taken over in form and content the whole of Indian English literature wouldn't survive its master. As far back as 1976 Uma Parameswaran noted a sharp decline in the creative powers of such novelists. To her, extinction obviously was round the corner.

Gandhi could only survive his own message if its universality were brought into light. The philosophical value of his teaching had to find a field of application in a context other than that of the fight for independence.

This is where Narayan, of all Indian English writers the least directly committed to violent social reforms subtly illustrates in his gentle novels of Malgudi that the quintessence of Gandhi's teaching is part and parcel of India's daily life; one might even be tempted to say of India's folklore.

The themes developed by Gandhian novelists are easily summed up because they are textbook applications of what the Mahatma ceaselessly repeated. The novelty they introduce into the literature of the sub-continent comes from the fact that they blend philosophy and art in their efforts to amend and reform people's mores.

To Gandhi, art could not exist for its own sake. It had to fulfil some kind of useful purpose and contribute to the general education of the people. Aesthetics could only be a means and not an end. If in a broader sense art had to educate, in a narrower and more temporal context it should help in the fight towards "swaraj" (self—rule or independence).

Indian English novelists taking to their pens have to be given credit for insisting on that aspect of Gandhi's philosophy which for obvious political reasons has often been underestimated and which links the accession to independence with a moral and spiritual revival of the country. To bring the Raj to an end was essential only because its existence forced Indians to regard themselves as an inferior and subdued race. Gandhi insisted upon the need for a moral revolution among his fellow countrymen, a revolution needed in itself regardless of the British presence and which would have to be carried on after the occupant's departure.

Three points stand out in Gandhi's philosophy and Narayan has repeatedly stressed these very points, in a way that puts him in a class of his own among other Indian-English novelists and that lifts the Mahatma's vision of India to loftier heights.

Life is a permanent and never ending quest for truth. That word has never been easy to define in the Gandhian context. It is generally equated with sincerity of heart or even 'soul force'. One must be true to oneself first of all. This necessarily implies a discovery of one's own self. Casting off social artefacts is a prerequisite to such a discovery. Man must question his place in society. He must be aware

of the vanity implicit in the holding of any public office and in the pursuit of any Cursus Honorum. Only then will he be able to re-establish the primitive and essential link with God necessary to answer the question "Who am I?" and hence the question that naturally ensues: "What am I?"

Individual peace can only be achieved within a well-defined social context. Village life as opposed to town life is what brings out the very best in man. Gandhi definitively dichotomized his approach to society. Town is evil and a great destroyer of families. Village life should develop a brotherly feeling among men. The head of the family should be responsible for the production of the essentials: food and cotton. As a way out of India's spiritual and physical misery Gandhi advocated production by the masses as opposed to mass production. It is, however, essential to remember that the village Gandhi had in mind was an ideal one, remote from the actual Indian village where exploitation by the Zamindars, money-lenders, religious intolerance and the rejection of Harijans were daily reality. Things may have been different in the past. Years back when the Governor General of the East India Company, brilliant administrators such as Elphinstone and Metcalfe wrote reports in praise of the Indian village which they described as the only unit of civilization on the sub-continent able to withstand unaltered all the political changes that were taking place at a higher level. In turn Maine, Stuart Mill or even Tocqueville were impressed by the capacity to self-perpetuation ingrained in such a social structure.

Finally Gandhi had to justify his use of the English language. The Indian National Congress was born of Macaulay's success in imposing English as the language of higher education in India and when Bentinck officialized this decision by signing the minutes of a meeting of his Council dated March 7th, 1835, he indirectly created an intelligentsia that would eventually be the prime mover in the fight for independence.

There is little doubt that having to use the master's language to communicate was a thorn in the foot of the extremists. In India English became the only possible tool with which to communicate. It was as such that Gandhi used it. Being a tool its perfection lay in its functional skill. Style became totally irrelevant. If the message in English had to be indianized to get across, then, so be it. Gandhi's addresses to the Viceroy and the speeches delivered during the Congress sessions became direct, straight-to-the-point-efforts.

Almost overnight the English used by the Indian-English writers was to become realistic in theme and style alike. In his preface to *Kanthapura* Raja Rao clearly worded the new gospel of Indian English writers.

One has to convey in a language that is not one's own

the spirit that is one's own. One has to convey the various shades and omissions of a certain thought moment that looks maltreated. . . . We cannot write like the English. We should not. We cannot write only as Indians. We have come to look at the large world as part of us. Our method of expression therefore has to be a dialect distinctive and colourful as the Irish or the American. Time only will justify it.

From then on things were never to be the same again. Gandhi unwittingly dictated a style and a theme from which no writer in English was to depart until Rushdie broke away in the early 1980s. Yet Narayan would seem to have been the only one to introduce a sort of personal vision of Gandhism in the art of novel writing, though he respected every canon of it.

Such a new approach to literature raised enthusiasm among a whole generation of novelists. From the 1930s on and well into the 50s these writers helped popularize in their novels those basic Gandhian ideals, thus contributing to the birth of a nation. But the nation did not come up to expectations, neither on a governmental level (massive industrialisation, wars, emergency powers . . .) nor on a village or individual one (organised exploitation of the weaker members of society, religious intolerance leading to nation-wide riots . . .). All those who had dreamt of an Indian renaissance became bitter critics of an establishment which proved very forgetful of old ideals.

In the post-independence years, artists rose in anger and cried traitor at the politicians holding office. From advocating a cause they came to criticize a situation they had in a way helped bring about:

> Most of the Indian writers writing in English today are in revolt against traditional Hinduism. They believe they have got a mission, that a novel's function should be seeing through society. . . . They are more or less writing a social criticism of that Hindu society.

As the years went by it became clear that the Gandhian flame was slowly being smothered under a heavy bureaucratic system and under the development of a technology which was otherwise meant to pave the way to social progress. What Nehru called revolution had triumphed over Gandhi's vision of the same thing.

Indeed it looked for a while as if the Gandhian school of literature had only prolonged by half a century the life of the larger group of Indian English writers, themselves a creation of the British presence in India. Once again fiction would either come to India from abroad or be written in the vernacular languages.

Among the few writers who have proved able to live by their pens, Narayan has always been regarded as being in a class of his own, steering clear of India's major problems to concentrate on Malgudi's quiet and seemingly unconcerned life. Yet, below the surface, this great painter of India has been a steady advocate of the Mahatma and of his ideals.

Gandhi himself appears as a character in many Gandhian novels, usually in those written before or immediately after independence. Anand, for instance, makes him a character in two of his books of fiction. *Untouchable* and *The Sword and the Sickle.* This might explain why such a serious critic as Professor Iyengar admits Narayan amongst the Gandhian novelists. **Waiting for the Mahatma** a novel in which Gandhi himself is a character certifies Narayan as one of them.

Despite appearances to the contrary it can be said that most of Narayan's characters are literary incarnations of the Gandhian ideal. They are people in quest of truth, discarding the social illusions that fettered them and reverting to the essentials of religion. What's more Narayan's heroes embody the greatest virtues of the Hindu way of life at the man in the street level: exactly where Gandhi wanted them to be. One could easily find fault with the orthodoxy of Narayan's Gandhism and point to the fact that Malgudi with its cinema studios, insurance companies and its University College cannot possibly be one of Gandhi's India's 700,000 villages. This is true up to a point only because we shall see, Gandhism is a humanism that can be practised anywhere provided the heart be willing. In line with those critics we could say that there is very little British presence in Narayan's novels and that the Indian characters do not react violently to it. Yet, unlike Forster's, Narayan's characters have no illusion as to which side of the great divide they belong. British teachers at the Albert Mission are oddities, definitely not enemies. Very little reference is made to the civil disobedience movement or to periodic but important events such as the Stafford Cripps proposals before independence, the Calcutta riots or the Bangladesh War at the time of Narayan's later novels. References to actual facts which were frequent in the earlier Gandhian literature are not necessary parts in a work of fiction.

To crown it all Narayan's English is most unaffected and flows easily. What W. Walsh said almost twenty years ago still holds true:

> This complicated cargo is carried on an English style which is limpid, simple, calm and unaffected, natural in its run and tone, and beautifully measured to its purposes.

> It has neither the American purr of the combustion engine nor the thick marmalade quality of British English

and it communicates with complete ease a different, an Indian, sensibility.

All this would seem to disqualify Narayan from being a Gandhian novelist unless we can prove that he has in fact added another dimension to Gandhism, a dimension in which only the essence of the Mahatma's philosophy has been kept and moulded to fit an India Gandhi himself could not have ignored: that of small provincial towns and of nondescript civil servants in the post-independence days.

Gandhi wanted to raise India out of the routine of tradition and religious superstition he believed it had fallen into. He wanted to revive the spirit of Ramakrishna and of Vivekananda. Only if Indians felt morally equal to the British would they feel they could be politically so.

At the start of the novel[, *The English Teacher,*] Krishnan, the English Teacher is the victim of two illusions which he is to discard one after the other: a social illusion linked to his status as a college lecturer and a spiritual illusion deriving from his belief that happiness in this life can be an end in itself. As a lecturer Krishnan doesn't take long to become aware that he is a fraud although he doesn't actually cheat either his head teacher or his students. Everyone is pleased with the work he does but he himself knows that what he delivers is only a very superficial message. The essence of teaching is missing from his lectures. He feels that he is only an in-between feeding back to his students what he himself has been fed. Proper teaching is something quite different. It is the work of a Guru imparting to his disciples not only his knowledge but also his way of thinking, his philosophical approach to life. This feeling of fulfilment in one's job, of full contentment, Krishnan eventually finds in a kindergarten school. What social downfall and what irony from the author! The lecturer's true place is down at the very bottom of the school system.

Social integration as opposed to the illusion of social vanity is not enough. Life is to be interpreted in religious terms. Religion makes man aware of his position in the universe, and make him transcend life itself until he be at one with the Being and the non-Being. Until one has reached such a stage in Hindu philosophy one is a mere victim of illusions, such as Krishnan was at the start of the novel just after his wife's death:

> There is no escape from loneliness and separation. I told myself often "wife, child, brothers, parents, friends . . . we come together only to part again. It is one continuous movement. They move away from us as we move away from them. They law comes into operation the moment we detach ourselves from our mother's womb."

Krishnan attains happiness because he strips himself bare of such illusions, because he feels "grateful to life and death." Isolation just cannot exist because man is part of society which itself is part of nature and of a universe which encompasses past, present, future, life and death.

There is little doubt that this interpretation of life as part of a larger religious experience, are as a quest for the discovery of one's true self is the corner stone of Gandhi's philosophy, itself part of India's religious past through its Vedantic origin.

Even more striking is Jagan's philosophical and religious itinerary [in *The Vendor of Sweets*]. At the start of the story he is quite a happy man, successful in his business and deeply convinced that he lives according to Gandhi's principles which he has always adhered to and for which he was imprisoned as a Freedom Fighter. Yet the reader is soon made aware of the fact that Jagan deludes himself and is the very embodiment of everything Gandhi fought against. He goes by the word but his heart is dead. His would be a philosophical system based on religion turns out to be nothing but mere idiosyncrasy. There is nothing Gandhian in his simplicity of life, only sheer hypocrisy and routine. Hypocrisy because he hoards his money in the loft, keeps two account books, one for himself and the other for the income-tax inspector. He abdicates his responsibilities as a father when he turns a blind eye to his son's mischief. Routine because his daily habits are ruled by superstition, his diet is pure nonsense and even charity is something planned.

Late in life Jagan becomes aware of his religious pharisaism and this produces salutory change in him. Jagan's reaction is an illustration of what Gandhi expected from his countryfellows. He reverts to the essentials of Hinduism and now lives by the spirit of the Gandhian message, which means that he enters a new life (could this be a symbolic representation of a possible post-independence India?)

> One enters a new life at the appointed time and it's foolish to resist. He was no longer the father of Mali, the maker of sweets and gatherer of money each day: he was gradually becoming something else, perhaps a supporter of bearded sculptor or was he really his ward.

Jagan's story may be read as a parable of contemporary India which through moral deprivation brought evil upon herself.

"Who am I?" The only question worth being answered is twice seriously debated during the first thirteen pages of *Mr. Sampath* by Srinivas, the hero of the novel. It is only when one can answer it that the next question "What am I?" can in turn be asked. With Srinivas we obtain confirmation that the Gandhian ideal of the discovery of the self and of its achievements is no easy quest. It is a great mental effort which requires training but which when reached gives one a new psychological dimension: one feels above the general rabble or, in Hardy's words "Far from the madding crowd".

> In this maze (human vanity and folly) Srinivas walked about unscathed because he had trained himself to view it all as a mere spectator.

He had trained himself: this is the important part of the quotation. Nothing comes by itself: everything is an effort that trains the mind.

Any man can be turned into a saint when properly trained. Two novels of Narayan's illustrate this theme which is also Gandhian if we understand by training not the mere acquisition of a physical or mental routine but the opening of a mind to the dedication of a good cause. *The Guide* and *A Tiger for Malgudi* both make this point clear.

Having served a prison sentence (a traditionally self-imposed Gandhian trial) Raju [in *The Guide*] comes out a new man ready to embark upon a new life. The cynic who took advantage of Rosie's talent and who drank and gambled her money away in Malgudi becomes devoted to a cause which is not even his but that of his adoptive village community. This cause he will defend unto death.

> For the first time in his life he was making an earnest effort, for the first time he was learning the drill of full application outside money and love, for the first time he was doing a thing in which he was not personally interested. He felt suddenly so enthusiastic that it gave him a new strength to go through with the ordeal.

The fact that he tried to achieve something in which he was not personally interested is precisely what gave him the strength necessary to succeed. Sincerity is always a prerequisite for success and that sincerity goes with unselfishness. Chandran [in *The Bachelor of Arts*] fails as a sanyasi because his heart is not in it, because his final intent in wearing the ochre robe is purely selfish: he is turned inwards instead of being opened to the world.

In *A Tiger for Malgudi* the message is even more distinctly spelt out. The tiger, man's arch-enemy has only known two masters. One who lived by the sword and so logically met his death at the tiger's claws. The relationship he tried to establish rested on force or fear only, when food was given in exchange for obedience and work. The

other master spoke of love only and radiating it only brought about more love.

In the only introduction Narayan has written to any of his novels he made his philosophy clear:

> **Now, in my story the "Tiger Hermit" employs his powers to save the tiger and transform it inwardly working on the basis that, deep within, the core of personality is the same, in spite of differing appearances and categories, an with the right approach you could expect the same response from a tiger as from any normal human being.**
> *--Michel Pousse*

Narayan's heroes are ordinary people whose lives take on a religious dimension. They revolutionize their inner selves to become better Indians and in that way the author reminds us that Gandhi's message appealed to the spiritual in man and that in this respect it remains valid today and will so for ever.

Gandhian novelists of the first period took great care to locate their novels in villages and to portray rural types (among others: Nagarajan's *Chronicles of Kedaram*, Rao's *Kanthapura*, Venkataramani's *Murugan the Tiller*). More so in the post independence years they pointed out unavoidable evils large concurbations lead to and in which individuals and families alike are destroyed (Desai's *Voices in the City*, Bhattacharya's *He who Rides a Tiger*). Narayan was faced with the problem of finding a location for his novels. He could neither locate them in the country (from the little he ventured to write it is clear that he knows nothing about it) nor in a large town (for the same reason, with the possible exception of Madras). Paradoxical as it might seem Narayan had to invent a fictional town to be faithful to the reality of India. Malgudi then is an ideal town belonging to the world of fiction and peopled by characters who also belong there. As a painter of India Narayan had to remain faithful to the social changes within the country and to the growth of an urban middle class living in middle-sized towns. In such towns people do not lose their personalities because everything remains on a human scale.

Narayan is a gentle novelist who deeply loves his country and his countrymen. His criticism even when it is bitter and far reaching can never be violent and what we get in his novels perfectly illustrates what Nehru called "the tender humanity of India."

As a humanist Narayan could not possibly accept the dichotomy of town and country. Men are the same everywhere, each born with his own qualities, be they good or bad, and each only fractionally moulded by his environment. Everything to be found in Narayan's villages: good, evil, murders even if we are to believe the "circle" [in *The Man-Eater of Malgudi*] patrolling the area on the hills where Vasu stalks his prey.

In India this town-village dichotomy originates with Gandhi, but what the Mahatma objected to mostly was the uprooting that necessarily went with the move from country to town. Malgudi itself is no better or worse than any ordinary village. Officials are corrupt and inefficiency is to be found at every level. Narayan masters sufficiently the art of novel writing not to make an in-depth study of corruption. He merely drops remarks here and there and this gives them strength as it makes corruption seem a perfectly normal part of life.

Malgudi is a microcosm upon which the outside world still has little impact even if the intrusion of the West is not to be belittled. Malgudi's problems are India's problems at large and in that respect the society shown is a long way away from the one Gandhi saw in his dreams. Belonging to the right caste is what makes the right marriage and pulling the right strings is what gets one a good job.

Yet balancing the effects of corruption and faithful to the traditional rhythm of Siva we find that many Gandhian principles are put into practice and what is more important, this is done as a normal way of life. Narayan uses the technique of sprinkling his novels with casual remarks. It is not the function that makes the man: good policemen exist and are humane. One of them buys disinfectant for the cells with his own pocket money; another one not minding the law allows relatives to see the body of a deceased person out of principle and whatever the inspector might say, People live simply. They may practice "Swadesi" out of necessity but money is never foremost in their minds. A quiet family life is depicted as the highest ideal and the greatest happiness upon this earth. While the religious sincerity of some of the major characters can be doubted at times, the feelings of the supporting ones are sincere. Religion is kept within the people as is illustrated by Sastri [in *The Man-Eater of Malgudi*] who is used by Nataraj as a reference book and whose optimism knows no limits because he has faith. Pujas are never forgotten and sanyasis are respected even when they help themselves to other people's flowers. Religious tolerance is something practised and not just boasted about. One of Nataraj's best friends is a Muslim. This we learn through a casual remark when others would have thought fit to write a novel to prove inter-religious friendship possible in the sub-continent.

In Narayan's novels Gandhi's preaching is echoed on every page. Faith is what will save India in the end and faith just

cannot be defeated. Daisy [in *The Painter of Signs*] believes in her mission which is to encourage birth control in the country. She can explain the whys of her scientific mission very clearly to every villager, and it makes so much sense. But when she meets the old temple ward, an incarnation of eternal India (he has been around for more than one hundred and twenty years) who can achieve wonders (he built the temple himself and can talk cobras back into their holes) she is left speechless. There is no arguing with faith and she has to leave that particular village in the hands of the old man.

Religious reassessment opens man's outlook and leads to tolerance and broadmindedness. Religion is not good in itself, only a certain approach is good for man, otherwise it may be evil. In Narayan's novels this is made clear through the character of Ebenezer, the Bible teacher, who illustrates a point B. Russell was to develop in his philosophy: religion creates hatred and the religion which does so in India is the one which has been imported by foreign powers because it is taught in a sectarian way.

Narayan's crowd is a contented lot and in their way, which is not ideal but is at a human level which implies human frailty they illustrate a concretization of the Gandhian ideal. Possibly a new form of it which does not insist on cotton spinning but which is a modern and faithful version of the Gandhian original.

Gandhian Literature came to life with a new language or, to be more accurate, it gave a new dimension to an old language, though it is true that at times Indian-English looks like a new language with a morphology, syntax and vocabulary of its own.

Up to Gandhi's appearance on the political scene English used by Indians was no different from "English English", as good as the King's English if one could possibly speak it. Gandhi's notion that the English language should be used in India as a tool to communicate and only for the sake of convenience implied a new approach. No longer having to model itself on Cambridge English it could accommodate Indianisms whenever needed. While many of his literary fellows obviously worked at creating a new style at times at the cost of artificiality, Narayan made a point of writing his novels in the same English as he spoke. He seems never to have consulted a dictionary or even a thesaurus. In the same way as he describes the India he knows well he uses the vocabulary he masters well, in that respect staying in line with Gandhi's wish. He makes no effort to improve upon a style that has remained the same throughout half a century of creative writing. By European standards his vocabulary is poor and fairly repetitive. It is by no means a faithful account of the language spoken in India and yet it is very Indian. From college lecturer down to village idiot everyone uses the same language: clear, direct, purposeful. Mali's English has remained unaffected by a year's stay in America [in **The Vendor of Sweets**]. Indianisms either in the syntax or morphology are scarce if we allow for the well established "me and you" and for such impossible to-translate-words as "sanyasi", "garuda", "jutka". . . . Technical vocabulary is carefully avoided (with the exception of the printing word but the author is known to be familiar with it through his own personal experience) and hardly ever is there fun made of his country fellows' approximate knowledge of English, such as indulged in by Narayan in **Waiting for the Mahatma.**

> "As a soldier I will not cry over split milk."
> "Is it split milk?" Sriram asked nervously.
> "Of course it is," asserted Jagadish.
> "When milk goes bad it splits into water and solid you know."

Puns like Chandran's [in **The Bachelor of Arts**] also are most infrequent:

> "My father would cast me out if I married out of caste."

All along Narayan uses his own English and this serves his purpose to perfection.

As far as the novel itself is concerned it looks as if Gandhian novelists have done nothing but shroud in Indian clothing what basically remains a western form of literature. Until fairly recently the novel was as alien in India as it was in Africa or in the rest of Asia, places where the oral tradition was all important. Many Gandhian novelists (for instance Anand in *The Sword and the Sickle*) departed from the oral tradition and wrote long novels swarming with characters. From the start Narayan decided to stick to the Indian tradition. His novels would be nothing but a written tale fully complying to the norms and composition of what is offered by the village story teller. As a result his novels were bound to be short and of a very linear structure. With the exception of **The Guide** there are no flashbacks unless one considers Raja the tiger's autobiography as falling within the flashback technique. The art of story-telling has its own rules: long descriptions have to be avoided because they tire the audience which may lose the thread of the story. Only the main characters must be given lives and personalities of their own, the supporting ones appearing when needed and being dropped immediately after. The plot (any subplot might confuse the listener) must build up slowly to a climax and then be drawn to a prompt conclusion.

All these characteristics are recurrent in Narayan's novels and account for the fact that as a novelist he has often been misunderstood by European critics. Narayan must be judged by his own standards which are those of the oral tale.

While other Indian English writers of the Gandhian school only Indianized the style while keeping to the original form of the novel, Narayan gave it not only Indian content but also an Indian form.

Narayan penetrated the heart of Gandhi's teaching. He separated the obviously ephemeral implications of his philosophy from what was eternal in it and he gave literary existence to the latter. This probably accounts for the fact that he can ceaselessly renew his inspiration while drawing from only one spring. His contemporaries have increasingly become mere social critics unable to detach themselves from the momentous events that preceded, and followed, accession to independence. They could not long outlive the Mahatma's passage upon this earth.

As a humanist rather than a revolutionary Narayan only flirted with the fight for independence. Preferring to bear witness to the universality of the Mahatma he took up his pen to show that like Shakespeare according to Ben Jonson his bond was with all time and all places.

Balbir Singh (essay date 1990)

SOURCE: "Theme of Art and Immortality in R. K. Narayan's *The Guide*," in *Literary Criterion*, Vol. XXV, No. 2, 1990, pp. 36-46.

[In the following essay, Singh analyzes the place of art and immortality in Narayan's The Guide.*]*

The desire for immortality which in Jungian terms is a "primordial affirmation" in human beings and which has its "origin in a peculiar feeling of extension in space and time" is realised to the highest degree by a perfect identification and expression of what Jung calls the "collective unconscious." This "collective unconscious," in turn, is realised in its full dimension by its approximation to what F. A. Wilson describes as "the qualitative aspect of the creativity of the universe . . . the transcendental universe programmed to become aware of itself". Now this becoming of the Universe completely aware of itself is presented in Indian thought as Shiva or Vishnu as representative of "Absolute Consciousness." Indian Vedanta also expresses a similar view. According to this philosophy "the Real self is called Atman. As an infinite conscious reality (Satyam, Jnanam, Anantam) the self for a man is identical with the self of all beings and, therefore, with God. . . ." Jung's "Collective unconscious" which is almost the same thing as "servabhutam" becomes a reflection of the "absolute consciousness."

Art as a representative of life, reflects a co-ordination between man's inner urges and the evolutionary tendency in man and nature. While reflecting on these phenomena an artist perceives the self of all beings in his own being and becomes an image of absolute consciousness. The process develops in him a humanising tendency, and since he deals with an hyperasthetic situation, he becomes a great inspirational source for the excessively beautiful aspect of life. This way he becomes one of the most effective and significant means for the survival of mankind. In giving an aesthetic expression to the creativity of the universe, an artist's self becomes identical with that of God and partakes of God's immortality with the only difference that the material in the hands of God for manipulation is supposed to be the whole of the universe while in the hands of an artist, as is pointed out by James Joyce, it is only "the daily bread of experience which he transmutes into the radiant body of ever living life". Such a transmutation can be brought about only by a mind capable of giving expression to consciousness in its entirety. D. H. Lawrence says that "any creative act occupies the whole consciousness of man". Using Coleridge's term 'androgynous mind' to imply the 'whole consciousness', Virginia Woolf says that it is this which enables an artist to "pass from outer to inner (sic) and inhabit eternity".

Like every art, dance is an act of creation. It recreates a new situation and arouses in the dancer new and higher personality. Like yoga, dance induces realisation of one's own secret nature through the concentration of psychic energies and gives expression to the meaning of existence in its uninterrupted sequence. In Hindu mythology Shiva, the arch yogi, is also Nataraja, "King of Dancers". His dance represents the cosmic drama and symbolises nature's aesthetic principle. His graceful dancing gestures "precipitate the cosmic illusion; (and) produce . . . the continuous creation—destruction of the universe". So Shiva is Maha Kala, "The Black One", "Eternity". The Indian classical dances show a preoccupation with eternity "with the dancer constantly trying to achieve the perfect pose to convey a sense of timelessness". The artist is naturally filled with the desire to achieve this "timelessness" or eternity in his own being.

R. K. Narayan's greatness lies in the fact that he weaves the theme of art and immortality into the very texture of his novel *The Guide.* All the three major characters of the novel represent one or the other aspect of art. Rosie represents art. Her name signifies art in its inception, for when her art is perfected she becomes a "gorge rose". The dancing aspect of Lord Shiva gets manifested in her when she gets an urge to dance at the sight of a cobra, an emblem of Lord Shiva. As the cobra sways its hood from side to side, she makes a dance-like motion of her body in imitation of it just for a second, and that reveals her to be "the greatest dancer of the century." This act of Rosie is symbolic of the casting off of the first slough on art. When Rosie perfects her art, it induces in her the realisation of her own

secret nature, "the divine essence". In her last performance before Raju, she performs the snake dance and becomes like one who resides "in the ever-radiant home of the gods in Kailas", and the songs she sings becomes "the song that elevated the serpent and brought out its mystic quality". At this time she becomes a perfect identity of Lord Shiva and of "Eternity".

Rosie, thus, represents the spirit of art that enkindles every heart to some degree and which, in India, had become stifled during the centuries of foreign rule. As a result, the Indian society during this period had become taboo-ridden and spiritually dead. Under such circumstances the art of dancing especially suffered suppression and became restricted to a few families and the devadasis (temple girls). Rosie's mother is such a devadasi. Rosie tells Raju, "I belong to a family traditionally dedicated to the temples as dancers; my mother, grandmother, and before her, her mother . . . We are viewed as public women". Rosie, thus, belongs to a family which has, through countless generations, helped in preserving the cult of the art of dancing in India and has formed a link between the ancient glory of this art and its modern counterpart. Referring to the artistic achievements of courtesans and temple girls in ancient times Moti Chandra in his preface to *The World of Courtesons* says that "in spite of their perfidies. . . . (they) gave an impetus to art". Again quoting I. W. Hauer he refers to "the ascetic element of yoga" in Pamshchali, "a sacred prostitute" in the vedic period. Now the ancient artistic talent and "the ascetic element of Yoga" lie dormant in Rosie. She gets a constant urge to develop this art in her, and works with a fully concentrated effort to do so when she gets an opportunity.

But, as we see, during the whole period of foreign rule there was no encouragement, no incentive, no schools of art to carry forward the tradition of dancing. There was no organisation to interpret, to preserve or to communicate to the people the rich inheritance of art we had received from the past. The sculptural art and the paintings in fresco, wherever they existed, were left to the foreigners to discover and interpret them for us. The western critics were, no doubt, enthusiastic about discovering the sources of art and culture in India but were little interested in developing the potential for art that was in India. Marco, Rosie's husband, represents such an attitude in the novel and, with his ability to give wide publicity to anything, seems to possess the power to grant immortality to art. Since the spirit of art is for ever wedded to immortality, Rosie is wedded to Marco, the western-looking, the western-oriented art critic. With his analytical aesthetics, he is concerned with only the tangible manifestation of art and not with the spirit that lies behind art. Narayan gives him the name of foreign adventurer because he seems very alien to the spirit of India. Raju himself represents that spirit to the extent it survived under the long foreign rule; and the absence of any patronage for developing the vast potential for art that was in India, the burden naturally fell on amateurish men like him. So in the novel he represents forces which groom art; while Marco, even though alien to the spirit of India, represents forces that lead to the preservation of art.

In this context the reference to the 'Peak House' is significant. The caves are located near the Peak House and contain art at its peak. Marco, who is interested in art at its peak, feels at home here, and can work with dedication to study and reinterpret the history of the place. In the hotel down the hill, Rosie is unwilling to go to the Peak House with Marco because she has not gone up even a single step in her art and cannot think of ascending to the peak in a single effort; but with Raju, who can guide her, direct her to achieve the heights in her art, she willingly agrees to go. On the top Rosie, though herself aspiring to be an artist, finds the paintings in fresco beyond her comprehension. It is at the Peak House that Rosie is filled with the utmost passion to achieve the heights through her art, and feels no scruples in enticing Raju to see that she has a great potential for art. But, for a coalescence of these two forces, symbolized in the two characters, both Raju and Rosie must come down hill where they can find their starting point. Rosie, on some pretext, comes down hill with him, and when they come to the hotel, Raju takes control of her and, as he says, "with her, lock[s] the door on the world".

Here Raju's comment is very significant in moulding the future events of the novel. Undeveloped art can be kept hidden from the world as it has been kept during the centuries of foreign rule, but the question arises whether it is possible to confine fully developed art to oneself. Can a healthy seed buried underground remain hidden from the world for long? It is bound to sprout sooner or later. By perfecting her art Rosie is bound to open her door to the world, and any attempt on the part of Raju to keep her confined to himself is bound to meet with failure and perhaps with some sort of punishment too.

At the Peak House Rosie's imperfections look stark naked to an expert eye, and any attempt on the part of imperfect art to expect recognition and patronage from an art critic is bound to meet with rebuff. When Marco comes to know that Rosie has flirted with a "fervid art lover" like Raju and has pitted his scholarship and experience against Raju's naive appreciation, he cannot but be prompted to sever all relations with her. He deserts her, and she has to come to Raju for shelter and to be groomed by him. At this juncture when Gaffur asks them if he should drive them to the Peak House, Rosie becomes very alert and says, "No, no . . . I have had enough of it". She is scared of going to the Peak House, not because there is any Marco there now, but because now she becomes too conscious of the fact that she

is far from the heights of her art. It is only perfect art, maybe in the form of wall paintings in the caves, which can stay on the Peak. Referring to Marco she says, "we were not meant to be in each other's Company" for at this stage her inhert art could have no hope of getting recognition from an experienced art critic.

At this stage Narayan presents a conflict between the traditional attitude to art and the awakening that came with the independence of India. The traditional attitude to art is represented by Raju's mother and his "uncle-in-law" (sic) while the new awakenings shows itself in Rosie and Raju. A point comes where the two attitudes come into direct conflict. Neither yields the ground for sometimes for being too sure of itself. Ultimately Raju's mother leaves the house to stay with her brother in the village.

Raju does everything in his power to see that Rosie blossoms into a full rose and that she shines as an artist. For Rosie, Raju's "Guidance [is] enough. She [accepts] it in absolutely unquestioning faith" and very soon perfects her art.

Though Raju makes love to her constantly, she does not feel interested in the love aspect of their relationship thus belying Freudian psychological dictum that sexual immaturity or repression is the sole cause generating the creative urge. The creative urge in Rosie is instigated by her desire to present the universal and timeless fascination felt in art to be able to transcend time which is the main objective of nature and art. Very soon she gets tired of the all absorbing love which Raju can give her, and after a few months of training asks him about his plans: "I have now had good practice. I can manage a show of four hours". Now she is no longer 'Rosie signifying art in its inception'. She is now a mature artist and requires to be given a new name "which could have significance, poetry and university".

With Raju's help she soars "rocket like" and becomes famous all over the place. She gets so many engagements that Raju has a great difficulty in preparing her itinerary. Other artists come to see her. She likes their company. In no way she considers herself to be superior to them. She tells Raju that "they are good people" and have the "blessings of Goddess Saraswati" and that they serve the purpose of art. As an artist she is interested only in achieving perfection in art through regular practice and an exchange of views with other artists and scholars. "At one corner of the room she would always keep a bronze figure of Nataraj, the god of dancers", whose dance represents the ultimate art in nature. Rosie feels keen to develop such perfection in her art as is represented in the dance of Shiva. She enjoys the company of other "art folk". The urge in her at the sub-conscious level is to develop an art which would, through its aesthetising influence, bring about a transformation in society so that it breaks itself free of all the shackles that have bound it so long. We can "educate the public taste" by exposing society to art. But to reduce dancing to "mechanical actions day in and day out" would be to destroy the creative aspect in art. Creative art enables an artist to reach the gates of eternity. Every artist aspires to achieve this end and so does Rosie.

When Rosie rises so high in the world of art, Raju's function as a force grooming art ends there. In the company of others artists he begins to look like an "Inter-loper". Though a great impresario, he refuses to grow into a force which can lead to the preservation of art and lend it immortality, for the only model before him of such a force is Marco, whom he hates so much. So he develops a perverted philosophy of earning money through Rosie. He says, "My philosophy was that while it lasted the maximum money had to be squeezed out". Such an approach again puts great constraints on the development of art. Rosie begins to feel troubled and very much ill at ease. Raju's perversion prevents him from understanding what exactly she suffers from. He tries to laugh it off but in vain. The urge in Rosie to transcend all limitations on art is too strong to be put aside. Then comes another turning point in her life. One day in *The Illustrated Weekly* of Bombay she reads about Marco's book *The Cultural History of South India* with the comment that it was an 'epoch-making discovery in Indian cultural history.' It stirs up her whole "unconscious personality" or excites what Ram Dial calls "her inner cravings". Raju again fails to understand her mood: "I felt bewildered and unhappy. I didn't understand her sudden affection for her husband. What was this sudden mood that was coming over her?" Now that her art is at its peak Marco is the man who can win her immortality symbolized in his acceptance of her art and in his ability to eternize it by publishing about it. She is filled with the desire to go back to him. To Raju's query if he would take her back she says, "He may not admit me over the threshold, in which event it is far better to end one's life on his door steps".

Art as a replication of the Nature's purpose develops its inherent capacity to transcend time and with this breaks all the constraints on it. In the last dance she performs before Raju she becomes an abstraction, a vision like the snake "that resides on the locks of Shiva himself . . . . and in the ever radiant home of the gods in Kailas", and with this dance the final slough on art is cast off. The highest art does not require forces grooming art or the forces preserving art. It has its own sustaining power. So says Raju, "Neither Marco nor I had any place in her life, which had its own sustaining vitality and which she herself had underestimated all alone".

Now the question arises as to why Narayan turns his chief exponent into a yogi. Raju's development from a "fervid" lover of art to a yogi is not an unrelated phenomenon. The difference between an art lover, an artist and a yogi is only of degree and not of kind. The art lover and the artist have a similar sort of creative involvement. While the artist literally expresses this involvement, the art lover only 'empathises with the work of art and seeks an aesthetic experience through it". Art, as is suggested by James Joyce, enables the artist "to forge in the smithy of his soul the uncreated conscience of the race". Yoga achieves the same end in an indirect way. Yoga, as Zimmer says, enables the yogin "to gain control over the forces of one's own being . . . chiefly to attain union with . . . the Universal Spirit". A union with the Universal Spirit, in turn, leads to a complete identification with the whole mankind, and, thus, enables the yogin to create in his soul "the uncreated conscience of the race." This way both art and yoga go to reconcile a highly emotionalised mind to a world too often devoid of all emotional meaning, and both aid in the transformation of that world to meet the human requirement, one through its aesthetising influence, and the other through a strict spiritual discipline. Art and yoga are so closely related that the Hindu view, as Ananda Coomaraswami says, "treats the practice of art as a form of yoga". To support his point he quotes Shankaracharya:

> Let the imager establish images in temples by meditation on the deities who are the objects of his devotion. For the successful achievement of this yoga, the lineaments of the image are described in books to be dwelt upon in detail. In no other way, not even by direct and immediate vision of actual object, is it possible to be so absorbed in contemplation, as thus in the making of images.

So Raju's conversion from an art lover to a yogi forms a natural process of development. Conforming to such a view P. S. Sundram writes: "It is a curious evolution . . . but one thing grows naturally out of another, and there is not a single false not anywhere".

Velan and the villagers in the novel represent "the traditional India" and are made of the stuff "disciples are made of". Narayan here emphasizes their great need for spiritual guidance. After centuries of spiritual slumber they have become incapacitated to respond to the aesthetising influence of art. At first Raju tries to indoctrinate them into the art of yoga: "Well, that is why I say reflect, recollect . . . I want all of you to think independently, of your own accord, and not allow yourself to be led about by nose as if you were cattle". But when he fails in his initial attempts, he exhibits to them through his personal example, at first hesitantly and then very decisively, the spiritual force they can generate through the exercise of yoga. It is through this spiritualizing force of yoga that society can be transformed so that it becomes a society in which spiritual reawakening becomes a self-sustaining phenomenon. In such a society art will for ever prosper.

In Hindu mythology Shiva, "the all containing omniscient supra-consciousness", is also Niskala Shiva, "the unchanging sterile Absolute, devoid of every urge or energy towards procreation and cosmogenic transmutation". Shiva is also Natraja, the god of dancers. Referring to this R. K. Narayan says that he is "the god whose primal dance created the vibrations that set the world in motion." Shiva's dance, thus symbolises the cosmic drama with its creative, destructive and evolutionary forces at work trying to achieve the state of "super-consciousness." That is what F. A. Wilson means when he says that the universe is "programmed to become aware of itself." Art thus represents the aesthetic urge to achieve the state of complete consciousness, the state of eternity, which is also the state of yoga (yoga is the concentration which restricts the fluctuations of mind stuff.) The artist thus embodies in himself the niskala state (potential art or energy) which becoming animated and efflorescent, grows into the skala state (the creative state of art).

As we have already seen, the facets of art referred to already are beautifully manifested in the novel in the figures of Rosie and Raju personifying art and consciousness respectively. The latter had been seen reduced to the niskala state during the centuries of foreign rule, but are now shown to work their way up gradually to the resplendence of the skala state.

Just as the beholder is not under any compelling necessity to go in quest for the Absolute in and by itself, for the energy of the Absolute pervades us, so we are not led by any overt necessity to search for the ultimate in art; the seeds of the creative art are there in us. We need only to perceive and develop it. The novel, therefore, is a powerful plea for the revival of Indian classical arts, so that the beholder stands elevated in the process of the perception of it through participation in it which makes him partake of immortality.

Chitra Sankaran (essay date 1991)

SOURCE: "Patterns of Story-telling in R. K. Narayan's *The Guide*," in *Journal of Commonwealth Literature,* Vol. XXVI, No. 1, 1991, pp. 127-50.

[*In the following essay, Sankaran analyzes Narayan's fusing of traditional Indian myth and the English novel form, focusing on* The Guide.]

The novel as a genre, especially in the twentieth century,

has undergone a great deal of change. In The West, one can witness a movement away from the Victorian Novel form of the nineteenth century. This movement can, to an extent, be seen reflected in commonwealth countries too, where during the middle and latter half of the twentieth century, we observe a shift away from previously established western modes.

In India for instance, the earlier fascination with Western form and theory, reflected in the works of Rabindranath Tagore and Sarojini Naidu, is replaced by the increasingly experimental works of the later writers. This change can be seen in the fiction of Raja Rao, as in the poetry of A. K. Ramanujam, the drama of Girish Karnad and many other writers. In the works of these writers, we notice a harking back to traditional native literatures. Thus poetry in Indo-Anglian writing very frequently incorporates the techniques of the Sanskrit *kavyas,* prose works adopt the ornate style of the *Puranas,* and dramas feature the poetics of Sanskrit *natakas.* Very often these works, we find, deliberately draw attention to their experiments. This is certainly true of Raja Rao, whose works have all demonstrated a greater affinity to Sanskrit forms than to the English novel form. With Narayan's works however, the deceptive simplicity of his fiction very often obscures his superb capacity to blend traditional Indian modes with the English novel form. Narayan's instinctive assimilation of his native literature together with what appears to be a natural affinity to the English novel form has led to the creation of a class of fiction which appears simple only on a superficial level. And concerted effort at analysis seems to lead us into increasing difficulties, for his works combine the distilled essences of western and eastern forms and yet each novel appears to be a completely homogeneous entity.

Though this mixed loyalty to two literary modes is a feature that can be seen in all his fiction, a complex patterning is especially to be seen in such novels as **The Man-Eater Of Malgudi, Mr. Sampath,** and **The Guide.** In these novels, beneath the standard paradigm of the English novel form, we glean teasing glimpses of an archaic alien pattern that seems to blend well with, yet modify the paradigm. In **The Guide,** a complex creation of Narayan's the pattern is more diffused and is apparent in many layers.

The Guide, generally acclaimed by critics as being perhaps the best of Narayan's novels, is a gently ironic tale which, to borrow Alastair Niven's phrase, "depicts the human dilemma by blending irony and pathos with great delicacy". The tale is told from a double perspective: from the point of view of the third person omniscient author and the first person narrative of the protagonist, Raju. These two perspectives alternate with each other allowing the use of what Keith Garebian calls "the braided time-scheme". The narrative opens in the present and moves to the past, and throughout the story we witness this forward and backward movement in time. Another feature of the double narrative is the distinctly different narrative tones that the two carry. The authorial voice describes the present and adopts an ironic expository tone, whereas Raju's narrative is in the form of an apologia. Also this part of the narrative is episodic and resembles the oral story-telling tradition of ancient India—a feature we see Raja Rao use to such good effect in *Kanthapura*. All these traits point to a pattern analogous to the ancient Sanskrit genre, the *katha* or tale.

In some ways *The Guide* can be read as a complex allegory satirising the process by which gods and demi-gods came to be established within the religion . . . the centuries myths and stories came to be built around a man until he gradually attained the stature of a god and joined the ranks of celestial beings as a divine incarnation.
—*Chitra Sankaran*

"The Tale" as a literary genre has always had an indefinite origin and a dubious ancestry. By definition, tales mean "the stories handed down by oral tradition from an unknown antiquity among savage and civilized peoples". But popular tales won their way subsequently into literature. Thus the Homeric epics contain many popular tales as also the *Rig Veda*. But essentially in these versions, as in the original, the tales set out in simple narrative, most often in prose but also in verse, stories about demi-gods, gods, supernatural beings, heroes, kings and saints. The purpose of the ancient tales was most often entertainment and edification.

In Sanskrit, tales and fables were an essential part of its classical literature. Kunhan Raja in his *Survey of Sanskrit Literature* talks of Vedic and later Buddhistic literature in Sanskrit, rich in fables and tales, which are classified as *kathas*. Though the ancient *itihasas* and *puranas* contain most of the tales and fables, the tales developed into a separate literary genre at a later stage. The earliest work of the nature is considered by most scholars of Sanskrit to have been *Brhat-Katha* (the big story book) of Gunadya. The work is now lost, but the several commentaries that exist on the work indicate to us that the collection of tales were about heroes, kings and gods, and fables with animal and bird stories. Despite this lack of earlier distinction between stories dealing with animals and others dealing with men and gods, the later *Katha*, devoted to describing the life of a hero or a saint, was well established. In *The Guide* we perceive features from the *katha* of ancient Sanskrit literature.

In some ways *The Guide* can be read as a complex alle-

gory satirising the process by which gods and demi-gods came to be established within the religion, wherein through the centuries myths and stories came to be built around a man until he gradually attained the stature of a god and joined the ranks of celestial beings as a divine incarnation. In this view, *The Guide* would be a satire, albeit a gentle one, about the system of worship within Hinduism. Interpreting the book in this way would bring us to the interesting subject of authorial intention and execution. Given the sophisticated irony, evident in the third-person narrative, this is a very possible interpretation. But what strikes us most in the novel is the pattern of the *Katha* that is incorporated into the structure.

The most prominent characteristic of the *Katha* is discussed by Arthur Mcdonell in his book, *A History of Sanskrit Literature*.

> A distinguishing feature of the Sanskrit collection of fairy stories and fables. . . . is the insertion of a number of different stories within the framework of a single narrative. The characters of the main story in turn relate various tales to edify one another.

In Somadeva's *Katha Sarith Sagara* (ocean of streams of stories), the most popular adaptation of *Brhat-Katha*, this structure is well evident.

The style of the *katha* mimics the oral tradition of antiquity. There is a straightforward story related by a strong narrative voice. However, the overall structure of a *katha* is cyclical and more important, the pattern of story-telling is layered. The story opens with the narrative mentioning some characters, who then become independent narrators in their own right, and so forth.

The Guide demonstrates all these patterns of story-telling. The novel begins with the authorial voice relating the present. Two characters, Raju and Velan, are introduced, and their interaction with each other, we realize, is the basis for the beginning of the second narrative by Raju. This follows the *Katha* paradigm. In *Katha Sarith Sagara*, for instance, the authorial narrative sets the initial scene between Shiva and Parvathi and their *vidyadhara*, Pushpadanta. This in turn leads to a set of events which begins the second narrative by Pushpadanta. Pushpadanta's narrative is biographical and retrospective. He meets his friend Kanabhuti, and at his request begins to tell the story of his life. The similarity to Raju's narrative, also biographical and retrospective, is striking. Furthermore, the structure is cyclical in that it starts at a point and comes back to the same point after a series of stories are related. Thus, we get the "essentially non-linear style" that G. P. Gemill talks about in relation to *The Cat and Shakespeare*. This in effect is a feature typical to the *Katha*.

The Katha Sarith Sagara begins with the authorial voice recounting the curse of the *Vidyadharas,* Pushpadanta and Malyavan, by goddess Parvathi and relates the meeting of the two on earth in their birth as humans. Then Pushpadanta alias Vararuchi relates his own and friends' adventures to Kanabhuti, but the story always returns to the point where Vararuchi is telling his tale to the attentive Kanabhuti. The structure of the text is layered, in that, while there is chronological progression in Vararuchi's narrative, this does not imply a movement forward in the main story line.

In *The Guide* too, Raju relates his life-story to Velan and though the secondary narrative progresses chronologically, tracing Raju's life from childhood onwards up to the point when Velan meets him, this does not imply a progress in the third person narrative, which moves independently. However, it is noteworthy that the primary narrative relating the events that are occurring at that point cannot, after a certain stage, proceed to the end until the secondary narrative is completed. This is in fact made a dictum in the *Katha* genre. Thus is *Katha Sarith Sagara,* Parvathi, when she curses the two Vidyadharas, Pushpadanta and Malyavan, puts in a clause that Pushpadanta will be born as Kararuchi and will accidentally meet Malyavan who will be born as Kararuchi and that, though on meeting they will remember their curse, they will be released from it *only after Kanabhuti has fully related his life story* and Malyavan has heard it completely. Hence, the complete narration of Pushpadanta's life becomes essential for the main story to proceed to its end, when the two characters will be finally released from their curse.

A similar pattern can also be perceived in *The Guide.* At a point when Raju finds himself cornered and needs to confess the truth to Velan, it is vital that Velan learn the whole truth and signal to Raju that he still considers him a saint before the main story can proceed to its final enigmatic conclusion.

Techniques in the narrative too, subtly reflect the ancient techniques present in the *Kathas.* Thus Raju's narrative to Velan in the middle of the first chapter is interrupted by the phrase, "Raju said, in the course of narrating his life-story to this man who was called Velan. . .". From a novelistic view-point, as M. K. Naik points out, this might appear to be a clumsy interruption, but it is nevertheless interesting that Narayan is deliberately indicating a transition to a second level of narrative, set in the past, signalling to the reader that there are two distinct narratives in the novel. This effectively draws our attention to the older *katha* form. In the *Katha Sarith Sagara* we find phrases similar to this quite frequently:

> Then Vararuchi, to gratify Kanabhuti . . . told all his history from his birth at full length, in the following words.

or again,

> Having thus spoken while Kanabhuti was listening with intent mind, Vararuchi went on to tell his tale. . . .

Thus in *The Guide,* several features of the ancient *katha* or tale are subtly incorporated into the English novel form. Our increasing familiarity with the experimentation in the West with form and technique in the novel perhaps makes Narayan's own experiments less conspicuous. But Narayan's incorporation of the techniques from Indian tradition are not only evident in the structure of the narrative, but can be perceived even beneath the narrative level in myth-motifs that subtly influence our perception of the characters.

The novel is built around the character of Raju, a tourist guide who is forced by circumstances to assume the mantle of sagehood for a small village community. The novel traces his transformation from a 'guide' to a 'guru'. At one superficial level this transformation can be justified by applying the philosophy of *Bhakthi Prapatti,* where Raju's transformation can be interpreted as genuine and as the consequence of an act of free and undeserved grace from God. The *bhakthi* cult can also perhaps help define Velan's and the villagers' adulation of Raju more clearly. "*Bhakthi*", as T. W. Organ points out, "is a vague and elastic term coming from the root *bhaj* meaning to be attached to, to be devoted to, or to resort to . . . the basic *bhakthi* emotion is a complete mixture of fear, awe, fascination, love and dependence." It is not too difficult to identify all these emotions in Velan's or the villagers' deference for Raju. At their very first meeting, Velan's awe and fascination for Raju is conveyed to us: "The man stood gazing reverentially on his face." Velan's attitude is one of humility: "The villager on the lower step looked up at his face with devotion, which irked Raju." Gradually, successive events in their lives contrive toward establishing Raju in his role. *Bhakthi* explains this attitude well: "one may confer divinity or semi-divinity upon an object, and then take a *bhakthi* attitude towards it". Through the course of the narrative, we find that Raju comes to be established as the object of the villagers' devotion. We learn that, "they brought him huge chrysanthemum garlands, jasmine and rose petals in baskets. . . He protested to Velan. . . . "I'm a poor man and you" are poor men; why do you give me all this? You must stop it. But it was not possible to stop the practice; they loved to bring him gifts. He came to be called Swami by his congregation and where he lived was called the Temple." This is directly in line with the *bhakthi* mode of worship. "One may express *bhakthi* toward a revered object by means of the traditional artefacta of worship: flowers, fruit, incense, fire, water, etc."

We find that the people of Mangala start reposing greater

trust in Raju progressively. They not only expect Raju to solve their social problems, ". . . people brought him their disputes and quarrels over the division of ancestral property. He had to set apart several hours of his afternoon for these activities," but he also takes on a semi-divine stature: "It was believed that when he stroked the head of a child, the child improved in various ways."

T. W. Organ stresses that "*Bhakthi* is more than an attitude of deference; it also implies the taking of refuge in a god for protection, for assistance, or for special benefits, with confidence that the god is approachable and that he reciprocates with the same love that the devotee has for god." To the people of Mangala Raju's continued presence in their midst and his interest in their activities is positive proof of his love for them; as such he becomes more worthy of adulation. Velan's affection for "swami" is completely devoid of any kind of criticism or analysis that one brings to bear upon most human relationships. His humble, unquestioning acceptance of Raju, even after the latter's confession, is one of the typical traits of *bhakthi marga*. As Walsh remarks, Velan "takes the confession simply as a piece of singular condescension on Raju's part". The truth in no way reduces his belief in the saviour, and when Raju embarks on his final fast, Velan, we are told, was "keeping a sympathetic fast, he was now eating on alternate days, confining his diet to saltless boiled greens". The whole relationship between the villagers and Raju fits in neatly into the pattern of the *bhakthi* cult. Thus, once again, an understanding of a traditional concept of worship clarifies aspects of the novel. But at a more fundamental level the very conception of characters is subtly dictated by traditional considerations.

Raju is that rare novelistic creation—a personality that is completely realistic, yet lacking any definable characteristics. This is because Raju is, in a sense, a distillation of a type of character that has existed in Hindu mythology for nearly five centuries—the 'trickster sage'. But despite a long lineage Raju is special because he is also quite definitely a twentieth century novelistic personality. In Raju, we find that Narayan has, with his usual artistry, attempted to fuse two infinitely different variables: a typical character of eastern literatures with a complex novelistic personality. Raju emerges as an authentic character on two levels, on the mythic level and on the narrative level. This is because in his narrative technique Narayan resorts to a subtle method, wherein on one level he presents a straightforward novelistic character through the narrative line, but on an underlying level he reinforces the mythic personage by introducing motifs and symbols from Hindu mythology. These are well-worn motifs which are recognisable to those accustomed to the traditional literatures. It is on this level that he appeals to Velan and to the others at Mangala. Narayan makes this possible by integrating into the texture of the narrative, as well as into the characters in the novel,

several features that are typical to ancient Hindu archetypes. Thus, in a sense, the archetype of the trickster-sage is reinforced by these other features that surround him.

Though critics have recognised *The Guide* as the most remarkable of Narayan's achievements and have discussed at length its narrative technique, there has been little or no mention about the innumerable myth-motifs that have been built into the work. Narayan, fusing together an authentic novelistic character and an eastern archetype, has accomplished his end with such artistry that we can safely say that his design for the most part has gone unnoticed. Therefore, to fully appreciate the essence of this character and indeed the novel itself, it becomes essential to trace the genealogy of the 'trickster-sage'. It also becomes important to identify the symbols and motifs underlying the conception of the other characters, to which end one has to enter the labyrinthine maze of Hindu mythology.

In order to comprehend the pre-eminence of the 'trickster-sage' figure in Hindu mythology, and indeed to understand the indispensability of this archetype, it becomes essential to establish hierarchy within the Hindu cosmos. Hindu mythology, having to an extent absorbed the speculative aspects of the various philosophical schools, depicts no created life-form as immortal. Brahman, the universal essence, is the only eternal substance. Within this realm of created beings the Gods are the superior beings with life-spans ranging over several million celestial years. Almost as powerful as the gods are some of the *rishis* or sages who have attained their powers through intense meditation. There are many ranks of rishis from the uppermost Brahma rishis, to Raja rishis, and so on down the line. Ranged against the Gods and rishis are the *Rakshasas* or *Asuras,* the evil demons who are capable of obtaining great powers through intense meditation, which they then use to evil ends. In the midst of this endless power struggle is the hapless "*Manusha*" or man. The sages, usually of human extraction, but also sometimes possessing divine or semi-divine origins, also have long life-spans lasting up to sixty or seventy human generations or more, and are capable of as many divine acts as the Gods themselves; for instance, sage Visvamitra creates a private paradise for king Trishanku in the sky.

But perhaps the most vital function of the sages is that they act as a link between the Gods and humans, moving freely between heaven and earth. Visvamitra might visit the earthly king Dasaratha and report of a conversation he had shared with god Brahma the previous week. In this way, the gods mingle with the men and the sages bring the heavenly abodes very close to home, a feature that Raja Rao mentions in his preface to *Kanthapura*. A noteworthy feature of these sages is that, though the sage-figure forms an archetype, yet the sages are also definite individuals. It is perhaps the strange mixture of the archetype and the individual existing in Hindu mythology that has inspired Narayan to create his protagonist to fit well into the ancient archetype and yet exist as a definite individual.

Thus, though Vasishta, Visvamitra and Narada are all sages, Vasishta is serene, detached and wise; Visvamitra is arrogant, quick-tempered and impulsive; Sage Narada, the son of god Brahma and Saraswathy (the goddess of learning), is gossipy, prone to creating mischief among the gods for his own amusement. These distinctly individual figures, however, share all the *t*ypical features of their kind, that is, of rishis. Another salient feature of the sages, which is vital to an understanding of the prototype itself, is that, though a sage might at the end of a thousand years of meditation amass great spiritual merit and acquire tremendous powers, he is very often shown to have begun life as a mere *manusha* or man with more than his fair share of human imperfections. The *shastras* or holy books record that the great sage Valmiki began life as a highwayman.

Thus the trickster-sage, a figure deeply familiar to those intimately acquainted with Hindu myths, is one that goes back to ancient Sanskrit and Tamil literatures. In Tamil literature, apart from the *Thala-purana* (legendary history) of temples, which is full of the figures of trickster-sages, *Saiva-Siddhantha* literature, contains within it the *Thiruvilaiyadar Purana* where Shiva is treated as the *Pithan*. Within the system the devotees adulate Shiva as the trickster or divine madman. Another equally popular Tamil poem, *Vallithirumanam,* describes the courtship of Lord Subramanya (Shiva's son) with Valli—a gypsy. The god assumes the form of a lecherous sage making advances to the girl. It is noteworthy that this myth is unique to the Tamils, binding this god to their homeland. Shulman points this out in his book *Tamil Temple Myths:* "In the Sanskrit tradition, Skanda is either an eternal *brahmacarin* or the husband of the army of the gods—Devasena. But in Tamil the earliest reference to a bride is to Valli. . . . The story of the wooing of Valli ranks among the most intricate and beautiful passages of the entire Tamil puranic literature. It also contains some of the oldest indigenous fragments of myth to survive". The figure of Lord Muruga as the trickster-sage is one dear to the hearts of the Tamils. During temple festivals, touring drama troupes regularly present this episode of Murugan *as a sage* wooing the gypsy girl, interspersed with spicy dialogues and, needless to say, a great deal of ribaldry. Hence to the people of Narayan's homestate, and therefore by implication to the villagers of Mangala, the trickster-sage is a familiar figure. In Tamil-Nadu, because of the unique place given to the divine play tales of Shiva and to *Valli thirumanam* or the marriage of Valli, the trickster-sage remains a popular figure, and in the northern states 'the sage' has perhaps not retained the same status. The figure, however, can be traced right from the *itihasas*

and *Puranas* in Sanskrit. A knowledge of these facts about the sages, therefore, greatly enhances our study of the myth-motifs built into Raju's character.

In Hindu mythology, the sages and even the gods themselves are shown to be fallible, and no one is considered perfect or sunk so low as to be incapable of reaching great spiritual heights. Also, in Hindu theology, transformation in a person can occur due entirely to an outside agency without the volition of the individual. Raju would, in this light, be eminent 'sage material'.

Throughout the narrative two levels of the story present themselves. One is the sophisticated ironical level which appeals to the intellect. At this level a deep rooted irony operates, exposing the gullibility of the Indian people. This is the level where, as Alastair Niven points out, there is a "general sense that Indian people too readily escape from reality by creating false gods". Beneath this level of sophisticated irony there exists another layer which operates on the level of faith. This harnesses for its end a number of symbols, allegories and motifs from Hindu mythology. William Walsh, examining the thread of the story line, catches a glimpse of this underlying layer. He realizes that "Velan's attitude of submissive respect" is "prompted in part by the temple itself, in part by his own traditional expectations, in part by Raju's bearing and appearance." All these factors are deeply entrenched in myth and would certainly play a major role in influencing Velan and his community. But they are introduced into the texture of the novel very subtly and by various means. The double narrative within the novel is one such efficient means of dividing these two levels. However, it must be stressed that both narrative levels operate without distinction on the novelistic and the mythic matrixes of the book. Thus the third-person narrative reveals the inner tumult, scepticism, weakness, and indeed the inadequacies of Raju to successfully carry off the part that he is forced to take on. Raju's narration to Velan is also designed to reveal Raju's deplorable past and his inadequacies consequent to those events which make his present role as saint appear incongruous.

However, beneath these two narratives, there can be perceived a counter-narrative which undermines the scepticism present in the narratives. This is achieved by subtly introducing various features and archetypes from Hindu myths which reinforce the central image of 'trickster-sage'. The interpretation of this figure, however, varies on the two narrative levels. On the straightforward story line Raju is depicted as the trickster who assumes the mantle of sagehood because it suits his purposes. His motive is to deceive and is entered into after a lot of calculation at the beginning.

He had to decide on his future today. He should either

go back to the town of his birth, bear the giggles and stares for a few days, or go somewhere else. Where could he go? He had not trained himself to make a living out of hard work. Food was coming to him unasked now . . . He realized that he had no alternative: he must play the role that Velan had given him.

Here the term 'trickster-sage' assumes an ironical overtone and becomes a parody of the archetype portrayed in the myths, wherein divine beings or sages very often assume the form of a human or even an animal in order to trick a devotee. One such archetype is clearly delineated in the myth of Harishchandra, as narrated by Narayan in his collection *Gods, Demons and Others.*

Two sages Vashishta and Visvamitra we are told, debated over the many good attributes of king Harishchandra. While Vasishta extolled his steadfast adherence to truth, Visvamitra in a spirit of argument declares that no human is beyond corruption given the necessary circumstances. The Gods sighting a chance for entertainment press Visvamitra to take on the challenge of corrupting Harishchandra. The sages descend to earth and Visvamitra, assuming the form of a terrible monster ravages Harishchandra's kingdom. The king hunting down the beast gets lost in the forest, overcome with hunger and thirst. Visvamitra then appears before him in the guise of a venerable sage and offers him food and water. The guileless king is overcome with gratitude and promises to give the sage anything he desires. The sage then declares that he would like to have Harishchandra's kingdom and all his worldly possessions and those of his wife's and son's. The King renowned for his regard for truth, immediately relinquishes all his worldly goods and leaves the kingdom in rags along with his wife and son. He is made to face endless tribulations, but through it all, Harishchandra steadfastly holds on to the truth. At last, the gods moved by his plight right all his reversals, return his kingdom and shower their blessings on the noble king.

The story attempts to place *maya* at the centre of the tale. It stresses the fact that all worldly misfortunes may be designed by the Gods for a purpose and that being deceived by illusion is part of the human predicament. The belief that very often appearances can deceive is one that is central not only to Hinduism but to the novel. This belief is the basis for the peasants' faith in Raju. The peasants discuss the concept of illusion:

"I don't think he is that kind of yogi," said another.

"Who can say? Appearances are sometimes misleading", said someone.

To the peasants, Raju embodies the ancient archetype, a mystical figure worthy of reverence, perhaps because, unlike the readers who are aware of Raju's inner thoughts, they can only judge by outward appearances: "He has renounced the world, he does nothing but meditate."

This double presentation of the 'trickster-sage' image is woven into the texture of the novel very subtly. Raju himself is shown to operate on the level of scepticism and reason. He views his own predicament with complete honesty and yet, being human, is amused and flattered by the situation. His reactions at all times are entirely natural. At times he is annoyed by the adulation directed at him.

Velan rose, bowed low and tried to touch Raju's feet. Raju recoiled at the attempt. "I'll not permit anyone to do this. God alone is entitled to such a prostration."

Again Raju "felt irritated at the responsibility that Velan was thrusting on him. . . . " But gradually, we find that he comes "to view himself as a master of these occasions". All these emotions and uncertainties of Raju are presented at the level of the narrative—a level which is open to reason. But at an underlying level, the counter-narrative working on suggestion advances an altogether different approach to Raju and the role he assumes. At this level in which Velan and his friends operate, Raju's sagehood emerges as something authentic despite Raju's own misgivings. Raju's words themselves subtly introduce this view of a mysterious pattern which asserts itself over existence, despite or irrespective of a puny individual. This is evident time and again in the narrative. For instance, when the village teacher remarks, "I'll do anything . . . under your guidance," Raju replies, "I'm but an instrument accepting guidance myself." There is deep irony on the narrative level, for though Raju is here playing a role (as the passage makes clear) and is not in any sense sincere, yet ironically we can read his disingenuous words as expressing a truth. Though we are conscious of the humour in the situation, we realize that on an underlying level the passage is weighted with mythic implications—what in Sanskrit is termed *alaukika* (loka—world; aloka—not of the world).

Alaukika is defined variously by critics. Here, it is used in the sense of a supernatural agency which imposes a pattern not immediately apparent to human eyes, but which becomes evident when all the facts are presented. This *alaukika* level can be perceived as a recurring device through the text. Raju remarks at one point "we generally do not have a correct measure of our own wisdom". This is manifestly an indication of the *alaukika* pattern built into the novel's texture. Gradually, as the narrative progresses, a feeling of inevitability about the events overtakes the reader. Raju's inexplicable behaviour in forging Rosie's signature, his subsequent imprisonment and his arrival at Mangala, all seem to form a pattern, just as Harishchandra's story does, when viewed from this level. The authorial voice stresses this feature: "Something was happening on a different plane over which one had no control or choice and where a philosophical attitude made no difference". The *alaukika* level which presents Raju's transformation from a charlatan to a saint, despite his own scepticism, is subtly revealed by sentences which mark his gradual departure from his established self-image. Raju, we are told, "lost count of the time that passed in these activities . . . Several months (or perhaps years) had passed . . . He realized that it was unnecessary to maintain a calendar." Raju, like the sages, is shown to move away from the dominating preoccupation with temporal concerns. Raju progresses to a stage, when "He seemed to belong to the world now." By this time he has "lost interest in accumulation" and, furthermore, "His eyes shown with softness and compassion, the light of wisdom emanated from them." Thus, as the narrative reveals Raju's limitations and deceptions on the rational level, a counterdepiction diminishes these limitations and establishes his correspondence with the archetypal sage figure. This affiliation is further strengthened by the incorporation of a number of myth-motifs.

The first of these is evident in the opening passage of the novel. In Sanskrit poetics, a description of certain salient features of a place immediately indicates to the reader the nature of the place and the kind of people who would inhabit it. This is called the *svabhava* of the place. The abode of a Sage, or *ashrama,* would therefore have certain features which would indicate its holy *svabhava,* which would differ markedly from that of, say, a crematorial ground, which in turn would have certain other characteristic features. R. K. Narayan in his book, ***Gods, Demons and Others,*** distils this quality from Sanskrit poetics. In his description of the *ashramas* (hermitages) of sage Kanva and sage Vasishta, the passages are remarkably similar. The *ashramas* are usually on the banks of a beautiful river, away from human habitation, shaded by tall cool trees which serve as retreats for animals, birds and insects. The *ashrama* of sage Kanva on the banks of the Malini river and Vasishta's *ashrama,* which the ruler of Chedi enters, both possess the attributes of a holy place. We read that

> during his trip he (the ruler of Chedi) came upon a hermit's camp. The king looked about the scene stretching away in valleys and uplands, trees towering above, multicoloured blooms everywhere, creepers and shrubs and greenery; the cry of birds and the chant of sacred verse; . . . and the scent of sandalwood and flowers pervading the air. The king who had seen and experienced the finest surroundings asked his minister "what place is this, combining in it so much physical beauty and the aura of spiritual essences." "It's the ashrama of sage Vasishta".

By now, alert as we are to Narayan's subtle art, we can discover several features of an ashrama incorporated into Raju's lonely retreat. The place is quiet, and this is indicated by Raju's reaction to Velan: "Raju welcomed the intrusion, something to relieve the loneliness of the place". It is on a river bank, and the river itself is holy, for the villager significantly uses it for his ritual purification before approaching 'the august personage'.

> The other . . . went down the river steps to wash his feet and face . . . and took his seat two steps below the granite slab on which Raju was sitting cross-legged as if it were a throne.

Raju's position, it is noteworthy, is the traditional position of a guru; sitting on a stone slab as befits a sage who has renounced worldly comforts; on a higher level subtly indicative of his spiritual superiority over the pupil—here the peasant Velan; and most significant of all it is situated beside an ancient shrine. The place has every feature of an *ashrama:* "The branches of the trees canopying the river course rustled and trembled with the agitation of birds and monkeys settling down for the night." This is a clear indication of the good portents of a place—for a tree is considered auspicious which gives shelter to numerous life-forms. This is well brought out in a passage in the *Katha Sarith Sagara.*

> Near the himalayas . . . There is a rohini tree, which resembles the Vedas, in that many birds take refuge in its branches that extend through the heaven, as brahmins in the various branches of the sacred tradition.

The shrine itself contains all the necessary ingredients for a myth to be perpetrated from that spot. There is an inner sanctum with a stone image of ". . . a tall god with four hands, bearing a mace and wheel, with a beautifully chiseled head".

As the tale progresses, more details are added, so that the setting matches the archetype. With the start of the evening classes, "The pillared hall was bright with the lanterns the villagers had brought with them. It looked like a place where a great assembly was about to begin." Further on, we are told that "The ancient ceiling echoed with the voices of men, women and children repeating sacred texts in unison." The resemblance to the chant of sacred texts, one of the definite presages for locating an *ashram,* cannot be overlooked. The temple itself is the centre of the unfolding tale, and Raju becomes indelibly associated with it, for, except on one occasion when he goes to inspect the dead cow, he never leaves its mystical precincts. The third person narrative gently underlines this point: "He came to be called Swami by his congregation and where he lived was called the Temple." Like Pai's house in *The Cat and Shakespeare* "with its ochre bands on it almost as on a temple", this shrine too, which "the people loved . . . so much that they lime-washed its walls and drew red bands on them", becomes a powerful central-motif deeply symbolic to the unfolding tale.

Raju's appearance also incorporates many myth-motifs. At one level the narrative presents with sympathy and humour Raju's predicament and his agile improvisations to rise up to it.

> Raju soon realized that his spiritual status would be enhanced if he grew a beard and long hair to fall on his nape. A clean-shaven, close-haired saint was an anomaly. He bore the various stages of his make-up with fortitude, not minding the prickly phase he had to pass through before a well-authenticated beard could cover his face and come down his chest.

While Raju consciously strives to match his face to the archetype, at a deeper level, Narayan harnesses several motifs from myths to increase the likeness. A knowledge of these myth-motifs then enhance our appreciation of how closely Raju fits the image of the 'trickster-sage'. This can be gleaned using Narayan's own retelling of Hindu myths from *Gods, Demons and Others*. In the myth of "Lavana", a 'trickster-sage' arrives at the court of the king.

> He was a bare gaunt man, his forehead was blazoned with holy marks and his shawl was a rare kashmir one, declaring to one and all that he was an honoured man . . . his head covered with white hair falling on his nape, struck awe in anyone beholding him. They seated him amidst learned men.

The description here bears a similarity to Raju's physical appearance. But the resemblance does not end there. The physical appearance is usually emphasized in order to reveal how this has a powerful effect on the people surrounding him. We read that "the king could not take his eyes off him". It is noteworthy, that Raju has a very similar effect on the people of Mangala: "They just sat there on the lower step and looked at Raju and kept looking at him." Very often the myths describe the seer's piercing eyes. In *Lavana* this is taken a step further, for this eyes are the direct tools of his 'magic trade'.

The seer in the myth comes to the king's court in the guise of a magician. King Lavana, bored with the usual round of magic tricks, declares: "Let it be something new." Reassured by the sage on that point, the king declares:

> "Now proceed. Bring out your bag."

> "I have no bag."

> "That is a good sign. No bag of tricks. Then what have you?"

> "Only these", said the magician, indicating his own eyes and opening them wide.

> "Only what"? asked the king, looking up.

> When his eyes met the other's eyes—everything changed.

The similarity between this passage and the one in the text where Velan's sister claims to have been transformed after her meeting with Raju is striking. We read that,

> The girl herself seemed to have spoken to Raju as her saviour. She had told everyone "He doesn't speak to anyone, but if he looks at you, you are changed."

Motifs from Hindu myths are used not only to increase the mythic overtones in the central character but are extended to include other characters as well. The most significant among these is the motif of the dancing girl.

In Hindu literature, the archetypal image of "woman" as seductress, who is constantly attempting to distract a man and wean him away from his aspired path of spiritual discipline, is one that has persisted from Vedic times onwards right down to the Indian literatures of the late nineteenth and early twentieth centuries. During the later classical ages, however, owing perhaps to the increasing influence of Buddhist literature, we find that in Hindu literature a particular class of women who came to be termed as *devadasis,* literally 'women of God', were usually assigned the role of seductresses. These women, accomplished in classical music and dance, were in theory reared to perform in temples during temple festivals, but in practice came to be viewed as women of questionable morality. These women who claimed descent from the celestial nymphs or *apsaras* who danced in heaven for the entertainment of the gods, replaced their progenitors as archetypal figures of seduction in literatures.

In *The Guide,* the narrative is careful to establish this fact about Rosie's background. Raju relates it to Velan.

> "You see", she began . . . "Can you guess to what class I belong?" I looked her up and down and ventured, "the finest, whatever it may be, and I don't believe in class or caste . . ."

> "I belong to a family traditionally dedicated to the temples as dancers; my mother, grandmother and, be-

fore her, her mother. Even as a young girl, I danced in our village temple. You know how our caste is viewed?" "It's the noblest caste on earth," I said. "We are viewed as public women," she said plainly. . . ."

The passage is crucial to placing Raju in the 'trickster-sage' model. The passage itself follows a traditional pattern which establishes the origins of the woman, firmly placing her in the role of the enchantress who seduces 'the potential sage'. The image of the celestial nymph, sent down by the Gods to disturb a meditating sage, is a fairly common motif in Hindu mythology. Many a time a sage attempts by his meditation to amass a lot of spiritual energy, the Gods feel threatened and dispatch a celestial nymph to distract him! The nymph, more often than not, succeeds in her mission and begets a child. The sage then, returning to his senses after the infatuation, would spurn the seductress and redouble his efforts at meditation. The nymph would invariably leave the baby on earth to be tended by humans and return to her celestial abode. Thus even the great sage Visvamitra is seduced by the celestial nymph Maneka. After a thousand years of sport with her he returns to his meditation, his spiritual powers reduced but his image as sage undamaged. John Dowson in his *Classical Dictionary of Hindu Mythology and Religion,* describes the myth in spare terms:

> "The Mahabharata and Ramayana tell the story of Visvamitra's amour with Maneka. His austerities had so alarmed the Gods that Indra sent this Apsaras to seduce 'Visvamitra' by the display of her charms and the exercise of all her allurements". She succeeded and the result was the birth of Sakuntala. Visvamitra at length became ashamed of his passion and dismissing the nymph with gentle accents he retired to the northern mountains where he practised severe austerities for a thousand years. He is said also to have had an amour with the nymph Rambha.

Neither Rosie herself with her dubious origins nor Raju with his obsessive involvement with her fits into the ordered life at Malgudi, but seem more akin to the prototypes of the ancient myths. Raju's obsession of Rosie, and his needless forgery, all seem totally outside the normal pattern of life. In the narrative time and time again, Rosie's origins and the differences in background between Rosie and Raju are emphasized, as for instance in Raju's mother's admonition: ". . . don't have anything to do with these dancing women. They are all a bad sort." Her question to Rosie shortly after, highlights the crux of the matter, when she asks Rosie, "what is your father's name?" Raju is deeply embarrassed on her behalf and remarks, "It was a dreadful question for the girl. She knew only her mother." His mother's repeated remonstrations against Rosie's stay is centred around the argument, "You can't have a dancing girl

in your house . . . What is the home coming to?" And her reaction is one that is shared by the community, by Gaffur, by the Sait and by others. The Sait, who comes to ask Raju for his dues, is taken aback on hearing the sound of Rosie's dance. Raju narrates the incident: "Dance practice! He was astounded. It was the last thing he expected in a home like mine." And finally Raju's brutally forthright uncle states the difference without mincing words.

> "Hey, wench!" he cried to Rosie, addressing her in the singular, or something even lower than singular. Now stop your music and all those gesticulations and listen to me . . . Are you of our caste? No. Our class? No. Do we know you? No . . . In that case, Why are you here? After all, you are a dancing girl. We do not admit them in our families."

Rosie gets further entrenched in the role of the enchantress with the very first symbol associated with her—the snake. 'The snake-women' or *naga-kannikas* of the nether world are again archetypal symbols of seduction. The great sage Valmiki, we are told, was born of one.

> Valmiki's next birth . . . was from the womb of a *naga-kannika,* a beauty from the nether world of serpents, who had enticed a sage in the forests and gone back to her world.

Once again the pattern is set. The very first mention that Raju makes of Rosie associated her with this image: "There was a girl who had come all the way from Madras and who asked the moment she set foot in Malgudi 'Can you show me a cobra—a king cobra it must be'. . . ." The girl, whose name at this point Raju does not know, is shown to have a morbid attraction to snakes.

> . . . the cobra raised itself and darted hither and thither and swayed. The whole thing repelled me, but it seemed to fascinate the girl.

The symbol gets better defined when Raju's mother dubs Rosie as the 'serpent-girl'.

> She flew straight at the sobbing Rosie, crying, "Are you now satisfied with your handiwork, you she-devil, you demon. Where have you dropped on us from? Everything was so good and quiet—until you came; you came in like a viper. Bah! I have never seen anyone work such havoc on a young fool! What a fine boy he used to be! The moment he set his eyes on you, he was gone. On the very day I heard him mention the 'serpent girl' my heart sank."

The placing of Rosie in the role of the dancing girl or the snake girl is crucial to the theme of the 'trickster-sage'.

As soon as Rosie is identified in the role of 'the celestial nymph' and the *naga-kannika,* the pattern of the archetype emerges, and it becomes easier to envisage Raju in the role of the seduced sage. This certainly would be the way the situation would present itself to the peasant Velan, bred on thousands of such tales from his childhood. This would be one reason why his faith in Raju is not shaken after Raju narrates his story to him.

> "I don't know why you tell me all this Swami. It's very kind of you to address at such length your humble servant."

Even as the threads of the narrative enumerate the various inadequacies and misgivings of Raju, the counter-narrative, which works through symbols and motifs, suggests an alternative reading of the details, subtly establishing Raju in the image of the archetype. Velan's acceptance of Raju as the Guru is not surprising, when one takes into account the fact that Raju is carefully built up to correspond to the archetype.

Furthermore, the climate of *Rasa* (delight, emotion, pleasure), an intrinsic aspect of Hinduism, while standing opposed to *Tapas* (austerity, withdrawal, mortification,) does not denigrate worldly, even sensuous, experiences, provided they ultimately lead to spiritual discipline. Rasa is an acknowledged path of spiritual training within the religion. Raju, at the end of the book, if one followed the trend of the pattern set by the myth, would have been a yogi all his life, if one took 'yogi' in the broadest sense of the term to mean a spiritual aspirant. This is probably the spirit of the American filmmaker's question "Have you always been a yogi?" to which Raju replies, "Yes, more or less". Raju speaks the truth, though even at this point he may not be aware of it. His answer set at the end of the novel is one sure clue to the mythic perspective that the novel advanced so consistently through the text. Therefore, M. K. Naik's comment, that Raju even at the end is "alert enough to tell a brazen-faced lie to the American film producer", does not perhaps reflect adequately the significance of the counter-narrative.

This may also be the reason for his remark that Velan, even after hearing the confession, "refuses to accept that the saint is a charlatan", for gradually, as the tale progresses, the counter-narrative gains ascendance over the straightforward story line, and the clear line that divides the charlatan from a saint slowly gets blurred, until finally the two merge to leave behind the strange enigma that is Raju.

The enigma of Raju's transformation gradually takes shape, artfully crafted in through the counter-narrative. Seemingly insignificant details add up to its suggestive value by subtly introducing powerful myth-motifs. One such insignificant detail, which incorporates a whole world of symbolism, is Raju's artless musing after one of his grandiose statements to Velan: "Have I been in prison or in some sort of transmigration?"

In Hindu religious literature, there is always evident beneath the surface a continuous friction between religious and secular powers. One very often comes across instances where great sages are imprisoned by kings or other secular powers for deeds which appear illegal or heretical. But the sages develop their yogic powers within the prison walls, and when released, usually through divine intervention, become more saintlike. A good example to illustrate this allusion would be the story of sage "Abhirama", author of an *anthathi* by that name.

Legend has it that the sage, a firm devotee of Goddess Abhirami, was a *jivan-muktha* and true to the tradition of *jivan-mukthas* was oblivious to mere worldly conventions.

> On a festive new-moon day when the temple was being cleared for a visit by king Sarabojhi, the sage, immersed in deep meditation, is indifferent to all implorations to leave the temple. The priests at last give up in despair deeming it easier to explain to the king than persuade the "mad-sage". The king, on being told, is curious to meet this sage. He approaches Abhirama and wishing to test his sanity inquires of him the day. The *jivan-muktha,* unconcerned about mere temporal cycles, murmurs abstractedly that it is the day of the full-moon. Convinced of his insanity, the king attempts to correct him, at which the sage calmly replies, "If my mother, Goddess Abhirami wills she can change a new moon into a full moon". The king enraged at this piece of impertinence orders his arrest and declares that, if there is not a full moon in the evening sky, then Abhirama will be hanged for all to see. Vast crowds gather to see the sage being led to prison. In prison, the sage, completely unruffled launches into a song of praise (anthathi) on the goddess. The people marvel at the sage, half in wonder and half in pity at his fate. Finally, darkness falls, and the sage is led out, still singing, to witness the moonless sky. At last, the goddess, moved by the plight of her devotee and in order to teach the arrogant king a lesson, removes one of her jewels and flings it into the sky, where, to human eyes, it shines brighter than a hundred moons! The astonished king finally realizes his folly and prostrates himself at the feet of the sage.

Thus the prison always features in stories where the sages confront worldly arrogance, and it remains a powerful symbol in Hindu mythology. It is no accident that Lord Krishna himself is born in a prison cell, where his parents are imprisoned by his evil uncle Kamsa. Again Prahlada, the great devotee of Lord Vishnu, is imprisoned by his evil father Hiranya Kasipu.

The prison or indeed confinement of any kind is a powerful symbol viewed as precipitating spiritual growth. In *The Cat and Shakespeare* too, we find this symbol present although at a relatively minor level, when Nair is sent to prison and his stay seems, in a curious way to add to his mystical powers. Nair's words ". . . what is jail but a philosophical illness?" succinctly sums up this viewpoint. Within the religious tradition it is believed that great sages, toward the end of their spiritual quest, ordered that they be sealed within four walls while alive. They were termed as attaining *samadhi*. This was believed to precipitate the release of their soul from their useless material bodies. In presenting Raju as an ex-prisoner, once again Narayan harnesses a very powerful symbol within Hinduism.

Narayan's considerable talent in subtly introducing traditional patterns and motifs into his novels perhaps requires more recognition than has been accorded to it. But this should not blind us to what has been the chief cause of his considerable popularity, namely, his ability to portray with insight the peculiar twists and turns of a human mind and furthermore, to accomplish this with a gentle sophisticated irony, which is detached yet astute in its grasp of essential human follies. Raju's character is a case in point. The portrayal of Raju as the mystic by no means intrudes upon the narrative line which depicts Raju's predicament authentically and with considerable humour. Raju's obsessive love of Rosie is presented with characteristic realism. Right from the start, his infatuation with Rosie is presented with a measure of irony in Narayan's "uncluttered and immediate" prose. Raju's growing obsession with the girl, his total disregard of the social norms which govern the Malgudian society leading up to his forgery and arrest are presented with insight and understanding. Raju seems to be transformed by apparent wealth and glamour for a brief period. The first-person narrative of Raju clearly delineates the details of his involvement with Rosie, his act of forgery and his subsequent imprisonment. Raju's decision to play the role of a saint then appears as a natural consequence of his former character. Thus, while at the underlying level his archetypal image is being reinforced, we are also made aware of his adroit manoeuvres to keep up his image. That the two levels co-exist without diminishing the considerable influence that each brings to bear upon the text is a testimony to Narayan's skill. It is this very lucid presentation of the naive, well-meaning protagonist in whom, as Walsh points out, "there is developed to the point of extremity what exists in all of us to some degree—the quality of suggestibility to the desires of others", that perhaps makes it more difficult for us to imbibe the equally distinct portrayal of him as the mythic archetype. The clever and resourceful Raju with his dexterity and connivance in

attempting to turn his unexpected predicament to his advantage, is a very endearing figure. Narayan communicates the various shades and nuances of Raju's feelings such as his bombast, "We cannot force vital solutions. Every question must bide its time"; or his petty anxieties, "I wish I had asked him what the age of the girl was. Hope she is uninteresting. I have had enough trouble in life", and his occasional guilt at "dragging those innocent men deeper and deeper into the bog of unclear thoughts" in a natural and clear prose. As the story progresses, Raju's reactions, as he feels himself manipulated into a position beyond his power to rectify, are portrayed realistically. At the height of his fast he watches with envy the pilgrims eating.

> He wondered what they might be eating—rice boiled with a pinch of saffron, melted ghee—and what were the vegetables? . . . the sight tormented him.

Here Raju's decision to attempt the fast whole-heartedly, with complete sincerity, is central to his change from a charlatan to, if not a saint, at least to a figure worthy of respect.

> With a sort of vindictive resolution he told himself, I'll chase away all thoughts of food. . . . This resolution gave him a peculiar strength.

But here there is nothing mystical in his resolution. It is portrayed as the natural reaction of a cornered man who decides ultimately to do his best given the lack of choice.

A little deliberation will help us realize that there is a profound difference in this version of Raju's change and its mythic version, where Raju is the mystic, a yogi who intercedes with the gods for the sake of humanity. To Velan and the villagers at Mangala, Raju appears only in this uncomplicated perspective. To them he is a presence in their midst from an archetypal world whose function is self-evident. Narayan's greatest skill lies in making it feasible to interpret Raju's fate in both these lights.

Roland Barthes, discussing the nature and function of Myth, isolates its essential quality: "In passing from history to nature, myth makes a saving: it abolishes the complexity of human action, gives it an elemental simplicity, . . . it organises a world without contradictions. . . . Myth creates a happy clarity."

Barthes maintains that it is this elemental patterning implicit in a mythic view of life which imbues most human activities with significance. From the knowledge that events are to follow a certain predestined course arises a sense of security and power which, according to Barthes, is the greatest contribution that myth can offer to humanity. In the novel, it is this elemental simplicity, this happy clarity of vision that Velan and the villagers share, which is shown to be strangely more powerful and indestructible than all the complex perspectives that Raju, and the readers with their ironic view of him, possess. Yet again we find that Narayan in his unobtrusive manner intimates a further dimension to our understanding of myth.

Alpana Sharma Knippling (essay date Winter 1993)

SOURCE: "R. K. Narayan, Raja Rao and Modern English Discourse in Colonial India," in *Modern Fiction Studies,* Vol. 39, No. 1, Winter, 1993, pp. 169-86.

[*In the following essay, Knippling discusses Indian novels written in English and the implications of colonialism and nationalism on these novels, specifically focusing on Narayan's* The English Teacher *and Raja Rao's* Kanthapura.]

Indigenous Indian novel-writing in English dates back to at least the mid-nineteenth century. Its "origin" owes as much to the educational reforms called for by both the 1813 Charter Act and the ensuing 1835 English Education Act of William Bentinck as to the circulation, representation, and purchase of English literature and culture among members of the Indian upper classes in nineteenth-century India. While we are not at liberty to assume that novel production in Britain and colonial India underwent simply parallel routes, we may still argue for the possibility, in the case of English-writing in India, of a nascent space in which British and Indian social codes and value systems began to intersect and mutually determine one another. More specifically, the translation of certain progressive British social codes and cultural values of the Enlightenment into Indian terms entailed something like a new episteme, within whose rigor Indian writers started to produce novels assuming a critical stance towards what were now viewed as "backward" Indian social and cultural practices. Bankim Chandra Chatterjee's 1864 novel, *Rajmohun's Wife,* for instance, utilizes a social reformer's zeal in its depiction of a middle-class Hindu woman's abuse by her husband. However, by the early twentieth century, many writers began to insist on the *Indian* "content" of their material, an increasingly prevalent tendency no doubt informed by the corresponding rise of nationalism and all the organized movements of civil disobedience.

It is within the folds of this complex history that we may understand the imbrications of the discourses of nationalism, colonialism, and modernity in the Indian colonial context. I would argue that, in order to effectively read early Indian literature in English (for the purposes of this essay, "early" signifies the period of the 1930s and 1940s), one needs to see how, in this period, the alliance of nationalism and colonialism produced India's modern "moment" and how the writing of a certain kind of fiction participated in this inauguration of modernity. Indeed, the uneven terrain of Indian colonial history, on which numerous nationalist struggles for independence were played out in the mid- to late-nineteenth century, yields nothing more startling than a picture of this very alliance between nationalism and colonialism, which, in a sense, secured India's modernity in the early twentieth century.

However, the alliance of nationalism and colonialism will not seem quite so startling if we remember that both these ideological formations had a shared stake in the larger Western bourgeois discourse of progressive liberal humanism, emerging as a symptom of modernity in the 1930s and 1940s. In their studies of the strategic exclusion of the subaltern from national narratives of emancipation, such Indian Marxist historians and theorists as the Subaltern Studies historians and Gayatri Chakravorty Spivak have pointed out that nationalism, or the organized resistance to imperialism, will itself always participate in "the cultural aspects of imperialism" as long as organized resistance to imperialism is a bourgeois movement. Bourgeois liberatory discourses of nationalism, in other words, cannot function in oppositional ways to discourses of imperialism because they are already aligned with discourses of imperialism, even contained within them. That discourses of nationalism did not evolve oppositionally to the British colonial apparatus; that the social determinations of class are such that the indigenous bourgeoisie participated in all "the cultural aspects of imperialism," from attending British universities to producing a nationalist rhetoric which came right out of the Western rational tradition: these are the crucial formulations that many Anglophone Indian authors and critics have not yet found themselves articulating in their expression of Indian national identity. What is "Indian" is seen as oppositional to or a corrective of what is "British," when, in fact, what is (bourgeois) "Indian" has effectively already been contained by what is "British." As for the subaltern classes, they may be positioned precariously at the margins of both nationalist and colonial discourse, "not situated outside the civilizing project but . . . caught in the path of its trajectory."

R. K. Narayan (b. 1906) and Raja Rao (b. 1908), two early Indian writers in English, productively demonstrate how the literary project participated in the modern "moment" inaugurated by the complicitous embrace of the discourses of nationalism and colonialism. Narayan's *The English Teacher* (1945) and Rao's *Kanthapura* (1938) are novels produced at a time when the most volatile political imperative concerned the need for Indian subjects to position themselves vis-à-vis British colonialism and Indian nationalism. But with the exception of *Waiting for the Mahatma,* neither colonialism nor nationalism occupies a central position in Narayan's novels of this or, for that matter, any later period. Conversely, questions regarding colonialism and nationalism do occupy a large part of Raja Rao's *Kanthapura,* but they are treated in such a way that they are deferred rather than addressed. In both Narayan's *The English Teacher* and Rao's *Kanthapura,* then, aspects of colonialism and nationalism are engaged in a sidewise fashion, indirectly and obliquely.

I would like to suggest that what seems to be most responsible for the curious lingering of questions regarding colonialism and nationalism at the threshold of these early modern novels is the regular and systematic function of English discourse within these fictional narratives. That is to say, English discourse functions in these novels as a way to both allow and authorize certain statements, while disallowing and de-authorizing others. In formulating such an argument, I have in mind Michel Foucault's project in *The Archaeology of Knowledge,* which can be described as conceiving a methodological account that does not automatically ground its "truth" in a self-willing and autonomous human agency, but instead looks at the particular conditions which govern and regulate the truth value of statements. Archaeology, thus conceived, is an examination of statements as worthy of study in and of themselves; but, remaining at the surface of those statements, it is also a method which tries to lay bare the conditions which make possible and perpetuate certain discursive formations. As Ian Hacking puts it, Foucault's project is to analyze discourse "not in terms of who says what but in terms of the conditions under which those sentences will have a definite truth value, and hence are capable of being uttered."

Of course, starting with *Discipline and Punish: The Birth of the Prison,* Foucault's attention was to move from the surface of words to their materiality in everyday practice. But his formulation, that discourse functions in ways that do not necessarily or always implicate human intention, which is itself only possible because of the terms which a certain discourse allows and disallows, is productive. It allows me to say that Narayan and Rao do not autonomously or willfully choose to be heavily influenced by English discourse and thereby prove to be individually culpable in the whole Westernizing process. Rather, I wish to point to how it was that English discourse came to hold such a sway among certain members of the Indian elite classes, that is, how many educated Indians were in the position to receive British discourse in the way that they did. This essay wishes to engage the systematic and insistent function of English discourse in the early modern texts of Narayan and Rao, with the assumption that this discourse is not willed into existence by these writers, that they are not simply or negatively persuaded by it; rather, it is the discourse which regulates the manner of its use by these writers.

I use the term "English discourse" as shorthand for all the Western discourses of progressive liberal humanism underpinning emergent conditions of modernity in colonial India. But English discourse in the colonial context cannot function in the same way as at "home." In colonial India, it cannot be separated from its institutional status—that is to say, its "body of anonymous, historical rules"; its everyday practices, as evidenced in British colonial administration; its hegemonic restructuring of the Indian social classes; its codification in Indian education in 1835; its traces in the English literature received by Indian readers, and so on. By English discourse, then, is conveyed the discursive functioning of everything "English" in India, with discourse itself viewed as a textual practice—a systematic way of "reading" and ordering—which, through historical repetition and institutional insertion in the colonial context, gains in authority and value.

The In-/Ex-citement of English Discourse: R. K. Narayan's The English Teacher

The first Indian novelist in English to secure international recognition, R. K. Narayan began his prolific career in the 1930s during the heyday of Indian political mobilization and the campaign of civil disobedience against British imperialism. But what takes the place of an overt nationalist agenda in Narayan's fiction are scattered allusions directed at both the British in India and the contemporary struggle for independence. These allusions, casually recorded, as it were, in the margins of his texts, seem to tell a profoundly ambivalent story about Narayan's relation to the political and nationalist movements that were popular across India during his early writing period. This ambivalence, however, perhaps owes less to Narayan's conscious engendering than to the particular functions released by English discourse in the space of his writing. On the one hand, in the guise of the canonical British literary tradition to which Narayan was and is intensely affiliated, English discourse acts as the *seducteur,* instituting desire and exciting Narayan and his male protagonists with the promise of plenitude and the "alchemy of inexplicable joy." On the other hand, in its institutional, more obviously colonial capacity, it plays the *provocateur,* inciting them to an aggression and frustration whose intensity is rarely expressed, let alone relieved.

Published two years before formal Indian independence, Narayan's *The English Teacher* mobilizes both these functions of English discourse. Not very well known in either India or in the Anglo-U.S., *The English Teacher* constitutes one of Narayan's earlier, semi-autobiographical attempts at writing. Its protagonist, Krishna—a disgruntled teacher of English literature and language at the Albert Mission College and an aspiring poet—suffers the sudden demise of his young wife. Thereafter, the narrative shifts from the public realm to the private, domestic one, in which Krishna grieves the loss of Susila and takes on the care of his small daughter, Leela. To his delight, he discovers a supernatural "medium" through which he begins communicating with Susila. In addition, Krishna befriends a man who runs an experimental, alternative school for children, to which Krishna sends Leela. Persuaded by this school's "Leave Alone System," according to which the innocence and purity of children's visions may be preserved, Krishna decides to resign from his own teaching job and assist his friend in experimental education. The end of *The English Teacher* has him united with a vision of his wife in a full "moment for which one feels grateful to Life and Death."

This bare outline cannot speak to the complexities of the narrative. For instance, one cannot simply oppose the two pedagogical approaches to education offered by the text and say that some essentially Indian way of knowing and learning pits itself against some essentially British one. Both systems of education are inflected with and participate in English discourse. Although the Albert Mission College is obviously a British institution run by the British principal, Mr. Brown, the experimental school run by Krishna's friend is described by him in a language that cannot be extricated from its Wordsworthian traces:

> "This is the meaning of the word joy—in its purest sense. We can learn a great deal watching [children] and playing with them. When we are qualified we can enter their life. . . . When I watch them, I get a glimpse of some purpose in existence and creation."

The Indian headmaster's words echo Krishna's own earlier statements, in which a similarly Wordsworthian trace occurs.

> Nature, nature, all our poets repeat till they are hoarse. There are subtle, invisible emanations in nature's surroundings; with them the deepest in us merges and harmonizes. I think it is the highest form of joy and peace we can ever comprehend.

Thus, in both its institutional and literary articulations, English discourse underpins the narrative. In fact, read problematically, the entire narrative demonstrates how English discourse regulates its reception by and influence upon Krishna/Narayan and, in particular, how its in-/ex-citement, its simultaneous play of provocation and seduction, is a function of that discourse.

The opening pages of *The English Teacher* offer a nightmarish look at the conditions under which Krishna teaches English literature at the Albert Mission College to distracted and bored students. Narayan describes Krishna's daily routine in a characteristically comic, ironic, and disengaged way:

> I got up at eight every day, read for the fiftieth time

Milton, Carlyle and Shakespeare, looked through compositions, swallowed a meal, dressed, and rushed out of the hostel . . . four hours later I returned to my room; my duty in the interval had been admonishing, cajoling and browbeating a few hundred boys of Albert Mission College so that they might mug up Shakespeare and Milton and secure high marks and save me adverse remarks from my chiefs at the end of the year. For this pain the authorities kindly paid me a 100 Rs. on the first of every month and dubbed me a lecturer.

Gauri Viswanathan's findings in "The Failure of English," in *Masks of Conquest: Literary Study and British Rule in India,* are proven most persuasively through this passage and the first section of Narayan's *The English Teacher,* where there seems to emerge a picture that evokes all "the unfulfilled promises of English literary education" for the British colonial administration:

> The study of English literature had merely succeeded in creating a class of Babus (perhaps the Indian equivalent of the English Philistines of whom Matthew Arnold wrote so scathingly) who were intellectually hollow and insufficiently equipped with the desirable amount of knowledge and culture. English education came to be criticized for its imitativeness and superficiality and for having produced an uprooted elite who were at once apostates to their own national tradition and imperfect imitators of the West.

In this passage, Viswanathan is concerned with the state of affairs for the British administration in the late nineteenth century. By the 1930s and 1940s, of course, the "uprooted apostates" and "imperfect imitators" she mentions have turned out to be either active nationalists or effective and, in some cases, subversive mimics (of the West), or both, depending upon the dispersal of particular discursive functions when English discourse is refracted through a modern lens.

In Narayan's text, the provocation of English discourse for the young teacher is its injunction to "stuff Shakespeare and Elizabethan metre and Romantic poetry . . . into young minds and feed them on the dead mutton of literary analysis and theories and histories" at the expense of "lessons in the fullest use of the mind." Time and again, this portrait of the relentless rules of discourse emerges:

> I spent the rest of the period giving a general analysis of the mistakes I had encountered in this batch of composition—*rather very, as such, for hence,* split infinitives, collective nouns, and all the rest of the traps that the English language sets for foreigners. I then set [the students] an exercise in essay-writing on the epigram "Man is the master of his own destiny." [sic] "An idi-

otic theme," I felt, "this abstract and confounded meta-physics;" [sic] but I could not help it. I had been ordered to set this subject to the class.

In this passage, the subject-position of the teacher, or the set of rules enabling him to inhabit structures of power in the classroom, is most powerfully and ironically underwritten by both the colonial agency that assigns authority ("I had been ordered to set this subject") and the "theme" of the composition topic ("Man is the master of his own destiny").

We learn that the colonial agent in question is the British principal, Mr. Brown. Brown exacerbates Krishna's provocation, reminding Krishna of the predicament of having to occupy intimately a discourse of power within which he himself seems disempowered. For instance, when Brown convenes a meeting of the teachers, he voices his anger at learning from an English honors student that the student did not know "honors" was spelt with the obligatory British "u." In private, Krishna responds to this sarcastically: "Brown's thirty years in India had not been ill-spent if they had opened the eyes of Indians to the need for speaking and writing correct English! The responsibility of the English department was indeed very great." In dialogue with a colleague who sides with Brown, Krishna poses the question:

> "Let us be fair. Ask Mr. Brown if he can say in any one of the two hundred Indian languages: 'The cat chases the rat.' He has spent thirty years in India."

> "It is all irrelevant," said Gajapathy.

> "Why should he think the responsibility for learning is all on our side and none on his? Why does he magnify his own importance?"

Here, Krishna interestingly effects a turning of the tables on Brown by showing the ignorance masked by the school principal's apparent knowledge. But he does not answer his own plaintive question ("'Why does he think the responsibility for learning is all on our side and none on his?'"); nor is his question actually answered by the novel itself. The conversation with Gajapathy comes to an end, and Krishna concludes, after some agitated thinking, that "[a]ll this trouble was due to lack of exercise and irregular habits." In just such an oblique manner this incident—centered on the spelling of a word (which to exacerbate the situation is, in an American edition, "correct" in any case)— stages a contemporary nationalist debate over the status of English in colonial India.

What, then, keeps Krishna in a profession which affords so little satisfaction? Here, we might invoke the complementary play of English discourse as excitement. Specifically,

the articulation of an emphatic position on the ideological practices of colonialism and nationalism is pre-empted by the ability of the British literary tradition to excite Krishna. When, at the end of the novel, Krishna resolves to resign from his job, he plays with the idea of stating anti-colonial motives in his resignation letter: "I was going to attack a whole century of false education. . . . This education had reduced us to a nation of morons; we were strangers to our own culture and camp followers of another culture, feeding on leavings and garbage." Significantly, however, he cannot actually mobilize these anti-colonial statements in his letter of resignation because they are like a rabid attack on all English writers, which was hardly my purpose. "What fool could be insensible to Shakespeare's sonnets or the 'Ode to the West Wind' or 'A thing of beauty is a joy forever'?" I reflected.

This question poignantly rewrites Krishna's attempted negotiation of nationalist issues. Indeed, the appeal of the British literary canon is articulated throughout the text, and everywhere its function is to forestall a radical political critique. The liberal humanist assumptions at work here are clear: we see the characteristic celebration of the human imagination, which is seen to function autonomously and independently of the public and political domains. Yet these very assumptions release immense complications when they are received as supposedly self-evident truths by Krishna. For, recast in colonial India, the aesthetics of liberal humanism cannot be divested of their political weight. Yet it is exactly the extrication of the political content of (liberal humanist) literature that is absent in Narayan's text. Krishna simply cannot distinguish the literature's colonial, ideological traces in his liberal humanist reception of it. Later, I will show how this inability was historically inflected and produced rather than a mark of some sort of self-willed failure on Krishna's or Narayan's part. Momentarily locating, then, but never quite fixing the repetitious habits of attempted negotiations and extrications, *The English Teacher* remains in what appears to be a moment which endlessly enacts, without resolving, the play of in-/ex-citement. Producing a certain measure of ambivalence, this play tends effectively to foreclose upon the terms of its critique

Narayan's own subjectivity, described by him with characteristic reticence in some of its twists and turns in the autobiography *My Days: A Memoir,* enacts a similar play of the in-/ex-citement of English discourse. On one hand, there is its ability to frustrate and incite in its colonial, ideological, and official capacity; on the other hand, its public capacity covered over, there is its ability to please and excite through its literary articulations. Perhaps owing to the logic of this simultaneous play, Narayan was to heed a friend's advice about not entering the graduate program in English literature ("a friend turned me back arguing that this would be a sure way to lose interest in literature") even as he decided to be a writer.

Owing to a similar logic, Narayan was to fail in English in his university entrance exams in high school, well aware that proficiency in English was "a social hallmark," even as his reading at this time was prolific. In 1925, one year before he enrolled in the B.A. program in English in Maharaja College, Mysore, the nineteen-year-old Narayan had read the poetry of Pope, Keats, Shelley, Byron, and Browning; the novels of Walter Scott, Dickens, Hardy, Tolstoy, Marie Corelli, Mrs. Henry Wood, Rider Haggard, and H. G. Wells; Palgrave's *Golden Treasury* and Long's *English Literature;* and the plays of Moliere, Marlowe, and Shakespeare. He also scoured dozens of British and American literary journals, newspapers, and monthlies: *Little Folks, Nineteenth Century and After, Cornhill,* the *Boys' Own Paper,* the *Strand Magazine,* the *Bookman, Harper's,* the *Atlantic, American Mercury,* the *London Mercury, John o' London, T. P.'s Weekly,* the *Spectator, The Times Literary Supplement,* and the Manchester *Guardian.*

This prolific reading was possible because Narayan's father was an administrator and headmaster at several government schools, and his position of authority gave Narayan full access at all times to college libraries. In **My Days,** we learn of other pertinent details, such as the Officers' club where Narayan's tweed-suited father customarily stopped by to play tennis before he came home. As a child in 1916, when nationwide protests were underway against the Rowlatt Act, Narayan, "entranced," joined the Madras march, only to be scolded by his uncle for doing so because the uncle "saw no logic in seeking a change of rulers." Upon being introduced to Biblical stories in his childhood Lutheran Mission School, Narayan was "enchanted":

> I loved the Rebeccas and Ruths one came across. When one or the other filled her pitcher from the well and poured water into the mouth of Lazarus or someone racked with thirst, I became thirsty too and longed for a draught of that crystal-clear, icy water. I stood up to be permitted to go out for a drink of water at the back-yard tap.

I mention these details in order to draw attention to the contradictory yet determining aspects which contribute, willy-nilly, to the simultaneous functions of provocation and seduction of English discourse in Narayan's "life" and "work."

What seems to ensure the more or less uniform maintenance and regulation of this double play of English discourse in colonial India is the historical excision of the "contaminant," British colonialism, from English literature. Interpreting Gauri Viswanathan, Rajeswari Sunder Rajan uses the history of this excision to argue for its problematic effects upon current academic practice in India:

> English literature was not indicted on ideological or historical grounds by association with the English ruler. Rather, it became the surrogate—and also the split—presence of the Englishman, or a repository of abstract and universal values freely available to the colonized as much as to the colonizer.
>
> It is this dissociation of English literature from its national origins that has made possible its unproblematic retention and continuance in the post-Independence education syllabus in India.

In other words, the controlled production and reception of English literature in the colonies was such that any ideological traces of imperialist power relations were excised from the literature, which then proceeded to circulate as a universal, trans-historical category in the colonies. What facilitated this sort of production and circulation was the "dissociation of English literature from its national origins." Rajan reminds us that Britain's local colonies—Wales, Scotland, Ireland—did manage to contest the nationalist rise of the British canon in the nineteenth century; but "[a]way from its scene of production, Britain, English literature could, in the colonies, assume a fixed and more homogeneous nationalist cast."

To some extent, these explanations help to contextualize and explain why and how English discourse could regulate its play in Narayan's identification with and reception of it. It must be added, however, that in the modern 1940s, *The English Teacher* assumes a particular global, geopolitical dimension in its project to represent "India" to the West and the West-like in the West's own terms. Such a solidified materialist project would not have been possible in nineteenth-century India, where more fluid, contradictory and, correspondingly, more resistant readings of English discourse were occurring. The figure of Henry Derozio (1809-1831), for instance, comes to mind. A popular poet and teacher of English at the Hindu College in Calcutta, Derozio was a self-proclaimed practitioner of progressive Western ideals: he attacked outmoded Hindu religious practices and lauded both the Christian missionary work in India and the French Revolution. Fired by the Romantic ideals of Byron, Derozio reportedly rode through the streets of Calcutta on an Arab horse. Yet he was also a patriotic zealot: anti-British and outspokenly nationalist, he did not distinguish the political content of his penchant for Romantic poetry, did not ask how one might at once oppose and admire the British. His own poetry drew equally on Wordsworth and Hindu mythology.

The (De)nativization of English: Raja Rao's Kanthapura

Raja Rao is perhaps best known for the 1938 novel, *Kanthapura,* in which he undertakes an experiment with the English language, nativizing it to produce the rhythm and cadence of his mother tongue, Kannada. Unlike Narayan, Raja Rao directly engages the issues of nationalism and colonialism, whose imbrications produce the ground for conditions of modernity in the novel. In it, the occupants of a fictional village, Kanthapura, are catapulted into modern conditions of existence, due to the progressive elements of both Gandhi's noncooperation movement and his philosophy regarding the upper-caste practice of untouchability. In the postcolonial context, there is much of interest in this rambling yet experimental narrative. For instance, we see the deployment of a radical politics which reveals its own class-, caste-, and gender-based privilege as it mobilizes subaltern resistance to the colonial apparatus. We also see the complications of a liberatory discourse which reinscribes the power relations it has set out to undo, thereby mimicking, in advance, the conditions of neo-colonialism. Indeed, the novel's original scene of writing, the French Alps, and its subsequent appearances and (dis)locations—first, in 1938, nine years before Indian Independence, in London; second, in 1947, the year of Indian Independence, in Bombay; third, in 1967, in New York—testify to the significant discursive shifts within colonial and postcolonial exigencies.

But what is important here is the effective retainment of Rao's text within English determinants. Specifically, Rao's project to rewrite English gets (dis)placed onto what one may call the material scenes or sites of his text: publication, translation, reception, and glossing. Hence, the text marks a deferral of Rao's engagement with aspects of nationalism and colonialism; alternatively, one may say that his engagement with those aspects can only be understood as operating within the parameters of English discourse. As with Narayan, what needs emphasizing is the symptomatic way in which English discourse regulates its modern articulation in the period under question.

Embedded in a rural peasant past, the story of *Kanthapura* is narrated in the oral traditional style by a pious old Brahmin woman, whose "native" speech displays Rao's experimentation with English. The more or less predictable life of the villagers, their social hierarchies enforced by the topography of their village, are interrupted when the young Brahmin man, Moorthy, begins to spread Gandhi's non-violence campaign among them. Moorthy is especially adept at using Hindu scripture to awaken the villagers' political sensibilities. Interestingly, the characters he influences most are the upper-caste women, who not only come to forgive Moorthy his excommunicatory act in entering the houses of the "untouchables" but also join with him in trying to liberate the "untouchables" from their bonded labor. The end of the novel sees the village's ultimate disruption

and the dispersion of the villagers in other villages and towns, but the text implies that once the spark of justice and equality has been lit, there will be no turning back.

Outlined in this way, the text seems to espouse a radical position, according to which, as Anindyo Roy puts it, the "theme of social awakening combines aspects of Greek tragedy uniquely adapted to record one of the most significant moments in modern Indian history." Roy seems usefully to problematize this very statement as he introduces the conditions of displacement which interrupt the "meaning" of Rao's text: "Written in the French Alps, the novel reflects the diasporic consciousness of a writer yearning to capture the reawakened spirit of a real India, striving to establish its modern identity." Here, Roy highlights the particular desires—as opposed to their fulfillment—released within a diasporic space that is itself removed from the imagined source, "a real India."

A similar deferred transaction is evidenced almost as equivocation in Rao's famous foreword to the novel, in which he states: "We cannot write like the English. We should not. We cannot write only as Indians. We have grown to look at the large world as a part of us." English both is and isn't "an alien language"; it is the language of Indians' "intellectual make-up" but not of their "emotional make-up." Caught in the impossible space of a strained articulation which both is and isn't English, but which nonetheless is *in* English, Rao's text defers the promise of delivering a nativized English that is "really" Indian.

A representative passage from the text demonstrates the problematic nature of Rao's experimentation with English. The narrator speaks:

> Three days later, when we were just beginning to say Ram-Ram after the rice had been thrown back into the rice granary, the cradle hung back to the roof, and the cauldron put back on the bath fire, and the gods put back in their sanctum, and all the houses washed and swept and adorned and sanctified, and when one by one our men were slipping in and then hurrying back to their jungle retreats, what should we see on that Saturday . . . but one, two, three cars going up the Bebbur mound, one, two, three crawling cars going up the Bebbur mound like a marriage procession, and we all said, "why, whose marriage now, when we are beating our mouths and crying?"

We cannot help noticing that this entire passage consists of one long, prolix sentence. It utilizes repetition (e.g., "cradle hung back . . . cauldron put back . . . gods put back"; "one, two, three cars going up . . . three crawling cars going up") and, simultaneously, a generous scattering of Bakhtinian socioideological heteroglossia (e.g., the chanting of "Ram-Ram," the "rice granary," "the gods put in their sanctum," "beating our mouths," etc.) which highlight the native, rural, and cultural practices of the village.

No doubt Rao intends such passages to be comprehended as translations from the Kannada, both literally and figuratively. But larger theoretical questions engage this kind of experimentation by a writer who is himself geographically, socially, and epistemologically distanced from the subaltern characters he is attempting to represent: Who, for instance, is the "native" in Rao's text, and what is being nativized? Further, we may ask, who recognizes this nativization? Klaus Steinvorth points out that Indianizations are perhaps meaningful only in a Indian, not a Western, context. The narrator, who in an empirical context would not even speak English, is made to utter startlingly refined poetic phrases, with stylized alliteration ("crunch—cough—cane"; "paste—pickles"; "pit—plant"), assonance ("side"—"sign"—"mainstri"—"lime"; "much"—"crunch"—"touch"), symmetrically balanced phrases ("telling story after story"—"looking to this side and that"; "lime their betel leaves"—"twist the tobacco leaves"), and so on. Hence, Steinvorth suggests that by deploying a sophisticated, stylized English, Rao means to target a Western audience for whom his nativizations will work.

According to Feroza Jussawalla, Rao's nativizations are not only geared towards a Western audience but also problematic for that very audience. For Jussawalla, Rao's experimentation fails because Rao does not take into account India's actual multicultural and multilingual situation of *spoken* English and the fact that his English can never *be* Kannada itself. She relates an experimental study in which Professor K. S. Narayana Rao of the University of Wisconsin asked an American and an Indian in turn to read aloud from *Kanthapura.* The American reading registered a loss in the "meaning" of the passage, due to the American reader's unfamiliarity with the rhythms of Kannada; the Indian reading flowed more smoothly but was flat in its inflection and could "put off" a Western listener.

For our purposes, both Steinvorth and Jussawalla usefully highlight the material sites—of translation and reception—which situate English in relation to its larger discursive functioning. Hence, we may productively ask: Who or what constitutes the readership of early Indian literature in English? How is meaning produced in hegemonic contexts? However, in posing these questions, I depart from Steinvorth's and Jussawalla's implicit assumption that literature functions in a space that is susceptible to full meaning, that language is somehow adequate to both itself and its meaning. In fact, the mark of writing is such that it institutes both the grounds for its possibility in utterance and, simultaneously, its impossibility to fully or actually utter. As such, Rao's project to nativize English is, from the start, already implicated in and delimited by its failure. For in order to nativize English, he must also provide the de-nativizing indices which will render intelligible those instances of nativization to Western readers. Specifically, he must engage a nationalist agenda by nativizing English, but he must also provide a fifty-nine page glossary of terms as an appendix to the book which de-nativizes his nativizations.

What can be understood as a failure that always already inheres in language itself·is also what de-politicizes Rao's project. His extensive translations from Kannada *back* to English work to contradict and negate his experimentation; his nativizations prove, after all, to be de-nativizations offered for their anthropological curiosity to American readers. Prior to New Direction's American publication of the novel in 1967, its earlier editions (one in London, the other in Bombay) did not include this glossary. I gather this from New Direction's note at the beginning of the novel: "The author's notes on Indian terms and references . . . may be unfamiliar to American readers." With the fifty-nine-page glossary added on in a later, postcolonial, distinctly American moment, not only does *Kanthapura* retrospectively correct and qualify its experimental premise and nationalist agenda, it also tends to reproduce the sorts of Orientalist gesture that Edward Said examined in *Orientalism:* it puts the "East" at the service of the "West." Specifically, the glossary fosters a kind of anthropological curiosity on the part of American readers, according to which "alien" cultures are deciphered in Western terms. With regard to the discipline of anthropology itself, such appropriating gestures bear a particular charge, because the ideological position of the anthropologist is allowed a certain suspect invisibility in his or her study of other, "alien" cultures.

Quite unlike Narayan in **The English Teacher,** Rao directly engages the issues of nationalism and colonialism in *Kanthapura.* He poses these issues in his modern and modernist project to nativize English which, in a sense, is to claim English as his own "proper" language when it is adapted to the rhythm and cadence of Kannada. But when this avowedly nationalist project gets (dis)placed onto the material scenes or sites of publication, translation, glossing, and reception, Rao's political agenda is deferred and postponed, awaiting a resolution that itself can be seen as infinitely deferred. What emerges, instead, is the way in which his Orientalizing project persists within the domains of English and the material scenes of the project's production and reproduction.

It may seem that I have sketched a worst-case scenario for early Indian literature and that I have done so circuitously. But if my analysis seems at all negative, it is because I wish to avoid an uncritical celebration of these texts. It should not follow that the literature of the colonized is automatically exempt from the sort of critique one may apply to the literature of the colonizer. This is an especially valid statement when we take into account that the category "Indian literature in English" is caught up in the same systems of signification and currency as is the category "English literature." But this is not to say that early Indian literature does not suggest the possibility for resistance against the dominant paradigm. It certainly carries with it the trace of its difference from "English literature," and, if read actively, this trace would yield the ground for a critical intervention in the narrative of imperialism. Indeed, a continuation of this study of Narayan and Rao would dwell on the resistant moments in their texts. I will only indicate a few of these here.

Krishna/Narayan's tendency to indulge in not only the Western classics but also Indian literatures indicates a disorganized and indiscriminate reading, which productively opens up a site of difference (that is, the text is and isn't English). As well, Narayan's understated and distinctly ironic writing style consistently interrupts his narrative, always ensuring it more than one interpretation; in fact, a variety of interpretations, mutually contradictory, seem to be produced simultaneously. With Rao, a locus of resistance may reside in the very (dis)placements of his text, as it moves from one site of production and circulation to another. Further, the glossary which is intended to facilitate access to Rao's "alien" material itself produces difficulties: it is awkwardly organized, so that the text defies quick consumption; also, the glossary is by no means exhaustive, so that it highlights the nonglossed aspects of an immensely stratified Hindu culture.

If my argument seems at all circuitous, this is owing, in part, to the sign of modernity under examination: modernity is or implies both a condition of certain possibilities and the ways in which those possibilities might be realized. With Narayan and Rao, modernity is both a desirable condition of "being" and a method that is written into the process of achieving that condition. In other words, it is both the means and the end, and, as such, it is a category that is to be understood as overdetermined.

Perhaps we may posit that the relation of those Indian writers who were closest to colonialism and nationalism is mediated in greater or lesser degrees by their proximity to modern English discourse. It may even be said that their modernity is constituted precisely to the extent to which their colonial and nationalist identifications converge in the "field" of English discourse. This generalization prompts us to ask: what currently passes for nationalism, colonialism, and English discourse in the subcontinent and what counts for modernity there? If such formations as Hindu fundamentalism, neocolonialism, capitalist commodity production, and cable TV immediately come to mind, do

we pose the question of a violent disjuncture within post-Independence Indian history, or a re-enactment of the original "epistemic fracture of imperialism"? In any case, one may say that the determining aspects of imperialism in early modern Indian literature allow us to see precisely what is, in our own postcolonial, global moment, increasingly difficult to map out: namely, the linkages of a discourse to the dominant ideological and cultural practices of a nation and its institutions.

Teresa Hubel (essay date 1994)

SOURCE: "Devadasi Defiance and *The Man-Eater of Malgudi*," in *Journal of the Commonwealth Literature,* Vol. XXIX, No. 1, 1994, pp. 15-28.

[*In the following essay, Hubel explores the changing role of the devadasis caste in India by tracing Narayan's portrayal of them through the character of Rangi.*]

In 1947, after over 50 years of agitation and political pressure on the part of a committed group of Hindu reformers, the Madras legislature passed an act into law that would change forever the unique culture of the professional female temple dancers of South India. It was called the "Madras Devadasis (Prevention of Dedication) Act". Despite having the wholehearted support of the Indian women's movement of the time, the Act represented the imposition of androcentric values on a matrifocal and matrilineal tradition, a tradition which had for centuries managed to withstand the compulsions of Hindu patriarchy. The devadasis were eventually forced to give up their profession and their unusual way of life. But the dance itself was not lost. It was, instead, reconstructed as a national treasure. One of the consequences of the 1947 Act is that, today in India and all over the world, the temple dance, once exclusively performed by devadasis, is dominated by women of the upper castes.

What I intend to do in the following pages is to explore the much suppressed history of the devadasis through a reading of R. K. Narayan's novel *The Man-Eater of Malgudi.* It might seem strange to readers that I should press this wonderfully funny book into the service of my historical rescue because it is generally interpreted as a story about two male characters, Nataraj and Vasu. These characters are frequently understood as antagonists, with Nataraj symbolizing the harmony that Narayan is supposed to prefer and Vasu the chaos he apparently dislikes. There are alternative explanations. Fakrul Alam sees *The Man-Eater of Malgudi* as a "narrative of identification" in which Nataraj struggles to incorporate the aggressiveness and spontaneity of Vasu into his own personality until he is able to emerge at the end of the tale, after Vasu destroys himself, as a "new, self-assured protagonist". M. M. Mahood focuses on the novel's politics, reading the encounter between Vasu and Nataraj as one that re-enacts the social and psychological processes of neo-imperialism. And L. P. Sinha explicates its mythic dimensions. All of these writers offer us legitimate and exciting approaches to *The Man-Eater of Malgudi,* and my intention is not to supplant these readings. But I would like to join the conversation by shifting the perspective from the masculine to that of the typically neglected feminine as it is articulated by the novel's devadasi character, Rangi.

The history of the temple dancers infiltrates this novel through Rangi. Although never actually called a devadasi, she is alternately identified as a "public woman", "a woman of the temple", "a temple prostitute", "a dedicated woman", and "a dancing woman", all of which epithets point to this South Indian profession and heritage. These are, of course, some of the more neutral definitions of Rangi that the novel offers. She is also described as "irresistible", a "notorious character", "a perfect female animal", "the woman to avoid", "a goddess carved out of cinder", "the awful fleshy creature whom Sastri considered it a sin to look at", and in that unapologetic hyperbole so typical of Narayan's humour, "the worst woman who had ever come back to Malgudi". *The Man-Eater of Malgudi* is wildly ambivalent about Rangi, and it is by investigating this ambivalence, by tracing its foundations both inside and outside the text, that I hope to demonstrate the potential of this devadasi character to unsettle the dominant mythic, a historical, conservative and patriarchal flow of Narayan's narrative.

The devadasi, a Sanskrit term that literally means "servant or slave of god", has fuelled the erotically charged imagination of Western man for about 400 years. Her appearance in Western writing is congruent with Europe's imperialist expansion into India. We see her, therefore, in early imperialist travel memoirs often as an emblem of the wealth to be found in the East. This is certainly how Domingos Paes chooses to describe the devadasis he encountered while accompanying the Portuguese envoy to the court of Krishnaraya at Vijayanagar, a kingdom which ruled over South India in the sixteenth century. His gaze fixes on the gold and precious gems that these women display on their bodies when they dance, attend on the god, or sit and chew betel in the presence of the king's wives. This latter activity, he informs us, is apparently an honour granted only to the devadasis of Vijayanagar. These women obviously amaze him. He writes,

> It surely is a marvel that women of such a profession should obtain such wealth; for there are some among them who have had lands presented to them and litters and maid-servants without number. One woman

in this city is said to possess 100,000 parados, about £25,000, and I can believe this from what I have seen.

It is clear from this passage that for Paes the temple dancers were extraordinary not only for their prosperity, since the king's wives also displayed such extravagant affluence, but for the prosperity that they achieved by means of what seems to him to be prostitution. Paes was one of the first of a long line of writers—European and Indian—to label the devadasis prostitutes. That this label does not fit snugly the community of devadasis that he saw in Vijayanagar is evident from his expressions of astonishment.

Towards the end of the eighteenth century, when, after thirty years of residence in South India, Abbé Dubois wrote his *Description of the Character, Manners, and Customs of the People of India,* he was undoubtedly following Paes's lead, for he too unabashedly assumes that the devadasis are prostitutes. And because of his ecclesiastical leanings, his assessment of their sexual behaviour is necessarily contemptuous. He calls them "strumpets" and "loose females" and uses adjectives like "lascivious" and "obscene" to characterize their singing. But there's more than simple disdain at work here, for at times the tone of his writing approaches bafflement:

> They [the devadasis] are bred to this profligate life from their infancy. They are taken from any cast [sic], and are frequently of respectable birth. It is nothing uncommon to hear of pregnant women, in the belief that it will tend to their happy delivery, making a vow, with the consent of their husbands, to devote the child then in the womb, if it should turn out a girl, to the service of the Pagoda. And, in doing so, they imagine they are performing a meritorious duty. The infamous life to which the daughter is destined brings no disgrace on the family.

Although the Abbé seems loathe to admit it, implicit in his depiction of the temple dancers is their honorable acceptance by the greater Hindu community of the late eighteenth century. And even the Abbé himself ultimately concedes that these women have their excellences. They are, he tells us, graceful dancers, they are elegant and refined in their public conduct and "decently clothed". When he compares them with "women of their stamp in Europe", whose "gross indecencies" and "lascivious airs" are "capable of inspiring the most determined libertine with disgust", the reader begins to suspect that the devadasis represent a much more alien experience than his Christian belief structures can accommodate.

Although an equally but differently complicated figure for many Indian observers, the devadasi was nevertheless accorded a significant role in Hindu society prior to the mid-twentieth century. Texts on classical Indian dance from the 1950s up to the present day assure the reader that her profession was a highly regarded one. The typical picture of the devadasi in these books shows her fulfilling her temple duties—dancing, singing, and performing various religious rituals—while living out her life in a house inherited from her mother and situated in one of the four streets surrounding the temple. The devadasi was also granted tax-free land in exchange for her temple service, and it was from the cultivation of this land by agricultural labourers that much of her income was derived. We also see her as the glamorous and skilfully seductive companion (and sexual partner) of men of the upper classes. Reginald Massey and Rina Singha construct her along these lines in their history of Indian dance:

> It is plain . . . that these devadasis were women of means. But this was not their only valuable possession. They were highly educated and polished in their manners and so able to provide their patrons with intellectual stimulation. This is the main reason why men of rank and learning resorted to them, as their own wives, being mainly confined to hearth and home, were sadly lacking in those qualities. It was, therefore, the accepted thing for these gentlemen to support such women privately, or to hire them from the temples:

The devadasis, then, are often depicted as the rivals of more conventional women, particularly Hindu wives. Before we endorse such an image, however, we should also acknowledge that the patriarchal structures in place during the centuries long history of the temple dancers' culture affected the polished mistresses as well as the stay-at-home wives. Both groups of women had their choices and rewards determined by an overarching paternalist ideology and authority, and both contrived their own resistances to it. The scope for resistance and the possibility of self-sufficiency was, however, wider for the devadasis because their tradition was matrilineal, a situation which inevitably leads to the unusual valuing of the female over the male. Still, it would be shortsighted to assume that any group existing within an economy dedicated to the preservation of the interests of upper class men would be able to evade entirely its masculine priorities.

My essay has, until this moment, presented the devadasi culture as homogeneous. Beryl De Zoete writes that there were, in fact, many categories of devadasis. Some categories designated the manner of their dedication to the temple—whether they offered themselves for service, were sold to the temple, or "given as an endowment . . . covered in jewels and rich in accomplishments"—and others indicated that they were paid regular wages as dancers, singers, and musicians. Massey and Singha delineate two other

devadasi distinctions, *valangai* or right-hand and *idangai* or left-hand. The *valangai* were permitted by custom to consort with or dance for only the upper or right-hand castes, while the *idangai* catered to left-hand castes, which Massey and Singha identify as artisans. The devadasis, then, did not constitute a perfectly uniform people. They differentiated themselves according to their function in the temple, their status at the time of their dedication, their prescribed sexual partners and audiences, and even their regional affiliations. It is important to recognize the diversity existing in the devadasi community so that we do not fall into the error of assuming that they were all wealthy and privileged women who consorted solely with the affluent classes of the Hindu elite. Although neither De Zoete nor Massey and Singha ventures into the bleaker world of the kidnapped girl sold to the temple against her will or the devadasi who eked out a living among poorer peoples whose fortunes, along with hers, rose and fell in accordance with apparently uncontrollable forces such as droughts, floods, and wars, these presences hover below the surfaces of their historical reconstructions. Any inquiry into the practices of these women must be careful not to see only those devadasis that the early imperialists saw—the immensely advantaged ones. For by doing so we erase those disadvantaged people whose lives are so often forgotten in our academic texts and discussions, and this is surely an act of intellectual imperialism, which reinscribes the hierarchies established by all previous imperialist projects.

We can say with some certainty, however, that devadasis, whatever their station or circumstance, shared a reputation for auspiciousness. Married to the deity of the temple in a ceremony that often resembled an upper-caste wedding, the devadasi acquired the title of *nitya sumangali*, which dance historian Ragini Devi translates as "eternally married". The significance of that special position in Hindu society has been examined by Amrit Srinivasan in a recent article, the focus of which is the more privileged devadasis of Tamil Nadu who at one time had liberal access to the elite classes and perhaps could be said to belong to those classes themselves. She maintains that the temple dancer entered secular society as *nitya sumangali*, which meant that she could expect to be received with respect and courtesy into the Hindu community outside the temple precincts. Not only did she pursue her dance career in this environment, but she was also invited to the homes of the wealthier families of her locality, where she participated in those ceremonies that were usually reserved only for the *sumangalis* or married women of the household, that is, she sang songs at weddings and puberty ceremonies, received new bridegrooms and their relatives, and tied the customary red beads on to the marriage necklaces of the families' daughters: "As a picture of good luck, beauty and fame the devadasi was welcome in all rich men's homes on happy occasions of celebration and honour. Her strict professionalism made her an adjunct to conservative domestic society not its ravager." Srinivasan further asserts that being *nitya sumangali* and dedicated to the temple deity also meant that the devadasi was not expected to perform those household tasks that were the province of her conventional counterpart in the society at large. She did not cook or clean for any men, not for her own brothers and uncles, who frequently lived in the same house as she, nor for her male dance guru.

Srinivasan's decidedly positive depiction of the temple dancers, and her determination, evident from the above quotation, to reclaim that tradition from those who would condemn the devadasi as the "ravager" of her people obviously has a history. Indeed, she wrote her ground-breaking essay as a reaction to the currently popular conception of the historical devadasi as a corrupted woman performing a degraded art form, a conception that had been propagated, moreover, by the very circles that initiated the destruction of this profession in the late nineteenth century, the English-educated Hindu middle and upper classes. It was this section of the population that had been most influenced by the Western perception of the devadasi as prostitute, which was doubtless the legacy of such writers and judges as Paes and Dubois.

In 1892 a group from these classes, which called itself the Madras Hindu Social Reform Association, launched the Anti-Nautch campaign, the purpose of which was to abolish all forms of professional dancing traditionally practised by women. (The word "nautch" is an anglicized version of a number of Indian vernacular terms derived from the Sanskrit root *nac,* meaning dance.) These reformers had clearly been persuaded by the Western/Christian classification of dancing women as prostitutes, and were further responding to pressure from the British government in India, which had (in spite of its official policy of non-interference at the time) also denounced the dancers during a number of publicized court cases involving devadasis. Moreover, they were products of an increasingly powerful social and political community that was determined to eliminate from Indian and particularly Hindu society those practices which they believed were detrimental to India's development as a nation: many of these reformers were, not surprisingly, nationalists as well. It is significant that most of the customs they attacked—child marriage, polygamy, sati, the Hindu convention of disallowing widow remarriage, and the devadasi tradition—involved what they perceived as the mistreatment of women and girls. While there is no doubt that most of these customs constituted serious gender oppressions, their refusal to distinguish between the culture of the temple dancers and such horrendous acts as the marrying of prepubertal girls to grown men is, nevertheless, questionable. For what this tendency to lump together all manner of feminine activities and func-

tions suggests is that the reformers were, consciously or unconsciously, passing their judgments from a stance that homogenized women. That stance was a staunchly androcentric one, and I would argue that the success of their efforts, at least in regard to the devadasis, was the result of the emergence of a new kind of patriarchy, which was becoming more and more prevalent in India as the nineteenth century drew to a close.

This new patriarchy, unlike the older variety alongside which it existed, not only narrowed the roles that women were permitted to play in society, valorizing their positions as wives and mothers, it also paved the way for the ascendancy of an urban middle-class prototype of woman. Coming as it did from the husbands and fathers of middle-class women who lived in cities, this growing ideology was interested in the feminine merely as it existed in relation to the masculine: its purpose was to produce wives and mothers who would be better companions for the young, English-educated men of the rising middle class. Women's alliances with one another, their relationships to god, their personal commitments to their physical, moral, spiritual and professional selves were relegated to the realm of the unimportant as the priorities of the predominantly male, urban, middle-class social reformers began to hold sway. Thus, although the reformers insisted that they were dedicated to freeing women and girls from the cruel customs of the older and more established Hindu patriarchy, they had simply invented a new male-centred system into which women of all castes and traditions would be made to fit. In *Feminism and Nationalism in the Third World* Kumari Jayawardena arrives at a similar hypothesis: "Since all area of social reform concerned the family, the effect of the reforms may have been to increase conservatism and, far from liberating women, merely to make conditions within the family structure less deplorable, especially for women of the bourgeoisie."

The last thing I would want to do is to glorify the Hindu patriarchy that existed during the ages before the middle class rose to power in the nineteenth century. A belief structure that called for the burning of widows or their permanent withdrawal from the joys of life is hardly commendable. But this pre-modernization patriarchy did seem to acknowledge and tolerate a broader range of roles for women. Within it, some women flourished who were not wives or who chose to live outside the paternalism of conventional domestic arrangements, such as the wandering ascetic and poet Mirabai, the female bhakti saints, the girls and women from the nayar matrilineal caste of Kerala and, of course, the devadasis. One of the problems with any patriarchy is that the good fortune and freedom of some women is often predicated on the abuse of others.

The dilemma that the devadasis faced when confronted by

the reformers and anti-Nautch campaigners was that they were *not* "women of the bourgeoisie". They did not share the middle-class belief in patrilineal descent nor its sexual mores nor even its conception of women as primarily keepers and managers of households. As I have already mentioned, the acts of dedication to the temple and marriage to god precluded the performing of domestic tasks. So extraordinary were the devadasis in terms of the construction of woman engendered by the reformers that they could not be made to conform to this paradigm without their distinctive ways of life being entirely destroyed. That the complete eradication of the devadasi culture was, in fact, the aim of the reformers is evident in a statement made by women's activist Muthulakshmi Reddy in 1927 when she first moved a bill in the Madras legislature to outlaw temple dedication. She said that she hoped that once they were released from their service to the temple, the devadasis "would become virtuous and legal wives, affectionate mothers and useful citizens." Her basic assumptions here demonstrate her allegiance to the middle-class doctrines of the anti-Nautch campaign. She suggests that, given devadasi practices, they could not possibly be "affectionate mothers and useful citizens" and, furthermore, that it is preferable to be a "legal" wife than to be a god's wife. In Reddy's estimation, "legal" wives have the monopoly on virtue.

Although the anti-Nautch campaign had seriously discredited the temple dancing women of South India, causing a public suppression of their culture decades before the Act actually became law in 1947, the passing of the "Madras Devadasis (Prevention of Dedication) Act" marked the end of the devadasi tradition. Disgraced and thrown out of the temples, the devadasis watched as the women from the high castes took over their dance on behalf of a newly independent Indian society that was eager to preserve its ancient artistic heritage.

When Narayan published *The Man-Eater of Malgudi* in 1961, the devadasis had been officially dispossessed for 14 years. Through the character of Rangi, the novel charts the effects of that dispossession. Narayan's devadasi is a woman on the very edges of Malgudi's Hindu society. Living "in the shadows of Abu Lane", Rangi is clearly from a family that has come down in the world, and she herself is the symbol of that decline. We are told by Nataraj, the narrator and protagonist, that her mother, Padma, was a dancer attached to Malgudi's Krishna temple: "Padma herself had been an exemplary, traditional dedicated woman of the temple, who could sing and dance, and who also took one or two wealthy lovers: she was now old and retired." Though there is some attempt to depict Padma as ruined in her old age, the narrator's tone is generally approving or neutral when he speaks of her. But her daughter, despite having inherited her mother's profession, is considered "notorious", Rangi's personal biography is filtered through the

double mediation of Nataraj recounting details that he has learned from his employee. Sastri, who lives not in the "shadows" but in Abu Lane proper:

> . . . she had studied in a school for a while, joined a drama troupe which toured the villages, and come back to the town after seducing all the menfolk she had set eyes on. According to Sastri, she was the worst woman who had ever come back to Malgudi. She was the subject of constant reference in Abu Lane, and was responsible for a great deal of the politics there.

The story of Rangi raises a number of uncertainties. First, we immediately suspect its veracity and the appropriateness of its implicit attitudes because it is so obviously exaggerated and is delivered to us by Rangi's greatest opponent, the ultra conservative Sastri. Second, the novel gives us no explanation for the difference between the town's denunciation of Rangi and its acceptance of Padma. Neither woman is married, both are or have been dancers associated with the temple, and both have taken more than one lover, and yet Rangi is unquestionably a pariah in a way that Padma is not. It is only when we have recourse to the history of the devadasis that this part of the story makes any sense.

Rangi is a product of the reformers' campaign to eradicate temple dancing in South India, which means that the ancient institutionalized protections of devadasi ways of life are no longer operating in Abu Lane. Having lost the support of the Hindu society in general, Rangi has consequently become this middle-class neighbourhood's victim. Her practices are the subject of disparaging gossip and her life's experiences are mocked. As a fatherless woman who is not a wife or a mother and because she chooses to conduct her sexual life without the social sanction of marriage, Rangi is a marginalized figure in Malgudi, and it is this circumstance, created by a combination of history and intolerance, that makes her available to Vasu, the rakshasa whose lawlessness comprises the principal theme of the novel. But while Vasu is clearly an outsider, Rangi is not. Her status is liminal; she belongs to Malgudi, but only just. The result of this positioning is that, unlike Vasu, Rangi has a stake in the town's future and past. And this stake adds weight to her significance in the text. The novel is not able to shrug off the implications of this temple dancer's defiance and degradation as easily as it dismisses the threat that Vasu poses. Moreover, what we can tease out through an analysis of the representation of Rangi is a critique of Nataraj's middle-class community and its values.

The prevalence of marriage stories in the novel suggests that, for the people of Malgudi, wedlock is a state of much importance. Nataraj is constantly concerned with the condition of his marriage as one event after another leads him to fear for its survival, and Muthu, the mahout, and Vasu, all have some opinion on the subject. Even the poet's monosyllabic epic about Krishna and his milkmaid lover Radha ends with a wedding celebration, though this legend typically focuses on the god's passion for his human beloved to such an extent that marriage in the Krishna tales usually seems beside the point. (Some stories about Krishna assert that he never married Radha at all.) What the marriage stories have in common, other than the fact that they are all recounted by men, is that they construct marriage as a relationship involving the husband's dominance and the wife's submission.

Narayan does not, however, encourage the reader to believe that this is an acceptable situation, and the most potent criticism of marriage as it is practiced in Malgudi comes from Rangi the devadasi. Although she never explicitly condemns marriage, her refusal to participate in it makes her a living illustration of an alternative model for women. We know that this is indeed a refusal, and not simply an inability because of her staunch defence of her "*dharma*" (which can be understood here as duty or prescribed course of life) when Nataraj, believing the gossip about dancing women, accuses her of taking opium: "Sir, I am only a public woman, following what is my *dharma*. I may be a sinner to you, but I do nothing worse than what some of the so-called family women are doing. I observe our rules. Whatever I do, I don't take opium." Rangi is certain that the manner in which she lives is entirely in accordance with the rules of her tradition and that these rules are perfectly legitimate. Moreover, the novel lets her justification stand. Nataraj's conscience-stricken reaction to her indignation—"I felt apologetic for uttering so outrageous a remark"—seems to offer support to Rangi's convictions and, further, points to the possibility that there is or should be a place in Hindu community for a woman like her.

She has clearly, then, opted out of an institution that the middle class in the novel imposes on women unforgivingly and in doing so has escaped the oppressions inherent in being married in a androcentric society, though she has also incurred its disdain and suffered its punishment of marginalization. But there are rewards for rebellion: Rangi is independent in a way that the wives can never be. Not having to rely on men for shelter, protection, or emotional fulfilment, and having already received patriarchy's penalty for nonconformity, she is free from the stricture of such an insecurity-ridden passion as jealousy. When Vasu brings other women to his room, expecting her to "quarrel with them", Rangi simply dismisses his actions: "Let any man do what he fancies. I don't care what anyone does, so long as he doesn't dictate to me what I should do." If we contrast this reaction to infidelity with Nataraj's wife's fierce jealousy after Rangi visits them at their home, we come to

realize how exceptional Narayan means to make his temple dancer. She is truly a woman of radical differences.

There is a pattern, then, in the novel's treatment of Rangi: it enshrines these differences at the same time that it gently chides Hindu society for its assumptions about unusual, overtly sexual women like her. Nowhere is this more humorously achieved than in the scene where the "notorious" temple dancer confronts the strait-laced printer in the back room of his print shop in the middle of the night. She has crept down from the attic room, where Vasu is sleeping, to persuade Nataraj to stop the gun-toting rakshasa from shooting Kumar the elephant. The reader watches as Nataraj, who is exhausted from working late on the first edition of the poet's epic and who has already experienced strong stirrings of arousal in Rangi's presence, is tossed between desire and resistance. In Nataraj's mind, Rangi becomes a female figure of immense power, a woman "ready as it seemed to swallow me up wholesale, to dissolve within the embrace of her mighty arms all the monogamous chastity I had practised a whole lifetime." Here is where we begin to understand that perhaps Rangi is more of a threat to Nataraj than Vasu is. For she jeopardizes both his status in the community, as Vasu does, and the stability of the domestic world. We are left with no doubt that his wife would somehow punish him were he to have sex with the temple dancer.

The encounter between a highly sexualized woman and a man determined to resist her has a long history in ancient Hindu literature. In the *Puramas* and the epics, the *Mahabharata* and the *Ramayana,* time and again we see dangerously desirable women setting out to beguile men from their more significant pursuits. Surabhi D. Sheth describes the typical situation.

> The picture one gets from the Puranic literature is of a man awaiting his fate as a prey of woman's physical charms and lacking any kind of inner control. At the same time, the image of woman which is projected is of a seductress trapping the man as if against his will. . . . It is probably for this reason that greater emphasis is placed on external controls in these stories as well as in codes of sexual behaviour. . . . Internalised controls were considered too difficult to cultivate given the kind of attitude the Puranic man betrayed towards woman's sexuality. Hence woman is blamed for *causing* sexual desire in man. . . .

The "external controls" that the *Puranas* endorsed often involved the destruction or the victimization of the *femme fatale.* Rambha was turned to stone when she dared to tempt the sage Vishvamitra, and when the gods, Mitra and Varuna, lost some of their semen at the mere sight of

Urvahsi, she was cursed to be born on earth. Sheth argues that the foundations for India's current patriarchy were laid in ancient Indian literature and that, therefore, the lives of women today in India are partially controlled by entrenched paradigms like the one quoted above. If this is the case, then Narayan is replicating in his novel an archetypal situation that has a very powerful hold on the minds of Hindu people. But this allusion in *The Man-Eater of Malgudi* does not function merely as a signal to Indian readers that they are in the realm of myth and scripture. I would argue, in fact, that Narayan uses the paradigm in order to undermine it. And he does this by showing us that Nataraj's desire for Rangi does not have its *source* in the charms of the devadasi. Not once does Narayan suggest that Rangi is to blame for her admirer's attentions or lusty thoughts. On the contrary, he portrays her as absolutely indifferent to Nataraj's desire. Her only response to his sexual hysteria is "Are you going to save that elephant or not?" What the ancient authors missed about this repeated drama between various men and various sirens—that the problem was not women's sexuality but, in Sheth's words, "man's own obsession about his sexual autonomy"—Narayan recovers through the character of Rangi.

In her connection to the displaced devadasis of India's history and in her disrupted connection to the fabled temptresses from the ancient epics and *Puranas*, Rangi brings a historicity to *The Man-Eater of Malgudi* that calls into question a prevailing view among critics concerning Narayan's apolitical bent. It is true that a straining towards myth is evident in the manner in which Vasu, the modern-day rakshasa, is conveniently eliminated in the end, thereby freeing Nataraj and the town from having to come to terms with his anti-sociability, and that in his final treatment of Rangi, Narayan refuses to confront the political implications of his portrait of this temple dancer suffering from the vicissitudes of history. She is, when last we see her, an almost forgotten woman, who cringes in a corner during the police investigation into Vasu's death, looking "jaded in a dull sari, with unkempt hair." Earlier in the story, Rangi's perpetual state of "*déshabillé*" had elicited in Nataraj plenty of passion. Now it only contributes to the overall picture of her powerlessness and humiliation. The Bhasmasura myth is also rewritten on the novel's closing page and what is excised from it is any mention of woman's contribution to the annihilation of the demon. In its original rendering, Sastri acknowledges the cleverness and labour of the goddess Mohini (Vishnu in his seductive female form) in tricking Bhasmasura through a kind of "Simon says" game into touching his head with his world-destroying hand and thus destroying himself. The missing Mohini at the end of the novel corresponds to the degraded Rangi, and we can surmise from this that Narayan is not prepared to take his criticism of middle-class Malgudi to its farthest

extreme: he colludes, finally, in that society's dismissal of the temple dancer.

Nevertheless his earlier criticism stands. Rangi, the devadasi who lives "in the shadows of Abu Lane", who takes men as lovers rather than husbands, who refuses to play the role of willing seductress assigned to her by the ancient literature of her country, remains a figure of difference in the novel. And while Narayan in the end sends her back to the edges of her society, he cannot get rid of her altogether.

As an indicator of historical change, Rangi can be compared to others among Narayan's women characters—Daisy, Savitri, Rosie, and Bharati, all of whom share with her a responsibility to their particular historical moments. Through Savitri, we learn about the anguish of wifehood in the 1930s, when women began to ask for something better than what conservative Hindu marriage could offer them: Bharati is the new Indian woman emerging from out of the last years of colonial rule and the imperatives of the nationalist movement; Rosie, another devadasi, demonstrates the reconstruction of the temple dance in the wake of Independence, its transformation into an art for public stages; in Daisy we see a woman responding to the effects of overpopulation; and Rangi, as this essay has argued, presents the consequences of the anti-Nautch campaign and the prevention of dedication act. They are made to bear on their persons and in their experiences the marks of Indian history. Narayan's fiction is not, therefore, as repressively timeless as critics tend to suggest. It is just a matter of looking for the political and the historical in the right places.

This examination of *The Man-Eater of Malgudi* has attempted to recover the historical devadasi. But I must finally admit that she is not recoverable. I cannot make her speak to you, not with the texts of dance history and anthropology nor with Narayan's fiction, because although the devadasi did indeed exist and a number of them are still alive in India today, her presence is not reproducible in words. What you hear in these pages is not her but only me sympathetic to her. In her excellent review article entitled "Recovering the Subject: *Subaltern Studies* and Histories of Resistance in Colonial South Asia", Rosalind O'Hanlon uncovers and questions one of the predominant myths at the heart of academic study—that the struggle of the intellectual to understand and write about the forgotten or neglected peoples of history is coterminous with the struggles of these same people to be heard by us:

> We may wish in all faith for their freedom from marginality and deprivation, and do our best to cast our insights in a form which they will be able to use. But if we ask ourselves why it is that we attack

historiography's dominant discourses, why we seek to find a resistant presence which has not been completely emptied or extinguished by the hegemonic, our answer must surely be that it is in order to envisage a realm of freedom in which we ourselves might speak.

This essay has served for me as that "realm of freedom".

Tone Sundt Urstad (essay date Summer 1994)

SOURCE: "Symbolism in R. K. Narayan's 'Naga,'" in *Studies in Short Fiction,* Vol. 31, No. 3, Summer, 1994, pp. 425-32.

[*In the following essay, Urstad discusses Narayan's juxtaposition of modern life and Hindu mythology in the short story "Naga."*]

R. K. Narayan is generally acknowledged as the most outstanding of the three major Indian authors writing in English to emerge in the 1930s (R. K. Narayan, Mulk Raj Anand, Raja Rao). His works have been described as "an original blend of Western method and Eastern material." His material is "Eastern" not just in the sense that he describes Indian characters in an Indian setting, but in the way that he uses references to Hindu mythology and the Indian epics to lend depth to his own works. He has what Britta Olinder has called "a singular power of joining his fresh and humorous view of the ordinary world with the deeper meaning and larger perspectives he finds in the mythical treasures of his own religion." In *The Man-Eater of Malgudi,* for instance, the comic conflict between the good-natured but ineffectual Nataraj and Vasu, his taxidermist lodger, is on a deeper level a struggle between the forces that sustain life and those hostile to life. The struggle is brought to a happy conclusion because Vasu, like the *rakshasa* to which he is compared, carries within him the seeds of his own destruction.

Narayan's basic technique of ironically juxtaposing scenes of modern life with the exploits of gods, demons, and heroes of old, is well known and, in the case of some of his novels, well documented. **"Naga"** shows to what effective use Narayan can also put the same basic technique within the tighter form of the short story.

"Speaking for myself," Narayan has said, "I discover a story when a personality passes through a crisis of spirit or circumstances." A character "faces some kind of crisis and either resolves it or lives with it." **"Naga"** certainly conforms to this simple pattern. A young boy faces two crises. When the story begins, he has already lived through the first one. Abandoned by his father, he has been forced to face life on his own. He has discovered that he has sufficient knowledge to carry on the family trade of snake charming, performing with Naga, the cobra the father has left behind. The story starts at a point close to the second crisis, which occurs when Naga—old and tired—has become a burden. The boy tries unsuccessfully to rid himself of his dependent by setting him free, only to find that Naga cannot survive on his own. The boy finds that he is incapable of purchasing his own liberty at the price on Naga's life and resumes responsibility for the snake. This is a variation on a theme that often appears in Narayan's works: an individual's impulse towards greater independence or individuality is hampered by forces within his immediate or extended family. Naga is family, as the father has made clear: "He is now own of our family and should learn to eat what we eat."

> **A basic knowledge of Hindu mythology is indispensable to an understanding of most of Narayan's works. . . .**
> *—Tone Sundt Urstad*

When the father abandons his son, he takes with him the "strumpet in the blue sari" and the performing monkey, and leaves behind in the hut the wicker basket containing Naga. The interpretation of the short story hinges partly on the answer to one question: why does the father leave the serpent rather than the monkey for his son? After all, when they performed for people, the father and the cobra functioned as one team, and the boy and the monkey as another. One could, of course, see the father's decision in terms of a selfish act: he takes the monkey because its earning power is far superior to that of the cobra, leaving his son to fend for himself as best he can (whereas the monkey is "popular," the father has to go through with his snake act "unmindful of the discouragement" initially met with from householders). Somehow this interpretation of the father's motives does not quite agree with the facts as we know them. The father is not described as an evil man. Admittedly, when under the influence of alcohol, he handles his son roughly. He also, by all accounts, has bad taste in women. However, in the few brief glances that we are given of him at the beginning of the story, he is presented as a sympathetic character. He teaches his son respect for animals; he shows imagination in is conversations with the child and a certain amount of sensitivity in his dealings with the animals. He has taken care of his son during the years of total dependence and has taught the boy his own trade, thereby ensuring that the child will one day be able to stand on his own feet. That the boy can, in fact, manage on his own is proven by events.

How, then, are we to interpret the father's act of leaving Naga—already an old snake and soon to become a burden—for the boy, while making off with the commercially viable monkey himself? After all, we are told that "the boy never ceased to sigh for the monkey. The worst blow his father had dealt him was the kidnapping of his monkey." At this point, one of the story's most striking features takes on a deeper significance: the use of names, or lack of them. The main character is known simply as "the boy"; neither the father nor the father's new consort has a name; her former husband and/or pimp is described only as "a hairy-chested man"; the neighbor who informs the boy of what has happened and who tries to comfort him is simply "a woman," and so on. There is a significant contrast here between the human beings, none of whom has a name, and the animals, who do: Naga, the snake; Rama, the monkey; Garuda, the kite. This serves to focus attention on these names, forcing the reader to consider the special significance that attaches to them.

A basic knowledge of Hindu mythology is indispensable to an understanding of most of Narayan's works, and this short story is no exception. Naga means, quite simply, "snake." Since ancient times snake divinities, known as "nagas," have been worshipped in India. In Indian architecture nagas are represented as beings with halos consisting of an uneven number of expanded cobra hoods.

The nagas are basically benign deities. They are guardians of the life-giving moisture of the earth, and dwell at the bottom of ponds and rivers and seas, where they are thought to have their own underworld realm (*Nagaloka*) full of beautiful palaces. Nagas are also thought to live among the roots of trees, since a tree is living proof that there is water in the ground. Because of their connection with the moisture in the earth, nagas are also the guardians of all metals and precious stones in the ground.

The nagas have a reputation for wisdom and knowledge and are associated with the act of protection. On Hindu and Buddhist monuments—one of Narayan's special interests—nagas are often depicted as worshipping and even protecting the gods and their incarnations. There are several old myths that illustrate this protective function. When the Buddha, after the Enlightenment, fell into a state of meditation that lasted for several weeks, the great naga Muchalinda protected him from the inclemencies of the weather by coiling itself around him and spreading its hood over his head like an umbrella.

The nagas protect not only superior beings but also mere mortals. Nagas live close to humans and, in some areas, have become popular household patrons. They are numbered among "the guardians of life" who together have the power to bestow on human beings "all the boons of earthly happiness—abundance of crops and cattle, prosperity, offspring, health, long life."

From the beginning of the story, it is clear that the father looks upon Naga not just as an ordinary snake, but as a serpent deity. To his audience he describes a snake as "a part of a god's ornament, and not an ordinary creature," referring specifically to images of Vishnu, Shiva, and Parvati. Voicing a widespread popular belief, he asserts that a serpent is "a great soul in a state of penance." The father expects great things from Naga, telling the boy,

> We must not fail to give Naga two eggs a week. When he grows old, he will grow shorter each day; someday he will grow wings and fly off, and do you know that at that time he will spit out the poison in his fangs in the form of a brilliant jewel, and if you possessed it you could become a king?

Again the father is voicing popular beliefs. A naga was supposed to carry a precious jewel in its head, and was often willing to grant jewels and other boons to deserving mortals. There is no reason to think that the father does not literally believe that Naga will eventually provide for his son's material welfare.

This image of Naga as a future dispenser of wealth is later reinforced by that of Naga as the protector of precious metals when the father leaves 80 paise in small change for his son, placed—significantly—on the lid of Naga's wicker basket. Naga's function as protector of coins is ironically alluded to in the boy's plans to sell Naga's skin "to the pursemakers" if the snake dies. Even the location of the hut is significant. It belongs to a "colony of huts, which had cropped up around the water fountain," situated "beside the park wall, in the shade of a big tamarind tree"—just the kind of place where one might expect to find a naga. Since he functions as a kind of household deity, Naga must obviously remain with the property that he protects, even after the little household has split up.

Clearly the father's motive in leaving Naga with the boy was a wish to obtain protection, in every sense of the word, for his son. The associations of the naga with protection in one form or another are very strong in Hindu mythology. If Narayan had wished to avoid these associations, surely he would have found a more neutral name for the snake. Instead he actually named the story after this "character."

The irony of all this is, of course, that Naga is quite simply a snake and thus vulnerable, and once he becomes old and sluggish he proves incapable of protecting even himself, let alone the boy. This becomes evident when the boy tries to set him free. Naga is oblivious to the threat to his life from the Brahmani Kite Garuda flying high above, "its shadow almost trailing the course of the lethargic snake." The boy sees that Naga is incapable of surviving on his own and resumes responsibility for him. Thus the protector becomes the protected as the boy and the snake reverse roles, and the boy reaches a new stage in his development towards greater maturity when, no longer protected by his father, he takes on the involuntary role of protector of his dependent, Naga.

It is noteworthy that although the boy sees unblinkingly that Naga is just a worn-out old snake, he also sees Naga partially with his father's eyes, as something more than just that. The boy's last words to Naga show that he still thinks of the snake both as serpent and divinity: "If you don't grow wings soon enough, I hope you will be hit on the head with a bamboo staff, as it normally happens to any cobra. . . ." On a more subtle level, we notice it in the way the boy talks to Naga when he lets the snake loose in a lonely spot with many "mounds, crevasses and anthills":

> You could make your home anywhere there, and your cousins will be happy to receive you back into their fold. . . . You should learn to be happy in your own home. You must forget me. You have become useless, and we must part. I don't know where my father is gone. He'd have kept you until you grew wings and all that, but I don't care.

The mention of Naga's "cousins" and "their fold," the repeated references to Naga's "home," and, a little further on in the paragraph, to Naga's "world," do not merely allude to the fact that an attempt has been made to return Naga to nature. Within the context of the naga myths it is clear that the boy wishes the snake to return to the realm of the nagas, *Nagaloka,* with its bejeweled palaces and comfortable life, which, it is believed, can be reached via anthills and caves.

Notwithstanding the fact that the boy also thinks of Naga as a serpent deity, we see that Naga means two different things to the father and the boy. For the former, Naga represents protection for his son; but for the latter, the snake represents unwanted responsibility. Naga causes unnecessary expense in the form of food and stands between the boy and total liberty of movement. As long as the boy is responsible for Naga he will be unable to realize his dream of perhaps getting on a train "someday and out into the wide world."

For the boy there is an opposition between Naga and Rama, just as the two are described as incompatible because the snake terrifies the monkey when it rears itself up. While Naga means age and dependence to the boy, the monkey represents youth and freedom. When Rama first turns up he is described as "a tiny monkey gambolling amidst the branches of the tamarind tree," the boy watching "with open-mouthed wonder." He says, "Father, I wish I were a monkey. I'd never come down from the tree." Subsequently we hear of the monkey's "endless antics," and even after the monkey is caught, taught to perform, and made to wear clothes, he is described in terms of playfulness and spontaneity. In the evenings, when his clothes are removed, Rama does "spontaneous somersaults in sheer relief." Early in the mornings he performs "many fresh and unexpected pranks." Even during performances the monkey does not only act rehearsed scenes, but does "what was natural to him—tumbling and acrobatics on top of a bamboo pole."

What does the monkey represent to the father? Again, the man follows standard Hindu mythology when he says that Rama is "gentle and wise." Monkeys are also symbols of wealth and fertility, and it is therefore appropriate that the father, setting off for his new existence together with the new woman in his life, should bring the monkey with him. Significantly, in northern India, the monkey-warrior Hanuman "presides over every settlement, the setting up of his image being a sign of its establishment." Just as Naga protects the established household, the monkey protects the new settlement. Significantly, a new trained monkey features prominently in the boy's dreams for a new life.

The father names the monkey "Rama," after the avatar of Vishnu who is the hero of the *Ramayana,* explaining: "Rama, name of the master of Hanuman, the Divine Monkey. Monkeys love that name." In this way the basic story of the *Ramayana* is evoked: how Rama sets out to find and bring back his wife Sita, the model of wifely fidelity and modesty, who has been abducted by the evil king of Lanka, Ravana. In his quest Rama is joined and helped by Hanuman and his monkey warriors. Together they defeat Ravana and bring back the virtuous Sita. In **"Naga,"** one of the tricks that Rama the monkey performs for the spectators is to "demonstrate how Hanuman, the Divine Monkey of the *Ramayana,* strode up and down with tail ablaze and set Ravana's capital on fire." All of the references to the old epic, with its heroic tale of courage, ideal love and virtue, serve to create an ironic background to the sordid details of the father's relationship with the "strumpet in the blue sari." In this modern tale of love the hero, whose lack of courage makes him avoid any confrontation with the "hairy-chested man," sets out accompanied by his monkey to liberate a latter-day Sita who is a prostitute (she stands at the door of her house "like a fixture") from a Ravana who is her husband and/or pimp. This Sita, who calls her lover's child "bad mischievous devil, full of evil curiosity," is certainly no model of chastity and purity.

In the passages that describe the boy's attempt to set the snake free, Narayan alludes to other Hindu myths that help to deepen our understanding of the boy's predicament. The scene is Nallappa's Grove (In Tamil Nallappa means "good father," an implied compliment to the boy for his handling of his dependent). When the boy sees that Naga is in imminent danger of being killed by the bird Garuda, he offers this touching prayer: "You are a god, but I know you eat snakes. Please leave Naga alone."

In Hindu mythology Garuda, the sun bird, is constantly at war with the nagas, who symbolize the life-giving waters, acting out the unremitting conflict between the sun and the water in a hot climate. In this battle Garuda is the stronger since the sun dries up the moisture in the earth. On the other hand, the serpents are thought to be tenacious of life (typically, Naga refuses to die). One myth relates how Vishnu rescued an elephant captured by the nagas. He came on his mount Garuda, but no battle was necessary because the nagas immediately fell down and worshipped their lord. At Puri in Orissa people who have been bitten by snakes are brought to a pillar in the temple and made to embrace the figure of the Garuda.

Vishnu is thus the lord of Garuda, which carries him through the air, but also of the nagas since he reclines upon the cosmic serpent Ananta. As "the Absolute, the all-containing Divine Essence," Vishnu must take up into himself all dichotomous aspects of life.

In Hindu mythology the opposition between Garuda and the nagas is seen in terms of the opposition between the sun and the water. In Western thought, however, the bird symbolizes "father Heaven . . . the unfettered far-flying celestial bodies . . . the spirit freed from the bondages of earth . . . divine eternal being." The serpent, on the other hand, represents mother Earth and a life tethered to worldly considerations. This is an opposition that Narayan clearly makes use of to lend depth to the ending of the story. Naga and Garuda are acting out the age-old battle for survival, in which Naga would not stand a chance without the boy's protection. At the same time, the bird "sailing in the blue sky" symbolizes complete freedom, unhampered by responsibilities and other earthly considerations, while the snake, on the other hand, symbolizes a life bound to the earth. The boy is forced to make a choice at this point, and, since he is not ruthless enough to sacrifice Naga, he remains bound by the snake's dependence on him. He is unable to do to Naga what his father did to him because, unlike the boy, Naga is incapable of surviving alone, while, unlike his father, the boy is not driven by a sufficiently strong human need to override the consideration.

It is in this context that Narayan's decision to give names to the animals but not to the human beings must be seen. Through the ancient myths evoked by the names of the animals, Narayan constructs a mythical framework within which the humans merely act out age-old patterns and conflicts: the tension between the father's duty towards his offspring and his own sexual and (perhaps) emotional needs, differs only in degree from the conflict in the boy's

mind between duty toward a dependent and a desire for personal freedom from responsibility. These tensions are only variations of an eternal pattern of life in which there will always be a conflict between the Sun-bird and the snakes, and in which Vishnu is lord over both Garuda and the nagas.

Shashi Tharoor (review date 11 September 1994)

SOURCE: "Comedies of Suffering," in *New York Times Book Review,* September 11, 1994, p. 40.

[*Tharoor is the author of* The Great Indian Novel *and* Show Business. *In the following review, he praises the stories in Narayan's* The Grandmother's Tale *as "interesting and often pleasurable," but complains of the banality of the author's prose.*]

"Some time in the early 30s," Graham Greene recalled, "an Indian friend of mine called Purna brought me a rather traveled and weary typescript—a novel written by a friend of his—and I let it lie on my desk for weeks unread until one rainy day." The English weather saved an Indian voice: Greene didn't know that the novel "had been rejected by half a dozen publishers and that Purna had been told by the author . . . to weight it with a stone and drop it into the Thames." Greene loved the novel, **Swami and Friends,** found a publisher for it in London, and so launched India's most distinguished literary career of recent times, that of Rasipuram Krishnaswami Narayan.

The author, now 87, went on to publish 25 more books, including 12 more novels. This year he was awarded a literary prize in India for outstanding lifetime achievement by a South Asian writer. The jury's citation declared Mr. Narayan "a master storyteller whose language is simple and unpretentious, whose wit is critical yet healing, whose characters are drawn with sharp precision and subtle irony, and whose narratives have the lightness of touch which only a craftsman of the highest order can risk." In the West, Mr. Narayan is widely considered the quintessential Indian writer, whose fiction evokes a sensibility and a rhythm older and less familiar to Westerners than that of any other writer in the English language.

The Grandmother's Tale: And Selected Stories appears in this country at the culmination of Mr. Narayan's long literary career. Fortunately, it effectively showcases all of his many strengths, as well as his considerable limitations.

The title story was published in India in 1992, by the author's own press, Indian Thought Publications, as a novella with illustrations by his cartoonist brother, R. K.

Laxman. Mr. Narayan's American publisher, rightly judging that *The Grandmother's Tale* did not have the heft to stand on its own, has dispensed with the drawings and added instead a selection of Mr. Narayan's best short stories culled from the last five decades of his work.

The old favorites are all here: the classic tale **"An Astrologer's Day,"** perhaps his most famous and widely anthologized short story, about an astrologer coming face to face with the man he thought he had murdered years earlier; **"A Horse and Two Goats,"** a hilarious account of the encounter between an American tourist and a desperately poor and illiterate Indian peasant, though one in which the joke is stretched to the breaking point; **"The Blind Dog,"** about a blind man and his dog, a moving meditation on free will, dependence and greed; and **"Emden,"** an affecting story of an old man reaching out for elusive wisps of his past.

In other stories, an aspiring woman novelist finds that her husband's recipes are more publishable than her fiction; a judge acquits the defendants in a murder trial when a monkey in a temple makes off with his glasses; a village storyteller loses his narrative gift and summons his audience to hear his most important story. Though there are some that seem merely anecdotal or half-realized, this collection represents Mr. Narayan at his best as a consummate teller of timeless tales, a meticulous recorder of the ironies of human life, an acute observer of the possibilities of the ordinary: India's answer to Jane Austen.

But they, and the stories that accompany them in this collection, also point to the banality of Mr. Narayan's concerns, the narrowness of his vision, the predictability of his prose and the shallowness of the pool of experience and vocabulary from which he draws. Like Austen's, his fiction is restricted to the concerns of a small society portrayed with precision and empathy; unlike Austen's, his prose cannot elevate those concerns beyond the ordinariness of its subjects. Mr. Narayan writes of, and from, the mind set of the small-town South Indian Brahmin, but his writing does not suggest that he is capable of a greater range.

The gentle wit, the simple sentences, the easy assumption of the inevitabilities of the tolerant Hindu social and philosophical system, the characteristically straightforward plotting are all hallmarks of Mr. Narayan's charm and help make many of these stories interesting and often pleasurable.

Yet Mr. Narayan's metronomic style is frequently not equal to the demands of his plots. Intense and potentially charged situations are rendered pathetic by the inadequacy of the language used to describe them. The title story, an autobiographical account of the author's grandmother, abandoned by the man she had married as a child, who travels hundred of miles and brings him back 20 years later after befriending and betraying his second wife, hints at extraordinary possibilities. But it is told in flat, monotonous sentences that frustrate rather than convince, and in a tone that ranges from the clichéd to the flippant.

The author has said in interviews that he is indifferent to the wider canon of English fiction and to the use of the English language by other writers, Western or Indian; indeed, his indifference is something of which he is inordinately proud. He says he doesn't read modern fiction: "I avoid every kind of influence." This shows in his writing, but he is defiant: "What is style?" he asked one interviewer, "Please ask these critics to first define it. . . . Style is a fad."

The result is that he uses words as if unconscious of their nuances; a distraught girl, who faces social ostracism and fears her husband dead, "threw a word of cheer to her mother and flounced out of the house." "Flounced" is a favorite Narayanism; it recurs in a man "slapping a face and flouncing out in a rage." Flowers grow "wildly" when the author means "wild"; a man whose wife and daughter upbraid him in indignation protests, "Everyone heckles me"; a village medicine man is called a "local wiseacre," though Mr. Narayan does not intend to be disparaging. Clichés and banalities abound—"kith and kin," "spick and span," "odds and ends," "for aught it mattered," "caught his fancy" and a proliferation of "lest"—as if the author learned them in a school textbook and is unaware that they have been hollowed by repetition. Mr. Narayan's words are just what they seem; there is no hint of meanings lurking behind the surface syllables, no shadow of worlds beyond the words. Indeed, though he writes in English, much of his prose reads like a translation.

Such pedestrian writing diminishes the stories, underlines the characters, trivializes the concerns: it confines R. K. Narayan to the status of an exotic chronicler of the ordinary. And it is not only the language that seems impervious to the existence of a wider world. Mr. Narayan's writing is blissfully free of the political clashes, social conflicts and historic upheavals that dominated Indian life during the more than half a century of his career, yet it is authentic in reflecting faithfully the worldview of a self-obsessed and complacent Brahmin caste. "I write primarily for myself," Mr. Narayan has said. "And I write about what interests me, human beings and human relationships. . . . Only the story matters; that's all." Fair enough: one does not expect Austen to be Orwell. But one does expect an Austen to enrich the possibilities of language, to illuminate the tools as well as the craft. Mr. Narayan's is an impoverished English, limited and conventional, its potential unexplored, its bones bare.

And yet—and yet. How can one fail to be charmed by an

illiterate gardener's pride at mastering the telephone? ("In distinguishing the mouthpiece from the earpiece, he displayed the pride of an astronaut strolling in space.") Or by a storekeeper's prattle about baldness? ("God gives us the hair and takes it away when obviously it is needed elsewhere, that is all.") Or to admit the aptness of Mr. Narayan's un-self-conscious description of villagers who "never noticed their surroundings because they lived in a kind of perpetual enchantment"? There is enchantment in Mr. Narayan's world; his tales often captivate, and perhaps one should not pay too much attention to their linguistic surroundings.

The world that emerges from these stories is one in which the family—or the lack of one—looms as the defining presence in each character's life; in which the ordinary individual comes to terms with the expectations of society, and in which these interactions afford opportunities for wry humor or understated pathos. Because of this, and because of their simplicity, the stories have a universal appeal, and are almost always absorbing. They are also infused with a Hindu humanism that is ultimately Mr. Narayan's most valuable characteristic, making even his most poignant stories comedies of suffering rather than tragedies of laughter.

In this joyous and frustrating book, the author has given himself the last word. "The only way to exist in harmony with Annamalai," his narrator says of a servant, "was to take him as he was, to improve or enlighten him would only exhaust the reformer and disrupt nature's design." Even the most grudging critic would not deny R. K. Narayan this self-created epitaph.

Hilary Mantel (review date 16 February 1995)

SOURCE: "Real Magicians," in *New York Review of Books*, Vol. XLII, No. 3, February 16, 1995, pp. 9-11.

[*In the following excerpt, Mantel discusses the inhabitants of Narayan's* The Grandmother's Tale and Selected Stories *and how the author presents them with humor.*]

Some years ago, in an essay called **"A Writer's Nightmare,"** R. K. Narayan imagined himself a citizen of a strange country called Xanadu, where the government printer had made a grave error; five tons of forms meant for the controller of stores had been turned out with the heading "controller of stories." Five tons of paper is no mean amount, and an official must be invented to make use of it. Perhaps, indeed, this is a matter in which government should have interfered before?

The Government has observed that next to rice and water, stories are the most-demanded stuff in daily life. . . . Every moment someone or other is always asking for a story.

And so there is to be a Central Story Bureau, with four directorates, one each for plot, character, atmosphere, and climax. Authors contemplating a story would have to fill in a form, obtain a treasury certificate, submit a synopsis, and obtain authorization. Unauthorized story tellers would be fined. Bad story tellers would have their ink bottles smashed. . . .

R. K. Narayan is a writer of towering achievement who has cultivated and preserved the lightest of touches. So small, so domestic, so quiet his stories seem; but great art can be very sly. Born 1906, publishing his first book in 1935, he is generally acknowledged to be India's greatest living writer. His writings span an age of huge social change, and in his stories and novels, set in the imaginary town of Malgudi, he has built a whole world for his readers to live inside. Graham Greene said, "Narayan wakes in me a spring of gratitude, for he has offered me a second home. Without him I could never have known what it is like to be Indian."

Can we know, if we are not? For the non-Indian reader, part of the fascination of Narayan's work is that he can make his world familiar to us—and yet within that familiarity, the exotic is preserved. He can do this because he has such a sharp eye. He never takes anything for granted: that this must be so, should be so, has always been so. Life surprises him; he allows himself to be surprised. Any day, any street, any room in an accustomed house, any face known since childhood, can suddenly be fresh and strange and new; one reality peels away and shows another underneath.

Most of the nineteen stories in *The Grandmother's Tale* are set in or around Malgudi, or a place very like it. It is Anyplace, really: to villagers it is a vast metropolis, but of little account to those used to the sophistication of Madras. Luckily for us, it is peopled by gossips, bystanders, doorstep lurkers, and window-peerers. No one really has a private life; every street contains a by-the-way nephew, a remote uncle, or roundabout cousin, all of them with flapping ears and a loud mouth. The people of Malgudi are insurance clerks, photographers, shopkeepers, doctors, beggars, astrologers, and professional exorcists. Their wives rise at dawn to cook for them, scold and harry them through their days, and wait up at night to berate them and give them hot drinks.

One surprising wife, in **"Salt and Sawdust,"** writes a novel. The hero is to be a dentist—an original touch—who has trained in China, which accounts for many odd facets of his character. He falls in love with the heroine while he is making her a new set of teeth, though how she lost the originals is exterior to the text. Fact and fiction get mixed up in the nightly discussions Veena holds with her husband. They plan lavish meals for the characters and write out the recipes. Veena's novel finds no substantial public, but she becomes a best-selling author of cookbooks and travels the country giving popular demonstrations. It is a result gratifying and disappointing in equal measure.

Dreams, aspirations: that is what Narayan deals in. Small men, and small women, have great ambitions inside them. The illiterate knife-grinder in **"The Edge"** wants his daughter to be a "lady doctor." He lives on handouts of food and sleeps in a derelict building so that he can send money back to her, though his wife wants to take her away from school and get her earning a living in the fields. Another story, **"A Horse and Two Goats,"** is about Muni, a starving goatherd—who has only two goats left. He engages in a comical transaction with an American tourist, who wants to buy a statue of a horse and rider which stands on the outskirts of the poor man's village. Finding the goatherd crouching under the horse's belly seeking shade, the redfaced stranger decides that Muni must be the statue's owner. He offers money; Muni is at first baffled, but concludes the man is trying to buy his goats. After all, has he not fattened the animals against the day when some fool will come along with a wallet full of rupees, and make him an offer for them? It is a dream come true.

"Carry them off after I get out of sight, or they will never follow you, but only me. . . ," Muni advises; but since he and the American do not have a word of any language in common, the mutual mystification runs its course. While Muni is at home gloating over his money and boasting to his wife, the American carries off the statue in his truck. Muni is stunned when, that night, the unwanted and abandoned goats bleat their way home to his door. Next morning, when he wakes, he will have more, and less, and just the same, as yesterday.

It is an empty enterprise to single out stories in this collection, to claim that they do this or that in particular. Narayan does not bother to wrap up his tales neatly. Life goes on, the stories flow on, one into another, as if tributaries could loop back and feed the greater stream. Only the title story is a little disappointing. The narrator, a would-be writer, coaxes out of his grandmother the story of her own mother, Bala, married at seven to a boy of ten. The boy disappears, having followed a gang of pilgrims who were passing through his village; when Bala grows up she decides to track him down. She takes to the road, begging when necessary, surviving all manner of dangers, and at last finds him, a prosperous man married to another woman. The story of Bala's journey, and of how she traps and manipu-

lates her husband into coming home with her, has many piquant details, but it must be said that Grandmother is not a natural storyteller, and we grow impatient with her vagueness and the gaps in her memory, however true-to-life her deficiencies are.

Elsewhere, as ever, the master is in charge of his material—his hand delicate, his methods douce. His characters, self-absorbed, are often blind to real events, and stalk the town by the light of their own egos. They are touchy, raw-nerved people, yet often grossly insensitive to the feelings of others; perhaps we all suspect ourselves of this failing, and with some reason? Narayan is the bard of marital strife. Paradoxically, it is the details that make for universality. Are married people's quarrels the same, all the world over? Time after time, you come across conversations you could swear you have heard, from your neighbors beyond the bedroom wall. Then the horrible realization strikes: Have I myself, perhaps, said such things? And had them said to me? Such absurd things—so passionate and so meant and so howlingly funny?

Narayan's humor almost defies analysis—but not quite. He can make you laugh out loud, but he never imposes a joke—all the humor arises from character, and much of it from the self-importance and the affectations of his people. There is always someone lurking—a wife or a donkey, a cat or a dark room—that will cut the pompous down to size. Yet the fun is very gentle, and predicated on absurdity, on the careful observation of workaday human foolishness. Unforgettable is the old man—formidable in his day, but not feeble—who takes the same walk every afternoon:

> Before six-thirty, he would be back at his gate, never having to use his torch, which he carried in his shirt pocket only as a precaution against any sudden eclipse of the sun or an unexpected nightfall.

At the heart of Narayan's achievement is this: he respects his characters, respects their created natures. This is why he can make jokes about them and stay friends with them. In one story after another he offers them a change of fortune, a change of heart. He allows them insights, illuminations, epiphanies, yet he does not despise their unenlightened, less fortunate state. There is nothing cozy about his fiction. He may be gentle, but he is too clever to be bland. What he depicts is a complex, plural, ever-changing society. As his characters are so strange to each other, is it a wonder that they are fresh and new to us? In **"Annamalai"** a man employs a gardener who begs him to take down a signboard on his gate that bears his name:

> "All sorts of people read your name aloud while passing down the road. It is not good. Often urchins and tots just learning to spell shout your name and run off

when I try to catch them. The other day some women read your name and laughed to themselves. Why should they? I do not like it at all." What a different world was his where a name was to be concealed rather than blazoned forth in print, ether waves, and celluloid!

In Malgudi and environs, cause and effect do not operate as in the West. Reality looks quite different where horoscopes govern lives—yet fate is partly negotiable. Bureaucrats, too, have their own lunatic rules, yet each man and woman, self-willed and go-getting, is at one time or another a master or mistress of destiny. Seldom has an author been less of a puppet-master; within the country Narayan has invented for them, his people live freely. They live on close terms not only with their neighbors, with the stray dogs in the street, the donkeys who stand about the fountains, but with their memories and their gods. Celebrant of both the outer and inner life, he makes us feel the vulnerability of human beings and of their social bonds. Here is the town with its daylight bustle, its hawkers, beggars, shoppers, porters: outside, and within, are the deep forests, where tigers roar in the night.

FURTHER READING

Criticism

Alam, Fakrul. "Plot and Character in R. K. Narayan's *The Man-Eater of Malgudi:* A Reassessment." *Ariel* 19, No. 3 (July 1988): 77-92.
> Analyzes the relationship between Nataraj and Vasu in Narayan's *The Man-Eater of Malgudi* and its effect on the novel's plot.

D. B. "A World Filled With Love." *New York Times Book Review* (25 December 1955): 10.
> Favorably compares Narayan's *Swami and Friends* and *The Bachelor of Arts* to the work of other novelists, such as H. G. Wells.

Getlein, Frank. "The 'Little Life' of Everyman." *The Commonweal* LVIII, No. 5 (8 May 1953): 126.
> Discusses the everyday nature of life, with all its pitfalls, described in Narayan's *The Financial Expert.*

Hardin, Nancy Shields. "Mysore/Malgudi: R. K. Narayan's World of South India." *Missouri Review* VI, No. 3 (Summer 1983): 125-38.
> Discusses the relationship between Narayan's real home of Mysore with his fictional world of Malgudi, and the place of his Indian heritage in his work.

Kirpal, Viney Pal Kaur. "An Analysis of Narayan's Technique." *Ariel* 14, No. 4 (October 1983): 16-19.
> Explores the deceptive simplicity of Narayan's writing.

Mathur, O. P. "Two Modern Versions of the Sita Myth: Narayan and Anand." *Journal of Commonwealth Literature* XXI, No. 1 (1986): 16-25.
> Compares and contrasts the way Narayan and Mulk Raj Anand reinterpret the Sita myth of Indian mythology.

Moynahan, Julian. "India of the Imagination . . ." *New York Times Book Review* (15 July 1990): 8.
> Favorably reviews Narayan's *The World of Nagaraj* and asserts "R. K. Narayan's world conveys a deep humanism quite rare in contemporary writing."

Sunitha, K. T. "The Theme of Childhood in *In the Castle of My Skin* and *Swami and Friends.*" *World Literature* 27, No. 2 (Autumn 1987): 291-96.
> Analyzes the cultural differences which influenced Narayan and George Lamming and how the authors presented the childhood consciousness in *Swami and Friends* and *In the Castle of My Skin*, respectively.

"Well Met in Malgudi." *Times Literary Supplement* 57, No. 2932 (9 May 1958): 254.
> Praises Narayan's body of work, calling *The Guide* "one of his best" and asserting that much of Narayan's success derives from his skillful use of English.

Towers, Robert. "Breaking the Spell." *New York Review of Books* XXXIV, No. 15 (8 October 1987): 45-7.
> Complains that "One finishes [*Talkative Man*] with the impression that R. K. Narayan is relying upon his well-known charm and ease of manner to lull his reader into accepting a rather slight comic sketch in the place of a deeper, fuller work."

Additional coverage of Narayan's life and career is contained in the following sources published by Gale: *Contemporary Authors,* **Vols. 81-84;** *Contemporary Authors New Revision Series,* **Vols. 33, and 61;** *DISCovering Authors Modules: Novelists; Major Twentieth-Century Writers; Short Story Criticism,* **Vol. 25; and** *Something about the Author,* **Vol. 62.**

Robert Pinsky

1940-

American poet and essayist.

The following entry presents criticism of Pinsky's career through 1998. For further information on his life and works, see *CLC,* Volumes 9, 19, 38, and 94.

INTRODUCTION

Named poet laureate of the United States in 1997, Pinsky is a poet-critic whose writings resist the categories of American contemporary poetry. Admired for its blend of vivid imagery and clear, discursive language, his poems explore such themes as truth and memory, cultural and individual history, and the transcendence of seemingly ordinary acts. Pinsky strives to create an organized world view by confronting the past in terms that would bring clarity to the present. His moral tone and mastery of poetic meter have been favorably compared to that of eighteenth- and nineteenth-century poets, and his critical insights about the theoretical function of poetry in the world as presented in his analytical works squarely situate him in the tradition of such other poet-critics as Samuel Taylor Coleridge, Matthew Arnold, T. S. Eliot, and W. H. Auden. Pinsky's literary fame also derives in part from his accomplishments as a translator, whose version of the first part of Dante Alighieri's *Commedia* (c. 1370-c. 1314), entitled *The Inferno of Dante* (1994), has garnered wide acclaim and numerous awards. Katha Pollitt has remarked of Pinsky that "here is a poet who, without forming a mini-movement or setting himself loudly at odds with the dominant tendencies of American poetry, has brought into it something new."

Biographical Information

Pinsky was born October 20, 1940, in Long Branch, New Jersey. Since his grandfather owned the local tavern, and his father had an established optometric practice, the Pinsky family enjoyed a measure of local prestige. Although he was not an accomplished student in school, Pinsky attended Rutgers University, where he associated with other young writers and poets who considered their literary apprenticeships to be beyond the pale of creative writing programs and professors' judgments. After graduating from Rutgers in 1962, Pinsky entered Stanford University, where he held Woodrow Wilson, Wallace Stegner, and Fulbright fellowships. While there Pinsky studied with the noted poet, critic, and instructor Yvor Winters and earned a Ph.D. in 1966. He briefly taught humanities at the

University of Chicago before he accepted a position as associate professor of English at Wellesley in 1968. A Massachusetts Council on the Arts grant provided the impetus to publish his first book of poetry, *Sadness and Happiness* (1975), which promptly was followed by his first volume of critical commentary, *The Situation of Poetry* (1976). From 1978 to 1986 Pinsky also served as poetry editor of *The New Republic*. With the publication of the book-length poem *An Explanation of America* in 1980, Pinsky left Wellesley for an English professorship at the University of California at Berkeley, where he remained until 1988. During the 1980s Pinsky completed another poetry collection, *History of My Heart* (1984); collaborated on translations of Nobel Prize-winning Polish poet Czeslaw Milosz's *The Separate Notebooks* (1985) and on a computerized novel called *Mindwheel* (1985); and published another book of criticism, *Poetry and the World* (1988), which was nominated for the National Book Critics Circle award in criticism. After the publication of *The Want Bone* (1990), Pinsky finished *The Inferno of Dante,* which won the *Los Angeles Times* Book Award for poetry and the Howard Morton Landon Prize for translation. In

1996 Pinsky issued a collection of both old and new poetry, *The Figured Wheel.* Since 1989, Pinsky has taught creative writing at Boston University and currently serves as poetry editor of *Slate,* an online magazine.

Major Works

Both *The Situation of Poetry* and *Poetry and the World* articulate his belief in linguistic clarity as the means to expand the boundaries of poetic expression. These works also acknowledge the role and significance of literary tradition in modern poetry. *The Situation of Poetry* presents Pinsky's views on the nature of poetry which emphasize the continuity of contemporary poetry with the poetic tradition of the past. The essays comprising *Poetry and the World* expand his concept of poetry, including a series of articles on the impact words have had on his own life. Pinsky's poetry follows the principles outlined in his criticism. Characterized by vivid imagery and a clear, straightforward voice, his poetry covers diverse subjects by using expansive narratives which are both intellectually stimulating and optimistic in tone. Pollitt has suggested that among Pinsky's "greatest accomplishments is the way he recoups for poetry some of the pleasures of prose: storytelling, humor, the rich texture of a world filled with people and ideas." *Sadness and Happiness* contains short lyrics, reminiscences, semi-dream poems, and long meditations, the latter exemplifying the form at which Pinsky excels. Noteworthy in this collection is the 17-page poem "Essay on Psychiatrists," which alludes to various cultural and literary references to the modern science. Similarly, *An Explanation of America,* one of Pinsky's most ambitious and strongest poems, forms a long, unified meditation on American history. Addressing his daughter, the narrator attempts to describe America's past so that she could use his knowledge to fulfill the promise of the future. Pinsky's subsequent collections continue to examine history—sometimes national, sometimes personal. The title poem of *History of My Heart,* for instance, presents a lyrical evocation of memory and desire in the form of an autobiographical narrative that draws upon Pinsky's life experiences but refrains from sentimentality. The poems of *The Want Bone* feature a pastiche technique marked by overt word-play which symbolizes and reveals a lust for life and a desire for sensual experience. The volume also features mock biblical stories about Jesus's childhood, including an extended prose narrative in which a disguised Jesus enters the story of Tristan and Isolde so that he can learn about love. *The Inferno of Dante* simulates the terza rima rhyme scheme of the original by using "slant-rhymes," a scheme based on like-sounding consonants at the ends of lines in each tercet. Pinsky's translation attempts to preserve Dante's intended meanings by expanding or compressing a literal translation of the original Italian.

Critical Reception

Esteemed by most for his abiding respect of literary tradition, Pinsky has earned critical acclaim for his intelligent appraisals and knowledge of his subjects. Scholars have observed that the intellectual virtuosity of Pinsky's criticism challenges readers, obliging them to uncover the intricate arguments beneath his lucid, plain language and imagery, yet by adopting a common, almost conversational tone his theories are readily comprehensible. Often extolled for his grasp of traditional metrical forms and his evocation of universal meaning within the confines of contemporary idiom, critics have applauded Pinsky's ability to reveal the wonder of common images and the hidden order behind the accidental events of ordinary life. Reviewers also have admired his poetry for its juxtaposition of personal experiences with universal feelings, of the past with the present, and of the minutiae of the self with the largest philosophical concerns of history, culture, and art. Pollitt has noted that "the poems of his maturity manage their startling shifts and juxtapositions in ways that give intellectual and sensuous delight." Although most commentary about his translation skills has recognized the ease and accessibility of his language, particularly praising his evocation of Dante's "vulgar eloquence," some have found Pinsky's syntax stilted or, in the case of his Dante translation, that his slant-rhyme scheme lacks the "momentum" of the original terza rima. Still, critical opinion about Pinsky's writings seems to be indicated by his nomination as poet laureate. According to Elizabeth Mehern, "in Pinsky's view, poetry is the people's art form, and Pinsky, in turn, is content to bear the mantle of the people's poet."

PRINCIPAL WORKS

Landor's Poetry (essays) 1968
Sadness and Happiness (poetry) 1975
The Situation of Poetry: Contemporary Poetry and Its Traditions (essays) 1976
An Explanation of America (poetry) 1979
History of My Heart (poetry) 1984
Poetry and the World (poetry and essays) 1988
The Want Bone (poetry) 1990
The Inferno of Dante: A New Verse Translation [translator] (poetry) 1994
The Figured Wheel: New and Collected Poems, 1966-1996 (poetry) 1996

CRITICISM

Robert Pinsky with Harry Thomas, et al. (interview date 2 February 1993)

SOURCE: "A Conversation with Robert Pinsky," in *TriQuarterly,* Vol. 92, Winter, 1994-95, pp. 21-37.

[*In the following interview, which was conducted originally on February 2, 1993 in Thomas's classroom at Davidson College, Pinsky discusses the art of translation, the cultural ways Judaism affected him personally, the influence of Eastern philosophies in his poems, and the transformative, historical aspects of his poetics.*]

[Jim Knowles:] *There's an essay by Seamus Heaney called "The Impact of Translation" in which he starts out with a translation by you. He talks about the problem a poet writing in English might have when he realizes that the kind of poem he is struggling to write has been written already in some other part of the world.*

[Robert Pinsky:] The poem is "Incantation," by Czeslaw Milosz, with whom I worked on various translations. Not long after Czeslaw and I had done the translation, Seamus was over to the house and I read it to him. He was struck by the same quality in it that I was. The poem is very explicit and quite, one might say, moralistic or idealistic. Could a poet in English, I thought, particularly an American poet, write such a poem? It's quite short; I'll read it to you:

"Incantation"

Human reason is beautiful and invincible.
No bars, no barbed wire, no pulping of books,
No sentence of banishment can prevail against it.
It establishes the universal ideas in language,
And guides our hand so we write Truth and Justice
With capital letters, lie and oppression with small.
It puts what should be above things as they are,
Is an enemy of despair and a friend of hope.
It does not know Jew from Greek or slave from master,
Giving us the estate of the world to manage.
It saves austere and transparent phrases
From the filthy discord of tortured words.
It says that everything is new under the sun,
Opens the congealed fist of the past.
Beautiful and very young are Philo-Sophia
And poetry, her ally in the service of the good.
As late as yesterday Nature celebrated their birth,
The news was brought to the mountains by a unicorn and an echo.
Their friendship will be glorious, their time has no limit.

Their enemies have delivered themselves to destruction.

Seamus has quite complex things to say about this poem. First, he admires it rather eloquently, and then he says something like, on the other hand, this is a poem that one can imagine being written by a prelate or somebody at the seminary on the hill, some literate and bromidic Catholic: someone of intelligence and good will who isn't really hip to poetry.

Instead, "Incantation" is, somehow, a truly wonderful poem. In a way, you can say that the most difficult thing to do in a poem is to present ideas, abstract ideas of this kind, this explicitly, and attain strong emotion. And perhaps the implication is that parts of the world that have experienced totalitarian regimes are fertile ground for this kind of direct approach, while our own good fortune in not having experienced war on our terrain for over a hundred years, nor having experienced a totalitarian regime or a police state, makes us less capable of such writing.

I don't think Seamus says that, in fact, although he takes up the idea. Milosz's own opinion of that idea is interesting—he says this is like envying a hunchback his hump. He considers it a very silly sentimentality on the part of Western writers, romanticizing or idealizing the situation of the artist in extremely oppressive political circumstances. Certainly, if there is a kind of writing we admire and would like to emulate in relation to our own woes and desires, that is up to us. A lot of American poets were disappointed, as I was, that the first poet to read at a presidential inauguration since Robert Frost, Maya Angelou, read something that lacked exactly the kind of cogency or depth or impact or precision that distinguishes the abstractions and noble sentiments of "Incantation" from the clichés of journalism or from what Seamus's imaginary seminarian might write. Ms. Angelou's poem was on the side of goodness, but lacked the passion of art; considered as a work of art it had the vagueness and figurative muddle of plausible journalism at some times and the awkwardness of mere public speaking at others. But that doesn't mean it can't be done who knows, by Ms. Angelou next time out, or by the poet laureate Mona Van Duyn, or whoever. Like everything else in art, it can't be done only until someone does it.

And the Heaney essay is quite subtle on the question, as I remember, and not easily paraphrased—he says something like, such writing depends immensely upon context. He says I read it aloud to him—he describes the house, he describes the moment, he's a Catholic writer of one generation thinking about Milosz, a Catholic writer of another generation; Seamus is from a country torn by violence and Milosz is from another country torn by violence, in short there's a whole context that made him especially receptive to the poem: and I think he's raising a question about context, rather than proposing to envy the hunchback his hump. It's a good essay, a wonderful essay, and I would not attempt to summarize it. I see you're nodding, so you'd agree with me that he doesn't exactly say we can or we can't write in this way.

[Jim Knowles:] *Right. I don't think the essay says that it's impossible to write a poem like this, but Heaney does seem to say that there's a trap we fall into when we try to write a poem that sounds like a translation.*

Yes. Yes. But I think we did a good enough job of translating "Incantation" that this translation doesn't sound like a translation, which therefore makes me think about this poem in some of the ways that I think about any poem in English that I admire. That first sentence and line—"Human reason is beautiful and invincible"—I believe I thought something like: damn it, I wish I had thought of that: and "that" could hardly mean the idea or sentiment. It must mean something more like, I wish I had found that mode and written that sentence; or, I wish I had heard that imagined music of meaning, I wish I had played that, made that sound. Which again I take to mean that it was possible: it was there to be written. The reason I couldn't have written this poem has to do with all the same reasons that I didn't write "Sailing to Byzantium" or didn't write "At the Fishhouses" but not to do with the fact that I am a Western writer or American or that I write in English. I couldn't have written this in the same sense that I couldn't have written "Sailing to Byzantium."

[Harry Thomas:] *On this same subject, though, near the end of his book,* Czeslaw Milosz and the Insufficiency of Lyric, *Donald Davie quotes your translation of Milosz's poem "The Father" from the sequence "The World," and he calls your translation a "brilliant" translation, he's full of praise for it, but when Milosz came to put together his* Collected Poems *he decided to use his own flatter, more trotlike version of the poem rather than yours.*

This is a complicated issue. Strictly speaking, the *Collected Poems* version is not entirely Czeslaw's own translation: it's largely word-for-word a trot, originally prepared by the scholar Lillian Vallee, though the note in the *Collected* says "translated by the author." Some arbitrariness of this kind in crediting translations is common, and more or less inevitable when many hands share the task. Lillian (who had very ably translated Milosz's *Bells in Winter*) generously provided her literal version of "The World," from which Bob Hass and I worked to make our translation for *The Separate Notebooks.*

I think sometimes a translation enters so much into the spirit of the new language that by a kind of luck it forms a new aesthetic whole; and if the author who first forged the poem deep in the furnace of the original language, and who fueled it with his heart, happens to know this new language well enough to perceive that new aesthetic whole, then it may seem to him in its formal spirit to be too much itself even though it may be extremely close, even more or less literal: he may prefer something that is not a poem in English, that is a mere rendering, even if the rendering is not particularly more accurate, even though it may be less literal. That is the interesting part: it has nothing to do with loose or free, literal or approximate, because the issue is not accuracy or maybe even not formal equivalence—but the issue of life, an alien aesthetic life. The translation that crosses over into the poetry of the new language may be so good it is bad.

Possibly something a little like this may have occurred with Czeslaw and "The World." I remember how the spirit of that project was reflected by the way we worked, in a committee: the poet Milosz, who is bilingual; Renata Gorczynski, who is not a poet but who is also bilingual, English and Polish; and then Hass and me, neither one of us bilingual, American poets dependent upon the other two and occasional helpers like Lillian Vallee as informants. I've discovered a new phrase I like: Bob and I were the metrical engineers! Also, I guess, idiom experts. This committee or writing troupe met in various combinations—two or three or four. Czeslaw used to joke about crediting the translations to The Grisly Peak collaborative, named after his street in Berkeley, or maybe crediting them to a single, pseudonymous translator, Dr. Grisleigh Peake. I remember one day Renata said Czeslaw can't make it today. His Korean translators had come to town, and he was meeting with them, she explained. Bob and I looked at one another and started to grin. Renata said, "What's so funny?" And I said, we were just envying his Korean translators, thinking how lucky they are. She said, what do you mean? He doesn't know Korean, was the answer. So he's not there looking over your shoulder, having a view and all the authority there is.

The translations from the "The World" we did in that period were much praised. People sometimes requested Czeslaw to read from them at public occasions, and reviewers singled them out when *The Separate Notebooks* appeared. This was all complicated by the fact that the originals are written in a form that doesn't exist in English. In Poland, for decades children learned to read by the use of rhymed primers. Not exactly an old-fashioned American primer, not exactly Stevenson's *A Child's Garden of Verses,* not exactly the didactic poems of Isaac Watts. Bob Hass describes the problem very well in *Ironwood's* Milosz issue. And the poems of "The World," though the sequence is subtitled "A Naive Poem," are a sophisticated response to World War II: "The World" is about Europe destroying itself. But in this "naive poem," what you see on the surface at the outset is the children, sister and brother, walking peacefully to school together. In separate poems, the children draw pictures; the mother carries a candle in a dark stairwell; the family have dinner. In another the father shows them the world, saying here's the global map, that's Europe, this is Italy, beyond the forest is Germany. He shows them the world, with a certain tone that by implication and context—making Seamus's point again—becomes in its overtones sinister and heartbreaking.

And these poems involve very simple, hard rhymes. In working with our translation committee, trying to get some of that formal note, thinking about the predominance in Polish of feminine rhymes, I made a thing that had a certain kind of rhyme in it, slanted or blunted feminine rhymes, and a certain sound, and to some degree it works, a compromise that does some little thing in English. But it does become another creature, another monster. So I can identify with Czeslaw in saying, well, this thing that has slouched and slanted its way into our committee is living and breathing in some kind of half-assed way; the sense is pretty literal, but there is also this smell of an alien, English-speaking animal, and I don't want to listen to it inhaling and exhaling and grunting around in its cage, I want something more like a telephone or a conduit.

[Harry Thomas:] *To the original's explicit abstract language?*

Yeah, The other thing made him nervous.

[Harry Thomas:] *But he seems to suggest that the tone you got through the peculiar feminine rhymes and so forth prevented you from rendering the abstract language and statements of the poems explicitly enough.*

Yes, but I think it was more "technical" than that. The rhymes in Polish are plain, like the cat sat on the mat. Virtually all endings in Polish are "feminine": they end on an unstressed syllable, so it's more like the kitty felt pity. They're like that, very hard and exact, and they're very simple. The rain fell on the garden and froze and the ice began to harden. They're just very, very plain, and the ones I cooked up for the version of "The World" printed in *The Separate Notebooks* are more like—well, Czeslaw called them "modern rhymes." Here is the opening poem of the sequence in *The Separate Notebooks* version:

"The Path"

Down where the green valley opens wider,
Along the path with grass blurring its border,
Through an oak grove just broken into flower,
Children come walking home from school together.

In a pencil case with a lid that slides open,
Bits of bread roll around with stumps of crayon,
And the penny hidden away by all children
For spring and the first cuckoo in the garden.

The girl's beret and her brother's school-cap
Bob, as they walk, above the fringe of bushes.
A jay screams, hopping in a treetop;
Over the trees, clouds drift in long ridges.

Now, past the curve, you can see the red roof:
Father leans on his hoe in the front garden,
Then bends down to touch a half-opened leaf;
From his tilled patch, he can see the whole region.

"Roof/garden, leaf/region" that is our version, with the consonantal rhymes, mostly feminine. Here is the same poem in the *Collected Poems:*

"The Road"

There where you see a green valley
And a road half-covered with grass,
Through an oak wood beginning to bloom
Children are returning home from school.

In a pencil case that opens sideways
Crayons rattle among crumbs of a roll
And a copper penny saved by every child
To greet the first spring cuckoo.

Sister's beret and brother's cap
Bob in the bushy underbrush,
A screeching jay hops in the branches
And long clouds float over the trees.

A red roof is already visible at the bend.
In front of the house father, leaning on a hoe,
Bows down, touches the unfolded leaves,
And from his flower bed inspects the whole region.

I think that the rhymed version is fairly close, and that it's just as abstract—the literal meaning is not much different. It is not a matter of abstractions. But the *Collected* doesn't attempt the rhymes; you can just be informed that they were in the original. I think that it is the rhythms and rhymes that help create an aesthetic creature—a kind of art-organism—and it is the breathing of such a creature that perhaps must make any author nervous simply by being *other*. I think it would make me nervous.

[Susan Wildey:] *Something that came up in class is that we were wondering in what way, if any, Judaism has affected your writing.*

I'm certain that it must have, in many ways. For instance, I talked last night about my interest in things that are made, made up: I am deeply interested in the subject of creation—high and low, great and small. And religions are notable makings, religion itself is. For one kind of religious person creation itself is an episode in the career of God. For me God is an important episode in the history of creation. Possibly having been raised as an Orthodox Jew, which is to say with considerable separation from the majority culture, has contributed to my interest in making. Not sharing such creations as Christmas or Easter or the—our, your—Saviour, and at the same time having other creations like the kosher laws or the prohibition against saying or writing the word for "God": that is a richly interesting conflict. It may have increased the impact upon me of the fact that we creatures—we mammals, we colony-insects, whatever we are—have invented not only language, but Christianity and Judaism and the United States of America and the violin and the blues and so forth.

> **The experience of a gorgeous, fading European reality—the rich, lower-class Eastern European Judaism and its culture, which were still present and very European in my childhood—must have had an impact on me that I can't fully understand.**
> —*Robert Pinsky*

The experience of a gorgeous, fading European reality—the rich, lower-class Eastern European Judaism and its culture, which were still present and very European in my childhood—must have had an impact on me that I can't fully understand. I grew up in a nominally orthodox family. My parents were quite secular people. They were good dancers, my father was a celebrated local athlete, they didn't go to synagogue except on the high holy days. We did have two sets of dishes—that is, we did "keep kosher." And as the oldest child, the oldest son in the family, I was expected to go to synagogue every Saturday. The *musaf,* the orthodox service, lasts three, maybe three and a half hours. Imagine for a moment being eleven years old: you don't like school; it's Saturday morning; you spend nearly four hours every Saturday morning in the company mainly of old men, chanting prayers in a language you don't understand, in a prolonged, accreted liturgy that is not dramatic. What happens is an accumulation of prayers and rituals, a liturgy that feels medieval. It does not have the drama of Mass: you don't eat God. It just happens. It comes time for "*Adon' olam,*" so everybody stands up and sings "*Adon' olam,*" and then you sit down again. Time for the *Shema,* you open the curtains, look at the Torah, sing the *Shema,* close it, and sit down again. And then you sing some other prayers. Three, three-and-a-half hours. And for the old men, it's picnic,

they love it. It's a social club for them. And afterwards everybody goes down to the basement and drinks schnapps and eats *kichele.* You aren't supposed to drive on the Sabbath, so it may be one o'clock, one-thirty, before you get home. Meanwhile, outside it is the great era of American baseball and the great formative era of rock and roll; across the street is a Catholic church, where they come and go, sometimes girls in First Communion dresses, they are doing something over there, something relatively brief and one may suspect dramatic, and relatively included by the majority culture.

And you just . . .well, I believe that for many people with Christian upbringings there's this thing I have read about in Joyce and others called a "crisis of faith" or "crisis of belief." That is not what happens in relation to Judaism, in my experience. You don't have a crisis of belief. Faith in any such sense was not something I could apprehend as a great concept in the religion. The religion is kind of a surrounding reality, no more "losable" in its own terms than the color of your eyes, or the force of gravity. It's like having faith in the universe, for the Jew to have "faith in" Judaism: it's just there. And there's only the vaguest idea of an afterlife. There's not a state of sin or a state of grace; everybody's kind of culpable vaguely and chosen vaguely. There's a merit system. You get *mitzvahs,* that is you get credited with good points, while waiting for the Messiah. Or you are credited with sins, bad points.

So you don't have a crisis of faith. You look over at the Church across the street, and you say to yourself, *hmmm,* Catholic girls and communion dresses and Jerry Lee Lewis and Jackie Robinson: it's the whole world out there, the splendid *traif* [non-kosher] cookie jar of the world. So you just turn to the world as soon as you get a chance. Or so you do if you are a child like me then. And I made a vow, I promised that little child: *once you don't have to do this, you aren't going to do it again.* They are making you do this, but when you are autonomous and you don't have to do this again, I promise you that you won't have to do it. And I am still keeping that promise. So Judaism was in large measure a powerful boredom for me, but it was a very powerful boredom: a serious and for me stilling force. And the force of that boredom, no mere ennui but a desperate, animal sense of being caged and trapped, left me, I think, with a feeling about the majority culture that makes me both feel more inside it than I might have been otherwise—because I *chose* it, I might not have, but I chose the majority culture and I like it—yet by the same process also more outside it, in my feelings, than I might be otherwise. There are special ways in which a secularized Jew feels both additionally in the new culture, compared to others, and outside it. Terms like "assimilation," or numbering generations from the first act of immigration, do not begin to deal with these intricacies.

So that's a quick sketch of my guess of what cultural ways I might have been affected by Judaism, to which I feel loyal in ways that have more to do with, say, the stories of Isaac Babel than the celebration of Passover. On the more purely religious aspects of the subject, I'd prefer to be silent right now. But to think of it theologically, exclusively theologically, would be wrong. That would neglect something else, a kind of tear-laden and enriching cultural struggle.

[Ed Breman:] *In the conclusion of a review of* **The Want Bone** *in the* New Republic, *the poem "At Pleasure Bay" is mentioned, and the reviewer says that in that poem you cash in your debts to Eastern philosophy that had been accumulating throughout* **The Want Bone.** *I was just wondering what your familiarity with Eastern philosophy was and how it might have influenced your poems.*

Oh, Eastern philosophy: I'm even less of a scholar of it than Judaism or Christianity. I lived in Berkeley, California, for nine years. I've done some superficial reading. Zimmerman's books about Hinduism and art are fascinating to me. I am attracted by the Hindu conception of time in the many parables where, say, Shiva will come, and then while he's talking there's a parade of ants and each ant is carrying a world, and each world has a thousand Shivas in it, and each of those Shivas is gesturing at a column of ants. They have many little parables or images like that, trying to enforce the immensity of the great cyclicalness—how everything comes back and comes back literally more times than you can imagine. And you give yourself games like that figure of the ants, as you try to imagine as best you can.

And I guess that at some point the idea I was talking to you about last night, about the way that culture is itself a kind of possession by the dead, coming back—at some point that idea illuminated for me the idea of metempsychosis, the transmigration of souls. And the way that the genetic inheritance is comparable to the cultural inheritance, each of them a constant shifting and combining of so many variables, as many variables as ants and Shivas, got connected in my mind with the migration of souls.

It is a trickle or thread that runs through this book. I suppose you could say I mock Buddha in **"The Hearts."** In an early draft of **"The Hearts,"** I can remember one line that I took out was, "Easy for Buddha to say." There's that tone in the poem still, of "Easy for Buddha to say" this or that. And as I understand it, there is a considerable Buddhist tradition of mocking Buddha. It's one of the things I like about Buddhism. A Zen saying I have heard is: "Buddha is a very good stick to pick up shit with." That's one Buddha saying, and there is something awfully admirable about it; I don't know, I suppose I do think Judaism or Christianity might be better off if they had that spirit. The Torah is a good stick to pick up shit with! It would transform the religion if you

could say that, if the religion were capacious enough and calm enough to embrace that.

[Oma Blaise:] *In your essay, "Responsibilities of the Poet," you talk about the poet needing to transform a subject. Can you say more about that?*

Bad art does what you expect. To me, it's not truly a poem if it merely says what most intelligent, well-meaning people would say. In the other direction, total surprise is babble, it's meaningless; I don't mean to say that one is on a quest simply for novelty. But your responsibility is, even if it's only to versify something you perceive as truth, to put that truth or homily into a rhyme in such a way that you are transforming it. Your job is to do something that the reader didn't already have. And this does not mean simply the lazy reader. One kind of popular fiction just spins out explicitly and doggedly the most vague, generalized fantasies the reader already has—the least individuated fantasies. The reader, on his or her own, has vague, perhaps commercially provoked fantasies of having quite a lot of money and many a sexual adventure; but the nature of these dreams or of the reader as a person makes him or her a little lazy imaginatively. So someone else puts in a lot of industry, and makes up specific names of characters, and puts them in rooms and buildings and airplanes, and flies them around, and has them have illegitimate children and meet them again twenty years later, and goes through all of the laborious spinning out of the plot.

This is an art, in the old broad sense, but it is not what I mean by the art of poetry. As I understand it, soap operas take the kind of fantasy people have in common and do the work—quite skillfully—of making such fantasy material explicit, without depriving it of a vague, dreamy generality that is part of the appeal. And the reason *Anna Karenina* has a loftier reputation, dealing with very similar material to the material of soap opera, is that the material is transformed by a powerful individual imagination. It is changed by not just anybody's imagination, but by that of a great, particular transformer. The result is that the material, the adultery and money and so forth, smells and feels like something that's both recognized and strange. Somewhere in that recognition and strangeness lies your job as an artist.

For instance, a lot of people have the notion that totalitarianism contains the seeds of its own destruction, and that art is somehow linked to truth, and therefore is the opposite of totalitarianism. According to such a belief, Fascist poetry at some level would become a contradiction in terms, as in Montale's essay on the subject. And one such person with notions of that—what is the word, let's say of that humanistic kind—Czeslaw Milosz wrote in the poem we were talking about earlier: "Beautiful and very young are

Philo-Sophia / And poetry, her ally in the service of the good . . .The news was brought to the mountains by a unicorn and an echo." That changes it; the unicorn and the echo, for example, transform the idea with a peculiar blend of irony and astonishment. And it's your job, if you are an artist, to find that moment of transformation. In contrast, sometimes people really. like clichés, they really like being told what they already think.

[Wyman Rembert:] *Can you tell us a little bit about* **Mindwheel***? Something we have says it's an electronic novel or complex interactive computer game. Does it have anything to do with poetry?*

It is a text adventure game, and I did put a lot of poetry into it, mostly borrowed. There are many poems in the game, and it was a great pleasure to see the playtesters at the company I wrote it for say, about some two- or three-hundred-year-old piece of writing, "that's neat." For example, there's a wonderful Walter Ralegh poem that you could call a riddle; it's in the form of a prophecy. It says, "Before the sixth day of the next new year . . .Four kings shall be assembled in this isle" and there shall be "the sound of trump" and "Dead bones shall then be tumbled up and down." What's being described, but never named, are the playing cards and dice. The charm of the poem is that it sounds like a mystical, rather frightening prophecy, and it's the cards and dice. At the end the poem says,

> this tumult shall not cease
> Until an Herald shall proclaim a peace,
> An Herald strange, the like was never born
> Whose very beard is flesh, and mouth is horn.

Until a Herald calls: " . . .the like was never born / Whose very beard is flesh, and mouth is horn." Well, *Mindwheel* is a narrative game where text appears on the screen; and in response to each bit of narrative, which ends with a prompt, you decide whether to go north or to look around a room, say. You type in an imperative or complete the sentence "I want to. . . ." and the machine responds by giving you more text on the screen. Early on in *Mindwheel,* a winged person is trapped behind bars, and you—the reader-protagonist—can free this person by solving a riddle. The riddle is, "an herald . . .the like was never born / Whose very beard is flesh, and mouth is horn." Has anybody guessed it yet? There is a hint in the expression of insult popular when I was in grade-school: "You weren't born, you were hatched." The answer is, a rooster. They play cards all night until the rooster calls: a morning herald which isn't born, but comes out of an egg; it has a beard of flesh and a mouth of horn.

This exemplifies a basic form of transformation, because the little riddle takes the extremely ordinary perception—

that the cock crows in the morning and the night is over—and gives it a mystical aura: its "very beard is flesh, and mouth is horn." Ralegh's poem is a commentary on mysticism, and indeed on poetry, perhaps more than it is on the cards and dice. It is a delighted, somewhat sardonic commentary on rhetoric.

[Ursula Reel:] *In your essay on T. S. Eliot you write: "True poetry is never really misunderstood or discarded, because its basis is in pleasure. Explanations and theories are misunderstood; pleasures are either had, or not." Can you elaborate a little bit on that and talk about the effect you want when you write a poem?*

It's very much involved with the sounds of the words. I hope that such an answer does not seem disappointing to you, or simple-minded. I have a conviction that if you write whatever it is well enough—Wallace Stevens is a good author to demonstrate this with—the reader will put up with quite a lot of incomprehension. Look at the rooster. I think, I hope, that you all recognize that there is something appealing about the sound of those lines. "Whose very beard is flesh, and mouth is horn" is a good line, one whose appeal may come not only before you think *it's a chicken,* but before you even think *it's a riddle.* You can sense that it's something, you get a little frisson of something interesting from it, though you don't "understand" it in the sense that you don't have "an answer" to it. You understand what kind of thing it is. Possibly before you "understand" that it's a riddle, you "understand" that it has a mystical quality, or that it sounds impressive. You come to understand *how* it's meant to make you think.

It sounds good, and it sounds good as a syntax, as well as an arrangement of consonant and vowels, and it sounds good as an unformulated recognition of other kinds of fact: the fact that "flesh" and "horn" are good words here, and the fact that horn means the substance of fingernails as well as the bony process of, say, a ram's horn, and that the ram's horn makes a pleasing connection with "herald," because it's the same word—to blow into a horn, a goat's or a ram's horn. That's how we have the word "horn," which we now apply to a sax or a trumpet, instruments made not of horn but brass. And a jazz musician will call his piano or drum set his "horn"! And so forth, through innumerable chimes and associations. A horny thing is a callous, a hardening of flesh. There is a sexual component to the flesh and horn and born and morning and certainly to the buried image of the rooster.

All of that is operating, operating and alive in you long before you think "rooster"—or else if it isn't operating, then no amount of cleverness or profundity will make it good, will make it poetry. So that "I don't get it" is a more damaging thing than "I don't understand it," because I think often you get it long before you understand it. We are familiar with this phenomenon in music. A record comes out, and part of the pleasure of it may be that the first five or six times you hear it you don't know what the words are; then you gradually find out what the words are. But you know whether you like it or not before you understand it. The words seem to be going very well with the tune, with what the chord changes and the harmony and the instrumentation and the singer's voice sound like, and you half-perceive whether you like these words, already. It is the same with a poem by Stéphane Mallarmé.

And I don't think these things are forgotten. I think that once something really gets under somebody's skin—is recognized as really good, in the way of art—it tends to remain, always a source of what I have to call the art-emotion: whatever that feeling is that art gives to us. And this happens in the culture in general, too. Eliot is rather out of style now, particularly with academics. But he's too good, the pleasure is too solid, for his work to truly fade. Kids are still reading "Prufrock" in high school, memorizing parts of it without meaning to. It's there forever, for everybody.

[Will Anderson:] *When you were talking about transformation earlier, I believe you used the word mystic or mystical, and it reminded me of, in **"The Refinery,"** the idea of refined from "oil of stone," and it seemed like the imagery is sort of chemical there, but there is a sense of a wondrous transformative power. Is that the same idea?*

Yes, it is the same idea. As I said last night, I always seek a way to experience these ideas as part of what's very ordinary. And "oil of stone" is a literal translation of "petroleum." You know, if something is petrified, it is turned into stone. And Peter is the rock you found your church on. So petroleum simply means stone-oil, oil of stone. The idea in that poem, that the transformations of petroleum—into gasoline, benzine, naphtalene, and motor oil and heating oil and all the other things it makes—WD40 and margarine and whatever else—is comparable to the transformations of language. I mean the way language itself changes, the way it changes other things, the way it illuminates our life, and in some ways is very toxic, quite poisonous and dangerous.

[Will Anderson:] *It's a pretty volatile mix.*

Yes, that is the sort of thinking the poem invites. It was a metaphor or comparison I liked so well that, maybe uncharacteristically, I based the whole poem upon it. The proposition is that language is like petroleum: it is dead life; it was once alive in a different way; in some other sense it remains stubbornly alive; it comes to us from the past, and we do gorgeous things with it—we wear these clothes, these fine woven stuffs and subtle colors, we have light, we

have music—and there is also something terrifying about it. You are tapping an energy that can feel supremely ordinary, yet that can also associate itself with mysterious awe. Explosion, gusher, leak—energy, as in a word like *fuck* or *Jesus* or *vendetta*.

[Will Anderson:] *I believe you said last night that you like the mix of the high and the low. Towards the end of that same poem, "The Refinery," it seems like there's that idea, the apposition of "Loveeries and memorized Chaucer."* . . .

. . .to me, contrast, maybe even more than the richness of some single word, is a gorgeous, living part of language, like contrast in music or cuisine.
—*Robert Pinsky*

Yes—and "lines from movies / And songs hoarded in mortmain." Varying texture in language is a pleasure partly as a reflection of the variety in oneself. My terminology of "high" and "low" oversimplifies this variety, or whatever I was trying for with "smeared keep" or "a gash of neon: Bar," or pairing "pinewoods" and "divinity"—to me, contrast, maybe even more than the richness of some single word, is a gorgeous, living part of language, like contrast in music or cuisine. The degrees and kinds of crunchy and smooth, high and low, the degrees of pungency or volume or hotness. In the refinery, they have that whole chemistry, as I understand it, that tunes a kind of hierarchy of degrees of refining. They call it "cracking" petroleum, breaking it into its components. And that is sort of like language too, maybe especially English, and maybe especially in America.

[Ann Brooke Lewis:] *It seems that in **"Window"** you use the word "Window" as an artifact or, as you talked about last night, as a matrix of its own, with its own history, its own part in the culture. How do you feel about the language that you grew up with personally? Do you feel that, as your Irish mother says, your house has a "windhole"? How much history or culture actually is in your language?*

Ideally, I would like to have it all in there. I would like to speak and write a language that does not deny either my lower-middle-class childhood or all the books I've read. I am what is called an educated person as these things go. That does not negate the way I spoke when I was a child, or the way the people around me spoke in what I suppose was a small town slum—so my mother would call it when she lamented our living there, and was certainly a working-class, racially mixed kind of a neighborhood. Just as the history of the language is in the language, the history of any person's language is in that person's speech and writing, and should be honored. One doesn't want to be limited to a pose or mode as either a pure street kid or as a pure professor, because one is not pure, and the pose or mode is a confinement. As an ideal, I would like to have it all together.

And sometimes you discover the plainness in the learnedness. It is delightful to discover that the origin of a word like "window" may be something as homely or simple as "windhole." Is that a "learned etymology"? In a way, but what could be more down-home, what could be plainer? It's [pointing] the windhole, the hole where wind comes in. Is that a piece of arcane learning, or a bit of fundamental, funky information about these brutal Anglo Saxons in their hut with its windhole?

Something comparable is found in the lovely language of the trades, for which I have considerable affection. A carpenter won't even call it a "window." Those separate panes are the "lights" to any builder or carpenter, and the whole is also a light. And these things, the vertical members in here, are "mullions." That piece of wood, the flat piece against the bottom below the sill, is the skirt, and the movable unit with the separate lights in it is the sash. This one has an upper sash and a lower sash. And there's a parting bead between the two sashes. And a head jamb and the side jambs. And they'll use these words very unself-consciously, in the interest of clarity and precision. Hand me some more of the parting beam and the four-penny nails. Because you need to be precise. Go to the lumber store and bring me back some 3 5/8" head jamb. Or I forget what this other thing is called, face molding or something. There's some other kind of jamb that goes this way. The word j-a-m-b: is that a high word or a low word?

One more pleasing example. I went to the hardware store and bought some fertilizer. The guy says, you could buy one of these little whirling things to spread it with, but really you could just strew it broadcast. And I realized what someone from a farming background might have always known, that "broadcast" was not invented by television or radio. The word was there: it's what you do with, say, seeds. If you have a sack slung around your shoulder, and you do this [swings his arm forward], you're broadcasting. The word existed before Marconi and before TV, and for me it had been an unrecognized, dead metaphor. it's just a homey word—not archaic, for farmers, I would guess, nor for the guy in my hardware store.

[Susan Wildey:] *Did you write **The Want Bone** from the picture by Michael Mazur that is reproduced on the book's jacket or did you actually see a shark's jaw?*

The image is tied to a weave of friendships that pleases me.

I saw one that my friend, the poet Tom Sleigh, had given Frank Bidart. It was on Frank's mantle, and I saw it shortly before I was going on vacation to the beach—a vacation where I saw something of Mike and Gail Mazur, in fact. And I wrote the poem at the beach, remembering the bone on Frank's mantle. When Tom saw the poem, he generously gave me a jawbone too!

Later, when I needed a jacket for the book, I couldn't find an image: the ones The Ecco Press liked, I didn't like, and the ones I liked, Ecco didn't. And Mike, working from the poem and from Tom's present to me, made the picture—a monotype, a form of which he is one of the contemporary masters. I happened to be in the studio when he pulled this monotype from his press-it's a wonderful, sensuous thing to see a monotype pulled: it is a one-of-a-kind print, the plate gooey with color pressed against paper by powerful rollers, a big surface, and a motor drives the roller across the sandwich of wet plate and paper, *shhhhh*. There's a certain amount of chance in the medium. If you're an expert, you can make textures that look like water or hair or smoke or these bubbles here. But you don't know exactly what it's going to look like. Maybe that is a model for what it is like to make any work of art?

James Longenbach (essay date Summer 1994)

SOURCE: "Robert Pinsky and the Language of Our Time," in *Salmagundi*, No. 103, Summer, 1994, pp. 157-77.

[*In the essay below, Longenbach traces Pinsky's artistic development in terms of the poet's "deep awareness—sometimes wariness, sometimes worship"—of historical, linguistic, and literary forces at work in his art.*]

Robert Pinsky has always stood apart from the various schisms used to map the world of American poetry. He not only admires both the formal terseness of Cunningham and the capacious waywardness of O'Hara; his poems also seem to partake of both these qualities. Formal and free, open and closed, Olson and Wilbur—however the twentieth-century American poetry is divided, Pinsky remains unplaceable in the best sense of the word. He has recently said that Seamus Heaney seems legitimately "post-modernist" because in his work, "formal freedom feels assumed, and matters of technique no longer fighting issues in the old modernist sense." This quality seems to me even stronger in Pinsky's own work. If he is a postmodern poet it is not because he opposes modernism in the way that some modern poets rejected their Romantic forebears; the label sticks because he has understood that opposition itself is what holds other poets down.

A poet's mark may be measured by his or her ability to expand the language (which is to say the culture) available to poetry. The effort is usually subtle (we don't need to think of Shakespeare as a formally innovative writer), and it always depends on an openness to a variety of poetries, both past and present. Unlike other writers who seem, mostly because of their formal choices, more programmatically postmodern, Pinsky has slowly become the more truly innovative poet—the poet who increases the possibilities open to poetry. By being both completely distinctive and completely undogmatic, Pinsky reminds me of the idiosyncratic pianist Glen Gould, who was known as a champion of twelve-tone music and who consequently affronted his admirers by publishing a gorgeously tonal string quartet. Gould replied that he was simply a "student"—as he called himself—whose "enthusiasms were seldom balanced by antagonisms." What's striking here is that Gould's performances are unmistakably unique: his originally came from an embrace of everything that music had to offer him.

I think it's important to make this point about Pinsky because his criticism has been used to widen the poetic canon's artificial oppositions. This is in part understandable, since Pinsky is a writer with clear opinions; but he is not a writer who would say that he is "denying the hegemony of such dominant twentieth-century conventions as the subjective modernist lyric." Pinsky is too sophisticated a critic to put together the words subjective, modernist, and lyric, secure that the phrase means something coherent enough to deny. It's true that Pinsky has criticized what I might call (though it makes me nervous to do so) a strain of attenuated modernism—much smaller than the practice of any modernist poet—that privileges the "image" to the exclusion of other kinds of poetic discourse. But to capitalize polemically on this aspect of Pinsky's work is to diminish the scope of what he's doing. Pinsky did not set out to replace one orthodoxy with another; his goal is to resist any vocabulary for poetry that becomes exclusionary and taken-for-granted. The point of *The Situation of Poetry* is that all poetic language is more or less arbitrary, none of it closer to the heart than any other. Pinsky has his preferences, but his argument is not with the "image" as such but with the unquestioned acceptance of its values.

Throughout *The Situation of Poetry* Pinsky discusses this issue in what seem like purely formal terms. But as the title of his most recent critical work—*Poetry and the World*—suggests, Pinsky understands that any formal issue in poetry is simultaneously a social issue: "The poet's first social responsibility, to continue the art, can be filled only through the second, opposed responsibility to change the terms of the art given—and it is given socially, which is to say politically." Except that it's not afraid of the word *art*, this statement is similar to many current "New Historicist" ideas about poetry. (In fact, the essay it's taken from, **"Responsibilities of the Poet,"** was first published in a special issue of *Critical Inquiry* on politics and poetic value: unlike most poet-critics, Pinsky seems in touch with academic literary criticism in profitable ways.) But the wisdom of this statement also resonates beyond critical fashion. Over the course of his career, Pinsky has made his finest poems not by harnessing beautiful language but by forcing the language of his time (the language that didn't yet seem beautiful) into poetry. This skill, discovered in the poems of *Sadness and Happiness* and perfected in those of *The Want Bone,* is the product of Pinsky's strong sense of poetry's historicity. Like the poets of his past, Wordsworth or Elizabeth Bishop, Pinsky resists not subjectivity itself but the dramatization of subjectivity uncomplicated by an awareness of the subject's social nature: this is Pinsky's inheritance, romantic and modern.

Pinsky was born and raised in Long Branch, New Jersey, a town that by 1940 was already a dilapidated resort. Graduating from Rutgers University in 1962, he wrote his senior thesis on T. S. Eliot. Then he enrolled as a graduate student at Stanford, and, quite by accident, became aware of Yvor Winters. During his first semester, after he read Robert Lowell's review of Winter's *Selected Poems,* Pinsky was impressed enough to show Winters his poems. On more than one occasion Pinsky has described this meeting with a delicately self-depreciating irony.

> He asked me to sit down, and he thumbed through the manuscript while I was there. It took him perhaps four minutes, stopping once or twice at certain ones. Then he looked up at me, and said, "You simply don't know how to write."
>
> He added that there was some gift there, but because I was ignorant of what to do with it, he could not estimate how much of a gift it was. If it was blind luck or happy fate or smiling Fortune that must be thanked for leading me to Stanford, let me congratulate myself for having the sense not to leave the room when he said that.

Pinsky stayed in the room for several years, taking directed reading courses with Winters and writing poems. He has subsequently expressed his debt to Winters many times (most wonderfully in the penultimate section of his **"Essay on Psychiatrists"**), but unlike other writers who identify with Winters, Pinsky has never seemed like a Wintersian, repeating the old man's idiosyncratic take on literary history. While Pinsky inherited Winter's preference for a Jonsonian clarity of statement in poetry, I think Winters was important to him as a poet-critic who stressed the necessity of coming to terms with the entire history of poetry: it was Winter's generosity rather than his crankiness that made an impression on the young Pinsky. In addition,

I think Winters stressed in usable terms what Pinsky probably knew intuitively: that the reading and writing of poetry was a moral act.

Three years after he showed Winters his work, Pinsky published his first poems in the October 1965 issue of the *Southern Review,* then a journal where many of Winter's students and friends appeared. These poems sound almost nothing like the work Pinsky would produce three or four years later, but they are distinguished by a formal clarity and ease. Of the four poems, Pinsky preserved only **"Old Woman"** in his first collection, *Sadness and Happiness.*

> Not even in darkest August,
> When the mysterious insects
> Marry loudly in the black weeds
> And the woodbine, limp after rain,
> In the cooled night is more fragrant,
> Do you gather in any slight
> Harvest to yourself. Deep whispers
> Of slight thunder, horizons off,
> May break your thin sleep, but awake,
> You cannot hear them. Harsh gleaner
> Of children, grandchildren—remnants
> Of nights now forever future—
> Your dry, invisible shudder
> Dies on this porch, where, uninflamed,
> You dread the oncoming seasons,
> Repose in electric light.

Like one of the poems that accompanied it in the *Southern Review* (another was set in rhymed couplets and the fourth in terza rima), **"Old Woman"** is organized syllabically, the eight syllables of each line variously accented. The subtlety of their rhythm does stand apart from the lines of the other poems ("The marriage bed awakes to hear / A voice reciting, without fear"), but **"Old Woman"** showed only half of what Pinsky would become: the expert craftsman.

Pinsky published no more poems until 1969-70, when he appeared again in the *Southern Review* and also in *Poetry:* all but one of these poems remain uncollected, as do three of the four additional poems that later appeared in the September 1971 issue of *Poetry.* The fourth poem, **"The Destruction of Long Branch,"** seems in retrospect like a breakthrough.

> When they came out with artificial turf
> I went back home with a thousand miles.
>
> I dug a trench by moonlight from the ocean
> And let it wash in quietly
>
> And make a brackish quicksand which the tide

> Sluiced upward from the streets and ditches.
> The downtown that the shopping centers killed,
> The garden apartments, the garages,
>
> The station, the Little Africa on (so help me)
> Liberty Street, the nicer sections
>
> All settled gently in a drench of sand
> And sunk with a minimum of noise.

It's tempting to say that the new power of these lines comes from Pinsky's focus on the peculiarity of his home town. In some sense, the poem does represent the finding of a "subject matter," and Pinsky has subsequently written in sophisticated ways about the importance of subject matter and of poems that are organized by the earnest presentation of their meaning. But this advance happened when it did because Pinsky broke through an earlier idea about poetic language. He has recently said that **"Old Woman"** represents a kind of poetry that no longer interests him because of its "overt lyricism of vocabulary and syntax." In contrast, the force of the language of **"The Destruction of Long Branch"** depends not on an extravagance of image or wit or metaphor—not even on the sonorous quality of lines like "Deep whispers / Of slight thunder, horizons off, / May break your thin sleep"—but on the unfolding of an argument that includes words like *shopping center.* Pinsky has joked that he tends to suspect a poet who hasn't gotten a shopping center into his poems: his point is to stress not only the place of the everyday world but the place of everyday language—language not yet poetic—in poetry. The phrase *shopping center* could never appear in **"Old Woman,"** just as Yeats could never have gotten the words *greasy till* into "To the Rose upon the Rood of Time"—even if he'd wanted to.

"The Destruction of Long Branch" sounds even more like the mature Pinsky because the introduction of phrases like *shopping center, artificial turf,* and *so help me* does not disrupt the formal clarity evident even in his earliest work. In **"American Poetry and American Life"** (collected along with **"Responsibilities of the Poet"** in *Poetry and the World*) Pinsky has described the social qualities of Anne Winter's poetry, and, like all influential poet-critics, he seems to account for aspects of his own poetry when he praises certain qualities in others'.

> I don't intend anything as quixotic or odious as prescribing a subject matter, or proscribing one. Rather, the point is that a certain kind of fluidity, a formal and moral quality, seems to have been demanded of American poets by their circumstance. . . . Winter's laundromat with its "*I mean to live*" seems simultaneously to challenge and embarrass poetic language,

and to incorporate it: to defy poetic form, and to demand it.

These sentences describe perfectly later poems like **"Pleasure Bay"** or **"The Hearts"** (the long, fluid poems that **"The Destruction of Long Branch"** looks forward to). They also describe the values that give those poems their idiosyncratic movement (Williams's diction plugged into Stevens's pentameters). Pinsky has no interest in the mysterious "freedom" often associated with the breaking of poetic forms, since he understands that forms are, as part of the historicity of his writing, unbreakable; but he is interested in bending them, testing them against the warp and woof of his experience.

Perhaps it isn't coincidental that **"The Destruction of Long Branch"** embodies thematically this double attitude toward history and culture—defying it and demanding it. The poem isn't about the slow decay of Long Branch; rather, it's about Pinsky's desire to flood the place and pave it over—an act which he accomplishes, like any romantic poet, "by moonlight." But the loving specificity of the poem's catalogue of everything that disappears belies his desire to destroy, and the poem ends not with destruction but with Pinsky's recreation—"cautiously elegiac"—of his home town. In the process, the words that threatened to make him what he is (*artificial turf, shopping mall*) become the words with which he names the world and makes it his own.

Comparing Elizabeth Bishop to Wordsworth, Pinsky has said that "her great subject is the contest—or truce, or trade-agreement—between the single human soul on the one side, and on the other side, the contingent world of artifacts and other people." This is Pinsky's great subject too, and it accounts for Pinsky's emphasis on the historicity of his language; it is only through the social structure of language that the single soul is constituted, and it is only through language that the soul asserts its power over the social structure. "Naming and placing things," says Pinsky apropos of Bishop (though he could have been talking about **"The Destruction of Long Branch"**), "is an approach to genuine liberty. This is true even though the very means of naming things . . .are also part of the terrain."

This concern unites the poems of *Sadness and Happiness.* If Bishop's "In the Waiting Room" is a poem that dramatizes the difficulty of realizing that the self is a social construction (the individual merely "one of them"), then the first poem in *Sadness and Happiness* is about the opposite difficulty of seeing the individual as anything but a product of the categories that constitute it—"an I." The opening stanzas of **"Poem About People"** offer a comfortable account of other people seen less as individuals

than as exemplars of a kind of Johnsonian "general nature." The difficulties begin here:

> But how love falters and flags
> When anyone's difficult eyes come
> Into focus, terrible gaze of a unique
> Soul, its need unlovable.

Pinsky offers several examples of this problem, the last of which explores the sentimentality of his earlier remark that it is "possible / To feel briefly like Jesus," crossing the "dark spaces" between individuals.

> In the movies, when the sensitive
> Young Jewish soldier nearly drowns
>
> Trying to rescue the thrashing
> Anti-semitic bully, swimming across
> The river raked by nazi fire,
> The awful part is the part truth:
>
> *Hate my whole kind,* but me,
> Love me for myself.

The truth is partial because single selves have meaning only as the parts of whole kinds; the difference is frightening, and difficult to calibrate. But it is not impossible, as the poem's final lines suggest, restating the opening stanzas' hope in darker, more tentative terms: "we / All dream it, the dark wind crossing / The wide spaces between us."

Two years after *Sadness and Happiness* appeared, Pinsky published *The Situation of Poetry.* But as his fugitive essays and reviews from the early seventies reveal, the book's argument had been in his mind for some time. Its thesis appeared in concentrated form in the June 1973 issue of *Poetry.*

> Some contemporary poems tend, pretty distinctly as such matters go, toward coolness: the aspect of modernism which effaces or holds back the warmth of authorial commitment to feeling or idea, in favor of a surface cool under the reader's touch.
>
> A previous generation sought coolness through concentration on objective images. But the techniques implied by the term "imagism" have come to look rhetorical and warmly committed. . . . When it fails, it resembles other forms of "poetic diction."

This was the problem. In the January 1974 issue of *Poetry* Pinsky offered a solution.

> Most people who read poetry have some loose idea of what the prose virtues are—a demanding,

unglamourous group, including perhaps Clarity, Flexibility, Efficiency. . .? This is a drab, a grotesquely puritanical bunch of shrews. They never appear in blurbs. And yet when they are courted by those who understand them—Williams, Bishop—the Prose Virtues, which sound like a supporting chorus, perform virtuoso marvels. They become not merely the poem's minimum requirement, but the poetic essence.

The only word missing here is *discursive:* the word is Pinsky's, but it has become the word most often used to describe his poems, especially those from *Sadness and Happiness* like "Essay on Psychiatrists" and "Tennis." Throughout these poems, Pinsky tries to recapture the pre-Romantic sensibility of Dryden or Virgil (the sensibility that was supposedly available, as Winters is made to say in "Essay on Psychiatrists," before "the middle / Of the Eighteenth Century" when "the logical / Foundations of Western thought decayed and fell apart"). If Virgil could write poems about the skills of farming, why not poems about the skills of tennis?

> Hit to the weakness. All things being equal
> Hit crosscourt rather than down the line, because
> If you hit crosscourt back to him, then he
> Can only hit back either towards you (crosscourt)
> Or parallel to you (down the line), but never
> Away from you, the way that you can hit
>
> Away from him if he hits down the line.

When these lines were first published, they seemed like an incredible breath of fresh air: nothing could have stood more at odds with the fashion for confessional poetry. But after almost twenty years, the more egregiously discursive poems don't seem to me to be the finest achievement in *Sadness and Happiness*—necessary though they were for Pinsky's development. While the textures of "Essay on Psychiatrists" or "Tennis" do encourage the expansion of poetic language, they do so programmatically, making the inclusion in poetry of phrases like *crosscourt* and *down the line* sound like a feat rather than an achievement that later poems will build on. Consequently, the poems seem more like attempts to write like Virgil (no more possible than it is to write like Keats) than efforts to adapt his pre-Romantic sensibility to the poetry of today. In contrast, that is exactly what poems like "Poem About People," "Discretions of Alcibiades," or "The Beach Women" do.

In retrospect, then, how dangerous it was for Pinsky to embark on the long poem *Explanation of America,* published in 1979. This poem is as plainly discursive as "Tennis," but unlike "Tennis" or even "Essay on Psychiatrists," *Explanation* is a poem in which Pinsky has something urgent to say. Halfway through, Pinsky offers this hope to his daughter, to whom the poem is addressed.

> The words—"*Vietnam*"—that I can't use in poems
> Without the one word threatening to gape
> And swallow and enclose the poem, for you
> May grow more finite; able to be touched.

This is what Pinsky had learned, writing his first book of poems. But the word that he chooses here, so much more charged than *shopping center,* reveals how much he feels is at stake in the expansion of the language of poetry. Pinsky begins *Explanation* by stressing the vast multiplicity of images in American culture ("Colonial Diners, Disney, films / Of concentration camps, the napalmed child / Trotting through famous newsfilm"), and he wants his daughter to see all these images—just as he wants to build a poem ample enough to contain them. Such a poem might satisfy Pinsky's smaller hope:

> The Shopping Center itself will be as precious
> And quaint as is the threadmill now converted
> Into a quaint and high-class shopping center.

But the larger hope—the larger word—is not dispatched with so easily:

> Someday, the War in Southeast Asia, somewhere—
> Perhaps for you and people younger than you—
> Will be the kind of history and pain
> Saguntum is for me; but never tamed
> Or "history" for me, I think.

J. D. McClatchy has called *An Explanation of America* Pinsky's "most capacious and aspiring work," but I agree with him when he says that *History of My Heart,* published in 1984, represents a turning point in Pinsky's career. Pinsky's great subject—the dialectical relationship of the self and the social structure—was necessarily at the center of his meditation on what the word "America" might mean. But while the poems of *History of My Heart* and *The Want Bone* continue this meditation, they do so dramatically, enacting the dialectic as well as explaining it. These poems retain the discursive clarity of the long poem, but their narratives seem (even within their smaller compass) more comprehensive and complex, more a dramatization of a mind thinking than the product of thought (to borrow a distinction Elizabeth Bishop favored).

The opening poem in *History of my Heart,* "The Figured Wheel," describes the rotation of a great wheel throughout history. A catalogue of culture, high and low, familiar and foreign, it begins with a *shopping mall* rather than a *center* and ends with the creation of Robert Pinsky's single self.

It is hung with devices
By dead masters who have survived by reducing
themselves magically

To tiny organisms, to wisps of matter, crumbs of soil,
Bits of dry skin, microscopic flakes, which is why
they are called "great,"
In their humility that goes on celebrating the turning
Of the wheel as it rolls unrelentingly over

A cow plodding through car traffic on a street in Iasi,
And over the haunts of Robert Pinsky's mother and
father
And wife and children and his sweet self
Which he hereby unwillingly and inexpertly gives up,
because it is
There, figured and pre-figured in the nothing-
transfiguring wheel.

These lines establish the terms in which the title *History of My Heart* must be understood. Virtually all of Pinsky's poems are autobiographical, but they recognize that an autobiography, like the self it narrates, is constituted by a wide array of cultural and historical forces. To get to the "heart" of these poems is not to find some essential core but to recognize that the heart is on the surface of everything the poet sees or speaks. Any distinctions between private and public "history" become difficult to sustain.

The second poem in *History of My Heart* adds a more plainly political charge to this history. **"The Unseen"** begins with a group of tourists in Krakow, touring the death camp. The scene is "unswallowable," both unbearably familiar and unbearably horrific: "We felt bored / And at the same time like screaming Biblical phrases." Stalled between these extremes, Pinsky remembers a "sleep-time game"—an insomniac's dream of heroic destruction: granted the power of invisibility, Pinsky roams the camp, saves the victims from the gas chamber, and, as a finale, flushes "everything with a vague flood / Of fire and blood." As in **"The Destruction of Long Branch,"** Pinsky dreams of having power over his history, remaking what made him.

It's not possible to take that dream too seriously in **"The Destruction of Long Branch,"** of course: its act of destruction serves as a kind of metaphor for the self's struggle with language and history. But in **"The Unseen"** the act is too literal, too historically charged, and Pinsky must back away from it more clearly.

I don't feel changed, or even informed—in that,
It's like any other historical monument; although
It is true that I don't ever at night any more

Prowl rows of red buildings unseen, doing
Justice like an angry god to escape insomnia.

Though he feels unchanged, Pinsky describes an important transformation here. Having imagined himself as the "unseen," Pinsky now recognizes a more potent invisible presence.

And so,
O discredited Lord of Hosts, your servant gapes

Obediently to swallow various doings of us, the most
Capable of all your former creatures . . .

I think this force could be called "history" as easily as "Lord of Hosts." Having earlier found the scene "unswallowable," Pinsky realizes that he has no choice but to take in the past. And as **"The Figured Wheel"** suggests, the past—however sordid—is already inside him: in this sense, the force could also be called "my heart."

This historical wheel rolls through all of Pinsky's work, but these lines from *The Want Bone* (his best and most recent book) point to a slight change in his attitude: "How can I turn this wheel / that turns my life?" Throughout *History of My Heart* Pinsky is amazed by the vast array of images that make up the self; throughout *The Want Bone* he is equally amazed by the images that the self can make. The desire—the want—to turn the wheel of history has certainly been present in Pinsky's work since **"The Destruction of Long Branch"**; but in *The Want Bone* Pinsky sometimes stands aghast at the potential hubris of the human imagination—or what in **"What Why When How Who"** he calls

The old conspiracy of gain and pleasure

Flowering in the mind greedily to build the world
And break it.

Behind these lines stand Old Testament injunctions against idolatry—"they worship the work of their own hands, that which their own fingers have made"—but in an essay on the prophet Isaiah Pinsky concludes that "all worship, even the most meticulous or elaborate, may be flawed by the spirit of idolatry." Since idolatry is in some way essential to human action, good or bad, Pinsky's fascination is less with greed as such than with the point where pleasure begins to conspire unhappily with gain.

The astonishing first poem in *The Want Bone,* **"From the Childhood of Jesus,"** is impatient with both Old and New Testament wisdom, both the laws of Judaism and Jesus' revision of them. Pinsky tells the apocryphal tale of a young Jesus who makes a little pond of mud and twigs and models twelve sparrows from clay. The scene seems innocent enough until "a certain Jew" (Pinsky incorporates the language of the anti-Semitic joke or story here) scolds the child for "making images." In response, Jesus makes the sparrows come to life, and, when the son of Annas accidentally ruins the little pond, Jesus makes the boy wither away. The petulant tone of Jesus' anger is familiar from the gospels ("what did the water / Do to harm you?"), but his actions are merciless, filled with the childish greed and self-importance that the tone suggests. (As Pinsky says in **"Lament for the Makers,"** worship is "tautological, with its Blessed / Art thou O Lord who consecrates the Sabbath . . . And then the sudden curt command or truth: / God told him, Thou shalt cut thy foreskin off.") **"From the Childhood of Jesus"** ends like a parable gone wrong.

> Alone in his cot in Joseph's house, the Son
> Of man was crying himself to sleep. The moon
>
> Rose higher, the Jews put out their lights and slept,
> And all was calm and as it had been, except
>
> In the agitated household of the scribe Annas,
> And high in the dark, where unknown even to Jesus
>
> The twelve new sparrows flew aimlessly through the
> night,
> Not blinking or resting, as if never to alight.

Jesus is resolutely human in this story, granted the powers of a god but the emotions of a child, and, like any man, he cannot control the things he has made: the poem's final image is more frightening than the child's petulance. **"From the Childhood of Jesus"** is astonishing because, while it is ultimately about the consequences of the simple human desire for power, it tells that profane story in the vocabulary of the sacred. Consequently, this poem about hubris is itself startlingly hubristic—a paradox that embodies Pinsky's uneasy double attitude toward the human imagination.

"From the Childhood of Jesus" exemplifies one of the two kinds of poems that make up *The Want Bone.* The other kind, rather than adapting Biblical rhetoric, combines a multiplicity of vocabularies and narratives into a shape that seems both wild and controlled, random and planned. Most of these poems are organized something like a Baroque concerto with a *ritornello* or repeating theme that returns (though in a different key) after each episode of new material. In **"The Uncreation"** various ideas of singing hold the poem's disparate materials together. In **"At Pleasure Bay"** some version of the phrase "never the same" recurs. And in **"The Shirt"** the repeated motif is neither a theme nor a phrase but simply a rhythm: "The back, the yoke, the yardage" or "The planter, the picker, the sorter." Similar to those of *History of My Heart* but even more accomplished, these poems are what **"The Destruction of Long Branch"** ultimately made possible.

In **"The Hearts"** the *ritornello* is an unsentimental image

of the heart, itself the sentimental image of desire, as "pulpy shore-life battened on a jetty."

> Slashed by the little deaths of sleep and pleasure,
> They swell in the nurturing spasms of the waves,
>
> Sucking to cling; and even in death itself—
> Baked, frozen—they shrink to grip the granite harder.

Between the recurrences of this image comes a catalogue of harsh desires. The victim of a suffocating lover is equated with a heroin addict who knows, the first time he shoots up, that he will suffer, go to prison, and probably die. But this knowledge doesn't stop the addict, whose consolation is that proposed by Enobarbus in *Antony and Cleopatra* when Antony laments "Would I had never seen her": "Then you would have missed / A wonderful piece of work." This passage, in turn, invokes a sentence from Stephen Booth's commentary on Shakespeare's sonnets: "Shakespeare was almost certainly homosexual, / Bisexual, or heterosexual, the sonnets / Provide no evidence on the matter." This link in the chain of associations provokes the poem's central question: why does human desire fuel, over and over again, the making of images—the singing of songs, the throwing of pots, the writing of poems?

All of these creative acts are invoked as the chain continues, one image leading metonymically to the next. The question of Shakespeare's sexuality invokes the rhetoric of courtly love (tears, crystals, hearts) which still infects the songs (Lee Andrews and The Hearts—"My tear drops are / Like crystals") we sing in the shower (falling like tears or crystals).

> To Buddha every distinct thing is illusion
> And becoming is destruction, but still we sing
> In the shower. I do. In the beginning God drenched
>
> The Emptiness with images: the potter
> Crosslegged at his wheel in Benares market
> Making mud cups, another cup each second
>
> Tapering up between his fingers, one more
> To sell the tea-seller at a penny a dozen,
> And tea a penny a cup. The customers smash
>
> The empties, and waves of traffic grind the shards
> To mud for new cups, in turn; and I keep one here
> Next to me: holding it awhile from out of the cloud
>
> Of dust that rises from the shattered pieces,
> The risen dust alive with fire, then settled
> And soaked and whirling again on the wheel that
> turns
>
> And looks on the world as on another cloud,

On everything the heart can grasp and throw away
As a passing cloud . . .

The image of the wheel returns here, but unlike **"The Figured Wheel"** the potter's wheel is turned by a man: the result of all human *making,* Pinsky suggests, is this absurd, this transient—not the potent images with which the Old Testament god drenches the emptiness but the mere images that the Buddha denounces as empty. And yet, as the poem continues to unfold, the wheel continues to turn—perhaps productively. The visions of the Old Testament are dismissed as "too barbarous for heaven / And too preposterous for belief on earth" (Pinsky rehearses the horrible vision in Isaiah 6, after which the prophet's unclean lips are purified by a live coal), and **"The Hearts"** ends by returning to Lee Andrews and The Hearts, their record spinning like the potter's wheel.

> As the record ends, a coda in retard:
> The Hearts in a shifting velvety *ah,* and *ah*
> Prolonged again, and again as Lee Andrews
>
> Reaches *ah* high for *I have to gain Faith, Hope*
> And Charity, God only knows the girl
> Who will love me—Oh! if we only could
> *Start over again*! Then The Hearts chant the chords
> Again a final time, *ah* and the record turns
> Through all the music, and on into silence again.

These lines of the poem answer the song: you can start again, though you'll end up in pretty much the same place. Finally, Pinsky's suggestion is that the turning itself—the longing, the singing, the making—must constitute our human value. If this seems like a paltry consolation, the empty images condemned by the Buddha, we should remember in contrast the uncontrollable, unsatisfying images conjured by the Son of Man.

The final lines of **"The Hearts"** cannot sound like too definitive a conclusion since, like so many of Pinsky's later poems, **"The Hearts"** eschews the normal kinds of progression or closure we associate with lyric poetry. Less than the final lines it is the *turning* of the poem itself that is most memorable. In his essay **"Poetry and Pleasure"** Pinsky praises the apparently random succession of thoughts and observations that a letter can accommodate, and in his quest to keep poetry open to all kinds of language and experience, Pinsky has tried to establish that kind of movement in poems like **"The Hearts," "Shirt,"** or **"Pleasure Bay."** He asks in **"Poetry and Pleasure"** the question implicit in his work since **"The Destruction of Long Branch"**: "if gorgeous, impressive language and profound, crucial ideas were all that poetry offered to engage us, would it seem—as it does to many of us—as necessary as food?" What engages us is not the product—the achieved

word or thought—but the process of a mind moving through those thoughts and words: "This movement—physical in the sounds of a poem, moral in its relation to the society implied by language, the person who utters the poem—is near the heart of poetry's mysterious appeal, for me." In its sinuous investigation of desire, **"The Hearts"** tries to describe this appeal: more profoundly, the poem enacts it.

I've quoted **"Poetry and Pleasure"** to elucidate Pinsky's poems, but of course Pinsky is trying to say something about the pleasures of poetry at large; the phrase "Death is the mother of beauty" is not particularly interesting except because it occurs within the idiosyncratic movement of thought and sound in Stevens's "Sunday Morning." In **"American Poetry and American Life"** Pinsky returns to this quality of movement, emphasizing that it is visible in a wide range of American poetries.

> One could exemplify this fluidity of tone, including the inseparable blend of comic and ecstatic, formal and vulgar, in an enormous range of American poets, John Ashbery and Elizabeth Bishop, George Oppen and James Merrill, Allen Ginsberg and Marianne Moore. (I think that the stylistic trait I mean also characterizes poems that do not explicitly take up American cultural material such as bus rides or movies.)

Pinsky is interested in developing categories for the discussion of American poetry that do not encourage the polemical oppositions of Oppen and Merrill, Ginsberg and Moore, or—even more culturally overdetermined—the high and the low. His strategy not only clarifies the position of his own work but helps to insure the future health and diversity of American literature: the segregation of poetic schools only limits the possibilities available to poetry.

> **Pinsky is interested in developing categories for the discussion of American poetry that do not encourage the polemical oppositions of Oppen and Merrill, Ginsberg and Moore, or—even more culturally overdetermined—the high and the low.**
> —*James Longenbach*

Even the most deeply entrenched battle positions of American poetry don't interest Pinsky. In an essay occasioned by the centennial of T. S. Eliot's birth, he has admitted that the subject of his undergraduate thesis first alerted him to the quality of movement he so values, the "clangorous, barely-harmonized bringing together of the sacred and profane."

Eliot is above all the pre-eminent poet of this clash or

yoking. . . . Because he identified and penetrated this dualism in the rhythms and noises and smells and surfaces of modern life, without simplifying what he saw into false ideas of squalor or perfection, Eliot remains entirely essential for us. He is not merely whatever we mean by "great poet," but precisely what Pound means by "an inventor." For this, Eliot's readers forgive him his mean side, his religio-authoritarian claptrap, the plushy grandiosity of "Ash Wednesday," the tetrameter anti-Semitism, the genteel trivialities of the late plays.

Today almost thirty years after Eliot's death, there still seems something daring about this expression of debt and affinity.

I began this essay by proposing that it is precisely through such acknowledgements of debt and affinity that Pinsky's originality is constituted. Tracing his artistic development, I think we can see that Pinsky's own work provides the terms in which my proposition must be understood. Since our selves are turned on the great wheel of history and language, we owe whatever combination of qualities that might distinguish us, formal and vulgar, comic and ecstatic, to mysterious forces we disregard at our own peril. Pinsky's is a poetry of acknowledgment, and its power grows from his deep awareness—sometimes wariness, sometimes worship—of the literary, linguistic, and historical precedents that continue to design his life even as he writes today. Acknowledging Eliot, Pinsky calls him an "inventor," which Pound defined as a writer who discovers "a particular process or more than one mode and process." Above inventors, said Pound, stands the small class of "masters," those "who, apart from their own inventions, are able to assimilate and co-ordinate a large number of preceding inventions." This, near the end of the twentieth century, in both his poetry and his prose, is what Robert Pinsky is doing.

Robert Pinsky (essay date March-April 1996)

SOURCE: "American Poetry in American Life," in *The American Poetry Review*, Vol. 25, No. 2, March-April, 1996, pp. 19-23.

[*In the essay below, Pinsky contemplates the social contexts of American poetry in contemporary America, tracing the development of its various manifestations and emphasizing the individual scale of its character.*]

What is the place of American poetry in American life?

Walt Whitman saw that the United States in its size and diversity, its relative freedom from aristocratic institutions and folk traditions, would need holding together. He thought it would be held together by poetry, by the American bard. He took that to be the meaning of American poetry: the machine created from words that would provide a form to hold us together, as other nations are held together by forms that hark back to old court cultures or to ancestral folk roots.

That has not been the case. You could make a stronger argument that such binding together of what threatens to come apart is accomplished by television, by twentieth-century popular music, and by professional sports, forms of the American genius which Whitman could not have predicted, and which he might have adored.

What then is poetry's actual place here, and what does the answer tell us about our country? For instance, is poetry in America today altogether an elite art: for, by and of the few? Or does it reflect some of the democratic ideals and vision—still powerfully appealing, however vague or unfulfilled—of Walt Whitman?

To put the question differently, do the various ways the art of poetry pops up in American life today suggest any historical meaning or coherence? I mean to include all the diverse social facts we see that might mean "poetry" to anyone: the *Norton Anthology of Modern Poetry* and the *Norton Anthology of Postmodern Poetry*; Poets in the Schools, in hospitals, residences for the elderly, prisons, and so forth. (Having occasionally visited prisons to teach or to attend readings by inmates, as many American poets have done, I have wondered if the prison system is at least one area of American life where poetry sometimes has central, unquestionable importance, both for individuals and as a good that helps bind various individuals together.) I include, also, the poems published in the *New Yorker* and *The New Republic* each week; rap music; poetry slams in bars; poetry readings; summer conferences; middle-aged nostalgia for the heyday of Bob Dylan; the importance of ethnic, gender, sexual-preference paradigms and audiences; the decline among academics of the old modernist idea of art as replacing religion; current highbrow movements like "language poetry" or "new formalism"; successful publishing phenomena ranging up and down the scale from Rod McKuen and Khalil Gibran, through Charles Bukowski, to Allen Ginsberg; the resurgence of regionalism; the ascendance of theory in scholarship and a dearth of serious, practical criticism of new work; and, along with the rise of creative writing as an academic discipline, magazine articles deploring that rise, associating it with a decline in the art itself.

As a practical matter, I am interested in the flourishing but much-criticized institution of university creative writing programs—a subject that has taken on heightened interest for me in recent years, since I joined such a program. (Like many writers of my generation who now teach in creative writing programs, I never attended one as a student.)

All these activities are a matter primarily not of art, but of culture. That is, poetry like any art has a complex social setting. And arts change, and their social setting changes, in related processes that affect the cultural meaning of any new work and the world that surrounds it, in the mind of the writer and in the mind of the reader.

When I was a child, in the nineteen-forties, many of the high-school-educated adults in lower-middle-class families like mine could recite some lines of poetry, often something sonorous and richly elegant purely as language: the opening stanza of Thomas Gray's "Elegy Written in a Country Churchyard," perhaps; or some of Portia's "The quality of mercy is not strained" speech from *The Merchant of Venice*; or one of the better known Shakespeare sonnets; or Wordsworth's "The world is too much with us" sonnet; or perhaps even part of Keats's "To Autumn," or part of Wordsworth's "Tintern Abbey" ode, which in a survey of English teachers conducted by the *American Mercury* magazine in the 1920's was voted the greatest poem in the English language.

Or in a different, but related vein, people of the older generations might have by heart some "philosophical" tags: stanzas of Edward Fitzgerald's gorgeously fatalistic and melancholy *Rubaiyat*; or some of the Victorian and post-Victorian poetry of existential, implicitly or explicitly, agnostic moral uplift, such as Kipling's "If," or W. E. Henley's "Invictus" ("Out of the night that covers me, / Black as the pit from pole to pole," said Mr. Poppik, the man who delivered seltzer to our apartment, "I thank whatever gods may be / For my unconquerable soul").

Finally, and more widely known than either of the first two categories, there were sentimental verse narratives, elegiac and nostalgic, like "The Old Oaken Bucket"—a copy of which is found on the body of the man who throws himself into the threshing-machine in Willa Cather's *My Antonia*. "Casey at the Bat," which is extremely elegiac and nostalgic toward its small-town past, is a journalistic and vaudeville example of the genre, and Longfellow's *Hiawatha* is a high-culture, literary example. (Robert Frost's poem "Directive" is the greatest modernist variation on this genre.)

I suppose that this presence of poetry, thin but distinct, in the minds of the adults I knew can be credited to an American conception of democracy: that is, to American public schools in the spirit of John Dewey. Practical yet highminded, those schools found a place for poetry in the education and social integration of the offspring of immigrants, farmers, and workers. Poetry functioned as

ornamental language, as medicinal, uplifting language to replace a waning religious certainty, and as a narrative expression, thereby containment, of grief for a lost, innocent past.

This cultural pond I have tried to sketch should not itself be the object of our nostalgia. Fairly shallow and quickly evaporating, it had become cut off from its sources in the nineteenth-century past. In the Protestant country's towns and cities, on the Fourth of July, in the nineteenth century, people used to gather around bandstands for the purpose of hearing not so much fireworks or band concerts as patriotic speeches—which invariably quoted and borrowed swatches of Milton's *Paradise Lost*. John Hollander's monumental recent anthology of nineteenth-century American verse shows how deeply poetry permeated the culture, and how entirely Milton permeated the poetry.

Cut off from that past, the backwater body of poetry I now and then heard was also severed in another way—being cut off, too, from the upper-middle-class culture. In the "high" culture of salons (still extant), and of quarterlies, galleries, and universities, the nineteenth-century canon of Mr. Poppik had already decades before, been displaced and discredited by the onslaught of modernism. The eloquence of Gray and FitzGerald, though it may have indelibly formed the taste of the Modernists Ezra Pound and T. S. Eliot themselves, had in another sense been banished, though we can of course hear its echo in the contemporary high-style writing of, say, W. S. Merwin, just as there may be some ghost of secular moral uplift in Gary Snyder or of nostalgia for lost innocence in John Ashbery. Styles in an art change more rapidly than the needs they fill.

In sweeping away sentimentality and softness, as I was taught in college that they did, Pound and Eliot do not appear to have had in mind the sweeping-away of the upper-middle-class audience. When Pound titled a prose piece "The Constant Preaching to the Mob"—the point of the piece is to discredit "the lie" that Anglo-Saxon poets or Homer performed their "lordly art" for the amusement of ordinary folk and warriors at dinnertime—he had in mind a large, if genteel, "mob" of cultivated readers. Pound's dictum that the artist supplies the antennae of the race implies such readers.

Whether such a "mob" of readers existed; whether Pound and Eliot had to leave America for London in order to find a cultural setting, rigidly stratified by class, where poetry was attended to by the upper classes; whether they went to London in order to invent the figment of such a culture; whether contemporary nostalgists are sentimental in imagining some supposed heyday of poetry in America—however you look at these questions, they suggest the way Pound and Eliot generated a powerful sense of social context, an idea of a poetry audience that affected my generation and perhaps later ones too.

The firm sense of a leisure-class poetry audience is more obvious in Eliot's essays, and in the Eliot persona, than in the case of Pound, who liked to boast that his ancestors the Loomises were very well known horse thieves in New York state. But Pound was also related to Longfellow, on his mother's side, and was taken to Venice at the age of twelve: that is, he was a member of the American provincial elite. The flamboyant rhetoric of his early journalism is that of an insurgent, but not an invader; it is a raucous insider who writes in 1918:

> As for the nineteenth century, with all respect to its achievements, I think we shall look back upon it as a rather blurry, messy sort of a period, a rather sentimentalistic, mannerish sort of a period. I say this without any self-righteousness, with no self-satisfaction.

Possibly this assumption—of being inside a literary culture in which poetry commands significant attention, and exerts considerable force—provides the story of modernism with some of its enduring power and allure, underlying the more obvious appeal in the idea of a revolution sweeping clean.

Power and allure such passages surely had for me when I first read them in college. Like many Americans, I read this modernist denunciation of the overthrown nineteenth century with a thrill of assent, as a knowing recruit, at virtually the same moment as I was beginning to acquaint myself with the thing overthrown—or maybe not at the same moment, maybe even a little before. To put it differently, many of us learned simultaneously to be intoxicated by the Yeats of "He Wishes for the Cloths of Heaven"—improvising an imagined former immersion in such art, like delighted millionaires buying the ancestors with the country home—and to be de-toxed by the later Yeats of "Sailing to Byzantium," a poem that for a time became poetry itself for me.

With a thrill perhaps related to the attraction of deconstruction for a later generation of students, at college in the late fifties and early sixties I discovered the great mainstream of Romantic eloquence behind the puddle of snatches and chestnuts I knew as a child, at the same time as I was in some imaginary way disclaiming that eloquence—"blurry, messy"—through the surrogates of Pound, Eliot, late Yeats, Williams, Stevens.

These are complicated transactions. The nineteenth century, for example, was about to be rehabilitated by critical fashion, and the nineteenth-century core of the modernists to be anatomized. Though the social attitudes of many modernists were reactionary—snobbish, anti-Semitic, provin-

cial, even fascistic—they could be perceived as welcoming first generation newcomers to "high culture" because they disrupted that culture by despising certain pillars of it, and because the gentility or complacency of the displaced Georgian poetry, especially to urban Americans, seemed inherently anti-democratic. The narrative of revision and overthrow, itself, lets air into the perceived culture.

Modernism offered a way to join the club, in a variation on Groucho's joke, and to disclaim it: or conversely, and more personally, a way to feel both loyal and superior to my father beaming as he chanted a forced-memorization fragment, "Great God! I'd rather be / A pagan suckled in a creed outworn!" (I wish I could remember which Jewish friend of mine recounts how while reading that poem one day he realized with a sudden shock that he was a pagan suckled in a creed outworn.) It seemed possible, in other words, to attempt to write a poem that might be both part of poetry in English, and part of oneself.

It is important to say at this point that none of this would have any meaning if it were not based on great works of art. When I was a freshman in college I typed out the poem "Sailing to Byzantium" and taped it to the wall over my toaster:

> *O sages standing in God's holy fire*
> *As in the gold mosaic of a wall*
> *Come from the holy fire, perne in a gyre,*
> *And be the singing-masters of my soul.*
> *Consume my heart away; sick with desire*
> *And fastened to a dying animal*
> *It knows not what it is; and gather me*
> *Into the artifice of eternity*

"Consume my heart away; sick with desire / And fastened to a dying animal / It knows not what it is; and gather me / Into the artifice of eternity." This retains a majesty not to be explained, but I think that part of its power for me was and is the universalizing gesture: the soul is tied to a dying thing, and does not itself know what it is, but those mortifications also betaken that the soul struggles toward a destiny unencompassed by any terms it has ever heard or seen: explosive as a meaning in American Sign Language bursting out of a body. That struggle, toward something specific but mysterious—"the artifice of eternity"—anchors the noble sweep of the triads near the beginning, "Whatever is begotten, born, and dies"; and at the end, "Of what is past, or passing, or to come."

Yeats's "holy city," being at least half pagan, embodies a spiritual center that is not Christian nor Jewish nor anything quite under the sun. It embodies the nineteenth-century religion of art, in other words, presented in modernist terms.

For English-speaking readers coming into the great literature of the language from groups previously outside it, outside by virtue of circumstances like geography or social class or race or politics, that holy city of art, in this work and in others—"Portrait of the Artist as a Young Man" for example—has been a transforming presence. This is an ideal fresh for all its ties to the remote past, exhilarating, made in part out of the language used every day since childhood as casually as dimes and nickels, yet austerely challenging—"lordly," to borrow another Poundian term—in ways independent of such matters as, for example, the this-worldly opinions and outlook of William Butler Yeats.

As an evocation of that lordly presence or holy city, "Sailing to Byzantium" contains the most cogent critique possible of creative writing courses:

> *Nor is there singing school but studying*
> *Monuments of its own magnificence.*

I think of these two lines whenever I think about my profession of teaching writing. These terms are quite absolute—as absolute as the neglect that in the country of begetting, birth and death is shown by "all" toward "monuments," a word whose repetition, especially in comparison to the delicate enameled gold bird, has an unsettling funerary or civic quality. The older poetry in Yeats's mind must have included Keats's "Ode to a Nightingale," a monument which was itself written by a member of the urban lower class who heard the nightingale singing not at an English country estate or in Fiesole, but outside a friend's house in Hampstead. Our first sense of Yeats's transformation may be to emphasize artifice, the change from Keats's hidden, live nightingale to a mechanical bird displayed on a branch. But another aspect of this transformation is to introduce the city omitted from Keats's poem: to make the bird part of a social space: official, splendid, courtly.

The formulation is not only uncompromising, then; it is awe-inspiring as well: the only singing school is studying monumental examples of magnificent singing. The delicate quality of the image of the bird, and the charming, intimate, Persian-miniature quality of the drowsy emperor are balanced by the idea of a school made of magnificent monuments with singing-masters who stand in the gold mosaic of a wall.

We can giggle a little in noting that Yeats does not say, there is no singing school but taking workshops with Derek Walcott, or there is no singing school but registering for the translation seminar, two literature courses and so forth. But in reminding me in my own belief that any study of art must depend upon attention to great examples of the practice of that art, Yeats's lines with their solemn air of the public, perhaps even the imperial, also remind me that art is not pure: the curator and transmitter of art is society.

Let me now present a small theory of creative writing, a relatively recent phenomenon, in relation to American society. When I began writing poems there were a few writing programs, at Iowa and some other schools, but they seemed a minor part of the scene. Like many of my poet friends born, like me, around 1940—Robert Hass, Frank Bidart—I attended a Ph.D. program. But beginning with people a little younger than us something changes.

To see this watershed clearly, consider the *Harvard Book of Contemporary Poetry,* edited by Helen Vendler and published by the Harvard University Press in 1985. Until the most recent generations you could have assembled quite a respectable anthology representing American poetry of this century by including only poets who went to Harvard. I mean not only graduates like T. S. Eliot and dropouts like Robert Frost and Wallace Stevens, but recent figures as diverse as John Ashbery, Robert Bly, Robert Creeley, Donald Hall, Frank O'Hara, and Adrienne Rich. An imaginary and aesthetically wide-ranging anthology that extended beyond Harvard would include such Ivy Leaguers as Allen Ginsberg (Columbia) and W. S. Merwin (Princeton), or in their generation Marianne Moore at Bryn Mawr and Ezra Pound and W. C. Williams at the University of Pennsylvania. Apparently, some kind of change occurs with the generation born after that of Adrienne Rich at Radcliffe and Sylvia Plath at Smith.

A remarkable fact about the *Harvard Book* is that of the younger poets represented, those born since 1935, not one attended college at Harvard or Radcliffe.

In fact, hardly any of the younger generation in the book attended an eastern private college or university. This is partly coincidence, no doubt, but just the same, I think that this sampling reflects the fact that American highbrow culture, though still very far from classless, is much less of a northeastern or Ivy League property than it was just twenty or thirty years ago. Since Vendler is a strong-minded critic, not particularly populist, who made her selections according to her literary judgement, the poets in her anthology represent a reasonable sampling—that is, one that could be considered "random" in this respect. Here are the alma maters of the eleven youngest poets included, born between 1935 and 1952: Davidson College; California State College in Los Angeles; N.Y.U.; University of California, Riverside; Rutgers, the State University of New Jersey; the University of Virginia; no college degree; the University of Illinois; the State University of New York at Binghamton; "a French *lycée* in Rome"; and the University of Miami. It would be laughable to suggest that this inventory represents some catalogue of the oppressed or the excluded. And no one ever said, "There is no singing school but Harvard." But I think the list does reflect a relatively subtle but distinct social change: in region and in class, poetry like much else has been dispersed—to Montana, to Iowa, to Illinois, to those prisons and schools for the blind, and to adult creative writing classes. It is a truism that factors like the expansion of state universities, the GI bill, and demographic movement have meant that many kinds of cultural goods are more widely distributed, less contained in traditional centers, than they were before World War II.

Along with many other aspects of American life, poetry is less concentrated in a region or an elite—and more professionalized—than it was before. In the absence of the folk traditions or the aristocratic traditions or the cultural homogeneity another society might have, we develop more or less professional, middle-class institutions to satisfy what seems to be a fundamental hunger for the art: the MFA, the summer conference where people can work on their writing skills as if on their tennis or violin technique. What once provided a center of taste in one region and class of the country—something slightly resembling the great European capitals—has been replaced by the newer institutions, spread around the country. In the spirit of Whitman, we ought to welcome this, even if it is equally true that in the spirit of—who? Mencken or Twain?—we ought to be wary and critical as well.

This dispersal or transformation—and a nostalgic, half-conscious snobbery that resents it—may underlie some of the peculiar scorn directed at creative writing programs, and at contemporary poetry. It is tempting merely to dismiss such scorn, especially insofar as it laments a vague or implausible good old days of poetry. Such lamenting of poetry's present state—sometimes sentimentalizing or inflating that vague utopian former day—has become a journalistic category.

The authors of these pieces rarely pay convincing attention to contemporary poems, nor to the supposedly longed-for poetry of the past. From that vagueness of attention I conclude that whatever they signify—and they certainly signify something—it probably has to do with some area of feeling, different from poetry itself, some social current or attitude. I will share one particularly silly example, a sentence written by Joseph Epstein in his article "Who Killed Poetry," published in *Commentary*:

> The crowds in London once stood on their toes to see Tennyson pass; today a figure like Tennyson probably would not like poetry and might not even read it.

Think about it—I dare you. Tennyson would not read Tennyson, if he were alive today? Is this a way of saying that Epstein does not read *In Memoriam*? Is the standing on toes of "the crowds" really Epstein's cultural touchstone? Or were they bums? How does he know what Tennyson "probably would not like"? What is "a figure like Tennyson"? If the crowds were standing around flatfooted when Hopkins or Hardy passed, does that mean the decline had set in by their day? Or—finally—did Tennyson perhaps draw a crowd for historical reasons not entirely to do with poetry? Perhaps that is what "a figure like Tennyson" means.

It is hard not to conclude that an important element here is a myth of the superior past, when edifying highbrow artifacts were popular, and their artificers rich and famous. This myth can be grafted onto crowds of Victorian celebrity-seekers or for that matter onto the sweet but unheroic quotations and fragments that were in the heads of my parents' generation. As a myth, this idea may have been more plausible in the days when American "high" culture was centered in a relatively small number of places and institutions. The author of the sentence seems to me to be half in love with the idea of popular taste as the measure of all things, and half terrified by that same idea. In the decline of an aristocratic standard of taste that he half loathes, half would like to rely on, he turns his scorn toward something that he calls "poetry nowadays."

Such gestures in other words may respond more to a half-conscious idea about the culture as a whole than they respond to actual poems, old or new. Insofar as they have to do with poetry, it may be that poetry's actual diffusion—into the often ungraceful or clumsy terrain of local adult education classes, summer conferences, creative writing classes at varying levels of distinction, poets encouraging the writing of blind or deaf children, etc.—offends the myth of its golden age.

On the other hand, however feeble or inauthentic the attacks on it may be, there are repellent elements in the institution of creative writing: valuable insofar as it makes the art available as a conduit for poetry from the past to the present, creative writing is a blight when it becomes a guild, implicitly limiting practice to certificate-bearing members, or when it becomes an Academy, promoting official styles and sanctioned authors. Certainly, there is something to resist as well as something to admire in the spirit of creative writing—a spirit which I'll summarize as dispersed in the provinces rather than centered in a capital, rhetorical and practical rather than scholarly, professional rather than hieratic, American rather than European, middle-class rather than aristocratic. The dispersion is in itself more noble than the elite it replaces; the guild, or an Academy with "poet" merely another job description, is more offensive than any elite.

As with many aspects of American life since World War

II, the fact that the university has become a harbor for art—even the arts of jazz and cinema!—seems part of an ambiguous bargain, where heightened possibility may be bartered for lost autonomy. Does the improvised or extended institution bring a cultural good to more of us, or merely feed us a cheap imitation? Does it keep alive what our artists have made, or officially embalm it—or briskly turn away from the past, from "monuments of its own magnificence," altogether?

We can hope that as the organism of culture generates an institution, it also makes antibodies of a kind to resist it. From this viewpoint, disparate phenomena like the rise of poetry bars, with their raucous contests, and the elevation of estimable foreign writers—Milosz, Akhmatova, Neruda, and Rilke seem to be the favorite poets of my students—can be seen as two responses counter to provincialism, to the potential for a dreary, Soviet-like poetry, chauvinistic and institutionally sanctioned.

. . . I insist: the medium of poetry is not words, not even lines, not even sounds; the medium of poetry is the vibrating column of air rising up from the chest of one person, shaped inside the voice-box and inside the mouth into meaning sounds, emerging one at a time and therefore in a certain order.

—Robert Pinsky

I take it to be a kind of sacred principle that the purpose of study is in part reverence for the thing studied—beyond any benefit to us who study. Creative writing is still adjusting its relation to that principle, and doing so at a time when it is inheriting responsibilities from older forms of study. I have heard that some universities no longer have a Department of English, or a Department of French, and so forth, but a new entity called the Department of Literary Theory. The next logical step is for creative writing to evolve into a Department of Literary Practice.

Leaving institutions aside, poetry's social place must also be understood in relation to poetry's form. In fact, if challenged to define what is most often or essentially lacking in the cultural institutions we Americans have improvised for poetry—from prisons to universities, from rock poetry to language poetry, from Creative Writing to Deconstruction—my answer would be an understanding of the form.

The form of an art is determined by its medium. I have said before in writing that poetry is the most bodily of all the arts—and my friends have gently suggested that I had gotten a bit carried away: "Uh, Robert—*dancing* has more to do with the body, doesn't it?"

But no, I insist: the medium of poetry is not words, not even lines, not even sounds; the medium of poetry is the vibrating column of air rising up from the chest of one person, shaped inside the voice-box and inside the mouth into meaning sounds, emerging one at a time and therefore in a certain order.

That is, the medium of poetry issues from an individual body—and not necessarily a gifted body, not necessarily the body of the artist. Because the medium comes from inside of the body, and because it is shaped by the artist for the ordinary person's physical presence and performance, I repeat that poetry is a physical art, indeed a bodily art, and indeed the most bodily of arts.

A poem is written to be said and heard, not necessarily by an impressive actor or by a poet who has studied self-presentation; it is a more intimate or personal form than theater, then. This explains why I have been so moved by certain performances of poems by undergraduate students in classes where I have asked everyone to have a poem ready to recite from memory. The sound of a young woman I had underestimated saying the words of Yeats's "Easter 1916" with understanding, or some student of an unlikely ethnicity shaping his breath to the intricate passion of Herbert's "Church Monuments" or Robert Hayden's "Those Winter Sundays" moves me not because I am sentimental about American students, but because I am witnessing this art in practice. The relation between the sounds of poetry and memory are especially clear when the author, like Yeats or Herbert or Hayden, is long dead—the immediate intimacy of breath is combined, at such times, with the long survival of the past.

In contrast, the same set of principles explains to me why I have felt covertly bored when friends play for me their recording of Sir John Gielgud reciting Shakespeare's sonnets, or when a poet skillfully infuses not very distinguished work with a lot of personal force, thrilling an audience with what is basically the art of monologue. I try to murmur politely, recognizing the performance skills, but feeling the absence of poetry's form in these presentations.

If I am right, the meaning of poetry's form is extremely intimate as well as bodily; the form is also related to memory, and not only personal memory: it is cultural and historical memory as well. At this intersection of inward and outward, the form of poetry is based on the sounds of the words—not as set to music or as pronounced in a special way, but as spoken—words arranged to make an art of their sounds; the conventional printed notation for that art is lines. (In his important book, *The Founding of English Meter,* John Thompson says that by the Aristotelian principle that all art is imitation, what poetic rhythm imitates is the utterances of a language; lines of verse imitate sentences.) The art is not dependent on large numbers of people or elaborate equipment—unlike, say, the movies. It tends toward the scale of one body, and as a result it may be limited by a certain resistance to some means of mass presentation, and to mixed media. (I am thinking of the high-minded TV show where while an actor reads Stevens's "The Snow Man," we are shown banally artistic footage of a snowman.)

There is a social meaning to poetry's form, worth thinking about in relation to our time. To take a dramatic example of such social meaning—I hope not a melodramatic example—Czeslaw Milosz relates that during the Nazi occupation of Poland poetry became more popular. Even the most timid soul could feel, by carrying in a pocket a copy of some poem in Polish—a poem perhaps not even particularly political in content—that this possession was an assertion of identity, and therefore of resistance. In the presence of that monolithic, violent, totalitarian menace, a form based on the sufficiency of the individual—the sufficiency not merely of the individual itself, but the individual as bearer and instrument of a culture, in this case of a national past—took on a heightened social significance.

On a less extreme level, I think that the presence of poetry, of even one poem, in a contemporary American life has comparable powers and associations: with something defiantly ungovernable, or something loyal to a certain vision of the past, or merely something personal—personal in scale, as well as in nature. This art that ranges from the lyrical to the heroic takes place in the modest, intimate theater of the reader's human voice.

Any art has social significance if only because works imply who the art belongs to; if I am right about the form of poetry, poetry belongs to communities as a form of memory, but to individuals as a form of existence: the read or memorized or recited poem refers to the sounds of words and sentences formed in one present person's body, yet it functions as a reminder of the past. Whitman makes the great statement of this insight: that poetry, in a single human body, can embrace multitudes and epochs.

What might such a form mean in the context of a culture in love with mass, technological phenomena, distributed and duplicated and made available by astoundingly elegant and impressive devices? I love my CDs, my television, my computer, all my modern dazzlements: what does the form of poetry mean for me in this context?

The answer is not "nothing." On the evidence of the many applications to the writing program where I work, and on the evidence of writers' conferences, Poets in the Schools, and so forth—and on the evidence of my own soul—I would guess that poetry, true to its form and to its peculiar history in American culture, embodies a particular appetite for the equivalent, in art, of individual speech. It embodies the idea that in someone's voice, forming the words and sentences we exchange all day, there is the model for a form of art, with its defining place among other arts.

Sometimes we read that American poetry is in "crisis"—maybe the crisis is general, and projected onto poetry at a moment when art in general is being redefined: professors are writing about music videos and network series; Sven Birkerts is worried that electronic media are pillaging the domain of fiction; film actors are giving readings of their poetry at Chateau Marmont; creative writing seems to be simultaneously marking the end of one elite and—at its worst—spawning another.

It is dizzy-making, maybe fruitless to contemplate this "crisis" of mass and individual, elite and popular, academic and demotic. Muddling at trying to think through such tangled immensities, I realize that what I crave to hear is a voice—a voice in a poem. The single human voice—which cannot match film for spectacle, or music for glamour, or drama for ready emotion—conveys something of all of those things, along with the precious sense of human scale. Contrary to the vision of *Leaves of Grass,* poetry may not hold us together in the mass; yet we seem to carry it as the vessel of some valuable property, the property, perhaps, of a singular imagination inside some one of us. Such imagination sometimes finds its actual voice in poetry. The time of its greatness is by no means over.

Katha Pollitt (review date 18 August 1996)

SOURCE: "World of Wonders," in *The New York Times Book Review,* August 18, 1996, p. 9.

[*Below, Pollitt admires the freshness of Pinsky's verse in* The Figured Wheel.]

Robert Pinsky's extraordinarily accomplished and beautiful volume of collected poems, **The Figured Wheel,** will remind readers that here is a poet who, without forming a mini-movement or setting himself loudly at odds with the dominant tendencies of American poetry, has brought into it something new—beginning with his first volume, **Sadness and Happiness** (1975), and gathering authority with each subsequent book. Call it a way of being autobiographical without being confessional, of connecting the particulars of the self—his Jewishness; his 1940's and 50's childhood in Long Branch, N.J.; his adult life as "professor or / Poet or parent or writing conference pooh-bah"—with the largest intellectual concerns of history, culture, psychology and art.

Poetry has become so disconnected from the other literary arts that we don't usually look for a poet to share important affinities except with other poets.
— *Katha Pollitt*

Poetry has become so disconnected from the other literary arts that we don't usually look for a poet to share important affinities except with other poets. But one of Mr. Pinsky's great accomplishments is the way he recoups for poetry some of the pleasures of prose: storytelling, humor, the rich texture of a world filled with people and ideas. In its free and vigorous play of mind, his **"Essay on Psychiatrists"** really is an essay, a witty, clear-eyed 21-part argument that moves from a group portrait of psychiatrists as a bourgeois social type (liberal politics, B'nai B'rith, "a place on the Cape with Marimekko drapes") to a large and fully earned conclusion: "But it is all bosh, the false / Link between genius and sickness."

A full accounting of his literary connections would have to include Saul Bellow, Bernard Malamud, Philip Roth and Cynthia Ozick—Jewish novelists with whom he shares a wide variety of concerns. There's the fascination with fables and rabbinic lore (**"The Rhyme of Reb Nachman," "From the Childhood of Jesus,"** the jewel-like prose tale **"Jesus and Isolt"**). There's the nostalgic love-hatred for the stifling familial urgencies of the now-vanished world of lower-middle-class Jewish immigrants and the celebration of the talismans—movies, pop music, comics, sports—by which those immigrants' children defined themselves as Americans. In **"The Night Game,"** Mr. Pinsky recalls himself as a child imagining a Jewish southpaw "Even more gifted / Than Whitey Ford" who refuses to pitch on Yom Kippur. The long poem **"History of My Heart"** begins with his mother remembering Fats Waller improvising on a piano "the size of a lady's jewel box or a wedding cake" in the toy department of Macy's, that symbol of democratic glamour. In **"A Woman,"** a grandmother figure attempts to instill in a child her own Old World suspicions and terrors as they walk through an ordinary Long Branch day that seems to range across centuries—from the "imbecile / Panic of the chickens" slaughtered in the market to the purchase of a uniquely American treat, a milkshake. Although the poem ends with the child's vow

"Never to forgive her" for holding him back from a Halloween parade, what it shows is that the woman's half-mad smotherings and warnings have awakened the child to self-awareness and a heightened perception of the world. As the title suggests, she's a muse.

It is not surprising that Mr. Pinsky, whose last book was a widely praised translation of Dante's *Inferno* into modern terza rima, should have large ambitions for his own poems. Even the titles of his books proclaim his intention to grapple with major themes: *Sadness and Happiness, An Explanation of America, History of My Heart, Poetry and the World.* One of the earliest poems collected here, **"Poem About People,"** is a tragicomic meditation on humanity itself:

> In the movies, when the sensitive
> Young Jewish soldier nearly drowns
> Trying to rescue the thrashing
> Anti-semitic bully, swimming across
> The river raked by nazi fire,
> The awful part is the part truth:
> Hate my whole kind, but me,
> Love me for myself.

The determination with which the early poems set themselves in opposition to the then-dominant confessional mode in favor of the ironic, the didactic, the "discursive" (to use Mr. Pinsky's own term) can make them seem dry or willed today, a bit like the benign and prudent therapists cautiously lauded in **"Essay on Psychiatrists."** It is really with *History of My Heart* (1984) that Mr. Pinsky finds a way of making a poem that is, well, poetical, that makes images and the connections—or gaps—between images bear a meaning whose emotional resonance derives in part from its indeterminacy. **"The New Saddhus"** imagines a multicultural assortment of middle-aged men, "Kurd, Celt, Marxist and Rotarian," setting out on a mysterious pilgrimage. Is it a rejection of breadwinning and family life, or a new bend in the masculine (and why only masculine?) life path? In the poem **"The Figured Wheel,"** what is that fantastically decorated juggernaut that rolls over teeming, unresisting humanity—language, culture, history? The way all three both create and destroy? These images have a vitality, a strangeness that overflows interpretation.

Similarly, **"Shirt"** is a kind of free-associative catalogue that encompasses technical sewing terms, Asian sweatshop workers "Gossiping over tea and noodles on their break," the Triangle factory fire, Hart Crane, the invention of tartans, Southern slavery and more. A shirt, it would seem, is a kind of poem:

> George Herbert, your descendant is a Black
> Lady in South Carolina, her name is Irma

And she inspected my shirt. Its color and fit
And feel and its clean smell have satisfied
Both her and me.

"Shirt" is a dazzling bravura performance, but it suggests a risk attached to the Whitman stance of "I am large, I contain multitudes." I'm not so sure that Irma is as happy to inspect that shirt as Mr. Pinsky is to wear it. There are times in these poems when one feels that Wordsworth's egotistical sublime is trying very hard—too hard—to be Keats's negative capability, and that what is presented as a kind of grand vision of humanity is a version of self-delight. As with Whitman, as with the Eastern philosophies that furnish him with so many gorgeous examples and metaphors, there's a potential for coldness in Mr. Pinsky's wide-angle vision.

Most of the time, though, the poems of his maturity manage their startling shifts and juxtapositions in ways that give intellectual and sensuous delight. You can read **"At Pleasure Bay"** a dozen times and still feel a kind of delicious surprise at the way Mr. Pinsky moves from the 1927 double suicide of "the Chief of Police and Mrs. W." through music and bootlegging and boats and Unity Mitford's infatuation with Hitler, all the way to reincarnation—the whole ultimately unfathomable round of violence, passion, beauty and sorrow that is human experience coming back always a little different, like the catbird in the willows singing "never the same phrase twice." Who else could have written **"The Refinery,"** in which ancient animal gods from the collective unconscious wake up and take a train to the factory of language (imagined as a kind of petroleum, pressed out of human history while they were sleeping)? Or the recent **"Impossible to Tell,"** which moves between the 17th-century Japanese poet Basho and a friend's sudden death, gives full-dress and very funny versions of two Jewish jokes and—while positing that human existence resembles a renga, a Japanese interlinked poetical form—is itself a kind of renga.

What makes Mr. Pinsky such a rewarding and exciting writer is the sense he gives, in the very shape and structure of his poems, of getting at the depths of human experience, in which everything is always repeated but also always new. The feathery and furry tribal gods, Jesus, Basho, the frail old people who came to his father for eyeglasses, Shiva and Parvati, the chief and Mrs. W. and Robert Pinsky himself are all characters in a story that has no end and possibly no ultimate meaning either but to which we listen spellbound because, like the figured wheel covered with mysterious symbols, it is our story.

Ralph Blumenthal (essay date 28 March 1997)

SOURCE: "A New Poet Laureate at Home with Dante, the Internet and Sometimes Both," in *The New York Times,* March 28, 1997, pp. C3.

[*In the following essay, Blumenthal provides an overview of Pinsky's life and career, reporting his response to being named poet laureate of the United States.*]

Robert Pinsky, a prize-winning poet who bridges Dante and the Internet, has been named the nation's next poet laureate. The selection is being announced today by the Librarian of Congress, James H. Billington, who cited Mr. Pinsky's mastery of computers as well as his translations and "his own probing poetry."

Like the last 8 of his 38 predecessors, the 56-year-old Mr. Pinsky will also carry the title of consultant in poetry, but there are few statutory duties for the pay ($35,000) outside of organizing several literary programs, readings and talks. Laureates, however, have used their two-year platform since 1937 to foster poetry in schools, workshops and cityscapes and to enhance the library's archives. The reigning laureate, Robert Hass, who bows out with a final lecture on May 1, crisscrossed the country taking the measure of literacy at citizen forums and Rotary Clubs and, not incidentally, collecting snippets of impromptu haiku from passers-by.

Mr. Pinsky, a professor of graduate writing at Boston University who propelled Dante onto the best-seller lists with his acclaimed 1994 verse translation of the *Inferno,* said in an interview in New York yesterday that he might take a tack from his classes and ask a broad spectrum of Americans, including powers that be in Washington, to read and record their favorite poems for the library. "What would President Clinton or Al Gore pick?" he asked. "Or Jesse Helms?"

"If people ask in 1,000 years who Americans were, this might help them figure it out," he said. Although poetry seems to be in some vogue, cropping up in movies and ever more popular public readings, Mr. Pinsky said it was still widely manhandled in schools.

"Teachers have pedagogically treated poems as an occasion to say something smart," he said. But poetry, he said, is as simple as art on an individual scale, its medium a single human voice. That, he said, is the secret of poetry's "immense power in an age of arts dominated by mechanical reproduction."

Not that Mr. Pinsky has anything against modern technology. He is the poetry editor of the Internet magazine *Slate* (at http://www.slate.com), and as a certifiable computer pioneer wrote a 1984 interactive "text adventure"

[*Mindwheel*] modeled loosely on the *Inferno*. "A side of me wants to try anything," he said.

In fact, he has commented, poetry and computers share two key attributes, speed and memory. "They share," he wrote, "the great human myth of trope, an image that could be called the secret passage: the discovery of large, manifold channels through a small ordinary-looking or all but invisible aperture."

And anyway, he asked, what is poetry but technology that uses the human body? He also likens poetry to ice-skating with its daring leaps and flashing vistas.

If Mr. Pinsky's translation of the *Inferno* popularized his name, the work becoming a selection of the Book of the Month Club and a best seller, he has long been highly regarded in literary circles for his five books of poetry since 1975 (*Sadness and Happiness, An Explanation of America, History of My Heart, The Want Bone, The Figured Wheel*); three books of prose (*Landor's Poetry, The Situation of Poetry, Poetry and the World*) and a translation of *The Separate Notebooks* by Czeslaw Milosz. He was at a Barnes & Noble bookstore in Boston last week giving a reading from *The Figured Wheel,* his latest collection, published last year and just now coming out in paperback, when calls reached him about his appointment.

He achieved his translation of Dante without a scholar's knowledge of Italian. "My work is not a work of scholarship," he said. "It's a work of metrical engineering."

Poetry gripped him from youth in Long Branch, N.J., he recalled, although his was not a literary family. His father was an optician and his grandfather, David Pinsky, was a small-time prizefighter, tavern-owner and bootlegger. But even before he know what poetry was, he said, he savored the sounds of words like the conductor's cry: "Passengers going to Hoboken, change trains at Summit."

At Rutgers University he wrote out Yeats's "Sailing to Byzantium" and taped it to a wall. Why? "It was the speed with which he covered the ground," Mr. Pinsky said. "Wow: 'artifice of eternity'!"

After college, he received a graduate fellowship at Stanford and taught English at the University of California at Berkeley before moving to Boston University, where, he said, he hopes to continue teaching after taking office in October. He and his wife, Ellen, a clinical psychologist, have three grown daughters.

He takes his poetic inspiration from everywhere and anything, he said. "If you look at this Tropicana container," he said, lifting it from the table, "when did they start putting paraffin on the carton and the fluttering banner here? If you could understand that, you might understand a lot of Western history." His poems seem hard to classify, ranging widely over Judeo-Christian themes, autobiography and genre scenes. "I like human artifacts," he said.

Being used to a noisy, crowded household, he says, he writes fast and almost anywhere, even in airports. "I can easily get a mass of clay on the table," he said, although he added that the last 20 percent could entail many drafts.

He plays the saxophone, and is an avid baseball fan and Red Sox rooter, by way of the Brooklyn Dodgers. "Being a Dodger fan is good preparation for being a Red Sox fan," he said.

Both teams, he said, exemplify "values deeper than success."

He said he was proud to follow many of his icons, including Robert Lowell, Elizabeth Bishop, Conrad Aiken, William Carlos Williams, Robert Frost and Robert Penn Warren. But he is also glad, he said, that the job description has expanded from just plain poet laureate to consultant in poetry as well.

"It's a greater distinction to be consulted than to be laureled," he said.

Elizabeth Mehren (essay date 10 June 1997)

SOURCE: "The Meter Is Running," in *Los Angeles Times*, June 10, 1997, pp. E1, E6.

[*In the essay below, Mehren summarizes the achievements of Pinsky's life and career, focusing on his passion for making poetry accessible to the masses.*]

A small smile brightened Robert Pinsky's face as he pondered the weekend's entertainment offerings. Listed in the newspaper—along with club happenings, flower shows, dinner theaters and the movie guide—were 16 separate poetry events.

Readings. Discussion groups. Open-mike poetry performances. Poetry slams, sort of like sports contests, but where 100 meters is not likely to induce a sweat.

"It's a truly popular art, an art everybody can enjoy," declared Pinsky, champion of odes on the Internet, advocate of everyday lyricism, believer in the simple certainty that a sonnet may dwell anywhere—for example, on the label of a catsup bottle. In Pinsky's view; poetry is the people's art form, and Pinsky, in turn, clearly is content to bear the mantle of the people's poet.

Which makes his official title, poet laureate of the United States, seem . . ."Kind of a paradox, isn't it?" he volunteered.

Raised in Long Branch, N.J., the 56-year-old professor of graduate writing at Boston University hardly seems the type to sport a crown of laurel leaves. He has a delicious sense of humor and an e-mail addiction issue. He haunts Fenway Park and cheers for the Red Sox, anyone's definition of a non-noble cause.

His father was an optician and amateur baseball player (for a team called the Jewish Aces); his grandfather was a tavern owner, bootlegger and small-time prizefighter. When he went off to Rutgers, Pinsky became the first member of his family ever to go to college. Even at graduate school at Stanford, his mother would call every week and beg him to take the optician's licensing exam, "something to fall back on." Pinsky would remind her he intended to become a university professor, a prospect from which his mother drew only scant comfort.

As the father of three grown daughters, Pinsky knows that "it's hard to say what makes a kid go a certain direction." But as a youth, even while playing sandlot baseball, he knew his own direction would be toward the arts. "Even my daydreams about being an athlete were rather theatrical," Pinsky remembered. He played the saxophone, moved by the rhythm as much as the sound. At Rutgers, he hand-wrote Yeats' "Sailing to Byzantium" and taped it to his dormitory wall. It remains his favorite poem.

His mother's fears notwithstanding, he found gainful academic employment. After Stanford, he taught at Wellesley before moving to the English department at UC Berkeley. But a feeling of intellectual smugness there made him uncomfortable, Pinsky said. His friends at Berkeley thought he was crazy when he uprooted his children and his wife, Ellen, a clinical psychologist, and headed for BU, a lesser-ranked school in a far colder place.

For Pinsky, it was a warm return to an active and prolific community of poets he had befriended during his Wellesley years, headed by his old friend Frank Bidart. "His literary ties, intellectual ties, spiritual ties, ties of direction were all here," poet Lloyd Schwartz, head of the creative writing program at the University of Massachusetts at Boston, said of Pinsky. "The center of Robert's writing life was here."

Like many in what Schwartz called "this strong circle of serious poets," Bidart and Pinsky were disciples of the late

Robert Lowell and followers also of the late Elizabeth Bishop. From his earliest days in this loose, but loyal group, Pinsky stood out as a speculative, abstract thinker. He took risks. He wrote a poetic essay about psychiatry. He forged a new translation of the *Inferno*—**The Inferno of Dante: A New Verse Translation** (1994)—and landed Dante on the bestseller list. Refusing to cede to the traditional aversion of some intellectuals to popular culture, he penned an ode to television and a poem about computers. One of his grand works, **An Explanation of America** (1979) is an epic poem written for his oldest daughter, now a manager at Borders Books in Los Angeles.

"There's a line, the last line, in **An Explanation of America,**" Schwartz said. "It reads: 'So large and strangely broken and unforeseen.' I think those phrases describe Robert's poetry. It's very ambitious, in the largest sense of the word. He deals with very big issues and themes. America! Poetry, and the world, what it means to be a humane person in the world. He deals with them not with the most traditional, logical, orderly and abstract, intellectual methods, but he uses a sort of intuition and psychological association. His mind in that poem is swinging wildly, in an unexpected and quite irrational, poetic way."

Pinsky's works combine "both a manic expressiveness and gesture, plus a very immediate and colloquial tone," agreed David St. John, a poet who teaches at the University of Southern California and who has lectured with Pinsky at the Napa Writers' Conference, where poetry readings are held amid the grapevines. "People feel very much at ease within one of his poems," St. John added. "They are very companionable poems."

Not only that, said St. John, but he is "absolutely enthralling to listen to. His sense of language is enacted in his own conversations."

Pinsky runs on megahertz energy, but even pausing for a *cafe latte* around the corner from his office, he speaks with dizzying eloquence. Here is Pinsky's explanation for why, in an increasingly mechanistic world, poetry is growing in popularity.

> The craving for it is even stronger in reaction to how powerful and brilliantly organized mass art has become. Mass art is being designed by talented experts, and being distributed and rapidly duplicated. The copy is the medium. The ultimate medium of the poem, even if the person reads the poem from a book that has been printed from 50,000 copies—the ultimate medium is one person's voice. Poetry is a vocal art. The medium of popular music is an album. It's an easily duplicable CD. In poetry, the mass distribution of the written word is only the means to an end.

As this country's 39th poet laureate, Pinsky follows on the poetic heels of his own icon, Lowell, as well as Randall Jarrell, Robert Frost and Robert Penn Warren. Most recently, Californian Robert Hass and Rita Dove held the post. Both said they came close to collapsing from the way they threw themselves into a job whose official duties are only to give one reading at the Library of Congress, to deliver one essay and to organize the library's literary programs.

But Hass and Dove took seriously the job's less carefully articulated mandate of increasing public awareness of poetry, and Pinsky can be expected to do the same. He plans to make mass access to poetry one of the primary planks of his platform. He envisions huge read-ins. He wants weekly poems on the Internet: Punch the right button and you can hear them read aloud. "One week it might be a contemporary poem, then a week later it might be a 16th century poem by Ben Jonson," Pinsky said.

Part of the $35,000-a-year poet laureate's job is to serve as a consultant to the Library of Congress, and already Pinsky is making plans for a giant poetry repository, videotaped readings, "25% to 30% by prominent Americans, and 70% to 75% the rest of us." Bill Clinton, Al Gore, Jesse Helms, Pinsky's tailor: "Everyone will read a favorite poem. The only thing that will be excluded is that you can't read your own work. My goal is to create an archive—what Americans do with the poems they love, what they do with their faces as they read them."

He also aims to broaden the teaching of poetry. By introducing small children to poems, he said, "you are teaching them the intellectual, physical coordination of ideas and meanings in a way that is fundamental to our nature as animals. Dr. Seuss is good for you."

There is little secret to his methodology for introducing young people to the wonders of verse. "I put it in two words. Read aloud," he said. "Not just when they are small. I still read aloud to my three daughters, who are 20 to 30 years old."

He is equally ferocious in his defense of the relationship between poetry and modern technology. Pinsky is the poetry editor of the weekly Internet magazine *Slate,* and feels fiercely that poetry online is "part of our time." He has little patience for the suggestion that posting poems in cyberspace might be construed in some circles as a cheap imitation.

"You might as well ask, did it cheapen poetry for poets to write odes celebrating the birthdays of kings in the 17th century?" Pinsky rejoined. The electronic revolution "is part of the world, and poetry is part of the world, too," he said.

His friend St. John sees Pinsky's passion for technology as one of his greatest virtues in his official role. "To Robert, to do something as ancient and as timeless as to write a poem, should not be at odds with the future, at odds with how consciousness is understood," he explained.

One way Pinsky said he interprets consciousness is by integrating humor and poetry. "For me, there's a kind of quickness, restlessness, surprise, vividness and sharpness that characterizes both poetry and comedy," he said. In the middle of **"Impossible to Tell,"** a poetic elegy that appears in Pinsky's major anthology, *The Figured Wheel* (1996), for example, Pinsky pauses to tell jokes, citing at one point—of all unpoetic references in an ode to a dead friend—Mel Brooks.

But there it is, Pinsky's sense that poetry knows no barriers, his belief that "poetry goes very, very deep," that it has "a mysterious power to assuage us and to bring us, together"—and that if, by some fluke, poetry is not in all of us, it should be.

Louise Glück (essay date July-August 1997)

SOURCE: "Story Tellers," in *The American Poetry Review,* July-August, 1997, pp. 9-12.

[*Below, Glück explains the ways a narrative impulse informs Pinsky's poetics, comparing his poetry with that of Stephen Dobyns.*]

The poet Stephen Dobyns, who is also the novelist Stephen Dobyns, once remarked with just irritation that the narrative, as a poetic strategy, is usually misread, or not taken for what in his opinion it is: a metaphor. As though when the poet couldn't think of anything interesting, he told a story.

Like Homer. Like the Bible.

Contemporary critics prefer, it appears, the static/rhapsodic, in which the translation of event to art is more literal: what is event in the world becomes, in the poem, luminous image. In fact, narrative is also transformation and recreation, and the use of stories managed in more ways, to more ends, than one. In the old battle to determine the greater form (a subject in itself) poet critics, eschewing the story, seem, like the Puritan fathers, to eschew entertainment, as though having a good time couldn't happen in the presence of sublime art. But the impulse to use narrative informs the work of some of our best (and certainly most original) poets. Dobyns, obviously, but also, in a quite different way, Robert Pinsky.

It is a standard misfortune of poets (and artists in general) that their work continues to be read according to whatever impressions or verdicts attended its debut. In consequence Robert Pinsky is often regarded as a poet of extensive dispassionate curiosity and wide learning, ethical by disposition, rational in bias, a maker of grids and systems, an organizer—the opposite of the fiery prophetic, the poet claimed by, overtaken by, emotion—and, in his calm, somehow disguised or withholding. Even when, as now, he is regularly and perceptively admired, he tends to be admired for his masterful interweavings of public and private, for his formal brilliance, for the extraordinary variety of his gifts (even passionately reverential notices sometimes digress with odd eagerness into Pinsky's work as a translator, his explorations of high-tech forms like computer games).

It is difficult to account exactly for the tone of this approbation. Pinsky is neither a poet of lyric compression nor a rhapsodist—the two forms to which readers habitually ascribe warmth, or intense feeling. And readers are, often, genuinely overwhelmed by the breadth of his erudition. But neither that erudition nor the poems' virtuosity completely explains the curious reticence and demurrals of even his most impassioned reviewers. It has sometimes seemed to me that he is read as though he were a cultural historian, in whose mind individual agony and enterprise are subsumed into, or emblematic of, panoramic history. Readers are, I suppose, distracted by Pinsky's considerable memory, his grasp of (and fascination with) data. But they mistake, I believe, the background for the foreground.

This problem with emphasis is in part a problem of expectation. In the ways we expect (at present) to see (or hear) the poet, Pinsky seems invisible, more the impresario than the coloratura. This preference for the heart-on-the-sleeve heart of lyric and rhapsodic poetry mistakes the performative nature of all art, mistakes performance for essence.

Moreover, there is, in Pinsky's human portraits, an even-handedness that can seem, by present standard of judgment, concealing. Unlike most of his peers, Pinsky is not especially interested in individual psychology. Like the parent of many children, determined to appear to love all equally, Pinsky seems, by this standard, either withholding, or (the explanation usually settled for) not interested in such things. We have been trained to distrust apparent absence of preference. And yet the same balanced affection informs everything Whitman ever did, though his work is, obviously, more effusive in manner. Human passion, human life—these seem, protected against the historical which is taken to be Pinsky's field of vision, merely the poignant laboring of tiny figures in a Bosch painting, or the stalwart repetitious efforts of valets and elevator boys, working hard for promotion. To the absence of visible bias, we impute either coolness of heart or, alternatively, larger, less immediate, aims, focuses.

None of these assumptions is correct. And yet, curiously, they are, none of them, exactly incorrect either. Pinsky truly is interested in history; he truly is not a poet of the struggling or transported first person. What is so strange is the persistence of my impression that Pinsky is, among poets singled out for highest praise, the poet read both most closely and most anxiously. The poet, perhaps, whose work makes most plain the limitation of the contemporary reader, even (perhaps especially) the trained reader.

For most of this century, poets have been divesting themselves of the arsenal of devices which had come to seem static or imprisoning. What remains is tone, the medium of the soul. Set aside, for the moment, the fact that very few poets are capable of evolving even a single unprecedented tone: the depressing corollary of this divestment has been marked atrophy of skills within the reader. Because Pinsky isn't using tone as an instrument of hasty self-portraiture, tone is hard to fix, fluid: for all their dazzling aural pleasure, these are not poems made to be acted out in Theater 101. Moreover, in Pinsky's art, form does what we have come to believe only tone can do. That is to say, form here is not intellectual construct but rather metaphor. For the poems to be understood at all they must be apprehended entire, as shapes.

I said earlier that readers have mistaken the background for the foreground. It may be more accurate to say that they miss the larger scrim against which history is projected, by which it is dwarfed. History, in these poems is a means not an end: to view it as an end is to miss the awe that permeates Pinsky's work.

History is what human action accumulates into. If Pinsky is not particularly interested in psychology, he is gripped by cause-and-effect. Hence (at the most obvious level) the mechanical figures. Hence, formally, the larger musical analogies, the way, in poem after poem, one figure answers another figure, like jazz improvisations: bird song, shard of narrative, shimmer of tree over water. The overwhelming preoccupation of the poems is less history than what lies beyond history: chaos, eternity. Projected against this unknowable void, history takes on the poignancy of what is (in other poets) the property of individual life. And the need to understand the shapes of history is driven by the hunger to know how chaos works: the poems try to outsmart, second guess human limitation: all their constructions are postulates, the single provable side of an algebraic equation, a seeking after parallel inference. Human life is to history as history is to chaos. Pinsky is less a synthesizer of data than a student of the great mysteries: against the background of the eternal, the void, stories are musical phrases, simultaneously completed formal shapes and inconclusive fragments.

Narrative elements, characteristically, figure in, but do not dominate the poems. Even when, as in **"From the Childhood of Jesus"** the story gives its shape to the whole, the poem invokes, in its closure, the shifting ground of the eternal, in a classic cinematic dissolve:

> . . .The moon
>
> Rose higher, the Jews put out their lights and slept,
> And all was calm and as it had been, except
>
> In the agitated household of the scribe Annas,
> And high in the dark, where unknown even to Jesus
>
> The twelve new sparrows flew aimlessly through the night,
> Not blinking or resting, as if never to alight.

Precisely because stories are not explored as psychological archetypes, Pinsky is free to use them as notes, or phrases, as a painter would use a wash of violet or sepia. A suggestion, a resonance. They fade in, fade out, unravel, and their long unwinding or unraveling is part of Pinsky's intent, and characteristic of his treatment of every element in the poem: don't shut it down, play it like a kite on a very long string, let its every implication, its every nuance, elaborate itself, express itself: if shape is metaphor, dangerous to impose it prematurely.

> In the willows along the river at Pleasure Bay
> A catbird singing, never the same phrase twice.

And then, answering the catbird, a swatch of story:

> Here under the pines a little off the road
> In 1927 the Chief of Police
> And Mrs. W. killed themselves together,
> Sitting in a roadster . . .

Layer after layer, the poem builds. The tenor in his clown costume finishing his aria, applause, cheers, other stories, all accumulate into the long trance, the held note of Pleasure Bay, our little errand in the world. The Chief and Mrs. W. come back again in the poem as they meant to, having died "to stay together, as local ghosts." No poem I can think of renders so indelibly the evanescence of the palpable:

> Here's where you might have slipped across the water
> When you were only a presence, at Pleasure Bay.

That the poem begins and ends with the same words, the first line echoed in the last line, makes it seem to have occurred in a heart beat, or less than a heart beat, all the stories, the war, the catbird, accumulating (in the absence of lyric compression) into the lyric moment: stopped time. Only in Pinsky's art, lyric time pulses and quivers, like the tenor's vibrato, shifting, adjusting. **"At Pleasure Bay"** (a title rich in itself in associative possibility) never undertakes to describe or fix the consciousness in which it occurs. Toward the poem's mid-point, "Shivers of a story that a child might hear / and half remember . . ." simulates the birth of awareness as much as it names a focus. In lesser hands, the poem would turn on itself here, the various elements reiterated, reconverging, as a mind forms itself around these details, sounds, mica-chips of narrative. But as Pinsky designs the poem, the emerging "you" who dominates its latter third presides over a movement increasingly spectral, non-concrete: the fixed verbs of the story, of the catbird's song, the "killed themselves together" of historical time, become the loose hypotheses of eternal speculation, as though individual mind and individual identity were the most, not least, elastic element:

> Here's where you might have slipped across the water
> When you were only a presence, at Pleasure Bay.

We don't respond to the narrative elements in Pinsky as we respond to stories, in part because outcome isn't an issue. The materials are either the materials of legend or, more typically, the narrative comes to us in pieces or summaries; these are, with the sensual data more common to poetry, components of developing perceptive life: one brain cell imprinted with a bird call, one with an old story, their apparently arbitrary juxtaposition less arbitrary than it initially seems—we have to back away a bit, so that perspective grows wide enough to accommodate diversity.

The visual correlative of a Pinsky poem would be an arc yearning upward. A poem by Stephen Dobyns is nothing like that: where Pinsky is essentially meditative, the poems elaborating themselves in coils and spirals, Dobyns's poems are a rapid downward trajectory, the poems' accumulating mass increasing their speed. Where Pinsky is speculative, Dobyns is apocalyptic, his use of narrative material much closer to what prose reading leads us to expect. Here, typically, the story shapes the poem; like the great novelists, Dobyns has a moral vision; he seems, sometimes, a cross between Jonathan Edwards and Quentin Tarantino, with something of Twain's slyness mixed in. The poems are fierce, impatient, judgmental, wildly funny. He has not been, as Pinsky has, praised and misunderstood. Neither has he received (except from other poets, among whom he has the status of the hero) the kind of attention his gifts deserve. His practice of several arts (and his staggering productivity) unnerve readers who have adopted a mantra concerning range: it bespeaks, they think, superficiality. Like all mantras, this simplifies judgments. In any case, the manifold examples of Dobyns's mastery continue to appear with stubborn frequency under various numbers in the Dewey decimal system.

Dobyns's range has cost him attention; so has his wit. Though the poems move like slalom runs, hair-raising, relentless, they are (many of them) too entertaining, too well written (to invoke Pound's notion) for classroom pieties. No one devises wilder, more unexpected occasions. But Dobyns's brilliance lies less in his initial inventiveness than in his sustained resourcefulness: in poem after poem, that resourcefulness builds, invention doubling and tripling like poker stakes.

His habit is to begin casually:

> This morning, because the snow swirled deep
> around my house, I made oatmeal for breakfast.

And the slight adjustments and modifications and amplifications that follow seem initially perfectly reasonable:

> At first it was runny so I added more oatmeal . . .

Within a few lines though the radio is "playing Spanish music," the speaker has become "passionate." And a great deal of oatmeal is being generated. Characteristically in Dobyns the casual occasion gets very quickly out of hand, the figurative taken too literally; even his wittiest poems generate, in their pacing, some flicker of dread.

It matters that this poem, in which the amassed pots of oatmeal become "souvenir ashtrays" and, eventually, an erotic Galatea, begins innocently; it matters that, once begun, its momentum is unstoppable. Life, Dobyns means us to see, is all momentum, speeding up as the end approaches; it won't (like poetry) stand still.

At a certain point in the poem, under the influence of that inspiring Spanish music, the impulse toward creation dislodges the impulse toward mass production (as in the evolution of mind or of civilization); the many pots of starchy clay become a woman made of oatmeal, and the poem reveals itself as parable, not anecdote. One of the conclusions you come to, after studying the work of Stephen Dobyns for a few decades, is that it is possible to be inventive and obsessive simultaneously (Frank Bidart's career offers another example of this phenomenon). Dobyns understands that the obsessive writer runs the risk of self imitation: he deals with this risk in several ways, partly by shrugging it off, knowing that in a career so monumentally fecund, larger architectural shapes must sooner or later be appar-

ent, and partly, crucially, through the combining of dramatic resourcefulness with a sort of tonal fearlessness. No one since Plath (and, before Plath, no one since D. H. Lawrence) has taken on the reader in such inspired and varied confrontations: this is one of poetry's genuinely thrilling tactics—impossible not to react (it is also, interestingly, the most dramatic way in which Dobyns is misunderstood, mainly by listeners who mistake the strategies of art for personal violence, personal aggression). As a tactic, combativeness of this kind must be inventive; we arm ourselves very quickly as readers; for combativeness to work, it must surprise us, throw us off guard. Too, there must be a sense of something more serious at work than simple misanthropy. Dobyns's confrontations are rooted in, fueled by, his insistence that we recognize our own taste for palatable falsehood, and, having recognized it, recognize its capacity to destroy feeling.

The diversity of Dobyns's scenarios has a second function (beyond what it accomplishes in service of tone), a function specifically connected to the obsessive core of his work. The story he tells, over and over, is the death of hope (or delusion), the death of innocence, an aspect of which becomes, through the endless variety of the poems' locales and circumstances, its omnipresence. By showing us the wall everywhere, the poems insist that we see it: the hope they hold out is not the false hope of evasion but the hope that there may be, after the devastations of accuracy, durable wisdom.

As contemporary prose fiction has grown more static, evolving mainly as exploration of voice or consciousness, it has grown less explicitly moral in its preoccupations. Perhaps more clearly than any other American poet, Dobyns knows why: as an artist driven by moral passions and imperatives, he sees that only narrative can adequately represent in art the insidious onset of harm. This is hardly the lyric's forte: with its commitment to the concluded, the archetypal, the timeless, the lyric can hardly hope to embody what is by definition both progressive and dramatic. Dobyns writes poems in which it is impossible to fix the turn, the moment: how do you say, in "Oatmeal Deluxe," when, in the elaborate comic turn that constitutes the poem's first, say, two-thirds, the red flag goes up? When the speaker turns to his lover, the point is already made, the poem has proven what is now asserted as self-evident, because it has been, as metaphor, richly enacted:

> . . .You ask me
> why I don't love you, why you can't
> live with me. What can I tell you? If I
> can make a woman out of oatmeal, my friend,
> what trouble would I make for you, a woman?

That "Oatmeal Deluxe" would not be grouped among

Dobyns's harrowing poems makes the structural point more tellingly. The poem parallels creation as invention with creation as self delusion: the woman in this poem cannot be spared suffering, but her insistence on self delusion will prolong that suffering, and complicate it. As the turn makes plain, she insists on seeing this confrontation as a conflict of will; the point, though, is that if she gets what she wants (a life with the speaker, the demonic creator) her suffering will begin *in* that life and culminate, after that life explodes, in a moment like the present moment, with the added bleakness of self accusation. Why hadn't she read the signs, why had she wasted so much time trying to effect impossible transformations? The alternative isn't freedom from pain, but the substitution of the pain that comes of facing truth for the prolonged pain of denial.

As in all the great Dobyns poems, it is possible to see, even at the level of the grammar, the single fascination Dobyns shares with Pinsky, a fascination with cause-and-effect. (In an interesting reversal of lyric, which freezes narrative into static archetypal configurations, Dobyns has dramatized this fascination in a book of poems based on paintings; *The Balthus Poems* construct, for that painter's riveting tableaus, dramas, story lines; they recreate the implications of stillness in a different, more volatile, contemplative mode.)

Under the poems warnings and chastisements and ferocities, there seems to me to be a core of deep tenderness, increasingly apparent. The turn at the end of "Oatmeal Deluxe," the direct address with its complex nuance, that phrase "my friend" has been more widely copied by young poets than any similar gesture by any poet in my generation. Ironic, distant, and yet informed also by helpless affection, the tribal affection of mortal for mortal, all of us flawed, doomed, embarked on courses of damaging affection, always ready to respond to Spanish music, in our foolish, desperate obsessions, all of us incipiently scarred. Dobyns's notion of the social is more immediate, more pressing than Pinsky's: he tracks damage; not surprising that among his myriad forms is the detective novel, the novel in which the self's collision with the world must, as a matter of form, involve punishable crime. But I think at bottom Dobyns means to spare and to save: the savagery of his poems is less a taunt than an intended deterrent. He is a poet appalled by human fate, appalled that what can be foreseen cannot be prevented.

My dictionary defines "moral" in a paragraph of ways, almost all of which unite the idea of character and the idea of action. In practical terms, it is difficult to separate the two; in life, character inevitably becomes behavior (though the translation is sometimes surprising and includes the various devices by which we try to avoid revealing ourselves—silence, withdrawal, and so on). Insofar as poets

have been concerned with the moral they have tended to be concerned with the speaking of, and discerning of, truth; that poetry has not been preoccupied with the moral as it is transformed into and by gesture owes in part to poetry's treatment of the issue of time.

This has always been poetry's special province, a charged and resonant object. But the terms in which time is regarded have been absolute: death, age, the loss of love. Sequential time, that enacts itself in gesture (as opposed to ritual) has no place in the world of extremes and archetypes. It as remained, though, to be reclaimed for poetry by forms more imperfect and more expansive than the lyric, forms more interested in vicissitude and ramifications.

Certainly it is Pinsky's implicit subject. Time is what lies beyond history, surrounds it—**"At Pleasure Bay"** makes of time an envelope, an enclosure; time, like the poem, becomes that medium in which we are suspended, curiously free of gravity (this is different from lyric suspension, in that lyric time disdains or opposes history). In **"At Pleasure Bay,"** the reiterated phrase, reintroduced at intervals in its multiple variations, that phrase is "never the same," while not *exactly* the same stands, in the poem, for that which recurs as sound and as gesture; it stands for recurrence even as it asserts the absence of perfect duplication. And time becomes like the physical universe, unknowable, infinite, shapely.

And for Dobyns, time is all gravity, irrevocable as Milton's fall but in slow motion, with error terrifyingly diffused. In Dobyns's time, nothing can be sustained, nothing is safe: the painful duration of a Dobyns poem is a protest against the fact of time even as, in its unfolding content, the poem embodies time's effects. Dobyns shares with the lyric a sense of the inescapable terminus; unlike the lyric, his poems simulate human guile and human labor, the endlessly poignant human attempt to avoid the end.

Ultimately, no attempt to distinguish narrative from lyric can depend simply on the presence of sequential action. Set aside the obvious objections to the inherently sequential language itself, whether written or spoken, which, in following sentence one with sentence two invokes or simulates chronology, so that even stationary outcry unfolds dramatically. Consider simply, visible or gestural action, of which there are, I think, two major types. When Apollo pursues Daphne and Daphne turns into a laurel tree something occurs that, despite its narrative structure, seems unmistakably the terrain of lyric: the story of Daphne enacts two states, linked by a hiatus of pursuit; it moves through time not as evolutionary unfolding but toward transformation, toward a condition independent of time, one thing or one state having become another. Said another way: when Daphne attains her true or ideal form, that transformation terminates action, time freezes into what the great lyric makes emblematic or paradigmatic and the lesser lyric makes merely pat. But emblem and paradigm are not the only forms by which the true, or eternal, or soulful can enter poetry. My use of the term narrative means to identify a type of art (or habit of mind) that seeks to locate in the endless unfolding of time not a still point but an underlying pattern or implication; it resists constriction and facile equations; it finds in shift and movement what lyric uses stopped time to manifest. Plainly, pattern cannot be inferred from two states or gestures; if pattern sketches in the paradigmatic, it doesn't do so by resisting mutation. It is precisely this relentless mobility that occurs in the work of both Dobyns and Pinsky, in the proliferating oatmeal shapes of "Oatmeal Deluxe" and in Pinsky's unstoppable river: an unfolding, a pattern, as opposed to the iconic stasis of which the laurel tree makes an example.

The glory of the lyric is that it does what life cannot do: this also means that it is less flexibly responsive to life, more defined by the poet's obsessions and associations. Over centuries, this can mean stagnation within the form, as the inventions of genius come to be stabilized, incorporated as norms. Neither Pinsky nor Dobyns has the look, on the page, of the cutting edge, the experimental: no showy contempt for grammar, no murky lacunae, no cult of illogic. And yet it seems to me that in the richest way, this is what they are: they enlarge the definition of the art.

FURTHER READING

Criticism

R. W. Flint. "Feeding the Hunger for Stories." *The New York Times Book Review* (8 April 1984): 14.
> Finds that Pinsky's "manifold talents have become better servants of memory" in *History of My Heart.*

Additional coverage of Pinsky's life and career is contained in the following sources published by Gale: *Contemporary Authors Autobiography Series,* Vol. 4; *Contemporary Authors,* Vols. 29-32R; *DISCovering Authors: Poets Module*; **and** *Dictionary of Literary Biography Yearbook,* 1982.

☐ Contemporary Literary Criticism

Indexes

Literary Criticism Series
Cumulative Author Index
Cumulative Topic Index
Cumulative Nationality Index
Title Index, Volume 121

How to Use This Index

The main references

Camus, Albert
1913-1960 . . . . . . .CLC 1, 2, 4, 9, 11,
14, 32, 69; DA; DAB; DAC; DAM
DRAM, MST, NOV; DC2; SSC 9;
WLC

list all author entries in the following Gale Literary Criticism series:

BLC = *Black Literature Criticism*
BLCS = *Black Literature Criticism Supplement*
CLC = *Contemporary Literary Criticism*
CLR = *Children's Literature Review*
CMLC = *Classical and Medieval Literature Criticism*
DA = *DISCovering Authors*
DAB = *DISCovering Authors: British*
DAC = *DISCovering Authors: Canadian*
DAM = *DISCovering Authors Modules*
  DRAM = *dramatists;* *MST* = *most-studied*
  authors; *MULT* = *multicultural authors;* *NOV* =
  novelists; *POET* = *poets;* *POP* = *popular/genre*
  writers; *DC* = *Drama Criticism*
HLC = *Hispanic Literature Criticism*
LC = *Literature Criticism from 1400 to 1800*
NCLC = *Nineteenth-Century Literature Criticism*
PC = *Poetry Criticism*
SSC = *Short Story Criticism*
TCLC = *Twentieth-Century Literary Criticism*
WLC = *World Literature Criticism, 1500 to the Present*
WLCS = *World Literature Criticism Supplement*

The cross-references

See also CA 89-92; DLB 72; MTCW

list all author entries in the following Gale biographical and literary sources:

AAYA = *Authors & Artists for Young Adults*
AITN = *Authors in the News*
BEST = *Bestsellers*
BW = *Black Writers*
CA = *Contemporary Authors*
CAAS = *Contemporary Authors Autobiography Series*
CABS = *Contemporary Authors Bibliographical Series*
CANR = *Contemporary Authors New Revision Series*
CAP = *Contemporary Authors Permanent Series*
CDALB = *Concise Dictionary of American Literary Biography*
CDBLB = *Concise Dictionary of British Literary Biography*

DLB = *Dictionary of Literary Biography*
DLBD = *Dictionary of Literary Biography Documentary Series*
DLBY = *Dictionary of Literary Biography Yearbook*
HW = *Hispanic Writers*
JRDA = *Junior DISCovering Authors*
MAICYA = *Major Authors and Illustrators for Children and Young Adults*
MTCW = *Major 20th-Century Writers*
NNAL = *Native North American Literature*
SAAS = *Something about the Author Autobiography Series*
SATA = *Something about the Author*
YABC = *Yesterday's Authors of Books for Children*

See also AAYA 20; CDALB 1865-1917; CLR 1, 38; DLB 1, 42, 79; DLBD 14; JRDA; MAICYA; SATA 100; YABC 1

Aldanov, M. A.
See Aldanov, Mark (Alexandrovich)

Aldanov, Mark (Alexandrovich) 1886(?)-1957 .... **TCLC 23**
See also CA 118

Aldington, Richard 1892-1962 .... **CLC 49**
See also CA 85-88; CANR 45; DLB 20, 36, 100, 149

Aldiss, Brian W(ilson) 1925- . **CLC 5, 14, 40; DAM NOV**
See also CA 5-8R; CAAS 2; CANR 5, 28, 64; DLB 14; MTCW 1, 2; SATA 34

Alegria, Claribel 1924- **CLC 75; DAM MULT; PC 26**
See also CA 131; CAAS 15; CANR 66; DLB 145; HW 1; MTCW 1

Alegria, Fernando 1918- .... **CLC 57**
See also CA 9-12R; CANR 5, 32, 72; HW 1, 2

Aleichem, Sholom .... **TCLC 1, 35; SSC 33**
See also Rabinovitch, Sholem

Alepoudelis, Odysseus
See Elytis, Odysseus

Aleshkovsky, Joseph 1929-
See Aleshkovsky, Yuz
See also CA 121; 128

Aleshkovsky, Yuz .... **CLC 44**
See also Aleshkovsky, Joseph

Alexander, Lloyd (Chudley) 1924- ... **CLC 35**
See also AAYA 1, 27; CA 1-4R; CANR 1, 24, 38, 55; CLR 1, 5, 48; DLB 52; JRDA; MAICYA; MTCW 1; SAAS 19; SATA 3, 49, 81

Alexander, Meena 1951- .... **CLC 121**
See also CA 115; CANR 38, 70

Alexander, Samuel 1859-1938 .... **TCLC 77**

Alexie, Sherman (Joseph, Jr.) 1966- **CLC 96; DAM MULT**
See also AAYA 28; CA 138; CANR 65; DLB 175, 206; MTCW 1; NNAL

Alfau, Felipe 1902- .... **CLC 66**
See also CA 137

Alger, Horatio, Jr. 1832-1899 .... **NCLC 8**
See also DLB 42; SATA 16

Algren, Nelson 1909-1981 **CLC 4, 10, 33; SSC 33**
See also CA 13-16R; 103; CANR 20, 61; CDALB 1941-1968; DLB 9; DLBY 81, 82; MTCW 1, 2

Ali, Ahmed 1910- .... **CLC 69**
See also CA 25-28R; CANR 15, 34

Alighieri, Dante
See Dante

Allan, John B.
See Westlake, Donald E(dwin)

Allan, Sidney
See Hartmann, Sadakichi

Allan, Sydney
See Hartmann, Sadakichi

Allen, Edward 1948- .... **CLC 59**

Allen, Fred 1894-1956 .... **TCLC 87**

Allen, Paula Gunn 1939- .... **CLC 84; DAM MULT**
See also CA 112; 143; CANR 63; DLB 175; MTCW 1; NNAL

Allen, Roland
See Ayckbourn, Alan

Allen, Sarah A.
See Hopkins, Pauline Elizabeth

Allen, Sidney H.
See Hartmann, Sadakichi

Allen, Woody 1935- **CLC 16, 52; DAM POP**
See also AAYA 10; CA 33-36R; CANR 27, 38, 63; DLB 44; MTCW 1

Allende, Isabel 1942- . **CLC 39, 57, 97; DAM MULT, NOV; HLC; WLCS**
See also AAYA 18; CA 125; 130; CANR 51, 74; DLB 145; HW 1, 2; INT 130; MTCW 1, 2

Alleyn, Ellen
See Rossetti, Christina (Georgina)

Allingham, Margery (Louise) 1904-1966 **CLC 19**
See also CA 5-8R; 25-28R; CANR 4, 58; DLB 77; MTCW 1, 2

Allingham, William 1824-1889 ...... **NCLC 25**
See also DLB 35

Allison, Dorothy E. 1949- .... **CLC 78**
See also CA 140; CANR 66; MTCW 1

Allston, Washington 1779-1843 .... **NCLC 2**
See also DLB 1

Almedingen, E. M. .... **CLC 12**
See also Almedingen, Martha Edith von
See also SATA 3

Almedingen, Martha Edith von 1898-1971
See Almedingen, E. M.
See also CA 1-4R; CANR 1

Almodovar, Pedro 1949(?)- **CLC 114; HLCS 1**
See also CA 133; CANR 72; HW 2

Almqvist, Carl Jonas Love 1793-1866 **N C L C 42**

Alonso, Damaso 1898-1990 .... **CLC 14**
See also CA 110; 131; 130; CANR 72; DLB 108; HW 1, 2

Alov
See Gogŏl, Nikolai (Vasilyevich)

Alta 1942- .... **CLC 19**
See also CA 57-60

Alter, Robert B(ernard) 1935- .... **CLC 34**
See also CA 49-52; CANR 1, 47

Alther, Lisa 1944- .... **CLC 7, 41**
See also CA 65-68; CAAS 30; CANR 12, 30, 51; MTCW 1

Althusser, L.
See Althusser, Louis

Althusser, Louis 1918-1990 .... **CLC 106**
See also CA 131; 132

Altman, Robert 1925- .... **CLC 16, 116**
See also CA 73-76; CANR 43

Alvarez, A(lfred) 1929- .... **CLC 5, 13**
See also CA 1-4R; CANR 3, 33, 63; DLB 14, 40

Alvarez, Alejandro Rodriguez 1903-1965
See Casona, Alejandro
See also CA 131; 93-96; HW 1

Alvarez, Julia 1950- .... **CLC 93; HLCS 1**
See also AAYA 25; CA 147; CANR 69; MTCW 1

Alvaro, Corrado 1896-1956 .... **TCLC 60**
See also CA 163

Amado, Jorge 1912- **CLC 13, 40, 106; DAM MULT, NOV; HLC**
See also CA 77-80; CANR 35, 74; DLB 113; HW 2; MTCW 1, 2

Ambler, Eric 1909-1998 .... **CLC 4, 6, 9**
See also CA 9-12R; 171; CANR 7, 38, 74; DLB 77; MTCW 1, 2

Amichai, Yehuda 1924- ... **CLC 9, 22, 57, 116**
See also CA 85-88; CANR 46, 60; MTCW 1

Amichai, Yehudah
See Amichai, Yehuda

Amiel, Henri Frederic 1821-1881 .... **NCLC 4**

Amis, Kingsley (William) 1922-1995 **CLC 1, 2, 3, 5, 8, 13, 40, 44; DA; DAB; DAC; DAM MST, NOV**
See also AITN 2; CA 9-12R; 150; CANR 8, 28, 54; CDBLB 1945-1960; DLB 15, 27, 100, 139; DLBY 96; INT CANR-8; MTCW 1, 2

Amis, Martin (Louis) 1949- **CLC 4, 9, 38, 62, 101**
See also BEST 90:3; CA 65-68; CANR 8, 27, 54, 73; DLB 14, 194; INT CANR-27; MTCW 1

Ammons, A(rchie) R(andolph) 1926- **CLC 2, 3, 5, 8, 9, 25, 57, 108; DAM POET; PC 16**
See also AITN 1; CA 9-12R; CANR 6, 36, 51, 73; DLB 5, 165; MTCW 1, 2

Amo, Tauraatua i
See Adams, Henry (Brooks)

Amory, Thomas 1691(?)-1788 .... **LC 48**

Anand, Mulk Raj 1905- .. **CLC 23, 93; DAM NOV**
See also CA 65-68; CANR 32, 64; MTCW 1, 2

Anatol
See Schnitzler, Arthur

Anaximander c. 610B.C.-c. 546B.C. **CMLC 22**

Anaya, Rudolfo A(lfonso) 1937- ..... **CLC 23; DAM MULT, NOV; HLC**
See also AAYA 20; CA 45-48; CAAS 4; CANR 1, 32, 51; DLB 82, 206; HW 1; MTCW 1, 2

Andersen, Hans Christian 1805-1875 **NCLC 7, 79; DA; DAB; DAC; DAM MST, POP; SSC 6; WLC**
See also CLR 6; MAICYA; SATA 100; YABC 1

Anderson, C. Farley
See Mencken, H(enry) L(ouis); Nathan, George Jean

Anderson, Jessica (Margaret) Queale 1916- **CLC 37**
See also CA 9-12R; CANR 4, 62

Anderson, Jon (Victor) 1940- .. **CLC 9; DAM POET**
See also CA 25-28R; CANR 20

Anderson, Lindsay (Gordon) 1923-1994 **C L C 20**
See also CA 125; 128; 146; CANR 77

Anderson, Maxwell 1888-1959 **TCLC 2; DAM DRAM**
See also CA 105; 152; DLB 7; MTCW 2

Anderson, Poul (William) 1926- .... **CLC 15**
See also AAYA 5; CA 1-4R; CAAS 2; CANR 2, 15, 34, 64; CLR 58; DLB 8; INT CANR-15; MTCW 1, 2; SATA 90; SATA-Brief 39; SATA-Essay 106

Anderson, Robert (Woodruff) 1917- **CLC 23; DAM DRAM**
See also AITN 1; CA 21-24R; CANR 32; DLB 7

Anderson, Sherwood 1876-1941 **TCLC 1, 10, 24; DA; DAB; DAC; DAM MST, NOV; SSC 1; WLC**
See also AAYA 30; CA 104; 121; CANR 61; CDALB 1917-1929; DLB 4, 9, 86; DLBD 1; MTCW 1, 2

Andier, Pierre
See Desnos, Robert

Andouard
See Giraudoux, (Hippolyte) Jean

Andrade, Carlos Drummond de .... **CLC 18**
See also Drummond de Andrade, Carlos

Andrade, Mario de 1893-1945 .... **TCLC 43**

Andreae, Johann V(alentin) 1586-1654 **LC 32**
See also DLB 164

Andreas-Salome, Lou 1861-1937 ... **TCLC 56**
See also DLB 66

Andress, Lesley

Author Index

15, 42, 98; DA; DAB; DAC; DAM MST, NOV, POP; SSC 29; WLC
See also AAYA 15; AITN 1, 2; CA 1-4R; CANR 2, 30, 75; CDALB 1968-1988; DLB 2, 8; MTCW 1, 2; SATA 11, 64

Bradford, Gamaliel 1863-1932 ...... **TCLC 36**
See also CA 160; DLB 17

Bradley, David (Henry), Jr. 1950- ... **CLC 23, 118; BLC 1; DAM MULT**
See also BW 1, 3; CA 104; CANR 26, 81; DLB 33

Bradley, John Ed(mund, Jr.) 1958- .. **CLC 55**
See also CA 139

Bradley, Marion Zimmer 1930-**CLC 30; DAM POP**
See also AAYA 9; CA 57-60; CAAS 10; CANR 7, 31, 51, 75; DLB 8; MTCW 1, 2; SATA 90

Bradstreet, Anne 1612(?)-1672**LC 4, 30; DA; DAC; DAM MST, POET; PC 10**
See also CDALB 1640-1865; DLB 24

Brady, Joan 1939- .... **CLC 86**
See also CA 141

Bragg, Melvyn 1939- .... **CLC 10**
See also BEST 89:3; CA 57-60; CANR 10, 48; DLB 14

Brahe, Tycho 1546-1601 .... **LC 45**

Braine, John (Gerard) 1922-1986**CLC 1, 3, 41**
See also CA 1-4R; 120; CANR 1, 33; CDBLB 1945-1960; DLB 15; DLBY 86; MTCW 1

Bramah, Ernest 1868-1942 .... **TCLC 72**
See also CA 156; DLB 70

Brammer, William 1930(?)-1978 .... **CLC 31**
See also CA 77-80

Brancati, Vitaliano 1907-1954 .... **TCLC 12**
See also CA 109

Brancato, Robin F(idler) 1936- .... **CLC 35**
See also AAYA 9; CA 69-72; CANR 11, 45; CLR 32; JRDA; SAAS 9; SATA 97

Brand, Max
See Faust, Frederick (Schiller)

Brand, Millen 1906-1980 .... **CLC 7**
See also CA 21-24R; 97-100; CANR 72

Branden, Barbara .... **CLC 44**
See also CA 148

Brandes, Georg (Morris Cohen) 1842-1927 **TCLC 10**
See also CA 105

Brandys, Kazimierz 1916- .... **CLC 62**

Branley, Franklyn M(ansfield) 1915-**CLC 21**
See also CA 33-36R; CANR 14, 39; CLR 13; MAICYA; SAAS 16; SATA 4, 68

Brathwaite, Edward (Kamau) 1930-**CLC 11; BLCS; DAM POET**
See also BW 2, 3; CA 25-28R; CANR 11, 26, 47; DLB 125

Brautigan, Richard (Gary) 1935-1984**CLC 1, 3, 5, 9, 12, 34, 42; DAM NOV**
See also CA 53-56; 113; CANR 34; DLB 2, 5, 206; DLBY 80, 84; MTCW 1; SATA 56

Brave Bird, Mary 1953-
See Crow Dog, Mary (Ellen)
See also NNAL

Braverman, Kate 1950- .... **CLC 67**
See also CA 89-92

Brecht, (Eugen) Bertolt (Friedrich) 1898-1956 **TCLC 1, 6, 13, 35; DA; DAB; DAC; DAM DRAM, MST; DC 3; WLC**
See also CA 104; 133; CANR 62; DLB 56, 124; MTCW 1, 2

Brecht, Eugen Berthold Friedrich
See Brecht, (Eugen) Bertolt (Friedrich)

Bremer, Fredrika 1801-1865 .... **NCLC 11**

Brennan, Christopher John 1870-1932**TCLC 17**
See also CA 117

Brennan, Maeve 1917-1993 .... **CLC 5**
See also CA 81-84; CANR 72

Brent, Linda
See Jacobs, Harriet A(nn)

Brentano, Clemens (Maria) 1778-1842**NCLC 1**
See also DLB 90

Brent of Bin Bin
See Franklin, (Stella Maria Sarah) Miles (Lampe)

Brenton, Howard 1942- .... **CLC 31**
See also CA 69-72; CANR 33, 67; DLB 13; MTCW 1

Breslin, James 1930-1996
See Breslin, Jimmy
See also CA 73-76; CANR 31, 75; DAM NOV; MTCW 1, 2

Breslin, Jimmy .... **CLC 4, 43**
See also Breslin, James
See also AITN 1; DLB 185; MTCW 2

Bresson, Robert 1901- .... **CLC 16**
See also CA 110; CANR 49

Breton, Andre 1896-1966**CLC 2, 9, 15, 54; PC 15**
See also CA 19-20; 25-28R; CANR 40, 60; CAP 2; DLB 65; MTCW 1, 2

Breytenbach, Breyten 1939(?)- . **CLC 23, 37; DAM POET**
See also CA 113; 129; CANR 61

Bridgers, Sue Ellen 1942- .... **CLC 26**
See also AAYA 8; CA 65-68; CANR 11, 36; CLR 18; DLB 52; JRDA; MAICYA; SAAS 1; SATA 22, 90; SATA-Essay 109

Bridges, Robert (Seymour) 1844-1930**TCLC 1; DAM POET**
See also CA 104; 152; CDBLB 1890-1914; DLB 19, 98

Bridie, James .... **TCLC 3**
See also Mavor, Osborne Henry
See also DLB 10

Brin, David 1950- .... **CLC 34**
See also AAYA 21; CA 102; CANR 24, 70; INT CANR-24; SATA 65

Brink, Andre (Philippus) 1935- **CLC 18, 36, 106**
See also CA 104; CANR 39, 62; INT 103; MTCW 1

Brinsmead, H(esba) F(ay) 1922- .... **CLC 21**
See also CA 21-24R; CANR 10; CLR 47; MAICYA; SAAS 5; SATA 18, 78

Brittain, Vera (Mary) 1893(?)-1970 . **CLC 23**
See also CA 13-16; 25-28R; CANR 58; CAP 1; DLB 191; MTCW 1, 2

Broch, Hermann 1886-1951 .... **TCLC 20**
See also CA 117; DLB 85, 124

Brock, Rose
See Hansen, Joseph

Brodkey, Harold (Roy) 1930-1996 .... **CLC 56**
See also CA 111; 151; CANR 71; DLB 130

Brodskii, Iosif
See Brodsky, Joseph

Brodsky, Iosif Alexandrovich 1940-1996
See Brodsky, Joseph
See also AITN 1; CA 41-44R; 151; CANR 37; DAM POET; MTCW 1, 2

Brodsky, Joseph 1940-1996 **CLC 4, 6, 13, 36, 100; PC 9**
See also Brodskii, Iosif; Brodsky, Iosif Alexandrovich
See also MTCW 1

Brodsky, Michael (Mark) 1948- .... **CLC 19**

See also CA 102; CANR 18, 41, 58

Bromell, Henry 1947- .... **CLC 5**
See also CA 53-56; CANR 9

Bromfield, Louis (Brucker) 1896-1956**T C L C 11**
See also CA 107; 155; DLB 4, 9, 86

Broner, E(sther) M(asserman) 1930- **CLC 19**
See also CA 17-20R; CANR 8, 25, 72; DLB 28

Bronk, William (M.) 1918-1999 .... **CLC 10**
See also CA 89-92; 177; CANR 23; DLB 165

Bronstein, Lev Davidovich
See Trotsky, Leon

Bronte, Anne 1820-1849 .... **NCLC 71**
See also DLB 21, 199

Bronte, Charlotte 1816-1855 **NCLC 3, 8, 33, 58; DA; DAB; DAC; DAM MST, NOV; WLC**
See also AAYA 17; CDBLB 1832-1890; DLB 21, 159, 199

Bronte, Emily (Jane) 1818-1848**NCLC 16, 35; DA; DAB; DAC; DAM MST, NOV, POET; PC 8; WLC**
See also AAYA 17; CDBLB 1832-1890; DLB 21, 32, 199

Brooke, Frances 1724-1789 .... **LC 6, 48**
See also DLB 39, 99

Brooke, Henry 1703(?)-1783 .... **LC 1**
See also DLB 39

Brooke, Rupert (Chawner) 1887-1915**T C L C 2, 7; DA; DAB; DAC; DAM MST, POET; PC 24; WLC**
See also CA 104; 132; CANR 61; CDBLB 1914-1945; DLB 19; MTCW 1, 2

Brooke-Haven, P.
See Wodehouse, P(elham) G(renville)

Brooke-Rose, Christine 1926(?)- .... **CLC 40**
See also CA 13-16R; CANR 58; DLB 14

Brookner, Anita 1928-**CLC 32, 34, 51; DAB; DAM POP**
See also CA 114; 120; CANR 37, 56; DLB 194; DLBY 87; MTCW 1, 2

Brooks, Cleanth 1906-1994 **CLC 24, 86, 110**
See also CA 17-20R; 145; CANR 33, 35; DLB 63; DLBY 94; INT CANR-35; MTCW 1, 2

Brooks, George
See Baum, L(yman) Frank

Brooks, Gwendolyn 1917- **CLC 1, 2, 4, 5, 15, 49; BLC 1; DA; DAC; DAM MST, MULT, POET; PC 7; WLC**
See also AAYA 20; AITN 1; BW 2, 3; CA 1-4R; CANR 1, 27, 52, 75; CDALB 1941-1968; CLR 27; DLB 5, 76, 165; MTCW 1, 2; SATA 6

Brooks, Mel .... **CLC 12**
See also Kaminsky, Melvin
See also AAYA 13; DLB 26

Brooks, Peter 1938- .... **CLC 34**
See also CA 45-48; CANR 1

Brooks, Van Wyck 1886-1963 .... **CLC 29**
See also CA 1-4R; CANR 6; DLB 45, 63, 103

Brophy, Brigid (Antonia) 1929-1995 **CLC 6, 11, 29, 105**
See also CA 5-8R; 149; CAAS 4; CANR 25, 53; DLB 14; MTCW 1, 2

Brosman, Catharine Savage 1934- ..... **CLC 9**
See also CA 61-64; CANR 21, 46

Brossard, Nicole 1943- .... **CLC 115**
See also CA 122; CAAS 16; DLB 53

Brother Antoninus
See Everson, William (Oliver)

The Brothers Quay
See Quay, Stephen; Quay, Timothy

Broughton, T(homas) Alan 1936- ..... **CLC 19**

See also CA 45-48; CANR 2, 23, 48
Broumas, Olga 1949- .... **CLC 10, 73**
See also CA 85-88; CANR 20, 69
Brown, Alan 1950- .... **CLC 99**
See also CA 156
Brown, Charles Brockden 1771-1810 **N C L C 22, 74**
See also CDALB 1640-1865; DLB 37, 59, 73
Brown, Christy 1932-1981 .... **CLC 63**
See also CA 105; 104; CANR 72; DLB 14
Brown, Claude 1937- **CLC 30; BLC 1; DAM MULT**
See also AAYA 7; BW 1, 3; CA 73-76; CANR 81
Brown, Dee (Alexander) 1908- .. **CLC 18, 47; DAM POP**
See also AAYA 30; CA 13-16R; CAAS 6; CANR 11, 45, 60; DLBY 80; MTCW 1, 2; SATA 5
Brown, George
See Wertmueller, Lina
Brown, George Douglas 1869-1902 **TCLC 28**
See also CA 162
Brown, George Mackay 1921-1996 **CLC 5, 48, 100**
See also CA 21-24R; 151; CAAS 6; CANR 12, 37, 67; DLB 14, 27, 139; MTCW 1; SATA 35
Brown, (William) Larry 1951- .... **CLC 73**
See also CA 130; 134; INT 133
Brown, Moses
See Barrett, William (Christopher)
Brown, Rita Mae 1944- **CLC 18, 43, 79; DAM NOV, POP**
See also CA 45-48; CANR 2, 11, 35, 62; INT CANR-11; MTCW 1, 2
Brown, Roderick (Langmere) Haig-
See Haig-Brown, Roderick (Langmere)
Brown, Rosellen 1939- .... **CLC 32**
See also CA 77-80; CAAS 10; CANR 14, 44
Brown, Sterling Allen 1901-1989 **CLC 1, 23, 59; BLC 1; DAM MULT, POET**
See also BW 1, 3; CA 85-88; 127; CANR 26; DLB 48, 51, 63; MTCW 1, 2
Brown, Will
See Ainsworth, William Harrison
Brown, William Wells 1813-1884 ... **NCLC 2; BLC 1; DAM MULT; DC 1**
See also DLB 3, 50
Browne, (Clyde) Jackson 1948(?)- .... **CLC 21**
See also CA 120
Browning, Elizabeth Barrett 1806-1861 **NCLC 1, 16, 61, 66; DA; DAB; DAC; DAM MST, POET; PC 6; WLC**
See also CDBLB 1832-1890; DLB 32, 199
Browning, Robert 1812-1889 . **NCLC 19, 79; DA; DAB; DAC; DAM MST, POET; PC 2; WLCS**
See also CDBLB 1832-1890; DLB 32, 163; YABC 1
Browning, Tod 1882-1962 .... **CLC 16**
See also CA 141; 117
Brownson, Orestes Augustus 1803-1876 **NCLC 50**
See also DLB 1, 59, 73
Bruccoli, Matthew J(oseph) 1931- ... **CLC 34**
See also CA 9-12R; CANR 7; DLB 103
Bruce, Lenny .... **CLC 21**
See also Schneider, Leonard Alfred
Bruin, John
See Brutus, Dennis
Brulard, Henri
See Stendhal

Brulls, Christian
See Simenon, Georges (Jacques Christian)
Brunner, John (Kilian Houston) 1934-1995 **CLC 8, 10; DAM POP**
See also CA 1-4R; 149; CAAS 8; CANR 2, 37; MTCW 1, 2
Bruno, Giordano 1548-1600 .... **LC 27**
Brutus, Dennis 1924- **CLC 43; BLC 1; DAM MULT, POET; PC 24**
See also BW 2, 3; CA 49-52; CAAS 14; CANR 2, 27, 42, 81; DLB 117
Bryan, C(ourtlandt) D(ixon) B(arnes) 1936- **CLC 29**
See also CA 73-76; CANR 13, 68; DLB 185; INT CANR-13
Bryan, Michael
See Moore, Brian
Bryant, William Cullen 1794-1878 . **NCLC 6, 46; DA; DAB; DAC; DAM MST, POET; PC 20**
See also CDALB 1640-1865; DLB 3, 43, 59, 189
Bryusov, Valery Yakovlevich 1873-1924 **TCLC 10**
See also CA 107; 155
Buchan, John 1875-1940 ..... **TCLC 41; DAB; DAM POP**
See also CA 108; 145; DLB 34, 70, 156; MTCW 1; YABC 2
Buchanan, George 1506-1582 .... **LC 4**
See also DLB 152
Buchheim, Lothar-Guenther 1918- .... **CLC 6**
See also CA 85-88
Buchner, (Karl) Georg 1813-1837 . **NCLC 26**
Buchwald, Art(hur) 1925- .... **CLC 33**
See also AITN 1; CA 5-8R; CANR 21, 67; MTCW 1, 2; SATA 10
Buck, Pearl S(ydenstricker) 1892-1973 **CLC 7, 11, 18; DA; DAB; DAC; DAM MST, NOV**
See also AITN 1; CA 1-4R; 41-44R; CANR 1, 34; CDALBS; DLB 9, 102; MTCW 1, 2; SATA 1, 25
Buckler, Ernest 1908-1984 .... **CLC 13; DAC; DAM MST**
See also CA 11-12; 114; CAP 1; DLB 68; SATA 47
Buckley, Vincent (Thomas) 1925-1988 **CLC 57**
See also CA 101
Buckley, William F(rank), Jr. 1925- **CLC 7, 18, 37; DAM POP**
See also AITN 1; CA 1-4R; CANR 1, 24, 53; DLB 137; DLBY 80; INT CANR-24; MTCW 1, 2
Buechner, (Carl) Frederick 1926- **CLC 2, 4, 6, 9; DAM NOV**
See also CA 13-16R; CANR 11, 39, 64; DLBY 80; INT CANR-11; MTCW 1, 2
Buell, John (Edward) 1927- .... **CLC 10**
See also CA 1-4R; CANR 71; DLB 53
Buero Vallejo, Antonio 1916- ..... **CLC 15, 46**
See also CA 106; CANR 24, 49, 75; HW 1; MTCW 1, 2
Bufalino, Gesualdo 1920(?)- .... **CLC 74**
See also DLB 196
Bugayev, Boris Nikolayevich 1880-1934 **TCLC 7; PC 11**
See also Bely, Andrey
See also CA 104; 165; MTCW 1
Bukowski, Charles 1920-1994 **CLC 2, 5, 9, 41, 82, 108; DAM NOV, POET; PC 18**
See also CA 17-20R; 144; CANR 40, 62; DLB 5, 130, 169; MTCW 1, 2
Bulgakov, Mikhail (Afanas'evich) 1891-1940

TCLC 2, 16; DAM DRAM, NOV; SSC 18
See also CA 105; 152
Bulgya, Alexander Alexandrovich 1901-1956 **TCLC 53**
See also Fadeyev, Alexander
See also CA 117
Bullins, Ed 1935- **CLC 1, 5, 7; BLC 1; DAM DRAM, MULT; DC 6**
See also BW 2, 3; CA 49-52; CAAS 16; CANR 24, 46, 73; DLB 7, 38; MTCW 1, 2
Bulwer-Lytton, Edward (George Earle Lytton) 1803-1873 .... **NCLC 1, 45**
See also DLB 21
Bunin, Ivan Alexeyevich 1870-1953 **TCLC 6; SSC 5**
See also CA 104
Bunting, Basil 1900-1985 ..... **CLC 10, 39, 47; DAM POET**
See also CA 53-56; 115; CANR 7; DLB 20
Bunuel, Luis 1900-1983 .. **CLC 16, 80; DAM MULT; HLC**
See also CA 101; 110; CANR 32, 77; HW 1
Bunyan, John 1628-1688 ... **LC 4; DA; DAB; DAC; DAM MST; WLC**
See also CDBLB 1660-1789; DLB 39
Burckhardt, Jacob (Christoph) 1818-1897 **NCLC 49**
Burford, Eleanor
See Hibbert, Eleanor Alice Burford
Burgess, Anthony **CLC 1, 2, 4, 5, 8, 10, 13, 15, 22, 40, 62, 81, 94; DAB**
See also Wilson, John (Anthony) Burgess
See also AAYA 25; AITN 1; CDBLB 1960 to Present; DLB 14, 194; DLBY 98; MTCW 1
Burke, Edmund 1729(?)-1797 **LC 7, 36; DA; DAB; DAC; DAM MST; WLC**
See also DLB 104
Burke, Kenneth (Duva) 1897-1993 **CLC 2, 24**
See also CA 5-8R; 143; CANR 39, 74; DLB 45, 63; MTCW 1, 2
Burke, Leda
See Garnett, David
Burke, Ralph
See Silverberg, Robert
Burke, Thomas 1886-1945 .... **TCLC 63**
See also CA 113; 155; DLB 197
Burney, Fanny 1752-1840 .... **NCLC 12. 54**
See also DLB 39
Burns, Robert 1759-1796 . **LC 3, 29, 40; DA; DAB; DAC; DAM MST, POET; PC 6; WLC**
See also CDBLB 1789-1832; DLB 109
Burns, Tex
See L'Amour, Louis (Dearborn)
Burnshaw, Stanley 1906- .... **CLC 3, 13, 44**
See also CA 9-12R; DLB 48; DLBY 97
Burr, Anne 1937- .... **CLC 6**
See also CA 25-28R
Burroughs, Edgar Rice 1875-1950 . **TCLC 2, 32; DAM NOV**
See also AAYA 11; CA 104; 132; DLB 8; MTCW 1, 2; SATA 41
Burroughs, William S(eward) 1914-1997 **CLC 1, 2, 5, 15, 22, 42, 75, 109; DA; DAB; DAC; DAM MST, NOV, POP; WLC**
See also AITN 2; CA 9-12R; 160; CANR 20, 52; DLB 2, 8, 16, 152; DLBY 81, 97; MTCW 1, 2
Burton, Sir Richard F(rancis) 1821-1890 **NCLC 42**
See also DLB 55, 166, 184
Busch, Frederick 1941- ..... **CLC 7, 10, 18, 47**
See also CA 33-36R; CAAS 1; CANR 45, 73;

See Hansen, Joseph

Colum, Padraic 1881-1972 .... **CLC 28**
See also CA 73-76; 33-36R; CANR 35; CLR 36; MAICYA; MTCW 1; SATA 15

Colvin, James
See Moorcock, Michael (John)

Colwin, Laurie (E.) 1944-1992**CLC 5, 13, 23, 84**
See also CA 89-92; 139; CANR 20, 46; DLBY 80; MTCW 1

Comfort, Alex(ander) 1920-**CLC 7; DAM POP**
See also CA 1-4R; CANR 1, 45; MTCW 1

Comfort, Montgomery
See Campbell, (John) Ramsey

Compton-Burnett, I(vy) 1884(?)-1969**CLC 1, 3, 10, 15, 34; DAM NOV**
See also CA 1-4R; 25-28R; CANR 4; DLB 36; MTCW 1

Comstock, Anthony 1844-1915 ...... **TCLC 13**
See also CA 110; 169

Comte, Auguste 1798-1857 .... **NCLC 54**

Conan Doyle, Arthur
See Doyle, Arthur Conan

Conde, Maryse 1937- .... **CLC 52, 92; BLCS; DAM MULT**
See also Boucolon, Maryse
See also BW 2; MTCW 1

Condillac, Etienne Bonnot de 1714-1780 **L C 26**

Condon, Richard (Thomas) 1915-1996**CLC 4, 6, 8, 10, 45, 100; DAM NOV**
See also BEST 90:3; CA 1-4R; 151; CAAS 1; CANR 2, 23; INT CANR-23; MTCW 1, 2

Confucius 551B.C.-479B.C. .. **CMLC 19; DA; DAB; DAC; DAM MST; WLCS**

Congreve, William 1670-1729 **LC 5, 21; DA; DAB; DAC; DAM DRAM, MST, POET; DC 2; WLC**
See also CDBLB 1660-1789; DLB 39, 84

Connell, Evan S(helby), Jr. 1924-**CLC 4, 6, 45; DAM NOV**
See also AAYA 7; CA 1-4R; CAAS 2; CANR 2, 39, 76; DLB 2; DLBY 81; MTCW 1, 2

Connelly, Marc(us Cook) 1890-1980 .. **CLC 7**
See also CA 85-88; 102; CANR 30; DLB 7; DLBY 80; SATA-Obit 25

Connor, Ralph .... **TCLC 31**
See also Gordon, Charles William
See also DLB 92

Conrad, Joseph 1857-1924**TCLC 1, 6, 13, 25, 43, 57; DA; DAB; DAC; DAM MST, NOV; SSC 9; WLC**
See also AAYA 26; CA 104; 131; CANR 60; CDBLB 1890-1914; DLB 10, 34, 98, 156; MTCW 1, 2; SATA 27

Conrad, Robert Arnold
See Hart, Moss

Conroy, Pat
See Conroy, (Donald) Pat(rick)
See also MTCW 2

Conroy, (Donald) Pat(rick) 1945-**CLC 30, 74; DAM NOV, POP**
See also Conroy, Pat
See also AAYA 8; AITN 1; CA 85-88; CANR 24, 53; DLB 6; MTCW 1

Constant (de Rebecque), (Henri) Benjamin 1767-1830 .... **NCLC 6**
See also DLB 119

Conybeare, Charles Augustus
See Eliot, T(homas) S(tearns)

Cook, Michael 1933-......................... **CLC 58**
See also CA 93-96; CANR 68; DLB 53

Cook, Robin 1940- .... **CLC 14; DAM POP**

See also BEST 90:2; CA 108; 111; CANR 41; INT 111

Cook, Roy
See Silverberg, Robert

Cooke, Elizabeth 1948- .... **CLC 55**
See also CA 129

Cooke, John Esten 1830-1886 .... **NCLC 5**
See also DLB 3

Cooke, John Estes
See Baum, L(yman) Frank

Cooke, M. E.
See Creasey, John

Cooke, Margaret
See Creasey, John

Cook-Lynn, Elizabeth 1930-.. **CLC 93; DAM MULT**
See also CA 133; DLB 175; NNAL

Cooney, Ray .... **CLC 62**

Cooper, Douglas 1960- .... **CLC 86**

Cooper, Henry St. John
See Creasey, John

Cooper, J(oan) California (?)-**CLC 56; DAM MULT**
See also AAYA 12; BW 1; CA 125; CANR 55; DLB 212

Cooper, James Fenimore 1789-1851**NCLC 1, 27, 54**
See also AAYA 22; CDALB 1640-1865; DLB 3; SATA 19

Coover, Robert (Lowell) 1932- **CLC 3, 7, 15, 32, 46, 87; DAM NOV; SSC 15**
See also CA 45-48; CANR 3, 37, 58; DLB 2; DLBY 81; MTCW 1, 2

Copeland, Stewart (Armstrong) 1952-**CLC 26**

Copernicus, Nicolaus 1473-1543 .... **LC 45**

Coppard, A(lfred) E(dgar) 1878-1957 **T C L C 5; SSC 21**
See also CA 114; 167; DLB 162; YABC 1

Coppee, Francois 1842-1908 .... **TCLC 25**
See also CA 170

Coppola, Francis Ford 1939- .... **CLC 16**
See also CA 77-80; CANR 40, 78; DLB 44

Corbiere, Tristan 1845-1875 .... **NCLC 43**

Corcoran, Barbara 1911- .... **CLC 17**
See also AAYA 14; CA 21-24R; CAAS 2; CANR 11, 28, 48; CLR 50; DLB 52; JRDA; SAAS 20; SATA 3, 77

Cordelier, Maurice
See Giraudoux, (Hippolyte) Jean

Corelli, Marie 1855-1924 .... **TCLC 51**
See also Mackay, Mary
See also DLB 34, 156

Corman, Cid 1924- .... **CLC 9**
See also Corman, Sidney
See also CAAS 2; DLB 5, 193

Corman, Sidney 1924-
See Corman, Cid
See also CA 85-88; CANR 44; DAM POET

Cormier, Robert (Edmund) 1925-**CLC 12, 30; DA; DAB; DAC; DAM MST, NOV**
See also AAYA 3, 19; CA 1-4R; CANR 5, 23, 76; CDALB 1968-1988; CLR 12, 55; DLB 52; INT CANR-23; JRDA; MAICYA; MTCW 1, 2; SATA 10, 45, 83

Corn, Alfred (DeWitt III) 1943- .... **CLC 33**
See also CA 104; CAAS 25; CANR 44; DLB 120; DLBY 80

Corneille, Pierre 1606-1684 .... **LC 28; DAB; DAM MST**

Cornwell, David (John Moore) 1931-**CLC 9, 15; DAM POP**
See also le Carre, John
See also CA 5-8R; CANR 13, 33, 59; MTCW

1, 2

Corso, (Nunzio) Gregory 1930- .... **CLC 1, 11**
See also CA 5-8R; CANR 41, 76; DLB 5, 16; MTCW 1, 2

Cortazar, Julio 1914-1984**CLC 2, 3, 5, 10, 13, 15, 33, 34, 92; DAM MULT, NOV; HLC; SSC 7**
See also CA 21-24R; CANR 12, 32, 81; DLB 113; HW 1, 2; MTCW 1, 2

CORTES, HERNAN 1484-1547 .... **LC 31**

Corvinus, Jakob
See Raabe, Wilhelm (Karl)

Corwin, Cecil
See Kornbluth, C(yril) M.

Cosic, Dobrica 1921- .... **CLC 14**
See also CA 122; 138; DLB 181

Costain, Thomas B(ertram) 1885-1965 **C L C 30**
See also CA 5-8R; 25-28R; DLB 9

Costantini, Humberto 1924(?)-1987 . **CLC 49**
See also CA 131; 122; HW 1

Costello, Elvis 1955- .... **CLC 21**

Costenoble, Philostene
See Ghelderode, Michel de

Cotes, Cecil V.
See Duncan, Sara Jeannette

Cotter, Joseph Seamon Sr. 1861-1949 **T C L C 28; BLC 1; DAM MULT**
See also BW 1; CA 124; DLB 50

Couch, Arthur Thomas Quiller
See Quiller-Couch, SirArthur (Thomas)

Coulton, James
See Hansen, Joseph

Couperus, Louis (Marie Anne) 1863-1923 **TCLC 15**
See also CA 115

Coupland, Douglas 1961-**CLC 85; DAC; DAM POP**
See also CA 142; CANR 57

Court, Wesli
See Turco, Lewis (Putnam)

Courtenay, Bryce 1933- .... **CLC 59**
See also CA 138

Courtney, Robert
See Ellison, Harlan (Jay)

Cousteau, Jacques-Yves 1910-1997 .. **CLC 30**
See also CA 65-68; 159; CANR 15, 67; MTCW 1; SATA 38, 98

Coventry, Francis 1725-1754 .... **LC 46**

Cowan, Peter (Walkinshaw) 1914- .... **SSC 28**
See also CA 21-24R; CANR 9, 25, 50

Coward, Noel (Peirce) 1899-1973**CLC 1, 9, 29, 51; DAM DRAM**
See also AITN 1; CA 17-18; 41-44R; CANR 35; CAP 2; CDBLB 1914-1945; DLB 10; MTCW 1, 2

Cowley, Abraham 1618-1667 .... **LC 43**
See also DLB 131, 151

Cowley, Malcolm 1898-1989 .... **CLC 39**
See also CA 5-8R; 128; CANR 3, 55; DLB 4, 48; DLBY 81, 89; MTCW 1, 2

Cowper, William 1731-1800 . **NCLC 8; DAM POET**
See also DLB 104, 109

Cox, William Trevor 1928- .... **CLC 9, 14, 71; DAM NOV**
See also Trevor, William
See also CA 9-12R; CANR 4, 37, 55, 76; DLB 14; INT CANR-37; MTCW 1, 2

Coyne, P. J.
See Masters, Hilary

Cozzens, James Gould 1903-1978**CLC 1, 4, 11, 92**

See also CA 9-12R; 81-84; CANR 19; CDALB 1941-1968; DLB 9; DLBD 2; DLBY 84, 97; MTCW 1, 2

Crabbe, George 1754-1832 .... **NCLC 26**
See also DLB 93

Craddock, Charles Egbert
See Murfree, Mary Noailles

Craig, A. A.
See Anderson, Poul (William)

Craik, Dinah Maria (Mulock) 1826-1887
NCLC 38
See also DLB 35, 163; MAICYA; SATA 34

Cram, Ralph Adams 1863-1942 ..... **TCLC 45**
See also CA 160

Crane, (Harold) Hart 1899-1932 **TCLC 2, 5, 80; DA; DAB; DAC; DAM MST, POET; PC 3; WLC**
See also CA 104; 127; CDALB 1917-1929; DLB 4, 48; MTCW 1, 2

Crane, R(onald) S(almon) 1886-1967**CLC 27**
See also CA 85-88; DLB 63

Crane, Stephen (Townley) 1871-1900 **T C L C 11, 17, 32; DA; DAB; DAC; DAM MST, NOV, POET; SSC 7; WLC**
See also AAYA 21; CA 109; 140; CDALB 1865-1917; DLB 12, 54, 78; YABC 2

Cranshaw, Stanley
See Fisher, Dorothy (Frances) Canfield

Crase, Douglas 1944- .... **CLC 58**
See also CA 106

Crashaw, Richard 1612(?)-1649 .... **LC 24**
See also DLB 126

Craven, Margaret 1901-1980 . **CLC 17; DAC**
See also CA 103

Crawford, F(rancis) Marion 1854-1909**TCLC 10**
See also CA 107; 168; DLB 71

Crawford, Isabella Valancy 1850-1887**N C L C 12**
See also DLB 92

Crayon, Geoffrey
See Irving, Washington

Creasey, John 1908-1973 .... **CLC 11**
See also CA 5-8R; 41-44R; CANR 8, 59; DLB 77; MTCW 1

Crebillon, Claude Prosper Jolyot de (fils) 1707-1777 .... **LC 1, 28**

Credo
See Creasey, John

Credo, Alvaro J. de
See Prado (Calvo), Pedro

Creeley, Robert (White) 1926-**CLC 1, 2, 4, 8, 11, 15, 36, 78; DAM POET**
See also CA 1-4R; CAAS 10; CANR 23, 43; DLB 5, 16, 169; DLBD 17; MTCW 1, 2

Crews, Harry (Eugene) 1935- **CLC 6, 23, 49**
See also AITN 1; CA 25-28R; CANR 20, 57; DLB 6, 143, 185; MTCW 1, 2

Crichton, (John) Michael 1942-**CLC 2, 6, 54, 90; DAM NOV, POP**
See also AAYA 10; AITN 2; CA 25-28R; CANR 13, 40, 54, 76; DLBY 81; INT CANR-13; JRDA; MTCW 1, 2; SATA 9, 88

Crispin, Edmund .... **CLC 22**
See also Montgomery, (Robert) Bruce
See also DLB 87

Cristofer, Michael 1945(?)- .... **CLC 28; DAM DRAM**
See also CA 110; 152; DLB 7

Croce, Benedetto 1866-1952 .... **TCLC 37**
See also CA 120; 155

Crockett, David 1786-1836 .... **NCLC 8**
See also DLB 3, 11

Crockett, Davy
See Crockett, David

Crofts, Freeman Wills 1879-1957 .. **TCLC 55**
See also CA 115; DLB 77

Croker, John Wilson 1780-1857 .... **NCLC 10**
See also DLB 110

Crommelynck, Fernand 1885-1970 .. **CLC 75**
See also CA 89-92

Cromwell, Oliver 1599-1658 .... **LC 43**

Cronin, A(rchibald) J(oseph) 1896-1981**C L C 32**
See also CA 1-4R; 102; CANR 5; DLB 191; SATA 47; SATA-Obit 25

Cross, Amanda
See Heilbrun, Carolyn G(old)

Crothers, Rachel 1878(?)-1958 ...... **TCLC 19**
See also CA 113; DLB 7

Croves, Hal
See Traven, B.

Crow Dog, Mary (Ellen) (?)- .... **CLC 93**
See also Brave Bird, Mary
See also CA 154

Crowfield, Christopher
See Stowe, Harriet (Elizabeth) Beecher

Crowley, Aleister .... **TCLC 7**
See also Crowley, Edward Alexander

Crowley, Edward Alexander 1875-1947
See Crowley, Aleister
See also CA 104

Crowley, John 1942- .... **CLC 57**
See also CA 61-64; CANR 43; DLBY 82; SATA 65

Crud
See Crumb, R(obert)

Crumarums
See Crumb, R(obert)

Crumb, R(obert) 1943- .... **CLC 17**
See also CA 106

Crumbum
See Crumb, R(obert)

Crumski
See Crumb, R(obert)

Crum the Bum
See Crumb, R(obert)

Crunk
See Crumb, R(obert)

Crustt
See Crumb, R(obert)

Cryer, Gretchen (Kiger) 1935- .... **CLC 21**
See also CA 114; 123

Csath, Geza 1887-1919 .... **TCLC 13**
See also CA 111

Cudlip, David R(ockwell) 1933- .... **CLC 34**
See also CA 177

Cullen, Countee 1903-1946**TCLC 4, 37; BLC 1; DA; DAC; DAM MST, MULT, POET; PC 20; WLCS**
See also BW 1; CA 108; 124; CDALB 1917-1929; DLB 4, 48, 51; MTCW 1, 2; SATA 18

Cum, R.
See Crumb, R(obert)

Cummings, Bruce F(rederick) 1889-1919
See Barbellion, W. N. P.
See also CA 123

Cummings, E(dward) E(stlin) 1894-1962**CLC 1, 3, 8, 12, 15, 68; DA; DAB; DAC; DAM MST, POET; PC 5; WLC**
See also CA 73-76; CANR 31; CDALB 1929-1941; DLB 4, 48; MTCW 1, 2

Cunha, Euclides (Rodrigues Pimenta) da 1866-1909 .... **TCLC 24**
See also CA 123

Cunningham, E. V.
See Fast, Howard (Melvin)

Cunningham, J(ames) V(incent) 1911-1985
CLC 3, 31
See also CA 1-4R; 115; CANR 1, 72; DLB 5

Cunningham, Julia (Woolfolk) 1916-**CLC 12**
See also CA 9-12R; CANR 4, 19, 36; JRDA; MAICYA; SAAS 2; SATA 1, 26

Cunningham, Michael 1952- .... **CLC 34**
See also CA 136

Cunninghame Graham, R(obert) B(ontine) 1852-1936 .... **TCLC 19**
See also Graham, R(obert) B(ontine) Cunninghame
See also CA 119; DLB 98

Currie, Ellen 19(?)- .... **CLC 44**

Curtin, Philip
See Lowndes, Marie Adelaide (Belloc)

Curtis, Price
See Ellison, Harlan (Jay)

Cutrate, Joe
See Spiegelman, Art

Cynewulf c. 770-c. 840 .... **CMLC 23**

Czaczkes, Shmuel Yosef
See Agnon, S(hmuel) Y(osef Halevi)

Dabrowska, Maria (Szumska) 1889-1965**CLC 15**
See also CA 106

Dabydeen, David 1955- .... **CLC 34**
See also BW 1; CA 125; CANR 56

Dacey, Philip 1939- .... **CLC 51**
See also CA 37-40R; CAAS 17; CANR 14, 32, 64; DLB 105

Dagerman, Stig (Halvard) 1923-1954 **T C L C 17**
See also CA 117; 155

Dahl, Roald 1916-1990**CLC 1, 6, 18, 79; DAB; DAC; DAM MST, NOV, POP**
See also AAYA 15; CA 1-4R; 133; CANR 6, 32, 37, 62; CLR 1, 7, 41; DLB 139; JRDA; MAICYA; MTCW 1, 2; SATA 1, 26, 73; SATA-Obit 65

Dahlberg, Edward 1900-1977 .. **CLC 1, 7, 14**
See also CA 9-12R; 69-72; CANR 31, 62; DLB 48; MTCW 1

Daitch, Susan 1954- .... **CLC 103**
See also CA 161

Dale, Colin .... **TCLC 18**
See also Lawrence, T(homas) E(dward)

Dale, George E.
See Asimov, Isaac

Daly, Elizabeth 1878-1967 .... **CLC 52**
See also CA 23-24; 25-28R; CANR 60; CAP 2

Daly, Maureen 1921- .... **CLC 17**
See also AAYA 5; CANR 37; JRDA; MAICYA; SAAS 1; SATA 2

Damas, Leon-Gontran 1912-1978 .... **CLC 84**
See also BW 1; CA 125; 73-76

Dana, Richard Henry Sr. 1787-1879**NCLC 53**

Daniel, Samuel 1562(?)-1619 .... **LC 24**
See also DLB 62

Daniels, Brett
See Adler, Renata

Dannay, Frederic 1905-1982 . **CLC 11; DAM POP**
See also Queen, Ellery
See also CA 1-4R; 107; CANR 1, 39; DLB 137; MTCW 1

D'Annunzio, Gabriele 1863-1938**TCLC 6, 40**
See also CA 104; 155

Danois, N. le
See Gourmont, Remy (-Marie-Charles) de

Dante 1265-1321 .... **CMLC 3, 18; DA; DAB; DAC; DAM MST, POET; PC 21; WLCS**

d'Antibes, Germain
See Simenon, Georges (Jacques Christian)
Danticat, Edwidge 1969- .... **CLC 94**
See also AAYA 29; CA 152; CANR 73; MTCW
1
Danvers, Dennis 1947- .... **CLC 70**
Danziger, Paula 1944- .... **CLC 21**
See also AAYA 4; CA 112; 115; CANR 37; CLR
20; JRDA; MAICYA; SATA 36, 63, 102;
SATA-Brief 30
Da Ponte, Lorenzo 1749-1838 .... **NCLC 50**
Dario, Ruben 1867-1916 .... **TCLC 4; DAM
MULT; HLC; PC 15**
See also CA 131; CANR 81; HW 1, 2; MTCW
1, 2
Darley, George 1795-1846 .... **NCLC 2**
See also DLB 96
Darrow, Clarence (Seward) 1857-1938**T C L C
81**
See also CA 164
Darwin, Charles 1809-1882 .... **NCLC 57**
See also DLB 57, 166
Daryush, Elizabeth 1887-1977 ...... **CLC 6, 19**
See also CA 49-52; CANR 3, 81; DLB 20
Dasgupta, Surendranath 1887-1952**TCLC 81**
See also CA 157
**Dashwood, Edmee Elizabeth Monica de la Pas-
ture** 1890-1943
See Delafield, E. M.
See also CA 119; 154
Daudet, (Louis Marie) Alphonse 1840-1897
NCLC 1
See also DLB 123
Daumal, Rene 1908-1944 .... **TCLC 14**
See also CA 114
Davenant, William 1606-1668 .... **LC 13**
See also DLB 58, 126
Davenport, Guy (Mattison, Jr.) 1927-**CLC 6,
14, 38; SSC 16**
See also CA 33-36R; CANR 23, 73; DLB 130
Davidson, Avram (James) 1923-1993
See Queen, Ellery
See also CA 101; 171; CANR 26; DLB 8
Davidson, Donald (Grady) 1893-1968**CLC 2,
13, 19**
See also CA 5-8R; 25-28R; CANR 4; DLB 45
Davidson, Hugh
See Hamilton, Edmond
Davidson, John 1857-1909 .... **TCLC 24**
See also CA 118; DLB 19
Davidson, Sara 1943- .... **CLC 9**
See also CA 81-84; CANR 44, 68; DLB 185
Davie, Donald (Alfred) 1922-1995 . **CLC 5, 8,
10, 31**
See also CA 1-4R; 149; CAAS 3; CANR 1, 44;
DLB 27; MTCW 1
Davies, Ray(mond Douglas) 1944- ... **CLC 21**
See also CA 116; 146
Davies, Rhys 1901-1978 .... **CLC 23**
See also CA 9-12R; 81-84; CANR 4; DLB 139,
191
Davies, (William) Robertson 1913-1995 **C L C
2, 7, 13, 25, 42, 75, 91; DA; DAB; DAC;
DAM MST, NOV, POP; WLC**
See also BEST 89:2; CA 33-36R; 150; CANR
17, 42; DLB 68; INT CANR-17; MTCW 1,
2
Davies, W(illiam) H(enry) 1871-1940**TCLC 5**
See also CA 104; DLB 19, 174
Davies, Walter C.
See Kornbluth, C(yril) M.
Davis, Angela (Yvonne) 1944- **CLC 77; DAM
MULT**

See also BW 2, 3; CA 57-60; CANR 10, 81
Davis, B. Lynch
See Bioy Casares, Adolfo; Borges, Jorge Luis
Davis, B. Lynch
See Bioy Casares, Adolfo
Davis, Harold Lenoir 1894-1960 ...... **CLC 49**
See also CA 89-92; DLB 9, 206
Davis, Rebecca (Blaine) Harding 1831-1910
TCLC 6
See also CA 104; DLB 74
Davis, Richard Harding 1864-1916**TCLC 24**
See also CA 114; DLB 12, 23, 78, 79, 189;
DLBD 13
Davison, Frank Dalby 1893-1970 ..... **CLC 15**
See also CA 116
Davison, Lawrence H.
See Lawrence, D(avid) H(erbert Richards)
Davison, Peter (Hubert) 1928- .... **CLC 28**
See also CA 9-12R; CAAS 4; CANR 3, 43; DLB
5
Davys, Mary 1674-1732 .... **LC 1, 46**
See also DLB 39
Dawson, Fielding 1930- .... **CLC 6**
See also CA 85-88; DLB 130
Dawson, Peter
See Faust, Frederick (Schiller)
Day, Clarence (Shepard, Jr.) 1874-1935
TCLC 25
See also CA 108; DLB 11
Day, Thomas 1748-1789 .... **LC 1**
See also DLB 39; YABC 1
Day Lewis, C(ecil) 1904-1972 . **CLC 1, 6, 10;
DAM POET; PC 11**
See also Blake, Nicholas
See also CA 13-16; 33-36R; CANR 34; CAP 1;
DLB 15, 20; MTCW 1, 2
Dazai Osamu 1909-1948 .... **TCLC 11**
See also Tsushima, Shuji
See also CA 164; DLB 182
de Andrade, Carlos Drummond 1892-1945
See Drummond de Andrade, Carlos
Deane, Norman
See Creasey, John
**de Beauvoir, Simone (Lucie Ernestine Marie
Bertrand)**
See Beauvoir, Simone (Lucie Ernestine Marie
Bertrand) de
de Beer, P.
See Bosman, Herman Charles
de Brissac, Malcolm
See Dickinson, Peter (Malcolm)
de Chardin, Pierre Teilhard
See Teilhard de Chardin, (Marie Joseph) Pierre
Dee, John 1527-1608 .... **LC 20**
Deer, Sandra 1940- .... **CLC 45**
De Ferrari, Gabriella 1941- .... **CLC 65**
See also CA 146
Defoe, Daniel 1660(?)-1731 ..... **LC 1, 42; DA;
DAB; DAC; DAM MST, NOV; WLC**
See also AAYA 27; CDBLB 1660-1789; DLB
39, 95, 101; JRDA; MAICYA; SATA 22
de Gourmont, Remy(-Marie-Charles)
See Gourmont, Remy (-Marie-Charles) de
de Hartog, Jan 1914- .... **CLC 19**
See also CA 1-4R; CANR 1
de Hostos, E. M.
See Hostos (y Bonilla), Eugenio Maria de
de Hostos, Eugenio M.
See Hostos (y Bonilla), Eugenio Maria de
Deighton, Len .... **CLC 4, 7, 22, 46**
See also Deighton, Leonard Cyril
See also AAYA 6; BEST 89:2; CDBLB 1960 to
Present; DLB 87

Deighton, Leonard Cyril 1929-
See Deighton, Len
See also CA 9-12R; CANR 19, 33, 68; DAM
NOV, POP; MTCW 1, 2
Dekker, Thomas 1572(?)-1632 .. **LC 22; DAM
DRAM**
See also CDBLB Before 1660; DLB 62, 172
Delafield, E. M. 1890-1943 .... **TCLC 61**
See also Dashwood, Edmee Elizabeth Monica
de la Pasture
See also DLB 34
de la Mare, Walter (John) 1873-1956**TCLC 4,
53; DAB; DAC; DAM MST, POET; SSC
14; WLC**
See also CA 163; CDBLB 1914-1945; CLR 23;
DLB 162; MTCW 1; SATA 16
Delaney, Franey
See O'Hara, John (Henry)
Delaney, Shelagh 1939-**CLC 29; DAM DRAM**
See also CA 17-20R; CANR 30, 67; CDBLB
1960 to Present; DLB 13; MTCW 1
Delany, Mary (Granville Pendarves) 1700-1788
LC 12
Delany, Samuel R(ay, Jr.) 1942-**CLC 8, 14, 38;
BLC 1; DAM MULT**
See also AAYA 24; BW 2, 3; CA 81-84; CANR
27, 43; DLB 8, 33; MTCW 1, 2
De La Ramee, (Marie) Louise 1839-1908
See Ouida
See also SATA 20
de la Roche, Mazo 1879-1961 .... **CLC 14**
See also CA 85-88; CANR 30; DLB 68; SATA
64
De La Salle, Innocent
See Hartmann, Sadakichi
Delbanco, Nicholas (Franklin) 1942- **CLC 6,
13**
See also CA 17-20R; CAAS 2; CANR 29, 55;
DLB 6
del Castillo, Michel 1933- .... **CLC 38**
See also CA 109; CANR 77
Deledda, Grazia (Cosima) 1875(?)-1936
TCLC 23
See also CA 123
Delibes, Miguel .... **CLC 8, 18**
See also Delibes Setien, Miguel
Delibes Setien, Miguel 1920-
See Delibes, Miguel
See also CA 45-48; CANR 1, 32; HW 1; MTCW
1
DeLillo, Don 1936- **CLC 8, 10, 13, 27, 39, 54,
76; DAM NOV, POP**
See also BEST 89:1; CA 81-84; CANR 21, 76;
DLB 6, 173; MTCW 1, 2
de Lisser, H. G.
See De Lisser, H(erbert) G(eorge)
See also DLB 117
De Lisser, H(erbert) G(eorge) 1878-1944
TCLC 12
See also de Lisser, H. G.
See also BW 2; CA 109; 152
Deloney, Thomas 1560(?)-1600 .... **LC 41**
See also DLB 167
Deloria, Vine (Victor), Jr. 1933- ..... **CLC 21;
DAM MULT**
See also CA 53-56; CANR 5, 20, 48; DLB 175;
MTCW 1; NNAL; SATA 21
Del Vecchio, John M(ichael) 1947- ... **CLC 29**
See also CA 110; DLBD 9
de Man, Paul (Adolph Michel) 1919-1983
CLC 55
See also CA 128; 111; CANR 61; DLB 67;
MTCW 1, 2

De Marinis, Rick 1934- .... **CLC 54**
  See also CA 57-60; CAAS 24; CANR 9, 25, 50
Dembry, R. Emmet
  See Murfree, Mary Noailles
Demby, William 1922-**CLC 53; BLC 1; DAM MULT**
  See also BW 1, 3; CA 81-84; CANR 81; DLB 33
de Menton, Francisco
  See Chin, Frank (Chew, Jr.)
Demijohn, Thom
  See Disch, Thomas M(ichael)
de Montherlant, Henry (Milon)
  See Montherlant, Henry (Milon) de
Demosthenes 384B.C.-322B.C. ...... **CMLC 13**
  See also DLB 176
de Natale, Francine
  See Malzberg, Barry N(athaniel)
Denby, Edwin (Orr) 1903-1983 .... **CLC 48**
  See also CA 138; 110
Denis, Julio
  See Cortazar, Julio
Denmark, Harrison
  See Zelazny, Roger (Joseph)
Dennis, John 1658-1734 .... **LC 11**
  See also DLB 101
Dennis, Nigel (Forbes) 1912-1989 ...... **CLC 8**
  See also CA 25-28R; 129; DLB 13, 15; MTCW 1
Dent, Lester 1904(?)-1959 .... **TCLC 72**
  See also CA 112; 161
De Palma, Brian (Russell) 1940- .... **CLC 20**
  See also CA 109
De Quincey, Thomas 1785-1859 ...... **NCLC 4**
  See also CDBLB 1789-1832; DLB 110; 144
Deren, Eleanora 1908(?)-1961
  See Deren, Maya
  See also CA 111
Deren, Maya 1917-1961 .... **CLC 16, 102**
  See also Deren, Eleanora
Derleth, August (William) 1909-1971**CLC 31**
  See also CA 1-4R; 29-32R; CANR 4; DLB 9; DLBD 17; SATA 5
Der Nister 1884-1950 .... **TCLC 56**
de Routisie, Albert
  See Aragon, Louis
Derrida, Jacques 1930- .... **CLC 24, 87**
  See also CA 124; 127; CANR 76; MTCW 1
Derry Down Derry
  See Lear, Edward
Dersonnes, Jacques
  See Simenon, Georges (Jacques Christian)
Desai, Anita 1937-**CLC 19, 37, 97; DAB; DAM NOV**
  See also CA 81-84; CANR 33, 53; MTCW 1, 2; SATA 63
Desai, Kiran 1971- .... **CLC 119**
  See also CA 171
de Saint-Luc, Jean
  See Glassco, John
de Saint Roman, Arnaud
  See Aragon, Louis
Descartes, Rene 1596-1650 .... **LC 20, 35**
De Sica, Vittorio 1901(?)-1974 .... **CLC 20**
  See also CA 117
Desnos, Robert 1900-1945 .... **TCLC 22**
  See also CA 121; 151
Destouches, Louis-Ferdinand 1894-1961**C L C 9, 15**
  See also Celine, Louis-Ferdinand
  See also CA 85-88; CANR 28; MTCW 1
de Tolignac, Gaston
  See Griffith, D(avid Lewelyn) W(ark)

Deutsch, Babette 1895-1982 .... **CLC 18**
  See also CA 1-4R; 108; CANR 4, 79; DLB 45; SATA 1; SATA-Obit 33
Devenant, William 1606-1649 .... **LC 13**
Devkota, Laxmiprasad 1909-1959 . **TCLC 23**
  See also CA 123
De Voto, Bernard (Augustine) 1897-1955
  TCLC 29
  See also CA 113; 160; DLB 9
De Vries, Peter 1910-1993 **CLC 1, 2, 3, 7, 10, 28, 46; DAM NOV**
  See also CA 17-20R; 142; CANR 41; DLB 6; DLBY 82; MTCW 1, 2
Dewey, John 1859-1952 .... **TCLC 95**
  See also CA 114; 170
Dexter, John
  See Bradley, Marion Zimmer
Dexter, Martin
  See Faust, Frederick (Schiller)
Dexter, Pete 1943- ... **CLC 34, 55; DAM POP**
  See also BEST 89:2; CA 127; 131; INT 131; MTCW 1
Diamano, Silmang
  See Senghor, Leopold Sedar
Diamond, Neil 1941- .... **CLC 30**
  See also CA 108
Diaz del Castillo, Bernal 1496-1584 .. **LC 31; HLCS 1**
di Bassetto, Corno
  See Shaw, George Bernard
Dick, Philip K(indred) 1928-1982**CLC 10, 30, 72; DAM NOV, POP**
  See also AAYA 24; CA 49-52; 106; CANR 2, 16; DLB 8; MTCW 1, 2
Dickens, Charles (John Huffam) 1812-1870
  NCLC 3, 8, 18, 26, 37, 50; DA; DAB; DAC; DAM MST, NOV; SSC 17; WLC
  See also AAYA 23; CDBLB 1832-1890; DLB 21, 55, 70, 159, 166; JRDA; MAICYA; SATA 15
Dickey, James (Lafayette) 1923-1997 **CLC 1, 2, 4, 7, 10, 15, 47, 109; DAM NOV, POET, POP**
  See also AITN 1, 2; CA 9-12R; 156; CABS 2; CANR 10, 48, 61; CDALB 1968-1988; DLB 5, 193; DLBD 7; DLBY 82, 93, 96, 97, 98; INT CANR-10; MTCW 1, 2
Dickey, William 1928-1994 .... **CLC 3, 28**
  See also CA 9-12R; 145; CANR 24, 79; DLB 5
Dickinson, Charles 1951- .... **CLC 49**
  See also CA 128
Dickinson, Emily (Elizabeth) 1830-1886
  NCLC 21, 77; DA; DAB; DAC; DAM MST, POET; PC 1; WLC
  See also AAYA 22; CDALB 1865-1917; DLB 1; SATA 29
Dickinson, Peter (Malcolm) 1927-**CLC 12, 35**
  See also AAYA 9; CA 41-44R; CANR 31, 58; CLR 29; DLB 87, 161; JRDA; MAICYA; SATA 5, 62, 95
Dickson, Carr
  See Carr, John Dickson
Dickson, Carter
  See Carr, John Dickson
Diderot, Denis 1713-1784 .... **LC 26**
Didion, Joan 1934-**CLC 1, 3, 8, 14, 32; DAM NOV**
  See also AITN 1; CA 5-8R; CANR 14, 52, 76; CDALB 1968-1988; DLB 2, 173, 185; DLBY 81, 86; MTCW 1, 2
Dietrich, Robert
  See Hunt, E(verette) Howard, (Jr.)
Difusa, Pati

  See Almodovar, Pedro
Dillard, Annie 1945- .. **CLC 9, 60, 115; DAM NOV**
  See also AAYA 6; CA 49-52; CANR 3, 43, 62; DLB 80; MTCW 1, 2; SATA 10
Dillard, R(ichard) H(enry) W(ilde) 1937-
  CLC 5
  See also CA 21-24R; CAAS 7; CANR 10; DLB 5
Dillon, Eilis 1920-1994 .... **CLC 17**
  See also CA 9-12R; 147; CAAS 3; CANR 4, 38, 78; CLR 26; MAICYA; SATA 2, 74; SATA-Essay 105; SATA-Obit 83
Dimont, Penelope
  See Mortimer, Penelope (Ruth)
Dinesen, Isak .... **CLC 10, 29, 95; SSC 7**
  See also Blixen, Karen (Christentze Dinesen)
  See also MTCW 1
Ding Ling .... **CLC 68**
  See also Chiang, Pin-chin
Diphusa, Patty
  See Almodovar, Pedro
Disch, Thomas M(ichael) 1940- .... **CLC 7, 36**
  See also AAYA 17; CA 21-24R; CAAS 4; CANR 17, 36, 54; CLR 18; DLB 8; MAICYA; MTCW 1, 2; SAAS 15; SATA 92
Disch, Tom
  See Disch, Thomas M(ichael)
d'Isly, Georges
  See Simenon, Georges (Jacques Christian)
Disraeli, Benjamin 1804-1881**NCLC 2, 39, 79**
  See also DLB 21, 55
Ditcum, Steve
  See Crumb, R(obert)
Dixon, Paige
  See Corcoran, Barbara
Dixon, Stephen 1936- .... **CLC 52; SSC 16**
  See also CA 89-92; CANR 17, 40, 54; DLB 130
Doak, Annie
  See Dillard, Annie
Dobell, Sydney Thompson 1824-1874 **N C L C 43**
  See also DLB 32
Doblin, Alfred .... **TCLC 13**
  See also Doeblin, Alfred
Dobrolyubov, Nikolai Alexandrovich 1836-1861
  NCLC 5
Dobson, Austin 1840-1921 .... **TCLC 79**
  See also DLB 35; 144
Dobyns, Stephen 1941- .... **CLC 37**
  See also CA 45-48; CANR 2, 18
Doctorow, E(dgar) L(aurence) 1931- **CLC 6, 11, 15, 18, 37, 44, 65, 113; DAM NOV, POP**
  See also AAYA 22; AITN 2; BEST 89:3; CA 45-48; CANR 2, 33, 51, 76; CDALB 1968-1988; DLB 2, 28, 173; DLBY 80; MTCW 1, 2
Dodgson, Charles Lutwidge 1832-1898
  See Carroll, Lewis
  See also CLR 2; DA; DAB; DAC; DAM MST, NOV, POET; MAICYA; SATA 100; YABC 2
Dodson, Owen (Vincent) 1914-1983 **CLC 79; BLC 1; DAM MULT**
  See also BW 1; CA 65-68; 110; CANR 24; DLB 76
Doeblin, Alfred 1878-1957 .... **TCLC 13**
  See Doblin, Alfred
  See also CA 110; 141; DLB 66
Doerr, Harriet 1910- .... **CLC 34**
  See also CA 117; 122; CANR 47; INT 122
Domecq, H(onorio Bustos)
  See Bioy Casares, Adolfo
Domecq, H(onorio) Bustos

See Bioy Casares, Adolfo; Borges, Jorge Luis

Domini, Rey
See Lorde, Audre (Geraldine)

Dominique
See Proust, (Valentin-Louis-George-Eugene-)
Marcel

Don, A
See Stephen, SirLeslie

Donaldson, Stephen R. 1947- **CLC 46; DAM POP**
See also CA 89-92; CANR 13, 55; INT CANR-13

Donleavy, J(ames) P(atrick) 1926-**CLC 1, 4, 6, 10, 45**
See also AITN 2; CA 9-12R; CANR 24, 49, 62, 80; DLB 6, 173; INT CANR-24; MTCW 1, 2

Donne, John 1572-1631**LC 10, 24; DA; DAB; DAC; DAM MST, POET; PC 1; WLC**
See also CDBLB Before 1660; DLB 121, 151

Donnell, David 1939(?)- .... **CLC 34**

Donoghue, P. S.
See Hunt, E(verette) Howard, (Jr.)

Donoso (Yanez), Jose 1924-1996**CLC 4, 8, 11, 32, 99; DAM MULT; HLC;SSC 34**
See also CA 81-84; 155; CANR 32, 73; DLB 113; HW 1, 2; MTCW 1, 2

Donovan, John 1928-1992 .... **CLC 35**
See also AAYA 20; CA 97-100; 137; CLR 3; MAICYA; SATA 72; SATA-Brief 29

Don Roberto
See Cunninghame Graham, R(obert) B(ontine)

Doolittle, Hilda 1886-1961**CLC 3, 8, 14, 31, 34, 73; DA; DAC; DAM MST, POET; PC 5; WLC**
See also H. D.
See also CA 97-100; CANR 35; DLB 4, 45; MTCW 1, 2

Dorfman, Ariel 1942- ...... **CLC 48, 77; DAM MULT; HLC**
See also CA 124; 130; CANR 67, 70; HW 1, 2; INT 130

Dorn, Edward (Merton) 1929- ... **CLC 10, 18**
See also CA 93-96; CANR 42, 79; DLB 5; INT 93-96

Dorris, Michael (Anthony) 1945-1997 .. **C L C 109; DAM MULT, NOV**
See also AAYA 20; BEST 90:1; CA 102; 157; CANR 19, 46, 75; CLR 58; DLB 175; MTCW 2; NNAL; SATA 75; SATA-Obit 94

Dorris, Michael A.
See Dorris, Michael (Anthony)

Dorsan, Luc
See Simenon, Georges (Jacques Christian)

Dorsange, Jean
See Simenon, Georges (Jacques Christian)

Dos Passos, John (Roderigo) 1896-1970 **C L C 1, 4, 8, 11, 15, 25, 34, 82; DA; DAB; DAC; DAM MST, NOV; WLC**
See also CA 1-4R; 29-32R; CANR 3; CDALB 1929-1941; DLB 4, 9; DLBD 1. 15; DLBY 96; MTCW 1, 2

Dossage, Jean
See Simenon, Georges (Jacques Christian)

Dostoevsky, Fedor Mikhailovich 1821-1881 **NCLC 2, 7, 21, 33, 43; DA; DAB; DAC; DAM MST, NOV; SSC 2, 33; WLC**

Doughty, Charles M(ontagu) 1843-1926 **TCLC 27**
See also CA 115; DLB 19, 57, 174

Douglas, Ellen .... **CLC 73**
See also Haxton, Josephine Ayres; Williamson, Ellen Douglas

Douglas, Gavin 1475(?)-1522 .... **LC 20**
See also DLB 132

Douglas, George
See Brown, George Douglas

Douglas, Keith (Castellain) 1920-1944**T C L C 40**
See also CA 160; DLB 27

Douglas, Leonard
See Bradbury, Ray (Douglas)

Douglas, Michael
See Crichton, (John) Michael

Douglas, (George) Norman 1868-1952**T C L C 68**
See also CA 119; 157; DLB 34, 195

Douglas, William
See Brown, George Douglas

Douglass, Frederick 1817(?)-1895**NCLC 7, 55; BLC 1; DA; DAC; DAM MST, MULT; WLC**
See also CDALB 1640-1865; DLB 1, 43, 50, 79; SATA 29

Dourado, (Waldomiro Freitas) Autran 1926- **CLC 23, 60**
See also CA 25-28R; CANR 34, 81; DLB 145; HW 2

Dourado, Waldomiro Autran
See Dourado, (Waldomiro Freitas) Autran

Dove, Rita (Frances) 1952-**CLC 50, 81; BLCS; DAM MULT, POET; PC 6**
See also BW 2; CA 109; CAAS 19; CANR 27, 42, 68, 76; CDALBS; DLB 120; MTCW 1

Doveglion
See Villa, Jose Garcia

Dowell, Coleman 1925-1985 .... **CLC 60**
See also CA 25-28R; 117; CANR 10; DLB 130

Dowson, Ernest (Christopher) 1867-1900 **TCLC 4**
See also CA 105; 150; DLB 19, 135

Doyle, A'. Conan
See Doyle, Arthur Conan

Doyle, Arthur Conan 1859-1930**TCLC 7; DA; DAB; DAC; DAM MST, NOV; SSC 12; WLC**
See also AAYA 14; CA 104; 122; CDBLB 1890-1914; DLB 18, 70, 156, 178; MTCW 1, 2; SATA 24

Doyle, Conan
See Doyle, Arthur Conan

Doyle, John
See Graves, Robert (von Ranke)

Doyle, Roddy 1958(?)- .... **CLC 81**
See also AAYA 14; CA 143; CANR 73; DLB 194

Doyle, Sir A. Conan
See Doyle, Arthur Conan

Doyle, Sir Arthur Conan
See Doyle, Arthur Conan

Dr. A
See Asimov, Isaac; Silverstein, Alvin

Drabble, Margaret 1939-**CLC 2, 3, 5, 8, 10, 22, 53; DAB; DAC; DAM MST, NOV, POP**
See also CA 13-16R; CANR 18, 35, 63; CDBLB 1960 to Present; DLB 14, 155; MTCW 1, 2; SATA 48

Drapier, M. B.
See Swift, Jonathan

Drayham, James
See Mencken, H(enry) L(ouis)

Drayton, Michael 1563-1631 ......**LC 8; DAM POET**
See also DLB 121

Dreadstone, Carl
See Campbell, (John) Ramsey

Dreiser, Theodore (Herman Albert) 1871-1945 **TCLC 10, 18, 35, 83; DA; DAC; DAM MST, NOV; SSC 30; WLC**
See also CA 106; 132; CDALB 1865-1917; DLB 9, 12, 102, 137; DLBD 1; MTCW 1, 2

Drexler, Rosalyn 1926- .... **CLC 2, 6**
See also CA 81-84; CANR 68

Dreyer, Carl Theodor 1889-1968 ...... **CLC 16**
See also CA 116

Drieu la Rochelle, Pierre(-Eugene) 1893-1945 **TCLC 21**
See also CA 117; DLB 72

Drinkwater, John 1882-1937 .... **TCLC 57**
See also CA 109; 149; DLB 10, 19, 149

Drop Shot
See Cable, George Washington

Droste-Hulshoff, Annette Freiin von 1797-1848 **NCLC 3**
See also DLB 133

Drummond, Walter
See Silverberg, Robert

Drummond, William Henry 1854-1907**T C L C 25**
See also CA 160; DLB 92

Drummond de Andrade, Carlos 1902-1987 **CLC 18**
See also Andrade, Carlos Drummond de
See also CA 132; 123

Drury, Allen (Stuart) 1918-1998 .... **CLC 37**
See also CA 57-60; 170; CANR 18, 52; INT CANR-18

Dryden, John 1631-1700**LC 3, 21; DA; DAB; DAC; DAM DRAM, MST, POET; DC 3; PC 25; WLC**
See also CDBLB 1660-1789; DLB 80, 101, 131

Duberman, Martin (Bauml) 1930- ..... **CLC 8**
See also CA 1-4R; CANR 2, 63

Dubie, Norman (Evans) 1945- .... **CLC 36**
See also CA 69-72; CANR 12; DLB 120

Du Bois, W(illiam) E(dward) B(urghardt) 1868-1963 .. **CLC 1, 2, 13, 64, 96; BLC 1; DA; DAC; DAM MST, MULT, NOV; WLC**
See also BW 1, 3; CA 85-88; CANR 34; CDALB 1865-1917; DLB 47, 50, 91; MTCW 1, 2; SATA 42

Dubus, Andre 1936-1999**CLC 13, 36, 97; SSC 15**
See also CA 21-24R; 177; CANR 17; DLB 130; INT CANR-17

Duca Minimo
See D'Annunzio, Gabriele

Ducharme, Rejean 1941- .... **CLC 74**
See also CA 165; DLB 60

Duclos, Charles Pinot 1704-1772 .... **LC 1**

Dudek, Louis 1918- .... **CLC 11, 19**
See also CA 45-48; CAAS 14; CANR 1; DLB 88

Duerrenmatt, Friedrich 1921-1990**CLC 1, 4, 8, 11, 15, 43, 102; DAM DRAM**
See also CA 17-20R; CANR 33; DLB 69, 124; MTCW 1, 2

Duffy, Bruce 1953(?)- .... **CLC 50**
See also CA 172

Duffy, Maureen 1933- .... **CLC 37**
See also CA 25-28R; CANR 33, 68; DLB 14; MTCW 1

Dugan, Alan 1923- .... **CLC 2, 6**
See also CA 81-84; DLB 5

du Gard, Roger Martin
See Martin du Gard, Roger

Duhamel, Georges 1884-1966 .... **CLC 8**
See also CA 81-84; 25-28R; CANR 35; DLB 65; MTCW 1

TCLC 57
See also CA 114; 149

Eisner, Simon
See Kornbluth, C(yril) M.

Ekeloef, (Bengt) Gunnar 1907-1968 **CLC 27;**
DAM POET; PC 23
See also CA 123; 25-28R

Ekelof, (Bengt) Gunnar
See Ekeloef, (Bengt) Gunnar

Ekelund, Vilhelm 1880-1949 .... **TCLC 75**

Ekwensi, C. O. D.
See Ekwensi, Cyprian (Odiatu Duaka)

Ekwensi, Cyprian (Odiatu Duaka) 1921-**CLC**
4; BLC 1; DAM MULT
See also BW 2, 3; CA 29-32R; CANR 18, 42,
74; DLB 117; MTCW 1, 2; SATA 66

Elaine .... **TCLC 18**
See also Leverson, Ada

El Crummo
See Crumb, R(obert)

Elder, Lonne III 1931-1996 .... **DC 8**
See also BLC 1; BW 1, 3; CA 81-84; 152;
CANR 25; DAM MULT; DLB 7, 38, 44

Elia
See Lamb, Charles

Eliade, Mircea 1907-1986 .... **CLC 19**
See also CA 65-68; 119; CANR 30, 62; MTCW
1

Eliot, A. D.
See Jewett, (Theodora) Sarah Orne

Eliot, Alice
See Jewett, (Theodora) Sarah Orne

Eliot, Dan
See Silverberg, Robert

Eliot, George 1819-1880 **NCLC 4, 13, 23, 41,**
49; DA; DAB; DAC; DAM MST, NOV; PC
20; WLC
See also CDBLB 1832-1890; DLB 21, 35, 55

Eliot, John 1604-1690 .... **LC 5**
See also DLB 24

Eliot, T(homas) S(tearns) 1888-1965**CLC 1, 2,**
3, 6, 9, 10, 13, 15, 24, 34, 41, 55, 57, 113;
DA; DAB; DAC; DAM DRAM, MST,
POET; PC 5; WLC
See also AAYA 28; CA 5-8R; 25-28R; CANR
41; CDALB 1929-1941; DLB 7, 10, 45, 63;
DLBY 88; MTCW 1, 2

Elizabeth 1866-1941 .... **TCLC 41**

Elkin, Stanley L(awrence) 1930-1995 **CLC 4,**
6, 9, 14, 27, 51, 91; DAM NOV, POP; SSC
12
See also CA 9-12R; 148; CANR 8, 46; DLB 2,
28; DLBY 80; INT CANR-8; MTCW 1, 2

Elledge, Scott .... **CLC 34**

Elliot, Don
See Silverberg, Robert

Elliott, Don
See Silverberg, Robert

Elliott, George P(aul) 1918-1980 .... **CLC 2**
See also CA 1-4R; 97-100; CANR 2

Elliott, Janice 1931-............................ **CLC 47**
See also CA 13-16R; CANR 8, 29; DLB 14

Elliott, Sumner Locke 1917-1991 ..... **CLC 38**
See also CA 5-8R; 134; CANR 2, 21

Elliott, William
See Bradbury, Ray (Douglas)

Ellis, A. E. .... **CLC 7**

Ellis, Alice Thomas .... **CLC 40**
See also Haycraft, Anna
See also DLB 194; MTCW 1

Ellis, Bret Easton 1964-**CLC 39, 71, 117; DAM**
POP
See also AAYA 2; CA 118; 123; CANR 51, 74;

INT 123; MTCW 1

Ellis, (Henry) Havelock 1859-1939 **TCLC 14**
See also CA 109; 169; DLB 190

Ellis, Landon
See Ellison, Harlan (Jay)

Ellis, Trey 1962- .... **CLC 55**
See also CA 146

Ellison, Harlan (Jay) 1934- ... **CLC 1, 13, 42;**
DAM POP; SSC 14
See also AAYA 29; CA 5-8R; CANR 5, 46; DLB
8; INT CANR-5; MTCW 1, 2

Ellison, Ralph (Waldo) 1914-1994.**CLC 1, 3,**
11, 54, 86, 114; BLC 1; DA;DAB; DAC;
DAM MST, MULT, NOV; SSC 26; WLC
See also AAYA 19; BW 1, 3; CA 9-12R; 145;
CANR 24, 53; CDALB 1941-1968; DLB 2,
76; DLBY 94; MTCW 1, 2

Ellmann, Lucy (Elizabeth) 1956- ..... **CLC 61**
See also CA 128

Ellmann, Richard (David) 1918-1987**CLC 50**
See also BEST 89:2; CA 1-4R; 122; CANR 2,
28, 61; DLB 103; DLBY 87; MTCW 1, 2

Elman, Richard (Martin) 1934-1997 **CLC 19**
See also CA 17-20R; 163; CAAS 3; CANR 47

Elron
See Hubbard, L(afayette) Ron(ald)

Eluard, Paul .... **TCLC 7, 41**
See also Grindel, Eugene

Elyot, Sir Thomas 1490(?)-1546 .... **LC 11**

Elytis, Odysseus 1911-1996 **CLC 15, 49, 100;**
DAM POET; PC 21
See also CA 102; 151; MTCW 1, 2

Emecheta, (Florence Onye) Buchi 1944-**C L C**
14, 48; BLC 2; DAM MULT
See also BW 2, 3; CA 81-84; CANR 27, 81;
DLB 117; MTCW 1, 2; SATA 66

Emerson, Mary Moody 1774-1863 **NCLC 66**

Emerson, Ralph Waldo 1803-1882 . **NCLC 1,**
38; DA; DAB; DAC; DAM MST, POET;
PC 18; WLC
See also CDALB 1640-1865; DLB 1, 59, 73

Eminescu, Mihail 1850-1889 .... **NCLC 33**

Empson, William 1906-1984**CLC 3, 8, 19, 33,**
34
See also CA 17-20R; 112; CANR 31, 61; DLB
20; MTCW 1, 2

Enchi, Fumiko (Ueda) 1905-1986 ..... **CLC 31**
See also CA 129; 121; DLB 182

Ende, Michael (Andreas Helmuth) 1929-1995
CLC 31
See also CA 118; 124; 149; CANR 36; CLR
14; DLB 75; MAICYA; SATA 61; SATA-
Brief 42; SATA-Obit 86

Endo, Shusaku 1923-1996 **CLC 7, 14, 19, 54,**
99; DAM NOV
See also CA 29-32R; 153; CANR 21, 54; DLB
182; MTCW 1, 2

Engel, Marian 1933-1985 .... **CLC 36**
See also CA 25-28R; CANR 12; DLB 53; INT
CANR-12

Engelhardt, Frederick
See Hubbard, L(afayette) Ron(ald)

Enright, D(ennis) J(oseph) 1920-**CLC 4, 8, 31**
See also CA 1-4R; CANR 1, 42; DLB 27; SATA
25

Enzensberger, Hans Magnus 1929- .. **CLC 43**
See also CA 116; 119

Ephron, Nora 1941- .... **CLC 17, 31**
See also AITN 2; CA 65-68; CANR 12, 39

Epicurus 341B.C.-270B.C. .... **CMLC 21**
See also DLB 176

Epsilon
See Betjeman, John

Epstein, Daniel Mark 1948- .... **CLC 7**
See also CA 49-52; CANR 2, 53

Epstein, Jacob 1956- .... **CLC 19**
See also CA 114

Epstein, Jean 1897-1953 .... **TCLC 92**

Epstein, Joseph 1937-......................... **CLC 39**
See also CA 112; 119; CANR 50, 65

Epstein, Leslie 1938- .... **CLC 27**
See also CA 73-76; CAAS 12; CANR 23, 69

Equiano, Olaudah 1745(?)-1797 **LC 16; BLC**
2; DAM MULT
See also DLB 37, 50

ER .... **TCLC 33**
See also CA 160; DLB 85

Erasmus, Desiderius 1469(?)-1536 ...... **LC 16**

Erdman, Paul E(mil) 1932- .... **CLC 25**
See also AITN 1; CA 61-64; CANR 13, 43

Erdrich, Louise 1954-**CLC 39, 54, 120; DAM**
MULT, NOV, POP
See also AAYA 10; BEST 89:1; CA 114; CANR
41, 62; CDALBS; DLB 152, 175, 206;
MTCW 1; NNAL; SATA 94

Erenburg, Ilya (Grigoryevich)
See Ehrenburg, Ilya (Grigoryevich)

Erickson, Stephen Michael 1950-
See Erickson, Steve
See also CA 129

Erickson, Steve 1950- .... **CLC 64**
See also Erickson, Stephen Michael
See also CANR 60, 68

Ericson, Walter
See Fast, Howard (Melvin)

Eriksson, Buntel
See Bergman, (Ernst) Ingmar

Ernaux, Annie 1940- .... **CLC 88**
See also CA 147

Erskine, John 1879-1951 .... **TCLC 84**
See also CA 112; 159; DLB 9, 102

Eschenbach, Wolfram von
See Wolfram von Eschenbach

Eseki, Bruno
See Mphahlele, Ezekiel

Esenin, Sergei (Alexandrovich) 1895-1925
TCLC 4
See also CA 104

Eshleman, Clayton 1935- .... **CLC 7**
See also CA 33-36R; CAAS 6; DLB 5

Espriella, Don Manuel Alvarez
See Southey, Robert

Espriu, Salvador 1913-1985 .... **CLC 9**
See also CA 154; 115; DLB 134

Espronceda, Jose de 1808-1842 ..... **NCLC 39**

Esse, James
See Stephens, James

Esterbrook, Tom
See Hubbard, L(afayette) Ron(ald)

Estleman, Loren D. 1952-**CLC 48; DAM NOV,**
POP
See also AAYA 27; CA 85-88; CANR 27, 74;
INT CANR-27; MTCW 1, 2

Euclid 306B.C.-283B.C. .... **CMLC 25**

Eugenides, Jeffrey 1960(?)- .... **CLC 81**
See also CA 144

Euripides c. 485B.C.-406B.C.**CMLC 23; DA;**
DAB; DAC; DAM DRAM, MST; DC 4;
WLCS
See also DLB 176

Evan, Evin
See Faust, Frederick (Schiller)

Evans, Caradoc 1878-1945 .... **TCLC 85**

Evans, Evan
See Faust, Frederick (Schiller)

Evans, Marian

See Eliot, George

Evans, Mary Ann
See Eliot, George

Evarts, Esther
See Benson, Sally

Everett, Percival L. 1956- .... **CLC 57**
See also BW 2; CA 129

Everson, R(onald) G(ilmour) 1903- . **CLC 27**
See also CA 17-20R; DLB 88

Everson, William (Oliver) 1912-1994 **CLC 1, 5, 14**
See also CA 9-12R; 145; CANR 20; DLB 212; MTCW 1

Evtushenko, Evgenii Aleksandrovich
See Yevtushenko, Yevgeny (Alexandrovich)

Ewart, Gavin (Buchanan) 1916-1995**CLC 13, 46**
See also CA 89-92; 150; CANR 17, 46; DLB 40; MTCW 1

Ewers, Hanns Heinz 1871-1943 ..... **TCLC 12**
See also CA 109; 149

Ewing, Frederick R.
See Sturgeon, Theodore (Hamilton)

Exley, Frederick (Earl) 1929-1992 **CLC 6, 11**
See also AITN 2; CA 81-84; 138; DLB 143; DLBY 81

Eynhardt, Guillermo
See Quiroga, Horacio (Sylvestre)

Ezekiel, Nissim 1924- .... **CLC 61**
See also CA 61-64

Ezekiel, Tish O'Dowd 1943- .... **CLC 34**
See also CA 129

Fadeyev, A.
See Bulgya, Alexander Alexandrovich

Fadeyev, Alexander .... **TCLC 53**
See also Bulgya, Alexander Alexandrovich

Fagen, Donald 1948- .... **CLC 26**

Fainzilberg, Ilya Arnoldovich 1897-1937
See Ilf, Ilya
See also CA 120; 165

Fair, Ronald L. 1932- .... **CLC 18**
See also BW 1; CA 69-72; CANR 25; DLB 33

Fairbairn, Roger
See Carr, John Dickson

Fairbairns, Zoe (Ann) 1948- .... **CLC 32**
See also CA 103; CANR 21

Falco, Gian
See Papini, Giovanni

Falconer, James
See Kirkup, James

Falconer, Kenneth
See Kornbluth, C(yril) M.

Falkland, Samuel
See Heijermans, Herman

Fallaci, Oriana 1930- .... **CLC 11, 110**
See also CA 77-80; CANR 15, 58; MTCW 1

Faludy, George 1913- .... **CLC 42**
See also CA 21-24R

Faludy, Gyoergy
See Faludy, George

Fanon, Frantz 1925-1961 ... **CLC 74; BLC 2; DAM MULT**
See also BW 1; CA 116; 89-92

Fanshawe, Ann 1625-1680 .... **LC 11**

Fante, John (Thomas) 1911-1983 ..... **CLC 60**
See also CA 69-72; 109; CANR 23; DLB 130; DLBY 83

Farah, Nuruddin 1945-**CLC 53; BLC 2; DAM MULT**
See also BW 2, 3; CA 106; CANR 81; DLB 125

Fargue, Leon-Paul 1876(?)-1947 ... **TCLC 11**
See also CA 109

Farigoule, Louis
See Romains, Jules

Farina, Richard 1936(?)-1966 .... **CLC 9**
See also CA 81-84; 25-28R

Farley, Walter (Lorimer) 1915-1989 **CLC 17**
See also CA 17-20R; CANR 8, 29; DLB 22; JRDA; MAICYA; SATA 2, 43

Farmer, Philip Jose 1918- .... **CLC 1, 19**
See also AAYA 28; CA 1-4R; CANR 4, 35; DLB 8; MTCW 1; SATA 93

Farquhar, George 1677-1707 ... **LC 21; DAM DRAM**
See also DLB 84

Farrell, J(ames) G(ordon) 1935-1979 **CLC 6**
See also CA 73-76; 89-92; CANR 36; DLB 14; MTCW 1

Farrell, James T(homas) 1904-1979**CLC 1, 4, 8, 11, 66; SSC 28**
See also CA 5-8R; 89-92; CANR 9, 61; DLB 4, 9, 86; DLBD 2; MTCW 1, 2

Farren, Richard J.
See Betjeman, John

Farren, Richard M.
See Betjeman, John

Fassbinder, Rainer Werner 1946-1982**CLC 20**
See also CA 93-96; 106; CANR 31

Fast, Howard (Melvin) 1914- **CLC 23; DAM NOV**
See also AAYA 16; CA 1-4R; CAAS 18; CANR 1, 33, 54, 75; DLB 9; INT CANR-33; MTCW 1; SATA 7; SATA-Essay 107

Faulcon, Robert
See Holdstock, Robert P.

Faulkner, William (Cuthbert) 1897-1962**CLC 1, 3, 6, 8, 9, 11, 14, 18, 28, 52, 68; DA; DAB; DAC; DAM MST, NOV; SSC 1, 35; WLC**
See also AAYA 7; CA 81-84; CANR 33; CDALB 1929-1941; DLB 9, 11, 44, 102; DLBD 2; DLBY 86, 97; MTCW 1, 2

Fauset, Jessie Redmon 1884(?)-1961**CLC 19, 54; BLC 2; DAM MULT**
See also BW 1; CA 109; DLB 51

Faust, Frederick (Schiller) 1892-1944(?) **TCLC 49; DAM POP**
See also CA 108; 152

Faust, Irvin 1924- .... **CLC 8**
See also CA 33-36R; CANR 28, 67; DLB 2, 28; DLBY 80

Fawkes, Guy
See Benchley, Robert (Charles)

Fearing, Kenneth (Flexner) 1902-1961 . **C L C 51**
See also CA 93-96; CANR 59; DLB 9

Fecamps, Elise
See Creasey, John

Federman, Raymond 1928- .... **CLC 6, 47**
See also CA 17-20R; CAAS 8; CANR 10, 43; DLBY 80

Federspiel, J(uerg) F. 1931- .... **CLC 42**
See also CA 146

Feiffer, Jules (Ralph) 1929- ..... **CLC 2, 8, 64; DAM DRAM**
See also AAYA 3; CA 17-20R; CANR 30, 59; DLB 7, 44; INT CANR-30; MTCW 1; SATA 8, 61

Feige, Hermann Albert Otto Maximilian
See Traven, B.

Feinberg, David B. 1956-1994 .... **CLC 59**
See also CA 135; 147

Feinstein, Elaine 1930- .... **CLC 36**
See also CA 69-72; CAAS 1; CANR 31, 68; DLB 14, 40; MTCW 1

Feldman, Irving (Mordecai) 1928- ..... **CLC 7**

See also CA 1-4R; CANR 1; DLB 169

Felix-Tchicaya, Gerald
See Tchicaya, Gerald Felix

Fellini, Federico 1920-1993 .... **CLC 16, 85**
See also CA 65-68; 143; CANR 33

Felsen, Henry Gregor 1916- .... **CLC 17**
See also CA 1-4R; CANR 1; SAAS 2; SATA 1

Fenno, Jack
See Calisher, Hortense

Fenollosa, Ernest (Francisco) 1853-1908 **TCLC 91**

Fenton, James Martin 1949- .... **CLC 32**
See also CA 102; DLB 40

Ferber, Edna 1887-1968 .... **CLC 18, 93**
See also AITN 1; CA 5-8R; 25-28R; CANR 68; DLB 9, 28, 86; MTCW 1, 2; SATA 7

Ferguson, Helen
See Kavan, Anna

Ferguson, Samuel 1810-1886 .... **NCLC 33**
See also DLB 32

Fergusson, Robert 1750-1774 .... **LC 29**
See also DLB 109

Ferling, Lawrence
See Ferlinghetti, Lawrence (Monsanto)

Ferlinghetti, Lawrence (Monsanto) 1919(?)- **CLC 2, 6, 10, 27, 111; DAM POET; PC 1**
See also CA 5-8R; CANR 3, 41, 73; CDALB 1941-1968; DLB 5, 16; MTCW 1, 2

Fernandez, Vicente Garcia Huidobro
See Huidobro Fernandez, Vicente Garcia

Ferrer, Gabriel (Francisco Victor) Miro
See Miro (Ferrer), Gabriel (Francisco Victor)

Ferrier, Susan (Edmonstone) 1782-1854 **NCLC 8**
See also DLB 116

Ferrigno, Robert 1948(?)- .... **CLC 65**
See also CA 140

Ferron, Jacques 1921-1985 ....**CLC 94; DAC**
See also CA 117; 129; DLB 60

Feuchtwanger, Lion 1884-1958 .... **TCLC 3**
See also CA 104; DLB 66

Feuillet, Octave 1821-1890 .... **NCLC 45**
See also DLB 192

Feydeau, Georges (Leon Jules Marie) 1862-1921 .... **TCLC 22; DAM DRAM**
See also CA 113; 152; DLB 192

Fichte, Johann Gottlieb 1762-1814**NCLC 62**
See also DLB 90

Ficino, Marsilio 1433-1499 .... **LC 12**

Fiedeler, Hans
See Doeblin, Alfred

Fiedler, Leslie A(aron) 1917- . **CLC 4, 13, 24**
See also CA 9-12R; CANR 7, 63; DLB 28, 67; MTCW 1, 2

Field, Andrew 1938- .... **CLC 44**
See also CA 97-100; CANR 25

Field, Eugene 1850-1895 .... **NCLC 3**
See also DLB 23, 42, 140; DLBD 13; MAICYA; SATA 16

Field, Gans T.
See Wellman, Manly Wade

Field, Michael 1915-1971 .... **TCLC 43**
See also CA 29-32R

Field, Peter
See Hobson, Laura Z(ametkin)

Fielding, Henry 1707-1754 ..... **LC 1, 46; DA; DAB; DAC; DAM DRAM, MST, NOV; WLC**
See also CDBLB 1660-1789; DLB 39, 84, 101

Fielding, Sarah 1710-1768 .... **LC 1, 44**
See also DLB 39

Fields, W. C. 1880-1946 .... **TCLC 80**
See also DLB 44

Fierstein, Harvey (Forbes) 1954- ... **CLC 33;
  DAM DRAM, POP**
    See also CA 123; 129
Figes, Eva 1932- .... **CLC 31**
    See also CA 53-56; CANR 4, 44; DLB 14
Finch, Anne 1661-1720 .... **LC 3; PC 21**
    See also DLB 95
Finch, Robert (Duer Claydon) 1900- **CLC 18**
    See also CA 57-60; CANR 9, 24, 49; DLB 88
Findley, Timothy 1930- . **CLC 27, 102; DAC;
  DAM MST**
    See also CA 25-28R; CANR 12, 42, 69; DLB
    53
Fink, William
    See Mencken, H(enry) L(ouis)
Firbank, Louis 1942-
    See Reed, Lou
    See also CA 117
Firbank, (Arthur Annesley) Ronald 1886-1926
  TCLC 1
    See also CA 104; 177; DLB 36
Fisher, Dorothy (Frances) Canfield 1879-1958
  TCLC 87
    See also CA 114; 136; CANR 80; DLB 9, 102;
    MAICYA; YABC 1
Fisher, M(ary) F(rances) K(ennedy) 1908-1992
  CLC 76, 87
    See also CA 77-80; 138; CANR 44; MTCW 1
Fisher, Roy 1930- .... **CLC 25**
    See also CA 81-84; CAAS 10; CANR 16; DLB
    40
Fisher, Rudolph 1897-1934 **TCLC 11; BLC 2;
  DAM MULT; SSC 25**
    See also BW 1, 3; CA 107; 124; CANR 80; DLB
    51, 102
Fisher, Vardis (Alvero) 1895-1968 ...... **CLC 7**
    See also CA 5-8R; 25-28R; CANR 68; DLB 9,
    206
Fiske, Tarleton
    See Bloch, Robert (Albert)
Fitch, Clarke
    See Sinclair, Upton (Beall)
Fitch, John IV
    See Cormier, Robert (Edmund)
Fitzgerald, Captain Hugh
    See Baum, L(yman) Frank
FitzGerald, Edward 1809-1883 .... **NCLC 9**
    See also DLB 32
Fitzgerald, F(rancis) Scott (Key) 1896-1940
  **TCLC 1, 6, 14, 28, 55; DA; DAB; DAC;
  DAM MST, NOV; SSC 6, 31; WLC**
    See also AAYA 24; AITN 1; CA 110; 123;
    CDALB 1917-1929; DLB 4, 9, 86; DLBD 1,
    15, 16; DLBY 81, 96; MTCW 1, 2
Fitzgerald, Penelope 1916- ... **CLC 19, 51, 61**
    See also CA 85-88; CAAS 10; CANR 56; DLB
    14, 194; MTCW 2
Fitzgerald, Robert (Stuart) 1910-1985 **CLC 39**
    See also CA 1-4R; 114; CANR 1; DLBY 80
FitzGerald, Robert D(avid) 1902-1987 **CLC 19**
    See also CA 17-20R
Fitzgerald, Zelda (Sayre) 1900-1948 **TCLC 52**
    See also CA 117; 126; DLBY 84
Flanagan, Thomas (James Bonner) 1923-
  CLC 25, 52
    See also CA 108; CANR 55; DLBY 80; INT
    108; MTCW 1
Flaubert, Gustave 1821-1880 **NCLC 2, 10, 19,
  62, 66; DA; DAB; DAC; DAM MST, NOV;
  SSC 11; WLC**
    See also DLB 119
Flecker, Herman Elroy
    See Flecker, (Herman) James Elroy

Flecker, (Herman) James Elroy 1884-1915
  TCLC 43
    See also CA 109; 150; DLB 10, 19
Fleming, Ian (Lancaster) 1908-1964 . **CLC 3,
  30; DAM POP**
    See also AAYA 26; CA 5-8R; CANR 59;
    CDBLB 1945-1960; DLB 87, 201; MTCW
    1, 2; SATA 9
Fleming, Thomas (James) 1927- .... **CLC 37**
    See also CA 5-8R; CANR 10; INT CANR-10;
    SATA 8
Fletcher, John 1579-1625 .... **LC 33; DC 6**
    See also CDBLB Before 1660; DLB 58
Fletcher, John Gould 1886-1950 .... **TCLC 35**
    See also CA 107; 167; DLB 4, 45
Fleur, Paul
    See Pohl, Frederik
Flooglebuckle, Al
    See Spiegelman, Art
Flying Officer X
    See Bates, H(erbert) E(rnest)
Fo, Dario 1926- **CLC 32, 109; DAM DRAM;
  DC 10**
    See also CA 116; 128; CANR 68; DLBY 97;
    MTCW 1, 2
Fogarty, Jonathan Titulescu Esq.
    See Farrell, James T(homas)
Folke, Will
    See Bloch, Robert (Albert)
Follett, Ken(neth Martin) 1949- ..... **CLC 18;
  DAM NOV, POP**
    See also AAYA 6; BEST 89:4; CA 81-84; CANR
    13, 33, 54; DLB 87; DLBY 81; INT CANR-
    33; MTCW 1
Fontane, Theodor 1819-1898 .... **NCLC 26**
    See also DLB 129
Foote, Horton 1916- **CLC 51, 91; DAM DRAM**
    See also CA 73-76; CANR 34, 51; DLB 26; INT
    CANR-34
Foote, Shelby 1916- **CLC 75; DAM NOV, POP**
    See also CA 5-8R; CANR 3, 45, 74; DLB 2,
    17; MTCW 2
Forbes, Esther 1891-1967 .... **CLC 12**
    See also AAYA 17; CA 13-14; 25-28R; CAP 1;
    CLR 27; DLB 22; JRDA; MAICYA; SATA
    2, 100
Forche, Carolyn (Louise) 1950- **CLC 25, 83,
  86; DAM POET; PC 10**
    See also CA 109; 117; CANR 50, 74; DLB 5,
    193; INT 117; MTCW 1
Ford, Elbur
    See Hibbert, Eleanor Alice Burford
Ford, Ford Madox 1873-1939 **TCLC 1, 15, 39,
  57; DAM NOV**
    See also CA 104; 132; CANR 74; CDBLB
    1914-1945; DLB 162; MTCW 1, 2
Ford, Henry 1863-1947 .... **TCLC 73**
    See also CA 115; 148
Ford, John 1586-(?) .... **DC 8**
    See also CDBLB Before 1660; DAM DRAM;
    DLB 58
Ford, John 1895-1973 .... **CLC 16**
    See also CA 45-48
Ford, Richard 1944- .... **CLC 46, 99**
    See also CA 69-72; CANR 11, 47; MTCW 1
Ford, Webster
    See Masters, Edgar Lee
Foreman, Richard 1937- .... **CLC 50**
    See also CA 65-68; CANR 32, 63
Forester, C(ecil) S(cott) 1899-1966 ... **CLC 35**
    See also CA 73-76; 25-28R; DLB 191; SATA
    13
Forez

    See Mauriac, Francois (Charles)
Forman, James Douglas 1932- .... **CLC 21**
    See also AAYA 17; CA 9-12R; CANR 4, 19,
    42; JRDA; MAICYA; SATA 8, 70
Fornes, Maria Irene 1930- **CLC 39, 61; DC 10;
  HLCS 1**
    See also CA 25-28R; CANR 28, 81; DLB 7;
    HW 1, 2; INT CANR-28; MTCW 1
Forrest, Leon (Richard) 1937-1997 .. **CLC 4;
  BLCS**
    See also BW 2; CA 89-92; 162; CAAS 7; CANR
    25, 52; DLB 33
Forster, E(dward) M(organ) 1879-1970 **C L C
  1, 2, 3, 4, 9, 10, 13, 15, 22, 45, 77; DA; DAB;
  DAC; DAM MST, NOV; SSC 27; WLC**
    See also AAYA 2; CA 13-14; 25-28R; CANR
    45; CAP 1; CDBLB 1914-1945; DLB 34, 98,
    162, 178, 195; DLBD 10; MTCW 1, 2; SATA
    57
Forster, John 1812-1876 .... **NCLC 11**
    See also DLB 144, 184
Forsyth, Frederick 1938- **CLC 2, 5, 36; DAM
  NOV, POP**
    See also BEST 89:4; CA 85-88; CANR 38, 62;
    DLB 87; MTCW 1, 2
Forten, Charlotte L. .... **TCLC 16; BLC 2**
    See also Grimke, Charlotte L(ottie) Forten
    See also DLB 50
Foscolo, Ugo 1778-1827 .... **NCLC 8**
Fosse, Bob .... **CLC 20**
    See also Fosse, Robert Louis
Fosse, Robert Louis 1927-1987
    See Fosse, Bob
    See also CA 110; 123
Foster, Stephen Collins 1826-1864 **NCLC 26**
Foucault, Michel 1926-1984 . **CLC 31, 34, 69**
    See also CA 105; 113; CANR 34; MTCW 1, 2
Fouque, Friedrich (Heinrich Karl) de la Motte
  1777-1843 .... **NCLC 2**
    See also DLB 90
Fourier, Charles 1772-1837 .... **NCLC 51**
Fournier, Henri Alban 1886-1914
    See Alain-Fournier
    See also CA 104
Fournier, Pierre 1916- .... **CLC 11**
    See also Gascar, Pierre
    See also CA 89-92; CANR 16, 40
Fowles, John (Philip) 1926- **CLC 1, 2, 3, 4, 6,
  9, 10, 15, 33, 87; DAB; DAC; DAM MST;
  SSC 33**
    See also CA 5-8R; CANR 25, 71; CDBLB 1960
    to Present; DLB 14, 139, 207; MTCW 1, 2;
    SATA 22
Fox, Paula 1923- .... **CLC 2, 8, 121**
    See also AAYA 3; CA 73-76; CANR 20, 36,
    62; CLR 1, 44; DLB 52; JRDA; MAICYA;
    MTCW 1; SATA 17, 60
Fox, William Price (Jr.) 1926- .... **CLC 22**
    See also CA 17-20R; CAAS 19; CANR 11; DLB
    2; DLBY 81
Foxe, John 1516(?)-1587 .... **LC 14**
    See also DLB 132
Frame, Janet 1924- **CLC 2, 3, 6, 22, 66, 96; SSC
  29**
    See also Clutha, Janet Paterson Frame
France, Anatole .... **TCLC 9**
    See also Thibault, Jacques Anatole Francois
    See also DLB 123; MTCW 1
Francis, Claude 19(?)- .... **CLC 50**
Francis, Dick 1920- **CLC 2, 22, 42, 102; DAM
  POP**
    See also AAYA 5, 21; BEST 89:3; CA 5-8R;
    CANR 9, 42, 68; CDBLB 1960 to Present;

DLB 87; INT CANR-9; MTCW 1, 2

Francis, Robert (Churchill) 1901-1987 **C L C 15**
See also CA 1-4R; 123; CANR 1

Frank, Anne(lies Marie) 1929-1945**TCLC 17; DA; DAB; DAC; DAM MST; WLC**
See also AAYA 12; CA 113; 133; CANR 68; MTCW 1, 2; SATA 87; SATA-Brief 42

Frank, Bruno 1887-1945 .... **TCLC 81**
See also DLB 118

Frank, Elizabeth 1945- .... **CLC 39**
See also CA 121; 126; CANR 78; INT 126

Frankl, Viktor E(mil) 1905-1997 ...... **CLC 93**
See also CA 65-68; 161

Franklin, Benjamin
See Hasek, Jaroslav (Matej Frantisek)

Franklin, Benjamin 1706-1790 .. **LC 25; DA; DAB; DAC; DAM MST; WLCS**
See also CDALB 1640-1865; DLB 24, 43, 73

Franklin, (Stella Maria Sarah) Miles (Lampe) 1879-1954 .... **TCLC 7**
See also CA 104; 164

Fraser, (Lady) Antonia (Pakenham) 1932- **CLC 32, 107**
See also CA 85-88; CANR 44, 65; MTCW 1, 2; SATA-Brief 32

Fraser, George MacDonald 1925- ...... **CLC 7**
See also CA 45-48; CANR 2, 48, 74; MTCW 1

Fraser, Sylvia 1935- .... **CLC 64**
See also CA 45-48; CANR 1, 16, 60

Frayn, Michael 1933-**CLC 3, 7, 31, 47; DAM DRAM, NOV**
See also CA 5-8R; CANR 30, 69; DLB 13, 14, 194; MTCW 1, 2

Fraze, Candida (Merrill) 1945- .... **CLC 50**
See also CA 126

Frazer, J(ames) G(eorge) 1854-1941**TCLC 32**
See also CA 118

Frazer, Robert Caine
See Creasey, John

Frazer, Sir James George
See Frazer, J(ames) G(eorge)

Frazier, Charles 1950-...................... **CLC 109**
See also CA 161

Frazier, Ian 1951- .... **CLC 46**
See also CA 130; CANR 54

Frederic, Harold 1856-1898 .... **NCLC 10**
See also DLB 12, 23; DLBD 13

Frederick, John
See Faust, Frederick (Schiller)

Frederick the Great 1712-1786 .... **LC 14**

Fredro, Aleksander 1793-1876 .... **NCLC 8**

Freeling, Nicolas 1927- .... **CLC 38**
See also CA 49-52; CAAS 12; CANR 1, 17, 50; DLB 87

Freeman, Douglas Southall 1886-1953**T C L C 11**
See also CA 109; DLB 17; DLBD 17

Freeman, Judith 1946-.....................**CLC 55**
See also CA 148

Freeman, Mary Eleanor Wilkins 1852-1930 **TCLC 9; SSC 1**
See also CA 106; 177; DLB 12, 78

Freeman, R(ichard) Austin 1862-1943**T C L C 21**
See also CA 113; DLB 70

French, Albert 1943- .... **CLC 86**
See also BW 3; CA 167

French, Marilyn 1929-**CLC 10, 18, 60; DAM DRAM, NOV, POP**
See also CA 69-72; CANR 3, 31; INT CANR-31; MTCW 1, 2

French, Paul

See Asimov, Isaac

Freneau, Philip Morin 1752-1832 ... **NCLC 1**
See also DLB 37, 43

Freud, Sigmund 1856-1939 .... **TCLC 52**
See also CA 115; 133; CANR 69; MTCW 1, 2

Friedan, Betty (Naomi) 1921- .... **CLC 74**
See also CA 65-68; CANR 18, 45, 74; MTCW 1, 2

Friedlander, Saul 1932- .... **CLC 90**
See also CA 117; 130; CANR 72

Friedman, B(ernard) H(arper) 1926- **CLC 7**
See also CA 1-4R; CANR 3, 48

Friedman, Bruce Jay 1930- ...... **CLC 3, 5, 56**
See also CA 9-12R; CANR 25, 52; DLB 2, 28; INT CANR-25

Friel, Brian 1929- .**CLC 5, 42, 59, 115; DC 8**
See also CA 21-24R; CANR 33, 69; DLB 13; MTCW 1

Friis-Baastad, Babbis Ellinor 1921-1970**C L C 12**
See also CA 17-20R; 134; SATA 7

Frisch, Max (Rudolf) 1911-1991**CLC 3, 9, 14, 18, 32, 44; DAM DRAM, NOV**
See also CA 85-88; 134; CANR 32, 74; DLB 69, 124; MTCW 1, 2

Fromentin, Eugene (Samuel Auguste) 1820-1876 .... **NCLC 10**
See also DLB 123

Frost, Frederick
See Faust, Frederick (Schiller)

Frost, Robert (Lee) 1874-1963**CLC 1, 3, 4, 9, 10, 13, 15, 26, 34, 44; DA; DAB; DAC; DAM MST, POET; PC 1; WLC**
See also AAYA 21; CA 89-92; CANR 33; CDALB 1917-1929; DLB 54; DLBD 7; MTCW 1, 2; SATA 14

Froude, James Anthony 1818-1894**NCLC 43**
See also DLB 18, 57, 144

Froy, Herald
See Waterhouse, Keith (Spencer)

Fry, Christopher 1907- **CLC 2, 10, 14; DAM DRAM**
See also CA 17-20R; CAAS 23; CANR 9, 30, 74; DLB 13; MTCW 1, 2; SATA 66

Frye, (Herman) Northrop 1912-1991**CLC 24, 70**
See also CA 5-8R; 133; CANR 8, 37; DLB 67, 68; MTCW 1, 2

Fuchs, Daniel 1909-1993 .... **CLC 8, 22**
See also CA 81-84; 142; CAAS 5; CANR 40; DLB 9, 26, 28; DLBY 93

Fuchs, Daniel 1934- .... **CLC 34**
See also CA 37-40R; CANR 14, 48

Fuentes, Carlos 1928-**CLC 3, 8, 10, 13, 22, 41, 60, 113; DA; DAB; DAC; DAM MST, MULT, NOV; HLC; SSC 24; WLC**
See also AAYA 4; AITN 2; CA 69-72; CANR 10, 32, 68; DLB 113; HW 1, 2; MTCW 1, 2

Fuentes, Gregorio Lopez y
See Lopez y Fuentes, Gregorio

Fugard, (Harold) Athol 1932-**CLC 5, 9, 14, 25, 40, 80; DAM DRAM; DC 3**
See also AAYA 17; CA 85-88; CANR 32, 54; MTCW 1

Fugard, Sheila 1932- .... **CLC 48**
See also CA 125

Fuller, Charles (H., Jr.) 1939-**CLC 25; BLC 2; DAM DRAM, MULT; DC 1**
See also BW 2; CA 108; 112; DLB 38; INT 112; MTCW 1

Fuller, John (Leopold) 1937-............. **CLC 62**
See also CA 21-24R; CANR 9, 44; DLB 40

Fuller, Margaret .... **NCLC 5, 50**

See also Ossoli, Sarah Margaret (Fuller marchesa d')

Fuller, Roy (Broadbent) 1912-1991**CLC 4, 28**
See also CA 5-8R; 135; CAAS 10; CANR 53; DLB 15, 20; SATA 87

Fulton, Alice 1952- .... **CLC 52**
See also CA 116; CANR 57; DLB 193

Furphy, Joseph 1843-1912 .... **TCLC 25**
See also CA 163

Fussell, Paul 1924-............................... **CLC 74**
See also BEST 90:1; CA 17-20R; CANR 8, 21, 35, 69; INT CANR-21; MTCW 1, 2

Futabatei, Shimei 1864-1909 .... **TCLC 44**
See also CA 162; DLB 180

Futrelle, Jacques 1875-1912 .... **TCLC 19**
See also CA 113; 155

Gaboriau, Emile 1835-1873 .... **NCLC 14**

Gadda, Carlo Emilio 1893-1973 .... **CLC 11**
See also CA 89-92; DLB 177

Gaddis, William 1922-1998**CLC 1, 3, 6, 8, 10, 19, 43, 86**
See also CA 17-20R; 172; CANR 21, 48; DLB 2; MTCW 1, 2

Gage, Walter
See Inge, William (Motter)

Gaines, Ernest J(ames) 1933- **CLC 3, 11, 18, 86; BLC 2; DAM MULT**
See also AAYA 18; AITN 1; BW 2, 3; CA 9-12R; CANR 6, 24, 42, 75; CDALB 1968-1988; DLB 2, 33, 152; DLBY 80; MTCW 1, 2; SATA 86

Gaitskill, Mary 1954- .... **CLC 69**
See also CA 128; CANR 61

Galdos, Benito Perez
See Perez Galdos, Benito

Gale, Zona 1874-1938**TCLC 7; DAM DRAM**
See also CA 105; 153; DLB 9, 78

Galeano, Eduardo (Hughes) 1940- . **CLC 72; HLCS 1**
See also CA 29-32R; CANR 13, 32; HW 1

Galiano, Juan Valera y Alcala
See Valera y Alcala-Galiano, Juan

Galilei, Galileo 1546-1642 .... **LC 45**

Gallagher, Tess 1943- ...... **CLC 18, 63; DAM POET; PC 9**
See also CA 106; DLB 212

Gallant, Mavis 1922- ... **CLC 7, 18, 38; DAC; DAM MST; SSC 5**
See also CA 69-72; CANR 29, 69; DLB 53; MTCW 1, 2

Gallant, Roy A(rthur) 1924- .... **CLC 17**
See also CA 5-8R; CANR 4, 29, 54; CLR 30; MAICYA; SATA 4, 68

Gallico, Paul (William) 1897-1976 ..... **CLC 2**
See also AITN 1; CA 5-8R; 69-72; CANR 23; DLB 9, 171; MAICYA; SATA 13

Gallo, Max Louis 1932- .... **CLC 95**
See also CA 85-88

Gallois, Lucien
See Desnos, Robert

Gallup, Ralph
See Whitemore, Hugh (John)

Galsworthy, John 1867-1933**TCLC 1, 45; DA; DAB; DAC; DAM DRAM, MST, NOV; SSC 22; WLC**
See also CA 104; 141; CANR 75; CDBLB 1890-1914; DLB 10, 34, 98, 162; DLBD 16; MTCW 1

Galt, John 1779-1839 .... **NCLC 1**
See also DLB 99, 116, 159

Galvin, James 1951- .... **CLC 38**
See also CA 108; CANR 26

Gamboa, Federico 1864-1939 .... **TCLC 36**

See also CA 167; HW 2

Gandhi, M. K.
See Gandhi, Mohandas Karamchand

Gandhi, Mahatma
See Gandhi, Mohandas Karamchand

Gandhi, Mohandas Karamchand 1869-1948 **TCLC 59; DAM MULT**
See also CA 121; 132; MTCW 1, 2

Gann, Ernest Kellogg 1910-1991 ...... **CLC 23**
See also AITN 1; CA 1-4R; 136; CANR 1

Garcia, Cristina 1958- .... **CLC 76**
See also CA 141; CANR 73; HW 2

Garcia Lorca, Federico 1898-1936**TCLC 1, 7, 49; DA; DAB; DAC; DAM DRAM, MST, MULT, POET; DC 2; HLC; PC 3; WLC**
See also CA 104; 131; CANR 81; DLB 108; HW 1, 2; MTCW 1, 2

Garcia Marquez, Gabriel (Jose) 1928-**CLC 2, 3, 8, 10, 15, 27, 47, 55, 68; DA; DAB; DAC; DAM MST, MULT, NOV, POP; HLC; SSC 8; WLC**
See also AAYA 3; BEST 89:1, 90:4; CA 33-36R; CANR 10, 28, 50, 75; DLB 113; HW 1, 2; MTCW 1, 2

Gard, Janice
See Latham, Jean Lee

Gard, Roger Martin du
See Martin du Gard, Roger

Gardam, Jane 1928- .... **CLC 43**
See also CA 49-52; CANR 2, 18, 33, 54; CLR 12; DLB 14, 161; MAICYA; MTCW 1; SAAS 9; SATA 39, 76; SATA-Brief 28

Gardner, Herb(ert) 1934- .... **CLC 44**
See also CA 149

Gardner, John (Champlin), Jr. 1933-1982 **CLC 2, 3, 5, 7, 8, 10, 18, 28, 34; DAM NOV, POP; SSC 7**
See also AITN 1; CA 65-68; 107; CANR 33, 73; CDALBS; DLB 2; DLBY 82; MTCW 1; SATA 40; SATA-Obit 31

Gardner, John (Edmund) 1926-**CLC 30; DAM POP**
See also CA 103; CANR 15, 69; MTCW 1

Gardner, Miriam
See Bradley, Marion Zimmer

Gardner, Noel
See Kuttner, Henry

Gardons, S. S.
See Snodgrass, W(illiam) D(e Witt)

Garfield, Leon 1921-1996 .... **CLC 12**
See also AAYA 8; CA 17-20R; 152; CANR 38, 41, 78; CLR 21; DLB 161; JRDA; MAICYA; SATA 1, 32, 76; SATA-Obit 90

Garland, (Hannibal) Hamlin 1860-1940 **TCLC 3; SSC 18**
See also CA 104; DLB 12, 71, 78, 186

Garneau, (Hector de) Saint-Denys 1912-1943 **TCLC 13**
See also CA 111; DLB 88

Garner, Alan 1934-**CLC 17; DAB; DAM POP**
See also AAYA 18; CA 73-76; CANR 15, 64; CLR 20; DLB 161; MAICYA; MTCW 1, 2; SATA 18, 69; SATA-Essay 108

Garner, Hugh 1913-1979 .... **CLC 13**
See also CA 69-72; CANR 31; DLB 68

Garnett, David 1892-1981 .... **CLC 3**
See also CA 5-8R; 103; CANR 17, 79; DLB 34; MTCW 2

Garos, Stephanie
See Katz, Steve

Garrett, George (Palmer) 1929-**CLC 3, 11, 51; SSC 30**
See also CA 1-4R; CAAS 5; CANR 1, 42, 67;

DLB 2, 5, 130, 152; DLBY 83

Garrick, David 1717-1779 .... **LC 15; DAM DRAM**
See also DLB 84

Garrigue, Jean 1914-1972 .... **CLC 2, 8**
See also CA 5-8R; 37-40R; CANR 20

Garrison, Frederick
See Sinclair, Upton (Beall)

Garth, Will
See Hamilton, Edmond; Kuttner, Henry

Garvey, Marcus (Moziah, Jr.) 1887-1940 **TCLC 41; BLC 2; DAM MULT**
See also BW 1; CA 120; 124; CANR 79

Gary, Romain .... **CLC 25**
See also Kacew, Romain
See also DLB 83

Gascar, Pierre .... **CLC 11**
See also Fournier, Pierre

Gascoyne, David (Emery) 1916- .... **CLC 45**
See also CA 65-68; CANR 10, 28, 54; DLB 20; MTCW 1

Gaskell, Elizabeth Cleghorn 1810-1865**NCLC 70; DAB; DAM MST; SSC 25**
See also CDBLB 1832-1890; DLB 21, 144, 159

Gass, William H(oward) 1924-**CLC 1, 2, 8, 11, 15, 39; SSC 12**
See also CA 17-20R; CANR 30, 71; DLB 2; MTCW 1, 2

Gasset, Jose Ortega y
See Ortega y Gasset, Jose

Gates, Henry Louis, Jr. 1950-**CLC 65; BLCS; DAM MULT**
See also BW 2, 3; CA 109; CANR 25, 53, 75; DLB 67; MTCW 1

Gautier, Theophile 1811-1872 .. **NCLC 1, 59; DAM POET; PC 18; SSC 20**
See also DLB 119

Gawsworth, John
See Bates, H(erbert) E(rnest)

Gay, John 1685-1732 ... **LC 49; DAM DRAM**
See also DLB 84, 95

Gay, Oliver
See Gogarty, Oliver St. John

Gaye, Marvin (Penze) 1939-1984 ..... **CLC 26**
See also CA 112

Gebler, Carlo (Ernest) 1954- .... **CLC 39**
See also CA 119; 133

Gee, Maggie (Mary) 1948- .... **CLC 57**
See also CA 130; DLB 207

Gee, Maurice (Gough) 1931-............. **CLC 29**
See also CA 97-100; CANR 67; CLR 56; SATA 46, 101

Gelbart, Larry (Simon) 1923- .... **CLC 21, 61**
See also CA 73-76; CANR 45

Gelber, Jack 1932- .... **CLC 1, 6, 14, 79**
See also CA 1-4R; CANR 2; DLB 7

Gellhorn, Martha (Ellis) 1908-1998 **CLC 14, 60**
See also CA 77-80; 164; CANR 44; DLBY 82, 98

Genet, Jean 1910-1986**CLC 1, 2, 5, 10, 14, 44, 46; DAM DRAM**
See also CA 13-16R; CANR 18; DLB 72; DLBY 86; MTCW 1, 2

Gent, Peter 1942- .... **CLC 29**
See also AITN 1; CA 89-92; DLBY 82

Gentlewoman in New England, A
See Bradstreet, Anne

Gentlewoman in Those Parts, A
See Bradstreet, Anne

George, Jean Craighead 1919- .... **CLC 35**
See also AAYA 8; CA 5-8R; CANR 25; CLR 1; DLB 52; JRDA; MAICYA; SATA 2, 68

George, Stefan (Anton) 1868-1933**TCLC 2, 14**
See also CA 104

Georges, Georges Martin
See Simenon, Georges (Jacques Christian)

Gerhardi, William Alexander
See Gerhardie, William Alexander

Gerhardie, William Alexander 1895-1977 **CLC 5**
See also CA 25-28R; 73-76; CANR 18; DLB 36

Gerstler, Amy 1956- .... **CLC 70**
See also CA 146

Gertler, T. .... **CLC 34**
See also CA 116; 121; INT 121

Ghalib ....**NCLC 39, 78**
See also Ghalib, Hsadullah Khan

Ghalib, Hsadullah Khan 1797-1869
See Ghalib
See also DAM POET

Ghelderode, Michel de 1898-1962**CLC 6, 11; DAM DRAM**
See also CA 85-88; CANR 40, 77

Ghiselin, Brewster 1903- .... **CLC 23**
See also CA 13-16R; CAAS 10; CANR 13

Ghose, Aurabinda 1872-1950 .... **TCLC 63**
See also CA 163

Ghose, Zulfikar 1935- .... **CLC 42**
See also CA 65-68; CANR 67

Ghosh, Amitav 1956- .... **CLC 44**
See also CA 147; CANR 80

Giacosa, Giuseppe 1847-1906 .... **TCLC 7**
See also CA 104

Gibb, Lee
See Waterhouse, Keith (Spencer)

Gibbon, Lewis Grassic .... **TCLC 4**
See also Mitchell, James Leslie

Gibbons, Kaye 1960-**CLC 50, 88; DAM POP**
See also CA 151; CANR 75; MTCW 1

Gibran, Kahlil 1883-1931 . **TCLC 1, 9; DAM POET, POP; PC 9**
See also CA 104; 150; MTCW 2

Gibran, Khalil
See Gibran, Kahlil

Gibson, William 1914- .. **CLC 23; DA; DAB; DAC; DAM DRAM, MST**
See also CA 9-12R; CANR 9, 42, 75; DLB 7; MTCW 1; SATA 66

Gibson, William (Ford) 1948- ... **CLC 39, 63; DAM POP**
See also AAYA 12; CA 126; 133; CANR 52; MTCW 1

Gide, Andre (Paul Guillaume) 1869-1951 **TCLC 5, 12, 36; DA; DAB; DAC; DAM MST, NOV; SSC 13; WLC**
See also CA 104; 124; DLB 65; MTCW 1, 2

Gifford, Barry (Colby) 1946- .... **CLC 34**
See also CA 65-68; CANR 9, 30, 40

Gilbert, Frank
See De Voto, Bernard (Augustine)

Gilbert, W(illiam) S(chwenck) 1836-1911 **TCLC 3; DAM DRAM, POET**
See also CA 104; 173; SATA 36

Gilbreth, Frank B., Jr. 1911- .... **CLC 17**
See also CA 9-12R; SATA 2

Gilchrist, Ellen 1935-**CLC 34, 48; DAM POP; SSC 14**
See also CA 113; 116; CANR 41, 61; DLB 130; MTCW 1, 2

Giles, Molly 1942- .... **CLC 39**
See also CA 126

Gill, Eric 1882-1940 .... **TCLC 85**

Gill, Patrick
See Creasey, John

Gosse, Edmund (William) 1849-1928 **TCLC 28**
  See also CA 117; DLB 57, 144, 184
Gotlieb, Phyllis Fay (Bloom) 1926- .. **CLC 18**
  See also CA 13-16R; CANR 7; DLB 88
Gottesman, S. D.
  See Kornbluth, C(yril) M.; Pohl, Frederik
Gottfried von Strassburg fl. c. 1210- **CMLC 10**
  See also DLB 138
Gould, Lois .... **CLC 4, 10**
  See also CA 77-80; CANR 29; MTCW 1
Gourmont, Remy (-Marie-Charles) de 1858-1915 .... **TCLC 17**
  See also CA 109; 150; MTCW 2
Govier, Katherine 1948- .... **CLC 51**
  See also CA 101; CANR 18, 40
Goyen, (Charles) William 1915-1983 **CLC 5, 8, 14, 40**
  See also AITN 2; CA 5-8R; 110; CANR 6, 71; DLB 2; DLBY 83; INT CANR-6
Goytisolo, Juan 1931- . **CLC 5, 10, 23; DAM MULT; HLC**
  See also CA 85-88; CANR 32, 61; HW 1, 2; MTCW 1, 2
Gozzano, Guido 1883-1916 .... **PC 10**
  See also CA 154; DLB 114
Gozzi, (Conte) Carlo 1720-1806 .... **NCLC 23**
Grabbe, Christian Dietrich 1801-1836 **NCLC 2**
  See also DLB 133
Grace, Patricia Frances 1937- .... **CLC 56**
  See also CA 176
Gracian y Morales, Baltasar 1601-1658 **LC 15**
Gracq, Julien .... **CLC 11, 48**
  See also Poirier, Louis
  See also DLB 83
Grade, Chaim 1910-1982 .... **CLC 10**
  See also CA 93-96; 107
Graduate of Oxford, A
  See Ruskin, John
Grafton, Garth
  See Duncan, Sara Jeannette
Graham, John
  See Phillips, David Graham
Graham, Jorie 1951- .... **CLC 48, 118**
  See also CA 111; CANR 63; DLB 120
Graham, R(obert) B(ontine) Cunninghame
  See Cunninghame Graham, R(obert) B(ontine)
  See also DLB 98, 135, 174
Graham, Robert
  See Haldeman, Joe (William)
Graham, Tom
  See Lewis, (Harry) Sinclair
Graham, W(illiam) S(ydney) 1918-1986 **CLC 29**
  See also CA 73-76; 118; DLB 20
Graham, Winston (Mawdsley) 1910- **CLC 23**
  See also CA 49-52; CANR 2, 22, 45, 66; DLB 77
Grahame, Kenneth 1859-1932 **TCLC 64; DAB**
  See also CA 108; 136; CANR 80; CLR 5; DLB 34, 141, 178; MAICYA; MTCW 2; SATA 100; YABC 1
Granovsky, Timofei Nikolaevich 1813-1855 **NCLC 75**
  See also DLB 198
Grant, Skeeter
  See Spiegelman, Art
Granville-Barker, Harley 1877-1946 **TCLC 2; DAM DRAM**
  See also Barker, Harley Granville
  See also CA 104
Grass, Guenter (Wilhelm) 1927- **CLC 1, 2, 4, 6,**

11, 15, 22, 32, 49, 88; DA; DAB; DAC; DAM MST, NOV; WLC
  See also CA 13-16R; CANR 20, 75; DLB 75, 124; MTCW 1, 2
Gratton, Thomas
  See Hulme, T(homas) E(rnest)
Grau, Shirley Ann 1929- . **CLC 4, 9; SSC 15**
  See also CA 89-92; CANR 22, 69; DLB 2; INT CANR-22; MTCW 1
Gravel, Fern
  See Hall, James Norman
Graver, Elizabeth 1964- .... **CLC 70**
  See also CA 135; CANR 71
Graves, Richard Perceval 1945- .... **CLC 44**
  See also CA 65-68; CANR 9, 26, 51
Graves, Robert (von Ranke) 1895-1985 **CLC 1, 2, 6, 11, 39, 44, 45; DAB; DAC; DAM MST, POET; PC 6**
  See also CA 5-8R; 117; CANR 5, 36; CDBLB 1914-1945; DLB 20, 100, 191; DLBD 18; DLBY 85; MTCW 1, 2; SATA 45
Graves, Valerie
  See Bradley, Marion Zimmer
Gray, Alasdair (James) 1934- .... **CLC 41**
  See also CA 126; CANR 47, 69; DLB 194; INT 126; MTCW 1, 2
Gray, Amlin 1946- .... **CLC 29**
  See also CA 138
Gray, Francine du Plessix 1930- ..... **CLC 22; DAM NOV**
  See also BEST 90:3; CA 61-64; CAAS 2; CANR 11, 33, 75, 81; INT CANR-11; MTCW 1, 2
Gray, John (Henry) 1866-1934 ...... **TCLC 19**
  See also CA 119; 162
Gray, Simon (James Holliday) 1936- **CLC 9, 14, 36**
  See also AITN 1; CA 21-24R; CAAS 3; CANR 32, 69; DLB 13; MTCW 1
Gray, Spalding 1941- **CLC 49, 112; DAM POP; DC 7**
  See also CA 128; CANR 74; MTCW 2
Gray, Thomas 1716-1771 **LC 4, 40; DA; DAB; DAC; DAM MST; PC 2; WLC**
  See also CDBLB 1660-1789; DLB 109
Grayson, David
  See Baker, Ray Stannard
Grayson, Richard (A.) 1951- .... **CLC 38**
  See also CA 85-88; CANR 14, 31, 57
Greeley, Andrew M(oran) 1928- ..... **CLC 28; DAM POP**
  See also CA 5-8R; CAAS 7; CANR 7, 43, 69; MTCW 1, 2
Green, Anna Katharine 1846-1935 **TCLC 63**
  See also CA 112; 159; DLB 202
Green, Brian
  See Card, Orson Scott
Green, Hannah
  See Greenberg, Joanne (Goldenberg)
Green, Hannah 1927(?)-1996 .... **CLC 3**
  See also CA 73-76; CANR 59
Green, Henry 1905-1973 .... **CLC 2, 13, 97**
  See also Yorke, Henry Vincent
  See also CA 175; DLB 15
Green, Julian (Hartridge) 1900-1998
  See Green, Julien
  See also CA 21-24R; 169; CANR 33; DLB 4, 72; MTCW 1
Green, Julien .... **CLC 3, 11, 77**
  See also Green, Julian (Hartridge)
  See also MTCW 2
Green, Paul (Eliot) 1894-1981 **CLC 25; DAM DRAM**

See also AITN 1; CA 5-8R; 103; CANR 3; DLB 7, 9; DLBY 81
Greenberg, Ivan 1908-1973
  See Rahv, Philip
  See also CA 85-88
Greenberg, Joanne (Goldenberg) 1932- **CLC 7, 30**
  See also AAYA 12; CA 5-8R; CANR 14, 32, 69; SATA 25
Greenberg, Richard 1959(?)- .... **CLC 57**
  See also CA 138
Greene, Bette 1934- .... **CLC 30**
  See also AAYA 7; CA 53-56; CANR 4; CLR 2; JRDA; MAICYA; SAAS 16; SATA 8, 102
Greene, Gael .... **CLC 8**
  See also CA 13-16R; CANR 10
Greene, Graham (Henry) 1904-1991 **CLC 1, 3, 6, 9, 14, 18, 27, 37, 70, 72; DA; DAB; DAC; DAM MST, NOV; SSC 29; WLC**
  See also AITN 2; CA 13-16R; 133; CANR 35, 61; CDBLB 1945-1960; DLB 13, 15, 77, 100, 162, 201, 204; DLBY 91; MTCW 1, 2; SATA 20
Greene, Robert 1558-1592 .... **LC 41**
  See also DLB 62, 167
Greer, Richard
  See Silverberg, Robert
Gregor, Arthur 1923- .... **CLC 9**
  See also CA 25-28R; CAAS 10; CANR 11; SATA 36
Gregor, Lee
  See Pohl, Frederik
Gregory, Isabella Augusta (Persse) 1852-1932 **TCLC 1**
  See also CA 104; DLB 10
Gregory, J. Dennis
  See Williams, John A(lfred)
Grendon, Stephen
  See Derleth, August (William)
Grenville, Kate 1950- .... **CLC 61**
  See also CA 118; CANR 53
Grenville, Pelham
  See Wodehouse, P(elham) G(renville)
Greve, Felix Paul (Berthold Friedrich) 1879-1948
  See Grove, Frederick Philip
  See also CA 104; 141; 175; CANR 79; DAC; DAM MST
Grey, Zane 1872-1939 .. **TCLC 6; DAM POP**
  See also CA 104; 132; DLB 212; MTCW 1, 2
Grieg, (Johan) Nordahl (Brun) 1902-1943 **TCLC 10**
  See also CA 107
Grieve, C(hristopher) M(urray) 1892-1978 **CLC 11, 19; DAM POET**
  See also MacDiarmid, Hugh; Pteleon
  See also CA 5-8R; 85-88; CANR 33; MTCW 1
Griffin, Gerald 1803-1840 .... **NCLC 7**
  See also DLB 159
Griffin, John Howard 1920-1980 ..... **CLC 68**
  See also AITN 1; CA 1-4R; 101; CANR 2
Griffin, Peter 1942- .... **CLC 39**
  See also CA 136
Griffith, D(avid Lewelyn) W(ark) 1875(?)-1948 **TCLC 68**
  See also CA 119; 150; CANR 80
Griffith, Lawrence
  See Griffith, D(avid Lewelyn) W(ark)
Griffiths, Trevor 1935- .... **CLC 13, 52**
  See also CA 97-100; CANR 45; DLB 13
Griggs, Sutton Elbert 1872-1930(?) **TCLC 77**
  See also CA 123; DLB 50
Grigson, Geoffrey (Edward Harvey) 1905-1985

See also Wight, James Alfred
See also AAYA 1; CA 148; CANR 40; MTCW
2; SATA 86
Herrmann, Dorothy 1941- .... **CLC 44**
See also CA 107
Herrmann, Taffy
See Herrmann, Dorothy
Hersey, John (Richard) 1914-1993**CLC 1, 2, 7,
9, 40, 81, 97; DAM POP**
See also AAYA 29; CA 17-20R; 140; CANR
33; CDALBS; DLB 6, 185; MTCW 1, 2;
SATA 25; SATA-Obit 76
Herzen, Aleksandr Ivanovich 1812-1870
NCLC 10, 61
Herzl, Theodor 1860-1904 .... **TCLC 36**
See also CA 168
Herzog, Werner 1942- .... **CLC 16**
See also CA 89-92
Hesiod c. 8th cent. B.C.- .... **CMLC 5**
See also DLB 176
Hesse, Hermann 1877-1962**CLC 1, 2, 3, 6, 11,
17, 25, 69; DA; DAB; DAC; DAM MST,
NOV; SSC 9; WLC**
. See also CA 17-18; CAP 2; DLB 66; MTCW 1,
2; SATA 50
Hewes, Cady
See De Voto, Bernard (Augustine)
Heyen, William 1940- .... **CLC 13, 18**
See also CA 33-36R; CAAS 9; DLB 5
Heyerdahl, Thor 1914- .... **CLC 26**
See also CA 5-8R; CANR 5, 22, 66, 73; MTCW
1, 2; SATA 2, 52
Heym, Georg (Theodor Franz Arthur) 1887-
1912 .... **TCLC 9**
See also CA 106
Heym, Stefan 1913- .... **CLC 41**
See also CA 9-12R; CANR 4; DLB 69
Heyse, Paul (Johann Ludwig von) 1830-1914
TCLC 8
See also CA 104; DLB 129
Heyward, (Edwin) DuBose 1885-1940 **T C L C
59**
See also CA 108; 157; DLB 7, 9, 45; SATA 21
Hibbert, Eleanor Alice Burford 1906-1993
CLC 7; DAM POP
See also BEST 90:4; CA 17-20R; 140; CANR
9, 28, 59; MTCW 2; SATA 2; SATA-Obit 74
Hichens, Robert (Smythe) 1864-1950 **T C L C
64**
See also CA 162; DLB 153
Higgins, George V(incent) 1939-**CLC 4, 7, 10,
18**
See also CA 77-80; CAAS 5; CANR 17, 51;
DLB 2; DLBY 81, 98; INT CANR-17;
MTCW 1
Higginson, Thomas Wentworth 1823-1911
TCLC 36
See also CA 162; DLB 1, 64
Highet, Helen
See MacInnes, Helen (Clark)
Highsmith, (Mary) Patricia 1921-1995**CLC 2,
4, 14, 42, 102; DAM NOV, POP**
See also CA 1-4R; 147; CANR 1, 20, 48, 62;
MTCW 1, 2
Highwater, Jamake (Mamake) 1942(?)- **C L C
12**
See also AAYA 7; CA 65-68; CAAS 7; CANR
10, 34; CLR 17; DLB 52; DLBY 85; JRDA;
MAICYA; SATA 32, 69; SATA-Brief 30
Highway, Tomson 1951-**CLC 92; DAC; DAM
MULT**
See also CA 151; CANR 75; MTCW 2; NNAL
Higuchi, Ichiyo 1872-1896 .... **NCLC 49**

Hijuelos, Oscar 1951- **CLC 65; DAM MULT,
POP; HLC**
See also AAYA 25; BEST 90:1; CA 123; CANR
50, 75; DLB 145; HW 1, 2; MTCW 2
Hikmet, Nazim 1902(?)-1963 .... **CLC 40**
See also CA 141; 93-96
Hildegard von Bingen 1098-1179 . **CMLC 20**
See also DLB 148
Hildesheimer, Wolfgang 1916-1991 .. **CLC 49**
See also CA 101; 135; DLB 69, 124
Hill, Geoffrey (William) 1932- **CLC 5, 8, 18,
45; DAM POET**
See also CA 81-84; CANR 21; CDBLB 1960
to Present; DLB 40; MTCW 1
Hill, George Roy 1921- .... **CLC 26**
See also CA 110; 122
Hill, John
See Koontz, Dean R(ay)
Hill, Susan (Elizabeth) 1942- .... **CLC 4, 113;
DAB; DAM MST, NOV**
See also CA 33-36R; CANR 29, 69; DLB 14,
139; MTCW 1
Hillerman, Tony 1925- . **CLC 62; DAM POP**
See also AAYA 6; BEST 89:1; CA 29-32R;
CANR 21, 42, 65; DLB 206; SATA 6
Hillesum, Etty 1914-1943 .... **TCLC 49**
See also CA 137
Hilliard, Noel (Harvey) 1929- .... **CLC 15**
See also CA 9-12R; CANR 7, 69
Hillis, Rick 1956- .... **CLC 66**
See also CA 134
Hilton, James 1900-1954 .... **TCLC 21**
See also CA 108; 169; DLB 34, 77; SATA 34
Himes, Chester (Bomar) 1909-1984**CLC 2, 4,
7, 18, 58, 108; BLC 2; DAM MULT**
See also BW 2; CA 25-28R; 114; CANR 22;
DLB 2, 76, 143; MTCW 1, 2
Hinde, Thomas .... **CLC 6, 11**
See also Chitty, Thomas Willes
Hindin, Nathan
See Bloch, Robert (Albert)
Hine, (William) Daryl 1936- .... **CLC 15**
See also CA 1-4R; CAAS 15; CANR 1, 20; DLB
60
Hinkson, Katharine Tynan
See Tynan, Katharine
Hinton, S(usan) E(loise) 1950- **CLC 30, 111;
DA; DAB; DAC; DAM MST, NOV**
See also AAYA 2; CA 81-84; CANR 32, 62;
CDALBS; CLR 3, 23; JRDA; MAICYA;
MTCW 1, 2; SATA 19, 58
Hippius, Zinaida .... **TCLC 9**
See also Gippius, Zinaida (Nikolayevna)
Hiraoka, Kimitake 1925-1970
See Mishima, Yukio
See also CA 97-100; 29-32R; DAM DRAM;
MTCW 1, 2
Hirsch, E(ric) D(onald), Jr. 1928- .... **CLC 79**
See also CA 25-28R; CANR 27, 51; DLB 67;
INT CANR-27; MTCW 1
Hirsch, Edward 1950- .... **CLC 31, 50**
See also CA 104; CANR 20, 42; DLB 120
Hitchcock, Alfred (Joseph) 1899-1980**CLC 16**
See also AAYA 22; CA 159; 97-100; SATA 27;
SATA-Obit 24
Hitler, Adolf 1889-1945 .... **TCLC 53**
See also CA 117; 147
Hoagland, Edward 1932- .... **CLC 28**
See also CA 1-4R; CANR 2, 31, 57; DLB 6;
SATA 51
Hoban, Russell (Conwell) 1925- . **CLC 7, 25;
DAM NOV**
See also CA 5-8R; CANR 23, 37, 66; CLR 3;

DLB 52; MAICYA; MTCW 1, 2; SATA 1,
40, 78
Hobbes, Thomas 1588-1679 .... **LC 36**
See also DLB 151
Hobbs, Perry
See Blackmur, R(ichard) P(almer)
Hobson, Laura Z(ametkin) 1900-1986**CLC 7,
25**
See also CA 17-20R; 118; CANR 55; DLB 28;
SATA 52
Hochhuth, Rolf 1931- .. **CLC 4, 11, 18; DAM
DRAM**
See also CA 5-8R; CANR 33, 75; DLB 124;
MTCW 1, 2
Hochman, Sandra 1936- .... **CLC 3, 8**
See also CA 5-8R; DLB 5
Hochwaelder, Fritz 1911-1986**CLC 36; DAM
DRAM**
See also CA 29-32R; 120; CANR 42; MTCW 1
Hochwalder, Fritz
See Hochwaelder, Fritz
Hocking, Mary (Eunice) 1921- .... **CLC 13**
See also CA 101; CANR 18, 40
Hodgins, Jack 1938- .... **CLC 23**
See also CA 93-96; DLB 60
Hodgson, William Hope 1877(?)-1918 **T C L C
13**
See also CA 111; 164; DLB 70, 153, 156, 178;
MTCW 2
Hoeg, Peter 1957- .... **CLC 95**
See also CA 151; CANR 75; MTCW 2
Hoffman, Alice 1952- ... **CLC 51; DAM NOV**
See also CA 77-80; CANR 34, 66; MTCW 1, 2
Hoffman, Daniel (Gerard) 1923-**CLC 6, 13, 23**
See also CA 1-4R; CANR 4; DLB 5
Hoffman, Stanley 1944- .... **CLC 5**
See also CA 77-80
Hoffman, William M(oses) 1939- ...... **CLC 40**
See also CA 57-60; CANR 11, 71
Hoffmann, E(rnst) T(heodor) A(madeus) 1776-
1822 .... **NCLC 2; SSC 13**
See also DLB 90; SATA 27
Hofmann, Gert 1931- .... **CLC 54**
See also CA 128
Hofmannsthal, Hugo von 1874-1929**TCLC 11;
DAM DRAM; DC 4**
See also CA 106; 153; DLB 81, 118
Hogan, Linda 1947- ... **CLC 73; DAM MULT**
See also CA 120; CANR 45, 73; DLB 175;
NNAL
Hogarth, Charles
See Creasey, John
Hogarth, Emmett
See Polonsky, Abraham (Lincoln)
Hogg, James 1770-1835 .... **NCLC 4**
See also DLB 93, 116, 159
Holbach, Paul Henri Thiry Baron 1723-1789
LC 14
Holberg, Ludvig 1684-1754 .... **LC 6**
Holden, Ursula 1921- .... **CLC 18**
See also CA 101; CAAS 8; CANR 22
Holderlin, (Johann Christian) Friedrich 1770-
1843 .... **NCLC 16; PC 4**
Holdstock, Robert
See Holdstock, Robert P.
Holdstock, Robert P. 1948- .... **CLC 39**
See also CA 131; CANR 81
Holland, Isabelle 1920- .... **CLC 21**
See also AAYA 11; CA 21-24R; CANR 10, 25,
47; CLR 57; JRDA; MAICYA; SATA 8, 70;
SATA-Essay 103
Holland, Marcus
See Caldwell, (Janet Miriam) Taylor (Holland)

See also AAYA 28; DLB 119, 192; SATA 47

Huidobro, Vicente
See Huidobro Fernandez, Vicente Garcia

Huidobro Fernandez, Vicente Garcia 1893-
1948 .... **TCLC 31**
See also CA 131; HW 1

Hulme, Keri 1947- .... **CLC 39**
See also CA 125; CANR 69; INT 125

Hulme, T(homas) E(rnest) 1883-1917 **T C L C
21**
See also CA 117; DLB 19

Hume, David 1711-1776 .... **LC 7**
See also DLB 104

Humphrey, William 1924-1997 .... **CLC 45**
See also CA 77-80; 160; CANR 68; DLB 212

Humphreys, Emyr Owen 1919- .... **CLC 47**
See also CA 5-8R; CANR 3, 24; DLB 15

Humphreys, Josephine 1945- ..... **CLC 34, 57**
See also CA 121; 127; INT 127

Huneker, James Gibbons 1857-1921**TCLC 65**
See also DLB 71

Hungerford, Pixie
See Brinsmead, H(esba) F(ay)

Hunt, E(verette) Howard, (Jr.) 1918- **CLC 3**
See also AITN 1; CA 45-48; CANR 2, 47

Hunt, Kyle
See Creasey, John

Hunt, (James Henry) Leigh 1784-1859**N C L C
1, 70; DAM POET**
See also DLB 96, 110, 144

Hunt, Marsha 1946- .... **CLC 70**
See also BW 2, 3; CA 143; CANR 79

Hunt, Violet 1866(?)-1942 .... **TCLC 53**
See also DLB 162, 197

Hunter, E. Waldo
See Sturgeon, Theodore (Hamilton)

Hunter, Evan 1926-. **CLC 11, 31; DAM POP**
See also CA 5-8R; CANR 5, 38, 62; DLBY 82;
INT CANR-5; MTCW 1; SATA 25

Hunter, Kristin (Eggleston) 1931- .... **CLC 35**
See also AITN 1; BW 1; CA 13-16R; CANR
13; CLR 3; DLB 33; INT CANR-13;
MAICYA; SAAS 10; SATA 12

Hunter, Mollie 1922- .... **CLC 21**
See also McIlwraith, Maureen Mollie Hunter
See also AAYA 13; CANR 37, 78; CLR 25; DLB
161; JRDA; MAICYA; SAAS 7; SATA 54,
106

Hunter, Robert (?)-1734 .... **LC 7**

Hurston, Zora Neale 1903-1960**CLC 7, 30, 61;
BLC 2; DA; DAC; DAM MST, MULT,
NOV; SSC 4; WLCS**
See also AAYA 15; BW 1, 3; CA 85-88; CANR
61; CDALBS; DLB 51, 86; MTCW 1, 2

Huston, John (Marcellus) 1906-1987**CLC 20**
See also CA 73-76; 123; CANR 34; DLB 26

Hustvedt, Siri 1955- .... **CLC 76**
See also CA 137

Hutten, Ulrich von 1488-1523 .... **LC 16**
See also DLB 179

Huxley, Aldous (Leonard) 1894-1963 **CLC 1,
3, 4, 5, 8, 11, 18, 35, 79; DA; DAB; DAC;
DAM MST, NOV; WLC**
See also AAYA 11; CA 85-88; CANR 44;
CDBLB 1914-1945; DLB 36, 100, 162, 195;
MTCW 1, 2; SATA 63

Huxley, T(homas) H(enry) 1825-1895 **N C L C
67**
See also DLB 57

Huysmans, Joris-Karl 1848-1907**TCLC 7, 69**
See also CA 104; 165; DLB 123

Hwang, David Henry 1957-... **CLC 55; DAM
DRAM; DC 4**

See also CA 127; 132; CANR 76; DLB 212;
INT 132; MTCW 2

Hyde, Anthony 1946- .... **CLC 42**
See also CA 136

Hyde, Margaret O(ldroyd) 1917- ..... **CLC 21**
See also CA 1-4R; CANR 1, 36; CLR 23; JRDA;
MAICYA; SAAS 8; SATA 1, 42, 76

Hynes, James 1956(?)- .... **CLC 65**
See also CA 164

Ian, Janis 1951- .... **CLC 21**
See also CA 105

Ibanez, Vicente Blasco
See Blasco Ibanez, Vicente

Ibarguengoitia, Jorge 1928-1983 ..... **CLC 37**
See also CA 124; 113; HW 1

Ibsen, Henrik (Johan) 1828-1906 **TCLC 2, 8,
16, 37, 52; DA; DAB; DAC; DAM DRAM,
MST; DC 2; WLC**
See also CA 104; 141

Ibuse, Masuji 1898-1993 .... **CLC 22**
See also CA 127; 141; DLB 180

Ichikawa, Kon 1915- .... **CLC 20**
See also CA 121

Idle, Eric 1943- .... **CLC 21**
See also Monty Python
See also CA 116; CANR 35

Ignatow, David 1914-1997 .. **CLC 4, 7, 14, 40**
See also CA 9-12R; 162; CAAS 3; CANR 31,
57; DLB 5

Ihimaera, Witi 1944- .... **CLC 46**
See also CA 77-80

Ilf, Ilya .... **TCLC 21**
See also Fainzilberg, Ilya Arnoldovich

Illyes, Gyula 1902-1983 .... **PC 16**
See also CA 114; 109

Immermann, Karl (Lebrecht) 1796-1840
NCLC 4, 49
See also DLB 133

Ince, Thomas H. 1882-1924 .... **TCLC 89**

Inchbald, Elizabeth 1753-1821 ...... **NCLC 62**
See also DLB 39, 89

Inclan, Ramon (Maria) del Valle
See Valle-Inclan, Ramon (Maria) del

Infante, G(uillermo) Cabrera
See Cabrera Infante, G(uillermo)

Ingalls, Rachel (Holmes) 1940- .... **CLC 42**
See also CA 123; 127

Ingamells, Reginald Charles
See Ingamells, Rex

Ingamells, Rex 1913-1955 .... **TCLC 35**
See also CA 167

Inge, William (Motter) 1913-1973 . **CLC 1, 8,
19; DAM DRAM**
See also CA 9-12R; CDALB 1941-1968; DLB
7; MTCW 1, 2

Ingelow, Jean 1820-1897 .... **NCLC 39**
See also DLB 35, 163; SATA 33

Ingram, Willis J.
See Harris, Mark

Innaurato, Albert (F.) 1948(?)- .. **CLC 21, 60**
See also CA 115; 122; CANR 78; INT 122

Innes, Michael
See Stewart, J(ohn) I(nnes) M(ackintosh)

Innis, Harold Adams 1894-1952 .... **TCLC 77**
See also DLB 88

Ionesco, Eugene 1909-1994**CLC 1, 4, 6, 9, 11,
15, 41, 86; DA; DAB; DAC; DAM DRAM,
MST; WLC**
See also CA 9-12R; 144; CANR 55; MTCW 1,
2; SATA 7; SATA-Obit 79

Iqbal, Muhammad 1873-1938 .... **TCLC 28**

Ireland, Patrick
See O'Doherty, Brian

Iron, Ralph
See Schreiner, Olive (Emilie Albertina)

Irving, John (Winslow) 1942-**CLC 13, 23, 38,
112; DAM NOV, POP**
See also AAYA 8; BEST 89:3; CA 25-28R;
CANR 28, 73; DLB 6; DLBY 82; MTCW 1,
2

Irving, Washington 1783-1859 . **NCLC 2, 19;
DA; DAB; DAC; DAM MST; SSC 2; WLC**
See also CDALB 1640-1865; DLB 3, 11, 30,
59, 73, 74, 186; YABC 2

Irwin, P. K.
See Page, P(atricia) K(athleen)

Isaacs, Jorge Ricardo 1837-1895 ... **NCLC 70**

Isaacs, Susan 1943- .... **CLC 32; DAM POP**
See also BEST 89:1; CA 89-92; CANR 20, 41,
65; INT CANR-20; MTCW 1, 2

Isherwood, Christopher (William Bradshaw)
1904-1986 .... **CLC 1, 9, 11, 14, 44; DAM
DRAM, NOV**
See also CA 13-16R; 117; CANR 35; DLB 15,
195; DLBY 86; MTCW 1, 2

Ishiguro, Kazuo 1954-.. **CLC 27, 56, 59, 110;
DAM NOV**
See also BEST 90:2; CA 120; CANR 49; DLB
194; MTCW 1, 2

Ishikawa, Hakuhin
See Ishikawa, Takuboku

Ishikawa, Takuboku 1886(?)-1912 **TCLC 15;
DAM POET; PC 10**
See also CA 113; 153

Iskander, Fazil 1929- .... **CLC 47**
See also CA 102

Isler, Alan (David) 1934- .... **CLC 91**
See also CA 156

Ivan IV 1530-1584 .... **LC 17**

Ivanov, Vyacheslav Ivanovich 1866-1949
TCLC 33
See also CA 122

Ivask, Ivar Vidrik 1927-1992 .... **CLC 14**
See also CA 37-40R; 139; CANR 24

Ives, Morgan
See Bradley, Marion Zimmer

Izumi Shikibu c. 973-c. 1034 .... **CMLC 33**

J. R. S.
See Gogarty, Oliver St. John

Jabran, Kahlil
See Gibran, Kahlil

Jabran, Khalil
See Gibran, Kahlil

Jackson, Daniel
See Wingrove, David (John)

Jackson, Jesse 1908-1983 .... **CLC 12**
See also BW 1; CA 25-28R; 109; CANR 27;
CLR 28; MAICYA; SATA 2, 29; SATA-Obit
48

Jackson, Laura (Riding) 1901-1991
See Riding, Laura
See also CA 65-68; 135; CANR 28; DLB 48

Jackson, Sam
See Trumbo, Dalton

Jackson, Sara
See Wingrove, David (John)

Jackson, Shirley 1919-1965 . **CLC 11, 60, 87;
DA; DAC; DAM MST; SSC 9; WLC**
See also AAYA 9; CA 1-4R; 25-28R; CANR 4,
52; CDALB 1941-1968; DLB 6; MTCW 2;
SATA 2

Jacob, (Cyprien-)Max 1876-1944 .... **TCLC 6**
See also CA 104

Jacobs, Harriet A(nn) 1813(?)-1897**NCLC 67**

Jacobs, Jim 1942- .... **CLC 12**
See also CA 97-100; INT 97-100

See also BW 2, 3; CA 142; CANR 79

Jones, Gayl 1949- .... **CLC 6, 9; BLC 2; DAM MULT**
See also BW 2, 3; CA 77-80; CANR 27, 66; DLB 33; MTCW 1, 2

Jones, James 1921-1977 ...... **CLC 1, 3, 10, 39**
See also AITN 1, 2; CA 1-4R; 69-72; CANR 6; DLB 2, 143; DLBD 17; DLBY 98; MTCW 1

Jones, John J.
See Lovecraft, H(oward) P(hillips)

Jones, LeRoi .... **CLC 1, 2, 3, 5, 10, 14**
See also Baraka, Amiri
See also MTCW 2

Jones, Louis B. 1953- .... **CLC 65**
See also CA 141; CANR 73

Jones, Madison (Percy, Jr.) 1925- .... **CLC 4**
See also CA 13-16R; CAAS 11; CANR 7, 54; DLB 152

Jones, Mervyn 1922- .... **CLC 10, 52**
See also CA 45-48; CAAS 5; CANR 1; MTCW 1

Jones, Mick 1956(?)- .... **CLC 30**

Jones, Nettie (Pearl) 1941- .... **CLC 34**
See also BW 2; CA 137; CAAS 20

Jones, Preston 1936-1979 .... **CLC 10**
See also CA 73-76; 89-92; DLB 7

Jones, Robert F(rancis) 1934- .... **CLC 7**
See also CA 49-52; CANR 2, 61

Jones, Rod 1953- .... **CLC 50**
See also CA 128

Jones, Terence Graham Parry 1942- **CLC 21**
See also Jones, Terry; Monty Python
See also CA 112; 116; CANR 35; INT 116

Jones, Terry
See Jones, Terence Graham Parry
See also SATA 67; SATA-Brief 51

Jones, Thom 1945(?)- .... **CLC 81**
See also CA 157

Jong, Erica 1942- . **CLC 4, 6, 8, 18, 83; DAM NOV, POP**
See also AITN 1; BEST 90:2; CA 73-76; CANR 26, 52, 75; DLB 2, 5, 28, 152; INT CANR-26; MTCW 1, 2

Jonson, Ben(jamin) 1572(?)-1637 .. **LC 6, 33; DA; DAB; DAC; DAM DRAM, MST, POET; DC 4; PC 17; WLC**
See also CDBLB Before 1660; DLB 62, 121

Jordan, June 1936- **CLC 5, 11, 23, 114; BLCS; DAM MULT, POET**
See also AAYA 2; BW 2, 3; CA 33-36R; CANR 25, 70; CLR 10; DLB 38; MAICYA; MTCW 1; SATA 4

Jordan, Neil (Patrick) 1950- .... **CLC 110**
See also CA 124; 130; CANR 54; INT 130

Jordan, Pat(rick M.) 1941- .... **CLC 37**
See also CA 33-36R

Jorgensen, Ivar
See Ellison, Harlan (Jay)

Jorgenson, Ivar
See Silverberg, Robert

Josephus, Flavius c. 37-100 .... **CMLC 13**

Josipovici, Gabriel 1940- .... **CLC 6, 43**
See also CA 37-40R; CAAS 8; CANR 47; DLB 14

Joubert, Joseph 1754-1824 .... **NCLC 9**

Jouve, Pierre Jean 1887-1976 .... **CLC 47**
See also CA 65-68

Jovine, Francesco 1902-1950 .... **TCLC 79**

Joyce, James (Augustine Aloysius) 1882-1941 **TCLC 3, 8, 16, 35, 52; DA; DAB; DAC; DAM MST, NOV, POET; PC 22; SSC 3, 26; WLC**
See also CA 104; 126; CDBLB 1914-1945;

DLB 10, 19, 36, 162; MTCW 1, 2

Jozsef, Attila 1905-1937 .... **TCLC 22**
See also CA 116

Juana Ines de la Cruz 1651(?)-1695 .... **LC 5; HLCS 1; PC 24**

Judd, Cyril
See Kornbluth, C(yril) M.; Pohl, Frederik

Julian of Norwich 1342(?)-1416(?) .... **LC 6**
See also DLB 146

Junger, Sebastian 1962- ....**CLC 109**
See also AAYA 28; CA 165

Juniper, Alex
See Hospital, Janette Turner

Junius
See Luxemburg, Rosa

Just, Ward (Swift) 1935- ....**CLC 4, 27**
See also CA 25-28R; CANR 32; INT CANR-32

Justice, Donald (Rodney) 1925- .. **CLC 6, 19, 102; DAM POET**
See also CA 5-8R; CANR 26, 54, 74; DLBY 83; INT CANR-26; MTCW 2

Juvenal c. 60-c. 13 .... **CMLC 8**
See also Juvenalis, Decimus Junius
See also DLB 211

Juvenalis, Decimus Junius 55(?)-c. 127(?)
See Juvenal

Juvenis
See Bourne, Randolph S(illiman)

Kacew, Romain 1914-1980
See Gary, Romain
See also CA 108; 102

Kadare, Ismail 1936- .... **CLC 52**
See also CA 161

Kadohata, Cynthia .... **CLC 59**
See also CA 140

Kafka, Franz 1883-1924 **TCLC 2, 6, 13, 29, 47, 53; DA; DAB; DAC; DAM MST, NOV; SSC 5, 29, 35; WLC**
See also CA 105; 126; DLB 81; MTCW 1, 2

Kahanovitsch, Pinkhes
See Der Nister

Kahn, Roger 1927- .... **CLC 30**
See also CA 25-28R; CANR 44, 69; DLB 171; SATA 37

Kain, Saul
See Sassoon, Siegfried (Lorraine)

Kaiser, Georg 1878-1945 .... **TCLC 9**
See also CA 106; DLB 124

Kaletski, Alexander 1946- .... **CLC 39**
See also CA 118; 143

Kalidasa fl. c. 400- .... **CMLC 9; PC 22**

Kallman, Chester (Simon) 1921-1975 **CLC 2**
See also CA 45-48; 53-56; CANR 3

Kaminsky, Melvin 1926-
See Brooks, Mel
See also CA 65-68; CANR 16

Kaminsky, Stuart M(elvin) 1934- ..... **CLC 59**
See also CA 73-76; CANR 29, 53

Kandinsky, Wassily 1866-1944 ...... **TCLC 92**
See also CA 118; 155

Kane, Francis
See Robbins, Harold

Kane, Paul
See Simon, Paul (Frederick)

Kane, Wilson
See Bloch, Robert (Albert)

Kanin, Garson 1912-1999 .... **CLC 22**
See also AITN 1; CA 5-8R; 177; CANR 7, 78; DLB 7

Kaniuk, Yoram 1930- .... **CLC 19**
See also CA 134

Kant, Immanuel 1724-1804 ...... **NCLC 27, 67**

See also DLB 94

Kantor, MacKinlay 1904-1977 .... **CLC 7**
See also CA 61-64; 73-76; CANR 60, 63; DLB 9, 102; MTCW 2

Kaplan, David Michael 1946- .... **CLC 50**

Kaplan, James 1951- .... **CLC 59**
See also CA 135

Karageorge, Michael
See Anderson, Poul (William)

Karamzin, Nikolai Mikhailovich 1766-1826 **NCLC 3**
See also DLB 150

Karapanou, Margarita 1946- .... **CLC 13**
See also CA 101

Karinthy, Frigyes 1887-1938 .... **TCLC 47**
See also CA 170

Karl, Frederick R(obert) 1927- .... **CLC 34**
See also CA 5-8R; CANR 3, 44

Kastel, Warren
See Silverberg, Robert

Kataev, Evgeny Petrovich 1903-1942
See Petrov, Evgeny
See also CA 120

Kataphusin
See Ruskin, John

Katz, Steve 1935- .... **CLC 47**
See also CA 25-28R; CAAS 14, 64; CANR 12; DLBY 83

Kauffman, Janet 1945- .... **CLC 42**
See also CA 117; CANR 43; DLBY 86

Kaufman, Bob (Garnell) 1925-1986 . **CLC 49**
See also BW 1; CA 41-44R; 118; CANR 22; DLB 16, 41

Kaufman, George S. 1889-1961 **CLC 38; DAM DRAM**
See also CA 108; 93-96; DLB 7; INT 108; MTCW 2

Kaufman, Sue .... **CLC 3, 8**
See also Barondess, Sue K(aufman)

Kavafis, Konstantinos Petrou 1863-1933
See Cavafy, C(onstantine) P(eter)
See also CA 104

Kavan, Anna 1901-1968 .... **CLC 5, 13, 82**
See also CA 5-8R; CANR 6, 57; MTCW 1

Kavanagh, Dan
See Barnes, Julian (Patrick)

Kavanagh, Julie 1952- .... **CLC 119**
See also CA 163

Kavanagh, Patrick (Joseph) 1904-1967 **C L C 22**
See also CA 123; 25-28R; DLB 15, 20; MTCW 1

Kawabata, Yasunari 1899-1972 **CLC 2, 5, 9, 18, 107; DAM MULT; SSC 17**
See also CA 93-96; 33-36R; DLB 180; MTCW 2

Kaye, M(ary) M(argaret) 1909- .... **CLC 28**
See also CA 89-92; CANR 24, 60; MTCW 1, 2; SATA 62

Kaye, Mollie
See Kaye, M(ary) M(argaret)

Kaye-Smith, Sheila 1887-1956 .... **TCLC 20**
See also CA 118; DLB 36

Kaymor, Patrice Maguilene
See Senghor, Leopold Sedar

Kazan, Elia 1909- .... **CLC 6, 16, 63**
See also CA 21-24R; CANR 32, 78

Kazantzakis, Nikos 1883(?)-1957 **TCLC 2, 5, 33**
See also CA 105; 132; MTCW 1, 2

Kazin, Alfred 1915-1998 ..... **CLC 34, 38, 119**
See also CA 1-4R; CAAS 7; CANR 1, 45, 79; DLB 67

See also CA 89-92; CANR 80; DLB 75

Leonard, Elmore (John, Jr.) 1925-**CLC 28, 34, 71, 120; DAM POP**
See also AAYA 22; AITN 1; BEST 89:1, 90:4; CA 81-84; CANR 12, 28, 53, 76; DLB 173; INT CANR-28; MTCW 1, 2

Leonard, Hugh .... **CLC 19**
See also Byrne, John Keyes
See also DLB 13

Leonov, Leonid (Maximovich) 1899-1994 **CLC 92; DAM NOV**
See also CA 129; CANR 74, 76; MTCW 1, 2

Leopardi, (Conte) Giacomo 1798-1837**NCLC 22**

Le Reveler
See Artaud, Antonin (Marie Joseph)

Lerman, Eleanor 1952- .... **CLC 9**
See also CA 85-88; CANR 69

Lerman, Rhoda 1936- .... **CLC 56**
See also CA 49-52; CANR 70

Lermontov, Mikhail Yuryevich 1814-1841 **NCLC 47; PC 18**
See also DLB 205

Leroux, Gaston 1868-1927 .... **TCLC 25**
See also CA 108; 136; CANR 69; SATA 65

Lesage, Alain-Rene 1668-1747 .... **LC 2, 28**

Leskov, Nikolai (Semyonovich) 1831-1895 **NCLC 25; SSC 34**

Lessing, Doris (May) 1919-**CLC 1, 2, 3, 6, 10, 15, 22, 40, 94; DA; DAB;DAC; DAM MST, NOV; SSC 6; WLCS**
See also CA 9-12R; CAAS 14; CANR 33, 54, 76; CDBLB 1960 to Present; DLB 15, 139; DLBY 85; MTCW 1, 2

Lessing, Gotthold Ephraim 1729-1781 . **LC 8**
See also DLB 97

Lester, Richard 1932- .... **CLC 20**

Lever, Charles (James) 1806-1872 **NCLC 23**
See also DLB 21

Leverson, Ada 1865(?)-1936(?) ...... **TCLC 18**
See also Elaine
See also CA 117; DLB 153

Levertov, Denise 1923-1997**CLC 1, 2, 3, 5, 8, 15, 28, 66; DAM POET; PC 11**
See also CA 1-4R; 163; CAAS 19; CANR 3, 29, 50; CDALBS; DLB 5, 165; INT CANR-29; MTCW 1, 2

Levi, Jonathan .... **CLC 76**

Levi, Peter (Chad Tigar) 1931- .... **CLC 41**
See also CA 5-8R; CANR 34, 80; DLB 40

Levi, Primo 1919-1987 . **CLC 37, 50; SSC 12**
See also CA 13-16R; 122; CANR 12, 33, 61, 70; DLB 177; MTCW 1, 2

Levin, Ira 1929- .... **CLC 3, 6; DAM POP**
See also CA 21-24R; CANR 17, 44, 74; MTCW 1, 2; SATA 66

Levin, Meyer 1905-1981 . **CLC 7; DAM POP**
See also AITN 1; CA 9-12R; 104; CANR 15; DLB 9, 28; DLBY 81; SATA 21; SATA-Obit 27

Levine, Norman 1924- .... **CLC 54**
See also CA 73-76; CAAS 23; CANR 14, 70; DLB 88

Levine, Philip 1928-**CLC 2, 4, 5, 9, 14, 33, 118; DAM POET; PC 22**
See also CA 9-12R; CANR 9, 37, 52; DLB 5

Levinson, Deirdre 1931- .... **CLC 49**
See also CA 73-76; CANR 70

Levi-Strauss, Claude 1908- .... **CLC 38**
See also CA 1-4R; CANR 6, 32, 57; MTCW 1, 2

Levitin, Sonia (Wolff) 1934- .... **CLC 17**
See also AAYA 13; CA 29-32R; CANR 14, 32,

79; CLR 53; JRDA; MAICYA; SAAS 2; SATA 4, 68

Levon, O. U.
See Kesey, Ken (Elton)

Levy, Amy 1861-1889 .... **NCLC 59**
See also DLB 156

Lewes, George Henry 1817-1878 ... **NCLC 25**
See also DLB 55, 144

Lewis, Alun 1915-1944 .... **TCLC 3**
See also CA 104; DLB 20, 162

Lewis, C. Day
See Day Lewis, C(ecil)

Lewis, C(live) S(taples) 1898-1963**CLC 1, 3, 6, 14, 27; DA; DAB; DAC; DAM MST, NOV, POP; WLC**
See also AAYA 3; CA 81-84; CANR 33, 71; CDBLB 1945-1960; CLR 3, 27; DLB 15, 100, 160; JRDA; MAICYA; MTCW 1, 2; SATA 13, 100

Lewis, Janet 1899-1998 .... **CLC 41**
See also Winters, Janet Lewis
See also CA 9-12R; 172; CANR 29, 63; CAP 1; DLBY 87

Lewis, Matthew Gregory 1775-1818**NCLC 11, 62**
See also DLB 39, 158, 178

Lewis, (Harry) Sinclair 1885-1951 . **TCLC 4, 13, 23, 39; DA; DAB; DAC; DAM MST, NOV; WLC**
See also CA 104; 133; CDALB 1917-1929; DLB 9, 102; DLBD 1; MTCW 1, 2

Lewis, (Percy) Wyndham 1882(?)-1957**TCLC 2, 9; SSC 34**
See also CA 104; 157; DLB 15; MTCW 2

Lewisohn, Ludwig 1883-1955 .... **TCLC 19**
See also CA 107; DLB 4, 9, 28, 102

Lewton, Val 1904-1951 .... **TCLC 76**

Leyner, Mark 1956- .... **CLC 92**
See also CA 110; CANR 28, 53; MTCW 2

Lezama Lima, Jose 1910-1976**CLC 4, 10, 101; DAM MULT; HLCS 2**
See also CA 77-80; CANR 71; DLB 113; HW 1, 2

L'Heureux, John (Clarke) 1934- .... **CLC 52**
See also CA 13-16R; CANR 23, 45

Liddell, C. H.
See Kuttner, Henry

Lie, Jonas (Lauritz Idemil) 1833-1908(?) **TCLC 5**
See also CA 115

Lieber, Joel 1937-1971 .... **CLC 6**
See also CA 73-76; 29-32R

Lieber, Stanley Martin
See Lee, Stan

Lieberman, Laurence (James) 1935- **CLC 4, 36**
See also CA 17-20R; CANR 8, 36

Lieh Tzu fl. 7th cent. B.C.-5th cent. B.C. **CMLC 27**

Lieksman, Anders
See Haavikko, Paavo Juhani

Li Fei-kan 1904-
See Pa Chin
See also CA 105

Lifton, Robert Jay 1926- .... **CLC 67**
See also CA 17-20R; CANR 27, 78; INT CANR-27; SATA 66

Lightfoot, Gordon 1938- .... **CLC 26**
See also CA 109

Lightman, Alan P(aige) 1948- .... **CLC 81**
See also CA 141; CANR 63

Ligotti, Thomas (Robert) 1953-**CLC 44; SSC 16**

See also CA 123; CANR 49

Li Ho 791-817 .... **PC 13**

Liliencron, (Friedrich Adolf Axel) Detlev von 1844-1909 .... **TCLC 18**
See also CA 117

Lilly, William 1602-1681 .... **LC 27**

Lima, Jose Lezama
See Lezama Lima, Jose

Lima Barreto, Afonso Henrique de 1881-1922 **TCLC 23**
See also CA 117

Limonov, Edward 1944- .... **CLC 67**
See also CA 137

Lin, Frank
See Atherton, Gertrude (Franklin Horn)

Lincoln, Abraham 1809-1865 .... **NCLC 18**

Lind, Jakov .... **CLC 1, 2, 4, 27, 82**
See also Landwirth, Heinz
See also CAAS 4

Lindbergh, Anne (Spencer) Morrow 1906- **CLC 82; DAM NOV**
See also CA 17-20R; CANR 16, 73; MTCW 1, 2; SATA 33

Lindsay, David 1878-1945 .... **TCLC 15**
See also CA 113

Lindsay, (Nicholas) Vachel 1879-1931 **TCLC 17; DA; DAC; DAM MST, POET; PC 23; WLC**
See also CA 114; 135; CANR 79; CDALB 1865-1917; DLB 54; SATA 40

Linke-Poot
See Doeblin, Alfred

Linney, Romulus 1930- .... **CLC 51**
See also CA 1-4R; CANR 40, 44, 79

Linton, Eliza Lynn 1822-1898 .... **NCLC 41**
See also DLB 18

Li Po 701-763 .... **CMLC 2**

Lipsius, Justus 1547-1606 .... **LC 16**

Lipsyte, Robert (Michael) 1938-**CLC 21; DA; DAC; DAM MST, NOV**
See also AAYA 7; CA 17-20R; CANR 8, 57; CLR 23; JRDA; MAICYA; SATA 5, 68

Lish, Gordon (Jay) 1934- ... **CLC 45; SSC 18**
See also CA 113; 117; CANR 79; DLB 130; INT 117

Lispector, Clarice 1925(?)-1977 ...... **CLC 43; HLCS 2; SSC 34**
See also CA 139; 116; CANR 71; DLB 113; HW 2

Littell, Robert 1935(?)- .... **CLC 42**
See also CA 109; 112; CANR 64

Little, Malcolm 1925-1965
See Malcolm X
See also BW 1, 3; CA 125; 111; DA; DAB; DAC; DAM MST, MULT; MTCW 1,2

Littlewit, Humphrey Gent.
See Lovecraft, H(oward) P(hillips)

Litwos
See Sienkiewicz, Henryk (Adam Alexander Pius)

Liu, E 1857-1909 .... **TCLC 15**
See also CA 115

Lively, Penelope (Margaret) 1933- .. **CLC 32, 50; DAM NOV**
See also CA 41-44R; CANR 29, 67, 79; CLR 7; DLB 14, 161, 207; JRDA; MAICYA; MTCW 1, 2; SATA 7, 60, 101

Livesay, Dorothy (Kathleen) 1909-**CLC 4, 15, 79; DAC; DAM MST, POET**
See also AITN 2; CA 25-28R; CAAS 8; CANR 36, 67; DLB 68; MTCW 1

Livy c. 59B.C.-c. 17 .... **CMLC 11**
See also DLB 211

Lizardi, Jose Joaquin Fernandez de 1776-1827
NCLC 30
Llewellyn, Richard
See Llewellyn Lloyd, Richard Dafydd Vivian
See also DLB 15
Llewellyn Lloyd, Richard Dafydd Vivian 1906-
1983 .... CLC 7, 80
See also Llewellyn, Richard
See also CA 53-56; 111; CANR 7, 71; SATA
11; SATA-Obit 37
Llosa, (Jorge) Mario (Pedro) Vargas
See Vargas Llosa, (Jorge) Mario (Pedro)
Lloyd, Manda
See Mander, (Mary) Jane
Lloyd Webber, Andrew 1948-
See Webber, Andrew Lloyd
See also AAYA 1; CA 116; 149; DAM DRAM;
SATA 56
Llull, Ramon c. 1235-c. 1316 .... CMLC 12
Lobb, Ebenezer
See Upward, Allen
Locke, Alain (Le Roy) 1886-1954 . TCLC 43;
BLCS
See also BW 1, 3; CA 106; 124; CANR 79; DLB
51
Locke, John 1632-1704 .... LC 7, 35
See also DLB 101
Locke-Elliott, Sumner
See Elliott, Sumner Locke
Lockhart, John Gibson 1794-1854 .. NCLC 6
See also DLB 110, 116, 144
Lodge, David (John) 1935- .... CLC 36; DAM
POP
See also BEST 90:1; CA 17-20R; CANR 19,
53; DLB 14, 194; INT CANR-19; MTCW 1,
2
Lodge, Thomas 1558-1625 .... LC 41
Lodge, Thomas 1558-1625 .... LC 41
See also DLB 172
Loennbohm, Armas Eino Leopold 1878-1926
See Leino, Eino
See also CA 123
Loewinsohn, Ron(ald William) 1937-CLC 52
See also CA 25-28R; CANR 71
Logan, Jake
See Smith, Martin Cruz
Logan, John (Burton) 1923-1987 .... CLC 5
See also CA 77-80; 124; CANR 45; DLB 5
Lo Kuan-chung 1330(?)-1400(?) .... LC 12
Lombard, Nap
See Johnson, Pamela Hansford
London, Jack . TCLC 9, 15, 39; SSC 4; WLC
See also London, John Griffith
See also AAYA 13; AITN 2; CDALB 1865-
1917; DLB 8, 12, 78, 212; SATA 18
London, John Griffith 1876-1916
See London, Jack
See also CA 110; 119; CANR 73; DA; DAB;
DAC; DAM MST, NOV; JRDA; MAICYA;
MTCW 1, 2
Long, Emmett
See Leonard, Elmore (John, Jr.)
Longbaugh, Harry
See Goldman, William (W.)
Longfellow, Henry Wadsworth 1807-1882
NCLC 2, 45; DA; DAB; DAC; DAM MST,
POET; WLCS
See also CDALB 1640-1865; DLB 1, 59; SATA
19
Longinus c. 1st cent. - .... CMLC 27
See also DLB 176
Longley, Michael 1939- .... CLC 29
See also CA 102; DLB 40

Longus fl. c. 2nd cent. - .... CMLC 7
Longway, A. Hugh
See Lang, Andrew
Lonnrot, Elias 1802-1884 .... NCLC 53
Lopate, Phillip 1943- .... CLC 29
See also CA 97-100; DLBY 80; INT 97-100
Lopez Portillo (y Pacheco), Jose 1920-CLC 46
See also CA 129; HW 1
Lopez y Fuentes, Gregorio 1897(?)-1966C L C
32
See also CA 131; HW 1
Lorca, Federico Garcia
See Garcia Lorca, Federico
Lord, Bette Bao 1938- .... CLC 23
See also BEST 90:3; CA 107; CANR 41, 79;
INT 107; SATA 58
Lord Auch
See Bataille, Georges
Lord Byron
See Byron, George Gordon (Noel)
Lorde, Audre (Geraldine) 1934-1992CLC 18,
71; BLC 2; DAM MULT, POET; PC 12
See also BW 1, 3; CA 25-28R; 142; CANR 16,
26, 46; DLB 41; MTCW 1, 2
Lord Houghton
See Milnes, Richard Monckton
Lord Jeffrey
See Jeffrey, Francis
Lorenzini, Carlo 1826-1890
See Collodi, Carlo
See also MAICYA; SATA 29, 100
Lorenzo, Heberto Padilla
See Padilla (Lorenzo), Heberto
Loris
See Hofmannsthal, Hugo von
Loti, Pierre .... TCLC 11
See also Viaud, (Louis Marie) Julien
See also DLB 123
Louie, David Wong 1954- .... CLC 70
See also CA 139
Louis, Father M.
See Merton, Thomas
Lovecraft, H(oward) P(hillips) 1890-1937
TCLC 4, 22; DAM POP; SSC 3
See also AAYA 14; CA 104; 133; MTCW 1, 2
Lovelace, Earl 1935- .... CLC 51
See also BW 2; CA 77-80; CANR 41, 72; DLB
125; MTCW 1
Lovelace, Richard 1618-1657 .... LC 24
See also DLB 131
Lowell, Amy 1874-1925 .... TCLC 1, 8; DAM
POET; PC 13
See also CA 104; 151; DLB 54, 140; MTCW 2
Lowell, James Russell 1819-1891 .... NCLC 2
See also CDALB 1640-1865; DLB 1, 11, 64,
79, 189
Lowell, Robert (Traill Spence, Jr.) 1917-1977
CLC 1, 2, 3, 4, 5, 8, 9, 11, 15, 37; DA; DAB;
DAC; DAM MST, NOV; PC 3; WLC
See also CA 9-12R; 73-76; CABS 2; CANR 26,
60; CDALBS; DLB 5, 169; MTCW 1, 2
Lowenthal, Michael (Francis) 1969-CLC 119
See also CA 150
Lowndes, Marie Adelaide (Belloc) 1868-1947
TCLC 12
See also CA 107; DLB 70
Lowry, (Clarence) Malcolm 1909-1957T C L C
6, 40; SSC 31
See also CA 105; 131; CANR 62; CDBLB
1945-1960; DLB 15; MTCW 1, 2
Lowry, Mina Gertrude 1882-1966
See Loy, Mina
See also CA 113

Loxsmith, John
See Brunner, John (Kilian Houston)
Loy, Mina .... CLC 28; DAM POET; PC 16
See also Lowry, Mina Gertrude
See also DLB 4, 54
Loyson-Bridet
See Schwob, Marcel (Mayer Andre)
Lucan 39-65 .... CMLC 33
See also DLB 211
Lucas, Craig 1951- .... CLC 64
See also CA 137; CANR 71
Lucas, E(dward) V(errall) 1868-1938 T C L C
73
See also CA 176; DLB 98, 149, 153; SATA 20
Lucas, George 1944- .... CLC 16
See also AAYA 1, 23; CA 77-80; CANR 30;
SATA 56
Lucas, Hans
See Godard, Jean-Luc
Lucas, Victoria
See Plath, Sylvia
Lucian c. 120-c. 180 .... CMLC 32
See also DLB 176
Ludlam, Charles 1943-1987 .... CLC 46, 50
See also CA 85-88; 122; CANR 72
Ludlum, Robert 1927-CLC 22, 43; DAM NOV,
POP
See also AAYA 10; BEST 89:1, 90:3; CA 33-
36R; CANR 25, 41, 68; DLBY 82; MTCW
1, 2
Ludwig, Ken .... CLC 60
Ludwig, Otto 1813-1865 .... NCLC 4
See also DLB 129
Lugones, Leopoldo 1874-1938 ...... TCLC 15;
HLCS 2
See also CA 116; 131; HW 1
Lu Hsun 1881-1936 .... TCLC 3; SSC 20
See also Shu-Jen, Chou
Lukacs, George .... CLC 24
See also Lukacs, Gyorgy (Szegeny von)
Lukacs, Gyorgy (Szegeny von) 1885-1971
See Lukacs, George
See also CA 101; 29-32R; CANR 62; MTCW 2
Luke, Peter (Ambrose Cyprian) 1919-1995
CLC 38
See also CA 81-84; 147; CANR 72; DLB 13
Lunar, Dennis
See Mungo, Raymond
Lurie, Alison 1926- .... CLC 4, 5, 18, 39
See also CA 1-4R; CANR 2, 17, 50; DLB 2;
MTCW 1; SATA 46
Lustig, Arnost 1926- .... CLC 56
See also AAYA 3; CA 69-72; CANR 47; SATA
56
Luther, Martin 1483-1546 .... LC 9, 37
See also DLB 179
Luxemburg, Rosa 1870(?)-1919 ..... TCLC 63
See also CA 118
Luzi, Mario 1914- .... CLC 13
See also CA 61-64; CANR 9, 70; DLB 128
Lyly, John 1554(?)-1606LC 41; DAM DRAM;
DC 7
See also DLB 62, 167
L'Ymagier
See Gourmont, Remy (-Marie-Charles) de
Lynch, B. Suarez
See Bioy Casares, Adolfo; Borges, Jorge Luis
Lynch, B. Suarez
See Bioy Casares, Adolfo
Lynch, David (K.) 1946- .... CLC 66
See also CA 124; 129
Lynch, James
See Andreyev, Leonid (Nikolaevich)

Lynch Davis, B.
See Bioy Casares, Adolfo; Borges, Jorge Luis
Lyndsay, Sir David 1490-1555 .... **LC 20**
Lynn, Kenneth S(chuyler) 1923- ...... **CLC 50**
See also CA 1-4R; CANR 3, 27, 65
Lynx
See West, Rebecca
Lyons, Marcus
See Blish, James (Benjamin)
Lyre, Pinchbeck
See Sassoon, Siegfried (Lorraine)
Lytle, Andrew (Nelson) 1902-1995 ... **CLC 22**
See also CA 9-12R; 150; CANR 70; DLB 6;
DLBY 95
Lyttelton, George 1709-1773 .... **LC 10**
Maas, Peter 1929- .... **CLC 29**
See also CA 93-96; INT 93-96; MTCW 2
Macaulay, Rose 1881-1958 .... **TCLC 7, 44**
See also CA 104; DLB 36
Macaulay, Thomas Babington 1800-1859
NCLC 42
See also CDBLB 1832-1890; DLB 32, 55
MacBeth, George (Mann) 1932-1992**CLC 2, 5,
9**
See also CA 25-28R; 136; CANR 61, 66; DLB
40; MTCW 1; SATA 4; SATA-Obit 70
MacCaig, Norman (Alexander) 1910-**CLC 36;
DAB; DAM POET**
See also CA 9-12R; CANR 3, 34; DLB 27
MacCarthy, Sir(Charles Otto) Desmond 1877-
1952 .... **TCLC 36**
See also CA 167
MacDiarmid, Hugh**CLC 2, 4, 11, 19, 63; PC 9**
See also Grieve, C(hristopher) M(urray)
See also CDBLB 1945-1960; DLB 20
MacDonald, Anson
See Heinlein, Robert A(nson)
Macdonald, Cynthia 1928- .... **CLC 13, 19**
See also CA 49-52; CANR 4, 44; DLB 105
MacDonald, George 1824-1905 .... **TCLC 9**
See also CA 106; 137; CANR 80; DLB 18, 163,
178; MAICYA; SATA 33, 100
Macdonald, John
See Millar, Kenneth
MacDonald, John D(ann) 1916-1986 **CLC 3,
27, 44; DAM NOV, POP**
See also CA 1-4R; 121; CANR 1, 19, 60; DLB
8; DLBY 86; MTCW 1, 2
Macdonald, John Ross
See Millar, Kenneth
Macdonald, Ross .... **CLC 1, 2, 3, 14, 34, 41**
See also Millar, Kenneth
See also DLBD 6
MacDougal, John
See Blish, James (Benjamin)
MacEwen, Gwendolyn (Margaret) 1941-1987
CLC 13, 55
See also CA 9-12R; 124; CANR 7, 22; DLB
53; SATA 50; SATA-Obit 55
Macha, Karel Hynek 1810-1846 .... **NCLC 46**
Machado (y Ruiz), Antonio 1875-1939**T C L C
3**
See also CA 104; 174; DLB 108; HW 2
Machado de Assis, Joaquim Maria 1839-1908
TCLC 10; BLC 2; HLCS 2; SSC 24
See also CA 107; 153
Machen, Arthur .... **TCLC 4; SSC 20**
See also Jones, Arthur Llewellyn
See also DLB 36, 156, 178
Machiavelli, Niccolo 1469-1527**LC 8, 36; DA;
DAB; DAC; DAM MST; WLCS**
MacInnes, Colin 1914-1976 .... **CLC 4, 23**
See also CA 69-72; 65-68; CANR 21; DLB 14;

MTCW 1, 2
MacInnes, Helen (Clark) 1907-1985 **CLC 27,
39; DAM POP**
See also CA 1-4R; 117; CANR 1, 28, 58; DLB
87; MTCW 1, 2; SATA 22; SATA-Obit 44
Mackenzie, Compton (Edward Montague)
1883-1972 .... **CLC 18**
See also CA 21-22; 37-40R; CAP 2; DLB 34,
100
Mackenzie, Henry 1745-1831 .... **NCLC 41**
See also DLB 39
Mackintosh, Elizabeth 1896(?)-1952
See Tey, Josephine
See also CA 110
MacLaren, James
See Grieve, C(hristopher) M(urray)
Mac Laverty, Bernard 1942- .... **CLC 31**
See also CA 116; 118; CANR 43; INT 118
MacLean, Alistair (Stuart) 1922(?)-1987**C L C
3, 13, 50, 63; DAM POP**
See also CA 57-60; 121; CANR 28, 61; MTCW
1; SATA 23; SATA-Obit 50
Maclean, Norman (Fitzroy) 1902-1990 **C L C
78; DAM POP; SSC 13**
See also CA 102; 132; CANR 49; DLB 206
MacLeish, Archibald 1892-1982**CLC 3, 8, 14,
68; DAM POET**
See also CA 9-12R; 106; CANR 33, 63;
CDALBS; DLB 4, 7, 45; DLBY 82; MTCW
1, 2
MacLennan, (John) Hugh 1907-1990 **CLC 2,
14, 92; DAC; DAM MST**
See also CA 5-8R; 142; CANR 33; DLB 68;
MTCW 1, 2
MacLeod, Alistair 1936-**CLC 56; DAC; DAM
MST**
See also CA 123; DLB 60; MTCW 2
Macleod, Fiona
See Sharp, William
MacNeice, (Frederick) Louis 1907-1963**C L C
1, 4, 10, 53; DAB; DAM POET**
See also CA 85-88; CANR 61; DLB 10, 20;
MTCW 1, 2
MacNeill, Dand
See Fraser, George MacDonald
Macpherson, James 1736-1796 .... **LC 29**
See also Ossian
See also DLB 109
Macpherson, (Jean) Jay 1931- .... **CLC 14**
See also CA 5-8R; DLB 53
MacShane, Frank 1927- .... **CLC 39**
See also CA 9-12R; CANR 3, 33; DLB 111
Macumber, Mari
See Sandoz, Mari(e Susette)
Madach, Imre 1823-1864 .... **NCLC 19**
Madden, (Jerry) David 1933- .... **CLC 5, 15**
See also CA 1-4R; CAAS 3; CANR 4, 45; DLB
6; MTCW 1
Maddern, Al(an)
See Ellison, Harlan (Jay)
Madhubuti, Haki R. 1942-**CLC 6, 73; BLC 2;
DAM MULT, POET; PC 5**
See also Lee, Don L.
See also BW 2, 3; CA 73-76; CANR 24, 51,
73; DLB 5, 41; DLBD 8; MTCW 2
Maepenn, Hugh
See Kuttner, Henry
Maepenn, K. H.
See Kuttner, Henry
Maeterlinck, Maurice 1862-1949 ... **TCLC 3;
DAM DRAM**
See also CA 104; 136; CANR 80; DLB 192;
SATA 66

Maginn, William 1794-1842 .... **NCLC 8**
See also DLB 110, 159
Mahapatra, Jayanta 1928- .... **CLC 33; DAM
MULT**
See also CA 73-76; CAAS 9; CANR 15, 33, 66
Mahfouz, Naguib (Abdel Aziz Al-Sabilgi)
1911(?)-
See Mahfuz, Najib
See also BEST 89:2; CA 128; CANR 55; DAM
NOV; MTCW 1, 2
Mahfuz, Najib .... **CLC 52, 55**
See also Mahfouz, Naguib (Abdel Aziz Al-
Sabilgi)
See also DLBY 88
Mahon, Derek 1941- .... **CLC 27**
See also CA 113; 128; DLB 40
Mailer, Norman 1923-**CLC 1, 2, 3, 4, 5, 8, 11,
14, 28, 39, 74, 111; DA; DAB; DAC; DAM
MST, NOV, POP**
See also AITN 2; CA 9-12R; CABS 1; CANR
28, 74, 77; CDALB 1968-1988; DLB 2, 16,
28, 185; DLBD 3; DLBY 80, 83; MTCW 1,
2
Maillet, Antonine 1929- . **CLC 54, 118; DAC**
See also CA 115; 120; CANR 46, 74, 77; DLB
60; INT 120; MTCW 2
Mais, Roger 1905-1955 .... **TCLC 8**
See also BW 1, 3; CA 105; 124; DLB 125;
MTCW 1
Maistre, Joseph de 1753-1821 .... **NCLC 37**
Maitland, Frederic 1850-1906 .... **TCLC 65**
Maitland, Sara (Louise) 1950- .... **CLC 49**
See also CA 69-72; CANR 13, 59
Major, Clarence 1936-**CLC 3, 19, 48; BLC 2;
DAM MULT**
See also BW 2, 3; CA 21-24R; CAAS 6; CANR
13, 25, 53; DLB 33
Major, Kevin (Gerald) 1949- .. **CLC 26; DAC**
See also AAYA 16; CA 97-100; CANR 21, 38;
CLR 11; DLB 60; INT CANR-21; JRDA;
MAICYA; SATA 32, 82
Maki, James
See Ozu, Yasujiro
Malabaila, Damiano
See Levi, Primo
Malamud, Bernard 1914-1986**CLC 1, 2, 3, 5,
8, 9, 11, 18, 27, 44, 78, 85; DA; DAB; DAC;
DAM MST, NOV, POP; SSC 15; WLC**
See also AAYA 16; CA 5-8R; 118; CABS 1;
CANR 28, 62; CDALB 1941-1968; DLB 2,
28, 152; DLBY 80, 86; MTCW 1, 2
Malan, Herman
See Bosman, Herman Charles; Bosman, Herman
Charles
Malaparte, Curzio 1898-1957 .... **TCLC 52**
Malcolm, Dan
See Silverberg, Robert
Malcolm X .... **CLC 82, 117; BLC 2; WLCS**
See also Little, Malcolm
Malherbe, Francois de 1555-1628 .... **LC 5**
Mallarme, Stephane 1842-1898 **NCLC 4, 41;
DAM POET; PC 4**
Mallet-Joris, Francoise 1930- .... **CLC 11**
See also CA 65-68; CANR 17; DLB 83
Malley, Ern
See McAuley, James Phillip
Mallowan, Agatha Christie
See Christie, Agatha (Mary Clarissa)
Maloff, Saul 1922- .... **CLC 5**
See also CA 33-36R
Malone, Louis
See MacNeice, (Frederick) Louis
Malone, Michael (Christopher) 1942-**CLC 43**

28, 59; DAM POET
See also CA 9-12R; 132; CANR 6, 33; MTCW 1; SATA 41; SATA-Obit 66

McGuane, Thomas (Francis III) 1939-CLC 3, 7, 18, 45
See also AITN 2; CA 49-52; CANR 5, 24, 49; DLB 2, 212; DLBY 80; INT CANR-24; MTCW 1

McGuckian, Medbh 1950- ..... CLC 48; DAM POET
See also CA 143; DLB 40

McHale, Tom 1942(?)-1982 .... CLC 3, 5
See also AITN 1; CA 77-80; 106

McIlvanney, William 1936- .... CLC 42
See also CA 25-28R; CANR 61; DLB 14, 207

McIlwraith, Maureen Mollie Hunter
See Hunter, Mollie
See also SATA 2

McInerney, Jay 1955-CLC 34, 112; DAM POP
See also AAYA 18; CA 116; 123; CANR 45, 68; INT 123; MTCW 2

McIntyre, Vonda N(eel) 1948- .... CLC 18
See also CA 81-84; CANR 17, 34, 69; MTCW 1

McKay, ClaudeTCLC 7, 41; BLC 3; DAB; PC 2
See also McKay, Festus Claudius
See also DLB 4, 45, 51, 117

McKay, Festus Claudius 1889-1948
See McKay, Claude
See also BW 1, 3; CA 104; 124; CANR 73; DA; DAC; DAM MST, MULT, NOV, POET; MTCW 1, 2; WLC

McKuen, Rod 1933- .... CLC 1, 3
See also AITN 1; CA 41-44R; CANR 40

McLoughlin, R. B.
See Mencken, H(enry) L(ouis)

McLuhan, (Herbert) Marshall 1911-1980
CLC 37, 83
See also CA 9-12R; 102; CANR 12, 34, 61; DLB 88; INT CANR-12; MTCW 1, 2

McMillan, Terry (L.) 1951- CLC 50, 61, 112; BLCS; DAM MULT, NOV, POP
See also AAYA 21; BW 2, 3; CA 140; CANR 60; MTCW 2

McMurtry, Larry (Jeff) 1936-CLC 2, 3, 7, 11, 27, 44; DAM NOV, POP
See also AAYA 15; AITN 2; BEST 89:2; CA 5-8R; CANR 19, 43, 64; CDALB 1968-1988; DLB 2, 143; DLBY 80, 87; MTCW 1, 2

McNally, T. M. 1961- .... CLC 82

McNally, Terrence 1939-.... CLC 4, 7, 41, 91; DAM DRAM
See also CA 45-48; CANR 2, 56; DLB 7; MTCW 2

McNamer, Deirdre 1950- .... CLC 70

McNeal, Tom .... CLC 119

McNeile, Herman Cyril 1888-1937
See Sapper
See also DLB 77

McNickle, (William) D'Arcy 1904-1977 C L C 89; DAM MULT
See also CA 9-12R; 85-88; CANR 5, 45; DLB 175, 212; NNAL; SATA-Obit 22

McPhee, John (Angus) 1931- .... CLC 36
See also BEST 90:1; CA 65-68; CANR 20, 46, 64, 69; DLB 185; MTCW 1, 2

McPherson, James Alan 1943-.. CLC 19, 77; BLCS
See also BW 1, 3; CA 25-28R; CAAS 17; CANR 24, 74; DLB 38; MTCW 1, 2

McPherson, William (Alexander) 1933-C L C 34

See also CA 69-72; CANR 28; INT CANR-28

Mead, George Herbert 1873-1958 . TCLC 89

Mead, Margaret 1901-1978 .... CLC 37
See also AITN 1; CA 1-4R; 81-84; CANR 4; MTCW 1, 2; SATA-Obit 20

Meaker, Marijane (Agnes) 1927-
See Kerr, M. E.
See also CA 107; CANR 37, 63; INT 107; JRDA; MAICYA; MTCW 1; SATA 20, 61, 99

Medoff, Mark (Howard) 1940- ... CLC 6, 23; DAM DRAM
See also AITN 1; CA 53-56; CANR 5; DLB 7; INT CANR-5

Medvedev, P. N.
See Bakhtin, Mikhail Mikhailovich

Meged, Aharon
See Megged, Aharon

Meged, Aron
See Megged, Aharon

Megged, Aharon 1920- .... CLC 9
See also CA 49-52; CAAS 13; CANR 1

Mehta, Ved (Parkash) 1934- .... CLC 37
See also CA 1-4R; CANR 2, 23, 69; MTCW 1

Melanter
See Blackmore, R(ichard) D(oddridge)

Melies, Georges 1861-1938 .... TCLC 81

Melikow, Loris
See Hofmannsthal, Hugo von

Melmoth, Sebastian
See Wilde, Oscar

Meltzer, Milton 1915- .... CLC 26
See also AAYA 8; CA 13-16R; CANR 38; CLR 13; DLB 61; JRDA; MAICYA; SAAS 1; SATA 1, 50, 80

Melville, Herman 1819-1891NCLC 3, 12, 29, 45, 49; DA; DAB; DAC; DAM MST, NOV; SSC 1, 17; WLC
See also AAYA 25; CDALB 1640-1865; DLB 3, 74; SATA 59

Menander c. 342B.C.-c. 292B.C. ..... CMLC 9; DAM DRAM; DC 3
See also DLB 176

Mencken, H(enry) L(ouis) 1880-1956 T C L C 13
See also CA 105; 125; CDALB 1917-1929; DLB 11, 29, 63, 137; MTCW 1, 2

Mendelsohn, Jane 1965(?)- .... CLC 99
See also CA 154

Mercer, David 1928-1980CLC 5; DAM DRAM
See also CA 9-12R; 102; CANR 23; DLB 13; MTCW 1

Merchant, Paul
See Ellison, Harlan (Jay)

Meredith, George 1828-1909 . TCLC 17, 43; DAM POET
See also CA 117; 153; CANR 80; CDBLB 1832-1890; DLB 18, 35, 57, 159

Meredith, William (Morris) 1919-CLC 4, 13, 22, 55; DAM POET
See also CA 9-12R; CAAS 14; CANR 6, 40; DLB 5

Merezhkovsky, Dmitry Sergeyevich 1865-1941 TCLC 29
See also CA 169

Merimee, Prosper 1803-1870NCLC 6, 65; SSC 7
See also DLB 119, 192

Merkin, Daphne 1954- .... CLC 44
See also CA 123

Merlin, Arthur
See Blish, James (Benjamin)

Merrill, James (Ingram) 1926-1995CLC 2, 3,

6, 8, 13, 18, 34, 91; DAM POET
See also CA 13-16R; 147; CANR 10, 49, 63; DLB 5, 165; DLBY 85; INT CANR-10; MTCW 1, 2

Merriman, Alex
See Silverberg, Robert

Merriman, Brian 1747-1805 .... NCLC 70

Merritt, E. B.
See Waddington, Miriam

Merton, Thomas 1915-1968CLC 1, 3, 11, 34, 83; PC 10
See also CA 5-8R; 25-28R; CANR 22, 53; DLB 48; DLBY 81; MTCW 1, 2

Merwin, W(illiam) S(tanley) 1927- CLC 1, 2, 3, 5, 8, 13, 18, 45, 88; DAM POET
See also CA 13-16R; CANR 15, 51; DLB 5, 169; INT CANR-15; MTCW 1, 2

Metcalf, John 1938- .... CLC 37
See also CA 113; DLB 60

Metcalf, Suzanne
See Baum, L(yman) Frank

Mew, Charlotte (Mary) 1870-1928 .. TCLC 8
See also CA 105; DLB 19, 135

Mewshaw, Michael 1943- .... CLC 9
See also CA 53-56; CANR 7, 47; DLBY 80

Meyer, June
See Jordan, June

Meyer, Lynn
See Slavitt, David R(ytman)

Meyer-Meyrink, Gustav 1868-1932
See Meyrink, Gustav
See also CA 117

Meyers, Jeffrey 1939- .... CLC 39
See also CA 73-76; CANR 54; DLB 111

Meynell, Alice (Christina Gertrude Thompson) 1847-1922 .... TCLC 6
See also CA 104; 177; DLB 19, 98

Meyrink, Gustav .... TCLC 21
See also Meyer-Meyrink, Gustav
See also DLB 81

Michaels, Leonard 1933- CLC 6, 25; SSC 16
See also CA 61-64; CANR 21, 62; DLB 130; MTCW 1

Michaux, Henri 1899-1984 .... CLC 8, 19
See also CA 85-88; 114

Micheaux, Oscar (Devereaux) 1884-1951 TCLC 76
See also BW 3; CA 174; DLB 50

Michelangelo 1475-1564 .... LC 12

Michelet, Jules 1798-1874 .... NCLC 31

Michels, Robert 1876-1936 .... TCLC 88

Michener, James A(lbert) 1907(?)-1997 C L C 1, 5, 11, 29, 60, 109; DAM NOV, POP
See also AAYA 27; AITN 1; BEST 90:1; CA 5-8R; 161; CANR 21, 45, 68; DLB 6; MTCW 1, 2

Mickiewicz, Adam 1798-1855 .... NCLC 3

Middleton, Christopher 1926- .... CLC 13
See also CA 13-16R; CANR 29, 54; DLB 40

Middleton, Richard (Barham) 1882-1911 TCLC 56
See also DLB 156

Middleton, Stanley 1919- .... CLC 7, 38
See also CA 25-28R; CAAS 23; CANR 21, 46, 81; DLB 14

Middleton, Thomas 1580-1627 LC 33; DAM DRAM, MST; DC 5
See also DLB 58

Migueis, Jose Rodrigues 1901- .... CLC 10

Mikszath, Kalman 1847-1910 .... TCLC 31
See also CA 170

Miles, Jack .... CLC 100

Miles, Josephine (Louise) 1911-1985CLC 1, 2,

2, 17, 38, 64; DLB 14; MTCW 1, 2; SATA
93

Moore, Brian 1921-1999 **CLC 1, 3, 5, 7, 8, 19,
32, 90; DAB; DAC; DAM MST**
See also CA 1-4R; 174; CANR 1, 25, 42, 63;
MTCW 1, 2

Moore, Edward
See Muir, Edwin

Moore, G. E. 1873-1958 .... **TCLC 89**

Moore, George Augustus 1852-1933 **TCLC 7;
SSC 19**
See also CA 104; 177; DLB 10, 18, 57, 135

Moore, Lorrie .... **CLC 39, 45, 68**
See also Moore, Marie Lorena

Moore, Marianne (Craig) 1887-1972 **CLC 1, 2,
4, 8, 10, 13, 19, 47; DA; DAB; DAC; DAM
MST, POET; PC 4; WLCS**
See also CA 1-4R; 33-36R; CANR 3, 61;
CDALB 1929-1941; DLB 45; DLBD 7;
MTCW 1, 2; SATA 20

Moore, Marie Lorena 1957-
See Moore, Lorrie
See also CA 116; CANR 39

Moore, Thomas 1779-1852 .... **NCLC 6**
See also DLB 96, 144

Morand, Paul 1888-1976 .... **CLC 41; SSC 22**
See also CA 69-72; DLB 65

Morante, Elsa 1918-1985 .... **CLC 8, 47**
See also CA 85-88; 117; CANR 35; DLB 177;
MTCW 1, 2

Moravia, Alberto 1907-1990 **CLC 2, 7, 11, 27,
46; SSC 26**
See also Pincherle, Alberto
See also DLB 177; MTCW 2

More, Hannah 1745-1833 .... **NCLC 27**
See also DLB 107, 109, 116, 158

More, Henry 1614-1687 .... **LC 9**
See also DLB 126

More, Sir Thomas 1478-1535 .... **LC 10, 32**

Moreas, Jean .... **TCLC 18**
See also Papadiamantopoulos, Johannes

Morgan, Berry 1919- .... **CLC 6**
See also CA 49-52; DLB 6

Morgan, Claire
See Highsmith, (Mary) Patricia

Morgan, Edwin (George) 1920- .... **CLC 31**
See also CA 5-8R; CANR 3, 43; DLB 27

Morgan, (George) Frederick 1922- .. **CLC 23**
See also CA 17-20R; CANR 21

Morgan, Harriet
See Mencken, H(enry) L(ouis)

Morgan, Jane
See Cooper, James Fenimore

Morgan, Janet 1945- .... **CLC 39**
See also CA 65-68

Morgan, Lady 1776(?)-1859 .... **NCLC 29**
See also DLB 116, 158

Morgan, Robin (Evonne) 1941- .... **CLC 2**
See also CA 69-72; CANR 29, 68; MTCW 1;
SATA 80

Morgan, Scott
See Kuttner, Henry

Morgan, Seth 1949(?)-1990 .... **CLC 65**
See also CA 132

Morgenstern, Christian 1871-1914 . **TCLC 8**
See also CA 105

Morgenstern, S.
See Goldman, William (W.)

Moricz, Zsigmond 1879-1942 .... **TCLC 33**
See also CA 165

Morike, Eduard (Friedrich) 1804-1875 **NCLC
10**
See also DLB 133

Moritz, Karl Philipp 1756-1793 .... **LC 2**
See also DLB 94

Morland, Peter Henry
See Faust, Frederick (Schiller)

Morley, Christopher (Darlington) 1890-1957
TCLC 87
See also CA 112; DLB 9

Morren, Theophil
See Hofmannsthal, Hugo von

Morris, Bill 1952- .... **CLC 76**

Morris, Julian
See West, Morris L(anglo)

Morris, Steveland Judkins 1950(?)-
See Wonder, Stevie
See also CA 111

Morris, William 1834-1896 .... **NCLC 4**
See also CDBLB 1832-1890; DLB 18, 35, 57,
156, 178, 184

Morris, Wright 1910-1998 **CLC 1, 3, 7, 18, 37**
See also CA 9-12R; 167; CANR 21, 81; DLB
2, 206; DLBY 81; MTCW 1, 2

Morrison, Arthur 1863-1945 .... **TCLC 72**
See also CA 120; 157; DLB 70, 135, 197

Morrison, Chloe Anthony Wofford
See Morrison, Toni

Morrison, James Douglas 1943-1971
See Morrison, Jim
See also CA 73-76; CANR 40

Morrison, Jim .... **CLC 17**
See also Morrison, James Douglas

Morrison, Toni 1931- **CLC 4, 10, 22, 55, 81, 87;
BLC 3; DA; DAB; DAC; DAM MST,
MULT, NOV, POP**
See also AAYA 1, 22; BW 2, 3; CA 29-32R;
CANR 27, 42, 67; CDALB 1968-1988; DLB
6, 33, 143; DLBY 81; MTCW 1, 2; SATA 57

Morrison, Van 1945- .... **CLC 21**
See also CA 116; 168

Morrissy, Mary 1958- .... **CLC 99**

Mortimer, John (Clifford) 1923- **CLC 28, 43;
DAM DRAM, POP**
See also CA 13-16R; CANR 21, 69; CDBLB
1960 to Present; DLB 13; INT CANR-21;
MTCW 1, 2

Mortimer, Penelope (Ruth) 1918- .... **CLC 5**
See also CA 57-60; CANR 45

Morton, Anthony
See Creasey, John

Mosca, Gaetano 1858-1941 .... **TCLC 75**

Mosher, Howard Frank 1943- .... **CLC 62**
See also CA 139; CANR 65

Mosley, Nicholas 1923- .... **CLC 43, 70**
See also CA 69-72; CANR 41, 60; DLB 14, 207

Mosley, Walter 1952- **CLC 97; BLCS; DAM
MULT, POP**
See also AAYA 17; BW 2; CA 142; CANR 57;
MTCW 2

Moss, Howard 1922-1987 **CLC 7, 14, 45, 50;
DAM POET**
See also CA 1-4R; 123; CANR 1, 44; DLB 5

Mossgiel, Rab
See Burns, Robert

Motion, Andrew (Peter) 1952- .... **CLC 47**
See also CA 146; DLB 40

Motley, Willard (Francis) 1909-1965 **CLC 18**
See also BW 1; CA 117; 106; DLB 76, 143

Motoori, Norinaga 1730-1801 .... **NCLC 45**

Mott, Michael (Charles Alston) 1930- **CLC 15,
34**
See also CA 5-8R; CAAS 7; CANR 7, 29

Mountain Wolf Woman 1884-1960 .. **CLC 92**
See also CA 144; NNAL

Moure, Erin 1955- .... **CLC 88**

See also CA 113; DLB 60

Mowat, Farley (McGill) 1921- **CLC 26; DAC;
DAM MST**
See also AAYA 1; CA 1-4R; CANR 4, 24, 42,
68; CLR 20; DLB 68; INT CANR-24; JRDA;
MAICYA; MTCW 1, 2; SATA 3, 55

Mowatt, Anna Cora 1819-1870 ..... **NCLC 74**

Moyers, Bill 1934- .... **CLC 74**
See also AITN 2; CA 61-64; CANR 31, 52

Mphahlele, Es'kia
See Mphahlele, Ezekiel
See also DLB 125

Mphahlele, Ezekiel 1919- .. **CLC 25; BLC 3;
DAM MULT**
See also Mphahlele, Es'kia
See also BW 2, 3; CA 81-84; CANR 26, 76;
MTCW 2

Mqhayi, S(amuel) E(dward) K(rune Loliwe)
1875-1945 **TCLC 25; BLC 3; DAM MULT**
See also CA 153

Mrozek, Slawomir 1930- .... **CLC 3, 13**
See also CA 13-16R; CAAS 10; CANR 29;
MTCW 1

Mrs. Belloc-Lowndes
See Lowndes, Marie Adelaide (Belloc)

Mtwa, Percy (?)- .... **CLC 47**

Mueller, Lisel 1924- .... **CLC 13, 51**
See also CA 93-96; DLB 105

Muir, Edwin 1887-1959 .... **TCLC 2, 87**
See also CA 104; DLB 20, 100, 191

Muir, John 1838-1914 .... **TCLC 28**
See also CA 165; DLB 186

Mujica Lainez, Manuel 1910-1984 ... **CLC 31**
See also Lainez, Manuel Mujica
See also CA 81-84; 112; CANR 32; HW 1

Mukherjee, Bharati 1940- **CLC 53, 115; DAM
NOV**
See also BEST 89:2; CA 107; CANR 45, 72;
DLB 60; MTCW 1, 2

Muldoon, Paul 1951- **CLC 32, 72; DAM POET**
See also CA 113; 129; CANR 52; DLB 40; INT
129

Mulisch, Harry 1927- .... **CLC 42**
See also CA 9-12R; CANR 6, 26, 56

Mull, Martin 1943- .... **CLC 17**
See also CA 105

Muller, Wilhelm .... **NCLC 73**

Mulock, Dinah Maria
See Craik, Dinah Maria (Mulock)

Munford, Robert 1737(?)-1783 .... **LC 5**
See also DLB 31

Mungo, Raymond 1946- .... **CLC 72**
See also CA 49-52; CANR 2

Munro, Alice 1931- .... **CLC 6, 10, 19, 50, 95;
DAC; DAM MST, NOV; SSC 3; WLCS**
See also AITN 2; CA 33-36R; CANR 33, 53,
75; DLB 53; MTCW 1, 2; SATA 29

Munro, H(ector) H(ugh) 1870-1916
See Saki
See also CA 104; 130; CDBLB 1890-1914; DA;
DAB; DAC; DAM MST, NOV; DLB 34, 162;
MTCW 1, 2; WLC

Murdoch, (Jean) Iris 1919- **CLC 1, 2, 3, 4, 6, 8,
11, 15, 22, 31, 51; DAB; DAC; DAM MST,
NOV**
See also CA 13-16R; CANR 8, 43, 68; CDBLB
1960 to Present; DLB 14, 194; INT CANR-
8; MTCW 1, 2

Murfree, Mary Noailles 1850-1922 ... **SSC 22**
See also CA 122; 176; DLB 12, 74

Murnau, Friedrich Wilhelm
See Plumpe, Friedrich Wilhelm

Murphy, Richard 1927- .... **CLC 41**

See also CA 110

Nizan, Paul 1905-1940 .... **TCLC 40**
See also CA 161; DLB 72

Nkosi, Lewis 1936- .... **CLC 45; BLC 3; DAM MULT**
See also BW 1, 3; CA 65-68; CANR 27, 81; DLB 157

Nodier, (Jean) Charles (Emmanuel) 1780-1844 **NCLC 19**
See also DLB 119

Noguchi, Yone 1875-1947 .... **TCLC 80**

Nolan, Christopher 1965- .... **CLC 58**
See also CA 111

Noon, Jeff 1957- .... **CLC 91**
See also CA 148

Norden, Charles
See Durrell, Lawrence (George)

Nordhoff, Charles (Bernard) 1887-1947 **TCLC 23**
See also CA 108; DLB 9; SATA 23

Norfolk, Lawrence 1963- .... **CLC 76**
See also CA 144

Norman, Marsha 1947- **CLC 28; DAM DRAM; DC 8**
See also CA 105; CABS 3; CANR 41; DLBY 84

Normyx
See Douglas, (George) Norman

Norris, Frank 1870-1902 .... **SSC 28**
See Norris, (Benjamin) Frank(lin, Jr.)
See also CDALB 1865-1917; DLB 12, 71, 186

Norris, (Benjamin) Frank(lin, Jr.) 1870-1902 **TCLC 24**
See also Norris, Frank
See also CA 110; 160

Norris, Leslie 1921- .... **CLC 14**
See also CA 11-12; CANR 14; CAP 1; DLB 27

North, Andrew
See Norton, Andre

North, Anthony
See Koontz, Dean R(ay)

North, Captain George
See Stevenson, Robert Louis (Balfour)

North, Milou
See Erdrich, Louise

Northrup, B. A.
See Hubbard, L(afayette) Ron(ald)

North Staffs
See Hulme, T(homas) E(rnest)

Norton, Alice Mary
See Norton, Andre
See also MAICYA; SATA 1, 43

Norton, Andre 1912- .... **CLC 12**
See also Norton, Alice Mary
See also AAYA 14; CA 1-4R; CANR 68; CLR 50; DLB 8, 52; JRDA; MTCW 1; SATA 91

Norton, Caroline 1808-1877 .... **NCLC 47**
See also DLB 21, 159, 199

Norway, Nevil Shute 1899-1960
See Shute, Nevil
See also CA 102; 93-96; MTCW 2

Norwid, Cyprian Kamil 1821-1883 **NCLC 17**

Nosille, Nabrah
See Ellison, Harlan (Jay)

Nossack, Hans Erich 1901-1978 .... **CLC 6**
See also CA 93-96; 85-88; DLB 69

Nostradamus 1503-1566 .... **LC 27**

Nosu, Chuji
See Ozu, Yasujiro

Notenburg, Eleanora (Genrikhovna) von
See Guro, Elena

Nova, Craig 1945- .... **CLC 7, 31**
See also CA 45-48; CANR 2, 53

Novak, Joseph
See Kosinski, Jerzy (Nikodem)

Novalis 1772-1801 .... **NCLC 13**
See also DLB 90

Novis, Emile
See Weil, Simone (Adolphine)

Nowlan, Alden (Albert) 1933-1983 **CLC 15; DAC; DAM MST**
See also CA 9-12R; CANR 5; DLB 53

Noyes, Alfred 1880-1958 .... **TCLC 7**
See also CA 104; DLB 20

Nunn, Kem .... **CLC 34**
See also CA 159

Nye, Robert 1939- .. **CLC 13, 42; DAM NOV**
See also CA 33-36R; CANR 29, 67; DLB 14; MTCW 1; SATA 6

Nyro, Laura 1947- .... **CLC 17**

Oates, Joyce Carol 1938- **CLC 1, 2, 3, 6, 9, 11, 15, 19, 33, 52, 108; DA; DAB; DAC; DAM MST, NOV, POP; SSC 6; WLC**
See also AAYA 15; AITN 1; BEST 89:2; CA 5-8R; CANR 25, 45, 74; CDALB 1968-1988; DLB 2, 5, 130; DLBY 81; INT CANR-25; MTCW 1, 2

O'Brien, Darcy 1939-1998 .... **CLC 11**
See also CA 21-24R; 167; CANR 8, 59

O'Brien, E. G.
See Clarke, Arthur C(harles)

O'Brien, Edna 1936- **CLC 3, 5, 8, 13, 36, 65, 116; DAM NOV; SSC 10**
See also CA 1-4R; CANR 6, 41, 65; CDBLB 1960 to Present; DLB 14; MTCW 1, 2

O'Brien, Fitz-James 1828-1862 ..... **NCLC 21**
See also DLB 74

O'Brien, Flann .... **CLC 1, 4, 5, 7, 10, 47**
See also O Nuallain, Brian

O'Brien, Richard 1942- .... **CLC 17**
See also CA 124

O'Brien, (William) Tim(othy) 1946- . **CLC 7, 19, 40, 103; DAM POP**
See also AAYA 16; CA 85-88; CANR 40, 58; CDALBS; DLB 152; DLBD 9; DLBY 80; MTCW 2

Obstfelder, Sigbjoern 1866-1900 ... **TCLC 23**
See also CA 123

O'Casey, Sean 1880-1964 **CLC 1, 5, 9, 11, 15, 88; DAB; DAC; DAM DRAM, MST; WLCS**
See also CA 89-92; CANR 62; CDBLB 1914-1945; DLB 10; MTCW 1, 2

O'Cathasaigh, Sean
See O'Casey, Sean

Ochs, Phil 1940-1976 .... **CLC 17**
See also CA 65-68

O'Connor, Edwin (Greene) 1918-1968 **CLC 14**
See also CA 93-96; 25-28R

O'Connor, (Mary) Flannery 1925-1964 **C L C 1, 2, 3, 6, 10, 13, 15, 21, 66, 104; DA; DAB; DAC; DAM MST, NOV; SSC 1, 23; WLC**
See also AAYA 7; CA 1-4R; CANR 3, 41; CDALB 1941-1968; DLB 2, 152; DLBD 12; DLBY 80; MTCW 1, 2

O'Connor, Frank .... **CLC 23; SSC 5**
See also O'Donovan, Michael John
See also DLB 162

O'Dell, Scott 1898-1989 .... **CLC 30**
See also AAYA 3; CA 61-64; 129; CANR 12, 30; CLR 1, 16; DLB 52; JRDA; MAICYA; SATA 12, 60

Odets, Clifford 1906-1963 **CLC 2, 28, 98; DAM DRAM; DC 6**
See also CA 85-88; CANR 62; DLB 7, 26; MTCW 1, 2

O'Doherty, Brian 1934- .... **CLC 76**
See also CA 105

O'Donnell, K. M.
See Malzberg, Barry N(athaniel)

O'Donnell, Lawrence
See Kuttner, Henry

O'Donovan, Michael John 1903-1966 **CLC 14**
See also O'Connor, Frank
See also CA 93-96

Oe, Kenzaburo 1935- **CLC 10, 36, 86; DAM NOV; SSC 20**
See also CA 97-100; CANR 36, 50, 74; DLB 182; DLBY 94; MTCW 1, 2

O'Faolain, Julia 1932- .... **CLC 6, 19, 47, 108**
See also CA 81-84; CAAS 2; CANR 12, 61; DLB 14; MTCW 1

O'Faolain, Sean 1900-1991 **CLC 1, 7, 14, 32, 70; SSC 13**
See also CA 61-64; 134; CANR 12, 66; DLB 15, 162; MTCW 1, 2

O'Flaherty, Liam 1896-1984 **CLC 5, 34; SSC 6**
See also CA 101; 113; CANR 35; DLB 36, 162; DLBY 84; MTCW 1, 2

Ogilvy, Gavin
See Barrie, J(ames) M(atthew)

O'Grady, Standish (James) 1846-1928 **T C L C 5**
See also CA 104; 157

O'Grady, Timothy 1951- .... **CLC 59**
See also CA 138

O'Hara, Frank 1926-1966 . **CLC 2, 5, 13, 78; DAM POET**
See also CA 9-12R; 25-28R; CANR 33; DLB 5, 16, 193; MTCW 1, 2

O'Hara, John (Henry) 1905-1970 **CLC 1, 2, 3, 6, 11, 42; DAM NOV; SSC 15**
See also CA 5-8R; 25-28R; CANR 31, 60; CDALB 1929-1941; DLB 9, 86; DLBD 2; MTCW 1, 2

O Hehir, Diana 1922- .... **CLC 41**
See also CA 93-96

Okigbo, Christopher (Ifenayichukwu) 1932-1967 **CLC 25, 84; BLC 3; DAM MULT, POET; PC 7**
See also BW 1, 3; CA 77-80; CANR 74; DLB 125; MTCW 1, 2

Okri, Ben 1959- .... **CLC 87**
See also BW 2, 3; CA 130; 138; CANR 65; DLB 157; INT 138; MTCW 2

Olds, Sharon 1942- .... **CLC 32, 39, 85; DAM POET; PC 22**
See also CA 101; CANR 18, 41, 66; DLB 120; MTCW 2

Oldstyle, Jonathan
See Irving, Washington

Olesha, Yuri (Karlovich) 1899-1960 .. **CLC 8**
See also CA 85-88

Oliphant, Laurence 1829(?)-1888 .. **NCLC 47**
See also DLB 18, 166

Oliphant, Margaret (Oliphant Wilson) 1828-1897 .... **NCLC 11, 61; SSC 25**
See also DLB 18, 159, 190

Oliver, Mary 1935- .... **CLC 19, 34, 98**
See also CA 21-24R; CANR 9, 43; DLB 5, 193

Olivier, Laurence (Kerr) 1907-1989 . **CLC 20**
See also CA 111; 150; 129

Olsen, Tillie 1912- **CLC 4, 13, 114; DA; DAB; DAC; DAM MST; SSC 11**
See also CA 1-4R; CANR 1, 43, 74; CDALBS; DLB 28, 206; DLBY 80; MTCW 1, 2

Olson, Charles (John) 1910-1970 **CLC 1, 2, 5, 6, 9, 11, 29; DAM POET; PC 19**
See also CA 13-16; 25-28R; CABS 2; CANR

See also AITN 2; BW 2, 3; CA 41-44R; CANR 26, 66; DLB 33; MTCW 2; SATA 8, 108

Parmenides c. 515B.C.-c. 450B.C. **CMLC 22**
See also DLB 176

Parnell, Thomas 1679-1718 .... **LC 3**
See also DLB 94

Parra, Nicanor 1914- ...... **CLC 2, 102; DAM MULT; HLC**
See also CA 85-88; CANR 32; HW 1; MTCW 1

Parrish, Mary Frances
See Fisher, M(ary) F(rances) K(ennedy)

Parson
See Coleridge, Samuel Taylor

Parson Lot
See Kingsley, Charles

Partridge, Anthony
See Oppenheim, E(dward) Phillips

Pascal, Blaise 1623-1662 .... **LC 35**

Pascoli, Giovanni 1855-1912 .... **TCLC 45**
See also CA 170

Pasolini, Pier Paolo 1922-1975 . **CLC 20, 37, 106; PC 17**
See also CA 93-96; 61-64; CANR 63; DLB 128, 177; MTCW 1

Pasquini
See Silone, Ignazio

Pastan, Linda (Olenik) 1932- **CLC 27; DAM POET**
See also CA 61-64; CANR 18, 40, 61; DLB 5

Pasternak, Boris (Leonidovich) 1890-1960 **CLC 7, 10, 18, 63; DA; DAB; DAC; DAM MST, NOV, POET; PC 6; SSC 31; WLC**
See also CA 127; 116; MTCW 1, 2

Patchen, Kenneth 1911-1972 ... **CLC 1, 2, 18; DAM POET**
See also CA 1-4R; 33-36R; CANR 3, 35; DLB 16, 48; MTCW 1

Pater, Walter (Horatio) 1839-1894 .. **NCLC 7**
See also CDBLB 1832-1890; DLB 57, 156

Paterson, A(ndrew) B(arton) 1864-1941 **TCLC 32**
See also CA 155; SATA 97

Paterson, Katherine (Womeldorf) 1932-**C L C 12, 30**
See also AAYA 1; CA 21-24R; CANR 28, 59; CLR 7, 50; DLB 52; JRDA; MAICYA; MTCW 1; SATA 13, 53, 92

Patmore, Coventry Kersey Dighton 1823-1896 **NCLC 9**
See also DLB 35, 98

Paton, Alan (Stewart) 1903-1988 **CLC 4, 10, 25, 55, 106; DA; DAB; DAC; DAM MST, NOV; WLC**
See also AAYA 26; CA 13-16; 125; CANR 22; CAP 1; DLBD 17; MTCW 1, 2; SATA 11; SATA-Obit 56

Paton Walsh, Gillian 1937-
See Walsh, Jill Paton
See also CANR 38; JRDA; MAICYA; SAAS 3; SATA 4, 72, 109

Patton, George S. 1885-1945 .... **TCLC 79**

Paulding, James Kirke 1778-1860 ... **NCLC 2**
See also DLB 3, 59, 74

Paulin, Thomas Neilson 1949-
See Paulin, Tom
See also CA 123; 128

Paulin, Tom .... **CLC 37**
See also Paulin, Thomas Neilson
See also DLB 40

Paustovsky, Konstantin (Georgievich) 1892-1968 .... **CLC 40**
See also CA 93-96; 25-28R

Pavese, Cesare 1908-1950 ... **TCLC 3; PC 13; SSC 19**
See also CA 104; 169; DLB 128, 177

Pavic, Milorad 1929- .... **CLC 60**
See also CA 136; DLB 181

Pavlov, Ivan Petrovich 1849-1936 . **TCLC 91**
See also CA 118

Payne, Alan
See Jakes, John (William)

Paz, Gil
See Lugones, Leopoldo

Paz, Octavio 1914-1998**CLC 3, 4, 6, 10, 19, 51, 65, 119; DA; DAB; DAC; DAM MST, MULT, POET; HLC; PC 1; WLC**
See also CA 73-76; 165; CANR 32, 65; DLBY 90, 98; HW 1, 2; MTCW 1, 2

p'Bitek, Okot 1931-1982 .... **CLC 96; BLC 3; DAM MULT**
See also BW 2, 3; CA 124; 107; DLB 125; MTCW 1, 2

Peacock, Molly 1947- .... **CLC 60**
See also CA 103; CAAS 21; CANR 52; DLB 120

Peacock, Thomas Love 1785-1866 . **NCLC 22**
See also DLB 96, 116

Peake, Mervyn 1911-1968 .... **CLC 7, 54**
See also CA 5-8R; 25-28R; CANR 3; DLB 15, 160; MTCW 1; SATA 23

Pearce, Philippa .... **CLC 21**
See also Christie, (Ann) Philippa
See also CLR 9; DLB 161; MAICYA; SATA 1, 67

Pearl, Eric
See Elman, Richard (Martin)

Pearson, T(homas) R(eid) 1956- .... **CLC 39**
See also CA 120; 130; INT 130

Peck, Dale 1967- .... **CLC 81**
See also CA 146; CANR 72

Peck, John 1941- .... **CLC 3**
See also CA 49-52; CANR 3

Peck, Richard (Wayne) 1934- .... **CLC 21**
See also AAYA 1, 24; CA 85-88; CANR 19, 38; CLR 15; INT CANR-19; JRDA; MAICYA; SAAS 2; SATA 18, 55, 97

Peck, Robert Newton 1928- ..... **CLC 17; DA; DAC; DAM MST**
See also AAYA 3; CA 81-84; CANR 31, 63; CLR 45; JRDA; MAICYA; SAAS 1; SATA 21, 62; SATA-Essay 108

Peckinpah, (David) Sam(uel) 1925-1984**C L C 20**
See also CA 109; 114

Pedersen, Knut 1859-1952
See Hamsun, Knut
See also CA 104; 119; CANR 63; MTCW 1, 2

Peeslake, Gaffer
See Durrell, Lawrence (George)

Peguy, Charles Pierre 1873-1914 .. **TCLC 10**
See also CA 107

Peirce, Charles Sanders 1839-1914 **TCLC 81**

Pena, Ramon del Valle y
See Valle-Inclan, Ramon (Maria) del

Pendennis, Arthur Esquir
See Thackeray, William Makepeace

Penn, William 1644-1718 .... **LC 25**
See also DLB 24

PEPECE
See Prado (Calvo), Pedro

Pepys, Samuel 1633-1703 **LC 11; DA; DAB; DAC; DAM MST; WLC**
See also CDBLB 1660-1789; DLB 101

Percy, Walker 1916-1990**CLC 2, 3, 6, 8, 14, 18, 47, 65; DAM NOV, POP**

See also CA 1-4R; 131; CANR 1, 23, 64; DLB 2; DLBY 80, 90; MTCW 1, 2

Percy, William Alexander 1885-1942**TCLC 84**
See also CA 163; MTCW 2

Perec, Georges 1936-1982 .... **CLC 56, 116**
See also CA 141; DLB 83

Pereda (y Sanchez de Porrua), Jose Maria de 1833-1906 .... **TCLC 16**
See also CA 117

Pereda y Porrua, Jose Maria de
See Pereda (y Sanchez de Porrua), Jose Maria de

Peregoy, George Weems
See Mencken, H(enry) L(ouis)

Perelman, S(idney) J(oseph) 1904-1979 **C L C 3, 5, 9, 15, 23, 44, 49; DAM DRAM; SSC 32**
See also AITN 1, 2; CA 73-76; 89-92; CANR 18; DLB 11, 44; MTCW 1, 2

Peret, Benjamin 1899-1959 .... **TCLC 20**
See also CA 117

Peretz, Isaac Loeb 1851(?)-1915 ... **TCLC 16; SSC 26**
See also CA 109

Peretz, Yitzhok Leibush
See Peretz, Isaac Loeb

Perez Galdos, Benito 1843-1920 ... **TCLC 27; HLCS 2**
See also CA 125; 153; HW 1

Perrault, Charles 1628-1703 .... **LC 2**
See also MAICYA; SATA 25

Perry, Brighton
See Sherwood, Robert E(mmet)

Perse, St.-John
See Leger, (Marie-Rene Auguste) Alexis Saint-Leger

Perutz, Leo(pold) 1882-1957 .... **TCLC 60**
See also CA 147; DLB 81

Peseenz, Tulio F.
See Lopez y Fuentes, Gregorio

Pesetsky, Bette 1932- .... **CLC 28**
See also CA 133; DLB 130

Peshkov, Alexei Maximovich 1868-1936
See Gorky, Maxim
See also CA 105; 141; DA; DAC; DAM DRAM, MST, NOV; MTCW 2

Pessoa, Fernando (Antonio Nogueira) 1888-1935**TCLC 27; DAM MULT; HLC; PC 20**
See also CA 125

Peterkin, Julia Mood 1880-1961 .... **CLC 31**
See also CA 102; DLB 9

Peters, Joan K(aren) 1945- .... **CLC 39**
See also CA 158

Peters, Robert L(ouis) 1924- .... **CLC 7**
See also CA 13-16R; CAAS 8; DLB 105

Petofi, Sandor 1823-1849 .... **NCLC 21**

Petrakis, Harry Mark 1923- .... **CLC 3**
See also CA 9-12R; CANR 4, 30

Petrarch 1304-1374 **CMLC 20; DAM POET; PC 8**

Petrov, Evgeny .... **TCLC 21**
See also Kataev, Evgeny Petrovich

Petry, Ann (Lane) 1908-1997 ... **CLC 1, 7, 18**
See also BW 1, 3; CA 5-8R; 157; CAAS 6; CANR 4, 46; CLR 12; DLB 76; JRDA; MAICYA; MTCW 1; SATA 5; SATA-Obit 94

Petursson, Halligrimur 1614-1674 .... **LC 8**

Peychinovich
See Vazov, Ivan (Minchov)

Phaedrus c. 18B.C.-c. 50 .... **CMLC 25**
See also DLB 211

Philips, Katherine 1632-1664 .... **LC 30**
See also DLB 131

Potok, Chaim 1929- ... **CLC 2, 7, 14, 26, 112; DAM NOV**
See also AAYA 15; AITN 1, 2; CA 17-20R; CANR 19, 35, 64; DLB 28, 152; INT CANR-19; MTCW 1, 2; SATA 33, 106

Potter, (Helen) Beatrix 1866-1943
See Webb, (Martha) Beatrice (Potter)
See also MAICYA; MTCW 2

Potter, Dennis (Christopher George) 1935-1994 **CLC 58, 86**
See also CA 107; 145; CANR 33, 61; MTCW 1

Pound, Ezra (Weston Loomis) 1885-1972
CLC 1, 2, 3, 4, 5, 7, 10, 13, 18, 34, 48, 50, 112; DA; DAB; DAC; DAM MST, POET; PC 4; WLC
See also CA 5-8R; 37-40R; CANR 40; CDALB 1917-1929; DLB 4, 45, 63; DLBD 15; MTCW 1, 2

Povod, Reinaldo 1959-1994 .... **CLC 44**
See also CA 136; 146

Powell, Adam Clayton, Jr. 1908-1972 **CLC 89; BLC 3; DAM MULT**
See also BW 1, 3; CA 102; 33-36R

Powell, Anthony (Dymoke) 1905- **CLC 1, 3, 7, 9, 10, 31**
See also CA 1-4R; CANR 1, 32, 62; CDBLB 1945-1960; DLB 15; MTCW 1, 2

Powell, Dawn 1897-1965 .... **CLC 66**
See also CA 5-8R; DLBY 97

Powell, Padgett 1952- .... **CLC 34**
See also CA 126; CANR 63

Power, Susan 1961- .... **CLC 91**

Powers, J(ames) F(arl) 1917- **CLC 1, 4, 8, 57; SSC 4**
See also CA 1-4R; CANR 2, 61; DLB 130; MTCW 1

Powers, John J(ames) 1945-
See Powers, John R.
See also CA 69-72

Powers, John R. .... **CLC 66**
See also Powers, John J(ames)

Powers, Richard (S.) 1957- .... **CLC 93**
See also CA 148; CANR 80

Pownall, David 1938- .... **CLC 10**
See also CA 89-92; CAAS 18; CANR 49; DLB 14

Powys, John Cowper 1872-1963 **CLC 7, 9, 15, 46**
See also CA 85-88; DLB 15; MTCW 1, 2

Powys, T(heodore) F(rancis) 1875-1953 **TCLC 9**
See also CA 106; DLB 36, 162

Prado (Calvo), Pedro 1886-1952 ... **TCLC 75**
See also CA 131; HW 1

Prager, Emily 1952- .... **CLC 56**

Pratt, E(dwin) J(ohn) 1883(?)-1964 **CLC 19; DAC; DAM POET**
See also CA 141; 93-96; CANR 77; DLB 92

Premchand .... **TCLC 21**
See also Srivastava, Dhanpat Rai

Preussler, Otfried 1923- .... **CLC 17**
See also CA 77-80; SATA 24

Prevert, Jacques (Henri Marie) 1900-1977 **CLC 15**
See also CA 77-80; 69-72; CANR 29, 61; MTCW 1; SATA-Obit 30

Prevost, Abbe (Antoine Francois) 1697-1763 **LC 1**

Price, (Edward) Reynolds 1933- **CLC 3, 6, 13, 43, 50, 63; DAM NOV; SSC 22**
See also CA 1-4R; CANR 1, 37, 57; DLB 2; INT CANR-37

Price, Richard 1949- .... **CLC 6, 12**

See also CA 49-52; CANR 3; DLBY 81

Prichard, Katharine Susannah 1883-1969 **CLC 46**
See also CA 11-12; CANR 33; CAP 1; MTCW 1; SATA 66

Priestley, J(ohn) B(oynton) 1894-1984 **CLC 2, 5, 9, 34; DAM DRAM, NOV**
See also CA 9-12R; 113; CANR 33; CDBLB 1914-1945; DLB 10, 34, 77, 100, 139; DLBY 84; MTCW 1, 2

Prince 1958(?)- .... **CLC 35**

Prince, F(rank) T(empleton) 1912- .. **CLC 22**
See also CA 101; CANR 43, 79; DLB 20

Prince Kropotkin
See Kropotkin, Peter (Aleksieevich)

Prior, Matthew 1664-1721 .... **LC 4**
See also DLB 95

Prishvin, Mikhail 1873-1954 .... **TCLC 75**

Pritchard, William H(arrison) 1932- **CLC 34**
See also CA 65-68; CANR 23; DLB 111

Pritchett, V(ictor) S(awdon) 1900-1997 **C L C 5, 13, 15, 41; DAM NOV; SSC 14**
See also CA 61-64; 157; CANR 31, 63; DLB 15, 139; MTCW 1, 2

Private 19022
See Manning, Frederic

Probst, Mark 1925- .... **CLC 59**
See also CA 130

Prokosch, Frederic 1908-1989 ...... **CLC 4, 48**
See also CA 73-76; 128; DLB 48; MTCW 2

Propertius, Sextus c. 50B.C.-c. 16B.C. **C M L C 32**
See also DLB 211

Prophet, The
See Dreiser, Theodore (Herman Albert)

Prose, Francine 1947- .... **CLC 45**
See also CA 109; 112; CANR 46; SATA 101

Proudhon
See Cunha, Euclides (Rodrigues Pimenta) da

Proulx, Annie
See Proulx, E(dna) Annie

Proulx, E(dna) Annie 1935- ... **CLC 81; DAM POP**
See also CA 145; CANR 65; MTCW 2

Proust, (Valentin-Louis-George-Eugene-) Marcel 1871-1922 **TCLC 7, 13, 33; DA; DAB; DAC; DAM MST, NOV; WLC**
See also CA 104; 120; DLB 65; MTCW 1, 2

Prowler, Harley
See Masters, Edgar Lee

Prus, Boleslaw 1845-1912 .... **TCLC 48**

Pryor, Richard (Franklin Lenox Thomas) 1940- **CLC 26**
See also CA 122; 152

Przybyszewski, Stanislaw 1868-1927 **TCLC 36**
See also CA 160; DLB 66

Pteleon
See Grieve, C(hristopher) M(urray)
See also DAM POET

Puckett, Lute
See Masters, Edgar Lee

Puig, Manuel 1932-1990 **CLC 3, 5, 10, 28, 65; DAM MULT; HLC**
See also CA 45-48; CANR 2, 32, 63; DLB 113; HW 1, 2; MTCW 1, 2

Pulitzer, Joseph 1847-1911 .... **TCLC 76**
See also CA 114; DLB 23

Purdy, A(lfred) W(ellington) 1918- **CLC 3, 6, 14, 50; DAC; DAM MST, POET**
See also CA 81-84; CAAS 17; CANR 42, 66; DLB 88

Purdy, James (Amos) 1923- **CLC 2, 4, 10, 28, 52**

See also CA 33-36R; CAAS 1; CANR 19, 51; DLB 2; INT CANR-19; MTCW 1

Pure, Simon
See Swinnerton, Frank Arthur

Pushkin, Alexander (Sergeyevich) 1799-1837 **NCLC 3, 27; DA; DAB; DAC; DAM DRAM, MST, POET; PC 10; SSC 27; WLC**
See also DLB 205; SATA 61

P'u Sung-ling 1640-1715 .... **LC 49; SSC 31**

Putnam, Arthur Lee
See Alger, Horatio, Jr.

Puzo, Mario 1920-1999 **CLC 1, 2, 6, 36, 107; DAM NOV, POP**
See also CA 65-68; CANR 4, 42, 65; DLB 6; MTCW 1, 2

Pygge, Edward
See Barnes, Julian (Patrick)

Pyle, Ernest Taylor 1900-1945
See Pyle, Ernie
See also CA 115; 160

Pyle, Ernie 1900-1945 .... **TCLC 75**
See also Pyle, Ernest Taylor
See also DLB 29; MTCW 2

Pyle, Howard 1853-1911 .... **TCLC 81**
See also CA 109; 137; CLR 22; DLB 42, 188; DLBD 13; MAICYA; SATA 16, 100

Pym, Barbara (Mary Crampton) 1913-1980 **CLC 13, 19, 37, 111**
See also CA 13-14; 97-100; CANR 13, 34; CAP 1; DLB 14, 207; DLBY 87; MTCW 1, 2

Pynchon, Thomas (Ruggles, Jr.) 1937- **CLC 2, 3, 6, 9, 11, 18, 33, 62, 72; DA; DAB; DAC; DAM MST, NOV, POP; SSC 14; WLC**
See also BEST 90:2; CA 17-20R; CANR 22, 46, 73; DLB 2, 173; MTCW 1, 2

Pythagoras c. 570B.C.-c. 500B.C. . **CMLC 22**
See also DLB 176

Q
See Quiller-Couch, SirArthur (Thomas)

Qian Zhongshu
See Ch'ien Chung-shu

Qroll
See Dagerman, Stig (Halvard)

Quarrington, Paul (Lewis) 1953- ..... **CLC 65**
See also CA 129; CANR 62

Quasimodo, Salvatore 1901-1968 ..... **CLC 10**
See also CA 13-16; 25-28R; CAP 1; DLB 114; MTCW 1

Quay, Stephen 1947- .... **CLC 95**

Quay, Timothy 1947- .... **CLC 95**

Queen, Ellery .... **CLC 3, 11**
See also Dannay, Frederic; Davidson, Avram (James); Lee, Manfred B(ennington); Marlowe, Stephen; Sturgeon, Theodore (Hamilton); Vance, John Holbrook

Queen, Ellery, Jr.
See Dannay, Frederic; Lee, Manfred B(ennington)

Queneau, Raymond 1903-1976 **CLC 2, 5, 10, 42**
See also CA 77-80; 69-72; CANR 32; DLB 72; MTCW 1, 2

Quevedo, Francisco de 1580-1645 .... **LC 23**

Quiller-Couch, SirArthur (Thomas) 1863-1944 **TCLC 53**
See also CA 118; 166; DLB 135, 153, 190

Quin, Ann (Marie) 1936-1973 .... **CLC 6**
See also CA 9-12R; 45-48; DLB 14

Quinn, Martin
See Smith, Martin Cruz

Quinn, Peter 1947- .... **CLC 91**

Quinn, Simon

See Smith, Martin Cruz
Quiroga, Horacio (Sylvestre) 1878-1937
TCLC 20; DAM MULT; HLC
See also CA 117; 131; HW 1; MTCW 1
Quoirez, Francoise 1935- .... **CLC 9**
See also Sagan, Francoise
See also CA 49-52; CANR 6, 39, 73; MTCW
1, 2
Raabe, Wilhelm (Karl) 1831-1910. TCLC 45
See also CA 167; DLB 129
Rabe, David (William) 1940- ... **CLC 4, 8, 33;**
DAM DRAM
See also CA 85-88; CABS 3; CANR 59; DLB 7
Rabelais, Francois 1483-1553LC 5; DA; DAB;
DAC; DAM MST; WLC
Rabinovitch, Sholem 1859-1916
See Aleichem, Sholom
See also CA 104
Rabinyan, Dorit 1972- .... **CLC 119**
See also CA 170
Rachilde 1860-1953 .... **TCLC 67**
See also DLB 123, 192
Racine, Jean 1639-1699 .LC 28; DAB; DAM
MST
Radcliffe, Ann (Ward) 1764-1823NCLC 6, 55
See also DLB 39, 178
Radiguet, Raymond 1903-1923 ...... **TCLC 29**
See also CA 162; DLB 65
Radnoti, Miklos 1909-1944 .... **TCLC 16**
See also CA 118
Rado, James 1939- .... **CLC 17**
See also CA 105
Radvanyi, Netty 1900-1983
See Seghers, Anna
See also CA 85-88; 110
Rae, Ben
See Griffiths, Trevor
Raeburn, John (Hay) 1941- .... **CLC 34**
See also CA 57-60
Ragni, Gerome 1942-1991 .... **CLC 17**
See also CA 105; 134
Rahv, Philip 1908-1973 .... **CLC 24**
See also Greenberg, Ivan
See also DLB 137
Raimund, Ferdinand Jakob 1790-1836NCLC
69
See also DLB 90
Raine, Craig 1944- .... **CLC 32, 103**
See also CA 108; CANR 29, 51; DLB 40
Raine, Kathleen (Jessie) 1908- ...... **CLC 7, 45**
See also CA 85-88; CANR 46; DLB 20; MTCW
1
Rainis, Janis 1865-1929 .... **TCLC 29**
See also CA 170
Rakosi, Carl 1903- .... **CLC 47**
See also Rawley, Callman
See also CAAS 5; DLB 193
Raleigh, Richard
See Lovecraft, H(oward) P(hillips)
Raleigh, Sir Walter 1554(?)-1618 . LC 31, 39
See also CDBLB Before 1660; DLB 172
Rallentando, H. P.
See Sayers, Dorothy L(eigh)
Ramal, Walter
See de la Mare, Walter (John)
Ramana Maharshi 1879-1950 .... **TCLC 84**
Ramoacn y Cajal, Santiago 1852-1934T C L C
93
Ramon, Juan
See Jimenez (Mantecon), Juan Ramon
Ramos, Graciliano 1892-1953 .... **TCLC 32**
See also CA 167; HW 2
Rampersad, Arnold 1941- .... **CLC 44**

See also BW 2, 3; CA 127; 133; CANR 81; DLB
111; INT 133
Rampling, Anne
See Rice, Anne
Ramsay, Allan 1684(?)-1758 .... **LC 29**
See also DLB 95
Ramuz, Charles-Ferdinand 1878-1947T C L C
33
See also CA 165
Rand, Ayn 1905-1982CLC 3, 30, 44, 79; DA;
DAC; DAM MST, NOV, POP; WLC
See also AAYA 10; CA 13-16R; 105; CANR
27, 73; CDALBS; MTCW 1, 2
Randall, Dudley (Felker) 1914-CLC 1; BLC 3;
DAM MULT
See also BW 1, 3; CA 25-28R; CANR 23; DLB
41
Randall, Robert
See Silverberg, Robert
Ranger, Ken
See Creasey, John
Ransom, John Crowe 1888-1974CLC 2, 4, 5,
11, 24; DAM POET
See also CA 5-8R; 49-52; CANR 6, 34;
CDALBS; DLB 45, 63; MTCW 1, 2
Rao, Raja 1909- ..... **CLC 25, 56; DAM NOV**
See also CA 73-76; CANR 51; MTCW 1, 2
Raphael, Frederic (Michael) 1931-CLC 2, 14
See also CA 1-4R; CANR 1; DLB 14
Ratcliffe, James P.
See Mencken, H(enry) L(ouis)
Rathbone, Julian 1935- .... **CLC 41**
See also CA 101; CANR 34, 73
Rattigan, Terence (Mervyn) 1911-1977CLC 7;
DAM DRAM
See also CA 85-88; 73-76; CDBLB 1945-1960;
DLB 13; MTCW 1, 2
Ratushinskaya, Irina 1954- .... **CLC 54**
See also CA 129; CANR 68
Raven, Simon (Arthur Noel) 1927- .. CLC 14
See also CA 81-84
Ravenna, Michael
See Welty, Eudora
Rawley, Callman 1903-
See Rakosi, Carl
See also CA 21-24R; CANR 12, 32
Rawlings, Marjorie Kinnan 1896-1953T CLC
4
See also AAYA 20; CA 104; 137; CANR 74;
DLB 9, 22, 102; DLBD 17; JRDA; MAICYA;
MTCW 2; SATA 100; YABC 1
Ray, Satyajit 1921-1992 .. CLC 16, 76; DAM
MULT
See also CA 114; 137
Read, Herbert Edward 1893-1968 ..... CLC 4
See also CA 85-88; 25-28R; DLB 20, 149
Read, Piers Paul 1941- .... **CLC 4, 10, 25**
See also CA 21-24R; CANR 38; DLB 14; SATA
21
Reade, Charles 1814-1884 .... **NCLC 2, 74**
See also DLB 21
Reade, Hamish
See Gray, Simon (James Holliday)
Reading, Peter 1946- .... **CLC 47**
See also CA 103; CANR 46; DLB 40
Reaney, James 1926- .. CLC 13; DAC; DAM
MST
See also CA 41-44R; CAAS 15; CANR 42; DLB
68; SATA 43
Rebreanu, Liviu 1885-1944 .... **TCLC 28**
See also CA 165
Rechy, John (Francisco) 1934- CLC 1, 7, 14,
18, 107; DAM MULT; HLC

See also CA 5-8R; CAAS 4; CANR 6, 32, 64;
DLB 122; DLBY 82; HW 1, 2; INT CANR-
6
Redcam, Tom 1870-1933 .... **TCLC 25**
Reddin, Keith .... **CLC 67**
Redgrove, Peter (William) 1932- .. CLC 6, 41
See also CA 1-4R; CANR 3, 39, 77; DLB 40
Redmon, Anne .... **CLC 22**
See also Nightingale, Anne Redmon
See also DLBY 86
Reed, Eliot
See Ambler, Eric
Reed, Ishmael 1938-CLC 2, 3, 5, 6, 13, 32, 60;
BLC 3; DAM MULT
See also BW 2, 3; CA 21-24R; CANR 25, 48,
74; DLB 2, 5, 33, 169; DLBD 8; MTCW 1,
2
Reed, John (Silas) 1887-1920 .... **TCLC 9**
See also CA 106
Reed, Lou .... **CLC 21**
See also Firbank, Louis
Reeve, Clara 1729-1807 .... **NCLC 19**
See also DLB 39
Reich, Wilhelm 1897-1957 .... **TCLC 57**
Reid, Christopher (John) 1949- .... **CLC 33**
See also CA 140; DLB 40
Reid, Desmond
See Moorcock, Michael (John)
Reid Banks, Lynne 1929-
See Banks, Lynne Reid
See also CA 1-4R; CANR 6, 22, 38; CLR 24;
JRDA; MAICYA; SATA 22, 75
Reilly, William K.
See Creasey, John
Reiner, Max
See Caldwell, (Janet Miriam) Taylor (Holland)
Reis, Ricardo
See Pessoa, Fernando (Antonio Nogueira)
Remarque, Erich Maria 1898-1970 CLC 21;
DA; DAB; DAC; DAM MST, NOV
See also AAYA 27; CA 77-80; 29-32R; DLB
56; MTCW 1, 2
Remington, Frederic 1861-1909 .... TCLC 89
See also CA 108; 169; DLB 12, 186, 188; SATA
41
Remizov, A.
See Remizov, Aleksei (Mikhailovich)
Remizov, A. M.
See Remizov, Aleksei (Mikhailovich)
Remizov, Aleksei (Mikhailovich) 1877-1957
TCLC 27
See also CA 125; 133
Renan, Joseph Ernest 1823-1892 ..NCLC 26
Renard, Jules 1864-1910 .... **TCLC 17**
See also CA 117
Renault, Mary .... **CLC 3, 11, 17**
See also Challans, Mary
See also DLBY 83; MTCW 2
Rendell, Ruth (Barbara) 1930- . CLC 28, 48;
DAM POP
See also Vine, Barbara
See also CA 109; CANR 32, 52, 74; DLB 87;
INT CANR-32; MTCW 1, 2
Renoir, Jean 1894-1979 .... **CLC 20**
See also CA 129; 85-88
Resnais, Alain 1922- .... **CLC 16**
Reverdy, Pierre 1889-1960 .... **CLC 53**
See also CA 97-100; 89-92
Rexroth, Kenneth 1905-1982 CLC 1, 2, 6, 11,
22, 49, 112; DAM POET; PC 20
See also CA 5-8R; 107; CANR 14, 34, 63;
CDALB 1941-1968; DLB 16, 48, 165, 212;
DLBY 82; INT CANR-14; MTCW 1, 2

Rodgers, Mary 1931- .... CLC 12
See also CA 49-52; CANR 8, 55; CLR 20; INT
CANR-8; JRDA; MAICYA; SATA 8
Rodgers, W(illiam) R(obert) 1909-1969CLC 7
See also CA 85-88; DLB 20
Rodman, Eric
See Silverberg, Robert
Rodman, Howard 1920(?)-1985 .... CLC 65
See also CA 118
Rodman, Maia
See Wojciechowska, Maia (Teresa)
Rodriguez, Claudio 1934- .... CLC 10
See also DLB 134
Roelvaag, O(le) E(dvart) 1876-1931TCLC 17
See also CA 117; 171; DLB 9
Roethke, Theodore (Huebner) 1908-1963CLC
1, 3, 8, 11, 19, 46, 101; DAM POET; PC 15
See also CA 81-84; CABS 2; CDALB 1941-
1968; DLB 5, 206; MTCW 1, 2
Rogers, Samuel 1763-1855 .... NCLC 69
See also DLB 93
Rogers, Thomas Hunton 1927- .... CLC 57
See also CA 89-92; INT 89-92
Rogers, Will(iam Penn Adair) 1879-1935
TCLC 8, 71; DAM MULT
See also CA 105; 144; DLB 11; MTCW 2;
NNAL
Rogin, Gilbert 1929- .... CLC 18
See also CA 65-68; CANR 15
Rohan, Koda .... TCLC 22
See also Koda Shigeyuki
Rohlfs, Anna Katharine Green
See Green, Anna Katharine
Rohmer, Eric .... CLC 16
See also Scherer, Jean-Marie Maurice
Rohmer, Sax .... TCLC 28
See also Ward, Arthur Henry Sarsfield
See also DLB 70
Roiphe, Anne (Richardson) 1935- .. CLC 3, 9
See also CA 89-92; CANR 45, 73; DLBY 80;
INT 89-92
Rojas, Fernando de 1465-1541LC 23; HLCS 1
Rolfe, Frederick (William Serafino Austin
Lewis Mary) 1860-1913 .... TCLC 12
See also CA 107; DLB 34, 156
Rolland, Romain 1866-1944 .... TCLC 23
See also CA 118; DLB 65
Rolle, Richard c. 1300-c. 1349 ...... CMLC 21
See also DLB 146
Rolvaag, O(le) E(dvart)
See Roelvaag, O(le) E(dvart)
Romain Arnaud, Saint
See Aragon, Louis
Romains, Jules 1885-1972 .... CLC 7
See also CA 85-88; CANR 34; DLB 65; MTCW
1
Romero, Jose Ruben 1890-1952 .... TCLC 14
See also CA 114; 131; HW 1
Ronsard, Pierre de 1524-1585 .. LC 6; PC 11
Rooke, Leon 1934- .. CLC 25, 34; DAM POP
See also CA 25-28R; CANR 23, 53
Roosevelt, Franklin Delano 1882-1945T C L C
93
See also CA 116; 173
Roosevelt, Theodore 1858-1919 ..... TCLC 69
See also CA 115; 170; DLB 47, 186
Roper, William 1498-1578 .... LC 10
Roquelaure, A. N.
See Rice, Anne
Rosa, Joao Guimaraes 1908-1967 .. CLC 23;
HLCS 1
See also CA 89-92; DLB 113
Rose, Wendy 1948-CLC 85; DAM MULT; PC

13
See also CA 53-56; CANR 5, 51; DLB 175;
NNAL; SATA 12
Rosen, R. D.
See Rosen, Richard (Dean)
Rosen, Richard (Dean) 1949- .... CLC 39
See also CA 77-80; CANR 62; INT CANR-30
Rosenberg, Isaac 1890-1918 .... TCLC 12
See also CA 107; DLB 20
Rosenblatt, Joe .... CLC 15
See also Rosenblatt, Joseph
Rosenblatt, Joseph 1933-
See Rosenblatt, Joe
See also CA 89-92; INT 89-92
Rosenfeld, Samuel
See Tzara, Tristan
Rosenstock, Sami
See Tzara, Tristan
Rosenstock, Samuel
See Tzara, Tristan
Rosenthal, M(acha) L(ouis) 1917-1996. C L C
28
See also CA 1-4R; 152; CAAS 6; CANR 4, 51;
DLB 5; SATA 59
Ross, Barnaby
See Dannay, Frederic
Ross, Bernard L.
See Follett, Ken(neth Martin)
Ross, J. H.
See Lawrence, T(homas) E(dward)
Ross, John Hume
See Lawrence, T(homas) E(dward)
Ross, Martin
See Martin, Violet Florence
See also DLB 135
Ross, (James) Sinclair 1908-1996 ... CLC 13;
DAC; DAM MST; SSC 24
See also CA 73-76; CANR 81; DLB 88
Rossetti, Christina (Georgina) 1830-1894
NCLC 2, 50, 66; DA; DAB; DAC; DAM
MST, POET; PC 7; WLC
See also DLB 35, 163; MAICYA; SATA 20
Rossetti, Dante Gabriel 1828-1882 . NCLC 4,
77; DA; DAB; DAC; DAM MST, POET;
WLC
See also CDBLB 1832-1890; DLB 35
Rossner, Judith (Perelman) 1935-CLC 6, 9, 29
See also AITN 2; BEST 90:3; CA 17-20R;
CANR 18, 51, 73; DLB 6; INT CANR-18;
MTCW 1, 2
Rostand, Edmond (Eugene Alexis) 1868-1918
TCLC 6, 37; DA; DAB; DAC; DAM
DRAM, MST; DC 10
See also CA 104; 126; DLB 192; MTCW 1
Roth, Henry 1906-1995 ..... CLC 2, 6, 11, 104
See also CA 11-12; 149; CANR 38, 63; CAP 1;
DLB 28; MTCW 1, 2
Roth, Philip (Milton) 1933-CLC 1, 2, 3, 4, 6, 9,
15, 22, 31, 47, 66, 86, 119; DA; DAB; DAC;
DAM MST, NOV, POP; SSC 26; WLC
See also BEST 90:3; CA 1-4R; CANR 1, 22,
36, 55; CDALB 1968-1988; DLB 2, 28, 173;
DLBY 82; MTCW 1, 2
Rothenberg, Jerome 1931- .... CLC 6, 57
See also CA 45-48; CANR 1; DLB 5, 193
Roumain, Jacques (Jean Baptiste) 1907-1944
TCLC 19; BLC 3; DAM MULT
See also BW 1; CA 117; 125
Rourke, Constance (Mayfield) 1885-1941
TCLC 12
See also CA 107; YABC 1
Rousseau, Jean-Baptiste 1671-1741 ...... LC 9
Rousseau, Jean-Jacques 1712-1778LC 14, 36;

DA; DAB; DAC; DAM MST; WLC
Roussel, Raymond 1877-1933 .... TCLC 20
See also CA 117
Rovit, Earl (Herbert) 1927- .... CLC 7
See also CA 5-8R; CANR 12
Rowe, Elizabeth Singer 1674-1737 ...... LC 44
See also DLB 39, 95
Rowe, Nicholas 1674-1718 .... LC 8
See also DLB 84
Rowley, Ames Dorrance
See Lovecraft, H(oward) P(hillips)
Rowson, Susanna Haswell 1762(?)-1824
NCLC 5, 69
See also DLB 37, 200
Roy, Arundhati 1960(?)- .... CLC 109
See also CA 163; DLBY 97
Roy, Gabrielle 1909-1983 CLC 10, 14; DAB;
DAC; DAM MST
See also CA 53-56; 110; CANR 5, 61; DLB 68;
MTCW 1; SATA 104
Royko, Mike 1932-1997 .... CLC 109
See also CA 89-92; 157; CANR 26
Rozewicz, Tadeusz 1921- .. CLC 9, 23; DAM
POET
See also CA 108; CANR 36, 66; MTCW 1, 2
Ruark, Gibbons 1941- .... CLC 3
See also CA 33-36R; CAAS 23; CANR 14, 31,
57; DLB 120
Rubens, Bernice (Ruth) 1923- .... CLC 19, 31
See also CA 25-28R; CANR 33, 65; DLB 14,
207; MTCW 1
Rubin, Harold
See Robbins, Harold
Rudkin, (James) David 1936- .... CLC 14
See also CA 89-92; DLB 13
Rudnik, Raphael 1933- .... CLC 7
See also CA 29-32R
Ruffian, M.
See Hasek, Jaroslav (Matej Frantisek)
Ruiz, Jose Martinez .... CLC 11
See also Martinez Ruiz, Jose
Rukeyser, Muriel 1913-1980CLC 6, 10, 15, 27;
DAM POET; PC 12
See also CA 5-8R; 93-96; CANR 26, 60; DLB
48; MTCW 1, 2; SATA-Obit 22
Rule, Jane (Vance) 1931- .... CLC 27
See also CA 25-28R; CAAS 18; CANR 12; DLB
60
Rulfo, Juan 1918-1986 ...... CLC 8, 80; DAM
MULT; HLC; SSC 25
See also CA 85-88; 118; CANR 26; DLB 113;
HW 1, 2; MTCW 1, 2
Rumi, Jalal al-Din 1297-1373 .... CMLC 20
Runeberg, Johan 1804-1877 .... NCLC 41
Runyon, (Alfred) Damon 1884(?)-1946T C L C
10
See also CA 107; 165; DLB 11, 86, 171; MTCW
2
Rush, Norman 1933- .... CLC 44
See also CA 121; 126; INT 126
Rushdie, (Ahmed) Salman 1947-CLC 23, 31,
55, 100; DAB; DAC; DAM MST, NOV,
POP; WLCS
See also BEST 89:3; CA 108; 111; CANR 33,
56; DLB 194; INT 111; MTCW 1, 2
Rushforth, Peter (Scott) 1945- .... CLC 19
See also CA 101
Ruskin, John 1819-1900 .... TCLC 63
See also CA 114; 129; CDBLB 1832-1890;
DLB 55, 163, 190; SATA 24
Russ, Joanna 1937- .... CLC 15
See also CANR 11, 31, 65; DLB 8; MTCW 1
Russell, George William 1867-1935

See Baker, Jean H.
   See also CA 104; 153; CDBLB 1890-1914;
      DAM POET
Russell, (Henry) Ken(neth Alfred) 1927- **C L C
   16**
   See also CA 105
Russell, William Martin 1947- .... **CLC 60**
   See also CA 164
Rutherford, Mark .... **TCLC 25**
   See also White, William Hale
   See also DLB 18
Ruyslinck, Ward 1929- .... **CLC 14**
   See also Belser, Reimond Karel Maria de
Ryan, Cornelius (John) 1920-1974 ..... **CLC 7**
   See also CA 69-72; 53-56; CANR 38
Ryan, Michael 1946- .... **CLC 65**
   See also CA 49-52; DLBY 82
Ryan, Tim
   See Dent, Lester
Rybakov, Anatoli (Naumovich) 1911-1998
      CLC 23, 53
   See also CA 126; 135; 172; SATA 79; SATA-
      Obit 108
Ryder, Jonathan
   See Ludlum, Robert
Ryga, George 1932-1987**CLC 14; DAC; DAM
   MST**
   See also CA 101; 124; CANR 43; DLB 60
S. H.
   See Hartmann, Sadakichi
S. S.
   See Sassoon, Siegfried (Lorraine)
Saba, Umberto 1883-1957 .... **TCLC 33**
   See also CA 144; CANR 79; DLB 114
Sabatini, Rafael 1875-1950 .... **TCLC 47**
   See also CA 162
Sabato, Ernesto (R.) 1911-**CLC 10, 23; DAM
   MULT; HLC**
   See also CA 97-100; CANR 32, 65; DLB 145;
      HW 1, 2; MTCW 1, 2
Sa-Carniero, Mario de 1890-1916 . **TCLC 83**
Sacastru, Martin
   See Bioy Casares, Adolfo
Sacastru, Martin
   See Bioy Casares, Adolfo
Sacher-Masoch, Leopold von 1836(?)-1895
      NCLC 31
Sachs, Marilyn (Stickle) 1927- .... **CLC 35**
   See also AAYA 2; CA 17-20R; CANR 13, 47;
      CLR 2; JRDA; MAICYA; SAAS 2; SATA 3,
      68
Sachs, Nelly 1891-1970 .... **CLC 14, 98**
   See also CA 17-18; 25-28R; CAP 2; MTCW 2
Sackler, Howard (Oliver) 1929-1982 **CLC 14**
   See also CA 61-64; 108; CANR 30; DLB 7
Sacks, Oliver (Wolf) 1933- .... **CLC 67**
   See also CA 53-56; CANR 28, 50, 76; INT
      CANR-28; MTCW 1, 2
Sadakichi
   See Hartmann, Sadakichi
Sade, Donatien Alphonse Francois, Comte de
   1740-1814 .... **NCLC 47**
Sadoff, Ira 1945- .... **CLC 9**
   See also CA 53-56; CANR 5, 21; DLB 120
Saetone
   See Camus, Albert
Safire, William 1929- .... **CLC 10**
   See also CA 17-20R; CANR 31, 54
Sagan, Carl (Edward) 1934-1996**CLC 30, 112**
   See also AAYA 2; CA 25-28R; 155; CANR 11,
      36, 74; MTCW 1, 2; SATA 58; SATA-Obit
      94
Sagan, Francoise .... **CLC 3, 6, 9, 17, 36**

See also Quoirez, Francoise
   See also DLB 83; MTCW 2
Sahgal, Nayantara (Pandit) 1927- .... **CLC 41**
   See also CA 9-12R; CANR 11
Saint, H(arry) F. 1941- .... **CLC 50**
   See also CA 127
St. Aubin de Teran, Lisa 1953-
   See Teran, Lisa St. Aubin de
   See also CA 118; 126; INT 126
Saint Birgitta of Sweden c. 1303-1373**C M L C
   24**
Sainte-Beuve, Charles Augustin 1804-1869
      NCLC 5
**Saint-Exupery, Antoine (Jean Baptiste Marie
   Roger) de** 1900-1944**TCLC 2, 56; DAM
   NOV; WLC**
   See also CA 108; 132; CLR 10; DLB 72;
      MAICYA; MTCW 1, 2; SATA 20
St. John, David
   See Hunt, E(verette) Howard, (Jr.)
Saint-John Perse
   See Leger, (Marie-Rene Auguste) Alexis Saint-
      Leger
Saintsbury, George (Edward Bateman) 1845-
      1933 .... **TCLC 31**
   See also CA 160; DLB 57, 149
Sait Faik .... **TCLC 23**
   See also Abasiyanik, Sait Faik
Saki .... **TCLC 3; SSC 12**
   See also Munro, H(ector) H(ugh)
   See also MTCW 2
Sala, George Augustus .... **NCLC 46**
Salama, Hannu 1936- .... **CLC 18**
Salamanca, J(ack) R(ichard) 1922-**CLC 4, 15**
   See also CA 25-28R
Sale, J. Kirkpatrick
   See Sale, Kirkpatrick
Sale, Kirkpatrick 1937- .... **CLC 68**
   See also CA 13-16R; CANR 10
Salinas, Luis Omar 1937- ...... **CLC 90; DAM
   MULT; HLC**
   See also CA 131; CANR 81; DLB 82; HW 1, 2
Salinas (y Serrano), Pedro 1891(?)-1951
      TCLC 17
   See also CA 117; DLB 134
Salinger, J(erome) D(avid) 1919-**CLC 1, 3, 8,
   12, 55, 56; DA; DAB; DAC; DAM MST,
   NOV, POP; SSC 2, 28; WLC**
   See also AAYA 2; CA 5-8R; CANR 39; CDALB
      1941-1968; CLR 18; DLB 2, 102, 173;
      MAICYA; MTCW 1, 2; SATA 67
Salisbury, John
   See Caute, (John) David
Salter, James 1925- .... **CLC 7, 52, 59**
   See also CA 73-76; DLB 130
Saltus, Edgar (Everton) 1855-1921 . **TCLC 8**
   See also CA 105; DLB 202
Saltykov, Mikhail Evgrafovich 1826-1889
      NCLC 16
Samarakis, Antonis 1919- .... **CLC 5**
   See also CA 25-28R; CAAS 16; CANR 36
Sanchez, Florencio 1875-1910 .... **TCLC 37**
   See also CA 153; HW 1
Sanchez, Luis Rafael 1936- .... **CLC 23**
   See also CA 128; DLB 145; HW 1
Sanchez, Sonia 1934- .... **CLC 5, 116; BLC 3;
   DAM MULT; PC 9**
   See also BW 2, 3; CA 33-36R; CANR 24, 49,
      74; CLR 18; DLB 41; DLBD 8; MAICYA;
      MTCW 1, 2; SATA 22
Sand, George 1804-1876**NCLC 2, 42, 57; DA;
   DAB; DAC; DAM MST, NOV; WLC**
   See also DLB 119, 192

Sandburg, Carl (August) 1878-1967**CLC 1, 4,
   10, 15, 35; DA; DAB; DAC; DAM MST,
   POET; PC 2; WLC**
   See also AAYA 24; CA 5-8R; 25-28R; CANR
      35; CDALB 1865-1917; DLB 17,54;
      MAICYA; MTCW 1, 2; SATA 8
Sandburg, Charles
   See Sandburg, Carl (August)
Sandburg, Charles A.
   See Sandburg, Carl (August)
Sanders, (James) Ed(ward) 1939- .. **CLC 53;
   DAM POET**
   See also CA 13-16R; CAAS 21; CANR 13, 44,
      78; DLB 16
Sanders, Lawrence 1920-1998**CLC 41; DAM
   POP**
   See also BEST 89:4; CA 81-84; 165; CANR
      33, 62; MTCW 1
Sanders, Noah
   See Blount, Roy (Alton), Jr.
Sanders, Winston P.
   See Anderson, Poul (William)
Sandoz, Mari(e Susette) 1896-1966 .. **CLC 28**
   See also CA 1-4R; 25-28R; CANR 17, 64; DLB
      9, 212; MTCW 1, 2; SATA 5
Saner, Reg(inald Anthony) 1931- .... **CLC 9**
   See also CA 65-68
Sankara 788-820 .... **CMLC 32**
Sannazaro, Jacopo 1456(?)-1530 .... **LC 8**
Sansom, William 1912-1976 **CLC 2, 6; DAM
   NOV; SSC 21**
   See also CA 5-8R; 65-68; CANR 42; DLB 139;
      MTCW 1
Santayana, George 1863-1952 .... **TCLC 40**
   See also CA 115; DLB 54, 71; DLBD 13
Santiago, Danny .... **CLC 33**
   See also James, Daniel (Lewis)
   See also DLB 122
Santmyer, Helen Hoover 1895-1986 . **CLC 33**
   See also CA 1-4R; 118; CANR 15, 33; DLBY
      84; MTCW 1
Santoka, Taneda 1882-1940 .... **TCLC 72**
Santos, Bienvenido N(uqui) 1911-1996 . **C L C
   22; DAM MULT**
   See also CA 101; 151; CANR 19, 46
Sapper .... **TCLC 44**
   See also McNeile, Herman Cyril
Sapphire
   See Sapphire, Brenda
Sapphire, Brenda 1950- .... **CLC 99**
Sappho fl. 6th cent. B.C.- ...... **CMLC 3; DAM
   POET; PC 5**
   See also DLB 176
Saramago, Jose 1922- ...... **CLC 119; HLCS 1**
   See also CA 153
Sarduy, Severo 1937-1993**CLC 6, 97; HLCS 1**
   See also CA 89-92; 142; CANR 58, 81; DLB
      113; HW 1, 2
Sargeson, Frank 1903-1982 .... **CLC 31**
   See also CA 25-28R; 106; CANR 38, 79
Sarmiento, Felix Ruben Garcia
   See Dario, Ruben
Saro-Wiwa, Ken(ule Beeson) 1941-1995**C L C
   114**
   See also BW 2; CA 142; 150; CANR 60; DLB
      157
Saroyan, William 1908-1981**CLC 1, 8, 10, 29,
   34, 56; DA; DAB; DAC; DAM DRAM,
   MST, NOV; SSC 21; WLC**
   See also CA 5-8R; 103; CANR 30; CDALBS;
      DLB 7, 9, 86; DLBY 81; MTCW 1, 2; SATA
      23; SATA-Obit 24
Sarraute, Nathalie 1900-**CLC 1, 2, 4, 8, 10, 31,**

WLC
See also CDBLB Before 1660; DLB 167

Spicer, Jack 1925-1965 **CLC 8, 18, 72; DAM POET**
See also CA 85-88; DLB 5, 16, 193

Spiegelman, Art 1948- .... **CLC 76**
See also AAYA 10; CA 125; CANR 41, 55, 74; MTCW 2; SATA 109

Spielberg, Peter 1929- .... **CLC 6**
See also CA 5-8R; CANR 4, 48; DLBY 81

Spielberg, Steven 1947- .... **CLC 20**
See also AAYA 8, 24; CA 77-80; CANR 32; SATA 32

Spillane, Frank Morrison 1918-
See Spillane, Mickey
See also CA 25-28R; CANR 28, 63; MTCW 1, 2; SATA 66

Spillane, Mickey .... **CLC 3, 13**
See also Spillane, Frank Morrison
See also MTCW 2

Spinoza, Benedictus de 1632-1677 .... **LC 9**

Spinrad, Norman (Richard) 1940- ... **CLC 46**
See also CA 37-40R; CAAS 19; CANR 20; DLB 8; INT CANR-20

Spitteler, Carl (Friedrich Georg) 1845-1924 **TCLC 12**
See also CA 109; DLB 129

Spivack, Kathleen (Romola Drucker) 1938- **CLC 6**
See also CA 49-52

Spoto, Donald 1941- .... **CLC 39**
See also CA 65-68; CANR 11, 57

Springsteen, Bruce (F.) 1949- .... **CLC 17**
See also CA 111

Spurling, Hilary 1940- .... **CLC 34**
See also CA 104; CANR 25, 52

Spyker, John Howland
See Elman, Richard (Martin)

Squires, (James) Radcliffe 1917-1993 **CLC 51**
See also CA 1-4R; 140; CANR 6, 21

Srivastava, Dhanpat Rai 1880(?)-1936
See Premchand
See also CA 118

Stacy, Donald
See Pohl, Frederik

Stael, Germaine de 1766-1817
See Stael-Holstein, Anne Louise Germaine Necker Baronn
See also DLB 119

Stael-Holstein, Anne Louise Germaine Necker Baronn 1766-1817 .... **NCLC 3**
See also Stael, Germaine de
See also DLB 192

Stafford, Jean 1915-1979 **CLC 4, 7, 19, 68; SSC 26**
See also CA 1-4R; 85-88; CANR 3, 65; DLB 2, 173; MTCW 1, 2; SATA-Obit 22

Stafford, William (Edgar) 1914-1993 **CLC 4, 7, 29; DAM POET**
See also CA 5-8R; 142; CAAS 3; CANR 5, 22; DLB 5, 206; INT CANR-22

Stagnelius, Eric Johan 1793-1823 . **NCLC 61**

Staines, Trevor
See Brunner, John (Kilian Houston)

Stairs, Gordon
See Austin, Mary (Hunter)

Stalin, Joseph 1879-1953 .... **TCLC 92**

Stannard, Martin 1947- .... **CLC 44**
See also CA 142; DLB 155

Stanton, Elizabeth Cady 1815-1902 **TCLC 73**
See also CA 171; DLB 79

Stanton, Maura 1946- .... **CLC 9**
See also CA 89-92; CANR 15; DLB 120

Stanton, Schuyler
See Baum, L(yman) Frank

Stapledon, (William) Olaf 1886-1950 **T C L C 22**
See also CA 111; 162; DLB 15

Starbuck, George (Edwin) 1931-1996 **CLC 53; DAM POET**
See also CA 21-24R; 153; CANR 23

Stark, Richard
See Westlake, Donald E(dwin)

Staunton, Schuyler
See Baum, L(yman) Frank

Stead, Christina (Ellen) 1902-1983 **CLC 2, 5, 8, 32, 80**
See also CA 13-16R; 109; CANR 33, 40; MTCW 1, 2

Stead, William Thomas 1849-1912 **TCLC 48**
See also CA 167

Steele, Richard 1672-1729 .... **LC 18**
See also CDBLB 1660-1789; DLB 84, 101

Steele, Timothy (Reid) 1948- .... **CLC 45**
See also CA 93-96; CANR 16, 50; DLB 120

Steffens, (Joseph) Lincoln 1866-1936 **T C L C 20**
See also CA 117

Stegner, Wallace (Earle) 1909-1993 **CLC 9, 49, 81; DAM NOV; SSC 27**
See also AITN 1; BEST 90:3; CA 1-4R; 141; CAAS 9; CANR 1, 21, 46; DLB 9, 206; DLBY 93; MTCW 1, 2

Stein, Gertrude 1874-1946 **TCLC 1, 6, 28, 48; DA; DAB; DAC; DAM MST, NOV, POET; PC 18; WLC**
See also CA 104; 132; CDALB 1917-1929; DLB 4, 54, 86; DLBD 15; MTCW 1, 2

Steinbeck, John (Ernst) 1902-1968 **CLC 1, 5, 9, 13, 21, 34, 45, 75; DA; DAB; DAC; DAM DRAM, MST, NOV; SSC 11; WLC**
See also AAYA 12; CA 1-4R; 25-28R; CANR 1, 35; CDALB 1929-1941; DLB 7, 9, 212; DLBD 2; MTCW 1, 2; SATA 9

Steinem, Gloria 1934- .... **CLC 63**
See also CA 53-56; CANR 28, 51; MTCW 1, 2

Steiner, George 1929- ... **CLC 24; DAM NOV**
See also CA 73-76; CANR 31, 67; DLB 67; MTCW 1, 2; SATA 62

Steiner, K. Leslie
See Delany, Samuel R(ay, Jr.)

Steiner, Rudolf 1861-1925 .... **TCLC 13**
See also CA 107

Stendhal 1783-1842 **NCLC 23, 46; DA; DAB; DAC; DAM MST, NOV; SSC 27; WLC**
See also DLB 119

Stephen, Adeline Virginia
See Woolf, (Adeline) Virginia

Stephen, SirLeslie 1832-1904 .... **TCLC 23**
See also CA 123; DLB 57, 144, 190

Stephen, Sir Leslie
See Stephen, SirLeslie

Stephen, Virginia
See Woolf, (Adeline) Virginia

Stephens, James 1882(?)-1950 .... **TCLC 4**
See also CA 104; DLB 19, 153, 162

Stephens, Reed
See Donaldson, Stephen R.

Steptoe, Lydia
See Barnes, Djuna

Sterchi, Beat 1949- .... **CLC 65**

Sterling, Brett
See Bradbury, Ray (Douglas); Hamilton, Edmond

Sterling, Bruce 1954- .... **CLC 72**
See also CA 119; CANR 44

Sterling, George 1869-1926 .... **TCLC 20**
See also CA 117; 165; DLB 54

Stern, Gerald 1925- .... **CLC 40, 100**
See also CA 81-84; CANR 28; DLB 105

Stern, Richard (Gustave) 1928- .... **CLC 4, 39**
See also CA 1-4R; CANR 1, 25, 52; DLBY 87; INT CANR-25

Sternberg, Josef von 1894-1969 .... **CLC 20**
See also CA 81-84

Sterne, Laurence 1713-1768 ... **LC 2, 48; DA; DAB; DAC; DAM MST, NOV; WLC**
See also CDBLB 1660-1789; DLB 39

Sternheim, (William Adolf) Carl 1878-1942 **TCLC 8**
See also CA 105; DLB 56, 118

Stevens, Mark 1951- .... **CLC 34**
See also CA 122

Stevens, Wallace 1879-1955 **TCLC 3, 12, 45; DA; DAB; DAC; DAM MST, POET; PC 6; WLC**
See also CA 104; 124; CDALB 1929-1941; DLB 54; MTCW 1, 2

Stevenson, Anne (Katharine) 1933- **CLC 7, 33**
See also CA 17-20R; CAAS 9; CANR 9, 33; DLB 40; MTCW 1

Stevenson, Robert Louis (Balfour) 1850-1894 **NCLC 5, 14, 63; DA; DAB; DAC; DAM MST, NOV; SSC 11; WLC**
See also AAYA 24; CDBLB 1890-1914; CLR 10, 11; DLB 18, 57, 141, 156, 174; DLBD 13; JRDA; MAICYA; SATA 100; YABC 2

Stewart, J(ohn) I(nnes) M(ackintosh) 1906-1994 .... **CLC 7, 14, 32**
See also CA 85-88; 147; CAAS 3; CANR 47; MTCW 1, 2

Stewart, Mary (Florence Elinor) 1916- **CLC 7, 35, 117; DAB**
See also AAYA 29; CA 1-4R; CANR 1, 59; SATA 12

Stewart, Mary Rainbow
See Stewart, Mary (Florence Elinor)

Stifle, June
See Campbell, Maria

Stifter, Adalbert 1805-1868 **NCLC 41; SSC 28**
See also DLB 133

Still, James 1906- .... **CLC 49**
See also CA 65-68; CAAS 17; CANR 10, 26; DLB 9; SATA 29

Sting 1951-
See Sumner, Gordon Matthew
See also CA 167

Stirling, Arthur
See Sinclair, Upton (Beall)

Stitt, Milan 1941- .... **CLC 29**
See also CA 69-72

Stockton, Francis Richard 1834-1902
See Stockton, Frank R.
See also CA 108; 137; MAICYA; SATA 44

Stockton, Frank R. .... **TCLC 47**
See also Stockton, Francis Richard
See also DLB 42, 74; DLBD 13; SATA-Brief 32

Stoddard, Charles
See Kuttner, Henry

Stoker, Abraham 1847-1912
See Stoker, Bram
See also CA 105; 150; DA; DAC; DAM MST, NOV; SATA 29

Stoker, Bram 1847-1912 **TCLC 8; DAB; WLC**
See also Stoker, Abraham
See also AAYA 23; CDBLB 1890-1914; DLB 36, 70, 178

Stolz, Mary (Slattery) 1920- .... **CLC 12**

See also AAYA 8; AITN 1; CA 5-8R; CANR 13, 41; JRDA; MAICYA; SAAS 3; SATA 10, 71

Stone, Irving 1903-1989 .. **CLC 7; DAM POP**
See also AITN 1; CA 1-4R; 129; CAAS 3; CANR 1, 23; INT CANR-23; MTCW 1, 2; SATA 3; SATA-Obit 64

Stone, Oliver (William) 1946- .... **CLC 73**
See also AAYA 15; CA 110; CANR 55

Stone, Robert (Anthony) 1937-**CLC 5, 23, 42**
See also CA 85-88; CANR 23, 66; DLB 152; INT CANR-23; MTCW 1

Stone, Zachary
See Follett, Ken(neth Martin)

Stoppard, Tom 1937-**CLC 1, 3, 4, 5, 8, 15, 29, 34, 63, 91; DA; DAB; DAC; DAM DRAM, MST; DC 6; WLC**
See also CA 81-84; CANR 39, 67; CDBLB 1960 to Present; DLB 13; DLBY 85; MTCW 1, 2

Storey, David (Malcolm) 1933-**CLC 2, 4, 5, 8; DAM DRAM**
See also CA 81-84; CANR 36; DLB 13, 14, 207; MTCW 1

Storm, Hyemeyohsts 1935- ...... **CLC 3; DAM MULT**
See also CA 81-84; CANR 45; NNAL

Storm, Theodor 1817-1888 .... **SSC 27**

Storm, (Hans) Theodor (Woldsen) 1817-1888 **NCLC 1; SSC 27**
See also DLB 129

Storni, Alfonsina 1892-1938 . **TCLC 5; DAM MULT; HLC**
See also CA 104; 131; HW 1

Stoughton, William 1631-1701 .... **LC 38**
See also DLB 24

Stout, Rex (Todhunter) 1886-1975 ..... **CLC 3**
See also AITN 2; CA 61-64; CANR 71

Stow, (Julian) Randolph 1935- .. **CLC 23, 48**
See also CA 13-16R; CANR 33; MTCW 1

Stowe, Harriet (Elizabeth) Beecher 1811-1896 **NCLC 3, 50; DA; DAB; DAC; DAM MST, NOV; WLC**
See also CDALB 1865-1917; DLB 1, 12, 42, 74, 189; JRDA; MAICYA; YABC 1

Strachey, (Giles) Lytton 1880-1932 **TCLC 12**
See also CA 110; DLB 149; DLBD 10; MTCW 2

Strand, Mark 1934- **CLC 6, 18, 41, 71; DAM POET**
See also CA 21-24R; CANR 40, 65; DLB 5; SATA 41

Straub, Peter (Francis) 1943- . **CLC 28, 107; DAM POP**
See also BEST 89:1; CA 85-88; CANR 28, 65; DLBY 84; MTCW 1, 2

Strauss, Botho 1944- .... **CLC 22**
See also CA 157; DLB 124

Streatfeild, (Mary) Noel 1895(?)-1986**CLC 21**
See also CA 81-84; 120; CANR 31; CLR 17; DLB 160; MAICYA; SATA 20; SATA-Obit 48

Stribling, T(homas) S(igismund) 1881-1965 **CLC 23**
See also CA 107; DLB 9

Stringer, Arthur 1874-1950 .... **TCLC 37**
See also CA 161; DLB 92

Stringer, David
See Roberts, Keith (John Kingston)

Stroheim, Erich von 1885-1957 ..... **TCLC 71**

Strugatskii, Arkadii (Natanovich) 1925-1991 **CLC 27**
See also CA 106; 135

Strugatskii, Boris (Natanovich) 1933-**CLC 27**
See also CA 106

Strummer, Joe 1953(?)- .... **CLC 30**

Strunk, William, Jr. 1869-1946 ...... **TCLC 92**
See also CA 118; 164

Stuart, Don A.
See Campbell, John W(ood, Jr.)

Stuart, Ian
See MacLean, Alistair (Stuart)

Stuart, Jesse (Hilton) 1906-1984**CLC 1, 8, 11, 14, 34; SSC 31**
See also CA 5-8R; 112; CANR 31; DLB 9, 48, 102; DLBY 84; SATA 2; SATA-Obit 36

Sturgeon, Theodore (Hamilton) 1918-1985 **CLC 22, 39**
See also Queen, Ellery
See also CA 81-84; 116; CANR 32; DLB 8; DLBY 85; MTCW 1, 2

Sturges, Preston 1898-1959 .... **TCLC 48**
See also CA 114; 149; DLB 26

Styron, William 1925-**CLC 1, 3, 5, 11, 15, 60; DAM NOV, POP; SSC 25**
See also BEST 90:4; CA 5-8R; CANR 6, 33, 74; CDALB 1968-1988; DLB 2, 143; DLBY 80; INT CANR-6; MTCW 1, 2

Su, Chien 1884-1918
See Su Man-shu
See also CA 123

Suarez Lynch, B.
See Bioy Casares, Adolfo; Borges, Jorge Luis

Suckow, Ruth 1892-1960 .... **SSC 18**
See also CA 113; DLB 9, 102

Sudermann, Hermann 1857-1928 .. **TCLC 15**
See also CA 107; DLB 118

Sue, Eugene 1804-1857 .... **NCLC 1**
See also DLB 119

Sueskind, Patrick 1949- .... **CLC 44**
See also Suskind, Patrick

Sukenick, Ronald 1932- .... **CLC 3, 4, 6, 48**
See also CA 25-28R; CAAS 8; CANR 32; DLB 173; DLBY 81

Suknaski, Andrew 1942- .... **CLC 19**
See also CA 101; DLB 53

Sullivan, Vernon
See Vian, Boris

Sully Prudhomme 1839-1907 .... **TCLC 31**

Su Man-shu .... **TCLC 24**
See also Su, Chien

Summerforest, Ivy B.
See Kirkup, James

Summers, Andrew James 1942- .... **CLC 26**

Summers, Andy
See Summers, Andrew James

Summers, Hollis (Spurgeon, Jr.) 1916-**CLC 10**
See also CA 5-8R; CANR 3; DLB 6

Summers, (Alphonsus Joseph-Mary Augustus) Montague 1880-1948 .... **TCLC 16**
See also CA 118; 163

Sumner, Gordon Matthew .... **CLC 26**
See also Sting

Surtees, Robert Smith 1803-1864 .. **NCLC 14**
See also DLB 21

Susann, Jacqueline 1921-1974 .... **CLC 3**
See also AITN 1; CA 65-68; 53-56; MTCW 1, 2

Su Shih 1036-1101 .... **CMLC 15**

Suskind, Patrick
See Sueskind, Patrick
See also CA 145

Sutcliff, Rosemary 1920-1992**CLC 26; DAB; DAC; DAM MST, POP**
See also AAYA 10; CA 5-8R; 139; CANR 37; CLR 1, 37; JRDA; MAICYA; SATA 6, 44, 78; SATA-Obit 73

Sutro, Alfred 1863-1933 .... **TCLC 6**
See also CA 105; DLB 10

Sutton, Henry
See Slavitt, David R(ytman)

Svevo, Italo 1861-1928 . **TCLC 2, 35; SSC 25**
See also Schmitz, Aron Hector

Swados, Elizabeth (A.) 1951- .... **CLC 12**
See also CA 97-100; CANR 49; INT 97-100

Swados, Harvey 1920-1972 .... **CLC 5**
See also CA 5-8R; 37-40R; CANR 6; DLB 2

Swan, Gladys 1934- .... **CLC 69**
See also CA 101; CANR 17, 39

Swarthout, Glendon (Fred) 1918-1992**CLC 35**
See also CA 1-4R; 139; CANR 1, 47; SATA 26

Sweet, Sarah C.
See Jewett, (Theodora) Sarah Orne

Swenson, May 1919-1989**CLC 4, 14, 61, 106; DA; DAB; DAC; DAM MST, POET; PC 14**
See also CA 5-8R; 130; CANR 36, 61; DLB 5; MTCW 1, 2; SATA 15

Swift, Augustus
See Lovecraft, H(oward) P(hillips)

Swift, Graham (Colin) 1949- ...... **CLC 41, 88**
See also CA 117; 122; CANR 46, 71; DLB 194; MTCW 2

Swift, Jonathan 1667-1745 ..... **LC 1, 42; DA; DAB; DAC; DAM MST, NOV, POET; PC 9; WLC**
See also CDBLB 1660-1789; CLR 53; DLB 39, 95, 101; SATA 19

Swinburne, Algernon Charles 1837-1909 **TCLC 8, 36; DA; DAB; DAC; DAM MST, POET; PC 24; WLC**
See also CA 105; 140; CDBLB 1832-1890; DLB 35, 57

Swinfen, Ann .... **CLC 34**

Swinnerton, Frank Arthur 1884-1982**CLC 31**
See also CA 108; DLB 34

Swithen, John
See King, Stephen (Edwin)

Sylvia
See Ashton-Warner, Sylvia (Constance)

Symmes, Robert Edward
See Duncan, Robert (Edward)

Symonds, John Addington 1840-1893 **NCLC 34**
See also DLB 57, 144

Symons, Arthur 1865-1945 .... **TCLC 11**
See also CA 107; DLB 19, 57, 149

Symons, Julian (Gustave) 1912-1994 **CLC 2, 14, 32**
See also CA 49-52; 147; CAAS 3; CANR 3, 33, 59; DLB 87, 155; DLBY 92; MTCW 1

Synge, (Edmund) J(ohn) M(illington) 1871-1909 ... **TCLC 6, 37; DAM DRAM; DC 2**
See also CA 104; 141; CDBLB 1890-1914; DLB 10, 19

Syruc, J.
See Milosz, Czeslaw

Szirtes, George 1948- .... **CLC 46**
See also CA 109; CANR 27, 61

Szymborska, Wislawa 1923- .... **CLC 99**
See also CA 154; DLBY 96; MTCW 2

T. O., Nik
See Annensky, Innokenty (Fyodorovich)

Tabori, George 1914- .... **CLC 19**
See also CA 49-52; CANR 4, 69

Tagore, Rabindranath 1861-1941TCLC 3, 53;
DAM DRAM, POET; PC 8
See also CA 104; 120; MTCW 1, 2

Taine, Hippolyte Adolphe 1828-1893. N C L C
15

Talese, Gay 1932- .... CLC 37
See also AITN 1; CA 1-4R; CANR 9, 58; DLB
185; INT CANR-9; MTCW 1, 2

Tallent, Elizabeth (Ann) 1954- .... CLC 45
See also CA 117; CANR 72; DLB 130

Tally, Ted 1952- .... CLC 42
See also CA 120; 124; INT 124

Talvik, Heiti 1904-1947 .... TCLC 87

Tamayo y Baus, Manuel 1829-1898 NCLC 1

Tammsaare, A(nton) H(ansen) 1878-1940
TCLC 27
See also CA 164

Tam'si, Tchicaya U
See Tchicaya, Gerald Felix

Tan, Amy (Ruth) 1952- . CLC 59, 120; DAM
MULT, NOV, POP
See also AAYA 9; BEST 89:3; CA 136; CANR
54; CDALBS; DLB 173; MTCW 2; SATA
75

Tandem, Felix
See Spitteler, Carl (Friedrich Georg)

Tanizaki, Jun'ichiro 1886-1965CLC 8, 14, 28;
SSC 21
See also CA 93-96; 25-28R; DLB 180; MTCW
2

Tanner, William
See Amis, Kingsley (William)

Tao Lao
See Storni, Alfonsina

Tarassoff, Lev
See Troyat, Henri

Tarbell, Ida M(inerva) 1857-1944 . TCLC 40
See also CA 122; DLB 47

Tarkington, (Newton) Booth 1869-1946TCLC
9
See also CA 110; 143; DLB 9, 102; MTCW 2;
SATA 17

Tarkovsky, Andrei (Arsenyevich) 1932-1986
CLC 75
See also CA 127

Tartt, Donna 1964(?)- .... CLC 76
See also CA 142

Tasso, Torquato 1544-1595 .... LC 5

Tate, (John Orley) Allen 1899-1979CLC 2, 4,
6, 9, 11, 14, 24
See also CA 5-8R; 85-88; CANR 32; DLB 4,
45, 63; DLBD 17; MTCW 1, 2

Tate, Ellalice
See Hibbert, Eleanor Alice Burford

Tate, James (Vincent) 1943- ..... CLC 2, 6, 25
See also CA 21-24R; CANR 29, 57; DLB 5,
169

Tavel, Ronald 1940- .... CLC 6
See also CA 21-24R; CANR 33

Taylor, C(ecil) P(hilip) 1929-1981 .... CLC 27
See also CA 25-28R; 105; CANR 47

Taylor, Edward 1642(?)-1729 ..... LC 11; DA;
DAB; DAC; DAM MST, POET
See also DLB 24

Taylor, Eleanor Ross 1920- .... CLC 5
See also CA 81-84; CANR 70

Taylor, Elizabeth 1912-1975 ..... CLC 2, 4, 29
See also CA 13-16R; CANR 9, 70; DLB 139;
MTCW 1; SATA 13

Taylor, Frederick Winslow 1856-1915 T C L C
76

Taylor, Henry (Splawn) 1942- .... CLC 44
See also CA 33-36R; CAAS 7; CANR 31; DLB

5

Taylor, Kamala (Purnaiya) 1924-
See Markandaya, Kamala
See also CA 77-80

Taylor, Mildred D. .... CLC 21
See also AAYA 10; BW 1; CA 85-88; CANR
25; CLR 9, 59; DLB 52; JRDA; MAICYA;
SAAS 5; SATA 15, 70

Taylor, Peter (Hillsman) 1917-1994CLC 1, 4,
18, 37, 44, 50, 71; SSC 10
See also CA 13-16R; 147; CANR 9, 50; DLBY
81, 94; INT CANR-9; MTCW 1, 2

Taylor, Robert Lewis 1912-1998 .... CLC 14
See also CA 1-4R; 170; CANR 3, 64; SATA 10

Tchekhov, Anton
See Chekhov, Anton (Pavlovich)

Tchicaya, Gerald Felix 1931-1988 .. CLC 101
See also CA 129; 125; CANR 81

Tchicaya U Tam'si
See Tchicaya, Gerald Felix

Teasdale, Sara 1884-1933 .... TCLC 4
See also CA 104; 163; DLB 45; SATA 32

Tegner, Esaias 1782-1846 .... NCLC 2

Teilhard de Chardin, (Marie Joseph) Pierre
1881-1955 .... TCLC 9
See also CA 105

Temple, Ann
See Mortimer, Penelope (Ruth)

Tennant, Emma (Christina) 1937-CLC 13, 52
See also CA 65-68; CAAS 9; CANR 10, 38,
59; DLB 14

Tenneshaw, S. M.
See Silverberg, Robert

Tennyson, Alfred 1809-1892 ... NCLC 30, 65;
DA; DAB; DAC; DAM MST, POET; PC
6; WLC
See also CDBLB 1832-1890; DLB 32

Teran, Lisa St. Aubin de .... CLC 36
See also St. Aubin de Teran, Lisa

Terence c. 184B.C.-c. 159B.C.CMLC 14; DC 7
See also DLB 211

Teresa de Jesus, St. 1515-1582 .... LC 18

Terkel, Louis 1912-
See Terkel, Studs
See also CA 57-60; CANR 18, 45, 67; MTCW
1, 2

Terkel, Studs .... CLC 38
See also Terkel, Louis
See also AITN 1; MTCW 2

Terry, C. V.
See Slaughter, Frank G(ill)

Terry, Megan 1932- .... CLC 19
See also CA 77-80; CABS 3; CANR 43; DLB 7

Tertullian c. 155-c. 245 .... CMLC 29

Tertz, Abram
See Sinyavsky, Andrei (Donatevich)

Tesich, Steve 1943(?)-1996 .... CLC 40, 69
See also CA 105; 152; DLBY 83

Tesla, Nikola 1856-1943 .... TCLC 88

Teternikov, Fyodor Kuzmich 1863-1927
See Sologub, Fyodor
See also CA 104

Tevis, Walter 1928-1984 .... CLC 42
See also CA 113

Tey, Josephine .... TCLC 14
See also Mackintosh, Elizabeth
See also DLB 77

Thackeray, William Makepeace 1811-1863
NCLC 5, 14, 22, 43; DA; DAB; DAC; DAM
MST, NOV; WLC
See also CDBLB 1832-1890; DLB 21, 55, 159,
163; SATA 23

Thakura, Ravindranatha

See Tagore, Rabindranath

Tharoor, Shashi 1956- .... CLC 70
See also CA 141

Thelwell, Michael Miles 1939- .... CLC 22
See also BW 2; CA 101

Theobald, Lewis, Jr.
See Lovecraft, H(oward) P(hillips)

Theodorescu, Ion N. 1880-1967
See Arghezi, Tudor
See also CA 116

Theriault, Yves 1915-1983 .... CLC 79; DAC;
DAM MST
See also CA 102; DLB 88

Theroux, Alexander (Louis) 1939-CLC 2, 25
See also CA 85-88; CANR 20, 63

Theroux, Paul (Edward) 1941- CLC 5, 8, 11,
15, 28, 46; DAM POP
See also AAYA 28; BEST 89:4; CA 33-36R;
CANR 20, 45, 74; CDALBS; DLB 2; MTCW
1, 2; SATA 44, 109

Thesen, Sharon 1946- .... CLC 56
See also CA 163

Thevenin, Denis
See Duhamel, Georges

Thibault, Jacques Anatole Francois 1844-1924
See France, Anatole
See also CA 106; 127; DAM NOV; MTCW 1,
2

Thiele, Colin (Milton) 1920- .... CLC 17
See also CA 29-32R; CANR 12, 28, 53; CLR
27; MAICYA; SAAS 2; SATA 14, 72

Thomas, Audrey (Callahan) 1935-CLC 7, 13,
37, 107; SSC 20
See also AITN 2; CA 21-24R; CAAS 19; CANR
36, 58; DLB 60; MTCW 1

Thomas, D(onald) M(ichael) 1935- . CLC 13,
22, 31
See also CA 61-64; CAAS 11; CANR 17, 45,
75; CDBLB 1960 to Present; DLB 40, 207;
INT CANR-17; MTCW 1, 2

Thomas, Dylan (Marlais) 1914-1953TCLC 1,
8, 45; DA; DAB; DAC; DAM DRAM,
MST, POET; PC 2; SSC 3; WLC
See also CA 104; 120; CANR 65; CDBLB
1945-1960; DLB 13, 20, 139; MTCW 1, 2;
SATA 60

Thomas, (Philip) Edward 1878-1917 . T C L C
10; DAM POET
See also CA 106; 153; DLB 98

Thomas, Joyce Carol 1938- .... CLC 35
See also AAYA 12; BW 2, 3; CA 113; 116;
CANR 48; CLR 19; DLB 33; INT 116;
JRDA; MAICYA; MTCW 1, 2; SAAS 7;
SATA 40, 78

Thomas, Lewis 1913-1993 .... CLC 35
See also CA 85-88; 143; CANR 38, 60; MTCW
1, 2

Thomas, M. Carey 1857-1935 .... TCLC 89

Thomas, Paul
See Mann, (Paul) Thomas

Thomas, Piri 1928- .... CLC 17; HLCS 2
See also CA 73-76; HW 1

Thomas, R(onald) S(tuart) 1913- CLC 6, 13,
48; DAB; DAM POET
See also CA 89-92; CAAS 4; CANR 30;
CDBLB 1960 to Present; DLB 27; MTCW 1

Thomas, Ross (Elmore) 1926-1995 ... CLC 39
See also CA 33-36R; 150; CANR 22, 63

Thompson, Francis Clegg
See Mencken, H(enry) L(ouis)

Thompson, Francis Joseph 1859-1907TCLC 4
See also CA 104; CDBLB 1890-1914; DLB 19

Thompson, Hunter S(tockton) 1939- CLC 9,

17, 40, 104; DAM POP
See also BEST 89:1; CA 17-20R; CANR 23, 46, 74, 77; DLB 185; MTCW 1, 2

Thompson, James Myers
See Thompson, Jim (Myers)

Thompson, Jim (Myers) 1906-1977(?)CLC 69
See also CA 140

Thompson, Judith .... CLC 39

Thomson, James 1700-1748 ..: LC 16, 29, 40;
DAM POET
See also DLB 95

Thomson, James 1834-1882 NCLC 18; DAM
POET
See also DLB 35

Thoreau, Henry David 1817-1862NCLC 7, 21, 61; DA; DAB; DAC; DAM MST; WLC
See also CDALB 1640-1865; DLB 1

Thornton, Hall
See Silverberg, Robert

Thucydides c. 455B.C.-399B.C. .... CMLC 17
See also DLB 176

Thurber, James (Grover) 1894-1961 . CLC 5, 11, 25; DA; DAB; DAC; DAM DRAM, MST, NOV; SSC 1
See also CA 73-76; CANR 17, 39; CDALB 1929-1941; DLB 4, 11, 22, 102; MAICYA; MTCW 1, 2; SATA 13

Thurman, Wallace (Henry) 1902-1934T C L C 6; BLC 3; DAM MULT
See also BW 1, 3; CA 104; 124; CANR 81; DLB 51

Ticheburn, Cheviot
See Ainsworth, William Harrison

Tieck, (Johann) Ludwig 1773-1853 NCLC 5, 46; SSC 31
See also DLB 90

Tiger, Derry
See Ellison, Harlan (Jay)

Tilghman, Christopher 1948(?)- .... CLC 65
See also CA 159

Tillinghast, Richard (Williford) 1940-CLC 29
See also CA 29-32R; CAAS 23; CANR 26, 51

Timrod, Henry 1828-1867 .... NCLC 25
See also DLB 3

Tindall, Gillian (Elizabeth) 1938- ...... CLC 7
See also CA 21-24R; CANR 11, 65

Tiptree, James, Jr. .... CLC 48, 50
See also Sheldon, Alice Hastings Bradley
See also DLB 8

Titmarsh, Michael Angelo
See Thackeray, William Makepeace

Tocqueville, Alexis (Charles Henri Maurice Clerel, Comte) de 1805-1859
.... NCLC 7, 63

Tolkien, J(ohn) R(onald) R(euel) 1892-1973
CLC 1, 2, 3, 8, 12, 38; DA; DAB; DAC; DAM MST, NOV, POP; WLC
See also AAYA 10; AITN 1; 45-48; CANR 36; CAP 2; CDBLB 1914-1945; CLR 56; DLB 15, 160; JRDA; MAICYA; MTCW 1, 2; SATA 2, 32, 100; SATA-Obit 24

Toller, Ernst 1893-1939 .... TCLC 10
See also CA 107; DLB 124

Tolson, M. B.
See Tolson, Melvin B(eaunorus)

Tolson, Melvin B(eaunorus) 1898(?)-1966
CLC 36, 105; BLC 3; DAM MULT, POET
See also BW 1, 3; CA 124; 89-92; CANR 80; DLB 48, 76

Tolstoi, Aleksei Nikolaevich
See Tolstoy, Alexey Nikolaevich

Tolstoy, Alexey Nikolaevich 1882-1945T C L C 18

See also CA 107; 158

Tolstoy, Count Leo
See Tolstoy, Leo (Nikolaevich)

Tolstoy, Leo (Nikolaevich) 1828-1910TCLC 4, 11, 17, 28, 44, 79; DA; DAB; DAC; DAM MST, NOV; SSC 9, 30; WLC
See also CA 104; 123; SATA 26

Tomasi di Lampedusa, Giuseppe 1896-1957
See Lampedusa, Giuseppe (Tomasi) di
See also CA 111

Tomlin, Lily .... CLC 17
See also Tomlin, Mary Jean

Tomlin, Mary Jean 1939(?)-
See Tomlin, Lily
See also CA 117

Tomlinson, (Alfred) Charles 1927-CLC 2, 4, 6, 13, 45; DAM POET; PC 17
See also CA 5-8R; CANR 33; DLB 40

Tomlinson, H(enry) M(ajor) 1873-1958TCLC 71
See also CA 118; 161; DLB 36, 100, 195

Tonson, Jacob
See Bennett, (Enoch) Arnold

Toole, John Kennedy 1937-1969 CLC 19, 64
See also CA 104; DLBY 81; MTCW 2

Toomer, Jean 1894-1967CLC 1, 4, 13, 22; BLC 3; DAM MULT; PC 7; SSC 1; WLCS
See also BW 1; CA 85-88; CDALB 1917-1929; DLB 45, 51; MTCW 1, 2

Torley, Luke
See Blish, James (Benjamin)

Tornimparte, Alessandra
See Ginzburg, Natalia

Torre, Raoul della
See Mencken, H(enry) L(ouis)

Torrey, E(dwin) Fuller 1937- .... CLC 34
See also CA 119; CANR 71

Torsvan, Ben Traven
See Traven, B.

Torsvan, Benno Traven
See Traven, B.

Torsvan, Berick Traven
See Traven, B.

Torsvan, Berwick Traven
See Traven, B.

Torsvan, Bruno Traven
See Traven, B.

Torsvan, Traven
See Traven, B.

Tournier, Michel (Edouard) 1924-CLC 6, 23, 36, 95
See also CA 49-52; CANR 3, 36, 74; DLB 83; MTCW 1, 2; SATA 23

Tournimparte, Alessandra
See Ginzburg, Natalia

Towers, Ivar
See Kornbluth, C(yril) M.

Towne, Robert (Burton) 1936(?)- ..... CLC 87
See also CA 108; DLB 44

Townsend, Sue .... CLC 61
See also Townsend, Susan Elaine
See also AAYA 28; SATA 55, 93; SATA-Brief 48

Townsend, Susan Elaine 1946-
See Townsend, Sue
See also CA 119; 127; CANR 65; DAB; DAC; DAM MST

Townshend, Peter (Dennis Blandford) 1945-
CLC 17, 42
See also CA 107

Tozzi, Federigo 1883-1920 .... TCLC 31
See also CA 160

Traill, Catharine Parr 1802-1899 .. NCLC 31

See also DLB 99

Trakl, Georg 1887-1914 .... TCLC 5; PC 20
See also CA 104; 165; MTCW 2

Transtroemer, Tomas (Goesta) 1931-CLC 52, 65; DAM POET
See also CA 117; 129; CAAS 17

Transtromer, Tomas Gosta
See Transtroemer, Tomas (Goesta)

Traven, B. (?)-1969 .... CLC 8, 11
See also CA 19-20; 25-28R; CAP 2; DLB 9, 56; MTCW 1

Treitel, Jonathan 1959- .... CLC 70

Tremain, Rose 1943- .... CLC 42
See also CA 97-100; CANR 44; DLB 14

Tremblay, Michel 1942- CLC 29, 102; DAC; DAM MST
See also CA 116; 128; DLB 60; MTCW 1, 2

Trevanian .... CLC 29
See also Whitaker, Rod(ney)

Trevor, Glen
See Hilton, James

Trevor, William 1928-CLC 7, 9, 14, 25, 71, 116; SSC 21
See also Cox, William Trevor
See also DLB 14, 139; MTCW 2

Trifonov, Yuri (Valentinovich) 1925-1981
CLC 45
See also CA 126; 103; MTCW 1

Trilling, Lionel 1905-1975 ...... CLC 9, 11, 24
See also CA 9-12R; 61-64; CANR 10; DLB 28, 63; INT CANR-10; MTCW 1, 2

Trimball, W. H.
See Mencken, H(enry) L(ouis)

Tristan
See Gomez de la Serna, Ramon

Tristram
See Housman, A(lfred) E(dward)

Trogdon, William (Lewis) 1939-
See Heat-Moon, William Least
See also CA 115; 119; CANR 47; INT 119

Trollope, Anthony 1815-1882NCLC 6, 33; DA; DAB; DAC; DAM MST, NOV; SSC 28; WLC
See also CDBLB 1832-1890; DLB 21, 57, 159; SATA 22

Trollope, Frances 1779-1863 .... NCLC 30
See also DLB 21, 166

Trotsky, Leon 1879-1940 .... TCLC 22
See also CA 118; 167

Trotter (Cockburn), Catharine 1679-1749L C 8
See also DLB 84

Trout, Kilgore
See Farmer, Philip Jose

Trow, George W. S. 1943- .... CLC 52
See also CA 126

Troyat, Henri 1911- .... CLC 23
See also CA 45-48; CANR 2, 33, 67; MTCW 1

Trudeau, G(arretson) B(eekman) 1948-
See Trudeau, Garry B.
See also CA 81-84; CANR 31; SATA 35

Trudeau, Garry B. .... CLC 12
See also Trudeau, G(arretson) B(eekman)
See also AAYA 10; AITN 2

Truffaut, Francois 1932-1984 .. CLC 20, 101
See also CA 81-84; 113; CANR 34

Trumbo, Dalton 1905-1976 .... CLC 19
See also CA 21-24R; 69-72; CANR 10; DLB 26

Trumbull, John 1750-1831 .... NCLC 30
See also DLB 31

Trundlett, Helen B.
See Eliot, T(homas) S(tearns)

CLC 3, 6, 9, 10, 15, 31, 42, 85; DA; DAB; DAC; DAM MST, MULT, NOV; HLC
   See also CA 73-76; CANR 18, 32, 42, 67; DLB 145; HW 1, 2; MTCW 1, 2

Vasiliu, Gheorghe 1881-1957
   See Bacovia, George
   See also CA 123

Vassa, Gustavus
   See Equiano, Olaudah

Vassilikos, Vassilis 1933- .... CLC 4, 8
   See also CA 81-84; CANR 75

Vaughan, Henry 1621-1695 .... LC 27
   See also DLB 131

Vaughn, Stephanie .... CLC 62

Vazov, Ivan (Minchov) 1850-1921 . TCLC 25
   See also CA 121; 167; DLB 147

Veblen, Thorstein B(unde) 1857-1929 **T C L C 31**
   See also CA 115; 165

Vega, Lope de 1562-1635 ..... LC 23; HLCS 2

Venison, Alfred
   See Pound, Ezra (Weston Loomis)

Verdi, Marie de
   See Mencken, H(enry) L(ouis)

Verdu, Matilde
   See Cela, Camilo Jose

Verga, Giovanni (Carmelo) 1840-1922**T C L C 3; SSC 21**
   See also CA 104; 123

Vergil 70B.C.-19B.C. ... CMLC 9; DA; DAB; DAC; DAM MST, POET; PC 12; WLCS
   See also Virgil

Verhaeren, Emile (Adolphe Gustave) 1855-1916 **TCLC 12**
   See also CA 109

Verlaine, Paul (Marie) 1844-1896**NCLC 2, 51; DAM POET; PC 2**

Verne, Jules (Gabriel) 1828-1905**TCLC 6, 52**
   See also AAYA 16; CA 110; 131; DLB 123; JRDA; MAICYA; SATA 21

Very, Jones 1813-1880 .... NCLC 9
   See also DLB 1

Vesaas, Tarjei 1897-1970 .... CLC 48
   See also CA 29-32R

Vialis, Gaston
   See Simenon, Georges (Jacques Christian)

Vian, Boris 1920-1959 .... TCLC 9
   See also CA 106; 164; DLB 72; MTCW 2

Viaud, (Louis Marie) Julien 1850-1923
   See Loti, Pierre
   See also CA 107

Vicar, Henry
   See Felsen, Henry Gregor

Vicker, Angus
   See Felsen, Henry Gregor

Vidal, Gore 1925-**CLC 2, 4, 6, 8, 10, 22, 33, 72; DAM NOV, POP**
   See also AITN 1; BEST 90:2; CA 5-8R; CANR 13, 45, 65; CDALBS; DLB 6, 152; INT CANR-13; MTCW 1, 2

Viereck, Peter (Robert Edwin) 1916- . CLC 4
   See also CA 1-4R; CANR 1, 47; DLB 5

Vigny, Alfred (Victor) de 1797-1863**NCLC 7; DAM POET; PC 26**
   See also DLB 119, 192

Vilakazi, Benedict Wallet 1906-1947**TCLC 37**
   See also CA 168

Villa, Jose Garcia 1904-1997 .... PC 22
   See also CA 25-28R; CANR 12

Villaurrutia, Xavier 1903-1950 ...... TCLC 80
   See also HW 1

Villiers de l'Isle Adam, Jean Marie Mathias Philippe Auguste, Comte de 1838-1889

NCLC 3; SSC 14
   See also DLB 123

Villon, Francois 1431-1463(?) .... PC 13
   See also DLB 208

Vinci, Leonardo da 1452-1519 ....LC 12

Vine, Barbara .... CLC 50
   See also Rendell, Ruth (Barbara)
   See also BEST 90:4

Vinge, Joan (Carol) D(ennison) 1948-**CLC 30; SSC 24**
   See also CA 93-96; CANR 72; SATA 36

Violis, G.
   See Simenon, Georges (Jacques Christian)

Virgil 70B.C.-19B.C.
   See Vergil
   See also DLB 211

Visconti, Luchino 1906-1976 .... CLC 16
   See also CA 81-84; 65-68; CANR 39

Vittorini, Elio 1908-1966 .... CLC 6, 9, 14
   See also CA 133; 25-28R

Vivekananda, Swami 1863-1902 .... TCLC 88

Vizenor, Gerald Robert 1934-**CLC 103; DAM MULT**
   See also CA 13-16R; CAAS 22; CANR 5, 21, 44, 67; DLB 175; MTCW 2; NNAL

Vizinczey, Stephen 1933- .... CLC 40
   See also CA 128; INT 128

Vliet, R(ussell) G(ordon) 1929-1984 CLC 22
   See also CA 37-40R; 112; CANR 18

Vogau, Boris Andreyevich 1894-1937(?)
   See Pilnyak, Boris
   See also CA 123

Vogel, Paula A(nne) 1951- .... CLC 76
   See also CA 108

Voigt, Cynthia 1942- .... CLC 30
   See also AAYA 3, 30; CA 106; CANR 18, 37, 40; CLR 13, 48; INT CANR-18; JRDA; MAICYA; SATA 48, 79; SATA-Brief 33

Voigt, Ellen Bryant 1943- .... CLC 54
   See also CA 69-72; CANR 11, 29, 55; DLB 120

Voinovich, Vladimir (Nikolaevich) 1932-**C L C 10, 49**
   See also CA 81-84; CAAS 12; CANR 33, 67; MTCW 1

Vollmann, William T. 1959- ..CLC 89; DAM NOV, POP**
   See also CA 134; CANR 67; MTCW 2

Voloshinov, V. N.
   See Bakhtin, Mikhail Mikhailovich

Voltaire 1694-1778 . LC 14; DA; DAB; DAC; DAM DRAM, MST; SSC 12; WLC

von Aschendrof, BaronIgnatz
   See Ford, Ford Madox

von Daeniken, Erich 1935- .... CLC 30
   See also AITN 1; CA 37-40R; CANR 17, 44

von Daniken, Erich
   See von Daeniken, Erich

von Heidenstam, (Carl Gustaf) Verner
   See Heidenstam, (Carl Gustaf) Verner von

von Heyse, Paul (Johann Ludwig)
   See Heyse, Paul (Johann Ludwig von)

von Hofmannsthal, Hugo
   See Hofmannsthal, Hugo von

von Horvath, Odon
   See Horvath, Oedoen von

von Horvath, Oedoen
   See Horvath, Oedoen von

von Liliencron, (Friedrich Adolf Axel) Detlev
   See Liliencron, (Friedrich Adolf Axel) Detlev von

Vonnegut, Kurt, Jr. 1922-**CLC 1, 2, 3, 4, 5, 8, 12, 22, 40, 60, 111; DA; DAB; DAC; DAM MST, NOV, POP; SSC 8; WLC**

See also AAYA 6; AITN 1; BEST 90:4; CA 1-4R; CANR 1, 25, 49, 75; CDALB 1968-1988; DLB 2, 8, 152; DLBD 3; DLBY 80; MTCW 1, 2

Von Rachen, Kurt
   See Hubbard, L(afayette) Ron(ald)

von Rezzori (d'Arezzo), Gregor
   See Rezzori (d'Arezzo), Gregor von

von Sternberg, Josef
   See Sternberg, Josef von

Vorster, Gordon 1924- .... CLC 34
   See also CA 133

Vosce, Trudie
   See Ozick, Cynthia

Voznesensky, Andrei (Andreievich) 1933-**CLC 1, 15, 57; DAM POET**
   See also CA 89-92; CANR 37; MTCW 1

Waddington, Miriam 1917- .... CLC 28
   See also CA 21-24R; CANR 12, 30; DLB 68

Wagman, Fredrica 1937- .... CLC 7
   See also CA 97-100; INT 97-100

Wagner, Linda W.
   See Wagner-Martin, Linda (C.)

Wagner, Linda Welshimer
   See Wagner-Martin, Linda (C.)

Wagner, Richard 1813-1883 .... NCLC 9
   See also DLB 129

Wagner-Martin, Linda (C.) 1936- .... CLC 50
   See also CA 159

Wagoner, David (Russell) 1926- CLC 3, 5, 15
   See also CA 1-4R; CAAS 3; CANR 2, 71; DLB 5; SATA 14

Wah, Fred(erick James) 1939- .... CLC 44
   See also CA 107; 141; DLB 60

Wahloo, Per 1926-1975 .... CLC 7
   See also CA 61-64; CANR 73

Wahloo, Peter
   See Wahloo, Per

Wain, John (Barrington) 1925-1994 . CLC 2, 11, 15, 46**
   See also CA 5-8R; 145; CAAS 4; CANR 23, 54; CDBLB 1960 to Present; DLB 15, 27, 139, 155; MTCW 1, 2

Wajda, Andrzej 1926- .... CLC 16
   See also CA 102

Wakefield, Dan 1932- .... CLC 7
   See also CA 21-24R; CAAS 7

Wakoski, Diane 1937- CLC 2, 4, 7, 9, 11, 40; DAM POET; PC 15**
   See also CA 13-16R; CAAS 1; CANR 9, 60; DLB 5; INT CANR-9; MTCW 2

Wakoski-Sherbell, Diane
   See Wakoski, Diane

Walcott, Derek (Alton) 1930-**CLC 2, 4, 9, 14, 25, 42, 67, 76; BLC 3; DAB; DAC; DAM MST, MULT, POET; DC 7**
   See also BW 2; CA 89-92; CANR 26, 47, 75, 80; DLB 117; DLBY 81; MTCW 1, 2

Waldman, Anne (Lesley) 1945- .... CLC 7
   See also CA 37-40R; CAAS 17; CANR 34, 69; DLB 16

Waldo, E. Hunter
   See Sturgeon, Theodore (Hamilton)

Waldo, Edward Hamilton
   See Sturgeon, Theodore (Hamilton)

Walker, Alice (Malsenior) 1944- CLC 5, 6, 9, 19, 27, 46, 58, 103; BLC 3; DA; DAB; DAC; DAM MST, MULT, NOV, POET, POP; SSC 5; WLCS**
   See also AAYA 3; BEST 89:4; BW 2, 3; CA 37-40R; CANR 9, 27, 49, 66; CDALB 1968-1988; DLB 6, 33, 143; INT CANR-27; MTCW 1, 2; SATA 31

Walker, David Harry 1911-1992 .... **CLC 14**
See also CA 1-4R; 137; CANR 1; SATA 8; SATA-Obit 71

Walker, Edward Joseph 1934-
See Walker, Ted
See also CA 21-24R; CANR 12, 28, 53

Walker, George F. 1947- . **CLC 44, 61; DAB; DAC; DAM MST**
See also CA 103; CANR 21, 43, 59; DLB 60

Walker, Joseph A. 1935- .... **CLC 19; DAM DRAM, MST**
See also BW 1, 3; CA 89-92; CANR 26; DLB 38

Walker, Margaret (Abigail) 1915-1998 **CLC 1, 6; BLC; DAM MULT; PC 20**
See also BW 2, 3; CA 73-76; 172; CANR 26, 54, 76; DLB 76, 152; MTCW 1, 2

Walker, Ted .... **CLC 13**
See also Walker, Edward Joseph
See also DLB 40

Wallace, David Foster 1962- ..... **CLC 50, 114**
See also CA 132; CANR 59; MTCW 2

Wallace, Dexter
See Masters, Edgar Lee

Wallace, (Richard Horatio) Edgar 1875-1932 **TCLC 57**
See also CA 115; DLB 70

Wallace, Irving 1916-1990 **CLC 7, 13; DAM NOV, POP**
See also AITN 1; CA 1-4R; 132; CAAS 1; CANR 1, 27; INT CANR-27; MTCW 1, 2

Wallant, Edward Lewis 1926-1962 **CLC 5, 10**
See also CA 1-4R; CANR 22; DLB 2, 28, 143; MTCW 1, 2

Wallas, Graham 1858-1932 .... **TCLC 91**

Walley, Byron
See Card, Orson Scott

Walpole, Horace 1717-1797 .... **LC 49**
See also DLB 39, 104

Walpole, Hugh (Seymour) 1884-1941 **TCLC 5**
See also CA 104; 165; DLB 34; MTCW 2

Walser, Martin 1927- .... **CLC 27**
See also CA 57-60; CANR 8, 46; DLB 75, 124

Walser, Robert 1878-1956 **TCLC 18; SSC 20**
See also CA 118; 165; DLB 66

Walsh, Jill Paton ... . **CLC 35**
See Paton Walsh, Gillian
See also AAYA 11; CLR 2; DLB 161; SAAS 3

Walter, Villiam Christian
See Andersen, Hans Christian

Wambaugh, Joseph (Aloysius, Jr.) 1937- **CLC 3, 18; DAM NOV, POP**
See also AITN 1; BEST 89:3; CA 33-36R; CANR 42, 65; DLB 6; DLBY 83; MTCW 1, 2

Wang Wei 699(?)-761(?) .... **PC 18**

Ward, Arthur Henry Sarsfield 1883-1959
See Rohmer, Sax
See also CA 108; 173

Ward, Douglas Turner 1930- .... **CLC 19**
See also BW 1; CA 81-84; CANR 27; DLB 7, 38

Ward, E. D.
See Lucas, E(dward) V(errall)

Ward, Mary Augusta
See Ward, Mrs. Humphry

Ward, Mrs. Humphry 1851-1920 .. **TCLC 55**
See also DLB 18

Ward, Peter
See Faust, Frederick (Schiller)

Warhol, Andy 1928(?)-1987 .... **CLC 20**
See also AAYA 12; BEST 89:4; CA 89-92; 121; CANR 34

Warner, Francis (Robert le Plastrier) 1937-
CLC 14
See also CA 53-56; CANR 11

Warner, Marina 1946- .... **CLC 59**
See also CA 65-68; CANR 21, 55; DLB 194

Warner, Rex (Ernest) 1905-1986 ...... **CLC 45**
See also CA 89-92; 119; DLB 15

Warner, Susan (Bogert) 1819-1885 **NCLC 31**
See also DLB 3, 42

Warner, Sylvia (Constance) Ashton
See Ashton-Warner, Sylvia (Constance)

Warner, Sylvia Townsend 1893-1978 **CLC 7, 19; SSC 23**
See also CA 61-64; 77-80; CANR 16, 60; DLB 34, 139; MTCW 1, 2

Warren, Mercy Otis 1728-1814 ..... **NCLC 13**
See also DLB 31, 200

Warren, Robert Penn 1905-1989 **CLC 1, 4, 6, 8, 10, 13, 18, 39, 53, 59; DA; DAB; DAC; DAM MST, NOV, POET; SSC 4; WLC**
See also AITN 1; CA 13-16R; 129; CANR 10, 47; CDALB 1968-1988; DLB 2, 48, 152; DLBY 80, 89; INT CANR-10; MTCW 1, 2; SATA 46; SATA-Obit 63

Warshofsky, Isaac
See Singer, Isaac Bashevis

Warton, Thomas 1728-1790 ..... **LC 15; DAM POET**
See also DLB 104, 109

Waruk, Kona
See Harris, (Theodore) Wilson

Warung, Price 1855-1911 .... **TCLC 45**

Warwick, Jarvis
See Garner, Hugh

Washington, Alex
See Harris, Mark

Washington, Booker T(aliaferro) 1856-1915 **TCLC 10; BLC 3; DAM MULT**
See also BW 1; CA 114; 125; SATA 28

Washington, George 1732-1799 .... **LC 25**
See also DLB 31

Wassermann, (Karl) Jakob 1873-1934 **TCLC 6**
See also CA 104; 163; DLB 66

Wasserstein, Wendy 1950- ... **CLC 32, 59, 90; DAM DRAM; DC 4**
See also CA 121; 129; CABS 3; CANR 53, 75; INT 129; MTCW 2; SATA 94

Waterhouse, Keith (Spencer) 1929- . **CLC 47**
See also CA 5-8R; CANR 38, 67; DLB 13, 15; MTCW 1, 2

Waters, Frank (Joseph) 1902-1995 .. **CLC 88**
See also CA 5-8R; 149; CAAS 13; CANR 3, 18, 63; DLB 212; DLBY 86

Waters, Roger 1944- .... **CLC 35**

Watkins, Frances Ellen
See Harper, Frances Ellen Watkins

Watkins, Gerrold
See Malzberg, Barry N(athaniel)

Watkins, Gloria 1955(?)-
See hooks, bell
See also BW 2; CA 143; MTCW 2

Watkins, Paul 1964- .... **CLC 55**
See also CA 132; CANR 62

Watkins, Vernon Phillips 1906-1967 **CLC 43**
See also CA 9-10; 25-28R; CAP 1; DLB 20

Watson, Irving S.
See Mencken, H(enry) L(ouis)

Watson, John H.
See Farmer, Philip Jose

Watson, Richard F.
See Silverberg, Robert

Waugh, Auberon (Alexander) 1939- .. **CLC 7**

See also CA 45-48; CANR 6, 22; DLB 14, 194

Waugh, Evelyn (Arthur St. John) 1903-1966 **CLC 1, 3, 8, 13, 19, 27, 44, 107; DA; DAB; DAC; DAM MST, NOV, POP; WLC**
See also CA 85-88; 25-28R; CANR 22; CDBLB 1914-1945; DLB 15, 162, 195; MTCW 1, 2

Waugh, Harriet 1944- .... **CLC 6**
See also CA 85-88; CANR 22

Ways, C. R.
See Blount, Roy (Alton), Jr.

Waystaff, Simon
See Swift, Jonathan

Webb, (Martha) Beatrice (Potter) 1858-1943 **TCLC 22**
See also Potter, (Helen) Beatrix
See also CA 117; DLB 190

Webb, Charles (Richard) 1939- .... **CLC 7**
See also CA 25-28R

Webb, James H(enry), Jr. 1946- .... **CLC 22**
See also CA 81-84

Webb, Mary (Gladys Meredith) 1881-1927 **TCLC 24**
See also CA 123; DLB 34

Webb, Mrs. Sidney
See Webb, (Martha) Beatrice (Potter)

Webb, Phyllis 1927- .... **CLC 18**
See also CA 104; CANR 23; DLB 53

Webb, Sidney (James) 1859-1947 .. **TCLC 22**
See also CA 117; 163; DLB 190

Webber, Andrew Lloyd .... **CLC 21**
See also Lloyd Webber, Andrew

Weber, Lenora Mattingly 1895-1971 **CLC 12**
See also CA 19-20; 29-32R; CAP 1; SATA 2; SATA-Obit 26

Weber, Max 1864-1920 .... **TCLC 69**
See also CA 109

Webster, John 1579(?)-1634(?) ... **LC 33; DA; DAB; DAC; DAM DRAM, MST; DC 2; WLC**
See also CDBLB Before 1660; DLB 58

Webster, Noah 1758-1843 .... **NCLC 30**
See also DLB 1, 37, 42, 43, 73

Wedekind, (Benjamin) Frank(lin) 1864-1918 **TCLC 7; DAM DRAM**
See also CA 104; 153; DLB 118

Weidman, Jerome 1913-1998 .... **CLC 7**
See also AITN 2; CA 1-4R; 171; CANR 1; DLB 28

Weil, Simone (Adolphine) 1909-1943 **TCLC 23**
See also CA 117; 159; MTCW 2

Weininger, Otto 1880-1903 .... **TCLC 84**

Weinstein, Nathan
See West, Nathanael

Weinstein, Nathan von Wallenstein
See West, Nathanael

Weir, Peter (Lindsay) 1944- .... **CLC 20**
See also CA 113; 123

Weiss, Peter (Ulrich) 1916-1982 **CLC 3, 15, 51; DAM DRAM**
See also CA 45-48; 106; CANR 3; DLB 69, 124

Weiss, Theodore (Russell) 1916- **CLC 3, 8, 14**
See also CA 9-12R; CAAS 2; CANR 46; DLB 5

Welch, (Maurice) Denton 1915-1948 **TCLC 22**
See also CA 121; 148

Welch, James 1940- ..... **CLC 6, 14, 52; DAM MULT, POP**
See also CA 85-88; CANR 42, 66; DLB 175; NNAL

Weldon, Fay 1931- . **CLC 6, 9, 11, 19, 36, 59; DAM POP**
See also CA 21-24R; CANR 16, 46, 63; CDBLB 1960 to Present; DLB 14, 194; INT CANR-

16; MTCW 1, 2

Wellek, Rene 1903-1995 .... **CLC 28**
See also CA 5-8R; 150; CAAS 7; CANR 8; DLB
63; INT CANR-8

Weller, Michael 1942- .... **CLC 10, 53**
See also CA 85-88

Weller, Paul 1958- .... **CLC 26**

Wellershoff, Dieter 1925- .... **CLC 46**
See also CA 89-92; CANR 16, 37

Welles, (George) Orson 1915-1985**CLC 20, 80**
See also CA 93-96; 117

Wellman, John McDowell 1945-
See Wellman, Mac
See also CA 166

Wellman, Mac 1945- .... **CLC 65**
See also Wellman, John McDowell; Wellman,
John McDowell

Wellman, Manly Wade 1903-1986 .... **CLC 49**
See also CA 1-4R; 118; CANR 6, 16, 44; SATA
6; SATA-Obit 47

Wells, Carolyn 1869(?)-1942 .... **TCLC 35**
See also CA 113; DLB 11

Wells, H(erbert) G(eorge) 1866-1946**TCLC 6,
12, 19; DA; DAB; DAC; DAM MST, NOV;
SSC 6; WLC**
See also AAYA 18; CA 110; 121; CDBLB 1914-
1945; DLB 34, 70, 156, 178; MTCW 1, 2;
SATA 20

Wells, Rosemary 1943- .... **CLC 12**
See also AAYA 13; CA 85-88; CANR 48; CLR
16; MAICYA; SAAS 1; SATA 18, 69

Welty, Eudora 1909- **CLC 1, 2, 5, 14, 22, 33,
105; DA; DAB; DAC; DAM MST, NOV;
SSC 1, 27; WLC**
See also CA 9-12R; CABS 1; CANR 32, 65;
CDALB 1941-1968; DLB 2, 102, 143;
DLBD 12; DLBY 87; MTCW 1, 2

Wen I-to 1899-1946 .... **TCLC 28**

Wentworth, Robert
See Hamilton, Edmond

Werfel, Franz (Viktor) 1890-1945 ... **TCLC 8**
See also CA 104; 161; DLB 81, 124

Wergeland, Henrik Arnold 1808-1845**N C L C
5**

Wersba, Barbara 1932- .... **CLC 30**
See also AAYA 2, 30; CA 29-32R; CANR 16,
38; CLR 3; DLB 52; JRDA; MAICYA; SAAS
2; SATA 1, 58; SATA-Essay 103

Wertmueller, Lina 1928- .... **CLC 16**
See also CA 97-100; CANR 39, 78

Wescott, Glenway 1901-1987**CLC 13; SSC 35**
See also CA 13-16R; 121; CANR 23, 70; DLB
4, 9, 102

Wesker, Arnold 1932- .... **CLC 3, 5, 42; DAB;
DAM DRAM**
See also CA 1-4R; CAAS 7; CANR 1, 33;
CDBLB 1960 to Present; DLB 13; MTCW 1

Wesley, Richard (Errol) 1945- .... **CLC 7**
See also BW 1; CA 57-60; CANR 27; DLB 38

Wessel, Johan Herman 1742-1785 .... **LC 7**

West, Anthony (Panther) 1914-1987 **CLC 50**
See also CA 45-48; 124; CANR 3, 19; DLB 15

West, C. P.
See Wodehouse, P(elham) G(renville)

West, (Mary) Jessamyn 1902-1984**CLC 7, 17**
See also CA 9-12R; 112; CANR 27; DLB 6;
DLBY 84; MTCW 1, 2; SATA-Obit 37

West, Morris L(anglo) 1916- .... **CLC 6, 33**
See also CA 5-8R; CANR 24, 49, 64; MTCW
1, 2

West, Nathanael 1903-1940 **TCLC 1, 14, 44;
SSC 16**
See also CA 104; 125; CDALB 1929-1941;

DLB 4, 9, 28; MTCW 1, 2

West, Owen
See Koontz, Dean R(ay)

West, Paul 1930- .... **CLC 7, 14, 96**
See also CA 13-16R; CAAS 7; CANR 22, 53,
76; DLB 14; INT CANR-22; MTCW 2

West, Rebecca 1892-1983 ... **CLC 7, 9, 31, 50**
See also CA 5-8R; 109; CANR 19; DLB 36;
DLBY 83; MTCW 1, 2

Westall, Robert (Atkinson) 1929-1993**CLC 17**
See also AAYA 12; CA 69-72; 141; CANR 18,
68; CLR 13; JRDA; MAICYA; SAAS 2;
SATA 23, 69; SATA-Obit 75

Westermarck, Edward 1862-1939 . **TCLC 87**

Westlake, Donald E(dwin) 1933- **CLC 7, 33;
DAM POP**
See also CA 17-20R; CAAS 13; CANR 16, 44,
65; INT CANR-16; MTCW 2

Westmacott, Mary
See Christie, Agatha (Mary Clarissa)

Weston, Allen
See Norton, Andre

Wetcheek, J. L.
See Feuchtwanger, Lion

Wetering, Janwillem van de
See van de Wetering, Janwillem

Wetherald, Agnes Ethelwyn 1857-1940**T C L C
81**
See also DLB 99

Wetherell, Elizabeth
See Warner, Susan (Bogert)

Whale, James 1889-1957 .... **TCLC 63**

Whalen, Philip 1923- .... **CLC 6, 29**
See also CA 9-12R; CANR 5, 39; DLB 16

Wharton, Edith (Newbold Jones) 1862-1937
**TCLC 3, 9, 27, 53; DA; DAB; DAC; DAM
MST, NOV; SSC 6; WLC**
See also AAYA 25; CA 104; 132; CDALB 1865-
1917; DLB 4, 9, 12, 78, 189; DLBD 13;
MTCW 1, 2

Wharton, James
See Mencken, H(enry) L(ouis)

Wharton, William (a pseudonym)CLC 18, 37
See also CA 93-96; DLBY 80; INT 93-96

Wheatley (Peters), Phillis 1754(?)-1784**LC 3,
50; BLC 3; DA; DAC; DAM MST, MULT,
POET; PC 3; WLC**
See also CDALB 1640-1865; DLB 31, 50

Wheelock, John Hall 1886-1978 .... **CLC 14**
See also CA 13-16R; 77-80; CANR 14; DLB
45

White, E(lwyn) B(rooks) 1899-1985 **CLC 10,
34, 39; DAM POP**
See also AITN 2; CA 13-16R; 116; CANR 16,
37; CDALBS; CLR 1, 21; DLB 11, 22;
MAICYA; MTCW 1, 2; SATA 2, 29, 100;
SATA-Obit 44

White, Edmund (Valentine III) 1940-**CLC 27,
110; DAM POP**
See also AAYA 7; CA 45-48; CANR 3, 19, 36,
62; MTCW 1, 2

White, Patrick (Victor Martindale) 1912-1990
CLC 3, 4, 5, 7, 9, 18, 65, 69
See also CA 81-84; 132; CANR 43; MTCW 1

White, Phyllis Dorothy James 1920-
See James, P. D.
See also CA 21-24R; CANR 17, 43, 65; DAM
POP; MTCW 1, 2

White, T(erence) H(anbury) 1906-1964 **C L C
30**
See also AAYA 22; CA 73-76; CANR 37; DLB
160; JRDA; MAICYA; SATA 12

White, Terence de Vere 1912-1994 ... **CLC 49**

See also CA 49-52; 145; CANR 3

White, Walter
See White, Walter F(rancis)
See also BLC; DAM MULT

White, Walter F(rancis) 1893-1955 **TCLC 15**
See also White, Walter
See also BW 1; CA 115; 124; DLB 51

White, William Hale 1831-1913
See Rutherford, Mark
See also CA 121

Whitehead, E(dward) A(nthony) 1933-**CLC 5**
See also CA 65-68; CANR 58

Whitemore, Hugh (John) 1936- .... **CLC 37**
See also CA 132; CANR 77; INT 132

Whitman, Sarah Helen (Power) 1803-1878
NCLC 19
See also DLB 1

Whitman, Walt(er) 1819-1892 . **NCLC 4, 31;
DA; DAB; DAC; DAM MST, POET; PC
3; WLC**
See also CDALB 1640-1865; DLB 3, 64; SATA
20

Whitney, Phyllis A(yame) 1903- ..... **CLC 42;
DAM POP**
See also AITN 2; BEST 90:3; CA 1-4R; CANR
3, 25, 38, 60; CLR 59; JRDA; MAICYA;
MTCW 2; SATA 1, 30

Whittemore, (Edward) Reed (Jr.) 1919-**CLC 4**
See also CA 9-12R; CAAS 8; CANR 4; DLB 5

Whittier, John Greenleaf 1807-1892**NCLC 8,
59**
See also DLB 1

Whittlebot, Hernia
See Coward, Noel (Peirce)

Wicker, Thomas Grey 1926-
See Wicker, Tom
See also CA 65-68; CANR 21, 46

Wicker, Tom .... **CLC 7**
See also Wicker, Thomas Grey

Wideman, John Edgar 1941- **CLC 5, 34, 36,
67; BLC 3; DAM MULT**
See also BW 2, 3; CA 85-88; CANR 14, 42,
67; DLB 33, 143; MTCW 2

Wiebe, Rudy (Henry) 1934- .. **CLC 6, 11, 14;
DAC; DAM MST**
See also CA 37-40R; CANR 42, 67; DLB 60

Wieland, Christoph Martin 1733-1813**N C L C
17**
See also DLB 97

Wiene, Robert 1881-1938 .... **TCLC 56**

Wieners, John 1934- .... **CLC 7**
See also CA 13-16R; DLB 16

Wiesel, Elie(zer) 1928- **CLC 3, 5, 11, 37; DA;
DAB; DAC; DAM MST, NOV; WLCS**
See also AAYA 7; AITN 1; CA 5-8R; CAAS 4;
CANR 8, 40, 65; CDALBS; DLB 83; DLBY
87; INT CANR-8; MTCW 1, 2; SATA 56

Wiggins, Marianne 1947- .... **CLC 57**
See also BEST 89:3; CA 130; CANR 60

Wight, James Alfred 1916-1995
See Herriot, James
See also CA 77-80; SATA 55; SATA-Brief 44

Wilbur, Richard (Purdy) 1921-**CLC 3, 6, 9, 14,
53, 110; DA; DAB; DAC; DAM MST,
POET**
See also CA 1-4R; CABS 2; CANR 2, 29, 76;
CDALBS; DLB 5, 169; INT CANR-29;
MTCW 1, 2; SATA 9, 108

Wild, Peter 1940- .... **CLC 14**
See also CA 37-40R; DLB 5

Wilde, Oscar 1854(?)-1900**TCLC 1, 8, 23, 41;
DA; DAB; DAC; DAM DRAM, MST,
NOV; SSC 11; WLC**

Literary Criticism Series
Cumulative Topic Index

This index lists all topic entries in Gale's *Classical and Medieval Literature Criticism, Contemporary Literary Criticism, Literature Criticism from 1400 to 1800, Nineteenth-Century Literature Criticism,* and *Twentieth-Century Literary Criticism.*

Topic Index

Topic Index

Contemporary Literary Criticism
Cumulative Nationality Index

Nationality Index

Nationality Index

Nationality Index

Nationality Index

Nationality Index

ISBN 0-7876-3196-5

90000
9 780787 631963